The Handbook of Communication and

Handbooks in Communication and Media

This series aims to provide theoretically ambitious but accessible volumes devoted to the major fields and subfields within communication and media studies. Each volume sets out to ground and orientate the student through a broad range of specially commissioned chapters, while also providing the more experienced scholar and teacher with a convenient and comprehensive overview of the latest trends and critical directions.

The Handbook of Communication and Corporate Reputation

Edited by

Craig E. Carroll

WILEY Blackwell

This paperback edition first published 2015
© 2013 John Wiley & Sons, Inc
Edition history: John Wiley & Sons, Inc (hardback, 2013)

Registered Office
John Wiley & Sons, Ltd, The Atrium, Southern Gate, Chichester, West Sussex, PO19 8SQ, UK

Editorial Offices
350 Main Street, Malden, MA 02148-5020, USA
9600 Garsington Road, Oxford, OX4 2DQ, UK
The Atrium, Southern Gate, Chichester, West Sussex, PO19 8SQ, UK

For details of our global editorial offices, for customer services, and for information about how to apply for permission to reuse the copyright material in this book please see our website at www.wiley.com/wiley-blackwell.

Library of Congress Cataloging-in-Publication Data
The handbook of communication and corporate reputation / Edited by Craig E. Carroll.
      pages cm. – (Handbooks in communication and media ; 46)
   Includes bibliographical references and index.
   ISBN 978-0-470-67098-9 (cloth) ISBN 978-1-119-06123-6 (pbk)
   1. Corporate culture.   2. Business ethics.   3. Mass media and business.   I. Carroll, Craig E., editor of compilation.
   HD58.7.H3345   2013
   659.2–dc23

                                                                                      2012037004

A catalogue record for this book is available from the British Library.

Cover image: © VisionsofAmerica/Joe Sohm/Getty Images

Set in 9/11.5pt Galliard by SPi Global, Pondicherry, India
Printed and bound in Malaysia by Vivar Printing Sdn Bhd

1   2015

Contents

About the Editor

Craig E. Carroll (PhD, The University of Texas at Austin) is a Visiting Scholar in Corporate Communication at New York University's Stern School of Business and Senior Research Fellow with the Reputation Institute. He previously taught at the University of North Carolina at Chapel Hill and the University of Southern California in the Annenberg School for Communication and Journalism. Carroll teaches on the adjunct faculty at IE Communication School (Madrid, Spain), Università della Svizzera italiana (Lugano, Switzerland), and the University of Florida. Dr. Carroll has been a visiting professor at Northwestern University, University of Amsterdam, Rotterdam School of Management, and the University of Cambridge. Carroll's research examines the role of communication in facets related to corporate reputation, organizational identity, and corporate social responsibility, including their relationships with the news media and the individual's role in their construction, meaning and management. His research in these areas has been presented in 16 countries outside of the United States.

Carroll is the editor of *Corporate Reputation and the News Media* (Routledge, 2011). His research has been published in *Communication Research, Corporate Reputation Review, Journal of Business Ethics, Journal of Business Research, Journalism and Communication Monographs* (China), *Management Learning, Public Relations Journal,* and *Public Relations Review.* He serves on the editorial boards for *Corporate Communications: An International Journal, Corporate Reputation Review, Journal of Communication, Journal of Public Relations Research, Public Relations Inquiry,* and *Public Relations Review.* He serves as the executive director of the Observatory on Corporate Reputation, LLC and was named *PR News'* Educator of the Year in 2008. Professor Carroll is past chair of the Public Relations division of the International Communication Association. He is a member of the International Association of Business Communicators and the Public Relations Society of America, as well as their local chapters in New York City and Nashville, Tennessee.

Notes on Contributors

Susan Westcott Alessandri (PhD, University of North Carolina at Chapel Hill, 2002) is Associate Professor in the Department of Communication and Journalism at Suffolk University. She is the author of *Visual Identity: Promoting and Protecting the Public Face of an Organization*. Her research has also been published in several textbooks and journals, including *Corporate Reputation Review*, *Corporate Communications: An International Journal*, *Education Review of Business Communication*, *Journal of Marketing for Higher Education*, *Journal of Advertising Education*, and *Journal of Employee Communication Management*. Alessandri serves on the editorial boards of *Corporate Reputation Review*, *Corporate Communications: An International Journal*, *Journal of Advertising Education*, and *Newspaper Research Journal*. She also serves on the executive committee of the Media Management and Economics Division of Association for Education in Journalism and Mass Communication (AEJMC).

Kathryn Anthony (MA, University of Kentucky) is a doctoral student in the Department of Communication at the University of Kentucky where she serves as a teaching assistant and a research assistant. Her research interests include risk and crisis communication, health communication, and organizational communication. She has served as a research assistant

for the Department of Homeland Security's National Center for Food Protection and Defense (NCFPD) and for the National Center for Risk and Economic Analysis of Terrorism Events (CREATE). She has published in the *Journal of Applied Communication Research* and *Argumentation and Advocacy*. Katie is also a member of the Lexington-Fayette county Community Emergency Response Team.

Jennifer L. Bartlett (PhD, Queensland University of Technology) is a senior lecturer in the School of Advertising, Marketing, and Public Relations at the Faculty of Business at Queensland University of Technology, Australia. Her research has been published in the *Public Relations Review*, *Asia Pacific Journal of Public Relations*, *Journal of Communication Management*, and *Australian Journal of Communication*. She serves on the editorial boards of *Prism: The Online Public Relations Journal* in Australia and New Zealand. Bartlett is the previous secretary and incoming vice chair of the International Communication Association's Public Relations division. She is also a fellow of the Public Relations Institute of Australia (PRIA).

William L. Benoit (PhD, Wayne State University) is Professor of Communication Studies at Ohio University. He developed the image repair theory and applied it in a number of case studies. He has published over 10 books (including *Accounts, Excuses, and Apologies*) and over 200 articles and book chapters. He has published in such journals as *Quarterly Journal of Speech, Communication Monographs, Human Communication Research, Public Relations Review, Journal of Applied Communication, Journalism and Mass Communication Review, Communication Education, Critical Studies in Media Communication,* and *Political Communication.* He is currently ranked as one of the most productive scholars in communication.

Bruce K. Berger (PhD, University of Kentucky) is Reese Phifer Professor of Advertising & Public Relations in the College of Communication & Information Sciences at the University of Alabama. His research interests include leadership in public relations practice and education, influence and power relations, and employee and organizational communications. He has coauthored a book about power relations in practice and published more than 40 articles and book chapters in academic and professional publications. He is a member of the Arthur W. Page Society and serves on the board of directors of The Plank Center for Leadership in Public Relations and the Institute for Public Relations. Previously, he was vice president of public relations for Whirlpool Corporation and president of the Whirlpool Foundation. He worked in international public relations for 20 years.

Peggy Simcic Brønn (DBA, Henley Management College) is Professor of Communication and Management in the Norwegian Business School's Department of Communication, Culture and Languages, and associate dean of the school's Bachelor in Public Relations. She is also director of the Center for Corporate Communication. Dr. Brønn has conducted research on relationship outcomes, reputation and reputation risk analysis, institutionalization of communication, motives for social engagement, and the strategic role of communication managers. Her works are published in the *European Journal of Marketing, Journal of Communication Management, Public Relations Review, Journal of Communication Management* (European editor), *Corporate Reputation Review* (editorial board), *Corporate Communication: An International Journal* (editorial board), *Journal of Business Ethics,* and *Business and Society Review,* among others. She is coeditor of *Corporate Communication: A Strategic Approach to Building Reputation* (second edition) and is coauthor of the first academic book on reputation in Norwegian. She is Norway's academic representative to the Reputation Institute and consults in the private, public, and nonprofit sectors in Norway.

Craig E. Carroll (PhD, The University of Texas at Austin) is a Visiting Scholar in Corporate Communication at New York University's Stern School of Business and Senior Research Fellow with the Reputation Institute. Professor Carroll is editor of the Handbook of Communication and Corporate Reputation.

Clarke L. Caywood (PhD, the University of Wisconsin-Madison) is Full Professor of Integrated Marketing Communications in the Medill School at Northwestern University. He published the second edition of the *Handbook of Strategic Public Relations & Integrated Marketing Communications* (McGraw-Hill, 2011). He was named by *PRWeek* as one of the most influential 100 PR people of the twentieth century (*PRWeek,* October 18, 1999), the top 10 outstanding educators in 2000 (*PRWeek,* February 7, 2000), and Educator of the Year by the Public Relations Society of America in 2002–2003. He has served as member of the Board of the Chicago Museum of Contemporary Art, the Advisory Board of the Chicago Symphony, the Direct Selling Education Foundation Board, and Co-Chair of the Awards Committee of the Public Relations Society of America. He is also a member and former trustee of the A.W. Page Society. He has worked for two past governors and the attorney general of the state of Wisconsin.

W. Timothy Coombs (PhD, Purdue University) is Full Professor in the Nicholson School of Communication at the University of Central Florida. Coombs is the 2002 recipient of Jackson, Jackson & Wagner Behavioral Science Prize from the Public Relations Society of American for his crisis research. His research has led to the development and testing of the situational crisis communication theory (SCCT). He has published widely in the areas of crisis management including articles in a variety of journals. His research includes the award-winning book *Ongoing Crisis Communication*. He has coauthored the award-winning books *It's Not Just Public Relations* with Sherry J. Holladay and *Today's Public Relations* with Robert L. Heath. He is also coeditor of *The Handbook of Crisis Communication* and coauthor of *PR Strategy and Application: Managing Influence*. Dr. Coombs had delivered presentations in Australia, Austria, Belgium, Denmark, Finland, Germany, Hong Kong, Norway, Sweden, and the United Kingdom.

Jeffrey L. Courtright (PhD, Purdue University) is Associate Professor of Communication at Illinois State University. With more than 20 years in public relations education and research, he investigates the relationship between corporate reputation and message design across a variety of contexts, from environmental communication to community relations to international public relations. He studies both for-profit and nonprofit organizations and has published multiple research articles, several with Dr. Peter Smudde as coauthor. He also has published with Dr. Smudde the books *Inspiring Cooperation and Celebrating Organizations* (2012) and *Power and Public Relations* (2007).

Sally Davenport (PhD, Victoria University of Wellington) is Professor of Management at Victoria University of Wellington and has a background in the physical sciences and research expertise in the areas of strategy, technology, innovation, and research management and policy. In April 2011, she was appointed as a commissioner with the New Zealand Productivity Commission. Her research interests center on organizational and stakeholder strategy and discourse surrounding the manage-

ment of science, technology, and innovation, with a particular focus on the growth of high-tech firms. She has been a principal investigator/leader on three major research grants. Sally is currently a member of the editorial boards of four international journals and is Deputy Chair of the Advisory Board of the International Society for Professional Innovation Management. Her articles have appeared in journals such as *Organization Studies, Human Relations, Research Policy, Discourse Studies, British Journal of Management, European Journal of Marketing, European Planning Studies, R&D Management, Technology Analysis & Strategic Management*, and *Science & Pubic Policy*.

Marcia W. DiStaso (PhD, University of Miami) is an Assistant Professor of Public Relations in the College of Communications at Pennsylvania State University. Her research has been published (or accepted for publication) in the *Journal of Public Relations Research, Public Relations Review, Public Relations Journal, Journalism Studies, Mass Communication & Society*, in many books and through the Institute for Public Relations. She is an Arthur W. Page Center Senior Research Fellow, chair of the Public Relations Society of America (PRSA) Financial Communications division, chair-elect of the PRSA Educator's Academy, co-chair of PRSA's National Research Committee, a board member for the International Public Relations Research Conference, and an associate editor for the Social Science of Social Media Research Center.

Melissa D. Dodd (PhD, University of Miami) is Assistant Professor of Public Relations at the State University of New York in Oswego. She is the (co)author of multiple refereed journal publications and has presented award-winning papers at top-tier academic conferences. Her research interests include social capital theory, individual/interpersonal variables, social media, reputation, ethics, and measurement as they relate to public relations. She serves as an Advisory Board Member for the International Public Relations Research Conference and

Book Review Editor for the Journal of the Association for Communication Administration. Dodd has held consulting positions with the Corporate Communication Department of Bacardi USA and the University of Miami's Emergency Management Department.

Mohan J. Dutta (PhD, University of Minnesota) is Professor and Head of the Department of Communications and New Media at the National University of Singapore and Courtesy Professor of Communication at Purdue University. At NUS, he is the Founding Director of the Center for Culture-Centered Approach to Research and Evaluation (CARE), directing research on culturally-centered, community-based projects of social change. He teaches and conducts research in international health communication, critical cultural theory, poverty in healthcare, health activism in globalization politics, indigenous cosmologies of health, subaltern studies and dialogue, and public policy and social change. Currently, he serves as Editor of the "Global Health Communication Book Series" with Left Coast Press and sits on the editorial board of seven journals. Before arriving to NUS, he served as Associate Dean of Research in the College of Liberal Arts at Purdue University, a Service Learning Fellow, and a fellow of the Entrepreneurial Leadership Academy. Also at Purdue, he served as the Founding Director of the Center for Poverty and Health Inequities (COPHI).

Sabine Einwiller (PhD, University of St. Gallen) is Professor of Corporate Communication at the Department of Communication, Johannes Gutenberg University of Mainz, Germany, where she is also responsible for a master's program in corporate communication. Her current research interests focus on causes and measurement of corporate reputation, integrated communication management, and the effects of negative publicity. Her research has been published in various international journals such as the *Corporate Communications: An International Journal, Corporate Reputation Review, Journal of the Academy of Marketing Science,* and *Journal of Consumer Psychology.*

Magnus Frostenson (PhD, Stockholm School of Economics) is an Associate Professor of Business Administration. His dissertation focused on issues of ethics and culture in newly internationalized Swedish firms. He is currently a researcher with the Department of Business Studies at Uppsala University and is also a senior lecturer at the Örebro University School of Business. He is the author of several journal articles, books, and book chapters, primarily in business ethics and corporate social responsibility. He has published in the *Journal of Business Ethics, Philosophy of Management,* and *Business Ethics: A European Review,* among other academic periodicals. In 2011, he published a monograph on business ethics, to be followed in 2012 by a new book on sustainability reporting.

Dawn R. Gilpin (PhD, Temple University) is an Assistant Professor at the Walter Cronkite School of Journalism and Mass Communication at Arizona State University. Her work has been published in the *Journal of Public Relations Research, Public Relations Review, Journal of Communication Management, Health Communication, E:CO Complexity & Organization, Studies in Communication Sciences, Global Media Journal,* and in several edited volumes. With Priscilla Murphy, she is coauthor of *Crisis Management in a Complex World* (Oxford University Press, 2008).

Karla K. Gower (PhD, University of North Carolina at Chapel Hill) is a Professor in the Department of Advertising and Public Relations and Director of the Plank Center for Leadership in Public Relations at the University of Alabama. She is the author of *The Opinions of Mankind: Racial Issues, Press, and Propaganda in the Cold War* (with R. Lentz), *Legal and Ethical Considerations for Public Relations, PR and the Press: The Troubled Embrace,* and *Liberty and Authority in Free Expression Law: The United States and Canada.* Her research has also been published in *Communication Law & Policy, Journalism and Mass Communication Quarterly, Journal of Public Relations Research, Public Relations Review, Journal of*

Communication Management, American Journalism, and *Journalism History*. She serves on the editorial boards of the *Journal of Public Relations Research* and *Journalism History*.

Robert J. Green (MA, Wake Forest University) is a doctoral student at the Brian Lamb School of Communication, Purdue University. His research has been published in *Communication Teacher*.

Anne Gregory (PhD, Leeds Metropolitan University) is Professor of Public Relations and Director of the Centre for Public Relations Studies at Leeds Metropolitan University, UK. She has authored over 70 publications publishing in *Public Relations Review, Journal of Marketing Management, Journal of Marketing Communications, Corporate Communications, International Journal of Communication Ethics, Journal of Public Affairs* and *Journal of Communication Management*. She is also, editor-in-chief of the *Journal of Communication Management*, and edits the globally available Chartered Institute of Public Relations (CIPR) series of 17 books, which she initiated. Anne also leads specialist commercial research and consultancy projects from the center working with public and private sector clients. Originally a broadcast journalist, Anne spent 10 years as a senior practitioner before moving on to academia. She was president of the CIPR in 2004, leading it to chartered status and was awarded the CIPR's Sir Stephen Tallents Medal for her outstanding contribution to public relations in 2010. Anne is a committed internationalist and, in May 2011, was voted chair-elect of the Global Alliance of Public Relations and Communications Management, the umbrella organization of over 60 public relations institutes from around the world.

James E. Grunig (PhD, University of Wisconsin–Madison) is a Professor Emeritus of Public Relations in the Department of Communication at the University of Maryland College Park. He is the coauthor of *Relações públicas: Teoria, contexto e relacionamentos (Public Relations: Theory, Context, and Relationships),*

Excellent Public Relations and Effective Organizations: A Study of Communication Management in Three Countries, Managing Public Relations, Public Relations Techniques, and *Manager's Guide to Excellence in Public Relations and Communication Management.* He is editor of *Excellence in Public Relations and Communication Management. Excellent Public Relations and Effective Organizations* received the 2002 PRIDE award of the Public Relations Division of the National Communication Association as the best book in public relations in the previous two years. In addition to his books, Grunig has written 246 other publications such as book chapters, journal articles, reports, and papers. He has won seven major awards in public relations: the Arthur W. Page Society Distinguished Service Award; the Pathfinder Award for excellence in public relations research of the Institute for Public Relations Research and Education; the Outstanding Educator Award of the Public Relations Society of America (PRSA); the Jackson, Jackson and Wagner Award for behavioral science research of the PRSA Foundation; the Alexander Hamilton Medal for Lifetime Contributions to Professional Public Relations of the Institute for Public Relations; the Lloyd Dennis Award for Distinguished Leadership in Public Affairs (with Larissa A. Grunig) from the Public Affairs and Government Section of PRSA; and the Dr. Hamid Notghi Prize for Career Achievement in Public Relations from the Kargozar Public Relations Institute, Tehran, Iran. He also won the most prestigious lifetime award of the Association for Education in Journalism and Mass Communication (AEJMC), the Paul J. Deutschmann Award for Excellence in Research. He was the forty-fifth Annual Distinguished Lecturer of the Institute for Public Relations in 2006. He has been awarded honorary doctorates by the Universidad San Martin de Porres in Peru, the University of Bucharest in Romania, Istanbul University in Turkey, and the University of Quebec at Montreal in Canada.

Kristen Guth (MA, University of Illinois at Urbana-Champaign) is a doctoral student in the Department of Communication at the

Annenberg School for Communication and Journalism at the University of Southern California (USC). Her recent scholarly interests include organizational communication and technology. Kristen's current research examines corporate social responsibility communicated on the Internet, Twitter sentiment analysis, and scenario planning for organizations. In 2012, Kristen researched youth, organizations, and information quality issues on the Internet with the Youth and Media Lab at the Berkman Center for Internet and Society at Harvard University. In addition to prior roles as a journalist for Fox and NBC, she has professional experience in corporate and non-profit public relations for digital and traditional media contexts. She has taught undergraduate courses in public speaking and communication technology and society at the University of Illinois at Urbana-Champaign. Kristen currently teaches undergraduate and graduate students in the experiential learning center at the USC Marshall School of Business.

Robert L. Heath (PhD, University of Illinois) is Professor Emeritus at the University of Houston, author of many books and articles on issues management, public relations, crisis communication, risk communication, organizational rhetorical theory, and narrative theory. Notable in the list of recent publications is the *SAGE Handbook of Public Relations* (2010), *Handbook of Risk and Crisis Communication* (2009, with H. Dan O'Hair), *Rhetorical and Critical Approaches to Public Relations II* (2009, with Elizabeth Toth and Damion Waymer), *Today's Public Relations* (2006, with W. Timothy Coombs), and *The Encyclopedia of Public Relations* (2005). He is the lead editor and author of the lead article in a special issue of *Management Communication Quarterly* addressing external organizational rhetoric (2011, 25/3).

Sherry J. Holladay (PhD, Purdue University) is a Professor at the Nicholson School of Communication at the University of Central Florida in Orlando. Dr. Holladay's research interests include crisis communication, corporate social responsibility, reputation management, activism, and stakeholder relations. Her work appears in the *Journal of Public Relations Research*, *Public Relations Review*, *Management Communication Quarterly*, *Journal of Communication Management*, and *International Journal of Strategic Communication*. She is coauthor of *It's Not Just PR: Public Relations in Society*, *Public Relations Strategies and Applications: Managing Influence*, and *Managing Corporate Responsibility: A Communication Approach*, and coeditor of the *Handbook of Crisis Communication*.

Alex D. Holt (BA, The George Washington University) was, at the time of this writing, an undergraduate honors student majoring in political communication.

Chun-ju Flora Hung-Baesecke (PhD, University of Maryland at College Park) is the Associate Director of the Center for Media and Communication Research and Assistant Professor of the Public Relations & Advertising Option in the Department of Communication Studies at Hong Kong Baptist University. Her research interests are relationship management, strategic management, reputation management, crisis communication, conflict resolution, negotiation, and corporate social responsibility. Dr. Hung published her research in book chapters and in international refereed journals, for example, *Journal of Public Relations Research*, *Journal of Communication Management*, *Public Relations Review*, and *International Journal of Strategic Communication*, and has presented research papers in international academic public relations conferences.

Øyvind Ihlen (dr.art., University of Oslo) is Professor at the Department of Media and Communication at the University of Oslo. He was previously Professor of Communication and Management at the Norwegian School of Management and at Hedmark University College. Ihlen has edited, written, and cowritten seven books, among them *Public Relations and Social Theory* (Routledge, 2009) and *Handbook of Communication and Corporate*

Social Responsibility (Wiley Blackwell, 2011). His award-winning research has appeared in numerous anthologies and in journals such as the *Journal of Public Relations Research, Public Relations Review, Journal of Public Affairs, International Journal of Strategic Communication, Journal of Communication Management, Corporate Communications, Management Communication Quarterly, International Journal of Organizational Analysis, Environmental Communication, Sustainable Development,* and *Business Strategy and the Environment.* He is on the editorial board of 9 journals and have reviewed for an additional 12 journals and publishing houses.

Laura Illia (PhD, Università della Svizzera Italiana) is Professor in Corporate Communication at IE University and Academic Director of the Master at the same University (ES). Her current research focuses on how issues of organizational identity, social responsibility, corporate communication and branding are involved in organizational management and change. She has been doing research at the University of Cambridge (UK), London School of Economics and Political Science (UK) and University of Lugano (CH). Her works are published in journals like *MIT Sloan Management Review, British Journal of Management, Journal of Business Research, Journal of Applied Behavioural Science, Corporate Reputation Review, Corporate Communication: An International Journal, Journal of Public Relations Research,* and others. She currently serves on the Editorial Board of *Business & Society* (Sage), *Corporate Reputation Review* (Palgrave) and *Corporate Communication: An International Journal* (Emerald).

Rajul Jain (MA, University of Florida) is a PhD candidate in Public Relations at the University of Florida. Prior to coming to the United States in 2007, Rajul worked as a business analyst and communication coordinator at a multinational telecommunication firm in India. Rajul is a recipient of the 2011 Ketchum Excellence in Public Relations Research Award. She has several years of professional experience in cor-

porate and nonprofit public relations, as well as teaching experience at the university level, which includes teaching public relations courses at DePaul University. Her research focus is on corporate and transnational public relations.

Pan Ji (PhD, University of South Carolina) is a postdoctoral research fellow at Nanyang Technological University (Singapore), his research interests relate to the effects and antecedents of mediated social connectivity, frame building within media organizations, as well as the behavioral or cognitive effects of media framing. Specifically, Ji examines the coverage of global events such as environmental crises, product safety issues or health perils, as well as the spread of related information and resources within established or emergent social networks. Current studies involve a social network analysis of blog hyperlink networks, framing of made-in-China products in Western media, and the impacts of SNS on job mobility and entrepreneurship among Singaporeans.

Hua Jiang (PhD, University of Maryland at College Park) is Assistant Professor at Towson University. She teaches both undergraduate and graduate public relations courses, including *Principles of Strategic Public Relations and Integrated Communication, Public Relations and Integrated Communication Campaigns, Mass Communication Research, Theories of Public Relations and Organizational Communication,* and *Practice of Public Relations and Organizational Communication.* Her research interests include work/life conflict issues in public relations, public relations leadership, relationship management, social media, public diplomacy, activism, and global public relations. Her work has been published or accepted to be published in peer-reviewed academic journals including *Journal of Public Relations Research, Journal of Health Communication, Public Relations Review, Asian Journal of Communication, Public Relations Journal, Journal of Public Affairs,* and *Public Relations Inquiry.* Dr. Jiang has also contributed book chapters to *Handbook of communication and corporate reputation, Handbook of public diplomacy,* and *Gender* *and public relations: Critical perspectives on voice, image and identity.*

Esben Karmark (PhD, Copenhagen Business School) is Associate Professor in the Department of Intercultural Communication and Management at Copenhagen Business School in Denmark. His research examines corporate communication, corporate branding (and particularly cultural dimensions and brand retail), organizational and corporate identity, and corporate culture. He has published his research and teaching cases in such edited books as *Media, Organizations, and Identity* and *Corporate Branding Purpose/People/Process.*

Robert Kerr (PhD, University of North Carolina at Chapel Hill) is Professor at the University of Oklahoma. His First Amendment research focuses on legal and public policy issues involved in maintaining a truly free marketplace of ideas for citizens in an age when corporate and government voices have grown more powerful than ever. He was the most honored participant over the past decade in national research competitions of the Association for Education in Journalism and Mass Communication, a 2010 Musambira and Nesta study documented. In 2008, he was named a Presidential Professor by OU and the winner of the National Communication Association's Franklyn S. Haiman Award for Distinguished Scholarship in Freedom of Expression. Kerr's latest book – *The Corporate Free-Speech Movement: Cognitive Feudalism and the Endangered Marketplace of Ideas* – foreshadowed the recent economic crisis in global markets, as well as the 2010 US Supreme Court ruling in *Citizens United v. FEC* that removed virtually all limits on corporate spending in political campaigns.

Jeong-Nam Kim (PhD, University of Maryland at College Park) is Associate Professor in the Brian Lamb School of Communication at Purdue University. His research areas are strategic management of public relations, public behaviors, health/risk communication, and online and offline communicative actions among publics. Jeong-Nam and James Grunig

of the University of Maryland developed a situational theory of problem solving (STOPS), a generalized version of the situational theory of publics. Currently, he is conducting research using the new situational theory in the areas of public relations, public opinion, and health, risk, and science communication.

Sookyong Kim (MS, Kansas State University) is a doctoral student in the Department of Advertising, Public Relations & Retailing at Michigan State University. She has worked as a research assistant at Michigan State University for the Advergame project funded by the National Institutes of Health. Sookyong's work focuses mainly on food marketing to children, social marketing, deceptive product placement in media, and implications for public policy. She is currently teaching social marketing to undergraduate students at Michigan State University.

Yungwook Kim (PhD, University of Florida) is a Professor and Chair for School of Communication at Ewha Womans University, where he teaches crisis management and public relations. His current research focuses on the role of communication and culture in the context of crisis management and conflict resolution. He taught at Illinois State University prior to the current position. He was also a Fulbright Scholar at Program on Negotiation at Harvard Law School. His research appears in the *Journal of Public Relations Research, Public Relations Review, Corporate Communications: An International Journal, Journal of Promotion Management, Journalism and Mass Communication Quarterly, Journal of Broadcasting and Electronic Media, Journal of Asia Pacific Communication, Journal of Business Ethics,* and many other Korean scholarly journals. He wrote Korean books titled *Understanding Crisis Management: Public Relationship and Crisis Communication; Public Relations Communication: Systems, Rhetorical and Critical Approaches; Risk, Crisis and Communication: Interpreting and Coping with Risks; Crises and Conflicts in Modern Society;* and *Nonprofit Communication: Communication Campaigns for the Powerless and Public Interest.*

John C. Lammers (PhD, University of California, Davis) is Professor in the Department of Communication at the University of Illinois at Urbana-Champaign, where he directs the Health Communication Online Masters of Science Program. He teaches courses in organizational communication and communication in health organizations, professions, and policy. His recent scholarly work has focused on a formal theory of institutional influences on organizational communication. In particular, he has worked on a merger of the sociological tradition of studying institutions with the communication tradition of focusing on messages. This has resulted in a theory of institutional messages that may be applied in a variety of cases including corporate reputation, the social media environment of organizations, and interprofessional communication. Currently, he is studying the role of professionalism among first responders to disasters in the United States and the Netherlands.

Alexander V. Laskin (PhD, University of Florida) is Associate Professor and director of graduate studies at the Department of Public Relations, Quinnipiac University. Laskin had most of his work experience in investor relations, international mergers and acquisitions, and marketing research. Today, Laskin's academic research focuses on investor relations, strategic corporate communications, social responsibility, and international communications. He is the author of two books and several book chapters. He also published his research in such journals as the *Journal of Business Communication, Journal of Public Relations Research, Journal of Communication Management*, and others. His research on the value of investor relations was recognized by the Institute for Public Relations with 2006 Ketchum Excellence in Public Relations Research Award.

Shirley Leitch (PhD, University of Auckland) leads the Socially Sustainable Technology Flagship within the Swinburne University Institute of Social Research. Prior to joining Swinburne, she was dean of commerce at the University of Wollongong, served as pro vice-chancellor of Public Affairs at the University of Waikato and held a personal chair in corporate communication. Professor Leitch is an A-ranked scholar under the New Zealand PBRF research assessment system. Professor Leitch is a member of research teams that have received over $4 million in national competitive grants. With over 100 publications to her name, her work appears in the *European Journal of Marketing, Journal of Management Studies, Organization Studies, Human Relations, Discourse Studies, Public Relations Review, Science and Public Policy, Australian Journal of Communication, International Studies in Management and Organization*, and *Journal of Brand Management*, among others. Her research is focused on public discourse and change, including science–society engagement in relation to controversial science.

Paul S. Lieber (PhD, Louisiana State University) recently served as the strategic communications advisor to Special Operations Command – Australia, preceded by stints as the command writer for US Special Operations Command, head of information operations research for US Central Command, and on the faculties of the University of Canberra (Australia), the University of South Carolina (US), and Emerson College (US), respectively. Paul's widely published research emphasis mirrors his several years of professional practice in global strategic communication, centered on creating valid, predictive models of persuasion within interactive and/or advanced technology environments.

Vilma Luoma-aho (PhD, University of Jyväskylä, Finland) is a researcher and scientific director of the research project What Is Expected of the Media at the Department of Communication at the University of Jyvaskyla, Finland. Her research has been published in *Public Relations Review, Corporate Reputation Review, Corporate Communications: An International Journal, Business History, Business Ethics: A European Review, The International Journal of Public Sector Management, Ethical Space: The International Journal of Communication Ethics*, and *Innovation Journalism.*

Luoma-aho serves as the secretary of the Strategic Communication – division of Nord Media.

Jarol B. Manheim (PhD, Northwestern University) is Emeritus Professor of Media and Public Affairs and of Political Science at The George Washington University, where he developed the world's first degree-granting curriculum in political communication and later served as the founding director of the School of Media and Public Affairs. In addition to numerous books, his research has been published in the *American Political Science Review, British Journal of Political Science, International Journal of Press/Politics, International Public Relations Review, Journal of Politics, Journal of Communication, Journalism and Mass Communication Quarterly, Political Communication, Presidential Studies Quarterly*, and *Public Relations Review*, and he has served in editorial positions or on the editorial boards of *International Journal of Press/Politics, Journal of Politics, Journalism and Mass Communication Quarterly, Policy Studies Journal*, and *Political Communication*. Manheim chaired the committees that founded the journal *Political Communication*, and later served as chair of the Political Communication Section of the American Political Science Association. He was named 1995 CASE/Carnegie District of Columbia Professor of the Year; his work has also been awarded the Donald McGannon Research Essay Award for Social and Ethical Relevance in Communication Policy and the American Library Association's Outstanding Reference Source of the Year.

Tina McCorkindale (PhD, University of Miami) is an Assistant Professor of Public Relations at Appalachian State University. Her research has been published in the *Public Relations Review, Journal of New Communications Research, Public Relations Journal, Journal of Hospitality and Leisure Marketing, Feedback*, and in several books. McCorkindale serves as the chair for the Public Relations Society of America (PRSA) Educators Academy, co-chair of PRSA's National Research Committee, a board member for the International Public Relations Research Conference, and an associate editor for the Social Science of Social Media Research Center. Her research focuses on social media, including transparency and authenticity, and measurement.

Linjuan Rita Men (PhD, University of Miami) is Assistant Professor at Southern Methodist University. Rita's research interests include reputation management, employee engagement, and social media public relations. Rita's work has appeared in refereed journals of the *Public Relations Review, International Journal of Strategic Communication, Public Relations Journal*, and *Journal of Research in Interactive Marketing*. She also coauthored book chapters in the *IABC Handbook of Organizational Communication* (second edition) and *New Media and Public Relations* (second edition). Rita won the Ketchum Excellence in Public Relations Research Award from the Institute for Public Relations in 2010 and Top Student Paper Award in the Public Relations Division of ICA in 2011. Rita's professional experience includes corporate communication (Alibaba Group, Inc.), marketing campaign planning (L'Oreal, Inc.), and public relations research (Ketchum, Inc.). Rita is the former coordinator of the International Public Relations Research Conference.

Juan Meng (PhD, University of Alabama) is currently Assistant Professor in Public Relations in the Grady College of Journalism and Mass Communication at the University of Georgia. Meng's current research interests include the quantitative measurement of strategic leadership in public relations, the theory development in the field of public relations leadership, the combined use of qualitative and quantitative methods to study participation in leadership development process from an international perspective, and multinational corporates' reputation and knowledge management strategies in emerging markets. Her most recent publications appear in *Public Relations Review, Journal of Public Relations Research, Public Relations Journal, Journal of World Business, Journal of Promotion Management, Journal of Communication Management, China Media Research,* and *Social Science Journal*. She teaches PR courses at both undergraduate and graduate levels at the University of Georgia.

Liz Merlot (PhD, Monash University) is Senior Research Assistant to Professor Leitch at the Swinburne University of Technology in Melbourne, Australia. Merlot has published in the *International Journal of Human Resource Development Management* and *The International Journal of Human Resource Management*. Her research has focused on strategic international human resource management, international nongovernmental organizations, the experience of higher degree research students, and more recently, issues around productivity, science policy, and discourse.

Rahul Mitra (MA, Bowling Green State University) is a doctoral candidate and Alan H. Monroe Graduate Scholar at the Brian Lamb School of Communication, Purdue University. His research has been published in the *Public Relations Review*, *Journal of Business Ethics*, *Journal of Business Communication*, *Journal of International and Intercultural Communication*, *Journal of Research Practice*, *Communication, Culture & Critique*, *Journal of Broadcasting & Electronic Media*, and *Journal of Communication Inquiry*. Mitra serves as the student board member of the International Communication Association.

Juan-Carlos Molleda (PhD, University of South Carolina) is Professor and Director of Global Strategic Communication of the Department of Public Relations, University of Florida's College of Journalism and Communications. He is a founding member of the Institute for Public Relations' Commission on Global Public Relations Research, 2012–2013 chair of the International Communication Association's Public Relations Division, and coordinator of the PR Landscape Project of the Global Alliance for Public Relations and Communication Management. Molleda's research interests are in global corporate public relations; professionalism and social roles in Latin America; transnational crises; and the interplay among identity,

authenticity, and reputation in a strategic communication environment.

Judy Motion (PhD, University of Waikato) is a member of the Journalism and Media Research Centre at the University of New South Wales (UNSW), Sydney, Australia. Professor Motion has written extensively on the power of public relations, public engagement processes, and branding. Funded research grants include leadership of a New Zealand research project titled "Socially and Culturally Sustainable Biotechnology" and membership of research projects titled "Building our Productivity: Understanding Sustainable Collective Productivity" and "National Demonstration Education and Engagement Program." Professor Motion's work has been published in numerous journals including *Public Relations Review*, *Journal of Public Relations Research*, *Media, Culture & Society*, *Organization Studies*, *Journal of Business Research*, *European Journal of Marketing*, *Public Understanding of Science*, and *Political Communication*. She has contributed chapters to the *SAGE Handbook of Public Relations*, *The Global Handbook of Public Relations*, and *The Encyclopedia of Public Relations*.

Priscilla Murphy (PhD, Brown University) is Professor Emerita of Strategic Communication at Temple University in Philadelphia, Pennsylvania. Her work has appeared in the *Journal of Public Relations Research*; *Public Relations Review*; *Chinese Journal of Communication*; *International Communication Gazette*; *Health Communication, Science, Technology & Human Values*; *Science Communication*; *Journal of Communication Management*; *Canadian Journal of Communication*; and *Journal of Applied Communication Research*. She is coauthor, with Dawn R. Gilpin, of *Crisis Management in a Complex World* (Oxford University Press, 2008). She has served on the editorial board of the *Journal of Public Relations Research*, *Public Relations Review*, *International Journal of Strategic Communication*, and *Communication Quarterly*.

James S. O'Rourke (PhD, Syracuse University) teaches management and corporate communication at the University of Notre Dame, where he is a teaching professor of management and the Arthur F. and Mary J. O'Neil Director of the Eugene D. Fanning Center for Business Communication. He is the author of numerous books, including *Management Communication: A Case Analysis Approach*, now in its fifth edition from Prentice-Hall, as well as *The Truth about Confident Presenting* from the Financial Times, and *Effective Communication* from Dorling Kindersley. He is the principal author or directing editor of more than 250 management and corporate communication case studies. O'Rourke is a trustee of both the Arthur W. Page Society and the Institute for Public Relations. He is a member of the Reputation Institute, and the Management Communication Association, and a regular consultant to *Fortune* 500 and midsize businesses throughout North America.

Josef Pallas (PhD, Uppsala University) is lecturer and researcher in the Department of Business Studies and the Department of Informatics and Media at Uppsala University. His research focuses mainly on the increased mediatization of the Western economy and the implications this has for the way modern organizations are governed. He is coauthor and coeditor of a number of books/book chapters as well as of journal articles and reports dealing with the topics of mediatization, corporate communications, and corporate governance.

Justin E. Pettigrew (MA, University of Georgia) is a former communications executive with 12 years of experience in both corporate and agency public relations. His corporate experience includes work for Turner Broadcasting Inc., The Weather Channel, The Travel Channel, and Landmark Communications. His work at Hill & Knowlton, Inc., a leading international communications consultancy, included clients such as Dornier Medical Systems, Inc., The Smithsonian Museum, Johnson & Johnson, and HP China. His research has been published in the *Journal of Public Relations Research* and *Public Relations Review*. He is currently a doctoral student in the Grady College of Journal-

ism and Mass Communication at the University of Georgia.

Magda Pieczka (PhD, Stirling University) is reader in public relations at Queen Margaret University in Edinburgh, Scotland. She is a joint coordinator of the QMUCentre for Dialogue. Magda's research interests are focused on professionalization of public relations and, more broadly, communication management. She has written about public relations theory, PR consultancy industry in the United Kingdom, professional narratives in public relations, as well as the use of dialog and deliberation in science communication and public policy making. Magda is a coeditor of *Journal of Communication Management*, European editor of *Public Relations Inquiry*, and a member of the editorial board of *Journal of Public Relations Research*.

Matthew W. Ragas (PhD, University of Florida) is an Assistant Professor of Public Relations in the College of Communication at DePaul University in Chicago. His research has been published in *Journalism & Mass Communication Quarterly*, *Mass Communication & Society*, *Public Relations Review*, *International Journal of Strategic Communication*, and *Web Journal of Mass Communication Research*. Ragas is a recipient of the Nafziger-White-Salwen Dissertation Award from the Association for Education in Journalism and Mass Communication.

Bryan H. Reber (PhD, University of Missouri, Columbia) is Associate Professor in the Department of Advertising and Public Relations, Grady College of Journalism and Mass Communication, at the University of Georgia. His research has been published in the *International Journal of Strategic Communication*, *Journal of Advertising Education*, *Journal of Broadcasting and Electronic Media*, *Journal of Communication Management*, *Journal of Public Relations Research*, *Journalism and Mass Communication Quarterly*, and *Public Relations Review*. He is the coauthor of *Gaining Influence in Public Relations: The Role* *of Resistance in Practice*, *THINK Public Relations 2e*, and *Public Relations Writing and Media Techniques 7e*. He serves on the editorial board of the *Journal of Public Relations Research*.

Robyn Remke (PhD, Purdue University) is an Associate Professor in the Department of Intercultural Communication and Management and the codirector of the EngAGE (Engaged, Applied, Global Education) Program at the Copenhagen Business School. Motivated by questions of social and organizational injustice and discrimination, her research uses a critical/feminist lens to explore the gendered nature of organizations and organizing. Her research focuses on the ways in which organizational members embody organizational practices such as leadership, diversity management programs, and parental leave policies through communication. In addition, she studies alternative forms of workplace organizational structures and gendered identity in the workplace. Robyn has published journal articles in *Communication Studies* and *Communication Monographs*, and is a coauthor of several book chapters on leadership and dissent, applied communication, and diversity. Robyn is also the president of the Organization for the Study of Communication, Language & Gender.

Nora J. Rifon (PhD, City University of New York) is a Professor in the Department of Advertising, Public Relations & Retailing at Michigan State University, and director of the Children's Central Research Collaborative. Professor Rifon uses cognitive processing paradigms to study consumer response to marketing communications. Her work focuses on cause-related sponsorships, the effectiveness of celebrity endorsers, consumer online privacy, food marketing, and public policy. Her research has been published in marketing, advertising, communication, computer science, and public policy journals, and has been funded by the National Science Foundation, the National Institutes of Health, Microsoft Research, and other foundations. She has served as consultant to industry and government including the Michigan Attorney General's Office and

the Department of Information Technology. Professor Rifon recently edited a special issue of *The Journal of Advertising* and serves on several editorial review boards. She lives in Okemos, Michigan, with her daughter Zoe.

Stefania Romenti (PhD, IULM University) is an Assistant Professor of Public Relations and Corporate Communication at IULM University (Milan, Italy) and Vice-Director of the Executive Master in Corporate Public Relations (IULM University). She teaches public relations at IULM University. She is also part of the teaching research commission of the PhD program on corporate communication at IULM University. Dr. Romenti centers her research on strategic communication, the influence of communication on corporate reputation, stakeholder management and engagement, dialogue, social media, measurement and evaluation. She published various academic articles in international journals on previous themes for *International Journal of Strategic Communication*, *Journal of Communication Management*, *Corporate Communication: an International Journal*, *Public Relations Review*, *Sloan Management Review*. She works as reviewer for the international journals *Corporate Communication: an International Journal* (Emerald) and *International Journal of Strategic Communication*, as well as for international conferences such as Euprera Annual Congress and The Annual Conference on Public Relations History.

Friederike Schultz (PhD, Free University, Berlin) is Assistant Professor in Organizational Communication and New Media at the Department for Communication Science at Free University of Amsterdam. She did her PhD (Dr.) at Free University Berlin and has been working as visiting scholar, lecturer, and assistant at several Europen universities (Cambridge, St. Gallen, Nottingham, Moscow). Her research has been published in the *Journal of Management Studies*, *Public Relations Review*, and *Corporate Communication: An International Journal*. She serves on the editorial board of *Corporate Communications: An International Journal* (CCIJ) and is coeditor of the Special

Issue on CSR Communication in CCIJ in 2012 and a Special Issue on Responsible Business in the Blogosphere in *Journal of Business Ethics*. Schultz is the Secretary of the International Communication Association's Public Relations division.

Craig R. Scott (PhD, Arizona State University) is an Associate Professor of Communication in the School of Communication & Information at Rutgers University. His research examines anonymity and identification in organizational and mediated communication contexts. His work related to anonymous communication specifically has been published in *Communication Theory, Management Communication Quarterly, Journal of Computer-Mediated Communication, Journal of Applied Communication Research, Communication Yearbook, Western Journal of Communication, Communication Quarterly*, and *Free Speech Yearbook*. Portions of this chapter are drawn from his forthcoming book *Anonymous Agencies, Backstreet Businesses, and Covert Collectives: Rethinking Organizations in the 21st Century* (Stanford University Press). Scott is vice chair of the Organizational Communication Division of the International Communication Association and is also a member of the National Communication Association and the Academy of Management.

Timothy L. Sellnow (PhD, Wayne State University) is Professor of Communication and Associate Dean for graduate programs in communication at the University of Kentucky. His primary research and teaching focus is on risk and crisis communication. Much of his recent research focuses on strategic communication for mitigating the impact of and maintaining resilience in response to potential terrorist attacks in the United States. He has coauthored four books and published many refereed journal articles focusing on strategies for effective risk and crisis communication. He currently serves as theme leader for the risk communication research team at the National Center for Food Protection and Defense, a Center of Excellence sponsored by the Department of Homeland

Security. He has also served on several occasions as a risk and crisis communication consultant for the Centers for Disease Control and Prevention.

Karen Smreker (MA, Michigan State University) a second year student in the Media and Information Studies Doctoral program at Michigan State University. She received a small grant from MSU's Children's Central, in conjunction with Michigan's Children's Trust Fund, to conduct research on cyberbullying. Last year, she was a research assistant on a grant funded by the National Institute of Health examining Advergames influence on children. She is now working as a teaching assistant and hopes to receive her PhD in Public Relations in 2014. Karen currently resides in East Lansing.

Peter M. Smudde (PhD, Wayne State University) is APR and Associate Professor of communication and public relations program coordinator at Illinois State University. He has published the books *Public Relations as Dramatistic Organizing* (2011) and *Humanistic Critique of Education* (2010). He has also published many articles, several with coauthor Dr. Jeffrey L. Courtright. With Dr. Courtright, he has published the books *Inspiring Cooperation and Celebrating Organizations* (2012) and *Power and Public Relations* (2007). His industry experience includes leading, planning, writing, editing, and evaluating a full range of public relations, marketing, executive, and technical communications for companies of various sizes and in many industries. He has held an executive-level position in public relations; worked in corporate, agency, and entrepreneurial enterprises; and has served numerous clients through his own consulting practice.

Don W. Stacks (PhD, University of Florida) has earned numerous academic and professional awards for teaching and research, including "Professor of the Year" and "Provost's Award for Scholarly Activity." His professional recognitions include the "Pathfinder Award" for programmatic research, the "Jackson Jackson and

Wagner Award" for applied research, and the Public Relations Society of America's "Educator of the Year" award. He has received the NCA's PRIDE Award for best textbook of the year twice. His background is based primarily in corporate/governmental public relations and consulting. He has authored or edited numerous books, book chapters, and articles. His most recent works are in the area of public relations measurement and evaluation and include the *Primer of Public Relations Research*, second edition (Guilford Press), the *Dictionary of Public Relations Research, Measurement, and Evaluation* (Institute for Public Relations), and several articles in *Public Relations Journal*.

Cees B.M. van Riel (PhD, Erasmus University) is Professor of Corporate Communication at the Rotterdam School of Management/ Erasmus University and is the vice chairman and cofounder of the Reputation Institute. Cees van Riel has published articles in *Academy of Management Journal, Long Range Planning, Journal of Management Studies*, and *Journal of Marketing*, and 10 books. His best known books are *Principles of Corporate Communication* (1996), *Fame & Fortune* (2004), and *Essentials of Corporate Communication* (2006). His most recent book is *The Alignment Factor. Leveraging Total Stakeholder Support* (2012), was published in four different languages.

Sarah VanSlette (PhD, Purdue University) is an Assistant Professor in the Department of Speech Communication at Southern Illinois University Edwardsville. VanSlette's research focuses on "communication of controversy" or "problematic PR," and she approaches her study of public relations and strategic communication from a rhetorical perspective.

Richard J. Varey (PhD, Manchester School of Management) is Professor of Marketing at The Waikato Management School, University of Waikato, New Zealand. His scholarly project is "Marketing in and for sustainable society," including Society and Marketing, Relationship Marketing, and 21st Century Marketing Inter-

action. He coedited (with Professor Barbara Lewis) *Internal Marketing: Directions for Management* (Routledge, 2000) and authored *Marketing Communication: Principles and Practice* (Routledge, 2002) and *Relationship Marketing: Dialogue and Networks in the E-Commerce Era* (Wiley, 2002). He has published conceptual and review articles widely in international research journals. He is an editorial board member for a number of specialist journals and associate editor (Asia-Pacific) of the *Journal of Customer Behaviour* and founding member of the Editorial Advisory Board and Book Reviews Editor for *Social Business*. He is a member of the expert panel of TechCast, the virtual technology forecasting think tank.

Shari R. Veil (PhD, North Dakota State University) is Director of the Division of Risk Sciences and Assistant Professor of Communication at the University of Kentucky where she coordinates research, funding, education, and training programs specific to risk and crisis communication and teaches courses in risk and crisis, organizational, and mass communication. Her research interests include organizational learning in high-risk environments, community preparedness, and communication strategies for crisis management. Her research has been funded by the United States Department of Agriculture, the Environmental Protection Agency, and the Department of Homeland Security's National Center for Food Protection and Defense and National Center for Risk and Economic Analysis of Terrorism Events.

Damion Waymer (PhD, Purdue University) is an Assistant Professor in the Department of Communication at Virginia Tech, where he teaches public relations, issues management, public relations campaigns, and organizational communication. His research uses issues management, public relations theory, and organizational rhetoric to explore issues of diversity in general and issues of race, class, and gender specifically. Representative works have been published in outlets such as the *Journal of Applied Communication Research, Management*

Communication Quarterly, Public Relations Review, Journal of Public Relations Research, Communication Quarterly, and *Journal of Communication Inquiry.*

Jungeun Yang (PhD, Ewha Womans University, 2012) is a lecturer and researcher for School of Communication at Ewha Womans University. Her research focuses on the influence of culture on Koreans' communication, especially in the context of conflict resolution. Also, she worked as a public relations practitioner at InComm Brodeur. Her publications include "The influence of Chemyon on facework and conflict styles," "The impact of cultural variables and third-party mediation on conflict resolution," and "The effect of cultural predictors on perceived ethicality of negotiation behavior."

Sung-Un Yang (PhD, University of Maryland) is Associate Professor at School of Journalism, Indiana University Bloomington. Dr. Yang's research focuses on organization–public relationship management; organization/country reputation management; and social media and communication effectiveness. Dr. Yang authored or coauthored numerous articles in leading refereed journals including *Communi-* *cation Research, Journal of Public Relations Research, Public Relations Review, Corporate Reputation Review, Journal of Communication Management, Public Relations Journal, Higher Education,* and *Journal of Marketing in Higher Education,* among others.

Theodore E. Zorn (PhD, University of Kentucky) is Pro Vice-Chancellor and Dean of the College of Business at Massey University in New Zealand. His teaching and research interests are organizational change processes, especially change-related communication and change discourses. Ted is the chair of the Organizational Communication Division of the International Communication Association (ICA), past editor of *Management Communication Quarterly,* and the 2006 recipient of ICA's Frederic Jablin Award for Outstanding Contribution to Organizational Communication. He has published more than 80 books, articles, and chapters, including recent articles in *Human Communication Research, Communication Yearbook, Public Understanding of Science, Journal of Applied Communication Research, Management Communication Quarterly, New Media & Society,* and *Media, Culture & Society.* He is also coauthor of the textbook *Organizational Communication in an Age of Globalization,* now in its second edition.

Acknowledgments

What an exciting project this was! It all started with a short meeting with Wiley-Blackwell senior editor Elizabeth Swayze in Singapore when we were at the annual meeting of the International Communication Association. Elizabeth demonstrated a perceptive ear and eye and immediately saw the value in the project.

The people writing the chapters for this project made this handbook such a valuable contribution to the field. With 36 hours of meeting with Elizabeth, most of the contributors of this book, who were present at the conference, signed on. They are dedicated scholars, kind and compassionate people, and fun people to be around. I appreciate their belief in the project, the speed at which they said yes to participating, the work they did, and their flexibility, patience, and accommodation they demonstrated in bringing this project to fruition. I also appreciate the eleventh hour contributors who helped round out our book to make it complete and an even stronger collection of essays. That they came through under such compressed time has my deepest respect and appreciation.

Each and every member of this handbook has earned a special place in my heart. They deserve to be mentioned by name. They are, in order of chapters Cees van Riel, Sherry Holladay, Robyn Remke, Nora Rifon, Karen Smreker, Sookyong Kim, Peggy Brønn, Judy Motion, Sally Davenport, Shirley Leitch, Liz Merlot, James O'Rourke IV, Anne Gregory, Clarke Caywood, Richard Varey, Susan Westcott Alessandri, Karla Gower, Mattew Ragas, Priscilla Murphy, Dawn Gilpin, Stefani Romenti, Laura Illia, Jeong-Nam Kim, Chun-ju Flora Hung-Baesecke, Sung-Un Yang, Jim Grunig, William Benoit, John Lammers, Kristen Guth, Timothy Sellnow, Shari Veil, Kathryn Anthony, Øyvind Ihlen, Timothy Coombs, Vilma Luoma-aho, Sabine Einwiller, Juan Meng, Bruce Berger, Hua Jiang, Justin Pettigrew, Bryan Reber, Pan Ji, Paul Lieber, Friederike Schultz, Alexander Laskin, Bob Heath, Peter Smudde, Jeffrey L. Courtright, Jarol Manheim, Alex Holt, Juan-Carlos Molleda, Rajul Jain, Esben Karmark, Robert Kerr, Damion Waymer, *Sarah VanSlette*, Rahul Mitra, Mohan Dutta, Robert Green, Tina McCorkindale, Marcia DiStaso, Magda Pieczka, Ted Zorn, Jennifer Bartlett, Josef Pallas, Magnus Frostenson, Craig Scott, Don Stacks, Melissa Dodd, Linjuan Rita Men, Yung-wook Kim, and Jungeun Yang.

In addition to Elizabeth, Julia Kirk's time, energy, responsiveness, gentleness, and attention to detail helped bring this volume together. Caitlin Selle served as an editorial assistant and provided diligence, conscientiousness, focus, speed, and responsiveness making the coordination and orchestration of such a large global project an expedited and pleasurable one! She has a bright future ahead of her. Aileen Castell and Wesley Weed provided attention to detail and a close reading of the text, helping to make it a stronger volume.

At New York University's Stern School of Business, Irv Schenkler has been a fantastic host and colleague. I'm grateful for Irv making the time, space, and resources available for me to concentrate on this handbook. At the Reputation Institute, I am grateful to Charles Fombrun, Seth Kerker and Cees van Riel.

I am blessed by a number of mentors who have shaped me in various ways over the years: George Cheney, Rod Hart, Cees van Riel, Charles Fombrun, Stephen Greyser, Felix Gutierrez, Max McCombs, Donald Shaw and Lamar Reinsch. Twenty years later, Buddy Goodall (who recently passed away) and Eric Eisenberg still inspire me with their original creativity, ingenuity, and most importantly, their friendliness, accessibility, and willingness to engage a young graduate student that first got me started down this path. Sandy Green has been a faithful friend and trusted colleague over the years. He is a constant and daily source of inspiration, radical ideas, and social support. Sandy has my deepest respect for his character, his relentless pursuit of knowledge, wisdom, and excellence, and his devotion to family and friends, and to living a balanced and full life. Nell Huang-Horowitz and Sun Young Lee deserve special mention for their friendship, collaboration, and insights over the years.

In Nashville and New York, I have found a special place and good mixture of thought leaders, experienced professionals, and colleagues: Amber Beckham, Geneva Brignolo, Beth Curley, Julie Davis, Marcia Dawkins, Stan Knott, Heather McDonald, Kay McDowell, Kimberly Pace, Gene Policinski, Bonnie Riechert, Vic Rivera, Irv Schenkler, Amy Seigenthaler, John Seigenthaler, Sr., Debbie Turner, Steve Tippens, Doreen Wade, and Tim Webb for making Nashville, Tennessee, the town I now call home, a joyous place to be. Thank you for your friendship, counsel, example, inspiration, and camaraderie. I am particularly indebted to to Daniel LeBreton from Peter Rock Consulting and Julie Davis for their valuable insights and counsel.

Out-of-town and out-of-the-country sources of support and inspiration deserving special mention during the completion of this project include Alan Kelly, Reid Walker, Sixtus Oechsle, Stephen Greyser, Elliot Schreiber, Rod Hart, Donald Shaw, Laura Illia, Friederike Schultz, Sabine Einwiller, Peter Kowalski, and Spiro Kiousis.

And finally, to mom, dad, and the fam. In the words of poet Gary Morris, "We may no longer live in the same house, but you're always in my heart." Thank you for home.

Corporate Reputation and the Multi-Disciplinary Field of Communication

Craig E. Carroll
New York University, USA

Corporate reputation's development as a concept has been an interesting one to follow. Compared to most other communication concepts I am familiar with, it is one whose entry into the field began around the same time I was preparing to begin graduate work. Most of the other concepts I have enjoyed thinking about (organizational identity and identification, for instance) have rich histories with scholars and research that predate my time in the field.

When I was in high school and college, I enjoyed reading business histories and business reference books on organizational leadership and the best companies to work for. Peters and Waterman's (1982) *In Search of Excellence* and Deal and Kennedy's (1982) *Corporate Culture* were some of the early ones, and they happened to lead me into the study of organizational communication as an undergraduate. I also read various reference books on the best companies to work for so I could know where to look when pursuing summer internships, and I was fascinated by biographies written by company founders, entrepreneurs, and CEOs. Later in my career, I had the opportunity to work with business historian and entrepreneur Gary Hoover, founder of Hoover's, Inc., in Austin, Texas, moving volumes of his business reference books online to the Internet and creating a searchable database of corporate histories that was updated on a daily basis.

The business books I read as an undergraduate were generally about topics other than corporate reputation, and I read them for other purposes: to learn about how to create visionary leadership, organizational excellence, and competitive corporate cultures, or simply how to get a job or an internship at one of these great companies. In these volumes, well-known companies and *un*known companies were heralded in the anecdotes as case studies illustrating leadership, excellence, innovation, and employee and customer satisfaction. And with just one such mention, unknown companies were turned into corporate celebrities, offering best practices for wannabe entrepreneurs to master and held up as exemplars in textbooks for undergraduates in business, marketing, and communication who wanted to learn how to manage or communicate better. The focus, however, was never on the companies themselves, but on what the companies could offer or demonstrate in the way of codifiable knowledge about how things should be done.

Indeed, the companies mentioned, featured, or highlighted in the media during the 1980s

The Handbook of Communication and Corporate Reputation, First Edition. Edited by Craig E. Carroll.
© 2013 John Wiley & Sons, Inc. Published 2015 by John Wiley & Sons, Inc.

were often used as examples to illustrate other points, topics, and ideas of concern: organizational excellence, corporate culture, innovation, or total quality management, for instance. The reputations of these companies (while the companies themselves might have disagreed) were not the focus of the articles or media attention.

In retrospect, these books helped create corporate reputations for the companies involved. Ironically, however, Waterman (1987) wrote later that many of the companies from *In Search of Excellence* were no longer in existence. But they had their heyday – and their reputations – for a time.

And in fact, it was in 1983 when *Fortune* Magazine produced a special topic issue devoted to the "Most Admired Companies of the Year." Deephouse (2000) tells the story of how the special issue was not originally conceived as an annual issue and the methodology used in selecting and rating the firms was not very scientifically rigorous. Once the publication saw the sales of the special issue explode, however, *then* it began to take a more thoughtful, regimented, and methodical approach to the rankings. But scholarly interest in corporate reputation would not arise for several more years.

The scholarly article generally regarded as the tipping point that made corporate reputation a central topic of engagement was Fombrun and Shanley's (1990) investigation of *Fortune*'s Most Admired Companies published in the *Academy of Management Journal* in 1990. Many other disciplines – economics, sociology, psychology, and marketing, for instance – had also engaged the concept, but they did not have the same effect as this management article. Moreover, scholars of corporate social responsibility (CSR) (e.g., Chakravarthy, 1986; Conine and Madden, 1986; McGuire *et al.*, 1988) had also used the *Fortune* ratings. What made the Fombrun and Shanley study different was that the previous studies focused on a single dimension of reputation (CSR) rather than the overall concept, whereas Fombrun and Shanley focused on multiple dimensions of reputation.

The next major development in the scholarly business literature devoted to corporate reputa-

tion studies was Fombrun's (1996) treatise, *Reputation: Realizing Value from the Company Image*, issued by the Harvard Business Press. Many of the ideas still gaining currency today within what is now a field devoted to corporate reputation have their roots in this volume.

The following year saw additional major developments. First, New York University Stern School of Business Professor Charles Fombrun and Erasmus University/Rotterdam School of Management Professor Cees van Riel launched an international and interdisciplinary conference on corporate reputation, identity, and competitiveness made up of scholars from business, management, finance, accounting, marketing, and a number of subfields within the communication discipline.

The conference gave rise to a second development that year, the publication of the academic/ practitioner journal *Corporate Reputation Review*, which has now evolved into a full scholarly journal. In the inaugural issue, Fombrun and van Riel (1997) reviewed six academic business-related disciplines that had paid attention to corporate reputation: economics, strategic management, marketing, organizational behavior, sociology, and accounting. Communication, however, was not among them.

The third development, also that year, was van Riel's (1997) argument that corporate communication, which at the time was viewed as an emerging field, should be responsible for corporate reputation as one of its duties. Van Riel (1995) had previously published *Principles of Corporate Communication*, but it was not until the international corporate reputation conference that management and communication researchers started to commingle.

Clearly, the wave of scholarly attention to corporate reputation can be credited to the business disciplines. The first work on corporate reputation began in public relations in the 1950s (Eells, 1959). Because the practice of public relations itself had such a poor reputation within the scholarly community and the concept of image had a poor image (Avenarius, 1993), the initial thinking on corporate reputation received little traction and was soon buried within the archives as scholars moved on to other endeavors. Indeed, scholars' devoting attention to helping organizations form more favorable images was frowned upon. For many, the concepts of organizational image and corporate reputation were conflated or treated as equivalents. But the separation and distinction of these two concepts (image = unflattering; reputation = more noble) over time enabled scholars to advance work on corporate reputation and scholars have not looked back.

As noted earlier, most of the literature on corporate reputation resides within the business schools, evidenced by the recently released *Oxford Handbook of Corporate Reputation* (Barnett and Pollock, 2012), which discusses scholarly developments from a number of business-related disciplines, including management, sociology, economics, finance, history, marketing, and psychology. The communication discipline is noticeably absent, leaving many central questions about the concept unaddressed. This handbook by Barnett and Pollock may satisfy those who are content with an understanding of corporate reputation from a management or organizational perspective, but for those who want to understand corporate reputation in greater depth, communication perspectives must be included.

Overview

The purpose of the present book is to come to a deeper understanding of corporate reputation – the concept, its antecedents, its dimensions, its consequences, and its measurement, management, and valuation – from the perspective of communication, and then, from multiple disciplinary perspectives found within this field.

This chapter begins by examining corporate reputation from a uniquely communication perspective. The first section defines corporate reputation from a communication perspective, identifies and reviews a number of ways that corporate reputation is conceptualized in practice, and then, using the most basic communication model, draws attention to corporate reputation as an object of communication. Reframing corporate reputation from the perspective of

multiple communication elements (messages, noise, and feedback) helps to more clearly see what communication brings to the study of corporate reputation.

The first section of this handbook introduces and describes what a number of subfields within communication offer for the understanding of corporate reputation. In previous writings, I have outlined the developments and contributions to corporate reputation from a mass communication perspective (Carroll, 2004, 2011). Van Riel (1995, 1997) has made similar contributions from the perspective of corporate communication. Still others (e.g., Hutton *et al.*, 2001) have done so from the perspective of public relations. What is still lacking, however, is a comprehensive view from the perspective of communication, which is itself a wide-ranging field and considered by many still to be multidisciplinary. This is one purpose of this compendium.

Not all disciplines need to study corporate reputation, but corporate reputation scholars would be remiss not to consider the full variety of contributions that the study of communication can make to the phenomenon. We consider a few.

The second section of the book reviews a number of prominent and emerging theories related to communication that deepen our insights into corporate reputation. Some are established, some are recent. The list is not exhaustive.

The third section of the book outlines the various corporate reputation attributes that are typically studied, and then reviews the literature on them for what the field of communication offers. The most commonly studied corporate reputation attributes are covered. The section concludes with a chapter on message design.

The fourth section of the book proposes new directions for corporate reputation research – new domains, unchartered territories.

Finally, the fifth section of the book addresses questions of research methodology, evaluation, and valuation.

The final chapter extracts key points and questions arising from the previous handbook chapters and plots out a research agenda for communication scholars interested in learning more about corporate reputation and offers corporate reputation scholars avenues through which to delve more deeply into communication literature. As much as I would like to claim that this is a definitive volume, at best it could be described as a snapshot of the state of the art of the study of corporate reputation in the field of communication.

Corporate Reputation as an Object of Communication

Corporate reputation as communication messages

Organizations can have multiple types of corporate reputations. The AC⁴ID Reputation Framework (Carroll *et al.*, 2011, p. 467) identifies a number of them:[1]

- The actual reputation ("what we really are") consists of the current attributes of the company, as privately understood by individuals. These may be tacit and unexplored.
- The communicated reputation ("what we say we are"), whether through controllable media (advertising, marketing, public relations, or sponsorships) or uncontrollable media (word of mouth, news reports, commentary, or social media).
- The conceived (or perceived) reputation ("what we are seen to be") is how the company is seen by various constituents.
- The construed reputation ("what we think others see") is top management's view of a(nother) stakeholder's views (e.g., consumers' or customers') of the organization's reputation.
- The covenanted reputation ("what the brand stands for") refers to what the brand promises and the stakeholders expect.
- The ideal reputation ("what we ought to be") consists of the optimum positioning of the organization in its market within a given timeframe.

- The desired reputation ("what we wish to be") is analogous to the ideal reputation, but it resides in the hearts and minds of organizational leaders.

This framework by Carroll *et al.* (2011) illustrates the fundamental role that communication plays in the conceptualizing, messaging, and interpretation of corporate reputation. A *corporate reputation* is broadly defined as a widely circulated, oft-repeated *message* of minimal variation about an organization revealing something about the organization's nature. From an information-transfer perspective, the meaning of the widely shared, oft-repeated message of minimal variation resides with the sender. From a transactional-process perspective, the person or audience receiving the widely circulated, oft-repeated message of minimal variation constructs the meaning. Meanings include the thoughts in the mind of the sender and receiver as well as the interpretations each makes of the other's messages. Thus, as messages with minimal variation, corporate reputations can carry meanings that can vary from person to person or be widely shared and oft-repeated, giving them an air of objectivity. What each of the AC⁴ID corporate reputation types have in common is that they contain messages about "who the organization is," the difference being whether the source is the organization, stakeholders, or third parties and what channel they use. See Table 1.1 for a description.

Not all messages about organizations are about their corporate reputations. The challenge for organizations is to create sufficient communication channels, environments, and opportunities for unobtrusively receiving messages and cues about how their behaviors and policies affect those in their environment – whether from stakeholders, third parties, or research – and then categorizing, cataloging, and then distributing the incoming messages to the appropriate organizational members without creating information overload, so that the messages are appropriately classified as *noise* or *feedback* and appropriate and reasonable organizational learning and growth can occur.

Table 1.1 Corporate reputations as communication messages, noise, and feedback.

Reputation	Description	Source	Message reference	Receiver	Channel	Reputation as
Actual "what we really are"	The impressions, perceptions, and experiences of individuals	Stakeholders	Organization	Stakeholders	Interpersonal Controlled and uncontrolled media	Message Feedback Noise
Communicated "what we say we are"	Through controllable or uncontrollable media	Organization	Organization	Stakeholders Organization	Controlled and uncontrolled media	Message Message Noise
Conceived "what we are seen to be"	How company is seen by various stakeholders	Stakeholders	Organization	Stakeholders Organization	Interpersonal Intrapersonal Research Interpersonal	Feedback Noise Feedback Noise
Construed "what we think others see"	Top management's views of another stakeholder's views	Organization	Stakeholders	Organization	Intrapersonal	Noise
Covenanted "what the brand stands for"	Brand promises stakeholders expect	Stakeholders	Organization	Stakeholders Organization	Intrapersonal Research	Noise Feedback
Ideal "what we ought to be"	Optimum positioning of the organization	Top management	Industry and market research	Top management	Intrapersonal	Feedback
Desired "what we wish to be"	Hearts and minds of organizational leaders	Top management	Top management	Stakeholders Employees	Interpersonal	Message

Note: Carroll *et al.* (2011) examine multiple types of corporate reputation based on Balmer's (Balmer and Greyser, 2002; Balmer *et al.*, 2009) work with organizational identity. The framework by Carroll, Greyser, and Schreiber is augmented here to illustrate the fundamental role that communication plays in the conceptualizing, messaging, and interpretation of corporate reputation and the multiple roles corporate reputation plays in feedback and noise management.

The goal is to move from learning of the messages to learning from the messages while the message source is a nonpublic or latent, and the issue is latent rather than manifest.[2] During this formative stage, the message source may share an issue with an organization but have no self-awareness of how or whether the situation or potential they experience is shared by others. If this public perceives that corrective action is needed and it is not taken by the organization, the public may become either apathetic or aware. If the public becomes aware and perceives that nothing is still done about their message, their message has the potential to be widely publicized often repeated, thus becoming part of the organization's corporate reputation. For this reason, the proper classification of messages as noise or feedback becomes important.

The AC[4]ID Reputation Framework is grounded in the premise that when organizations are aware of these multiple reputations, they can use insights from the field of communication to

- appropriately categorize messages as feedback or noise;
- clarify and reduce the organization's contribution to the noise they, their stakeholders, and third parties experience; and
- more adequately respond to feedback and create organizational learning, growth, and development.

The following two sections examine corporate reputation from the perspective of communication noise and feedback.

Corporate reputations as communication noise

Noise is any stimulus that distracts from a message at hand. Noise affects the receiver's ability to process the message and the sender's ability to be heard. It can block, distort, negate, bias, change, or confuse the meaning of any message. Noise can also be a message itself – a message that interferes with the transmission and attendance to other messages.

When organizational members receive an incoming message, they assess its importance or relevance in light of personal or organizational goals or objectives and the importance of the message for the sender in light of the sender's relationship with the organization. A message may be classified as physical noise if the message does not relate to these goals or if the message is not allocated to the correct person or department. *Physical noise* occurs when stimuli in the environment, such as sight or sound, draws people's attention away from a message. In the example here, the messages of concern are those having nothing to do with organizational goals or objectives. In cases where messages do relate to organizational goals or objectives, semantic noise may still interfere. *Semantic noise* refers to the distractions caused by certain symbols that take our attention away from a message, for example, if the language used has different meanings for the sender and receiver, and thus the message is not given proper attendance. In both cases, the messages may have implications for the organization's reputation if the sender perceives that improper action was taken.

The more common type of noise relating to corporate reputation is psychological noise. *Psychological noise* refers to the distracting messages produced by internal thoughts or feelings that interfere with message attendance. Psychological noise includes preconceived notions, expectations, prejudices, and other ingrained biases that affect one's attendance to messages. Psychological noise limits people's ability to attend to messages because everyone has perceptions of how things are and how they ought to be, including perceptions of what organizations are and how they should be.

There are several examples of corporate reputation that can serve as psychological noise. See Table 1.1. The construed reputation refers to top management's views of another stakeholder's reputation views. This largely intrapersonal message refers to "what we think others see." Likewise, communicated reputation may function as autocommunication where organizational members are also the audiences (Christensen, 1997; Christensen and Cheney,

2000). In both cases, these reputations may serve as noise that leads to the filtering, tuning out, or disconfirming of incongruent incoming messages from stakeholders, which leads to organizational neglect or defensiveness and a misallocation of resources in response (Dukerich and Carter, 2000).

On the other hand, stakeholders have their own views of corporate reputation that serve as noise. For example, the covenanted reputation – the brand promises stakeholders expect – serves as an intrapersonal message stakeholders hear when they are processing the firm's actual or conceived reputations from other stakeholders, the communicated reputation from the organization, and the desired reputation from top management. If audience members consider the conceived reputation of the organization to be controversial or not to coincide with their beliefs as to what the organization should be about (the covenanted reputation), the noise produced will have a large bearing on whether they will listen effectively to the organization's communicated reputation. Moreover, listeners may unknowingly use selective hearing and selective retention to screen out statements that contradict their preconceived ideas about the organization and selectively attend only to those messages that reinforce their preconceived notions. This in turn further alters the organization's actual reputation, the impressions, perceptions, and experiences of individuals.

In addition, organizations can also think of their reputations as *secondhand noise*. Secondhand noise is put into the environment by others who are not involved in the communication exchange, and it affects other audiences and publics without the organization's or their public's consent. In this sense, second noise is like secondhand smoke, having negative impacts on people without anyone's consent. Those putting forward their views in public may be disregarding the rights of others and claiming rights that may not be theirs to claim.

In sum, the challenge for organizations is to appropriately categorize messages as feedback or noise and to clarify and reduce the organization's contribution to the noise that they, their stakeholders, and third parties experience. The next section focuses on corporate reputation as feedback.

Corporate reputation as communication feedback

Feedback contains information about the value or influence of a particular message for an organization or its stakeholders. Feedback messages reveal how others view an organization's past and present behavior or performance, not the future. Feedback may be shared with an organization or with other stakeholders.

Feedback is critical for organizational learning, growth, and development, but it should be *for* learning, not just *of* learning. For organizations to improve their performance, they have to break the "doing" by considering what is working and what is not. Feedback is usually about the gap between an actual level and some reference level. Feedback helps the organization adjust its current and future behavior to improve organizational performance, decision making, communication, and public relationships, and in the end, increase its likelihood of survival.

When organizations treat messages as feedback, the organization is provided with information about how its identities, messages, actions, or policies are received, often deviating from the intentions of the organization. Deviation is not inherently bad. Argyris and Schon (1978) describe *deviation-counteracting feedback* as that which enlightens organizations to pursue, continue, or adhere to an established message, action, policy, or strategy that is in line with public norms and expectations. In such a case, organizations continue ahead.

On the other hand, *deviation-amplifying feedback* encourages the organization to *better explain* its messages, actions, policies, and strategies, or to *consider and pursue corrective alternatives*, thereby bringing the organization in line with public norms and expectations. Organizations should care about these feedback loops, because the feedback has the potential to *become* their reputations if organizations do not respond at all, if they do not explain themselves adequately, or they do not pursue corrective alternatives.

Examples of corporate reputation that serve as feedback for an organization are the conceived, covenanted, and ideal reputations. See Table 1.1. The conceived reputation tells organizations how they are currently seen by their various stakeholders, while the covenanted reputation tells organizations what stakeholders expect. These forms of feedback are usually arrived at by stakeholder research. On the other hand, the organization's ideal reputation is based on feedback from financial analysts, consultants, regulatory and legislative entities. This feedback comes from in-depth interviews, archival research, competitive intelligence, and so on, which helps determine the optimum positioning of the organization.

Feedback provides meaningful information to more than just the focal organization. Stakeholders regularly incorporate feedback from other stakeholders into their views of organizations, and this is not without consequence. For instance, third parties with no organizational relationship history use reputational feedback to decide whether they *want* a relationship. Those with existing organizational relationships use reputation as feedback to authenticate and validate their own relationships with the organization. Then finally, third parties such as regulatory or legislative entities may also use public feedback to decide how and when to penalize organizations through financial penalties, monitoring, compliance programs, regulation, legislation, or investigations. Employees may experience turnover, while activists and consumer groups may recommend protests or boycotts.

Organizations face several challenges when it comes to incorporating feedback. They must create an accessible and available climate where messages can be received unobtrusively, without altering their intended meaning, and without resulting in information overload. Moreover, organizations should strive to incorporate feedback in an open, observable, and timely way while it is at the latent stage and strive to avoid creating publics galvanized around the feedback.

Reputation as feedback or noise

The last major observation to make in this section is that messages about corporate reputation can be either feedback or noise, depending on the choice the receiver makes, whether the receiver is the organization or a stakeholder group. When stakeholders read or hear about an organization's actual reputation from other stakeholders in controlled or uncontrolled media, they choose whether to view the message as noise or feedback. Likewise, when organizations hear from stakeholders about how the company is seen, they too may decide whether the messages are noise or feedback. If the messages come from research, organizations are likely to view the messages as feedback. On the other hand, if the messages are informal and unsolicited, organizations may view the messages as noise to their own peril. Lastly, failing to give organizations feedback sends a nonverbal signal itself. It leads to mixed messages, false assessment by observers, confusion, and lack of trust.

In sum, organizations also need to be aware of the impact that messages have for corporate reputation. They must appropriately categorize messages as feedback or noise; clarify and reduce the organization's contribution to the noise that they, their stakeholders, and third parties experience; and more adequately respond to feedback so as to create organizational learning, growth, and development.

Understanding how to manage corporate reputation as noise and feedback, as well as having effective strategies and techniques for dealing with noise and feedback, can help organizations improve their communication, relationships, and reputations.

The rest of the volume

The first section of this handbook introduces and describes what a number of subfields within communication offer for the understanding of corporate reputation. In Chapter 2, Cees B.M. van Riel examines public opinion. In Chapter 3, Sherry J. Holladay examines interpersonal communication. In Chapter 4, Robyn Remke examines organizational communication. In Chapter 5, Nora J. Rifon, Karen Smreker, and Sookyong Kim examine advertising. In Chapter 6, Peggy Simcic Brønn examines corporate communication. In Chapter 7, Judy Motion, Sally Davenport, Shirley Leitch, and Liz Merlot examine public relations. In Chapter 8, James O'Rourke IV examines management communication. In Chapter 9, Anne Gregory examines communication management. In Chapter 10, Clarke L. Caywood examines integrated marketing communications. In Chapter 11, Richard Varey examines marketing communication. In Chapter 12, I examine journalism and mass communication. In Chapter 13, Susan Westcott Alessandri examines visual communication. In Chapter 14, Karla K. Gower examines corporate communication law.

In Section 2, "Theoretical Perspectives," Matthew W. Ragas examines agenda-building and agenda-setting theory in Chapter 15. In Chapter 16, Priscilla Murphy and Dawn R. Gilpin examine complexity theory. In Chapter 17, Stefania Romenti and Laura Illia communicatively constituted organization theory. In Chapter 18, Jeong-Nam Kim, Chun-ju Flora Hung-Baesecke, Sung-Un Yang, and James E. Grunig examine the research heritage of the excellence theory. In Chapter 19, William Benoit examines image repair theory. In Chapter 20, John C. Lammers and Kristen Guth examine institutionalization theory. In Chapter 21, Timothy L. Sellnow, Shari R. Veil, and Kathryn Anthony examine organizational learning. In Chapter 22, Øyvind Ihlen examines rhetorical theory. In Chapter 23, W. Timothy Coombs examines the situational theory of crisis. Then finally, in Chapter 24, Vilma Luoma-aho examines the theory of social capital.

In Section 3, "Attributes of Reputation," starting with Chapter 25, Sabine Einwiller introduces the section on corporate attributes and associations. In Chapter 26, Juan Meng and Bruce K. Berger examine executive leadership. In Chapter 27, Hua Jiang examines workplace environment. In Chapter 28, Justin Pettigrew and Bryan H. Reber examine corporate governance. In Chapter 29, Pan Ji and Paul S. Lieber examine products and services.

In Chapter 30, Friederike Schultz examines corporate social responsibility. In Chapter 31, Alexander V. Laskin examines financial performance. In Chapter 32, Robert L. Heath examines issue management and risk management. In Chapter 33, Peter M. Smudde and Jeffrey L. Courtright round out the section by examining the issues of message design.

In Section 4, "Contexts of Reputation," starting with Chapter 34, Jarol B. Manheim and Alex D. Holt examine activism. In Chapter 35, Juan-Carlos Molleda and Rajul Jain examine organizational identity and authenticity. In Chapter 36, Esben Karmark examines corporate branding. In Chapter 37, Robert Kerr examines corporate speech. In Chapter 38, Damion Waymer and Sarah VanSlette examine organizational diversity. In Chapter 39, Rahul Mitra, Mohan J. Dutta, and Robert J. Green examine emerging markets. In Chapter 40, Tina McCorkindale and Marcia W. DiStaso examine social media. In Chapter 41, Magda Pieczka and Theodore E. Zorn examine corporate reputation as a management fad. In Chapter 42, Jennifer L. Bartlett, Josef Pallas, and Magnus Frostenson link corporate reputation to legitimacy by examining accreditation and rankings. Then finally, in Chapter 43, Craig R. Scott examines how hidden organizations deal with corporate reputation.

In Section 5, "Communication Research and Evaluation," starting with Chapter 44, Don W. Stacks, Melissa D. Dodd, and Linjuan Rita Men examine measurement and evaluation. Then in Chapter 45, Yungwook Kim and Jungeun Yang examine corporate reputation's link to return on investment (ROI). Finally, in Chapter 46, I outline a research agenda for future communication research in corporate reputation studies.

Notes

1 This framework is based on Balmer's (Balmer and Greyser, 2002; Balmer *et al.*, 2009) work on multiple identities.
2 See Grunig and Hunt (1984) for their description of the stages of developments for publics: non-public, latent, apathetic, aware, and active.

References

Argyris, C. and Schon, D.A. (1978) *Organizational Learning: A Theory of Action Perspective*. Reading, MA: Addison-Wesley.

Avenarius, H. (1993) Introduction: Image and public relations practice. *Journal of Public Relations Research*, 5(2), 65–70.

Balmer, J.M.T. and Greyser, S.A. (2002) Managing the multiple identities of the corporation. *California Management Review*, 44(3), 72–86.

Balmer, J.M.T., Stuart, H., and Greyser, S.A. (2009) Aligning identity and strategy: Corporate branding at British Airways in the late 20th century. *California Management Review*, 51(3), 6–23.

Barnett, M.L. and Pollock, T.G. (2012) *The Oxford Handbook of Corporate Reputation*. Oxford, UK: Oxford University Press.

Carroll, C.E. (2004) *How the mass media influence perceptions of corporate reputation: Exploring agenda-setting effects within business news coverage*. Unpublished doctoral dissertation, The University of Texas at Austin, Austin, TX.

Carroll, C.E. (2011) *Corporate Reputation and the News Media: Agenda-Setting within Business News in Developed, Emerging, and Frontier Markets*. New York: Routledge.

Carroll, C.E., Greyser, S.A., and Schreiber, E. (2011) Building and maintaining reputation through communications. In C. Caywood (ed.), *The International Handbook of Strategic Public Relations & Integrated Communications*. New York: McGraw-Hill, pp. 457–476.

Chakravarthy, B.S. (1986) Measuring strategic performance. *Strategic Management Journal*, 7, 437–458.

Christensen, L.T. (1997) Marketing as auto-communication. *Consumption, Markets and Culture*, 1(3), 197–227.

Christensen, L.T. and Cheney, G. (2000) Self-absorption and self-seduction in the corporate identity game. In M. Schultz, M.J. Hatch, and M. Larsen (eds), *The Expressive Organization: Linking Identity, Reputation, and the Corporate Brand*. Oxford, UK: Oxford University Press, pp. 246–270.

Conine, T.F. and Madden, G.P. (1986) Corporate social responsibility and investment value. In W.D. Guth (ed.), *Handbook of Business Strategy*. Boston: Warren, Gorham, & Lamont.

Deal, T.E. and Kennedy, A.A. (1982) *Corporate Culture: The Rites and Symbols of Corporate Life*. Harmondsworth: Penguin.

Deephouse, D.L. (2000) Media reputation as a strategic resource: An integration of mass communication and resource-based theories. *Journal of Management*, 26(6), 1091–1112.

Dukerich, J.M. and Carter, S.M. (2000) Distorted images and reputation repair. In M. Schulz, M.J. Hatch, and M.H. Larsen (eds), *The Expressive Organization: Linking Identity, Reputation, and the Corporate Brand*. Oxford, UK: Oxford University Press, pp. 97–112.

Eells, R. (1959) The corporate image in public relations. *California Management Review*, 1(4), 15–23.

Fombrun, C.J. (1996) *Reputation: Realizing Value from the Corporate Image*. Boston: Harvard Business School Press.

Fombrun, C.J. and Shanley, M. (1990) What's in a name? Reputation building and corporate strategy. *Academy of Management Journal*, 33(2), 233–258.

Fombrun, C.J. and van Riel, C.B.M. (1997) The reputational landscape. *Corporate Reputation Review*, 1(1/2), 5–13.

Grunig, J.E. and Hunt, T. (1984) *Managing Public Relations*. Fort Worth, TX: Harcourt Brace & Company.

Hutton, J.G., Goodman, M.B., Alexander, J.B., and Genest, C.M. (2001) Reputation management: The new face of corporate public relations? *Public Relations Review*, 27(3), 247.

McGuire, J.B., Sundgren, A., and Schneweiss, T. (1988) Corporate social responsibility and firm financial performance. *Academy of Management Journal*, 31(4), 854–872.

Peters, T. and Waterman, R. (1982) *In Search of Excellence*. New York: Harper & Row.

van Riel, C.B.M. (1995) *Principles of Corporate Communication*. London: Prentice Hall.

van Riel, C.B.M. (1997) Research in corporate communication: An overview of an emerging field. *Management Communication Quarterly*, 11(2), 288–309.

Waterman, R.H. Jr. (1987) *The Renewal Factor – How the Best Get and Keep the Competitive Edge*. New York: Bantam Books.

Section 1

Communication Disciplines of Reputation

2

Corporate Reputation and the Discipline of Public Opinion

Cees B.M. van Riel

Rotterdam School of Management, Erasmus University, The Netherlands

This chapter examines corporate reputation from the disciplinary perspective of public opinion. The chapter begins with a history of public opinion research, followed by a brief review of theories of public opinion. A brief comparison is made to the concept of reputation, followed by a description of how each stakeholder group has different antecedents.

Introduction

Creating alignment with external stakeholders requires a basic understanding of their beliefs about the organization. This can be achieved by tracking perceptions of those relevant stakeholders, which is essentially the firm's reputation. However, we know from research that the assessment of an individual organization is also impacted by other sets of beliefs, such as product evaluations, industry reputation, and public opinion.

In contrast to reputation, public opinion research is not specifically focused on one organization, but on individuals and organizations that dominate a public opinion debate, such as media and leaders of advocacy groups. Public opinion and reputation research are strongly related. Reputation can be seen as a subset of public opinion. As a consequence,

research in reputation can find many inspiring ideas in public opinion theory. In this chapter, I will present an overview of some key findings in public opinion research that can be used as a source of inspiration in reputation studies. In the next section, I will focus on the concept and the theory on reputation. In the concluding part of this chapter, the similarities and differences between public opinion and reputation will be discussed.

Public opinion: history

Discussions about public opinion can be found in various publications of philosophers such as Locke, prominent in the seventeenth century, who labeled "divine laws, civil laws, and laws of fashion" not very positively, as public opinion (Locke, 1988). Rousseau (1750) was more positive and recognised public opinion as "a

The Handbook of Communication and Corporate Reputation, First Edition. Edited by Craig E. Carroll.
© 2013 John Wiley & Sons, Inc. Published 2015 by John Wiley & Sons, Inc.

tool used by society to force groups (individuals) to become a follower of 'correct' behavior, laws embedded in the hearts of people, not in legal documents." Finally, Alexis de Tocqueville (1969) saw "public opinion as tyranny: it forces people to attune personal opinions to majority views. The more equal people are, the less they tend to believe one group (social powerful people) and the more they tend to support generally accepted opinions." This pressure has impact not only for individuals, but also for the government and other representatives of power.

A boost in public opinion research took place in the middle of the nineteenth century with the launch of the representative survey technique. This quantification of public opinion trends was used in debates about what a government should do or should not do. The next accelerator in the field came in the 1930s, with the creation of the academic journal *Public Opinion Quarterly*, stimulating academics to contribute to the further development of public opinion research. In the opening article of this journal, Allport defined public opinion as "interpretations of topics of national interest that can be expressed freely by individuals outside the government, intended to influence decision making by the dominant powers in a specific society."

According to Allport (1937), people express an opinion because they expect others will confirm their points of view; that is, "You start cleaning the snow in front of your door because you expect others to do the same" (Allport, 1937). Another reason people express opinions publicly is their fear of isolation, a punishment for not joining the dominant stream of social thought. In addition to these individual needs, public opinion is also affected by context factors, more precisely by the influence of a social group on opinion formation such as a family, school, church, work environment, and last but not least, the media (Childs, 1965).

Public opinion: theory

Originally, most authors writing about the effects of mass media on public opinion typified the impact of the press as "a giant hypodermic needle influencing the masses quite easily." However, the assumed power of newspapers, magazines, radio, and television was overestimated, as later studies showed. The dominant belief today is that media are only effective in confirming existing public trends and are not able to change them radically. According to Brouwer (1962), the creation of public opinion works like a mycelium: one sees the upstanding mushrooms – the media – and not the network of roots below the ground. In reputation circles, we call what moves round that network "informal communication." But it is the most important element of the mycelium's survival.

Brouwer stresses that mass media are the most visible and spectacular part of opinion creation. The real driver of opinion creation, though, is informal communication, and the negotiations between members of the public that leads to a dominant opinion. Research of Carroll and McCombs (2003) showed that the impact of media is larger when a medium devotes time and space to an issue. This is the media's so-called agenda-setting function. That is, the more attention is paid to an issue, the higher the likelihood it will become relevant in the minds of the medium's readers or viewers.

Recent research into the impact social media holds over public opinion indicates that such avenues are more powerful than we have assumed in the past (Hunter *et al.*, 2009). A key characteristic of social media is that interest groups that want something specific to happen drive the issues. In the past, pressure groups were forced to depend on attention from conventional media. Now, they communicate directly. And the impact of their interventions increases tremendously when their messages make their way into and are echoed by old-style media like television or newspapers, which still carry influence. Old media give third-party validation to what is appearing in the new media.

The basic principles of the creation and development of public opinion can be found in the so-called spiral of silence theory of Noelle-Neumann (1977). The basic notions of her theory can be summarized as follows:

- Individuals have a strong need to be accepted by the group of which they want to be part, and strongly fear isolation over expressing a point of view that is not aligned with the (perceived) dominant opinion. That is why most people are opinion followers, instead of opinion leaders.
- People who consider their opinion to be part of the dominant logic in society tend to express it loud and clearly, while people who consider their personal view as a minority point of view have a tendency to stay silent.
- Choosing to be part of the silent majority is driven by individual characteristics – the fear of isolation – combined with group pressure, resulting from repeated messaging by the media and peer groups stressing the same dominant opinions while avoiding the minority views.
- This mixture of personal and group characteristics results in the "bandwagon effect" and the spiral of silence mechanism that reduces public discussions of minority topics; as the majority point of view gets more attention, the number of its supporters increases.
- Dominance in public opinion, however, is never forever. If an opponent group is excluded from public debate over a period of time, they will strengthen and sharpen their opinions, and their repression will be eventually followed by a larger degree of popularity, due to the underdog effect. If they persevere, their vision might become the new dominant public opinion. After that, the opinion formation and control process described here repeats again.

Reputation

Reputation derives from the Latin words "re," which means over and over, and "putare," which is calculating. Reputation literally means calculating over and over again the pros and cons of a subject, a person, an organization, or its products. This is a rational process that also holds an emotional component. Reputation is a perception about the degree of admiration, positive feelings, and trust an individual has for another person, an organization, an industry, or even a country.

Reputation is the result of information processes impacted by cues from the organization itself, from peers, media, and last but not least, from personal experience. Assessment of an organization's reputation is rooted in an assessment of the performance of a firm or institution over time, including in the past and with expectations about the future. Reputations only matter in the context of an object with which it is compared. However, reputations are not fixed forever. They tend to be volatile depending on what the organizations do or what happens in the context in which they operate.

Reputation matters, but antecedents differ per stakeholder group

A positive reputation matters greatly, if only because it substantially reduces an organization's costs. There are piles of studies showing that a solid reputation decreases costs in the labor market, since it is easier to attract and retain new employees; that it decreases costs of attracting capital and simplifies finding potential joint venture partners; and last but not least, it lowers the costs of litigation, simply because these types of organizations are trusted more and sued less. An excellent reputation also gives a firm certain advantages with specific stakeholder groups. For example:

Financial Audiences. A good reputation with these stakeholders mitigates financial damage in a stock market crisis. Moreover, having a good corporate reputation positively impacts security analysts' earnings forecasts (Cordeiro and Sambharya, 1997). Future profitability is associated with higher reputation, since evidence has shown that corporate reputation has beneficial implications for future profitability, by helping organizations attain superior performance outcomes (Roberts and Dowling, 1997).

Two types of financial audiences are especially important in reputation-building activities: securities analysts and institutional investors (Roberts and Dowling, 1997). Analysts who study stocks have shown a certain "herd mentality," meaning they are influenced by opinion leaders within their own field of work. Reputation appears to affect investment decisions by institutional and individual investors too. From an organizational perspective, maintaining a good corporate reputation with institutional shareholders is most critical, given the financial power they can exert.

A recent study by Wang *et al.* (2011) provides evidence on the reputation–equity performance relationship. By comparing firms with high and low rankings in a reputation ranking list, as well as with firms not being mentioned in a reputation list, Wang *et al.* found that simply being listed in a reputation ranking increases appreciation for a firm by investors, while a high reputation ranking appears to have an even more positive effect and is a competitive advantage (Wang *et al.*, 2011).

Governments. Building favorable relations with government institutions has a positive payoff as it allows the organization to attain, maintain, or enhance cooperation with public sector institutions (Grunig, 1992). However, data providing "evidence" about the degree to which a sound reputation makes a difference in the public sector are hard to find and mainly anecdotal. The explanation is obvious: civil servants and politicians never admit that they are influenced by excellent reputations, just as they claim to be immune to the whispers and contributions of lobbyists (Fombrun and van Riel, 2004; Grunig and Hunt, 1984).

Customers. A good reputation among consumers increases the likelihood of favorable purchase decisions. Advertising claims about being best in class are credible only if the organization has a good reputation (Goldberg and Hartwick, 1990). A good reputation pays off especially in high-risk purchase situations. In these risk assessments, corporate reputation associations with especially innovation and trustworthiness become more prevalent when evaluating the product,

thereby tipping the scale in favor of purchasing goods from a high-reputation organization (Gürhan-Canli and Batra, 2004; Thompson, 2000).

Companies with a good reputation are also able to charge higher prices and build a customer base that is more loyal, and which buys a broader range of products and services (Eccles *et al.*, 2007). When faced with a new product, the customer will take into account the reputation of the parent behind the brand; if an organization has built a good reputation based on its abilities, this will spill over into positive perceptions of new products offered by that organization (Brown and Dacin, 1997). It must be noted that these effects are likely to be most prevalent when the organization uses a monolithic branding strategy (Berens *et al.*, 2005).

Labor Market. A company's reputation as employer is based on its past actions and jobseekers' expectations of the organization's future behavior (Carmichael, 1984). An organization with a good workplace reputation is seen as having an increased ability to efficiently attract the most talented employees (Chauvin and Guthrie, 1994; Gatewood *et al.*, 1993; Judge and Cable, 1997). In times when there is full employment and ample opportunities for high potential talent, they are more willing to react to recruitment ads from admired organizations (Gatewood *et al.*, 1993). Research has shown that jobseekers are more willing to pursue jobs with organizations that have a reputation for social responsibility (Greening and Turban, 2000). Coldwell *et al.* (2008) posit that a jobseeker builds an opinion of an ethical fit with an organization based on perceptions of the organization's corporate social responsibility-derived reputation. Not only is an organization with a good reputation able to attract a larger number of applicants, but under certain circumstances, it can also even select higher-quality jobseekers (Cable and Turban, 2003). Having a good reputation increases the influx of executives from other blue chip companies.

Hence, companies should safeguard their reputation around employment, because it is likely that a negative reputation will bring trouble in hiring employees in the future (Carmichael, 1984). Formulated more positively, having a reputation of preferred employer will not only positively impact the organization's hiring process, but also have a positive effect on the organization's stock market valuation (Chauvin and Guthrie, 1994).

Nongovernmental Organizations (NGOs). A favorable reputation with NGOs is critical for organizations, especially for those of substance and international scale. Mostly self-appointed watchdog or advocacy groups, NGOs typically operate on charitable donations from foundations and individuals, and focus on issues such as human rights, the environment, certain diseases, child development, and corporate behavior. While a cynic might suggest that a good protest issue is a fine way to raise more funds, these groups play an increasing important and needed role in both local and global societies, often addressing issues that governments overlook and which hold no interest for business. Because their motives appear ethical, NGOs can make life difficult for corporations in their crosshairs. Building cooperative alignments therefore reduces the chance of contentious or hostile interactions.

For example, when Starbucks received criticism from an NGO regarding its coffee purchasing activities, the Seattle-based firm decided to switch to fair trade coffee (Argenti, 2004), rather than fight. Since an NGO may attack an organization's network of customers, financers, insurers, and suppliers, such nonprofits often have surprising power. In some ways, their very existence depends on how frequently and effectively they apply it (Greening and Turban, 2000).

Public opinion and reputation: A comparison

Public opinion can be described as the complex of preferences expressed by a significant number of persons on *issues* of *national interest* that they want the *government* to take care of. Reputation on the other hand can be typified as an overall assessment of an *organization*, predicting support by constituents that depend or want to depend on organizational performance, impacting the license to operate for the firm.

Public opinion research has a long tradition, is rooted in solid philosophical foundations and methodologies, and expressed in interesting theoretical explanations. Nearly all the examples in this chapter described theoretical notions about public opinion can also be used to explain the creation and development of reputation. The consequences of public opinion research for the practice of corporate communication officers are twofold:

1   Organizations should scan carefully those issues that might impact them when crucial groups in society consider a topic in the firm's domain as highly important, and push for actions by a governmental institution aimed at "solving" the perceived problem through legislation.

2   Awareness of the issue is one thing; taking adequate actions is a different challenge. A key point corporate communication managers should take into consideration is avoiding as much as possible, becoming the public's opinion object of irritation. In other words, avoid at all prices that a general trend in public opinion is primarily focused on your own organization, resulting in a reputation problem of gigantic proportion. Consider for example, the negative sentiments about obesity in the Western world as a dominant issue of public opinion. Pressure groups purposely selected McDonald's as the epitome of the problem, a smart choice from their point of view. For McDonald's, not so much. The US government now requires restaurants to publish calorie counts in foods, and while this may not deter anyone from eating two Big Macs and a large serving of french fries, it does reflect negatively on all companies that serve high-calorie meals, broadening the accusations to an industry level.

Conclusions

A key point of differentiation with reputation research is that in public opinion studies, the emphasis lies on the impact of issues on the political decision-making process, including legislation and later litigation. Discussions about public opinion are nearly always focused in the end on governmental decisions. In contrast, discussions about reputations result in a variety of stakeholder demands granting – or limiting – a license to operate to a specific organization. Reputation problems are not easy to solve; however, when organizations are attacked as the main responsible actor for a public opinion issue, and in other words, public opinion merges with an organizational reputation problem, real serious challenges open up for corporate communication managers. Avoiding these situations is clearly crucial.

References

Allport, G.W. (1937) *Personality: A Psychological Interpretation*. New York: Holt, Rinehart and Winston.

Argenti, P.A. (2004) Collaborating with activists: How Starbucks works with NGOs. *California Management Review*, 47, 91–116.

Berens, G.A.J.M., van Riel, C.B.M., and van Bruggen, G.H. (2005) Corporate associations and consumer product responses: The moderating role of corporate brand dominance. *Journal of Marketing*, 69(3), 35–48.

Brouwer, M. (1962) Mass communication and the social sciences: Some neglected areas. *International Social Science Journal*, 14(2), 303–319. (Reprinted in Dexter, A.L. and White, D.M. (eds) (1964) *People Society and Mass Communications*. New York: The Free Press/Collier-Macmillan.)

Brown, T.J. and Dacin, P.A. (1997) The company and the product: Corporate associations and consumer product responses. *Journal of Marketing*, 61(1), 68–84.

Cable, D.M. and Turban, D.B. (2003) The value of organizational image in the recruitment context: A brand equity perspective. *Journal of Applied Social Psychology*, 33, 2244–2266.

Carmichael, H.L. (1984) Reputations in the labor market. *American Economic Review*, 74(4), 713–725.

Carroll, C.E. and McCombs, M. (2003) Agenda-setting effects of business news on the public's images and opinions about major corporations. *Corporate Reputation Review*, 6(1), 36–46.

Chauvin, K.W. and Guthrie, J.P. (1994) Labor market reputation and the value of the firm. *Managerial and Decision Economics*, 15, 543–552.

Childs, H.L. (1965) *Public Opinion: Nature, Formation, and Role*. Princeton, NJ: D. Van Nostrand.

Coldwell, D.A., Billsberry, J., van Meurs, N., and Marsh, P.J.G. (2008) The effects of person-organisation ethical fit on employee attraction and retention: Towards a testable explanatory model. *Journal of Business Ethics*, 78, 611–622.

Cordeiro, J. and Sambharya, R. (1997) Do corporate reputations influence security analyst earnings forecasts? *Corporate Reputation Review*, 1, 94–98.

de Tocqueville, A. (1969) *Democracy in America (1835)*. Garden City, NY: George Lawrence.

Eccles, R.G., Grant, R.M., and van Riel, C.B.M. (2007) Reputation and transparency: Lessons from a painful period in public disclosure. *Long Range Planning*, 69(4), 353–359.

Fombrun, C.J. and van Riel, C.B.M. (2004) *Fame and Fortune. How the World's Top Companies Develop Winning Reputations*. New York: Pearson Publishing and the Financial Times.

Gatewood, R.D., Gowan, M.A., and Lautenschlager, G.J. (1993) Corporate image, recruitment image, and initial job choice decisions. *Academy of Management Journal*, 36(2), 414–427.

Goldberg, M. and Hartwick, J. (1990) The effects of advertising reputation and extremity of advertising claim on advertising effectiveness. *Journal of Consumer Research*, 17(2), 172–179.

Greening, D.W. and Turban, D.B. (2000) Corporate social performance as a competitive advantage in attracting a quality workforce. *Business and Society*, 39, 254–280.

Grunig, J.E. (ed.) (1992) *Excellence in Public Relations and Communication Management*. Hillsdale, NJ: Lawrence Erlbaum Associates.

Grunig, J.E. and Hunt, T. (1984) *Managing Public Relations*. New York: Holt, Rinehart and Winston.

Gürhan-Canli, Z. and Batra, R. (2004) When corporate image affects product evaluations: The moderating role of perceived risk. *Journal of Marketing Research*, 41(May), 197–205.

Hunter, M.L., van Wassenhove, L.N., and Besiou, M. (2009) Stakeholder media: The Trojan horse of corporate responsibility. Working Paper, INSEAD.

Judge, T.A. and Cable, D.M. (1997) Applicant personality, organizational culture and organizational attraction. *Personnel Psychology, 50*, 359–394.

Locke, J. (1988) *Two Treatises of Government, a Critical Edition with an Introduction and Apparatus Criticus by Peter Laslett.* Cambridge, UK: Cambridge University Press.

Noelle-Neumann, E. (1977) Turbulences in the climate of opinion: Methodological applications of the spiral of silence theory. *Public Opinion Quarterly, 41*(2), 143–158.

Roberts, P.W. and Dowling, G.R. (1997) The value of a firm's corporate reputation: How reputation helps attain and sustain superior profitability. *Corporate Reputation Review, 1*, 72–76.

Rousseau, J.J. (1750) *A Discourse: Has the Restoration of the Arts and Sciences Had a Purifying Effect upon Morals?* Geneva, Switzerland: Barillot & fils.

Thompson, J.B. (ed.) (2000) *Political Scandal: Power and Visibility in the Media Age.* Cambridge, UK: Polity.

Wang, Y., Berens, G., and van Riel, C.B.M. (2011) Managing reputation rankings: A crucial step for attracting equity investors? Working Paper, ERIM.

3

Corporate Reputation and the Discipline of Interpersonal Communication

Sherry J. Holladay
University of Central Florida, USA

This chapter reviews ways in which approaches to the study of interpersonal communication have influenced conceptualizations of reputation and reputation management, and identifies interpersonal communication's potential to contribute additional insights. Three interpersonal communication approaches – social cognition, social exchange theory, and impression management – are discussed as primary contributors to the study of reputation. Implications for future research in reputation are presented.

Introduction

Although interpersonal communication (IC) might seem like a somewhat unlikely contributor to the study of corporate reputation, the influence of interpersonal communication theories is evident in much of the language used to describe reputations. Interpersonal communication has been defined as "dyadic communication in which two individuals, sharing the roles of sender and receiver, become connected through the mutual activity of creating meaning" (Trenholm and Jensen, 2008, p. 29). The assumption is that this interpersonal communication process creates a relationship. Reputation literature often invokes concepts from interpersonal communication such as rela-

tionships, attitudes and cognitions, disclosure, and trust. This selective review highlights ways in which interpersonal communication has infiltrated discussions of reputation and identifies interpersonal communication's potential to contribute additional insights.

This chapter begins with a brief orientation to the origins of interpersonal communication. Definitions of reputation then are introduced to demonstrate how ideas from interpersonal communication are reflected in those definitions. Next, three major theoretical orientations in interpersonal communication are described along with selected implications for the study of corporate reputation. The final section identifies the limitations of applying interpersonal communication theory to the study of reputation.

The Handbook of Communication and Corporate Reputation, First Edition. Edited by Craig E. Carroll.
© 2013 John Wiley & Sons, Inc. Published 2015 by John Wiley & Sons, Inc.

Origins of Interpersonal Communication: A Brief Overview

Interpersonal communication grew out of more general theories of communication that sought to conceptualize the communication process (for reviews, see Cappella, 1987; Heath and Bryant, 1992; Thomlison, 2000). Theories of interpersonal communication emerged from the shadows of public communication and mass communication theories and drew on more established disciplines like psychology and sociology to map its identity. Interpersonal communication's dyadic focus distinguished it from other forms of communication. The "levels approach" (Littlejohn and Foss, 2005) uses the situation and number of interactants to distinguish between communication contexts (e.g., mass communication involved communication from one source to many receivers and often required the use of technology; small group communication typically occurred among three or more people in a face-to-face setting).

Ideas about relationship qualities that distinguished impersonal from interpersonal relationships emerged from the work of Knapp (1978) and Miller and Steinberg (1975). Miller and Steinberg's (1975) developmental view of interpersonal communication posited that the types of information shared in a relationship are distinguished between impersonal and interpersonal relationships. Most relationships do not progress beyond impersonal because people exchange only general cultural level and sociological level knowledge. In contrast, sharing psychological level knowledge allows people to communicate with others as unique individuals. The implication is that although a person may develop many interpersonal relationships, each one is qualitatively different. *Trust* was identified as the key to sharing psychological level information and to the development of interpersonal relationships. Knapp's (1978) "staircase model" offered a more fine-grained view of communication within relationships by focusing on development and deterioration processes. He described qualitative and quantitative differences in the communication that marked the 10 stages of coming together and coming apart.

This early work on interpersonal communication work holds implications for conceptualizations of reputation. Definitions of reputation often use the language of interpersonal communication, and this seems especially true for studies of reputation that are grounded in the public relations literature, most likely because public relations views relationship management as its primary function (see, e.g., Ferguson, 1984; Ledingham and Bruning, 2000). Relationships described in definitions of reputation seem to be more impersonal, rather than interpersonal, due the quality of information shared between the organization and constituents.

The interpersonal communication models also suggest that relationships are not static and can intensify or deteriorate depending on the communication that constitutes the relationship. The implication for the reputation literature is the need to clarify the types of relationship that are desirable and possible and to capture those features in measurement instruments. The common practice of aggregating data from all constituent groups (see, e.g., Fombrun, 1996) treats all relationships in the same way. Some have suggested that a more effective measurement practice would be to more precisely identify which constituent group and which issue (e.g., financial performance, innovation, corporate social responsibility (CSR)) are assessed (Lewellyn, 2002; Walker, 2010). Although this approach to assessment obviously does not consider dyadic relationships, aggregating data within constituent groups would more closely parallel interpersonal communication's concerns with qualitatively different relationships.

Trust has been identified as a central quality of interpersonal relationships as well as reputations (Edelman, 2012; Fombrun and van Riel, 2004; van Riel and Fombrun, 2007). For instance, Ponzi *et al.* (2011) recently developed a short form of the popular RepTrak™ measure, RepTrak™ Pulse, that contains the item "X is a company I can trust." However, the meanings of the term "trust" differ markedly between interpersonal communication and reputation. The reputation literature often uses trust as a proxy for credibility, competency, or honesty as in "I can believe what the organization claims." Within the interpersonal communication context, trust is viewed quite differently. Trust is assumed to develop slowly over time because trusting someone entails taking a risk by becoming vulnerable to the other. Trust also entails behaving in a trustworthy way by protecting the vulnerability of the other (Trenholm and Jensen, 2008). This interpersonal communication definition of trust implicates an interdependency that is incommensurate with the unidirectional conceptualization of trust assessed in reputation measures. Why do we not ask if the organization trusts the constituents?

Conceptualizations of Corporate Reputation

This section briefly highlights how interpersonal communication concepts are evident in approaches to reputation by drawing on influential works by Fombrun and associates. Fombrun (1996) encourages us to remember that to "acquire a reputation that is positive, enduring, and resilient requires managers to invest heavily in building and maintaining good relationships with their company's constituents" (p. 57). Fombrun and van Riel (1997) suggest that reputations involve appraisals of "the firm's ability to deliver valued outcomes to multiple stakeholders" (p. 10). More recently, Fombrun and associates have described corporate reputations as "beliefs about companies' past and future actions that shape how stakeholders interact with them" (Ponzi *et al.*, 2011, p. 30).

These explanations raise a number of questions related to interpersonal communication. For example, what constitutes "good relationships" within this context and how will corporations "invest" in relationships? Will similar relationships be cultivated with all constituent groups? How do organizations learn about expectations

and what constitutes "valued outcomes?" How do they understand constituent beliefs about past actions and predictions concerning future actions? These questions can be addressed through the various lenses of interpersonal communication.

Three Major Approaches to Interpersonal Communication

The social cognition approach

The social cognition approach to interpersonal communication involves "the study of the cognitive structures and processes that influence perceptions of people and social events" (Trenholm and Jensen, 2008, p. 148). Social cognition examines the interpretive frameworks, or schemata, people draw upon when making sense of themselves, other people, events, and situations. Social cognition also underpins expectations for behavior and relationships as well as formulation of goals and actions that can help them reach desired outcomes (Fiske and Taylor, 1991; Kelley, 1972). Hence, this internal sensemaking is presumed to affect relationships by guiding the interpretation, planning, and production of messages that comprise interaction.

The domain of social cognition encompasses numerous ideas that are important to the study of reputation, including perceptions, attitudes, attributions, and expectations. Petty and Cacioppo (1986) explain that attitudes are "general evaluations people hold in regard to themselves, other people, objects, and issues" (p. 4), and these "attitudes can be based on a variety of behavioral, affective, and cognitive experiences and are capable of guiding behavioral, affective, and cognitive processes" (p. 5). Reputation is a type of schema composed of cognitions and attitudes (Grunig, 1993). In this case, "reputation" would refer to schema, or cognitive associations, about reputable organizations in general. Reputation, then, can be viewed as a collection of attributes, both descriptive and evaluative, that are perceived as related to one another. Reputation measures attempt to operationalize the schema's essential features and assess constituent attitudes about specific organizations along those dimensions. However, some reputation researchers have pointed out the need to recognize that reputation is often issue specific (e.g., issues might include financial performance, innovation, use of capital) and stakeholder group specific (Lewellyn, 2002; Walker, 2010). This means that a single, general schema cannot capture the specific attributes that may drive constituent assessments of reputation.

Reputation schemata guide perceptual processes and inferences. The fact that schemata are resistant to change (Fiske and Taylor, 1991) is consistent with the idea that reputations are stable and enduring (Gray and Balmer, 1998; Mahon, 2002; Roberts and Dowling, 2002). In addition, attitudes persist unless there is a reason to change. Perceptual processes including selective exposure, selective attention, and selective interpretation are influenced by prior attitudes and help to explain why attitudes persist (Fiske and Taylor, 1991). The challenge for corporations that need to improve a poor reputation is to find ways to circumvent information-processing defaults and encourage constituents to review more favorable information.

In spite of the fact that schemata and attitudes are interconnected and are resistant to change, the language of "reputation management" suggests that organizations should communicate with constituents to influence the development of or reinforce positive associations and positive reputation evaluations. Cues such as the credibility of a source of information may be important to attitude change for people lacking strong involvement in the issue (Petty and Cacioppo, 1986). Hence, favorable reputation rankings by credible organizations such as *Fortune* Magazine's "Most Admired Companies" might prompt a shift in attitudes toward a company's reputation. A family of theories called cognitive consistency theories (e.g., Festinger, 1957; Heider, 1958; Newcomb, 1953) seek to explain how attitudes may shift when inconsistent cognitions cause discomfort.

For example, someone who strongly supports CSR initiatives may find his or her negative attitude toward a specific organization becomes more positive upon learning that the organization's CSR record is award winning. Other theories of persuasion can lend insight into the persuasion process but are beyond the scope of this chapter.

Another significant research domain within social cognition involves people's motivation to "make sense" of actions and the environment in which they operate by supplying causal attributions (Heider, 1958; Jones and Davis, 1965; Kelley, 1972; Weiner, 1986). Heider (1958) characterized people as "naive psychologists" who seek causal explanations for their own and others' behaviors. People draw upon preexisting schema when constructing these causal explanations.

Corporations should be concerned with the kinds of attributions constituents make about the organization and the consequences of those attributions for attitudes toward the organization. In the case of reputation, the parallel is that constituents will try to make sense of a corporation's actions by supplying a causal explanation. Attributions answer the question: "Why did the organization do that?" Although this attributional process is inevitable, organizations can actively attempt to shape people's attributions by supplying explanations for behavior. This is especially important in cases where the behavior and the organization are likely to be evaluated negatively unless some reframing of the situation is provided. For example, the media may report that the organization's CEO acted unethically by embezzling. An individual might attribute the unethical behavior to the organization's "culture of corruption." However, the organization could try to change the attribution by explaining that the CEO embezzled because of financial problems in his or her personal life. This account could alter attributions about the origins of the unethical behavior to better exonerate the organization. Accounts are explanations designed to reconstruct interpretations in a way that benefits the account giver (Goffman, 1967; Schlenker, 1980). This topic is closely related to the idea of impression management and is elaborated later.

Tenets of attribution theory claim that the absence of information to explain behavior tends to be psychologically uncomfortable, and people are motivated to reduce uncertainty. When people lack information about the other, for example, people are motivated to reduce uncertainty to a level that is comfortable for them (Berger and Calabrese, 1975). This can involve making causal attributions about one's own and the other's behavior or engaging in information-seeking behaviors to collect additional information. Although initial interaction with strangers was the original focus of uncertainty reduction theory, principles of uncertainty reduction can be extended to many other situations. As is the case in addressing people's tendency to make causal attributions, organizations can supply information to reduce the uncertainty of constituents. Uncertainty often plagues organizations during times of financial turbulence, CEO and management changes, restructuring, and crises, for example. Active communication with constituents should help to reduce uncertainty and preserve positive attitudes toward the organization.

The literature on social cognition is vast and holds many implications for reputation research. Other social cognition approaches that are relevant to reputation are reviewed elsewhere (e.g., Thomlison, 2000) and include co-orientation theory (Broom and Dozier, 1990; McLeod and Chaffee, 1973; Newcomb, 1953), metaperspectives (Laing, 1969), and information processing and persuasion (Dillard and Pfau, 2002; Heath and Bryant, 1992; Petty and Cacioppo, 1986).

The social exchange approach

Two theories grounded in social psychology but embraced by interpersonal researchers are social penetration theory and social exchange theory. The theories rely on concepts from social cognition to explain how people evaluate costs and rewards associated with their relationships and decide whether to maintain, intensify, or de-escalate relationships.

Social penetration theory (Altman and Taylor, 1973; Taylor and Altman, 1987) focuses on self-disclosure to explain the process of relational development. Self-disclosure varies in breadth (number of topics discussed) and depth (degree of "personalness" of the information). The model proposes that people are likely to disclose more public information before revealing more "risky," intimate information. The norm of reciprocity of disclosure tends to characterize relationships that become more intimate (Derlega *et al.*, 1993). However, most relationships do not become deeper and are comfortably maintained at a more impersonal level.

A parallel of self-disclosure in reputation research could be information about operations supplied by the organization. Some organizations strive to be more transparent, while others are more closed. What kinds of information are sufficient for making constituents believe they are receiving high-quality information (the equivalent of "personal-" or psychological-level data) and how does that impact perceptions of relational quality and reputation assessments?

Social exchange theory has been integrated with social penetration theory to explain how individuals make relationship management decisions. Social exchange theory (Thibaut and Kelley, 1959; see Roloff, 1981, for various social exchange theories) evokes an economic metaphor to explain why some relationships develop into intimate, stable relationships; others remain at a more superficial, impersonal level; and others are dissolved. The economic metaphor driving the conceptualization of processes casts people as rational calculators of the costs (contributions to the relationship, unpleasant experiences, etc.) and rewards (outcomes, benefits derived from the relationship) accrued through relational exchanges. It moves beyond positioning self-disclosure as the primary driver of relationship development by including other behaviors and cognitions in the equation. Like social penetration theory, social exchange theory seeks to explain dyadic-level behavior (relationships) but focuses on individuals as decision makers who assess the ratio of benefits to costs.

People will remain in a relationship when the costs do not exceed the rewards (Taylor and Altman, 1987). Trust is also an important component because relational partners must trust each other to honor their obligations. Knowledge of the self and of the other within the relational context ties social cognition to the social exchange process. People are motivated to acquire information that will help them understand and predict behaviors of the other to determine if the exchange is likely to meet expectations.

Both theories presume that cognitive elements described in the section on social cognition are important to the relationship process. For example, evaluations of costs and rewards are subjective because different people assign different values to those costs and rewards. The theories also help us understand that although each relationship is unique, relationships exist within a web of past and possible future relationships. Contributions to and benefits derived from relationships are gauged not only against the current relationship but also against previous relationships that contribute to that individual's context of evaluation (comparison level). Evaluations of costs and rewards are also made for possible alternative relationships that could be developed (comparison level of alternatives). In this way, the theory extends its focus beyond a single relationship to acknowledge the potential influence of a larger network of relationships.

The social exchange approach encourages reputation researchers to consider the negotiation of the exchange relationship, including what constituents identify as costs and rewards in supporting the organization and how these affect relationship behaviors and reputation evaluations. In addition, how does the organization see the exchange relationship and fulfill the implicit exchange contract? Overall, how is the nature of the organization–constituent relationship defined by the exchanges? Fombrun's (1996) proposition that reputations are comparative evaluations made against competitors parallels social exchange theory's concepts of comparison level and comparison level of alternatives and suggests the need to look beyond a single relationship.

Research on turning points could lend insight into specific events that constituents believe have altered their relationships with the organization or their perception of the reputation. A turning point is "any event or occurrence that is associated with a change in a relationship" (Baxter and Bullis, 1986, p. 470). Understanding what types of events are likely to be seen as turning points and the impact of turning points on reputation evaluations could enable organizations to better manage relationships and reputations. Research in crisis communication, for example, demonstrates that crises can function as turning points because they can threaten reputations and even an organization's survival (Coombs, 2012). Research could reveal more common events that constituents perceive as significant enough to alter their relationships with and evaluations of organizations.

Rusbult (1987) and Rusbult and colleagues (1982, 1988) used the social exchange approach to conceptualize relational investments, interdependency, and responses to unsatisfactory exchange relationships. They adapted Hirschman's (1970) exit–voice–loyalty model to characterize responses to relational decline in romantic and organizational relationships. The responses include exit, leaving the relationship; voice, trying to make improvements in the relationship; and loyalty, waiting and hoping for improvements. Rusbult found that people who experience high relational satisfaction and high investment will engage in voice and loyalty. People are more likely to exit when they have attractive alternatives beyond the current relationship.

Although Hirschman's original model pertained to employee reactions to dissatisfaction in organizations, Rusbult has demonstrated its applicability to various types of exchange relationships. For example, the model could inform an organization's understanding of constituent reactions to reputation management efforts. Dissatisfied constituents may elect to exit the relationship even when they have invested previously in the relationship because they perceive attractive alternatives to the relationship. Constituents' choice to voice concerns through protests about an organization's practices demonstrates a willingness to remain engaged even when changes are needed.

The impression management approach

The theoretical perspective of Erving Goffman (1959, 1974), a sociologist, was embraced by interpersonal communication scholars, and his ideas are reflected in contemporary approaches to reputation. Among his significant contributions is the focus on strategic impression management. Goffman employed a dramaturgical metaphor to describe how interaction is much like a play, where characters produce the "self" through verbal and nonverbal communication to craft believable performances that audiences will endorse as credible and appropriate within a particular context. Goffman's idea of *face* refers to the self that is presented to others within an interaction. The concept of facework (see also Cupach and Metts, 1994; Schlenker, 1980) parallels contemporary conceptions of tactics and strategies in reputation management.

Interactants coordinate actions with others to create impressions that are consonant with the role requirements and expectations arising from the situation and that are designed to make the interactants appear competent. This requires some degree of shared understanding and the desire to coordinate behaviors with others. Social cognition comes into play because effective performances require understanding of the self, the other(s), the situation, expectations, acceptable ways of pursuing goals, and so forth. Effective performance necessitates interdependency with relevant others because each must support the others' faces. In the case of reputations, organizations often benefit from the endorsements of third parties who support the organization's facework. Reputation research could examine how constituents weigh these endorsements. As studies of attitude change have demonstrated, the impact of endorsements may depend on the extent to which constituents perceive the third party to be credible.

The goals of impression management are similar to that of reputation management. We can ask "What does an organization's competent communication look like and how does that influence reputation evaluations?" Like reputation itself, competent interpersonal communication is a multifaceted attribution (Spitzberg and Cupach, 1984). Competent communication requires both flexibility in knowledge and behavior because communication must be adapted to the communication demands of myriad situations. Competent interpersonal communication is associated with positive outcomes like relationship management, satisfaction, and effective conflict management (Spitzberg and Cupach, 1984, 2002).

However, successful impression management is not a given. Missteps in performance, such as failing to perform facework effectively or confronting identity challenges from others, mean that the actor has failed to meet others' expectations. Missteps can pose reputational threats that must then be addressed through remediation strategies designed to promote more desirable interpretations of the behavior or atone for the faux pas. Accounts may be used to explain, excuse, or justify behavior (Goffman, 1967; Schlenker, 1980), and are examples of repair strategies that are presumed to hold important implications for successful recovery from problematic behavior. Literature on reputation management (e.g., see Allen and Caillouet, 1994; Benoit, 1995; Coombs, 2012, for reputation repair strategies) helps organizations identify and respond to reputational threats stemming from organizational behaviors such as poor decision making, defective product design, CEO misbehavior, legitimacy challenges, or equipment failures.

A primary challenge confronting organizations is the need to recognize the numerous ways in which they engage in self-presentation. Individuals should be aware of and be able to control the number of tools they use to engage in impression management (e.g., face-to-face interaction, Facebook, Twitter). In contrast, an organization's impression management is more complex and relies on many communication tools as well as different authors and performers in orchestrating face. Numerous performers (the CEO, spokespersons, employees, etc.) are responsible for impression management, making consistent coordination of the content of performance problematic. While an individual should be able to more tightly control facework, an organization will likely find it extremely challenging.

Limitations of the Alliance

Although this brief review has identified numerous areas where interpersonal communication approaches can inform reputation research, there are also limitations to this partnership. This discussion highlights two significant limitations. The most serious limitation is the incommensurate relationship between organization–constituent relationships and interpersonal dyadic relationships. Equating the two relationships ignores the fact that the "constituent" component is actually composed of an aggregate of *many* constituents who are unlikely to share common schemata, relational expectations, and so on. It is unwise to equate an aggregate of many with a single individual. Additionally, in most reputational research, it is not a single organization that is being evaluated. This problem challenges researchers to offer conceptualizations of interpersonal communication phenomena and pose questions that are sensitive to these fundamental differences.

The second limitation concerns the use of the term "relationship." At best, the relationship is typically an impersonal one. Also, it is not the relationship itself as a whole that is studied. Rather, reputation measurements assess constituent perceptions of the organization, not the other way around. A one-way transmission view of communication dominates the research approach. The organization engages in impression management activities through various communication modalities and constituents evaluate the performances. This research approach is inconsistent with the idea of a relationship.

In conclusion, although the potential for an alliance between interpersonal communication and reputation exists, researchers would be wise to consider whether and how interpersonal communication approaches can be accurately and fruitfully adapted to accommodate the realities of popular approaches to reputation measurement and reputation management.

References

Allen, M.W. and Caillouet, R.H. (1994) Legitimation endeavors: Impression management strategies used by an organization in crisis. *Communication Monographs*, 61, 44–62.

Altman, I. and Taylor, D.A. (1973) *Social Penetration: The Development of Interpersonal Relationships*. New York: Holt, Rinehart and Winston.

Baxter, L.A. and Bullis, C. (1986) Turning points in developing romantic relationships. *Human Communication Research*, 12(4), 469–493.

Benoit, W.L. (1995) *Accounts, Excuses, and Apologies. A Theory of Image Restoration*. Albany, NY: State University of New York Press.

Berger, C.R. and Calabrese, R.J. (1975) Some explorations in initial interaction: Toward a developmental theory of interpersonal communication. *Human Communication Research*, 1, 99–112.

Broom, G.M. and Dozier, D.M. (1990) *Using Research in Public Relations: Applications to Program Management*. Englewood Cliffs, NJ: Prentice Hall.

Cappella, J.N. (1987) Interpersonal communication: Definitions and fundamental questions. In C.R. Berger and S.H. Chaffee (eds), *Handbook of Communication Science*. Newbury Park, CA: Sage.

Coombs, W.T. (2012) *Ongoing Crisis Communication: Managing, Planning, and Responding* (3rd ed.). Los Angeles, CA: Sage.

Cupach, W.R. and Metts, S. (1994) *Facework*. Thousand Oaks, CA: Sage.

Derlega, V.J., Metts, S., Petronio, S., and Margulis, S.T. (1993) *Self-Disclosure*. Newbury Park, CA: Sage.

Dillard, J.P. and Pfau, M. (2002) *The Persuasion Handbook: Developments in Theory and Practice*. Thousand Oaks, CA: Sage.

Edelman (2012) Trust Barometer Global Results. Retrieved from http://trust.edelman.com/trust-download/global-results/ (last accessed October 9, 2012).

Ferguson, M.A. (1984) Building theory in public relations: Interorganizational relationships. Paper presented to the Association for Education in Journalism and Mass Communication, Gainesville, FL, August.

Festinger, L. (1957) *A Theory of Cognitive Dissonance*. Stanford, CA: Stanford University Press.

Fiske, S.T. and Taylor, S.E. (1991) *Social Cognition*. New York: Random House.

Fombrun, C.J. (1996) *Reputation: Realizing Value from the Corporate Image*. Boston: Harvard Business School Press.

Fombrun, C.J. and van Riel, C.B.M. (1997) The reputational landscape. *Corporate Reputation Review*, 1(1/2), 5–13.

Fombrun, C.J. and van Riel, C.B.M. (2004) *Fame & Fortune: How Successful Companies Build Winning Reputations*. New York: Prentice Hall Financial Times.

Goffman, E. (1959) *The Presentation of Self in Everyday Life*. Garden City, NY: Anchor.

Goffman, E. (1967) *Interaction Ritual: Essays in Face-to-Face Behavior*. New York: Doubleday.

Goffman, E. (1974) *Frame Analysis: An Essay on the Organization of Experience*. New York: Harper Collins.

Gray, E.R. and Balmer, J.M.T. (1998) Managing corporate image and corporate reputation. *Long Range Planning*, 31(5), 695–702.

Grunig, J.E. (1993) Image and substance: From symbolic to behavioral relationships. *Public Relations Review*, 19(2), 121–139.

Heath, R.L. and Bryant, J. (1992) *Human Communication Theory and Research: Concepts, Contexts, and Challenges*. Hillsdale, NJ: Lawrence Erlbaum Associates.

Heider, F. (1958) *The Psychology of Interpersonal Relations*. New York: Wiley.

Hirschman, A. (1970) *Exit, Voice, and Loyalty*. Cambridge, MA: Harvard University Press.

Jones, E.E. and Davis, K.E. (1965) From acts to dispositions: The attribution process in person perception. In L. Berkowitz (ed.), *Advances in Experimental Social Psychology* (Vol. 2). New York: Academic Press, pp. 219–266.

Kelley, H.H. (1972) Causal schemata and the attribution process. In E.E. Jones, D.E. Kanouse, H.H. Kelley, R.E. Nisbett, S. Valins, and B. Weiner (eds), *Attribution: Perceiving the Causes of Behavior*. Morristown, NJ: General Learning Press, pp. 151–174.

Knapp, M. (1978) *Social Intercourse: From Greeting to Goodbye*. Boston: Allyn & Bacon.

Laing, R.D. (1969) *Self and Others*. London: Tavistock.

Ledingham, J.A. and Bruning, S.D. (eds) (2000) *Public Relations as Relationship Management: A Relational Approach to the Study and Practice of Public Relations*. Mahwah, NJ: Lawrence Erlbaum Associates.

Lewellyn, P.G. (2002) Corporate reputation: Focusing the Zeitgeist. *Business and Society*, 41(4), 446–455.

Littlejohn, S.W. and Foss, K.A. (2005) *Theories of Human Communication* (8th ed.). Belmont, CA: Thomson Wadsworth.

Mahon, J.F. (2002) Corporate reputation: A research agenda using strategy and stakeholder literature. *Business and Society*, 41, 415–455.

McLeod, J.M. and Chaffee, S.H. (1973) Interpersonal approaches to communication research. *American Behavioral Scientist*, 16, 469–499.

Miller, G.R. and Steinberg, M. (1975) *Between People: A New Analysis of Interpersonal Communication*. Chicago, IL: Science Research Associates.

Newcomb, T.M. (1953) An approach to the study of communicative acts. *Psychological Review*, 60, 393–404.

Petty, R.E. and Cacioppo, J.T. (1986) *Communication and Persuasion: Central and Peripheral Routes to Attitude Change*. New York: Springer-Verlag.

Ponzi, L.J., Fombrun, C.J., and Gardberg, N.A. (2011) RepTrak™ Pulse: Conceptualizing and validating a short-form measure of corporate reputation. *Corporate Reputation Review*, 14(1), 15–35.

Roberts, P.W. and Dowling, G.R. (2002) Corporate reputation and sustained superior financial performance. *Strategic Management Journal*, 23(12), 1077–1093.

Roloff, M.E. (1981) *Interpersonal Communication: The Social Exchange Approach*. Beverly Hills, CA: Sage.

Rusbult, C.E. (1987) Responses to dissatisfaction in close relationships: The exit-voice-loyalty-neglect model. In D. Perlman and S. Duck (eds), *Intimate Relationships: Development, Dynamics, and Deterioration*. Thousand Oaks, CA: Sage, pp. 209–237.

Rusbult, C.E., Zembrod, I.M., and Gunn, L.K. (1982) Exit, voice, loyalty and neglect: Responses to dissatisfaction in romantic involvements. *Journal of Personality and Social Psychology*, 43(6), 1230–1242.

Rusbult, C.E., Farrell, D., Rogers, C.E., and Mainous, A.G. (1988) Exit, voice, loyalty and neglect: An integrative model of responses to declining job satisfaction. *Academy of Management Journal, 33*(3), 599–627.

Schlenker, B.R. (1980) *Impression Management: The Self-Concept, Social Identity, and Interpersonal Relations.* Monterey, CA: Brooks/Cole Publishing.

Spitzberg, B.H. and Cupach, W.R. (1984) *Interpersonal Communication Competence.* Beverly Hills, CA: Sage.

Spitzberg, B.H. and Cupach, W.R. (2002) Interpersonal skills. In M.L. Knapp and J.A. Daly (eds), *Handbook of Interpersonal Communication* (3rd ed.). Thousand Oaks, CA: Sage, pp. 564–611.

Taylor, D.A. and Altman, I. (1987) Communication in interpersonal relationships: Social penetration processes. In M. Roloff and G.R. Miller (eds), *Interpersonal Processes: New Directions in Communication Research.* Newbury Park, CA: Sage, pp. 257–277.

Thibaut, J.W. and Kelley, H.H. (1959) *The Social Psychology of Groups.* New York: John Wiley & Sons.

Thomlison, T.D. (2000) An interpersonal primer with implications for public relations. In J.A. Ledingham and S.D. Bruning (eds), *Public Relations as Relationship Management: A Relational Approach to the Study and Practice of Public Relations.* Mahwah, NJ: Lawrence Erlbaum Associates, pp. 177–203.

Trenholm, S. and Jensen, A. (2008) *Interpersonal Communication* (6th ed.). New York: Oxford University Press.

van Riel, C.B.M. and Fombrun, C.J. (2007) *Essential of Corporate Communication.* London: Routledge.

Walker, K. (2010) A systematic review of the corporate reputation literature: Definition, measurement, and theory. *Corporate Reputation Review, 12*(4), 357–387.

Weiner, B. (1986) *An Attributional Theory of Motivation and Emotion.* New York: Springer-Verlag.

4

Corporate Reputation and the Discipline of Organizational Communication

Robyn Remke

Copenhagen Business School, Denmark

Corporate reputation and organizational communication research share some points of theoretical and conceptual overlap, even if the term "corporate reputation" is rarely used within organizational communication scholarship. These shared interests align around theoretical and empirical questions related to the core corporate reputation concept. This chapter will attempt to highlight these overlaps and offer suggestions as to how organizational communication research can contribute to our understanding of corporate reputation. Specifically, the chapter focuses on the noteworthy overlap of empirical interests within organizational communication and corporate reputation research that relates to organizational identity and identification and leadership. Arguing an organizational communicative framework explicates theoretical aspects of corporate reputation that more traditional management and business frameworks miss, the chapter provides researchers and practitioners with additional explanatory resources to enhance our knowledge of corporate reputation.

Introduction

A chapter summarizing the research on corporate reputation in organizational communication research could be quite easy to write, in part because there is very little research on the topic. Although van Riel (1997) lists corporate reputation as one of three key concepts within *corporate* communication scholarship, there are very few mentions of corporate reputation within organizational communication literature – a related, albeit, different research perspective. Searches in multiple academic search engines reveal few articles in management and business journals that focus on communication as a tool for developing and maintaining a corporate reputation (cf. Gotsi and Wilson, 2001; Gray and Balmer, 1998). Other studies highlight the ways in which employee communication impact or shape corporate reputation (cf. Smidts *et al.*, 2001). While these studies demonstrate an undeniable link between communication and corporate reputation, these articles limit their conceptualization of communication to the transmission model whereby communication becomes a medium or conduit for information

The Handbook of Communication and Corporate Reputation, First Edition. Edited by Craig E. Carroll.

transmission. This is not an incorrect use of the communication concept. However, this conceptualization is more often used by scholars of corporate and strategic communication. There are other ways in which an organizational communication perspective could reveal new insights into corporate reputation.

The theoretical boundaries between corporate communication, organizational rhetoric, and strategic communication research are often blurred, sometimes permeable and always dynamic (Boyd and Waymer, 2011; Christensen and Cornelissen, 2011; Meisenbach and McMillan, 2006; van Riel, 1997). There is no doubt that organizational communication scholars and corporate and strategic communication scholars engage in similar empirical contexts, are driven by similar research questions, and even read the same theoretical literature. But, there are significant, if subtle, differences between these communicative disciplines, which shed some light on why the organizational communication field has been slow to consider corporate reputation as a research construct.

We will explore these differences in finer detail later in the chapter. To begin, I borrow Mumby's (2006) oft-cited definition of organizational communication, which he argues includes the

> various and complex communication practices of humans engaged in collective, coordinated, and goal-oriented behavior. In simple terms, organizational communication scholars study the dynamic relationships between communication processes and human organizing. (p. 3290)

At first glance, it seems like corporate reputation would be a natural point of inquiry for organizational communication scholars. In fact, there are already some points of theoretical and conceptual overlap, even if the term "corporate reputation" is rarely used in their texts. For example, organizational communication scholars and rhetoricians acknowledge the importance of corporate reputation: Boyd and Waymer (2011) suggest that a negative reputation can nullify a corporation's philanthropic efforts, and Kuhn and Ashcraft (2003) maintain that "reputation and anticipation of future regula-

tory problems can have intangible impacts on firm activity" (p. 31). However, neither of these articles delves any deeper into the communicative processes by which the corporate reputation negatively impacts the organization. The effect is taken for granted and the communicative process left unexplored.

Admittedly, the previously mentioned research does not focus explicitly on the concept of corporate reputation. However, a closer look reveals points of overlap where organizational communication research concerns and interests are aligned around theoretical and empirical questions related to the corporate reputation concept. This chapter will attempt to highlight these overlaps and offer suggestions as to how organizational communication research can contribute to our understanding of corporate reputation. The chapter begins by defining both corporate reputation and organizational communication. It then highlights two areas of study where organizational communication and corporate reputation research overlap – organizational identity and leadership. However, before moving to our definitions, we must consider a simple question: why should we study corporate reputation?

Why Corporate Reputation?

The fact that so little organizational communication research is dedicated to studying corporate reputation could serve as an indication that it is not a relevant or important topic. However, this interpretation is misguided if for no other reason because corporate reputation is a growing concern for organizational members and especially managers and leaders. There are compelling empirically based reasons that help explain why the business world cares about and has dedicated resources toward developing a strong and positive corporate reputation (Greyser, 1999). Most economists and business leaders agree that there are benefits to having a strong corporate reputation. A strong corporate reputation can positively persuade customers to conduct their business with the company, even if there are other competing companies with similar products or services. In fact, Greyser (1999) suggests that customer loyalty may allow a company to charge a premium for their goods or services; their strong corporate reputation continues to support the customer's initial decision to give the company their business. Moreover, a strong reputation also helps protect an organization during a controversy or down-economy by maintaining customer/client loyalty. Given the increased level of competition as well as the increased access consumers have to multiple companies, organizations cannot simply assume they have consumer loyalty.

The market-based business case for investing in a strong and positive corporate reputation may seem obvious or commonsensical – not necessarily worthy of further theoretical investigation. Moreover, contemporary organizational communication scholars tend to be drawn to issues related to workplace equality, work/life balance, or social justice, and less by a company's increased profit or "bottom line." Therefore, the business case for studying corporate reputation may not be a motivating rationale for many organizational communication scholars. However, organizational communication research has long focused on alternative types of organizations including feminist organizations, hybrid organizations, government organization, universities, nonprofit organizations, health providers, and public service groups, all of which depend on some sort of organizational reputation to maintain consumer/client respectability and legitimacy. To that end, communication scholars also focus on the communicative processes of organizing, which could be useful in understanding the rather complex ways in which corporate reputations are created, maintained, and even destroyed, as well as help explain how they influence organizational members and other stakeholders. Therefore, more attention should be paid to corporate reputation. To better detail how organizational communication can approach and study corporate reputation, I begin with a brief section that defines corporate reputation.

Definition of Corporate Reputation

Acknowledging that corporate reputation is not one simple concept, I offer this brief overview. Thankfully, because there will be no shortage of definitions of corporate reputation provided in these chapters, my goal is not to provide an exhaustive conceptualization of this idea. However, I think it will be useful to establish a starting point or working definition in order to draw parallels and points of intersection with organizational communication research.

Corporate reputation is a multidimensional construct in part because it is shared by scholars from different academic fields who represent varied theoretical perspectives. The "underlying theoretical pluralism" (Lange *et al.*, 2011, p. 163) of the concept contributes to its interdisciplinarity scope and heuristic value. While the diffuse disciplinary and theoretical interest in corporate reputation provides a rich knowledge base and empirical examples, it comes as no surprise that there is no one final or unified definition of corporate reputation. However, having surveyed much of the corporate reputation literature, Barnett *et al.* (2006) determined that there are three key points that are central to the concept of corporate responsibility. The first point defines reputation *as a state of awareness*. In these cases, observers or stakeholders have a general awareness of a firm but do not make judgments about the organization. Much of the research utilizing this definition centers on the perceptions of the corporate reputation. The second key point defines reputation *as an assessment*. Corporate reputation functions as a judgment, estimate or evaluation of the particular organization. Finally, the third point positions corporate reputation *as an asset*. From this perspective, a reputation is something of value or significance and can function as an intangible resource and economic asset.

Similarly, Lange *et al.* (2011) determine that three key conceptualizations, to use their term, dominate the corporate reputation research, particularly in recent management scholarship. These three conceptualizations define corporate reputation as (1) *being known*, which considers the "generalized awareness or visibility of the organization"; (2) *being known for something*, which is the "perceived predictability of organizational outcomes and behavior relevant to specific audience interests"; and (3) generalized favorability. An organization's generalized favorability is determined by the "perceptions or judgments of the overall organization as good, attractive, and appropriate" (p. 155).

For the purposes of this chapter, I borrow Barnett *et al.*'s (2006) definition for corporate reputation: the "observers' collective judgments of a corporation based on assessments of the financial, social, and environmental impacts attributed to the corporation over time" (p. 34). This definition seems to capture the key elements found in much of the corporate reputation literature.

Interestingly, at the heart of this definition and aforementioned conceptualizations are the practices of perception and awareness. Perception and awareness are fundamentally communicative phenomenon. Therefore, corporate reputation is, in some ways, a communicative construct. To be clear, however, as noted earlier, the conceptual overlap between corporate reputation and organization communication is not merely limited to the process of communicating a corporate reputation message to relevant stakeholders. Indeed, an organizational communication lens highlights the process by which a corporate reputation is constructed through the perceptions of all organizational members and related stakeholders. In order to develop this idea further, I begin by defining organizational communication.

Definitions of Organizational Communication

Organizational communication is similar to corporate and strategic communication and even organizational rhetoric. While these similarities can often lead to fruitful interdisciplinary research, it is important to establish what conceptual attributes are unique to organizational communication studies (Redding, 1985; Tompkins and Wanca-Thibault, 2001). There are several ways one can define or categorize organizational communication. Deetz (2001) describes three of the most commonly used conceptualizations for organizational communication: as a (1) specific subset within the communication discipline; (2) specific "phenomenon that exists in organizations" (p. 5); or (3) particular way of explaining organizations and organizational processes. The latter two conceptualizations highlight possible points of intersection with corporate reputation research, so I will briefly consider each of these approaches in the following sections.

Communication as a Phenomenon within Organizations

The second of Deetz's (2001) perspectives defines organizational communication as communication that occurs within an organization. This definition is commonly used in textbooks and by practitioners because of its simplicity and accurately describes much of the early organizational communication research. However, this definition provides little theoretical clarification as to what is *communicative* about the phenomenon being studied. This perspective assumes all communication that takes place within an organization is organizational communication. This presumes that there is one definition for communication and that all communication is similar. It also fails to make explicit how a communicative approach to understanding organizations is unique, particularly when compared to strategic or corporate communication theories.

Cheney and Christensen (2001) find this definition problematic as well:

> With few exceptions, the eternally directed communications of organizations have been defined by organizational communication

scholars as activities outside the province of their concerns. Because the study of organizational communication traditionally has been focused on acts of communication between senders and receivers within the "container" of the organization – that is, within clearly defined organizational borders – most communication aimed at *external* audiences, and markets in particular, has been regarded as alien to the field. (pp. 231–232, italics in the original)

Cheney and Christensen acknowledge the failure to account for external audiences' perspectives in research that defined organizations as bounded entities. More contemporary research considers organizational boundaries to be flexible, permeable, or even nonexistent, thus acknowledging that organizations do not exist in vacuums and are impacted by environmental factors (Morgan *et al.*, 2004; Sutcliffe, 2001).

Communication as a Way to Describe and Explain Organizations

Alternatively, organizational communication can be a way to *describe* and/or *explain* organizations (Ashcraft *et al.*, 2009). Deetz (2001) argues that organizational communication "can be used to explain the production of social structures, psychological states, member categories, knowledge, and so forth rather than being conceptualized as simply one phenomenon among these others in organizations" (p. 5). Notice the focus on the *production* of the organizational phenomenon; communication moves from being merely a part of an organization to constituting the meaning-making process of organizing (Putnam and Pacanowsky, 1983). Mumby (2006) elaborates on this definition by explaining that "communication is conceived as foundational to, and constitutive of, organizations, while organizations are viewed as relatively enduring structures that are both medium and outcome of communication processes" (p. 3290). Clearly, this definition of organizational communication moves beyond the earliest definitions that relied on the transmission model of communication (Axley, 1984) to examine communicative causality or efficiency. In light of the linguistic turn, now much organizational communication research focuses on the ways in which we use communication to make sense of every day.

To that end, more contemporary organizational communication research examines the ways in which communication brings organizational life into reality. In short, "communication generates, not merely expresses, key organizational realities" (Ashcraft *et al.*, 2009, p. 2). These organizational realities include corporate reputation. In fact, this definition helps us understand how something seemingly intangible such as corporate reputation has the full power of influence as something tangible. This perspective explicates

> how the exchange [communication] itself activates hierarchy, breathing life into organizational charts and policy manuals. And by putting abstract structures into live motion, communication subjects them to real-time improvisation and negotiation. (Ashcraft *et al.*, 2009, p. 4).

Both of these definitions provide rarely sought insights into the phenomenon of corporate reputation. What follows are two areas of organizational communication research that is relevant or related to corporate communication research.

Identity/Image/Identification

Both organizational communication and corporate reputation scholars are interested in issues of organizational identity/image/identification. In defining corporate reputation, several scholars acknowledged the "muddy" nature of the concept, noting that the terms organizational identity and image are often used interchangeably with corporate reputation (Melewar and Jenkins, 2002). In fact, Fombrun and van Riel (1997) situate organizational identity and image as subsets or building blocks for corporate reputation. From their perspective, identity describes the ways in which the internal stakeholders perceive the organization with image used to describe the perception held by external stakeholders. Combined, organizational identity and image create corporate reputation. While this may be a rather simplistic description of the corporate reputation creation process, it highlights the attributes about corporate reputation that are mirrored in organizational communication research on organizational identity, identification, and image.

Organizational communication scholars are asking questions similar to those found in the organizational studies and management disciplines (of which corporate reputation research is often situated) about identity and identification (cf. Albert and Whetten, 1985; Alvesson, 2000, 2001; Ashforth and Mael, 1989; Du Gay, 1996, 2007; Dutton and Dukerich, 1991; Gioia *et al.*, 2000; Hatch and Schultz, 2002; Schultz *et al.*, 2000; Scott and Lane, 2000; Sveningsson and Larsson, 2006). For scholars who define organizational communication as communication bounded within an organization, concern for unity of message between internal and external stakeholders is of keen interest:

> Many organizations have begun to realize the difficulties of convincing an external audience about their deeds (e.g., their protection of the environment of defense of human rights) if the *internal* audience does not accept the message – and vice versa. (Cheney and Christensen, 2001, p. 232)

One could argue that the *message* Cheney and Christensen reference is or is at least directly related to the organization's reputation. Communication practitioners face the challenge of developing communication strategies that extend beyond message transmission and consider the ways in which diverse audiences, including internal and external stakeholders, perceive and then cocreate the corporate reputation. This focus stems from a realization that

an organization's primary management challenge is not only to provide quality, cost-effective goods and services. Contemporary organizations must do all these things with a particular distinctiveness that gives the organization legitimization through an advantageous profile (Cheney and Christensen, 2001). This profile or identity must remain consistent with all stakeholders or "the organization of today will have difficulties sustaining and confirming a coherent sense of 'self' necessary to maintain credibility and legitimacy in and outside the organization" (Cheney and Christensen, 2001, p. 232). Therefore, the focus on a coherent and consistent organizational identity is shared by corporate reputation scholars as well as communication practitioners and organizational communication scholars alike. For example, Frandsen and Johansen (2011) highlight two different *corporate identity management* strategies – the American and Scandinavian – that address climate change within the automotive industry. Corporate identity management strategies function very similarly to corporate reputation. In addition, Meisenbach and Bonewits Feldner (2011) indirectly hint at the importance of studying corporate reputation from an organizational rhetorical perspective when they write "2010 will be remembered in part for the rhetorical successes and failures of the Toyota Corporation and British Petroleum (BP) as both sought to manage their identities and rebuild their legitimacy in the wake of their current crises" (p. 561).

Alternatively, scholars who adopt a more discourse-based definition of organizational communication study the ways in which organizational identity – reputation – is constructed and becomes meaningful to individual organizational members:

> If we accept the idea that organizational communication is essentially a process through which meaning is essentially created, negotiated, and managed, we should expect to find identity at issue in most organizing processes, especially in those explicitly concerned with addressing external audiences. (Cheney and Christensen, 2001, 2001, p. 241)

Cheney (Cheney, 1983a,b; Cheney and Tompkins, 1987) was one of the first organizational communication scholars to use rhetorical identification theory to explore organizational membership and commitment as a means of identification. At the heart of this research is a concern for how the organization comes to be defined, understood, and conceptualized – identified – by a diverse group of stakeholders. This research acknowledges the importance of organizational identity as well as its communicatively constructed origins.

Organizational identity and identification continue to be a central concern for communication scholars (Alvesson *et al.*, 2008; Stuart, 1999), but the focus shifts to the communicative practices that constitute the identity/identification process (Eisenberg, 2001; Holmer-Nadesan, 1996; Tracy and Trethewey, 2005). Using this perspective, we better understand the ways in which individual workers create organizational and professional identities (Ashcraft, 2005, 2007, 2008; Cheney and Ashcraft, 2007; Tracy, 2000; Wieland, 2010). Other research uncovers the discursive practices that workers use to negotiate their individual identities around workplace and everyday-life realities such as time management (Kuhn, 2006), financial responsibilities (Meisenbach, 2010), and family responsibilities (Edley, 2004). Frandsen (2012), Meisenbach (2008), and others examine the ways in which workers in stigmatized occupations or low-reputation organizations make sense of their role and develop coping strategies that buffer them from the downsides of the stigma or low reputation. Finally, scholars investigate how individual personal identities, which include one's sex, gender, race, and class, come to be constructed through organizational communication (Allen, 2011; Ashcraft, 1996; Kondo, 1990; Lucas, 2011; Trethewey, 1997, 1999). These research examples appear only indirectly linked to corporate reputation, but when understood as a related communicative process, organizational identity and identification become key factors in understanding how corporate reputation is co-constructed among organizational members.

Leadership

Leadership, another interdisciplinary concept, provides an additional point where organizational communication and corporate reputation research intersect. Much leadership research draws on psychological perspectives that focus on the qualities and traits of individual leaders. More recently, however, influenced by theories rooted in social constructivist perspectives, leadership scholars are challenging the psychological perspective and focusing more on the communicative *practices* of leadership (Grint and Jackson, 2010). Specifically, moving beyond merely studying the speeches of great leaders, organizational communication scholars provide alternative conceptualizations of leadership that focus on the discourses of leaders. This scholarship highlights how discourse creates leadership: "Discursive approaches tend to focus on *how* leadership is achieved or 'brought off' in discourse" (Fairhurst, 2007, p. 5). Leadership is dynamic and must adapt to different contextual and environmental needs and expectations (Barge and Fairhurst, 2008). This perspective helps managers understand the importance of developing flexible and responsive leadership styles. In addition, this perspective provides a more democratic approach to leadership by disconnecting leadership from particular positions or individuals; leadership can be practiced or performed by anyone at any time, if they meet the expectations and needs of those who follow (Fairhurst, 2011; Fairhurst and Grant, 2010).

Leadership ties directly to corporate reputation, because reputation is, in part, determined by the corporate leadership (Gray and Balmer, 1998). Greyser (1999) argued that managers and leaders affect their company's reputation either negatively or positively. The organizational leadership play an active role in developing and maintaining the corporate reputation through strategic organizational communication. Fairhurst and Grant (2010), however, remind us that it is not only formal managers who influence corporate reputation; others can assume a leadership position and use skilled communication to persuade stakeholders of alternative reputations. One type of strategic communication a leader should consider in regard to corporate reputation is framing.

Framing is a communication tool that enables leaders to create realistic and positive corporate reputations that make sense to stakeholders. As noted earlier, corporate reputation depends on the perception of multiple stakeholders who collectively come to a shared understanding about the corporation's reputation. And, while a leader cannot control all the circumstances an organization will face, he or she can "control the context under which events are seen if they recognize a framing opportunity" (Fairhurst, 2011, p. 2). Stakeholders and organizational members look to managers and leaders to frame or define "the situation here and now" (Fairhurst, 2011, p. 3) in a way that corresponds to their organizational experience. In other words, the managers demonstrate leadership when they actively engage in communicative practices that help shape a corporate reputation that ultimately "sticks" with the organizational members. A loss of corporate reputation or a bad reputation may result in management's failure to frame the organizational image and identity in a way that matches the stakeholder's experiences (Greyser, 1999).

An organizational communicative perspective helps explain how individual organizational members demonstrate leadership, even if they are not officially designated as managers. Moreover, a communicative definition of leadership helps explain how the influence of key individuals, both internal and external to the company, can shape corporate reputation.

Conclusion

Questions concerning corporate reputation are rarely entertained by organizational communication researchers. However, upon further consideration, there is noteworthy overlap of empirical interests within organizational communication and corporate reputation research that relates to organizational identity and identification and leadership. Moreover, an organizational communicative framework explicates

theoretical aspects of corporate reputation that more traditional management and business frameworks miss. An organizational communication perspective, therefore, provides the researcher and practitioner with additional explanatory resources to enhance our knowledge of corporate reputation.

References

Albert, S. and Whetten, D.A. (1985) Organizational identity. In L.L. Cummings and B.M. Staw (eds), *Research in Organizational Behavior*. Greenwich, UK: JAI.

Allen, B.J. (2011) *Difference Matters: Communicating Social Identity* (2nd ed.). Long Grove, IL: Waveland Press.

Alvesson, M. (2000) Social identity and the problem of loyalty in knowledge-intensive companies. *Journal of Management Studies, 37*, 1101–1122.

Alvesson, M. (2001) Knowledge work: Ambiguity, image, and identity. *Human Relations, 54*, 863–886.

Alvesson, M., Ashcraft, K.L., and Thomas, R. (2008) Identity matters: Reflections on the construction of identity scholarship in organization studies. *Organization, 15*, 5–28.

Ashcraft, K.L. (1996) "A woman's worst enemy": Reflections on a narrative of organizational life and female identity. *Journal of Applied Communication Research, 24*, 217–239.

Ashcraft, K.L. (2005) Resistance through consent? Occupational identity, organizational form, and the maintenance of masculinity among commercial airline pilots. *Management Communication Quarterly, 19*, 67–90.

Ashcraft, K.L. (2007) Appreciating the "work" of discourse: Occupational identity and difference as organizing mechanisms in the case of commercial airline pilots. *Discourse & Communication, 1*, 9–36.

Ashcraft, K.L. (2008) Bringing the body back to work, wherever that is: Professionalization, segregation, and occupational identity. Unpublished manuscript.

Ashcraft, K.L., Kuhn, T., and Cooren, F. (2009) Constitutional amendments: "Materializing" organizational communication. *The Academy of Management Annals, 3*, 1–64.

Ashforth, B.E. and Mael, F. (1989) Social identity theory and the organization. *Academy of Management Review, 14*, 20–39.

Axley, S. (1984) Managerial and organizational communication in terms of the conduit metaphor. *Academy of Management Review, 9*, 428–437.

Barge, J.K. and Fairhurst, G.T. (2008) Living leadership: A systemic constructionist approach. *Leadership, 4*, 227–251.

Barnett, M.L., Jermier, J.M., and Lafferty, B.A. (2006) Corporate reputation: The definitional landscape. *Corporate Reputation Review, 9*, 26–38.

Boyd, J. and Waymer, D. (2011) Organizational rhetoric: A subject of interest(s). *Management Communication Quarterly, 25*, 474–493.

Cheney, G. (1983a) The rhetoric of identification and the study of organizational communication. *Quarterly Journal of Speech, 69*, 143–158.

Cheney, G. (1983b) On the various and changing meanings of organizational membership: A field study of organizational identification. *Communication Monographs, 50*, 342–362.

Cheney, G. and Ashcraft, K.L. (2007) Considering "the professional" in communication studies: Implications for theory and research within and beyond the boundaries of organizational communication. *Communication Theory, 17*, 146–175.

Cheney, G. and Christensen, L.T. (2001) Identity at issue: Linkages between "internal" and "external" organizational communication. In F.M. Jablin and L.L. Putnam (eds), *New Handbook of Organizational Communication*. Thousand Oaks, CA: Sage Publications, pp. 231–269.

Cheney, G. and Tompkins, P.K. (1987) Coming to terms with organizational identification and commitment. *Central States Speech Journal, 38*, 1–15.

Christensen, L. and Cornelissen, J. (2011) Bridging corporate and organizational communication: Review, development and a look to the future. *Management Communication Quarterly, 25*, 383–414.

Deetz, S.A. (2001) Conceptual foundations. In F.M. Jablin and L.L. Putnam (eds), *The New Handbook of Organizational Communication*. Thousand Oaks, CA: Sage Publications, pp. 3–46.

Du Gay, P. (1996) *Consumption and Identity at Work*. Thousand Oaks: Sage Publications.

Du Gay, P. (2007) *Organizing Identity*. Los Angeles, CA: Sage Publications.

Dutton, J.E. and Dukerich, J.M. (1991) Keeping an eye on the mirror?: Image and identity in organizational adaptation. *Academy of Management Journal, 34*, 517–554.

Edley, P.P. (2004) Entrepreneurial Mothers' Balance of Work and Family: Discursive Constructions of Time, Mothering, and Identity. In Pm. Buzzanell, H. Sterk, and L. Turner (eds), *Gender in Applied Communication Contexts*. Thousand Oaks, CA: Sage Publications, pp. 225–273.

Eisenberg, E. (2001) Building a mystery: Toward a new theory of communication and identity. *Journal of Communication, 51*, 534–552.

Fairhurst, G.T. (2007) *Discursive Leadership: In Conversation with Leadership Psychology*. Los Angeles, CA: Sage Publications.

Fairhurst, G.T. (2011) *The Power of Framing: Creating the Language of Leadership*. San Francisco, CA: Jossey-Bass.

Fairhurst, G.T. and Grant, D. (2010) The social construction of leadership: A sailing guide. *Management Communication Quarterly, 23*, 171–210.

Fombrun, C. and van Riel, C. (1997) The reputation landscape. *Corporate Reputation Review, 1*, 5–13.

Frandsen, F. and Johansen, W. (2011) Rhetoric, climate change, and corporate identity management. *Management Communication Quarterly, 25*(3), 511–530.

Frandsen, S. (2012) Organizational image, identification, and cynical distance prestigious professionals in a low-prestige organization. *Management Communication Quarterly, 26*, 351–376.

Gioia, D.A., Schultz, M., and Corley, K.G. (2000) Organizational identity, image, and adaptive instability. *Academy of Management Review, 25*, 63–81.

Gotsi, M. and Wilson, A.M. (2001) Corporate reputation: Seeking a definition. *Corporate Communications: An International Journal, 6*, 24–30.

Gray, E.R. and Balmer, J.M.T. (1998) Managing corporate image and corporate reputation. *Range Planning, 31*, 695–702.

Greyser, S.A. (1999) Advancing and enhancing corporate reputation. *Corporate Communications: An International Journal, 4*, 177–181.

Grint, K. and Jackson, B. (2010) Toward "socially constructive" social constructions of leadership. *Management Communication Quarterly, 24*, 348–355.

Hatch, M.J. and Schultz, M. (2002) The dynamics of organizational identity. *Human Relations, 55*, 989–1018.

Holmer-Nadesan, M. (1996) Organizational identity and space of action. *Organization Studies, 17*, 49–81.

Kondo, D.K. (1990) *Crafting Selves: Power, Gender and Discourses of Identity in a Japanese Workplace*. Chicago, IL: The University of Chicago Press.

Kuhn, T. (2006) A "demented work ethic" and a "lifestyle firm": Discourse, identity, and workplace time commitments. *Organization Studies, 27*, 1339.

Kuhn, T. and Ashcraft, K. (2003) Corporate scandal and the theory of the firm. *Management Communication Quarterly, 17*, 20–57.

Lange, D., Lee, P.M., and Dai, Y. (2011) Organizational reputation: A review. *Journal of Management, 37*, 153–184.

Lucas, K. (2011) Blue-collar discourses of workplace dignity: Using outgroup comparisons to construct positive identities. *Management Communication Quarterly, 25*, 353–374.

Meisenbach, R.J. (2008) Working with tensions: Materiality, discourse, and (dis)empowerment in occupational identity negotiation among higher education fund-raisers. *Management Communication Quarterly, 22*, 258–287.

Meisenbach, R.J. (2010) The female breadwinner: Phenomenological experience and the gendered identity in work/family spaces. *Sex Roles, 62*, 2–19.

Meisenbach, R.J. and Bonewits Feldner, S. (2011) Adopting an attitude of wisdom in organizational rhetorical theory and practice: Contemplating the ideal and the real. *Management Communication Quarterly, 25*, 560–568.

Meisenbach, R.J. and McMillan, J.J. (2006) Blurring the boundaries: Historical developments and future directions in organization rhetoric. *Communication Yearbook, 30*, 99–141.

Melewar, T.C. and Jenkins, E. (2002) Defining the corporate identity construct. *Corporate Reputation Review, 5*, 76–90.

Morgan, J.M., Reynolds, C.M., Nelson, T.J., Johanningmeier, A.R., Griffin, M., and Andrade, P. (2004) Tales from the fields: Sources of employee identification in agribusiness. *Management Communication Quarterly, 17*, 360–395.

Mumby, D.K. (2006) Organizational communication. In G. Ritzer (ed.), *Blackwell Encyclopedia of Sociology*. London: Wiley-Blackwell, pp. 3290–3299.

Putnam, L.L. and Pacanowsky, M.E. (eds) (1983) *Communication and Organizations: An Interpretive Approach*. Beverly Hills, CA: Sage Publications.

Redding, W.C. (1985) Stumbling toward identity: The emergence of organizational communication as a field of study. In R.D. McPhee and P.K. Tompkins (eds), *Organizational Communication: Traditional Themes and New Directions*. Beverly Hills, CA: Sage Publications, pp. 15–54.

Schultz, M., Hatch, M.J., and Larsen, M.H. (eds) (2000) *The Expressive Organization: Linking Identity, Reputation, and the Corporate Brand*. Oxford, UK: Oxford University Press.

Scott, S.G. and Lane, V.R. (2000) A stakeholder approach to organizational identity. *Academy of Management Review, 25*, 43–62.

Smidts, A., Pruyn, A.T.H., and van Riel, C. (2001) The impact of employee communication and perceived external prestige on organizational identification. *Academy of Management Journal, 44*, 1051–1062.

Stuart, H. (1999) Towards a definitive model of the corporate identity management process. *Corporate Communications: An International Journal, 4*, 200–207.

Sutcliffe, K.M. (2001) Organizational environments and organizational information processing. In F.M. Jablin and L.L. Putnam (eds), *The New Handbook of Organizational Communication*. Thousand Oaks, CA: Sage Publications.

Sveningsson, S. and Larsson, M. (2006) Fantasies of leadership: Identity work. *Leadership, 2*, 203–224.

Tompkins, P.K. and Wanca-Thibault, M. (2001) Organizational communication: Prelude and prospects. In F.M. Jablin and L.L. Putnam (eds), *The New Handbook of Organizational Communication*. Thousand Oaks, CA: Sage Publications, pp. xvii–xxxi.

Tracy, S.J. (2000) Becoming a character for commerce: Emotion labor, self-subordination, and discursive construction of identity in a total institution. *Management Communication Quarterly, 14*, 90–128.

Tracy, S.J. and Trethewey, A. (2005) Fracturing the real-self – fake-self dichotomy: Moving toward "crystallized" organizational discourses and identities. *Communication Theory, 15*, 168–195.

Trethewey, A. (1997) Resistance, identity, and empowerment: A postmodern feminist analysis of clients in a human service organization. *Communication Monographs, 64*, 281–301.

Trethewey, A. (1999) Discipline bodies: Women's embodied identities at work. *Organization Studies, 20*, 423–450.

van Riel, C.B.M. (1997) Research in corporate communication. *Management Communication Quarterly, 11*, 288–309.

Wieland, S.M.B. (2010) Ideal selves as resources for the situated practice of identity. *Management Communication Quarterly, 24*, 503–528.

5

Corporate Reputation and the Discipline of Advertising

Nora J. Rifon, Karen Smreker, and Sookyong Kim

Michigan State University, USA

Enhancing corporate reputation, once the province of public relations executives, is an important advertising objective. This chapter discusses how advertising can be used to enhance corporate reputation among personal consumers. It is assumed that consumers are more likely to be concerned with a company's product offerings, social responsibility, and sincerity than other dimensions of corporate reputation. Essentially, little research has directly addressed the question of how advertising can effectively enhance corporate reputation. Thus, the chapter reviews and integrates concepts and research findings from a variety of more substantive advertising domains. Studies of advertising effects on consumers' brand and advertiser perceptions, particularly perceptions of credibility, and research on cause-related marketing and celebrity endorser effects are reviewed, as their results help us to paint a picture of how advertising can influence corporate reputation. The chapter concludes with a short case study that illustrates the concepts presented.

Enhancing corporate reputation, once the province of public relations executives, is an important advertising objective. Advertising can carry messages that speak directly to a company's image, but it can also indirectly influence corporate reputation by leveraging a company's assets such as brands and corporate activities. Brand advertising, advertising that communicates brand and corporate sponsorships, and ads that tout other corporate behaviors can influence stakeholder perceptions of a company's reputation. In fact, brand and corporate reputation appear linked through some form of reciprocal determinism. Corporate reputation has been cited as essential for brand building and the wide-ranging success of a company. According to Jim Copeland, retired CEO of Deloitte Touche Tohmatsu, "A good reputation creates demand, and demand can command premium pricing . . . it also defines the markets' expectations of everything you offer" (Donlon, 2001, p. 44). According to Morris Denton, Executive Vice President and General Manager at Edelman and past Vice President of Corpo-

The Handbook of Communication and Corporate Reputation, First Edition. Edited by Craig E. Carroll.
© 2013 John Wiley & Sons, Inc. Published 2015 by John Wiley & Sons, Inc.

rate Marketing at AMD, "In the absence of corporate credibility, it really doesn't matter what your product strategy is" ("Passion readies Denton," 2003).

Research on corporate reputation has focused mainly on financial or managerial concepts of reputation, viewing reputation as an intangible asset of interest to the investment community (Cravens *et al.*, 2003; Fombrun and Shanley, 1990; Melewar and Jenkins, 2002; Pruzan, 2001). In most studies of corporate reputation, the samples have been drawn from corporations and/or investment analysts, the stakeholders of primary interest to management. However, if corporate reputation influences demand and brand perceptions, then it is critical for advertisers to embrace the importance of consumer perceptions of a brand's parent company in order to attain brand success. In fact, several dimensions of corporate reputation, product and services, social responsibility, and sincerity stand out as company characteristics consumers care about. Thus, advertising to consumers should be included in a plan to enhance corporate image.

This chapter discusses how advertising can be used to enhance corporate reputation among personal consumers. It is assumed that consumers are more likely to be concerned with a company's product offerings, social responsibility, and sincerity than other dimensions of corporate reputation. Also, because corporate reputation is an intangible resource, advertising to support reputation enhancement in consumers may require different executions and styles than advertising of tangible brands. Essentially, little research has directly addressed the question of how advertising can effectively enhance corporate reputation. Consequently, the chapter will review and integrate concepts, research, and findings from a variety of more substantive advertising domains. Select studies of advertising effects on consumers' brand and advertiser perceptions, particularly perceptions of advertiser credibility, and of cause-related marketing (CRM) effects are reviewed, as their results help us to paint a picture of how advertising can influence corporate reputation.

Corporate Reputation Dimensions for Consumers

Corporate reputation has been defined as a perceptual representation of a company's past actions and future prospects that describes the firm's overall appeal to all of its key constituents when compared to other leading rivals, or a stakeholder's global assessment of a company based on performance characteristics salient to that stakeholder (Fombrun, 1996). The salient dimensions of a company's reputation may differ across stakeholders (e.g., employees, investors, or consumers) who are likely to be concerned with different corporate performance characteristics (Rifon *et al.*, 2005).

Perhaps the most well-known of the corporate reputation indices is the RepTrak used by the Reputation Institute. The Reputation Institute's RepTrak™ scorecard provides a reasonable representation of the dimensions addressed by most studies and appear in Table 5.1.

Using these dimensions, we can address how advertising can enhance consumer perceptions of corporate reputation. *Products and services*, *social responsibility* and *sincerity* are likely to be more salient to consumers than *performance*, *leadership*, and *workplace*. Among the dimensions proposed by Ponzi *et al.* (2011). The RepTrak™ "Pulse", is an emotion-based measure of the corporate reputation construct that untangles the drivers of corporate reputation from measurement of the construct itself. This four-item measure is considered to reflect global feelings or affective state toward the company rather than perceptions or judgments of its specific performances or characteristics. This is akin to the affect or global evaluative dimension of an attitude toward an object, the focus of studies in several areas of persuasive communication. Attitude toward a company's brand is the focus of many studies of advertising effects that offer a substantial body of evidence that we can use to understand reputation enhancement through the *products and services* dimension.

Finally, *citizenship* and/or *corporate social responsibility* has become more important to

Table 5.1 Reputation Institute's RepTrak™ Scorecard.

Products/Services	High Quality
	Value for Money
	Stand Behind
	Meets Customer Needs
Innovation	Innovative
	First to Market
	Adapts Quickly to Change
Workplace	Rewards Employees Fairly
	Employee Well-being
	Offers Equal Opportunities
Governance	Open and Transparent
	Behaves Ethically
	Fair in the way it does Business
Citizenship	Environmentally Responsible
	Supports Good Causes
	Positive Influence on Society
Leadership	Well Organized
	Appealing Leader
	Excellent Management
	Clear Vision for its Future
Performance	Profitable
	Better Results than Expected
	Strong Growth Prospects

consumers, many of whom report that social responsibility can swing their brand choice in favor of the "good" company. Studies of CRM strategies offer evidence that CRM, when implemented appropriately, can enhance corporate reputation. Targeting consumers with strategies to enhance perceptions of citizenship and social responsibility has the potential to enhance the overall public esteem of a company and its global reputation. Figure 5.1 summarizes the factors that play a role in changing consumer perceptions of corporate reputation and the outcomes that may be influenced.

How Advertising Works

Traditionally, advertising has been defined as a paid for, product-related message through the mass media by an identified sponsor. With today's rapidly changing media environment, the traditional mass media no longer limit the

form an ad can take and mass customization is becoming the norm. But the general principles of what advertising can and should do have not really changed.

Advertising can achieve a variety of objectives and ad managers are likely to define them in sales and temporal terms. But if we seek to enhance corporate reputation, then it is useful to understand what types of consumer response can be altered and how. A simple model of advertising effects consists of the following primary concepts, the source of the message, the content of the message, the medium of message transmission, and consumer response. In addition, there are characteristics of the consumer that we need to comprehend in order to understand consumer reaction to any ad.

At the outset, we should note that companies, as intangible entities to many consumers, may be considered credence goods; that is, goods for which consumers may have little factual knowledge or experience. Advertising is thought to have greater potential to create a product image for experience and credence

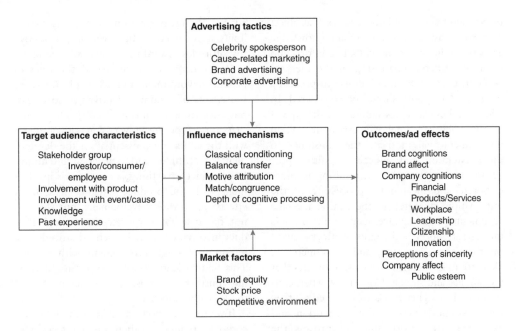

Figure 5.1   Model of factors in corporate reputation advertising effects.

goods, as compared to search goods (Darby and Karni, 1973; Nelson, 1974). Search goods are those that consumers can easily evaluate before purchase (e.g., a computer, a piece of furniture or clothing). On the other hand, experience goods (e.g., health care service, wine) must be used to observe their characteristics and quality. Credence goods (e.g., vitamins, expert services such as a physician or plumber) are difficult to evaluate even after their consumption, since their benefits often cannot be seen. Because credence goods are difficult to evaluate prior to or after use, advertisers may offer the only product knowledge a consumer can obtain prior to use. Thus, advertising may be effectively used to create images that do not already exist and can enhance reputation.

In general, we can classify consumer response into three categories: cognitive, affective, and conative. Cognitive response refers to the beliefs that consumers develop in response to an ad, this is also considered the "thinking" response. Beliefs are different than feelings and are considered to be informational in nature.

Beliefs can be about a brand in an ad, the ad itself, and/or the source of the message. Affective response is considered to be the "feeling" response with the two dimensions of intensity and valence. Affect can be positive or negative, and the nature of affect also changes with its intensity. An intense experience of affect is considered to be strong emotion, such as joy and love or fear and guilt; less intense affect can be a globalized mood of feeling relaxed and calm, or perhaps bored and restless; and the least intense affect is considered to be an evaluation of an object in terms of it being good or bad, or liked or disliked. Most models of consumer response use the lowest level of affect and often consider it to be a cognitive evaluation of feelings rather than an experience of a feeling. Finally, the conative response is a consumer's intention to behave, often as intention to purchase the brand, based on the ad's message.

The consumer characteristics that are most important to consumer response are the personal relevance of the product or issue in the ad, the consumer's involvement with the ad itself, the consumer's attitude toward that object, and the level of knowledge of that object prior to exposure. Involvement and knowledge are key predictors of the cognitive effort, and resulting in-depth processing of the message content, that a consumer will use to process a message. Thus, both should be considered. In addition, these factors will influence the type of response the consumer will experience. High involvement will motivate the consumer to focus attention and allocate cognitive processing resources to the ad, resulting in more elaborate and meaningful processing of the information presented in the central message arguments. Less involvement results in less interest, attention, and cognitive effort focused on the central message, and consumers are likely to utilize heuristic processing of cues that are familiar and simple. Conversely, when consumers have higher levels of knowledge, they have less motivation to focus attention and exert cognitive effort, but can process the message more efficiently (cf. Bettman and Park, 1980; Celsi and Olson, 1988).

In contrast to the cognitive information models, pure affect models can explain the role of familiarity and feelings evoked by advertising (Aaker *et al.*, 1986; Peterson *et al.*, 1986). According to pure affect models, consumers shape their preferences based on liking, feelings, and emotions evoked by mere exposure to the advertisement, not by the cognitive attribution of the product or brand information (e.g., Zajonc, 1980).

When consumers view an ad, they not only develop beliefs and feelings about the brand advertised, but they can also have thoughts and feelings about the ad and the advertiser. In a classic study of advertising effects, Lutz *et al.* (1983) found that a consumer's attitude toward the ad had a strong influence on attitude toward the brand. Subsequent studies confirm the validity of that finding and suggest that attitude toward the ad has a stronger influence on brand attitudes under conditions of low involvement (Brown and Stayman, 1992). Furthermore, MacKenzie and Lutz (1989) discovered that a consumer's perceptions about the advertiser had an unexpectedly significant influence on the development of attitude toward the

ad. Specifically, perceptions of advertiser credibility were linked to the development of positive attitudes toward the ad and ad credibility.

One notable study compared the roles of product involvement and ad involvement for the effects of product advertising and corporate advertising (Kim *et al.*, 2009). They found that for corporate advertising, involvement with the ad itself was essential for the development of attitudes and behavioral intentions. For product advertising, a consumer's involvement with the product category had direct effects on attitude development, but this was not the case for corporate advertising. Product involvement only influenced attitude and intention through involvement with the ad. This finding suggests that corporate advertising must create consumer engagement with the ad to be effective.

If we focus on how advertising can influence corporate reputation, then source effects in ad messages are critical to understand. In any one ad, there can be several sources. The vehicle of the ad's placement, the medium of transmission, the spokesperson, if present, and the advertiser are all sources in an ad. Ad credibility refers to the degree of perceived truthfulness and believability of the advertised claims about the brand. Ad credibility consists of perceived advertiser credibility and advertising credibility (MacKenzie and Lutz, 1989, p. 51).

Sincerity: Advertiser/Company Credibility

Corporate sincerity is a dimension that is remarkably similar to that of source credibility, a concept that pervades models and empirical studies of message effects. Several sources exist in most advertisements and include the medium of message transmission, the vehicle of the message's placement, the model, the spokesperson or endorser in the message, the brand, and the advertiser/company marketing the brand. There is a growing body of empirical evidence that sources credibility, and increasingly, advertiser/corporate credibility (Goldberg and Hartwick, 1990) is important for a message's effectiveness under conditions of high as well as low involvement.

Highly credible sources are valuable because they generate more positive attitudes and behaviors (Craig and McCann, 1978) and gain more attention (Sternthal *et al.*, 1978) than sources that lack credibility. MacKenzie and Lutz (1989) found attitude toward an advertiser, and advertiser credibility played unexpectedly significant roles in determining attitude toward the ad. Few advertising scholars would argue the importance of a consumer's attitude toward an ad in determining an advertisement's effectiveness. Mitchell and Olson (1981) first provided this evidence, and the results of dozens of subsequent studies confirmed the mediating influence of ad attitude in a variety of contexts, thereby supporting the view that better-liked ads lead to more positive evaluations of the advertised brand (Chattopadhyay and Nedungadi, 1992). Thus, corporate credibility appears to be essential for effective brand advertising. However, can advertising strategy effect corporate credibility and reputation? Several scholars would say yes. Corporate reputation is considered by some to be driven by the company's source credibility in a message (Goldberg and Hartwick, 1990; Goldsmith *et al.*, 2000).

Studies investigating the source credibility of celebrities and other endorsers provide the foundation for the study of corporate credibility. Three dimensions, expertise, trustworthiness, and attractiveness (Haley, 1996; Ohanian, 1990), have typically been cited for their facilitation of advertising effects. The first two dimensions are applicable both to individuals and companies as sponsors or endorsers. Attractiveness, however, is problematic as a construct when applied to organizations or corporations (Goldsmith *et al.*, 2000). Goldsmith *et al.* (2000) distinguish between reputation and credibility, stating that "corporate credibility is the perceived expertise and trustworthiness of a firm; reputation, on the other hand, is much broader in scope and includes, but is not limited to, the dimensions of expertise and trustworthiness" (p. 44).

There is empirical evidence that CRM activities can be effectively leveraged through advertising to enhance the credibility of and attitudes toward the advertiser, in addition to perceived social responsibility.

Social Responsibility and Sincerity: CRM

Often referred to as "doing well, by doing good," CRM is a form of cause–brand alliance. A cause–brand alliance creates an association between company selling a product and a social cause or issue. CRM links the consumer purchase of the brand to the support of a cause or not for profit organization. It offers consumers who desire to support the cause a means to offer that support with little effort or sacrifice while engaging in everyday purchase behaviors. Consumers report being less sensitive to price and product attribute differences after exposure to a CRM campaign (Pracejus and Olsen, 2004), and that support of a cause can be a deciding factor in brand decisions, particularly under conditions of product parity (Holmes and Kilbane, 1993). The Cone Cause Evolution Study (Cone Communications, 2010) reports that given product parity, 93% of "Moms" and 85% of "Millennials" are likely to switch brands based on the support of a cause.

CRM campaigns enhance consumer perceptions of corporate credibility (Berger *et al.*, 1999; Chaney and Dolli, 2001; Hajjat, 2003; Lafferty *et al.*, 2004; Trimble and Rifon, 2006; Yechaim *et al.*, 2003). However, CRM campaigns have the potential to create unintended consequences and backlash (Barone *et al.*, 2000; Dahl and Lavack, 1995), as consumers may doubt the sincerity of the sponsoring company and have eroded perceptions of company credibility (Rifon *et al.*, 2004). Consumer acceptance of the alliance is essential for consumers to respond positively to CRM (Trimble and Rifon, 2006) and several characteristics of the CRM matter.

American Express has been widely cited for its introduction of the first CRM campaign. In the early 1980s, American Express tried out a new marketing concept to increase use of their card and the cards' acceptance at retail outlets (Andreason, 1996). For every purchase a consumer made using an American Express card, American Express Co. would make a donation to charity. First, American Express used this marketing practice in San Francisco, and following the success of that campaign, the company developed a national campaign that supported the renovation of Ellis Island and the Statue of Liberty. American Express had hit on a marketing concept so innovative they were able to copyright the term they developed to describe it: cause-related marketing.

The choice of the social cause, based on its "fit" to the sponsoring company, may be the most widely studied element of CRM (Brown and Dacin, 1997; Ellen *et al.*, 2000; Hajjat, 2003; Mizerski *et al.*, 2001; Porter and Kramer, 2002; Pracejus and Olsen, 2004; Trimble and Rifon, 2006). The fit between a cause and a sponsoring company has the potential to create consumer perceptions of the compatibility between the company and cause, and generate subsequent positive corporate credibility and attitude perceptions (Trimble and Rifon, 2006). The most widely studied, and believed to be the most essential, is functional fit or congruence between the pair. A functional fit may exist when the core competencies of the company clearly support the sponsored cause (Brown and Dacin, 1997; Porter and Kramer, 2002). For example, if a computer software company donated a part of their profits or products to school computing programs, or if a bottled water manufacturer donated to victims of a drought, consumers could functionally experience the core competence of the company in support of the cause. Fit, or the lack of fit, appears to drive consumer attributions of the company's motive for supporting the cause. When there is a lack of fit, it may trigger a consumer's "why is that" reaction, causing more thought and skepticism for the alliance. Rifon *et al.* (2004) found that the lower the fit, the more likely consumers were to make attributions of a profit motive for

the alliance resulting in a weakening of credibility perceptions.

The longevity of the alliance can also influence consumer response and compensate for a lack of functional fit. When a company maintains a relationship with a cause or not for profit over time, the longevity of the sponsorship creates a behavioral pattern that the consumer is more likely to accept over time. In 1978, in Burlington, Vermont, Ben Cohen and Jerry Greenfield began a small ice cream company called Ben & Jerry's. From its earliest inception, the company incorporated social responsibility in its mission statement; the ice cream manufacturer committed to social responsibility and environmental sustainability (http://www.benjerry.com/).

The consumer's relationship with the cause is another important element. Consumers may identify with some causes more than others. As an example, individuals stricken with an illness, and friends and family of that person, may identify with efforts to raise money to fight that disease.

In addition, some causes have wide appeal and for any audience and most companies when chosen for their CRM campaigns. This may be due to the widespread effects of an issue, touching the lives of a majority of consumers, or perhaps due to a cultural norm. For example, breast cancer and, notably, the not-for-profit Susan G. Koman Breast Cancer Research Foundation have become very popular causes receiving support from companies ranging from the NFL to Avon. St. Jude's Children's Research Hospital in Memphis Tennessee, founded by Danny Thomas, is devoted to curing childhood cancers and offers care to all regardless of ability to pay. Many companies align with St. Jude's through their annual Thanks and Giving campaign, donating money to St. Jude's based on customer purchases. A variety of retailers participate and benefit through supporting a cause that, regardless of functional fit or core competencies, appeals to most people (Anonymous, 2012). In 2012, St. Jude raised over $64 million through its retail partners, including Kmart, CVS, and K Jewelers.

There is some evidence that a cause–brand alliance with a functional fit does not insure success (Ellen *et al.*, 2000; Mizerski *et al.*, 2001; Pracejus and Olsen, 2004; Trimble and Rifon, 2006). Some executives have reported concerns about consumer perceptions of corporate greed if the connection between the corporation and the cause are too obvious or too close (Webb and Mohr, 1998). The gender of the target market also matters. Women report more positive responses to CRM campaigns than men (Berger *et al.*, 1999; Ross *et al.*, 1990, 1992; Trimble and Rifon, 2006), but it is not clear why.

Celebrity Spokespersons

Because corporations are not tangible human entities, giving the corporation human qualities may help consumers to see them not as cold, distant, and uncaring profiteers, but as sincere and compassionate friends with souls. One way to accomplish this is through the use of a celebrity spokesperson. A celebrity spokesperson is typically defined as a recognizable person who uses this recognition to promote a consumer good through an advertisement. A recognizable personality can anthropomorphize a company by putting a "face" on the company and humanizing it. The idea of anthropomorphizing the company is not new and can be seen through history in the use of trade characters invented to embody and communicate the personality of the product or company (Aggarwal and McGill, 2007). Famous examples include Betty Crocker and the Pillsbury Doughboy. From 1979 to 1986, the Smith Barney brokerage firm used John Houseman to communicate the qualities of their firm. At the time, John Houseman played a Harvard Law school professor, Professor Kingsfield, made famous in the movie *The Paper Chase* and in the television series of the same name (Elliott, 1985). In the voice of his character, Houseman stated in the ad, "Smith Barney, they make money the old fashioned way, they *earn* it."

Houseman's character efficiently personifies the brokerage firm and embodies it with credibility, authority, expertise, and engendering trust.

There is evidence that individuals spontaneously infer and attribute personality traits to organizations (Slaughter *et al.*, 2004). Using a celebrity spokesperson can facilitate this process and demonstrate the traits that are desired. A celebrity spokesperson works through a process of meaning transfer. The characteristics of the celebrity transfer to a product, and in this case, the corporation (McCracken, 1989). This transfer process helps explain some of the appeal of a celebrity endorser; a person will purchase a product endorsed by a celebrity in the hopes of becoming more like that celebrity.

As noted earlier, Ohanian (1990) identified three global characteristics that can make a celebrity more effective: attractiveness, credibility, and expertise. Choi and Rifon (2007) elaborated on Ohanian's work using traits identified in marketing, psychology, and advertising. They identified genuineness, competence, excitement, and sociability as desirable endorser traits. However, these global factors do not account for the unique characteristics that any one celebrity might possess and are thought to transfer to the products they ally with (McCracken, 1989), and when using a celebrity spokesperson, care must be taken to identify the proper set of traits.

A celebrity spokesperson can help a product to stand out among its competitors (Dean and Biswas, 2001). Empirical evidence supports the use of a celebrity that fits the product for greater credibility and ad effects (Koernig and Boyd, 2009). For example, an attractive celebrity would be more effective at selling beauty products than an unattractive celebrity. Or a race car driver would be more effective at selling tires than a golfer. To increase effectiveness further, the celebrity should be seen as both physically attractive and as having some expertise regarding the product (Eisend and Langner, 2010). Expertise indicates that the celebrity is competent, knowledgeable, has experience, and is qualified (Tantiseneepong *et al.*, 2012).

A celebrity spokesperson is often hired from outside the company, but when anthropomorphizing a company, history shows that some of the best personalities came from inside the company. Lee Iacocca is the perfect example of an endorser from within the company, having been ranked the eighteenth best CEO of all time by Portfolio (Portfolio.com, 2009). His no-nonsense attitude made him a trustworthy and believable spokesperson. Iacocca became CEO of Chrysler when the company was about to go bankrupt. The company was having problems with high costs, poor quality, high interest rates, inflation, and inefficiency (Thorpe, 1988). Iacocca had been notoriously fired from Ford Motor Company after a fall out with Henry Ford II (before being hired by Chrysler). In an attempt to make over Chrysler's image, Iacocca became the company's spokesman. He spoke directly to the consumer and owned up the mistakes Chrysler had made that led to their current financial situation. Over the next few years, Iacocca did over 60 spots informing the public of Chrysler's progress (Coleman, n.d.). In these spots, Iacocca focused on the American dream, Chrysler as a company, and how these American-made cars could meet the needs of the American consumer. He focused on the fact that if Chrysler fell, it could affect the rest of the economy and hurt the American worker. To the public, Iacocca represented the underdog that was able to accomplish the American dream (Thorpe, 1988).

One reason Iacocca may have been so influential as a spokesperson for Chrysler was that as the CEO, he personified the expert, shown in past research to be essential for positive ad effects. Research has shown that CEOs are seen as more knowledgeable (Freiden, 1984) and can improve a consumer's perception of trustworthiness (Rubin *et al.*, 1982). While not all CEOs will be viewed as trustworthy, Iacocca was. He used tactics that have been shown to be more persuasive than one-sided communications. By acknowledging some of the mistakes Chrysler made, he added credibility to his message and himself.

While there is no one formula for selecting a celebrity spokesperson, some (*several*) factors should be considered. Overall, research shows that consumers tend to prefer a celebrity endorser to a CEO or president spokesperson. In comparison studies, celebrities seem to perform better across the board than do CEOs (Maronick, 2005). When selecting a celebrity, results show that attractiveness is more important than familiarity, as is likability (Erdogan *et al.*, 2001), and the appearance of being knowledgeable about the product creates expertise (Tantiseneepong *et al.*, 2012).

When a celebrity has too many different endorsements, the relationship between the celebrity and the brand can become diluted. Consumers begin to sense the reason for the endorsement is payment rather than a sincere feeling or support for the brand. It is also possible that a celebrity suddenly disappears from the spotlight or changes his or her image (Erdogan *et al.*, 2001). For this reason, many companies include morality clauses or death and disgrace insurance in the endorser's contract. Death and disgrace insurance simply says that the company can void the contract if the endorser dies, is disabled, or is disgraced. In addition to having insurance, a morality clause can be included in the contract. If the spokesperson transgresses, this allows the company to break the contract without penalty. However, splitting with a spokesperson is not a desired outcome. So the selection of a celebrity spokesperson to personify the company bears great risk, but it is a risk that might pay off (Erdogan and Drollinger, 2008).

Bringing It All Together: The American Express Members Project

In 2007, American Express introduced its latest CRM campaign, its Members Project, an illustration of the successful incorporation of several tactics into one campaign to enhance corporate reputation. The Members Project was not a traditional CRM campaign, and American Express showed its forward thinking and innovativeness in this area with every element of the campaign. The engagement of card members in the selection of the cause to support, the use of social media, the use of a unique collection of celebrity spokespeople, and the use of pathos and humor all played a role in this campaign standing out for its creativity and finesse in execution.

The cause

While other companies select and present a cause, issue, or not for profit to sponsor and highlight their CRM campaigns, American Express asked its customers which cause to sponsor. Over 7000 projects were put forward at the beginning of the campaign, and cardholders were asked to discuss and vote on the projects that they thought were worthy. Over a period of about three months, the projects were narrowed down to 50, then 25, then 5, and the winning project was announced on August 3. In traditional CRM practice, American Express linked its donation to customer participation, guaranteeing a $1 donation to the winning project for each person who registered during the program. The number of registrants was approximately 186,500, but American Express went beyond their original commitment and donated $2 million to the winning project, "Children's Safe Drinking Water," devoted to providing safe drinking water for children in Africa, administered by UNICEF. The other four finalists included a wide range of initiatives: global reforestation, the restoration of US national parks, investment in US schools, and alternative energy, and each received $100,000 (Quinton, 2008).

Social media

Social media served as the dominant platform for the campaign that was supported by advertising across other media, and since its inception, the campaign has been completely moved to Facebook. Card members were directed to the Members Project web site where they could read about the many not-for-profit seeking support. Voting occurred at the web site as well. Presently, American Express has put the campaign completely within the Facebook network, utilizing its affordances such as "liking" and of course, the essential word of mouse (mouth), "sharing."

Celebrities

The campaign used a collection of celebrities to metaphorically communicate the member's theme with personality and humor. In one notable ad for the first campaign (available at http://www.youtube.com/watch?v=BV6U_ujddnE), a collection of celebrities present the Members Project in traditional ad form, until the fourth wall is broken, and the audience is shown Martin Scorsese behind the scenes directing the commercial. Ellen DeGeneres, Shaun White, Andre Agassi, Alicia Keys, and Sheryl Crow present a serious description of the Members Project until they are interrupted by an unknown young man, who appears to unintentionally walk through the commercial. Martin Scorsese says cut and the young man presents his vote for a worthy project, and Ellen DeGeneres makes a self-deprecating joke. The slogan "you don't have to be famous to make a difference," is illustrated by the action in this ad, and the serious subject matter is tempered with a joke by DeGeneres. Also supporting the theme is that each celebrity was a card member who previously had been in an ad for American Express. The varied personalities in this group offered an appeal to a variety of target markets using celebrities who were well known, from different entertainment domains (music, tennis, snowboarding, television, and film), representing success in each of their areas.

Clearly, American Express did "good," but did they do well? Amex and Digitas thought so and considered the campaign to be the most recognizable of all American Express campaigns to date, reaching an estimated 1.5 million people and "greater than 50% recognition among both current and prospective card members" (Quinton, 2008). The 2008 campaign generated greater member participation with over 400,000 registrants, and over 1.8 million unique visitors to the project web site (Meyers, 2008). However, there appears to be no report of the campaign's actually increasing the number of card members as was the case with their first Statue of Liberty campaign.

Conclusions

Advertising can indeed be used to enhance corporate reputation. For it to be effective, the company must engage in activities that can be positively leveraged to consumers and other stakeholders. Since advertiser credibility is essential for the creation of positive brand advertising effects, maintaining corporate credibility should be a top priority for communication.

References

Aaker, D., Stayman, D.M., and Hagerty, M.R. (1986) Warmth in advertising: Measurement, impact and sequence effects. *Journal of Consumer Research*, 12(March), 365–381.

Aggarwal, P. and McGill, A. (2007) Is that car smiling at me?: Schema congruity as a basis for evaluating anthropomorphized products. *Journal of Consumer Research*, 34, 468–479.

Andreason, A.R. (1996) Profit for nonprofits: Find a corporate partner. *Harvard Business Review*, 74, 47–59.

Anonymous (2012) St. Jude thanks and giving campaign raises more than $64 million to save lives of children battling cancer and other deadly diseases. St. Jude Fundraising and Donor News. Retrieved from http://www.stjude.org/stjude/v/index.jsp?vgnextoid=d6dae1537af25310VgnVCM100000290115acRCRD&rss=latest_news (last accessed September 11, 2012).

Barone, M.J., Miyazaki, A.D., and Taylor, K.A. (2000) The influence of cause-related marketing on consumer choice: Does one good turn deserve another? *Journal of the Academy of Marketing Science*, 28(2), 248–262.

Berger, I.E., Cunningham, P.H., and Kozinets, R.V. (1999) Consumer persuasion through cause-related advertising. *Advances in Consumer Research*, 26, 491–497.

Bettman, J.R. and Park, W.C. (1980) Effects of prior knowledge and experience and phase of the choice process on consumer decision processes: A protocol analysis. *Journal of Consumer Research*, 7(3), 234.

Bhattacharya, C.B. and Sen, S. (2003) Consumer-company identification: A framework for understanding consumers' relationship with companies. *Journal of Marketing*, 67(April), 76–88.

Brown, S.P. and Stayman, D.M. (1992) Antecedents and consequences of attitude toward the AD: A meta-analysis. *Journal of Consumer Research*, 19(1), 34–51.

Brown, T.J. and Dacin, P.A. (1997) The company and the product: Corporate associations and consumer product responses. *Journal of Marketing*, 61(January), 68–84.

Celsi, R.L. and Olson, J.C. (1988) The role of involvement in attention and comprehension process. *Journal of Consumer Research*, 15 (September), 210–224.

Chaney, I. and Dolli, N. (2001) Cause-related marketing in New Zealand. *International Journal of Nonprofit and Voluntary Sector Marketing*, 6(2), 145–163.

Chattopadhyay, A. and Nedungadi, P. (1992) Does attitude toward the ad endure? The moderating effects of attention and delay. *Journal of Consumer Research*, 19(2), 25–33.

Choi, S.M. and Rifon, N.J. (2007) Who is the celebrity in advertising? Understanding dimensions of celebrity images. *The Journal of Popular Culture*, 40(2), 304–324.

Coleman, J.W. (n.d.) Choosing the company spokesperson part 8. Retrieved from MCAI Media Community http://mcai-oc.org/index.php?option=com_content&view=article&id=604:choosing-the-company-spokesperson-part-8&catid=9:articles (last accessed September 11, 2012).

Cone Communications (2010) Cone Cause Evolution Study. Retrieved from http://www.coneinc.com/2010-cone-cause-evolution-study (last accessed September 11, 2012).

Craig, C.S. and McCann, J.M. (1978) Assessing communication effects on energy conservation. *Journal of Consumer Research*, 5(2), 82–88.

Cravens, K., Goad Oliver, E., and Ramamoorti, S. (2003) The reputation index: Measuring and managing corporate reputation. *European Management Journal*, 21(2), 201–212.

Dahl, D.W. and Lavack, A.M. (1995) Cause-related marketing: Impact of size of cause-related promotion on consumer perceptions and participation. In D.W. Stewart and N.J. Vilcassim (eds), *1995 AMA Winter Educators Conference: Marketing Theory and Applications, VI*. Chicago, IL: American Marketing Association, pp. 476–481.

Darby, M.R. and Karni, E. (1973) Free competition and the optimal amount of fraud. *Journal of Law and Economics*, *16*(April), 67–86.

Dean, D.H. and Biswas, A. (2001) Third-party organization endorsement of products: An advertising cue affecting consumer prepurchase evaluation of goods and services. *Journal of Advertising*, *30*(4), 41–57.

Donlon, J.P. (2001) Guess who's the chief reputation officer? *Chief Executive*, *165*, 44–48.

Eisend, M. and Langner, T. (2010) Immediate and delayed advertising effects of celebrity endorsers attractiveness and expertise. *International Journal of Advertising*, *29*(4), 527–546.

Ellen, P.S., Mohr, L.A., and Webb, D.J. (2000) Charitable programs and the retailer: Do they mix? *Journal of Retailing*, *76*(3), 393–406.

Elliott, S. (1985) Smith Barney summons the ghost of a haughty John Houseman in a revival of its "timeless" ads. The New York Times, August 25, Business Day.

Erdogan, B.Z., Baker, M.J., and Tagg, S. (2001) Selecting celebrity endorsers: The practitioner's perspective. *Journal of Advertising Research*, *41*, 39–48.

Erdogan, B.Z. and Drollinger, T. (2008) Death and disgrace insurance for celebrity endorsers: A luxury or necessity? *Journal of Current Issues and Research in Advertising*, *30*(1), 71–77.

Fombrun, C.J. (1996) *Reputation: Realizing Value from the Corporation.* Boston: Harvard Business School Press.

Fombrun, C.J. and Shanley, M. (1990) What's in a name? Reputation building and corporate strategy. *Academy of Management Journal*, *33*(2), 233–258.

Freiden, J. (1984) Advertising spokesperson effects: An examination of endorser type and gender of two audiences. *Journal of Advertising Research*, *24*, 33–41.

Goldberg, M.E. and Hartwick, J. (1990) The effects of advertiser reputation and extremity of advertising claim on advertising effectiveness. *Journal of Consumer Research*, *17*, 172–179.

Goldsmith, R.E., Lafferty, B.A., and Newell, S.J. (2000) The impact of corporate credibility and celebrity credibility on consumer reaction to advertisements and brands. *Journal of Advertising*, *29*(3), 43–54.

Hajjat, M.M. (2003) Effect of cause-related marketing on attitudes and purchase intentions: The moderating role of cause involvement and donations size. *Journal of Nonprofit & Public Sector Marketing*, *11*(1), 93–109.

Haley, E. (1996) Exploring the construct of organization as source: Consumers' understandings of organizational sponsorship of advocacy advertising. *Journal of Advertising*, *25*(2), 19–35.

Harris Interactive (2003) Reputation Quotient(sm). Retrieved from Harrisinteractive.com (last accessed September 11, 2012).

Holmes, J.H. and Kilbane, C.J. (1993) Cause-related marketing: Selected effects of price and charitable donations. *Journal of Nonprofit & Public Sector Marketing*, *1*(4), 67–83.

Kim, S., Haley, E., and Koo, G.-Y. (2009) Comparison of the paths from consumer involvement types to AD responses between corporate advertising and product advertising. *Journal of Advertising*, *38*(3, Fall), 67–80.

Koernig, S. and Boyd, T. (2009) To catch a tiger or let him go: The match-up effect and athlete endorsers for sport and non-sport brands. *Sport Marketing Quarterly*, *18*(1), 25–37.

Lafferty, B.A., Goldsmith, R.E., and Hult, G.T.M. (2004) The impact of the alliance on the partners: A look at cause-brand alliances. *Psychology and Marketing*, *21*(7), 509–531.

Lutz, R.J., MacKenzie, S.B., and Belch, G.E. (1983) Attitude toward the ad as a mediator of advertising effectiveness: Determinants and consequences. *Advances in Consumer Research*, *10*(1), 532–539.

MacKenzie, S.B. and Lutz, R.J. (1989) An empirical examination of the structural antecedents of attitude toward the AD in an advertising pretesting context. *Journal of Marketing*, *53*(April), 48–65.

Maronick, T.J. (2005) Celebrity versus company president as endorsers of high risk products for elderly consumers. *Journal of Promotion Management*, *11*(4), 63–80.

McCracken, G. (1989) Who is the celebrity endorser? Cultural foundations of the endorsement process. *The Journal of Consumer Research*, *16*(3), 310–321.

Melewar, T.C. and Jenkins, E. (2002) Defining the corporate identity construct. *Corporate Reputation Review*, *5*(1), 76–90.

Meyers, T. (2008) American Express Members Project: A marketing 50 case study. Advertising Age, November 17.

Mitchell, A.A. and Olson, J.C. (1981) Are product attribute beliefs the only mediator of advertising effects on brand attitude? *Journal of Marketing Research*, *18*(August), 318–332.

Mizerski, D., Mizerski, K., and Sandler, O. (2001) A field experiment comparing the effectiveness of "ambush" and cause related AD appeals for social marketing causes. *Journal of Nonprofit & Public Sector Marketing, 9*(4), 25–45.

Nelson, P. (1974) Advertising as information. *Journal of Political Economy, 82*(July/August), 729–754.

Ohanian, R. (1990) Construction and validation of a scale to measure celebrity endorsers' perceived expertise, trustworthiness and attractiveness. *Journal of Advertising, 19*(3), 39–52.

Passion readies Denton for AMD's comms challenges. (2003) PRWeek, September 24, p. 13.

Peterson, R.A., Hoyer, W.D., and Wilson, W.R. (1986) Reflections on the role of affect in consumer behavior. In R.A. Peterson, W.D. Hoyer, and W.R. Wilson (eds), *The Role of Affect in Consumer Behavior: Emerging Theories and Applications.* Lexington, MA: Lexington Books, pp. 141–159.

Ponzi, L.J., Fombrun, C.J., and Gardberg, N.A. (2011) RepTrak™ pulse: Conceptualizing and validating a short-form measure of corporate reputation. *Corporate Reputation Review, 14*(1), 15–35.

Porter, M. and Kramer, M.R. (2002) The competitive advantage of corporate philanthropy. *Harvard Business Review, 80,* 57–68.

Portfolio (2009) Portfolio's Best American CEOs of All Time. http://www.cnbc.com/id/ 30391313/page/4 (last accessed December 24, 2012).

Pracejus, J.W. and Olsen, G.D. (2004) The role of brand/cause fit in the effectiveness of cause-related marketing campaigns. *Journal of Business Research, 57,* 635–640.

Pruzan, P. (2001) Corporate reputation: Image and identity. *Corporate Reputation Review, 4*(1), 50–64.

Quinton, B. (2008) American Express lets cardmembers nominate social betterment ideas. Promo-Magazine, November 1. Retrieved from http:// promomagazine.com/interactivemarketing/ 1101-amex-digitas-campaign/ (last accessed September 11, 2012).

Rifon, N.J., Choi, S.M., Trimble, C., and Li, H. (2004) Congruence effects in sponsorship: The mediating role of sponsor credibility and consumer attributions of sponsor motive. *Journal of Advertising, 33*(1), 29–42.

Rifon, N.J., Choi, S.M., and Quilliam, E.T. (2005) Corporate reputation and source credibility in

persuasive messages. American Marketing Association Summer Educator's Conference, August.

Ross, J.K. III, Stutts, M.A., and Patterson, L.T. (1990) Tactical considerations for the effective use of cause-related marketing. *The Journal of Applied Business Research, 7*(2), 58–65.

Ross, J.K. III, Patterson, L.T., and Stutts, M.A. (1992) Consumer perceptions of organizations that use case-related marketing. *Journal of the Academy of Marketing Science, 20*(1), 93–97.

Rubin, V., Mager, C., and Friedman, H. (1982) Company president versus spokesperson in television commercials. *Journal of Advertising Research, 22,* 31–33.

Slaughter, J.E., Zicker, M.J., Highhouse, S., and Mohr, D. (2004) Personality trait inferences about organizations: Development of a measure and assessment of construct validity. *Journal of Applied Psychology, 89,* 85–103.

Sternthal, B., Phillips, L.W., and Cholakia, R. (1978) The persuasive effect of scarce credibility: A situational analysis. *Public Opinion Quarterly, 42*(3), 285–314.

Tantiseneepong, N., Gorton, M., and White, J. (2012) Evaluating responses to celebrity endorsements using projective techniques. *Qualitative Market Research, 15*(1), 57–69.

Thorpe, J.M. (1988) Lee Iacocca and the generation of myth in the spokesman advertising campaign for Chrysler from 1980–1984. *Journal of American Culture, 11*(2), 41–45.

Trimble, C. and Rifon, N.J. (2006) Effects of consumer perceptions of match in cause-related marketing message. *International Journal of Nonprofit & Voluntary Sector Marketing, 11*(1), 29–47.

Webb, D.J. and Mohr, L.A. (1998) A typology of consumer responses to cause-related marketing: From skeptics to socially concerned. *Journal of Public Policy & Marketing, 17*(Fall), 226–238.

Yechaim, E., Barron, G., Erev, I., and Erez, M. (2003) On the robustness and the direction of the effect of cause-related marketing. *Journal of Consumer Behavior, 2*(4), 320–332.

Zajonc, R.B. (1980) Feeling and thinking: Preferences need no inferences. *American Psychologist, 35*(February), 151–175.

6

Corporate Reputation and the Discipline of Corporate Communication

Peggy Simcic Brønn

Norwegian Business School (BI), Norway

This chapter looks at reputation through the lens of corporate communication starting with an overview of the historical development of corporate communication and the three dominant views: as a management discipline, as integrated communication, and as another term for public relations. This is followed by a discussion of the core concepts of image and corporate identity that provide the foundation of understanding corporate communication. The conclusion is that at its heart, corporate communication is all about reputation. Present and future research combining corporate communication is addressed along with trends impacting the field. The chapter concludes with a discussion on criticisms of some of the accepted principles supporting the field.

Introduction

Corporate communication has been around for a while, but it is only in the last 15–20 years that it has become firmly established as a field of academic research and study. David Bernstein (1984) is credited with being the leading pioneer within the field of corporate communication (Balmer, 2009). Bernstein articulated the "strategic necessity for senior executives to adopt an overarching corporate-wide communication program" (p. 553). Bernstein was stimulated to write his book *Company Image and Reality: A Critique of Corporate Communication* because he felt that few organizations realized that everything they do sends a message. He also felt that communication was an underappreciated resource, one that in fact should be the responsibility of the chief executive. He developed a communication wheel with the organization in the center of the hub (he included here also industry and country of origin), communication channels comprising the spokes, and stakeholders the rim of the wheel. The wheel illustrated that organizations have many stakeholders and many communication options, not just public relations, and/or advertising. Balmer and Greyser (2003) later added corporate branding covenant, partnerships, and the effect of environmental factors to the communication wheel. Their model, which consists of 11 stakeholder and interest

The Handbook of Communication and Corporate Reputation, First Edition. Edited by Craig E. Carroll.
© 2013 John Wiley & Sons, Inc. Published 2015 by John Wiley & Sons, Inc.

groups, multiplied by 11 communication channels, generates an overwhelming 121 communication configurations and demonstrates the complexity of an organization's communication challenges.

The fact that a practitioner is given credit as a pioneer of the field corresponds to the viewpoint of Argenti (1996), who asserts that corporate communication "evolved within the business world more quickly and more thoroughly" (p. 74) in contrast to its academic development. Argenti (2009) sees corporate communication as a better integration of those functions normally consigned to public relations. These embrace media relations, financial relations, crisis communication, and so on. He includes marketing communication as a function under corporate communication, but his description is typically marketing PR, product publicity, and customer relations.

Steyn (2004) sees no theoretical differences between corporate communication and public relations. She prefers to use the term corporate communication due to the "negative connotation that 'public relations' has for some members of management/the public" (p. 169). Argenti's (2009) view is also that the field of public relations has given way to corporate communication because PR is too associated with press relations or what he calls "flak." Corporate communication is thus perceived as removing the stigma from PR. This is not dissimilar to Bernstein, who saw public relations as possibly corporate communication but in reality as primarily press relations. Hutton *et al.* (2001) defined corporate communication as the overall internal/external communication function of the organization while noting that in some firms, it was also called public relations or corporate relations.

Van Riel (1995) is recognized as writing the first academic book on corporate communication (Balmer, 2009). Van Riel makes a point to use communication without an "s." As he explains, communication with an "s" implies integration of methods (tactics), while communication without an "s" denotes the communication function. In van Riel's view, corporate communication is an

instrument of management by means of which all consciously used forms of internal and external communication are "harmonized" as effectively and efficiently as possible, so as to create a favourable basis for relationships with groups upon which the company is dependent. (van Riel, 1995, p. 26)

Van Riel and Fombrun (2007) credit Jackson's (1987) definition of corporate communication as among the first to appear in international literature. His definition that "corporate communication is the total communication activity generated by a company to achieve its planned objectives" (Jackson, 1987, cited in van Riel and Fombrun, 2007, p. 25) is reflected in van Riel's (1995) definition.

Van Riel (1995) places three broad categories of communication under the umbrella of corporate communication: marketing communication, management communication, and organizational communication. Marketing communication is defined as activities that support the sale of goods and services, of which advertising is generally regarded as the dominant element, and where most of the communications budget is spent, at least in commercial organizations. The consumer is the primary stakeholder. Management communication is considered communication from senior management to internal and external groups. The goal of internal management communication is to develop a common vision for the company/organization, to establish and maintain confidence in the leadership, to implement and manage change processes, and to empower and motivate employees. Management communication may include personal communications between virtually anyone in the organization, but also with external stakeholders. The last category is organizational communication, which for van Riel includes all other forms of communication used by the organization, focused primarily on the stakeholders who are not customers. It also reflects a more traditional public relations viewpoint as opposed to what we today understand as organizational communication, which is primarily internally focused. Van Riel's organizational communication function in this sense often has a long-term perspective and is not designed to directly generate sales (in the private sector). Included here are financial communication (investor relations), government relations, public relations, and media relations. The approach advocated by van Riel was suggested by public relations professors Toth and Trujillo (1986) when they proposed a redefinition of corporate communication through integrating concepts from public relations, organizational communications, and management research.

According to Kitchen (1997), corporate communication consists of three dimensions – public relations, marketing, and human resource (HR) management. Adding HR to the mix acknowledges the role that employees play in influencing perceptions of the organization. Thus, HR in this sense comprises internal marketing to employees.

Cornelissen (2008) describes corporate communication from an integrated perspective. This is explored through the work of Kotler and Mindak and their 1978 seminal piece on integrating public relations and marketing (some authors place its beginnings as early as the 1930s, others as in the 1960s). Depending on the "class of an organization," the two functions might be two separate but equal functions, equal but overlapping functions, marketing or PR as the dominant function, and marketing and PR as the same function.

Since the 1980s, there has been a realization that "silo thinking" is not productive. Bernstein (1984) even viewed corporate communication as the no man's land between advertising and public relations. Greater emphasis was being placed on the complementary nature of the two functions as well as on the areas where they overlap. The subsequent development in the 1990s of integrated marketing communication and integrated communication were thus viewed as a more strategic approach to communication (see Cornelissen and Thorpe, 2001). Researchers promoting this philosophy include Duncan and Moriarty (1997), Grønstedt (1996), Schultz and Kitchen (2001), and Schultz *et al.* (1994). However, the focus was still primarily on marketing communication, consumers, and products.

The integrated approach does not mean that there is no longer a need for separate public relations and marketing functions. The expectation is that corporate communication as a field may include expertise and experience from many communication disciplines including public relations, marketing, organizational communication and human resources management, in order to manage and integrate different messages under a single umbrella (Christensen *et al.*, 2007, p. 655).

Finally, Christensen *et al.* (2008) view corporate communication as a mind-set. Because its ultimate goal is to "manage all communications that involve the organization as a whole" (p. 3), all communication is thus covered by one perspective.

Image and Corporate Identity

It is impossible to discuss corporate communication and reputation without first taking up two important concepts: image and corporate identity. It must be acknowledged that the early writings in corporate communication were more concerned about the *image* of the organization. Bernstein (1984) asserts that "reputation is another term loosely trading places with image" (p. 18). Van Riel's (1995) groundbreaking book has an entire chapter on image and its measurement, barely mentioning reputation. This focus on image in the early writings on reputation is supported by Gotsi and Wilson (2001), who found that most of the authors they surveyed defined image in a way that was synonymous with reputation. They also found that many contemporary academics still support this position. It is proposed that the reason for this is that the authors mentioned in Gotsi and Wilson's article have backgrounds from public relations (Rindova, 1997) where the emphasis is on image as something created by the organization. The move from emphasizing image to reputation can be viewed as a strategic one. Image can be seen as something that can be constructed or manipulated and that is externally focused (Hatch and Schultz, 1997). A more internal–external approach is necessary where image is influenced by the organization's communication and by organizational members, arguably the behavior element of corporate identity, defined as who, or what, the organization tells others they are. People recognize and form perceptions (images) of the organization through its identity elements, the signals sent by the organization through symbols, communication and behavior (Dowling 2001).

For Fombrun and Shanley (1990), publics construct a *reputation* of the organization from information that originates from the organization itself. Watson and Kitchen (2008) believe that images contribute to the reputation of the organization. Reputations are formed, according to Balmer and Gray (1999), through a process that they call corporate communication. By communicating a clear image based on a positive identity, firms can build an "enviable" reputation (p. 131). Therefore, what an organization says about itself, and how they say it, is an extremely important part of any discussion of reputation.

According to Schraiger (2004), reputation is more influenced by perceptions rather than real knowledge, and thus managing corporate reputation is a primary task of corporate communication. Argenti (2009) supports this view as he sees reputation strategy, along with organizational identity and image, as the most critical part of the corporate communication function.

For Cornelissen (2008), corporate communication's overarching goal is to establish and maintain a favorable reputation among stakeholder groups. Fombrun and Rindova (1998, p. 210) note that "communications that make a firm transparent enable shareholders to appreciate the firm's operations better, and so facilitate ascribing it a better reputation." Burke (1998, p. 8) has a similar understanding and finds that the most important functions of corporate communication are to "sustain, foster and develop an organization's reputation."

Corporate communication has three roles that according to Dowling (2006) can help "to substantiate and amplify stakeholders' opinions of a company's reputation" (p. 64). First is raising awareness and generating understanding and appreciation of the organization, second is defending or explaining an organization's actions, and third is internal communication about the organization.

Van Riel's (2003) subsequent definition of corporate communication embraces corporate identity, stakeholders, and reputation. According to van Riel, corporate communication can be described as

> the orchestration of all the instruments in the field of organization identity (communication, symbols and behavior of organizational members) in such an attractive and realistic manner as to create or maintain a positive reputation for groups with which the organization has a dependent relationship. (p. 163)

For Schultz and de Chernatony (2002), reputation means creating a solid bond between the organization and stakeholder groups through a clear set of values. Key for building reputation is thus aligning organizational identity, corporate identity, and image. In other words, is who we say we are and how we are perceived anchored in who we really are? Furthermore, alignment, expressiveness, and reputation are produced by integrating the communication functions, according to van Riel and Fombrun (2007). These authors state quite clearly that the benefits of a corporate communication campaign should be reputation building.

Present and Future Research

Research that brings together corporate communication and reputation is rather sparse and in addition has given mixed results. Hutton *et al.* (2001) found a modest correlation between spending on corporate communication and reputation when studying *Fortune*'s Most Admired Companies. After adjusting the results for company size, the correlation dropped. Larger firms tended to have higher reputations but not necessarily larger communication budgets. These results appear to contradict research from Harris/Impulse Research (1999) that indicated a clear and consistent correlation between communication spending and reputation.

Wiedmann and Prauschke (2006) hypothesized that the higher the perceived quality of corporate communication, the higher the reputation of the firm. They measured the quality of corporate communication as (1) informing the public in a sincere way, (2) feeling well informed, and (3) the communication from the firm is reliable. Not only was there a direct correlation between quality of corporate communication and reputation, but the quality of corporate communication also impacted perceptions of value for money, customer orientation, innovativeness, and CEO competence.

Fombrun and van Riel (2004) investigated five communication variables that are correlated with high reputation rankings: authenticity, visibility, transparency, distinctiveness, and consistency. Responsiveness was later added (van Riel and Fombrun, 2007). *Visibility* is comprised of public prominence and market prominence. Public prominence occurs when an organization has high "street" exposure. Market prominence occurs when there is powerful brand equity from a strong corporate brand or product brand portfolio. Market prominence also comes from being listed on a public stock exchange and highly exposed corporate citizenship. *Distinctiveness* occurs when firms distinguish themselves from their rivals based on their unique characteristics. *Transparency* allows stakeholders access to information that enables them to make an accurate assessment of the organization. *Responsiveness* is the heart of dialog, which is built on the premise that the organization will adjust its stance or behavior based on feedback from the environment. This is also one of the core principles in much of the research on strategic communication, where two-way symmetrical communication is a critical component (Grunig, 2001). *Authenticity* is what makes the organization real, genuine, accurate, reliable, and trustworthy.

As noted previously, the integrated approach to corporate communications promotes an umbrella function assembling the various communication functions in an organization. While there is a large literature on the organization of communication and communication functions, there is little empirical research (Cornelissen *et al.*, 2006). One study by Einwiller and Will (2002) looked at how the functions responsible for relating with stakeholders were organized, concentrating on corporate communication functions. Their findings indicated that the size of the communication department tended to be dependent on the philosophy of centralization versus autonomous business units, and there was no common view of integration or similarities between marketing and corporate communication. The research offered no evidence that the firms' way of managing their communication function was effective or not or if reputations were better or worse.

Cornelissen *et al.* (2006) take exception to the traditional view of measuring reputation as a strategic outcome of corporate communication and the development of best practices based on reputation scores. They suggest that future research must link management practices with outcomes in order to truly understand corporate communication and its influence.

Elving (2010), reflecting on the 15-year history of the journal *Corporate Communications: An International Journal*, noted the tendency for papers to come from the United Kingdom, Europe, or North America, with 40% from the United Kingdom alone. However, the percentage of papers from Europe rose to nearly 45% in the three years between 2006 and 2009. And there are clear indications that more articles are being submitted from Asia and Africa. Elving interprets this trend as evidence that corporate communication as a field of practice and science is spreading. Interestingly, while Cornelissen *et al.* (2006) are calling for more insight into management practices, Elving found that this emphasis was popular in the first half of the decade starting in 2000, but almost completely vanished after 2005. Interest is rather moving toward corporate social responsibility, reputation, and corporate identity. It is worth noting that the majority of the papers still remain loyal to internal and change communication as well as external communication processes including branding and public relations.

Bernstein (2009) in his reflections on the development of corporate communication raises concerns that he feels deserve more attention. One of these is trust. As he observes, trust is at all times low for all sectors: governments, the media, business, and in particular the financial sector. Obvious questions raised here are: how do organizations restore trust and what is the role of corporate communication? However, Bernstein is more interested in the rhetoric of corporate communication and the behavior of the organization, meaning people in the organization. He believes that organizational behavior does not in general match what is being said. Courtright and Smudde (2009) believe that the reputation literature has in general ignored the rhetorical and discursive aspects of communication (they specifically say public relations). They view reputation management and public relations as "the measured and ethical use of language and symbols to inspire cooperation between an organization and its publics" (Courtright and Smudde, 2007, p. 4). Future research would link analyses of what organizations are saying to reputation and behavior.

Another area of increasing importance is that of social media. For example, Facebook and Twitter have stimulated a revived interest in social networks because of their power to fully allow two-way communication. The development of these media has been instrumental in bringing people together in conversations, that is, social networks. They also present an entirely new and different, not to mention powerful, challenge to reputation and corporate communication as they allow stakeholders to take control of the conversation:

> To safeguard their reputations in this highly nuanced digital landscape, then, all brands must ensure their social media presence is both "globally" consistent and "locally" relevant by developing scalable social engagement strategies. (iMedia Connection, 2010, November 9, in *Reputation Intelligence*, Winter 2010–2011)

Zerfass (2008) identifies three challenges facing communicators regarding Web 2.0 that need investigating: (1) the structuring of the process of communication management, (2) communicating effectively with social media, and (3) linking social web communication to corporate strategies. These broad areas raise additional issues of how to implement social web applications for knowledge management, organizational participation in popular platforms and channels (who and how?), and what are the best scorecards and strategy maps?

The third area, linking to corporate strategies, may be the most difficult as studies and interest in social media can rapidly focus on the tool itself and not the outcome.

The next question is: what outcomes should be measured for corporate communication efforts involving social media? It seems that the biggest interest at the moment is sales related. As noted by iMedia Connection (2010), "the connection of social media to sales, sales indicators, promotions, and other measurable or valued marketing and sales conversions is fueling the investment in social media." But social networks also support creativity and innovation *within* the organization. These are part of the firm's processes and products but are, at least in the formative stages, intangible and difficult to measure directly. It seems that a "corporate communication approach" (integrated) is critical if the organization is to take advantage of the true benefits of computer-mediated communication and the reputation benefits that can accrue from it. Obviously, there is a dire need for interdisciplinary research that can shed light on the critical factors related to engaging employees and stakeholders in a manner that encourages learning and not the least innovation.

Conclusion

It has been suggested that the function of corporate communication is to influence stakeholders' perceptions of the organization (Forman and Argenti, 2005). The function should be used to "form support groups' interpretation and perceptions and socialize the support groups into the organization's own culture." Using words like form and influence may give the impression that organizations can somehow make people believe what they want them to believe. This is in sharp contrast to variables that invite dialog – real dialog based on stakeholder involvement. This includes words like transparency, authenticity, and responsiveness, the building blocks of good reputations.

Harmonizing communication through a corporate communication department responsible for both marketing communication and traditional PR activities sounds reasonable but is difficult to put into practice. As discussed earlier, discussions on marketing communication and PR structural and role differences have been prevalent since the 1970s. Today, there is evidence that PR managers may report to the CEO but are still not viewed as formal members of the top management team providing input into strategic decision making (Cornelissen *et al.*, 2006). In such situations, communication can rapidly become a one-way tool to convince stakeholders of the organization's position instead of a strategic instrument in relationship building that can lead to good reputations. Research indicates that marketing and PR do often work together but the relationship is often more informal than formal, and is often dependent on the relationship between members of the departments. Cornelissen and Thorpe (2001) suggest that organizations should consider a more flexible and less structural approach to their external communication activities.

Questions have also been raised if the concepts of corporate identity and corporate communication can be applied to all organizations. For example, some researchers believe that applying corporate branding and what they perceive as its demands for a precise definition of identity and consistency in communication is problematic for the public sector (Wæraas, 2008). According to Wæraas, the public sector's contradictory and inconsistent values and multiple identities make it impossible for them to promote one set of values or one identity (p. 205). Most organizations are made up of a numerous of individuals and numerous subcultures and identities, and consistency does not imply dogma. It means that organizations need to understand who they are, and if they are complex with multiple identities, then that is who they say they are. Doing otherwise sets the stage for a reputational crisis.

There are also some researchers who point out that consistency cannot always be an overriding value (Christensen *et al.*, 2008). Their seemingly paradoxical argument is as follows: if an organization is always looking for consistency, it will not necessarily be able to adapt to the environment when needed. Inconsistency can be a necessity in a transitional period. The focus should not necessarily be on the gap between words and action, but organizations should rather applaud any experimentation that can lead to improvement. These researchers twist the adage of "walk the talk." For them, it is more correct that good leaders "talk the walk."

Organizations need to take a long-term approach to reputation building that involves different functions such as strategy, marketing, design, HR, and communication. The research community might also take note of this recommendation. Those studying reputation in different disciplines need to reach out to communication scholars and vice versa. Reputation is an organization-wide phenomenon and an organization's communication is often the first, and sometimes the only, basis on which stakeholders base their impression of an organization. There is ample evidence that the responsibility for building reputation with a strategic focus resides, if not wholly then substantially, within the corporate communication function.

References

Argenti, P. (1996) Corporate communication as a discipline: Toward a definition. *Management Communication Quarterly*, 10(1), 73–97.

Argenti, P. (2009) *Corporate Communication* (5th ed.). New York: McGraw-Hill.

Balmer, J. (2009) Corporate marketing: Apocalypse, advent and epiphany. *Management Decision*, 47(4), 544–572.

Balmer, J. and Gray, E.R. (1999) Corporate identity and corporate communications: Creating a competitive advantage. *Corporate Communications: An International Journal*, 4, 171–176.

Balmer, J. and Greyser, S. (2003) Managing the multiple identities of the organization. In S. Greyser and J. Balmer (eds), *Revealing the Corporation: Perspectives on Identity, Image, Reputation.* London: Routledge.

Bernstein, D. (1984) *Company Image and Reality: A Critique of Corporate Communications.* Eastbourne, NY: Holt, Rinehart and Winston.

Bernstein, D. (2009) Rhetoric and reputation: Some thoughts on corporate dissonance. *Management Decision*, 47(4), 603–615.

Burke, T. (1998) Risks and reputations: The economics of transaction costs. *Corporate Communications*, 3(1), 5–10.

Christensen, L., Cornelissen, J., and Morsing, M. (2007) Corporate communications and its receptions: A comment on Llewellyn and Harrison. *Human Relations*, 60(4), 653–661.

Christensen, T., Morsing, M., and Cheney, G. (2008) *Corporate Communications: Convention, Complexity, and Critique.* London: Sage.

Cornelissen, J.P. (2008) *Corporate Communication: A Guide to Theory and Practice.* London: Sage.

Cornelissen, J.P. and Thorpe, R. (2001) The organization of external communication disciplines in UK companies: A conceptual and empirical analysis of dimensions and determinants. *Journal of Business Communication*, 38, 413–438.

Cornelissen, J.P., van Bekkum, T., and van Ruler, B. (2006) Corporate communication: A practice-based theoretical conceptualization. *Corporate Reputation Review*, 9(2), 114–133.

Courtright, J.L. and Smudde, P.M. (eds) (2007) *Power and Public Relations.* Cresskill, NJ: Hampton Press.

Courtright, J.L. and Smudde, P.M. (2009) Leveraging organizational innovation for strategic reputation management. *Corporate Reputation Review*, 12(3), 245–269.

Dowling, G. (2006) Communicating corporate reputation through stories. *California Management Review*, 49(1), 62–81.

Duncan, T. and Moriarty, S. (1997) *Driving Brand Value: Using Integrated Marketing to Manage Profitable Stakeholder Relationships.* New York: McGraw-Hill.

Einwiller, S. and Will, M. (2002) Towards an integrated approach to corporate branding – An empirical study. *Corporate Communication: An International Journal*, 7(2), 100–109.

Elving, W. (2010) Trends and developments within corporate communication: An analysis of ten years of CCIJ. *Corporate Communications: An International Journal*, 15(1), 5–8.

Fombrun, C.J. and Rindova, V.P. (1998) Constructing competitive advantage: The role of firm-constituent interactions. *Strategic Management Journal*, 20, 691–710.

Fombrun, C.J. and Shanley, M. (1990) What's in a name? Reputation building and corporate strategy. *Academy of Management Journal*, 33(2), 233–258.

Fombrun, C.J. and van Riel, C.B.M. (2004) *Fame & Fortune: How Successful Companies Build Winning Reputations.* Upper Saddle River, NJ: Financial Times Prentice Hall.

Forman, J. and Argenti, P. (2005) How corporate communication influences strategy implementation, reputation and the corporate brand: An exploratory qualitative study. *Corporate Reputation Review*, 8(3), 245–264.

Gotsi, M. and Wilson, A.M. (2001) Corporate reputation: Seeking a definition. *Corporate Communications: An International Journal*, 6(1), 24–30.

Grønstedt, A. (1996) Integrating marketing communication and public relations: A stakeholder relations model. In E. Thorson and J. Moore (eds), *Integrated Communication: Synergy of Persuasive Voices.* Mahwah, NJ: Lawrence Erlbaum Associates, pp. 287–304.

Grunig, J. (2001) Two-way symmetrical public relations: Past, present and future. In R.L. Heath (ed.), *Handbook of Public Relations.* Thousand Oaks, CA: Sage, pp. 11–30.

Harris/Impulse Research (1999) Corporate communications spending & reputations of Fortune 500 companies. Project Report sponsored by the Council of Public Relations Firms, Impulse Research Corporation, California.

Hatch, M.J. and Schultz, M. (1997) Relations between organizational culture, identity and image. *European Journal of Marketing*, 31(5/6), 356–365.

Hutton, J.G., Goodman, M.B., Alexander, J.B., and Genest, C.M. (2001) Reputation management: The new face of corporate public relations? *Public Relations Review*, 27, 247–261.

iMedia Connection (2010) Socialization through Glocalization: Engaging audiences in the modern digital landscape. Reputation Intelligence, November 9, Winter 2010–2011, pp. 4–10.

Jackson, P. (1987) *Corporate Communication for Managers.* London: Pitman.

Kitchen, P. (1997) Was public relations a prelude to corporate communications? *Corporate Communications: An International Journal*, 2(1), 22–30.

Kotler, P. and Mindak, W. (1978) Marketing and public relations; should they be partners or rivals? *Journal of Marketing, 42*, 13–20.

Rindova, V.P. (1997) The image cascade and the formation of corporate reputations. *Corporate Reputation Review, 1*(1 and 2), 188–194.

Schraiger, M. (2004) Components and parameters of corporate reputation – An empirical study. *Schmalenbach Business Review, 56*, 46–71.

Schultz, D. and Kitchen, P. (2001) *Raising the Corporate Umbrella. Corporate Communications in the 21st Century*. London: Palgrave.

Schultz, D., Tannenbaum, S.I., and Lauterborn, R.F. (1994) *The New Marketing Paradigm: Integrated Marketing Communication*. Chicago, IL: NTC Business Books.

Schultz, M. and de Chernatony, L. (2002) Introduction: The challenges of corporate branding. *Corporate Reputation Review, 5*(2/3), 105–123.

Steyn, B. (2004) From strategy to corporate communication strategy: A conceptualisation. *Journal of Communication Management, 8*(2), 168–183.

Toth, E.L. and Trujillo, N. (1986) Reinventing corporate communication. *Public Relations Review, 13*(4), 42–53.

van Riel, C.B.M. (1995) *Principles of Corporate Communication*. Hemel Hempstead, UK: Prentice Hall.

van Riel, C.B.M. (2003) The management of corporate communication. In S. Greyser and J. Balmer (eds), *Revealing the Corporation: Perspectives on Identity, Image, Reputation*. London: Routledge, pp. 163–170.

van Riel, C.B.M. and Fombrun, C.J. (2007) *Essentials of Corporate Communication*. London: Routledge.

Wæraas, A. (2008) Can public sector organizations be coherent corporate brands? *Marketing Theory, 8*, 205–221.

Watson, T. and Kitchen, P. (2008) Corporate communication: Reputation in action. In T.C. Melawar (ed.), *Facets of Corporate Identity, Communication and Reputation*. London: Taylor & Francis, pp. 121–140.

Wiedmann, K.-P. and Prauschke, C. (2006) How do stakeholder alignment concepts influence corporate reputation? The role of corporate communication in reputation building. Paper presented at the 10th Reputation Institute Conference on Reputation, Identity, Image & Competitiveness, New York, May 25–28.

Zerfass, A. (2008) Social Web, interactive communication and open innovation: Joining forces to contribute to the bottom line. Paper presented at the EuroBlogg International Research Symposium, Brussels, Belgium, March.

7

Corporate Reputation and the Discipline of Public Relations

Judy Motion
University of New South Wales, Australia

Sally Davenport
Victoria University of Wellington, New Zealand

Shirley Leitch
Swinburne University, Australia

Liz Merlot
Swinburne University, Australia

Public relations offers the study of corporate reputation a rich tradition of communication scholarship that highlights issues of meaning and sensemaking. The chapter outlines various schools of thought in public relations and their impact on definitional issues, and examines the multidisciplinary, multidimensional paradigmatic shift that is taking place in public relations. Symbolic capital and positioning theories are proposed as salient resources for corporate reputation work along with fundamental public relations principles.

Introduction

During a recent interview for a lecturer position, an experienced practitioner who was asked to define public relations responded that public relations is reputation management. At first glance, this definition may seem perfectly acceptable. Conflating public relations and corporate reputation is, however, a somewhat naïve definitional approach which does not engage with the complexity and richness of each discipline. Public relations and corporate reputation are not interchangeable – they are interdependent. Retention of distinctions

The Handbook of Communication and Corporate Reputation, First Edition. Edited by Craig E. Carroll.
© 2013 John Wiley & Sons, Inc. Published 2015 by John Wiley & Sons, Inc.

between disciplines and their discrete epistemological and conceptual orientations is important. However, while a nascent discipline is evolving, scholarship and practice from another discipline may be "borrowed" and retheorized in accordance with the emergent discipline's rationale, purpose, and values. Our aim in this chapter is to explain how the discipline of public relations may inform the study of corporate reputation. In line with the handbook theme, we focus on the communicative dimensions of corporate reputation and concentrate on meaning as the fundamental nexus between the two disciplines. Our discussion outlines definitional issues, examines a paradigmatic shift in understandings of public relations, and suggests how the study of corporate reputation may be advanced by consideration of public relations concepts, in particular, the concepts of positionality and symbolic capital. A case study on the discourse of productivity is presented as a vehicle to apply key public relations concepts to corporate reputation.

The Definitional Terrain: Public Relations and Corporate Reputation

Definitional tensions emerge from the subjective nature of the multiple ontological, epistemological, paradigmatic, and theoretical orientations of various schools of thought. Within public relations, there is tacit agreement that the discipline is concerned with persuasive communication (Heath, 2001). Although multiple schools of thought compete and thrive in the discipline of public relations, the two main approaches that dominate the definitional terrain may be broadly categorized as meaning production and sensemaking (Heath, 2001) or relational (Ferguson, 1984; Hutton, 1999; Ledingham and Bruning, 1999). Increasingly the boundaries between these two approaches are blurring and shifting as scholars work across multiple theories and themes.

Although corporate reputation is a nebulous term to define and explain, like public relations,

it is also broadly concerned with how meanings are produced and interpreted through multiple relationships. Perhaps because the "definitional landscape of corporate reputation has continued to expand drawing upon multiple literatures and disciplines" (Barnett *et al.*, 2006, p. 26), corporate reputation has yet to reach any general definitional consensus. Early definitional work focused on the identity and image aspects of corporate reputation. Dowling (1994) defined corporate reputation as "the evaluation (respect, esteem, estimation) in which an organizations image is held by people" (p. 8). Argenti and Druckmiller (2004) expanded on the identity definitional dimensions and referred to reputation as "the collective representation of multiple constituencies' images of a company, built up over time and based on a company's identity programs, its performance and how constituencies have perceived its behavior" (p. 369). Drawing together these definitions, Watson (2010, p. 340) suggested that reputation is a "collective representation" of images and perceptions – "the sum of predictable behaviours, relationships, and two way communication undertaken by an organization as judged affectively and cognitively by its stakeholders over a period of time" (Watson, 2010, p. 340). Watson's definition offers a public relations-oriented lens for understanding corporate reputation as a communicative function concerned with organizational identity, and relational and perceptual issues. Gray and Balmer's (1998) definition of corporate reputation as "the perception of a firm" may be integrated with Watson's definitional explanation to form a working definition of corporate reputation for this chapter.

Barnett *et al.* (2006) classified the definitions of corporate reputation into thematic clusters termed "awareness," "assessment," and "asset," which simplified the range of definitional understandings of corporate reputation. The definitional approach we adopt above fits within the awareness definitional cluster. Provocatively, Barnett *et al.* (2006, p. 36) suggested that it may be time to move away from definitions that relate to *awareness* (images, perceptions) to define reputation in terms of *assessment* (estimation, judgment, evaluation, and opinion). Preferences for quasi-scientific definitions that address quantitative issues of measurement, assessment, and evaluation do not, however, actually explain what a discipline is – they are, instead, linked to the need for nascent disciplines to establish academic rigor and legitimacy. Another definitional issue is that too often academics try to develop compound definitional statements that summarize every possible dimension of a discipline. However, we eschew the need for a single common definition and suggest, instead, that it is crucial that scholars and practitioners develop and select definitions that are based on "research concerning what organizations are actually doing" (Hutton *et al.*, 2001, p. 248) and take into account definitional context, relevance, and salience.

We also advocate for a tentative new definitional cluster that concentrates on meaning as a defining feature of corporate reputation. Corporate reputation, we argue, is simultaneously a meaning creation and sensemaking construct. Rhetorical (Heath, 1992, 2001; Ihlen, 2002) and discursive (Leitch and Motion, 2010; Motion and Leitch, 1996) approaches in public relations focus our attention on meaning, language, and change, and have much to offer corporate reputation. Discourse, with its associated concept of positioning, offers significant potential for extending the conceptual underpinning of corporate reputation. In later sections of this chapter, we expand on how public relations offers a set of discursive applications that may be used to enhance corporate reputations by communicating the complex realities of an organization and aligning behavior with societal expectations.

Development of a cluster of relational definitions is also important for corporate reputation. Definitions that assume an organization may control its reputation are deeply problematic (Brønn, 2010). Relationships may perhaps be managed, but they cannot be controlled (Leitch and Neilson, 2001). Power, too, has not featured prominently in the corporate reputation definitional landscape – contemporary public relations research is rapidly advancing research

in this area (see, e.g., Edwards, 2006; Heath *et al.*, 2010).

Moving beyond narrow constrained quasi-scientific orientations to seek public relations contributions for meaning and relation-oriented corporate reputation definitional clusters has the potential to open up rather than close down the development of corporate reputation as a discipline.

Paradigmatic Shifts: Public Relations

There has been a recent shift on how we understand the paradigmatic foundations of the rapidly evolving discipline of public relations. Early work by Trujillo and Toth (1987) suggested that we could classify public relations processes and practices into functional, interpretive, and critical paradigms according to the goals or intentions of an organization. *Functionalist public relations* was concerned with "measurable, quantifiable indicators of organizational effectiveness and efficiency." Grunig and Hunt's (1984) systems work is often cited as an early example of such work which then later evolved into the "excellence" approach. *Interpretive public relations*, as suggested by Trujillo and Toth (1987), is concerned with the symbolic aspects of organizational communication and concentrates on meaning-related issues. Work within this paradigm includes sensemaking, and rhetorical and cultural approaches. Heath's (1992, 2001) work on rhetoric is a well-established leader within this paradigmatic framework as is the pioneering work of Sriramesh (1992) on culture and public relations. The third paradigm that Trujillo and Toth (1987) identified is the *critical public relations* approach that "treats organizations as ideological and material arenas for power, influence and control" (p. 216). Issues of power, change, and politics dominate this paradigm, which critique inequitable power relations, opaque or dishonest communicative efforts, and manipulative public relations practices and argue for radical social change. The critical paradigm is emerging as an increasingly popular and productive field of research that owes much to the early works of Ewen (1996) and L'Etang and Pieczka (1996).

The Trujillo and Toth (1987) paradigmatic framework has provided an extremely useful approach for categorizing public relations orientations and may also apply to corporate reputation scholarship. However, the paradigmatic framework was derived from organizational studies work and therefore reflected organizational imperatives. A significant quantum of public relations research now focuses beyond the organization to individual, national, and societal imperatives. Corporate reputation should also take into account the expectations of civil society (Taylor, 2010). Another limitation of the Trujillo and Toth (1987) framework for public relations is that emergent public relations schools of thought and theoretical orientations may traverse paradigmatic boundaries and will not easily fit within the framework. Perhaps these observations of the limitations of a paradigmatic framework constitute a useful insight for the study of corporate reputation – it is fine to borrow from other disciplines, but in time, externally derived theories, frameworks, and models need to be adapted or redeveloped to reflect disciplinary progress.

Heath (2010, p. 1) suggests that the three dominant paradigms of public relations may now be redefined as "management adjustive, discourse engagement and normative/critical/ethical." These categories offer more scope for accommodating approaches that sit outside the organizationally derived framework and cross-paradigmatic schools of thought, such as the study of public relations of nations (see, e.g., L'Etang, 2004; Toledano, 2005).

Management Adjustive

Heath (2010) explains that the systems approach to public relations may now be subsumed within a management adjustive paradigm that takes into account developments in managerial theory and practice. He suggests that a proactive philosophy has now developed through issues management that guides organizational responsiveness to complexity and chaos. The aim is to align interests and to develop mutually beneficial relationships through managerial processes. Corporate reputation work must also be proactive and future focused, scanning for potential issues, managing meaning, and responding in accordance with societal expectations (see Coombs, 2010; Coombs and Holladay, 2002; Heath, 1997). A full discussion of this approach and the implications for corporate reputation is presented within the chapter by Robert Heath in this handbook.

Discourse Engagement

Within the discourse engagement paradigm, there is a focus on participative and collaborative communication. Discourses may be understood as sets of meanings or systems of knowledge that construct how we know, understand, and talk about the world. Fairclough (1992) identified those who actively attempt to manage discourse as "professional technologists who research, design and provide training in discourse practices" (p. 8). Public relations practitioners and their meaning production work function as discourse technologists (Motion and Leitch, 1996) who seek to develop, popularize, and transform discourse by introducing "new ways of thinking" (Leitch and Motion, 2010, p. 103) and by influencing how we think about objects, subjects, and strategies (Foucault, 1972). Those who attempt to shape and manage corporate reputation in an effort to create positive identification with and legitimacy for particular organizations may also be thought of as discourse technologists or "reputation management advocates" (Hutton *et al.*, 2001, p. 249).

Attempts to manage reputation are concerned with what an organization means, how it is positioned in relation to other organizations, and stakeholder interpretations of corporate behavior. Discourse offers a strategic resource that individuals and organizations may deploy in their corporate reputation work. Change may be legitimated, drawing upon discursive legitimization strategies to conform with, circumvent, or contest existing power/knowledge relations and to produce truth (Foucault, 1980) in relation to their corporate reputations. Efforts to gain acceptance for a desired corporate reputation strategy need to be implemented in such a way that associated communicative and behavioral practices are accepted as the ethical, approved norm. Increasingly, engagement and participative communication processes (De Bussy, 2010; Hughes and Demetrious, 2006; Motion and Leitch, 2008) are developed to cocreate shared meanings and agreements about stakeholder and societal expectations and establish acceptable practice (Botan and Taylor, 2004; Taylor, 2010). At the heart of all reputational efforts is the attempt to fix certain meanings and overturn others – a discourse engagement orientation offers corporate reputation advocates and scholars a rich resource for advancing understanding of a meaning-oriented paradigm.

Normative/Critical/Ethical Paradigm

The normative/critical/ethical paradigm, as suggested by Heath (2010), focuses on responsibility and societal obligations. The aim of public relations is viewed as building harmony and resolving discord. A myriad of approaches may be identified within this paradigm that includes, for example, postmodern (Holtzhausen, 2000; McKie, 2001, 2010), poststructuralist (Motion and Leitch, 2009), and postcolonial critiques (McKie and Munshi, 2007), themes of power, globalization, diversity and change (Bardhah and Weaver, 2011; Curtin and Gaither, 2007; Edwards and Hodges, 2011; Heath et al., 2010; Sriramesh and Verčič, 2009), and ethics and corporate responsibility (Cheney and Christensen, 2001; L'Etang, 1995). Bardhah and Weaver (2011)

and Heath (2010) pointed to an emergent multidisciplinary and multidimensional blending of paradigmatic approaches. For Heath (2010), guiding principles for pubic relations emphasize proactive adjustment, collaborative communication, and responsible behavior. Simply stated, Heath suggests that an organization should adjust its behavior to focus on mutual interests and benefits that meet societal ideals and expectations, communicate collaboratively through discourse to develop shared meanings, and behave ethically. This philosophy provides guidelines for organizations and offers a neat fit with the objectives of corporate reputation work.

Theoretical Resources

Within this section, we highlight several germane, meaning-related theories within public relations that are potential resources for the study of corporate reputation. Significant work has been undertaken in public relations to apply social theory to public relations (Ihlen et al., 2009), focusing on "reflexivity and reflective modes rather than emphasizing effectivity or efficiency" (Bentele and Wehmeier, 2009). This work is a valuable resource for the study of corporate reputation because public relations efforts directly impact on and partially create corporate reputations. One possible application of social theory that may readily contribute to the study of corporate reputation is Bourdieu's (1986) theory of capital, which has been applied within public relations (Edwards, 2006, 2009; Ihlen, 2005, 2009). The concept of *symbolic capital*, we argue, is highly salient for the study of corporate reputation. Symbolic capital provides those that have it (whether individuals, organizations, or nations), the power to determine and impose a version of the world through language (Bourdieu, 1977, 1987). We propose that a useful way of understanding symbolic capital is that it is concerned with the power of meanings and that some meanings convey significant value. Symbolic capital is therefore inextricably linked with discourse, and attention should focus on the discursive formation, modification, and transformation of meaning, as well as focus on the rules that underpin corporate reputation work. Corporate reputation work is also concerned with normalizing and legitimizing certain ideas and defining positions and functions. Positive reputations and the meanings associated with an organization are a form of symbolic capital for organizations.

Organizations may attempt to deliberately manage their reputation and maximize their symbolic capital by adopting and claiming *positions* in relation to identity or issues. An organization's corporate reputation will partly evolve from and reflect promotional strategies and the products or service it sells. Positioning strategies in relation to competitors and market context are a significant consideration for corporate reputation work. Within a market, reputation may be assessed in relation to competitors and contextualized in terms of, for example, temporality or global politics.

Positioning may also be considered in relation to discourse and identity formation. Organizations may adopt or claim positions within a discourse that carry identity implications that offer "a conceptual repertoire and a location" (Davies and Harré, 1990, p. 46) within and across a complex network of discourses which align with a particular worldview. Positions, however, are not only linked to identity. They may also be political in nature and issue related (Roper, 2005). This type of positioning is understood as the adoption of a "discourse" position because it is a declaration of where an organization is locatesd in relation to an issue. Claiming or advocating a particular discourse position has significant reputational effects and implications when a particular worldview is advocated, interest in an issue is declared, and the stakes are identified (Motion, 1999). Those seeking to advocate particular reputational strategies have a number of positioning options to consider including identity formation, meaning creation, competitive differentiation, and promotional possibilities,

which will maximize symbolic capital in the market and more broadly in civil society.

Case Study: Corporate Reputation – A Productivity Perspective

Productivity is a significant public relations issue for government and corporate reputational work. Within this section, we offer a case study that examines how New Zealand organizations respond to a government-driven public relations effort to increase productivity. The aim of the case study is to offer insights into how discursive, symbolic, and positioning strategies are played out and offer a praxis-oriented platform to discuss and theorize corporate reputation. The research outlined in this case study is part of a larger funded program that explores the ways in which firms from the New Zealand food and beverage sector help to build productivity. The case study is based on interviews with key informants, typically organizational managers, CEOs, and/or owners, from 15 food and beverage case organizations in New Zealand. New Zealand's food and beverage firms employ one in five New Zealanders, contribute half of the total exports, and comprise 10% of gross domestic product ("Backing our strengths," 2008; Evans, 2007; Winger, 2005).

New Zealand managers explained that they adopted a "niche" positioning strategy and built reputations differentiated by quality, innovation, or philosophy. Niche positioning addressed some of the factors that limit productivity, in particular, the size of the firm (in terms of resources available and competitive strategy) and country attributes (the size of the New Zealand market). New Zealand firms struggle to choose an appropriate positioning strategy for international markets: "I didn't want to look like a New Zealand company overseas, I wanted to look more local, but the feedback was 'push the fact that you are from New Zealand, we love it over here'." New Zealand ·

organizations rarely have internationally well-established reputations that will make an impact in global markets – New Zealand's identity and reputation as "clean and green" has greater potential leverage and impact.

Reputational advantages that provide some power to negotiate the global marketplace may also be derived from communicating how smaller size can be an advantage. For example, one informant notes that "the fact that we are a smaller company, we run smaller drives; we can be a bit nimble so if somebody wants a hundred tonne of this or that, we'll change specification for them." Adaptability, then, presents communicative possibilities for corporate reputation.

Clever positioning allowed particular meanings to be established that may potentially increase reputational value in terms of being perceived as an innovative firm. The meanings associated with a firm have a significant impact on reputation and may be sourced from preexisting aspects of the organization rather than something new. Research and development, production method, the way you treat your workforce, how you choose what goes in your product (quality), nutritional value, medicinal property, aesthetic property, safety dimensions, and country of origin all impact on reputation and may offer possibilities for generating symbolic capital. The meanings that a consumer associates with an organization, for example, production methods, may be leveraged for promotional and reputational purposes:

> **Interviewee 1:** There is some differentiation coming in terms of the way our cattle are farmed – they're grass fed versus grain fed . . . there are more health issues [benefits] that are being discovered about that method of farming that we use in New Zealand.
> **Interviewee 2:** [It's] a selling point: the health, the grass fed thing, free range as opposed to intensively farmed. They're what the consumer wants to hear . . . .

Symbolic capital evolved from promoting the method of production and offered significant reputational advantages. In this next example,

messages about food safety generate reputational advantages:

> We've gone out with a branded programme where we're wrapping a very strong food safety story or putting together a food safety brand. . . . We've got New Zealand MAF that certify every paddock. . . . In the Japanese market they're most concerned about food safety. So we can . . . promote a food safety programme that our competitors haven't been able to do.

These approaches offered alternative ways of generating symbolic capital and focused attention on meaning creation processes. Positioning strategies impacted on the meanings associated with an organization's reputation and suggest that a more nuanced mode of interpreting productivity, market possibilities, and constraints is vital. Reexamining all the elements of an organization's practices and adjusting them in accordance with societal norms and ethics may successfully reposition an organization's reputation in the marketplace and generate symbolic capital.

Conclusion

Within this chapter, we have offered insights on how the study of corporate reputation may benefit from the discipline of public relations. The discussion centered primarily on the importance of meaning as a foundational concept for understanding and working with corporate reputation. Within public relations scholarship, as Heath (2010, p. 1) points out, a thorough discussion of meaning is now taking place in order to "cocreate enactable collective sense making and interest alignment." Corporate reputation advocates would find a rich source for theory building by exploring the meaning and relationship schools of thought and adopting the paradigmatic public relations principles of adjustment, collaborative communication, and ethical behavior.

References

Argenti, P.A. and Druckmiller, B. (2004) Reputation and the corporate brand. *Corporate Reputation Review*, *7*(4), 368–374.

Backing our strengths: Areas of focus to support economic transformation. (2008) New Zealand Government, May.

Bardhah, N. and Weaver, C.K. (eds) (2011) *Public Relations in Global Cultural Contexts: Multi-Paradigmatic Perspectives*. New York: Routledge.

Barnett, M.L., Jermier, J.M., and Lafferty, B.A. (2006) Corporate reputation: The definitional landscape. *Corporate Reputation Review*, *9*(1), 26–38.

Bentele, G. and Wehmeier, S. (2009) Commentary: Linking sociology with public relations – Some critical reflections in reflexive times. In Ø. Ihlen, B. van Ruler, and M. Fredriksson (eds), *Public Relations and Social Theory: Key Figures and Concepts*. New York: Routledge, pp. 341–361.

Botan, C.H. and Taylor, M. (2004) Public relations: The state of the field. *Journal of Communication*, *54*, 641–661.

Bourdieu, P. (1977) *Outline of a Theory of Practice*. Melbourne, Australia: Cambridge University Press.

Bourdieu, P. (1986) The forms of capital. In J.G. Richardson (ed.), *Handbook of Theory and Research for the Sociology of Education*. Westport, CT: Greenwood Press, pp. 241–258.

Bourdieu, P. (ed.) (1987) Social space and symbolic power. In *Other Words: Essays towards a Reflexive Sociology*. Stanford, CA: Stanford University Press, pp. 122–139.

Brønn, P.S. (2010) Reputation, communication and the corporate brand. In R.L. Heath (ed.), *The Sage Handbook of Public Relations* (2nd ed.). Thousand Oaks, CA: Sage, pp. 307–320.

Cheney, G. and Christensen, L.T. (2001) Public relations as contested terrain: A critical response. In R.L. Heath (ed.), *Handbook of Public Relations*. Thousand Oaks, CA: Sage, pp. 167–182.

Coombs, W.T. (2010) Crisis communication: A developing field. In R.L. Heath (ed.), *The Sage Handbook of Public Relations* (2nd ed.). Thousand Oaks, CA: Sage, pp. 477–487.

Coombs, W.T. and Holladay, S.J. (2002) Helping crisis managers protect reputational assets: Initial tests of the situational crisis communication theory. *Management Communication Quarterly*, *16*(2), 165–186.

Curtin, P.A. and Gaither, T.K. (2007) *International Public Relations: Negotiating Culture, Identity, and Power*. Thousand Oaks, CA: Sage.

Davies, B. and Harré, R. (1990) Positioning: The discursive production of selves. *Journal for the Theory of Social Behavior*, *20*(1), 43–63.

De Bussy, N. (2010) Dialogue as a basis for stakeholder engagement: Defining and measuring the core competencies. In R.L. Heath (ed.), *The Sage Handbook of Public Relations* (2nd ed.). Thousand Oaks, CA: Sage, pp. 127–144.

Dowling, G. (1994) *Corporate Reputations: Strategies for Developing the Corporate Brand*. Melbourne: Longman Cheshire.

Edwards, L. (2006) Rethinking power in public relations. *Public Relations Review*, *32*, 229–231.

Edwards, L. (2009) Symbolic power and public relations practice: Locating individual practitioners in their social context. *Journal of Public Relations*, *21*(3), 251–272.

Edwards, L. and Hodges, C.E.M. (eds) (2011) *Public Relations, Society and Culture: Theoretical and Empirical Explorations*. Oxford, UK: Routledge.

Evans, L. (2007) NZ food and beverages: Challenges and opportunities. Food Magazine, November 20–23.

Ewen, S. (1996) *PR! A Social History of Spin*. New York: Basic Books.

Fairclough, N. (1992) *Discourse and Social Change*. Cambridge, UK: Polity.

Ferguson, M.A. (1984). Building theory in public relations: Interorganizational relationships as a public relations paradigm. Paper presented to the Public Relations Division, Association for Education in Journalism and Mass Communication Annual Convention, Gainesville, FL, August.

Foucault, M. (1972) *The Archaeology of Knowledge* (A.M. Sheridan Smith, trans.). London: Routledge.

Foucault, M. (1980) *Power/Knowledge: Selected Interview and Other Writings 1972–1977* (C. Gordon, L. Marshall, J. Mepham, and K. Soper, trans.). New York: Pantheon.

Gray, E.R. and Balmer, J.M.T. (1998) Managing corporate image and reputation. *Long Range Planning*, *31*(5), 695–702.

Grunig, J.E. and Hunt, T. (1984) *Managing Public Relations*. New York: Holt, Rinehart and Winston.

Heath, R.L. (1992) The wrangle in the marketplace: A rhetorical perspective of public relations. In

E.L. Toth and R.L. Heath (eds), *Rhetorical and Critical Approaches to Public Relations*. Hillsdale, NJ: Lawrence Erlbaum, pp. 17–36.

Heath, R.L. (1997) *Strategic Issues Management: Organizations and Public Policy Challenges*. Thousand Oaks, CA: Sage.

Heath, R.L. (ed.) (2001) A rhetorical enactment rationale for public relations: The good organization communicating well. In *Handbook of Public Relations*. Thousand Oaks, CA: Sage, pp. 31–50.

Heath, R.L. (ed.) (2010) Mind, self, society. In *The Sage Handbook of Public Relations* (2nd ed.). Thousand Oaks, CA: Sage, pp. 1–4.

Heath, R.L., Motion, J., and Leitch, S. (2010) Power and public relations: Paradoxes and programmatic thoughts. In R.L. Heath (ed.), *The Sage Handbook of Public Relations* (2nd ed.). Thousand Oaks, CA: Sage, pp. 191–204.

Holtzhausen, D.R. (2000) Postmodern values in public relations. *Journal of Public Relations Research*, *12*(1), 93–114.

Hughes, P. and Demetrious, K. (2006) Engaging with stakeholders or constructing them? Attitudes and assumptions in stakeholder software. *Journal of Corporate Citizenship*, *23*, 93–101.

Hutton, J.G. (1999) The definition, dimensions and domain of public relations. *Public Relations Review*, *25*(2), 199–214.

Hutton, J.G., Goodman, M.B., Alexander, J.B., and Genest, C.M. (2001) Reputation management: The new face of corporate public relations? *Public Relations Review*, *27*, 247–261.

Ihlen, Ø. (2002) Rhetoric and resources: Notes for a new approach to public relations and issues management. *Journal of Public Affairs*, *2*(4), 259–269.

Ihlen, Ø. (2005) The power of social capital: Adapting Bourdieu to the study of public relations. *Public Relations Review*, *31*(4), 492–496.

Ihlen, Ø. (2009) On Bourdieu: Public relations in field struggles. In Ø. Ihlen, B. van Ruler, and M. Fredriksson (eds), *Public Relations and Social Theory: Key Figures and Concepts*. New York: Routledge, pp. 62–82.

Ihlen, Ø., van Ruler, B., and Fredriksson, M. (eds) (2009) *Public Relations and Social Theory: Key Figures and Concepts*. New York: Routledge.

Ledingham, J.A. and Bruning, S.D. (1999) Relationship management in public relations: Dimensions of an organization-public relationship. *Public Relations Review*, *24*(1), 55–65.

Leitch, S. and Motion, J. (2010) Publics and public relations: Effecting change. In R.L. Heath (ed.), *The Sage Handbook of Public Relations* (2nd ed.). Thousand Oaks, CA: Sage, pp. 99–110.

Leitch, S. and Neilson, D. (2001) Bringing publics into public relations: New theoretical frameworks for practice. In R.L. Heath (ed.), *The Sage Handbook of Public Relations*. Thousand Oaks, CA: Sage, pp. 127–138.

L'Etang, J. (1995) Ethical corporate social responsibility: A framework for managers. *Journal of Business Ethics*, *14*(2), 125–132.

L'Etang, J. (2004) *Public Relations in Britain: A History of Professional Practice in the Twentieth Century*. Mahwah, NJ: Lawrence Erlbaum.

L'Etang, J. and Pieczka, M. (eds) (1996) *Critical Perspectives in Public Relations*. Boston: Thomson.

McKie, D. (2001) Updating public relations: "New science" research paradigms, and uneven developments. In R. Heath (ed.), *Handbook of Public Relations*. Thousand Oaks, CA: Sage, pp. 75–91.

McKie, D. (2010) Signs of the times: Economic sciences, futures and public relations. In R.L. Heath (ed.), *The Sage Handbook of Public Relations* (2nd ed.). Thousand Oaks, CA: Sage, pp. 85–97.

Mckie, D. and Munshi, D. (2007) *Reconfiguring Public Relations: Ecology, Equity and Enterprise*. Oxford, UK: Routledge.

Motion, J. (1999) Personal public relations: Identity as a public relations commodity. *Public Relations Review*, *25*(4), 465–479.

Motion, J. and Leitch, S. (1996) A discursive perspective from New Zealand: Another worldview. *Public Relations Review*, *22*(3), 297–309.

Motion, J. and Leitch, S. (2008) The multiple discourses of science-society engagement. *Australian Journal of Communication*, *35*(3), 29–40.

Motion, J. and Leitch, S. (2009) On Foucault: A toolbox for public relations. In Ø. Ihlen, B. van Ruler, and M. Fredriksson (eds), *Public Relations and Social Theory: Key Figures and Concepts*. New York: Routledge, pp. 83–102.

Roper, J. (2005) Organizational identities, identification and positioning: Learning from political fields. *Public Relations Review*, *31*(1), 139–148.

Sriramesh, K. (1992) The impact of societal culture on public relations: Ethnographic evidence from India. *Public Relations Review*, *18*(2), 201–211.

Sriramesh, K. and Verčič, D. (eds) (2009) *The Global Public Relations Handbook: Theory, Research and Practice* (2nd ed.). New York: Routledge.

Taylor, M. (2010) Public relations in the enactment of civil society. In R.L. Heath (ed.), *The Sage Handbook of Public Relations* (2nd ed.). Thousand Oaks, CA: Sage, pp. 5–15.

Toledano, M. (2005) Challenging accounts: Public relations and a tale of two revolutions. *Public Relations Review*, *31*(4), 463–470.

Trujillo, N. and Toth, E.L. (1987) Organizational perspectives for public relations research and practice. *Management Communication Quarterly*, *1*(2), 199–281.

Watson, T. (2010) Reputation models, drivers, and measurement. In R.L. Heath (ed.), *The Sage Handbook of Public Relations*. Thousand Oaks, CA: Sage, pp. 339–351.

Winger, R. (2005) A study into the level of value-added products in New Zealand food and beverage exports. A report for New Zealand Trade and Enterprise, Institute of Food, Nutrition and Human Health, Massey University.

8

Corporate Reputation and the Discipline of Management Communication

James S. O'Rourke

University of Notre Dame, USA

This chapter focuses on management communication as a key discipline, essential in advancing the goals of an organization and forming its reputation. It answers the intriguing question "What do managers do all day?" and outlines the skill set they need to thrive in a modern work environment. Talking and listening, paramount to communication, are viewed as opportunities rather than obligations. The author also emphasizes writing – both as a means of documentation and as an integral part of a manager's climb up the career ladder. The chapter explains how communication helps managers create and share meaning with employees and customers as well as shareholders. Readers will learn how messages are often the product of social circumstances both within and beyond their control. Managers will be challenged to improve their existing communication skills and develop new ones to prepare for changes in the workforce and their own ascension up the career ladder.

This chapter will argue that management communication is a central discipline in the study of communication and corporate reputation. An understanding of language and its inherent powers, combined with the skill to speak, write, listen, and form interpersonal relationships, will determine whether companies succeed or fail, and are rewarded or penalized for their reputations.

At the midpoint of the twentieth century, Peter Drucker (1954) wrote, "Managers have to learn to know language, to understand what words are and what they mean. Perhaps most important, they have to acquire respect for language as [our] most precious gift and heritage.

The manager must understand the meaning of the old definition of rhetoric as 'the art which draws men's hearts to the love of true knowledge.'"

Later, Eccles and Nohria (1992) reframed Drucker's (1954) view to offer a perspective of management that few others have seen: "To see management in its proper light, managers need first to take language seriously" (p. 205). In particular, they argue, a coherent view of management must focus on three issues: the use of rhetoric to achieve a manager's goals, the shaping of a managerial identity, and taking action to achieve the goals of the organizations that employ us. Above all, they say, "the essence

The Handbook of Communication and Corporate Reputation, First Edition. Edited by Craig E. Carroll.
© 2013 John Wiley & Sons, Inc. Published 2015 by John Wiley & Sons, Inc.

of what management is all about [is] the effective use of language to get things done" (p. 211). One of the things managers get done is the creation, management, and monitoring of corporate reputation.

The job of becoming a competent, effective manager thus becomes one of understanding language and action. It also involves finding ways to shape how others see and think of *the manager and his or her role*. A number of noted researchers have examined the important relationship between communication and action within large and complex organizations and conclude that the two are inseparable. Without the right words, used in the right way, it is unlikely that the right reputations develop. "Words do matter," write Eccles and Nohria (1992, p. 209), "they matter very much. Without words we have no way of expressing strategic concepts, structural forms, or designs for performance measurement systems." Language, they conclude, "is too important to managers to be taken for granted or, even worse, abused."

So, if language is a manager's key to corporate reputation management, the next question is obvious: how good are managers at using language? Managers' ability to take action – to hire a talented workforce, to change an organization's reputation, to launch a new product line – depends entirely on how effectively they use management communication, both as a speaker and as a listener. Managers' effectiveness as a speaker and writer will determine how well they are able to manage the firm's reputation. And their effectiveness as listeners will determine how well they understand and respond to others and can change the organization in response to their feedback.

This chapter will examine the role management communication plays in corporate reputation formation, management and change, and the position occupied by rhetoric in the life of business organizations. In particular, though, this chapter will focus on the skills, abilities, and competencies for using language, attempting to influence others, and responding to the requirements of peers, superiors, stakeholders, and the organization in which managers and employees work.

Management communication is about the movement of information and the skills that facilitate it – speaking, writing, listening, and processes of critical thinking. It is also about understanding who the organization is (identity), who others think the organization is (reputation), and the contributions individuals can make to the success of their business in light of their organization's existing reputation. It is also about confidence – the knowledge that one can speak and write well, listen with great skill as others speak, and both seek out and provide the feedback essential to creating, managing, or changing their organization's reputation.

This chapter will first look at the nature of managerial work, examining the roles managers play and the characteristics of the jobs they hold. The chapter will also look at what varies in a manager's position, what is different from one manager's job to another and the management skills needed to succeed. At the heart of this chapter, though, is the notion that communication, in many ways, is the work of managers. This chapter goes on to examine the roles of writing and speaking in **the life of a manager**, as well as other specific applications and challenges managers face as they play their role in the creation, maintenance, and change of corporate reputation.

What Do Managers Do All Day?

Most management textbooks would say that managers spend their time engaged in planning, organizing, staffing, directing, coordinating, reporting, and controlling. These activities, as Hannaway (1989) found in her study of managers at work, "do not, in fact, describe what managers do" (p. 39). At best, they seem to describe vague objectives that managers are continually trying to accomplish. The real world, however, is far from being that simple. The world in which most managers work is a "messy and hectic stream of ongoing activity" (Eccles and Nohria, 1992, p. 47).

Managers are in constant action. Virtually every study of managers in action has found that they "switch frequently from task to task, changing their focus of attention to respond to issues as they arise, and engaging in a large volume of tasks of short duration" (Hannaway, 1989, p. 37; Kotter, 1982). Mintzberg (1973, p. 31) observed CEOs on the job to get some idea of what they do and how they spend their time. He found, for instance, that they averaged 36 written and 16 verbal contacts per day, almost every one of them dealing with a distinct or different issue. Most of these activities were brief, lasting less than nine minutes.

Kotter (1999) studied a number of successful general managers over a five-year period and found that they spend most of their time with others, including subordinates, their bosses, and numerous people from outside the organization. Kotter's study found that the average manager spent just 25% of his or her time working alone, and that time was spent largely at home, on airplanes, or commuting. Few of them spend less than 70% of their time with others, and some spend up to 90% of their working time this way.

Kotter (1999) also found that the breadth of topics in their discussions with others was extremely wide, with unimportant issues taking time alongside important business matters. His study revealed that managers rarely make "big decisions" during these conversations and rarely give orders in a traditional sense. They often react to others' initiatives and spend substantial amounts of time in unplanned activities that are not on their calendars. He found that managers will spend most of their time with others in short, disjointed conversations. "Discussions of a single question or issue rarely last more than ten minutes," he notes. "It is not at all unusual for a general manager to cover ten unrelated topics in a five-minute conversation." More recently, managers studied by Sproull (1984) showed similar patterns. During the course of a day, they engaged in 58 different activities with an average duration of just nine minutes.

Interruptions also appear to be a natural part of the job. Stewart (1967) found that the managers she studied could work uninterrupted for half an hour only nine times during the four weeks she studied them. Managers, in fact, spend very little time by themselves. Contrary to the image offered by management textbooks, they are rarely alone drawing up plans or worrying about important decisions. Instead, they spend most of their time interacting with others – both inside and outside the organization. If casual interactions in hallways, phone conversations, one-on-one meetings, and larger group meetings are included, managers spend about two-thirds of their time with other people (Eccles and Nohria, 1992). As Mintzberg (1973) has pointed out, "Unlike other workers, the manager does not leave the telephone or the meeting to get back to work. Rather, these contacts are his work."

The interactive nature of management means that most management work is conversational (Pondy, 1978). When managers are in action, they are talking and listening. Studies on the nature of managerial work indicate that managers spend about two-thirds to three-quarters of their time in verbal activity (Mintzberg, 1973). These verbal conversations, according to Eccles and Nohria (1992), are the means by which managers gather information, stay on top of things, identify problems, negotiate shared meanings, develop plans, put things in motion, give orders, assert authority, develop relationships, and spread gossip. In short, they are what the manager's daily practice is all about. "Through other forms of talk, such as speeches and presentations," they write, "managers establish definitions and meanings for their own actions and give others a sense of what the organization is about, where it is at, and what it is up to" (pp. 47–48).

Major Characteristics of the Manager's Job

Time is fragmented. Managers have acknowledged from antiquity that they never seem to have enough time to get all those things done that need to be done. In the latter years of the twentieth century, however, a new phenomenon arose: demand for time from those in leadership roles increased, while the number of hours in a day remained constant. Increased work hours was one reaction to such demand, but managers quickly discovered that the day had just 24 hours and that working more of them produced diminishing marginal returns. According to one researcher, "Managers are overburdened with obligations yet cannot easily delegate their tasks. As a result, they are driven to overwork and forced to do many tasks superficially. Brevity, fragmentation, and verbal communication characterize their work" (Mintzberg, 1990, p. 167).

Values compete and the various roles are in tension. Managers clearly cannot satisfy everyone. Employees want more time to do their jobs; customers want products and services delivered quickly and at high-quality levels. Supervisors want more money to spend on equipment, training, and product development; shareholders want returns on investment maximized. A manager caught in the middle cannot deliver to each of these people what each most wants; decisions are often based on the urgency of the need and the proximity of the problem.

The job is overloaded. In recent years, many North American and global businesses were reorganized to make them more efficient, nimble, and competitive. For the most part, this reorganization meant decentralizing many processes along with the wholesale elimination of middle management layers. Many managers who survived such downsizing found that their number of direct reports had doubled. Classical management theory suggests that seven is the maximum number of direct reports a manager can reasonably handle. Today, high-speed information technology and remarkably efficient telecommunication systems mean that many managers have as many as 20 or 30 people reporting to them directly.

Efficiency is a core skill. With less time than they need, with time fragmented into increasingly smaller units during the workday, with the workplace following many managers out the door and even on vacation, and with many more responsibilities loaded onto managers in downsized, flatter organizations, efficiency has become the core management skill of the twenty-first century.

What Varies in a Manager's Job? The Emphasis

The entrepreneur role is gaining importance. Managers must increasingly be aware of threats and opportunities in their environment. Threats include technological breakthroughs on the part of competitors, obsolescence in a manager's organization, and dramatically shortened product cycles. Opportunities might include product or service niches that are underserved; out-of-cycle hiring opportunities, mergers, purchases, or upgrades in equipment; space; or other assets. Managers who are carefully attuned to the marketplace and competitive environment will look for opportunities to gain an advantage.

So is the leadership role. Managers must be more sophisticated as strategists and mentors. A manager's job involves much more than simple caretaking in a division of a large organization. Unless organizations are able to attract, train, motivate, retain, and promote good people, they cannot possibly hope to gain advantage over the competition. Thus, as leaders, managers must constantly act as mentors to those in the organization with promise and potential. When organizations lose a highly capable worker, all else in their world will come to a halt until they can replace that worker. Even if they find someone ideally suited and superbly qualified for a vacant position, they must still train, motivate, and inspire that new recruit, and live with the knowledge that productivity levels will be lower for a while than they were with their previous employee.

Managers must create a local vision as they help people grow. The company's annual report and those slick-paper brochures their sales force hands to customers may articulate the vision, values, and beliefs of the company. But what do those concepts really mean to workers at their location? What does a competitive global strategy mean to their staff at 8:00 a.m. on Monday? Somehow, managers must create a local version of that strategy, explaining in practical and understandable terms what their organization or unit is all about and how the work of their employees fits into the larger picture.

Management Skills Required for the Twenty-First Century

The twenty-first century workplace requires three types of skills, each of which will be useful at different points in a manager's career:

Technical skills. These are most valuable at the entry level, but less valuable at more senior levels. Organizations hire people for their technical expertise: can managers assess the market value of a commercial office building? Can they calculate a set of net present values? Are they experienced in the use of C++ or SAP/R3 software? These skill sets, however, constantly change and can become quickly outdated. What gets recruits in the door of a large organization will not necessarily get them promoted.

Relating skills. These are valuable across the managerial career span and are more likely to help managers progress and be promoted to higher levels of responsibility. These skills, which help managers to form relationships, are at the heart of what management communication is about: reading, writing, speaking, listening, and thinking about how they can help as the demands of their job shift and increase at the same time.

Conceptual skills. These skills are least valuable at the entry level, but more valuable at senior levels in the organization. They permit managers to look past the details of today's work assignment and see the bigger picture. Successful managers who hope to become executives in the highest levels of a business must begin, at a relatively early age, to develop the ability to see beyond the horizon and ask long-term questions. If managers have not

formed the relationships that will help them get promoted, however, they may not be around long enough to have an opportunity to use their conceptual skills.

Talk Is the Work

Managers across industries, according to Deirdre Borden, spend about 75% of their time in verbal interaction (Borden, 1995). Those daily interactions include the following:

One-on-one conversations. Increasingly, managers find that information is passed orally, often face-to-face in offices, hallways, conference rooms, cafeterias, restrooms, athletic facilities, parking lots, and literally dozens of other venues. An enormous amount of information is exchanged, validated, confirmed, and passed back and forth under highly informal circumstances.

Telephone conversations. Managers spend an astounding amount of time on the telephone these days. Curiously, the amount of time per telephone call is decreasing, but the number of calls per day is increasing. With the nearly universal availability of cellular and satellite telephone service, very few people are out of reach of the office for very long. The decision to switch off a cellular telephone, in fact, is now considered a decision in favor of work–life balance.

Video teleconferencing. Bridging time zones as well as cultures, videoconferencing facilities make direct conversations with employees, colleagues, customers, and business partners across the nation or around the world a simple matter. Carrier Corporation, the air-conditioning manufacturer, is now typical of firms using desktop videoconferencing to conduct everything from staff meetings to technical training. Engineers at Carrier's Farmington, Connecticut, headquarters can hook up with service managers in branch offices thousands of miles away to explain new product developments, demonstrate repair techniques, and update field staff on matters that would, just recently, have required extensive travel or expensive, broadcast-quality television programming. Their exchanges are informal, conversational, and not much different than they would be if both people were in the same room (Ziegler, 1994).

Presentations to small groups. Managers frequently find themselves making presentations, formal and informal, to groups of three to eight people for many different reasons: They pass along information given to them by executives; they review the status of projects in process; they explain changes in everything from working schedules to organizational goals. Such presentations are sometimes supported by PowerPoint decks or printed outlines, but they are oral in nature and retain much of the conversational character of one-to-one conversations.

Public speaking to larger audiences. Most managers are unable to escape the periodic requirement to speak to larger audiences of several dozen or, perhaps, several hundred people. Such presentations are usually more formal in structure and are often supported by PowerPoint or Corel software that can deliver data from text files, graphics, and photos, and even motion clips from streaming video. Despite the more formal atmosphere and sophisticated audiovisual support systems, such presentations still involve one manager talking to others, framing, shaping, and passing information to an audience.

nication time either talking or listening to others who are talking.

According to Werner (1975) and others who study the communication habits of postmodern business organizations, managers are involved in more than just speeches and presentations from the dais or teleconference podium. They spend their days in meetings, on the telephone, conducting interviews, giving tours, supervising informal visits to their facilities, and at a wide variety of social events.

Each of these activities may look to some managers like an obligation imposed by the job. Shrewd managers see them as opportunities to hear what others are thinking, to gather information informally from the grapevine, to listen in on office gossip, to pass along viewpoints that have not yet made their way to the more formal channels of communication, or to catch up with a colleague or friend in a more relaxed setting. No matter what the intention of each manager who engages in these activities, the information they produce and the insight that follows from them can be put to work the same day to achieve organizational and personal objectives. "To understand why effective managers behave as they do," writes Kotter (1999), "it is essential first to recognize two fundamental challenges and dilemmas found in most of their jobs." Managers must first figure out what to do, despite an enormous amount of potentially relevant information (along with much that is not), and then they must get things done "through a large and diverse group of people despite having little direct control over most of them" (Kotter, 1999, pp. 145–159).

The Major Channels of Management Communication Are Talking and Listening

A series of scientific studies, beginning with Nichols and Stevens (1957), Rankin (1952), and Wolvin and Coakley (1982) confirm that most managers spend the largest portion of their day talking and listening. Werner's (1975) thesis, in fact, found that North American adults spend more than 78% of their commu-

The Role of Writing

Writing plays an important role in the life of any organization. In some organizations, it becomes more important than in others. At Procter & Gamble (P&G), for example, brand managers cannot raise a work-related issue in a team meeting unless the ideas are first circulated in writing. For P&G managers, this approach means explaining their ideas in explicit detail in a standard one- to three-page memo, complete with background, financial discussion, implementation details, and justification for the ideas proposed.

Other organizations are more oral in their traditions – 3M Canada comes to mind as a "spoken" organization – but the fact remains: the most important projects, decisions, and ideas end up in writing. Writing also provides analysis, justification, documentation, and analytic discipline, particularly as managers approach important decisions that will affect the profitability and strategic direction of the company.

Writing is a career sifter. If managers demonstrate their inability to put ideas on paper in a clear, unambiguous fashion, they are not likely to last. Stories of bad writers who have been shown the door early in their careers are legion. Managers' principal objective, at least during the first few years of their career, is to keep their names out of such stories. Remember, those who are most likely to notice the quality and skill in managers' written documents are the very people likely to matter to a manager's future.

Managers do most of their own writing and editing. The days when they could lean back and thoughtfully dictate a letter or memo to a skilled secretarial assistant are mostly gone. Some senior executives know how efficient dictation can be, especially with a top-notch administrative assistant taking shorthand, but how many managers have that advantage today? Very few, mostly because buying a computer and printer is substantially cheaper than hiring another employee. Managers at all levels of most organizations draft, review, edit, and dispatch their own correspondence, reports, and proposals.

Documents take on lives of their own. Once it is gone from the manager's desk, it is not his or hers anymore. When they sign a letter and put it in the mail, it is no longer the manager's letter – it is the property of the person or organization it was sent to. As a result, the recipient is free to do as he or she sees fit with your writing, including using it against the author. If the author's ideas are ill-considered or not well expressed, others in the organization who are not especially sympa-

thetic to the manager's views may head for the copy machine with the manager's work in hand. The advice for managers is simple: do not mail the first draft, and do not ever sign your name to a document you are not proud of.

Communication Is Invention

Without question, communication is a process of invention. Managers literally create meaning through communication. A company, for example, is not in default until a team of auditors sits down to examine the books and review the matter. Only after extended discussion do the accountants come to the conclusion that the company is, in fact, in default. It is their discussion that creates the outcome. Until that point, default was simply one of many possibilities.

The fact is managers create meaning through communication. It is largely through discussion and verbal exchange – often heated and passionate – that managers decide who they wish to be: market leaders, takeover artists, innovators, or defenders of the economy. It is only through communication that meaning is created for shareholders, for employees, for customers, and others. Those long, detailed, and intense discussions determine how much the company will declare in dividends this year, whether the company is willing to risk a strike or labor action, and how soon to roll out the new product line customers are asking for. Additionally, it is important to note that managers usually figure things out by talking about them as much as they talk about the things they have already figured out. Talk serves as a wonderful palliative: justifying, analyzing, dissecting, reassuring, and analyzing the events that confront managers each day.

Information Is Socially Constructed

If we are to understand just how important human discourse is in the life of a business, several points seem especially important.

Information is created, shared, and interpreted by people. Meaning is a truly human phenomenon. An issue is only important if people think it is. Facts are facts only if we can agree upon their definition. Perceptions and assumptions are as important as truth itself in a discussion about what a manager should do next (Berger and Luckmann, 1967; Searle, 1995). Information never speaks for itself. It is not uncommon for a manager to rise to address a group of his colleagues and say, "Gentlemen, the numbers speak for themselves." Frankly, the numbers never speak for themselves. They almost always require some sort of interpretation, some sort of explanation or context. Do not assume that others see the facts in the same way you do and never assume that what is seen is the truth. Others may see the same set of facts or evidence but may not reach the same conclusions. Few things in life are self-explanatory.

Context always drives meaning. The backdrop to a message is always of paramount importance to the listener, viewer, or reader in reaching a reasonable, rational conclusion about what he or she sees and hears. What's in the news these days as we take up this particular subject? What moment in history do we occupy? What related or relevant information is under consideration as this new message arrives? We cannot possibly derive meaning from one message without considering everything else that surrounds it.

A messenger always accompanies a message. It is difficult to separate a message from its messenger. We often want to react more to the source of the information than we do to the information itself. That is natural and entirely normal. People speak for a reason, and we often judge their reasons for speaking before analyzing what they have to say. Keep in mind that, in every organization, message recipients will judge the value, power, purpose, intent, and outcomes of the messages they receive by the source of those messages as much as by the content and intent of the messages themselves. If the messages managers send are to have the impact hoped for, they must come from a source the receiver knows, respects, and understands.

Managers' Greatest Challenge

Every manager knows communication is vital, but every manager also seems to "know" that he or she is great at it. Managers' greatest challenge is to admit to flaws in their skill set and work tirelessly to improve them. First, managers must admit to the flaws.

Larkin and Larkin (1994) write that "Deep down, managers believe they are communicating effectively. In ten years of management consulting, we have never had a manager say to us that he or she was a poor communicator. They admit to the occasional screw-up, but overall, everyone, without exception, believes he or she is basically a good communicator" (p. X).

Managers' Task as Professionals

As a professional manager, the first task is to recognize and understand one's strengths and weaknesses as a communicator. Until these communication tasks at which you are most and least skilled are identified, you will have little opportunity for improvement and advancement.

Foremost among managers' goals should be to improve existing skills. Improve one's ability to do what is done best. Be alert to opportunities, however, to develop new skills. Managers should add to their inventory of abilities to keep themselves employable and promotable.

Two other suggestions come to mind for improving managers' professional standing. First, acquire a knowledge base that will work for the years ahead. That means speaking with and listening to other professionals in their company, industry, and community. They should be alert to trends that could affect their company's products and services, as well as their own future.

It also means reading. Managers should read at least one national newspaper each day, including the *Wall Street Journal*, *The New York Times*, or the *Financial Times*, as well as a local newspaper. Their reading should include weekly news magazines, such as *U.S. News & World Report, Business Week,* and the *Economist.* They should subscribe to monthly magazines such as *Fast Company* and *Fortune.* And they should read at least one new hardcover title a month. A dozen books each year is the bare minimum on which one should depend for new ideas, insights, and managerial guidance.

The final challenge is to develop the confidence needed to succeed as a manager, particularly under conditions of uncertainty, change, and challenge.

References

Berger, P.L. and Luckmann, T. (1967) *The Social Construction of Reality.* New York: Doubleday.

Borden, D. (1995) *The Business of Talk: Organizations in Action.* New York: Blackwell.

Drucker, P.F. (1954) *The Practice of Management.* New York: Harper & Row.

Eccles, R.G. and Nohria, N. (1992) *Beyond the Hype: Rediscovering the Essence of Management.* Boston: The Harvard Business School Press.

Hannaway, J. (1989) *Managers Managing: The Workings of an Administrative System.* New York: Oxford University Press.

Kotter, J.P. (1982) *The General Managers.* New York: The Free Press.

Kotter, J.P. (1999) What effective general managers really do. *Harvard Business Review,* 60, 145–159.

Larkin, T.J. and Larkin, S. (1994) *Communicating Change: Winning Employee Support for New Business Goals.* New York: McGraw-Hill.

Mintzberg, H. (1973) *The Nature of Managerial Work.* New York: Harper & Row.

Mintzberg, H. (1990) The manager's job: Folklore and fact. *Harvard Business Review,* 68, 166–167.

Nichols, R.G. and Stevens, L. (1957) *Are You Listening?* New York: McGraw-Hill.

Pondy, L.R. (1978) Leadership is a language game. In M.W. McCall, Jr. and M.M. Lombardo (eds), *Leadership: Where Else Can We Go?* Durham, NC: Duke University Press, pp. 87–99.

Rankin, P.T. (1952) The measurement of the ability to understand spoken language. Unpublished PhD dissertation, University of Michigan (1926). Dissertation Abstracts 12, No. 6 (1952), pp. 847–848.

Searle, J.R. (1995) *The Construction of Social Reality.* New York: The Free Press (see also Berger, P.L. and Luckmann, T. (1967) *The Social Construction of Reality.* New York: Doubleday).

Sproull, L.S. (1984) The nature of managerial attention. In L.S. Sproull (ed.), *Advances in Information Processing in Organizations.* Greenwich, CT: JAI Press.

Stewart, R. (1967) *Managers and Their Jobs.* London: Macmillan.

Werner, E.K. (1975) A study of communication time. Unpublished Master's thesis, University of Maryland, College Park, MD.

Wolvin, A.D. and Coakley, C.G. (1982) *Listening.* Dubuque, IA: William C. Brown and Co.

Ziegler, B. (1994) Video conference calls change business. *Wall Street Journal,* October 13, pp. B1, B12.

9

Corporate Reputation and the Discipline of Communication Management

Anne Gregory

Leeds Metropolitan University, UK

This chapter looks at the management process of organizing and managing communication within organizations. It looks at this from three perspectives. First, it examines the organizational context that sets the backcloth for organizing and managing communication. Second, it looks at the contribution of communication at four strategic levels: societal, organizational, program, and individual. Finally, it looks at the structural options for communication departments. The chapter argues that a well-structured and managed communication function in itself is an indicator of how seriously an organization takes the specialism that has formal responsibility for managing relationships and corporate reputation. It also argues that the way communication is organized and managed has an impact on how effectively communication can undertake its work: this too can make a significant contribution to the reputation of the organization as a whole.

Introduction

This chapter explores how communication management can contribute to corporate reputation. Here, communication management is not seen as an alternative name to public relations, corporate communication, or any other label that is ascribed to the functional specialism formally charged with relationship building and reputation management in organizations. Rather, it is seen as the process which determines how communication is organized and managed. This process requires a deep level of analysis and, if done with rigor and integrity,

will ensure that the communication function is structured and focused on activities that matter. A necessary consequence of this will be an enhanced reputation for the organization.

Communication management is considered from three perspectives in this chapter: first, context which determines overall communication needs; second, the contribution of communication at four strategic levels within the organization; and third, the structure of the communication function. Before exploring these areas in detail, two distinct roles for communication are defined. They are broadly similar to those described by Putnam and

The Handbook of Communication and Corporate Reputation, First Edition. Edited by Craig E. Carroll.
© 2013 John Wiley & Sons, Inc. Published 2015 by John Wiley & Sons, Inc.

Nicotera (2009) and Zerfass (2008) who labeled them enabling and constituting, but here are called enabling and transforming:

- *Communication as enabler.* This is the traditional way of viewing the contribution of communication. Many of the definitions of corporate communication (e.g., Christensen *et al.*, 2008; Cornelissen, 2011; Jackson, 1987; van Riel and Fombrun, 2007) describe it as the integration of all the internal and external communication of an organization whose purpose is "establishing and maintaining favorable reputations with stakeholder groups upon which the organization is dependent" (Cornelissen, 2011, p. 5). Simplifying the more sophisticated arguments of these authors, the essence of corporate communication is projecting the identity of the organization, through consistent symbols, communication, and behavior (Dowling, 2001) in a coordinated way so that stakeholders form a particular image which is supportive of and builds its reputation. Its focus is the organization presenting itself in a favorable light with communication enabling this to happen through the deployment of professional expertise.
- *Communication as transformer.* As transformational force, communication is seen as part of the organizational DNA. It is not just concerned with communication per se, but it can transform the very nature of the organization – its culture, its values, and how they are determined, and is based on an appreciation that communication is not neutral; it has inherent agency. It also means a recognition that everything the organization has, does, and says has impact. For example, the organization's systems and processes, organizational structure, and physical assets are a narrative and pointer as to whether communication is embedded as a core competence. Communication seen in this light translates from being a corporate messenger, to a corporate agent where the decisions made are informed by and seen through a communication lens. Much of

this is acknowledged in the corporate communication literature quoted earlier, but finds even stronger resonance in the organizational literature (e.g., Hatch and Schultz, 2008), which stresses the importance of communication within organizations themselves as they seek to negotiate, define, and enact corporate identity. It is more than the integration mind-set that Christensen *et al.* (2008) suggest for corporate communication, it is a mind-set that transforms ways of thinking and working as organizational decisions are imbued with stakeholder intelligence and performed with a full understanding of the communication implications.

With these perspectives in mind, the communication context is now discussed in detail.

The Context of Communication

Klaus Schwab, founder and Executive Chairman of the World Economic Forum (WEF), speaking at the World Public Relations Forum in Stockholm, Sweden, 2010, listed five driving factors in a globalizing world which he asserted had just witnessed the first truly global crisis: the financial meltdown in Western countries. These drivers are as follows:

- *Time compression.* The world has experienced as much change in one generation as in the whole of the last century. A pertinent example is the advances in genetics, which now means insurance companies can predict health risks more accurately.
- *Complexity.* WEF has identified over 78 different global opportunities and threats. This is an astounding number in itself, but complexity is compounded because many of these factors are intertwined, making their resolution more difficult. For example, water shortages, mass migration, and armed conflict are all interlinked and can threaten organizational supply chains.

- *Interconnectivity of issues.* In the past, politics, the social sphere, and technology operated in relatively separate silos; now they are interconnected. For example, technological developments designed for mainly social applications have implications in autocratic countries.
- *Interdependence.* There are no boundaries in the global village. The local, national, and international are all linked. A local financial crisis in America affected the whole world and threatens the employment and housing prospects of millions.
- *Context.* The context in which the world and work is operating is changing: the focus of economic power is shifting – geographically from north to south and from west to east. Organizationally, power is moving from organizational leaders to stakeholders, including employees (top-down to bottom-up).

The WEF's conclusion is that these issues are too large to be faced individually by organizations or nations. Schwab (2010) also recognizes the essential role of communication in stimulating and facilitating debate about these issues and drawing collaborative communities together.

So what has all this to do with communication management? These issues set the contextual backcloth for organizational life and can have far-reaching repercussions which demand a communication response. For example, threatened supply chains may mean relocation. Mass migration may mean changes to employment regulations. Interdependence requires more proactive issues management.

In addition to these *macro* issues (Grant, 2005), there are the issues, challenges, and opportunities that are specific to each organization and which shape the role of communication. Finally, there are developments which have forceful impact on communication directly, for example, social media are changing the balance of power and the nature of the relationship organizations have with their stakeholders. As the Arthur W. Page Society (2007) states in "The Authentic Enterprise," an examination of

these issues of globalization, empowered stakeholders, and the development of a global digital commons forces the conclusion that organizations have reached a point of "strategic inflection" which requires a new way of operating. The solution has communication at its heart and authenticity as its defining characteristic. These contextualizing factors have a significant impact on how communication is managed in organizations. They have to be more ubiquitous, responsive, agile, and transparent.

Having set the context for communication management, the levels of communication within organizations are now addressed. Understanding how the function contributes at these levels is important because it has impact on where the communication function is located and how it is managed.

The Levels at Which Communication Should Be Managed

The way organizations are structured and work organizationally dictates how communication can be deployed effectively. The South African academic Benita Steyn (2007) first mapped the role of communication against the different strategic levels within private sector organizations. She identified five strategic levels where communication has a key role to play: enterprise, corporate, business unit, functional, and operational. A more generic approach that can be used by all organizations, including the public, private, and not-for-profit sectors is supported by the UK Chartered Institute of Public Relations (Gregory and White, 2008) and identifies four levels at which communication can make a contribution. These are the societal, organizational, program, and the individual levels. They are discussed in the following sections.

Societal level

Here organizations strive to obtain and maintain their legitimacy or "license to operate" by seeking the approval of society as a whole for their operations (what they do) and activities (how they do what they do). At this level, organizations attempt to determine their purpose and place in the world and whether their endeavors will gain support. The societal legitimacy test can apply to whole industries as well as individual organizations. For example, the nuclear accident in Fukushima in Japan in March 2011 following an earthquake and tsunami is now provoking a global discussion on the legitimacy of civil nuclear programs, with Germany stating it will close all its 17 plants by 2037 (Evans, 2011).

Critically important at this level, even if an organization is deemed to be legitimate, is its overall standing and reputation among its peers. The higher this is, the more likely it is to attract advocates and supporters, the greater its value, and in times of crisis, a good reputation offers a measure of protection (Argenti, 2009; Balmer and Gray, 1999; Cornelissen, 2011).

In its enabling role, communication will assist the organization in promoting its corporate identity, and undertaking communication with relevant stakeholder groups to demonstrate fulfillment of its wider social obligations, through, for example, corporate social responsibility programs.

In its transforming role, communication will assist the organization in clarifying its mission and values, not just in promoting those that are already decided. Communication management involves bringing into the organization contextual intelligence about what is acceptable in society, about whether the proposed or ongoing mission and values will engender support, or if realignment is needed because societal and hence stakeholder expectations are changing. This dual role of promotion (and sometimes defense) of the organization and intelligence gathering is usually called *boundary spanning* (White and Dozier, 1992). It involves a managed process of engagement with stakeholders and other sources of information about the wider issues that will shape societal attitudes and concerns such as those indicated in the first part of this chapter.

Ultimately, organizations are judged by their ability to live up to the standards and values that they themselves declare. Communication management at this societal level involves clear communication of organizational purpose (or mission) and values and the provision of evidence that demonstrates consistent performance against them. Society's judgment on overall performance is the reputation that the organization actually has.

Organizational level

Beneath the societal level, at senior management level, executives seek to implement the mission and values of the organization by making strategic and operational decisions. These decisions often entail how the organization will marshal and deploy its resources to assist in it realizing its strategy – the route to achieving its mission. Unfortunately, it is often financial concerns that dominate organizational decision making, despite this sometimes having adverse impacts on reputation. For example, in the interests of cost saving, many domestic banks have closed local branches and rely on electronic transaction systems, but this has led to criticisms that banks have become remote, impersonal, and insensitive to individual needs.

In its enabling role, communication management is about ensuring that there are effective and efficient means of relaying organizational decisions both inside and outside the organization and about facilitating discussions prior to those decisions if appropriate.

In its transformational role, communication management requires that senior managers are assisted to make properly informed decisions by bringing the multiple views of stakeholders into the decision-making process. These stakeholders are different from, but also form part of the stakeholders mentioned at societal level. Whereas these last might be regarded as the "general public," at the organizational level, stakeholders are those with a much more direct stake in the organization, such as employees, suppliers, regulators, and regular customers.

The implication for communication management is important. On occasion, communication managers will advocate for stakeholders who are less powerful, but nonetheless have legitimate concerns which should be taken into account. It is also the role of communication management at this level to advise senior managers on the likely impact of their decisions based on the intimate knowledge of stakeholder communities. For example, local hospital managers may wish to increase car-parking charges for visitors to raise much needed revenue, but may not be aware of the impact that may have on vulnerable stakeholders or of the wider reputational risks. Over time, this more expanded and enlightened thinking, which ultimately also builds and sustains reputation, becomes a mind-set (Christensen *et al.*, 2008) which forms part of the organizational DNA and is and of itself transformative: shaping the organizational culture and the nature of the relationships with stakeholders.

It is interesting to note at this stage how the contribution of managed communication is perceived in the strategic management literature. The resource-based view of strategy began to gain prominence in the 1990s when Barney (1991), building on Wernerfelt's (1984) earlier work, argued that an organization's internal resources were critical to success and indeed could be the source of competitive advantage. The skills and knowledge embedded within the organization and upon which corporate strategy was built were seen as "core competencies" Prahalad and Hamel (1990). Leonard-Barton (1992) saw not only skills and knowledge, but also the organization's administrative and technical systems, and its values and norms as core capabilities which could be levered for success. Fiol (1991) first identified corporate identity (or reputation) as an organizational resource rather than a cost, and this argument has been supported by later strategic management authors (e.g., Agerwal and Helfat, 2009; Winter, 2007). Communication, managed well at the organizational level, is a positive asset which can be used to build reputational capital.

Program level

At the program level, it is the responsibility of the communication function to liaise with other functions in the organization and with senior managers about the contribution it can make to help the organization realize its mission and objectives. This will take two forms: first, it will assist other parts of the organization with their communication efforts (enabling). Second, it will train managers and those others responsible for stakeholder contact how to be "communicatively competent" (Hamrefors, 2010) or, at a minimum, communicatively aware. It is not possible now in the age of social media, not that it ever was, for communication to be "managed" by one function (although it does need to be coordinated), neither should it be if others are competent. Part of the work of communication management is educative: building expertise throughout the organization so that other key individuals and functions can undertake their own communication management while being aware of when they need to draw on expert help. Hence, throughout the organization, members become sensitized to the issues and skills and knowledge required in communication management and of their responsibilities whether they are part of the formal communication management process or not. This transformative work can have a profound effect on the culture of the organization. It can be liberating, creative, and a force for innovation and unity if done well with organization members understanding that they have a contribution to make as co-creators of the organizational DNA. Done badly, communication can be seen as an organizational straightjacket where members find it difficult to express their own personalities and opinions because of a rigorously enforced corporate identity regime which requires rote responses and behavior (Christensen *et al.*, 2008).

Second, at the program level, communication programs are researched, designed, planned, implemented, and evaluated preferably using the templates and methodologies

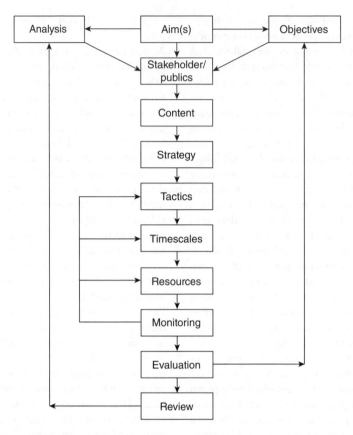

Figure 9.1 Gregory's planning template.

recommended by public relations and communication academics such as Ferguson (1999), Gregory (2010), Harrison (2011), McElreath (1997), and Smith (2009). This is largely an enabling function, but the results can be transformational.

Gregory's (2010) template (Figure 9.1) is shown, but all follow the same basic pattern. Planning templates are not to be used as static and purely processes driven. The fast moving context and communication tools that characterize modern practice means that these templates should be used iteratively and flexibly. For example, as Pal and Dutta (2008) say, it becomes increasingly difficult to define what a stakeholder group is, given that millions of people from across the world can take a stake in an organization, often without that organization realizing:

groups form and reform as their stake changes. Furthermore, these planning templates are positivist in design and do not properly accommodate the subtleties of communication as co-constructed meaning, sensemaking, and sensegiving (Putnam and Boys, 2006; Weick, 1995; Weick *et al.*, 2005); however, since this chapter is focused on communication management, that is what is emphasized here.

While all the steps of the planning template are important, four are picked out as requiring the special attention of the communication manager:

• *Analysis* where both the macro and micro organizational context should be investigated using techniques like PESTLE and SWOT to gain a deep understanding of the issues and opportunities the organization faces. This should be accompanied by an investigation of the organization itself to understand any internal issues. Finally, there should be an analysis of the organization's stakeholders and publics to understand their current attitudes both toward the organization and toward the issues that are pertinent to it. This analysis not only forms the basis of information that will inform organizational decision making, but sets a benchmark against which communication activities can be measured.

- *Objectives* which need to be separated into *outcome* aims – the measurable cognitive, affective, and conative changes that are desired in and with stakeholders; and *process* objectives which are the activities the practitioner will implement to achieve the aims, such as to organize an event to which 500 people will be attracted.

- *Strategy* is the underlying rationale behind the program upon which the tactics are built. Strategy addresses the question "how is the issue to be approached?", but does not explain the detailed tactics. Effective communication management relies on a strong strategy which provides coherence and a sense of direction.

- *Evaluation* demonstrates the effectiveness of each program by measuring how objectives have been met. The cumulative effects of communication programs should also show a demonstrable effect as reputation is tracked over time.

It is still the case that many communication departments are measured just on the basis of their competence in communication program planning (De Santo and Moss, 2004; Hogg and Doolan, 1999; Murray and White, 2005) and are not involved substantially at the societal and organizational levels. Part of the reason for that is that they do not display the correct management competencies (Gregory, 2008; Hogg and Doolan, 1999; Moss *et al.*, 2005), hence the consideration of individual performance in communication management in this next section.

Individual level

The competence of individual practitioners underpins their capability to undertake the roles outlined earlier. Much work has been done on conceptualizing the roles of public relations practitioners (e.g., Broom, 1982; Broom and Smith, 1979; De Santo and Moss, 2004; Dozier, 1992; Dozier and Broom, 1995; Moss *et al.*, 2000; Toth *et al.*, 1998). There is far too much in the literature to do it justice in the space available, but work largely in America defined two main roles, which have been the focus of much of the ensuing scholarship (Dozier and Broom, 1995; Moss *et al.*, 2000, 2005): the communication technician, who is an implementer of programs researched and planned by others (an enabling role) and the communication manager who sets policy, undertakes research, and plans and evaluates programs (elements of the transforming role). Moss *et al.* (2005), in their empirical work in the United Kingdom and United States, identified five elements to the communication manager role; four relate to managerial responsibility: monitor and evaluator, key policy and strategy advisor, troubleshooter/problem solver, and issues management expert. It seems that senior communication managers are also personally involved in implementing what might be regarded as high-risk or complex technician work, for example, media relations on corporate earnings. The key role of the senior practitioner in environmental scanning, issues identification, and evaluative research is also a recurring theme in the literature (e.g., Dozier and Broom, 1995; Grunig *et al.*, 2002).

Clearly, to undertake the responsibilities assigned to their role, practitioners need the requisite range and depth of knowledge and skills. Again, it is outside the scope of this chapter to review these since they are more than adequately covered by the professional bodies (e.g., Chartered Institute of Public Relations, 2012; Public Relations Society of America, 1993, 1999, 2006) and the many textbooks on the subject (e.g., Broom, 2009; Harrison, 2011; Newsom *et al.*, 2012; Tench *et al.*, 2009).

There is also research on the personal characteristics and behaviors required of public relations professionals. Numerous textbooks (e.g., Black, 2001; Newsom *et al.*, 2012) typically mention wide interests, enthusiasm, energy, drive, intellectual curiosity, creativity, flexibility, judgment, honesty, decision-making abilities, and problem solving. In 2008, Gregory (2008) undertook the first comprehensive study of the behavioral repertoires, or competencies, of senior practitioners which identified 10 each in the private and public sectors, many held in common such as taking a strategic, long-term view; making decisions and acting; investigating and analyzing; taking responsibility for high standards; networking and communication capabilities; and leading and supporting others.

The individual capabilities of practitioners are critical to the performance of the communication function as a whole. Unfortunately, there is significant evidence (Arthur W. Page Society, 2007; Murray and White, 2005) that chief executive officers (CEOs) struggle to find professionals of the right caliber. This in turn affects the level at which communication can operate in the organization. Expert practitioners do much to enhance corporate reputation; inexpert ones can do untold damage.

In concluding this section, the author suggests that there are three main reasons why it is important to articulate and organize the contribution of communication in levels within organizations:

- It clarifies and confirms the contribution that communication can play as an enabling and transforming force throughout the organization, including at the most senior decision-making table.
- It demonstrates that communication contributes more than purposeful programs and campaigns.
- Understanding that communication operates at various levels enables communication professionals to enact different roles as appropriate: sometimes as senior councilor and mentor, sometimes as technician.

Having looked at the contribution of communication as enabler and transformative force throughout the organization, it follows that the location and structure of the function should be the next considerations.

The Location and Structure of the Communication Function

There have been many debates about the location of the communication function. The *Excellence study* (Dozier *et al.*, 1995; Grunig *et al.*, 2002) argued that the most senior communicator should report directly to the CEO and be part of the *dominant coalition*, that is, the senior decision-making group in the organization. They also stated that the public relations department should be autonomous (able to take decisions without constant referral to senior management) and independent of control by other functions such as marketing and human resources. The corporate communication scholars (e.g., Cornelissen, 2011; van Riel and Fombrun, 2007) support this view, their contention being that there has to be a coordinated effort to align all the communicative efforts of the organization both internally and externally, including marketing and management communication, in order to present a consistent corporate identity that is a critical element in reputation building. The rationale put forward earlier in this chapter on the levels of contribution is a powerful argument for the communication team being influential at all levels, and this would include the most senior tables.

In addition, there is a drive toward integration of all the communicative functions (Cornelissen, 2011; Zerfass *et al.*, 2011), with a senior director leading it, and if that is not the formal organizational arrangement, there is certainly a recognition that there has to be greater coordination between communicative functions so that they can be managed strategically. Many functions share the same channels and tools, for example, social media networks and the interactivity and speed of such media

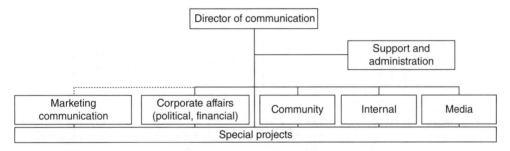

Figure 9.2   A communication department structured according to functions.

requires a managed and strategically coordinated response.

Furthermore, given the accountabilities of the CEO and other senior managers to multiple stakeholders and the risks involved when organizational reputation is put at risk, it is advisable that communication is among what are called the *staff* functions that support the executive and board and ideally should be a part of the executive or board. CEOs themselves recognize the need to have expert communication advice (Arthur W. Page Society, 2007), and the European Communication Monitor (Zerfass *et al.*, 2011) reports that 60% of top communication managers report to the CEO, with 18% reporting to another board member or function, and 18% have a place on the board themselves. The communication function also has *line* responsibilities; that is, it supports other functional areas such as human resources, the legal department, and operations with their communication efforts.

Bearing these things in mind therefore, there are three main ways that communication is usually structured in organizations (Gregory, 2010). The first, and increasingly more typical, is along functional lines. That is, the main communication activities are packaged up into recognizable specialist areas, and those people assigned to these areas undertake all the tasks relating to it such as counseling, online, and publications (see Figure 9.2).

There are two obvious problems associated with such a structure. First, those working within particular specialisms become siloed in their own areas of expertise and could become an inflexible resource unable to operate in other

specialized areas of communication, and sometimes unable to respond to shifting organization requirements. The special projects team or consultancy assistance may mitigate this. Second, significant effort has to be made to coordinate activities between groups so that there is no unnecessary duplication either of work internally or in communicating with internal and external stakeholders.

Some communication departments are organized along task lines; that is, tasks requiring particular skills, knowledge, and experience are bundled together and given to small groups or individuals to perform. An example of a task-based structure is given in Figure 9.3. Again, there are potential problems associated with this structure. Apart from the two identified earlier, a task-based structure raises a third issue which can be an overfocus on technical expertise and a lack of opportunity or interest in a more strategic approach.

A third way to structure and manage communication is that professionals are organized as if they were an internal consultancy. In this situation, they will work on short- and long-term projects that require both tasks and functions to be undertaken. The communication department will therefore consist of a number of project teams where any one individual may belong to several depending on their individual capabilities and the requirements of the project (see Figure 9.4).

Project (or matrix) working can displace some of the problems endemic in task or function-based teams. It also allows professionals to undertake a variety of work and in mixed teams where there are opportunities to learn

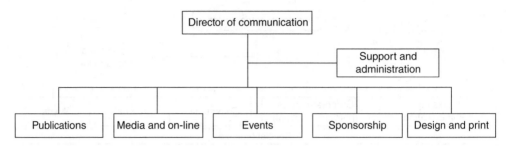

Figure 9.3 A communication department structured according to tasks.

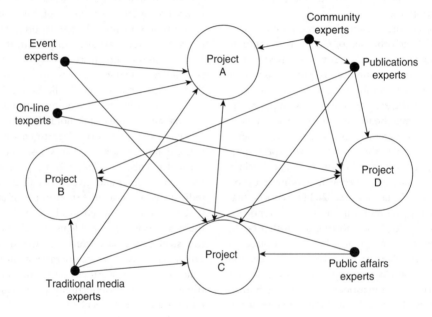

Figure 9.4 A communication department with a matrix structure.

skills and knowledge from other team members. However, there is one significant issue with project working: it is difficult to keep a coherent view of the overall picture for the organization. Project teams are often constituted as a result of a perceived need by particular departments or managers and gaps can appear in the portfolio of work where some significant need remains unidentified. These are more likely to be the crosscutting issues and activities which form parts of the overall tapestry of organizational life, but which at an individual depart-

mental and manager level are not large enough to warrant commissioning a specific project.

The way communication departments are structured depends on the needs of the individual organization. However, of overriding importance is that the structure allows communicators access to and facilitates working with senior management and at all levels within the organization, and that they are able to communicate in a timely and sophisticated manner with internal and external stakeholders. The structure should be located where the most senior communicator is "wired in" to the organization in such a way that they are able to take a holistic overview of the organization and of the context in which it operates. Then, they will be able to advise and counsel senior managers in the most appropriate way. If these requirements are taken into account, there will be no unnecessary structural barriers to communication professionals undertaking their roles effectively and efficiently, which in turn impacts on corporate reputation.

Conclusions

This chapter has sought to do three things. First, to provide an overview of some of the contextual factors that are affecting organizations and therefore their communication functions. This has a profound impact on how communication has to be managed both currently and in the future. Second, to describe and demonstrate the enabling and transforming role that properly managed communication can contribute at all levels within an organization. Third, to provide some examples of how the communication function can be structured in order for it to be effective.

Focusing on communication management is vital. The professionalism with which the organization and management of communication is undertaken speaks volumes about the wider professionalism of the leaders of the communication function. Its location and its relationship with senior managers speak volumes about the standing of the communication function within the organization as a whole. Communication management undertaken seriously and with due regard for the highest possible standards is an indicator that reputation itself is taken seriously within the organization.

References

Agerwal, R. and Helfat, C. (2009) Strategic renewal of organizations. *Organization Science*, 20(2), 281–293.

Argenti, P. (2009) *Corporate Communication*. New York: McGraw-Hill.

Arthur W. Page Society (2007) The authentic enterprise. Retrieved from http://www.awpagesociety.com/insights/authentic-enterprise-report/ (last accessed September 12, 2012).

Balmer, J.M.T. and Gray, E.R. (1999) Corporate identity and corporate communications: Creating a competitive advantage. *Corporate Communications: An International Journal*, 4(4), 171–177.

Barney, J.B. (1991) Firm resources and sustained competitive advantage. *Journal of Management*, 17, 9–120.

Black, C. (2001) *The PR Practitioners Desktop Guide*. London: Hawkesmere Plc.

Broom, G.M. (1982) A comparison of sex roles in public relations. *Public Relations Review*, 5(3), 47–59.

Broom, G.M. (2009) *Cutlip and Center's Effective Public Relations* (8th ed.). Upper Saddle River, NJ: Prentice Hall.

Broom, G.M. and Smith, G.D. (1979) Testing the practitioner's impact on clients. *Public Relations Review*, 5, 47–59.

Chartered Institute of Public Relations (2012) Syllabii for the advanced certificate and diploma. Retrieved from http://www.cipr.co.uk/sites/default/files/CIPR%20course%20recognition%20final.pdf (last accessed October 10, 2012).

Christensen, L., Morsing, M., and Cheney, G. (2008) *Corporate Communication: Convention, Complexity and Critique*. London: Sage.

Cornelissen, J.P. (2011) *Corporate Communication: A Guide to Theory and Practice* (3rd ed.). London: Sage.

De Santo, B. and Moss, D.A. (2004) Rediscovering what PR managers do: Rethinking the measurement of managerial behavior in the public relations context. *Journal of Communication Management*, 9(2), 179–196.

Dowling, G.R. (2001) *Creating Corporate Reputations: Identity, Image, and Performance*. Oxford, UK: Oxford University Press.

Dozier, D.M. (1992) The organizational roles of communicators and public relations practitioners. In J.E. Grunig (ed.), *Excellence in Public Relations and Communications Management*. Hillsdale, NJ: Lawrence Erlbaum Associates, pp. 327–355.

Dozier, D.M. and Broom, G.M. (1995) Evolution of the manager role in public relations practice. *Journal of Public Relations Research*, 7(1), 3–26.

Dozier, D.M., Grunig, L.A., and Grunig, J.E. (1995) *Manager's Guide to Excellence in Public*

Relations and Communication Management. Mahwah, NJ: Lawrence Erlbaum Associates.

Evans, S. (2011) Japan disaster reopens nuclear debate in Europe and US. Retrieved from http://www.bbc.co.uk/news/world-europe-12730393 (last accessed September 12, 2012).

Ferguson, S.D. (1999) _Communication Planning_. Thousand Oaks, CA: Sage.

Fiol, C.M. (1991) Managing culture and a competitive resource: An identity-based view of sustainable competitive advantage. _Journal of Management, 17_, 191–211.

Grant, R.M. (2005) _Contemporary Strategy Analysis_. Malden, MA: Blackwell Publishing.

Gregory, A. (2008) The competencies of senior practitioners in the UK: An initial study. _Public Relations Review, 34_(3), 215–223.

Gregory, A. (2010) _Planning and Managing Public Relations Campaigns_. London: Kogan Page.

Gregory, A. and White, J. (2008) Introducing the Chartered Institute of Public Relations work on research and evaluation. In B. van Ruler, A. Tkalac Vercic, and D. Vercic (eds), _Public Relations Metrics: Research and Evaluation_. London: Routledge, pp. 307–317.

Grunig, L.A., Grunig, J.E., and Dozier, D.H. (2002) _Excellent Public Relations and Effective Organisations: A Study of Communications Management in Three Countries_. Mahwah, NJ: Lawrence Erlbaum Associates.

Hamrefors, S. (2010) Communicative leadership. _Journal of Communication Management, 14_(2), 141–152.

Harrison, K. (2011) _Strategic Public Relations_. South Yarra, VIC: Palgrave Macmillan.

Hatch, M.J. and Schultz, M. (2008) _Taking Brand Initiative: How Companies Can Align Strategy, Culture, and Identity through Corporate Branding_. San Francisco, CA: Jossey-Bass.

Hogg, G. and Doolan, D. (1999) Playing the part: Practitioner roles in public relations. _European Journal of Marketing, 33_(5/6), 597–611.

Jackson, P. (1987) _Corporate Communication for Managers_. London: Pitman.

Leonard-Barton, D. (1992) Core capabilities and core rigidities: A paradox in making new product development. _Strategic Management Journal, 13_, 111–125.

McElreath, M.P. (1997) _Managing Systematic and Ethical Public Relations Campaigns_. Madison, WI: Brown & Benchmark.

Moss, D.A., Warnaby, G., and Newman, A. (2000) Public relations practitioner role enactment at the senior management level within UK compa-nies. _Journal of Public Relations Research, 12_(4), 277–307.

Moss, D.A., Newman, A., and DeSanto, B. (2005) What do communications managers do? Defining and refining the core elements of management in a public relations/communication context. _Journalism and Mass Communication Quarterly, 82_, 873–890.

Murray, K. and White, J. (2005) CEO's views on reputation management. _Journal of Communication Management, 9_(4), 348–358.

Newsom, D., Turk, J.V.S., and Kruckeberg, D. (2012) _This Is PR!_ (11th ed.). Belmont, CA: Wadsworth Publishing.

Pal, M. and Dutta, M.J. (2008) Public relations in a global context: The relevance of critical modernism as a theoretical lens. _Journal of Public Relations Research, 20_(2), 159–179.

Prahalad, C.K. and Hamel, G. (1990) The core competence of the corporation. _Harvard Business Review, 68_(3), 79–91.

Public Relations Society of America (1993) _Public Relations Professional Career Guide_. New York: PRSA Foundation.

Public Relations Society of America (1999) _A Port of Entry_. New York: PRSA.

Public Relations Society of America (2006) _The Professional Bond_. New York: PRSA.

Putnam, L.L. and Boys, S. (2006) Revisiting metaphors of organisational communication. In S.R. Clegg, C. Handy, T.B. Lawrence, and W.R. Nord (eds), _The Sage Handbook of Organizational Studies_. London: Sage, pp. 541–576.

Putnam, L.L. and Nicotera, A.M. (eds) (2009) _Building Theories of Organization. The Constitutive Role of Communication: Towards an Alternative Theory of Corporate Communication_. New York: Routledge.

Schwab, K. (2010) Speech at the world public relations forum. Stockholm, June 15.

Smith, R.D. (2009) _Strategic Planning for Public Relations_ (3rd ed.). Mahwah, NJ: Lawrence Erlbaum Associates.

Steyn, B. (2007) Contribution of public relations to organizational strategy formulation. In E. Toth (ed.), _The Future of Excellence in Public Relations and Communication Management_. Mahwah, NJ: Lawrence Erlbaum Associates.

Tench, R., D'Artrey, M., and Fawkes, J. (2009) Role of the public relations practitioner. In R. Tench and L. Yeomans (eds), _Exploring Public Relations_ (2nd ed.). London: Pearson, pp. 35–64.

Toth, E.L., Serini, S.A., Wright, D.K., and Emig, A.G. (1998) Trends in public relations roles:

1990–1995. *Public Relations Review*, *24*(2), 145–163.

van Riel, C.B.M. and Fombrun, C.J. (2007) *Essentials of Corporate Communication*. London: Routledge.

Weick, K.E. (1995) *Sensemaking in Organizations*. Thousand Oaks, CA: Sage.

Weick, K.E., Sutcliffe, K.M., and Obstfeld, D. (2005) Organizing and the process of sensemaking. *Organisational Science*, *16*(4), 409–421.

Wernerfelt, B. (1984) A resource-based view of the firm. *Strategic Management Journal*, *5*, 171–180.

White, J. and Dozier, D.M. (1992) Public relations and management decision making. In J.E. Grunig (ed.), *Excellence in Public Relations and Communication Management*. Hillsdown, NJ: Lawrence Erlbaum Associates.

Winter, S.G. (2007) Management 223. Wharton School, University of Pennsylvania, Philadelphia.

Zerfass, A. (2008) Corporate communication revisited: Integrating business strategy and strategic communication. In A. Zerfass, B. van Ruler, and K. Sriramesh (eds), *Public Relations Research. European and International Perspectives*. Wiesbarden, Germany: VS Verlag Fur Sozialwissenschaften.

Zerfass, A., Verhoeven, P., Tench, R., Moreno, A., and Verčič, D. (2011) European Communication Monitor 2011. Empirical insights into strategic communication in Europe. Results of an empirical survey in 43 countries (chart version). Brussels: EACD, EUPRERA. Retrieved from http://www.communicationmonitor.eu (last accessed September 12, 2012).

10

Corporate Reputation and the Discipline of Integrated Marketing Communications

Clarke L. Caywood
Northwestern University, USA

This chapter explores how integrated marketing communications (IMC) has emerged as a reputation support force. It examines the development of IMC and the reputation-building process. The chapter examines reputational risks with certain types of products that pose a threat to consumers, users, and influential people, and discusses how communicating with consumers and dozens of other "protected status" stakeholders can be a high-risk professional action capable of building or ruining an organizational reputation. To overcome these negative factors, the chapter primarily addresses the IMC strategic means to reduce the risk to the reputation of an organization or individual.

Despite the inherent risk of communications tactics, using the framework of an integrated marketing communications (IMC) strategy with stakeholders may help prevent reputation damage. An integrated strategy can continuously build a positive reputation. As a managerial process, IMC has developed over the past two decades. It can support the creation of a more positive reputation for an organization and more positive brands of the activities, products, and services of the organizations (see Caywood, 2012a).

Definition of IMC

It is logical that an integrated strategy should be better than a "disintegrated" one. IMC is defined with the benefit of a global perspective in Kliatchko's (2008) definition, which is more parsimonious and based on his comprehensive analysis. He states, "IMC is an audience-driven business process of strategically managing stakeholders, content, channels, and results of brand communication programs" (Kliatchko, 2008). One weakness of this definition is its use of the word "business," which might detract for some readers from the value of IMC in many organizations including government, politics, nongovernmental organizations (NGOs), and more. However, a precise definition of IMC is not yet definitive. Even the logical and heralded integration of functional areas (sales, advertising, promotions, database marketing, and public relations) of marketing communications has not provided a clear path for IMC-based reputational management. The

The Handbook of Communication and Corporate Reputation, First Edition. Edited by Craig E. Carroll.
© 2013 John Wiley & Sons, Inc. Published 2015 by John Wiley & Sons, Inc.

intuitive sense of combining a mix of traditional areas of marketing communications does not prove its value. However, one business adage may apply: we continue to profitably use it so we believe it must work.

An academic literature search on integrated communications, integrated marketing, relationship marketing, and IMC does not demonstrate any substantial attention to the importance of reputation in IMC or related fields except in a limited application to product and services branding (Kondo and Caywood, 2011). The research suggests that relationship marketing and integrated marketing with IMC have made marketing more customer oriented and/or more stakeholder oriented. The value of any of these still partial theories is that marketing is becoming more holistic. And, a more holistic, coordinated marketing should require a greater attention to the building of a baseline positive reputation for the organization or baseline positive brands for the products or services of organizations.

Emergence of IMC as a Reputational Support Process

In 1992, the advertising, direct marketing, and public relations faculty at Northwestern University's Medill School of Journalism launched a comprehensive graduate program in a newly developing field. At the time, agencies or marketing communication's companies were traditionally labeled "advertising," "direct marketing," or "public relations." All these functional areas were (and still are) professional fields of practice. However, changes were coming (Duncan and Caywood, 1996).

The forward-looking agencies and their parent-holding companies were exploring how to combine the expertise and resources of these separate fields. One goal of these acquisitions was to build a larger revenue source from clients served by common agencies of the holding company rather than many independent agencies. One way to do this was to build

an integrated holding company of agencies and consultancies sharing clients and profits.

Northwestern's faculty and students were the beneficiaries of industry's search for new ideas on how to create a more formal integrated process. At the time, faculty and practitioners were searching for a label for what logically seemed the right outcome – something integrated rather than what had been disintegrated. One of the leading companies called it "holistic communications." Another called it a "symphony" referring to the complex instrumentation in an orchestral symphony. Some talked about "one voice, one look, one feel." Others branded their versions of the concept that seemed to take greatest hold at the beginning of, in the early 1990s, the last decade of the twentieth century as IMC (Caywood and Ewing, 1991).

It was not a wholly new idea. In fact, a number of marketing professors had been teaching a subject popularly referred to as marketing communications since the 1960s. One distinction was that schools of management teaching marketing communications typically had no other courses that advanced a single course in marketing communication. For the generalist degree in business, marketers needed to consider several channels of communications to promote their products and services. But since the same students had to take courses on other elements of marketing and management (pricing, distribution, and product development), there did not seem to be any room in the curriculum for additional courses in communications.

Marketing communications may have been one of the most undervalued elements of the classic description of the four Ps of marketing (e.g., product, price, place, promotion) (Perreault *et al.*, 2011). One reason for calling it marketing communications was a symbolic representation that it was not only mass advertising, usually taught in several courses (creative, campaigns, strategy, cases, media planning) in schools of journalism and mass communications.

By the mid-twentieth century, broadcast and print advertising were becoming dominant and expensive channels of promotion. However, to some critics, mass advertising seemed far less relevant to the large business-to-business economy. And, with the growth of the more focused integration concept and practice, mass advertising seemed to be increasingly less relevant to even the business-to-consumer marketing. The mass channels developed for most of the twentieth century that included television, newspaper, radio, and magazine advertising seemed threatened by more targeted and cost-effective message channels.

Development of IMC Brand and Reputation Process

The goal of IMC for agencies included an argument that offering a client a richer mix of tactics under a carefully integrated strategy not only made good business sense, but also made good sense for the holding company's specialist firms to coordinate the budget for marketing research and communications under a single umbrella. A notable failing of the assumption was that the client would increase its marketing communication budget by adding public relations or adding direct marketing. As it seems to have "played out," the clients also logically looked for ways the marketing communication specialties could be combined to save them promotional dollars in their budget. After all, the economy in parts of the 1980s and 1990s was a recessionary period in business. It was not as unstable as the present, dragged out recession in the second decade of the twenty-first century, but it was an economic reminder of the need for IMC-based numerator and denominator management.

It is a continuing battle, but IMC has gained some momentum fighting for more measured results. IMC teaches not only short-term outcomes but shows how to estimate realistic calculations of the "lifetime value" of a customer or stakeholder relationship. Along with several other variables, "lifetime value" is one of the advanced elements of what constitutes modern IMC. Six key elements are listed here:

1 IMC is a managerial process. IMC raises the stature of advertising, PR, and marketing communication from a creative staff and tactics function to an advanced *management* function. As a managerial process, it depends heavily on planning, implementation, and evaluation. Traditionally, marketing communication was driven by campaign implementation and some of the most creative tactics available to organizations.

Decisions could be analyzed at the higher policy, strategic and then tactical levels. Policy management included social-, political-, and environmental- and industry-level decisions. These policy management decisions affected the company-wide, market, and operations decisions and tactics. Strategic contributions under IMC became more feasible to implement as they influenced well-known tactics to sell products, build brands, and strengthen reputations. IMC must still reach for policy-level contributions.

2 IMC is a research-based decision process. For many decades, advertising, public relations, promotions, and perhaps most commonly direct marketing relied on research only about the audience or consumer. Advertising, PR, and promotions often relied heavily on the psychographic attitude, interest, and opinion factors of consumer/stakeholder attitudes, interests, and opinions to determine the message and offer content. For example, the psychographic profile of a consumer who likes the outdoors, sports, social interaction, or other activities would be appealed to with advertising or events matching those interests. The social sciences were strong partners with the marketing communication fields to profile the audience.

3 IMC is behaviorally determined. Direct marketing experts contributed to IMC target marketing precisely based on the previous purchase behaviors of the target. Fortunately, the direct marketing industry represented initially by catalog marketers, financial credit companies, and political and other NGO fund-raising were able to track

precisely the actions of the recipients who responded directly. This form of marketing, sometimes degradingly referred to as "junk mail," actually begat one of the most advanced marketing metric models of "behavioral marketing." It is based not simply on attitude models but on actual purchases or decisions regarding an offer of a product or service. Much of what is known about consumers and stakeholders today is based on relationships built by companies and other organizations with the customers, donors, and influential stakeholders.

4   IMC is stakeholder driven. This element of IMC raised the bar of IMC from simply a sales-driven tactical process selling and marketing to B2B customers or B2C consumers to a strategic communication process. Caywood in 2012 wrote extensively about the growing range of stakeholders (Caywood, 2012b, p. 121). The research and strategic focus of IMC becomes much broader going beyond the consumer orientation. The IMC program at Northwestern University added "and other stakeholders" to their course descriptions of IMC:

We use the phrase ("customers and other stakeholders") to be sure that in our definition and operation of IMC that we are not narrowly focused but broadly concentrated from the outside-in. The media (traditional journalism), the union, employees, geographic community, federal, regional, state and local governments, public and private interest groups and non-governmental organizations (NGO's and more), universities, etc. are significant stakeholders in the management and marketing processes in an organizations. They are stakeholders because that "have a stake in the success or failure" or another organization. Some IMC professional spend their lives defining, building, maintaining and saving relationships with stakeholders to build a more profitable company with a strong reputation and corporate brand. (http://www.medill.northwestern.edu/imc/page.aspx?id=63021)

The stakeholder function was not practiced broadly except by the field of public rela-

tions. With PR linked to IMC, the difference was more significant. The C-Suite was reintroduced to the power of using strategic marketing and communications to build brand and reputational relationships with many stakeholders.

5   IMC is both financially determined both in a short-term and long-term framework. The simple explanation was best used to illustrate how companies and other organizations could profit from more careful planning of their marketing and other program budgets. The company could, in some instances "cut its way to profits" by reducing the denominator. We use the equation R/E equals P (where R = gross revenues; E = gross operating expenses, including marketing, personnel, and equipment; and P = gross profits). Using the simple formula $R/E = P$, management can increase profits P in two ways: one, the management can cut staff and cut expenditures on advertising, PR, or direct marketing, and more by reducing the denominator, E. Or, two, management can increase the numerator, R, by raising prices, increasing sales volume, selling to more customers or fostering more sales to the same customers.

This battle of the numerator and denominator is not new to any budget-bound organization. The challenge for IMC proponents was to demonstrate how in both the short term, and even more surely in the long term, IMC could increase revenues (numerator) by efficient and effective expenditures on marketing communication (usually less of wasteful mass advertising) make the organization more profitable.

6   IMC also depends on calculations that illustrate the "lifetime customer value" of specific customers and even stakeholders. This calculation offers management a path to investing more in some customers than in others (Schultz and Walters, 1997). Over a period of time (metaphorically "lifetime"), IMC managers estimate the revenues and profits of a particularly key customer or a segment of consumers. The longer view of value allows the IMC team to determine

how much more or less they can invest in acquiring and retaining a client or customer.

All of the elements listed focus on utilizing all resources possible to consider future outcomes, focus on all stakeholders using research and behavioral science, avoid pitfalls of a societal or financial nature, and therefore, enhance the reputation of the company or organization.

Political examples of IMC

It was evident to some observers, including those managing and writing about political campaigns (Caywood and Laczniak, 1986; Caywood and Preston, 1989; Richards and Caywood, 1991), that direct mail advertising, public relations, promotions, and other channels of promoting the message of the product (a candidate, in this case) were gaining enormous momentum. The lifeblood of political marketing was communications (in addition to money). For over two decades, prior to the "invention" of IMC, political campaigns were run using voter behavior databases, later celebrated as "breakthroughs" in consumer marketing campaigns. The messages about the candidate (and his or her reputation) could be economically delivered via a wider range of channels – the channels to reach citizens who were most likely to vote or donate, those who would vote for a specific party, and then most likely to vote for a specific candidate (Thorson et al., 1991a,b).

The 1986 campaign for US Senate in Wisconsin by Scott McCallum (later Governor) used an early data management software version of dBase II "dbase" as its organizing process. In a 1988 latter race for Lieutenant Governor, McCallum's political advisors used later derivations of the software. Several congressional campaigns in the second district of Wisconsin in the 1980s were managed with software driving the messages that defined the positive reputations of the candidates using a wide range of integrated media.

The integrated logic held for events, speeches, door-to-door candidate efforts, and leaflet distribution. Some channels used mass and other media that were not paid (earned press). It was not free either since it took experienced professionals to persuade reporters and editors in news to report on the candidate's positive and sometimes negative contacts with voters and their speeches to targeted audiences. Part of the challenge of using public relations was that the channel was not "controllable" as mass advertisers had become used to in purchased media (Caywood and Laczniak, 1985; Laczniak and Caywood, 1987).

Another important channel, mined heavily long before digital communications spread widely in politics, is fondly called "snail mail" now, but was the most personal channel of delivery at the time. Catalog marketers, alumni associations, military recruiting offices, political campaigns, and charities depended on the US mail or "junk mail." Candidate fund-raising money by mail depended on the particularly popular use of mailing lists from donated sources including clubs, churches, political parties, and purchased mail house lists (magazine subscribers, hobby clubs, association memberships, country clubs, alumni lists, etc.). The software programs were carefully designed to allow follow-up of communications and contributions, which were tracked by database systems.

IMC eventually became the term applied to the Medill School of Journalism's Department of Advertising. Its goal, at the time, was to put the right tactics in the right place, at the right time (advertising, promotions, public relations, and direct marketing). This functional description later laid the groundwork for IMC. IMC became a managerial process that now strategically helps to define the product and service reputation and branding in marketing 20 years later. It also created an umbrella concept of reputation that helped holding companies (then called conglomerates) to make sense of their business strategy.

Corporate reputation-building examples

Over the past three decades, the Chicago global company Sara Lee has variously owned Hanes, Coach Leather, Ball Park Franks, Sara Lee baked goods, and many more companies. Each company in the holding company portfolio was selected for its strong, positive brand name and upward economic potential. Usefully, the parent company name of Sara Lee was recognized as having a strong reputation for financial management, leadership, and careful development of the companies it owned in the 1990s. In this way, the management of the reputation of the brands helped to build the reputation of the corporate brand and vice versa.

Similarly, IBM found it could create branded names of targeted technologies in the 1990s. Not all the products of IBM enjoyed equal brand reputations or even the same generally positive reputation of the parent company. For example, IBM's ThinkPad laptop (later sold to Lenovo in China) found the "ThinkPad" name could be favorably applied to a wider range of products and services. An advisory board, which I participated in, identified a wide range of products and services that could benefit from the ThinkPad moniker. RSC6000 and AS400 were highly desired mid-range computers for business but their names did not carry over as strong and positive marketing communication assets (Caywood and Bauer, 1986).

The Emerson Company in St. Louis, Missouri, in the early 1990s owned 40 different companies including InSinkErator. It took a decade to manage the moving target of new divisions, SBUs, and wholly owned companies to be recognized as part of Emerson. Early in the branding and reputation-building process using IMC and management training at Northwestern's Medill School, even business cards, used by managers of the 40 companies, did not usually acknowledge the parent company. At the parent company level, Wall Street fund managers clearly recognized and rewarded the positive reputation built by the managers of Emerson for its shareholders.

Reputation Management under Pressure

One test of the role of IMC in reputation protection, survival or maintenance is under pressure. Some organizations operate under a constant state of stakeholder-induced pressure.

There are two categories of organizations that fit this profile. One is makers of high-risk products and services that can cause fatal or great damage such as food, chemicals, health, cosmetics, transportation, and energy industries (Nowak *et al.*, 2002). The second category is organizations that target "unprotected" visible (e.g., children, infants) or invisible (e.g., poor, mentally ill) populations. The two categories in the following sections are dramatically influenced by stakeholders such as regulators, the press, social communities, consumers, competitors, government, and more.

For example, products and services marketed to children, the elderly, racial minorities, or even pet animals hold a particular level of reputational risk. Marketing, even social marketing, is not always prepared to address these issues (Caywood and Laczniak, 1989). The limited focus of marketing on branding to increase loyalty to sell the product or service does not address reputational risks except to gain loyalty for repurchase (Langrehr *et al.*, 1997). Sometimes the messages can be very subtle using racial, value, and age symbols that send unintended messages to the audience (Caywood and Langrehr, 1990; Langrehr and Caywood, 1989, 1995; Langrehr *et al.*, 1997). Instead, a more integrated approach led by public relations (corporate or strategic communications) provides the theoretical and practical support for organizational reputations (Caywood, 2005).

Because high-risk oriented industries produce and sell potentially high-risk products, the number of products and services that might be considered more risky than others is enormous (see the following list). All products and services might have some risk associated with them through poorly handled use or deliberate misuse. Managers concerned with managing their corporate reputation and SBU brand reputations are advised to begin to use IMC more quickly if they manage any of the following categories of organizations, products, and services.

At-risk industries

There are identifiable categories of products and services that have a potential to do severe damage or cause fatalities (e.g., poorly formulated or tested pharmaceuticals, undercooked food, and auto safety) (Table 10.1).

At-risk populations of targeted stakeholders

This category focuses on the targeted buyers (moms), users (children), and influentials (press or social media site). See Table 10.2. Some of the populations listed are simply perceived by society (depending on the exact culture) as more vulnerable. Organizations selling or working with such groups must use reputational management as a process to thwart the appearance of exploiting the targets.

The assumption is that some populations of citizens require or are owed more protection from avarice, illegal, and immoral organizational activities. In scientific research, for example, some cite the following: fetuses, children, prisoners, pregnant women, mentally disabled or cognitively impaired persons, terminally ill patients, the elderly, students and

Table 10.1 At-risk industries.

Pharmaceuticals
   Prescription drugs, over-the-counter drugs, natural supplement, medical record keeping
Food
   Foods for human consumption
   Animal (pet) foods
   Fresh or raw foods
   Packaged foods
   Prepared foods in restaurants, homes
Home
   Fire warning systems, smoke alarms
   Carbon monoxide alarms
   Product-building content (e.g., insulation)
   Fire hazard roofing materials, construction
   Plumbing supplies
   Water-saving equipment
Maintenance
   Chain saws, cleaning chemicals
   Ladders, shelving, dollies, other
   Heating systems in homes, public/private buildings, and transportation
Firewood-burning equipment
   Ventilation equipment
   Carbon monoxide emission monitors
   Asbestos-covered products and removal procedures
Propane tanks in rural homes and patios
   Gas explosions from pipes, leaks, street connection failure
   Fuel oil tanks and ground leaks
Transportation
   Airplanes, auto, trucks, ships, school buses, recreational boats, sailboats, snowmobiles, water jet skis, subways, bicycles, buses, trolleys
   General related transportation products/services
Instruction
Licensing
Product safety checkup
Flotation devices
   Fuel safety measures
   Design failure
   Seat belts

Table 10.1 (*Continued*)

Driver standards and background checks
   Night, early day schedules
Safety belts, airbags, padded dashes, breakaway mirrors, blind spot sensors, tire size issues, wheel design
Mass transit
   Travel security regarding terrorism
   New travel IDs for passengers
   Employee investigation, training
   Lighting, signage, warning messages
   Public messages for acceptance of rules
Skin and beauty products and services
   Cosmetics with risk to the elderly, young, pregnant
   Cosmetics with risk to the eyes
   Age-related treatments
   Any products with internal and external use
Medical elective surgery
   Lasik surgery, plastic surgery, tattoos, hair transplants
Age- and weight-related treatments – skin, chemical peels, and gastric bypass surgery
Entertainment
   Children's programs, advertising using entertainment characters
   Pornography, R- and X-rated movies for general distribution
   Movies, theater, music video games, comics, television (with regard to violence, racial issues, crime, sexual concerns)
   Parks including roller coasters and other rides, food, security
Sports – selling, playing, sponsoring
   Helmets, mouth guards, masks, metal bats
   Eye protection, clothing
   Speed (race track design, safety equipment)
   Medical (game rules, checkups)

Table 10.2 At-risk populations.

People with physical disabilities
Mentally ill
Lower IQ individuals
Low-income individuals
Racial minorities
Elderly
Children
Pregnant women
Infants
Fetuses
Military and former military personnel
Uneducated, less educated, illiterate populations
Recent immigrants
Any combination of the above excluding the next population
Pets

Note: The order is random since each product, service, or case will require very specific analysis regarding risks.

employees, survey research that involves AIDS information either with the general public or with vulnerable populations, or economically or educationally disadvantaged persons (St. Catherine's University, 2010).

Examples of protective legal and moral action taken to date are highly specific laws targeted at preventing the abuse of selling to a certain audience. Examples are the advertising of children's toys, marketing of financial services to the elderly, puffery-based advertising that misleads the less educated or common man, and contracts that are difficult to understand for the less educated or ESL customers, especially from agencies like the Food and Drug Administration (FDA), Federal Trade Commission (FTC), or Federal Reserve Board (FRB) (Federal Reserve Board, 2008).

Conclusion

The advanced metrics and elements of IMC offer marketers and communication professionals a superior strategy to manage reputations and brands. The IMC approach also offers a more broadly defined understanding of how crucial it can be to consider all stakeholders. Finally, IMC considers the fragility of some products and services and certain stakeholder groups (Caywood, 2009).

Caution seems reasonable when crafting a positive reputation for an organization under any circumstance. First, there is a level of distrust with which many communication efforts are regarded. Furthermore, when the products and services are labeled as higher risk by regulators or by society, the management of the reputation building process seems even more precarious. In the same way, when the analysis shows that the stakeholder groups targeted to purchase or be involved with the product or service is a high visibility, high-risk population, the reputation building process is, once again, more tenuous.

The risks are many and varied. The stakeholders are present; some vulnerable, some vigilant, all significant. IMC has been shown to use managerial, financial, research-based, and behaviorally determined means to guard and enhance reputations. With so many factors and stakeholders to consider, it seems advisable to do everything possible to protect your company or organization's greatest asset.

References

Caywood, C.L. (2005) "New metrics for public relations" for International Public Relations Research Conference. University of Miami, Miami, FL.

Caywood, C.L. (2009) The future of public relations. In B. Calder (ed.), *Kellogg on Advertising and Media*, pp. 196–207.

Caywood, C.L. (ed.) (2012a) *The Handbook of Strategic Public Relations and Integrated Marketing Communications*. New York: McGraw-Hill.

Caywood, C.L. (2012b) The stakeholder concept: Empowering public relations. In C.L. Caywood (ed.), *The Handbook of Strategic Public Relations and Integrated Marketing Communications*. New York: McGraw-Hill, pp. 121–130.

Caywood, C.L. and Bauer, C.L. (1986) An electronic bulletin board system for the sales profession. *Journal of Personal Selling and Sales Management*, 6, 85–90.

Caywood, C.L. and Ewing, R.P. (1991) Integrated marketing communications: A new master's degree concept. *Public Relations Review*, 17(3), 237–244.

Caywood, C.L. and Laczniak, G.R. (1985) Unethical political advertising: Decision considerations for policy and evaluation. American Marketing Association Winter Conference Proceedings and Presentation, Phoenix, AZ, pp. 37–41.

Caywood, C.L. and Laczniak, G.R. (1986) Ethics and personal selling: Death of a salesman as an ethical primer. *Journal of Personal Selling and Sales Management*, 6, 81–88.

Caywood, C.L. and Laczniak, G.R. (1989) The marketing of political candidates: Current tactics and future strategies. In S. Fine (ed.), *Social Marketing*. Boston: Allyn & Bacon, pp. 125–139.

Caywood, C.L. and Langrehr, F.W. (1990) Definitional issues related to using the seven sins and seven virtues as a model for advertising analysis. *Current Issues and Research in Advertising*, 12, 43–62.

Caywood, C.L. and Preston, I.L. (1989) The continuing debate on political advertising: Toward a jeopardy theory of political advertising as regulated speech. *The Journal of Public Policy and Marketing*, 8, 204–226.

Duncan, T. and Caywood, C.L. (1996) Integrated marketing communications – An evolutionary model. In E. Thorson (ed.), *Integrated Marketing Communications – Research and Theory*. Mahwah, NJ: Lawrence Erlbaum Associates.

Federal Reserve Board (2008) Report to the Congress on Credit Scoring and Its Effects on the Availability and Affordability of Credit. Submitted to the Congress pursuant to section 215 of the Fair and Accurate Credit Transactions Act of 2003 August 2007. Retrieved from http://federalreserve.gov/boarddocs/rptcongress/creditscore/differential.htm#toc10.2 (last accessed September 13, 2012).

Kliatchko, J. (2008) Revisiting the IMC construct: A revised definition and four pillars. *International Journal of Advertising*, 27, 133–160.

Kondo, K. and Caywood, C.L. (2011) IMC as an innovation: From integrated marketing communications to integrated marketing. 2011

International American Academy of Advertising, Perth, Australia.

Laczniak, G.R. and Caywood, C.L. (1987) The case for and against televised political advertising: Implications for research and public policy. *The Journal of Public Policy and Marketing*, 6, 16–32.

Langrehr, F.W. and Caywood, C.L. (1989) An assessment of the "sins" and "virtues" portrayed in advertising. *International Journal of Advertising*, 8, 391–403.

Langrehr, F.W. and Caywood, C.L. (1995) A semiotic approach to determining the sins and virtues portrayed in advertising. *Journal of Current Issues and Research in Advertising*, 17(Spring), 33–47.

Langrehr, F.W., Langrehr, V.B., and Caywood, C. (1997) A multi-meaning study of the value messages in print advertising. In R. Belk (ed.), *Research in Consumer Behavior*. Bradford, UK: Emerald Group Publishing Limited, pp. 173–208.

Nowak, G., Cole, G., Kirby, S., Freimuth, V. (all CDC), and Caywood, C. (2002) The application of "integrated marketing communications" to social marketing and health communication: Organizational challenges and implications. *Social Marketing Quarterly*, 4, 12–16. Special Issue in Innovative Social Marketing.

Perreault, W.D., Cannon, J.P., and McCarthy, E.J. (2011) *Essentials of Marketing*. New York: McGraw-Hill.

Richards, J.I. and Caywood, C.L. (1991) Symbolic speech in political advertising: Encroaching legal barriers. In F. Biocca (ed.), *Television and Political Advertising, Volume 2, Signs, Codes and Images*. Hillsdale, NJ: Lawrence Erlbaum Associates, pp. 231–256.

Schultz, D.E. and Walters, J.S. (1997) *Measuring Brand Communication ROI*. New York: Association of National Advertisers.

St. Catherine's University (2010) Are there any specially protected populations? Retrieved from http://minerva.stkate.edu/irb.nsf/pages/specialpopulations (last accessed September 13, 2012).

Thorson, E., Christ, W.G., and Caywood, C.L. (1991a) Effects of issue – Image strategies, attack and support appeals, music, and visual content in political commercials on attitudes, memory and voting content. *Journal of Broadcasting and Electronic Media*, 35(4), 465–486.

Thorson, E., Christ, W.G., and Caywood, C.L. (1991b) Selling candidates like tubes of toothpaste: Is the comparison apt? In F. Biocca (ed.), *Television and Political Advertising, Volume 1: Psychological Processes*. Hillsdale, NJ: Lawrence Erlbaum Associates, pp. 145–172.

11

Corporate Reputation and the Discipline of Marketing Communication

Richard J. Varey

University of Waikato, New Zealand

In this chapter, we consider how corporate reputation is conceived, understood, and investigated in the marketing communication field. We also acknowledge changing circumstances that indicate strongly to a revisioning of both branding, including corporate branding, and corporate reputation.

One way to look at this is to ask what is the management problem for marketing communication for which corporate reputation is the solution? Alternatively, what is the corporate reputation problem for which marketing communication is the solution? So, how does the marketing discipline and the specialism of marketing communication treat corporate reputation? How does corporate communication treat marketing communication? Of course, this is determined and underpinned by how the marketing and management disciplines treat marketing communication.

The discussion proceeds with an overview of concepts and applications, and considers the significance of the contemporary context of the sustainability imperative and the advent of the Internet. Finally, some future directions that seem important for researchers and educators in the field are raised.

Introduction

Defined as "information used to make a value judgment about an object or a person," reputation is widely regarded as quite obviously a strategic enduring intangible business asset in the form of corporate reputation. The reputation of a company is a differentiator and thus a source of strategic competitive advantage (see Davies *et al.*, 2003) inasmuch as it constitutes a distinctive appeal and signal of product (both good and service) quality, especially in service markets where this is particularly crucial.

Corporate reputation has received substantial research attention in marketing. A huge body of business research has conceived of reputation as equivalent to image, or as an element or aspect of image, or vice versa of image as an element or aspect of reputation. Corporate reputation is understood either as synonymous with corporate image, or they are understood to be mutually influencing. To get a sense of how marketing communication experts treat corporate reputation, an informal online search was conducted. It is evidently recognized as a crucial aspect of business strategy. Perhaps rather surprisingly, it is hard to get a sense that corporate reputation has been examined much by marketing communication specialists, that is, that it has been treated as a problem to be solved with communication.

In terms of management and student texts, Amazon.com currently lists over 3000 books with "corporate reputation" in the title or description, only about 20 of which are directly concerned with marketing communication (or public relations). Examples include Dowling (2002), Kitchen and Schultz (2001), Schultz *et al.* (2000), and Waddington and Earl (2012). A further 90 or so focus on corporate reputation and include a marketing perspective, and about 50 books address reputation and marketing communication. An informal browsing of recently published marketing communication textbooks reveals that the topic does not (yet) filter through to textbooks and thus presumably to student attention in college and university marketing departments. One exception is Rossiter and Bellman's (2005) *Marketing Communications: Theory and Applications* in which they discussed corporate brand preference and the effects of corporate image advertising. For them, marketing communications is nowadays about all possible points of contact (interaction seems a more useful concept) in which the brand can be communicated with potential and current customers.

In the academic research field, the *Journal of Marketing Communications*, now in its seventeenth volume, has so far published more than 300 articles, including just 19 that mention corporate reputation, and of them only 8 which substantively focus on the concept. The *International Journal of Advertising* (subtitled *The Quarterly Review of Marketing Communications*) seems to have never published on corporate reputation in its 20 volumes to date. The *Corporate Reputation Review* has specialized since 1997 in academic research and pro-

fessional analysis on reputations and reputation management. Just over 10% of articles published to date have addressed corporate reputation from the perspective of marketing communication or raised issues from this perspective. The *Journal of Marketing* has published just 18 articles since 1936, while the *European Journal of Marketing* has published some 248 articles since 1989 that mention corporate reputation, with just 21 addressing the field specifically in terms of marketing communication.

In the profession, the UK-based Chartered Institute of Marketing states that "marketing is all about stakeholder communications" (The Chartered Institute of Marketing, 2011), and their educational syllabus connects strategy, brand promise, and communication in regard to safeguarding reputation. Several attempts to locate details of such a focus on the American Marketing Association web site at the time of writing proved fruitless.

Given the variability of attention to corporate reputation in the marketing field, then why does it matter from the perspective of marketing communication? Isn't it simply obvious that marketing communication is meant, in part, to build positive reputation for commercial purposes?

Why Is Corporate Reputation a Marketing Issue?

It seems like common sense that familiarity leads to high regard, and therefore that reputation should be a central focus for marketing. What a company stands for and goodwill towards the company are closely linked to assessment of quality, and thus the salability of product offerings.

As an attributed character, a good reputation indicates credibility and collective esteem, and fosters trust and confidence. Earned "reputational capital" is similar to what accountants call "goodwill" and marketers call "brand equity" (Fombrun, 1996). Of course, reputation also creates responsibilities, since it is the exhibition of values (Travis, 2000): "Reputation is a concept with economic implications that defines the trust expressed toward a company by customers, influentials and others who ensure its survival and success" (Horton, 1995, p. 142). Respected companies experience elevated expectations for quality and reliability at any price point and have to deliver on their claims of "good character" to remain seen as credible, reliable, trustworthy, and responsible. The basis of reputation is in particular differentiating skills and capabilities, innovativeness, operational excellence, and closeness to customers – all attributes that distinguish a company from others. Businesses succeed when they accumulate economic wealth, so reputation is akin to a license to operate.

A favorable corporate reputation predisposes us to buy a company's products (van Riel, 1995) and can reduce the impact of unfavorable publicity by acting as a store of goodwill (O'Rourke, 1997). Positive reputation complements and supports marketing, in part helping to reduce postpurchase cognitive dissonance. Harris Interactive's 2009 survey in the United States found that 60% of people preferred to purchase from companies with strong reputations.

Acknowledged founding father of corporate reputation as a field of study and leading light in the development of management tools, Charles Fombrun (1996) identified the connection with marketing through stakeholder relationships, branding, and market interaction. The "reliability principle" simply observes that "The more reliable a company appears to its key constituents, the better regarded the company will be" (Fombrun, 1996, p. 64), although this is an unfortunate use of the term "appears" as this can be suggestive of inauthenticity, of appearance over substance. Perhaps *apparent* as in *evident* might be a clearer notion, yet we all realize that reputation may not be fully derived from full knowledge of established facts. Harris Interactive recognizes that "Reputation is not necessarily informed by any actual knowledge about, communication from, or interaction with the company" (The Chartered Institute of Marketing, 2011).

Corporate Reputation as a (Marketing) Communication Problem

How is corporate reputation a problem – or challenge – for marketing communication managers? Is corporate reputation a marketing problem or is it a public relations problem? For some specialists, the answer lies in the wider field of corporate communication in a holistic approach to orchestrating all communication, symbols, and behavior that construct and impact on corporate identity (Brønn and Berg, 2005; Langer and Varey, 2008; van Riel, 1995; van Riel and Fombrun, 2007; Varey, 1998, 2000).

Whereas marketing communication specialists might see corporate reputation as part of corporate brand, corporate communication specialists regard the corporate brand as part of corporate reputation – so does brand determine reputation, or vice versa? While some regard corporate reputation and corporate image as synonymous, most see corporate reputation as influencing and influenced by projected corporate images (Bickerton, 2000; Gotsi and Wilson, 2001).

To what extent is protecting and strengthening a corporate reputation a problem solvable with more and "effective" communication? Is most marketing communication concerned with (short-term) corporate image, leaving long-term corporate reputation untreated? Reputation is built on trust, authenticity, and integrity judgments that are not "communicated" in messages from the company.

Several marketing concerns are identified by Schultz and Walters (1997) that can be related to corporate reputation and corporate communication: a measure of loyalty, market share, and so on, that is, buying rate; customer retention; customer referrals (such advocacy indicates loyalty); price elasticity (such tolerance for increases reflects loyalty); and customer switching costs and barriers to competitor market entry (loyalty in the sense that customers are harder to "pull" to an alternative brand and an attractive reputation repels rivalry).

Spotts and Weinberger (2010) investigated the impact of marketing communications activities on corporate reputation, concluding that "The findings suggest that companies with different levels of brand evaluation (opinion and value) have distinct marketing communication profiles which can be labelled communication footprints. Further, this relationship is moderated by prior corporate reputation. Firms seeking to change stakeholder evaluations must pay particular attention to both the overall volume of publicity received, as well as the ratio of positive to negative publicity volume. Advertising spending plays an important supportive role in these evaluations" (p. 591).

A favorable and thus attractive image comes from the parts of the identity that show the company to be superior to competitors, expressed in "what we say we are" to generate awareness and preference, and thus create an emotional bond (at the company level, corporate image advertising is discussed later). We might experience inconsistencies in what the company does and what they say. Do you trust someone who tells you that you should trust them, especially when you realize that they benefit from such trust?

Strategically, Kay (1993) sees reputation as the most important commercial mechanism for conveying information to consumers, but it is not equally important in all markets. Much marketing communication is the act of promising – informing customers and consumers of the company's image as a supplier and server. How realistic is that as the primary focus? A company can inform the identity by expressing and projecting (i.e., positioning), but the image is an assessment made by observers who may or may not have direct experience as customers.

Marketing communication has largely been understood and practiced as expressing the voice of the company for the purpose of informing, persuading, and reminding people to buy the company's products (Keller, 2009). This is the stance taken in most textbooks. Thus, marketing communication is seen as comprising product advertising, product publicity, direct mail, personal selling, sponsorship activities, sales promotion activities, and packaging. Such activities and media content are used in support of sales with a customer/consumer (market) focus to create awareness and interest in products. Brand *positioning* is the concerted effort to create an image in the minds of consumers and customers.

Elsewhere, I have distinguished communicative and informative forms of interaction (Ballantyne and Varey, 2006; Varey, 2000, 2008). The former is practices of co-constructive collaboration, whereas the latter is the expressive distribution, usually selling, that is the more usual, narrow, conception of marketing communication in the practices of "decide–announce–persuade." Taking a holistic communication perspective, value creation is meaning making in communicative interaction. The informative conception of marketing interaction can explain corporate identity. This is an amalgam of characteristics chosen for promotion, producing the immediate, momentary meanings of behavior, symbols, and communication, in terms of impressions and recognition. Such attributes used to describe a company in answer to "who are you?" can be packaged in "messages" for transmission/dissemination to observers. Corporate image, on the other hand, is what someone believes about the company – "what do people think of you?" – in terms of the associations in mind to the company (Barich and Kotler, 1991). The total impression (Dichter, 1985) stems from an image assessment, for example, integrity, innovativeness, friendliness, and knowledge. Such an image review takes account of both the desirable and the sensed actual, observable primarily through action and change (Kotler and Armstrong, 1996), that is, through interaction.

Seen as a problem of managing communication, "A corporate reputation is a stakeholder's overall evaluation of a company over time. This evaluation is based on the stakeholder's direct experiences with the company, any other forms of communication and symbolism that provides information about the company's actions and/or a comparison with the action of other leading rivals" (Gotsi and Wilson, 2001, p. 29). Reputation is judgmental, dynamic, and relative, and supports choices of action in relation to potential partners (see also Vickers', 1983, appreciative system in explaining such "policy making" with regard to relationships).

Corporate reputation evolves over an extended period of time as an evaluation, in terms of esteem (approval, notability, respect, belief, cherishing, and so on) from past experiences (Balmer and Greyser, 2002), surfacing in "what can I expect your treatment of me to be and why should I deal with you?" Strong corporate reputation is not creatable through corporate communication programs alone – while image is susceptible to effects of communication campaigns, corporate reputation is a persisting and consistent assessment of the collective experience of those dealing with the company.

Customer influence is one area of managerial concern that is especially significant in service consumption. When the purpose of all business is understood to be service (in the service-dominant logic – see Vargo and Lusch, 2004, for the original argument), the company is at the core of the evaluation of benefits and costs. Corporate image may be the first thing that comes to mind. Outward appearance matters – a service business must be good *and* look good. While there may be allowance for imperfections, there can also be hypercritical assessment and negative reaction. Expectations are influenced by the image, and image is a dimension of quality in a service situation. Brand image supports tangible clues for abstract or intangible service. Since service experience evaluation is only possible after the event, reputation substitutes for quality assessment in search, inspection or immediate experience. Furthermore, service customers signal their own credibility and integrity through their associations with others of repute. *Market credibility* comes from credible market signaling of service quality, largely from credence in word-of-mouth recommendation.

How do image and reputation influence consumer attitudes and expectations in their assessments, aggregated over time? As a summary "collage" of past corporate behavior, reputation influences buying behavior. Citing the Reputations Corporation of Vancouver (a communication and reputation management agency), Mainwaring (2011, p. 135) points to the payback on reputation management: 72% of consumers are influenced in their buying decisions by reputation, while 89% use reputation to decide between products of equal merit. For Mainwaring, this is a brand issue. A positive reputation is an informative cue, indicating the likelihood of the company honoring promises, and a negative reputation stems from violation of expectations.

Several studies show that reputation assists in the creation of expectations (see Nguyen and Leblanc, 2001 and Yoon *et al.*, 1993). Response to service depends on attitude to reputation, and this is especially important in the absence of information and when there is uncertainty over performance. Marketers generally assume that communication builds reputation, and certainly reputation influences the effectiveness of marketing communication, primarily in terms of credibility of expressions, promises, and identity. Findings from these studies indicate that attractive corporate reputation is fostered through multiple channels of interaction, both informative and communicative. Corporate reputation is quite similar to brand equity and interacts with corporate image to influence customer loyalty.

Walsh and Beatty (2007) found that the most significant influences on customer satisfaction, loyalty, trust, and "word of mouth" were customer orientation, good employment, and product quality. Customer orientation seems to have the strongest influence on reputation for marketers. Customer care, understood as marketing communication (part of a relationship marketing strategy) impacts on corporate reputation. Indeed, marketing communications can create intense active loyal relationships (Keller, 2009) and thus strong and resilient market share.

Concepts and Perspectives

Now, a number of ideas found in the marketing communication literature with regard to reputation are outlined, resulting in the recognition of the convergence of two previously discrete conceptual fields: top-down strategic thinking on corporate reputation and bottom-up thinking on consumer response to branding (Bickerton, 2000). Although a matter of relative emphasis, whereas brand emphasizes associations, rational meaning, and position, reputation ("good name") rests on the emotional and irrational. In an era of mass marketing, image building is a primary aim, whereas in the present era of mass customization shifting to individuation, reputation matters in terms of core characteristics of the company, its people, and its products.

Branding has become a major concern for companies as brands are increasingly recognized as some of the most valuable company assets (Merz *et al.*, 2009). A brand can be thought of as a form of knowledge in part created by marketing activities, including "marketing communications." The benefits to the company of branding are quite similar to those indicated for corporate reputation in terms of enhancements in assessments of product performance, customer loyalty, resilience in the face of competitive marketing actions and marketing crises, profit margins, elasticity of customer response to price decreases and inelasticity of customer response to price increases, trade or intermediary cooperation and support, marketing communication effectiveness, and licensing and brand extension opportunities (Keller, 2009).

A strong brand increases the effectiveness of marketing communication, because consumers may be more willing to pay more attention to further brand communication, to judge more favorably and recall more readily media content and/or associated emotional or rational reactions. Building strong brands is thus a management priority (Aaker, 1992, 1996; Kapferer, 2004). Marketing communications can play a crucial role in shaping the knowledge needed to respond positively to brands (Keller, 2009): "brand knowledge is not the facts about the brand – it is all the thoughts, feelings, perceptions, images, experiences and so on that become linked to the brand in the minds of consumers (individuals and organizations). All of these types of information can be thought of in terms of a set of associations to the brand in consumer memory" (p. 143). The overall effect is both brand awareness, in terms of recall and recognition, and brand image in terms of evaluation and preference. What you think about a brand is both a meaning and an evaluation.

When you "have a brand in mind" you have one in your mind – brands are minded! A brand is both product and associations – marketing communication propagates visual and verbal benefit claims about attributes, subjective considerations, and emotions that contribute to the formation of brand images that influence beliefs and motivations. Such brand building arises among both customers and employees. The management problem is one of brand identity – what the company wants the brand to mean and stand for. A brand is no longer only a marketing communication means of differentiation and motivation.

The *corporate brand* is part of brand management (see Fombrun *et al.*, 2000, from the reputation perspective). In treating the company as a brand (see, e.g., de Chernatony and McDonald, 1998, from the marketing perspective), the purpose is to create awareness of the company name and distinguish the company as credible to buyers as a reliable specialist with expertise, experience, and relevant performance. The corporate brand thus supports relationships by expressing the values of the company, the added value in dealing with the company, along with trust and confidence. This augments product brands, providing efficiency gains in advertising spend, as strong corporate brands have little need to advertise beyond maintaining awareness.

Corporate reputation is a "super" brand (Dowling, 1995), the management of which is the responsibility of senior company managers, so marketing communication is strategic, in this sense. Aaker (1996) proposes a brand hierarchy, comprising the corporate brand, (in some cases) a product range brand, product line brand, sub-brand, and branded feature/component and/or service. At the apex of the nested hierarchy, the corporate brand – in the minds of both customers and employees – puts the company name at the heart of marketing. The corporate brand is part of that which is much bigger – the corporate reputation (see Balmer, 2001; Balmer and Gray, 2003; Knox and Bickerton, 2003).

Corporate brand management is emerging as a convergence of the company-centric, corporate strategy tradition of corporate reputation derived in past actions, and the market-centric corporate brand tradition of values and culture proposition translating into customer value premised on future promise (i.e., value positioning: see, e.g., Ballantyne *et al.*, 2011). Some part of marketing communications is becoming corporate brand management communications (Bickerton, 2000), in which corporate identity is an input, and the output (corporate image) may not be what was intended, and thus presents a communication problem.

Corporate associations are an alternative understanding to corporate identity in terms of beliefs, moods, emotions, and evaluations (Dacin and Brown, 2002). What a person knows about a company, primarily in product ability associations and social responsibility associations, results in its product brand being assessed in light of the corporate brand (Brown and Dacin, 1997). What comes to the fore is company product expertise and character in dealing with social issues (see also Berens *et al.*, 2005, and the discussion of social responsibility and sustainability later in this chapter).

Corporate-level marketing occurs when the focus and concern is for the company within networks of stakeholders and partnerships. This is a strategic perspective, focusing on integration of identity, image, reputation, communication, and corporate brand management, and it addresses marketing's power as an orchestrator or integrator in meeting stakeholder needs at a profit (Balmer and Greyser, 2002, 2006). This is a logical step in marketing's evolution to a company-wide focus in service to stakeholders; the integrative imperative is seen in integrated marketing communication and relationship marketing (discussed later), and more widely in the evolving corporate communication field. Perhaps surprisingly for the marketing special-

ist, this is not a new idea – Kenneth Boulding's economic treatment of the concept of corporate image as subjective knowledge in *The Image* (subtitled *Knowledge in Life and Society*) was published in 1956.

Corporate credibility is the extent to which consumers see a company willing and capable of meeting their needs with products. Keller and Aaker (1998) highlighted expertise/competence; trustworthiness in terms of honesty, dependability, and sensitivity to consumer needs; and likability.

Barich and Kotler (1991) introduced the notion of "marketing image" in an attempt to deal with the apparent conflict of interest between marketers and public relations specialists. This provides the marketer with a role in managing the corporate identity in order to foster the desired corporate image. Kotler (1986) argued that public relations should be part of "megamarketing" (social marketing). Then the marketer also takes responsibility for the supply of benefits to parties other than target consumers, for example, government, unions, or other interested third parties, who may act as gatekeepers. It is sometimes necessary to arrange additional incentives, inducements, or sanctions to gain desired responses from groups other than customers. This approach is the strategically coordinated application of economic, psychological, political, and public relations skills to gain the cooperation of a number of parties in order to enter and/or operate in a given "protected" market. This approach requires cooperation and coordination among marketers, company officers, public relations and public affairs specialists, and legal specialists. But public relations is seen as primarily a communication tool for influencing attitudes, whereas marketing aims to elicit specific behaviors and includes not only communication but needs assessment, product development, price setting, and the creation of distribution channels (Ehling *et al.*, 1992, p. 378). Thus, in this approach, public relations is not seen as involved in defining the goals of the company, but merely in making it easier to sell products and services, by "conditioning" the market.

White (1991) disagrees, arguing that public relations is a central management concern which complements marketing communications, and is firmly strategic, forward looking, and coordinating in scope and nature. Elsewhere in this book, no doubt, corporate reputation is claimed as a public relations problem and responsibility. Marketers can retain claim over *marketing reputation* – the company's reputation for marketing, as nicely illustrated in Sheth and Sisodia's (2006, p. 329) benefit-sharing matrix, which identifies exemplary marketing in which both marketers and customers prosper, and the three situations in which one or both lose out, that is, unethical marketing, wasteful marketing, and dumb marketing (in which costs exceed benefits).

Corporate image advertising arises when the focus is on promoting company contribution to society to tell the story of what the company stands for, beyond the purely economic (see, e.g., Biehal and Sheinin, 1998; Drumwright, 1996; Schumann *et al.*, 1991; and Sen and Bhattacharya, 2001).

Marketing communication often (usually, tactically) focuses overly on corporate image, when for certain stakeholders, corporate ability to produce economic and noneconomic benefit outcomes matters more. Corporate image and reputation is influenced by the mental picture investors have of a company as determined by the consistent performance and *effective communication*. According to Rossiter and Bellman (2005), corporate reputation is the corporate brand preference composed by a stakeholder from the subjective evaluative weighting and summing of benefit beliefs and emotional associations (p. 387), that is, from the corporate image. *Fortune* Magazine ranks the "most admired companies" in terms of corporate brand reputation.

Of course, such advertising-based activity is prone to skepticism among those who witness it and interpret motives and effects with cynicism (Pomering and Johnson, 2009). This is seen in so-called greenwashing, in which exaggerated claims about eco-efficiency and other aspects of social performance are revealed in inconsistencies of what is said and what is observed. Is the company's reputation all that it seems to be? Reputation is based on actions, whereas image is derived in appearances. Much of marketing communication's attention is to "positioning," that is, the creation of an image relative to consumer preferences and competing offerings.

Corporate personality is a metaphor for understanding the reaction, and interaction, of persons to company traits as if the company has "come to life" as another person. It emphasizes values and the emotional and expressive capacity of the company. The concept extends Aaker's brand personality scale (Aaker, 1996) from brand to company (Davies *et al.*, 2003), on dimensions of agreeableness, sincerity, competence, sophistication, sentimentality, excitement, enterprise, and so on.

Applications

Having established a general conceptual map, attention is now turned to particular areas of marketing practice in which the key ideas are deployed.

Integrated marketing communications (IMC) safeguards corporate identity, image, and reputation in the multiple channels of interaction by working to retain cohesiveness. IMC narrows the range of images among buyers, suppliers, and other stakeholders, and exploits the added value of the combined strategic roles of the various disciplines managing "communicating," to enhance clarity, consistency, and impact. *Image design* is the formulation of the communication of a positioning strategy that can partially determine consumer expectations, including ensuring that communication means are appropriate for buyer and seller needs, in media choices, company voice, and communication style.

The *relationship marketing* concepts of loyalty, word of mouth, and advocacy are consistent with the reputational notions of esteem, trust, commitment, and so on. Relationship marketing seems to imply something about reputation, although perhaps it is clear that a reputation is only invoked when someone does not know another, and is what is talked about in word-of-mouth communication. How does the "new paradigm" field of relationship marketing treat corporate reputation? A general search with Google Scholar produced not a single publication or citation. One consideration in selecting partners for relationship building is reputation by association. Reputation enables the enactment of relationships – "customer reputation" influences the company's reputations, as do the respective reputations of other associates.

For MacMillan *et al.* (2005) in studying reputation in relationships, communication includes how a business informs stakeholders about its activities as well as listening, sensing, evaluating, and responding to stakeholder concerns over changing needs (citing Duncan and Moriarty, 1998 and Ramsey and Sohi, 1997).

Internal marketing and corporate identification are concerned with the effects of motivation in the company on value creation capability and performance (see, e.g., Devine and Halpern, 2001). There is benefit from the marketing conditioning effect of corporate reputation for sales support, and there is also a contribution to reputation of the image and reputation among employees who can act as brand ambassadors with impact on other stakeholders. Ahmed and Rafiq (2003), for example, explain how competence-building internal marketing impacts on corporate reputation, and Smidts *et al.* (2001) examine the interactions of employee communication climate, "external prestige," and corporate identification. Varey (2005) proposed the internal marketing metaprocess as the dynamic communication structure that supports necessary interaction between subgroups that creates coherence and cooperation in a community of stakeholders. The internal marketing or internal relationship management system engenders corporate identification in terms of corporate image, personality, and reputation as a kind of glue which binds together knowledge workers into a coherent goal-oriented community with at least some sense of common purpose. Managers create the context of a climate of good service to foster commit-

ment to the business purpose as the currency of day-to-day work.

It is generally argued that service quality perceptions and market consciousness or business consciousness of customers, delivery staff, and managers can have a profound impact on the business performance of a company in terms of what strategy is designed, knowledge of achievement, and level of satisfaction and feelings about value for money. Internal marketing has been widely adopted as an approach to creating and maintaining a climate of good service. The task for managers in the people-intensive industries is to recruit and keep skilled, engaged people. Knowledge workers individually possess "know-how capital" (Lloyd, 1990), which is their skills, experience, and aptitudes, and their familiarity with the company's business idea, its style of operation, and its personality. *Corporate identification* is the cognitive connection that will ensure that some people join and make a commitment to stay and to contribute, while others come and go or do not choose to come in the first place. This term is synonymous with the popular notions of "buy-in" and "winning hearts and minds." It is no longer enough for an employee to perform tasks or obey orders. Each also needs to "believe" in the company and what it stands for and to "feel" for the work he or she is doing.

While markets/brands and publics/reputations are different, it is primarily because they are treated differently (Varey, 1997): marketing deals with markets and public relations deals with publics, for differing and complementary ends. It is helpful to distinguish *corporate public relations* from *marketing public relations*, the latter of which, like financial public relations and community public relations, serves a specific group – in this case, the marketing department. Kotler (1986) sees marketing public relations as a development of "publicity," which moves beyond "editorial column inches" to assistance in product launches, repositioning mature products, promoting product categories, influencing target groups, defending products under threat, and building corporate image – that is, creating an effect, and not just output.

Reputation is surely a relational concept. Cutlip *et al.* (1985) distinguish corporate public relations as "a function of management seeking to identify, establish and maintain mutually beneficial relationships between an organisation and the various publics on whom its success and failure depend," whereas marketing public relations is "not only concerned with organisational success and failure but also with specific publics: customers, consumers, and clients with whom exchange transactions take place."

Mercer (1992) sees public relations as the means by which the various significant "publics" of the company are identified and communicated with, to the advantage of the company, through personal and impersonal media. This publicizes a positive image of the company's achievements and leads to a good reputation. Mercer feels that publicity is the dominant form of public relations activity in practice. Others have argued that "public relations" is merely a form of consumer-oriented sales promotion. Then, marketing public relations is simply part of sales promotion – an information dissemination activity with persuasive intent.

Contemporary Contexts

Two mega changes in society – sustainability and online interaction – require awareness as they present challenges to rethink appreciation of reputation and brand. These combine to raise an alternative stakeholder perspective that takes a broader and deeper view than the (company-centric) prescribed "market."

The imperative for *social responsibility* in constructing a sustainable society recognizes the discourse of consumerism and affluent consumption, economic growth and the "new economy," environmental degradation and sustainable development, the market system, the marketing system, the social role of marketing, the "value" of marketing, and the marketing–consumption dynamic (Varey, 2010). Increasingly, corporate social responsibility qualifies corporate achievements (Becker-Olsen *et al.*,

2006), and a growing proportion of consumers want companies to minimize harm and maximize benefits (Haque, 2011; Mainwaring, 2011). Certain stakeholders are concerned with *how* products and profits are produced (see, e.g., Sisodia *et al.*, 2006). Contribution to society builds positive reputation for good corporate citizenship. Doing well by doing good builds a prosocial reputation that is becoming a license to operate as company policies and decisions with regard to stakeholders and corporate morality cumulatively impact on reputation (Jones, 1995), and the company is understood as a nexus of relationships among stakeholders.

Influencing factors in the reputational judgment or "appreciation" include social expectations, personality traits, trustworthiness, honesty, reliability, and benevolence (Berens and van Riel, 2004). As society is ever more conscious of a finite habitat and other quality of life issues, corporate social responsibility has become a key driver of reputation, ahead of goods and service quality. A reputation for social responsibility and corporate image enhanced by corporate social responsibility associations (Pomering and Johnson, 2009) provides competitive positioning in marketing interactions, as well as positive attitudes and emotions in buying and selling. Ethical brand reputations are differentiated in crowded markets and are tangibly rewarded because they are appealing to certain stakeholders. Tuston (2007) observes that "brands are no longer used only as marketing communication tools. Nowadays, branded companies seem well aware of stakeholders' concerns with non-financial business aspects and are responding through re-branding, improved customer relations and good corporate citizenship behaviour" (p. 140).

In *cause-related marketing*, strategic value-driven social partnering is intended to promote sales by supporting social causes, and can induce favorable attitudes to brands and partners, and favorable brand evaluations, leading to increased customer loyalty and catalyzing press coverage and enhanced corporate reputation. However, egoistic campaigns are not usually well received as good corporate citizenship (see Pomering and Johnson, 2009, for a helpful overview; see also Drumwright, 1996; Mainwaring, 2011; Sen and Bhattacharya, 2001; and Varadarajan and Menon, 1988).

Another major contextual force is discussed by Keller (2009) who highlights the change in society's interaction and communication brought about by *online facilities in the Internet.* In the age of social media, marketing information and communication (MIC) is no longer solely in the hands (and minds) of the company. Consumers converse with other consumers and publicly with the company, and have access to a huge range of information in various forms, such as descriptions, specifications, explanations, proposals, tests and trials, and evaluations. Tapscott and Ticoll (2003) and Tapscott and Williams (2006) called this condition "transparency," in which the company's behavior is on display in the Internet space, requiring and necessitating disclosure of information about products, company identity and history, and issues, and leading to a stronger reputation (see Hollender and Breen, 2010, for examples; see also Fombrun and Rindova, 1998).

Word of mouth is nothing more than *gossip,* and *word of mouse* is *upgraded* (and more generalized, distributed) gossip. *Word of mouth is* – just like a secret – passed from person to person, whereas *word of mouse – and just about all forms of consumer-generated media* – works differently. *Word of mouse* does not travel from person to person but to numerous "impersonal" persons – actually "impersonal readers," not listeners. Therefore, *word of mouse* has less power (of persuasion). Also, it is less attractive to the propagator – they are not instantly rewarded.

Another powerful side of this is the design of *online reputation systems,* in which reputation is constructed in the Internet through conversations about trust and confidence, publicly displayed as participatory, public, and aggregate assessments of honesty, concern shown for the customer in meeting commitments and treatment, and product quality and suitability. Examples are Amazon's product reviews, eBay's feedback profile, and TradeMe's auction feed-back user rating systems, in which system/community users are able to express their evaluations, and others see this collectively as reputation. It is interesting to observe that critical customer comments on Amazon.com are often about service rather than the purchased product. On the other hand, online corporate and personal reputation monitoring is booming with applications, with current examples including naymz.com personal brand management, rapleaf.com e-mail-based reputation lookup, reputation.com online judgment monitoring, trustplus.com trust scores in email, eBay, Facebook, LinkedIn and other social media sites, MonitorThis, and Trackur social media monitoring.

Reputation systems design is a major growth area in the burgeoning social media environment. The collective construction of reputation is now public and highly dynamic. Before the advent of the Internet, reputation was passed largely directly between people in direct conversation and written correspondence, through personal experience, and through media reporting – today, it is easy to observe what many others are saying about a company and products, and personally about you and others.

The Management of Corporate Reputation

The imperative for transforming our growth-driven society to a sustainable society when coupled with the expansive web of connectedness (in information and interaction) that is the Internet, brings the *stakeholder perspective* to the fore. Corporate reputation will be a driver for sustainable business, and openness will be the foundation for value creation.

Marketing, seen narrowly, adopts communication techniques as tools for sales support, to bring about opportunities for exchange and to consummate sales. In this view, the customer is the sole relevant stakeholder. The more holistic recognition of multiple and different stakes in business activities and outcomes ensures that people are not treated solely as customers and consumers. And, of course, people daily slip into and between multiple roles as workers, parents, students, and so on – not always consumers and customers, but still experiencing marketing and its effects. The communication problem is not limited to supporting sales. Reputation-enhancing processes and outcomes may be intended to indirectly promote sales, and there are other purposes and potentials. Reputation and brands engage publics and markets, recognizing the marketing value of brand and the societal value of brand, as evaluator and differentiator of products (both goods and service) and company. Strength in corporate reputation creates value (Devine and Halpern, 2001; Dolphin, 2004; Sanchez and Sotorrio, 2007), in terms of the social capital of recognition and trustworthiness, so strengthening and protecting reputation is clearly a management strategy. Merz *et al.* (2009) have highlighted the recent emergence of a stakeholder network perspective in understanding branding, and, again, the service-dominant logic for marketing seems to be a manifestation of the growing recognition of ecological interdependence.

Every company has a reputation whether actively managed or not. Even if the company remains unchanged (is that a realistic possibility?), a reputation can change simply because of changes in the related stakeholder groups. Reputation is a scarce commodity, reflecting the effects of competition in a field. A company has not one reputation but many – as an employer, in selling products, and in operational impact on the environment – reputation may differ among interests, issues, locations, cultures, and sociocultural groups.

A strong reputation built by serving stakeholders/constituents has paybacks that are in the self-interest of the company: premium prices when selling to customers, lower prices when buying from suppliers, high-performance employees when recruiting, pride of belonging and association when employing and partnering, elevated loyalty from both customers and employees, smoothed customer demand even in economic downturn, reduced risk of crisis, and a "halo" of increased latitude in dealings with stakeholders. All in all, companies with strong reputations get more and better support from their stakeholders/constituencies – value is created through strong (good) reputation and destroyed in antagonism or unrealized in indifference. Even no reputation is a negative (invoking lack of confidence, suspicion) when among well-known and highly regarded company of companies – and profile is unavoidable in the Internet.

Every company has a range of reputations, whether managed or not. Each observer holds some attitude towards the company, and this assessment of standing and personality may differ markedly from that intended by conscious cultivation through public relations, marketing, and selling efforts.

Walsh and Beatty (2007) define customer-based reputation (CBR) as "the customer's overall evaluation of a firm based on his or her reactions to the firm's goods, services, communication activities, interactions with the firm and/or its representatives or constituencies (such as employees, management, or other customers) and/or known corporate activities" (p. 129), identifying seven dimensions of corporate reputation including customers' appreciation of a company's communication activities and the appearance of company members in public.

The creation of a strong reputation requires a continuing investment of management time and other resources, and must reflect the company if it is to be successful. Reputations fade if not continually renewed (Emler, 1990). Reputation needs to be managed, and cultivation of a distinctive reputation needs to be active. Problems may be *real image* problems or *image communication* problems. There are two possible reasons for an image problem (Grönroos, 1990): the company is known but has a negative image (and the experiences of customers are probably bad) and the company is not well known, and thus has an unclear image or image based on out-of-date customer experiences. As observed by a professional practitioner: "If the image is false and our performance is good, it's our fault for being bad communicators. If the image is true and reflects our bad performance, it's our fault for being bad managers" (Bernstein, 1984).

When problems of technical and/or functional quality exist, a communication campaign alone is not going to work. At best, it will be a waste of money. Reality always wins in the long run. An *image advertising* campaign that is not based on reality only creates expectations. If expectations are higher as a result, but the experiences of reality are unchanged, the perceived service quality is affected in a negative way, and the image is damaged. Problems with service performance (technical and/or functional quality) cause an image problem, and internal actions that improve the performance of the company are needed if the bad image is to be improved. There is a *reputational risk* of reputation damage when promise keeping is not consistent, and marketing promotion over-promises, and the service system underdelivers. Image development or improvement efforts have to be based on reality. Reputation enhancement also requires consistency and persistence – sustainable image, if you like.

If the image is unknown, there is a communication problem. There is no in-depth image based on experience. Perhaps the performance has changed but insufficient interaction has taken place for the new reality to be experienced. Advertising can speed up the process of image improvement. It is important to realize that image is not what is communicated if the communicated image does not correspond with reality. When there is an inconsistency, reality wins and the company is perceived as untrustworthy – this damages image even more. What we believe to be is rarely factual reporting of what is.

A dialog of engagement between the company and its stakeholders must communicate ethics, mission, and values. Presentation of image will never suffice. The spheres of experience of all people with rights and responsibilities to the business must be understood. In managing reputation, it is necessary to cultivate different reputations in different groups, and to use appropriate methods in each. A communication planning process must be part of the managing system so that it involves managers

and communication facilitators daily as part of their primary work. Indeed, thinking holistically, some see marketing communication as part of corporate communication (van Riel, 1995; van Riel and Fombrun, 2007; Varey, 1998).

According to Cornelissen (2008), "Corporate communication is a management function that offers a framework for the effective coordination of all internal and external communication with the overall purpose of establishing and maintaining favourable reputations with stakeholder groups upon which the organization is dependent." In this holistic approach, marketing is integrated into a company communication management system (Varey, 2000) in a total stakeholder perspective and to integrate communication activities around constituent–constituent relationships. Marketing is described as a special case of human communication, in which all elements of the marketing mix are seen as communicative in action.

Reflection and Projection

This chapter closes in considering some conclusions and implications on which marketing communication specialists might direct their attention in understanding theory and practice. There is evidently a trend in the convergence of corporate brand and corporate reputation as increasingly "brand" implies "reputation," beyond the purely commercial sphere of buying and selling in society. With a strong business case for treating corporate reputation seriously as an asset, yet so little attention to corporate reputation in the marketing communication research literature, and consequently in marketing communication textbooks, the area seems ripe for further inquiry.

Corporate reputation is such an important business asset that the management of corporate reputation should be part of a strategic communication management agenda – but of course that is broader than marketing communication, and extends to corporate communication including public relations, and so on. Reputation provides the legitimizing basis for business – the "license to operate." Thus, the concept of corporate reputation spans marketing, public relations, management, and finance. It is notable that the Chartered Institute of Marketing now teaches corporate reputation to marketing specialists, and the noted British marketing communications specialist Chris Fill has recently coauthored a book on the subject for students of corporate reputation, branding, marketing communications, and public relations (Roper and Fill, 2012).

Brand reputation, along with intellectual property, human capital, and knowledge, is an intangible asset that accounts for most company value opportunity. It is the communication of values that people can connect with, realizing reputational benefit in the creation of value through reputation (Sanchez and Sotorrio, 2007). Corporate social responsibility impacts on social performance and ultimately on financial performance. Yet, sound responsible behavior is not sufficient. Performance needs to be communicated if a positive reputation is to be built and sustained. Communication is a responsibility – an issue of how the company relates to a stakeholder, sometimes proactively informing, other times listening, and engaging. Authentic good reputation comes from high purpose and deep respect. For many, reputation has emotional appeal – not simply a piece of objective information in rational choice. Corporate reputation is fundamentally significant in an interdependent ecology since it has the power to drive enhancement and to counter destructively pathological independent, often exploitative, behavior of individuals. The stakeholder perspective recognizes the significance of interaction. Ballantyne and Varey (2006) distinguish informative and communicative interaction. When marketing interaction is understood as informative and communicative, two complementary perspectives become apparent: the company voice and the value cocreation conversation. Indeed, with a service-dominant logic, marketing is inherently ethical and reputation is the effect and not merely the competitive treatment. There are implications

for understanding marketing communication purpose and form. A full appreciation necessitates a revisioning of the marketing communication agenda in the "online" society, otherwise, to paraphrase Marshall McLuhan, we will continue driving forward while looking in the rearview mirror!

References

Aaker, D.A. (1992) *Managing Brand Equity: Capitalizing on the Value of a Brand Name.* New York: The Free Press.

Aaker, D.A. (1996) *Building Strong Brands.* New York: The Free Press.

Ahmed, P.K. and Rafiq, M. (2003) Internal marketing and the mediating role of organizational competencies. *European Journal of Marketing,* 37(9), 1221–1241.

Ballantyne, D. and Varey, R.J. (2006) Creating value-in-use through marketing interaction: The exchange logic of relating, communicating and knowing. *Marketing Theory,* 6(3), 335–348.

Ballantyne, D., Frow, P., Varey, R.J., and Payne, A. (2011) Value propositions as communication practice: Taking a wider view. *Industrial Marketing Management,* 40(2), 202–210.

Balmer, J.M.T. (2001) Corporate identity, corporate branding and corporate marketing – Seeing through the fog. *European Journal of Marketing,* 35(3–4), 248–292.

Balmer, J.M.T. and Gray, E.R. (2003) Corporate brands: What are they? What of them? *European Journal of Marketing,* 37(7–8), 972–997.

Balmer, J.M.T. and Greyser, S.A. (eds) (2002) *Revealing the Corporation: Perspectives on Identity, Image, Reputation, Corporate Branding, and Corporate-Level Marketing.* London: Routledge.

Balmer, J.M.T. and Greyser, S.A. (2006) Corporate marketing: Integrating corporate identity, corporate branding, corporate communications, corporate image and corporate reputation. *European Journal of Marketing,* 40(7/8), 730–741.

Barich, H. and Kotler, P. (1991) A framework for marketing image management. *Sloan Management Review,* 32(2), 94–104.

Becker-Olsen, K.L., Cudmore, B.A., and Hill, R.P. (2006) The impact of perceived corporate social responsibility on consumer behaviour. *Journal of Business Research,* 59(1), 46–53.

Berens, G. and van Riel, C.B.M. (2004) Corporate associations in the academic literature: Three main streams of thought in the reputation measurement literature. *Corporate Reputation Review*, 7(2), 161–178.

Berens, G., van Riel, C.B.M., and van Bruggen, G.H. (2005) Corporate associations and consumer product responses: The moderating role of corporate brand dominance. *Journal of Marketing*, 69(3), 39–48.

Bernstein, D. (1984) *Company Image and Reality: A Critique of Corporate Communications*. London: Cassell Educational/Advertising Association.

Bickerton, D. (2000) Corporate reputation versus corporate branding: The realist debate. *Corporate Communications: An International Journal*, 5(1), 42–48.

Biehal, G.J. and Sheinin, D.A. (1998) Managing the brand in a corporate advertising environment: A decision-making framework for brand managers. *Journal of Advertising*, 27(2), 99–110.

Boulding, K.E. (1956) *The Image: Knowledge in Life and Society*. Ann Arbor, MI: The University of Michigan Press.

Brønn, P.S. and Berg, R.W. (eds) (2005) *Corporate Communication: A Strategic Approach to Building Reputation* (2nd ed.). Oslo, Norway: Gyldendal Akademisk.

Brown, T.J. and Dacin, P.A. (1997) The company and the product: Corporate associations and consumer product responses. *Journal of Marketing*, 61(1), 68–84.

Cornelissen, J. (2008) *Corporate Communication: A Guide to Theory and Practice* (2nd ed.). London: Sage Publications.

Cutlip, S., Center, A., and Broom, G. (1985) *Effective Public Relations* (6th ed.). Englewood Cliffs, NJ: Prentice Hall.

Dacin, P.A. and Brown, T.J. (2002) Corporate identity and corporate associations: A framework for future research. *Corporate Reputation Review*, 5(2–3), 254–263.

Davies, G., Chun, R., Vinhas Da Silva, R., and Roper, S. (2003) *Corporate Reputation and Competitiveness*. London: Routledge.

de Chernatony, L. and McDonald, M. (1998) *Creating Powerful Brands in Consumer, Service and Industrial Markets* (2nd ed.). Oxford, UK: Butterworth-Heinemann.

Devine, I. and Halpern, P. (2001) Implicit claims: The role of corporate reputation in value creation. *Corporate Reputation Review*, 4(1), 42–49.

Dichter, E. (1985) What's in an image. *Journal of Consumer Marketing*, 2(1), 75–81.

Dolphin, R.R. (2004) Corporate reputation – A value creating strategy. *Corporate Governance: The International Journal of Business in Society*, 4(3), 77–92.

Dowling, G.R. (1995) Corporate reputations – The company's super brand. *Journal of Brand Management*, 2(6), 377–385.

Dowling, G.R. (2002) *Creating Corporate Reputations: Identity, Image, and Performance*. Oxford, UK: Oxford University Press.

Drumwright, M. (1996) Corporate advertising with a social dimension: The role of noneconomic criteria. *Journal of Marketing*, 60, 71–87.

Duncan, T. and Moriarty, S.E. (1998) A communication-based marketing model for managing relationships. *Journal of Marketing*, 62(2), 1–13.

Ehling, W.P., White, J., and Grunig, J.E. (1992) Public relations and marketing practices. In J.E. Grunig (ed.), *Excellence in Public Relations and Communication Management*. Hillsdale, NJ: Lawrence Erlbaum Associates, pp. 357–394.

Emler, N. (1990) *A Social Psychology of Reputation*. Chichester: John Wiley & Sons.

Fombrun, C.J. (1996) *Reputation: Realizing Value from the Corporate Image*. Boston: Harvard Business School Press.

Fombrun, C.J. and Rindova, V.P. (1998) Reputation management in Global 1000 firms: A benchmarking study. *Corporate Reputation Review*, 1(3), 205–214.

Fombrun, C.J., Gardberg, N.A., and Sever, J.M. (2000) The Reputation Quotient[SM] index: A multistakeholder measure of corporate reputation. *Journal of Brand Management*, 7(4), 241–255.

Gotsi, M. and Wilson, A.M. (2001) Corporate reputation: Seeking a definition. *Corporate Communications: An International Journal*, 6(1), 24–30.

Grönroos, C. (1990) *Service Management and Marketing: Managing the Moments of Truth in Service Competition*. Lexington, MA: Lexington Books.

Haque, U. (2011) *The New Capitalist Manifesto: Building a Disruptively Better Business*. Boston: Harvard Business Review Press.

Hollender, J. and Breen, B. (2010) *The Responsibility Revolution: How the Next Generation of Businesses Will Win*. San Francisco, CA: Jossey-Bass.

Horton, J.L. (1995) *Integrating Corporate Communications: The Cost-Effective Use of Message and Medium*. London: Quorum Books.

Jones, T.M. (1995) Instrumental stakeholder theory: A synthesis of ethics and economics. *Academy of Management Review*, 20(2), 404–437.

Kapferer, J. (2004) *The New Strategic Brand Management* (3rd ed.). London: Kogan Page.

Kay, J. (1993) *Foundations of Corporate Success: How Business Strategies Add Value*. Oxford, UK: Oxford University Press.

Keller, K.L. (2009) Building strong brands in a modern marketing communications environment. *Journal of Marketing Communications*, 15(2–3), 139–155.

Keller, K.L. and Aaker, D.A. (1998) The impact of corporate marketing on a company's brand extensions. *Corporate Reputation Review*, 1(4), 356–378.

Kitchen, P.J. and Schultz, D.E. (2001) *Raising the Corporate Umbrella: Corporate Communications in the 21st Century*. London: Palgrave.

Knox, S. and Bickerton, D. (2003) The six conventions of corporate branding. *European Journal of Marketing*, 37(7–8), 998–1016.

Kotler, P. (1986) Megamarketing. *Harvard Business Review*, 64(2), 117–124.

Kotler, P. and Armstrong, G. (1996) *Principles of Marketing*. Englewood Cliffs, NJ: Prentice Hall.

Langer, R. and Varey, R.J. (2008) Corporations as storytellers – Stakeholders as image builders: Towards impressive corporate communication. In T.C. Melewar and E. Karaosmanoğlu (eds), *Contemporary Thoughts on Corporate Branding and Corporate Identity Management*. London: Palgrave Macmillan, pp. 205–226.

Lloyd, T. (1990) *The "Nice" Company: Why "Nice" Companies Make More Profits*. London: Bloomsbury Publishing.

MacMillan, K., Money, K., Downing, S., and Hillenbrand, C. (2005) Reputation in relationships: Measuring experiences, emotions and behaviors. *Corporate Reputation Review*, 8(3), 214–232.

Mainwaring, S. (2011) *We First: How Brands & Consumers Use Social Media to Build a Better World*. New York: Palgrave Macmillan.

Mercer, D. (1992) *Marketing*. Oxford, UK: Blackwell Business.

Merz, M.A., He, Y., and Vargo, S.L. (2009) The evolving brand logic: A service-dominant logic perspective. *Journal of the Academy of Marketing Science*, 37(3), 328–344.

Nguyen, N. and Leblanc, G. (2001) Corporate image and corporate reputation in customers' retention decisions in services. *Journal of Retailing and Consumer Services*, 8(4), 227–236.

O'Rourke, R. (1997) Managing in times of crisis. *Corporate Reputation Review*, 1, 1–12.

Pomering, A. and Johnson, L.W. (2009) Constructing a corporate social responsibility reputation using corporate image advertising. *Australasian Marketing Journal*, 17(2), 106–114.

Ramsey, R.P. and Sohi, R.S. (1997) Listening to your customers: The impact of perceived salesperson listening behavior on relationship outcomes. *Journal of the Academy of Marketing Science*, 25(2), 127–137.

Roper, S. and Fill, C. (2012) *Corporate Reputation: Brand and Communications*. London: Financial Times Prentice Hall.

Rossiter, J.R. and Bellman, S. (2005) *Marketing Communications: Theory and Applications*. Frenchs Forest, NSW: Pearson Education Australia.

Sanchez, J.L.F. and Sotorrio, L.L. (2007) The creation of value through corporate reputation. *Journal of Business Ethics*, 76(3), 335–346.

Schultz, D.E. and Walters, T. (1997) *Measuring Brand Communication ROI*. Chicago, IL: American Marketing Association.

Schultz, M., Hatch, M.J., and Larsen, M.H. (eds) (2000) *The Expressive Organization: Linking Identity, Reputation, and the Corporate Brand*. Oxford, UK: Oxford University Press.

Schumann, D.W., Hathcote, J.M., and West, S. (1991) Corporate advertising in America: A review of published studies on use, measurement, and effectiveness. *Journal of Advertising*, 20(3), 35–56.

Sen, S. and Bhattacharya, C.B. (2001) Does doing good always lead to doing better? Consumer reactions to corporate social responsibility. *Journal of Marketing Research*, 38, 225–243.

Sheth, J.N. and Sisodia, R.S. (eds) (2006) *Does Marketing Need Reform?: Fresh Perspectives on the Future*. New York: M.E. Sharpe.

Sisodia, R.S., Wolfe, D.B., and Sheth, J.N. (2006) *Firms of Endearment: How World-Class Companies Profit from Passion and Purpose*. Upper Saddle River, NJ: Prentice Hall.

Smidts, A., Pruyn, T.H., and van Riel, C.B.M. (2001) The impact of employee communication and perceived external prestige on organizational identification. *Academy of Management Journal*, 44(5), 1051–1062.

Spotts, H.E. and Weinberger, M.G. (2010) Marketplace footprints: Connecting marketing communication and corporate brands. *European Journal of Marketing*, 44(5), 591–609.

Tapscott, D. and Ticoll, D. (2003) *The Naked Corporation: How the Age of Transparency Will Revolutionize Business*. New York: The Free Press.

Tapscott, D. and Williams, A.D. (2006) *Wikinomics: How Mass Collaboration Changes Everything.* New York: Portfolio/Penguin.

The Chartered Institute of Marketing (2011) Retrieved from www.cim.co.uk (last accessed October 10, 2012).

Travis, D. (2000) *Emotional Branding: How Successful Brands Gain the Irrational Edge.* Roseville, CA: Prima Venture.

Tuston, D.H. (2007) Strategies moulding brand reputation building in the early 21st century. *Communicatio, 33*(2), 140–153.

van Riel, C.B.M. (1995) *Principles of Corporate Communication.* London: Prentice Hall.

van Riel, C.B.M. and Fombrun, C.J. (2007) *Essentials of Corporate Communication: Implementing Practices for Effective Reputation Management.* London: Routledge.

Varadarajan, P.R. and Menon, A. (1988) Cause related marketing: A coalignment of marketing strategy and corporate philanthropy. *Journal of Marketing, 52*, 58–74.

Varey, R.J. (1997) The external publics context. In P.J. Kitchen (ed.), *Public Relations: Principles and Practice.* London: International Thomson Business Press, pp. 89–108.

Varey, R.J. (1998) Locating marketing within the corporate communication managing system. *Journal of Marketing Communications, 4*(3), 177–190.

Varey, R.J. (2000) A critical review of conceptions of communication evident in contemporary business & management literature. *Journal of Communication Management, 4*(4), 328–340.

Varey, R.J. (2005) Identification in a co-operative community: Internal marketing to build corporate image and reputation. *International Journal of Applied Marketing, 1*(3).

Varey, R.J. (2008) Marketing as an interaction system. *Australasian Marketing Journal, 16*(1), 78–93.

Varey, R.J. (2010) Marketing means and ends for a sustainable society: A welfare agenda for transformative change. *Journal of Macromarketing, 30*(2), 112–126.

Vargo, S.L. and Lusch, R.F. (2004) Evolving to a new dominant logic for marketing. *Journal of Marketing, 68*(1), 1–17.

Vickers, G. (1983) *Human Systems Are Different.* London: Harper & Row.

Waddington, S. and Earl, S. (2012) *Brand Anarchy: Managing Corporate Reputation.* London: A&C Black Publishers.

Walsh, G. and Beatty, S. (2007) Customer-base corporate reputation of a service firm: Scale development and validation. *Journal of the Academy of Marketing Science, 35*, 127–143.

White, J. (1991) *How to Understand and Manage Public Relations: A Jargon-Free Guide to Public Relations Management.* London: Business Books Ltd.

Yoon, E., Guffey, H.J., and Kijewski, V. (1993) The effects of information and company reputation on intentions to buy a business service. *Journal of Business Research, 27*(3), 215–228.

12

Corporate Reputation and the Disciplines of Journalism and Mass Communication

Craig E. Carroll

New York University, USA

This chapter examines the journalism and mass communication disciplines for what they offer to the study of corporate reputation. Most of the early communication research devoted to corporate reputation began in the mass communication field (Carroll, 2011b). Only recently with the distinct body of research devoted to journalism have these efforts been extended.

Introduction

Journalism and mass communication are important to the study and understanding of corporate reputation because the mass media are the primary vehicle through which the public learns about organizations they are not familiar (Carroll and McCombs, 2003). Indeed, the news media enable existing organizational audiences to learn more about the organizations they already know something about and new audiences to gain cursory knowledge about organizations as they are attached to the issues of the day (Carroll, 2009). Moreover, the news media enable audiences to learn more about how the issues they care about that are difficult to personally observe (e.g., corporate social responsibility, innovation, environmental performance) or experience firsthand apply to specific companies, or learn about how companies they care about fall along the lines of issues (Einwiller *et al.*, 2010).

This chapter reviews the four primary research domains within journalism and mass communication for their primary focal points, noting along the way where existing corporate reputation research currently takes place and

where it could take place. The chapter begins with an overview of the major paradigms. Journalism and mass communication research has three major paradigms: the social science approach to media effects, the interpretive paradigm, and the critical/cultural paradigm (Pietilä, 1994; Potter *et al.*, 1993). Pietilä added the media's dependency on economic, political and ideological forces, uses and gratifications, and literary criticism to this list, but these three are the primary ones. Potter *et al.* observed that the social science media effects tradition (60%) and the interpretive paradigms (34%) accounted for most of the published mass communication research. If we were to restrict the topic to corporate reputation, we would likely find social science media effects research comprised a higher proportion.

This chapter charts the program of research in the field of journalism and mass communication, noting its theories and key findings where they occur. The focus is on generating new insights based on previous research that may guide future thinking and practice in corporate reputation research from a mass communication perspective.

The Handbook of Communication and Corporate Reputation, First Edition. Edited by Craig E. Carroll.
© 2013 John Wiley & Sons, Inc. Published 2015 by John Wiley & Sons, Inc.

Four Domains of Mass Communication Research

Journalism and mass communication research is classified into four domains: *media production, media content, media effects,* and *media audiences* (Potter, 2009; Shoemaker and Reese, 1996).

Media production

Media production concerns the influences on media content. Shoemaker and Reese (1996) developed a five-level hierarchy-of-influences model for explaining and landscaping the influences on media content. The lowest level, the media workers closest to raw materials, has less influence on the content, while further away levels "out of the hands" of individual media workers exert greater influence on content. The five levels, moving from that which is closest to media content to that which is further away, are the individual media workers, routines, the media organization, factors external to the media organization, and ideology.

From a media production perspective, Carroll and Deephouse (forthcoming) use the five-level hierarchy-of-influences framework (Shoemaker and Reese, 1996) to examine news media content characteristics about organizations. The media content outcomes Carroll and Deephouse seek to explain concern the volume, tone, topics, linkages, and timing of news reports. The linkages concern the associations journalists make between organizations and other objects and attributes, whether these are other organizations, issues, topics, individuals, or even other reference points. The media effects section describes how the volume (organizational media visibility), tone (media favorability), and linkages (media associations) as media content characteristics of organizations relate to corporate reputation.

Individual

The individual level is concerned with how journalists' demographic, psychological, and sociological characteristics influence and shape their reporting on the organizations they cover. For example, journalists' varying levels of math anxiety (cf. Curtin and Maier, 2001) may influence the type of company news stories journalists pursue. Indeed, one of the biggest issues organizational critics have with news reporting about their organizations concerns being misunderstood by journalists who do not understand business or finance (Ludwig, 2002). It was Bethany McLean's undergraduate degree in math that enabled this 31-year-old *Fortune* Magazine reporter (at the time) to have the skill sets required to review the numbers in Enron's 10-K statements and interview Enron executives in the news story many credit with bringing Enron down (Carroll, 2006). Most journalism and mass communication research and theory suggests that the level of the individual media worker has less influence than the four other levels above it, but it is not without its influence. Indeed, organizational, business, and management practice and research still ascribe great power to individuals, contending that media content reveals journalists' beliefs and feelings about organizations (Dowling, 2004), and encourages organizations to research, track, and monitor the journalists who write about them (Carroll, 2011d; Lerbinger, 2006).

Routines

The second level of influence is routines (Shoemaker and Reese, 1996). A routine refers to the regular courses of action, procedures, or processes one takes at regular intervals in order to be efficient or effective at accomplishing a goal or to maintain a system or environment so that one can efficiently or effectively function or operate to accomplish a goal. Journalistic heuristics for understanding what makes a good news story function as routines. Heuristics also help media workers avoid or deflect outside media criticism, public criticism, or embarrassment; tailor information to their audience needs and expectations; fit the demands of the channel, whether public relations, advertising, or news; and weigh how they gather and evaluate the raw information. Knowledge of how these dimensions of routines affects media content not only helps media workers in the construction of content, but also helps outside sources understand the creativity and constraints afforded by media workers, and thereby influence them within these confines. Carroll (2011b) describes how organizations' understanding of news values enables organizations to better understand when their messages should be pitched to the media or sent directly to their publics through other channels other than the news media. A considerable amount of research on information subsidies is devoted to understanding journalists' routines in order to know how to approach and pitch journalists.

Organization level

The organization level concerns more than understanding the news media as a social actor. It involves various organizational theories that impact the production of media. These include, for example, the impact of chain of command, organizational culture, how power and politics within organizations affect the decisions media workers make, or the implications of media organizations being businesses. For example, media workers are concerned with maximizing value for the media organization's owners and following organizational policies. Since media messages have high failure rates, media workers produce messages guaranteed to have higher degrees of commercial success. One way they do this is through polysemic messages, which appeal to different types of audiences. Media workers also work to reduce organizational expenses by relying on syndicated material and generating cross-promotional corporate synergies that benefit partners. Other manifestations include interlocking boards, the ownership structure (corporate vs. independent), and media conglomeration (Shoemaker and Reese, 1996).

Outside influences

The fourth level of influence concerns outside agenda-building influences such as those from information sources, other media organizations, wire services, revenue sources, other social institutional sources such as business and government, interest groups, the economic environment, technology, government controls, perceptions of "the market," and institutional affiliations such as interlocking boards (Shoemaker and Reese, 1996). At the external-to-the-news organization level, Westphal and Deephouse (2011) use social influence and social exchange theory to examine how CEOs can influence journalists to issue relatively positive reports about their firms through two mechanisms: ingratiatory behavior toward individual journalists (such as complimenting the journalist about his or her journalistic work, expressing agreement with the journalist's view on a business issue, or doing a personal favor for the journalist) and negative reciprocity that deters other journalists from issuing negative statements about the firm. Carroll (2011c) finds that corporate agenda building (working through the news media) is more effective than corporate agenda setting in attempting to shape firms' public prominence.

Ideology

Ideology is the highest level, residing at the societal level (Shoemaker and Reese, 1996), but other influences at this level that impact media content include the level of the media system for the country where the media operate (Carroll, 2011c; Sriramesh and Verčič, 2009). At the ideology level, Carroll compares the empirical findings of over 20 country case studies that examine media influence on corporate reputation within developed, emerging, and frontier markets for the role ideology plays in understanding this relationship.

Media content

Mass communication scholars studying content typically focus the characteristics of messages themselves. One of the central debates in mass communication content research concerns where the meaning of the message resides: in the text itself or in the minds of audience members. Experimental psychologists, for instance, infer meaning in media texts when they use them as treatments in their experiments predicting media effects in audiences (Potter, 2009).

Media content research is the least developed of the four domains and is generally considered descriptive, atheoretical, and fragmented. Message characteristics are of three types: manifest, latent patterned, and latent projective (Potter and Levine-Donnerstein, 1999), ranging on a quantitative to qualitative continuum. Manifest content is discrete, categorical, on the surface, and readily and easily observable. Manifest content is signified by the presence (or absence) of a unit of observation, such as the presence of a word in a sentence of a news article or the appearance of a particular source in a newscast interview. Quantitative characteristics include *objects* (e.g., persons, organizations, issues, or topics), *attributes* (substantive or evaluative), or *associations* (co-occurrences between any two objects, attributes, or objects and attributes). Theory is not often considered relevant when categorizing manifest content. Somewhere in the middle of the debate about the meaning of the message is *latent-patterned* content, which focuses on patterns in the content itself. Here, theory is the basis for deducing coding schemes. Qualitative characteristics include the appearance of objectivity, news frames, simplified conflict, dramatized hyperbole, sensationalism, deviance, polls, branding, personalization, and context (Potter, 2009). *Latent-projective* content shifts the focus more onto coders' interpretations of the meaning of the content (Potter and Levine-Donnerstein, 1999). Cultural and critical scholars argue that meaning resides with the audiences (Hall, 1980). Newcomb (1984) argued that texts do not speak for themselves and that we cannot predict an audience member's response by looking solely at the message. Latent-projective content allows the deductions of codes from weak theory inductions, resulting in a stronger theory.

There has been no systematic attempt to classify the range of mass media content and there are few meta-analyses of the studies that do exist. Riffe and Freitag (1997) found 486 content analysis studies in their literature review of 25 years of *Journalism & Mass Communication Quarterly* – and that was just one journal.

Potter (2009) observed that there are so many topics of interest compared to the number of media scholars that there are not enough resources to cover all the topics. He said we need to know how large the media content literature is and what topic areas are the most prevalent. He has called for future research to develop a topic-by-topic inventory of topics and critically analyze them so that we can map the phenomenon, identifying where the gaps are in our understanding of it. Park and Berger (2004) develop a baseline about news coverage on CEOs by examining the tone and topics that co-occur with CEOs in the press using four newspapers during the period from 1990 through 2000 to assess trends in the salience and valence of CEO press coverage and to examine dimensions of CEO images in the coverage.

Using Kiousis's (2004) explication of media salience as a guide, Carroll (2011d) breaks organizational news content down to identify four different dimensions of news media salience that relate to isolated dimensions of reputation: media visibility, *focal* media favorability, *peripheral* media favorability, and substantive media attributes such as company characteristics, news topics, and issues. Focal media favorability is concerned with how a focal organization is covered in a stream of news stories, and peripheral media favorability is concerned with the overall evaluative tone of the stream of news stories where an organization appears, regardless of how the organization itself is portrayed. The question about substantive media topics is how they are connected to the companies whose reputations are then implicated. In this sense, media associations becomes a more appropriate term. Media associations refer to the issues, topics, and attributes that co-occur with a particular organization. Carroll says these may be issues in the context of the organization, or a number of organizations considered in the context of one particular issue. But, it may be simply that organizations and issues co-occur, where each is given equal attention, but the attention of importance is their co-occurrence or linkage together.

Media effects

The media effects literature has undergone tremendous classification. A mass media effect is defined as "the occurrence of one of four patterns, when the shape of that pattern can be attributed to mass media influence. The four patterns are: (1) gradual alteration of a baseline, (2) reinforcement of a baseline, (3) sudden alteration of a baseline, and (4) sudden fluctuation from the baseline with a return to baseline" (Potter, 2009, p. 266). The most common media effects are cognitive, affective, behavioral, attitudinal, belief, and physiological.

Cognitive effects

The easiest to document is the acquisition of factual information. Examples of media effects research illustrating acquisition effects include *acquiring specific facts* about current events or political candidates' campaigns and the *triggering* of pattern constructions from media examples to the real world, such as about the prevalence of particular occupations (Vande Berg and O'Donnell-Trujillo, 1989) and the prominence of issues, political candidates, people, organizations, or their attributes or associations (Carroll, 2009, 2010, 2011a, 2011d; Golan and Wanta, 2001; McCombs and Shaw, 1972). They also include *triggering* the misjudgment of the media's general influence or their influence on public opinion; *altering* awareness, such as becoming aware of the environment as an issue; and *conditioning* one's intense video/computer game playing where one shifts the video game strategies from sequential to parallel (Potter, 2009).

Attitudinal effects

Attitudinal media effects include *acquiring attitudes* or value judgments about some object, attribute, or association. Examples of attitudinal media effects have been found about publicly traded companies (Carroll, 2009), government (Becker and Whitney, 1980), candidates, and campaigns (Kim *et al.*, 2005). They also include *acquiring criteria for judgment*, such as about current events. Attitudes

can also be *altered* or *conditioned* via media exposure, demonstrated by media effects found in research on cognitive consistency, elaboration likelihood, information integration, and media enjoyment (Potter, 2009).

Belief effects

Media exposure has led to faulty beliefs about the risks people have to media influence compared to other risks they may encounter (Potter, 2009). Media exposure has led to *triggering* the construction of beliefs about issues (McCombs and Shaw, 1972), political candidates (Weaver *et al.*, 1981), organizations (Carroll, 2010), and attributes (Golan and Wanta, 2001) that are most important in the real world; *altering beliefs* about the importance and weighting of certain issues such as environmental issues; and *conditioning beliefs* people have about politics (Potter, 2009).

Affect effects

Affect is different than attitudes or moods. Affective media effects concern the feelings people experience about a particular issue, object, attribute, association, or event, whether conscious or unconscious. They are the basis for attitudes, but not attitudes themselves. Moods, in contrast to affect, are not directed toward any particular object (Potter, 2009). Examples of media influencing the *acquisition* of affect include the media's role in learning appropriate emotional responses. Media may also *trigger* emotional reactions, such as fear, empathy, or humor. Media may also *alter* one's emotional reactions or *condition* one's emotional reactions (Potter, 2009).

Physiological effects

Physiological effects are ones that trigger an automatic bodily response, which may be purely or quasi-automatic. Examples of *triggered* physiological media effects are an increased heart rate and blood pressure, an example of a *conditioned* physical media effect transferring physiological arousal to other areas (Potter, 2009).

Behavioral effects

Behavioral effects are overt actions people take. Previous media effects research has recorded actual behavior, observation by a third party (coder/researcher), or self-report, with self-report data being the most suspect. *Acquired* behavior refers to learned behavior sequences learned through observation. Triggered behaviors include harmful behaviors, such as eating disorders, and prosocial behaviors, such as pro-environmental behavior and civic engagement. Media have been found to alter behaviors, such as reducing inhibitions to behave aggressively to conditioning behavior, such as using the media habitually, becoming more dependent on the media, and media addiction (Potter, 2009).

The media effects tradition has contributed the most to corporate reputation studies, particularly to the understanding of antecedents of corporate reputation. Carroll and McCombs (2003) use agenda-setting theory from media effects to conceptualize how the news media influence corporate reputation. One key finding from this media effects program of research is that the news media have *multiple* types of effects on corporate reputation – and that these specific effects *line up* individually to specific *dimensions* of corporate reputation rather than just to the global variable of corporate reputation, as suggested by Carroll (2011d). Specifically, the media effects tradition has revealed that media visibility is related to organizational prominence (Carroll, 2011b), media favorability is related to public esteem (Carroll, 2011b), and the salience of particular media topics match the associations audiences form of organizations connected to these topics (Einwiller *et al.*, 2010). The elaboration, isolation, and matching of these dimension findings help overcome the disparity and mixed results found in earlier research that simply linked media exposure to corporate reputation (e.g., Fombrun and Shanley, 1990; Wartick, 1992) and the minimal associations researchers have found between substantive attributes in the media and overall reputation (Kiousis *et al.*, 2007; Meijer and Kleinnijenhuis, 2006a) and affective attributes in the media and reputation (Meijer and Kleinnijenhuis, 2006b).

Gans (2004) identifies a number of media effects limited to the news media: the *social continuity effect* enables people to take for granted that the existing social order will continue with some degree of business as usual. The *informing effect* occurs most obviously through journalists seeking to inform their audiences, but also through audiences choosing which subjects to become informed about. The *legitimation and control effect* refers to the legitimation that comes from being newsworthy, and by exerting control by creating "mainstream" snapshots and downgrading competing snapshots. The news media also exert control over *opinions and activities*, and the *messenger effect* by exposing events through their reports that may otherwise go unnoticed. The *watchdog effect* works because institutions and organizations must protect their reputations. General *political effects* work by helping to shape the political climate or mood. The *electoral effect* works by giving the public information to evaluate candidates' character. The visibility effect provides a moment of fame. The *scapegoating effect* refers to reporting news that people may not want to hear but also the media themselves being blamed for the introduction of social changes or values that subgroups may disagree with. Even further, subgroups seeking to influence the public about their policies and positions and rely on the media to publicize their policies, blame the media when their audiences are not persuaded. Gans says that by the media absorbing accusations, they take the blame off of institutions and individuals who might otherwise be blamed.

Media audiences

Mass media research has viewed the audience through one of three points of view: organizational, sociological, and psychological. *Media organizational* scholars focus on attracting particular kinds of audiences and view audiences from a business perspective (Ettema and Whitney, 1992). The *media sociology* view (Hall, 1980) focuses on group affiliations, which they believe influence the media people use and how they interpret media messages.

Their research questions concern the degree to which group membership is reinforced or altered by media exposure and the degree to which group members interpret meaning from media content similarly, and under what conditions. The *media psychology* view (Webster and Phalen, 1997), the most prominent of the three, focuses on the individual and his or her motives for media exposure, with little to no attention to shared experience with other audience members.

Media psychology focuses extensively on audiences' information processing and what is meant by media exposure. Webster and Wakshlag (1985) articulate three views: exposure as choice, as attention, and as preference. "Choice" scholars follow an economic model, assuming that audience members follow a rational model where they think about their goals, weigh their options, and then think how to maximize the value of their limited resources. "Attention" scholars focus on an attention span continuum where audiences move from passivity to activity. "Preference" scholars (e.g., uses and gratifications research) focus on audiences who are active in their decision making, based on motives, needs, and preferences. Media psychology has a proliferation of terms for information processing: schema, frames, stereotypes, cognitive maps, cognitive structures, propositional networks, social scripts, memory association packets, and algorithms (Potter, 2009).

The primary theoretical perspective for studying audience exposures to media is uses and gratifications. The primary assumptions behind this program of research are that audiences are active in their media choices and that they are rational, knowing what is best for them in light of their available media choices and their needs. Contrasted with this line of research is the idea of automatic exposure, which reminds us that much of our media exposure is ritualistic and habitual, providing entertainment or mood enhancement rather than uncertainty reduction or environmental surveillance.

Limited audience research has been done on reputation. Using elaboration likelihood theory of persuasion, Carroll (2009) identified two types of audiences when it came to organizations and the news media: one audience follows the news to learn more about the companies they care about and evaluates the news for its implications for the covered organizations, and the other audience cares more about the issues of the day, learning about companies in a cursory way. Audiences who know something about an organization's attributes, such as its executive leadership, products and services, or financial performance, are more likely to read organizational news reports because the news reports cover organizations they know something about, and they want to learn more. For these audiences, a firm's focal media favorability has a stronger correlation to the firm's public esteem than for individuals who know less about the firm. On the other hand, some audiences only learn about organizations as a part of following the day's news, where these organizations then appear. For these audiences, a firm's peripheral media favorability (which is more tied to the overall evaluative tone of the news articles irrespective of how the firm is portrayed in a stream of news stories) has a stronger correlation to the firms' public esteem than peripheral media favorability does for audiences more familiar with the organizations.

Carroll and Lee (2008) examined the audience by considering how audiences' media recall and advertising recall of organizations' appearance in news and advertising affected their reputations. They found that both had a positive influence on corporate reputation. Furthermore, the impacts of each varied according to the level of the other. Future research should examine the reasons and the conditions for these interaction effects.

In sum, research on audiences, particularly from a uses and gratifications perspective, reminds us that people use media for a variety of purposes, and this line of research stands in contrast to previous research that presumes passive audiences.

Conclusions

Mass communication studies typically fall among one of these domains: production, content, effects, and audiences. Mass communication studies of corporate reputation do not engage the paradigmatic struggles typical of other topic areas in the field. Most of the journalism and mass communication research on corporate reputation concerns media effects, primarily from the agenda-setting and framing viewpoints. Future media effects research should move beyond cognitive, attitudinal, and affect effects to consider belief effects, physiological and behavioral (such as word of mouth). Much of the media effects literature has also considered the legitimation and control effects, opinions and activities, and watchdog effects, but the other effects (informing, political, and scapegoating) are worth exploring. In addition, audience research and media content research tied to corporate reputation is needed as well. Then finally, future research in journalism and mass communication should examine alternative paradigms such as the interpretive, critical/cultural perspectives, literary criticism, and reception analysis.

References

Becker, L.B. and Whitney, D.C. (1980) Effects of media dependencies audience assessment of government. *Communication Research*, 7(1), 95–120.

Carroll, C.E. (2006) Influences on the production of business news. Center for International Business and Management's Global Symposium on Business and Media, Judge Business School, University of Cambridge, UK.

Carroll, C.E. (2009) The relationship between media favorability and firms' public esteem. *Public Relations Journal*, 3(4), 1–32.

Carroll, C.E. (2010) Should firms circumvent or work through the news media? *Public Relations Review*, 36(3), 278–280.

Carroll, C.E. (2011a) *Corporate Reputation and the News Media: Agenda-Setting within Business News Coverage in Developed, Emerging, and Frontier Markets*. New York: Routledge.

Carroll, C.E. (2011b) International perspectives on agenda setting theory applied to business news. In C.E. Carroll (ed.), *Corporate Reputation and the News Media: Agenda-Setting within Business News in Developed, Emerging, and Frontier Markets*. New York: Routledge, pp. 3–14.

Carroll, C.E. (2011c) The state of agenda-setting research on corporate reputation and the news media around the globe: Conclusions, cautions, and contingent conditions. In C.E. Carroll (ed.), *Corporate Reputation and the News Media: Agenda-Setting within Business News in Developed, Emerging, and Frontier Markets*. New York: Routledge, pp. 423–441.

Carroll, C.E. (2011d) The role of the news media in corporate reputation management. In R.J. Burke, G. Martin, and C.L. Cooper (eds), *Corporate Reputation: Managing Threats and Opportunities*. Surrey, UK: Gower, pp. 199–216.

Carroll, C.E. and Deephouse, D.L. (forthcoming) What news is fit to print? A multi-level framework explaining the production of news about organizations. In L. Strannegård and J. Pallas (eds), *Organizing in New Media Landscape*. London: Routledge.

Carroll, C.E. and Lee, S.Y. (2008) The influence of audience recall and personal experience on corporate reputation. Association of Educators in Journalism and Mass Communication. Chicago, IL, August.

Carroll, C.E. and McCombs, M.E. (2003) Agenda-setting effects of business news on the public's images and opinions about major corporations. *Corporate Reputation Review*, 6(1), 36–46.

Curtin, P.A. and Maier, S.R. (2001) Numbers in the newsroom: A qualitative examination of a quantitative challenge. *Journalism & Mass Communication Quarterly*, 78(4), 720–738.

Dowling, G.R. (2004) Journalists' evaluation of corporate reputations. *Corporate Reputation Review*, 7(2), 196–205.

Einwiller, S., Carroll, C.E., and Korn, K. (2010) Under what conditions do the news media influence corporate reputation? The roles of media systems dependency and need for orientation. *Corporate Reputation Review*, 12(4), 299–315.

Ettema, J.S. and Whitney, D.C. (1982) *Individuals in Mass Media Organizations: Creativity and Constraint*. Thousand Oaks, CA: Sage Publications.

Fombrun, C.J. and Shanley, M. (1990) What's in a name? Reputation building and corporate strategy. *Academy of Management Journal*, 33(2), 233–258.

Gans, H.J. (2004) *Democracy and the News*. New York: Oxford University Press.

Golan, G. and Wanta, W. (2001) Second-level agenda setting in the New Hampshire primary: A comparison of coverage in three newspapers and public perceptions of candidates. *Journal-*

ism & Mass Communication Quarterly, 78(2), 247–259.

Hall, S. (1980) Encoding and decoding in the television discourse. In S. Hall, D. Hobson, A. Lowe, and P. Willis (eds), *Culture, Media, Language.* London, UK: Hutchinson, pp. 128–138.

Kim, S.-H., Scheufele, D.A., and Shanahan, J. (2005) Who cares about the issues? Issue voting and the role of news media during the 2000 US presidential election. *Journal of Communication, 55*(1), 103–121.

Kiousis, S. (2004) Explicating media salience: A factor analysis of New York Times issue coverage during the 2000 U.S. presidential election. *Journal of Communication, 54*(1), 71–87.

Kiousis, S., Popescu, C., and Mitrook, M.A. (2007) Understanding influence on corporate reputation: An examination of public relations efforts, media coverage, public opinion, and financial performance from an agenda-building and agenda-setting perspective. *Journal of Public Relations Research, 19*(2), 147–165.

Lerbinger, O. (2006) Proactive media relations. In O. Lerbinger (ed.), *Corporate Public Affairs: Interacting with Interest Groups, Media and Government.* Mahwah, NJ: Lawrence Erlbaum Associates, pp. 99–136.

Ludwig, M.D. (2002) Business journalists need specialized finance training. *Newspaper Research Journal, 23*(2/3), 129–141.

McCombs, M.E. and Shaw, D.L. (1972) The agenda-setting function of the mass media. *Public Opinion Quarterly, 36*(2), 176–187.

Meijer, M.-M. and Kleinnijenhuis, J. (2006a) The effects of issue news on corporate reputation: Applying the theories of agenda setting and issue ownership in the field of business communication. *Journal of Communication, 56*(4), 543–559.

Meijer, M.-M. and Kleinnijenhuis, J. (2006b) News and corporate reputation: Empirical findings from the Netherlands. *Public Relations Review, 32*(4), 341–348.

Newcomb, H. and Hirsch, P.M. (1984) Television as a cultural form: Implications for research. In W.D. Rowland and B. Watkins (eds), *Interpreting Television.* Beverly Hills, CA: Sage Publications, pp. 58–73.

Park, D.J. and Berger, B.K. (2004) The presentation of CEOs in the press, 1990–2000: Increasing salience, positive valence, and a focus on competency and personal dimensions of image.

Journal of Public Relations Research, 16(1), 93–125.

Pietilä, V. (1994) Perspectives on our past: Charting the histories of mass communication studies. *Critical Studies in Mass Communication, 11*(4), 346–361.

Potter, W.J. (2009) *Arguing for a General Framework for Mass Media Scholarship.* Thousand Oaks, CA: Sage Publications.

Potter, W.J., Cooper, R., and Dupagne, M. (1993) The three paradigms of mass media research in mainstream communication journals. *Communication Theory, 3*(4), 317–335.

Potter, W.J. and Levine-Donnerstein, D. (1999) Rethinking validity and reliability in content analysis. *Journal of Applied Communication Research, 27*(3), 258–284.

Riffe, D. and Freitag, A. (1997) A content analysis of content analyses: Twenty-five years of journalism quarterly. *Journalism & Mass Communication Quarterly, 74*(3), 515–524.

Shoemaker, P.J. and Reese, S.D. (1996) *Mediating the Message: Theories of Influences on Mass Media Content* (2nd ed.). White Plains, NY: Longman.

Sriramesh, K. and Verčič, D. (2009) *The Global Public Relations Handbook: Theory, Research, and Practice.* New York: Routledge.

Vande Berg, L.R. and O'Donnell-Trujillo, N. (1989) *Organizational Life on Television.* Norwood, NJ: Ablex.

Wartick, S.L. (1992) The relationship between intense media exposure and change in corporate reputation. *Business & Society, 31*(1), 33–49.

Weaver, D.H., Graber, D.A., McCombs, M.E., and Eyal, C. (1981) *Media Agenda Setting in a Presidential Election: Issues, Images, and Interest.* New York: Praeger.

Webster, J.G. and Phalen, P.F. (1997) *The Mass Audience: Rediscovering the Dominant Model.* Mahwah, NJ: Lawrence Erlbaum Associates.

Webster, J.G. and Wakshlag, J. (1985) Measuring exposure to television. In D. Zillmann and J. Bryant (eds), *Selective Exposure to Communication.* Hillsdale, NJ: Lawrence Erlbaum Associates, pp. 35–62.

Westphal, J.D. and Deephouse, D.L. (2011) Avoiding bad press: Interpersonal influence in relations between CEOs and journalists and the consequences for press reporting about firms and their leadership. *Organization Science, 22*(4), 1061–1086.

13

Corporate Reputation and the Discipline of Visual Communication

Susan Westcott Alessandri

Suffolk University, USA

This chapter focuses on visual identity as the heart of a brand or organization's reputation-building efforts and its central form of visual communication. This chapter will trace the history of visual identity and its relationship to reputation, and it will discuss how the strategic management of a visual identity can contribute to positive reputation-building efforts.

Brands and organizations – from businesses and nonprofits to universities and churches – have visual identities. On the most basic level, the brand or organization's visual identity differentiates the organization from others in the competitive marketplace. On a more strategic level, a visual identity serves the higher function of helping an organization achieve a positive image – and ultimately a positive reputation – in the minds of the public. When we see the Target Bullseye®, one or more of the associations we have with the Target brand will enter our consciousness, whether it is a memory of a positive or negative shopping experience or simply the recollection of an advertisement we saw on television. Since an organization's visual identity also includes sounds and scents, a positive or negative association might also be conjured when we hear a Harley-Davidson engine, or smell Johnson's® Baby Shampoo. Individual associations with a brand or an organization's visual identity communicate the image of that brand or organization, and over time, the collective impressions of the image form the brand or organization's reputation.

Today, there is a generally accepted distinction between identity (what the organization is) and image (what the organization is perceived to be). Over time, positive impressions of the organization's image can serve to promote a positive reputation. This happens through a relatively simple – though lengthy – process of association formation that begins with an organization's mission.

The practitioner literature on visual identity, which is found mostly in graphic design, advertising, and public relations trade publications, defines identity strictly in terms of a firm's visual identification – its name, logo, tagline, and color palette. This literature tends to focus on the importance of presenting the organization's visual identity in a consistent way – both in sub-

The Handbook of Communication and Corporate Reputation, First Edition. Edited by Craig E. Carroll.
© 2013 John Wiley & Sons, Inc. Published 2015 by John Wiley & Sons, Inc.

stance and over time (Ackerman, 1988, 1990; Carls, 1989; Gorman, 1994; LaRue, 1995; Pierson, 1993; Siegel, 1988, 1994). In an article focused on two firms that implemented new visual identities, Lorge (1998) interviewed one self-proclaimed "chief of logo police" that lamented the tedious work frequently associated with educating employees on the importance of presenting a consistent identity:

> I try desperately to have people understand they should follow the identity rules. If you don't, you're compromising the brand image. . . . It's a continuing task to get folks to understand why it's important. I simply explain that every time you see the Lear logo, it's an exposure. It works singly, but it also works cumulatively. Don't compromise it; [if you do,] you're destroying the synergy of the program.(p. 42)

Even while focusing on the more tactical issues associated with visual identity, many practitioners have advocated the use of strategic decision making for issues related to visual identity. Lambert (1989) integrated the tactical and strategic perspectives by offering two generalized definitions of visual identity – "all those manifestations of an organization that enable it to be distinctive" and "projecting who you are, what you do, and how you do it." Lambert advocated incorporating identity elements into every visual element a firm projects, including its architecture and building interior design.

Lambert's "iceberg" depicts identity in a two-level hierarchy: an upper level contains the elements that are seen by the public; the lower level contains the elements only seen or experienced by the firm. Appearing above the surface are the visual elements – name, logo, tagline, and color palette. This model implies that all things below the surface – such as the firm's in-house and public behavior – though invisible to the general public, are equal parts of the identity. This conceptual view provides a fitting segue into the scholarly, and often more strategic, view of visual identity.

Scholars have tended to view visual identity not as a singular outcome, but as the means to an end: a positive reputation. Schmitt *et al.*

(1995) presented a framework for the management of visual elements known as corporate aesthetics management (CAM). They contended that strategic management of a firm's aesthetic elements could aid the firm in achieving strategic competitive advantage. They built on the classic four P's of marketing – product, price, place, and promotion – by adding additional four P's: properties, products, presentations, and publications. These proposed additional four Ps help to account for all of a firm's aesthetic elements – from business cards to building architecture.

Van Riel (1997) joined the concepts of visual identity and reputation. He referred to them as two of the three key concepts in corporate communication research, with the third being the orchestration of communication. Viewed in a hierarchical way, this description supports the idea that an organization's visual identity is a building block to a positive reputation, but that the process of getting there involves an integrated and consistent message. Likewise, Balmer and Soenen (1999) conducted in-depth interviews and a content analysis in a study of the techniques used by 20 visual identity consultancies. They found that most consultancy projects employed what they refer to as a "vision-driven approach," based on the views of the chief executive or board of directors, which supports the assumption that visual identity is managed at the highest levels of the organization.

The present chapter focuses on visual identity, which is the core of a brand or organization's reputation-building efforts and its central form of visual communication. This chapter will trace the history of visual identity and its relationship to reputation, and it will discuss how the strategic management of a visual identity can contribute to positive reputation-building efforts.

Origins of Visual Identity

While there is no definitive origin of the field of visual identity, the history of symbols as a way to denote the source of an owner's goods dates back to ancient Egypt. Cattle owners in Egypt branded their cattle as a way of tracking their herds, and after the cattle were sold, the brand served as the mark of the seller (Ruston, 1955). Throughout history, markings have been used to denote source and identity, from the Hindus' use of marks in trade between India and Asia Minor from 1300 to 1200 BC to the use of coats of arms during medieval times. In fact, variations on ancient markings have found their way into modern commercial usage: the "orb and cross design" employed widely in Italy in the fifteenth century is very similar to the Nabisco trademark (Diamond, 1983).[1]

More modern use of "maker's marks" developed in prerevolutionary England as a way of identifying the source and quality of silversmiths' work. Rainwater (1966) defined a hallmark as "the official mark of the English Goldsmiths' Company used on articles of gold and silver to indicate their genuineness" (p. 210). In post-Revolutionary America, colonial artisans adopted the English silversmiths' tradition and used "pseudo hallmarks" to indicate their silver's origin. Bigelow (1948) observed that the number of silversmiths increased in proportion to the prosperity of the colonies, and "largely as an advertisement, many adopted the fashion of using a stamp with the surname often preceded by the initial of the Christian name which was usually enclosed in a plain rectangle or in one of irregular outline" (p. 18).

In the late nineteenth century, the US government brought structure to the use of marks when it codified federal trademark law with the Trademark Act of 1870. Just one year later, in 1871, the US Supreme Court heard *Canal Co. v. Clark*, which is said to be the US Supreme Court's first corporate identity case. The case dealt with using geographic terms as trademarks, and the court held that the plaintiff lacked the exclusive right to prevent others from using the term "Lackawanna" on coal mined in the Lackawanna Valley (McClure, 1979).

In 1876, the Trademark Act of 1870 was amended and was ultimately held unconstitutional by the US Supreme Court in 1879

(McClure, 1979). That was not the end of the use of trademarks, however. At the very end of the nineteenth century, the industrial revolution gave rise to the proliferation of trademarks to denote the origin and quality of goods. With the transition from handwork to machine work, mass production meant increased supplies and the need for merchants to make the public aware of the availability of their goods (Diamond, 1983). Between 1860 and 1920, the United States underwent a major transition – from a marketplace filled with bulk goods to a marketplace of goods bearing the identifiable marks – the trademarks – of their manufacturers. With increased competition to sell seemingly equivalent products, manufacturers began advertising their brand names and trademarks. Manufacturers also began to use product packaging as a medium for extolling a product's virtues. In 1887, Log Cabin maple syrup appeared on grocery-store shelves in cabin-shaped packages. Makers of Log Cabin syrup "soon found that customers willingly paid extra for the novelty, as well as for the convenience and product assurance they gained" (Sivulka, 1998, p. 52).

As early as the beginning of the twentieth century, the public's positive response to brand names was reflected in the financial valuations of trademarks. In 1905, the value of Royal Baking Powder's goodwill[2] was estimated at $5 million, and trademarks in general evolved into one of a firm's most valuable intangible assets (Drescher, 1992).

In a landmark trademark case in 1928, even before federal protection for trademarks existed, Justice Learned Hand eloquently articulated the idea of a trademark as an integral part of an organization's reputation. He wrote in an opinion for the Second Circuit Court of Appeals:

> [The merchant's] mark is his authentic seal; by it he vouches for the goods which bear it; it carries his name for good or ill. If another uses it, he borrows the owner's reputation, whose quality no longer lies within his own control. This is an injury, even though the borrower does not tarnish it, or divert sales by its use; for a reputation, like a face, is the

symbol of its possessor and creator, and another can use it only as a mark.

Disciplinary Limitations: Visual Identity and Reputation Defined

An early limitation in the literature associated with visual communication was one of semantics. There was a dearth of literature, and what existed often used the discipline's confusingly similar terminology – identity and image – interchangeably. Many studies employed "identity" in place of "image," and vice versa, when most scholars have come to see these as two constructs as related yet distinct. In addition, Balmer and Soenen (1997) conducted a major review of the literature and concluded that the research domain's limited empirical research added to confusion surrounding the terminology associated with the concept of identity.

Over the past two decades, however, the visual identity body of literature has matured to the point that there are now more consistent definitions across a broad range of studies, but the same issue that Balmer and Soenen highlighted in 1997 still persists today: there is a shortage of empirical studies, and specifically empirical studies that explore the all-important link between visual identity and reputation.

Another, and perhaps more long-term issue, is the context of identity. Management scholars have long published studies relating to organizational identity, while the visual communications and design disciplines study visual identity (sometimes called "corporate identity"). There have been scholars whose work has, whether by accident or design, bridged the gap between the two disciplines. For example, van Rekom delineated three criteria for a "corporate identity." He described a corporate identity as including those features considered the essence of an organization, the features that set an organization apart from others, and the continuity of these features over time. While these ideas mesh quite nicely with the ideal of always presenting a clear and consistent visual identity,

this view is also strikingly similar to the management discipline's widely accepted definition of "organizational identity" as that which is "core, distinctive, and enduring" about a firm (Albert and Whetten, 1985).

To alleviate confusion, and to further develop the body of literature related to visual identity specifically, it will be useful to define several related terms. These concepts are operationalized not only to give the reader a clearer view of their meaning, but also because the operationalizations may provide future researchers with a starting point for their own empirical research into the link between visual identity and reputation.

An organization's *visual, or corporate, identity* refers to the strategically planned and purposeful presentation of an organization. This includes all of the observable and measurable elements of an organization's identity manifest in its comprehensive visual presentation, including, but not limited to, its name, logo, tagline, color palette, and architecture. An organization's corporate identity also includes its public behavior, including, but not limited to, its reception of employees, customers, shareholders, and suppliers (Alessandri, 2001). In some cases, a corporate identity actually goes beyond the visual to employ the other senses: almost anything a person can see, smell, hear, or touch that is meant to market the organization or brand might become part of an organization's visual identity. For example, the perfumed scent of a Victoria's Secret store or the deep coffee smell at nearly any Starbucks has undoubtedly become a part of each of the brands' visual identities. And while Harley-Davidson has withdrawn its application for a trademark, many avid motorcyclists would attest to the sound a Harley makes as being an integral part of its corporate identity.

While it may be well within the control of an organization to develop a strategic visual identity, it is not a given that the organization's publics will notice or form associations with the visual identity. The average American consumer might see anywhere from hundreds to thousands of commercial messages per day, so the challenge is upon marketers to make their messages memorable. Marketing to today's sophisticated audiences means getting under the radar of many who are savvy enough to immediately spot a commercial message – and then perhaps turn away from it. When it is not immediately evident that a message is commercial, however, it may have the power to communicate more directly with consumers.

One way that organizations can communicate strategically and efficiently is through *nontraditional expressions of visual identity*. These occur when an organization explicitly uses one or more of its traditional identity elements (name, logo, tagline, or colors from its palette) in a unique way. This enables the organization to extend its traditional identity while reinforcing one or more of its individual identity elements (Alessandri, 2009). The deployment of these alternative forms of identity stems from an organization's overwhelming need to compete with more traditional messages, but organizations might also recognize the need to project a consistent identity that reaches consumers in a memorable way.

On a strategic level, the concept of nontraditional expressions of identity fits nicely within the realm of integrated marketing communications (IMC) because it allows organizations to project their identities in creative ways while still reinforcing the core message with consumers. On a more tactical level, however, nontraditional expressions of identity that are truly unique will help an organization cut through the proverbial message clutter – and perhaps spur positive word of mouth about the organization.

There are several examples of nontraditional expressions of identity around the world, and in varied organizations, including corporations, nonprofit organizations, and educational institutions. Generally, the concept of any kind of theme park is a nontraditional expression of identity. When visitors walk through the gates at Disney World or Legoland or Hersheypark, they are, in effect, subjecting themselves to a multisensory brand experience, and one that might last for days, all the while paying for the pleasure. Not all nontraditional expressions of visual identity need to be so grand, however.

Each July, the best cyclists in the world gather in France to compete in the Tour de France. French bank Credit Lyonnais is a major sponsor, and two different elements of the bank's visual identity are manifest throughout the tour: the bank's signature yellow color and its lion mascot. Each day following the race, the rider with the overall best time is awarded the *maillot jaune*, or the yellow jersey. The yellow jersey is adorned with several logos, but none are more prominent than those of Credit Lyonnais, and the yellow jersey itself is a reflection of the bank's signature color. In addition to the jersey, the race's leader is awarded a large stuffed lion, the bank's mascot. As might be expected, the awards ceremony following each day's ride is a highly popular event, and one that is always included in the daily international coverage of the race. In this way, Credit Lyonnais is able to reinforce its sponsorship of the Tour de France without explicitly advertising that sponsorship during the televised coverage of the race.

With their storied traditions and popular athletic programs, large US universities are often rife with nontraditional expressions of visual identity. Clemson University is an example of an organization that insinuated a signature element of its visual identity into a highly visible campus facility. Located in South Carolina, Clemson University is home to the Clemson Tigers. The university's athletic teams wear orange and rally around the school's mascot, a tiger, and the university's athletics logo, a tiger paw, which was designed based on the paw print of an actual tiger. In the years since the logo was designed, the university has incorporated it widely into its licensing program, and the logo appears on both the basketball court and football fields. Perhaps the most unique representation of the logo is on the university-affiliated public golf course, the Walker Golf Course, which opened in 1993. The Walker Golf Course's signature hole perfectly reflects Clemson's tiger paw logo. The seventeenth hole – the Tiger Paw, as it is known – is just that: the green is the shape of the large pad of the tiger's paw, and four sand traps, or bunkers, make up the remaining four pads of the paw.

Whether an organization chooses to communicate its visual identity, or elements of it, in a traditional or a nontraditional way, the visual identity must be managed strategically, in a way that aids the public in forming positive associations. These associations, in turn, form the *organizational image*, which is defined as the totality of a stakeholder's perceptions of the way an organization presents itself, either deliberately or accidentally. Organizations have several images, since perceptions vary widely among stakeholders. An organization manages its image by managing its identity (Alessandri, 2009; Markwick and Fill, 1997).

According to previous academic literature, the identity of an organization has an inseparable link with the organization's reputation (Alessandri, 2001; Balmer and Gray, 1999; Fombrun and Rindova, 2000; Markwick and Fill, 1997; van den Bosch *et al.*, 2005). Alessandri (2001), for example, proposed the following conceptual model: (1) interaction with an organizational *identity* can produce an organizational *image* and (2) repeated impressions of an organizational image can form a *reputation* of the organization over time. Similarly, Balmer and Gray (1999) suggested that corporate communication is a three-part process and maintained that the role of primary communication is to present a positive image of a firm for a strong reputation.

The concept of organizational reputation has been defined in multiple contexts, but, in general, as (1) assessments that multiple audiences make about the organization's ability to fulfill its expectations (Fombrun and Van Riel, 2003), (2) a collective system of perceptual beliefs among members of a social group (Bromley, 1993, 2000, 2002), (3) collective beliefs that exist about an organization's identity and prominence (Rao, 1994), and (4) collective representations shared in the minds of multiple audiences about an organization over time (Grunig and Hung, 2002; Yang and Grunig, 2005). The commonality among these definitions leads to the following definition: *organizational reputation* refers to perceptions of the organization shared by its multiple constituents over time (Alessandri *et al.*, 2006).

This definition supports the idea that an organization's image might change over time, depending on the management of the identity and the particular contextual circumstances, but that a reputation is enduring.

Visual Identity + Associations + Image = Reputation

The most basic tenet of trademark law, and the basic function of a visual identity, is to direct consumers to the source or origin of goods. Once basic source identification has been achieved, however, the visual identity serves the higher purpose, like many of its counterpart communication vehicles, of helping to maintain and strengthen the relationship between the organization and its publics. The visual identity can achieve this by aiding in the formation of associations that will ultimately produce a positive image and reputation of the organization, but any visual identity begins with the mission of the organization itself.

The organization's mission represents its philosophy (Abratt, 1989; Leuthesser and Kohli, 1997), its *raison d'etre*. Thus, every organization has a philosophy, whether tacit or codified, and whether it consciously projects it or lets it evolve naturally. Under the best circumstances, an organization will carefully develop and then nurture its identity, but even organizations that pay little attention to their identities are sending a message about their philosophy. Typically, a philosophy is exemplified through the behavior of the organization as well as in its visual presentation; these two complementary elements make up the organization's identity. The most important reality of the visual identity is that it is completely within the control of the organization: it can choose how to present itself visually, or through its behavior (Leitch and Motion, 1999; Topalian, 1984), which in turn aids the public in forming associations. Understanding *how* the public forms perceptions and associations, however, is key to understanding the best way to strategically manage a visual identity in a way that will most efficiently produce positive results.

Alessandri (2001) theorized that the "learning" of perceptions works in two stages: at a low-involvement level and, after an image of the identity has been formed, through classical conditioning. It seems appropriate to borrow theories from the psychological literature, since, as early as 1942, the United States Supreme Court recognized the psychological nature of symbols. Justice Felix Frankfurter wrote in a landmark trademark decision:

> The protection of trade-marks is the law's recognition of the psychological function of symbols. If it is true that we live by symbols, it is no less true that we purchase goods by them. A trade-mark is a merchandising shortcut which induces a purchaser to select what he wants, or what he has been led to believe he wants. (Frankfurter, 1942)

Frankfurter's recognition that symbolism is most successful if it is widely known supports the theoretical assumption that the public must first *recognize* the visual identity and then subsequently be conditioned to form a positive image of the visual identity.

Low involvement

The theory of low involvement explains how a consumer may actually come to recognize the visual identity of a firm. Krugman (1965) developed the theory of low involvement, asserting that a behavioral trigger may activate an awareness generated through repetition of a message. This behavior may then result in attitude change. Krugman described the process of attitude change through low involvement this way: repetition of a message will bring about two results – information will shift from short-term to long-term memory, and a change in the perception of the brand will occur (Krugman, 1965).

Krugman's theory is important to visual identity in two ways. First, this theory presents an alternative to the accepted "high-involvement" theory of attitude change, which states that attitude change prompts specific behaviors (Krugman, 1965). Secondly, the theory of low involvement provides an alternative to research that states that more than three exposures to a message are necessary before *any* awareness takes place (Krugman, 1972). Melewar and Saunders (2000) supported this theoretical view:

> As products and competitors proliferate, it is the names and images most repeated that will dominate. . . . Identical company name, similar symbol, consistent typography and standardized colors should appear . . . to enable the audience to view the organization as a single and unified entity. A high degree of standardization applied to the promotional tools projects a consistent global corporate visual identity.

Projecting a consistent visual identity is integral to forming a positive image through classical conditioning, the second phase of Alessandri's (2001) theoretical explanation of how visual identity works in the context of reputation building.

Classical conditioning

Visual identity consultant Clive Chajet provided a reporter with practical insight into the psychological nature of words when he said, "A name is an abstract tool. You make it what it is" (Townsend, 1990). Chajet's theory of attaching psychological meanings to words is an example of classical conditioning, when the public forms an attitude – in effect, learns a behavior – based on associations (Eagly and Chaiken, 1993, p. 393). The theory of classical conditioning asserts that systematically pairing a conditioned stimulus with an unconditioned stimulus over time will produce a particular emotion or attitude, which is the conditioned response. In the case of visual identity, the conditioned stimulus would be the presentation of the visual identity. The unconditioned stimulus would be the association – either positive or negative – paired with the visual identity. An example of a positive association might be an aesthetically pleasing visual presentation of the firm's logo, or a positive interaction with an organization's employee. After repeated pairings of the stimuli, the result – the conditioned response – will be a favorable attitude toward the organization when seeing an ad featuring an element of the visual identity, viewing the firm's logo, or hearing the name of the organization.

Using classical conditioning in a marketing context is not new, but this theory has an interesting connection to visual identity. The Latin root of the term identity is *idem*, which means "same." The Latin *identidem* means "repeatedly," or "the same each time" (Balmer, 1997).

Grossman and Till (1998) found support for the hypothesis that attitudes formed through classical conditioning are enduring, but they warned that repeated exposure to the visual identity without the unconditioned stimulus (a consistent and aesthetically pleasing visual presentation or positive behavior) is likely to erode the favorable attitude created through classical conditioning. For this reason, consistency and repetition are imperatives for organizations trying to gain favorable images – and ultimately positive reputations – in the minds of the public.

Relationship between Visual Identity and Reputation

Based on several scholars' principles of reputation formation (Bromley, 1993, 2000; Caruana, 1997; Fombrun and Shanley, 1990; Gotsi and Wilson, 2001; Grunig and Hung, 2002), an organization can only indirectly manage its reputation by directly managing its identity, which includes monitoring the direct or indirect (or mediated) experiences and information and/or symbols to which the audience may be exposed, and which may be received through a variety of communication channels. Because information is acquired from symbols (e.g., logos, architecture, taglines, and other visual attributes), an organization's reputation is thought to be related to the organization's visual identity. This further supports the idea that an organization, although it cannot directly manage its reputation, can directly manage its visual identity as a way of indirectly managing its reputation (Alessandri *et al.*, 2006).

Finally, Fombrun and van Riel (2003) proposed the following five dimensions of reputation: visibility, distinctiveness, authenticity, transparency, and consistency. *Visibility* refers to the organization itself, but extrapolating to the level of the visual identity, visibility refers to the pervasiveness of the visual identity (or elements thereof) in a variety of communication channels and contexts. The same is true of *consistency*: the organization must be consistent in its actions toward a variety of audiences, but the visual identity must also be presented consistently in a variety of media and communication channels. *Distinctiveness* refers to the unique position of the organization in the minds of its strategic constituents, according to Fombrun and van Riel (2003); they noted that distinctiveness can yield "top-of-mind" awareness of an organization's products and/or services in the public's minds. van den Bosch *et al.* (2005) claimed that the distinctive visual identity of an organization can be strongly related to the organization's distinctiveness in the minds of its stakeholders. For example, the more distinctive the Nike or Apple Computer logos are to their stakeholders, the more distinctively positioned are the companies and their products/services in the minds of stakeholders, which can contribute to the companies' favorable reputations.

Alessandri *et al.* (2006) also found empirical support for the relationship between visual identity and reputation in the context of universities. Study participants with a strong sense of the academic aspects of a university's visual identity tended to most positively evaluate the dimension of quality of academic performance. At the same time, it was the participants who most positively evaluated the dimension of emotional engagement who focused on the social aspect of the university's visual identity.

The Future: Further Empirical Evidence of Visual Identity + Image = Reputation

While the last decade has brought more recognition to the reputation discipline, the connection between visual identity and reputation remains more anecdotal than empirical. While there may be some solace in the reality that the body of literature on visual identity – and specifically the literature that links visual identity to reputation – is relatively young, the field needs to develop a more solid base of empirical research.

Building a body of literature that supports an empirical link between visual identity, image, and reputation would offer convincing proof of the efficacy of building, maintaining, and strategically managing a visual identity that directly supports reputation-building efforts. In this way, the literature on visual identity and reputation would become a go-to – as well as a benchmark – for any number of nonprofit and profit-seeking organizations that truly understand the importance of public perception and reputation.

Notes

1 In 1893, Nabisco's Adolphus Green was looking through a book that contained fifteenth-century Italian printers' symbols. He saw a cross with two bars and an oval, which represented "the triumph of the moral and spiritual over the evil and the material." The symbol had once been used as a printer's mark by the Society of Printers in Venice (Cahn, 1969).

2 A firm's goodwill reflects the value of the firm in excess of its asset value. Goodwill is treated as an intangible asset and is generally represented by the value of a well-respected corporate name, high employee morale, or other factors that are expected to translate into greater than normal earning power. See Downes, J. and Goodman,

J.E. (1995) *Dictionary of Finance and Investment Terms*. Hauppauge: Barron's Educational Series, Inc.

References

Abratt, R. (1989) A new approach to the corporate image management process. *Journal of Marketing Management*, 5(1), 63–76.

Ackerman, L.D. (1988) Identity strategies that make a difference. *The Journal of Business Strategy*, 9(May/June), 28–32.

Ackerman, L.D. (1990) Identity in action. *Communication World*, 7(September), 33–35.

Albert, S. and Whetten, D.A. (1985) Organizational identity. In R.F. Zammuto and K.S. Cameron (eds), *Research in Organizational Behavior*. Greenwich, CT: JAI Press, Inc., pp. 263–295.

Alessandri, S.W. (2001) Modeling corporate identity: A concept explication and theoretical explanation. *Corporate Communications: An International Journal*, 6(4), 173–182.

Alessandri, W.W. (2009) *Visual Identity: Promoting and Protecting the Public Face of an Organization*. Armonk, NY: M.E. Sharpe.

Alessandri, S.W., Yang, S.U., and Kinsey, D.F. (2006) An integrative approach to university visual identity and reputation. *Corporate Reputation Review*, 9(4), 258–270.

Balmer, J.M.T. (1997) Corporate identity: Past, present and future. Working Paper, University of Strathclyde International Centre for Corporate Identity Studies, Glasgow.

Balmer, J.M.T. and Gray, E.R. (1999) Corporate identity and corporate communications: Creating a competitive advantage. *Corporate Communications: An International Journal*, 4(4), 171–176.

Balmer, J.M.T. and Soenen, G.B. (1997) Operationalising the concept of corporate identity: Articulating the corporate identity mix and the corporate identity management mix. Working Paper, University of Strathclyde International Centre for Corporate Identity Studies, Glasgow.

Balmer, J.M.T. and Soenen, G.B. (1999) The acid test of corporate identity management. *Journal of Marketing Management*, 15(1), 69–92.

Bigelow, F.H. (1948) *Historic Silver of the Colonies and Its Makers*. New York: Tudor Publishing Company.

Bromley, D.B. (1993) *Reputation, Image, and Impression Management*. Chichester, UK: John Wiley & Sons.

Bromley, D.B. (2000) Psychological aspects of corporate identity, image and reputation. *Corporate Reputation Review, 3*(3), 240–252.

Bromley, D.B. (2002) Comparing corporate reputations: League tables, quotients, benchmarks, or case studies? *Corporate Reputation Review, 5*(1), 35–50.

Cahn, W. (1969) *Out of the Cracker Barrel, the Nabisco Story from Animal Crackers to ZuZus.* New York: Simon & Schuster.

Carls, K. (1989) Corporate coats of arms. *Harvard Business Review, 67*(May/June), 135–139.

Caruana, A. (1997) Corporate reputation: Concept and measurement. *Journal of Product & Brand Management, 6*(2), 109–118.

Diamond, S.A. (1983) The historical development of trademarks. *Trademark Reporter, 73*, 222–247.

Drescher, T.D. (1992) The transformation and evolution of trademarks – From signals to symbol to myth. *Trademark Reporter, 82*, 301–340.

Eagly, A.H. and Chaiken, S. (1993) *The Psychology of Attitudes.* Orlando, FL: Harcourt Brace College Publishers.

Fombrun, C.J. and Rindova, V. (2000) The road to transparency: Reputation management at Royal Dutch/Shell. In M. Schultz, M.J. Hatch, and M.H. Larsen (eds), *The Expressive Organization: Linking Identity, Reputation and the Corporate Brand.* Oxford, UK: Oxford University Press, pp. 77–96.

Fombrun, C.J. and Shanley, M. (1990) What's in a name? Reputation building and corporate strategy. *Academy of Management Journal, 33*(2), 233–258.

Fombrun, C.J. and van Riel, C.B.M. (2003) *Fame & Fortune: How Successful Companies Build Winning Reputations.* Upper Saddle River, NJ: Prentice Hall.

Frankfurter, F. (1942) U.S. Supreme Court. *Mishawaka Rubber & Woolen Manufacturing Co. v. S.S. Kresge Co.,* Washington, DC, U.S. LEXIS 1224.

Gorman, C. (1994) Developing an effective corporate identity program. *Public Relations Journal, 50*(7), 40–42.

Gotsi, M. and Wilson, A.M. (2001) Corporate reputation: Seeking a definition. *Corporate Communications: An International Journal, 6*(1), 24–30.

Grossman, R.P. and Till, B.D. (1998) The persistence of classically conditioned brand attitudes. *Journal of Advertising, 27*(1), 23–31.

Grunig, J.E. and Hung, C.F. (2002) The effect of relationships on reputation and reputation on

relationships: A cognitive, behavioral study. Paper presented at the PRSA Educator's Academy 5th Annual International, Interdisciplinary Public Relations Research Conference, Miami, FL, March.

Krugman, H.E. (1965) The impact of television advertising: Learning without involvement. *Public Opinion Quarterly, 29*(3), 349–356.

Krugman, H.E. (1972) Why three exposures may be enough. *Journal of Advertising Research, 12*(6), 11–14.

Lambert, A. (1989) Corporate identity and facilities management. *Facilities, 7*(12), 7–12.

LaRue, K. (1995) Don't shortchange your company with ineffective logo, trademark. *Houston Business Journal, 25*(September 15), 38.

Leitch, S. and Motion, J. (1999) Multiplicity in corporate identity strategy. *Corporate Communications: An International Journal, 4*(4), 193–199.

Leuthesser, L. and Kohli, C. (1997) Corporate identity: The role of mission statements. *Business Horizons, 40*(3), 59–66.

Lorge, S. (1998) Better off branded. *Sales & Marketing Management, 150*(March), 39–42.

Markwick, N. and Fill, C. (1997) Towards a framework for managing corporate identity. *European Journal of Marketing, 31*(5–6), 396–409.

McClure, D.M. (1979) Trademarks and unfair competition: A critical history of legal thought. *Trademark Reporter, 69*, 305–356.

Melewar, T.C. and Saunders, J. (2000) Global corporate visual identity systems: Using an extended marketing mix. *European Journal of Marketing, 34*(5/6), 538–550.

Pierson, J. (1993) When company logos detract from image. *Wall Street Journal,* June 18, p. B1.

Rainwater, D.T. (1966) *American Silver Manufacturers.* Hanover, Germany: Everybodys Press.

Rao, H. (1994) The social construction of reputation: Certification contests, legitimation, and the survival of organizations in the American automobile industry: 1985–1912. *Strategic Management Journal, 15*, 29–44.

Ruston, G. (1955) On the origin of trademarks. *Trademark Reporter, 45*, 127–144.

Schmitt, B.H., Simonson, A., and Marcus, J. (1995) Managing corporate image and identity. *Long Range Planning, 28*(5), 82–92.

Siegel, A. (1988) Common sense on corporate identity. *Across the Board, 25*(6), 27–32.

Siegel, A. (1994) Defining the corporate voice. *Across the Board, 31*(10), 56–57.

Sivulka, J. (1998) *Soap, Sex, and Cigarettes: A Cultural History of American Advertising.* Belmont, CA: Wadsworth Publishing Company.

Topalian, A. (1984) Corporate identity: Beyond the visual overstatements. *International Journal of Advertising, 3,* 55–62.

Townsend, B. (1990) Cashing in on corporate identity. *American Demographics, 12*(July), 42–43.

U.S. Congress, Federal Trademark Dilution Act 15 U.S.C. § 1127.

van den Bosch, A.L.M., De Jong, M.D.T., and Elving, W.J.L. (2005) How corporate visual identity supports reputation. *Corporate Communications: An International Journal, 10*(2), 108–116.

van Riel, C.B.M. (1997) Research in corporate communication: An overview of an emerging field. *Management Communication Quarterly, 11*(2), 288–309.

Yang, S.U. and Grunig, J.E. (2005) The effects of organization-public relationships outcomes on cognitive representations of organizations and overall evaluations of organizational performance. *Journal of Communication Management, 9*(4), 305–326.

14

Corporate Reputation and the Discipline of Corporate Communication Law

Karla K. Gower

University of Alabama, USA

This chapter begins with a discussion of the impact legal issues can have on corporate reputation. It then explores how the speech of corporations fits within the US Constitution's First Amendment, which traditionally has been used to protect the speech of individuals. The chapter discusses the different legal concepts of reputation and how those concepts are applied to corporations. Three specific areas of the law directly affecting corporate reputation are reviewed: defamation, false advertising, and privacy. Currently, corporations walk a line between being treated as individuals for purposes of the law and as public entities akin to a government agency. When equated with an individual, corporations are granted greater speech and privacy rights. When equated with the public sector, corporations are exposed to greater scrutiny. Transparency and honesty will be the keys to maintaining a corporate reputation in the future.

Communication law in the United States has traditionally focused on the First Amendment to the Constitution and its importance to print and broadcast journalism. As such, it is a twentieth-century phenomenon with the first US Supreme Court cases involving the constitutional right to free speech coming in 1919. It was not until 1978, however, that the Court held that corporations had speech rights under the First Amendment. Despite those rights, the government has long regulated the "speech" of corporations to protect individuals from being misled and deceived by unscrupulous businesses. For example, the Federal Trade Commission (FTC) is concerned with corporate misrepresentation and deception in advertising, while the Securities and Exchange Commission (SEC) deals with how, when, and to what extent the financial affairs of publicly traded companies are communicated to investors. News reports of companies running afoul of FTC or SEC regulations are highly damaging to the reputations of those corporations as well as to businesses in general.

According to the 2012 Edelman Trust Barometer, transparent and honest business practices are important factors impacting corporate reputation. In fact, 49% of informed

Backfire

publics between the ages of 25 and 64 who were surveyed agreed that government should regulate corporate activity to ensure that businesses behave responsibly. And governments often respond quickly to do so when it appears that the entire corporate world has lost its moral compass as happened during the Great Depression. In that instance, Congress reacted by enacting the Securities Act in 1933 and the Securities Exchange Act the following year to restore trust and confidence in the stock market. More recently, the financial scandals of 2001 and 2002 involving Enron, WorldCom, and Tyco among others led to the passage of the Sarbanes–Oxley Act, which requires greater financial transparency and accountability on the part of corporations. The 2009 banking collapse caused greater scrutiny of what appeared to be out-of-control CEO bonuses and companies that were "too big to fail."

Thus, wholesale moral lapses on the part of businesses lead to public mistrust and often legislation. Breaches of regulations mean the reputation of the company directly involved, as well as the reputations of all in that industry, is damaged. At the same time, corporate reputation can be impacted by lawsuits brought by private citizens, as was the case when activist Marc Kasky sued Nike, the multinational athletic goods marketer, for false advertising in California in 1998. Kasky alleged that Nike misled consumers about labor conditions in its overseas factories. Nike's reputation suffered as a result.

The "reputational penalties" imposed by the stock market on such companies are actually much greater than those imposed by regulatory agencies and civil settlements. In an empirical study of companies accused of financial fraud between 1978 and 2002, economists Karpoff *et al.* (2008) found that "for each dollar that a firm misleadingly inflates its market value when its books are cooked, on average, it loses this dollar when its misconduct is revealed, plus an additional $3.07. Of this additional loss, $0.36 is due to expected legal penalties and $2.71 is due to lost reputation" (p. 581).

Perhaps that is why corporations are quick to defend their reputations, sometimes via the courts, although even that strategy carries reputational risks. The fast-food chain McDonald's sued two environmental activists in England in 1990 for libel after they distributed a pamphlet claiming the company was complicit in rainforest destruction because of its use of soya in its livestock feed. McDonald's ultimately won the almost decade-long legal battle but lost in the court of public opinion because the media framed the case as Goliath taking on David. In the end, McDonald's announced that it had no plans to collect the £40,000 judgment.

Although many areas of communication law potentially affect corporate reputation, this chapter will examine only defamation, false advertising, and privacy because of their direct relation to corporate reputation. But it begins with a discussion of the relationship of corporations to the First Amendment.

Corporate Reputation and the First Amendment

While overall the First Amendment has been a powerful defender of speech and speakers from government interference, the US Supreme Court's protection of speech has waxed and waned over the years with the times and the makeup of the Court. As a result, scholars have attempted to develop theories that would lend consistency to the Court's decisions as well as explain why freedom of speech is so highly valued in American society.

Essentially, First Amendment theories tend to fall into one of two camps: societal or individual. Societal theorists argue that speech is protected because it is ultimately good for society. Open debate is necessary for the truth to emerge. It also allows for self-governance because citizens have the information necessary to make informed decisions and participate in the political process. And finally, the freedom to express ideas helps act as a safety valve. The belief is that if individuals are able to express themselves, their frustrations will not build, preventing violence and revolution.

Individual theorists, on the other hand, argue that the right to speak freely is protected because communication is what makes us human. Individuals who are deprived of their right to speak are devalued and lose dignity. Self-expression is what leads to self-realization and self-fulfillment. So where does that leave corporations?

Corporations have been held to have certain constitutional rights. They have been held to be "persons" for purposes of the Fifth Amendment's double jeopardy clause as well as the Fourteenth Amendment's equal protection and due process clauses. At the same time, however, corporations are not "citizens" within the privileges and immunities clause of the same amendment. Unlike the Fifth and Fourteenth Amendments, the First Amendment does not specify to whom the right belongs. It says simply that Congress shall not abridge the freedom of speech. The question then becomes, does the First Amendment protect the speech itself or the speaker's right to speak? If the latter, should corporations be granted the same protection under the First Amendment as individuals?

Scholars who take the position that freedom of expression is a personal right would not extend First Amendment rights to corporations because corporations are not persons; they are artificial entities created by law. In fact, a corporation cannot "speak" on its own; it can only, as one mass communication scholar notes, spend money for others to speak on its behalf (Kerr, 2010). Societal theorists, on the other hand, although concerned with democracy and political speech, would extend the protection of speech to corporations because their speech can help consumers make informed decisions in the marketplace. In their view, it is the speech itself rather than the speaker that is important.

The tension between the two perspectives – individual and societal – with respect to corporations can be clearly seen in the 1978 case, *First National Bank v. Bellotti* (1978), which was the first time the US Supreme Court specifically addressed the issue of corporate speech. First National had challenged a Massachusetts statute that prevented business corporations from spending money to affect the outcome of voter referenda unless the question before the voters concerned a corporation's property or its business. In finding in favor of First National, the Court stated that the lower court had asked the wrong question. "The proper question is not whether corporations 'have' First Amendment rights and, if so, whether they are coextensive with those of natural persons. Instead, the question must be whether [the statute] abridges expression that the First Amendment was meant to protect. We hold that it does" (p. 776). The Court here clearly was thinking of the societal value of speech.

Justice White, joined by Justices Brennan and Marshall, dissented strongly. "[W]hat some have considered to be the principal function of the First Amendment, the use of communication as a means of self-expression, self-realization, and self-fulfillment, is not at all furthered by corporate speech" (p. 804). While White acknowledged that some corporate speech deserved First Amendment protection on the basis that it was beneficial to consumers and employees, he was not willing to extend that protection to speech addressing a subject having no material effect on the corporation's business. His concern was that corporations, "which have been permitted to amass wealth as a result of special advantages extended by the State for certain economic purposes," would use "that wealth to acquire an unfair advantage in the political process" (p. 809).

The fear that corporate wealth will lead to undue influence during elections has led to a series of campaign finance laws. Overall, however, the Court has granted corporations First Amendment protection, although the common law has long protected them from the false speech of others.

Defamation

Defamation, which is also known as libel if the statement is written and slander if it is oral, is "the publication of a false and defamatory statement" regarding the plaintiff that harms the plaintiff's reputation (Langvardt, 1993, p. 7). In American law, two conceptions of reputation can be found: reputation as dignity and reputation as property (Post, 1986). With respect to the former understanding of the term, Justice Stewart perhaps described it best in his concurring opinion in *Rosenblatt v. Baer* (1966) when he said, "The right of man to the protection of his own reputation from unjustified invasion and wrongful hurt reflects no more than our basic concept of the essential dignity and worth of every human being" (p. 92). A corporation, of course, cannot experience emotions from a damaged reputation. "The business corporation has no personality, no dignity that can be assailed, no feelings that can be touched. Since it cannot suffer physical pain, worry or distress, it cannot lie awake nights brooding about a defamatory article" (Phelps and Hamilton, 1978, p. 80).

Although a corporation cannot "feel" pain when false statements are made about it, the common law does recognize that a corporation can be defamed and its reputation suffer as a result. Reputation in this sense is "a form of intangible property akin to goodwill" that exists in the marketplace and is earned over time (Post, 1986, p. 693). The definition of corporate reputation as "a collective representation of a firm's past actions and results that describes the firm's ability to deliver valued outcomes to multiple stakeholders" reflects the concept of reputation as property (Fombrun and van Riel, 1997, p. 10).

Whether individuals or corporations, plaintiffs in a defamation suit must prove six elements to be successful. First, the statement must be published, although widespread dissemination is not required. The statement merely has to be available to at least one other person. Plaintiffs must also show that the statement was about or concerning them and that others would recognize that it was. Third, plaintiffs must establish that the statement was defamatory; that is, it must hold the plaintiffs up to hatred, ridicule, and contempt; cause them to be shunned; or injure them in their business or trade. The statement must also be shown to be false. The law does not protect reputations from truthful allegations. And finally, plaintiffs have to establish fault and injury.

Fault and the First Amendment

The common law of defamation in the United States prior to 1964 reflected the belief that society had a "persuasive and strong interest in preventing and redressing attacks upon reputation" (*Rosenblatt v. Baer*, 1966, p. 86). Thus, once a plaintiff proved that the defamatory statement had been made, damages were presumed, and defendants, unless they could prove the statement was, in fact, true, were liable for those damages. But in the 1964 landmark case of *New York Times v. Sullivan* (1964), the US Supreme Court "constitutionalized" defamation, giving at least some libelous statements First Amendment protection.

The case arose from a full-page advertisement in the *Times* that criticized the conduct of Montgomery police in dealing with civil rights protestors. L.B. Sullivan, the public safety commissioner, sued, claiming his reputation had been damaged by the false allegations in the ad. The main defenses under the existing common law were truth and either conditional or qualified privilege. The *New York Times* could claim no such privileges in the case at hand, and the ad did in fact contain inaccuracies although the essence of the message was true. An Alabama jury found in favor of Sullivan and awarded him $500,000, which was upheld on appeal.

No doubt in part motivated by the tenor of the times, the US Supreme Court overruled the Alabama decision, declaring that there was a "profound national commitment" that public debate should be "uninhibited, robust, and wide-open" (p. 270). Some falsehoods were bound to arise, the Court held, in a full and free discussion of public issues. Public officials had to develop thick skins regarding statements related to their official conduct unless those statements were made with actual malice – "that is, with knowledge that it was false or with reckless disregard of whether it was false or not" (p. 280).

Over the next several years, the Court expanded the reach of its constitutional privilege to include defamations against public figures described as those who are "intimately involved in the resolution of important public questions or, by reason of their fame, shape events in areas of concern to society at large" (*Curtis Publishing Co. v. Butts*, 1967, p. 164). At its apex, in *Rosenbloom v. Metromedia* (1971), the Court extended the actual malice standard "to all discussion and communication involving matters of public or general concern" regardless of how public or private the plaintiff was.

Three years later, in *Gertz v. Robert Welch, Inc.* (1974), however, the Court backed away from the *Rosenbloom* public interest test, deciding instead to focus on the nature of the plaintiff rather than on the issue. The Court refined the concept of public figure into two categories: "all-purpose" and "limited." All-purpose public figures "occupy positions of such pervasive power and influence that they are deemed public figures for all purposes" (p. 345). Limited public figures, on the other hand, "have thrust themselves to the forefront of particular public controversies in order to influence the resolution of the issues involved" (p. 345). Such plaintiffs were only public figures to the extent that the defamatory statements related to that controversy. Otherwise, they were private figures. Public officials and public figures, whether all-purpose or limited, have to prove actual malice – knowledge of falsity – while private individuals have to prove a lesser standard of fault, usually negligence.

The Court's rationale for placing a heavier burden of proof on public figures was twofold. First, the Court said that public figures invite comment and scrutiny by virtue of their influential role in society. They not only expect attention, but in many cases they have also sought it out by their actions. That increased scrutiny leads to a greater chance of being defamed. Second, public figures have greater access to channels of communication through which to rebut false statements than do private individuals. Thus, the state has a greater interest in protecting the reputations of private individuals from defamation.

But what of corporations? What category of plaintiff do they fall into: public figure or private? Because the US Supreme Court has not addressed the status of corporate defamation plaintiffs, state and district courts vary in their approach. Some courts place great emphasis on the distinctions between corporations and individuals and the corresponding difference in their reputations (*Martin Marietta Corp. v. Evening Star Newspaper Co.*, 1976). These courts tend to find corporations to be public figures regardless of the situation, drawing on the *Rosenbloom* public interest test.

Other courts, however, take the position that *Gertz* is the standard to apply whether the plaintiff is a corporation or an individual. Although these courts are in agreement on the application of *Gertz*, they vary in the factors they use to determine whether a corporation is a public figure and thus carries the burden of proving actual malice or a private figure with a lesser burden of fault. Criticism of one's products has been considered a "public controversy" for the purposes of *Gertz* (*Bose Corp. v. Consumers Union*, 1982; *Steaks Unlimited, Inc. v. Deaner*, 1980) and other times not (*U.S. Healthcare v. Blue Cross of Greater Philadelphia*, 1990; *Vegod Corp. v. American Broadcasting Corp.*, 1979). Advertising campaigns are sometimes seen as evidence of access to channels of communication (*Steaks Unlimited, Inc. v. Deaner*, 1980; *Vegod Corp. v. American Broadcasting Corp.*, 1979), and the solicitation of product reviews as inviting public scrutiny (*Bose Corp. v. Consumers Union*, 1982).

In at least one case, a corporation has been found to be an all-purpose public figure, which requires, according to *Gertz v. Robert Welch, Inc.* (1974), "clear evidence of general fame or notoriety in the community, and pervasive involvement in the affairs of society" (p. 352). In *Reliance Insurance Co. v. Barron* (1977), the court held Reliance to be such a public figure because the company had corporate assets of more than $1 billion and at the time was making a public stock offering. Thus, the public had an interest in knowing about its business.

When dealing with a corporate client that has been defamed, it is probably best to work on the assumption that it will be found to be a public figure. It can be argued, of course, that one of the Court's rationales for the distinction between public and private figures, access to channels of communication, no longer applies. The Internet and social media have given everyone the ability to counter defamatory statements publicly. But the idea that public figures warrant greater scrutiny remains viable. Jackson (2001) has argued that "the corporation's inherent public character and power dictate that corporations be subject to a higher level of scrutiny as defamation plaintiffs" (p. 9). Others have noted that the increased focus by corporations on social responsibility has made the corporate form even more public (Fetzer, 1982).

Damages

Once a plaintiff successfully establishes the elements of defamation, the court turns to the question of damages. Individuals may be awarded general damages, an amount to compensate them for their pain and suffering; special damages, an amount based on financial loss as a result of the libel; and punitive damages, an amount to punish the defendant for its actions. In both Great Britain and Canada, neither of which have adopted the *New York Times v. Sullivan* (1964) actual malice standard, corporate plaintiffs typically receive nominal general damages unless they can show clear financial injury from the defamation, because "[a] company cannot be injured in its feelings, it can only be injured in its pocket. Its reputation can be injured by a libel but that injury must sound in money" (*Lewis v. Daily Telegraph*, 1964, p. 234). For example, in *Ho v. Ming Pao Newspapers (Western Canada) Ltd.* (2000), the corporation was awarded only $1000 in general damages although the court acknowledged that the result might have been different had the plaintiff been a natural person.

Recent decisions in Canada and Great Britain, however, suggest a trend toward granting corporate defamation plaintiffs more substantive general damages. In a 2007 Canadian case, the court awarded the plaintiffs a total of $250,000 in general damages (*WeGo Kayaking Ltd. v. Sewid*, 2007). Similarly, the House of Lords concluded, in *Jameel v. Wall Street Journal Europe SPRL* (2006), that "the good name of a company, as that of an individual, is a thing of value. A damaging libel may lower its standing in the eyes of the public and even its own staff, make people less ready to deal with it, less willing or less proud to work for it" (p. 10).

False Advertising

False advertising can impact a corporation's reputation in two ways. First, if consumers discover that an organization has been lying to them or at least misleading them through its advertising, those consumers will have a lower opinion of the organization. Second, competitors may mislead consumers about a corporation's business. Even if the corporation sues the competitor for false advertising, the damage may have already been done. In the United States, the FTC, the Lanham Act, state laws, and common law unfair competition laws all cover false advertising, but they vary in who can bring an action, the proof required, and the relief provided (Hines *et al.*, 2010).

Federal Trade Commission

The FTC protects consumers from "unfair or deceptive acts or practices" (Federal Trade Commission Act, 1995) on the part of businesses. Deception occurs when there is a material representation, omission, or practice that is likely to mislead a reasonable consumer. A material representation is a claim about the attributes of a product or service that would impact a consumer's purchase intention or behavior. Actual deception is not necessary; the issue for the FTC is the likelihood that the claim will mislead. And it must mislead a "reasonable consumer" within the specific target group. "A representation does not become 'false and deceptive' merely because it will be unreasonably misunderstood by an insignificant and unrepresentative segment of the class of persons to whom the representation is addressed" (*Heinz S. Kirchner*, 1963, p. 1290).

The FTC is particularly concerned about the use of endorsements and testimonials in advertisements because it believes they carry weight with consumers. The newest FTC guidelines on the topic require bloggers and other social media communicators to disclose any incentivized relationships they have with the advertisers before endorsing or reviewing products. Similarly, the European Commission has taken the position that undisclosed sponsorship is unfair to consumers even if the message conveyed is true (European Commission, 2009). As Tushnet (2010) has written, "Without some indication of the terms on which a 'user' is participating in a debate – as a fan, as a shill, or as some combination – audiences may lose trust in the medium, moving user reviews and blog posts from credible grassroots judgments to unbelievable 'astroturf'" (p. 12).

The Lanham Act

Section 43(a) of the federal Lanham Act, which is the common name for the Trademark Act of 1946, protects businesses from the deceptive practices of competitors. The deception can occur in two ways. First, a defendant can use, without consent, the plaintiff's trademark, essentially passing its own, typically inferior, products and services off as the plaintiff's. Claims under this part of Section 43(a) are for misrepresentations that are likely to cause confusion as to the origin, sponsorship, or approval of the goods or services by another person.

Second, a competitor can falsely or misleadingly represent the nature, character qualities, or origin of a plaintiff's goods, services, or business activities in an ad or promotion. Circuit courts have made it clear that the misrepresentations must be part of an overall strategic marketing plan and not just an isolated ad. In *Fashion Boutique of Short Hills, Inc. v. Fendi USA, Inc.* (2002), Fashion Boutique claimed that Fendi salespersons were telling consumers that the boutique sold fake merchandise. In dismissing the claim, the Second

Circuit held that the plaintiff had not established that the "contested representations are part of an organized campaign to penetrate the relevant markets. . . . [B]usinesses harmed by isolated disparaging statements do not have redress under the Lanham Act, but instead must seek redress under state law causes of action" (p. 56).

While actions under Section 43(a) are restricted to those arising from false statements made in commercial advertising or promotion, one advantage to using the section rather than suing for defamation is its strict liability approach. Once the plaintiff proves that customers were deceived and that they were harmed as a result, damages are presumed. In other words, the plaintiff does not have to prove "that the defendant knew of the contested statement's falsity, displayed reckless disregard for the truth, or failed to use reasonable care to ascertain the truth" (Langvardt, 1993, p. 5).

Privacy

Access to courts and information held by government agencies are two important areas of communication law because journalists cannot fulfill their role as watchdogs of government without such access. For corporations, the legal issue of access is really one of privacy. Corporate reputations are potentially vulnerable to the disclosure of financial and other proprietary records that have been filed with the courts pursuit to a civil lawsuit or with a governmental agency pursuant to that agency's regulations.

The Freedom of Information Act (FOIA), enacted in 1966, codifies the policy of disclosure of executive branch records, subject only to nine enumerated exemptions. The purpose of the act is to encourage the openness of government agencies as an acknowledgement of the public's right to know. At the same time, however, the exemptions signify the recognition that agencies may have possession of private and confidential information. To balance the two rights – the right to know and the right to privacy – the act places the burden on the governmental agency to establish that the records are covered by one of the nine exemptions; otherwise, the material must be disclosed to the requestor.

Although media outlets were the driving force behind the push to enact the legislation, corporations soon discovered that FOIA requests were a good way for them to gather information on their competitors. To thwart such access, the records must come within Exemption 4, which provides that "trade secrets and commercial or financial information obtained from a person and privileged or confidential" are exempt from disclosure.

Much of the case law on Exemption 4 concerns the question of what constitutes confidential commercial information. The current test was set out in 1976 by the D.C. Circuit Court in *National Parks & Conservation Association v. Kleppe* (1976). Under the test, information is "confidential" for the purposes of Exemption 4 if disclosure is likely to either "1) impair the government's ability to obtain necessary information in the future; or 2) cause substantial harm to the competitive position of the person from whom the information was obtained" (Radez, 2010, p. 646). The court in *National Parks* held that the agency need not prove competitive harm; the court would just use its judgment "in view of the nature of the material sought and competitive circumstances" of the business (p. 683). Courts tend to deny an exemption when the risk does not appear imminent or when it appears to be too speculative. In one case, the court rejected the argument that disclosure would lead to the public impression of financial instability.

Courts routinely reject the argument that disclosure of the information would harm a corporation's reputation, according to an analysis of 23 Exemption 4 cases (Radez, 2010). For example, the D.C. Circuit Court in 1987 held that the possibility of negative publicity and employee demoralization did not constitute sufficient competitive harm to prevent disclosure of affirmative-action data. But as Radez has argued, two cases filed as a result of the financial crisis of 2007 underscore the need for

the courts to reconsider the issue of reputational harm.

Bloomberg and the Fox News Network both brought suits within months of each other in 2008 against the Federal Reserve System (the Fed) after it refused to provide information about the Fed's expanded lending programs created to alleviate the financial crisis (*Bloomberg L.P. v. Bd. of Governors of the Fed. Reserve Sys.*, 2010; *Fox News Network v. Bd. of Governors of the Fed. Reserve Sys.*, 2010). The Fed took the position that the loan agreements, the identities of the parties to those agreements, and the collateral of the borrowers were confidential. It further argued that unless it "could guarantee the confidentiality of such loan agreements, its ability to act as a lender of last resort to increase liquidity and stabilize the financial markets would be impaired" (Radez, 2010, p. 7). In other words, the Fed's own reputation was at risk if the information was disclosed as well as the reputations of the corporations involved. For their part, Bloomberg and Fox argued that the threat of reputational harm was too speculative and did not fit within the *National Parks* test.

When the two cases came before the courts of first instance, the judges reached opposite conclusions. In *Fox*, Judge Hellerstein ruled in favor of the Fed, agreeing that borrowers would suffer "competitive and reputational harm" upon disclosure and that the disclosure would interfere with the agency's "effective execution of its statutory responsibilities." But Judge Preska in *Bloomberg* rejected the Fed's argument that reputational harm could amount to substantive competitive harm. On appeal, the Second Circuit Court of Appeals sidestepped the issue of reputation, deciding the cases without addressing it. As Radez (2010) noted, "The government's increasingly active role in the financial markets in response to the financial crisis presents unique challenges related to the security of financial institution records. Unfortunately, the Second Circuit's opinion leaves those records vulnerable when disclosure would trigger reputational, rather than more traditional, competitive harm" (p. 8).

Limitations and Future Directions

As indicated at the outset of this chapter, the focus in communication law is on the First Amendment and its relationship with journalists. With the growth of advertising and public relations curricula within journalism schools, topics such as advertising law and commercial speech have been added to media law courses. But there remains a gap in the literature on corporate reputation. Most of the work in this area involves campaign finance reform and the efforts to control the influence of corporations in the political process. But the concept of reputation itself remains unexplored for the most part. More studies need to be conducted on the effects of laws and regulations on corporate reputation and on how corporations can defend themselves and repair their reputations through free expression and the courts.

More work also needs to be done on defining terms. What is meant by "corporate reputation" in the legal and public relations disciplines? Are the definitions the same? Understanding, for example, how the law views corporate reputation will help us explain court decisions impacting corporate speech.

Currently, corporations walk a line between being treated as individuals for the purposes of the law and as public entities akin to a government agency. When essentially equated with an individual, corporations are allowed greater speech rights and privacy from intrusive examination. When equated with the public sector, corporations are given less leeway to respond to critics and are exposed to greater scrutiny. Increasingly, corporations are seen as public and as accountable to the public for their actions, which means legal means to redress critics will be curtailed. Transparency and honesty will be the keys to maintaining a corporate reputation in the future.

References

Bloomberg L.P. v. Bd. of Governors of the Fed. Reserve Sys., 649 F. Supp. 2d 262 (S.D.N.Y. 2009), aff'd, No. 08-4083-cv, No. 09-4097-cv (CON), 2010 WL 986527 (2nd Cir. March 19, 2010).

Bose Corp. v. Consumers Union, 692 F. 2d 189 (1st Cir. Mass. 1982).

Curtis Publishing Co. v. Butts, 388 US 130 (1967).

Edelman Trust Barometer (2012) Retrieved from http://trust.edelman.com/trust-download/executive-summary (last accessed October 10, 2012).

European Commission (2009) Guidance on the implementation/application of directive 2005/29/EC on unfair commercial practices. Retrieved from http://europa.eu/legislation_summaries/consumers/consumer_information/l32011_en.htm (last accessed October 12, 2012).

Fashion Boutique of Short Hills, Inc. v. Fendi USA, Inc., 134 F. 3d 48 (2nd Cir. 2002).

Federal Trade Commission Act. 15 U.S.C. §45 (West Supp. 1995).

Fetzer, P.N. (1982) The corporate defamation plaintiff as First Amendment "public figure": Nailing the jellyfish. *Iowa Law Review*, 68, 35.

First National Bank v. Bellotti, 435 US 765 (1978).

Fombrun, C. and van Riel, C. (1997) The reputational landscape. *Corporate Reputation Review*, 1, 6.

Fox News Network v. Bd. of Governors of the Fed. Reserve Sys., 639 F. Supp. 2d 384 (S.D.N.Y. 2008), vacated and remanded, No. 09-3795-cv, 2010 WL 986665 (2nd Cir. March 19, 2010).

Gertz v. Robert Welch, Inc., 418 US 323 (1974).

Heinz S. Kirchner, 63 F.T.C. 1282 (1963).

Hines, J.L., Kubow, J.D., Lenthall, E., and Berg, L. (March 8, 2010) Social media in action in commercial litigation. Retrieved from http://www.legalbytes.com/tags/lanham-act/#_ednref2 (last accessed September 14, 2012).

Ho v. Ming Pao Newspapers (Western Canada) Ltd., B.C.J. No. 7 (S.C.) (2000).

Jackson, D.M. (2001) The corporate defamation plaintiff in era of SLAPPs: Revisiting *New York Times v. Sullivan. William & Mary Bill of Rights Journal*, 9, 491.

Jameel v. Wall Street Journal Europe SPRL, UKHL 44 (2006).

Karpoff, J.M., Lee, D.S., and Martin, G.S. (2008) The cost to firms of cooking the books. *Journal of Finance & Quantitative Analysis*, 43, 581.

Kerr, R.L. (2010) Naturalizing the artificial citizen: Repeating Lochner's error in Citizens United v. Federal Election Commission. *Communication Law & Policy*, 15, 311–363.

Langvardt, A.W. (1993) Section 43(a), commercial falsehood, and the First Amendment: A proposed framework. *Minnesota Law Review*, *78*, 309.

Lewis v. Daily Telegraph, A.C. 235 (1964).

Martin Marietta Corp. v. Evening Star Newspaper Co., 417 F. Supp. 947 (D.D.C. 1976).

National Parks & Conservation Association v. Kleppe, 547 F. 2d 673 (D.C. Cir. 1976).

New York Times v. Sullivan, 376 US 254 (1964).

Phelps, R. and Hamilton, E. (1978) *Libel: Rights, Risks, Responsibilities* (2nd ed.). New York: Dover Publications.

Post, R.C. (1986) The social foundations of defamation law: Reputation and the constitution. *California Law Review*, *74*, 691.

Radez, K.V. (2010) The Freedom of Information Act Exemption 4: Protecting corporate reputation in the post-crash regulatory environment. *Columbia Business Law Review*, *2010*, 632.

Reliance Insurance Co. v. Barron, 442 F. Supp. 1341 (S.D.N.Y. 1977).

Rosenblatt v. Baer, 383 US 75 (1966).

Rosenbloom v. Metromedia, 403 US 29 (1971).

Steaks Unlimited, Inc. v. Deaner, 623 F. 2d 264 (3rd Cir. 1980).

Tushnet, R. (2010) Attention must be paid: Commercial speech, user-generated ads, and the challenge of reputation. *Buffalo Law Review*, *58*, 721.

U.S. Healthcare v. Blue Cross of Greater Philadelphia, 898 F. 2d 414 (1990).

Vegod Corp. v. American Broadcasting Corp., 25 Cal. 3d 763 (1979).

WeGo Kayaking Ltd. v. Sewid, B.C.J. No. 56 (S.C.) (2007).

Section 2

Theoretical Perspectives

15

Agenda-Building and Agenda-Setting Theory: Which Companies We Think About and How We Think About Them

Matthew W. Ragas

DePaul University, USA

The ubiquitous nature of the news media today often means that the media plays a consequential role in shaping both *which* companies the public think about (i.e., organizational prominence) and *how* the public thinks about these firms, in terms of their organizational esteem and organizational attributes. Guided by the mass communication theories of agenda building and agenda setting, a growing body of research indicates that corporate communication efforts and news media coverage influence the public's impressions of companies. Of course, these effects on corporate reputation are not universal or all-powerful, but rather are moderated by various contingent conditions. This chapter reviews the agenda-building and agenda-setting literature in this domain, specifically the linkages between the various dimensions of corporate reputation and media content; synthesizes these findings; and then outlines paths for future research.

Agenda-Building and Agenda-Setting Theory

Near the height of the financial crisis, as the US automotive industry stared into the abyss, Ford Motor Co. made a bold announcement: it would not burden American taxpayers by requesting federal bailout funding as part of its plan to regain profitability. Rivals General Motors (GM) and Chrysler, on the other hand, both requested and received government assistance. Sensing that this decision provided Ford with a comparative advantage over its rivals, the automaker significantly ramped up its media

relations efforts and advertising spending (LaReau, 2010), emphasizing a message of "accountability" and a commitment to "shared sacrifice during this difficult economic period" (Ford Motor Company, 2008, para. 16). Ford also highlighted its new product line of more fuel-efficient, environmentally friendly vehicles ("PR power list," 2009; Shah, 2009).

The taxpayer-funded bailout of Detroit quickly became a salient issue on the media agenda, with media coverage often highlighting Ford's decision to break from its peers and restructure its operations – without government intervention. Amidst a sea of negative media coverage surrounding the bailouts, Ford

The Handbook of Communication and Corporate Reputation, First Edition. Edited by Craig E. Carroll.
© 2013 John Wiley & Sons, Inc. Published 2015 by John Wiley & Sons, Inc.

was often portrayed in media reports as a company that was determined to stand on its own two feet ("Corporate branding," 2010; Shah, 2009). The results of the 2009 US Reputation Quotient (RQ) study, a leading annual survey of corporate reputation, suggest that Ford benefited significantly from its decision and the ensuing positive media attention. Ford's RQ score saw the biggest annual gain in the previous nine years of conducting the survey, checking in at #37 on the RQ rankings, while GM and Chrysler were stuck back farther in the pack at #54 and #55, respectively.

Fast forwarding a few years, the 2012 Harris RQ data tell a similar story. Ford has moved up to #25 on the RQ list, still well ahead of GM and Chrysler, which rank #44 and #50, respectively. With Ford continuing to emphasize its financial independence and commitment to innovation both directly and through the news media (Bruell, 2011; LaReau, 2010), the American public's perception of Ford has further improved, while perceptions of GM and Chrysler remain slow to change. This apparent linkage between the amount and type of media attention an organization receives and the organization's reputation does not come as a surprise to media effects researchers, particularly agenda-setting scholars.

Theoretical Foundation of Agenda Setting

"The pictures in our heads"

Inspired by Walter Lippmann's (1922) notion of the media influencing the "pictures in our heads" of "the world outside," scholars have spent the past four decades exploring the agenda-setting function of the news media and its role in the shaping of public opinion. In the initial agenda-setting study during the 1968 presidential election, McCombs and Shaw (1972) found a near-perfect rank-order correlation between the placement of public affairs issues on the media agenda, as measured by the amount of media attention each issue received, and the public agenda, as measured by the percentage of undecided voters that thought each issue was important. This initial study suggested that the public learned the relative importance of issues from the salience cues transmitted by the media.

The seminal Chapel Hill study (McCombs and Shaw, 1972) was followed by a series of more complex longitudinal field studies that sought to determine whether the media set the public agenda or vice versa. The accumulated field research over the years generally indicates that the flow of influence is most often from the media to the public (e.g., Behr and Iyengar, 1985; Funkhauser, 1973; Shaw and McCombs, 1977; Weaver *et al.*, 1981; Winter and Eyal, 1981). A series of controlled laboratory experiments conducted by Iyengar and Kinder (1987) corroborated these findings.

Now into its fourth decade, agenda-setting theory remains one of the most researched theories in the mass communication field, with over 400 empirical studies published around the world examining an increasingly diverse range of objects (issues, political candidates and elected officials, countries, brands, corporations, and the like) competing for attention on the media agenda and, in turn, influencing public perceptions of these objects (McCombs, 2006). While the agenda-setting perspective has expanded in breadth and scope over the years to encompass investigations into the origins of the media agenda, contingent conditions, attribute agenda setting, and the consequences of these processes, the core theoretical proposition has remained constant: *the transfer of salience from one agenda to another.*

First- and second-level effects

Cohen's (1963) classic dictum, "the media may not be successful much of the time in telling people what to think, but it is stunningly successful in telling its readers what to think about," (p. 13) is helpful in understanding what contemporary agenda-setting researchers have termed first- and second-level agenda-setting effects (McCombs *et al.*, 1997, 2000).

The first level is concerned with how the salience of objects in media messages influence "*what* we think about," while the second level is concerned with how the salience of attributes used in media messages to describe these objects shapes "*how* we think about" them.

At the second level of agenda setting, two classes of attributes that aid in the comprehension of media content are *substantive attributes* and *affective attributes* (McCombs *et al.*, 1997, 2000). Substantive attributes are the cognitive characteristics that journalists use to describe objects discussed in media content, while affective attributes refer to the tenor or tone used by journalists when describing these objects (Kiousis *et al.*, 2006, 2007).

The Mass Media and Corporate Reputation

A mediated experience

The public have several ways that they learn about a company. This includes potentially having a direct personal experience with the company as a stakeholder, whether that means being a customer, employee, investor, supplier, or a member of a community where the company has a large presence. An individual can also learn about a company through what family members, friends, or colleagues might have to say about the company. For a large segment of the public, though, what they learn about many companies is largely the result of a mediated experience. This includes forming impressions based on the information disseminated by information intermediaries, such as the news media, as well as through company-controlled advertising, public relations, and related communication efforts (Bromley, 2000; van Riel and Fombrun, 2007).

Given this backdrop, early corporate reputation scholarship (e.g., Fombrun and Shanley, 1990) identified the news media as a potential antecedent of corporate reputation. As explained by Fombrun (1996), "since few of us have direct access to companies' inner workings, we often rely on reporters and analysts who act as intermediaries. They screen, spin, and broker information for us; they help us make sense of companies' complex activities – and so affect company reputations" (p. 139). This being said, it was not until the past decade that systematic and sustained research programs focused specifically on the mass media's impact on reputation began in earnest (Carroll, 2011a; Carroll and McCombs, 2003). Agenda-setting theory has often served as the framework for guiding these investigations, and even when the theory has not been explicitly invoked, the concept of media salience has been implicit in research examining the linkage between presentations of firms in the mass media and corporate reputation.

Dimensions of reputation

In his doctoral dissertation Carroll (2004) first applied first and second level agenda-setting theory to various dimensions of corporate reputation, including companies' top-of-mind awareness, favorability and various reputational attributes. Firms' top-of-mind awareness has since been relabeled as *organizational prominence* (Carroll, 2010, 2011; Rindova, *et al.* 2005). Favorability, concerned with affect, has since been relabeled as firms' public esteem – the degree to which the public likes, trusts, admires, and respects an organization (Carroll, 2009, 2011).

Other empirical studies applied the agenda-setting concept to corporate reputation but using corporate reputation as a global variable. Fombrun and Shanley (1990) found a negative relationship between media attention and corporate reputation, yet Wartick (1992) found a positive relationship, but only for companies with "average" reputations – not those with "good" or "bad" reputations. Meijer and Kleinnijenhuis (2006) found a relationship for some organizations, but not for others, while Kiousis *et al.* (2007) found none at all. Carroll (2011b) explained these mixed findings by noting their use of reputation and media attention as global variables, rather than as multi-dimensional variables.

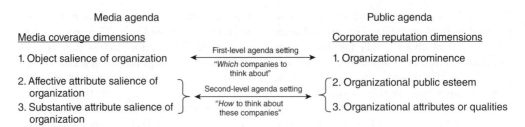

Figure 15.1 Media agenda-setting influences on corporate reputation.
Source: Adapted from Carroll (2011b).

The explication of media salience and corporate reputation in terms of individual dimensions, and then matching the appropriate dimensions of media salience to reputation, becomes important for seeing agenda-setting's explanatory power in shaping corporate reputation. Carroll (2011a) outlines the expected relationships between the dimensions of media coverage and the dimensions of reputation regarding "which companies to think about" (first-level agenda setting) and "how to think about those companies" (second-level agenda setting). See Figure 15.1.

An international team examined the following propositions result from this explication:

1 *Organizational prominence (first-level agenda setting).* There will be a positive relationship between the salience of organizations in media coverage and the level of organizational prominence among the public.

2 *Organizational public esteem (second-level affective agenda setting).* There will be a positive relationship between the salience of affective attributes of organizations (i.e., media favorability) in media coverage and the level of organizational public esteem.

3 *Organizational qualities or attributes (second-level substantive agenda setting).* There will be a positive relationship between the salience of substantive attributes of organizations (i.e., firm attributes or issues) in media coverage and the perceived salience of these organizational attributes in public opinion.

First-level agenda setting

A company must achieve some degree of visibility for the public to "think about" the firm and form an overall impression of it (Fombrun and van Riel, 2004). Research by Carroll (2004, 2010; replicated internationally (Carroll, 2011)) provides compelling evidence that the volume of news reports about a company impacts its level of top-of-mind awareness among the public. Using the 2000 US Harris RQ data, Carroll (2004, 2010) found that the more visibility RQ-ranked firms received in *The New York Times*, the greater the firms' subsequent level of organizational prominence, even after controlling for the effects of firm-issued news releases and the firms' prior level of prominence. Solid support for similar linkages between the amount of media attention directed toward a firm and its prominence have been found in a range of international settings as well, including Denmark (Kjaer and Morsing, 2011), Finland (Luoma-Aho et al., 2011), Norway (Ihlen and Brønn, 2011), Spain (Arrese and Baigorri, 2011), and Korea (Cha and Yang, 2011).

Of course, not all companies wish to maximize the amount of media attention they receive and may instead already be satisfied with the level of prominence they have achieved, particularly in the case of large firms. As argued by Fombrun and van Riel (2004), "Visibility is a two edged sword: on the one hand, it can be leveraged to achieve enhanced reputation. . . . On the other hand, visibility can have enduring negative effects on reputation" (p.

88). Indeed, public relations firms are tasked at times with trying to *minimize* the amount of attention an organization receives (Kiousis and Wu, 2008). Regardless of the strategic decision a company may make to try and raise or lower its media profile, this research indicates that, at its most basic level, the sheer volume of coverage about a firm often increases its level of prominence.

Second-level affective agenda setting

Shifting to reputation research exploring the second level of agenda setting, research indicates that the extent of favorable media tenor toward a company (Carroll, 2009, 2011d; Dalpiaz and Ravasi, 2011) is positively associated with the firm's level of public esteem, an affective dimension of reputation. Using the 2000 US Harris RQ poll paired with a content analysis of coverage in *The New York Times*, Carroll (2009) found that the level of media favorability toward RQ-ranked firms was significantly associated with the firms' level of public esteem, as measured using the three-item emotional appeal dimension of the RQ instrument (Fombrun *et al.*, 2000). An investigation by Dalpiaz and Ravasi (2011) of highly visible Italian companies, based on a content analysis of Italian print media coverage juxtaposed with the 2002 Harris RQ survey data, using the same measure of emotional appeal (Carroll, 2011a), revealed that media favorability was a significant predictor of organizational public esteem. Carroll (2009) unpacked media favorability into two dimensions. A firm's focal media favorability refers to the overall evaluation of a firm presented in a stream of media stories. A firm's peripheral media favorability refers to the overall evaluative tone accumulating from a stream of media stories where a firm is mentioned, yet is independent of how the focal firm is portrayed relative to the content. He found that firms' focal media favorability was correlated with their public esteem for respondents with more knowledge of the firms' attributes. Firms' peripheral media favorability correlated with public esteem for respondents having little to no knowledge about the firms' attributes.

Second-level substantive agenda setting

The news media provide varying levels of attention to various organizational attributes or qualities, such as company products and services, vision and leadership, workplace environment, financial performance, and social responsibility (Carroll and McCombs, 2003). Some cognitive attributes of a company are frequently highlighted in media coverage of the firm, some attributes receive modest attention, and other attributes may be ignored almost entirely in reporting about companies. The accumulating research (Carroll, 2004; Meijer, 2005; Meijer and Kleinnijenhuis, 2006) suggests that the salience of substantive company attributes in the news is modestly linked with the attributes that stakeholders perceive as most important and associate cognitively with companies when forming impressions of them.

As part of his analysis of the 2000 US RQ data, Carroll (2004) found that there was a correspondence between the amount of attention *The New York Times* dedicated to the attributes of "executive performance" and "workplace environment" for the RQ companies and the usage of these attributes by respondents for assessing firms' reputations. However, other attributes (financial performance, products and services, social responsibility) were *not* positively associated. An investigation using the 2005 US RQ data linked with content analyses of coverage in *The New York Times* and *The Wall Street Journal* found only minimal associations between company substantive attribute salience in media coverage and respondents' perceptions (Kiousis *et al.*, 2007).

Stronger support for second-level substantive agenda setting is provided by a study of issue news and reputation among large Dutch firms (Meijer and Kleinnijenhuis, 2006). This multiyear content analysis of media coverage in the Netherlands along with a panel survey of the public found that the amount of news about a certain organizational issue influenced the perceived salience of that issue (in regard to the issue's association with a specific organization) among the public. For example, the more Royal Dutch Shell was in the news in relation to the issue of the environment, the more the public associated Shell with the environment. Organizational issues are essentially treated as organizational attributes in this creative conceptualization of second-level substantive agenda setting in a corporate context.

Using issue ownership theory (Petrocik, 1996; Petrocik *et al.*, 2003), which finds that political parties have certain issues that they "own" and are judged more favorably on, Meijer and Kleinnijenhuis (2006) received support for this perspective in regard to corporate reputation. Respondents who associated an organization with an "owned" issue assigned a higher reputation score to the organization than those who associated the organization with a "not owned" issue. For example, the environment is an issue for which energy companies, such as Shell, are generally viewed unfavorably on; so an increase in media coverage on the environment – and if the public cognitively associates that issue with Shell – would lead to a lower reputation. These findings can also be thought of as evidence of "attribute priming" (Kim and McCombs, 2007; Kim *et al.*, 2002), in which the patterns of coverage help "prime" the attributes that individuals use to assess objects in the public eye. Then, using need for orientation Einwiller *et al.* (2010) found that the news media mattered more for determining firms' reputations when audiences depended upon the news media for information on attributes like *innovation* or *CSR* that are difficult for audience members to personally observe.

Building the Media Agenda

Agenda building and information subsidies

Since the mass media often set the public agenda or at least shape aspects of it, including influencing public opinion toward corporations, the next logical question then becomes, "who sets the media agenda?" (Gandy, 1982).

Agenda-setting research that specifically focuses on how the interactions between sources and journalists "build the media agenda" is known as agenda building (Turk, 1985; Turk and Franklin, 1987). News values dictate that journalists seek out official and authoritative sources that provide them with newsworthy information (Carroll, 2011e; Iyengar and McGrady, 2007). As powerful actors in society, corporations often fit these parameters and frequently serve in this role. While the relationship between the news media and business is strained at times, they both have what the other wants. Corporations have a stockpile of a commodity (newsworthy information) that the media often needs, while these same firms often seek the reach and legitimization that earned media coverage can provide (Carroll and McCombs, 2003; Carroll, 2010).

Crucial to the explication of agenda building is information subsidies, which are prepackaged, source-provided materials, such as news releases, speeches, and interviews, which attempt to increase the consumption of the source agenda by reducing journalists' cost, time, and complexity of news gathering (Berkowitz and Adams, 1990). Corporations invest tens of millions of dollars each year producing and disseminating information subsidies as part of media strategies designed to earn coverage, and in turn, influence public opinion. While the news media does not simply march dutifully to the drumbeat of corporations, the growing stream of corporate agenda-building research demonstrates that firms' efforts generally have a meaningful impact on the media coverage associated with them (e.g., Ohl *et al.*, 1995; Ragas, 2010; Ragas and Roberts, 2009; Ragas *et al.*, 2011).

Starting with first-level agenda-building evidence, based on the 2005 US RQ data, Kiousis *et al.* (2007) found that the use of wire-issued corporate news releases stimulated the amount of news stories written about these firms. Agenda-building (working through the news media) has also been examined for its impact on public prominence. Carroll examined whether corporate public agenda setting or corporate agenda building exerted a stronger influence. After controlling for the effects of firms' advertising expenditures and existing levels of prominence, results showed that in the absence of media salience, firms' corporate public agenda-setting efforts had no influence on their change in prominence. In the presence of media salience, however, firms' public agenda-setting efforts had a negative influence on their change in prominence. Turning to second-level agenda-building evidence, the same aforementioned Kiousis *et al.* (2007) study found modest evidence that the content of firms' releases and media coverage were generally associated regarding substantive and affective attribute salience, suggesting a deeper level of corporate influence on media content. Research into brand agenda setting found a similar transfer of attribute salience between a firm's brand communication efforts and customer perceptions of the brand (Ragas and Roberts, 2009).

Moving on to corporate issues, companies have also been found to successfully build coverage during mergers and acquisitions and proxy contests, two events in which firms serve as the primary source of information. Regional and national newspapers during a hostile takeover battle were found to adopt the key message points and general tone provided in the two dueling firms' news releases (Ohl *et al.*, 1995). Research into communication during proxy contests found agenda-building associations among the issues emphasized in company news releases and in elite business media coverage of the contests (Ragas, 2010; Ragas *et al.*, 2011). Cross-lag correlation analyses indicate that there was often reciprocal influence between the agendas of the companies and media during the contests, suggesting a give-and-take relationship. Einwiller *et al.* (2010) found strong support in the context of corporate social responsibility.

Congruence of company words and deeds

While companies that devote more resources to corporate communication activities, such as media relations, tend to have better reputations

(Hutton *et al.*, 2001; Kim, 2001), a firm's projected image should be congruent with its underlying actions and behaviors. To revisit the example provided by Ford Motor in the introduction, the automaker's increase in positive media coverage, and subsequent boost in public perception, was not simply a result of the firm ramping up its public relations and advertising, but rather that it was communicating a compelling message grounded in real firm policies – the refusal to take bailout dollars and a commitment to more fuel-efficient, environmentally friendly automobiles. On the other hand, while BP plc cultivated the image of an environmentally responsible corporate citizen, this was ultimately undermined by its Gulf oil spill performance (Rudolf, 2010).

The Arthur W. Page Society, an organization comprised of senior communication executives, states the following as a guiding principle: "prove it with action. Public perception of an organization is determined 90 percent by what it does and 10 percent by what it says" (Arthur W. Page Society, 2011, para. 3). The exact ratio of communication-to-action is debatable, but the point is clear – corporate communication efforts that are grounded in company policies and decisions do the most to enhance reputations (Fombrun, 1996; Fombrun and Shanley, 1990; Fombrun and van Riel, 2004). When company words and deeds become disjointed, a firm is particularly at risk of suffering a reputational decline. This sentiment is echoed by Deephouse (2000), who noted that news stories often include reports of firm actions; therefore, public relations "should have a foundation in actual actions throughout the firm" (p. 1108).

Contingent Conditions of Agenda Setting

The general public and an organization's stakeholders are certainly not automatons waiting to be programmed by the mass media, nor are the effects of the media agenda on the public uniform (McCombs, 2006). Rather, the media has a stronger impact on reputations under some conditions more than others. Research into the moderator variables that help explain the magnitude of agenda-setting effects is known as the contingent conditions of agenda setting (McCombs, 2005, 2006). Generally, these contingent conditions fall under two categories – media characteristics and audience characteristics (Winter, 1981).

Media and audience characteristics

Starting with media characteristics, research shows that not all media outlets are created equal in terms of agenda setting. Elite, national media outlets, such as *The New York Times*, have repeatedly been shown to drive the overall media agenda and have the greatest influence on public opinion (Danielian and Reese, 1989; Golan, 2006; Reese and Danielian, 1994). *The Wall Street Journal* (Ragas, 2010; Ragas *et al.*, 2011) has also been shown to play a lead role in shaping public opinion of corporations and business topics. The prominence of a story (Behr and Iyengar, 1985; Iyengar and Kinder, 1987), such as the lead of a television broadcast or the front page or section of a newspaper (Kiousis, 2004), has also been shown to strengthen agenda-setting effects. The characteristics of a country's media system also enhance or inhibit agenda setting. Effects are strongest in countries in which media penetration rates are fairly high and the public perceives the media as being a credible and independent source (Carroll, 2011d).

Turning to audience characteristics, the impact of the news on reputation has been found to be most pronounced for company attributes that individuals deem relevant and important, and for which they are likely unable to experience directly (Einwiller *et al.*, 2010). The perspectives of need for orientation (Weaver, 1977, 1980) and media system dependency (Ball-Rokeach, 1985) suggest that stakeholders are most likely to attend to the media, and in turn have their opinion shaped by it, when they seek orientation on a company attribute or issue and are largely dependent on the media for information on that attribute or issue. For example, Einwiller *et al.* (2010) found that the respondents' perceptions of an organization's social and environmental responsibility was shaped by media coverage. This is an attribute the respondents stated was important, but which they could largely learn about only through the media. Other audience characteristics identified as moderators include issue obtrusiveness/unobtrusiveness (Zucker, 1978) and interpersonal communication (Lasorsa and Wanta, 1990; Wanta and Wu, 1992).

Firm and source characteristics

Contingent conditions have also been identified, which help explain why some companies are more successful than others at building the media agenda. In addition to taking steps to bolster the newsworthiness of information subsidies (Carroll, 2011e), the accessibility and responsiveness of a company to media requests has also been found to enhance coverage (Ohl *et al.*, 1995). The demographic characteristics of a company may also enhance or diminish its agenda-building effects. For example, larger companies, as measured by size, revenue, or profits, are likely to receive more media attention than smaller companies (Ragas, 2010), given that news values gravitate toward covering stories with the widest audience impact (Becker and Vlad, 2009). On a related note, with elite news personnel often clustered in large cities and more likely to cover events that are close at hand rather than distant (Molotoch and Lester, 1974), companies headquartered or with sizable operations in large cities are at a potential advantage.

The perceived favorability, credibility, and reputation of organizational spokespeople can also impact an organization's efforts to manage their reputation through the news media. Political agenda-setting research finds that the president's approval rating moderates the influence that White House communication efforts have on the media (Blood and Phillips, 1997) and public opinion (Wanta, 1991). These effects are stronger when presidential approval is higher. Applying these findings to the corporate sphere, a CEO is often the most public face of a company and is frequently in the media spotlight (Park and Berger, 2004). Therefore, a spokesperson, such as a CEO, with high credibility may enjoy more success in shaping the media agenda (Fombrun and van Riel, 2004).

Paths for Future Research

In addition to devoting more research to the contingent conditions of agenda building and agenda setting on reputation, the following paths for future research are offered:

- *More diversity in media sources and types.* Most research to date has focused on the influence of coverage in elite national newspapers and broadcast news on reputation. Much less attention has been paid to the newswires, such as the AP, Reuters, Dow Jones News, and Bloomberg News, even though they are major providers of business news, with their content syndicated to thousands of outlets and increasingly accessible directly via the Web (Ragas, 2010; Weaver and Bimber, 2008). The effects of Web-only media outlets, including top blogs and trade publications, should also be investigated, particularly how these specialized sources may influence specific stakeholder groups.
- *Unbundling stakeholder opinion.* Perceptions of corporate reputation may vary by stakeholder group (Wartick, 1992). While the reputation construct has been unbundled into various dimensions, it has often been measured in only two ways – based on the collective opinion of the general public or of financial publics (i.e., executives, investors, analysts). Much less is known about how the media shapes perceptions among additional stakeholder groups, such as customers, employees, suppliers, and policy makers (Freeman, 1984).
- *Relative influence of mass media.* An open question is whether firm-provided information or news media-provided information has a greater influence on reputation. While the initial evidence suggests that reputation

is more credibly built by working through the media rather than with company advertising (Carroll, 2004; Fombrun and Shanley, 1990; Fombrun and van Riel, 2004) or wire-issued news releases (Carroll, 2010) direct to the public, this question needs to be explored more fully given the low-cost and wide reach provided by social media.

- *Social media and active publics.* The "rumor mill" (Fombrun, 1996) has long been acknowledged as a source of information about companies that can have reputational consequences. Active, vocal publics share their opinions about companies and corporate issues through social media, such as online forums, blogs, Twitter, Facebook, and at the end of online articles (Kim *et al.*, 2011). Corporations spend millions of dollars each year on social media monitoring programs, tracking, responding, and adapting firm policies based on what is being said through social media. Journalists follow these conversations and even use these vocal publics as sources. Given this backdrop, what influence may this modern rumor mill have on reputation?
- *Controlling for "the world outside".* Whenever possible, future research should continue to control for the effect of "the world outside" on reputation so that media effects are not inadvertently overstated (Behr and Iyengar, 1985). As demonstrated by the seminal work of Fombrun and Shanley (1990), while intermediaries such as the media shape the "pictures in our heads" of companies, so does direct or indirect exposure to real-world indicators such as financial performance, market valuation, charitable giving, corporate communication spending, and other objective indicators.

Conclusion

In sum, the ubiquitous nature of the mass media today often means that the media plays a consequential role in shaping both *which* companies the public think about (i.e., organizational prominence) and *how* the public thinks about these firms, in terms of their organizational esteem and organizational attributes (Carroll and McCombs, 2003). Of course, the agenda-setting effect of media coverage on reputation is not universal or all-powerful, but rather varies in strength and duration relative to other forces depending on the presence of various contingent conditions, such as organization, media, and audience characteristics. The media plays a particularly important role in shaping perceptions of companies and corporate issues when individuals have a need for orientation and the media serve as the principal source of information (Einwiller *et al.*, 2010).

Corporate agenda-building research demonstrates that, through public relations efforts, companies can help establish, grow, and protect their reputation in the media, and by extension, among the public and their stakeholders. In a time of shrinking newsrooms and reporting budgets, a case can be made that firms have more opportunities than ever to use information subsidies to shape how they are portrayed in the media. However, there are obvious limits to these efforts if company words and deeds are not aligned. At the end of the day, while the media presents a socially constructed reality, rather than a mirror reflection of the real world, there are aspects of reality at the core of the news. Business news is often grounded at least in part in company actions and policies – *what firms do* (or are failing to do), besides *what they say*.

Agenda-setting theory has proven to be a fruitful perspective for stimulating research into the media's role in public opinion formation for four decades. There is still much to learn about the media's effect on corporate reputation, but this growing line of inquiry is off to a running start. It is hoped that this chapter provides a useful synthesis and framework for advancing knowledge of the forces influencing, and being influenced by, reputation in the years ahead.

References

Arrese, A. and Baigorri, M. (2011) Corporate reputation and the news media in Spain. In C.E. Carroll (ed.), *Corporate Reputation and the News Media:* *Agenda-Setting within Business News Coverage in Developed, Emerging, and Frontier Markets.* New York: Routledge, pp. 168–191.

Arthur W. Page Society (2011) The Page principles. Retrieved from http://www.awpagesociety.com/about/the-page-principles/ (last accessed October 10, 2012).

Ball-Rokeach, S.J. (1985) The origins of individual media system dependency: A sociological framework. *Communication Research*, *12*(4), 485–510.

Becker, L.B. and Vlad, T. (2009) News organization and routines. In K. Wahl-Jorgensen and T. Hanitzsch (eds), *The Handbook of Journalism Studies.* New York: Routledge, pp. 59–72.

Behr, R.L. and Iyengar, S. (1985) Television news, real-world cues, and changes in the public agenda. *Public Opinion Quarterly*, *49*(1), 38–57.

Berkowitz, D. and Adams, D.B. (1990) Information subsidy and agenda-building in local television news. *Journalism Quarterly*, *67*(4), 723–731.

Blood, D.J. and Phillips, P.C.B. (1997) Economic headlines news on the agenda: New approaches to understanding causes and effects. In M. McCombs, D.L. Shaw, and D. Weaver (eds), *Communication and Democracy: Exploring the Intellectual Frontiers in Agenda-Setting Theory.* Mahwah, NJ: Erlbaum, pp. 97–114.

Bromley, D.B. (2000) Psychological aspects of corporate identity, image, and reputation. *Corporate Reputation Review*, *3*(3), 240–252.

Bruell, A. (2011) Automakers take a different route to highlight innovation. *PRWeek*, *14*(4), April, p. 14.

Carroll, C.E. (2004) How the mass media influence perceptions of corporate reputation: Exploring agenda-setting effects within business news coverage. Unpublished doctoral dissertation, University of Texas, Austin, TX.

Carroll, C.E. (2009) The relationship between firms' media favorability and public esteem. *Public Relations Journal*, *3*(4), 1–32.

Carroll, C.E. (2010) Should firms circumvent or work through the news media? *Public Relations Review*, *36*(3), 278–280.

Carroll, C.E. (2011a) *Corporate reputation and the news media: Agenda setting within business news in developed, emerging, and frontier markets.* New York: Routledge.

Carroll, C.E. (2011b) International Perspectives on Agenda Setting Theory Applied to Business News. In C.E. Carroll (Ed.), *Corporate reputation and the news media: Agenda setting within business news in developed, emerging, and frontier markets* (pp. 3–14). New York: Routledge.

Carroll, C.E. (2011c) Corporate reputation and the news media in the United States. In C.E. Carroll (ed.), *Corporate Reputation and the News Media: Agenda-Setting within Business News Coverage in Developed, Emerging, and Frontier Markets.* New York: Routledge, pp. 221–239.

Carroll, C.E. (2011d) The State of Agenda-Setting Research on Corporate Reputation and the News Media around the Globe: Conclusions, Cautions, and Contingent Conditions. In C.E. Carroll (Ed.), *Corporate reputation and the news media: Agenda setting within business news in developed, emerging, and frontier markets* (pp. 423–441). New York: Routledge.

Carroll, C.E. (2011e) The role of the news media in corporate reputation management. In R.J. Burke, G. Martin, and C.L. Cooper (eds), *Corporate Reputation: Managing Threats and Opportunities.* Surrey, UK: Gower, pp. 199–216.

Carroll, C.E. and McCombs, M. (2003) Agenda-setting effects of business news on the public's images and opinions about major corporations. *Corporate Reputation Review,* 6(1), 36–46.

Cha, H. and Yang, S. (2011) Corporate reputation and the news media in South Korea. In C.E. Carroll (ed.), *Corporate Reputation and the News Media: Agenda-Setting within Business News Coverage in Developed, Emerging, and Frontier Markets.* New York: Routledge, pp. 340–262.

Cohen, B. (1963) *The Press and Foreign Policy.* Princeton, NJ: Princeton University Press.

Corporate branding campaign of the year (2010) *PRWeek,* April, p. 25.

Dalpiaz, E. and Ravasi, D. (2011) Corporate reputation and the news media in Italy. In C.E. Carroll (ed.), *Corporate Reputation and the News Media: Agenda-Setting within Business News Coverage in Developed, Emerging, and Frontier Markets.* New York: Routledge, pp. 105–128.

Danielian, L. and Reese, S. (1989) A closer look at intermedia influences on agenda-setting: The cocaine issue of 1986. In P. Shoemaker (ed.), *Communication Campaigns about Drugs: Government, Media and the Public.* Hillsdale, NJ: Erlbaum, pp. 47–66.

Deephouse, D.L. (2000) Media reputation as a strategic resource: An integration of mass communication and resource based theories. *Journal of Management,* 26(6), 1091–1112.

Einwiller, S.A., Carroll, C.E., and Korn, K. (2010) Under what conditions do the news media influ-

ence corporate reputation? The roles of media dependency and need for orientation. *Corporate Reputation Review,* 12(4), 299–315.

Fombrun, C.J. (1996) *Reputation: Realizing Value from the Corporate Image.* Boston: Harvard Business School Press.

Fombrun, C.J., Gardberg, N.A., and Sever, J.M. (2000) The Reputation Quotient[sm]: A multi-stakeholder measure of corporate reputation. *Journal of Brand Management,* 7(4), 241–255.

Fombrun, C.J. and Shanley, M. (1990) What's in a name? Reputation building and corporate strategy. *Academy of Management Journal,* 33(2), 233–258.

Fombrun, C.J. and van Riel, C.B.M. (2004) *Fame & Fortune: How Successful Companies Build Winning Reputations.* Upper Saddle River, NJ: FT Prentice Hall.

Ford Motor Company (2008) Ford Motor Company submits business plan to Congress; profit target, electric car strategy among new details [Press release]. Retrieved from http://media.ford.com/article_print.cfm?article_id=29505 (last accessed September 17, 2012).

Freeman, R.E. (1984) A stakeholder theory of the modern corporation. In R.E. Freeman (ed.), *Stakeholder Theory and Organizational Ethics.* Boston: Pitman, pp. 38–48.

Funkhauser, G.R. (1973) The issues of the sixties: An exploratory study in the dynamics of public opinion. *Public Opinion Quarterly,* 37(1), 62–75.

Gandy, O.H. (1982) *Beyond Agenda Setting: Information Subsidies and Public Policy.* Norwood, NJ: Ablex.

Golan, G. (2006) Inter-media agenda setting and global news coverage: Assessing the influence of the New York Times on three television evening news programs. *Journalism Studies,* 7(2), 323–334.

Hutton, J.G., Goodman, M.B., Alexander, J.B., and Genest, C.M. (2001) Reputation management: The new face of corporate public relations? *Public Relations Review,* 27(3), 247–261.

Ihlen, Ø. and Brønn, P.S. (2011) Corporate reputation and the news media in Norway. In C.E. Carroll (ed.), *Corporate Reputation and the News Media: Agenda-Setting within Business News Coverage in Developed, Emerging, and Frontier Markets.* New York: Routledge, pp. 153–167.

Iyengar, S. and Kinder, D.R. (1987) *News That Matters: Television and American Opinion.* Chicago, IL: University of Chicago Press.

Iyengar, S. and McGrady, J.A. (2007) *Media Politics: A Citizen's Guide*. New York: Norton.

Kim, J.Y., Kiousis, S.K., and Xiang, Z. (2011) Agenda-building and agenda-setting in business: Effects of public relations on media and customers' online opinion. Paper presented at the Annual Meeting of the International Communication Association, Boston, May.

Kim, K. and McCombs, M.E. (2007) News story descriptions and the public's opinions of political candidates. *Journalism & Mass Communication Quarterly*, *77*(2), 273–291.

Kim, S.H., Scheufele, D.A., and Shanahan, J. (2002) Think about it this way: Attribute agenda-setting function of the press and the public's evaluation of a local issue. *Journalism & Mass Communication Quarterly*, *79*(1), 7–25.

Kim, Y. (2001) Measuring the economic value of public relations. *Journal of Public Relations Research*, *13*(1), 3–26.

Kiousis, S. (2004) Explicating media salience: A factor analysis of New York Times issue coverage during the 2000 U.S. presidential election. *Journal of Communication*, *54*(1), 71–87.

Kiousis, S. and Wu, X. (2008) International agenda-building and agenda-setting: Exploring the influence of public relations counsel on US news media and public perceptions of foreign nations. *International Communication Gazette*, *70*(1), 58–75.

Kiousis, S., Mitrook, M., Wu, X., and Seltzer, T. (2006) First- and second-level agenda-building and agenda-setting effects: Exploring the linkages among candidate news releases, media coverage, and public opinion during the 2002 Florida gubernatorial election. *Journal of Public Relations Research*, *18*(3), 265–285.

Kiousis, S., Popescu, C., and Mitrook, M. (2007) Understanding influence on corporate reputation: An examination of public relations efforts, media coverage, public opinion, and financial performance from an agenda-building and agenda-setting perspective. *Journal of Public Relations Research*, *19*(2), 147–165.

Kjaer, P. and Morsing, M. (2011) Corporate reputation and the news media in Denmark. In C.E. Carroll (ed.), *Corporate Reputation and the News Media: Agenda-Setting within Business News Coverage in Developed, Emerging, and Frontier Markets*. New York: Routledge, pp. 17–35.

LaReau, J. (2010) Dealer ads polish Ford image. *Automotive News*, *84*(6397), February 1, 8, 25.

Lasorsa, D.L. and Wanta, W. (1990) Effects of personal, interpersonal and media experiences on issue saliences. *Journalism Quarterly*, *67*(4), 804–813.

Lippmann, W. (1922) *Public Opinion*. New York: MacMillan.

Luoma-Aho, V., Uskali, T., Heinonen, J., and Ainamo, A. (2011) Corporate reputation and the news media in Finland. In C.E. Carroll (ed.), *Corporate Reputation and the News Media: Agenda-Setting within Business News Coverage in Developed, Emerging, and Frontier Markets*. New York: Routledge, pp. 36–61.

McCombs, M. (2005) A look at agenda-setting: Past, present and future. *Journalism Studies*, *6*(4), 543–557.

McCombs, M. (2006) *Setting the Agenda: The Mass Media and Public Opinion*. Malden, MA: Polity Press.

McCombs, M., Llamas, J.P., Lopez-Escobar, E., and Rey, F. (1997) Candidate images in Spanish elections: Second-level agenda-setting effects. *Journalism & Mass Communication Quarterly*, *74*(4), 703–717.

McCombs, M., Lopez-Escobar, E., and Llamas, J.P. (2000) Setting the agenda of attributes in the 1996 Spanish general election. *Journal of Communication*, *50*(2), 77–93.

McCombs, M.E. and Shaw, D.L. (1972) The agenda-setting function of mass media. *Public Opinion Quarterly*, *36*(2), 176–187.

Meijer, M. (2005) *Does Success Breed Success? Effects of News and Advertising on Corporate Reputation*. Amsterdam: Aksant.

Meijer, M. and Kleinnijenhuis, J. (2006) News and corporate reputation: Empirical findings from the Netherlands. *Public Relations Review*, *32*(4), 341–348.

Molotoch, H. and Lester, M. (1974) News as purpose behavior: On the strategic use of routine events, accidents, and scandals. *American Sociological Review*, *39*(1), 101–112.

Ohl, C.M., Pincus, J.D., Rimmer, T., and Harrison, D. (1995) Agenda-building role of news releases in corporate takeovers. *Public Relations Review*, *21*(2), 89–101.

Park, D. and Berger, B.K. (2004) The presentation of CEOs in the press, 1990–2000: Increasing salience, positive valence, and a focus on competency and personal dimensions of image. *Journal of Public Relations Research*, *16*(1), 93–125.

Petrocik, J.R. (1996) Issue ownership in presidential elections, with a 1980 case study. *American Journal of Political Science*, *40*, 825–850.

Petrocik, J.R., Benoit, W.L., and Hansen, G.J. (2003) Issue ownership and presidential campaigning, 1952–2000. *Political Science Quarterly, 118*, 599–626.

PR power list (2009) *PRWeek*, June, pp. 26–34.

Ragas, M.W. (2010) Agenda-building and agenda-setting in corporate proxy contests: Exploring influence among public relations efforts, financial media coverage and investor opinion. Unpublished doctoral dissertation, University of Florida.

Ragas, M.W. and Roberts, M.S. (2009) Agenda setting and agenda melding in an age of horizontal and vertical media: A new theoretical lens for virtual brand communities. *Journalism & Mass Communication Quarterly, 86*(1), 45–64.

Ragas, M.W., Kim, J., and Kiousis, S. (2011) Agenda-building in the corporate sphere: Analyzing influence in the 2008 Yahoo!-Icahn proxy contest. *Public Relations Review, 37*(3), 257–265.

Reese, S.D. and Danielian, L.H. (1994) Intermedia influence and the drug issue: Converging on cocaine. In P. Shoemaker (ed.), *Communication Campaigns against Drugs: Government, Media and the Public*. Hillsdale, NJ: Erlbaum, pp. 47–66.

Rudolf, J.C. (2010) Slogans and facts. NYTimes.com: Green, May 4. Retrieved from http://green.blogs.nytimes.com/2010/05/04/bps-green-credentials/ (last accessed September 17, 2012).

Shah, A. (2009) Newsmaker: Ray Day. *PRWeek*, November, pp. 44–45.

Shaw, D. and McCombs, M. (1977) *The Emergence of American Political Issues*. St. Paul, MN: West.

Turk, J.V. (1985) Information subsidies and influence. *Public Relations Review, 11*(3), 10–25.

Turk, J.V. and Franklin, B. (1987) Information subsidies: Agenda-setting traditions. *Public Relations Review, 13*(4), 29–41.

van Riel, C.B.M. and Fombrun, C.J. (2007) *Essentials of Corporate Communication: Implementing Practices for Effective Reputation Management*. New York: Routledge.

Wanta, W. (1991) Presidential approval ratings as a variable in the agenda-building process. *Journalism Quarterly, 68*(4), 672–679.

Wanta, W. and Wu, Y. (1992) Interpersonal communication and the agenda-setting process. *Journalism Quarterly, 69*(4), 847–855.

Wartick, S.L. (1992) The relationship between intense media exposure and change in corporate reputation. *Business and Society, 31*(1), 33–49.

Weaver, D., Graber, D., McCombs, M., and Eyal, C. (1981) *Media Agenda Setting in a Presidential Election: Issues, Images and Interest*. Westport, CT: Greenwood.

Weaver, D.A. and Bimber, B. (2008) Finding news stories: A comparison of searches using LexisNexis and Google News. *Journalism & Mass Communication Quarterly, 85*(3), 515–530.

Weaver, D.H. (1977) Political issues and voter need for orientation. In D.L. Shaw and M.E. McCombs (eds), *The Emergence of American Political Issues: The Agenda-Setting Function of the Press*. St. Paul, MN: West, pp. 107–119.

Weaver, D.H. (1980) Audience need for orientation and media effects. *Communication Research, 7*(3), 361–376.

Winter, J.P. (1981) Contingent conditions in the agenda-setting process. In G.C. Wilhoit and H. de Bock (eds), *Mass Communication Review Yearbook 2*. Beverly Hills, CA: Sage, pp. 235–243.

Winter, J.P. and Eyal, C. (1981) Agenda setting for the civil rights issue. *Public Opinion Quarterly, 45*(3), 376–383.

Zucker, H. (1978) The variable nature of news media influence. In B. Ruben (ed.), *Communication Yearbook 2*. New Brunswick, NJ: Transaction.

16

Complexity Theory and the Dynamics of Reputation

Priscilla Murphy
Temple University, USA

Dawn R. Gilpin
Arizona State University, USA

This chapter applies basic concepts of complexity theory to the process of constructing or deconstructing reputation. Complex systems are made up of individual agents who interact locally to adapt to their immediate situation. These myopic adjustments accumulate into large-scale patterns that affect the larger society, often in unanticipated, unstable, and uncontrollable ways. We look at central concepts of complexity theory – interactivity, adaptability, self-organization, instability, history, permeability, and constraints – pointing out their bearing on the dynamics of reputation. Next, we look at complexity-based methodologies to model reputational issues, currently case studies and network analyses. We view theories of complexity as part of an overall trend in public relations theory and practice toward a local, participatory approach that is flexible and adaptive, rather than an organization-centric approach that tries to control reputation by ascertaining public sentiment and applying corrective tactics.

Complexity theory, which once occupied an obscure corner of social science scholarship, has increasingly emerged as a useful way to explore topics that range from models of financial markets, traffic jams, and war strategies to commentary on science fiction novels (Johnston, 2001). A growing number of complexity-related publications during the past few years bear witness to the rapid development of theory and applications, specifically in communication. Recently, complexity-based approaches have shown special potential in studies of corporate and executive reputation (Gilpin, 2010; Murphy, 2010).

This chapter explains some basic concepts of complexity theory, focusing particularly on its relevance to reputation. We begin with complexity theory's transition from the natural to the social sciences. We then look at central concepts of complexity theory, pointing out their bearing on the dynamics of reputation. Next, we look at complexity-based methodologies to model reputational issues. We consider implications for practice, and we end with suggestions for future research.

The Emergence of Complexity Theory in the Social Sciences

Theories about complex systems originated first in the hard sciences, where they were taken up

The Handbook of Communication and Corporate Reputation, First Edition. Edited by Craig E. Carroll.
© 2013 John Wiley & Sons, Inc. Published 2015 by John Wiley & Sons, Inc.

by researchers in disciplines as disparate as brain architecture, the population cycles of wild animals, and the Internet. (For an overview of the emergence of complexity theory in the natural sciences, see Capra, 2005.)

Some authors (e.g., Miller and Page, 2007) have claimed that social science writings based on complexity go back in time as far as Adam Smith's *Wealth of Nations* in 1776, in which an "invisible hand" guides individuals to make self-interested decisions that lead to a coherent marketplace. Despite such singular forbears, for most scholars, complexity theory is still relatively new in the social sciences; according to Nowotny (2005), complexity-based thinking did not receive much attention in the social sciences until the 1970s. Given this recency, many of the concepts surrounding complexity theory are still in flux, including its definition. Various scholars have advanced their own definitions according to their own interests.

For our purposes, we focus on definitions that favor complexity's societal implications. Among this group, Miller and Page (2007) described complex systems as "composed of interacting, thoughtful (but perhaps not brilliant) agents" who "find themselves enmeshed in a web of connections with one another and, through a variety of adaptive processes, . . . must successfully navigate through this world" (pp. 3, 10). Emphasizing the micro–macro relationship, Murphy (2000) defined complexity theory as

> the study of many individual actors who interact locally in an effort to adapt to their immediate situation. These local adaptations, however, accumulate to form large-scale patterns that affect the greater society, often in ways that could not have been anticipated. (p. 450)

Unpredictability was also emphasized by Richardson and Cilliers (2001) who defined complex systems as "comprised of a large number of entities that display a high level of nonlinear interactivity" (p. 8). Connectivity and interdependence were accentuated in the parsimonious definition of van Uden *et al.* (2001): "Complexity science basically tells us that everything is connected to everything else" (p. 57).

Despite these different emphases, most scholars agree that complexity theory is the study of adaptive systems with components which we will describe in detail in the next section: individual agents who interact myopically, creating a dynamic, unstable system with ill-defined and permeable boundaries, a system that self-organizes into a new entity that cannot then be reduced to its parts (Gilpin and Murphy, 2008). (For in-depth discussions of the development of complexity theory in the social sciences, see Miller and Page, 2007; Urry, 2005.)

Since complexity theory originated in the natural sciences, its use in a communication context has raised issues of nomenclature and questions about suitable research approaches. For example, chaos theory is often defined in terms similar to complexity theory, especially in public relations studies where chaos theory has been used to talk about crisis situations (e.g., Murphy, 1996; Seeger *et al.*, 2001; Sellnow *et al.*, 2002). Chaos and complexity theories do share certain assumptions and interests (such as nonlinearity, positive feedback, and bifurcations), but complexity is not precisely the same as chaos. Some authors view chaos theory as an earlier term for complexity theory (Nowotny, 2005). Others view chaos and complexity as a duality, with chaos representing the disorderly potential of systems and complexity emphasizing systems' emergence into order (Smith and Jenks, 2005). More precisely, Goldberg and Markóczy (2000, p. 4) noted that "the study of chaos generally involves the study of extremely simple non-linear systems which lead to extremely complicated behavior" – the creation of disorder out of regimented repetition – whereas complexity moves in the opposite direction, being "generally about the (simple) interactions of many things (often repeated) leading to higher level patterns" of coherence. Therefore, "complexity science aims to explain the emergence of order – it is really *order-creation science*" (McKelvey, 2003, p. 108; italics in the original). In public relations scholarship, work currently continues in crisis research that uses the terminology of chaos rather than complexity. Nonetheless, for our purposes here – to discuss the emergence of a coherent order, such as reputation, rather than the devolution of order, such as crisis – complexity theory appears to be the most appropriate paradigm. This evolution of recognizable patterns makes complexity especially appealing to the social scientist interested in studying emergent phenomena such as the evolution of a coherent reputation from a myriad of individual perceptions.

Another issue resulting from the migration of complexity theory from the hard sciences to the social sciences has been the question of incommensurability, or the extent to which principles from natural science can meaningfully be adopted in social science (Introna, 2003). For example, MacKenzie (2005, p. 45) described a conflict between the hard sciences' "literal, non-metaphorical" vision of complexity as "a general social or historical physics," as opposed to the tendency of social scientists to treat complexity "as a source of new metaphors or tropes to be used in theory-building." As a result, she asked, "Can there be a critical social or historical physics that is not a world-view and that does not treat science as a source of metaphors?" Similarly, Miller and Page (2007) remarked that "complex systems have become a darling of the popular press and a rapidly advancing scientific field. Unfortunately, this creates a gap between popular accounts that rely on amorphous metaphors and cutting-edge research that requires a technical background" (p. 6), a dilemma they resolved through agent-based modeling of social arenas.

Others, such as McKie (2001, p. 81), have argued that adopting the rigid rules and quantitative bias of the hard sciences has actually worked to "retard" the social sciences. From this perspective, scholars contend that a complexity-based approach provides a more accurate view of both natural and social sciences than traditional reductionist science does. Urry (2005) also argued that "nature turns out to be more like human nature – unpredictable, sensitive to the surrounding world, influenced by small fluctuations" (p. 7). This confluence "suggests enormous interdependencies, paral-

lels, overlaps and convergences between analyses of physical *and* of social worlds. Indeed the very division between the 'physical' and the 'social' is a socio-historical product and one that is dissolving" (Urry, 2005, p. 7; see also Capra, 2005). Bridging the natural and social sciences thus involves seeing both domains as expressions of the same underlying worldview, not "conceiving of humanity as mechanical, but rather instead conceiving of nature as active and creative" (Wallerstein, 1996, quoted in Urry, 2003, pp. 12–13). This point of view creates a middle ground between the use of complexity theory strictly as metaphor and the requirement that it be quantitatively operationalized, a middle ground that is becoming increasingly populated by social scientists who use computer models of social systems (e.g., Axelrod, 1997; Miller and Page, 2007) or network studies that quantitatively represent social systems. (See Morçöl and Wachhaus, 2009, for a comparative discussion of network and complexity theories.)

In communication studies, this combination of quantitative, empirical data with qualitative, complexity-based interpretation has led to research founded on complexity as the theoretical construct and network analysis as the quantitative method. For example, Murphy (2010) used semantic network analysis to analyze the declining reputation of celebrity executive Martha Stewart. Gilpin (2010) used semantic network analysis to show subtle differences in the use of social media to communicate company image by Whole Foods.

Principles of Complexity Theory and Applications to Reputation

Although relatively few empirical studies to date have used complexity theory to explore the process of constructing or deconstructing reputation, there is considerable potential in doing so. Certain fundamentals of complexity theory indicate a natural affinity between the components of complex systems in general and reputation in particular. These principles form the basis for the following discussion: interactivity, adaptability, self-organization, instability, history, permeability, and constraints. (For fuller discussion of these principles in relation to crisis management, see Gilpin and Murphy, 2008.)

Interactions

Complex systems are composed of individual, interacting agents. In the social sciences, these agents are often construed as human beings; however, they need not be. For example, proponents of actor network theory (see Callon, 1986; Latour, 2005; Law, 1999) maintain that agents engaged in interactions within adaptive systems can range from humans to such non-human beings as microbes or computers. In the case of reputation, studies have generally been limited to human stakeholders. However, nonhuman interactions that possess power to shape a reputation might include, for example, crises or business associations affecting other organizations in the same industry; words and images sharing space, perhaps by chance, in media coverage; or modes of communication that might favor or delay transmission of information.

At the same time, simply having multiple individual elements engaged in a discursive space is not in itself sufficient to constitute a complex system. A system comprised of huge numbers of interacting elements may be merely complicated, not complex, although this is truer of a mechanical system such as a computer than a human social system. As Miller and Page (2007) pointed out, "In a complicated world, the various elements that make up the system maintain a degree of independence from one another," so that removing one element "does not fundamentally alter the system's behavior aside from that which directly resulted from the piece that was removed" (p. 9). This independence of elements makes it possible to study a complicated system in a reductionist manner, "using traditional tools that rely on reducing the system to its atomic elements" (p. 10). In contrast, "complexity arises when the depend-

ence among the elements becomes important" (p. 9) so that each agent in a complex system depends on the actions or influence of other agents in that system. Complexity-based thinking, therefore, "means thinking in terms of relationships, patterns, processes and context" (Capra, 2005, p. 33).

Adaptability

The agents in a complex system interact in ways that alter the system itself over time. These interactions are local and short range, primarily affecting neighboring agents. In addition, these interactions are myopic: no individual agent has complete knowledge about the behavior of the system as a whole, only the information received locally. Nonetheless, as Cilliers (1998) noted, local interaction "does not preclude wide-ranging influence"; as interactions accrete, their substance "gets modulated along the way. It can be enhanced, suppressed or altered in a number of ways" (p. 4). The behavior of the system does not directly result from the number of interactions among individual elements so much as from the patterns that emerge from these interactions. As Byrne (2005) observed,

> Complexity science is inherently dynamic. It is concerned with the description and explanation of change and one of its most powerful terms, imported from general dynamic theory, is trajectory—the account of the actual pattern of change of a system. (p. 97)

The principle of adaptability brings to the foreground certain challenges facing an organization that attempts to manage its reputation. It implies that, viewed as a complex system, a reputation does not directly result from the production of advertisements, the distribution of news releases, or the placement of interview spokespersons – the battery of tactical tools traditionally considered important in shaping public perceptions. Rather, interactions between these various modes of communication, further transformed by idiosyncratic audience reception and the intrusion into the same marketplace of other, unanticipated issues, create patterns and expectations that sum up to a reputation but remain subtle, even elusive, when scrutinized at the level of isolated indicators such as a customer survey or an instance of media coverage.

Complexity theory thereby captures the multifarious origins of, and influences on, organizations' reputations. Christensen and Askegaard (2001) explored a similar theme from a semiotic perspective, arguing against the existence of an objective organizational identity or image. Instead, they viewed these attributes as "social-historical simulations of organizational realities – simulations whose quality cannot be simply judged on the basis of their 'fit' with reality but must understood on the basis of their rhetorical power vis-à-vis . . . various audiences" (pp. 311–312). Although they used a different theoretical basis, the authors' sense of the social construction of image is shared by a complexity-based view of reputation as a compendium of local perspectives that collide with others to form an overall pattern.

Indeed, without invoking the principles of complexity theory, other scholars currently working in reputation describe similar processes of local interaction and adaptability. For example, the account by Kiousis *et al.* (2007, p. 149) of agenda-building theory in reputation follows a logic comparable to a complexity-based view of interaction among agents: "the process of salience formation [is] one involving reciprocal influence among multiple groups in addition to media and public opinion, such as policymakers, interest groups, and corporations," similar to the mutually adapting, multifarious agents of a complex system. Entman (2003) proposed a similar process in the formation of public opinion, which he called "cascading activism," whereby, through news framing, "ideas activate and spread" through "the existence of *networks of association*, among ideas, among people, and among the communicating symbols (words and images)" (p. 419; italics in the original). Like the "perhaps not brilliant" agents in a complex system (Miller and Page, 2007, p. 3), the "cognitive misers" who comprise public opinion in Entman's model

"operate under uncertainty and pressure, with mixed motives and varying levels of competence and understanding . . . in accordance with established mental maps and habits" (p. 420). They are local optimizers whose interactions eventually compose larger social patterns of belief.

Entman (2003) focused on ways in which government elites manage public opinion. However, the accretion of reputation by means of local, individual interactions often raises another problem familiar to issues managers and other trackers of reputation: these interactions tend to be impervious to external influence as they develop dynamically among the agents themselves. One reason why the patterns in complex systems resist efforts to regulate them has to do with the effects of recurrent interactions. Effects of interaction are "looped," meaning they can feed back at any point in the system, either positively (to encourage change) or negatively (to encourage stability). The type of feedback can be beneficial or harmful to corporate reputation. For example, Mitleton-Kelly (2003) pointed out that overvigilant surveillance can function as a repressively stabilizing form of negative feedback: "Although the intention of change management interventions is to create new ways of working, they may block or constrain emergent patterns of behaviour if they attempt to excessively design and control outcomes" (p. 35).

The concept of feedback loops could shed considerable light on the dynamics of reputation, although it would take further research to understand the effects fully. A brief example shows how feedback might work: Murphy (2010) applied the concept of positive feedback in her complexity-based study of the reputation of Martha Stewart; she maintained that the negative coverage of Stewart was set into motion by the efforts of her own public relations staff, "which adopted increasingly ambitious characterizations of Stewart in order to maintain the support of customers and investors as her business ventures grew." However, "once set in motion, the ever-expanding scope of these portrayals attracted unwanted corollaries that proved unstoppable" (p. 232). Stewart's reputation – as mean-minded, tough, and eventually criminal – took on a life of its own.

At the same time, the context of the interaction – organizational, economic, cultural – provides some constraints for the local interactions. Sets of constraints in complex systems form subsystems referred to as *attractor basins* (van Uden *et al.*, 2001). Attractors can be thought of as poles of a magnet that exert a pull on the system as it evolves, limiting or influencing the direction of change (Richardson *et al.*, 2001; van Uden *et al.*, 2001). At some points, certain constraints or combinations of constraints become dominant, forming an attractor basin characterized by localized patterns of behavior. As a given system evolves, it may "leap" across the volatile boundary zone between neighboring attractor basins (van Uden *et al.*, 2001, p. 61), taking on an entirely different set of values or characteristics.

If we conceive of reputation as a complex system, we might see attractor basins as the domains of influence by the various interested parties: the organization, the media, and various stakeholders. For example, Gilpin (2007) found that news releases issued by retailer Wal-Mart and mainstream media coverage of the company could be divided into two distinct attractor basins with regard to the organization's reputation, with a narrow boundary zone of mutual influence. Furthermore, each domain might in turn contain a number of minor attractors. For instance, different media sources may interact differently with the organization, and stakeholder groups may be highly differentiated by their different perceptions and patterns of behavior with regard to the organization (Sha, 2006).

A complex system thus accommodates multiple attractor basins that coexist and contend with each other. In contrast to general systems theory, complexity-based thinking does not view change as simply a response to an outside environment. Instead, the parts of the whole complex system – all the elements involved in producing a reputation – adapt to one another in an ongoing process. In a reputation study,

those interacting parts could include media, policy makers, interest groups, consumers, and other target audiences, influenced in turn by other actors, human and nonhuman, in the form of technologies, cultural norms, and institutional and legal structures.

At its best, adaptability can generate new patterns of behavior that enable an organization to operate more effectively than it would have by maintaining invariable behaviors. For example, Murphy (2000) pointed out that, faced with the original Tylenol poisonings in 1982, Johnson & Johnson preserved its reputation by adapting quickly to a dynamic news environment:

> First, it established some parameters – a kind of system constraint – by determining that its corporate credo, which gave priority to needs of the medical community and customers, would inform all its responses. Second, it ceded control of the poisoning investigation to public officials operating in partnership with internal tactical crisis teams. . . . In public relations forums, this behavior is symmetrical; in complexity terms, it is a fortuitous local adaptation. (p. 454)

Self-organization

In complex systems, adaptability can also be viewed in terms of the principle of self-organization. Agents are "perhaps not brilliant" (Miller and Page, 2007, p. 3), but they learn from their interactions, responding to each other's feedback in an ongoing process known as *coevolution*. What they learn cannot be specifically predicted or controlled, as it emerges from individual and shared history as well as ongoing interaction. Eventually, these small local moves amount to patterns. Theorists often refer to the outcome of coevolution as "emergence" – that is, unpredictable patterns of order that appear through a process of self-organization. Varela (1995), for example, asserted that emergence refers to the point at which a system's local interactions become global patterns encompassing all individual agents. This feature of emergence – of unpredictable self-organization – accounts for the often-made observation that if a system is truly complex, it is more than the sum of its parts because of the interaction among those parts (van Uden *et al.*, 2001). Complex systems are irreducible because their most valuable information consists of relationships between the agents; if the agents are considered in isolation, that information is lost.

The concept of self-organization further emphasizes the troublesome question of control, or in the context of reputation, of inability to manage the interpretations that stakeholders attribute to the behavior of organizations and individuals. One example of the imperviousness to change of historical patterns in complex systems is the continuing reputational woes of the powdered drink mix, Kool Aid. Since 1978, the mix has been linked to the mass suicide, through cyanide, of more than 900 members of a religious cult in Jonestown, Guyana. Even though the actual medium for the cyanide was a less well-known competitor named Flavor Aid, the Kool Aid/Jonestown link has remained so strong that decades later it has solidified into aphoristic advice for dealing with mistrusted groups: "Don't drink the Kool Aid."

The emergence of global patterns from local interactions can be visually expressed in terms of "fractals." Fractal mathematics is a type of nonlinear calculation that uses recursive iterations to reveal patterns that remain invariable regardless of scale, such as water droplets that might form steam from a teapot, clouds, or major weather systems captured in satellite photographs. Despite these identifiable patterns, the specific direction in which the fractal will develop can be predicted only to a limited degree. In terms of social behavior, fractals can represent a map of the various possible actions or attitudes available at any given point in time. They show how even minor changes in direction at those points can lead to very different outcomes over time by changing the path of successive arrays of possible behaviors, and eventually, of large-scale social patterns (Black *et al.*, 2005; Klenk *et al.*, 2000; Stacey, 2001).

While seemingly erudite and arcane, the concept of fractals offers a useful way to think about the construction of reputation. Built into the idea of fractals is "a remarkable discovery: if different points of view produce different results, this is not a problem to solve, but an opportunity to use" (Suteanu, 2005, p. 116). The "opportunity" consists of incorporating multiple perspectives and multiple scales when addressing multifaceted problems. As Suteanu pointed out, faced with complex situations, a fractal approach "revealed the importance of promoting not just one – the arguably 'best' – point of view, but of considering the same problem from multiple perspectives" (p. 117). Fractal approaches help to explain how diverse audiences play a role in constructing reputation. Fractals provide one model of the process of image creation that fits collaboratively, or interacts cooperatively, with audience perspectives rather than operating through image campaigns with specific goals that come from outside and are targeted at segmented stakeholders.

Instability and bifurcations in dissipative systems

The use of fractal patterns to map change over time evokes an additional characteristic of complex systems: they are unstable and constantly evolving. Complexity theorists capture this concept when they talk about "dissipative" systems – that is, systems that drift toward instability rather than settle in a state of equilibrium. As Morçöl and Wachhaus (2009) pointed out, "social organizations, like organizational forms in nature, are dissipative structures: they may decay into disorganization or transform into different (higher) forms of organization" (p. 54). Generally, dissipative systems do transmute into a higher form of organization rather than devolve into chaos, another sign that complexity is an order-seeking system.

Regardless of its outcome, instability is another aspect of complex systems that makes it difficult to fully specify their potential directions, let alone to exert control over them. Like many complexity theorists, Nowotny (2005) emphasized this lack of control as one sign of a larger paradigm shift whereby "high modernity with its unshakeable belief in planning (in society) and predictability (in science) is long past," along with "belief in simple cause–effect relationships. . . . In their place is an acknowledgement that many – perhaps most – relationships are non-linear and subject to ever changing patterns of unpredictability" (p. 16). One important consequence of nonlinearity is that cause and effect are disproportional, so that small causes can have a profound impact on the system and large events may have minimal effect.

Nonlinearity appears especially destabilizing when an organization is operating in conditions that take it "far from equilibrium" – that is, far from stable norms. This characteristic suggests why, in terms of reputation, small events often appear to tip public opinion into a negative range despite an organization's efforts to stem the momentum of public opinion through communication. One look at the Middle East revolutions of 2011 shows how abrupt, unexpected, and radical such a reversal of fortune can be. In a less sudden but equally dramatic turn of reputation, this disproportionate relationship between cause and effect underlies persistent public fears about "Death Panels" in health care reform in the United States. A phrase dropped by Republican Sarah Palin to describe Democratic proposals to pay for medical counseling about end-of-life care and living wills, the term tapped into such public anxiety that eventually the entire idea of end-of-life counseling was struck from future health care proposals. These "small, volitional beginnings" (Weick, 2001, p. 228) can therefore spiral into surprisingly powerful messages if they tap into broader cultural trends.

The instability and nonlinearity of public attitudes also provide a new perspective on the difficulties involved in reputation management noted by researchers who do not use complexity theory. Gotsi and Wilson (2001) emphasized that a corporate reputation is not "a static element that can only be influenced and hence managed through impressive logos and well planned formal communication activities." Rather, reputations are "dynamic constructs,

which influence and are influenced by all the ways in which a company projects its images: its behavior, communication and symbolism" (p. 29). As Murphy (2010) noted, public relations researchers have reached similar conclusions about the instability of reputation, pointing out that an entity has only limited control over its reputation – that a reputation is constantly tested, negotiated, and defended. It is inherently unstable and only partially controlled by its possessor. Among others, Berger (1999), Botan and Soto (1998), Coombs and Holladay (2001), Hallahan (1999), Ran and Duimering (2007), Vasquez (1996), and Williams and Moffitt (1997) have proposed social constructionist views of reputation as a shifting, recurrent process whereby an organization and its publics negotiate meaning through dynamic exchange between sender and receiver, organization and public. Although these theorists have not invoked complexity theory as such, they have all engaged the notions of multiple influences on reputation, and noted a process of dynamic negotiation over meaning that neither sender nor receiver can fully control.

Influence of history

Complex systems are not only unstable; they are also dynamic in that their history is an essential feature of their emergent patterns. Because the evolution of the system is the result of repeated interaction among its agents, history helps to produce present behavior. The history of a complex system is recorded at the level of individual elements, such as the experiences, values, and opinions of members of the public and organizational members, as well as at the macroscopic level in the rituals and other features of a shared culture (Richardson *et al.*, 2000).

Despite their dependence on their history, dissipative systems are nonetheless not predictable, mainly because of their nonlinearity. Fractal representations show that repeated interactions between agents allow variations to build up over time. Lamertz *et al.* (2003) described the potential of these variations to incite a public issue: "an issue is . . . not simply . . . a social problem that receives a predictable fluctuating share of public attention, but is a socially constructed discontinuity . . . or jolt . . . that disrupts an organizational field by interfering with the established meanings attributed to actors and their patterned interactions" (p. 84). From a complexity standpoint, organizations are always embedded in their context and cannot choose to separate themselves from it by acting in a way that denies or violates contextual patterns. It is this recursive dependence between actors and context that causes actors to lose control of crises in the first place. Reputations are constrained by the fact that "organizational actors, through their actions, create their own context. Once initiated, the context tends to develop a dynamic of its own, which escapes the control of the organizational actors" (Thiétart and Forgues, 1997, p. 119). Organizational patterns evolve in a fractal manner, in which similar assumptions, activities, and actors, interacting over time, repeat similar patterns in which subtle changes enter locally, get built in, and become part of a grander social pattern that expresses organizations' essential identity – whether they like it or not. One might see the "jolt" administered to the Catholic Church's reputation by the priestly abuse scandals in this way: the movement of abusive clergy from parish to parish represented small local adjustments that after decades amounted to such visible social patterns that they transformed the reputation and public character of the Church.

Permeable boundaries

In speaking of organizational identity and image, Hatch and Schultz (1997) noted "the breakdown of the boundary between their internal and external aspects," so that organizational members are not only "insiders," or employees, but simultaneously "outsiders" such as consumers or community members; as a result, "internal and external relations are collapsing together" (p. 356). They defined "identity" as traditionally internal, a collective understanding of organizational values by its employees, and "image" as a conscious formu-

lation of corporate identity for external consumption, but noted that "the relationships between culture, image and identity form circular processes involving mutual interdependence" so that "organizational identity is a self-reflexive product of the dynamic processes of organizational culture" (p. 361).

Although they did not use the nomenclature of complexity per se, the phenomena noted by these researchers can be understood and interpreted from the standpoint of the permeable and ill-defined boundaries characteristic of complex systems. Complexity-based thinking does not assume the existence of distinct borders between a system and its environment, even though systems are constantly adapting to their changing environments. This adaptation allows complex systems to evolve their own rules, as component agents make local decisions using information from the environment as part of the decision-making mix. These decisions in turn bring about changes in the environment. In this sense, the environment is not external to the system but integral to the system itself. Hatch and Schultz (1997) characterized this internal/external permeability in terms of a cultural arena in which organizational norms furnish "a symbolic context within which interpretations of organizational identity are formed and intentions to influence organizational image are formulated" (p. 360). They concluded that because it is constantly negotiated in a cultural arena, corporate identity can never be wholly managed. Murphy (2010) similarly concluded that some public relations practitioners' belief that reputation can be "managed" through traditional public relations campaigns (Budd, 1993; Fombrun, 1996; Fombrun and van Riel, 2004) is largely illusory. Using complexity-based models, she argued that reputation often takes on a life of its own, self-organizing in ways that defy organizations' attempts to manipulate it from the outside in directions of their own choosing.

Bifurcation

Further mitigating against efforts to control complex systems is the phenomenon known as *bifurcation*. This phenomenon refers to the tendency of complex systems to accumulate, over time, noise in the form of changes, imperfections, or inconsistencies that culminate in a dramatic disintegration of the system, a crisis that leads the system in a direction one could not necessarily anticipate. Indeed, the elements comprising a complex system are so interconnected that disorders easily cascade throughout the system. Rumors afford many examples of the ways in which unintended, unwanted, and often inaccurate information can quickly take over an information marketplace, often resulting in a dramatic reputational reversal. The rapidity and shock of calamitous rumors results from the ability of public opinion to bifurcate – to leap from one attractor basin of opinion parameters into another, which then self-organizes into a different, equally coherent set of perceptions.

Similar patterns have been observed in the dynamic shaping of reputation. For example, Bromley (1993) described the evolution of public perceptions as a tightly coupled network of mutual influences: "The behavior of individuals and their relationships with other people set in motion a widely spreading pattern of consequences and reactions – consequences that interact and produce further consequences, often of an unpredictable sort" (p. 7). Treadwell and Harrison (1994) also discerned this pattern among individuals seeking to make sense of an organization's reputation: "a variety of portrayals of the organization may emerge. [But] when a particular portrayal catches the attention and imagination of the group, it sets up a 'chain reaction of fantasy' and may become even more widely accepted" (p. 68). The same process characterizes the behavior of a complex system, with the emergence and diffusion of a new representation of that system. As an example, Murphy (2010) and Gilpin and Murphy (2008) described a cascade of illogical public opinion in 1999 that seriously damaged the reputation of Coca-Cola in Europe. Two unrelated batches of ill-smelling but nontoxic Coke in France and Belgium became associated in public opinion, and acquired further negative associations with a prior Belgian food scare

involving sheep, which led to connections with the sheep disease scrapie and thence mad cow disease. Events, media coverage, and public anxieties about genetically altered foods all interacted in complex ways to affect Coke's reputation in ways it could not control. The Coca-Cola case typifies the interaction of all the elements of a complex system that we identify as influencing reputation: interactivity, adaptability, self-organization, instability, history, permeability, and constraints.

Methods for the Study of Reputation as a Complex System

Because complexity theory is so new to communication, and especially to public relations, methods for its application have been relatively sparse. To date, complexity-based articles in public relations have used two methods: case study and network analysis.

Case studies

The case study approach has been particularly useful in projects that use complexity theory to explain both the process of change and the reputational aftermath of crises. For example, Gilpin and Murphy (2008) included case studies of the national spinach contamination crisis of 2006, NASA's Challenger disaster of 1986, and the 2007 tainting of Chinese-produced pet food. Complexity theory also structured the case histories used by van Ginneken (2003) to study market rumors, panics, and changes in reputation involving Benetton, Shell Oil, and the British beef industry.

Complexity theory has also been used to structure case studies involving reputation in popular writing, such as Gladwell's (2002) *Tipping Point* or Li and Bernoff's (2008) *Groundswell: Winning in a World Transformed by Social Technologies*. Although popular accounts do not necessarily invoke complexity theory by name, the central idea of many such books is that social changes are transmitted like epidemics in which "a small number of people started behaving differently and that behavior somehow spread" in rapid fashion, and in which "little changes had big effects" (Gladwell, 2002, p. 8), amounting to large-scale patterns that explain social phenomena ranging from the fad for Hush Puppies shoes to the drop in New York City crime.

Qualitative methods such as the case study approach are particularly useful for theory development. Quantitative study of longitudinal change brought about multiple interacting agents demands computing power that was not available until recently (and is still somewhat nascent). A few researchers, however, have begun to study reputation as a complex system by quantitative means, and particularly, network analyses.

Reputations, complex systems, and networks

A network is a graph comprised of nodes that represent members of that network and lines between nodes that show relationships between the members. Social networks may connect people, organizations, or machines; semantic networks may connect concepts, themes, and words. For people and organizations, networks serve as conduits for new ideas. As Monge and Contractor (2003) explained, communication networks "serve as a mechanism that exposes people, groups, and organizations to information, attitudinal messages, and the behavior of others," and this exposure, in turn, "increases the likelihood that network members will develop beliefs, assumptions, and attitudes that are similar to those of others in their network" (p. 465). This sequence of network contagion described by Monge and Contractor suggests a process similar to that by which complex systems coevolve through repeated interaction among the various agents that comprise them. This association between networks and complex systems is particularly useful for the study of reputation because it calls attention to the fact that reputation is a product of all the elements associated in a network – sources, themes,

people, other news – whether the associations are intentional or not.

For example, Yu and Lester (2008) explored the phenomenon of "reputation spillover" whereby stakeholders frame mental associations between organizations based on two heuristics derived from social network theory. The first is proximity, or direct ties between organizations such as strategic alliances; the second is structural equivalence, in which organizations have similar ties to others, such as serving the same sorts of customers or making the same types of products. One result of such linkage is that when one organization undergoes a reputational crisis, "information about this disruptive event is likely to spread quickly in the public domain, which will greatly facilitate and accelerate the reputational crisis spreading to others" (p. 101). Although Yu and Lester used network theory rather than complexity theory, the principle of interactions spreading into larger patterns that cannot be well managed is similar. Research by Gilpin (2010) and Murphy (2010) has combined the use of network and complexity theories to study the evolution of reputation.

Implications for Practice

The notion that reputations, like complex systems, self-determine their content and their outcomes, and resist attempts to influence their development, appears on the face of it to be less than good news for the public relations profession. Practices of the field – practitioner conferences and continuing education forums, textbooks, and professional accrediting bodies like the Public Relations Society of America (PRSA) – have long taken the position that public relations professionals should follow a linear planning process to achieve goals and objectives such as the improvement of reputation, and proceed with strategies and tactics that will achieve those objectives. Complexity theory appears, then, to contradict the public relations community's professional advice accumulated over several decades. Indeed, some would say that complexity theory presents a rather fatalistic worldview where planning and strategy make little difference.

In fact, that darker view is not the case, for several reasons. First, at its best, adaptability can generate new patterns of behavior that enable an organization to operate more effectively than it would have by maintaining invariable behaviors. As previously discussed, for years after the 1982 Tylenol poisonings, Johnson & Johnson continued to benefit from the reputational halo that came from its adaptability to that crisis. In addition, complex systems allow organizations to guide and influence (if not determine) the path of their reputation. We have repeatedly argued that complexity models show that it does little good for an organization to attempt to define its reputation by means external to audiences, as exemplified by such traditional public relations techniques as news releases and special events. Instead, an organization must occupy the same participatory plane as its stakeholders; it must be embedded in, rather than directing, the circumstances that add up to its reputation. Luoma-Aho and Vos (2009) expressed a similar idea, arguing that organizational reputations tend to be mutually negotiated with stakeholders in "issue arenas." Even though "previous literature on stakeholders is mostly organization centered . . . organizations today are rarely at the center of stakeholder attention" because issues "are not owned by one single organization, but several players" (pp. 120–121). Therefore, an organization concerned about issues management and reputation needs to pay attention, not to a defined roster of stakeholders or even to a singular issue, but rather to "the interrelatedness of the various issue arenas" in which the company operates (p. 121), and which refract off of each other to shape public perceptions and impel issue controversies to less-than-controllable outcomes.

Similarly, complexity theorists such as Prigogine and Stengers (1984; cited in Morçöl and Wachhaus, 2009) have argued from a phenomenological position that "the knowledge of a complex system is constricted not only by nonlinearity, but also by our cognitive apparatuses and our situatedness, or embeddedness,

in the world we observe" (p. 52). Complexity theory thus urges replacement of communication from an external organization, no matter how benign, with a local, "participatory" knowledge of the world by an observer who is situated in it. Such a system is "an invitation to a less-control-oriented management philosophy" in which managers "should be open to change, even transformational change and the kind of change they may not like" (p. 50). As Morçöl and Wachhaus pointed out, networks are not hierarchical: they "have the capability to regulate themselves and . . . they do not need [to] be centrally controlled to function" (p. 48). Therefore, Gilpin and Murphy (2008) argued that managers should approach public relations situations, including reputation change, looking to improvise and influence, to be "flexible rather than rigid, situated rather than sweeping, suggestive rather than prescriptive" (p. 176). This type of complexity-based thinking comes close to the concept of cocreation of meaning advocated by Heath and others (e.g., Heath *et al.*, 2006).

In terms of reputation management efforts, a complexity approach strongly suggests that some revision of public relations' traditional assumptions is in order. In common with other communication approaches that emphasize contingency, a complexity approach would recommend a move away from an organization-centric to a public-centric focus, or insist on the importance of context. As Murphy's (2010) complexity-based examination of Martha Stewart's reputation showed, messages imposed on consumers from Stewart's company consistently lost ground because they did not take into account the general perception that there was something inauthentic about Stewart, so that her actual jail time merely played out that underlying sense of illegitimacy in literal terms. Instead of the traditional approach used by Stewart's public relations team, the dependence of complex systems on local agent interactions emphasizes that it is necessary to engage with publics on a local level, rather than attempt to manipulate reputation by ascertaining public sentiment, then sending in news releases or other tactical actions to sway public opinion.

Hence, Gilpin (2010) pointed out that the social media environment opens up new opportunities for organizations to communicate directly with stakeholders, through multiple channels and even using multiple voices. Her study of Whole Foods' use of online news releases, a corporate blog, and microblogging via Twitter showed significant message differentiation among the channels, due in large part to the high degree of interaction with different stakeholders in each of these social media. Given this participatory environment, organizations can no longer seek to influence publics with sweeping messages, even though they may relinquish some control. As Gilpin noted, "the immediacy, mutuality, and public nature of Twitter make it a risky venue for organizations who are unwilling to engage in real-time public dialogue with stakeholders, or who fear missteps" (p. 280). Social media essentially introduce additional elements of complexity to the image construction process, as organizations are forced to recognize and adapt their core messages to stakeholder needs and engage in dialog that shapes the overall direction of the organization's reputation through co-construction of meaning. The sheer volume of local interaction that can occur via social media can give these channels significant weight compared to institutional messages issued through traditional media.

Being local means not being a distant expert: Nowotny (2005) argued that chaos theory was enthusiastically adopted in the 1970s by a lay public in part because it

> had a double significance, political and scientific. First, because "experts" who previously had pretended to know (almost) everything were shown not to know as much as they claimed, the political distance between governors and governed was reduced; traditional hierarchies of deference were eroded. (p. 16)

This type of close involvement with constituencies is a long-term strategy that can give organizations a role in shaping reputational outcomes. In circumstances of crisis or rapid change, however, organizations have the additional ability to exert leverage at critical points.

Hence, Murphy (1996) maintained that the very instability of complex systems means that " 'there are no inevitabilities' but rather a multiplicity of choices" and that it may be possible to influence those choices if one intervenes

> when dissonances have accumulated to the point of destabilizing the existing order so that rapid change to a new order is inevitable. Thus, "the issue for change becomes one of careful identification of such leverage points and an understanding of the proper application of 'force' (i.e., resources) at such points." (p. 109; see also Young, 1991, p. 443)

Even with such leverage, however, one can influence but not control potential outcomes.

Directions for Future Research

In this chapter, we have suggested a number of reasons why complex systems theory constitutes a promising model for how reputations emerge, with or without organizational presence, and how organizations can participate in the evolution of their own reputation. Like complex systems, reputations are cumulative and time based: they evolve and have a history. Reputations accumulate through a variety of stakeholders rather than through regulation by an overarching mechanism like news subsidies. Reputations are not entirely predictable: no matter how complete our familiarity with the components of a firm's reputation, we cannot foresee with certainty how or in what direction that reputational system as a whole will develop. The evolution of reputation depends on often-unpredictable interactions and associations among a network of perceivers – customers, the media, employees, other companies – rather than on linear or rational design. Finally, complex systems are dissipative: They may build to a point of bifurcation, after which they self-organize into some form that may restore earlier elements or lead in an entirely new direction.

These facets of reputation research brought out by complexity theory are also highly compatible with other current research approaches to reputation. The possibilities for cross-referencing these studies are many, and we have pointed out only a few in this chapter, among them network theories, issue arenas, and the cocreation of meaning. In this respect, complexity theory is part of an emerging group of related perspectives on reputation that insist on the ineffectiveness of traditional attempts at reputation control, the importance of a participatory perspective, and tolerance for change, even when it is unwanted change.

Although complexity theory and reputation studies are highly compatible, little work has been done in these areas, and numerous avenues for future research remain. We see two spheres that would particularly profit from researchers' attention: first, network-based studies; and second, reputation studies that collect all the new theoretical work, cited throughout this chapter, that emphasizes the contingent, the uncertain, the interdependent, and the poorly controlled aspects of communication.

In part, these recommendations for future research return to complexity theory's past roots in the natural sciences. As discussed earlier, the use of complex systems terminology by popular authors and social scientists has been criticized for reliance on "amorphous metaphors" rather than being "cutting-edge research that requires a technical background" (Miller and Page, 2007, p. 6). As summarized in this chapter, a number of studies, including several of our own, have explored complexity theory as a metaphor for crises, for reputation, or for issues management. The use of complexity as a metaphor is one important step in building a theoretical foundation. At this point, however, it is at least as important to further develop the use of complexity theory beyond metaphor. One way to do so is through network studies. Many of the complexity principles outlined earlier invoke the idea of networks as a way to visualize or analyze interactions among elements of complex adaptive systems. In fact, it is difficult to talk about such systems without expressing them in terms of networks. Network analysis offers an existing means to quantify the mutual influence of factors that shape reputation.

The second direction in which complexity theory might develop would place it more in the social science mainstream rather than introducing it as a borrowed theory from the natural sciences. Most articles on complexity theory in public relations (including this one) have had to explain the theory afresh each time, unlike theories that originated in public relations or closely allied social sciences. Complexity theory thus has a different stature from such widely known communication theories as exchange theory or the spiral of silence, which require little exegesis or justification to readers. This chapter has tried to point out ways in which complexity theory fits within a cohesive family of new, open-ended approaches to public relations. To that end, we have sought not only to explain the relevance of complexity theory specifically for reputation studies, but also to place the theory in context with other public relations theorizing that emphasizes the shifting, the unpredictable, and the local, so that complexity-based approaches support an overall changing paradigm of reputation within the field. Perhaps more important, looking at reputation from the standpoint of complexity theory makes it possible to take fresh perspectives and ask new questions that may help communication researchers to better understand that phenomenon.

In the end, complexity-based approaches to reputation point in two useful research directions. The first is to complement other approaches to changing the paradigm of reputation within the field. The second, and perhaps more important, is that they simultaneously make it possible to take fresh perspectives and ask new questions that may help communication researchers to better understand complexity theory in general as well as in specific manifestations.

References

Axelrod, R.M. (1997) *The Complexity of Cooperation*. Princeton, NJ: Princeton University Press.

Berger, B.K. (1999) The Halcion affair: Public relations and the construction of ideological world view. *Journal of Public Relations Research*, *11*(3), 185–203.

Black, J.A., Fabian, F., and Hinrichs, K.T. (2005) Fractals, stories, and the development of coherence in strategic logic. In R. Sanchez and A. Heene (eds), *Advances in Applied Business Strategy*. Oxford, UK: Elsevier Science, pp. 3–28.

Botan, C.H. and Soto, F. (1998) A semiotic approach to the internal functioning of publics: Implications for strategic communication and public relations. *Public Relations Review, 24*(1), 21–44.

Bromley, D.B. (1993) *Reputation, Image and Impression Management*. New York: Wiley.

Budd, J.F. (1993) *CEO Credibility: The Management of Reputation*. Lakeville, CT: Turtle Publishing Co.

Byrne, D. (2005) Complexity, configurations and cases. *Theory, Culture & Society, 22*(5), 95–111.

Callon, M. (1986) Some elements of a sociology of translation: Domestication of the scallops and the fishermen of St. Brieuc bay. In J. Law (ed.), *Power, Action and Belief: A New Sociology of Knowledge*. London: Routledge & Kegan Paul, pp. 196–233.

Capra, F. (2005) Complexity and life. *Theory, Culture & Society, 22*(5), 33–44.

Christensen, L.T. and Askegaard, S. (2001) Corporate identity and corporate image revisited: A semiotic perspective. *European Journal of Marketing, 35*(3/4), 292–315.

Cilliers, P. (1998) *Complexity and Postmodernism*. London: Routledge.

Coombs, W.T. and Holladay, S.J. (2001) An extended examination of the crisis situations: A fusion of the relational management and symbolic approaches. *Journal of Public Relations Research, 13*(4), 321–340.

Entman, R.M. (2003) Cascading activation: Contesting the White House's frame after 9/11. *Political Communication, 20*, 415–432.

Fombrun, C.J. (1996) *Reputation: Realizing Value from the Corporate Image*. Cambridge, MA: Harvard Business School Press.

Fombrun, C.J. and van Riel, C.B.M. (2004) *Fame & Fortune: How Successful Companies Build Winning Reputations*. Upper Saddle River, NJ: Prentice Hall.

Gilpin, D.R. (2007) A complexity perspective on reputation: Wal-Mart and the media. Paper presented to the Public Relations Division of the International Communication Association, San Francisco, CA, May 24–28.

Gilpin, D.R. (2010) Organizational image construction in a fragmented online media environment. *Journal of Public Relations Research, 22*(3), 265–287.

Gilpin, D.R. and Murphy, P. (2008) *Crisis Management in a Complex World*. New York: Oxford University Press.

Gladwell, M. (2002) *The Tipping Point: How Little Things Can Make a Big Difference*. Boston: Little, Brown and Company.

Goldberg, J. and Markóczy, L. (2000) Complex rhetoric and simple games. *Emergence, 2*(1), 72–100.

Gotsi, M. and Wilson, A.M. (2001) Corporate reputation: Seeking a definition. *Corporate Communications: An International Journal, 6*(1), 24–30.

Hallahan, K. (1999) Seven models of framing: Implications for public relations. *Journal of Public Relations Research, 11*(3), 205–242.

Hatch, M.J. and Schultz, M. (1997) Relations between organizational culture, identity and image. *European Journal of Marketing, 31*(5/6), 356–365.

Heath, R.L., Pierce, W.B., Shotter, J., Taylor, J.T., Kerstein, A., and Zorn, T. (2006) The processes of dialogue: Participation and legitimation. *Management Communication Quarterly, 19*(3), 341–375.

Introna, L.D. (2003) Complexity theory and organizational intervention? Dealing with (in)commensurability. In E. Mitleton-Kelly (ed.), *Complex Systems and Evolutionary Perspectives on Organisations: The Application of Complexity Theory to Organisations*. New York: Pergamon Press, pp. 205–219.

Johnston, J. (2001) Distributed information: Complexity theory in the novels of Neal Stephenson and Linda Negata. *Science Fiction Studies, 28*(2), 223–245.

Kiousis, S., Popescu, C., and Mitrook, M. (2007) Understanding influence on corporate reputation: An examination of public relations efforts, media coverage, public opinion, and financial performance from an agenda-building and agenda-setting perspective. *Journal of Public Relations Research, 19*(2), 147–165.

Klenk, J., Binnig, G., and Schmidt, G. (2000) Handling complexity with self-organizing fractal semantic networks. *Emergence, 2*(4), 151–162.

Lamertz, K., Martens, M.L., and Heugens, P.M.A.R. (2003) Issue evolution: A symbolic interactionist perspective. *Corporate Communication Review, 6*(1), 82–93.

Latour, B. (2005) *Reassembling the Social: An Introduction to Actor-Network Theory*. New York: Oxford University Press.

Law, J. (1999) After ANT: Complexity, naming and complexity. In J. Law and J. Hassard (eds), *Actor Network Theory and After*. Oxford, UK: Blackwell, pp. 1–14.

Li, C. and Bernoff, J. (2008) *Groundswell: Winning in a World Transformed by Social Technologies*. Cambridge, MA: Harvard Business School Press.

Luoma-Aho, V. and Vos, M. (2009) Monitoring the complexities: Nuclear power and public opinion. *Public Relations Review*, 35, 120–122.

Mackenzie, A. (2005) The problem of the attractor: A singular generality between sciences and social theory. *Theory, Culture & Society*, 22(5), 45–65.

McKelvey, B. (2003) Emergent order in firms: Complexity science vs. the entanglement trap. In E. Mitleton-Kelly (ed.), *Complex Systems and Evolutionary Perspectives on Organisations: The Application of Complexity Theory to Organisations*. New York: Pergamon Press, pp. 99–125.

McKie, D. (2001) Updating public relations: "New science," research paradigms, and uneven developments. In R.L. Heath and G. Vasquez (eds), *Handbook of Public Relations*. Thousand Oaks, CA: Sage Publications, pp. 75–91.

Miller, J.H. and Page, S.E. (2007) *Complex Adaptive Systems: An Introduction to Computational Models of Social Life*. Princeton, NJ: Princeton University Press.

Mitleton-Kelly, E. (2003) Ten principles of complexity and enabling infrastructures. In E. Mitleton-Kelly (ed.), *Complex Systems and Evolutionary Perspectives on Organisations: The Application of Complexity Theory to Organisations*. New York: Pergamon Press, pp. 23–50.

Monge, P.R. and Contractor, N.S. (2003) *Theories of Communication Networks*. Oxford, UK: Oxford University Press.

Morçöl, G. and Wachhaus, A. (2009) Network and complexity theories: A comparison and prospects for a synthesis. *Administrative Theory & Praxis*, 31(1), 44–58.

Murphy, P. (1996) Chaos theory as a model for managing issues and crises. *Public Relations Review*, 22(2), 95–113.

Murphy, P. (2000) Symmetry, contingency, complexity: Accommodating uncertainty in public relations theory. *Public Relations Review*, 26(4), 447–462.

Murphy, P. (2010) The intractability of reputation: Media coverage as a complex system in the case of Martha Stewart. *Journal of Public Relations Research*, 22(2), 209–237.

Nowotny, H. (2005) The increase of complexity and its reduction: Emergent interfaces between the natural sciences, humanities and social sciences. *Theory, Culture & Society*, 22(5), 15–31.

Prigogine, I. and Stengers, I. (1984) *Order Out of Chaos: Man's New Dialogue with Nature*. New York: Bantam.

Ran, B. and Duimering, P.R. (2007) Imaging the organization: Language use in organizational identity claims. *Journal of Business and Technical Communication*, 21(2), 155–187.

Richardson, K.A. and Cilliers, P. (2001) What is complexity science? A view from different directions. *Emergence*, 3(1), 5–22.

Richardson, K.A., Mathieson, G., and Cilliers, P. (2000) The theory and practice of complexity science: Epistemological considerations for military operational analysis. *SysteMexico*, 1(1), 25–66.

Richardson, K.A., Cilliers, P., and Lissack, M.R. (2001) Complexity science: A "gray" science, for the "stuff in between." *Emergence*, 3(2), 6–18.

Seeger, M., Sellnow, T., and Ulmer, R. (2001) Public relations and crisis communication: Organizing and chaos. In R.L. Heath (ed.), *Handbook of Public Relations*. Thousand Oaks, CA: Sage Publications, pp. 155–166.

Sellnow, T., Seeger, M., and Ulmer, R.R. (2002) Chaos theory, informational needs and the North Dakota floods. *Journal of Applied Communication Research*, 30, 269–292.

Sha, B.-L. (2006) Cultural identity in the segmentation of publics: An emerging theory of intercultural public relations. *Journal of Public Relations Research*, 18(1), 45–65.

Smith, J. and Jenks, C. (2005) Complexity, ecology and the materiality of Information. *Theory, Culture & Society*, 22(5), 141–163.

Stacey, R.D. (2001) *Complex Responsive Processes in Organizations: Learning and Knowledge Creation*. London: Routledge.

Suteanu, C. (2005) Complexity, science and the public: The geography of a new interpretation. *Theory, Culture & Society*, 22(5), 113–140.

Thiétart, R.A. and Forgues, B. (1997) Action, structure, and chaos. *Organization Studies*, 18(1), 119–143.

Treadwell, D.F. and Harrison, T.M. (1994) Conceptualizing and assessing organizational image: Model images, commitment, and communication. *Communication Monographs*, 61, 63–85.

Urry, J. (2003) *Global Complexity*. Cambridge, UK: Polity.

Urry, J. (2005) The complexity turn. *Theory, Culture & Society*, 22(5), 1–14.

van Ginneken, J. (2003) *Collective Behavior and Public Opinion*. Mahwah, NJ: Lawrence Erlbaum Associates.

van Uden, J., Richardson, K.A., and Cilliers, P. (2001) Postmodernism revisited? Complexity science and the study of organisations. *Tamara: Journal of Critical Postmodern Organization Science*, 1(3), 53–67.

Varela, F.J. (1995) The re-enchantment of the concrete. In L. Steels and R. Brooks (eds), *The Artificial Life Route to Artificial Intelligence: Building Embodied, Situated Agents*. Mahwah, NJ: Lawrence Erlbaum Associates, pp. 11–20.

Vasquez, G. (1996) Public relations as negotiation: An issue development perspective. *Journal of Public Relations Research*, 8(1), 57–77.

Wallerstein, I. (1996) *Open the Social Sciences: Report of the Gulbenkian Commission on the Restructuring of the Social Sciences*. Stanford, CA: Stanford University Press.

Weick, K. (2001) *Making Sense of the Organization*. Oxford, UK: Blackwell.

Williams, S.L. and Moffitt, M.A. (1997) Corporate image as an impression formation process: Prioritizing personal, organizational, and environmental audience factors. *Journal of Public Relations Research*, 9(4), 237–258.

Young, T.R. (1991) Chaos theory and symbolic interaction theory: Poetics for the postmodern sociologist. *Symbolic Interaction*, 14, 327.

Yu, T. and Lester, R.H. (2008) Moving beyond firm boundaries: A social network perspective on reputation spillover. *Corporate Reputation Review*, 11(1), 94–108.

17

Communicatively Constituted Reputation and Reputation Management

Stefania Romenti

IULM University, Italy

Laura Illia

IE University, Spain

Following organizational communication theory, organizations are communicatively constituted because the communication (often conceptualized as discourse) is the means by which human beings coordinate actions, create relationships, and constitute or maintain organizations. The communicatively constituted organization approach offers stimulating insights for corporate reputation development. The chapter examines the four communication pillars that constitute the becoming of the reputation, here named *communicatively constituted reputation (CCR)*. First, self-structuring deals with a well-defined and enduring corporate identity. Second, membership negotiation develops authenticity and trust assured by employees. Third, activity coordination assures continuous alignment among corporate values and daily collective behaviors. Fourth, institutional positioning deals with stakeholder engagement and community building. The chapter illustrates how each of the four flows of constitutive communication is connected to corporate reputation development; then, managerial implications and research agenda are analyzed.

Constitutive communication theory has a long tradition within organizational communication studies. Since Karl Weick (1979) argued that communication is the essence of organizations, a broad body of work started to examine how organizations are communicatively constituted. Constitutive communication belongs to the so-called context-centered approaches to the study of communication. More precisely, this approach goes beyond the classical functional approach to organizational communication, focused on messages, networks, and channels,

as well as the meaning-centered approach, focused on sensemaking, influence, and culture (Shockley-Zalaback, 2009).

Adopting a context-centered approach to the study and the practice of organizational communication means to recognize the growing interconnectedness among organizations and their stakeholders due to the exponential rise of turbulence and complexity which affect organizational settings as well as the pervasivity of new information and communication technologies. This approach is also in line with the

The Handbook of Communication and Corporate Reputation, First Edition. Edited by Craig E. Carroll.
© 2013 John Wiley & Sons, Inc. Published 2015 by John Wiley & Sons, Inc.

emerging perspectives on postmodernism, critical studies, global cultures, and institutions.

Our exploration is divided into two main sections. First, we briefly discuss what is meant with "communication constitutes organizations." Second, we consider the four main flows of constitutive communication, and we discuss how these are linked to reputation management. Third, we discuss the main opportunities for future research on topic.

The Constitutive Function of Organizational Communication

Following organizational communication theory, organizations are communicatively constituted because the communication (often conceptualized as discourse) is the means by which human beings coordinate actions, create relationships, and constitute or maintain organizations (Christensen and Cornelissen, 2011, p. 16; Putman *et al.*, 2009, p. 1). As Deetz (1992) noted, "communication cannot be reduced to an informational issue where meanings are assumed to be already existing, but must be seen as a process of meaning development and social production of perceptions, identities, social structures, and affective responses" (p. 4). There are four main processes of communication which permit organizing (McPhee and Zaug, 2009, p. 33) and testimony how communication constitutes organization (CCO): *self-structuring, membership negotiation, activity coordination, institutional positioning.*

The first one, *self-structuring* (McPhee and Zaug, 2009), refers to communication processes among organizational members (role holders and internal groups) which builds organization with "boundaries and loci that constitute the organizational identity that agents refer to" (p. 10). Through reflexive self-structuring activity, organizations gain control over complexity, design regular activity patterns, define internal connections and work processes, develop norms and trust internal relationships, set up hierarchical structures

as well as governance system, and legitimize authority. Through self-structuring, organizations become formally controlled entities which are deeply distinguished from informal groups. Self-structuring activity consists of communication that steers the organization toward a specific direction, which solidifies inside collaboration networks in order to shape the organization as a whole dealing with its own stakeholders. The main instruments for organizational self-structuring are written documents, such as mission statements, organizational charts, policies, minutes of meetings, budgeting, as well as decision-making and planning forums. Without this type of communication, one might consider it unthinkable to efficiently organize daily work (McPhee, 1985). Although a central position is given to channels, flows, who sends the information and who receives it, fidelity, noise, barriers, breakdowns, and gatekeepers (Krone *et al.*, 1987), organizational scholars conceive self-structuring activity as a flow of constitutive communication, which fundamentally shapes the identity through which the organization wants to be referred to by internal members and positioned by external stakeholders (McPhee and Zaug, 2009).

The second communication process is *membership negotiation* (McPhee and Zaug, 2009, p. 33). Organizations exist when they draw members in and let them take part of who the organization is (Tompkins and Cheney, 1985). A number of communication activities – formal and informal – are aimed at increasing the membership feeling among employees so to make them ambassadors of the company's values from the early socialization process. According to Smidts *et al.* (2001), internal communication needs to inform members on what is expected from them (information about "me"), and how their role fits within organizational broader objectives (information about "we"). This type of communication is oriented to the receiver and its psychological perspective (Krone *et al.*, 1987). Managing this type of communication requires specifically focus on how characteristics of individuals affect their communication, and how the receiver's attitudes, cognition, and perceptions will function as filters to the information they process. As conceptual filters are internal and not observable objectively, explanations of communication concepts are restricted to direct observations of inputs and outputs only, such as, for example, member's perceptions, level of identification, nonverbal behavior (McGovern *et al.*, 1978), and level of vocal activity (Diboye and Wiley, 1978). Membership negotiation as a flow of constitutive communication deals with the cultivation of internal networks of relationships, which enhances employees' commitment and their identification with the organization. If employees feel committed, they become strong advocates of organization and support it during crisis times.

The third communication process constituting organizations is *activity coordination* (McPhee and Zaug, 2009, p. 38). Cooperation is the basis of organizing (Mintzberg, 1979). However, to have a good environment to cooperate, it is essential to keep managing how the individual behaves in the group and how the group behaves with the individual (Krone *et al.*, 1987). Said in other words, one does not need to manage the individual and its psychological perspective, but the behavior and how he or she performs in relations to others. When one manages communication with this focus, one treats communication as an act of participation (Fisher, 1978). As Birdwhistell (1959) observed, when one focuses on cooperative acts, "an individual doesn't do communication, he/she becomes a part of communication" (p. 104). The key element is to bring the individual to participate in the organization and to promote his or her openness (Smidts *et al.*, 2001). Activity coordination is a flow of constitutive communication, which deals with solving practical problems, connecting work processes, and organizing work through communication. In other words, it is a step that completes the accomplishments of flows of communication previously described, because it adjusts policies and norms created by self-structuring processes. Activity coordination values the employees' cooperative networks, which affect the experience of empowerment, involvement, and collective participation at work.

The fourth communication process is *institutional positioning* (McPhee and Zaug, 2009, p. 41), which aims at negotiating organizational identity among the larger societal system. Organizations exist in a societal context that is already organized in a system of regulation, routines, and so on, and need to become legitimized as reliable partners of suppliers, customers, competitors, and governments. Societal subjects allow each organization to draw on other organizations for the variety of resources that it needs to accomplish its goals and maintain itself. Given this, there are a number of external communications activities such as, for example, public affairs, media relations, issue and risk management, or any sort of external communication that links the organization with the political, cultural, economic, and social environment in which organizations operate. The shared meaning emerging from any company interaction with its stakeholders and any symbolic communication of the company (Blumer, 1969; Mead, 1934) is the focus of this way of communicating (Krone *et al.*, 1987). Managing organizational communication with this institutional positioning perspective means to consider that the organization does not have symbols, but is constitutive part of the symbolic communication. Institutional positioning is a flow of constitutive communication, which establishes organizational identity and develops legitimacy. In other words, communication builds "institutions" recognized as such by peer and related organizations.

Flows of constitutive communication are deeply interconnected. "All of these flows are required, and a constituted organization is not just a set of flows but a complex relationships of them" (McPhee and Zaug, 2009, p. 42). Self-structuring focuses on organization as "a unique and formalized whole"; membership negotiation supports employees' identification and commitment; activity coordination allows collective participation at work; and finally, institutional positioning describes the organization as a legitimate partner within the social setting. But the question is: how do these interconnected flows can be conceptualized as the building blocks on which reputation is built?

How Organizational Communication Constitutes of Reputation

Corporate reputation is an enduring collective representation of a firm's past behavior (Cornelissen, 2008; Fombrun *et al.*, 2000). This collective representation builds audiences social expectations about a company and comes out from an indirect experience of the company (Berens and van Riel, 2004). In a way, it represents a relatively stable, long-term and collective, overall judgment of externals about an organization, its actions and achievements (Fombrun, 1996; Fombrun and Shanley, 1990).

A good reputation adds value. It buffers the negative impacts of a corporate crisis and is a competitive advantage, an intangible asset that helps to perform better in share value and market shares (Fombrun and Shanley, 1990; Kitchen, 2004; Rindova and Fombrun, 1999). Even though a company's reputation is an important mean of corporate persuasion and provides the credibility that pays off in time of turbulence, however, a company's reputation is also a weak asset, full of risks and pitfalls (Eccles *et al.*, 2006, 2007). A common error arises

from the failure to recognize that image and reputation are social constructions arising from continuous interchange between numerous internal and external perceptions of the organization (Hatch and Schultz, 2008). Appropriate management requires understanding these interchanges, to project a company in a way that fits its day-to-day reality, and thus avoiding false expectations.

When it comes to managing reputation, managers adopting a constitutive communication perspective need to take into account that reputation emerges from at least four main pillars. First is a well-defined and enduring corporate identity (self-structuring) (Roberts and Dowling, 2002; Stuebs and Li, 2009). Second is authenticity and trust assured by employees being ambassadors of a company's mission, vision, values, and brand (membership negotiation) (van Rekom *et al.*, 2006; van Riel *et al.*, 2009). Third is continuous alignment between corporate values and daily collective behaviors (activity coordination) (Doorley and Garcia, 2011). Fourth is stakeholder engagement and community building, which legitimates an organization as a social partner (institutional positioning) (Doorley and Garcia, 2011; Heat and Heat, 2007; Romenti, 2010). As Figure 17.1 illustrates, each of the four flows of con-

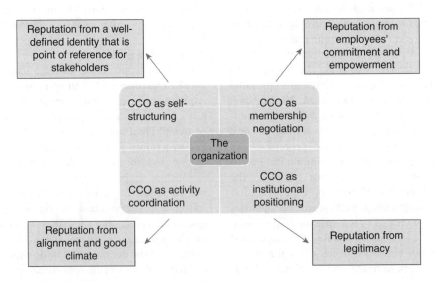

Figure 17.1 Model of how communication constitutes reputation.

stitutive communication is connected to a single component of corporate reputation.

Reputation comes out from self-structuring

Scholars highlight the need for senior managers to manage effectively their organization's corporate identity to improve reputation (Balmer and Gray, 1999; van Riel and Fombrun, 2007). A distinctive corporate identity is the backbone of reputation (van Riel and Fombrun, 2007) because it reflects managers' and employees' perceptions about the organizational core (Hatch and Schultz, 2008). Corporate identity influences the way in which stakeholders form their judgments (Dowling, 2006) – on the one hand, through visible symbols (i.e., architecture, office layouts, uniforms, dress codes, language, logos), which reflect organizational self-representation (Dowling, 2004), and on the other, through the expression of the deeper personality of the organization, which is the result of the shared values and beliefs of all organizational members. Corporate identity strengthens reputation when it is unequivocal, clear, and explicit, such as when it drives corporate behavior, so reinforcing the organizations' temporal consistency in the eyes of the stakeholders. To enhance reputation, all the communication contents by and about an organization should be consistent with its distinctive corporate identity over a given period of time (Balmer and Gray, 1999; Illia et al., 2004; van Riel and Fombrun, 2007). Constitutive communication perspective emphasizes the concept of reputation as a bundle of external perceptions of a distinctive corporate identity, and underlines the importance of involving employees (Dutton and Dukerick, 1991). The whole company communicates and the final goal is promoting the distinctiveness of the organization (Rindova and Fombrun, 1999). The formation of an "organization as a whole" is characterized by a well-defined organizational identity, which permits to the company to become a point of reference for employees as well as for external stakeholders (Illia and

Lurati, 2006). van Riel and Fombrun (2007) underline the importance of developing a reputation platform, which "describes the root positioning that a company adopts when it presents itself to internal and external observers" (p. 136). The reputation platform becomes the input for plotting and implementing a corporate story or narrative, which represents the frame for communication activities all over the organization. If communication is inherently a part of the organization's activities and strategies for future development, it strengthens reputation because it highlights the distinctiveness of the organization in the eyes of its stakeholders (Keh and Xie, 2009). The focus on an organization's expressiveness as a means of developing a strong reputation demands that the effects of communication strategy on stakeholders' perceptions and their consequent supporting should be measured. In this case, reputation models adopt a two-way model of communication, by listening to stakeholders' expectations and dealing with the gap between the actual and desired reputation among constituencies.

Reputation comes out from membership negotiation

Employees' cognitions and emotions have an important role for building a company's reputation. Among other reasons, this is important because employees become ambassadors of a company's core values (Illia et al., 2011; van Rekom et al., 2006). There are a number of decisions to be taken on communications constituting membership negotiation within organizations. These decisions affect the way membership is negotiated within the company. For example, one important decision is to choose the content of internal communication so that employees receive, on one level, the information on the organization and, on the other level, information on the function of the individual in the organization (van Riel and Fombrun, 2006; van Riel et al., 2009). Information on the organizational "we" level is key for membership negotiation because it enhances employees' social categorization within the organization (Smith, 2007). Examples of messages on the "we" level include information on organizational goals, mission, and vision as well as other communication that tells employees who the organization for which they work is, what the organization is doing, and where it is going (van Riel and Fombrun, 2006), such as information about new market entrances, alliances, financial investments, and future strategy and positioning. Differently, information on the "me" level is key to enhance employees' self-categorization within the organization (Smith, 2007). Examples of messages at the "me" level include job tasks, performance feedback, job opportunities in the organization, and all other messages that tell employees about their roles/ functions in the organization and how they perform these roles/performances. Managing internal communication through communications on these two levels permits managers to focus on how the receiver's attitudes, cognition, emotions, and perceptions function as filters to the information employees process (Goldhaber *et al.*, 1979). In this way, internal communication helps managers to cope with information overload and keep employees receptive toward internal communication messages (Katz and Kahn, 1966). Also, this permits to a certain extent to increase employees' identification with the organization (Smith, 2007) and assure that employees' cognitions and emotions have a positive role in building a company's reputation.

Reputation comes out from activity coordination

Balmer and Gray (1999) state that communication "form the nexus between an organisation's corporate identity and the coveted strategic objective of acquiring a favourable corporate reputation" (p. 172). These authors offer a broader view of communication by defining three forms of it: primary, secondary, and tertiary. The most interesting characteristic of this typology is that primary communication consists of organizational behaviors and their meanings transmitted to stakeholders. In other

words, whatever the organization does (e.g., in terms of product and services delivered, human resource policies, employees' behaviors to other stakeholders) is the fundamental component of corporate reputation (Balmer, 1998; Bromley, 1993; Fombrun, 1996; Fombrun and Shanley, 1990; Gray and Balmer, 1998). Above all, behaviors may contribute to reinforce reputation when they are linked to ethical and sustainable principles of management, and when they are consistent with organizational core values embedded in corporate identity. The central role assigned to behaviors within the reputation management process is the reason why the most commonly used corporate reputation measurement models (i.e., Fombrun's Reputation Quotient[SM], *Financial Times'* Reputational Rankings) evaluate stakeholder perceptions of a wide range of organizational elements: product and service quality, financial performance, social responsiveness, innovation, work-environment quality, and effectiveness of management. Fostering strategically aligned behaviors of employees so to assure that everyday employees' actions are consistent with the organization's strategy is of imperative importance to companies (van Riel *et al.*, 2009). Doorley and Garcia (2011) identify two kinds of aligning activities. The first one is aligning employees' behaviors in order to make them operate within appropriate boundaries coherent with organizations' stated values and reputation interests (Doorley and Garcia, 2011). The second one is aligning employee performance with the aim to drive employees' energies along with organizational strategies, long-term results, and customers' expectations (Doorley and Garcia, 2011). The continuous alignment between organizational values and daily behaviors needs to be driven by a strong leadership, sometimes taken by the CEO of the company who should be front-and-center on the topic. Organizations should encourage and facilitate the cultivation of collaboration networks, which promote employees' engagement in dialog about the gaps between "what we say" and "what we do" (Davenport, 2005). Employees are in fact very sensitive to misalignment, that is, when a company declares to make efforts to follow a mission and stated guiding values, but it takes actions which come into conflict with them. Internal communication activities which promote commitment, empowerment, and collective participation at work are crucial to the enhancement of alignment, as the constitutive communication perspective states. Commitment is promoted by a clear accountability system, which highlights the contribution of each single employee to the strategic alignment (Heat and Heat, 2007). Empowerment is enforced by internal communication centered on "rules of thumb," which are more useful of abstract concepts to employees who are deciding what to do when they do not know what to do (Doorley and Garcia, 2011). Collective participation at work is supported by engagement, which moves beyond merely listening to employees' needs and expectations. It means implementing co-decisional processes and partnerships about the reputation drivers themselves. Employees can be crucial in this process. They can be involved in the process of disseminating and implementing the organizational values and the corporate identity, as well as in work groups in order to implement shared solutions to make for instance the working environment and the internal climate better, and to debate the future challenges that the company would face (Romenti, 2010). Activity coordination allows the organization to be consistent and maintain a temporal alignment between stakeholders' expectations and organizational behavior, and ultimately enhance corporate reputation and performance results.

Reputation comes out from institutional positioning

The reputation of a company depends to a certain extent from communication aiming at positioning institutionally the company. The way the company presents itself to its audiences (Etang, 2008; Hatch and Schultz, 2008; van Riel, 1995; van Riel and Fombrun, 2007) through external communications that give positive impressions influence the level of legitimization and reputation of the company

(Carter, 2006; Dhalla, 2007; Elsbach, 1994; Elsbach and Sutton, 1992; King and Whetten, 2008; Lounsbury and Glynn, 2001; Price and Gioia, 2008). Also, corporate expressions inform how a company fits an industry's minimum and desired standards (King and Whetten, 2008, p. 201). Expressions communicate how the company conforms to social expectations associated with a particular population or industry, thereby enabling the company to gain legitimization by achieving minimum standards of the industry; expressions also communicate how the company distinguishes itself from its competitors and peers, thereby building the company's reputation in the industry.

Legitimacy is "a general perception or assumption that the actions of an entity are appropriate within some socially constructed system of norms, values, beliefs, and definitions" (Suchman, 1995, p. 574). As Pfeffer and Salancik (1978) indicate, a company does not need support from all segments of a society; rather, it needs endorsements from those segments that provide the organization with broader legitimacy. Legitimacy occurs when a company is able to conform to social expectations associated with a particular group of companies (Deephouse and Carter, 2005), to fulfill their social contact by operating within the norms of society (Brown and Deegan, 1998), to fit shared systems of rules that privilege some groups and avoid sanctions for not performing according to norms and rules settled in an industry (Powell and DiMaggio, 1991), and to avoid violating institutional identity codes (Hsu and Hannan, 2005). Reputation strictly interrelates with legitimacy as the more a company is legitimated, the more it differentiates itself from its competitors (Rindova and Fombrun, 1999). To a certain extent, this permits companies to build a collective enduring representation about themselves (Berens and van Riel, 2004; Cornelissen, 2008; Fombrun *et al.*, 2000) and to assure a positive, relatively stable, collective, and long-term judgments of audiences (Fombrun and Shanley, 1990).

Constitutive communication assures legitimacy through the engagement of stakeholders, which allow organizations to develop their ability to deliver value more efficiently (Fombrun *et al.*, 2000) and, consequently, to enhance their ability to satisfy the needs of multiple categories of stakeholders (Freeman, 1984). That means going beyond merely listening to stakeholders and addressing information to them. The objective of stakeholder engagement is to find mutually beneficial solutions, to create alliances and partnerships and to share responsibility with stakeholders (Gregory, 2007). This approach allows the organization to create a support network that can be used as a resource during times of crisis. Different categories of stakeholders, beyond employees, may be motivated to behave as "advocates" for organizations by supporting behavior, which seems to enhance reputation and performance results. Adopting a two-way symmetrical approach to communication means considering stakeholders as partners in the reputation development process, rather than judges of organizational performance. Putting stakeholder engagement at the center of a model of corporate reputation development offers two main opportunities. First, stakeholder engagement acts as lever that can propel and translate corporate identity into concrete organizational behavior. Second, it allows the organization to be consistent and maintain a temporal alignment between stakeholders' expectations and organizational behavior (Romenti, 2010). To assist in achieving business goals, stakeholder engagement should activate co-decisional processes, build partnerships, and stimulate supporting behavior from stakeholders. Activating co-decisional processes, for example, through ad hoc stakeholder meetings and multi-stakeholder workshops, means incorporating stakeholders' points of view in managerial decision making. The result is shared choices which should be more aligned to meeting stakeholders' expectations. Building partnerships means working together with stakeholders to devise, plan, and develop new business solutions. Stimulating supporting behavior transforms stakeholders into real advocates for organizational projects.

Building a Research Agenda on Communicatively Constituted Reputation (CCR)

The reputation of an organization depends to a certain extent from communication because "communication constitutes organizations," as an emergent perspective within the organizational communication field states. Constitutive communication consists of four flows that develop the building blocks on which reputation can be built. First, activity coordination assures the formation of an "organization as a whole," characterized from a well-defined organizational identity which permits to the company to become a point of reference for employees as well as for external stakeholders. Second, membership negotiation enhances employees' motivation and their empowerment in the organization so that the whole organization communicates in a consistent way. Third, activity coordination enables employees to align all behaviors within organizations with internal values and policies, as well as to enhance employees' commitment and empowerment. Besides, it drives trustworthiness and openness of information being disseminated in the organization, to increase the feeling of having a voice in the organization (participation in decision making), and the feeling of being taken seriously (supportiveness) Fourth, institutional positioning assures that organization through stakeholder engagement becomes a legitimate partner of social actors, beyond employees.

In the next paragraphs, we explore how future research can develop these four perspectives on reputation management, which start from a perspective that communication constitutes organization. Basically, our argument is that a strategic reputation management, which is based on the "communication constitutes organization" theoretical perspective, requires an appropriate management of various gaps and misalignment among image, reputation, and identity of the company (van Riel, 1995; van Riel and Fombrun, 2007). These gaps and misalignments offer important insights as they constitute the moments of truth for the corporation (Balmer and Greyser, 2002). In line with this perspective, we propose that it is important to abandon the assumption that communication is information. Communication is a process of meaning that is construed together with stakeholders. In this case, communication is not a "reality" or "truth" to communicate; it is enacted in each conversation that stakeholders have about the company (or with the company). The company cannot define "a priori" what meaning to communicate to stakeholders. The meaning about who the organization is, what its image and reputation is in constant definition, and any communication addressing a gap or misalignment constitute a communicational moment of truth about the company.

Activity patterns and leadership models for self-structuring

Self-structuring flow has to do with mechanisms that shape organization as a distinctive entity to which both internal and external members could be referred to. It does not concern the contents of work and the daily practices themselves, but the skeleton of work processes. It focuses on internal relations, norms, and social entities that connect the different parts of an organization and shape it. Self-structuring communication is about widespread responsibility, instead of centralized authority. This means that communication constitutes organization through internal collaborative networks, trust internal relations, norms of collaboration, and social coherence. Collaborative networks develop trust, which plays a more crucial role than top-down rules in steering the organization toward a specific direction. A major topic of research in this area would be the effective design of work processes as well as activity patterns which can develop collaborative internal networks. This leads to the conclusion that communication should be studied as something that a firm does, as a strategic practice that constitutes the becoming

of a company. Scholars should search for patterns of symbolic discourses to develop trust among employees and should assume a practice-oriented approach to research on communication topics. Another interesting area that could be examined from the "communication constitutes organization" perspective is the role of hierarchical structures and of governance system in developing collaborative internal networks. The adequacy and effectiveness of organizing structures and systems can be evaluated by how well organizational members perform their task, and feel involved and committed. A final avenue for research could be the practice of authority and leadership in self-structuring activity and its impact on the reputation-making process. Leadership takes place through communication, is part of the sensemaking activities of the organization, influences decision making, and charts the course of action for the organization (Shockley-Zalaback, 2009). Scholars should also search for framing mechanism enacted by leaders that are more effective within first self-structuring activity and then reputation making processes.

Management of collective identities for membership negotiation

The key issue here is to let members of a company be part of who the organization is (Tompkins and Cheney, 1985). Membership negotiation ought to be viewed as a flow of constitutive communication which deals with the cultivation of internal networks of relationships, which enhances employees' commitment and their identification with the organization. If employees feel committed, they become strong advocates of organization and support it during crisis times. Here, two key areas of research inquiry will be ones providing an accurate representation of organizational identity for managerial purposes, and a more accurate understanding of how to manage different identities in the organization. With regard to the first, considering organizational identity as a dynamic interplay between the essential characteristics and their plural interpretations will enable scholars to completely understand why an organization that seems fragmented is, in fact, a single, coherent organization (Corley *et al.*, 2006, p. 96). Consequently, it would be possible to use employees' perceptions of who the organization is to guide strategic decision making especially during times of change (Corley and Gioia, 2004). This would also be crucial to develop a common ground in the organization, which turns members into key ambassadors of the organization's long-lasting character (Gioia *et al.*, 2000; van Rekom *et al.*, 2006). With regard to the second insight, studies contributing to understand how a communicative perspective of the organization helps to manage reputation will be those exploring how one is able to manage the organization's essence as it permeates within members' daily identity understandings (Ravasi and Schultz, 2006; van Rekom *et al.*, 2006) that occur on an individual level. Said otherwise, will be those studies which will explore how to manage the organization according to the claims that are meaningful to members, therefore motivating them.

Problem-solving skills and communicative behaviors for activity coordination

Activity coordination flow focuses on the contents of work and daily activities themselves. It has to do with the adjustment of patterns, models, structures, and norms created through self-structuring activity. Activity coordination consists of communication which solves practical problems and organizes work effectively and efficiently, adapting to specific circumstances of the organizational environment. Interesting research areas here will be those developing a deep knowledge of which communication and technical competencies are required for effective problem-solving and decision-making processes. Another topic of research in this area would be the effective design of communities of practice, which are networks of individuals who interact regularly to work on innovating and improving with regard to their particular

problems. The key issue is to understand under which conditions communities of practice activate activity coordination processes and develop corporate reputation (Shockley-Zalaback, 2009). If employees feel empowered by the organizational communicative approach, they become strong advocates of a continuous problem-solving approach which adapts work processes and routines to changing reality. An avenue for research could be the practice of employees' engagement, how it can be stimulated, and how its results can be properly exploited by organizations (Doorley and Garcia, 2011).

Co-decisional processes and identity stories for institutional positioning

The key issue here is to assure stakeholder engagement and create the conditions by which different categories of stakeholders might be motivated to behave as advocates for organizations by supporting behavior, which seems to enhance reputation and performance results. Also, the key issue here is to assure that the company is legitimated as a good partner of social actors, beyond employees. Thus, related research studies here will be ones providing an accurate analysis of how one can activate co-decisional processes with key stakeholders (Gregory, 2007; Romenti, 2010). Further interesting research areas will be those developing an accurate analysis of how companies are able to be accommodating and loyal to partners (teaming up with others) and promote an inter-organizational identity to legitimize the organization at the collective level (fencing with others). This means that here, key studies will be those exploring how a company can have a collective strategy (Barnett and Hoffman, 2008) and work on its identity orientation with the whole organization (Brickson, 2005). Developing a "communication constitutes organization" perspective in this direction requires exploring how the identity statements of companies, different than other corporate statements, can be considered narratives providing institutional messages (Lammers, 2011;

Lammers and Barbour, 2006). As such, these stories do not provide a commercial spot informational univocal message. Contrariwise, they represent a communication constitutive part of the organization (McPhee and Zaug, 2009; Taylor and van Every, 2000). These identity stories express an institutional voice carrying out the core values at least nominally meant to be meaningful to everyone in and outside the company (Lammers, 2011). These identity stories are pervasive of the growing interconnectedness among the organizations and its stakeholders. As such, identity stories are influenced by the multiple identities enacted by organizations as a whole, both in a vertical sense (e.g., strategic groups, industries) and in the horizontal sense (interindustry groups, project-based groups, etc.).

Conclusions

Communication represents one of the most crucial components of reputation, as the interdisciplinary literature points out. The communicatively constituted organization approach offers stimulating insights for corporate reputation development. Communication through its four flows (self-structuring, membership negotiation, activity coordination, institutional positioning) constitutes the becoming of the reputation. Reputation comes out from self-structuring communication activity through the development of internal collaborative networks, trust relationships, and effective leadership models. Reputation comes out from membership negotiation activity through communication that enhances organizational identity and legitimacy. Reputation comes out from activity coordination through the diffusion of problem-solving skills and the widespread of effective communicative behaviors. Finally, reputation comes out from institutional positioning through developing identity stories and stakeholder engagement processes. Numerous streams of research can be identified in order to improve knowledge about reputation management.

References

Balmer, J.M.T. (1998) Corporate identity and the advent of corporate marketing. *Journal of Marketing Management*, 14(8), 963–996.

Balmer, J.M.T. and Gray, E.R. (1999) Corporate identity and corporate communications: Creating a competitive advantage. *Corporate Communications: An International Journal*, 4(4), 171–176.

Balmer, J.M.T. and Greyser, S.A. (2002) *Revealing the Corporation*. London: Routledge.

Barnett, M. and Hoffman, A. (2008) Beyond corporate reputation: Managing reputational interdependence. *Corporate Reputation Review*, 11(1), 1–9.

Berens, G. and van Riel, C.B.M. (2004) Corporate associations in the academic literature: Three main streams of thought in the reputation measurement literature. *Corporate Reputation Review*, 7(2), 161–178.

Birdwhistell, R.L. (1959) Contributions of linguistic-kinesic studies to understanding of schizophrenia. In A. Aurback (ed.), *Schizophrenia: An Integrated Approach*. New York: Ronald Press Company, pp. 99–123.

Blumer, H. (1969) *Symbolic Interactionism: Perspective and Method*. Englewood Cliffs, NJ: Prentice Hall.

Brickson, S.L. (2005) Organizational identity orientation: Forging a link between organizational identity and organizations' relations with stakeholders. *Administrative Science Quarterly*, 50(4), 576–609.

Bromley, D.B. (1993) *Reputation, Image, and Impression Management*. Chichester: John Wiley & Sons.

Brown, N. and Deegan, C. (1998) The public disclosure of environmental performance information – A dual test of media agenda setting theory and legitimacy theory. *Accounting and Business Research*, 29(1), 21.

Carter, S.M. (2006) The interaction of top management group, stakeholder, and situational factors on certain corporate reputation management activities. *The Journal of Management Studies*, 43(5), 1145.

Christensen, L.T. and Cornelissen, J.P. (2011) Bridging corporate and organizational communication. *Management Communication Quarterly*, 25(3), 383–414.

Corley, K.G. and Gioia, D.A. (2004) Identity ambiguity and change in the wake of a corporate spin-off. *Administrative Science Quarterly, 49,* 173–208.

Corley, K.G., Hartquail, C.V., Pratt, M.G., Glynn, M.A., Fiol, C.M., and Hatch, M.J. (2006) Guiding organizational identity through aged adolescence. *Journal of Management Inquiry, 15*(2), 85–99.

Cornelissen, J. (2008) *Corporate Communication: A Guide to Theory and Practice.* London: Sage Publications.

Davenport, T. (2005) *Thinking for a Living. How to Get Better Performances and Results from Knowledge Workers.* Boston: Harvard Business Press.

Deephouse, D.L. and Carter, S.M. (2005) An examination of differences between organizational legitimacy and organizational reputation. *The Journal of Management Studies, 42*(2), 329.

Deetz, S. (1992) Building a communication perspective in organization studies I: Foundations. Speech Communication Association, Chicago, IL.

Dhalla, R. (2007) The construction of organizational identity: Key contributing external and intra-organizational factors. *Corporate Reputation Review, 10*(4), 245.

Diboye, R.L. and Wiley, J.W. (1978) Reactions of male raters to interviewee self-presentation style and sex: Extension of previous research. *Journal of Vocational Behavior, 13,* 192–203.

Doorley, G. and Garcia, H.F. (2011) *Reputation Management. The Key to Successful Public Relations and Corporate Communication.* London: Routledge.

Dowling, G. (2004) Corporate reputations: Should you compete on yours. *California Management Review, 46*(3), 19–36.

Dowling, G. (2006) How good corporate reputations create corporate value. *Corporate Reputation Review, 9*(2), 134–143.

Dutton, J.E. and Dukerick, J. (1991) Keeping an eye on the mirror: Image and identity in organizational adaptation. *Academy of Management Review, 34*(3), 517–554.

Eccles, G., Grant, R.M., and van Riel, C.B.M. (2006) Reputation and transparency: Lessons from a painful period in public disclosure. *Long Range Planning, 39*(4), 353–359.

Eccles, R.G., Newquist, S.C., and Schatz, R. (2007) Reputation and its risks. *Harvard Business Review, 85*(2), 104–114.

Elsbach, K.D. (1994) Managing organizational legitimacy in the California cattle. *Administrative Science Quarterly, 39*(1), 57.

Elsbach, K.D. and Sutton, R.I. (1992) Acquiring organizational legitimacy through illegitimate actions: A marriage of institutional and impression management theories. *Academy of Management Journal, 35*(4), 699–738.

Etang, J. (2008) *Public Relations: Concepts, Practice and Critique.* Los Angeles, CA: Sage Publications.

Fisher, B.A. (1978) *Perspectives on Human Communication.* New York: Macmillan.

Fombrun, C.J. (1996) *Reputation. Realizing Value from the Corporate Image.* Boston: Harvard Business School Press.

Fombrun, C.J. and Shanley, M. (1990) What's in a name? Reputation building and corporate strategy. *Academy of Management Journal, 33*(2), 233–258.

Fombrun, C.J., Gardberg, N.A., and Sever, J.M. (2000) The Reputation Quotient^{SM}: A multi-stakeholder measure of corporate reputation. *The Journal of Brand Management, 7*(4), 241–255.

Freeman, R.E. (1984) *Strategic Management: A Stakeholder Approach.* Boston: Pitman.

Gioia, D.A., Shultz, M., and Corley, K.G. (2000) Organizational identity, image, and adaptive instability. *Academy of Management Review, 25*(1), 63–81.

Goldhaber, G.M., Dennis, H., Richetto, G., and Wiio, O. (1979) *Information Strategies: New Pathways to Corporate Power.* Englewood Cliffs, NJ: Prentice Hall.

Gray, E.R. and Balmer, J.M.T. (1998) Managing corporate image and corporate reputation. *Long Range Planning, 31*(5), 695–702.

Gregory, A. (2007) Involving stakeholders in developing corporate brands: The communication dimension. *Journal of Marketing Management, 23*(1–2), 59–73.

Hatch, M.J. and Schultz, M. (2008) *Taking the Brand Initiative.* San Francisco, CA: Jossey-Bass.

Heat, C. and Heat, D. (2007) *Made to Stick. Why Some Ideas Survive and Others Die.* New York: Random House.

Hsu, G. and Hannan, M.T. (2005) Identities, genres, and organizational forms. *Organization Science, 16*(5), 474–490.

Illia, L. and Lurati, F. (2006) Stakeholder perspective to organization's identity: Searching for a relationship approach. *Corporate Reputation Review, 8*(4), 293–304.

Illia, L., Schmid, E., Fishbach, I., Hantgartner, R., and Rivola, R. (2004) An issues management perspective to corporate identity: The case of a governmental agency. *Corporate Reputation Review*, 7(1), 10–24.

Illia, L., Bonaiuto, M., Pugliese, E., and van Rekom, J. (2011) Managing membership threats through collective efficacy. *Journal of Business Research*, 64(6), 631–639.

Katz, D. and Kahn, R.L. (1966) *The Social Psychology of Organizations*. New York: Wiley.

Keh, H.T. and Xie, Y. (2009) Corporate reputation and customer behavioral intentions: The roles of trust, identification and commitment. *Industrial Marketing Management*, 38(7), 732–742.

King, B. and Whetten, D. (2008) Rethinking the relationship between reputation and legitimacy: A social actor conceptualization. *Corporate Reputation Review*, 11(3), 192–207.

Kitchen, P.J. (2004) Corporate reputation. In S.S.A. Oliver (ed.), *Handbook of Corporate Communication and Public Relations: Pure and Applied*. London: Routledge, pp. 265–277.

Krone, J.K., Jablin, F.M., and Putnam, L.L. (1987) Communication theory and organizational communication: Multiple perspectives. In F.M. Jablin, L.L. Putnam, K.H. Roberts, and L.W. Porter (eds), *Handbook of Organizational Communication*. Newbury Park, CA: Sage Publications.

Lammers, J.C. (2011) How institutions communicate: Institutional messages, institutional logics, and organizational communication. *Management Communication Quarterly*, 25(1), 154–182.

Lammers, J.C. and Barbour, J.B. (2006) An institutional theory of organizational communication. *Communication Theory*, 16(3), 356–377.

Lounsbury, M. and Glynn, M.A. (2001) Cultural entrepreneurship: Stories, legitimacy, and the acquisitions of resources. *Strategic Management Journal*, 22(6/7), 545–564.

McGovern, T.V., Tinsley, E.A., and Howard, E.A. (1978) Interviewer evaluations of interviewee non verbal behavior. *Journal of Vocational Behavior*, 13, 163–171.

McPhee, R.D. (1985) Formal structure and organizational communication. In R.D. McPhee and P.K. Tompkins (eds), *Organizational Communication: Traditional Themes and New Directions*. Beverly Hills, CA: Sage Publications.

McPhee, R.D. and Zaug, P. (2009) The communicative constitution of organizations: A framework for explanation. In L.L. Putnam and A.M. Nicotera (eds), *Building Theories of Organization: The Constitutive Role of Communication*. New York: Routledge.

Mead, G.H. (1934) *Mind, Self, and Society*. Chicago, IL: University of Chicago Press.

Mintzberg, H. (1979) Patterns is strategy formation. *International Studies of Management and Organisation*, 9(3), 67–86.

Pfeffer, J. and Salancik, G.R. (1978) *The External Control of Organizations: A Resource Dependence Perspective*. New York: Harper & Row.

Powell, W.W. and DiMaggio, P.J. (1991) *The New Institutionalism in Organizational Analysis*. Chicago, IL: The University of Chicago Press.

Price, K. and Gioia, D. (2008) The self-monitoring organization: Minimizing discrepancies among differing images of organizational identity. *Corporate Reputation Review*, 11(4), 208–221.

Putman, L.L., Nicotera, A.M., and McPhee, R.D. (2009) Communication constitutes organization. In L.L. Putnam and A.M. Nicotera (eds), *Building Theories of Organization: The Constitutive Role of Communication*. New York: Routledge, pp. 1–20.

Ravasi, D. and Schultz, M. (2006) Responding to organizational identity threats: Exploring the role of organizational culture. *Academy of Management Journal*, 49(3), 433–458.

Rindova, V.P. and Fombrun, C.J. (1999) Constructing competitive advantage: The role of firm-constituent interpretation. *Strategic Management Journal*, 20(8), 691–710.

Roberts, P.W. and Dowling, G.R. (2002) Corporate reputation and sustained superior financial performance. *Strategic Management Journal*, 23(12), 1077–1093.

Romenti, S. (2010) Reputation and Stakeholder engagement: An Italian case study. *Journal of Communication Management*, 14(4), 306–318.

Shockley-Zalaback, P.S. (2009) *Fundamentals of Organizational Communication. Knowledge, Sensitivity, Skills Values*. Boston: Pearson.

Smidts, A., Pruyn, A., and van Riel, C.B.M. (2001) The impact of employee communication and perceived external prestige on organizational identification. *Academy of Management Journal*, 49(5), 1051–1062.

Smith, S. (2007) Why employees are more trusted than the CEO. *Strategic Communication Management*, 11(3), 7.

Stuebs, M. and Li, S. (2009) Corporate reputation and technical efficiency: Evidence from the chemical and business services industries. *Journal of Applied Business Research*, 25(5), 21–29.

Suchman, M.C. (1995) Managing legitimacy: Strategic and institutional approaches. *Academy of Management Review*, 20(3), 571–610.

Taylor, J.R. and van Every, E. (2000) *The Emergent Organization: Communication as Its Site and Surface*. Mahwah, NJ: Erlbaum.

Tompkins, P.K. and Cheney, G. (1985) Communication and unobtrusive control in contemporary organizations. In R.D. McPhee and P.K. Tompkins (eds), *Organizational Communication: Traditional Themes, and New Directions*. Beverly Hills, CA: Sage Publications, pp. 179–210.

van Rekom, J., Cees, B.M., van Riel, C.B.M., and Wierenga, B. (2006) A methodology for assessing organizational core values. *Journal of Management Studies*, 43(2), 175–201.

van Riel, C.B.M. (1995) *Principles of Corporate Communications*. London: Prentice Hall.

van Riel, C.B.M. and Fombrun, C.J. (2006) *Fame and Fortune*. London: FT Press.

van Riel, C.B.M. and Fombrun, C.J. (2007) *Essentials of Corporate Communication*. London: Routledge.

van Riel, C.B.M., Berens, G., and Dijkstra, M. (2009) Stimulating strategically aligned behavior among employees. *Journal of Management Studies*, 46(7), 1197–1227.

Weick, K.E. (1979) *The Social Psychology of Organizations* (2nd ed.). Reading, MA: Addison-Wesley.

18

A Strategic Management Approach to Reputation, Relationships, and Publics: The Research Heritage of the Excellence Theory[1]

Jeong-Nam Kim
Purdue University, USA

Chun-ju Flora Hung-Baesecke
Hong Kong Baptist University, China

Sung-Un Yang
Indiana University, USA

James E. Grunig
University of Maryland, USA

The Excellence theory developed from a program of research conducted from 1985 to 2002 on 327 organizations in the United States, Canada, and the United Kingdom. The research combined a number of middle-range theories of public relations and showed that public relations creates value for organizations and society through relationships and that public relations is most valuable when it is managerial, strategic, symmetrical, diverse, integrated, socially responsible, ethical, and global. Today, Excellence theory has evolved into a strategic management theory of public relations, which contrasts to the symbolic–interpretive paradigm that characterizes many theories of reputation. Research based on this strategic management paradigm shows that reputation is largely a byproduct of organizational behaviors and organization–public relationships – the well-known idea that actions speak louder than words. Both relationships and reputation differ for low-involvement and high-involvement publics, and strategic communicators should emphasize experiential relationships with high-involvement publics more than reputational relationships with low-involvement publics when they participate in organizational governance.

The Handbook of Communication and Corporate Reputation, First Edition. Edited by Craig E. Carroll.
© 2013 John Wiley & Sons, Inc. Published 2015 by John Wiley & Sons, Inc.

The research tradition that culminated in the Excellence theory conceptualizes public relations as a strategic management function rather than as a messaging, publicity, and media relations function. James Grunig began the tradition at the University of Maryland in the 1960s when he developed the situational theory of publics (e.g., J. Grunig, 1966, 1971, 1978, 1997), applied organizational theory to public relations (J. Grunig, 1976), identified the symmetrical model of public relations (J. Grunig, 1989), and introduced methods for the evaluation of communication programs (J. Grunig, 2008). The Excellence study, which began in 1985, brought these middle-level theories together with other prominent, middle-range public relations theories of the time. Since the completion of the Excellence study, scholars in this research tradition have continued to conduct research to help public relations professionals participate in strategic decision processes – research on environmental scanning and publics, scenario building, empowerment of public relations, ethics, relationships, the value of public relations, evaluation, relationship cultivation strategies, specialized areas of public relations, and global strategy (for a review of this research, see J. Grunig, 2006; Toth, 2007).

The Excellence theory, as it stands today, both describes and prescribes the role of public relations in strategic management. It is a general theory that explains how the public relations function should be structured and managed to provide the greatest value to organizations, publics, and society. Specifically, the theory

- explains how public relations contributes value to organizations, publics, and society;
- explains how an empowered public relations function makes a unique contribution to strategic management and distinguishes its role from that of other management functions, especially marketing;
- prescribes techniques that public relations managers can use to fulfill their role in strategic management;
- explains the critical role of relationships in the planning and evaluation of public relations programs;

- identifies different models of communication and explains which models are the most effective strategies for cultivating relationships with publics;
- incorporates ethics into the strategic role of public relations;
- explains how to apply the theory globally.

Beginning in 1985, a team of six researchers conducted a long-term study, funded by the International Association of Business Communicators (IABC) Research Foundation, on the characteristics of excellent public relations departments and on how such departments make their organizations more effective. The studied 327 organizations in the United States, Canada, and the United Kingdom to identify how organizations practice public relations in an excellent way – practices that are most likely to make organizations effective.

The first phase of the Excellence study consisted of quantitative survey research on the 327 organizations. Questionnaires were completed by 407 senior communication officers (some organizations had more than one public relations department), 292 CEOs or other executive managers, and 4631 employees (an average of 14 per organization). The organizations included corporations, government agencies, nonprofit organizations, and trade and professional associations.

The research team consisted of five scholars and a practitioner from the United Kingdom and the United States. James Grunig and Larissa Grunig were professors at the University of Maryland, and David Dozier was a professor at San Diego State University. William Ehling then was a professor at Syracuse University and now is retired. Jon White, then of the Cranfield School of Management in the United Kingdom, is now an independent consultant and teacher in London. Finally, Fred Repper, who is now deceased, was a distinguished senior public relations practitioner who had recently retired as vice president of public relations for Gulf States Utilities in Beaumont, Texas.

After collecting the quantitative survey data, the team analyzed it, first, by reducing as much of the data as possible into a single numerical index of excellence in communication management. The survey research was followed by qualitative interviews with heads of public relations, other public relations practitioners, and CEOs in 25 organizations with the highest and lowest scores on this index of excellence. The qualitative information provided insights on how excellent public relations came about in different organizations as well as detail on the outcomes produced by excellence and the value of public relations to an organization as seen by CEOs and senior public relations practitioners.

The Excellence study integrated most of the prominent middle-level theories of communication management that were available in the discipline at the time the study began. These middle-range theories included public relations roles and models, corporate social responsibility, and the relationship of public relations to marketing and other management functions. The goal of the research team was not to impose a single theory on public relations but to try to bring both complementary and competing theories together in a way that would answer questions and solve problems of concern to most public relations practitioners and scholars. The Excellence study eventually resulted in three books (Dozier *et al.*, 1995; J. Grunig, 1992; L. Grunig *et al.*, 2002).

The first book, *Excellence in Public Relations and Communication Management* (J. Grunig, 1992), reported the results of an extensive review of literature in public relations, communication, management, organizational sociology and psychology, social and cognitive psychology, feminist studies, political science, operations research, and culture. The team conducted this review to identify characteristics of public relations programs and departments and of the organizations in which they are found that make public relations more effective. The team also searched the literature for concepts that would explain the value of individual public relations programs and the value of the overall public relations function to an organization (Ehling, 1992; L. Grunig *et al.*, 1992). It then linked these two sets of theories

to identify the characteristics of a public relations function that are most likely to increase organizational effectiveness.

The second book, *Manager's Guide to Excellence in Public Relations and Communication Management* (Dozier *et al.*, 1995), summarized the literature review and presented a short, reader-friendly version of the theory and results of the study in a format intended mostly for practitioners rather than scholars. The third book, *Excellent Public Relations and Effective Organizations: A Study of Communication Management in Three Countries* (L. Grunig *et al.*, 2002), reviewed and updated the theories from the first book and presented the complete results of the quantitative and qualitative portions of the study.

The comprehensive theory of public relations that resulted from this extensive literature review and analysis of research data began with a premise of why public relations has value to an organization. That premise allowed the team to identify and connect attributes of the public relations function and of the organization that logically would be most likely to make the organization effective. This general theory consists of several generic principles that seem to apply throughout the world, although it specifies that these concepts must be applied differently in different cultures and political–economic systems. The theory also applies in different organizational settings such as government agencies, corporations, nonprofit organizations, and associations. In short, the theory offers a conceptual framework for the professional practice of public relations, which, with appropriate applications and revisions in different organizational and national cultures, is a fundamental component of effective management throughout the world.

The Excellence study provided evidence that there is a correlation between achieving short-term communication effects and maintaining quality long-term relationships (see, especially, Dozier *et al.*, 1995, chapter 16). The senior communicators in excellent departments reported more often than those in less-excellent departments that their departments had *outcome objectives* for their short-term programs aimed at the media, employees, community, customers, members, government, and investors. They also reported that their departments engaged in all forms of short-term evaluation more than did the less-excellent communicators – especially *scientific* evaluation but also *media placement* and *seat-of-the-pants* evaluation.

At the same time, the excellent communicators more often reported that their programs had *change-of-relationship* effects such as changes in behavior of a public, greater cooperation between the organization and public, and the development of a stable long-term relationship. They also reported more frequent *conflict avoidance* effects, such as avoiding litigation, fewer complaints from publics, and less interference by government. As a result, the Excellence study provided evidence that public relations departments that had set objectives and measured the outcomes of their short-term communication programs also believed that they experienced greater success in building long-term relationships with publics.

In-depth interviews of the most excellent public relations departments in the Excellence study showed that *good communication changes behavior of both management and publics* and, therefore, *results in good relationships.* If public relations managers help management to understand that certain decisions might have adverse consequences on a public, then management might make a different decision and behave in a different way than it might have otherwise, that is, a behavioral change by management that should lead to a behavioral change by a public. For example, a public would be more likely to accept a new road or building in its neighborhood, buy a product that is now more acceptable, or support a reduction in the number of employees that takes employee interests into account. There are also times when communication helps a public to trust management and to accept a decision that management wanted to make before communication took place.

The Excellence study, therefore, identified the importance of a strategic management role for public relations as well as the importance of relationships in explaining the value of public relations to organizations and society. At the beginning of the study, the researchers searched the management and sociological literature on organizational effectiveness for ideas that could explain the value of public relations. They found that effective organizations choose and achieve appropriate goals because they develop relationships with their stakeholder publics. Ineffective organizations cannot achieve their goals, at least in part, because their publics do not support and typically oppose management efforts to achieve what publics consider illegitimate goals. Poor relationships cost the organization a great deal of money – as a result of litigation, regulation, legislation, negative publicity, strikes, boycotts of products, loss of sales or donations, and public opposition. As a result, the process of developing and maintaining relationships with strategic publics is a crucial component of strategic management, issues management, and crisis management.

The Excellence study concluded, therefore, that public relations makes an organization more effective when it identifies the most strategic publics of the organization as part of strategic management processes and conducts communication programs to cultivate effective long-term relationships with those publics. As a result, we can determine the value of public relations by measuring the quality of relationships with strategic publics. And, we should be able to evaluate communication programs by measuring the effects of these programs and correlating them with relationship indicators.

Since the completion of the Excellence study, James Grunig and two of his former students, Yi Hui Huang now of Chinese University of Hong Kong and Chun Ju Hung now of Hong Kong Baptist University, searched the literature on interpersonal communication to identify characteristics of relationships that could be applied to organization–public relationships and to develop measures of these relationships (Huang, 1997; Hung, 2002). They identified four qualities of a good long-term relationship: trust (the level of confidence that an organization and public have in each other and their willingness to open themselves to the other), control mutuality (the degree to which both organization and public are satisfied with the amount of control they have over the relationship), commitment by both to the relationship, and satisfaction with the relationship (see Hon and J. Grunig, 1999).

As part of this same program of research, J. Grunig and Hung (2002) examined the concept of reputation, which became popular in the management literature at about the time the Excellence study was ending, to determine where that concept might fit into the theoretical structure of the Excellence study. That research produced an understanding of reputation that is somewhat different from that prevailing in the management literature. Whereas most reputation researchers seem to think of public relations as an interpretative messaging activity, researchers in the Excellence tradition isolated the importance of organizational behavior and organization–public relationships in explaining the nature of an organization's reputation. Before explaining the role of reputation in a strategic management approach to public relations, therefore, we examine two competing ways in which public relations scholars and practitioners, management scholars and practitioners, and people in general think about public relations

Symbolic and Behavioral Paradigms of Public Relations

We have named these differing views about public relations the *symbolic, interpretive* paradigm and the *strategic management, behavioral* paradigm. Those who embrace the symbolic paradigm generally assume that public relations strives to influence how publics interpret the behaviors of organizations after they occur and that its purpose is to secure the power of the decision makers who chose those behaviors. These cognitive interpretations are typically embodied in such concepts as image, reputation, brand, impressions, and identity. Practitioners who follow the interpretive paradigm emphasize messages, publicity, media relations,

and media effects, which they believe create an impression in the minds of publics that allow the organization to *buffer* itself from its environment, to use the words of Van den Bosch and van Riel (1998). Such organizations believe favorable impressions created by public relations can obscure their decisions and actions and, in turn, that they can behave in the way that managers with power want without interference from publics.

In contrast, the behavioral, strategic management paradigm focuses on the participation of public relations executives in strategic decision making so that they can help manage the behavior of organizations rather than only interpret it to publics. Van den Bosch and van Riel (1998) defined this type of public relations as a *bridging*, rather than a buffering, function. Public relations as a bridging activity is designed to build relationships with stakeholders. The strategic management paradigm of public relations emphasizes two-way communication of many kinds to provide publics a voice in management decisions and to facilitate dialog between management and publics both before and after decisions are made. The strategic management paradigm does not exclude traditional public relations activities such as media relations and the dissemination of information. Rather, it broadens the number and types of communication activities and fits them into a framework of environmental scanning, research, and listening. As a result, messages reflect the information needs of publics as well as the advocacy needs of organizations.

Public relations has value in this perspective because it brings a different set of problems and possible solutions to the attention of strategic managers. Public relations executives counsel members of top management about the likely consequences of policy decisions on publics. They give voice to and empower publics in organizational decision making by identifying strategic publics, conducting research to understand their problems and interests, and then communicating their views to senior management.

The strategic approach also accepts the presence of subjectivity in both theorizing and communicating, the central assumption of the symbolic–interpretive approach. However, it goes beyond the use of communication in *negotiating meaning* to enhance the power of organizations and managers and also plays a role in *negotiating the behavior* of both organizations and publics. Public relations educates and persuades publics by advocating corporate interests, but it also negotiates with publics when a collision of interests arises. In doing so, public relations benefits organizations by helping them make decisions, develop policies, provide services, and behave in ways that are accepted by and sought out by their stakeholder publics – thus increasing the organization's revenue, reducing its costs, and reducing its risk.

We believe, therefore, that it is important to view public relations as a strategic management function rather than as a purely interpretative function by explaining its role in strategic management and organizational governance. Concepts such as brand and reputation are symbolic in nature: a brand is what an organization tries to get stakeholders to think about the organization, and a reputation is what they actually think and say about it. What people think about an organization is important, and it does affect their behavior. However, most scholars and practitioners who embrace the symbolic paradigm seem to believe that messages or the media alone create a reputation. Our research, in contrast, shows that what stakeholders think (i.e., the cognitive structures such as reputations that are in their minds) reflect more the behavior of the organization and the actual relationships that stakeholders have with an organization than it reflects messages organizations send out. To put it simply: actions speak louder than words.

To truly "manage" a reputation, therefore, public relations professionals must participate in making management decisions and managing an organization's behavior. We can explain how that is done by examining the strategic role of public relations and the linkages among organizational behavior, relationships, and reputation.

A Strategic Management Role for Public Relations: How Organizational Behavior and Relationships Shape Reputation

The practice of a strategic management role for public relations and knowledge in the public relations department of how to practice it emerged in the Excellence study as the characteristics that most distinguished excellent from less-excellent public relations functions. The Excellence study showed that the most effective public relations departments participated in the making of overall strategic decisions in organizations. Less-effective departments generally had the less-central role of disseminating messages about strategic decisions made by others in the organization.

By participating in organizational decisions, excellent public relations departments were in a position to identify the stakeholders who would be affected by organizational decisions or who would affect those decisions. Once they had identified stakeholders, excellent public relations departments strategically developed programs to communicate with them. They conducted formative research to identify potential issues and define objectives for programs to communicate with the stakeholders, they specified measurable objectives for the communication programs, and they used both formal and informal methods to evaluate whether the objectives had been accomplished. Less-excellent departments conducted no formative or evaluative research and generally had only vague objectives that were difficult to measure.

Figure 18.1 depicts the roles of excellent public relations at two organizational levels, the organizational and the program levels – how the senior communication executive participates in the overall strategic management process of an organization and the strategic management of public relations programs themselves. The central concepts in Figure 18.1 are *management decisions* at the top, *stakeholders* and *publics* on the right, and *relationship*

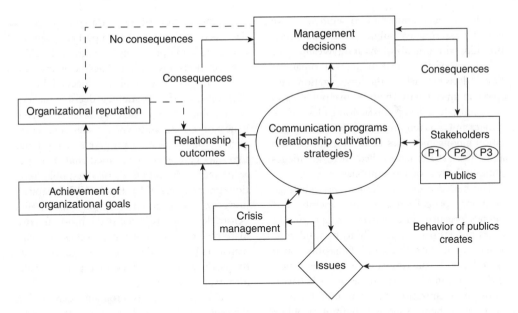

Figure 18.1 Model of strategic management of public relations. Reproduced with permission of James Grunig.

outcomes on the left. Connecting management and publics are the consequences that the behavior of each has on the other – the interdependence between an organization and its environment that creates the need for public relations.

The double arrows between management decisions and stakeholders at the upper right of Figure 18.1 show that strategic decision makers of an organization should interact with stakeholders through the public relations function because their decisions have consequences on publics or because the organization needs supportive relationships with stakeholders in order to make responsible decisions as well as to implement decisions and achieve organizational goals. Stakeholders might also seek a relationship with an organization in order to attain a consequence from the organization to solve a problem it recognizes – such as an environmental group that seeks a reduction in pollution from a chemical plant or nuclear laboratory or a community that seeks additional jobs for its residents. Thus, the consequences of organizational decisions (and behaviors resulting from those decisions) define

the stakeholders of an organization and, therefore, the stakeholders with whom the organization needs a relationship.

We define stakeholders as broad categories of people who might be affected by management decisions or who might affect those decisions – such as employees, customers, or community residents. When a strategic public relations manager scans the environment, therefore, his or her first step should be to think broadly in terms of stakeholder categories. Then, he or she should use a theory of publics (e.g., J. Grunig's, 1997, situational theory of publics; Kim *et al.*, 2010; Kim and J. Grunig's, 2011, situational theory of problem solving) to identify and segment active, passive, and latent publics from the nonpublics that might also be present in the stakeholder category. It is important to recognize that the publics that are segmented are not permanent or stable. Rather, they come and go as situations and organizational consequences change. Thus, a public relations manager typically must continually resegment publics as organizational decisions and consequences change.

It is especially important to segment active publics because active publics actually have relationships with organizations and typically make issues out of the consequences of organizational decisions when the organization fails to communicate with them. Active publics also communicate their dissatisfaction to less-active publics and thus tend to create a negative reputation among members of those publics. Kim and Rhee (2011) have called this the "megaphoning" effect of active publics.

The behavior of a public may be individual or it may be collective – when members of publics organize into activist groups. Sometimes publics react negatively to harmful consequences of an organization's behaviors – such as pollution or discrimination. At other times, they act positively to try to secure a behavior from an organization that has useful consequences for them – such as a community public that wants cleaner rivers and streams or a health-related public that might want a pharmaceutical company to produce an unprofitable orphan drug. At still other times, publics collaborate with organizations to secure consequences of benefit to both.

If an organization communicates effectively with publics before decisions are made or during the implementation of decisions, issues and crises may never occur and good relationships should be secured – an outcome depicted by an arrow from *communication programs* to *relationship outcomes* in Figure 18.1. Figure 18.1 then shows that good relationships generally result in a good reputation for the organization. This is because publics tend to have good relationships with and to think well of organizations that make decisions and behave in ways that publics approve of.

Figure 18.1 shows, however, that publics that cannot stop the consequences that harm them or secure the consequences that benefit them generally make issues out of the consequences. Issues, in turn, can become crises if they are not handled well. When issues or potential issues are discussed and negotiated with publics through communication, however, the result should be improved relationships with publics.

At the center of the strategic processes described in Figure 18.1 is an oval representing communication programs – programs to cultivate relationships with publics. Communication with potential publics is needed before decisions are made by strategic decision makers, when publics have formed but have not created issues or crises, and when issues and crises occur. Communication programs at the latter two stages are generally termed *issues management* and *crisis communication* by public relations practitioners. What Figure 18.1 illustrates, however, is that communication with publics before decisions are made is the most effective in resolving issues and crises because it helps managers to make decisions that are less likely to produce consequences that publics make into issues and crises.

The public relations programs depicted in the center oval should be managed strategically themselves. These programs should be developed from strategies to cultivate relationships with publics. Most communication techniques, programs, or campaigns conducted by public relations professionals can be classified as relationship cultivation strategies. Communication programs should begin with formative research, then develop achievable and measurable objectives, implement the program, and end with evaluation of whether the objectives have been met.

We have used the concept of cultivation strategies as the successor to J. Grunig's four models of public relations (press agentry, public information, two-way asymmetrical, and two-way symmetrical). In the Excellence study, we first replaced the models of public relations with four underlying characteristics of communication strategy: direction (one way or two way), purpose (symmetrical or asymmetrical), mediated or interpersonal, and ethical or unethical (L. Grunig *et al.*, 2002, chapter 8). Hon and J. Grunig (1999) identified a preliminary list of cultivation strategies, and Hung (2007) has modified and added to this list considerably as a result of her research. Men and Hung (2012) integrated the literature on strategic management to explore how organization–public relationships contribute to each stage of strategic management.

The final path in Figure 18.1 can be found in the dotted lines from *management decisions* to *organizational reputation* to *relationship outcomes* – a path labeled *no consequences*. This path depicts the approach taken by interpretive scholars who seem to believe that positive messages about management decisions – mostly disseminated through the mass media – can by themselves create a positive organizational reputation. Such a path might produce what we call a *reputational relationship* – a relationship based only on secondary sources and not based on an actual relationship between the organization and a public (J. Grunig and Hung, 2002).

Therefore, we have labeled the dotted line *no consequences* because we believe that organizations have reputational relationships only with people for whom the organization has few consequences. Such people can be defined as *audiences* because they are not truly *publics*. These audiences have little importance to an organization. As soon as an organization or public has consequences on the other, it begins to develop an involving behavioral relationship rather than a low-involvement reputational relationship. It is at that point that a group of people becomes an active and strategic public rather than a passive audience.

The public relations process depicted by Figure 18.1, therefore, provides a theoretical framework for a strategic management approach to public relations and explains how an intangible corporate asset such as reputation is produced through organizational governance and the cultivation of organization–public relationships.

Research on Reputation from a Behavioral, Strategic Management Perspective

Reputation and relationships

J. Grunig and Hung (2002) were the first to study how relationships affect an organization's reputation. They compared definitions of reputation with similar concepts such as brand,
image, goodwill, and impressions and concluded that all of these terms actually describe a single concept that cognitive psychologists call a *cognitive representation*. Definitions and measures of reputation, both in the psychological and business literature and in the professional public relations literature, suggest that reputation consists of what members of publics remember about an organization and talk about among themselves. In the research literature, Bromley (1993) defined reputation as "what is collectively said or believed about a person or thing." In the first issue of the journal *Corporate Reputation Review*, business scholars Fombrun and van Riel (1997) defined it as the "collective representation of a firm's past actions and results" (p. 10).

Nevertheless, J. Grunig and Hung found that most popular measures of reputation – such as the *Fortune* reputation index or Fombrun's Reputation Quotient[SM] – measure attitudes toward corporations rather than reputations. Attitudes are cognitions (thoughts) with an evaluative judgment attached to them. Most measures of reputation consist of the averaged evaluations of a number of areas of corporate performance (such as ethical behavior, treatment of employees and workplace conditions, financial performance, leadership, quality of management, social responsibility, customer focus, quality, reliability, and emotional appeal) as rated by several quite different publics (such as financial analysts, CEOs, and the "general" public). Because of the wide differences in publics and in the areas evaluated, the single average measure of reputation produced by most of the reputational surveys seems to have limited value as a measure of reputation.

In contrast to these grossly averaged measures, most writers about reputation (such as Fombrun, 1996) do actually argue that reputation is a product of organizational *behavior* and of *relationships* with publics. Yet, they measure neither the behaviors that publics recall nor the relationships. As we showed in our previous discussion of Figure 18.1, we do not believe that reputation can be *managed* directly. Rather, it can be *influenced* by affecting the behavior of management – when public relations executives participate in the strategic decision-making processes of an organization. We also believe that reputation is a by-product of organization–public relationships and that relationships should be used as the focal variable for measuring the value of public relations activities.

Research conducted by public relations scholars has provided support for this reasoning. Studies have shown that public relations has a greater long-term effect on relationships than on reputation and that reputation is largely a by-product of management behavior and the quality of organization–public relationships (Yang, 2007; Yang and J. Grunig, 2005). These findings show that attending to relationships will ultimately improve an organization's reputation. Reputation, however, cannot be managed directly; it is managed through the cultivation of relationships.

In contrast, writers about reputation generally believe that public relations serves a symbolic–interpretive, or *strategic messaging*, function rather than a *strategic management* function. For example, in his book on reputation, Fombrun (1996) discussed public relations in the chapter on "Shaping Consistent Images," which contains headings such as "Spin Doctoring," "Swayed by the Media," and "Public Facades." In contrast, we believe that public relations can help shape management behaviors. The role of public relations goes beyond communicating messages after decisions are made. Reputations are shaped by organizational behavior, and messages alone cannot change the way publics interpret these behaviors.

To support this theory, J. Grunig and Hung (2002) used the work of Bromley (1993) and other cognitive psychologists to develop an open-end question to measure the cognitive structures that people hold in their minds about organizations. They defined reputation as a *distribution* of different kinds of cognitive representations (rather than an average score) held by members of a collectivity – such as the general population or a specific public of an organization. These representations may or may not include an evaluation – an attitude. To measure this concept of reputation, they asked

a sample of the general population to "describe in a sentence or two what comes to mind when you think of" five organizations that were chosen for different reasons – General Electric, the National Rifle Association, the US Social Security Administration, Microsoft, and the American Red Cross. They coded these responses into different categories and then compared the means of six relationship variables for participants who mentioned each category with those who did not mention it.

The results confirmed that organizational behaviors and relationships were strongly related to reputation. Although organizational behaviors that people remembered were not always the most frequent cognitive structures (reputations) that people held for all of the organizations studied, they were at the top for organizations that were particularly popular or unpopular. The recall of either good or bad behaviors, in turn, had the most significant effect on the way research participants viewed the type and quality of relationships with an organization.

At the same time, J. Grunig and Hung (2002) found evidence that there can be a reputational relationship between an organization and a less-involved public. People who do not have experience with an organization can, and do, evaluate their relationship with it solely on what they have read or heard from others. In the case of the National Rifle Association, this reputational relationship led people to stigmatize or shun the organization – even though they did not perceive an involvement with it or did not have more than superficial knowledge about the organization.

Although this research suggests that public relations professionals should emphasize relationships as the focus of their work, it also showed that J. Grunig and Hung's (2002) definition and measure of reputation has value as a public relations metric. When reputation is defined as a distribution of cognitive representations, their open-end measure can reveal how members of a public think about an organization without forcing responses to fixed-end questions or the computing of a meaningless average score for many groups across many criteria. With this measure, it is possible to see what people do indeed think and say about an organization even when they know very little.

Communication behaviors of publics, reputation, and relationships

Although organizational efforts to influence reputation through strategic messaging are likely to be ineffective or fail altogether, the behavior of publics does influence the reputation of an organization. As defined earlier, reputation is the distribution of cognitive knowledge about an organization. Active publics are most likely to be the primary source of this distribution of cognitive knowledge – active publics' perception, cognition, motivation, and communicative actions will determine the content, amount, and tonality of what people remember and talk about with regard to an organization.

The aspects or actions of an organization that people remember and talk about is what constitutes reputation, and active publics are most likely to engage in communicative behaviors about their experiences and expectations with an organization. Information behaviors of active publics, therefore, become the mediating or the moderating variables that influence reputation. The quality or type of relationships between an organization and its publics are for the most part shaped by previous organizational behaviors. The resulting relationships then trigger or contextualize the communicative actions of members of publics. To understand the formation and evolution of reputation, it is necessary to understand the causes, processes, and consequences of communicative behaviors of active publics or highly involved behavioral relationship holders. However, the concept of reputation as defined earlier is not just limited to the cognitions held by active publics; rather, reputation encompasses the spectrum of publics and stakeholders that an organization may have. It is therefore necessary to account for when, why, and how nonpublics or passive stakeholders may arise and be motivated to produce cognitive representations about organizational decisions and behaviors

and how these cognitive representations are then communicated and reproduced in the minds of passive publics or the less-involved reputational relationship holders.

The situational theory of problem solving (Kim and J. Grunig, 2011) explains how a distribution of cognitive representations (reputation) can be formed and circulated in social communicative networks by the information behaviors among those individuals who recognize a problem. Figure 18.2 depicts this theory and compares it with J. Grunig's (1997) situational theory of publics, which the newer theory extends. As individuals recognize the discrepancies between what they expect and what they experience from an organization and its behaviors, they become members of an active public and are motivated to produce, select, and circulate information about their problems and the organization. The more active the members of an active public, the more they will select (information forfending) and circulate selected information (information forwarding) to mobilize attention, legitimacy, and resources toward their problem-solving efforts.

The cognitive representations of an organization that passive publics develop are likely to be the result of active publics' communicative behaviors. J. Grunig and Hung (2002) found that less-involved publics tend to evaluate an organization and their relationships with the organization based solely on hearsay rather than actual interaction or experience. Less-involved publics derive evaluative conclusions about the organization based on the cognitive representations resulting from the information seeking, selecting, and sharing activities that active, motivated publics engage in. It follows that the development of the content and direction (valence) of the cognitions about the organization will be similar to those held by active publics and will be influenced by the frequency and availability of information circulated by the active publics and the strength of the social communicative networks within which the publics are situated. In this way, the communicative actions of active publics are most likely to determine the cognitive representations about

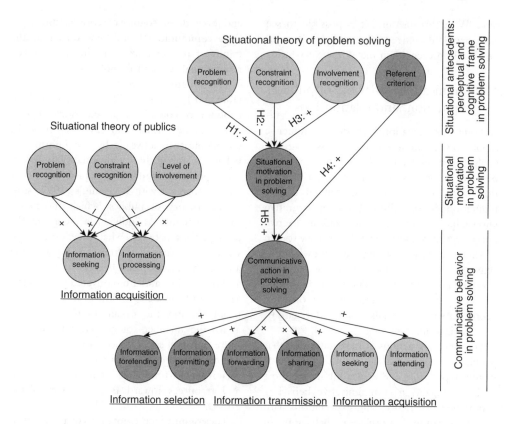

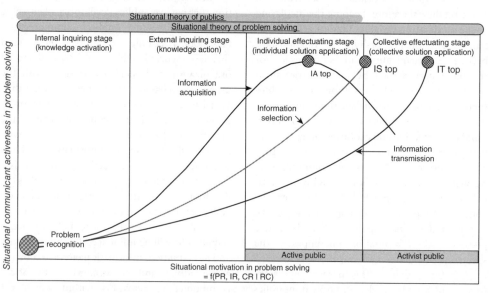

Figure 18.2   Situational theory of problem solving and sequential illustration of communicative actions. IA, information acquisition; IS, information selection; IT, information transmission; PR, problem recognition; IR, involvement recognition; CR, constraint recognition; RC, referent criterion.

an organization held by passive publics or less-involved reputational relationship holders.

The concepts of positive and negative mega-phoning by active publics, as defined by Kim and Rhee (2011), discuss the content, direction, or tonality of communicative behaviors of these publics as influenced by their perceived relationships with organizations. This is particularly important considering that the communicative environment has changed from mass-mediated communication to a digitalized, networked society. As noted earlier, the behavioral relationship holders are of utmost importance in this regard as their communicative behaviors are responsible for the amount, direction, and tonality of reputational information, as well as the distribution of such information to reputational relationship holders and other less-involved stakeholders or publics. Based on the cues received from behavioral relationship holders and whatever they can recall at that instant, reputational relationship holders make cursory evaluative judgments about the organization (cf. knowledge activation; Higgins, 1996).

It is commonplace for less-involved publics (reputational relationship holders) to be lacking in cognitive details that warrant their strong evaluative judgment or the attitudinal conclusion they form and hold. In the digitalized, networked society of today, there is a greater risk of such judgments and opinions being expressed and spread rapidly over social networking sites. This risk exists not just for active and aware publics but for passive publics as well. Although passive publics may not initiate conversation or give information themselves, they may express their ideas and opinions when solicited. The danger for organizations lies in the fact that the opinions held by these publics may be strong but not necessarily based on fact. The consequences of the spread of such strong but factually inaccurate opinions, enabled by the digitalized networks, could be dire for the organization.

The cognitive representations of less-involved, latent publics or nonpublics are also influenced by various consumer rants and employees' voluntary information behaviors about their organizations that are made available to them by digitalized networks. These bits of information are added to the distribution of cognitive representations in the hasty cognitive mills of those less-involved, latent publics or nonpublics. Thus, publics' communicative behaviors are a critical link and a more immediate precursor of the reputation that an organization will enjoy. The threats and opportunities that communicative actions by publics and stakeholders present for organizations can be observed from various publics and organizational contexts, and are increasingly gaining importance for the understanding of the dynamic process of reputation formation and evolution in the era of digitalized communication and networked information behaviors of publics (for detailed studies, see Kim, 2012).

Managing Reputations

Our explanation of the strategic management role of public relations and our review of research on how organizational behavior and relationships affect cognitive representations – that is, reputations – show that reputation management involves much more than managing messages distributed through the mass media to the general population. An organization is "branded" by its behavior, and bad behavior damages its reputation. A cognitive representation such as a reputation, therefore, can be managed only by managing the behavior of the organization. Public relations professionals, of course, do not manage organizational behaviors by themselves; but they can participate in the strategic decision-making process that produces those behaviors. Public relations professionals should play an important role in organizational governance, and they should focus on relationships as an indicator of both the value and the success of their work. If they do, the organization's reputation will take care of itself.

In most cases, we believe public relations people should emphasize active, strategic publics when they involve stakeholders in management decision making and measure the quality of relationships with those publics when they evaluate the success of public relations. Nevertheless, the indicators of relationships we have developed can also be used to evaluate reputational relationships with less-involved publics.

Brand and reputation for involved strategic publics are, for the most part, by-products of relational interactions with an organization. For less-involved publics, these cognitive representations are rough, shaky conjectures based on whatever cues are available to them. Notably, however, involved publics (behavioral relationship holders) influence less-involved groups (reputational relationship holders) through their witnessing, ranting, and recommendations (i.e., their communicative actions). Thus, the most important way to influence corporate brand or reputation for all publics is to identify behavioral relationship holders and incorporate their interests into management decisions and thus indirectly influence reputational relationship holders.

The threats or opportunities to a brand or reputation created by behavioral relationship holders have become amplified because of the current digitalization of new communication media. As Phillips and Young (2009) said in their book on online public relations, "your reputation . . . will increasingly depend on what comes up when you are Googled" (p. 157). Many "communicative actions" among strategic, active constituencies are now "digitally encoded" and "spread" through the extended social relationships that individuals form through social media. Specifically, negative or positive witnessing (what Kim and Rhee, 2011, called the "megaphoning" effect of active publics) now spreads faster and remains accessible "almost forever" – retrievable in digitized form in a networked society. Thus, less-involved groups have a greater chance of encountering negative (or positive) witnessing when they use digital media.

For example, a potential customer might search the Internet to check the experiences of others before making buying decisions. If he or she encounters substantially more negative than positive witnessing, this new customer will hesitate to buy the product or services. For another example, many online communities provide a customer forum to share experiences with products or services. An organization's relationship with "behavioral relationship holders," therefore, creates threats and opportunities to corporate branding and reputation for active publics but also among "reputational relationship" holders.

In conclusion, we believe that public relations has an important strategic role in organizational governance. Its role is more than influencing how publics interpret the behavior of an organization. Its role is to help shape that behavior. "Actions speak louder than words."

Note

1   Portions of this chapter have been modified from portions of J. Grunig (2011), J. Grunig *et al.* (2009), and J. Grunig and Kim (2011).

References

Bromley, D.B. (1993) *Reputation, Image, and Impression Management.* Chichester, UK: John Wiley & Sons.

Dozier, D.M., Grunig, L.A., and Grunig, J.E. (1995) *Manager's Guide to Excellence in Public Relations and Communication Management.* Mahwah, NJ: Lawrence Erlbaum Associates.

Ehling, W.P. (1992) Estimating the value of public relations and communication to an organization. In J.E. Grunig (ed.), *Excellence in Public Relations and Communication Management.* Hillsdale, NJ: Lawrence Erlbaum Associates, pp. 617–638.

Fombrun, C.J. (1996) *Reputation: Realizing Value from the Corporate Image.* Boston: Harvard Business School Press.

Fombrun, C.J. and van Riel, C.B.M. (1997) The reputational landscape. *Corporate Reputation Review, 1,* 5–13.

Grunig, J.E. (1966) The role of information in economic decision making. *Journalism Monographs, 3,* 1–51.

Grunig, J.E. (1971) Communication and the economic decision making processes of Colombian peasants. *Economic Development and Cultural Change, 19,* 580–597.

Grunig, J.E. (1976) Organizations and publics relations: Testing a communication theory. *Journalism Monographs*, 46, 1–59.

Grunig, J.E. (1978) Defining publics in public relations: The case of a suburban hospital. *Journalism Quarterly*, 55, 109–118.

Grunig, J.E. (1989) Symmetrical presuppositions as a framework for public relations theory. In C. Botan and V.T. Hazelton (eds), *Public Relations Theory*. Hillsdale, NJ: Lawrence Erlbaum Associates, pp. 17–44.

Grunig, J.E. (ed.) (1992) *Excellence in Public Relations and Communication Management*. Hillsdale, NJ: Lawrence Erlbaum Associates.

Grunig, J.E. (1997) A situational theory of publics: Conceptual history, recent challenges and new research. In D. Moss, T. MacManus, and D. Vercic (eds), *Public Relations Research: An International Perspective*. London: International Thomson Business Press, pp. 3–46.

Grunig, J.E. (2006) Furnishing the edifice: Ongoing research on public relations as a strategic management function. *Journal of Public Relations Research*, 18, 151–176.

Grunig, J.E. (2008) Conceptualizing quantitative research in public relations. In B. Van Ruler, A. Tkalac Verčič, and D. Verčič (eds), *Public Relations Metrics*. New York and London: Routledge, pp. 88–119.

Grunig, J.E. (2011) Public relations and strategic management: Institutionalizing organization-public relationships in contemporary society. *Central European Journal of Communication*, 41(6), 11–31.

Grunig, J.E. and Hung, C.R. (2002) The effect of relationships on reputation and reputation on relationships: A cognitive, behavioral study. Paper presented at the PRSA Educator's Academy 5th Annual International, Interdisciplinary Public Relations Research Conference, Miami, FL, March 8–10.

Grunig, J.E. and Kim, J.-N. (2011) Actions speak louder than words: How a strategic management approach to public relations can shape a company's brand and reputation through relationships. *Insight Train*, 1, 3–51 (SK Marketing & Company, Korea).

Grunig, J.E., Ferrari, M.A., and França, F. (2009) *Relações públicas: Teoria, contexto e relacionamentos* [Public Relations: Theory, Context, and Relationships]. São Paulo, Brazil: Difusao Editora.

Grunig, L.A., Grunig, J.E., and Ehling, W.P. (1992) What is an effective organization? In J.E. Grunig (ed.), *Excellence in Public Relations and Communication Management*. Hillsdale, NJ: Lawrence Erlbaum Associates, pp. 65–90.

Grunig, L.A., Grunig, J.E., and Dozier, D.M. (2002) *Excellent Public Relations and Effective Organizations: A Study of Communication Management in Three Countries*. Mahwah, NJ: Lawrence Erlbaum Associates.

Higgins, E.T. (1996) Knowledge activation, application, and salience. In E.T. Higgins and A.W. Kruglanski (eds), *Social Psychology: Handbook of Basic Principles*. New York: Guilford, pp. 133–168.

Hon, L.C. and Grunig, J.E. (1999) Guidelines for measuring relationships in public relations. Gainesville, FL: The Institute for Public Relations, Commission on PR Measurement and Evaluation. Retrieved from http://www.instituteforpr.org/wp-content/uploads/Guidelines_Measuring_Relationships.pdf (last accessed September 19, 2012).

Huang, Y.-H. (1997) Public relations strategies, relational outcomes, and conflict management strategies. Unpublished doctoral dissertation, University of Maryland, College Park, MD.

Hung, C.J. (2002) The interplay of relationship types, relationship cultivation, and relationship outcomes: How multinational and Taiwanese companies practice public relations and organization-public relationship management in China. Unpublished doctoral dissertation, University of Maryland, College Park, MD.

Hung, C.J. (2007) Toward the theory of relationship management in public relations: How to cultivate quality relationships. In E.L. Toth (ed.), *The Future of Excellence in Public Relations and Communication Management: Challenges for the Next Generation*. Mahwah, NJ: Lawrence Erlbaum Associates, pp. 443–476.

Kim, J.-N. (ed.) (2012) Strategic values of relationships and the communicative actions of publics and stakeholders [special issue]. *International Journal of Strategic Communication*, 6(1).

Kim, J.-N. and Grunig, J.E. (2011) Problem solving and communicative action: A situational theory of problem solving. *Journal of Communication*, 61, 120–149.

Kim, J.-N. and Rhee, Y. (2011) Strategic thinking about employee communication behavior (ECB) in public relations: Testing the models of megaphoning and scouting effects in Korea. *Journal of Public Relations Research*, 23, 248–263.

Kim, J.-N., Grunig, J.E., and Ni, L. (2010) Reconceptualizing the communicative action of publics: Acquisition, selection, and transmission of information in problematic situations. *International Journal of Strategic Communication, 4*, 126–154.

Men, L.J.R. and Hung, C.J.F. (2012) Exploring the roles of organization-public relationships in the strategic management process: Towards an integrated framework. *International Journal of Strategic Communication, 6*(2), 151–173.

Phillips, D. and Young, P. (2009) *Online Public Relations: A Practical Guide to Developing an Online Strategy in the World of Social Media*. London and Philadelphia: Kogan Page.

Toth, E.L. (ed.) (2007) *The Future of Excellence in Public Relations and Communication Management*. Mahwah, NJ: Lawrence Erlbaum Associates.

Van den Bosch, F.A.J. and van Riel, C.B.M. (1998) Buffering and bridging as environmental strategies of firms. *Business Strategy and the Environment, 7*, 24–31.

Yang, S.-U. (2007) An integrated model for organization-public relational outcomes, organizational reputation, and their antecedents. *Journal of Public Relations Research, 19*, 91–121.

Yang, S.-U. and Grunig, J.E. (2005) Decomposing organizational reputation: The effects of organization-public relationship outcomes on cognitive representations of organizations and evaluations of organizational performance. *Journal of Communication Management, 9*, 305–326.

19

Image Repair Theory and Corporate Reputation

William L. Benoit
Ohio University, USA

This chapter explicates image repair theory. It begins with the history and background of the theory, showing how it integrated several diverse approaches to repairing a damaged image. Image repair theory has been applied in a variety of contexts, including political, corporate, sports/entertainment, and international cases. The chapter lays out the assumptions of the theory, discusses the two key elements of a threat to an image (responsibility, offensiveness), describes image repair strategy, discusses the importance of perceptions and of the audience, and sketches future areas for research.

History/Origins of Image Repair Theory

Reputation (image, face) is important for several reasons. Corporations need to maintain a positive image in order to attract investors and customers. They must also avoid trouble with federal regulators, which can be a threat in some crisis situations. Benoit *et al.* (1991) reviewed the literature on persuasive defense, *apologia*, and accounts. Rhetorical theorists had not articulated a comprehensive approach to the question of how people, groups, and organizations (including corporations) can respond to threats to their image. The seeds of this theory can be found in a study of President Nixon's rhetorical responses to the Watergate

crisis (Benoit, 1982); political candidates seem particularly susceptible to political attacks (e.g., when Newt Gingrich surged in popularity before the 2012 Iowa caucuses, other candidates attacked him).

Image repair theory (initially called "image restoration theory") was first applied to political discourse (President Reagan's Iran-Contra discourse; Benoit *et al.*, 1991; other case studies using political discourse include Benoit, 2006a,b; Benoit and Henson, 2009; Benoit and McHale, 1999; Benoit and Nill, 1998a; Blaney and Benoit, 2001; Kennedy and Benoit, 1997; and Len-Rios and Benoit, 2004). For example, Benoit *et al.* (1991) reviewed existing literature and developed image repair theory. They applied this to President Reagan's rhetoric on the Iran-Contra affair (primarily whether

The Handbook of Communication and Corporate Reputation, First Edition. Edited by Craig E. Carroll.
© 2013 John Wiley & Sons, Inc. Published 2015 by John Wiley & Sons, Inc.

he traded arms for hostages). He denied trading arms for hostages until the Tower Commission Report made it clear that he had done so. At that point, he engaged in mortification and corrective action. His generally declining popularity began to recover at that point.

In February of 2004, President Bush gave an interview on *Meet the Press* as candidates vigorously attacked him during the Democratic presidential primaries, primary on the economy (jobs and the deficit), and the allegedly unjustified war in Iraq. He employed transcendence, framing himself as a "war president" (whose record on the economy must be judged by different standards from peacetime presidents). He also shifted blame for the economy to his predecessor, President Bill Clinton. His denials that the Iraq war was unjustified were relatively weak (Hussein was dangerous) and he relied on defeasibility (if Hussein secretly destroyed weapons of mass destruction (WMD), then Bush could not have known the weapons were gone). Defeasibility is a risky strategy because (even though it is true that there are limits to a president's powers) this strategy intentionally creates the impression that the president is not in control. President Bush also held a press conference in April of 2004; his popularity had declined as casualties mounted in Iraq. He denied making any mistakes – and thus did not apologize for any of his actions. His use of transcendence appealed mainly to partisans, and reaction was largely split along party lines. He failed to return his popularity to earlier, higher levels (Benoit, 2006a). President Bush also discussed Hurricane Katrina, using bolstering, defeasibility, and corrective. His discourse did little to counter the accusation that the response to Hurricane Katrina was slow. Defeasibility is risky for presidents to use because they ordinarily do not want to undermine perceptions of their power. Corrective action was too little too late (Benoit and Henson, 2009).

Judge Clarence Thomas's attempt to repair his image from accusations that he had sexually harassed Professor Anita Hill during his confirmation hearing was examined by Benoit and Nill (1998a). He denied the accusation and bolstered his reputation. He also accused his detractors in the Senate of racism; this made it difficult for the Senate to vote against him; he even accused them of "lynching" him metaphorically. Benoit and McHale (1999) argued that Kenneth Starr's repair of his image during an interview on *20/20* about allegations that he had engaged in a personal and political vendetta against President Clinton. However, his denials were unpersuasive and his attempt at bolstering relied on values his audience may not have shared. Len-Rios and Benoit (2004) analyzed Gary Condit's image repair after the disappearance of his intern, Chandra Levy. An apparent lack of candor, unpersuasive denials, and failure to accept any responsibility undermined the effectiveness of his discourse.

Soon thereafter, it was used to examine corporate crisis communication: AT&T's discourse after a service interruption (Benoit and Brinson, 1994). *Accounts, excuses, and apologies* (Benoit, 1995a) included three chapters on corporate image repair: Union Carbide and the deadly gas release at Bhopal, the Exxon *Valdez* oil spill, and messages from Coke and Pepsi. In 1984, a Union Carbide plant in Bhopal, India, released a deadly gas that killed 200 and injured thousands more (Benoit, 1995a). Union Carbide relied heavily on bolstering and corrective action. However, widespread belief that it was responsible for the leak kept these strategies from being effective. The Exxon *Valdez* oil tanker hit a reef and released over 10 million gallons of oil in 1989. Exxon shifted blame to the captain for the spill – whom Exxon had selected for the position – and to the state of Alaska and the Coast Guard for the slow response. Images on television showed the cleanup crew playing cards (instead of cleaning the oil) and undermined this strategy. In 1991, AT&T suffered a service interruption. This not only affected telephone calls, but also disrupted air travel because air traffic controllers relied on landlines: many flights were cancelled. AT&T effectively used mortification, corrective action, and bolstering to repair its image (Benoit and Brinson, 1994). Coke and Pepsi exchanged attacks and image repair in the trade publication *Nation's Restaurant News* from 1990 to 1992

(Benoit, 1995a). Pepsi claimed Coke charged its largest customer (McDonald's) less than other customers. Coke effectively denied that charge and stated that Pepsi ran the ad attacking Coke a second time after Coke had informed Pepsi that it was false. Coke argued that Pepsi competes for the customers of its clients because Pepsi owns Taco Bell, Pizza Hut, and Kentucky Fried Chicken. Pepsi could not deny this accusation. Benoit (1995a) offered evidence that some customers switched from Pepsi to Coke because Pepsi owned restaurants.

Image repair was employed to analyze Sears' defense against auto repair fraud (Benoit, 1995b), messages from Dow Corning about the dangers of breast implants (Brinson and Benoit, 1996), US Air's defense after one of its airplanes crashed, lobbying firm the Tobacco Institute responded to attacks on the dangers of smoking (Benoit and Hirson, 2001), and Firestone's defense against allegations that its unsafe tires had been responsible for accidents, deaths, and injuries (Blaney *et al.*, 2002). Sears was accused of auto repair fraud. The California Department of Consumer Affairs documented fraud (a pattern of replacing parts that were almost new) in Sears' auto repair stores. Sears denied that they replaced good parts – and then argued that when it happened it was preventative maintenance (obviously inconsistent). It ineffectually attacked the bureau. Then, a similar report of fraud was reported in New Jersey, and Sears was forced to implement corrective action (although it refused to admit wrongdoing). Dow Corning was attacked for producing unsafe silicone breast implants (Brinson and Benoit, 1996). Initially, it denied that they were harmful. Secret documents eventually emerged revealing that Dow Corning had not fully tested implants despite concerns of their own scientists. Then, Corning admitted they should have handled the documents differently. It also used corrective action to warn the women who had received implants of potential dangers and stopped making implants. Benoit and Czerwinski (1997) analyzed US Air's image repair after its jet crashed in 1994, killing 132 people – its fifth crash in five years. It published three full-page advertisements:

one from the CEO, one from pilots, and one from flight attendants (given the fact that poor maintenance was blamed, the lack of a letter from US Air's repair crews was conspicuous). The letters used bolstering, denial, and what can best be described as "pseudo-corrective action." The CEO appointed General Robert C. Oaks to administer US Air's safety efforts. However, his brief was not to make US Air's planes safer, but to convince the public that they were safe. This effort was not particularly successful. Firestone tires experienced blowouts that were blamed for over 270 deaths (Blaney *et al.*, 2002). It tried to blame Ford (most of the blowouts occurred in Ford Explorers). The company apologized and recalled the tires but also denied that the tires were defective (obviously conflicting strategies).

This approach has also been applied to sports and entertainment (Benoit, 1997; Benoit and Hanczor, 1994; Benoit and Nill, 1998b; Wen *et al.*, 2009). Actor Hugh Grant was arrested with a prostitute (Benoit, 1997). He appeared on several talk shows, using mortification. He appeared to be honest and remorseful. He did not attempt to justify his behavior. He did, however, attack elements of the British press for harassing his girlfriend (Elizabeth Hurley) and his family – but not for attacking Grant. This effort was evaluated as effective. Benoit and Hanczor (1994) examined Tonya Harding's defense after the attack on fellow-skater Nancy Kerrigan, which kept her from competing in the US Skating Championships (and the Olympics), an attack planned by Harding's bodyguard and ex-husband. Harding used bolstering, denial, and attacking her accusers. Although these strategies were appropriate, they were not developed persuasively and her defense was ineffective. Filmmaker Oliver Stone's movie "JFK," which argued for a conspiracy to kill the president, was attacked (for inaccuracy, Stone's directing techniques, his sources, and the conspiracy theory). Benoit and Nill (1998b) argued that Stone effectively defended himself, his sources, and the conspiracy theory (and attacked his accusers). Research has also examined image repair concerning other countries (Drumheller and Benoit, 2004; Wen *et al.*, 2009; Zhang and

Benoit, 2004, 2009). Drumheller and Benoit (2004) looked at image repair after the USS Greeneville collided with the Japanese trawler, the Ehime Maru, in 2001, killing nine people. The Nacy's image repair effort relied heavily on mortification, which was appropriate particularly given the Japanese culture. However, an important cultural expectation, that Captain Waddle apologizes directly to the victims' families in Japan, was unmet, undermining the defense. After the terrorist attacks of 9/11, Saudi Arabia was criticized for allegedly supporting the terrorists (some of whom were from Saudi Arabia) and for failing to adequately support the US invasion of Iraq (Zhang and Benoit, 2004). Saudi Arabia used press releases and other statements, speeches, and television and radio ads to answer the accusations with denial and bolstering. The defense was better at answering the accusation that the country had supported the 9/11 terrorists than that it had adequately supported the US military action. Zhang and Benoit (2009) investigated image repair from Chinese Health Minister Zhang Wenkang on SARS. He faced several accusations: the SARS outbreak was increasing, the government had downplayed the severity of the problem, the government ignored the Taiwanese who suffered from SARS, and the Health Ministry provided poor information. He used several strategies (denial, defeasibility, bolstering, minimization, differentiation, attack accuser, and corrective action). However, his messages were contradictory and apparently related on false information, so his defense was ineffective. Wen *et al.* (2009) contrasted image repair from Taiwanese-born American pitcher Wang and from Taiwanese newspapers. Wang used mortification and corrective action; the newspapers used evading responsibility (including blaming Wang's teammates) and reducing offensiveness (including minimization). Defenses by others (third-party defenses; in this case, newspapers) can use strategies (such as blaming teammates) that the accused cannot or should not use. Other approaches to corporate crisis communication include Coombs (2012), Hearit (2006), and Ulmer *et al.* (2011).

The Theory of Image Repair Discourse

Image repair theory (Benoit, 1995a) assumes that face, image, or reputation is important to individuals and organizations and that, when this key asset is threatened, image repair discourse is a resource for repairing that image. Attacks, criticisms, or complaints have two essential elements: an offensive act and responsibility for that act (Pomerantz, 1978). If no offensive act has been committed – or more accurately, if no relevant audience believes that an offensive act has been committed – no threat to reputation can occur. Furthermore, if an organization is not believed (by a pertinent audience) to be responsible, that organization's reputation is not at risk. Of course, responsibility or blame can appear in many guises. One may be held accountable for performing an act, for encouraging an act, or for permitting that act to occur. Only if both elements are present, offensiveness and blame, does a threat to reputation exist. Example, President Bush could not be held responsible for the devastation caused by Hurricane Katrina; he cannot control storms. However, if the federal response was unreasonably slow, he could be blamed for the slow response.

Note the emphasis on perceptions here: an organization's image is at risk when relevant audiences *believe* (perceive) that it should be blamed for an offensive act. The organization may in fact be innocent (and, if so, that fact could be an important part of an image repair effort – although the truth may not necessarily or automatically overcome misperceptions). However, if that company is thought to be guilty of an untoward action, that corporation's image is clearly at risk. Note also the importance of communication here. For example, British Petroleum's (BP) guilt in the gulf oil spill of 2010 is widely assumed (only 3% said BP and its drilling partners were not to blame for the spill; CBS News/*New York Times Poll*, 2011); for almost everyone, these attitudes were based on messages (news, Internet) rather than firsthand knowledge of BP and the spill. However, just as messages containing attacks or criticism can threaten an image, messages from the target have the potential to repair damaged images.

Image repair theory keys in on these two elements of threat to an image, offensiveness and blame. Some of the strategies for repairing a damaged reputation attempt to reduce offensiveness of the act in question; other strategies attempt to deny blame or evade responsibility. Still other strategies admit committing the offensive act and beg forgiveness or attempt to prevent recurrence of the problem or alleviate the effects of the offensive act. The fact that image repair theory develops responses (image repair discourse) out of the attack means that understanding the nature of the threat (attack, criticism, complaint) is essential to the process of image repair. See Table 19.1 for a list of strategies with definitions and examples of each strategy.

The first general strategy is *denial*, which has two variants. First, one accused of wrongdoing can *simply deny* committing the wrongful act or deny that the act performed was offensive. Second, the accused can *shift the blame* to the "real" culprit. This may be more effective at times than simple denial because it provides another target to blame. Of course, any persuasive message, including denial, cannot be assumed to work. One must provide a believable denial or a reasonable target for shifting blame (of course, this is true of all strategies; using any strategy or group of strategies in a message does not guarantee success). This strategy attempts to eliminate blame for the offensive act.

The next general strategy is *evading responsibility*. This approach has four variants. *Provocation* argues that another (person or organization) caused the accused to perform the offensive act. Committing the act is portrayed as a reasonable

Table 19.1 Corporate image repair strategies.

Strategy	Key characteristic	Example
Denial		
Simple denial	Did not perform act	Tylenol: did not poison capsule
Shift the blame	Another performed act	Tylenol: a "madman" poisoned capsules
Evasion of responsibility		
Provocation	Responded to act of another	Firm moved because of new taxes
Defeasibility	Lack of information or ability	Executive not told meeting changed
Accident	Mishap	Tree fell on tracks causing train wreck
Good intentions	Meant well	Sears wants to provide good auto repair service
Reducing offensiveness of event		
Bolstering	Stress good traits	Exxon's "swift and competent" cleanup of oil spill
Minimization	Act not serious	Exxon: few animals killed in oil spill
Differentiation	Act less offensive than similar acts	Sears: unneeded repairs were preventative maintenance, not fraud
Transcendence	More important values	Helping humans justifies testing animals
Attack accuser	Reduce credibility of accuser	Coke: Pepsi owns restaurants, competes directly with you for customers
Compensation	Reimburse victim	Disabled moviegoers given free passes after denied admission to movie
Corrective action	Plan to solve/prevent recurrence of problem	AT&T long-distance upgrades, promised to spend billions more to improve service
Mortification	Apologize	AT&T apologized for service interruption

Derived from Benoit (1995a, 1997).

reaction to the provocation. *Defeasibility* claims that the accused lacked information about or control over the offensive act. For example, I could say that I did not know that a deadline had been moved up (lack of information), so I should not be blamed for missing that deadline. An *accident* is a mishap, a misfortune. *Good intentions*, the final form of evading responsibility, admit performing the offensive act but the accused claims to have meant well. "I gave him the wrong medicine, but I was trying to help." This strategy attempts to reduce (rather than eliminate) blame for the offensive act.

The third general strategy for image repair is reducing offensiveness of the act. This strategy has six forms. *Bolstering* mentions good qualities or deeds of the accused, hoping that good will outweigh the offensive act. *Minimization* argues that the offensive act is not as bad as it seems: for example, one can argue the offensive act was smaller, shorter in duration, less harmful, or affected fewer people. *Differentiation* suggests that the offensive act, while bad, is not as bad as other, similar acts. For example, I might argue that I did not *steal* your car; I *borrowed it without asking first*. *Transcendence* claims that act was justified by something more important. "Yes, I stole a loaf of bread, but I did it to feed my starving child." *Attacking accuser* is an attempt to reduce the credibility of the source of accusations against the accused (one can also say the victim deserved what happened). *Compensation* attempts to counterbalance the offensive act by offering money, goods, or services to the victim. Unlike the first two general strategies, which deal with blame, this strategy tries to reduce perceived offensiveness of the act in question.

Corrective action does not address blame. This strategy can take two forms. The accused can attempt to repair the damage caused by the offensive act. It is also possible to take actions to prevent the offensive act from recurring. Usually, corrective action is undertaken by those who are guilty of committing the offensive act. However, exceptions can occur. For example, Tylenol was not responsible for the poison placed in their capsules. Still, the company introduced tamper-resistant packaging to try to prevent others from poisoning their products in the future (Benoit and Lindsey, 1987).

The final general strategy is *mortification*, which admits blame and asks for forgiveness. This general strategy can take several forms. The accused can explicitly apologize, admit wrongdoing, or express regret or remorse. One ambiguity in English is the statement "I'm sorry." This can be an instance of an apology, admitting to a transgression. However, it can also be an expression of sympathy without any admission of guilt. Corporations in particular must realize that an admission of guilt can make it difficult to win lawsuits asking for damages from wrongdoing (individuals can face lawsuits, of course, but this seems to be even more of a potential problem for corporations).

These strategies can be used singly or in combination. I do not claim that more strategies are necessarily better or more effective than fewer strategies. Effectiveness depends on the accusations, the audience, and how the strategies are enacted in the message (e.g., all denials are not persuasive). It is important to realize that some strategies (or some strategies as operationalized in a message) can be contradictory. It makes little sense to say, "I did nothing wrong (simple denial) and I apologize for doing it (mortification)." Similarly, if one denies committing an act, it is difficult to see how minimizing the offensiveness would help. Nixon's Cambodia speech (Benoit, 1995b) used differentiation and transcendence. These two strategies are not inherently contradictory. However, he used differentiation to argue that current military offensives as continuation of past policy (he differentiated them from the accusation that he was invading another country). Then, he used transcendence to argue that his military offensive was a new strategy that will end the war. It cannot be both the same as in the past and new.

It is important to say something about the audience – or audiences – for image repair discourse. Audiences can be very different, so messages that might be persuasive for one audience could be a disaster for another audience.

For example, consider a business operating a manufacturing plant accused of releasing dangerous pollutants into the environment. This company faces several different audiences, each with different concerns and interests. The environmental group which exposed the pollution is one potential audience. The news media which reported the situation is another audience. People who live near the plant constitute a third audience. Employees of the company, and particularly those who work at the plant in question, are yet another group. Governmental regulators are another important group. Stockholders are another potential audience. Notice that a message one group, local residents, would presumably like to hear – "We will spare no expense to eliminate pollution" – probably would not be very welcome to stockholders. A corporation attempting to repair an image under threat must identify relevant audiences and consider their interests. It may not be possible to repair an image with all possible audiences, or to achieve the same success in repairing an image with every audience: one may have to make choices about which audiences are most important and, perhaps, which are more amenable to persuasion.

Description of Theoretical Relevance to Corporate Reputation

As noted earlier, corporations must be very concerned about their image with pertinent audiences. Benoit (1995a) argues that threats to reputation are inevitable for several reasons: conflict over scarce resources, conflicting goals, accidents, and human error. Image repair theory illuminates the crisis situation, discussing several important ideas: communication can threaten and repair an image, perceptions of images are key, the relationship between threat (criticism) and defense is important, understanding the relevant audience(s) is vital, and potential strategies for repairing a damaged reputation have been identified. This theory

has been applied widely in the area of corporate reputation, as Kim *et al.* (2009) explain: "Over the past 18 years Benoit's Image Restoration Theory and Coombs' Situational Crisis Communication Theory have provided dominant paradigms for crisis communication research in public relations" (p. 446). This theory can help understand reputation for organizations generally and corporations specifically as well as for individuals in the corporate world. The studies cited earlier provide illustrations of the method.

Future Directions of Research

Additional case studies of image repair would be helpful, particularly as the world changes (new communication technology, such as the Internet, Facebook, or Twitter; globalization of trade; new technologies used by businesses change commerce). Businesses can reply to accusations on the Internet (including Facebook) or Twitter. The fact that trade is even more international today than in the past complicates image repair efforts – the audiences can have diverse knowledge and interests. Researchers can select case studies that illuminate these issues. Quantitative research on image repair strategies would also be useful. For example, Huang (2005) used the survey method to understand corporate image repair. She asked executives to recall a crisis situation and then rate how likely they were to use a particular strategy. Factor analysis yielded five groups of strategies: concession (mortification), justification (reduce offensiveness), excuse (evade responsibility), diversion (shift attention to other topics), and denial. Dardis and Haigh (2009) employed an empirical approach to image repair. They created image repair messages, which varied the defensive strategy used. Participants read press releases about a product recall for a fictitious company and their perception of the company's reputation was measured. Reducing offensiveness was more effective than denial, evading responsibility, corrective action, or mortification.

References

Benoit, W.L. (1982) Richard M. Nixon's rhetorical strategies in his public statements on Watergate. *Southern Speech Communication Journal, 47,* 192–211.

Benoit, W.L. (1995a) *Accounts, Excuses, Apologies: A Theory of Image Restoration Strategies.* Albany, NY: State University of New York Press. Selected as an Outstanding Academic Book by *Choice.*

Benoit, W.L. (1995b) Sears' repair of its auto service image: Image restoration discourse in the corporate sector. *Communication Studies, 46,* 89–105.

Benoit, W.L. (1997) Hugh Grant's image restoration discourse: An actor apologizes. *Communication Quarterly, 45,* 251–267.

Benoit, W.L. (2006a) Image repair in President Bush's April 2004 news conference. *Public Relations Review, 32,* 137–143.

Benoit, W.L. (2006b) President Bush's image repair effort on *Meet the Press*: The complexities of defeasability. *Journal of Applied Communication Research, 34,* 285–306.

Benoit, W.L. and Brinson, S.L. (1994) AT&T: Apologies are not enough. *Communication Quarterly, 42,* 75–88.

Benoit, W.L. and Czerwinski, A. (1997) A critical analysis of US Air's image repair discourse. *Business Communication Quarterly, 60,* 38–57.

Benoit, W.L. and Hanczor, R.S. (1994) The Tonya Harding controversy: An analysis of image repair strategies. *Communication Quarterly, 42,* 416–433.

Benoit, W.L. and Henson, J.R. (2009) President Bush's image repair discourse on Hurricane Katrina. *Public Relations Review, 35,* 40–46.

Benoit, W.L. and Hirson, D. (2001) *Doonesbury* versus the tobacco institute: The smoke Starters' Coupon. *Communication Quarterly, 49,* 279–294.

Benoit, W.L. and Lindsey, J.J. (1987) Argument strategies: Antidote to Tylenol's poisoned image. *Journal of the American Forensic Association, 23,* 136–146.

Benoit, W.L. and McHale, J.P. (1999) Kenneth Starr's image repair discourse viewed in *20/20. Communication Quarterly, 47,* 265–280.

Benoit, W.L. and Nill, D.M. (1998a) A critical analysis of Judge Clarence Thomas's statement before the Senate Judiciary Committee. *Communication Studies, 49,* 179–195.

Benoit, W.L. and Nill, D.M. (1998b) Oliver Stone's defense of *JFK. Communication Quarterly, 46,* 127–143.

Benoit, W.L., Gullifor, P., and Panici, D.A. (1991) President Reagan's defensive discourse on the Iran-Contra affair. *Communication Studies, 42,* 272–294.

Blaney, J.R. and Benoit, W.L. (2001) *The Clinton Scandals and the Politics of Image Restoration.* Westport, CT: Praeger.

Blaney, J.R., Benoit, W.L., and Brazeal, L.M. (2002) Blowout! Firestone's image restoration campaign. *Public Relations Review, 28,* 379–392.

Brinson, S.L. and Benoit, W.L. (1996) Dow Corning's image repair strategies in the breast implant crisis. *Communication Quarterly, 44,* 29–41.

CBS News/*New York Times Poll* (2010) Americans, Gulf residents, and the oil spill. http://www.cbsnews.com/htdocs/pdf/poll_oil_spill_062110.pdf (last accessed December 7, 2012).

Coombs, W.T. (2012) *Ongoing Crisis Communication: Planning, Managing, and Responding* (3rd ed.). Thousand Oaks, CA: Sage.

Dardis, F. and Haigh, M.M. (2009) Prescribing versus describing: Testing image restoration in a crisis situation. *Corporate Communications: An International Journal, 14,* 101–118.

Drumheller, K. and Benoit, W.L. (2004) USS Greeneville collides with Japan's Ehime Maru: Cultural issues in image repair discourse. *Public Relations Review, 30,* 177–185.

Hearit, K.M. (2006) *Crisis Management by Apology: Corporate Response to Allegations of Wrongdoing.* Mahwah, NJ: Lawrence Erlbaum.

Huang, Y.-H. (2005) Crisis communication strategies in Taiwan: Category, continuum, and cultural implication. *Public Relations Review, 31,* 229–238.

Kennedy, K.A. and Benoit, W.L. (1997) Newt Gingrich's book deal: A case study in self-defense rhetoric. *Southern Communication Journal, 63,* 197–216.

Kim, S., Avery, E.J., and Lariscy, R.W. (2009) Are crisis communicators practicing what we preach? An evaluation of crisis response strategy analyzed in public relations research from 1991–2009. *Public Relations Review, 35,* 446–448.

Len-Rios, M. and Benoit, W.L. (2004) Gary Condit's image repair strategies: Squandering a golden opportunity. *Public Relations Review, 50,* 95–106.

Pomerantz, A. (1978) Attributions of responsibility: Blamings. *Sociology, 12,* 115–121.

Ulmer, R.R., Sellnow, T.L., and Seeger, M.W. (2003) *Effective Crisis Communication: Moving from Crisis to Opportunity* (2nd ed.). Thousand Oaks, CA: Sage.

Wen, J., Yu, J., and Benoit, W.L. (2009) Our hero can't be wrong: A case study of collectivist image repair in Taiwan. *Chinese Journal of Communication, 2,* 174–192.

Zhang, J. and Benoit, W.L. (2004) Message strategies of Saudi Arabia's image restoration campaign after 9/11. *Public Relations Review, 30,* 161–167.

Zhang, W. and Benoit, W.L. (2009) Former Minister Zhang's discourse on SARS: Government's image restoration or destruction. *Public Relations Review, 35,* 240–246.

20

The Institutionalization of Corporate Reputation

John C. Lammers and Kristen Guth[1]

University of Illinois, USA

The literatures on corporate reputation and institutional theory have grown together over the last 30 years as organizational environments have become increasingly complex, competitive, and global. This chapter identifies the major concepts and areas of work in institutionalism including legitimacy, rational myths, isomorphism and the development of institutional fields, institutional logics, institutional work and entrepreneurship, and the processes of institutionalization and deinstitutionalization. For each of these areas, we review representative research on corporate reputation, and we discuss the implications in each area of viewing corporate reputation as an institutional message. We conclude with a discussion of the extent to which the business of corporate reputation itself has become institutionalized.

The management literatures on institutionalism and corporate reputation have accumulated rapidly since the 1980s, as globalization and competition have intensified the environment of organizations everywhere. Just as corporate survival and success depend on managing relatively fixed institutional environments, success also has come to depend on firms' reputations as perceived by employees, customers, and wider audiences in rapidly evolving competitive environments. As a number of authors have observed (Kraatz and Love, 2006; Rao, 1998; Walker, 2010), studies of reputation and institutions implicate each other. While corpora-

tions' reputations are generally understood as perceived, aggregated, comparative, and mutable (Fombrun, 1996; Fombrun and Shanley, 1990; Walker, 2010), institutions are fixed, formal, working rules applying to many organizations (Commons, 1934; Lammers and Barbour, 2006). Organizations may earn or lose their reputations independently of whether they conform to established rules, but conformity to rules is one aspect of reputation. It is at this intersection of perceived status (reputation) and fixed status (institution) that institutional theory has begun to make a contribution to our understanding of corporate reputation.

The Handbook of Communication and Corporate Reputation, First Edition. Edited by Craig E. Carroll.
© 2013 John Wiley & Sons, Inc. Published 2015 by John Wiley & Sons, Inc.

Institutional theory informs corporate reputation broadly in several ways. First, there is the legitimacy paradox: in order to have a positive reputation, an organization must generally conform to standards of legitimacy (King and Whetten, 2008; Whetten, 1997), but in order to have a strong reputation, an organization must also distinguish itself by sometimes challenging standards (Wartick, 2002). Institutional research concerns the identification of standards and the ways in which they are sustained or changed. Second, industry membership is an important moderator of reputation, as both corporate activities and institutional standards tend to be field specific. Institutional theory concerns itself with the development and nature of fields (DiMaggio and Powell, 1983). Third, once reputational rankings become part of the information environment, managers treat them as institutional pressures (Martins, 2005). Thus, we may speak of the institutionalization of reputation as a general phenomenon. Fourth, however, we may also speak of reputation as institutionalized at the firm level, as when specific firms' reputations become relatively fixed, or "sticky" (Schultz *et al.*, 2001). The process by which an organization becomes institutionalized – or in this case, how reputation contributes to legitimacy – is one of the oldest concerns of institutionalism (Selznick, 1949). Fifth, in the global political economy, organizations may earn reputations in one environment that do not easily transfer or apply in another environment. This institutional pluralism is also a concern of researchers working in the tradition of institutional theory (Kraatz and Block, 2008). Finally, the business of corporate reputation measurement and management may itself be institutionalized. In sum, then, corporate reputation may be seen as an important aspect of the institutionalized information environment of organizations.

The linkages between reputation and institutionalism also raise an additional issue, however. Reputation is an inherently communicative phenomenon, while institutional theory has only recently been articulated explicitly in terms of organizational communication[2] (Lammers, 2011; Lammers and Barbour, 2006; Phillips *et al.*, 2004). The mechanisms by which reputations are conceived and institutional standards persist or change involve communication dynamics. Moreover, while the outcomes may vary by industry or institutional fields, we would expect the communication processes to be similar across fields. Similarly, the communication processes by which an individual organization becomes institutionalized should be similar across organizations. And of course, the means by which a reputation built in one environment is received and accepted or rejected in another is also inherently communicative. Thus, in thinking about reputation from an institutional view, we require a communicatively inflected intuitionalism.

We suggest that one way to develop such an inflection is to consider corporate reputation as an institutional message. Lammers (2011) explicated the idea of the institutional message as a "collation of thoughts that takes on a life independent of senders and recipients. It may have the force of rules and is spread intentionally or unintentionally via multiple channels to narrow or wider audiences" (p. 171). We believe that considering reputation as a message opens opportunities for researchers in the institutional tradition to more carefully specify how institutional processes develop.[3] Thinking about reputation as a message may also sharpen the activities of managers who are charged with the responsibility of navigating the information environment of their organizations. Finally, the message approach increases the likelihood that we can actually develop strong explanations of how institutions develop, persist, or decline.

The purpose of this chapter is to review literature at the intersection of institutionalism and corporate reputation with an eye toward a communicatively inflected institutionalism. In order to accomplish that, we first outline briefly the major tenets and concepts of institutionalism. Then, for each of these areas, we review representative research on corporate reputation and we discuss the implications of viewing corporate reputation as an institutional message. We conclude with a discussion of the extent to which the business of corporate reputation itself has become institutionalized.

Institutional Research and Corporate Reputation

Institutionalism is an approach to organization studies that emphasizes rules, norms, and beliefs in the wider external environment of organizations. Most commentators date the rise of institutional theory from the publication of Meyer and Rowan's (1977) article on formal organizational structure as myth and ceremony. It was published at a time when the external environment of organizations – competitive pressures, globalization, and rising regulations – was increasingly recognized as a source of influence on organizations. Meyer and Rowan (1977) represented a lynch pin between Phillip Selznick's institutional studies in the 1940s and 1950s (Selznick, 1949, 1957), which focused on single organizational entities, and the many papers that followed, which tended to focus on institutionalized fields of organization (DiMaggio and Powell, 1983). Today, thousands of papers cite and employ institutional theory – just those at the intersection of institutional theory and corporate reputation number in the hundreds – but Greenwood *et al.* (2008) provide the most current and concise review of the field. For present purposes, we wish to draw attention to the research and implications that cohere around concerns for institutions, communication, and corporate reputation. As we identify the key features of institutions (as they are presently understood) and institutional research, we hope the reader will see their relevance for corporate reputation.

An institution is "more-or-less taken-for-granted repetitive social behaviour that is underpinned by normative systems and cognitive understandings that give meaning to social exchange and thus enable self-reproducing social order" (Greenwood *et al.*, 2008, p. 4). This definition contains the most frequently cited elements of the institutional view, including peoples' fairly rote acceptance of appropriate behaviors consistent with prevailing beliefs and expectations, reinforced by explicit, if rarely examined, laws and regulations (Scott, 2001). One aspect that is implied but not men-

tioned explicitly is that their "repetitive" and "self-reproducing nature" (Greenwood *et al.*, 2008, p. 4) contributes to slow change, or what we perceive as establishment. Attending to institutions draws attention to trans-organizational phenomena: beliefs, routines, norms, and rules that have lives independent of particular organizations (Lammers and Barbour, 2006).

The major concepts developed in institutional theory include legitimacy as rational myths (Deephouse and Suchman, 2008; Meyer and Rowan, 1977); isomorphic pressures in the development of institutional fields (DiMaggio and Powell, 1983); institutional logics (Friedland and Alford, 1991; Thornton and Ocasio, 2008); institutional work (Lawrence and Suddaby, 2006); institutional entrepreneurship (DiMaggio, 1988; Maguire *et al.*, 2004); and the processes of institutionalization and deinstitutionalization (Oliver, 1992; Tolbert and Zucker, 1996). Meyer and Rowan (1977) observed that elements of rationality are so widely available for organizations to employ that they have become substitutes for functional reasoning. For example, Lammers (2003) observed that high pay for executives is awarded in the absence of a functional explanation linking earnings or productivity to pay. DiMaggio and Powell (1983) observed that organizational fields develop as a result of competitive and regulatory pressures, and firms' tendency to adopt similar forms via professional norms, coercive rules, or rivalrous mimicry. Friedland and Alford (1991) posited that institutional logics were a field's "organizing principles . . . available to organizations and individuals to elaborate" (p. 248). Lawrence and Suddaby (2006) defined institutional work as the "purposive action of individuals and organizations aimed at creating, maintaining, and disrupting institutions" (p. 215). Over time, such work could lead to institutionalization (a process by which "social processes, obligations, or actualities come to take on a rule-like status in social thought and action," Meyer and Rowan, 1977, p. 342) or deinstitutionalization ("the process by which the legitimacy of an established or institutionalized organizational practice erodes or discontinues," Oliver, 1992, p. 264). In the next section, we review the use of these institutional concepts in the literature on corporate reputation.

Legitimacy and rational myths

Of all the concepts developed in the institutionalists' repertoire, the idea of legitimacy is the most closely associated with corporate reputation, and is implicated in much of what institutionalists study. In their initial articulation of the rational myth, Meyer and Rowan (1977) did not distinguish between legitimacy and reputation, but pointed out that "reputational gains" could result from engaging in institutionalized "ceremonial activities" (p. 355). Both legitimacy and reputation are frequently measured as stakeholders' perceptions of approval of an organization's actions (Deephouse and Carter, 2005; Elsbach, 2006; Lawrence, 1998; Rao, 1994; Ruef and Scott, 1998). Meyer and Scott (1983), for example, defined a completely legitimate organization as one "about which no question would be raised" (p. 201).

However, several researchers have sought to distinguish between reputation and legitimacy (Deephouse and Carter, 2005; King and Whetten, 2008). Deephouse and Carter (2005) carefully define the two concepts:

> legitimacy [may be understood to be] the social acceptance resulting from adherence to regulative, normative or cognitive norms and expectations. In contrast, we view reputation as a social comparison among organizations on a variety of attributes, which could include these same regulative, normative or cognitive dimensions. (p. 332)

In addition, Deephouse and Carter (2005) found that past financial performance and conformity to norms (in institutional terms, isomorphism – see the following section) differentially predicted reputation and two types of legitimacy (public and financial regulatory).

In some research, the norm-adherence versus peer-ranking distinction between legitimacy and reputation has been blurred. In the case of the adoption of practices for the purposes of symbolic conformity, legitimation and reputational practices are similar. Superficial adherence to rules to gain either the appearance of legitimacy or enhanced reputation or both has been the subject of a number of research papers. For example, Boiral (2007) reported that adherence to the industrial ISO 14001 standards appeared to be undertaken by the Canadian organizations he studied for ceremonial purposes, leading him to refer to their adoption as "corporate greening" (p. 127). Indeed, social and environmental corporate responsibility activities are often analyzed as attempts to improve reputation. In a study of accounting professionals' assessments of the legitimacy of environmental disclosures among chemical firms, Milne and Patten (2002) noted "that all attempts at legitimation are likely to form part of a 'myth system' that is loosely or entirely de-coupled (Weick, 1969) from the organization's 'operational code'" (p. 375).

Considering reputation as one kind of legitimacy message, we can see that firms endeavor to signal to their environments that their activities are consistent with prevailing beliefs, standards, and rules. In a study of the stakeholder decision-making process, Puncheva (2007) found that when stakeholders lack direct experience with a company, they will rely first on the reputation, second on the perceived social legitimacy, and finally, on the pragmatic legitimacy of the company before deciding to engage in any exchange with that company. Rao (1994) examined the US automobile industry from 1895 to 1912 and the role of credentials as institutionalized and social symbols of organizational capabilities that embody standards for that industry. Rindova *et al.* (2005) bolstered the idea that certifications, such as media rankings, certifications of achievement, and affiliation with high-status actors improve the prominence of organizational reputations. They proposed a model that attributes the perceived quality of organizational reputations to resource signals, including quality of inputs and productivity assets. Thus, institutionalists have contributed to the development of the concept of reputation by showing how legitimacy is connected to it, and offered support for the perceived aspect of the concept. But the power of legitimacy and reputation lie in field dynamics, which we discuss next.

Isomorphic pressures in the development of institutional fields

DiMaggio and Powell's (1983) insight about similarities among organizations sharing an institutional field followed closely Meyer and Rowan's (1977) arguments about rational myths. As Milne and Patten (2002) pointed out,

> "institutionalists tend to emphasize the collective structuration (DiMaggio and Powell, 1983) of entire *fields* or *sectors* of organizational life" (Suchman, 1995, p. 576; emphasis in the original). Much management behavior, including attempts to legitimate, may be controlled not by managers but by institutional pressures that produce an "iron cage" and create tendencies towards isomorphism within the organizational field (DiMaggio and Powell, 1983). These pressures, however, may be subtle, pervasive, yet powerful, myths of why organizations ought to exist, and how they ought to behave.

Note that the isomorphic pressures, whether mimetic, normative, or coercive (DiMaggio and Powell, 1983), concern organizations' search for legitimacy in their environments.

Despite institutionalism's emphasis on fields, reputation research employing institutional ideas tends to measure effects at the level of individual organizations. For example, Deephouse and Carter (2005), in examining the difference between reputation and legitimacy in banking practices, confirmed "that legitimacy emphasizes the social acceptance resulting from adherence to social norms and expectations whereas reputation emphasizes comparisons among organizations" (p. 329; see also Lawrence, 1998). However, their analysis tended to devolve to a focus on particular banks rather than the field as a whole; their strategy for analyzing strategic isomorphism was to assign values to banks' asset strategies (Deephouse

and Carter, 2005, p. 343). They found that isomorphism (approximating industry averages in investment portfolios) improves legitimacy but that its effects on reputation were mediated by the company's prior reputation. Moreover, stronger financial performance improved reputation but not legitimacy. In the end, their study found that "[i]somorphism appears critical for legitimacy but may have more complex relationships with reputation" (p. 353), reinforcing the idea that reputation may require elements of nonconformity.

A number of studies have employed the idea of isomorphic pressures as conformity moves on the part of organizations (Wright and Rwabizambuga, 2006). Westphal *et al.* (1997) found evidence of conformity bestowing legitimacy in a sample of hospitals, as did Staw and Epstein (2000), who linked the adoption of popular management methods to both external and internal reputation in a sample of large US corporations. Zyglidopoulos (2003) made the point that as issues evolve, corporations' behavior that was once successful must change to "match societal expectations because of competitive or institutional isomorphism forces" (p. 72). Levis (2006) observed isomorphic pressures at work in multinational corporations' adoption of corporate social responsibility (CSR) codes: "mimesis . . . explains how the adoption of CSR Codes by a number of MNCs sends a signal to others that they should act similarly" (p. 52). Glynn and Abzug (2002) studied symbolic isomorphism by examining corporate name changes. Controlling for the level of reputation, they found that "name changes in organizational conformity to institutionalized constitutive rules concerning name ambiguity and specificity increased legitimacy" (p. 275). Marquis *et al.* (2007) proposed a view of corporate actions regarding reputation as an outgrowth of isomorphic institutionalization processes at the level of specific geographical communities.

The aforementioned studies all provide support for the theoretical argument that firms adopt similar strategies for the sake of their reputations. The thrust of the institutionalists' arguments is that isomorphism results from conformity pressures from which few can escape. With respect to conformity, viewing reputation as an institutional message helps us see how the reproduction of specific messages (e.g., adoption of industrial standards) drowns out other messages, and becomes part of the information load with which managers must cope. Institutionalism sees those messages as driven by powerful underlying logics, to which we now turn.

Institutional logics

Friedland and Alford's (1991) original definition of institutional logics is fairly broad, applying to large swaths of institutional life, such as markets or democracy. As such, its relevance to corporate reputation may seem vague. However, Dunn and Jones (2010) provided the more succinct definition of institutional logics as "cultural beliefs and rules that shape the cognitions and behaviors of actors" (p. 114; see also Jackall, 1988; Scott, 2001; Thornton, 2002). Using that definition in a meta-analysis of studies of corporate social performance and corporate financial performance, Orlitzky (2011) found substantial differences between accounting journals, general management journals, and social issue management (SIM) journals. In studies published by economics, finance, or accounting journals, the average correlations of social and financial performances were only about half the size of the values reported by the SIM journals, while general management journals' findings fell in the mid-range. In other words, the institutional logic of a journal's discipline played some role in the size of the relationship between economic and social performances, both strong correlates of reputation.

Metzger *et al.* (1993) argued that corporations' codes of ethics that do not take account of the institutional logic of the corporation (such as incentives for making risky loans in a mortgage company), may do little to protect a company's reputation. Similarly, Herremans *et al.* (2009) found that competing logics within the Canadian petroleum industry differentiated companies' environmental policies

despite "shifting societal level logics for improved corporate environmental performance" (p. 449). At the field level, Levy *et al.* (2008) make the case that the rise and subsequent decline of nonfinancial reporting was a manifestation of competing institutional logics. Thus, institutional logics as the "belief systems and associated practices that predominate in an organizational field" (Scott *et al.*, 2000, p. 170) are predictive of firms' behaviors vis-à-vis their reputations.

Lammers (2011) suggested that institutional messages carry institutional logics in their audience reach, duration, and incumbency (the extent to which they obligate receivers to take certain actions). The most powerful reputations indeed reach wide audiences, have staying power, and are persuasive in obtaining (if not requiring) stakeholder loyalty and support. Certainly, the extant research shows that corporate reputations must be consistent with field-level logics. But the question of how reputations as messages are sustained, reach new audiences, or increase the likelihood of actions on the parts of receivers is institutional work, to which we now turn.

Institutional work

The idea of institutional work (Lawrence and Suddaby, 2006) is an explicit recognition that managers consciously seek to reconcile the actions of their firms – including managing their firms' reputations – with the institutional environments within which they work. While the idea has not been developed into a taxonomy of specific activities, a number of authors have alluded to the idea, especially as it concerns the evolving area of CSR. For example, Bertels and Peloza (2008) charted the activities of managers who responded to an "expectation gap" (pp. 58, 66) created by the adoption of CSR policies by elite firms in a geographic area. Geographic proximity, elite status, and visibility create the circumstances where policies leap across industry boundaries and then spread within industries through mimetic forces (p. 56). Similarly, Winn *et al.* (2008) identified the activities of industry and trade groups as institutional work in their study of collective industry reputation management. This focus on the institutional level of analysis lifts reputation studies beyond the concerns of the managers of individual organizations. A similar industry-level study of the Australian CSR movement was undertaken by Truscott *et al.* (2009). Once again, they identified the cross-organizational field activities of advocates of CSR as institutional work, which in this case was influenced by the infancy of the CSR movement. Wry (2009) associates business and society scholarship on CSR and reputation with institutional work, implying that even texts such as the one in which this chapter is published represent a facet of the institutional environment.

Institutional work concerns the activities of managers who must navigate their firms through complex institutional environments. Positioned on the boundaries between organization and environment, those managers are involved in what Sahlin and Wedlin (2008) referred to as the editing of institutional ideas. In considering the circulation, translation, and editing of institutional ideas, they are implicitly concerned with institutional messages. Useful studies could focus on the near simultaneous receipt and transmission of such messages in the adoption of policies and the broadcast of image and identity. A compelling problem is how firms and their managers can innovate under the pressures of conformity and reputation management we have discussed. That innovation is referred to as institutional entrepreneurship, which we discuss next.

Institutional entrepreneurship

As a special case of institutional work, institutional entrepreneurship was first identified by DiMaggio (1988) to refer to the activities associated with changing institutional logics. Institutional entrepreneurs should be rare, because institutionalized arrangements by definition become part of the taken-for-granted landscape of work and alternative routines are quite literally unknowable. Maguire *et al.* (2004) defined institutional entrepreneurship as the "activities of actors who . . . leverage resources to create new institutions or to transform existing ones"

(p. 657). Thus, the activities of individuals with respect to the management of corporate or industry reputation may be understood as institutional entrepreneurship. For example, Campbell (2007) incorporated the idea of institutional entrepreneurship into his theorizing about CSR: "the creation and enforcement of effective state regulations turn in part on the capacity of external actors, such as environmentalists, unions, consumers, and other stakeholders, to participate in and monitor these regulatory processes" (p. 955; see also Troast *et al.*, 2002). Such institutional entrepreneurs in turn create additional institutional constraints that managers must take into account in protecting or improving their own companies' reputations. Greenwood and Suddaby (2006) showed how corporate actors with elite reputations – in the case of leading accounting firms – can shift field logics.

If we think of institutional entrepreneurs as inventors of institutional messages, or more profoundly logics, we might develop an understanding of how field logics and their underlying beliefs and values create the possibility for corporate reputations. Retrospectively, we can analyze the success of certain firms (Apple or Starbucks, for example) as instances of the invention of new logics and the creation of the basis for new reputations. Additional research, however, is needed not only on successful institutional entrepreneurship, but also on failure as well. Ultimately, both failure and success contribute to what we think of as institutionalization or deinstitutionalization, the subject of the next section.

Processes of institutionalization and deinstitutionalization

Processes of institutionalization and deinstitutionalization have obvious implications for the study of corporate reputation. Specifically, managers aim to establish reputations that stakeholders will take for granted and not question whether the reputations should be challenged or reevaluated. In this sense managers may be said to be in the business of institutionalization. But because the process is usually understood at a larger scale than that of the single firm (at least in the new institutionalists' frame; see DiMaggio and Powell, 1991), reputation may be better understood as a *function* of institutionalization processes. That is, reputations depend on the establishment of certain sets of beliefs, norms, and rules. Thus, Den Hond and De Bakker (2007) showed how activist organizations, in attempting to institutionalize their agendas, may attack reputations or lend reputations to corporations in the process of deinstitutionalizing one issue frame and reinstitutionalizing another.

Applying the concept of the institutional message to institutionalization processes in the case of corporate reputation allows us to consider how reputations as messages endure or fail. The phenomena of activist organizations lending reputations to firms (Den Hond and De Bakker, 2007) raises the provocative idea that firms exist in interdependent relationships with social activist organizations, which were formerly thought of as part of an independent sector of the organizational world. From the institutional point of view, corporate reputations exist in an information environment of legitimacy pressures toward conformity, undergirded by stable logics which managers must navigate. Moreover, this view suggests that while legitimacy and reputation may not be the same thing, they both reflect a stable, relatively obdurate set of environmental conditions. This means that corporate reputation itself may be considered a feature of the institutional environment.

To What Extent Is Corporate Reputation Institutionalized?

The phenomenon of corporate reputation as a feature of individual organizations, industries, and markets bears some of the hallmarks of an institution. Lammers and Barbour (2006) offered a communicative definition of institution that serves our purposes. Institutions are seen as (1) constellations (i.e., relatively fixed patterns) of established practices; (2) manifested in beliefs; (3) carried by people; (4) of an enduring nature; (5) formal, that is, recorded

or archived; and (6) rational, that is, goal oriented.

To what extent are these characteristics of the field of corporate reputation? Over the last 20 years, the reputation business has taken on the appearance of a relatively established and enduring pattern of activities. As a general phenomenon, we can say that corporate reputation is indeed manifested in practices such as the *Fortune* Magazine's annual report on the Most Admired Companies. The widespread reliance on and attention given to this and other ranking systems (Fombrun *et al.*, 1999) and even the existence of the Reputation Institute and its affiliated journal *Corporate Reputation Review* confirm that indeed reputation is manifested in practices. Moreover, the well-documented moves toward total quality management (TQM), common human resource (HR) practices, CSR, and other industry standards are all evidence that reputation issues are believed to be important to the success of firms over and above economic efficiency.

That reputation is now an industry with its own population of consultants, careers, organizations, and experts is certainly true. A small number of companies focus solely on the use of human analysts to code journalist sentiment and research stakeholders (e.g., Prime Research, KDPaine, Cision, Reputation Institute, Report International, Cubit Media Research, and Cymfony) and a few large public relations firms with departments devoted to corporate reputation (such as Weber Shandwick, Waggener Edstrom Worldwide, and Edelman). However, the majority of organizations in the corporate reputation field conduct automated media sentiment analysis, and this area is unproven, unregulated, and of very uneven quality (J. Wethall, personal communication, February 28, 2012). As such, it represents an as yet uninstitutionalized media arena.

Like other firms that measure corporate reputation, the Reputation Institute belongs to an industry association of survey researchers (the Council of American Survey Research Organizations) and subscribes to its code of ethics (http://www.reputationinstitute.com/). Other industry groups include the International Association of Business Communicators (which has a research foundation and an annual conference devoted to corporate reputation); the Institute for Public Relations (which has a Measurement Commission); and the Public Relations Society of America, which has a committee devoted to corporate reputation (J. Wethall, personal communication, February 28, 2012). Each of these organizations has developed codes and procedures suggesting that the field is becoming formally rational, with a constellation of relatively fixed practices, positions, and beliefs.

Another way to view the institutionalization of corporate reputation is through the lens of the professions. Lammers and Garcia (2009) found that the term refers to

> an occupation the conduct of which is characterized by emotional neutrality, command over a body of knowledge, formal standards of conduct, a service orientation, elevated social status, extended training and education, self- and social control, and the establishment of formal associations. (p. 362)

The extent to which practitioners of corporate reputation manifest these features is an empirical question, but the presence of a journal, codes of ethics maintained by the several associations mentioned earlier, and the establishment of formal associations speak to partial professionalization. However, the absence of dedicated academic programs, particularly elevated social status, and a well-established service orientation suggests that professionalization is far from complete.

Conclusion: A Communicatively Inflected Institutional Approach to Corporate Reputation

Institutional theory has substantially contributed to our understanding of corporate reputation at the firm, industry, and field levels. Many of the concepts of institutional theory, from rational myths and isomorphic pressures to institutional work and entrepreneurship, have been employed in studies of corporate reputation. The evidence suggests that institutional theory can continue to assist researchers in understanding how corporate reputation influences corporate behavior in areas including CSR, HR, TQM, and field-specific policies and behaviors in industries as diverse as banking and salmon fishing. In this concluding section, we note three opportunities for researchers working at the intersection of institutional theory, communication, and corporate reputation.

First, researchers should consider reputations as messages that contribute to and draw from institutional logics. While reputation researchers generally attempt to develop (even multidimensional) metrics by which to gauge comparative reputations with fields, it is also the case that institutional fields are governed by distinctive logics that could be understood in terms of institutional messages. This means that there may be field-distinctive means of gaining, improving, losing, or resisting the messages that carry reputations. The survival of large financial institutions that have been implicated in the international banking crisis suggests an opportunity to study reputation message resistance.

Second, the burgeoning area of business in online reputation management, both as a problem for organizations and as a business enterprise in its own right, represents a new and unsettled frontier for studying corporate reputation from an institutional perspective. The role of social media in developing, maintaining, protecting, or attacking reputations is still being discovered. The durability and rapid transmission of electronic messages gives a whole new meaning to the idea that organizations "attain a life of their own and often overshadow, constrain, and manipulate their members" (Poole and McPhee, 1983, p. 195). The new media will give researchers an opportunity to study in real time the establishment of reputations.

Finally, institutions ultimately concern the established routines to which organizations conform in order to be perceived as legitimate. As corporate reputation becomes more institutionalized, and as its work occupations become more professionalized, it may be that reputation (perceived status) and legitimacy (institutional status) will come to mean the same thing. A core question then for researchers is how something as malleable as reputation becomes codified and formalized. We suggest that considering reputation as a message or signal (Kraatz and Love, 2006) is a useful approach, and we encourage researchers to develop the ideas of signal and message in studies of corporate reputation and institutional environments.

Notes

1 The authors are grateful to Sean Willett for tireless and excellent bibliographic work.
2 Actually, DiMaggio and Powell (1983) make reference to increased information load on organizations as a concomitant of the structuration of institutional fields, but this idea has not been developed by researchers.
3 This is similar to the approach taken by Kraatz and Love (2006), who referred to reputations as signals to stakeholder audiences. There is an important difference between signals (the meaning of which is agreed upon) and messages (which mean something to the sender but must be interpreted by audiences). We prefer the concept of the message because it implies complexity and captures the human element of meaning making.

References

Bertels, S. and Peloza, J. (2008) Running just to stand still? Managing CSR reputation in an era of ratcheting expectations. *Corporate Reputation Review, 11*, 56–73.

Boiral, O. (2007) Corporate greening through ISO 14001: A rational myth? *Organization Science, 18*, 127–146.

Campbell, J.L. (2007) Why would corporations behave in socially responsible ways? An institutional theory of corporate social responsibility. *Academy of Management Review, 32*, 946–967.

Commons, J.R. (1934) *Institutional Economics.* New York: Macmillan.

Deephouse, D. and Carter, S.M. (2005) An examination of differences between organizational legit-

imacy and organizational reputation. *Journal of Management Studies, 42*, 3–23.

Deephouse, D. and Suchman, M. (2008) Legitimacy in organizational institutionalism. In R. Greenwood, C. Oliver, R. Suddaby, and K. Sahlin-Andersson (eds), *The Handbook of Organizational Institutionalism.* Thousand Oaks, CA: Sage, pp. 49–77.

Den Hond, F. and De Bakker, F.G.A. (2007) Ideologically motivated activism: How activist groups influence corporate social change activities. *Academy of Management Review, 32*, 901–924.

DiMaggio, P.J. (1988) Interest and agency in institutional theory. In L.G. Zucker (ed.), *Institutional Patterns in Organizations. Culture and Environment.* Cambridge, MA: Ballinger Publishing Co., pp. 3–21.

DiMaggio, P.J. and Powell, W.W. (1983) The iron cage revisited: Institutional isomorphism and collective rationality in organization fields. *American Sociological Review, 48*, 147–160.

DiMaggio, P.J. and Powell, W.W. (1991) Introduction. In W.W. Powell and P.J. DiMaggio (eds), *The New Institutionalism in Organizational Analysis.* Chicago, IL: University of Chicago Press, pp. 1–38.

Dunn, M.B. and Jones, C. (2010) Institutional logics and institutional pluralism: The contestation of care and science logics in medical education, 1967–2005. *Administrative Science Quarterly, 55*, 114–149.

Elsbach, K.D. (2006) *Organizational Perception Management.* Mahwah, NJ: Lawrence Erlbaum.

Fombrun, C.J. (1996) *Reputation: Realizing Value from the Corporate Image.* Boston: Harvard Business School Press.

Fombrun, C.J. and Shanley, M. (1990) What's in a name? Reputation building and corporate strategy. *Academy of Management Journal, 33*, 233–258.

Fombrun, C.J., Gardberg, N.A., and Sever, J.M. (1999) The Reputation Quotient[SM]: A multi-stakeholder measure of corporate reputation. *The Journal of Brand Management, 7*, 241–254.

Friedland, R. and Alford, R.R. (1991) Bringing society back in: Symbols, practices, and institutional contradictions. In W.W. Powell and P.J. DiMaggio (eds), *The New Institutionalism in Organizational Analysis.* Chicago, IL: University of Chicago Press, pp. 232–263.

Glynn, M.A. and Abzug, R. (2002) Institutionalizing identity: Symbolic isomorphism and organizational names. *Academy of Management Journal, 45*, 267.

Greenwood, R. and Suddaby, R. (2006) Institutional entrepreneurship in mature fields: The Big Five accounting firms. *Academy of Management Journal, 49,* 27–48.

Greenwood, R., Oliver, C., Sahlin, K., and Suddaby, R. (2008) Introduction. In R. Greenwood, C. Oliver, K. Sahlin, and R. Suddaby (eds), *The Sage Handbook of Organizational Institutionalism.* Thousand Oaks, CA: Sage, pp. 1–46.

Herremans, I.M., Herschovis, M.S., and Bertels, S. (2009) Leaders and laggards: The influence of competing logics on corporate environmental action. *Journal of Business Ethics, 89,* 449–472.

Jackall, R. (1988) *Moral Mazes.* New York: Oxford Press.

King, B.G. and Whetten, D.A. (2008) Rethinking the relationship between reputation and legitimacy: A social actor conceptualization. *Corporate Reputation Review, 11,* 192–208.

Kraatz, M.S. and Block, E.S. (2008) Organizational implications of institutional pluralism. In R. Greenwood, C. Oliver, K. Sahlin, and R. Suddaby (eds), *The Sage Handbook of Organizational Institutionalism.* Thousand Oaks, CA: Sage, pp. 243–275.

Kraatz, M.S. and Love, E.G. (2006) Studying the dynamics of reputation: A framework for research on the reputational consequences of corporate actions. In D.J. Ketchen and D. Bergh (eds), *Research Methodology in Strategy and Management* (Vol. 3). Bingley, UK: Emerald Group Publishing Limited, pp. 343–383.

Lammers, J.C. (2003) An institutional perspective on communicating corporate responsibility. *Management Communication Quarterly, 16,* 618–624.

Lammers, J.C. (2011) How institutions communicate: Institutional messages, institutional logics, and organizational communication. *Management Communication Quarterly, 25,* 154–182.

Lammers, J.C. and Barbour, J.B. (2006) An institutional theory of organizational communication. *Communication Theory, 16,* 356–377.

Lammers, J.C. and Garcia, M.A. (2009) Exploring the concept of "profession" for organizational communication research: Institutional influences in a veterinary organization. *Management Communication Quarterly, 22,* 357–384.

Lawrence, T.B. (1998) Examining resources in an occupational community: Reputation in Canadian forensic accounting. *Human Relations, 51,* 1103–1131.

Lawrence, T.B. and Suddaby, R. (2006) Institutions and institutional work. In S.R. Clegg, C. Hardy, T.B. Lawrence, and W.R. Nord (eds), *Handbook of Organization Studies* (2nd ed.). London: Sage, pp. 215–254.

Levis, J. (2006) Adoption of corporate social responsibility codes by multinational companies. *Journal of Asian Economics, 17,* 50–55.

Levy, D.L., Brown, H., and de Jong, M. (2008) NGO strategies and the politics of corporate governance: The case of the Global Reporting Initiative. Paper for Third Colloquium on Corporate Political Activity, Paris, May.

Maguire, S., Hardy, C., and Lawrence, T. (2004) Institutional entrepreneurship in emerging fields: HIV/AIDS treatment advocacy in Canada. *Academy of Management Journal, 47,* 654–679.

Marquis, C., Glynn, M.A., and Davis, G.F. (2007) Community isomorphism and corporate social action. *Academy of Management Review, 32,* 925–945.

Martins, L.L. (2005) A model of the effects of reputational rankings on organizational change. *Organization Science, 16,* 701–720.

Metzger, M., Dalton, D., and Hill, J.W. (1993) The organization of ethics and the ethics of organizations: The case for expanded organizational ethics audits business. *Ethics Quarterly, 3,* 27–43.

Meyer, J.W. and Rowan, B. (1977) Institutionalized organizations: Formal structure as myth and ceremony. *American Journal of Sociology, 83,* 340–363.

Meyer, J.W. and Scott, W.R. (1983) Centralization and the legitimacy problems of local government. In J.W. Meyer and W.R. Scott (eds), *Organizational Environments: Ritual and Rationality.* Beverly Hills, CA: Sage, pp. 199–215.

Milne, M.J. and Patten, D.M. (2002) Securing organizational legitimacy: An experimental decision case examining the impact of environmental disclosures. *Accounting, Auditing & Accountability Journal, 15,* 372–405.

Oliver, C. (1992) The antecedents of deinstitutionalization. *Organization Studies, 13,* 563–588.

Orlitzky, M. (2011) Institutional logics in the study of organizations: The social construction of the relationship between corporate social and financial performance. *Business Ethics Quarterly, 21,* 409–444.

Phillips, N., Lawrence, T.B., and Hardy, C. (2004) Discourse and institutions. *Academy of Management Review, 29,* 635–652.

Poole, M.S. and McPhee, R.D. (1983) A structural analysis of organizational climate. In L.L. Putnam and M. Pacanowsky (eds), *Communication and Organizations: An Interpretive Approach*. Newbury Park, CA: Sage, pp. 195–219.

Puncheva, P. (2007) The role of corporate reputation in the stakeholder decision-making process. *Business & Society*, *47*, 272–290.

Rao, H. (1994) The social construction of reputation: Certification contests, legitimation, and the survival of organizations in the American automobile industry, 1895–1912. *Strategic Management Journal*, *15*, 29–44.

Rao, H. (1998) Caveat emptor: The construction of nonprofit consumer watchdog organizations. *American Journal of Sociology*, *103*, 912–961.

Rindova, V.P., Williamson, I.O., Petkova, A.P., and Sever, J.M. (2005) Being good or being known: An empirical examination of the dimensions, antecedents, and consequences of organizational reputation. *The Academy of Management Journal*, *48*, 1033–1049.

Ruef, M. and Scott, W.R. (1998) A multidimensional model of organizational legitimacy: Hospital survival in changing institutional environments. *Administrative Science Quarterly*, *43*, 877–904.

Sahlin, K. and Wedlin, L. (2008) Circulating ideas: Imitation, translation and editing. In R. Greenwood, C. Oliver, K. Sahlin, and R. Suddaby (eds), *The Sage Handbook of Organizational Institutionalism*. Los Angeles, CA: Sage, pp. 218–242.

Schultz, M., Mouritsen, J., and Gabrielsen, G. (2001) Sticky reputation: Analyzing a ranking system. *Corporate Reputation Review*, *4*, 24–41.

Scott, W.R. (2001) *Institutions and Organizations*. Thousand Oaks, CA: Sage.

Scott, W.R., Ruef, M., Mendel, P.J., and Caronna, C.A. (2000) *Institutional Change and Healthcare Organizations*. Chicago, IL: University of Chicago Press.

Selznick, P. (1949) *TVA and the Grass Roots: A Study in the Sociology of Formal Organization*. Berkeley, CA: University of California Press.

Selznick, P. (1957) *Leadership in Administration: A Sociological Interpretation*. Evanston, IL: Row, Peterson.

Staw, B.M. and Epstein, L.D. (2000) What bandwagons bring: Effects of popular management techniques on corporate performance, reputation, and CEO pay. *Administrative Science Quarterly*, *45*, 523–556.

Suchman, M.C. (1995) Managing legitimacy: Strategic and institutional approaches. *Academy of Management Review*, *20*, 571–610.

Thornton, P. (2002) The rise of the corporation in a craft industry: Conflict and conformity in institutional logics. *Academy of Management Journal*, *45*, 81–101.

Thornton, P. and Ocasio, W. (2008) Institutional logics. In R. Greenwood, C. Oliver, K. Sahlin, and R. Suddaby (eds), *The SAGE Handbook of Organizational Institutionalism*. Thousand Oaks, CA: Sage, pp. 99–129.

Tolbert, P.S. and Zucker, L.G. (1996) The institutionalization of institutional theory. In S.R. Clegg, C. Hardy, and W.R. Nord (eds), *Handbook of Organization Studies*. Thousand Oaks, CA: Sage, pp. 175–190.

Troast, J.G., Hoffman, A.J., Riley, H.C., and Bazerman, M.H. (2002) Institutions as barriers and enablers to negotiated agreements: Institutional entrepreneurship and the Plum Creek Habitat Conservation Plan. In A.J. Hoffman and M.J. Ventresca (eds), *Organizations, Policy, and the Natural Environment*. Stanford, CA: Stanford University Press, pp. 235–261.

Truscott, R.A., Bartlett, J.L., and Tywoniak, S. (2009) The reputation of the corporate social responsibility industry in Australia. *Australasian Marketing Journal*, *17*, 84–91.

Walker, K. (2010) A systematic review of the corporate reputation literature: Definition, measurement, and theory. *Corporate Reputation Review*, *12*, 357–387.

Wartick, S.L. (2002) Measuring corporate reputation: Definition and data. *Business & Society*, *41*, 371–392.

Weick, K. (1969) *The Social Psychology of Organizing*. New York: McGraw-Hill.

Westphal, J.D., Gulati, R., and Shortell, S.M. (1997) Customization or conformity? An institutional and network perspective on the content and consequences of TQM adoption. *Administrative Science Quarterly*, *42*, 366–394.

Whetten, D.A. (1997) Part II: Where do reputations come from? Theory development and the study of corporate reputation. *Corporate Reputation Review*, *1*, 25–34.

Winn, M.I., MacDonald, P., and Zietsma, C. (2008) The dynamic tension between collective and competitive reputation management strategies. *Corporate Reputation Review*, *11*, 35–55.

Wright, C. and Rwabizambuga, A. (2006) Institutional pressures, corporate reputation, and voluntary codes of conduct: An examination of the Equator Principles. *Business and Society Review, 111,* 89–117.

Wry, T.E. (2009) Does business and society scholarship matter to society? Pursuing a normative agenda with critical realism and neoinstitu-

tional theory. *Journal of Business Ethics, 89,* 151–171.

Zyglidopoulos, S.C. (2003) The issue life-cycle: Implications for reputation for social performance and organizational legitimacy. *Corporate Reputation Review, 6,* 70–81.

21

Experiencing the Reputational Synergy of Success and Failure through Organizational Learning

Timothy L. Sellnow, Shari R. Veil, and Kathryn Anthony

University of Kentucky, USA

When unforeseeable crises occur, the tendency to place blame and assign punishment is fitting with human nature. Yet, while salvaging reputation in the short term, these backward-looking responses produce few opportunities for learning. This chapter examines the link between organizational preservation and learning. Specifically, we discuss how organizational learning impacts organizational legitimacy and reputation and provide strategies for learning in advance of major failures such as crises. Reactive learning strategies are also described as motivation for embracing a learning culture. We suggest that these strategies can enhance mindfulness and create renewed organizations and industries that are more dedicated to and better prepared for engaging in proactive learning.

Learning is a necessity, not an option, for organizations. If organizations fail to learn from their experiences and environments, they cannot undertake the essential adaptations needed to maintain a competitive and respected position in society. Organizations adapt through learning in order to establish or maintain social legitimacy and a favorable public reputation. Failure to learn will inevitably lead to a decline in both legitimacy and reputation. In this chapter, we further explore this link between organizational preservation and learning. We begin with an overview of organizational legitimacy and reputation and explore their connection to organizational learning. Next, we contrast single-, double-, and triple-loop learning. Proactive strategies for learning are then discussed as a means for learning in advance of major failures such as crises. Reactive learning strategies are also described as motivation for embracing a learning culture. Finally, we offer conclusions and a discussion of future research focusing on corporate reputation through the lens of communication and organizational learning.

Organizational Legitimacy and Reputation

As previewed, organizations must learn from and adapt to failure and environmental change

The Handbook of Communication and Corporate Reputation, First Edition. Edited by Craig E. Carroll.
© 2013 John Wiley & Sons, Inc. Published 2015 by John Wiley & Sons, Inc.

if they are to maintain organizational legitimacy and favorable reputations. Organizational legitimacy is defined as "an organization's right to exist and conduct operations" (Metzler, 2001, p. 322). Legitimacy is bestowed when stakeholders perceive that the organization is in line with socially and politically appropriate practices (Finet, 1993). For an organization to achieve and maintain legitimacy, its stakeholders must believe that the organization's actions are compatible with their norms or social standards.

Dowling and Pfeffer (1975) outline three broad strategies for establishing legitimacy. First, an organization can adapt its goals to conform to the greater social norms. Aligning organizational aspirations with key issues valued by stakeholders evidences a commonality between the viewpoints of the organization and its stakeholders. An organization may also try to change or persuade stakeholders to change their social norms to make them a more precise reflection of the organization's practices. Depending on their size and voice, organizations can bring to light social practices that may be supported by stakeholders once identified by the organization. Finally, organizations may attempt to become identified with symbols or institutions that already elicit a strong sense of legitimacy, allowing the organization to share in the partner organization's reputational glow.

As noted in previous chapters, a positive reputation is bestowed when a legitimate organization is held in high regard relative to its peer organizations (Fombrun, 1996; Fombrun and van Riel, 2004; Heugens *et al.*, 2004). Highly esteemed organizations are often perceived to have desirable character traits (Dowling, 2001; Fombrun, 1996; Fombrun and van Riel, 2004). These traits may include trustworthiness, social responsibility, and leadership, among others.

Another means for an organization to be deemed reputable is through evaluating and adapting its organizational culture to more closely align with broader society (Rao, 1994). Much like organizational legitimacy, reputation is assigned according to the organization's conformity to societal and cultural expectations.

Finally, reputation is determined based on compared ability to deliver quality products and profits (Fombrun and van Riel, 2004; Shapiro, 1982, 1983). For an organization to establish a positive reputation, its stakeholders must perceive the organization to align itself with higher standards and greater competence in these areas than its peer organizations.

Rao (1994) posits that reputation and legitimacy are complementary aspects of creating an organizational identity, and suggests that "reputation becomes an outcome of the process of legitimation" (p. 31). If an organization is not considered legitimate, it will not be held in high standing among its peers. However, an organization can have a poor reputation while still maintaining legitimacy. Therefore, suffering from an imperfect reputation is less dire than suffering from an organizational legitimacy crisis. Being held in lower esteem does not necessarily mean a company will lose access to markets (Deephouse and Carter, 2005). A loss of reputation may, however, signify an organization's inability to compare favorably with its peers and thereby diminish legitimacy. Thus, reputational threats can threaten both reputation and legitimacy.

Reputation Management

Reputational threats are essentially expectation gaps whereby stakeholders' expectations of corporate behavior do not match the stakeholders' perceptions of actual corporate behavior (Nigh and Cochran, 1987). As news of an issue or crisis spreads, the gap is often increased by media and other stakeholders who publicly compare the organization with its peers. Negative publicity damages an organization's perceived reliability, expertise, and attractiveness (Renkema and Hoeken, 1998), thereby further damaging corporate reputation.

There is a wealth of research on how an organization can repair its image and even bolster its reputational standing in the midst of failure through the communicative action of apologia (Benoit, 1995a,b, 1997, 2000; Dionisopoulos and Vibbert, 1988; Hearit, 1994, 1995a,b, 2001; Scott and Lyman, 1968; Ware and Linkugel, 1973). Apologia is typically invoked to place blame on another and absolve the organization of blame (Hearit, 1994). Responsibility for a failure is often transferred to another entity through apologia. However, if organizations are to recover from issues and crises, they must also maintain or regain their legitimacy (Finet, 1994; Hearit, 1995a; Sellnow, 1993).

Sellnow (1994) argues that routine image repair solutions, such as shifting blame and scapegoating, may salvage an organization's image in the short term, but the actions do little to avert fears that similar crises will occur in the future. Apologia is typically enacted out of concern for reputational maintenance, rather than reestablishment of organizational legitimacy. Original solutions that signal change within an organization can often "enhance a perception of preventive, long-term change and renewed social legitimacy" (Sellnow and Seeger, 1989, p. 17). As part of the organizational learning process, enacting these solutions, or taking corrective action, demonstrates to stakeholders that the organization has learned from the situation and sought to resolve the problem.

Organizational Learning

Organizational learning in its simplest form is a process of detecting and correcting error (Argyris, 1982). Organizational learning occurs when errors are shared and analyzed and the experience is distributed as a lesson learned by the organization in order to enact changes in routine process (Popper and Lipshitz, 2000). Organizations are able to collect, analyze, store, disseminate, and use information retrieved in the learning process (Popper and Lipshitz, 1999, 2000; Somech and Drach-Zahavy, 2004). To salvage reputation in the midst of failure, organization members need to not only extract knowledge from the situation to engender learning, but also respond outwardly so external stakeholders can see that the organization is

attempting to move beyond the crisis and implement new practices to prevent future failures (Elliot, 2009). Organizations must engage in responsible actions that promote public confidence and display "corporate responsiveness" (Ulrich, 1995, p. 3). In effect, to manage corporate reputation in the wake of a failure or crisis, an organization must demonstrate learning. The form and degree of learning, however, can vary widely. Next, we discuss the means by which learning can escalate from the single-loop to double- and triple-loop levels.

Single-loop learning

Argyris' (1982) single-loop learning identifies the potential to correct errors without correcting the underlying policies. Single-loop learning leads to a first-order type of change, in which small adjustments are made so current practices can function more effectively (Bartunek and Moch, 1987). Rhee (2009) assessed the influence of market reputation, whether positive or negative, on an organization's motivation to learn from product or operational deficiencies. Rhee (2009) postulated that organizations with poor reputations should be motivated to reduce its number of product defects. On the other hand, firms with historically strong reputations should be motivated to keep the number of product defects low so as to maintain a positive reputation. As projected, Rhee discovered that firms with good and poor reputations are more motivated to reduce errors than firms with intermediate reputations. Specifically, Rhee observed a U-shaped curve, where firms with more positive and negative reputations were more motivated to engage in organizational learning to achieve desirable reputation standing.

Double-loop learning

While reputation may be a motivation for correcting product defects, learning that ends in the correction of errors may not necessarily prevent future issues or crises from occurring again. Senge (1990) posits that learning organizations should capitalize on feedback to "change the thinking that produced the problem in the first place" (p. 95). "To overlook the events that led to a crisis only opens the door for a similar, possibly more devastating or even deadly crisis to occur" (Veil, 2011, p. 5). Double-loop learning is a more extensive form of learning than single loop. Not only are new actions taken to rectify organizational error, but the underlying governing policies and corporate values are also reconsidered and altered to prevent future occurrences of the problem. Thus, double-loop learning creates second-order change.

Organizational leaders can adequately address organizational change when access to organizational feedback is available. Extensive intra-organizational dialog and experimentation are necessary conditions for double-loop learning. Thus, managers who do not promote a *culture* of organizational dialog will likely restrict learning to the single-loop level or preclude learning altogether. To achieve both single- and double-loop learning, organizational leaders must allow or even encourage constructive criticism of the organization's status quo and maintain an openness to experiment with new ideas (Schimmel and Muntslag, 2009).

Reputational rankings of organizations are an increasingly influential and motivational source of feedback. Martins (2005) analyzed the effects of rankings assigned to an organization versus perceived identity in the minds of top administrators and managers. In an assessment of graduate schools, Martins (2005) revealed that institutions whose rankings did not compare favorably with the positive perceptions held by top managers were more likely to institute change. Top managers' perceptions of the impact of the rankings and organizational identity were more likely to determine change than the perceived validity of the rankings. Martins (2005) suggests that, through the rankings, the public is purportedly able to receive a "positional status" on the organization. Reputations are positively or negatively affected by rankings and therefore exert great influence in the public eye. Whether rankings are deemed a reliable reflection of legitimacy and reputation or not, they have unquestionably become a powerful motivator for learning and change.

Triple-loop learning

Nielsen (1993) argues that double-loop learning considers the integrity and ethical implications of the underlying organizational policies in an effort to change them. However, the values of the underlying social systems are outside the consideration of single- and double-loop learning (Argyris, 1982). Nielsen extends single- and double-loop learning to include triple-loop learning, which considers the social structure in which the organization's policies are embedded. According to Nielsen, double-loop action learning still "frames organizational ethics and integrity issues as individual phenomena, while for the most part, ignoring or at least not explicitly treating embedded social tradition as a partner in mutual action learning" (p. 122). Spitzeck (2009) suggests that organizational learning, specifically moral learning, is necessary to successfully manage the reputation of an organization. Moral learning refers to "a change in the dominant values of the organization in making or defending decisions" (p. 161).

Bartunek and Moch (1987) contend that third-order change allows organizational members to see the benefits and limitations of their shared understandings and make the cultural adjustments needed. Argyris and Schön (1996) argued that culture change is the central process by which an organization learns. A culture of learning allows for new insights and lasting behavioral changes instead of mere rituals of learning (Popper and Lipshitz, 1999). Most importantly, Veil (2011) maintains that "without generating learning as an essential outcome in the organization's culture, few changes will occur that could prevent a future crisis" (p. 23). When incorporated into an organization's culture and practice, learning can, and often does, occur proactively. In the next section, we detail several means for learning proactively.

Proactive Learning Strategies

Organizations learn proactively when they anticipate problems before they manifest into major failures or crises. Previous research identifies environmental scanning, issue management, and actional legitimacy as conceptual frameworks for engaging in proactive learning. We discuss each of these frameworks in this section.

Environmental scanning

Organizational leaders engage in environmental scanning to learn from their environments and implement changes in organizational routines based on the information acquired (Choo, 2001; Choo and Auster, 1993). Environmental scanning bolsters an organization's strategic planning process and enables the organization to be proactive rather than reactive toward its environment. Environmental scanning contributes to organizational learning by increasing knowledge and thereby enhancing an organization's capacity to change.

The external environmental scanning process allows organizations to learn vicariously from the failures and crises experienced by other organizations (Ulmer *et al.*, 2007). Weick and Ashford (2001) suggest that "by watching what happens to individuals when they engage in different behavior patterns, the learner comes to understand that a certain strategy leads to success while another leads to failure, without engaging in either strategy personally" (p. 712). Similarly, organizations can learn what practices to adopt and which to expunge through the achievements and blunders of parallel organizations.

Boin *et al.* (2005) admit that "it is virtually impossible to predict with any sort of precision when and where a crisis will strike"; however, improved systems of internal environmental scanning "may help to spot emerging vulnerabilities before it is too late" (p. 19). Addressing small failures as they are identified in environmental scanning allows for "small doses of experience to discover uncertainties unpredict-

able in advance" (Wildavsky, 1988, p. 26). Weick and Suttcliffe (2001) argued that the recognition of small failures as "near misses," can act as vaccinations that allow the organization to learn to defend against the recurrence of another failure (p. 165).

Mitroff and Anagnos (2001) suggest that "organizations need to constantly scan their entire operations and internal and external environments for early warning signals of potential 'ticking time bombs'" (p. 8). Recognition of warning signals depends crucially on both the capacity of organizational members and the organization's system of signal detection. Unfortunately, organizations "often fail to observe that their system is failing" (Boin *et al.*, 2005, p. 20). Mitroff and Anagnos (2001) identified denial as the number one barrier to recognizing warning signals.

Veil (2011) adds mindless classification and response, trained incapacity, and reliance on success to the list of barriers to recognizing warning signals. She argued that organizational members go on autopilot to "get the job done" by classifying new experiences with previous experiences and ignoring variations from the expected outcome. Veil (2011) contends further that training can cause blindness to warning signals by encouraging organizational members to follow protocol simply because "that's the way things are done around here," even though alternative strategies may decrease errors. Finally, she posits that success is actually a barrier to learning through environmental scanning precrisis. Each warning signal that is ignored but does not cause a catastrophe solidifies the misguided belief that failure cannot occur.

Dillon and Tinsley (2008) found that individuals are surprised by the outcome of near misses, but, instead of creating an urgency to address the risk and resolve the problem created by a near miss, individuals often respond with complacency. In fact, they found repeated evidence that near misses decrease perceived risk and actually promote riskier decisions. Success leads to persistence at the expense of adaptability by sending a reinforcing signal that no corrective action is necessary (Levinthal and

March, 1981; March, 1978; Sitkin, 1996). Unfortunately, as Smith (1993) suggests, "A failure to learn is a precursor to crisis at another point and time" (pp. 292–293).

Mitroff and Anagnos (2001) provide a clear explanation of how organizational learning through environmental scanning can affect corporate reputation:

> The slogan "If it ain't broke, don't fix it" needs to be replaced with a new attitude: "If it ain't broke, it soon will be"; therefore fix it now when you can still be the good guy, or fix it later and risk being labeled the bad guy. (p. 8)

Veil (2011) suggests that "The sooner warnings, failures, or crises are recognized, the less damaging they will be to the organization" (p. 26). Environmental scanning can assist organizations in recognizing warning signals in time to learn and adjust organizational practices, especially for single-loop learning. However, classification, training, and continued success make it easy to deny the potential for failure. As small failures and near misses escalate and become public, broader issues can develop.

Issue management

Issue management concerns "the identification, monitoring, and analysis of trends in key public's opinions that can mature into public policy and regulative or legislative constraint" (Heath, 1997, p. 6). More than a process of detecting warning signals, a proper utilization of issues management can help organizations build longtime relationships, and act in a responsible way to serve the interests of a variety of stakeholders (Heath, 1997). Scholars suggest that effective issue management does not result in quick responses to periodic environmental scanning, but should instead be the foundation for long-term organizational decision making (Veil and Kent, 2008).

Issue management, as opposed to crisis management, follows an issue as it develops. The decisions made or not made to manage an issue can affect whether the issue eventually becomes a crisis (Coombs, 2007). The five stages of the issue life cycle include pre-issue, potential issue, public issue, critical issue, and dormant issue (Botan and Taylor, 2004). The identification of the life cycle is meaningful to issue management because it allows an organization to develop different strategies according to an issue's stage. For example, Crable and Vibbert (1985) suggested that instead of reacting to an issue at its critical stage, corporations should identify an issue in its early stages. Defining the nature of an issue in its early stages gives the organization a better chance to reposition the issue or influence public policy. Resolving an issue before it escalates into a crisis is vital to an organization's future.

Heugens *et al.* (2004) note that issues and crises "play a different role in organizational learning and change processes" (p. 1350). Issues allow organizations to engage in learning processes like comparing, analyzing, explaining, and devising analogies (Heugens *et al.*, 2004). However, crisis "shocks organizational systems out of complacency," thereby, stimulating learning and legitimizing the need for immediate change (Veil and Sellnow, 2008, p. 12). Heugens *et al.* (2004) suggest that the slow development of issues and immediacy of crises encourage organizations to establish "multiple reputation management capabilities, each geared specifically towards crises or issues" (p. 1350). As a proactive learning strategy, issue management can effectively prevent crises from occurring, thereby protecting organizational legitimacy and corporate reputation.

Actional legitimacy

Actional legitimacy is a proactive learning strategy that is effective in addressing a reputational threat, with or without the existence of an actual crisis. Boyd (2009) sees legitimacy as "the foundation of all effective communication with publics – without it, any organizational messages or actions will be looked upon with skepticism" (p. 157). He explains that "whether an organization is looking to its overall persona (organizational legitimacy) or to a particular policy (actional legitimacy), it must attend to its public's expectations for responsible execution" (p. 164). This execution must demonstrate actions taken in response to the reputational threat. Actional legitimacy "extends well beyond traditional discourse, to include a wide range of meaning-laden actions and nonverbal displays" (Suchman, 1995, p. 586). Finet (1993) adds that legitimacy management is "related to both notions of external turbulence and the use of organizationally adaptive devices to deal with it" (p. 39).

Organizations can facilitate relegitimation through strategic restructuring (Suchman, 1995). Without apologizing for wrongdoing, "the organization can selectively confess that limited aspects of its operations were flawed and can then act decisively and visibly to remedy those specific faults" (Suchman, 1995, p. 598). Suchman describes two types of restructuring: (1) creating monitors and watchdogs, to symbolize contrition and change; and (2) symbolically distancing the organization from those who contributed to the crisis.

Heath and Millar (2004) explain that the "exigencies created by a crisis center on the organization's actions and statements to regain control of the circumstances" (p. 10). As such, the response must provide an explanation to stakeholders about what happened, and ultimately, provide a solution or a process for identifying a solution for the problem (Heath and Millar, 2004). Through actional legitimacy, organizations acknowledge the problem, articulate intent to solve the problem, take observable actions, and, finally, maintain an ongoing commitment to issue resolution (Boyd, 2000). Actional legitimacy may be achieved when an action is in the corporation's domain of authority; is performed appropriately, responsibly, and conscientiously; contributes to corporate goals; and inspires public confidence (Brummer, 1991).

Environmental scanning, issue management, and actional legitimacy are all proactive learning strategies that can assist organizations in engaging in single- and double-loop learning. Despite these well-known management strategies, some organizations still cannot see the warning signals of impending crisis until it is too late. Once hit with the recalcitrance of crisis, the missed opportunities for learning are revealed retrospectively.

Organizational Learning and Crisis

Recalcitrance describes a point in which our perceived reality is contradicted by an experience (Burke, 1954). Once the experience occurs, we can never go back to the worldview held before the experience. Veil (2011) likens organizational crisis to recalcitrance. The warning signals that lead to the crisis can suddenly be seen because the recalcitrance of the crisis forces a reframing of all information. Crisis "shocks organizational systems out of complacency" (Veil and Sellnow, 2008, p. 12), because the organization's collective worldview is forever changed by the crisis. Recalcitrant learning occurs once the organization begins to view itself through the new frame. The existing system is rendered ineffective and cannot be maintained (Venette *et al.*, 2003). Resistance to change is diminished and strategies that may not have been considered viable before are suddenly available to the organization because the range of its potential behaviors is changed (Huber, 1991; Lerbinger, 1997). The recalcitrance of crisis has the potential to force an organization into learning.

Madsen and Desai (2010) investigated the effects of organizational successes and failures on organizational learning to discover which experiences are more motivating for organizations. Like Sitkin (1996), they suggest that organizational failure typically engenders organizational learning to a much greater level than does organizational success. In addition, organizational learning obtained from success depreciates at a much quicker rate than lessons acquired from organizational failures. The memories of organizational failures also tend to linger with the members of the organization, and thus, the knowledge acquired is more powerful among organizational members than the knowledge acquired from success. Madsen and Desai (2010) suggest that organizations tend to learn more and implement more change from large-scale failures than from small-scale ones. Such findings point to crises as unique, and potentially positive, opportunities for learning.

Organizations can actually benefit from crises, when they are viewed prospectively as opportunities to learn (Mitroff, 2005; Ulmer *et al.*, 2007, 2011; Veil, 2011). Mitroff (2005) offers a framework of seven lessons that can help an organization emerge stronger from a crisis including the emotional, creative, social and political, integrative, technical, aesthetic, and spiritual development that occurs in a crisis. Seeger *et al.* (2003) claim that "if organizations embrace the opportunity to acquire new knowledge and to enact new strategies, they can emerge from crises with renewed vitality" (p. 266).

The radical learning that occurs postcrisis can assist the organization in regaining legitimacy and reputational standing immediately following the crisis by demonstrating corrective action. If the experience is committed to the organization's memory, proactive learning strategies like environmental scanning, issue management, and actional legitimacy to prevent another crisis from occurring in the future can be realized. However, if the organization cannot move beyond first-order change to engage in triple- or at least double-loop learning, the culture and policies that lead to the crisis will continue to plague the organization long after the proverbial bandage has been applied to fix the error rather than address its underlying cause. Even more, sometimes the challenge is not learning, but unlearning the policies and practices that initially lead to the crisis.

Organizational memory

Organizational memory can be defined as "an accumulation of knowledge based on the observation of successes and failures, both within the company and through vicarious learning" (Ulmer *et al.*, 2011, p. 178). Organizational memory is achieved through three phases. First, organizations must acquire knowledge of previous and potential failures. Second, the knowledge must be disseminated throughout the organization. If the knowledge is held by only a few, the loss of those members over time will result in the eventual loss of the

acquired knowledge. Finally, organizational members must be willing to act on the knowledge. If organizational members are unwilling to change their practices to implement the disseminated knowledge, then the organization risks incurring repeated failures or even crises.

Accumulation of knowledge is meaningless if organizations cannot rely on it to inform future behavior. Ulmer *et al.* (2011) describe the Union Carbide leak in Bhopal, India, as one of the most notorious examples of failed organizational memory. The Union Carbide plant in Bhopal was on the verge of permanent closure. As the highly trained, veteran employees were transferred from Bhopal to more profitable units, the Bhopal plant was reduced to a staff with subpar knowledge of the workings of the plant. Vital knowledge was neither maintained nor disseminated to lower employees, an organizational oversight resulting in an inconceivably detrimental failure.

One potential explanation for a lack of organizational memory may stem from barriers in the knowledge diffusion process. Elliot (2009) attributes the failure of organizational learning from crises to a lack of understanding of policy translation, policy implementation, and the obstacle of organizational barriers. While organizational leaders may attempt to acquire knowledge and engender organizational learning in the wake of crises, little information may exist regarding the translation of policy innovations into practice within the organization. Coupled with the often-negative effects of organizational barriers to adopting new practices, it seems that organizational failure to learn is directly related to the diffusion process of policies. A lack of open dialog to promote translation limits the potential for double-loop learning (Schimmel and Muntslag, 2009), and without addressing the underlying governing policies, second-order change will not occur.

Elliot (2009) depicts the problematic nature of failed organizational learning from crises through two case studies pertaining to a child protection agency. The agency experienced a crisis through the death of a child resulting from inefficient regulatory methods of the organization, and then another child perished from similar causes a mere seven years later. Despite specific recommendations made to the agency by the governmental education office, the organization was unable to adequately implement the recommendations and failed to learn from its initial crisis.

Unlearning

Following some crises, the most important changes may not be for organizations to learn new policies and practices, but to unlearn others. The process of organizational unlearning is much more complex than simply replacing old knowledge with new knowledge. Argyris *et al.* (1985) suggest that individuals will continue to engage in the same unproductive behaviors that lead to negative consequences rather than question the governing beliefs that drive the unproductive behaviors.

Nystrom and Starbuck (1984) agreed:

> People in organizations rarely abandon their current beliefs and procedures merely because alternatives might offer better results: They know that their current beliefs and procedures have arisen from rational analyses and successful experiences, so they have to see evidence that these beliefs and procedures are seriously deficient before they will even think about major changes. (p. 55)

Nystrom and Starbuck (1984) contend that organizational leaders are often oblivious to problems that develop in their organizations because either they choose not to heed the warnings of their subordinates or the warnings never reach them due to a top-down organizational hierarchy. The manifestation of crises, many of which are avoidable, are often attributed to the flawed cognitive frameworks of organizational leaders (Nystrom and Starbuck, 1984).

Nystrom and Starbuck (1984) provide three suggestions for managers committed to improving their organizations via organizational unlearning. First, top managers should listen and take seriously the dissent voiced by their subordinates; far too often, top managers

encounter multiple indications or problems during the gestation of crises, but are not always willing to heed these warnings. Second, top managers should exploit opportunities for change in their organizations. When unanticipated events or innovations occur, managers should look for new ways to adapt that engender unlearning of old protocols and procedures. Finally, organizational leaders should accept opportunities to experiment with new ideas from other individuals in the organization; trial implementation of novel ideas may prove much more efficient than routine means of accomplishing the same tasks. Ultimately, to improve organizational learning, managers should actively pursue opportunities to engage in unlearning those routines or interpretations that have dilapidated over time.

In nearly all cases, crises necessitate learning and change. All of the learning (and unlearning) strategies identified thus far in this chapter have pointed to opportunities and barriers to enacting first- or second-order change. Triple-loop learning goes beyond the rituals of learning to enact lasting behavioral change through establishing a learning culture (Argyris and Schön, 1996; Popper and Lipshitz, 1999).

Core Values and Organizational Learning

The following section discusses learning that impacts the foundation or core of the organization. Learning of this magnitude requires learning at the cultural level where the organization is reintroduced to the values and virtues upon which social legitimacy is based. In this section, we discuss the role mindfulness plays in triple-loop learning. We also discuss how, when organizations engage in discourse of renewal, they strip away distractions and self-interest to reacquaint the organizational member with the core values of the organization. Through the process of renewal, the organization can reemerge from the crisis as a stronger, more resilient organization than it was before the crisis.

Mindful learning

Langer (1989) explains mindfulness as a *continual* process of reframing to avoid examining issues from a single perspective. She suggests that "To catch the early warnings of trouble, we must be alert to new information, to subtle deviations from the way things typically go" (Langer, 1989, p. 134). Mindfulness involves a certain level of creativity to look beyond one's expectations and consider situations that do not fit a preconceived frame of reference. Langer and Moldoveanu (2000) claim that mindfulness is the process of drawing "novel distinctions," as long as the distinctions are new to the viewer. They argue that drawing novel distinctions from one's environment enables individuals to create new categories and not rely on categories formed in the past. Drawing distinctions is imperative as it enables individuals to become more knowledgeable of their surroundings, more competent in creating new categories for organizing information, more capable in processing information, and more aware of multiple approaches to handling discrepancies in their cognitive categories.

Veil (2011) postulates that by noticing the elements of an organizational environment that do not fit a preconceived classification, organizations are capable of engaging in mindful learning. She advances the mindful learning model, which reveals a continuous cycle of recognizing warning signs that are out of place through reframing, extracting knowledge from these signals, and implementing this knowledge into organizational practice. As a reoccurring recalcitrance, mindful learning forces us to reframe our worldview to create "an awareness that filters through the routines and training to draw attention to what does not match our expectations" (p. 19).

In order for an organization to maintain operations that reflect the mindful learning model, the organizational culture must encourage mindfulness among its members. "In adopting a mindful culture, organizations have a collective motive to watch for deviants from the norm and recognize, question, and replace assumptions that underpin current practices"

(Veil, 2011, p. 27). Weick and Sutcliffe (2001) observe that "a well-developed capability for mindfulness catches the unexpected earlier, when it is smaller, comprehends its potential importance despite the small size of the disruption, and removes, contains, or rebounds from the effects of the unexpected" (p. 17–18). Organizations with a mindful culture have the potential to reach the highest level of learning in response to crises – renewal.

Renewal

Unlike image repair strategies employed to deflect blame, the discourse of renewal is a unique approach that views crises as an opportunity to improve the organization and the trust of its stakeholders. The foundations of renewal discourse can be found in the value-based, postcrisis responses of organizational leaders intent on rebuilding their businesses following a crisis (Seeger and Ulmer, 2001, 2002). As a natural and immediate response to crisis, renewal discourse concentrates on healing, reconnecting to core values, and embracing learning opportunities brought to light by the crisis (Hurst, 2002; Ulmer *et al.*, 2007).

Reierson *et al.* (2009) link the work of Hurst (2002) and Seeger and Ulmer (2002) to describe renewal discourse as "connecting with core values, establishing the importance of the past in the present, and spurring efforts and energy toward process and the future" (p. 116). Toelken *et al.* (2005) suggest that through renewal "crises can serve as the underlying source" for learning and change (p. 47). As a process of learning, renewal discourse "can point out fallacious assumptions or unforeseen vulnerabilities" while reestablishing core values and precipitating "consensus, cooperation, and support" (p. 47).

By returning an organization to its base values, renewal discourse allows organizations to truly engage in triple-loop learning by enacting culture change (Argyris and Schön, 1996). If learning is positioned as an integral component of an organizational culture, the potential to identify warning signals and prevent failures is increased exponentially (Veil, 2011). Renewal provides the cultural realignment and moral learning needed to engage in mindful learning.

Future Directions for Organizational Learning and Reputation Management

The most respected and resilient organizations are constantly engaged in the learning process. Insensitivity to or discounting failure may, in the short term, allow an organization to avoid the discomfort of change. In the long-term, however, organizations that are unwilling to learn from failure are destined to struggle with maintaining social legitimacy and reputational standing.

The link between learning and organizational success inspires continued research revealing the conditions in which organizations learn best. Ideally, organizations afford themselves the capacity and impetus to learn proactively. Although beneficial in all settings, the value of proactive learning in cases where failure is devastating to lives and livelihood is inestimable. For example, failures in areas such as underground mining, air transportation, nuclear power, and national security have such disparaging consequences that retrospective learning is not an option. Research focusing on mindfulness and the development of a learning culture can empower organizations in industries such as these to recognize warning signs and respond to them before a crisis occurs. Thus, continued research focusing on proactive learning is essential to the well-being of modern society.

Despite a constant dedication to learning, crises will continue to occur. In fact, the number of major industry accidents causing 50 deaths or more rose sharply over the previous two decades (Mitroff and Anagnos, 2001), while the last decade saw overwhelming financial losses across multiple sectors. Surely irresponsibility is to blame for many of these crises. For others, organizations have responded to the best of their abilities. Increasing risk is inherent in an increasingly global society whose industries are facing unprecedented complexity and interactivity (Perrow, 1999).

When unforeseeable crises occur, the tendency to place blame and assign punishment is fitting with human nature. Yet, while salvaging reputation in the short term, these backward-looking responses can, at best, produce single-loop learning. The more justified objective should be to explore the way crises can be viewed as learning opportunities. Such opportunities can enhance mindfulness and create renewed organizations and industries that are more dedicated to and better prepared for engaging in proactive learning. With the increasing risk of major organizational failures at all levels of society, organizations have no choice but to actively engage in the learning process to maintain legitimacy and attain positive reputational standing.

References

Argyris, C. (1982) *Reasoning, Learning and Action: Individual and Organizational.* San Francisco, CA: Jossey-Bass.

Argyris, C. and Schön, D. (1996) *Organizational Learning II: Theory, Method and Practice.* Reading, MA: Addison-Wesley.

Argyris, C., Putman, R., and Smith, D.M. (1985) *Action Science: Concepts, Methods and Skills for Research and Intervention.* San Francisco, CA: Jossey-Bass.

Bartunek, J.M. and Moch, M.K. (1987) First-order, second-order and third-order change and organization development interventions: A cognitive approach. *Journal of Applied Behavioral Science, 23,* 483–500.

Benoit, W.L. (1995a) *Accounts, Excuses, Apologies: A Theory of Image Restoration Strategies.* Albany, NY: State University of New York Press.

Benoit, W.L. (1995b) An analysis of Sears' repair of its auto repair image: Image restoration discourse in the corporate sector. *Communication Studies, 46,* 89–105.

Benoit, W.L. (1997) Image restoration discourse and crisis communication. *Public Relations Review, 23,* 177–186.

Benoit, W.L. (2000) Another visit to the theory of image restoration strategies. *Communication Quarterly, 48,* 40–43.

Boin, A., Hart, P., Stern, E., and Sundelius, B. (2005) *The Politics of Crisis Management: Public Leadership under Pressure.* Cambridge, UK: Cambridge University Press.

Botan, C.H. and Taylor, M. (2004) Public relations: State of the field. *Journal of Communication,* 54, 645–661.

Boyd, J. (2000) Actional legitimation: No crisis necessary. *Journal of Public Relations Research,* 12(4), 341–353.

Boyd, J. (2009) 756*: The legitimacy of a baseball number. In R.L. Heath, E.L. Toth, and D. Waymer (eds), *Rhetorical and Critical Approaches to Public Relations II.* New York: Routledge, pp. 154–169.

Brummer, J.J. (1991) *Corporate Responsibility and Legitimacy: An Interdisciplinary Analysis.* New York: Greenwood.

Burke, K. (1954) *Permanence and Change: An Anatomy of Purpose.* Berkeley, CA: University of California Press.

Choo, C.W. (2001) *Information Management for the Intelligent Organization: The Art of Scanning the Environment* (3rd ed.). Medford, NJ: Information Today, Inc.

Choo, C.W. and Auster, E. (1993) Environmental scanning: Acquisition and use of information by managers. In M.E. Williams (ed.), *Annual Review of Information Science and Technology.* Medford, NJ: Learned Information, Inc. For the American Society for Information Science.

Coombs, W.T. (2007) *Ongoing Crisis Communication: Planning, Managing, and Responding* (2nd ed.). Thousand Oaks, CA: Sage.

Crable, R.E. and Vibbert, S.L. (1985) Managing issues and influencing public policy. *Public Relations Review,* 11, 3–16.

Deephouse, D.L. and Carter, S.M. (2005) An examination of differences between organizational legitimacy and organizational reputation. *Journal of Management Studies,* 42(2), 329–360.

Dillon, R.L. and Tinsley, C.H. (2008) How near-misses influence decision making under risk: A missed opportunity for learning. *Management Science,* 54(8), 1425–1440.

Dionisopoulos, G.N. and Vibbert, S.L. (1988) CBS vs. Mobil Oil: Charges of creative bookkeeping in 1979. In H.R. Ryan (ed.), *Oratorical Encounters: Selected Studies and Sources of Twentieth Century Political Accusations and Apologies.* New York: Greenwood Press, pp. 241–251.

Dowling, G.R. (2001) *Creating Corporate Reputations.* Oxford, UK: Oxford University Press.

Dowling, J. and Pfeffer, J. (1975) Organizational legitimacy: Social values and organizational behavior. *Pacific Sociological Review,* 18(1), 122–136.

Elliot, D. (2009) The failure of organizational learning from crisis – A matter of life and death? *Journal of Contingencies and Crisis Management,* 17, 157–168.

Finet, D. (1993) Effects of boundary spanning communication on the sociopolitical delegitimation of an organization. *Management Communication Quarterly,* 7(1), 36–66.

Finet, D. (1994) Interest advocacy and the transformation in organizational communication. In B. Kovacic (ed.), *New Approaches to Organizational Communication.* Albany, NY: State University of New York Press, pp. 169–190.

Fombrun, C.J. (1996) *Reputation: Realizing Value from the Corporate Image.* Cambridge, MA: Harvard Business School Press.

Fombrun, C.J. and van Riel, C.B.M. (2004) *Fame & Fortune: How Successful Companies Build Winning Reputations.* Upper Saddle River, NJ: Financial Times/Prentice Hall.

Hearit, K.M. (1994) Apologies and public relations crises at Chrysler, Toshiba, and Volvo. *Public Relations Review,* 20, 113–125.

Hearit, K.M. (1995a) Mistakes were made: Organizational apologia and crisis of social legitimacy. *Communication Studies,* 46, 1–17.

Hearit, K.M. (1995b) From "we didn't do it" to "it's not our fault": The use of apologia in public relations crises. In W.N. Elwood (ed.), *Public Relations Inquiry as Rhetorical Criticism.* Westport, CT: Praeger, pp. 117–131.

Hearit, K.M. (2001) Corporate apologia: When an organization speaks in defense of itself. In R.L. Heath (ed.), *Handbook of Public Relations.* Thousand Oaks, CA: Sage, pp. 595–605.

Heath, R.L. (1997) *Strategic Issues Management.* Thousand Oaks, CA: Sage.

Heath, R.L. and Millar, D.P. (2004) A rhetorical approach to crisis communication: Management, communication processes, and strategic responses. In R.L. Heath and P.D. Millar (eds), *Responding to Crisis: A Rhetorical Approach to Crisis Communication.* Mahwah, NJ: Lawrence Erlbaum Associates, pp. 1–18.

Heugens, P.P., van Riel, C.B., and van den Bosch, F.A. (2004) Reputation management capabilities as decision rules. *Journal of Management Studies,* 41(8), 1349–1377.

Huber, G.P. (1991) Organizational learning: The contributing processes and the literatures. *Organizational Science*, 2, 88–115.

Hurst, D. (2002) *Crisis and Renewal.* Boston: Harvard Business School Press.

Langer, E.J. (1989) *Mindfulness.* Cambridge, MA: Perseus.

Langer, E.J. and Moldoveanu, M. (2000) The construct of mindfulness. *Journal of Social Issues*, 56(1), 1–9.

Lerbinger, O. (1997) *The Crisis Manager: Facing Risk and Responsibility.* Mahwah, NJ: Lawrence Erlbaum Associates.

Levinthal, D. and March, J.G. (1981) A model of adaptive organizational search. *Journal of Economic Behavior and Organization*, 2, 307–333.

Madsen, P.M. and Desai, V.D. (2010) Failing to learn? The effects of failure and success on organizational learning in the global orbital launch vehicle industry. *Academy of Management Journal*, 53, 451–476.

March, J.G. (1978) Bounded rationality, ambiguity, and the engineering of choice. *Bell Journal of Economics*, 9, 587–608.

Martins, L.L. (2005) A model of the effects of reputational rankings on organizational change. *Organization Science*, 16, 701–720.

Metzler, M.B. (2001) The centrality of organizational legitimacy to public relations practice. In R.L. Heath (ed.), *Handbook of Public Relations.* Thousand Oaks, CA: Sage, pp. 321–334.

Mitroff, I.I. (2005) *Why Some Companies Emerge Stronger and Better from a Crisis: 7 Essential Lessons for Surviving Disaster.* New York: AMACOM.

Mitroff, I.I. and Anagnos, G. (2001) *Managing Crisis Before They Happen: What Every Executive and Manager Needs to Know about Crises Management.* New York: AMACOM.

Nielsen, R.P. (1993) Woolman's "I am we" triple-loop action-learning: Origin and application in organization ethics. *Journal of Applied Behavioral Science*, 29, 117–138.

Nigh, D. and Cochran, P.L. (1987) Issues management and the multinational enterprise. *Management International Review*, 1, 4–12.

Nystrom, P.C. and Starbuck, W.H. (1984) To avoid organizational crises, unlearn. *Organizational Dynamics*, 12(4), 53–65.

Perrow, C. (1999) *Normal Accidents: Living with High-Risk Technologies.* Princeton, NJ: Princeton University Press.

Popper, M. and Lipshitz, R. (1999) Organizational learning mechanisms, culture, and feasibility.

Journal of Applied Behavioral Science, 34, 161–179.

Popper, M. and Lipshitz, R. (2000) Organizational learning mechanisms, culture, and feasibility. *Management Learning*, 31, 181–196.

Rao, H. (1994) The social construction of reputation: Certification contests, legitimation, and the survival of organizations in the American automobile industry: 1895–1912. *Strategic Management Journal*, 15, 29–44.

Reierson, J.L., Sellnow, T.L., and Ulmer, R.R. (2009) Complexities of crisis renewal over time: Learning from the case of tainted Odwalla apple juice. *Communication Studies*, 60, 114–129.

Renkema, J. and Hoeken, H. (1998) The influence of negative newspaper publicity on corporate image in the Netherlands. *Journal of Business Communication*, 32(4), 262–382.

Rhee, M. (2009) Does reputation contribute to reducing organizational errors? A learning approach. *Journal of Management Studies*, 46, 676–703.

Schimmel, R. and Muntslag, D.R. (2009) Learning barriers: A frame-work for the examination of structural impediments to organizational change. *Human Resource Management*, 48, 399–416.

Scott, M.B. and Lyman, S.M. (1968) Accounts. *American Sociological Review*, 33, 46–62.

Seeger, M.W., Sellnow, T.L., and Ulmer, R.R. (2003) *Communication and Organizational Crisis.* Westport, CT: Praeger.

Seeger, M.W. and Ulmer, R.R. (2001) Virtuous responses to organizational crisis: Aaron Feuerstein and Milt Cole. *Journal of Business Ethics*, 31, 369–376.

Seeger, M.W. and Ulmer, R.R. (2002) A post-crisis discourse of renewal: The cases of Malden Mills and Cole Hardwoods. *Journal of Applied Communication Research*, 30, 126–142.

Sellnow, T.L. (1993) Scientific argument in organizational crisis communication: The case of Exxon. *Argumentation and Advocacy*, 30(1), 28–43.

Sellnow, T.L. (1994) Speaking in defense of Chrysler: Lee Iacocca's crisis communication. In M.W. Seeger (ed.), *I Gotta Tell You: Speeches of Lee Iacocca.* Detroit, MI: Wayne State University Press.

Sellnow, T.L. and Seeger, M.W. (1989) Crisis messages: Wall Street and the Reagan administration after Black Monday. *Speaker and Gavel*, 26, 9–18.

Senge, P.M. (1990) *The Fifth Discipline: The Art and Practice of the Learning Organization.* New York: Doubleday.

Shapiro, C. (1982) Consumer information, product quality, and seller reputation. *Bell Journal of Economics, 13,* 20–35.

Shapiro, C. (1983) Premiums for high quality products as returns to reputations. *Quarterly Journal of Economics, 98,* 659–679..

Sitkin, S.B. (1996) Learning through failure: The strategy of small losses. In M.D. Cohen and L.S. Sproull (eds), *Organizational Learning.* Thousand Oaks, CA: Sage, pp. 541–578.

Smith, D. (1993) Crisis management in the public sector: Lessons from the prison service. In J. Wilson and P. Hinton (eds), *Public Service and the 1990s: Issues in Public Service Finance and Management.* London: Tudor Press, pp. 141–170.

Somech, A. and Drach-Zahavy, A. (2004) Exploring organizational citizenship behavior from an organizational perspective: The relationship between organizational learning and organizational citizenship behaviour. *Journal of Occupational & Organizational Psychology, 77,* 281–298.

Spitzeck, H. (2009) Organizational and moral learning: What, if anything, do corporations learn from NGO critique? *Journal of Business Ethics, 88,* 157–173.

Suchman, M.C. (1995) Managing legitimacy: Strategic and institutional approaches. *Academy of Management Review, 20,* 571–610.

Toelken, K., Seeger, M.W., and Batteau, A. (2005) Learning and renewal following threat and crisis: The experience of a computer services firm in response to Y2K and 9/11. Proceedings of the 2nd International ISCRAM Conference, B. Van de Walle and B. Carle (eds), Brussels, Belgium, pp. 43–51.

Ulmer, R.R., Sellnow, T.L., and Seeger, M.W. (2007) *Effective Crisis Communication: Moving from Crisis to Opportunity.* Thousand Oaks, CA: Sage.

Ulmer, R.R., Sellnow, T.L., and Seeger, M.W. (2011) *Effective Crisis Communication: Moving from Crisis to Opportunity* (2nd ed.). Thousand Oaks, CA: Sage.

Ulrich, P. (1995) Introduction. In P. Ulrich and C. Sarasin (eds), *Facing Public Interest: The Ethical Challenge to Business Policy and Corporate Communications.* Dordrecht: Kluwer, pp. 1–8.

Veil, S.R. (2011) Mindful learning in crisis management. *Journal of Business Communication, 48*(2), 1–32.

Veil, S.R. and Kent, M. (2008) Issues management and inoculation: Tylenol's responsible dosing advertising. *Public Relations Review, 34,* 399–402.

Veil, S.R. and Sellnow, T.L. (2008) Organizational learning in a high-risk environment: Responding to an anthrax outbreak. *Journal of Applied Communications, 92*(1), 75–93.

Venette, S.J., Sellnow, T.L., and Lang, P.A. (2003) Metanarration's role in restructuring perceptions of crisis: NHTA's failure in the Ford-Firestone crisis. *Journal of Business Communication, 40,* 218–236.

Ware, B.L. and Linkugel, W.A. (1973) They spoke in defense of themselves: On the generic criticism of apologia. *Quarterly Journal of Speech, 59,* 273–283.

Weick, K.E. and Ashford, S.J. (2001) Learning in organizations. In F.M. Jablin and L.L. Putnam (eds), *The New Handbook of Organizational Communication: Advances in Theory, Research, and Methods.* Thousand Oaks, CA: Sage, pp. 704–731.

Weick, K.E. and Suttcliffe, K.M. (2001) *Managing the Unexpected.* San Francisco, CA: Jossey-Bass.

Wildavsky, A.B. (1988) *Searching for Safety.* New Brunswick, NJ: Transaction Books.

22

Relating Rhetoric and Reputation

Øyvind Ihlen

University of Oslo, Norway

A strong reputation can be an asset for rhetoric, but how can rhetoric be an asset for reputation? This chapter explores how rhetorical concepts and techniques can improve corporate reputation, as well as scholars' understanding of such corporate attempts. The notions of ethos and identification are discussed in particular detail. It is also argued that rhetoric offers an epistemological perspective that is needed to cope with construction of identity, image, and reputation.

Your speech has the best effect, if your life matches the lessons you preach. [Author's translation].

The above quote stems from a moral fable written by the seventeenth-century essayist and playwright Ludvig Holberg (1971). In this particular fable, the Stork and the Hawk compete to present the most profound speech on moral matters. While both birds speak very eloquently, the judges finally award the prize to the Stork. The reason is that a moral speech given by an innocent Stork is better than a moral speech presented by a bird of prey. In other words, a solid reputation can be an asset for rhetoric and can help the goals of a rhetor. In this chapter, the converse relationship is explored – the ways in which *rhetoric* can be an asset for reputation are discussed. The chapter focuses particularly on the rhetorical concepts of *ethos* and *identification*, and on techniques used to strengthen ethos and create identification. Ethos and iden-tification can improve the understanding of how corporations attempt to manage their reputation.

The chapter is structured as follows. First, a brief discussion of the notion of corporate reputation is needed and a call for attention to the role of language is issued. Second, a short overview of the Western rhetorical tradition is presented. Third, the ways in which rhetoric can be used to study corporate discourse are discussed. Fourth, the concept of ethos is explained and linked to corporate rhetoric. Fifth, a discussion of the concept of identification is presented, as it has been suggested that the act of creating identification is the key activity of rhetoric. The final part of the chapter presents some ideas for a research agenda on rhetoric and corporate reputation.

The Handbook of Communication and Corporate Reputation, First Edition. Edited by Craig E. Carroll.
© 2013 John Wiley & Sons, Inc. Published 2015 by John Wiley & Sons, Inc.

Identity, Image, and Reputation

Corporate reputation can be briefly defined as the general estimation the public has of a corporation (Gotsi and Wilson, 2001). A premise for the following discussion is that reputation has to be seen in relation to the dialectic pair, organizational and corporate identity, as well as in relation to image. In order for corporations to improve their reputation, a first step is for managers to ask "who or what are we as a corporation?" or "who or what do we say we are as a corporation?" Organizational identity can be described as an internally oriented concept that focuses on what the members of an organization think the organization is about. Corporate identity, on the other hand, is influenced primarily by management's articulation of the vision and mission for the organization (Hatch and Schultz, 1997; Ihlen, 2010a). The Coca Cola Company, for instance, presents its mission in the following way: "To refresh the world . . . To inspire moments of optimism and happiness . . . To create value and make a difference" (http://www.thecoca-colacompany.com/ourcompany/mission_vision_values.html, accessed July 7, 2011). Whether or not Coca Cola employees hold a similar view of what the company is about is an empirical question. One hypothesis could be that they see the company as primarily providing a sought-after soft drink.

The identity of an organization can be contrasted with its image, which can be defined as the immediate impression that stakeholders form of the organization. The Coca Cola Company, for instance, attracted criticism when it became known that it had given the American Academy of Family Physicians a grant to "enhance educational information about nutrition" and "focus on the role of beverages and sweeteners in a healthy diet" (http://latimes-blogs.latimes.com/booster_shots/2009/10/american-academy-family-physicians-coca-cola-.html, accessed July 7, 2011). Calling attention to this alliance could create an image of the Coca Cola Company as a corporation trying to prevent physicians from criticizing its product. The image, in turn, forms the reputation, which is seen as the long-term collective judgments observers have of an organization based on their assessments of the financial, social, and/or environmental impacts of the corporation (Barnett et al., 2006). The reputation of the Coca Cola Company is created not only by the alliance with the American Academy of Family Physicians, but also by its history as a brand positioned in more than 200 countries. A whole section on the Wikipedia website is dedicated to criticism of the company (http://en.wikipedia.org/wiki/Criticism_of_Coca-Cola, accessed July 7, 2011).

Stakeholders have first- and second-hand experience with the goods or services of the organization, which also influence the reputation of a corporation (Ihlen, 2010a). First-hand experience would include drinking Coke, living near a Coke plant, being exposed to Coke advertising, and/or doing business with the company. Second-hand experience would for instance be what your friends and relatives tell you about the same matters.

As pointed out elsewhere in this volume, reputation is considered an asset for corporations. Although demonstrating the economic value of a strong reputation has proved to be difficult, most of the literature points to how a strong reputation can help to increase sales, attract investors, increase the ability to hold on to and recruit employees, and gain favorable media coverage, and that it helps organizations during crises (e.g., Fombrun and van Riel, 2004; van Riel and Balmer, 1997). Others have argued that both image and reputation reside in the minds of the stakeholders, making *management* of image and reputation problematic. Thus, theorists argue that corporations should focus on their identity, which they *can* control through the way they present themselves. A consistent and pleasing corporate identity leads to a positive image, and this, in turn, is thought to create a good reputation (Campbell et al., 2006; Ihlen, 2010a).

Nevertheless, it is important to remember that there is no simple relation between corporate identity and corporate image, as both are social constructs. This also means that the concepts should be judged on how well they work rhetorically and not only on their fit with "actual reality" (Christensen and Askegaard, 2001; Christensen and Cheney, 2000).

The latter phrase is emphasized to call attention to the difficulty of social mediation of both material and immaterial structures, as will be discussed in the next section. Rhetors always make selections, or as Burke believed: "Even if a given terminology is a *reflection* of reality, by its very nature as a terminology it must be a *selection* of reality; and to this extent it must function also as a *deflection* of reality" (Burke, 1966, p. 45). Social constructionism places language in the central role as our vehicle for understanding the world, and notions such as identity are seen as things that are constantly being negotiated and changed in a social context (Tsetsura, 2010). From this perspective, language becomes not just a communication tool but a way of seeing and generating knowledge. Constructionism also sees the discipline of rhetoric takes center stage, as witnessed by the interest from scholars working in such areas as communication, public relations, organizational communication, management, law, political science, history, anthropology, and other areas (Ihlen, 2010b; Lucaites *et al.*, 1999; Meisenbach and McMillian, 2006; Sillince and Suddaby, 2008). Before discussing how rhetoric can be used for the analysis of corporate reputation, however, a brief overview of the Western rhetorical tradition and its epistemology is necessary to give some background understanding.

The Western Rhetorical Tradition and its Epistemology

This section firstly defines rhetoric and points to some of the crucial contributions from the Western tradition. Secondly, it highlights the epistemological perspective mentioned briefly in the preceding section.

The Western rhetorical tradition has its roots in ancient Greece and Rome and in works by such scholars as Aristotle, Isocrates, Cicero, and Quintilian. Aristotle defined rhetoric as "an ability, in each [particular] case, to see the available means of persuasion" (Aristotle, trans. 2007, 1.2.1). For Isocrates, the epistemic quality of rhetoric was important, as he stated that "we use the same arguments by which we persuade others in our own deliberations" (Isocrates, trans. 2000, 15.256).

In everyday use, *rhetoric* is often applied as a contrast to "substantial action" and "reality." The term is reserved for empty words and deception. A blog looking at climate science, for instance, juxtaposes what the natural gas industry says with "extensive evidence showing their claims are pure rhetoric, and not reality" (http://www.desmogblog.com/natural-gas-industry-rhetoric-versus-reality, accessed July 7, 2011). In other words, what is implied is that it is only the natural gas industry that engages in rhetoric, whereas its critics rely on facts and information that is imparted straightforwardly. Incidentally, while I sympathize with the cause of this particular blog post, I would maintain that rhetoric involves attempts to persuade and/or convince people, which is something that everyone engages in every day. Everyone uses rhetoric, not least the anti-rhetoricians.

In the twentieth century, a renewed interest for rhetoric was expressed by leading figures such as Burke (1950/1969) and Perelman and Olbrechts-Tyteca (1969/1971). Burke's goal was to rediscover and restore rhetorical elements that he felt had been obscured and even vandalized by the emphasis on aesthetics. Perelman and Olbrechts-Tyteca shared these sentiments and were particularly interested in reinstating matters of rationality. The new rhetoricians expanded the scope of rhetoric to include all forms of symbol use, including mass media use.

The new rhetoric was partly driven by epistemological debates, and rhetoric was seen as something more than intellectual history. The basic philosophical underpinnings of the rhetorical tradition were discussed: rhetoric is involved in all human behavior and helps some ideas to be accepted and others to be rejected.

Some have argued that classical rhetoric typically saw truth as something that the rhetor had arrived at previously, and that rhetoric should merely help to communicate this truth (Lunsford and Ede, 1994; Ohmann, 1994). A clearly defined relationship existed between the rhetor, the audience, and the world, which was mediated by language. In modern rhetoric, however, there is no fully confident or generally accepted epistemological stance that articulates the relationship of the knower and the known (Lunsford and Ede, 1994; Ohmann, 1994). Nevertheless, one widespread position is that truth is inseparable from discourse; that is, it is inseparable from the way we use language and interact. Rhetoric is not seen as something that decorates or disguises truth; rhetoric is a way of *creating* truths rest upon some kind of human consensus (Farrell, 1999; Scott, 1999). At one point in time, "everyone" knew that the world was flat.

In 1967, taking his lead from Stephen E. Toulmin (1958), Robert L. Scott (1999) argued that rhetoric is epistemic; it is a way of knowing. This *social–epistemic rhetoric* understands rhetoric as constructing and modifying reality, social conditions, and relationships. Rhetoric is implicated in all human behavior and constructs social knowledge that is situated materially and historically. It is through rhetoric that ideas are accepted or rejected. Rhetorical interaction is involved when something is declared to be a fact, in the interpretation of that fact as well as in how it is used to justify action. This also extends to discourse communities that often try to deny that rhetoric plays a role – for instance, economics and branches of science dealing with "objective facts" (McCloskey, 1998). Nevertheless, all types of knowledge must rest upon some kind of human consensus, and thus there is a need for rhetoric (Farrell, 1999; Scott, 1999).

In a sense, then, truth might be conceived as being created moment by moment. This has brought about a renewed interest in the works of the sophistic tradition and its emphasis on contingency – how something is probable, rather than certain (e.g., Jarratt, 1991; Poulakos, 1999). Scott later regretted the use of the word "epistemic," since he saw no way of being certain. According to Scott, rhetoric is *a* way

of knowing, or rather understanding, not *the* way of knowing or understanding. Most importantly, however, positivism's notion of grand truths should be ignored (Scott, 1993).

Different labels have been used for the various versions of the epistemological stance sketched above: *intersubjectivity, rhetorical subjectivism, rhetorical relativism*, and so forth. These stances can be shown to have a modern counterpart, which is alternately called *rhetorical objectivism, rhetorical dialectic*, or *critical rationalism*. The general view held by scholars operating with such mind-sets is that truth is discovered with the help of rhetoric. This debate has clear parallels with the sociological debate between realists and constructionists (e.g., Berger & Luckmann, 1966). In the realm of environmental sociology, for instance, realists think that objective knowledge about the environment is possible. In the radical version of social constructionism, however, there is no way of concluding that environmental problems actually do exist (Hannigan, 1995). Some have sought to bridge the problematic duality by placing the two positions on a continuum, and by introducing different mixtures of the two positions (Cherwitz and Hikins, 1999).

Taking the latter course, mixing the two positions, it is possible to argue for the view that "reality" is a product of a synthesis between material structures and practices on the one side, and the use of symbols that reinforce or question those structures and practices on the other (Sandmann, 1996). The position taken in this chapter inclines toward such a synthesis view. It rejects the most radical version of the "rhetoric is epistemic" stance, as that seems to have little room for material existence. This leads into discussions of ontological matters, that is, thoughts of what exists – kinds of being and the relationship between them. While acknowledging the existence of material structures, this chapter argues that rhetoric is necessary for the social mediation of this knowledge. It is not possible to communicate without rhetoric, and rhetoric is crucial for human understanding. In this sense, rhetoric is epistemic, and referring back to Isocrates (trans. 2000), it seems most fruitful to comprehend it as having a dialectic relationship to the ontological. This epistemological position also has importance for the discussion of corporate rhetoric; however, the next section will also examine how the individual-oriented rhetorical theory discussed above can be moved into the sphere of a collective like a corporation.

Rhetoric and the Corporation

This section discusses some of the differences between the situation of the ancient, individual orator and the corporation as a modern day rhetor. The direct transfer of ancient rhetorical theory to the study of corporate discourse might be awkward, particularly in light of how an organization is a collectivity with many selves and many realities (Cheney, 1992; McMillian, 2007). Rhetorical theory has always been primarily geared toward individuals, exemplified through, for instance, how Quintilian's (trans. 1920/1996) used Cato the Elder's maxim that an orator is a good man speaking well. Isocrates (trans. 2000, trans. 2004) maintained that only a good man could truly succeed with rhetoric. Roman scholars like Cicero (trans. 2001) and Quintilian (trans. 1920/1996) also spoke about the ideal rhetor as having certain qualities. The latter argued that the orator should possess "genuine wisdom and excellence of character" (Quintilian, trans. 1920/1996, 3.8.13). Taking his lead from this work, Heath (2001) proposed an ethical and pragmatic ideal for public relations as being "the good organization communicating well" (p. 39).

Elsewhere (Ihlen, 2010b), I have pointed to a number of particular differences between ancient and modern rhetoric. First of all, rhetors of today mostly represent organizations, and as such they are inseparable from these entities (Crable, 1990). Representing a collective can prove to be an asset as well as liability for both the individual and the organization. In times of crisis, individuals can be scapegoated in order to diffuse or deny crisis responsibility (Burke, 1945/1969; Seeger *et al.*,

1998). Conversely, the individual can be absolved if the organization as such takes the blame for the crisis. An individual rhetor representing an organization will also be able to draw on the history and credibility of the organization. A serious corporation could be expected to appoint a competent spokesperson. An example of the reverse would be corporations hiring, for instance, well-known journalists or politicians to be their figureheads or public relations directors. The credibility of the individual can then be transferred to the, perhaps, less well-known organization.

Second, there is a need for a revamped rhetorical theory, as the new rhetoric encourages the study of all forms of media, forms that the modern organization certainly has at its disposal. Examples range from television appearances, streaming videos, press releases, and Twitter messages to buildings and uniforms. A modern rhetoric must be adapted to reflect the understanding that the object of study includes "text" in this broad sense.

A third distinction is that a modern rhetoric has to account for the fact that time and place of the rhetorical encounter may be very different from the classical setting where a rhetor was standing in front of an audience. The audience may be dispersed in time and place, thus making immediate reaction and adaptation difficult or impossible for the rhetor. Furthermore, the mass audience is often more diverse, with differing values and multiple organizational identifications (Cheney *et al.*, 2004; Conrad and Lair, 2004; Crable, 1990). A strategy that is appropriate for one group of stakeholders can easily alienate another (Ice, 1991).

Rhetors are also agencies for organizations. They have become actors in the Hollywood sense: the "words we hear are someone else's: the understanding or emotions generated are controlled by forces off-stage. The actor in the Hollywood sense 'appears' and the actor in Burke's sense remains behind the scenes, not a part of the scene" (Crable, 1990, p. 123).

Finally, much of the identity and reputation literature seemingly urges corporations to ignore their collectivist basis and speak with one voice. Consistency is often presented as a goal in itself, while the value of having multiple identities has been ignored (Christensen and Askegaard, 2001; Christensen and Cheney, 2000; Leitch and Motion, 1999). People often hold multiple and contradictory images of an organization, but they are not necessarily uncomfortable with this situation. Therefore, some scholars have attempted to reconcile the concepts of consistency and multiplicity (van Riel, 1992; van Riel and Balmer, 1997). The *theory of common starting points* has been suggested, arguing that the starting point should be the central values that an organization uses, but that it is not necessary to make all communication from the organization uniform (van Riel, 1992; van Riel and Balmer, 1997). Importantly, clarity and consistency are not goals that should override the multiplicity of identities, diversity, and voices in organizations (Ihlen, 2010a).

While huge discrepancies between what is said and what is done might hurt the reputation of a corporation, it should be emphasized that aspirational talk does have a legitimate role and may help bring about social change in organizations. Rhetoric also alerts us to the fact that communication and action are interrelated and co-construct one another: "talk *is* action and, as a result, the power of discourse to constitute organizing practices should not be understated" (Ihlen *et al.*, 2011, p. 566). In other words, corporate rhetoric is not *just* rhetoric.

The Concept of Ethos

This section discusses the concept of ethos and ethos strategies at some length, before making the explicit connection to corporate rhetoric. Ethos is of particular importance when discussing reputation. First, however, it needs to be mentioned that classical rhetoric emphasized how the rhetor can use three types of proof for the purpose of persuasion: *logos*, or logical arguments, either through inductive reasoning, such as use of examples, or through deductive reasoning, using premises that lead to certain conclusions; *pathos*, or emotional appeals to the

audience; and finally, *ethos*, or ethical appeals that strengthen the credibility of the rhetor. These types of proof are linked to the message, the audience, and the rhetor, respectively. In a given discourse, "these are at all times coordinate and interact mutually, distinguishable but not separable from one another, although one may occasionally take precedence over the others" (Conley, 1990/1994, p. 15).

Ethos is of particular importance when discussing reputation. Aristotle argued that ethos – or character – is "almost, so to speak, the most authoritative form of persuasion" (Aristotle, trans. 2007, 1.2.4). Since rhetoric deals with areas where no exact knowledge exists, the character of the speaker becomes all-important. Ethos can thus be shown to trump logos, as we do not automatically adhere to valid logical arguments, but we have no choice other than to trust or not to trust the rhetor (Jasinski, 2001).

Following Aristotle, ethos is "character as it emerges in language" (Baumlin, 2001, p. 263). In other words, it is considered as the elements of a speech or a text that present the rhetor as trustworthy. In addition to direct ethos, there is also an indirect route through other aspects of discourse (Kinneavy and Warshauer, 1994). Emotional appeal might strengthen ethos as "the hearer suffers along with the pathetic speaker, even if what he says amounts to nothing" (Aristotle, trans. 2007, 3.7.5). Similarly, using enthymemes and maxims – certain logical appeals – can work well because audiences "are pleased if someone in a general observation hits upon opinions that they themselves have about a particular instance" (Aristotle, trans. 2007, 21.15).

While Aristotle argued that invented ethos was the province of rhetoric, other ancient scholars, like Isocrates, Cicero, and Quintilian pointed to the importance of the rhetor's reputation *prior* to the speech: "The character, the customs, the deeds, and the life, both of those who do the pleading and of those on whose behalf they plead, make a very important contribution to winning the case" (Cicero, trans. 2001, 2.182). Ethos permeates utterances, or as Quintilian put it, "whatever relates to the pleader of the cause relates to the cause itself" (Quintilian, trans. 1920/1996, 4.1.12).

For Aristotle, however, it was important that rhetors did not rely on their reputation alone, as ethos is put in play in each rhetorical situation (Aristotle, trans. 2007, 1.2.4). Aristotle argued that the rhetor should possess qualities that the community defines as virtue. Some thus argue that the rhetor is triggering the "audience's projection of authority and trustworthiness onto the speaker" (Baumlin and Baumlin, 1994, p. 99). In line with this, Smith (2004) argued that ethos "dwells in the character of the audience; and . . . in the speaker's style" (p. 3). Smith urged us to see ethos as tied, not only to the rhetor, but also to the text and to the audience of the rhetorical situation.

Aristotle argued that a rhetor could strengthen ethos in three ways:

> There are three reasons why speakers themselves are persuasive; for there are three things we trust other than logical demonstration. These are practical wisdom [*phronesis*] and virtue [*arete*] and good will [*eunoia*]; for speakers make mistakes in what they say through [failure to exhibit] either all or one of these. (Aristotle, trans. 2007, 2.1.5)

Practical wisdom, virtue, and good will will have a complex interrelation and correspond to the theme, the speaker, and the audience, respectively. In more detail, practical wisdom is understood as knowledge of *the right action*, something "that is distinct from technical knowledge and that cannot be learned in the same way as technical knowledge" (Kinneavy and Warshauer, 1994, p. 179). *Phronesis* is also bolstered by the use of logos and stylistic appeals. The latter entails, for instance, choice of grammatical person, verb tense, and voice.

Attempts to demonstrate virtue – justice, courage, self-control, liberality, magnanimity, magnificence, prudence – can include citing approval from respected authorities (Cicero, trans. 2001). This "third-party technique" is a well-known reputation-building technique today and was also extolled by Aristotle: "Since there are sometimes things to be said about

oneself that are invidious or prolix or contradictory . . . it is best to attribute them to another person" (Aristotle, trans. 2007, 3.17.16). The virtues were seen as "moving targets established by the audience" (Smith, 2004, p. 7). This again points to how the rhetor has to adapt to the audience; virtues valued by one audience might be despised by another. In general, however, the virtues most appreciated by the audience are often those that are most useful to society (Kinneavy and Warshauer, 1994).

Exhibiting goodwill should be understood as wishing good for others for their own sake. As Aristotle writes in *The Nicomachean Ethics*, "Goodwill is inoperative friendship, which when it continues and reaches the point of intimacy may become friendship proper – not the sort of friendship whose motive is utility or pleasure, for these do not arouse goodwill" (Aristotle, trans. 1996, 9.5.3). If the audience detects a friendship that requires reciprocation, the credibility of the rhetor is not enhanced (Smith, 2004). To demonstrate goodwill, the rhetor should "somehow identify with the audience, by for instance holding some of their basic aspirations, speaking their language, and if necessary sharing and affirming their prejudices" (Kinneavy and Warshauer, 1994, p. 177). Goodwill might thus be indirectly supported by pathos.

"These are the only possibilities," Aristotle added after pointing to the three strategies for strengthening ethos (2.1.6). In today's society, however, we know that character and credibility are also closely tied to what is perceived to be authentic, real, and genuine (e.g., Johansen, 2002). The rhetor has to be perceived as being him- or herself. The rhetor should avoid coming across as scripted or strategic; he or she should appear intimate and sharing, but also appear to be a consistent and consequent actor (Kjeldsen, 2004). Research on rhetoric as well as persuasion has highlighted other credibility factors also: scholars have pointed to the importance of power (the audience perceiving that the rhetor might reward or punish them), idealism (the audience members seeing qualities in the rhetor to which they aspire), and similarity (the audience seeing the rhetor resemble themselves) (Hart and Daughton, 2005).

Several of the insights presented above can be adapted to the study of corporate rhetoric. The notion of ethos has also been used to analyze corporate rhetoric, for instance, on environmental issues. Ihlen (2009) argued that corporations rely on a set of archetypical ethos strategies to appear as environmentally friendly: first of all, corporations tend to argue that they make the world better with their product or the positive leadership that they offer; secondly, corporations point to how they have cleaned up their own house by actions such as recycling or curbing emissions; thirdly, corporations use the third-party strategy, citing authorities or nongovernmental organizations (NGOs), that approve of their environmental efforts; and, finally, corporations argue that they care about their stakeholders and share their interests (Ihlen, 2009).

Corporate rhetors could also pay attention to how the roots of ethos can be traced back to *ethea*, which means "haunts," and thus that ethos is formed in the places where one "hangs out" (Jarratt and Reynolds, 1994, p. 48). McMillian (2007) sees the creation of *mutual dwelling places* as replacing corporate monolog with dialog; including *all* stakeholders, not only a few privileged ones; adding new measures of success, such as human and social capital; "replacing external attribution with corporate accountability and disclosure"; and fundamentally altering and decentering the corporation's "self-adoring gaze" (p. 25). The fundamental reorientation advocated by McMillian might in turn also help organizations obtain a reputation as a "good organization communicating well" (Heath, 2001, p. 31). As always, however, reputation can only be a by-product of a corporation's work with its identity. One of the paradoxes of corporate reputation is that attempts to strengthen often fail when it becomes the goal itself. The attempt to come across as credible, however, is a more feasible task. Still, ethos is situation bound; it deals specifically with the judgment of a rhetor's character *at a specific time*. Ethos is in play in every communication situation, and thus some argue that it might be better likened to image and not to the more long-term reputation (Kjeld-

sen, 2004). Still, in line with the argument that reputation has to be seen in relation to identity and image, ethos remains a crucial concept for the analysis of corporate reputation. The next section suggests another vital notion, that of identification.

Rhetoric as Identification

This section first briefly discusses identification as conceptualized by Burke (1950/1969), and then moves on to discuss techniques for creating identification.

Identification becomes essential for the rhetor, because people can only be persuaded if the rhetor can communicate with, for instance, speech, gestures, tone, ideas, and attitudes; in short, if the rhetor can identify his or her ways with those of the audience. In order to achieve this, both the rhetor and his or her audience have to "die" and be "reborn" a little. A rhetor might be able to change the audience's opinion in one respect, but will only succeed insofar as he or she yields to the audience's opinions in other respects (Burke, 1937/1984, 1950/1969).

There is, however, a crucial problem: although identification may be achieved, the division is not lifted. Total identification cannot exist; people are still physically separate beings. Instead, there is a situation of being both joined and separate. This is the *paradox of substance* and the reason that rhetoric is needed. The basic rhetorical situation is characterized by the concepts of congregation and segregation, cooperation and competition. Identification will always suggest a *we* and a *they* (Burke, 1950/1969, 1973).

In the context of corporate reputation, it is primarily ways of creating identification that are of interest. Cheney (1983, 1991) argued that organizations "assist" in identification processes with their employees and other stakeholders in order to induce cooperation and/or reduce the range of decisions to those alternatives that benefit the organization. The organization seeks to promote oneness with its members. While Cheney focuses on internal organizational communication, the three rhetorical techniques he identified for creating identification can also be extended to external corporate rhetoric:

1   *The common ground technique.* The corporation emphasizes common ground between itself and its members or stakeholders in terms of sharing values and/or interests, much like the ethos strategy of showing goodwill towards the audience. In this way, the rhetor attempts to create a direct, associative process whereby the rhetor says, in effect, "I am like you" or "I have the same interests as you." In an organizational context, the management might rely on an associational process and express concern for individual members or highlight the contributions made by individuals or groups. The organization might point to how "all" share the same interests and values, and want to achieve the same goals. The organization could advocate the benefits of pursuing the same goals, and also seek praise from others. A corporation might underscore values of freedom and democracy, which the public is likely to share (Crable & Vibbert, 1983). A corporation like ExxonMobil uses the common ground technique in the following way: "We will continue to advocate for an integrated set of solutions to today's major energy challenges ... help address climate change risks, and develop all economical energy sources to meet the needs of today and future generations" (ExxonMobil, 2010, p. 1). The implied idea is that *we are all in this together*. Here there is also a parallel with the idea that corporations need to create mutual dwelling places (McMillian, 2007).

2   *Antithesis.* The management of the corporation presents a common enemy, for instance urging employees to unite against hostile takeovers from a foreign company or government bureaucracy. The antithesis technique is thus a strategy of congregation by segregation; it is a disassociative technique that establishes new associations indirectly. The shared perspective of a "threat from outsiders" creates identification between the corporation and its stakeholders. Responding to signals that US tax breaks would be revoked for corporate jets, the National Business Aviation Association responded: "The president is vilifying an entire industry . . . This is an attempt to score some cheap political points on the back of an industry that employs 1.2 million people" (Lichtblau, 2011, p. A13). In other words, everyone concerned about jobs and a healthy economy should rally behind this cause.

3   *The transcendent.* We corporations could also attempt to create identification by explicitly using personal nouns like "we." The use of this noun takes identification for granted and works particularly well when it is not questioned. It then can work on a subtle unconscious level. Corporations typically seem to use this technique when addressing global challenges like climate change. Here is an example from Volkswagen: "there is an urgent need to step up *our* efforts regarding alternative sources of energy" [emphasis added] (Volkswagen AG, 2009, p. 18). As already indicated, the use of personal nouns can also strengthen the two techniques mentioned above: *we* share the same interests, we need to stand together against the enemy, and so forth.

To foster identification is to induce stakeholders to have the best interests of the organization in mind when they make decisions, to encourage them to think that things are a certain way, and, not least, to make them believe that this is the way the stakeholders want them to be. To create identification can thus be a fundamental way of creating a strong reputation; it moves beyond "just" being held in high esteem, as witnessed by the following that brands like Mac achieve (e.g., http://www.i-love-mac.com/). Still, the ways in which corporations set about creating identification to foster reputation form one of many areas that deserve closer attention from scholars. In the concluding section, I develop some ideas for other research avenues concerning rhetoric and corporate reputation.

Conclusion and Research Agenda

In this chapter, I have discussed the relationship between rhetoric and reputation. I have pointed to how a strong reputation can be an asset for rhetoric, but also to some particular ways in which rhetoric can help strengthen reputation. A rhetorical approach to reputation indicates strategies for appearing credible and for creating identification with the audience, both types of activities that can be said to help foster a strong reputation in the long run by means of enhancing an organization's image. A main point has also been to emphasize the fundamental epistemological role that rhetoric plays in constructing identity, image, and reputation: in constructing knowledge in general. A rhetorical approach to reputation provides a valuable epistemological platform alerting us to the crucial role of language in understanding the world. Rhetoric is enacting and creating the environment, and facts are being conditioned by social agreement. In this way rhetoric also has the power to constitute organizational practices. While a case has been made for studying corporate rhetoric, it is, however, also acknowledged that the direct transfer of knowledge from the individually oriented rhetorical theory is problematic in the context of the collective of the corporation.

The concept of ethos has been discussed along with the ways in which corporate rhetors have set out to strengthen ethos. Several of the corporate strategies in this respect can be recognized from the ancient literature, but new techniques have also been introduced, driven by for instance the modern desire to appear authentic. Given the premise that ethos is situation-specific, it has been likened to image, which in turn may influence corporate reputation (Kjeldsen, 2004). An even more profound way of improving corporate reputation is

through the route of creating identification between the corporation and its stakeholders. Some of the rhetorical strategies for this endeavor have been discussed and exemplified. The ability to create identification between a corporation and its stakeholders is also expressed in the relationship between some of the more famous brands like Mac or Harley Davidson and their respective customers.

The behavior of a corporation is key for a good reputation, but the corporate *communication* behavior is very important too, because we often have no first-hand experience with a corporation, and furthermore, opinions are formed in a social context. Reputation, for instance, has been defined as the degree to which stakeholders feel respect, admiration, trust, and good feelings towards a corporation. These attributes have been measured against dimensions such as financial standing, products and services, innovation, management, working conditions, ethics, and corporate social responsibility (see, Fombrun & van Riel, 2004; van Riel & Fombrun, 2007). It would be interesting to see rhetorical studies tied to each of these dimensions. How are corporations trying to create respect, admiration, trust, and good feelings regarding their products and services? The ability to come across as a credible provider is important, but this is obviously only one aspect. Further research could be conducted on how corporations use logos and pathos, the two other types of proof, when they are trying to build a good reputation as measured against these dimensions.

As mentioned, more research is also needed to gain a better grasp of how corporations attempt to create identification and how this relates to reputation. Furthermore, a fully developed rhetoric for corporate reputation would also have to take into account the situational aspect of rhetoric. Building on Cheney *et al.* (2004), it may be argued that rhetoric can be useful in the study of how reputation is influenced and created when organizations 1) *respond* to existing rhetorical situations; 2) attempt to *anticipate* future rhetorical situations; 3) attempt to *shape rhetorical situations*; and 4) try to *shape their own identities*.

A premise that has been furthered in this chapter is that reputation building has to start with the corporation taking a good look at itself, and asking some crucial questions about the central, lasting, and unique qualities of the corporation (Albert and Whetten, 2004). When the corporation understands its own identity, it might stand a better chance of understanding how its image is perceived. Rhetoric might also assist in grasping the words and perceptions of the stakeholders, which in turn should have an influence on the identity work and the behavior of the organization. The epistemological perspective offered by rhetoric should also make it easier for corporations to accept that there are many truths, also relating to identity, image, and reputation.

References

Albert, S. and Whetten, D.A. (2004) Organizational identity. In M.J. Hatch and M. Schultz (eds), *Organizational Identity: A Reader*. New York: Oxford University Press, pp. 89–118.

Aristotle (trans. 1996) *The Nicomachean Ethics* (H. Rackham, trans.). London: Wordsworth.

Aristotle (trans. 2007) *On Rhetoric: A Theory of Civic Discourse* (G.A. Kennedy, trans., 2nd ed.). New York: Oxford University Press.

Barnett, M.L., Jermier, J.M., and Lafferty, B.A. (2006) Corporate reputation: The definitional landscape. *Corporate Reputation Review*, 9(1), 26–38.

Baumlin, J.S. (2001) Ethos. In T.O. Sloane (ed.), *Encylopedia of Rhetoric*. New York: Oxford University Press, pp. 263–277.

Baumlin, J.S. and Baumlin, T.F. (1994) On the psychology of the *pisteis*: Mapping the terrains of mind and rhetoric. In J.S. Baumlin and T.F. Baumlin (eds), *Ethos: New Essays in Rhetorical and Critical Theory*. Dallas, TX: Southern Methodist University Press, pp. 91–112.

Berger, P. and Luckmann, T. (1966) *The Social Construction of Reality: A Treatise in the Sociology of Knowledge*. London: Penguin Books.

Boulding, K. (1956) *The Image: Knowledge in Life and Society*. Ann Arbor, MI: University of Michigan Press.

Burke, K. (1937/1984) *Attitudes Towards History* (3rd ed.). Berkeley, CA: University of California Press.

Burke, K. (1945/1969) *A Grammar of Motives*. Berkeley, CA: University of California Press.

Burke, K. (1950/1969) *A Rhetoric of Motives*. Berkeley, CA: University of California Press.

Burke, K. (1966) *Language as Symbolic Action: Essays on Life, Literature, and Method*. Berkeley, CA: University of California Press.

Burke, K. (1973) The rhetorical situation. In L. Thayer (ed.), *Communication: Ethical and Moral Issues*. London: Gordon and Breach Science Publishers, pp. 263–275.

Campbell, F.E., Herman, R.A., and Noble, D. (2006) Contradictions in "reputation management". *Journal of Communication Management*, 10(2), 191–196.

Cheney, G. (1983) The rhetoric of identification and the study of organizational communication. *Quarterly Journal of Speech*, 69, 143–158.

Cheney, G. (1991) *Rhetoric in an Organizational Society: Managing Multiple Identities*. Columbia, SC: University of South Carolina Press.

Cheney, G. (1992) The corporate person (re)presents itself. In E.L. Toth and R.L. Heath (eds), *Rhetorical and Critical Approaches to Public Relations*. Hillsdale, NJ: Lawrence Erlbaum Associates, pp. 165–183.

Cheney, G., Christensen, L.T., Conrad, C., and Lair, D.J. (2004) Corporate rhetoric as organizational discourse. In D. Grant, C. Hardy, C. Oswick, and L.L. Putnam (eds), *The Sage Handbook of Organizational Discourse*. London: Sage, pp. 79–103.

Cherwitz, R.A. and Hikins, J.W. (1999) Rhetorical perspectivism. In J.L. Lucaites, C.M. Condit, and S. Caudill (eds), *Contemporary Rhetorical Theory: A Reader*. New York: Guilford Press, pp. 176–193.

Christensen, L.T. and Askegaard, S. (2001) Corporate identity and corporate image revisited: A semiotic perspective. *European Journal of Marketing*, 35(3/4), 292–315.

Christensen, L.T. and Cheney, G. (2000) Self-absorption and self seduction in the corporate identity game. In M. Schultz, M.J. Hatch, and M. Holten Larsen (eds), *The Expressive Organization: Linking Identity, Reputation, and the Corporate Brand*. New York: Oxford University Press.

Cicero (trans. 2001) *On the Ideal Orator* (J.M. May and J. Wisse, trans.). New York: Oxford University Press.

Conley, T.M. (1990/1994) *Rhetoric in the European Tradition*. Chicago, IL: The University of Chicago Press.

Crable, R.E. (1990) "Organizational rhetoric" as the fourth great system: Theoretical, critical, and pragmatic implications. *Journal of Applied Communication Research, 18*(2), 115–128.

Crable, R.E. and Vibbert, S.L. (1983) Mobil's epideictic advocacy: "Observations" of Prometheus-bound. *Communication Monographs, 50*(4), 380–394.

ExxonMobil, (2010) *2009 Corporate Citizen Report: Adressing the Sustainability Challenge.* Irving, Texas: ExxonMobil.

Farrell, T.B. (1999) Knowledge, consensus, and rhetorical theory. In J.L. Lucaites, C.M. Condit, and S. Caudill (eds), *Contemporary Rhetorical Theory: A Reader.* New York: Guilford Press, pp. 140–152.

Fombrun, C.J. and van Riel, C.B.M. (2004) *Fame & Fortune: How Successful Companies Build Winning Reputations.* Upper Saddle River, NJ: Financial Times Prentice Hall.

Gotsi, M. and Wilson, A.M. (2001) Corporate reputation: Seeking a definition. *Corporate Communications: An International Journal, 6*(1), 24–30.

Hannigan, J.A. (1995) *Environmental Sociology: A Social Constructionist Perspective.* London: Routledge.

Hart, R.P. and Daughton, S. (2005) *Modern Rhetorical Criticism* (3rd ed.). Boston: Allyn & Bacon.

Hatch, M.J. and Schultz, M. (1997) Relations between organisational culture, identity and image. *European Journal of Marketing, 31*(5/6), 356–365.

Heath, R.L. (2001) A rhetorical enactment rationale for public relations: The good organization communicating well. In R.L. Heath (ed.), *Handbook of Public Relations.* Thousand Oaks, CA: Sage, pp. 31–50.

Holberg, L. (1971) *Ludvig Holberg værker i tolv bind [The Work of Ludvig Holberg in Twelve Volumes].* Gentofte, Denmark: Rosenkilde og Bagger.

Ice, R. (1991) Corporate publics and rhetorical strategies: The case of Union Carbide's Bhopal crisis. *Management Communication Quarterly, 4*(3), 341–362.

Ihlen, Ø. (2009) Good environmental citizens? The green rhetoric of corporate social responsibility. In R.L. Heath, E.L. Toth, and D. Waymer (eds), *Rhetorical and Critical Approaches to Public Relations II.* New York: Routledge, pp. 360–374.

Ihlen, Ø. (2010a) Corporate identity. In R.L. Jackson (ed.), *The Encyclopedia of Identity.* Thousand Oaks, CA: Sage, pp. 140–145.

Ihlen, Ø. (2010b) The cursed sisters: Public relations and rhetoric. In R.L. Heath (ed.), *The SAGE Handbook of Public Relations* (2nd ed.). Thousands Oaks, CA: Sage, pp. 59–70.

Ihlen, Ø., Bartlett, J., and May, S. (2011) Conclusions and take away points. In Ø. Ihlen, J. Bartlett, and S. May (eds), *Handbook of Communication and Corporate Social Responsibility.* Oxford, UK: Wiley-Blackwell.

Isocrates (trans. 2000) *Isocrates I* (D.C. Mirhady and Y.L. Too, trans.). Austin, TX: University of Texas Press.

Isocrates (trans. 2004) *Isocrates II* (T.L. Papillion, trans.). Austin, TX: University of Texas Press.

Jarratt, S.C. (1991) *Rereading the Sophists: Classical Rhetoric Refigured.* Carbondale, IL: Southern Illinois University Press.

Jarratt, S.C. and Reynolds, N. (1994) The splitting image: Contemporary feminisms and the ethics of ethos. In J.S. Baumlin and T.F. Baumlin (eds), *Ethos: New Essays in Rhetorical and Critical Theory.* Dallas, TX: Southern Methodist University Press, pp. 37–64.

Jasinski, J. (2001) *Sourcebook on Rhetoric: Key Concepts in Contemporary Rhetorical Studies.* Thousand Oaks, CA: Sage.

Johansen, A. (2002) *Talerens Troverdighet: Tekniske og Kulturelle Betingelser for Politisk Retorikk* [The Credibility of the Speaker: Technical and Cultural Conditions for Political Rhetoric]. Oslo, Norway: Universitetsforlaget.

Kinneavy, J.L. and Warshauer, S.C. (1994) From Aristotle to Madison Avenue: *Ethos* and the ethics of argument. In J.S. Baumlin and T.F. Baumlin (eds), *Ethos: New Essays in Rhetorical and Critical Theory.* Dallas, TX: Southern Methodist University Press, pp. 171–190.

Kjeldsen, J.E. (2004) *Retorikk i Vår Tid* [Rhetoric in Our Time]. Oslo, Norway: Spartacus Forlag.

Leitch, S. and Motion, J. (1999) Multiplicity in corporate identity strategy. *Corporate Communications: An International Journal, 4*(4), 193–199.

Lichtblau, E. (2011) Industry set for fight to keep corporate jet tax breaks. *New York Times,* p. A13.

Lucaites, J.L. and Condit, C.M. (1999) Introduction. In J.L. Lucaites, C.M. Condit, and S. Caudill (eds), *Contemporary Rhetorical Theory: A Reader.* New York: Guilford Press, pp. 1–18.

Lunsford, A.A. and Ede, L.S. (1994) On distinctions between classical and modern rhetoric. In T. Enos and S.C. Brown (eds), *Professing the New Rhetorics: A Sourcebook.* Upper Saddle River, NJ: Prentice Hall, pp. 397–411.

McCloskey, D.N. (1998) *The Rhetoric of Economics* (2nd ed.). Madison, WI: The University of Wisconsin Press.

McMillian, J.J. (2007) Why corporate social responsibility: Why now? How? In S.K. May, G. Cheney, and J. Roper (eds), *The Debate over Corporate Social Responsibility.* New York: Oxford University Press, pp. 15–29.

Ohmann, R. (1994) In lieu of a new rhetoric. In T. Enos and S.C. Brown (eds), *Professing the New Rhetorics: A Sourcebook.* Upper Saddle River, NJ: Prentice Hall, pp. 298–306.

Perelman, C. and Olbrechts-Tyteca, L. (1969/1971) *The New Rhetoric: A Treatise on Argumentation* (J. Wilkinson and P. Weaver, trans.). London: University of Notre Dame.

Poulakos, J. (1999) Toward a sophistic definition of rhetoric. In J.L. Lucaites, C.M. Condit, and S. Caudill (eds), *Contemporary Rhetorical Theory: A Reader.* New York: Guilford Press, pp. 25–34.

Quintilian (trans. 1920/1996) *Institutio Oratoria: Books I-XII* (H.E. Butler, trans.). Cambridge, MA: Harvard University Press.

Sandmann, W. (1996) The rhetorical function of "Earth in Balance". In S.A. Muir and T.L. Veenendall (eds), *Earthtalk: Communication Empowerment for Environmental Action.* Westport, CT: Praeger, pp. 119–134.

Scott, R.L. (1967) Rhetoric as epistemic. *Central States Speech Journal, 18,* 9–16.

Scott, R.L. (1993) Rhetoric is epistemic: What difference does that make? In T. Enos and S.C. Brown (eds), *Defining the New Rhetorics.* London: Sage, pp. 120–136.

Scott, R.L. (1999) On viewing rhetoric as epistemic. In J.L. Lucaites, C.M. Condit, and S. Caudill (eds), *Contemporary Rhetorical Theory: A Reader.* New York: Guilford Press, pp. 131–139.

Seeger, M.W., Sellnow, T.L., and Ulmer, R. (1998) Communication, organization, and crisis. *Communication Yearbook, 21,* 231–275.

Sillince, J.A.A. and Suddaby, R. (2008) Organizational rhetoric: Bridging management and communication scholarship. *Management Communication Quarterly, 22*(1), 5–12.

Smith, C.R. (2004) Ethos dwells pervasively: A hermeneutic reading of Aristotle on credibility. In M.J. Hyde (ed.), *The Ethos of Rhetoric.* Columbia, SC: University of South Carolina, pp. 1–19.

Toulmin, S.E. (1958) *The Uses of Argument.* London: Cambridge University Press.

Tsetsura, K. (2010) Social construction and public relations. In R.L. Heath (ed.), *The SAGE Handbook of Public Relations.* Thousand Oaks, CA: Sage, pp. 163–175.

van Riel, C.B.M. (1992) *Principles of Corporate Communication.* London: Prentice Hall.

van Riel, C.B.M. and Balmer, J.M.T. (1997) Corporate identity: The concept, its measurement and management. *European Journal of Marketing, 31*(5/6), 340–355.

van Riel, C.B.M. and Fombrun, C.J. (2007) *Essentials of Corporate Communication.* London: Routledge.

Volkswagen AG (2009) *Driving Ideas: Sustainability Report 2009/2010.* Wolfsburg, Germany: Volkswagen AG.

23

Situational Theory of Crisis: Situational Crisis Communication Theory and Corporate Reputation

W. Timothy Coombs
University of Central Florida, USA

There is a strong bond between crisis communication and corporate reputation management. In general, crises damage corporate reputations while the corporate reputation can be an asset or a liability to crisis managers. This chapter uses situational crisis communication theory (SCCT) to examine the connection between crisis communication and corporate reputation. SCCT provides a useful perspective on the connection between the two areas because corporate reputation is a primary outcome studied in SCCT and SCCT uses experimental methods to build its knowledge base. The chapter details SCCT, explores the relationship between SCCT and corporate reputation, and concludes with future research direction. By the end of the chapter, the reader has a greater understanding of how research in crisis communication and corporate reputation can inform one another.

The primary focus during a crisis situation is public safety. All communication efforts and resources should be concentrated on protecting people from the hazards of a crisis. But what comes after public safety? Sturges (1994) argued that once public safety is addressed, crisis managers can turn their attentions to repairing the reputational damage inflicted by the crisis. Crisis management has long held that reputational damage is a by-product of a crisis (e.g., Barton, 2001). Moreover, crisis communication experts argue that crisis communication is essential to reputation repair (e.g., Benoit, 1995; Coombs, 1995; Hearit, 1994).

Communication is essential throughout the crisis management process and can be divided into two broad categories: (1) managing information and (2) managing meaning. Managing information involves the collection and analysis of information and the dissemination of the knowledge created by analyzing crisis information. Managing meaning includes attempts to manage perceptions of the crisis and/or the organization in crisis (Coombs, 2009). The crisis communication research concentrates on crisis response strategies (Coombs, 2009, 2010a). Crisis response strategies are what managers say and do after a crisis occurs and

The Handbook of Communication and Corporate Reputation, First Edition. Edited by Craig E. Carroll.
© 2013 John Wiley & Sons, Inc. Published 2015 by John Wiley & Sons, Inc.

are a subset of crisis communication. The crisis response strategy research emphasizes reputation repair and protection (e.g., Benoit, 1995; Hearit, 1995). Crisis response strategies attempt to cultivate a postcrisis corporate reputation that is as strong as possible. Essentially, crisis response strategies are the public face of the crisis response and have a direct connection to corporate reputations.

A number of theories have been developed to explain the use of crisis response strategies to protect or repair corporate reputations, including corporate apologia (Dionisopolous and Vibbert, 1988; Hearit, 2001, 2006), image restoration theory (Benoit, 1995), and focusing events (Fishman, 1999). The present chapter focuses on situational crisis communication theory (SCCT). SCCT posits that the situation heavily influences the choices crisis managers make about crisis response strategies. Situational factors indicate which crisis response strategies will be more or less successful in protecting organizational assets such as reputation. The chapter begins with a discussion of SCCT's origins and then moves to an elaboration of the theory. The chapter concludes by examining the close connection between SCCT and corporate reputation, as well as directions for future research involving the two concepts.

Origins of SCCT

By the late 1980s, crisis communication was emerging as a distinct line of research within crisis communication. The literature often discussed different types of crises and different crisis response strategies. Crisis types are essentially frames that tell people how to interpret the crisis event (Coombs and Holladay, 2006). In 1988, Benson suggested that there should be a connection between crisis types and the crisis response. Rhetoricians had long held that the situation did influence the success or failure of communication strategies (e.g., Bitzer, 1968). Benson was drawing on this idea of situational influence to speculate on the future direction of crisis communication research.

At this time, crisis communication was primarily corporate apologia. Corporate apologia focused on how crisis managers could use crisis response strategies to protect or repair a corporation's public persona. A public persona is essentially corporate reputation – how people perceive the organization. Hence, corporate reputation was an important outcome from the beginning of crisis response research. All later crisis response strategy research is in one way or another derived from corporate apologia and a concern for corporate reputation.

SCCT was in part a reaction to Benson's (1988) call to connect the situation to the crisis response. The problem was finding a way to theoretically link the crisis types (descriptions of the crisis situation) to the crisis response strategies. SCCT drew on attribution theory to develop the connection. Attribution theory holds that people search for the causes of events, especially negative events, and choose the causal attribution that seems most satisfying to them. In general, people attribute events to external factors (the environment) or to internal factors (the person involved in the event). These attributions influence how people feel about and react to the event (Kelley, 1971; Weiner, 1986, 2006). Attributions for events occur naturally, and people will make these attributions based on very little evidence.

Crises are events highly likely to trigger attributions. Crises are negative events, and people want to know why they happened (Coombs, 1995, 2007a,c). A key element of attribution theory is responsibility for the event. People view those involved in a negative event more negatively if those involved are more responsible for the event – if there is an internal attribution. This is very logical. If a person is late to pick you up because he or she had a flat tire (low responsibility), you are not too upset and sympathetic. But if the person is late to pick you up because he or she forgot, you are upset and unsympathetic. Similarly, stakeholders are more upset when a crisis is caused by the organization in crisis than when some external event, such as a terrorist attack, prompted the crisis.

SCCT uses responsibility to link the crisis situation and crisis response strategies. SCCT examines the responsibility created by the crisis situation (crisis responsibility) and the acceptance of crisis responsibility found in the crisis response strategy. The basic premise is that as attributions of crisis responsibility increase, crisis managers must use crisis response strategies that increasingly accept responsibility for the crisis. Crisis managers can maximize the reputational benefits of crisis response strategies by matching them to the level of perceived crisis responsibility (Coombs, 1995, 2007b,c). SCCT treats corporate reputation as a primary outcome for crisis response strategies: the effectiveness of crisis response strategies is defined, in part, by how well they protect or repair corporate reputation. The next section describes the elements of SCCT.

Explication of SCCT

SCCT began as a set of propositions presented in the form of a decision tree. The propositions were guided by theory, and served to link crisis type and crisis response strategy through crisis responsibility. This section begins by defining the key variables and relationships in SCCT and then reviews the implications from the empirical tests and issues with operationalizing the variables.

Articulation and development of SCCT

A crisis situation is a constellation of factors that shape attributions of crisis responsibility. It is by anticipating how stakeholders are making attributions of crisis responsibility that crisis managers select the appropriate crisis response strategies for maximizing reputational protection. Currently, research has identified three variables that significantly affect attributions of crisis responsibility: crisis type, crisis history, and performance history.

Crisis type is the initial factor to assess. As noted earlier, a *crisis type* is the frame that is being used to define the crisis. Media, traditional and social, will give indications of how the crisis is being framed (Coombs and Holladay, 2010). Each crisis type has defining characteristics. Table 23.1 lists and defines the crisis types examined in SCCT. Each crisis type gen-

Table 23.1   Crisis types.

Victim crisis cluster (very low attributions of crisis responsibility)
  Natural disaster: acts of nature that can damage an organization or disrupt operations such as a hurricane.
  Rumors: false and harmful information is circulating about the organization.
  Workplace violence: a current or former employee harms current employees at the workplace.
  Product tampering/malevolence: an external actor purposefully damages the organization by actions such as product tampering or computer hacking.
Accidental crisis cluster (minimal attributions of crisis responsibility)
  Challenges: some stakeholders claim the organization is acting in an inappropriate or irresponsible fashion. The public challenge is based on moral or ethical grounds, not legal concerns.
  Technical error accidents: an industrial accident is cause by a technological or equipment failure.
  Technical error product harm: a product is produced improperly through a technological or equipment failure. The defective product then poses a threat to consumers.
Intentional crisis cluster (strong attributions of crisis responsibility)
  Human error accidents: an industrial accident is caused by human error. An employee causes the accident because of improper job performance.
  Human error product harm: a defective product is created due to human error. An employee's improper job performance causes the defect and the defective product poses a threat to consumers.
  Organizational misdeed: management knowingly violates laws or regulations or purposefully places stakeholders at risk. This would include knowingly selling a product that is dangerous or engaging in risky behaviors that could harm stakeholders in some way.

---

erates specific attributions of crisis responsibility. Research has shown that the crisis types can be grouped according the crisis responsibility each generates. Table 23.1 organizes the crisis types into three categories: (1) victim – very little attribution of crisis responsibility; (2) accidental – minimal attributions of crisis responsibility; and (3) intentional – strong attribution of crisis responsibility.

After the initial assessment of crisis type, crisis managers then consider the intensifying factors of crisis history and performance history. *Crisis history* is whether or not an organization has had similar crises in the past. *Performance history* is how well or poorly the organization has treated stakeholders in the past. Performance history is a variation of prior reputation – perceptions of the organization that stakeholders have before the crisis occurs. Similar crises or a negative prior reputation creates the impression that the crisis is part of a pattern of poor behavior. According to attribution theory, a pattern of poor behavior is an indicator of stability and will intensify attributions of personal control (Weiner, 1986) – that is, it will increase attributions of crisis responsibility.

If either intensifier is present, the attributions of crisis responsibility increase. A victim crisis with intensifiers will be viewed as an accidental crisis (minimal attribution of crisis responsibility), while an accident crisis will be viewed as an intentional crisis (strong attribution of crisis responsibility). Empirical research has found support for both crisis history and performance history intensifying attributions of crisis responsibility (Coombs, 2007c; Coombs and Holladay, 2002). It has been argued that a positive performance history/prior reputation should produce a halo effect – that the positive prior reputation protects an organization from reputational damage because the "halo" influences how people interpret the information about the crisis. However, empirical data to support a halo effect is sparse. Rather, a "Velcro effect" has been found. A history of crises or unfavorable performance history/prior reputation attracts additional reputational damage much like Velcro attracts lint (Coombs and Holladay, 2002, 2006). Instead of finding that positive crisis histories repelled reputational damage (halo effect), the negative crisis histories were generating additional reputational damage (Velcro effect).

Severity of damage has been considered as a possible intensifier as well, but the research thus far has been inconclusive (Coombs and Holladay, 2010). However, a promising reinterpretation of severity as susceptibility has been presented, and early tests are encouraging (Laufer *et al.*, 2005). Once further research is completed, the SCCT model may require revision. Figure 23.1 presents the current conceptualization of the SCCT model.

The last major variable in SCCT is the crisis response strategies. SCCT drew heavily on Benoit's (1995) work on crisis response strategies but integrated his work with other lists to create a composite list of crisis response strategies. Table 23.2 presents the crisis response strategies used in SCCT research. The order and grouping of crisis response strategies reflect how stakeholders perceive the strategies. The crisis response strategies reflect an accommodation continuum: as one moves from *denial* to *diminish* to *rebuild*, the crisis response strategies become increasingly accommodative to the needs of the victims. In turn, this focus on victim concerns increases the perception that the organization is taking responsibility for the crisis (Coombs, 2006).

SCCT views the crisis response strategies dedicated to reputation repair/protection as one of three categories of crisis response strategies based on the work of Sturges (1994). The first two categories of crisis response strategies are instructing information and adjusting information. *Instructing information* helps stakeholders to cope physically with the crisis; it tells stakeholders how to protect themselves from the crisis threat and includes calls to evacuate or shelter in place and directions on how to identify and return a hazardous product (recall guidance). *Adjusting information* helps stakeholders to cope psychologically with a crisis; it can include expressions of sympathy or concern, reports of actions to prevent a repeat of the crisis, and information about the cause of the crisis (Coombs, 2007b; Sturges, 1994).

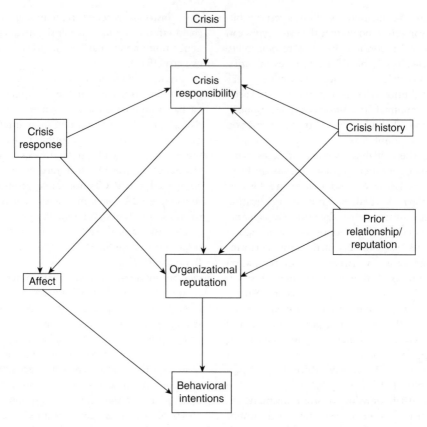

Figure 23.1   Situational crisis communication theory variables.

Table 23.2   Crisis response strategies.

Denial crisis response strategies
  Denial: managers claim that no crisis occurred.
  Attack the accuser: managers confront the person or group that claims the organization is in a crisis.
  Scapegoat: managers blame some outside person or group for the crisis.
Diminish crisis response strategies
  Excuse: managers minimize the organization's responsibility for the crisis by denying any intent to do
  harm and/or claiming an inability to control events that led to the crisis.
  Justification: managers minimize the perceived damage caused by the crisis.
Rebuild crisis response strategies
  Compensation: managers offer money or other gifts to victims.
  Apology: managers accept responsibility for the crisis and ask stakeholders to forgive them.
Bolstering crisis response strategies (supplemental strategies)
  Reminder: managers tell stakeholders about past good works of the organization.
  Ingratiation: managers thank stakeholders and/or praise stakeholders for their help during the crisis.
  Victimage: managers remind stakeholders that the organization is a victim of the crisis as well.

Instructing and adjusting information should come first, and reflect the need to make public safety the number one priority during a crisis. SCCT refers to the communication of instructing and adjusting information as the base response, the first messages to be communicated by crisis managers (Coombs, 2007c; Huang *et al.*, 2005).

SCCT began as a conference presentation in 1994. The first published work using the core ideas appeared in 1995. At that time, however, the theory did not yet have a name, as it was in the early stages of development. Attribution theory was used to construct a 2 × 2 matrix of crisis types. The dimensions were *internal–external control* and *intentional–unintentional*. The four crisis types were *faux pas* (external–unintentional), *terrorism* (external–intentional), *accidents* (internal–unintentional), and *transgressions* (internal–intentional). Additional situation factors included *veracity* of evidence a crisis exists (true, ambiguous, or false), *severity* of the damage from the crisis (major or minor), and *performance history* (prior reputation). Finally, crisis managers needed to consider whether they were addressing victims of the crisis or nonvictims. Decision trees were created for each crisis type; these started with crisis types, followed by evidence, damage, victim status, performance history, and culminated in recommended strategies for each branch in the decision tree.

The decision trees were analyses of the crisis situation. The focal point of such analysis was the crisis responsibility. The crisis response recommendations reflected the crisis responsibility each crisis situation was likely to generate. When crisis responsibility was believed to be high, the decision tree led to a crisis response strategy that took responsibility, such as mortification. For crises with low crisis responsibility, distance strategies such as justification could be used. Coombs' (1995) initial article articulated the foundational ideas that would become SCCT, a title that was first used in 2002 (Coombs and Holladay, 2002). The first empirical test of the foundational ideas was published in 1996.

Operationalizing the key variables

Quantitative research demands that variables be measured. Hence, it was critical to operationalize the key variables in SCCT by developing reliable measures. The key variables at the start of the SCCT's development were personal control, crisis blame, and corporate reputation. *Personal control* was derived from attribution theory and is one of the variables that influences attributions about events. The more people perceive personal control, the more likely they are to associate the crisis with the organization in crisis. Similarly, *blame* was an assessment of control from attribution theory. The more blame people assign to the organization, the more they hold the organization responsible for the crisis.

Personal control was assessed using a five-item personal control scale from McAuley *et al.*'s (1992) revised causal dimension scale with the wording of the items revised to reflect organizations rather than individuals. The reliabilities were acceptable, ranging from 0.84 to 0.89 (Coombs, 1999; Coombs and Holladay, 2001). Initially, external control was measured along with personal control using a scale developed by McAuley *et al.* (1992). However, external control added virtually nothing to explanations of the variance, so it was dropped. Blame was assessed using a three-item blame scale developed by Griffin *et al.* (1992), with the items again modified to reflect organizations rather than individuals. The reliabilities were acceptable, ranging from 0.80 to 0.91 (Coombs, 1999; Coombs and Holladay, 2001, 2002). Initially, personal control and blame were treated as separate concepts. Consistent with other attribution-based studies, however, the data revealed a significant overlap between the two variables. As a result, personal control and blame were collapsed into one variable called *crisis responsibility*. The new variable was measured using the three items from the blame scale and adding two items from the personal control scale. The reliability for the crisis responsibility measure was consistently around 0.81 (Coombs and Holladay, 2007). The crisis responsibility measure is critical to assessing how people are reacting to the crisis type, crisis history, and performance history/prior reputation.

Corporate reputation was measured using the Organizational Reputation Scale (ORP) (Coombs, 2007c). The ORP is based on the character subscale of McCroskey's (1966) credibility measure, modified to reflect organizations rather than individuals. The modifications are the reason the ORP is considered a separate scale. Character was selected as the focus because of its use of trust. Trust is a common element in most corporate reputation assessment instruments. For the SCCT research, a generic corporate reputation scale was needed so that it could be applied to a variety of organizations in a number of different situations. Because trust was the common element in reputation measures, it was selected as the basis for a generic corporate reputation scale (Coombs, 2007c). The ORP illustrates how corporate reputation research has influenced SCCT research. A key measure in SCCT was developed in accordance with how the corporate reputation research has conceptualized reputation assessment.

Initially, the ORP used a 10-item scale. The reliabilities were acceptable, ranging from 0.82 to 0.92 (Coombs and Holladay, 2002). A five-item version was developed to shorten the length of the surveys being used in the SCCT research. As the research progressed, other variables were added increasing the length of the survey. The various scales were reviewed to see if they could be shortened to reduce respondent fatigue yet maintain the reliability of the scale. The five-item version of the ORP showed consistent and acceptable reliability ranging from 0.82 to 0.87 (Coombs and Holladay, 2002, 2006, 2007). The ORP is critical to assessing the dominant dependent variable in SCCT – corporate reputation.

The independent variables in SCCT include crisis type, crisis history, performance history/prior reputation, and crisis response strategy. The independent variables are manipulated through the crisis scenarios that the respondents read or viewed. Most stakeholders learn about and experience a crisis through mediated reports of the crisis (Deephouse, 2000), which is why news stories are used as the stimuli for the SCCT experiments. Each study includes manipulation checks to ensure that respondents understood the designated differences between the manipulations of the independent variables.

SCCT research results and implications

Early SCCT research focused on identifying whether the variables were related as prescribed in the theory; this included verifying how people perceived the various crisis types. Initially, the crisis types were arrayed using the 2×2 matrix. As noted earlier, research confirmed that respondents did perceive crises according to matrix, but *personal control* and *intention* (*blame*) overlapped and thus were combined to form *crisis responsibility; external control* was eliminated because it added little to explanations of the variance. When SCCT shifted to crisis responsibility, the matrix was converted to a continuum. Crisis types were now arrayed according to attributions of crisis control. Cluster analysis was used to form the three categories of crisis types reported in Table 23.1 (Coombs and Holladay, 2002). Tests in later studies support this initial category system, as people consistently viewed victim, accidental, and intentional crises differently in terms of crisis responsibility (e.g., Claeys *et al.*, 2010).

The attributions of crisis responsibility are meaningful. The experimental studies demonstrate a consistent relationship between crisis responsibility and corporate reputation (Coombs, 2007c). Stronger attributions of crisis responsibility have been shown to be related to lower ratings of corporate reputation. Studies have consistently found correlations of over −0.30 between crisis responsibility and corporate reputation. The evidence is more than correlations, it is causal. Using experimental designs with random assignment, the manipulation of crisis responsibility (independent variable) does change the assessment of corporate reputation (dependent variable) (Coombs and Holladay, 2001). The crisis responsibility–

corporate reputation relationship is the central relationship for the initial conceptualization of SCCT.

The intensifiers become relevant once the relationship between crisis responsibility and corporate reputation has been established. Why bother to examine intensifiers if crisis responsibility has little or no effect on corporate reputation? Research results provide evidence for both *crisis history* and *performance history/prior reputation* as intensifiers. Crisis history was examined by comparing the same company in the same crisis but varying the crisis history. Respondents in the condition with a history of crises reported a reputation that was significantly lower than respondents with either no crisis history or a positive crisis history. The positive crisis history noted the organization had never had an event like the current crisis, while the no crisis history condition gave no mention of past crises (Coombs, 2004; Elliot, 2010). Moreover, crisis history had both an indirect effect (through crisis responsibility) and a direct effect on reputation. Coombs (2004) found effects in both the accidental and victim crisis categories.

Performance history has a logical connection to corporate reputation, as it is a form of reputation and is heavily influenced by corporate reputation research. It is logical that if an organization comes into a crisis with a favorable reputation, its reputation should remain strong after the crisis. A variety of corporate reputation and crisis experts posit that a favorable prior reputation is an asset during a crisis (Dowling, 2002; Fombrun and van Riel, 2004; Ulmer, 2001). There are two possible explanations for the benefit of a favorable prior reputation: the bank account and the halo effect. The bank account explanation argues that any crisis will cost an organization some of its reputational credits. Therefore, an organization should bank reputational credits prior to a crisis. If an organization has strong reserve of reputational credits, spending a few during a crisis hurts it less than it hurts an organization that has limited reputational credits before a crisis (Coombs and Holladay, 2006).

The halo effect suggests that positive perceptions of the organization deflect the negative information generated by a crisis and that stakeholders will be willing to give the organization in crisis the benefit of the doubt (Fombrun, 1996). SCCT research has found limited support for the halo effect. In instances where the prior reputation is extremely favorable, at least a 6 on a 7-point scale, a halo effect is found in technical-error accidents. There was also evidence to support the bank account interpretation of prior reputations. Moreover, performance history was found to have an indirect (through crisis responsibility) and direct effect on corporate reputation (Coombs and Holladay, 2001, 2006). The halo effect research in crisis communication is a direct result of ideas presented in the corporate reputation literature. Currently, research shows limited support for the halo effect and more support for the bank account analogy. Strong reputations are unlikely to completely deflect reputational damage but do provide strong account when crisis prompt withdrawals from the reputational account.

More recently, SCCT has begun to look at a broader range of independent variables including affect, negative word of mouth, and purchase intention (e.g., Coombs and Holladay, 2005). Early crisis research in marketing made links between attributions of crisis responsibility and both purchase intention and affect, so it was a logical extension for SCCT (Jorgensen, 1996; Mowen, 1980). The study of affect has concentrated on anger and how it acts as a motivator. For instance, research has shown how anger increases the likelihood of a person engaging in negative word of mouth after a crisis. This phenomenon has been called the negative communication dynamic. Anger is also a mediator between crisis responsibility and purchase intention (Coombs and Holladay, 2007).

Implications of the research for crisis communicators

SCCT is a form of evidence-based crisis communication information. An evidence-based

Table 23.3 Recommendations from SCCT.

1. Informing and adjusting information should be the initial response for a crisis that has victims or potential victims.
2. The base response is effective for victim and accidental crises with no intensifying factors.
3. Diminish crisis response strategies can be used for accidental crises with no intensifying factors.
4. Rebuild crisis response strategies should be used for intentional crises and accidental crises that have intensifying factors.
5. Denial crisis response strategies should be reserved for rumor and challenge crises.
6. The victimage crisis response strategy can be used with the base response for victim crises.
7. The reminder crisis response strategy may be useful when an organization has past good works but risks creating the impression of the organization as egocentric. Reminder is not recommended when attributions of crisis responsibility are strong.
8. The ingratiation crisis response strategy can be used anytime stakeholders have helped in addressing the crisis.

approach means that managers draw on the best available evidence when making decisions (Rousseau, 2006). SCCT uses empirical methods, driven by theory, to generate evidence used to understand the selection of crisis response strategies (Coombs, 2010b). The research from SCCT has been used to develop a set of prescriptive guidelines for crisis managers. Table 23.3 presents a quick summary of the advice provided by SCCT.

The SCCT research using crisis response strategies (e.g., Claeys et al., 2010; Coombs and Holladay, 1996, 2009) has confirmed that matching the level of crisis responsibility attributions to the perceived level of accepting responsibility in the crisis response does maximize reputational benefits during a crisis. SCCT provides a set of tools for evaluating crisis situations in terms of how people will perceive crisis responsibility. From that assessment, crisis managers then know which crisis response strategies will be more or less effective in protecting reputational assets. Crisis managers must combine the SCCT information with any financial or legal constraints they face (Tyler, 1997) to select their crisis response strategies, and at times, constraints may prevent crisis managers from employing the ideal crisis response strategies. SCCT helps crisis managers understand what benefits can be derived from the remaining crisis response strategy options by explaining how the "nonrecommended" crisis response strategies are likely to affect stakeholder perceptions of the crisis and/or organization in crisis.

Limitations

SCCT has used lab experiments, and as a result, the research has the limitations of any lab experiments in that the setting is artificial. However, the artificial nature of the experiments is a trade-off for the control needed to establish causal relationships (Stacks, 2002). Moreover, the majority of the experiments have used undergraduate students as respondents. When crisis managers have been used, however, the findings were no different from those using student populations (Coombs, 1999). Similarly, when consumers were used, again there was no difference in the findings (Claeys et al., 2010). SCCT is interested in nonvictims for crises and in testing basic human attribution and perception processes. Therefore, the student respondents fit within the parameters of the desired population and are viable respondents.

SCCT and Corporate Reputation

Since its earliest incarnation, SCCT has been intricately linked to corporate reputation. The initial outcome/dependent variable for SCCT has been corporate reputation. From the start,

SCCT was interested in understanding how crisis response strategies could be used to protect or repair the reputation damage associated with a crisis. Hence, SCCT drew on the corporate reputation research and added to that body of knowledge as well. The preceding discussion of SCCT has illustrated the connection with corporate reputation, but the following section expands upon that association.

Definition of crisis and corporate reputation

A crisis can be defined as "the perception of an unpredictable event that threatens important expectations of stakeholders and can seriously impact an organization's performance and generate negative outcomes" (Coombs, 2007b, pp. 2–3). One of the negative outcomes associated with a crisis is damage to the corporate reputation. Furthermore, the definition is influenced by the weight corporate reputation research was placing on stakeholder perceptions. A corporate reputation can be defined as how positively or negatively stakeholders perceive an organization. Corporate reputations are evaluative and developed through direct and indirect experience with an organization (Brown and Roed, 2001). Media reports can play a critical role in reputation formation. As noted earlier, most of the information stakeholders learn about a corporation is derived from media reports (Deephouse, 2000). Media reports give salience to particular information, thereby helping to shape reputations (Deephouse, 2000; Wartick, 1992). Stakeholders often draw on small bits of salient information when making reputation judgments (Carroll and McCombs, 2003).

When stakeholders process media reports and other information about a crisis, that crisis information becomes part of the indirect experience used to construct a corporate reputation. Crises stand out and are memorable because they are unexpected and negative (Fishman, 1999). This characteristic of standing out among other pieces of information gives crises the potential to have a significant impact on reputation formation. Well-formed positive corporate reputations, however, offer some protection from a crisis. As noted earlier, some crisis research has shown a limited halo effect for strong, positive corporate reputations (Coombs and Holladay, 2006). Nevertheless, the halo effect from a corporate reputation is limited. Stakeholders often do not dismiss the new negative information from a crisis; the negative information does affect their view of the organization, resulting in a tarnishing of the corporate reputation. Therefore, crisis response strategies are used to prevent and/or repair the damage a crisis inflicts on the corporate reputation.

Insights into corporate reputation from SCCT

The corporate reputation is a valuable, intangible asset for an organization. A great deal of time and effort can go into developing a favorable corporate reputation. Crises are a very real danger for any organization. Crises are a matter of when, not if, in corporate life. Any managers who believe that their organization is immune to crises are delusional and are creating unnecessary risk for their organizations and stakeholders. When a crisis does occur, it is a threat to the reputation of the corporation involved. SCCT was developed as a way to understand how best to use crisis response strategies for reputational protection during a crisis. SCCT has offered insights into how crises can affect the corporate reputation and how communication can be used to protect corporate reputation during a crisis.

As the previous section detailed, SCCT has identified a number of crisis factors that can negatively affect corporate reputations during a crisis. By modeling the effects of the crisis situation on corporate reputation, we gain insights into how crises may negatively impact corporate reputations. Consistent with early research, SCCT has documented a strong, negative relationship between crisis responsibility and corporate reputation (e.g., Jorgensen, 1996). Crises become more harmful to a corporate reputation as attributions of crisis responsibility increase. SCCT developed a set of crisis types that can be used to predict how much crisis responsibility stakeholders are likely to attribute to an organization during a crisis. Crisis history and performance history/prior reputation can intensify attribution of crisis responsibility. Moreover, histories or a negative performance history/prior reputation has a direct, negative effect on corporate reputation as well. By understanding how the crisis situation affects the corporation, managers can more effectively employ crisis response strategies for reputational protection. If managers know why crises are having a negative effect on corporate reputation, they are in a better position to use communication to prevent or to lessen that negative effect.

SCCT considers a number of ways to use crisis response strategies for reputation protection based on how a crisis affects the corporate reputation. The ways in which SCCT uses communication for reputation protection are related to the categories of crisis response strategies presented in Table 23.2. The *denial* crisis response strategies attempt to establish that either there is no crisis or that the organization is in no way responsible for the crisis. For instance, the *denial* strategy says there is no crisis, and the *scapegoating* strategy claims someone else is responsible for the crisis. The denial crisis response strategies seek to eliminate crisis responsibility. If the organization is not responsible for the crisis or if no crisis exists, there should be no reputational damage from the crisis. It should be noted, however, that denial is a dangerous crisis response strategy. If it is proven that the organization has some responsibility for the crisis, denial will intensify the reputational damage from the crisis (Ferrin *et al.*, 2007; Kim *et al.*, 2004).

The *diminish* strategies seek to establish a minimal level of responsibility for the crisis. They communicate that a crisis did happen and the organization is involved, but that stakeholders should attribute only minimal crisis responsibility to the organization. For instance, the *excuse* crisis response strategy tries to establish that the organization had little control over the crisis event and/or did not intend to create a harmful situation. Given the relationship

between crisis responsibility and corporate reputation, minimizing attributions of crisis responsibility also serves to minimize the damage the crisis can inflict on the corporate reputation. A corporate reputation is protected when attributions of crisis responsibility can be minimized.

For many crisis situations, however, denial and diminish will not provide effective reputation protection. Frequently, the organization is involved in the crisis and attributions of crisis responsibility will be high – intentional crises and accidental crises plus an intensifier. In high-crisis-responsibility crises, there will be damage to the corporate reputation. *Rebuild* crisis response strategies are used to repair some of the reputational damage. For instance, *compensation* and *apology* are perceived by stakeholders as the organization's taking responsibility for the crisis and addressing the needs of victims. Such positive actions help to replenish the reputational bank account. However, apology should not be a default response. Apology can be an over-response to a crisis when there is minimal or no responsibility for a crisis, and stakeholders can actually react negatively to the misuse of an apology (Ferrin *et al.*, 2007; Siomkos and Shrivastava, 1993).

Finally, the *bolstering* crisis response strategies represent a set of supplementary responses. The bolstering crisis response strategies are not to be used by themselves but rather in combination with other crisis response strategies. Using only the bolstering crisis response strategies could create the impression that the organization is trying to avoid the crisis by focusing on other factors. However, the bolstering strategies can work well with other crisis response strategies by highlighting positive factors or reminding people that the organization is a victim of the crisis too.

Crisis response strategies do not affect stakeholder perceptions, and ultimately, the postcrisis corporate reputation, by only one means. Crisis response strategies may seek to alter perceptions of the crisis situation itself through denial or diminish strategies or perceptions of the organization in crisis through rebuild and/or bolstering strategies.

Future Research Directions

A number of future research directions in SCCT are relevant to corporate reputation. This section will review four future research topics involving the intersection of SCCT and corporate reputation: (1) the relationship between affect and reputation following a crisis, (2) the value of "other" crisis response strategies, (3) the application of additional ideas from the attribution theory, and (4) the connection between SCCT and the contingency theory.

SCCT examines the affect – primarily anger – generated by a crisis. Corporate reputation and anger are both affected by a crisis. The question becomes how to order these two variables following a crisis. There are three options: (1) anger affects the postcrisis corporate reputation, (2) the postcrisis corporate reputation affects anger, or (3) anger and the postcrisis corporate reputation are formed simultaneously. Figure 23.2 illustrates the three options. The order does matter, as SCCT explores the effect of crisis response strategies on anger. For instance, if anger shapes the postcrisis corporate reputation, then efforts to reduce anger have an effect on corporate reputation. It is important to consider how anger and postcrisis corporate reputation are related in order to appreciate how attempts to mitigate anger from a crisis will impact corporate reputations (Fediuk *et al.*, 2010). Again, corporate reputation research is influencing crisis communication research. Insights that corporate reputation research is providing into the relationship between affect and corporate reputation are essential to SCCT research.

The study of crisis response strategies has been heavily skewed toward apologies. Consider the 2010 special issue of *Corporate Communication*, which was devoted to apologies in crisis management. In that special issue, Frandsen and Johansen (2010) examined the complexity of an apology within a global context, while Pace *et al.* (2010) compared the effects of apology and expressing regrets on corporate reputation and anger. Additional crisis response strategies that have received attention include compensation, concern/sympathy, and denial (e.g., Coombs and Holladay, 2008). From this research, we know how these strategies are likely to affect postcrisis corporate reputations across a variety of crisis types.

However, there are a number of "other" crisis response strategies that have received little if any attention from researchers. As a result, we know little about the effects of these "other" crisis response strategies on postcrisis corporate reputations and their value to reputation protection. In particular, we know very little about the bolstering (secondary) crisis response strategies. Bolstering is a recognized strategy in rhetoric (Ice, 1991), but we know little about its effectiveness in reputation protection and what situational factors increase or decrease its effectiveness. For example, does victimage work equally well for an organization with a positive prior reputation and one with a negative prior reputation? It could be that stakeholders engage

Figure 23.2 Anger and postcrisis corporate reputation.

in schadenfreude – taking joy in the failures of a disliked organization. Perhaps prior reputation is critical to the ability of bolstering crisis response strategies to protect corporate reputations. Increasing our understanding of the effectiveness and proper use of additional crisis response strategies would improve the advice we can offer to crisis managers seeking to protect reputational assets.

Turning to another direction for research, although SCCT is rooted in the attribution theory, it has used a limited set of ideas from this base theory. A number of principles from the attribution theory could be translated to crisis communication and tested for their relevance. Schwarz's (2008) application of covariation to SCCT is an example of how other principles from the attribution theory can be adapted for use in crisis communication. The fundamental attribution error principle and the discounting principle (Kelley, 1971) could have potential application to crisis communication through the SCCT lens. Such new principles could provide greater insight into how a crisis affects corporate reputations. In turn, the knowledge we gain about how a crisis affects a corporate reputation could be used to improve the application of crisis response strategies for reputation protection.

Another theoretical approach, the contingency theory, overlaps with SCCT in its treatment of crisis communication (Coombs, 2010b; Holtzhausen and Roberts, 2009). The contingency theory is a grand theory of public relations that focuses on the degree to which an organization uses an advocacy or accommodative response when in conflict with stakeholders (Cameron *et al.*, 2008; Cancel *et al.*, 1997; Pang *et al.*, 2010). Grand theories seek to explain an entire discipline and can be applied to all subdisciplines as well. Stance is a key variable in the contingency theory: stance is the organizational response to conflict and ranges from advocacy to accommodation. In total, there are over 80 variables in the contingency theory (Cancel *et al.*, 1997). One of those variables that has been applied to crisis communication is threat appraisal, which concentrates on whether the threat is internal or

external to an organization; internal threats are considered to be the greater threat (Jin, 2009; Jin and Cameron, 2007).

SCCT and the contingency theory are similar in two critical areas: responses and crisis types. As with the contingency theory, the crisis response strategies in SCCT are arranged on an accommodation continuum. SCCT focuses on concern for the victim (accommodation) and how that is translated into perceptions of taking responsibility for the crisis. The contingency theory emphasizes advocacy and accommodation in relation to a conflict situation. Both theories share an underlying accommodation dimension to their crisis communication options.

SCCT views crisis types primarily through crisis responsibility, while the contingency theory uses external–internal threat when applying the theory to crisis communication through the integrated crisis mapping model (Jin and Pang, 2010). The use of internal and external threat has similarities to SCCT's original conceptualization of crisis types as a 2×2 matrix that included internal and external control from the attribution theory. While they are based in different theories and using different names, the consistency between the two theories for crisis types is remarkable. With some concerted effort, SCCT and the contingency theory could be integrated. SCCT would supply the more crisis-specific focus grounded in the attribution theory, while the contingency theory would supply a wide array of additional variables that could be important to shaping perceptions of the crisis situation and the organization in crisis (Coombs, 2010b). These new variables could add insights to improve the reputation protection potential of crisis response strategies.

All four of the research lines outlined earlier have the potential to shed new light on the intersection of crisis communication and corporate reputation. Each can provide new insights about understanding the crisis situation and how crisis response strategies affect people's reactions to crisis, including the effect on postcrisis corporate reputation. Whatever new directions in research are pursued, a strong link will remain between SCCT research and corporate reputation.

Conclusion

SCCT was created with corporate reputation as a key variable. Because of this close connection, SCCT has been influenced by research in corporate reputation as well as contributing to the corporate reputation literature. SCCT has sought to understand how to use crisis response strategies to protect corporate reputations from a crisis. Crises are a natural part of an organization's life and can be a significant threat to the corporate reputation (Barton, 2001). The primary objective in crisis communication is public safety. Once public safety is addressed, crisis managers can consider the corporate reputation. Crisis communication can seek to insure that the postcrisis corporate reputation is as strong as the precrisis corporate reputation or suffers as little reputational damage as possible during a crisis. SCCT continues to examine how crisis response strategies can be used to prevent and to repair reputational damage inflicted by a crisis – to unpack the reputation protection potential of crisis response strategies. SCCT demonstrates the intersection of crisis communication and corporate reputation by illustrating the effect each area has on the other. Continued SCCT research will extend our understanding of the crisis situation and how crisis response strategies can be used most effectively to protect and to repair corporate reputations.

References

Barton, L. (2001) *Crisis in Organizations II* (2nd ed.). Cincinnati, OH: College Divisions South Western.

Benoit, W.L. (1995) *Accounts, Excuses, and Apologies: A Theory of Image Restoration*. Albany, NY: State University of New York Press.

Benson, J.A. (1988) Crisis revisited: An analysis of the strategies used by Tylenol in the second tampering episode. *Central States Speech Journal*, 38, 49–66.

Bitzer, L.F. (1968) The rhetorical situation. *Philosophy and Rhetoric*, 1, 165–168.

Brown, K.C. and Roed, B. (2001) Delahaye Medilink's 2001 media reputation index results. *The Gauge*, 16, 1–2. Retrieved from http://www.thegauge.com/v16n3laydownlawprint.thm (last accessed September 23, 2001).

Cameron, G.T., Pang, A., and Jin, Y. (2008) Contingency theory. In T.L. Hansen-Horn and B.D. Neff (eds), *Public Relations: From Theory to Practice*. New York: Pearson, pp. 134–157.

Cancel, A.E., Cameron, G.T., Sallot, L.M., and Motrook, M.A. (1997) It depends: A contingency theory of accommodation in public relations. *Journal of Public Relations Research*, 9, 31–63.

Carroll, C.E. and McCombs, M. (2003) Agenda-setting effects of business news on the public's image and opinions about major corporations. *Corporate Reputation Review*, 16, 36–46.

Claeys, A.S., Cauberghe, V., and Vyncke, P. (2010) Restoring reputations in times of crisis: An experimental study of the situational crisis communication theory and the moderating effects of locus of control. *Public Relations Review*, 36, 256–262.

Coombs, W.T. (1995) Choosing the right words: The development of guidelines for the selection of the "appropriate" crisis response strategies. *Management Communication Quarterly*, 8, 447–476.

Coombs, W.T. (1999) Information and compassion in crisis responses: A test of their effects. *Journal of Public Relations Research*, 11, 125–142.

Coombs, W.T. (2004) Impact of past crises on current crisis communications: Insights from situational crisis communication theory. *Journal of Business Communication*, 41, 265–289.

Coombs, W.T. (2006) The protective powers of crisis response strategies: Managing reputational assets during a crisis. *Journal of Promotion Management*, 12, 241–260.

Coombs, W.T. (2007a) Attribution theory as a guide for post-crisis communication research. *Public Relations Review*, 33, 135–139.

Coombs, W.T. (2007b) *Ongoing Crisis Communication: Planning, Managing, and Responding* (2nd ed.). Los Angeles, CA: Sage.

Coombs, W.T. (2007c) Protecting organization reputations during a crisis: The development and application of situational crisis communication theory. *Corporate Reputation Review*, 10(3), 163–177.

Coombs, W.T. (2009) Conceptualizing crisis communication. In R.L. Heath and H.D. O'Hair (eds), *Handbook of Crisis and Risk Communication*. New York: Routledge, pp. 100–119.

Coombs, W.T. (2010a) Parameters for crisis communication. In W.T. Coombs and S.J. Holladay (eds), *Handbook of Crisis Communication*. Malden, MA: Blackwell Publishing, pp. 17–53.

Coombs, W.T. (2010b) Pursuing evidence-based crisis communication. In W.T. Coombs and S.J. Holladay (eds), *Handbook of Crisis Communication*. Malden, MA: Blackwell Publishing, pp. 719–725.

Coombs, W.T. and Holladay, S.J. (1996) Communication and attributions in a crisis: An experimental study of crisis communication. *Journal of Public Relations Research*, 8(4), 279–295.

Coombs, W.T. and Holladay, S.J. (2001) An extended examination of the crisis situation: A fusion of the relational management and symbolic approaches. *Journal of Public Relations Research*, 13, 321–340.

Coombs, W.T. and Holladay, S.J. (2002) Helping crisis managers protect reputational assets: Initial tests of the situational crisis communication theory. *Management Communication Quarterly*, 16, 165–186.

Coombs, W.T. and Holladay, S.J. (2005) Exploratory study of stakeholder emotions: Affect and crisis. In N.M. Ashkanasy, W.J. Zerbe, and C.E.J. Hartel (eds), *Research on Emotion in Organizations: Volume 1: The Effect of Affect in Organizational Settings*, New York: Elsevier, pp. 271–288.

Coombs, W.T. and Holladay, S.J. (2006) Unpacking the halo effect: Reputation and crisis management. *Journal of Communication Management*, 10(2), 123–137.

Coombs, W.T. and Holladay, S.J. (2007) The negative communication dynamic: Exploring the impact of stakeholder affect on behavioral intentions. *Journal of Communication Management*, 11, 300–312.

Coombs, W.T. and Holladay, S.J. (2008) Comparing apology to equivalent crisis response strategies: Clarifying apology's role and value in crisis communication. *Public Relations Review*, 34, 252–257.

Coombs, W.T. and Holladay, S.J. (2009) Further explorations of post-crisis communication: Effect of media and response strategies on perceptions and intentions. *Public Relations Review*, 35, 1–6.

Coombs, W.T. and Holladay, S.J. (2010) Examining the effects of mutability and framing on perceptions of human error and technical error crises: Implications for situational crisis communication theory. In W.T. Coombs and S.J. Holladay (eds), *Handbook of Crisis Communication*. Malden, MA: Blackwell Publishing, pp. 181–204.

Deephouse, D.L. (2000) Media reputation as a strategic resource: An integration of mass communication and resource-based theories. *Journal of Management*, 26, 1091–1112.

Dionisopolous, G.N. and Vibbert, S.L. (1988) CBS vs. Mobil Oil: Charges of creative bookkeeping. In H.R. Ryan (ed.), *Oratorical Encounters: Selected Studies and Sources of 20th Century Political Accusation and Apologies*. Westport, CT: Greenwood, pp. 214–252.

Dowling, G. (2002) *Creating Corporate Reputations: Identity, Image, and Performance*. New York: Oxford University Press.

Elliot, J.D. (2010) How do past crises affect publics' perceptions of current events? An experiment testing corporate reputation during an adverse event. In W.T. Coombs and S.J. Holladay (eds), *Handbook of Crisis Communication*. Malden, MA: Blackwell Publishing, pp. 205–220.

Fediuk, T.A., Coombs, W.T., and Botero, I.C. (2010) Exploring crisis from a receiver perspective: Understanding stakeholder reactions during crisis events. In W.T. Coombs and S.J. Holladay (eds), *Handbook of Crisis Communication*. Malden, MA: Blackwell Publishing, pp. 635–656.

Ferrin, D.L., Kim, P.H., Cooper, C.D., and Dirks, K.T. (2007) Silence speaks volumes: The effectiveness of reticence in comparison to apology and denial for responding to integrity-and competence-based trust violations. *Journal of Applied Psychology*, 92, 893–908.

Fishman, D.A. (1999) ValuJet flight 592: Crisis communication theory blended and extended. *Communication Quarterly*, 47(4), 345–375.

Fombrun, C.J. (1996) *Reputation: Realizing Value from the Corporate Image*. Boston, MA: Harvard Business School Press.

Fombrun, C.J. and van Riel, C.B.M. (2004) *Fame & Fortune: How Successful Companies Build Winning Reputations*. New York: Prentice Hall Financial Times.

Frandsen, F. and Johansen, W. (2010) Apologizing in a globalizing world: Crisis communication and apologetic ethics. *Corporate Communi-*

cations: An International Journal, 15(4), 350–364.

Griffin, M., Babin, B.J., and Darden, W.R. (1992) Consumer assessments of responsibility for product-related injuries: The impact of regulations, warnings, and promotional policies. *Advances in Consumer Research, 19,* 870–877.

Hearit, K.M. (1994) Apologies and public relations crises at Chrysler, Toshiba, and Volvo. *Public Relations Review, 20*(2), 113–125.

Hearit, K.M. (1995) "Mistakes were made": Organizations, apologia, and crises of social legitimacy. *Communication Studies, 46,* 1–17.

Hearit, K.M. (2001) Corporate apologia: When an organization speaks in defense of itself. In R.L. Heath (ed.), *Handbook of Public Relations.* Thousand Oaks, CA: Sage, pp. 501–511.

Hearit, K.M. (2006) *Crisis Management by Apology: Corporate Response to Allegations of Wrongdoing.* Mahwah, NJ: Lawrence Erlbaum Associates.

Holtzhausen, D.R. and Roberts, G.F. (2009) An investigation into the role of image repair theory in strategic conflict management. *Journal of Public Relations Research, 21,* 165–186.

Huang, Y.H., Lin, Y.H., and Su, S.H. (2005) Crisis communicative strategies in Taiwan: Category, continuum, and cultural implication. *Public Relations Review, 31,* 229–238.

Ice, R. (1991) Corporate publics and rhetorical strategies: The case of Union Carbide's Bhopal crisis. *Management Communication Quarterly, 3,* 41–362.

Jin, Y. (2009) The effects of public's cognitive appraisal of emotions in crises on crisis coping and strategy assessment. *Public Relations Review, 35*(3), 310–313.

Jin, Y. and Cameron, G.T. (2007) The effects of threat type and duration on public relations practitioner's cognitive, affective, and conative responses to crisis situations. *Journal of Public Relations Research, 19,* 255–281.

Jin, Y. and Pang, A. (2010) Future directions of crisis communication research: Emotions in crisis – The next frontier. In W.T. Coombs and S.J. Holladay (eds), *Handbook of Crisis Communication.* Malden, MA: Blackwell Publishing, pp. 677–682.

Jorgensen, B.K. (1996) Components of consumer reaction to company-related mishaps: A structural equation model approach. *Advances in Consumer Research, 23,* 346–351.

Kelley, H.H. (1971) *Attribution in Social Interaction.* New York: General Learning Press.

Kim, P.H., Ferrin, D.L., Cooper, C.D., and Dirks, K.T. (2004) Removing the shadow of suspicion: The effects of apology versus denial for repairing competence- versus integrity-based trust violations. *Journal of Applied Psychology, 89,* 104–118.

Laufer, D., Gillespie, K., McBride, B., and Gonzalez, S. (2005) The role of severity in consumer attributions of blame: Defensive attributions in product harm crises in Mexico. *Journal of International Consumer Marketing, 17*(2/3), 33–50.

McAuley, E., Duncan, T.E., and Russell, D.W. (1992) Measuring causal attributions: The revised causal dimension scale (CDII). *Personality and Social Psychology Bulletin, 18,* 566–573.

McCroskey, J.C. (1966) *An Introduction to Rhetorical Communication.* Englewood Cliffs, NJ: Prentice Hall.

Mowen, J.C. (1980) Further information on consumer perceptions of product recalls. *Advances in Consumer Research, 8,* 519–523.

Pace, K.M., Fediuk, T.A., and Botero, I.C. (2010) The acceptance of responsibility and expressions of regret in organizational apologies after a transgression. *Corporate Communications: An International Journal, 15*(4), 410–427.

Pang, A., Jin, Y., and Cameron, G.T. (2010) Contingency theory conflict management: Directions for the practice of crisis communication from a decade of theory development, discovery, and dialogue. In W.T. Coombs and S.J. Holladay (eds), *Handbook of Crisis Communication.* Malden, MA: Blackwell Publishing, pp. 527–549.

Rousseau, D.M. (2006) Is there such a thing as "evidence-based management"? *Academy of Review, 31,* 256–269.

Schwarz, A. (2008) Covariation-based causal attributions during organizational crises: Suggestions for extending situational crisis communication theory. *International Journal of Strategic Communication, 2,* 31–53.

Siomkos, G. and Shrivastava, P. (1993) Responding to product liability crises. *Long Range Planning, 26*(5), 72–79.

Stacks, D.W. (2002) *Primer of Public Relations Research.* New York: Guilford Publications.

Sturges, D.L. (1994) Communicating through crisis: A strategy for organizational survival. *Management Communication Quarterly, 7*(3), 297–316.

Tyler, L. (1997) Liability means never being able to say you're sorry: Corporate guilt, legal constraints, and defensiveness in corporate communication. *Management Communication Quarterly, 11,* 51–73.

Ulmer, R.R. (2001) Effective crisis management through established stakeholder relationships. *Management Communication Quarterly, 14,* 590–615.

Wartick, S. (1992) The relationship between intense media exposure and change in corporate reputation. *Business & Society, 31,* 33–49.

Weiner, B. (1986) *An Attributional Theory of Motivation and Emotion.* New York: Springer-Verlag.

Weiner, B. (2006) *Social Motivation, Justice, and the Moral Emotions: An Attributional Approach.* Mahwah, NJ: Lawrence Erlbaum Associates.

24

Corporate Reputation and the Theory of Social Capital

Vilma Luoma-aho

University of Jyväskylä, Finland

Social capital as a theory has only in the recent decades received widespread attention though its roots date back to early theorizing on communities and social collaboration. The links between social capital and communication have been established, but social capital is most often viewed as a mere by-product of a well-working community, not an aim in itself. This chapter takes the concept one step further and introduces the theory behind social capital and examines the different ways in which it contributes to corporate reputation. The chapter argues that social capital can explain how reputation works in practice. The proposition made in this chapter is that corporate reputation affects the amount of social capital available for a corporation or its representatives via trust. The interrelations of social capital and reputation are two way: a good reputation enables the formation of social capital, while at the same time social capital may help in establishing a good reputation.

Introduction

Links between social capital and communication require clarification, and corporate reputation provides an entry point that has previously been much overlooked. The theory of social capital can help explain how reputation works in practice: social capital via communication enforces the virtuous circle of good experiences and collaboration. Trust becomes central, as much of communication depends on the relationship and its attributes. In fact, the proposition made in this chapter is that corporate reputation affects the amount of social capital available for a corporation or its representatives. As new and social media make corporate social capital visible, communication becomes critically important, and social capital is becoming the "reputation of the future."

This chapter is organized as follows: first, the history and origins of social capital are presented, and the links to corporate reputation are viewed. Second, the theoretical roots of social capital are explained, and the concept is defined. The links between social capital and communication are analyzed, and the focus is on different types of social capital. The question whether social capital is an individual or an

The Handbook of Communication and Corporate Reputation, First Edition. Edited by Craig E. Carroll.
© 2013 John Wiley & Sons, Inc. Published 2015 by John Wiley & Sons, Inc.

organizational gain is also posed, and previous studies on social capital are both introduced and criticized. Third, the theoretical relevance of social capital to corporate reputation in practice is described through a model of "the cycle of social capital." To end, future directions of research in this area are discussed.

History/Origins of Social Capital

Social capital owes its origin to such concepts as social connectedness, referring to formal memberships as well as informal social networks, and generalized reciprocity, social trust, and tolerance. Social capital describes the relational resources attainable through networks of social relationships (Coleman, 1990; Lin, 2001; Portes, 1998; Putnam, 1995): it enables people to collaborate, socialize, establish communities, and live together. Social capital can be understood as a form of intangible capital, a metaphor derived from other types of capital: "Whereas physical capital refers to physical objects and human capital refers to the properties of individuals, social capital refers to connections among individuals – social networks and the norms of reciprocity and trustworthiness that arise from them. In that sense, social capital is closely related to what some have called 'civic virtue'" (Putnam, 2000, p. 19).

The central idea behind social capital is collaboration, and Portes (1998) points out that already the works of the French sociologist Durkheim in the nineteenth century note the importance of being connected in a community as an antidote against anomie and self-destruction. Similarly, the sociologists of the twentieth-century Chicago School theorized about possible ways of recreating and building the sense of community that had been lost during the formation of the big cities in the United States. Communication, they argued, was central for creating and maintaining a sense of community (Cooley, 1909, 1918; Damico, 1978; Dewey, 1916/1963; McDermott, 1981; Mead, 1934); some even saw society to exist purely through the processes of communication. The Chicago School dreamed of "the Great Community" where a strong sense of community would reign through the means of communication and the media (Dewey, 1916/1963, 1938/1963). Interestingly, almost a centennium later, scholars on social capital (Putnam, 1993) have blamed the media, more specifically television, for destroying the sense of community that comes from meeting people and working together in informal clubs and associations. When the sense of community is lost, so is social capital, as people no longer have the connections and relationships they would need to thrive and feel part of a community.

As a concept, social capital was identified by Bourdieu (1986) and later given a clearer theoretical framework and subjected to scholarly research by Coleman (1988, 1990). The concept has since been popularized through the studies and writings of the political scientist Putnam (1993, 1995, 2000). Woolcock (2001) notes that the sources of social capital are more important than the consequences. Coleman and Bourdieu consider social capital to be an attribute of an individual, whereas Putnam views it as an attribute of communities. Coleman distinguishes three forms of social capital: obligations and expectations based on the trustworthiness of the social environment; flow and sharing of information through the social structure enabling social action; and norms along with sanctions to maintain them. Nahapiet and Ghoshal (1998) consider social capital to consist of network position (a structural component) and trust in the relationships within the network (relational component).

Social relations have both positive and negative outcomes: Coleman's (1988) self-interest paradigm demonstrated how a social system consists of actors acting based on self-interest but are simultaneously embedded in and limited by interdependent relationships. For Putnam, social capital consists of "features of social organization, such as trust, norms, and networks that can improve the efficiency of society by facilitating coordinated actions" (Putnam et al., 1993, p. 167). According to his thinking, social capital benefits not only those involved, but also bystanders and society at large, as the benefits vary in nature from decreased tribal conflict to voter turnout, lower transaction costs, and satisfied citizens (Putnam et al., 2003). Kruckeberg and Starck (1988) write of "communitarianism" and note the importance of community building through communication. In short, social capital enables collaboration and maintains a thriving community, and it is social capital that decreases as a sense of society is lost.

Links to corporate reputation

There are no original links to the concept of corporate reputation when it comes to the theory of social capital, but many writings on social capital understand the role of reputation for an individual. Bourdieu (1980/1995) and Lin (2001) view reputation mostly as a personal asset that helps others distinguish one's status. According to this thinking, reputation could be seen as a form of social capital. Bourdieu writes of "the capital of trust that stems from a reputation for honor as well as wealth" and argues that trust is the mechanism through which social capital can be utilized: "Because of trust they enjoy the capital of social relations they have accumulated" (Bourdieu, 1980/1995, p. 119). Putnam et al. (1993, p. 170) uses the concept similarly: "For example, my reputation for trustworthiness benefits you as well as me, since it enables us both to engage in mutually rewarding cooperation." In a similar manner, Putnam (1993, p. 173) cites Ostrom and concludes: "norms are reinforced by the network of relationships that depend on the establishment of a reputation for keeping promises and accepting the norms of the local community regarding behavior." As Putnam's approach is best matched for the corporate level, this chapter builds strongest on his theorizing.

Theoretical Description

Social capital can be seen as a metaphor derived from other types of capital: "Whereas physical capital refers to physical objects and human capital refers to the properties of individuals,

social capital refers to connections among individuals – social networks and the norms of reciprocity and trustworthiness that arise from them . . . The difference is that 'social capital' calls attention to the fact that civic virtue is most powerful when embedded in a dense network of reciprocal social relations. A society of many virtuous but isolated individuals is not necessarily rich in social capital" (Putnam, 2000, p. 19).

What makes social capital interesting are the many benefits it has been shown to provide. Previous research has been able to establish links between social capital and increased economic investments and lower transaction costs (Fukuyama, 1995), less corrupt and more effective government (Putnam et al., 1993), lower crime rate (Halpern, 1999; Putnam, 2000), longer life and better health (Hyyppä and Mäki, 2001; Wilkinson, 1996), improved overall child welfare (Cote and Healy, 2001), and increased educational achievement (Coleman, 1988), as well as better income equality (Kawachi et al., 1997; Wilkinson, 1996). The World Bank's definition of social capital builds on Putnam's thinking and highlights societal gains: "Social capital refers to the institutions, relationships, and norms that shape the quality and quantity of a society's social interactions . . . Social capital is not just the sum of the institutions which underpin a society – it is the glue that holds them together."

"The volume of social capital possessed by a given agent . . . depends on the size of the network of connections that he can effectively mobilize" (Bourdieu, 1986, p. 249). If social capital is understood as beneficial connections between individuals, then the logic behind social capital formation is straightforward: social capital is created as a by-product of people working together (Putnam et al., 1993). Social capital is productive, but it can deplete if it is not used: Healy (2001) describe it as "social ozone" that needs maintenance. Once created, however, social capital feeds on itself: "Effective collaborative institutions require interpersonal skills and trust, but those skills and that trust are also inculcated and reinforced by organized collaboration" (Putnam et al., 1993, p. 180).

Social capital defined

For Coleman (1988, 1990), rational action is central, and social capital is defined by its function: "It is not a single entity, but a variety of different entities having characteristics in common: they all consist of some aspect of a social structure, and they facilitate certain actions of individuals who are within the structure" (Coleman, 1990, p. 302). Coleman (1988) summarizes social capital to consist of obligations, trust, networks, norms, information channels, and social organization. Similarly, the Organisation for Economic Co-operation and Development (OECD) defines social capital as "networks together with shared norms, values and understandings that facilitate co-operation within or among groups" (Cote and Healy, 2001, p. 41). This definition highlights associations between people. Halpern (1999) introduces a "virtuous Catherine wheel" of social capital where at the hub are internalized values such as social trust, at the rim are certain mediating causal variables such as vibrant community, and the products or common goods such as low crime are the sparks that fly off.

Similarly, Bourdieu (1986) links social capital with societal issues as he represents a neo-Marxist perspective, where emphasis is based on access to resources and issues of power in society (Davies, 2001). Those with resources such as social capital have also access to power in society. Bourdieu understands social capital to work through strengthening other intangibles, such as symbolic capital. Social capital thus acts as a mediator for other types of capital, and it is possible that by controlling social capital may explain different degrees of profits or influence yielding from economic and cultural capital, and may even multiply the influence of these (Bourdieu, 1986; Coleman, 1988).

Social capital and communication

The theory of social capital is closely tied with theories of social networks and social relations. Relationships are mainly shaped via the structures of interpersonal interaction and communication (Henttonen, 2009; van Emmerik and Brenninkmeijer, 2009). In fact, communication is the mechanism through which social capital can be accessed, whether on an individual or organizational level. Communication is central for social capital as human messaging and symbolic activity are the basis on which social relationships are formed. In fact, "communication characteristics influence the potential for social capital formation, maintenance, and expenditure" (Fussell *et al.*, 2006, p. 151).

Aula (2011) views social capital as one reputational advantage, along with relationships and position, resulting from communication. He argues that (Aula, 2011, p. 35) "communication can strengthen stakeholder relationships and positions and build social capital for an organization." Hazelton and Kennan (2000, p. 83) list four communication functions that provide the mechanism for exploiting the stock of social capital in organizations: information exchange, problem/solution identification, behavior regulation, and conflict management. Of these, information exchange refers to organizational ability and trust available to deal with relevant information and symbols. Problem/solution identification refers to organizational ability to interpret the changes and potential problems relevant to them, whereas behavior regulation refers to aligning individual behavior and corporate image in line with organizational goals. Conflict management notes how conflict is in fact normal and valuable organizational activity is in need of management (Hazelton and Kennan, 2000, p. 83). While these all are important, they fail to emphasize the long-term nature of social capital as well as its positive nature. Hence, the list could be implemented with network-related functions such as "relationship maintenance"; the ability to connect and work together with individuals inside and outside the organization and create cohesion through positive experiences of working together and "innovation enabling" referring to the trust encouraging risk taking and using acquired information in novel ways. Also, the role of networks is so central for social capital.

Trust and trustworthiness (Coleman, 1990; Fukuyama, 1995) are central concepts for social capital, as social capital is beneficial only in a setting where trust abounds. Some link social capital directly with trust and its benefits such as competitive advantage: Fukuyama (1995, p. 27) sees trustworthiness as a form of social capital that increases "the capacity to form new associations." For Fussell *et al.* (2006, p. 151), trust is "an expectation that individuals will exhibit behavior that is consistent with expectations." They note that strong connections between people or organizations require time, emotional intensity, intimacy, and reciprocity. The logic also works in the reverse: Putnam *et al.* (1993) see informal clubs and collaboration as learning grounds for democracy: they claim that learning to trust people on a small scale will enable trust even on the societal level. Similarly, Rothstein (2003) notes how in ideal cases social capital generalizes trust into society at large. This learning to collaborate and formation of trust, however, are not quick processes, but take place gradually over time. In practice, trustworthiness signals others whether collaboration would be fruitful and reflects the likelihood of opportunistic behavior (Chiles and McMackin, 1996; Granovetter, 1985).

Bridging and bonding social capital

Two different types of relationships can be established through which social capital flows: bridging or inclusive (see, e.g., Burt, 1992; Putnam, 2000), and bonding or exclusive (see, e.g., Coleman, 1988; Putnam, 1993). Both of these have inspired their own research traditions. For bonding social capital, the focus has been on the density of networks, in-group cohesion, changing of identity toward a we feeling, norms, and reciprocity (Coleman, 1988; Johnson *et al.*, 2000; Putnam, 1993), whereas for bridging social capital, researchers have paid attention to network location, access to information, control, boundary spanning relationships, and individual gains (Burt, 1992; Leana and Van Buren, 1999; Putnam, 2000). Bonding social capital is the type that furthers in-group cohesion, whereas bridging social capital is understood as relationships with those outside the group. Previous studies have proven the value of both. For example, the relationship

between job satisfaction and bonding relationships has been established (Lucius and Kuhnert, 1997), as well as the link between bridging social capital and group effectiveness (breadth of knowledge as a mediator; Wong, 2007). Moreover, both types of social capital have been noted to be important in the organizational context of teams and R&D (Reagans and Zuckerman, 2001), where both collective action inside the team as well as external information transfer are needed.

In considering the value of social capital for corporate reputation, special interest should be placed on bridging social capital as it describes how information is accessed through less tight social relations. Bridging social capital, the kind that is the most beneficial for a healthy but diverse society, is difficult to create (Putnam *et al.*, 2003, p. 3). Bridging social capital is like oil for groups and societies; it smoothes relations between groups and individuals. Bridging social capital is close to what Granovetter (1973) calls weak ties, and related to what Burt (2002) calls structural holes. Structural holes in a network note that often distant or infrequent relationships are beneficial, as they provide access to new information. Bridging social capital hence identifies networks that bridge social divides and promote heterogeneity in groups and societies. It reinforces inclusive identities, and thus runs less risk of excess.

Individual or organizational gain?

Most of research on social capital focuses on the role it plays for an individual, such as personal access to different resources such as power (Brass, 1992), professional status and occupational gains (Lin, 2001), welfare, and health (Putnam *et al.*, 1993). In network terms, an individual centrally located in a network may gain unique access to certain resources or actors. The more central a position an individual holds within a network, the better the access and place in status hierarchy (Ibarra, 1993).

Nahapiet and Ghoshal (1998) note that social capital can create new value also for organizations, and they distinguish between structural, relational, and cognitive dimensions of social capital. Burke *et al.* (2011) mention social capital as an organizational asset that results from a harmonious culture, and investments in social capital (along with other forms of capital) eventually contribute to reputational capital of the organization. They note social capital to be of special value in human resource (HR) activities, where it enforces employee engagement and identification. Similarly, Preston (2004) links a positive corporate reputation with social capital, and a negative reputation with inherent liabilities.

In the online environment, Aula (2011, p. 30) suggests especially the cognitive dimension to matter as it is related to stories formed by stakeholders and spread within networks: he sees reputation as "an integral part of an organization's social-cognitive capital." Organizations can be seen as markets where people trade goods and ideas, and good networks improve success in this trade (Henttonen, 2009). In fact, Oh *et al.* (2006) call it "group social capital" where the key argument is that groups high in social capital are also more effective. The emphasis on Oh *et al.*'s definition of social capital is on resources accessible through different relationships inside an organization. Ihlen (2005, p. 495) argues that social capital may even be more important for organizations than individuals: "The vast number of connections gathered by most organizations points to how they are socially embedded in a much stronger sense than individuals." In fact, interorganizational studies have suggested that prior relationships also affect future relationships (Gulati, 1995), and organizational units centrally located in a network are often highly visible and sharers of information for others, making them attractive partners of collaboration to others (Tsai, 2000).

Social capital is important for corporations as its presence makes possible a kind of "action that is beneficial and which can be highly advantageous to those individuals, groups, or organizations that possess it in sufficient quantity" (Fussell *et al.*, 2006, p. 149). It facilitates the flow of information, and through a sense of belonging and social obligations, it may exert influence on others. For Lin (2001), success for organizations is linked with social capital. He differentiates between two motives for actions: expressive actions that aim at maintaining resources and instrumental actions that aim at obtaining resources.

Previous studies on social capital

Fukuyama (1995) has been able to link social capital with economic prosperity: he compared the relative economic performances of different nations on the basis of levels of trust apparent. In Fukuyama's research, the level of trust inherent in a given society determines its economic prosperity and ability to compete economically, and even affects its degree of democracy. Due to its many manifestations, both qualitative and quantitative approaches can be found in studies focusing on social capital. Coleman (1990) recommends qualitative methods or qualitative indicators to measure social capital, whereas Bourdieu (1991) argues for quantitative approach. Putnam's studies have applied both, though the focus is on quantitative. Ihlen (2005) suggests that both approaches are needed together to map corporate social capital and its influence, and suggests a combination of thinking from Lin to Coleman. The operationalization applied in these studies is most often based on the societal level on statistical comparisons, whereas trust and welfare are often self-rated measures. The samples are very case dependent, and much criticism has been targeted at the vagueness of the concept.

Criticism of the theory of social capital

As social capital is intangible in nature, it is easy to question whether it actually exists or not. Recent studies have also questioned its importance. In fact, Cowan and Jonard (2009) note that a certain degree of commonality among corporations in their knowledge is enough for successful alliances and social capital may not be needed. The theory of social capital has also been criticized for being naïve: critics claim that big societal problems cannot be explained by social capital alone. Also, critics think the message social capital brings is a forlorn one: once a community is set onto its level of social capital, research argues that little can be done to increase it (Putnam *et al.*, 1993; Rothstein, 2003). Another focus of critics has been its ignorance of the importance of individual discovery in knowledge creation (Locke, 1999). Adler and Kwon (2002) point out that there are also risks associated with social capital, such as overcommitment, cliques, and limited flow of new ideas. Moreover, critics have noted that there is little convincing empirical evidence that getting people to work together and trust each other on a smaller scale would result in social capital for the whole community (DeFilippis, 2001; Patulny, 2004).

What previous research on social capital has failed to explain in practice is how social capital is created on the individual and organizational level. This chapter suggests that the concept of reputation could help explain this missing link. Community does not happen by accident and neither does it prosper where it is not cultivated. This logic of social capital is similar to corporate reputation: the cultivation of stakeholder relations and a good reputation among stakeholders ensures organizational survival (Freeman, 1984). In fact, organizations with reciprocal, trusting stakeholder networks can be understood as having high amounts of social capital (Luoma-aho, 2009).

Description of Theoretical Relevance to Corporate Reputation

The proposition made in this chapter is that corporate reputation affects the amount of social capital available for a corporation or its representatives. The interrelations of social capital and reputation are two way: a good reputation enables the formation of social capital, while at the same time social capital may help in establishing a good reputation. The theory of social capital is especially timely for corporations during the ongoing switch to

business online, as realms such as social media make corporate social capital visible for masses and through it affect corporate reputation. When a corporation's business and private connections are mapped, shared experiences are documented almost in real time and direct feedback is visible for all; corporate reputation is no longer something that could be "managed" but instead focus is shifting toward maintaining the social relations and establishing high amounts of social capital.

Lin (2002) links organizational success directly with the amount of social capital available to it. According to Lin (2001), public recognition within the network spreads reputation, and he defines reputation as "favorable/unfavorable opinions about an individual in a social network" (Lin, 2001, p. 19). Lin differentiates between expressive actions that aim at maintaining resources, and instrumental actions that aim at obtaining resources. Corporate reputation is in Lin's thinking one of three returns of instrumental action: of the economic, political, and social gains, reputation is an indication of social gain. Corporate reputation one could argue, however, could also be applicable as an expressive action, as a good reputation could engender organizational legitimacy (Deephouse and Carter, 2005).

Group social capital

The notion of "group social capital" (Oh *et al.*, 2006) is a good starting point for linking social capital with corporate reputation as social capital is all about resources accessible through social relationships. Social capital is what gives value to corporate reputation as it provides a credible network within which reputation spreads. Walker *et al.* (1997) have noted how social capital influences network formation that proceeds through the establishment of new relationship. Networks are the embodiment of past success at collaboration. In fact, reputation can be described as the value of public awareness in the social networks important to the organization; "an intertemporal identity" (Pizzorno, 2004), a record of trustworthy or untrustworthy behavior in the eyes of the

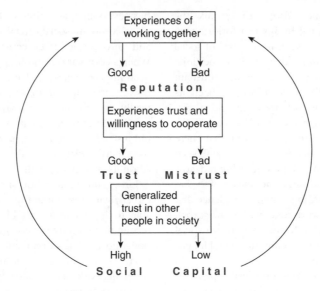

Figure 24.1 Model of the extremes of social capital creation (Luoma-aho, 2009, p. 243).

various stakeholders (Luoma-aho, 2009). Trust becomes a central concept, as emphasis is placed on "particularly the historical trustworthiness of parties in previous interactions with others, and it is the social context that makes reputational effects possible" (Rousseau *et al.*, 1998, p. 397). Previous experiences of working together create expectations for the future (Luoma-aho, 2009).

Reputation in practice

The theory of social capital explains how reputation works in practice. Tsai (2000, p. 928) sums how trustworthiness and reputation are connected inside organizations: "An organizational unit's reputation for trustworthiness is mainly determined by other units' perceptions and evaluations of the unit's integrity and reliability in interunit exchange. Such a reputation for trustworthiness is an important factor that will influence a unit's preferences in selecting its exchange partners, as a unit will be more willing to exchange resources with the units that it perceives as trustworthy." The same logic can also be applied to the external stakeholder relations of corporations; corporate reputation is assessed through perceptions and evaluations.

Social capital advances the understanding of corporate reputation as it provides a larger societal context in which corporate reputation is a central piece. Figure 24.1 illustrates how social capital is created on the societal level, and the logic is similar for corporations: good experiences of working with a corporation create a positive reputation and foster trust which in turn creates new social capital for the corporation. Social capital is also helpful for understanding the emergence and functions of networks: networks not only foster reciprocity, but also facilitate coordination and communication and amplify information about the trustworthiness of individuals or organizations, that is, their reputation.

Figure 24.1 describes the process of how social capital is created. The process is cyclic, and starts with experiences, whether of a person, group, or organization. The model is based on communication on both intrapersonal as well as the interpersonal level, as individuals make sense and share their experiences. These experiences (whether mediated or personal) of working together, either good or bad, form a reputation. This reputation is communicated to others consciously or unconsciously, and it carries with it certain expectations and facilitates willingness to trust (Luoma-aho, 2006; Misztal, 1996; Putnam *et al.*, 1993; Sztompka, 2000). The level of trust results in high or low amounts of social capital, which in turn shapes experiences and expectations and thus the possibilities for working together (Putnam, 2000; Putnam *et al.*, 1993, 2003). The model has both instrumental and theoretical value, as it demonstrates how experiences become expectations, which contribute to reality (Putnam *et al.*, 1993). For the process to work, however, a society is needed in which various voices are enabled and allowed to be heard. Fostering such a society requires communication.

The cycle of social capital

Once created, the cycle of social capital feeds on itself. Aula and Mantere (2008) call it a "circle of good." However, it is important to remember that reputation may be either positive or negative: a good reputation creates trust, whereas a bad reputation may diminish trust. When this established trust is communicated to others, its effects multiply. Trust is here understood as unequivocal: it exists to some degree or it is lacking. The organization – stakeholder relationship develops over time and a good reputation is formed through trustworthy conduct. Untrustworthy conduct or a bad reputation can be amended and improved over time with positive experiences. Research has shown, however, that it is much harder to reverse a negative reputation and poor trust than to repair damage done to a hitherto good reputation and high levels of trust (Sjovall and Talk, 2004).

In the process of social capital creation, the role of the different stakeholders is central. In fact, stakeholders with positive experiences and willingness to share those can be understood as "faith holders" or "social capitalists" for corporations: they spread the goodwill and maintain a positive reputation (Luoma-aho, 2005). Stakeholders as social capitalists are also a credible source as they often have personal experiences of the corporation. Similarly, Hunt (2009) borrows a concept from Cory Doctorow's science fiction and writes of a new

kind of reputation she calls whuffie: how noteworthy, nice, and networked an individual or a corporation is. In short, whuffie represents the amount of social capital gained among social networks, and in Doctorow's fiction, the amount of whuffie is decisive for whether people are willing to conduct business with one or not. Though fiction based, Hunt (2009) argues that the logic of whuffie is already reality in the online realm, where a trader's reputation and past deeds are clearly visible for potential business partners through the public feedback they have received.

The proposition made in this chapter is that corporate reputation affects the amount of social capital available for a corporation or its representatives. The interrelations of social capital and reputation are in fact two way: a good reputation enables the formation of social capital, while at the same time, social capital may help in establishing a good reputation. A bad reputation may hinder a corporation's relations with its stakeholders as well as limit its networking abilities. On the other hand, a good reputation may create new social capital and maintain the virtuous circle portrayed on the left of Figure 24.1.

Future Directions of Research

The central ideas behind social capital, collaboration, communities, networks, and trust are not new, but rather date back to the roots of sociology. The theory of social capital is timely as business and interaction move increasingly online, and past deeds become visible for everyone. One could say that social media makes corporate social capital visible, and that social capital is thus becoming the "reputation of the future." In fact, it could be stated that in the future, as whuffie will make or brake business, social capital will become foundational for corporations. Thus far, only few studies have tried to test and measure social capital in the corporate realm, possibly due to the challenges brought about by the intangible nature of social capital.

As sustainability and green values take over business, corporations are moving from one-time interactions to building lasting relationships with different stakeholders. This can be seen as an increase in social capital. Along with the increase in social capital, its influence to corporate reputation is also increased. This could lead to investments and losses in social capital becoming more tangible and eventually reportable (Lev, 2001). For such reporting to be accurately conducted, the nature and logic behind social capital and communication need to be better understood.

What previous research has failed to yet prove is the connection between social capital and behavioral outcomes. A central concept for social capital is trust, and the interrelations of reputation and trust should also be better studied. Is it possible to have a good reputation but lack stakeholder trust? And moreover, is it possible to have good relations with stakeholders and still have a poor reputation? The proposition made in this chapter is that corporate reputation affects the amount of social capital available for a corporation or its representatives. The interrelations of social capital and reputation were argued to be two way: a good reputation enables the formation of social capital, while at the same time, social capital may help in establishing a good reputation. Future studies should address whether this in fact is true, and if yes, which influencer is stronger.

As the two concepts of social capital and corporate reputation have so far not been clearly linked together, future studies should further incorporate social capital with network theories in the hope of defining which types of social relationships are relevant for corporate reputation. Research on social capital could also help in understanding the context and relationships in which corporate reputation matters. Future studies have to clarify the role of group social capital (Oh et al., 2006), whuffie, and whether social capital is actually needed or not. In fact, Cowan and Jonard (2009) note that a certain degree of commonality among firms in their knowledge is enough for successful alliances and social capital may not be needed.

Future studies should also focus on whether social capital can be created on the organizational level as distinguishable from teams and groups inside organizations, and what kind of contribution reputation has in practice for social capital.

References

Adler, P. and Kwon, S.-K. (2002) Social capital: Prospects for a new concept. *Academy of Management Review*, 27, 17–40.

Aula, P. (2011) Meshworked reputation: Publicists' views on the reputational impacts of online communication. *Public Relations Review*, 37(1), 28–36.

Aula, P. and Mantere, S. (2008) *Strategic Reputation Management*. New York: Routledge.

Bourdieu, P. (1980/1995) *The Logic of Practice*. Cambridge, UK: University Press.

Bourdieu, P. (1986) The forms of capital. In J. Richardson (ed.), *Handbook of Theory and Research for the Sociology of Education*. New York: Greenwood, pp. 241–258.

Bourdieu, P. (1991) *Language and Symbolic Power*. Cambridge, UK: Polity Press.

Brass, D.J. (1992) Power in organizations: A network perspective. In G. Moore and J. Whitt (eds), *Research in Politics and Society* (Vol. 4). Greenwich, CT: JAI Press, pp. 295–323.

Burke, R., Martin, G., and Cooper, C. (2011) *Corporate Reputation, Managing Opportunities and Threats*. Farnham, UK: Gower.

Burt, R. (1992) *Structural Holes: The Social Structure of Competition*. Cambridge, MA: Harvard University Press.

Burt, R. (2002) The social capital of structural holes. In M. Guillén, R. Collins, P. England, and M. Meyer (eds), *New Dimensions of Economic Sociology*. New York: Russell Sage Foundation, pp. 148–190.

Chiles, T.H. and McMackin, J.F. (1996) Integrating variable risk preferences, trust, and transaction cost economics. *Academy of Management Review*, 21(1), 73–99.

Coleman, J.S. (1988) Social capital in the creation of human capital. *American Journal of Sociology*, 94, 95–120.

Coleman, J.S. (1990) *Foundations of Social Theory*. Cambridge, MA: Harvard University Press.

Cooley, C.H. (1909) *Social Organization*. New York: Charles Scribner's Sons.

Cooley, C.H. (1918) *Social Process*. New York: Charles Scribner's Sons.

Cote, S. and Healy, T. (2001) *The Well-Being of Nations. The Role of Human and Social Capital*. Paris: Organisation for Economic Co-operation and Development.

Cowan, R. and Jonard, N. (2009) Knowledge portfolios and the organization of innovation networks. *Academy of Management Review*, 34(2), 320–342.

Damico, A.J. (1978) *Individuality and Community: The Social and Political Thought of John Dewey*. Gainesville, FL: University Press of Florida.

Davies, A. (2001) But we knew that already! – A study into the relationship between social capital and volunteering. Conference paper, Home Start. Sheffield, UK.

Deephouse, D. and Carter, S. (2005) An examination of differences between organizational legitimacy and organizational reputation. *Journal of Management Studies*, 42(2), 329–360.

DeFilippis, J. (2001) The myth of social capital in community development. *Housing Policy Debate*, 12(4), 781–806.

Dewey, J. (1916/1963) *Democracy and Education*. New York: The Macmillan Company.

Dewey, J. (1938/1963) *Experience and Education*. New York: Collier Books.

Freeman, R.E. (1984) *Strategic Management: A Stakeholder Approach*. Boston: Pitman.

Fukuyama, F. (1995) *Trust: The Social Virtues and the Creation of Prosperity*. New York: Free Press.

Fussell, H., Harrison-Rexrode, J., Kennan, W., and Hazleton, V. (2006) The relationship between social capital, transaction costs, and organizational outcomes. A case study. *Corporate Communications: An International Journal*, 11(2), 148–161.

Granovetter, M. (1973) The strength of weak ties. *American Journal of Sociology*, 78(6), 1360–1379.

Granovetter, M. (1985) Economic action and social structure: The problem of embeddedness. *American Journal of Sociology*, 91, 481–510.

Gulati, R. (1995) Social structure and alliance formation patterns: A longitudinal analysis. *Administrative Science Quarterly*, 40, 619–652.

Halpern, D. (1999) Social capital: the new golden goose. Unpublished review, Faculty of Social and Political Sciences, Cambridge University.

Hazelton, V. and Kennan, W. (2000) Social capital: Reconceptualizing the bottom line. *Corporate Communications: An International Journal*, 5(2), 81–86.

Healy, T. (2001) Health promotion and social capital. Conference Paper. International Evidence for the impact of Social Capital on Well Being. National University of Ireland, Galway.

Henttonen, K. (2009) The effects of social networks on work-team effectiveness. Doctoral dissertation, Lappeenranta University of Technology, Digipress. Retrieved from https://oa.doria.fi/bitstream/handle/10024/50526/isbn%209789522148704.pdf (last accessed September 23, 2012).

Hunt, T. (2009) *The Whuffie Factor. Using the Power of Social Networks to Build Your Business*. New York: Crown Business.

Hyyppä, M. and Mäki, J. (2001) Why do Swedish-speaking Finns have longer active life? An area for social capital research. *Health Promotion International*, 16, 55–64.

Ibarra, H. (1993) Network centrality, power and innovation involvement: Determinants of technical and administrative roles. *Academy of Management Journal*, 36(3), 471–501.

Ihlen, Ø. (2005) The power of social capital: Adapting Bourdieu to the study of public relations. *Public Relations Review*, 31, 492–496.

Johnson, O.E., Smith, M.L., and Gambill, D.Y. (2000) Reconstructing "we": Organizational identification in dynamic environment. In C.R. Leana and D.M. Rousseau (eds), *Relational Wealth: The Advantages of Stability in Changing Economy*. New York: Oxford University Press, pp. 153–168.

Kawachi, I., Kennedy, B., Lochner, K., and Prothrow-Stith, D. (1997) Social capital, income inequality, and mortality. *American Journal of Public Health*, 87(9), 1491–1498.

Kruckeberg, D. and Starck, K. (1988) *Public Relations & Community: A Reconstructed Theory*. New York: Praeger.

Leana, C.R. and Van Buren, H.J. III (1999) Organisational social capital and employment practices. *Academy of Management Review*, 24, 538–555.

Lev, B. (2001) *Intangibles. Management, Measurement and Reporting*. Washington, DC: Brookings Institution.

Lin, N. (2001) Building a network theory of social capital. In N. Lin, R.S. Burt, and K. Cook (eds), *Social Capital: Theory and Research*. New York: Aldine de Gruyter, pp. 3–30.

Lin, N. (2002) *Social Capital: A Theory of Social Structure and Action*. Cambridge, UK: Cambridge University Press.

Locke, E.A. (1999) Some reservations about social capital. *Academy of Management Review*, 24(1), 8–9.

Lucius, R.H. and Kuhnert, K.W. (1997) Using sociometry to predict team performance in the work place. *Journal of Psychology*, 131, 21–32.

Luoma-aho, V. (2005) *Faith-Holders as Social Capital of Finnish Public Organizations*. Jyväskylä: Jyväskylä University of Jyväskylä Press.

Luoma-aho, V. (2006) Intangibles of public organizations: Trust and reputation. In V. Luoma-aho and S. Peltola (eds), *Public Organizations in the Communication Society*. Jyväskylä: University of Jyväskylä Press, pp. 11–58.

Luoma-aho, V. (2009) Bowling together – Applying Robert Putnam's theories of community and social capital to public relations. In Ø. Ihlen and M. Fredriksson (eds), *Social Theory on PR*. London: Routledge/Lawrence Erlbaum, pp. 231–251.

McDermott, J.J. (1981) *The Philosophy of John Dewey*. Chicago, IL: University of Chicago Press.

Mead, G.H. (1934) *Mind, Self, and Society*. C.W. Morris (ed.). Chicago, IL: University of Chicago Press.

Misztal, B. (1996) *Trust in Modern Societies*. Padstow: Polity Press.

Nahapiet, J. and Ghoshal, S. (1998) Social capital, intellectual capital, and the organizational advantage. *Academy of Management Review.*, 22(2), 242–266.

Oh, H., Labianca, G., and Chung, M.-H. (2006) A multilevel model of group social capital. *Academy of Management Review*, 31(3), 569–582.

Patulny, R. (2004) Bonding, bridging and investment: Important aspects of a national social capital policy strategy. *Melbourne Journal of Politics*, 29, 68–81.

Pizzorno, A. (2004) Resources of social capital: Reputation and visibility. Keynote speech, ECSR Summer School on Social Capital, Trento, Italy, August.

Portes, A. (1998) Social capital: Its origins and applications in modern sociology. *Annual Review of Sociology*, 24, 1–25.

Preston, L.E. (2004) Reputation as a source of corporate social capital. *Journal of General Management*, 30(2), 43–49.

Putnam, R.D. (1993) The prosperous community. Social capital and public life. *The American Prospect*, 4(13), 11–18.

Putnam, R.D. (1995) Bowling alone: America's declining social capital. *Journal of Democracy*, 6, 65–78.

Putnam, R.D. (2000) *Bowling Alone: The Collapse and Revival of American Community*. New York: Simon & Schuster.

Putnam, R.D., Leonardi, R., and Nanetti, R.Y. (1993) *Making Democracy Work: Civic Traditions in Modern Italy*. Princeton, NJ: Princeton University Press.

Putnam, R.D., Feldstein, L., and Cohen, D. (2003) *Better Together: Restoring the American Community*. New York: Simon & Schuster.

Reagans, R. and Zuckerman, E.W. (2001) Networks, diversity, and productivity: The social capital of corporate R&D teams. *Organization Science*, 12(4), 502–517.

Rothstein, B. (2003) *Sociala fällor och Tillitens Problem*. Stockholm: SNS Förlag.

Rousseau, D.M., Sitkin, S.B., Burt, R.S., and Camerer, C. (1998) Not so different after all. A cross-discipline view of trust. *Academy of Management Review*, 23, 393–404.

Sjovall, A. and Talk, A. (2004) From actions to impressions: Cognitive attribution theory and the formation of corporate reputation. *Corporate Reputation Review*, 7(3), 269–281.

Sztompka, P. (2000) *Trust. A Sociological Theory*. Port Chester, NJ: Cambridge University Press.

Tsai, W. (2000) Social capital, strategic readiness and the formation of intraorganizational linkages. *Strategic Management Journal*, 21(9), 925–939.

van Emmerik, I.J.H. and Brenninkmeijer, V. (2009) Deep-level similarity and group social capital: Associations with team functioning. *Small Group Research*, 40(6), 650–669.

Walker, G., Kogut, B., and Shan, W. (1997) Social capital, structural holes and the formation of an industry network. *Organization Science*, 8, 108–125.

Wilkinson, R. (1996) *Unhealthy Societies: The Afflictions of Inequality*. London: Routledge.

Wong, S.-S. (2007) Task knowledge overlap and knowledge variety: The role of advice network structures and impact on group effectiveness. *Journal of Organizational Behavior*, 29(5), 591–614.

Woolcock, M. (2001) The place of social capital in understanding social and economic outcomes. *ISUMA Canadian Journal of Policy Research*, 2(1), 11–17.

Section 3

Attributes of Reputation

25

Corporate Attributes and Associat~~

Sabine Einwiller

Johannes Gutenberg-University Mainz, Germany

The strength of stakeholders' collective judgments of a company, its corporate reputation, is influenced by individuals' knowledge about a company, specifically their awareness of it as well as their associations with the firm and assessment of its various attributes. Based on theoretical underpinnings deduced from cognitive psychology and conceptualizations in marketing, the chapter provides a detailed discussion of the elements of stakeholder company knowledge: awareness, associations, and attributes. There are a variety of sources influencing the formation of stakeholder knowledge and eventually reputation, comprising direct experiences through personal encounters with the firm and/or its products and indirect experiences through communication from company-dominated and company-independent sources.

Introduction

There is common accord in academia and practice that there is a relationship between the way people perceive and judge a company and the success it achieves (e.g., Fombrun, 1996; van Riel and Fombrun, 2004). Essential for the form and strength of this relationship is the knowledge and the judgments a person holds in association with a company. These corporate associations, the links between the company and attributes stored in a person's memory, may be influenced by how a company presents itself and communicates about its attributes and

also by a variety of outside sources that are not directly manageable (Brown *et al.*, 2006), for example, the news media or online communications in social media. Both, corporate attributes and associations are inherent in the concept of corporate reputation which Barnett and colleagues (2006) based on a literature review and 49 prior definitional statements of corporate reputation defined as "[o]bservers' collective judgments of a corporation based on assessments of the financial, social, and environmental impacts attributed to the corporation over time" (p. 34). According to this definitional statement, the strength of a company's

The Handbook of Communication and Corporate Reputation, First Edition. Edited by Craig E. Carroll.
© 2013 John Wiley & Sons, Inc. Published 2015 by John Wiley & Sons, Inc.

reputation is influenced by people's assessment of its various attributes that, in aggregation, make up the collective judgments of a corporation.

Even though the corporate attributes are the properties of the company (e.g., financial performance, products and services), corporate reputation is very much a perceptual phenomenon as it depends on how these attributes are perceived and judged by those individuals who observe the firm. Among these observers, it is the company's stakeholders whose judgments are particularly relevant because they are the ones "that contribute, either voluntarily or involuntarily, to its wealth-creating capacity and activities (. . .)" (Post *et al.*, 2002, p. 19). Corporate reputation is important as it influences the amount and quality of stakeholders' contributions to the firm's wealth-creating capacity and activities, for example, their buying or investment intensity, their work commitment, or their willingness to defend the firm against opposers.

This chapter gives an overview of the two essential building blocks of corporate reputation: corporate associations and corporate attributes. It serves as an introduction to the chapters in this section of the reputation handbook that deal with specific corporate attributes like executive leadership, products and services, and corporate social responsibility. The chapter first provides theoretical underpinnings deduced from cognitive psychology and previous conceptualizations in marketing followed by a more detailed discussion of the concepts corporate associations and corporate attributes. The last part of the chapter deals with the role of communication in the formation of corporate awareness, attributes, and associations.

Theoretical Foundation

Conceptualizations of "associations" generally refer to memory models of cognitive psychology that involve some type of associative model formulation (e.g., Anderson, 1983b; Anderson and Bower, 1973; Quillian, 1966; Raaijmakers and Shiffrin, 1981) as theoretical foundation. In the marketing literature, associations have been widely discussed and explored, particularly in the context of branding and brand equity. Aaker (1991) suggests that brand associations represent the category of a brand's assets and liabilities that include anything linked in memory to a brand. According to Keller (1998), "[c]ustomer-based brand equity occurs when the consumer is familiar with the brand and holds some favorable, strong, and unique brand associations in memory" (p. 2).

Cognitive psychologists proposed associative network models (also called semantic or propositional network models) to understand how propositions are stored in memory (Eagly and Chaiken, 1993). An association denotes a relationship between two pieces of information, or knowledge nodes, in memory. For the consumer context, Krishnan (1996) remarked that "[l]inks between any two nodes suggest an association in the consumer's mind" (p. 391). A knowledge node can represent any piece of information, for example, a company name (e.g., Apple), a manager's name (e.g., Steve Jobs), a product (e.g., smartphone), or a characteristic (e.g., innovative), while the association represents the link between any two nodes, here for example, between Steve Jobs and innovative. A collection of knowledge nodes associated with each other may form a category. Categories capture the common meaning and the distinctive features of a class of objects thereby making the world more predictable (Bless *et al.*, 2004). When recognizing a new stimulus object, for example, a new Apple smartphone, as belonging to a particular category, Apple products, a person can infer many properties of the new stimulus object from the category. Complex knowledge structures that involve multiple categories and connections can be referred to as associative networks.

The extent of encoding and retrieval of information is determined by "spreading activation" (e.g., Anderson, 1983a; Collins and Loftus, 1975; Raaijmakers and Shiffrin, 1981). The process starts by the activation of a knowledge node or a set of nodes and then iteratively spreading that activation out to other nodes linked to the source nodes. The strengthening of associations is generally believed to happen when two or more nodes in memory are simultaneously active. Thus, items that co-occur more often in the activation process are more strongly associated, and the strength of association between activated nodes determines the particular information that can be retrieved from memory. For example, in considering an investment in an innovative company, an investor may think of Apple because of its strong association with the node containing the attribute "innovative."

Referring to the associative network memory model, Keller (1993) conceptualized the knowledge structure about a brand as consisting of a brand node in memory to which multiple associations are linked. Keller identified different dimensions of brand knowledge that affect consumer response. The first dimension is brand *awareness*, which is related to the strength of the brand node or trace in memory as reflected by recall and recognition. The second dimension consists of the *associations*, also referred to as the brand image, which Keller defined "as perceptions about a brand as reflected by the brand associations held in consumer memory" (p. 3). Keller's concept of brand knowledge was developed for product brands as the focal knowledge objects and one type of stakeholders, customers, or consumers, as knowledge subjects. The corporate entity plays a marginal role here and can be subsumed under the category of non-product-related associations.

Similar to Keller's (1993) conceptualization of customer-based brand knowledge at the level of the individual consumer, Rindova and colleagues (2005) proposed to differentiate two dimensions of reputation on the level of the firm's collective of stakeholders. Drawing on the institutional perspective of the firm, Rindova and colleagues proposed the collective awareness and recognition that an organization has accumulated in its organizational field as the first dimension of reputation. This *prominence* dimension parallels Keller's awareness dimension of consumer brand knowledge. For their second dimension, Rindova and colleagues

draw on the economics perspective, which addresses how stakeholders evaluate a particular organizational attribute. This *perceived quality* dimension of reputation is closely related to Keller's association or image dimensions of brand knowledge.

Stakeholder Company Knowledge

Referring to Keller's (1993) model of brand knowledge and the notion of reputation advocated by Rindova *et al.* (2005), it is helpful to develop an overarching basic concept of an individual stakeholder's company knowledge, consisting of a person's corporate awareness, the corporate associations as well as the associated corporate attributes. Different from Keller's concept where the focus is on consumers' knowledge of the product brand, the focus here is on the awareness, associations, and associated attributes all stakeholders (including customers and consumers) have stored in their memories with relation to the corporate entity.

Corporate awareness

Corporate awareness refers to the strength of the knowledge nodes representing the core elements of the company in stakeholders' memories. Although knowledge about a company can be encoded and retrieved through many company-related knowledge items, there are only few that make the company clearly recognizable without any further knowledge. Above all, this is the company name, but it may also be the logo or the top manager/founder clearly symbolizing the firm. A node's strength as reflected by easier recall and recognition of the knowledge item is the residue of prior activation history. It depends on the quantity of activation, that is, how often the node has been activated, and on the quality of activation (Keller, 1993). According to the levels-of-processing approach proposed by Craik and Lockhart (1972), activation quality is dependent on the depth of mental processing where a deeper level of processing (e.g., semantic processing) results in a more enduring memory trace than a shallow level of processing (e.g., phonemic processing). Corporate awareness is furthermore enhanced when the node representing the company name has many connections to other encoded memory items. In the marketing literature, the prominence or level of activation of a brand in memory has also been referred to as the "salience" of a brand (Alba and Chattopadhyay, 1986).

Corporate awareness is important for various reasons. Awareness is the essential prerequisite for all other steps in the communication process, because without awareness, no other communication effects can occur (Rossiter and Percy, 1998). Fombrun and colleagues (2000) remark that "without awareness, reputation could not exist" (p. 248). Keller (1993) notes that raising awareness of the brand – or in our case the company – in people's memories increases the likelihood that the company will be a member of the consideration set. This might imply not only to be among the brands a consumer considers buying (Narayana and Markin, 1975) but also to be among the companies the jobseeker considers applying for or the investor considers investing in. Clearly, without any awareness of a company's existence, the likelihood of being considered by potential stakeholders for any form of interaction is reduced to pure chance. Alba and Chattopadhyay (1986) furthermore found that increasing the salience of a single brand can significantly impair unaided recall of competing brands.

Enhanced application of the recognition heuristic is another important effect of awareness. Goldstein and Gigerenzer (2002) define the recognition heuristic as follows: "If one of two alternatives is recognized and the other is not, then infer that the recognized alternative has the higher value with respect to the criterion" (p. 76). Thus, investors who had to choose between a company that they recognize and one they do not recognize would value the known company higher; this increases the likelihood of investing their money in the recognized firm. Finally, awareness of the company

is not only influenced by the number of connections to other knowledge items; it also influences the formation and strength of corporate associations. An established company node is a necessary condition for associations to form, and the stronger the company node, the more easily different kinds of information can become attached to it in memory (Keller, 1993).

Corporate associations

As outlined earlier, an association denotes the relationship between two knowledge nodes in memory. Following this notion, corporate associations may be considered the links between those knowledge nodes that represent the company in essence (above all, the company name) and any other knowledge items stored in stakeholders' memories in relation herewith. Drawing on the reasoning of attitude scholars, the concept of corporate associations can be further specified. Attitude theory provides some helpful approaches to describe the potential forms of corporate associations, as a number of attitude scholars have long interpreted beliefs and attitudes in terms of associations in an associative knowledge network (see Eagly and Chaiken, 1993, p. 101ff).

Fishbein and Ajzen (1975) represent beliefs in a propositional form that links an attitude object (e.g., a company) to some other knowledge node (e.g., pollution) by means of a verb (e.g., creates). Thus, "[t]he attitude object and the entities with which it is associated, traditionally interpreted as 'beliefs', can be regarded as linked nodes in a propositional network" (Eagly and Chaiken, 1993, p. 103). Beliefs are viewed as cognitive representations[1] that can express evaluative responses to a greater or lesser extent. If the attitude object is linked with a negative attribute (e.g., pollution), the resulting evaluation is unfavorable; if the linked attribute carries a positive connotation (e.g., safe jobs), the evaluation will be favorable. Apart from relations of the cognitive type, people can experience feelings and emotions in connection with an attitude object. The affective response can range from extremely negative (e.g., anger, fear) to extremely positive (e.g., hope, joy). Individuals may also link representations of their past behavior they have exhibited with relation to the attitude object to this knowledge node. This can also take different evaluative manifestations, ranging from favorable (e.g., purchase) to unfavorable (e.g., boycott).

Correspondingly, Fazio (e.g., Fazio, 1995, 2007; Fazio *et al.*, 1982) proposed an attitude model that views attitudes as associations between a given object and a given summary evaluation of the object. The evaluative summaries are viewed as potentially stemming from beliefs, affect, and/or behavioral information. Thus, the attitude may be based on appraisals of the attributes that characterize the object; it can stem from emotional reactions that the attitude object evokes; it can be based on a person's past behaviors and experiences with the object; or it can also be based on some combination of these potential sources of evaluative information (Fazio, 2007).

Drawing on this reasoning in attitude theory, corporate associations shall be considered more specifically as the links between knowledge nodes representing the company in essence and other knowledge items stored in stakeholders' memories and the herein implicated evaluations as well as summary evaluations in the form of attitudes. These evaluations can range from extremely positive over a point that is more or less neutral to extremely negative. An attitude object, for example, a company, can also infer mixed evaluations, positive with regard to one aspect and negative with regard to another. In general, however, Eagly and Chaiken (1993) note that "people who evaluate an attitude object favorably are likely to associate it with positive attributes and unlikely to associate it with negative attributes, whereas people who evaluate an attitude object unfavorably are likely to associate it with negative attributes and unlikely to associate it with positive attributes" (p. 11).

This conceptualization of corporate associations coincides with Keller (1993), who regards brand attitudes as one type of brand association, and Brown and Dacin (Brown, 1998; Brown and Dacin, 1997) who view beliefs, evaluations, and summary evaluations as forms of corporate associations. Unlike these authors, however, who subsume the relations not only between the knowledge nodes but also the knowledge nodes themselves under the label associations, the associated knowledge items shall be considered separately here. Knowledge items that are linked to the essential corporate nodes can take various forms; however, most important for the context of corporate reputation are those representing corporate attributes.

Corporate attributes

An attribute, in general, is a quality or characteristic of an object, for example, of a company, a product, or a person. The verb "to attribute" implies the assignment of a quality or characteristic to someone or something. Thus, corporate attributes shall be considered those qualities or characteristics linked to the essential corporate knowledge nodes in stakeholders' memories. Scholars in marketing have come up with a number of typologies for brand and product attributes. Finn (1985) provides a comprehensive summary of 11 different attribute typologies. What is common to all these different approaches is that there is a distinction between the concrete, physical, objectively verifiable attributes and the abstract, beneficial, or subjective attributes of a product. Applied to the corporate context, a similar differentiation is applicable. The attributes of a company that are concrete and (more or less) objectively verifiable are those relating to its behavior, the corporate conduct. These include, for example, the firm's strategy, its leadership, and also its products and services. The attributes that are abstract and subjective in nature are those that are largely the result of a person's inference or attribution processes. Among these attributes are the inferred personality characteristics or traits associated with a company, like innovative or honest.

Berens and van Riel (2004), in their comprehensive review of the reputation measurement literature, unveil three main streams of thought differentiating the attributes people associate with companies:[2] (1) social expectations, which are "the expectations that people have regarding the behavior of companies" (Berens and van Riel, 2004, p. 161); (2) corporate personality, "the personality traits that people attribute to companies" (Berens and van Riel, 2004, p. 161); and (3) trust, "the perception of a company's honesty, reliability and benevolence" (Berens and van Riel, 2004, p. 161), where trust can as well be subsumed under the second category of attributed personality traits. In communication research, these attributes representing behavior and personality traits have been subsumed under the term substantive attributes (e.g., McCombs et al., 2000). Next, the two types of substantive attributes, corporate conduct attributes and corporate personality attributes, will be discussed.

Corporate conduct attributes

These attributes represent the knowledge nodes or categories comprising various knowledge items that carry stakeholders' perceptions of the corporate conduct. The definition of corporate reputation quoted at the beginning, "[o]bservers' collective judgments of a corporation based on assessments of the financial, social, and environmental impacts attributed to the corporation over time" (Barnett et al., 2006, p. 34), hints at some of the relevant areas of corporate conduct. In their literature review, Berens and van Riel (2004) summarize an even broader spectrum of behaviors. By using the term "social expectations," the authors indicate that people expect companies to perform certain behaviors in society like producing good products, supporting social causes, or treating their employees well. Although expectations are considered to vary over time, the notion in academic literature on what people expect from companies are rather coherent according to Berens' and van Riel's literature review. Table 25.1 gives an overview of the corporate conduct attributes discussed in the academic literature on corporate reputation and image measurement developed for multiple industries and published since 1990.

A clustering of the corporate conduct attributes discussed in the literature yields eight attribute categories of varying abstractness.

While the category *financial performance* comprises the specific expectation of stakeholders that the economic activity of a company ought to be profitable, the super-category *corporate ability* addresses the broad range of expectations concerning a company's ability to develop, produce, and deliver products and services, to be successful at that and leading in the market (e.g., Brown, 1998). Thus, the eight categories are not distinctly separate, just as knowledge in human memory is interconnected and not stored in silos. A category overlap as it occurs between *corporate ability* and the *financial performance* and *products and services* categories is, for example, also evident in the case of *social and environmental responsibility* and *management and leadership*. The overview furthermore shows that corporate conduct attributes appear with varying frequency in the academic literature. While the attribute categories *products and services, financial performance, social and environmental responsibility*, and *treatment of employees* are frequently included in the measurements or corporate reputation and image, others like *management and leadership, treatment of exchange partners*, and *marketing considerations* are considered less often by scholars.

Stakeholders' perceptions of a company's behavior and the degree to which their expectations regarding this behavior are fulfilled influence the way corporate conduct attributes are stored and evaluated in stakeholders' memories. In general, an expectation's fulfillment would imply a positive evaluation, while failure to fulfill the expectation goes along with an unfavorable evaluation (Berens and van Riel, 2004). The network structure of knowledge also enables inferences from one attribute and category to another. As illustrated earlier by the example of Apple, people use their associated knowledge to infer one attribute from the value of another. This way, even if much information about a company may not be encoded in memory, people derive the missing pieces logically from their network of positive and negative connections in memory (Bless et al., 2004). According to balance theory (e.g., Heider, 1946), cognitive structures tend toward consistency,

Table 25.1 Corporate conduct attributes (adapted from Berens and van Riel, 2004).

Corporate conduct attribute/category	Label used by author(s)	Author(s)	Handbook chapter
Corporate ability	Corporate ability/ies and success	Brown (1998); Brown and Dacin (1997)	
	Success	Aaker (1996); Helm (2005)	
	Economic responsibilities	Maignan and Ferrell (2003)	
	Market leadership	Saxton (1998)	
Financial performance	Financial performance	Fombrun et al. (2000); Fryxell and Wang (1994); Helm (2005); Saxton (1998)	Chapter 31 on financial performance (A.V. Laskin)
		Schwaiger (2004)	
	Performance	Johnson and Zinkhan (1990)	
	Company as investment	Maignan and Ferrell (2003)	
	Investor responsibilities		
Management and leadership	Vision and leadership	Fombrun et al. (2000)	Chapter 26 on leadership (J. Meng and B.K. Berger); Chapter 28 on corporate governance (J. Pettigrew and B.H. Reber)
	Qualification of management	Helm (2005)	
Products and services	Products and services	Fombrun et al. (2000)	Chapter 29 on products and services (P. Ji and P.S. Lieber)
	Product quality capabilities	Fryxell and Wang (1994)	
	Product considerations	Brown (1998)	
	Quality	Aaker (1996); Schwaiger (2004)	
	Product quality	Frank (1996); Helm (2005); Saxton (1998)	
	Service quality	Saxton (1998)	
	Value for money for customers	Helm (2005)	
	Concern for customers	Aaker (1996)	
	Customer orientation	Helm (2005)	
	Customer responsibilities	Maignan and Ferrell (2003)	
	Innovativeness	Aaker (1996)	
Marketing considerations	Marketing considerations	Brown (1998)	
	Credibility of advertising claims	Helm (2005)	
	Brand image through advertising	Saxton (1998)	

(*Continued*)

Table 25.1 (Continued)

Corporate conduct attribute/category	Label used by author(s)	Author(s)	Handbook chapter
Treatment of exchange partners	Company as seller	Johnson and Zinkhan (1990)	
	Supplier treatment	Frank (1996)	
	Interaction with exchange partners	Brown (1998)	
Treatment of employees	Company as employer	Johnson and Zinkhan (1990)	Chapter 27 on workplace environment (H. Jiang)
	Workplace environment	Fombrun et al. (2000)	
	Employee treatment	Frank (1996); Helm (2005)	
	Interaction with employees	Brown (1998)	
	Employee responsibilities	Maignan and Ferrell (2003)	
Social and environmental responsibility	Corporate social responsibility (CSR)	Brown and Dacin, (1997); Frank (1996); Fryxell and Wang (1994)	Chapter 30 on corporate social responsibility (F. Schultz)
	Responsibility	Schwaiger (2004)	
	Social responsibility and contributions	Brown (1998)	
	Social performance	Saxton (1998)	
	Company as citizen	Johnson and Zinkhan (1990)	
	Commitment to charitable and social issues	Helm (2005)	
	Philanthropic responsibilities	Maignan and Ferrell (2003)	
	Community orientation/responsibilities	Aaker (1996); Maignan and Ferrell (2003)	
	Social and environmental responsibility	Fombrun et al. (2000)	
	Environmental sensitivity	Aaker (1996)	
	Commitment to protecting environment	Helm (2005)	

and balanced relations in memory were shown to be remembered easier (DeSoto, 1960). Thus, stakeholders may infer that the company of which they know that it acts responsibly toward the environment may also treat its employees well. Stakeholders furthermore tend to make inferences from the perception of how a company behaves in the market and with respect to society to the underlying character-istics and stable traits of the company, the "cor-porate personality."

Corporate personality attributes

Personality has been defined as "the set of psy-chological traits and mechanisms within the individual that are organized and relatively enduring and that influence his or her interac-tions with, and adaptations to, the intrapsychic, physical, and social environments" (Larsen and Buss, 2005, p. 4). Berens and van Riel (2004) point to the early applications of the personality metaphor in conceptualizations of corporate image (Spector, 1961), brand (King, 1973), and corporate identity (Lux, 1986). In the 1990s, Jennifer Aaker (1997) developed a con-ceptualization and measurement instrument for brand personality. Aaker defines brand person-ality as "the set of human characteristics associ-ated with the brand" (p. 347), drawing on research on the "Big Five" human personality structure (Costa and McCrae, 1992).[3] Aaker developed the brand personality construct and the number and nature of its dimensions. From her research, she derived the following five dimensions: sincerity, excitement, competence, sophistication, and ruggedness.

In corporate reputation research, Davies and colleagues (2001, 2003) developed a corporate personality scale using Aaker's brand personal-ity scale as a starting point. An important inno-vation of Davies' approach was the development of an instrument suitable to measure the per-ception of external stakeholders as well as inter-nal ones (employees), which allows for assessing the gaps between employee and customer views (Davies *et al.*, 2004). The seven superordinate dimensions derived by Davies and colleagues are agreeableness, enterprise, competence, ruthlessness, chic, informality, and machismo.

For each dimension, there is a list of 3–12 specific personality attributes.

In psychology, the "process through which we seek to identify the causes of others' behav-ior and so gain knowledge of their stable traits and dispositions" (Baron *et al.*, 2006, p. 92) is termed attribution. Attribution processes have various functions for individuals (Forsyth, 1980) of which the control function appears particularly important in the context of stakeholder–company interaction. Understand-ing the causes of behaviors and events, even if erroneous, gives an individual a sense of per-sonal control by providing explanations of behavior and environmental outcomes, and facilitating the prediction of these types of out-comes (Forsyth, 1980). Forming knowledge of the stable traits of a company or brand helps people in selecting their interaction partners. From knowing the personality attributes of a company, stakeholders can infer whether they can relate to it, feel comfortable with it, and whether they can trust it. Particularly in uncer-tain situations that involve some kind of risk, it is helpful for an individual to gain some control over the situation by finding out whether the interaction partner is trustworthy, meaning that he or she will not exploit the other's exchange vulnerabilities (Barney and Hansen, 1994).

Trust has been emphasized as a central stra-tegic asset for organizations (e.g., Mayer *et al.*, 1995; Mishra, 1996). A person's trusting intention, his or her willingness to rely on an exchange partner (Moorman *et al.*, 1993), is based on inference about the other person's traits and intentions (e.g., Yamagishi and Yam-agishi, 1994) that imply trustworthiness. Those traits have been discussed and studied intensely in various disciplines. Mayer *et al.* (1995) argue that three personality traits of the trustee – ability, benevolence, and integrity – appear as antecedents of trust. Based on a meta-analysis of 80 trust definitions, McKnight and Chervany (1996) come up with a somewhat longer list of attributes (see Table 25.2). McKnight and Chervany posit that a person's trusting inten-tion is based on a person's confidence that an exchange partner has those attributes. Together, these attributes linked to an exchange partner

Table 25.2 Overview of the attributes implying trustworthiness (McKnight and Chervany, 1996, p. 85).

Broad category	Corporate personality attributes implying trustworthiness	Appearance in literature (count)
Competence	Competence	10
	Expertness	3
	Dynamism	3
Predictability	Predictability	6
Benevolence	Goodness/morality	6
	Goodwill/intentions	10
	Benevolent/caring/concern	14
	Responsiveness	4
Honesty	Honesty	7
	Credibility	1
	Reliability	6
	Dependability	5
Other	Openness/open-minded	2
	Careful/safe	2
	Shared understanding	0
	Personal attraction	1
		Total: 80

and the confidence with which they are held form the concept of "trusting beliefs."

Comparing the personality attributes implying trustworthiness with the conceptualization of corporate personality developed by Davies *et al.* (2003), we can identify various overlapping positions: trustworthiness in general and the specific attributes implying trustworthiness – above all competence, concern, honesty, reliability, and openness – are also attributes that are part of the comprehensive concept of corporate personality. Thus, trustworthiness serves not only as one dimension within the concept of trust but also as an integral part of the broader concept of corporate personality.

The perception of a company's personality traits influences stakeholders' evaluations. Whether the relation of an attribute with a company implies a positive or a negative evaluation, however, is dependent on the company and the situation, as well as the stakeholder's personality. The attribute "easygoing" for example, might entail a favorable evaluation in the case of a technology venture, but it might go along with an unfavorable evaluation in the case of an insurance company. Or, a young

fashion-conscious woman might favorably evaluate the firm to which she ascribes the attribute trendy. The same association made by an elderly conservative man would likely result in a negative evaluation of the company.

Formation of Corporate Awareness, Attributes, and Associations: The Role of Communication

The formation of stakeholder company knowledge – the awareness, associations, and attributes – is influenced by various sources. A basic distinction in sources is between direct experiences with a company (e.g., personal interaction with employees, product usage) and indirect experiences through communication from company-dominated impersonal sources (e.g., advertising, corporate web site), independent personal sources (e.g., word of mouth from friends), or independent impersonal sources (e.g., news media, rating agencies) (e.g., Engel *et al.*, 1995; Murray, 1991). Since many stakeholders do not have regular direct contact with a firm, they rely on independent impersonal sources or "information intermediaries" (Fombrun and Shanley, 1990), such as the news media, to help them find out about and understand a company's complex activities.

The spreading of information is essential as reputation emerges as a result of social network effects when information on an object in one relation spreads to others via an information network (Granovetter, 1985). Apart from the news media, communication platforms that may exert strong network effects are online social media like *Youtube, Facebook,* or *Twitter.* These company-independent sources are of growing importance for corporate reputation management. They may deliver insights into emerging issues which might potentially hamper or strengthen the corporate reputation and provide the opportunity for stakeholders to communicate openly about a company and for companies to openly join into the conversation.

Successfully managing the corporate reputation is a process that starts with listening and gauging stakeholder knowledge, externally but also internally, to find out about people's awareness of the firm, their associations, and stored or derived attributes. The internal perspective is particularly important in order to learn about the corporate identity (van Rekom, 1997) and to detect which attributes of the firm are central, enduring, and distinctive for its members (Albert and Whetten, 1985; Whetten, 2006). These insights along with the superordinate corporate strategy help define the strategy on what and to whom to communicate about which attributes of the firm. And eventually, monitoring communications in the media as well as in online (social) media above and beyond gauging the knowledge stakeholders have formed is key to evaluate and adjust the strategy for a successful corporate reputation management.

Notes

1 Eagly and Chaiken (1993) remark that beliefs have been given a variety of other names, "includ-ing cognitions, knowledge, opinions, information, and inferences" (p. 11). Here, the term "belief" shall be used for this type of cognitive representation in memory.

2 Berens and van Riel (2004) refer to the attributes associated with the company as corporate associations. However, in line with the definition of associations and attributes suggested here, the associated attributes are to be discussed under the label "corporate attributes."

3 The Big Five factors are openness, conscientiousness, extraversion, agreeableness, and neuroticism.

References

Aaker, D.A. (1991) *Managing Brand Equity: Capitalizing on the Value of a Brand Name.* New York: The Free Press.

Aaker, D.A. (1996) *Building Strong Brands.* New York: The Free Press.

Aaker, J.L. (1997) Dimensions of brand personality. *Journal of Marketing Research, 34*(3), 347–356.

Alba, J.W. and Chattopadhyay, A. (1986) Salience effects in brand recall. *Journal of Marketing Research, 23*(4), 363–359.

Albert, S. and Whetten, D.A. (1985) Organizational identity. In B.M. Staw and L.L. Cummings (eds), *Research in Organizational Behavior* (Vol. 7). Greenwich, CT: JAI Press Inc., pp. 263–295.

Anderson, J.R. (1983a) A spreading activation theory of memory. *Journal of Verbal Learning and Verbal Behavior, 22*(3), 261–295.

Anderson, J.R. (1983b) *The Architecture of Cognition* (3rd ed.). Cognitive Science Series: Vol. 5. Cambridge, MA: Harvard University Press.

Anderson, J.R. and Bower, G.H. (1973) *Human Associative Memory.* New York: Wiley.

Barnett, M.L., Jermier, J.M., and Lafferty, B.A. (2006) Corporate reputation: The definitional landscape. *Corporate Reputation Review, 9*(1), 26–38.

Barney, J.B. and Hansen, M.H. (1994) Trustworthiness as a source of competitive advantage. *Strategic Management Journal, 15*(Special Issue, Winter), 175–190.

Baron, R.A., Byrne, D.E., and Branscombe, N.R. (2006) *Social Psychology* (11th ed.). Boston: Pearson/Allyn & Bacon.

Berens, G. and van Riel, C.B.M. (2004) Corporate associations in the academic literature: Three main streams of thought in the reputation measurement literature. *Corporate Reputation Review, 7*(2), 161–178.

Bless, H., Fiedler, K., and Strack, F. (2004) *Social Cognition: How Individuals Construct Social Reality*. Hove, UK: Psychology Press.

Brown, T.J. (1998) Corporate associations in marketing: Antecedents and consequences. *Corporate Reputation Review*, 1(3), 215–233.

Brown, T.J. and Dacin, P.A. (1997) The company and the product: Corporate associations and consumer product responses. *Journal of Marketing*, 61(1), 68–84.

Brown, T.J., Dacin, P.A., Pratt, M.G., and Whetten, D.A. (2006) Identity, intended image, construed image, and reputation: An interdisciplinary framework and suggested terminology. *Journal of the Academy of Marketing Science*, 34(2), 99–106.

Collins, A.M. and Loftus, E.F. (1975) A spreading-activation theory of semantic processing. *Psychological Review*, 82(6), 407–428.

Costa, P.T. and McCrae, R.R. (1992) *Revised NEO Personality Inventory (NEO PI-R) and NEO Five-Factor Inventory (NEO-FFI): Professional Manual*. Odessa, FL: Psychological Assessment Resources.

Craik, F.I.M. and Lockhart, R.S. (1972) Levels of processing: A framework for memory research. *Journal of Verbal Learning and Verbal Behavior*, 11(6), 671–684.

Davies, G., Chun, R., DaSilva, R.V., and Roper, S. (2001) The personification metaphor as a measurement approach for corporate reputation. *Corporate Reputation Review*, 4(2), 113–127.

Davies, G., Chun, R., DaSilva, R.V., and Roper, S. (2003) *Corporate Reputation and Competitiveness* (1st ed.). London: Routledge.

Davies, G., Chun, R., DaSilva, R.V., and Roper, S. (2004) A corporate character scale to assess employee and customer views of organization reputation. *Corporate Reputation Review*, 7(2), 125–146.

DeSoto, C.B. (1960) Learning a social structure. *Journal of Abnormal and Social Psychology*, 60, 417–421.

Eagly, A.H. and Chaiken, S. (1993) *The Psychology of Attitudes*. Fort Worth, TX: Harcourt Brace Jovanovich College Publishers.

Engel, J.F., Blackwell, R.D., and Miniard, P.W. (1995) *Consumer Behavior* (8th ed.). The Dryden Press Series in Marketing. Forth Worth, TX: Dryden Press.

Fazio, R.H. (1995) Attitudes as object-evaluation associations: Determinants, consequences, and correlates of attitude accessibility. In R.E. Petty and J.A. Krosnick (eds), *Attitude Strength.*

Antecedents and Consequences. Mahwah, NJ: Lawrence Erlbaum Associates, pp. 247–282.

Fazio, R.H. (2007) Attitudes as object–evaluation associations of varying strength. *Social Cognition*, 25(5), 603–637.

Fazio, R.H., Chen, J.-M., McDonel, E.C., and Sherman, S.J. (1982) Attitude accessibility, attitude-behavior consistency and the strength of the object-evaluation association. *Journal of Experimental Social Psychology*, 18(4), 339–357.

Finn, A. (1985) A theory of the consumer evaluation process for new product concepts. In J.N. Sheth (ed.), *Research in Consumer Behaviour* (Vol. 1). Greenwich, CT: JAI Press Inc., pp. 35–65.

Fishbein, M. and Ajzen, I. (1975) *Belief, Attitude, Intention and Behavior: An Introduction to Theory and Research*. Addison-Wesley Series in Social Psychology. London: Addison-Wesley.

Fombrun, C.J. (1996) *Reputation: Realizing Value from the Corporate Image*. Boston: Harvard Business School Press.

Fombrun, C.J. and Shanley, M. (1990) What's in a name? Reputation building and corporate strategy. *Academy of Management Journal*, 33(2), 233–258.

Fombrun, C.J., Gardberg, N.A., and Sever, J.M. (2000) The Reputation Quotient[SM]: A multi-stakeholder measure of corporate reputation. *The Journal of Brand Management*, 7(4), 241–255.

Forsyth, D.R. (1980) The functions of attributions. *Social Psychology Quarterly*, 43(2), 184–189.

Frank, R.H. (1996) Can socially responsible firms survive in a competitive environment? In D. Messick and A. Tenbrunsel (eds), *Codes of Conduct: Behavioral Research into Business Ethics*. New York: Russell Sage Foundation, pp. 86–103.

Fryxell, G.E. and Wang, J. (1994) The *Fortune* corporate "reputation index": Reputation for what? *Journal of Management*, 20(1), 1–14.

Goldstein, D.G. and Gigerenzer, G. (2002) Models of ecological rationality: The recognition heuristic. *Psychological Review*, 109(1), 75–90.

Granovetter, M. (1985) Economic action and social structure: The problem of embeddedness. *American Journal of Sociology*, 91(3), 481–510.

Heider, F. (1946) Attitudes and cognitive organization. *Journal of Psychology*, 21, 107–112.

Helm, S. (2005) Designing a formative measure for corporate reputation. *Corporate Reputation Review*, 8(2), 95–109.

Johnson, M. and Zinkhan, G.M. (1990) Defining and measuring company image. In B.J. Dunlap (ed.), Proceedings of the Thirteenth Annual Conference of the Academy of Marketing Science (pp. 346–350). New Orleans, LA, April.

Keller, K.L. (1993) Conceptualizing, measuring, and managing customer-based brand equity. *Journal of Marketing*, 57(1), 1–22.

Keller, K.L. (1998) *Strategic Brand Management: Building, Measuring and Managing Brand Equity.* Upper Saddle River, NJ: Prentice Hall.

King, S. (1973) *Developing New Brands. The Times Management Library.* London: Pitman.

Krishnan, H.S. (1996) Characteristics of memory associations: A consumer-based brand equity perspective. *International Journal of Research in Marketing*, 13(4), 389–405.

Larsen, R.J. and Buss, D.M. (2005) *Personality Psychology: Domains of Knowledge about Human Nature* (2nd ed.). Boston: McGraw-Hill.

Lux, P.G.C. (1986) Zur Durchführung von Corporate Identity Programmen. In K. Birkigt (ed.), *Corporate Identity. Grundlagen, Funktionen, Fallbeispiele* (3rd ed.). Landsberg/Lech: Verl. Moderne Industrie, pp. 515–537.

Maignan, I. and Ferrell, O.C. (2003). Nature of corporate responsibilities: Perspectives from American, French, and German consumers. *Journal of Business Research*, 56(1), 55–67.

Mayer, R.C., Davis, J.H., and Schoorman, F.D. (1995) An integrative model of organizational trust. *Academy of Management Review*, 20(3), 709–734.

McCombs, M., Lopez-Escobar, E., and Llamas, J.P. (2000) Setting the agenda of attributes in the 1996 Spanish general election. *Journal of Communication*, 50(2), 77–92.

McKnight, D.H. and Chervany, N.L. (1996) The meanings of trust. MISRC Working Paper Series No. 96-04. Retrieved from http://misrc.umn.edu/wpaper/WorkingPapers/9604.pdf (last accessed September 24, 2012).

Mishra, A.K. (1996) Organizational responses to crisis: The centrality of trust. In R.M. Kramer and T.R. Tyler (eds), *Trust in Organizations: Frontiers of Theory and Research.* Thousand Oaks, CA: Sage, pp. 261–287.

Moorman, C., Deshpandé, R., and Zaltman, G. (1993) Factors affecting trust in market research relationships. *Journal of Marketing*, 57(1), 81–101.

Murray, K.B. (1991) A test of services marketing theory: Consumer information acquisition activities. *Journal of Marketing*, 55(1), 10–25.

Narayana, C.L. and Markin, R.J. (1975) Consumer behavior and product performance: An alternative conceptualization. *Journal of Marketing*, 39(4), 1–6.

Post, J.E., Preston, L.E., and Sachs, S. (2002) *Redefining the Corporation: Stakeholder Management and Organizational Wealth. Stanford Business Books.* Stanford, CA: Stanford University Press.

Quillian, R. (1966) *Semantic Memory.* Cambridge, MA: Bolt, Beranek and Newman, Inc.

Raaijmakers, J.G.W. and Shiffrin, R.M. (1981) Search of associative memory. *Psychological Review*, 8(2), 98–134.

Rindova, V.P., Williamson, I.O., Petkova, A.P., and Sever, J.M. (2005) Being good or being known: An empirical examination of the dimensions, antecedents, and consequences of organizational reputation. *Academy of Management Journal*, 48(6), 1033–1049.

Rossiter, J.R. and Percy, L. (1998) *Advertising Communications and Promotion Management* (2nd ed.). Advertising and Marketing Series. New York: McGraw-Hill.

Saxton, M.K. (1998) Where do corporate reputations come from? *Corporate Reputation Review*, 1(4), 393–399.

Schwaiger, M. (2004) Components and parameters of corporate reputation–An empirical study. *Schmalenbach Business Review*, 56(January), 46–71.

Spector, A.J. (1961) Basic dimensions of the corporate image. *Journal of Marketing*, 25(6), 47–51.

van Rekom, J. (1997) Deriving an operational measure of corporate identity. *European Journal of Marketing*, 31(5/6), 410–422.

van Riel, C.B.M. and Fombrun, C.J. (2004) *Fame & Fortune: How Successful Companies Build Winning Reputations* (4th ed.). Upper Saddle River, NJ: Pearson Education.

Whetten, D.A. (2006) Albert and Whetten revisited: Strengthening the concept of organizational identity. *Journal of Management Inquiry*, 15(3), 219–234.

Yamagishi, T. and Yamagishi, M. (1994) Trust and commitment in the United States and Japan. *Motivation and Emotion*, 18(2), 129–166.

26

What They Say and What They Do: Executives Affect Organizational Reputation through Effective Communication

Juan Meng

University of Georgia, USA

Bruce K. Berger

University of Alabama, USA

The roles and functions of senior executives in managing their organization's reputation has become a popular area of study. Though senior executives sometimes fail to take the necessary steps to protect their organizations from reputational risk, CEOs nevertheless represent organizational values and are the faces and voices of organizations. Though they may rely on their top management teams for inputs regarding operational decisions and long-term actions, the outcomes of strategic initiatives are often attributed to the CEOs' leadership. Thus, this chapter explores the roles and dimensions of CEOs and executive leadership with respect to communication and reputation formation and management.

Chapter Overview

CEOs' public image is the organization in the mind of the audience and to its stakeholders. Internally, CEOs influence employee perceptions and attitudes, trust in management, performance, and job- and organization-related outcomes (Daily and Johnson, 1997). Externally, the CEO's image plays a significant role in determining a company's reputation. Gaines-Ross (2000) found that not only do CEO behaviors influence the marketing of the firm and products and services to consumers, but a CEO's image also impacts financial analysts' stock recommendations, investors' purchase decisions, and company reputation.

As a strong indication of positive corporate reputation, a solid link between CEOs' leadership and firm performance has also been demonstrated. While external factors such as the

The Handbook of Communication and Corporate Reputation, First Edition. Edited by Craig E. Carroll.
© 2013 John Wiley & Sons, Inc. Published 2015 by John Wiley & Sons, Inc.

organization's industry and macroeconomic conditions can dramatically affect organizational performance, CEOs still account for a significant percentage of the total variance in performance. With estimates of variance accounted for ranging from 8.7% to 14.5%, it is clear that CEOs impact profitability (Thomas, 1988). Often, an organization's image is determined by how the CEO is portrayed in the media, and these depictions can influence a company's success or failure (Foster, 1990; Gary, 1986). CEOs personify and represent their organizations through their visibility in media. In this way their leadership influences perceptions of the organization among stakeholders, and thereby organizational reputation and performance.

Therefore, this chapter focuses on strategic leadership at the senior executive level, and we discuss how CEOs (and top management teams (TMTs)) and their strategic leadership can support organizations in building and managing reputations. We review five trends in executive leadership research and focus on how chief executives impact organizational performance. We believe these trends are highly relevant to the role of communication in corporate reputation and performance.

The five trends are (1) the identification of the succession process of executive psychology and a complex set of psychological attributes and observable characteristics of executives; (2) the interactive relationships between chief executives and their TMTs and the corresponding implications for strategy formation and organizational development; (3) chief executives' unique roles and contributions in facilitating transformational change for their organizations; (4) the intertwined relationship between CEO leadership and power, with a specific focus on the soft power of attraction and persuasion; and (5) the independent and dependent roles of executive leadership in shaping organizational culture and being reshaped by it over time.

By considering these perspectives on executive leadership, we believe this review not only synthesizes contemporary strategic leadership research, but more importantly, also suggests a contingent view of strategic leadership and senior executives' active roles in leading organizational transformation and building corporate reputations through effective communication.

Individual-Based Executive Actions and Succession

Executive psychology is the basis from which executives filter, selectively perceive, and interpret information as they develop their own judgments about how their organizations should respond to the situation (Hambrick, 1989). Finkelstein *et al.* (2009) define executive psychology as "the person's interwoven set of psychological and observable characteristics . . . which in turn yields a construed reality, gives rise to strategic choices, and ultimately affects organizational performance" (p. 49). They further argue that such psychological properties are attributes that chief executives bring to their institutional situations.

Research in executive psychology explores three broad areas: executive values, cognitive models, and other elements of personality (e.g., Miller and Droge, 1986; Miller and Toulouse, 1986). The executive value system has been considered at both social and personal levels, and many value dimensions (including Hofstede's cultural dimensions and other dimensions like rationality, novelty, duty, and power) have been employed to explain differences in executives' actions (House *et al.*, 2004). For example, Geletkanycz (1997) found strong causal links between senior executives' national culture and their commitment to the status quo when initiating corporate strategies. In addition, the values of executives function as perceptual filters to exert indirect influences on their actions. These perceptual filters "allow the manager to see what he or she wants to see" (see Finkelstein and Hambrick, 1996, pp. 48–56) and ultimately reflect the personality of the CEOs in their selection of strategies.

Meng and associates recently identified several value dimensions associated with senior public relations executives that are linked to effective public relations leadership (Meng, 2009; Meng *et al.*, 2012). The dimensions include of self-dynamics (e.g., the leader's personality, attributes, and style), ethical orientation (e.g., the nature of being ethical and doing the right things in public relations practice), and relationship building (e.g., the value of facilitating mutually beneficial relationships between an organization and its key stakeholders). Though leadership qualities and natures can be quite similar across different industries or organizations, these value dimensions appeared to be highly relevant to public relations leaders' strategic decision making and actions.

The cognitive models employed by executives have also been studied extensively to ascertain cognitive limits and their contribution to strategic decision making. Research on executive cognition has focused on an executive's cognitive content (what they know, assume, and believe); cognitive structure (how the content has been organized in their mind); and cognitive style (how the structured content in the mind works) (Nutt, 1993). Tyler and Steensma (1998) found that executives with technical degrees are more likely to position their organizations in a complex technological environment and obtain technological alliances for the organizations than are executives with a weaker technical background. This supports the idea that executives' knowledge and cognitive styles affect their decision making.

Finkelstein and Hambrick (1996) also identified other characteristics that contribute to an executive's orientation. These factors include an executive's experience or tenure, formal education, functional background, and international experience. There has been a steady increase in the education levels of executives over the past two decades, and young executives tend to be more highly educated than their older counterparts (Wiersema and Bantel, 1992). Moreover, new chief executives recruited from outside the organization make more changes, or are more likely to initiate transformational changes, than are those promoted from within (Hambrick and Fukutomi, 1991). However, the relationship between these factors and organizational outcomes needs further scrutiny since chief executives tend to make more ambitious strategic changes and to be more proactive early in their tenures than they do at a later stage (e.g., Datta and Guthrie, 1994; Hambrick and Fukutomi, 1991; Miller, 1991).

The study of psychological constructs in senior executives helps clarify the leadership construct and can provide an explanation for executive behaviors. Finkelstein and Hambrick (1996) also acknowledged the contributions of individual-based leadership research, and they argued for the consideration of a two-way causality between executive psychological properties and experiences: "Executive psychological and experience characteristics cannot reliably be put one before the other" (p. 47). Executive experiences affect their psychological characteristics, and fundamental psychological qualities can also substantially affect individuals' experiences.

The CEO-TMT Interface and Group-Based Executive Actions

Research on the TMT emerged in the early 1980s. Hambrick and Mason proposed upper echelon theory to refer to the relatively small group of the most influential executives in an organization. This group usually consists of the CEO and their direct report employees (e.g., the president, chief financial officer, senior legal counsel, and senior human resources leadership).

Finkelstein and Hambrick (1996) stressed that "top management team" does not necessarily imply "a formalized management-by-committee arrangement, but rather simply the constellation of the top three to ten executives" (p. 8). These groups possess distinctive experience and more significantly are responsible for formulating adaptive responses to the changing environment, making strategic decisions to lead change, and implementing those responses and strategies. This research stream has provided compelling insights about the impact of senior leaders, at both individual and collective levels, on their organizations' strategic choices and subsequent organizational performance.

As a direct response to their responsibilities and consensus on organizational leadership strategy, CEOs and their TMT members have been consolidated into a single category called the "dominant coalition" (Cyert and March, 1963), or the "upper echelons" (Hambrick and Mason, 1984). Empirical research has indicated the complicated nature of their task and the profound impact they can have on the strategic direction and performance of their organizations. CEOs and the TMT members largely represent their organization's value, social conduct, and reputation as the level of organizational publicity increases or the environment changes. There is growing evidence that TMT dynamics are directly linked to organizational performance (Peterson *et al.*, 2003). Today, one can never ignore the interaction between CEOs and the TMT members as a salient intervening mechanism in affecting organizational outcomes and functions.

Research suggests that CEOs are uniquely responsible for selecting, evaluating, rewarding, motivating, and coaching members of their TMTs. Peterson *et al.* (2003) found that the CEO personality is significantly related to TMT group dynamics, which are further related to organizational performance. Thus, the CEOs' leadership style is assessed and interpreted by those TMTs with whom they work directly. CEOs' transformational proclivity directly affects the TMT members' engagement in corporate actions and reputation building (e.g., Hambrick, 1998; Peterson *et al.*, 2003; Zaccaro and Klimoski, 2002).

Research also highlights the important mediating role of the TMTs in the institutional environment. For example, Peterson *et al.* (2003) found that the relationship between the CEO personality and organizational performance is mediated by the decision-making environment of the TMTs. Transformational CEOs can encourage their TMTs to be more responsive to new opportunities and associated risks, and be more committed to initiating new actions

and supporting changes. Meanwhile, CEOs are also constrained in their ability to change the organization. Constraints grow not only out of managerial discretion throughout the organization, but also from practical bounds imposed by the actions of the TMTs with whom they work directly (Finkelstein and Hambrick, 1996).

Executive Leadership and Organizational Transformation

A growing body of leadership research focuses on the leader–follower relationship. Unlike traditional leadership approaches, the research trend in transformational leadership focuses more on charismatic and affective elements of leadership, and on the followers' intrinsic motivation and self-development. Topics such as how leaders can use leadership to engage followers, and how leaders can use this inspirational process to leverage followers and themselves to better citizens have been studied (e.g., Bass, 1985; Burns, 1978; Conger, 1999; Judge and Piccolo, 2004).

More recently, scholars have suggested that theories of transformational leadership should be integrated with executive leadership perspectives to increase understanding of the transformational process, since chief executives often lead the way of transformation. Research has indicated that a key feature of strategic leadership is the active role of senior executives in all phases of the organizational transformation process (e.g., Boal and Hooijberg, 2000; Colbert *et al.*, 2008).

According to Bass (1985), transformational leadership comprises four primary characteristics: *idealized influence* from the transformational leader, *inspirational motivation* of the compelling visions of the future, *intellectual stimulation* of the safe institutional environment, and *individualized consideration* of improvement recognition. Several specific behaviors of transformational leaders support those characteristics and lead the change process:

- *Envisioning.* Chief executives are able to articulate a clear and credible vision of the new strategic direction in overarching terms for the organization (Conger and Kanungo, 1998).
- *Energizing.* Executives must demonstrate personal excitement for the changes and model the behaviors that are expected of others (Conger and Kanungo, 1998).
- *Enabling.* Executives must provide the resources necessary for undertaking significant change and use rewards to reinforce new behaviors (Nutt and Backoff, 1997).

Moreover, most leadership scholars believe that the importance of a well-articulated vision exists in its power to clarify the direction in which an organization needs to move and to explain the strategy for the organization to achieve its vision. Thus, the ability to articulate a compelling vision to followers is the most important aspect of transformational leadership (Conger and Kanungo, 1998). Meanwhile, a series of balanced actions are also essential in the transformation process. Chief executives need to apply leadership skills to empower others and maintain the credibility of the change effort in a consistent way. This includes serving as a role model, making decisions, and exhibiting actions that support their words.

Specifically, Kotter (1996) has suggested six crucial actions for chief executives to perform as effective change agents. These actions include the following: (1) establish a sense of urgency about the organization's competitive situation and ensure that the majority see the need for a major change; (2) form powerful guiding coalitions based on TMT members' expertise, reputations, and relationships; (3) broadcast the vision by using all communication channels that are available; (4) remove both internal and external obstacles in the transformation process; (5) create short-term wins in order to build momentum and collect compelling evidence to show performance improvements; and (6) institutionalize new approaches to ensure leadership succession and development in the next generation of TMTs.

Meng and associates also found that it is vital for chief executives to learn to "walk the talk" to maintain credibility and support for the overall transformation process. Becoming a living symbol of the new organizational culture can motivate organizational members to learn and adopt the new approaches, systems, and behaviors and to believe they can, in fact, thereby improve organizational performance. When interviewed, most respondents agreed that all members of the dominant coalition are needed to lead change and that factors impacting the effectiveness of organizational leaders should be applied to the corporate communication function (Berger and Meng, 2010; Meng, 2009). The respondents specifically mentioned that the abilities to articulate a vision and to "walk the talk" are crucial for senior corporate communication executives to indicate a high level of involvement, even though the direct followers might be limited to a group of communication teams (e.g., Meng and Berger, 2010; Meng *et al.*, 2012).

Increasingly, public relations and corporate communication professionals are members of the dominant coalition or strategic decision-making process. In countries where the public relations industry is more advanced (e.g., Canada, the United Kingdom, and the United States), organizational leaders have improved their knowledge and appreciation for diverse public relations and corporate communication efforts. This improvement has enabled senior communication executives to reposition their significant roles in the organizational transformation process. Overall, transformation has become a key feature associated with strategic leadership, and leaders are a critical tool on which organizations rely in their efforts to cope with today's turbulent environment and global economy.

The Intertwined Relationship between Leadership and Power

In practice, effective leadership is a social action with three key components – leaders, followers, and the contexts in which they interact (Yukl, 2002). Contemporary leadership theorists often see leadership as a mixture of hard and soft power skills. Soft power skills refer to the chief executive's ability to attract or persuade their followers. Hard power refers to their ability to make the hiring, firing, and/or financial decisions (Nye, 2010). In studying strategic leadership and leadership effectiveness, researchers focus more on investigating chief executives' application of soft power skills: how they achieve objectives and gain the desired outcomes by attracting and motivating followers rather than manipulating or threatening them, or using material incentives (e.g., Bass, 1985; Conger and Kanungo, 1998; Yukl and Falbe, 1991).

From a political science perspective, Nye (2008, 2010) considers the relationship between power and leadership (especially the CEO leadership) to be "inextricably intertwined" (p. 305). He characterized power as having both a hard form (coercive; such as police and financial powers) and a soft form (attractive; such as buying into the values) and suggests that "In practice, effective leadership requires a mixture of soft and hard power skills," a combination that produces "smart power" (p. 305). Nye believes that both hard and soft power skills (especially different proportions of both forms) are exercised to a certain degree by every leader within a variety of contexts. Like transformational leaders, smart executives use strategies to attract followers to do what they want them to do, and they lead as the role models.

Organizational behavior research has indicated the importance of recognizing power sources and their links to leadership effectiveness. Yukl and Falbe (1991) found power sources can be associated with hierarchical positions in the organization, levels of information possession, or individual persuasiveness and charisma. By comparing managers' applications of downward and lateral powers, they found legitimate power, expert power, and persuasiveness were the most important ones for carrying out requests. They also found a general pattern in applying powers among managers: they

tended to have more position power over subordinates than over peers.

Berger and Reber (2006) identified five types of power sources that executives can develop and draw from. *Individual sources* include skills, personal characteristics, and professional expertise and knowledge. *Structural sources* refer to hierarchical position, presence in decision-making groups, and controllable resources. *Relational sources* refer to personal relationships, coalitions, and internal and external social networks. *Informational sources* refer to access to and control over information and political intelligence, and *systemic sources* include professional associations and associated reputations, codes and standards, and measures of professional value. Clearly, CEOs and TMT members possesses significant structural, informational, and relational power, and presumably, they also possess strong individual and systemic power through their clubs and associations.

Power may be the most valuable and important resource in organizations (Bolman and Deal, 1991), and the use of power by CEOs bears implications for reputation building, especially inside organizations. That CEOs and TMTs possess substantial power in various forms is a given, but what they do with that power and the extent to which they share and distribute it among others in the organization is a crucial factor in building reputation. More than anything, perhaps, how CEOs use their power affects the communication climate of organizations, the strength and quality of employee and member identification with their organizations, and the overall culture of the organization.

Executive Leadership Behavior and Organizational Culture

Organizational culture has captured the interest of a variety of leadership researchers. Research has largely focused on the impact of organizational culture on corporate outcomes, and scholars believe that executive leadership is the primary shaper and builder of organizational culture (e.g., Davis, 1984). Similarly, Porter and Nohria (2010) described the CEO as the one who "defines the roles of individuals in the organization, assigns them into units, establishes reporting relationships, and delineating how units will coordinate with each other" (p. 436).

It appears that only those cultures that enable organizations to anticipate and adapt to environmental change will be associated with high levels of performance over time (e.g., Kotter and Heskett, 1992; Waldman and Yammarino, 1999). Organizations that lack an adaptive culture may constrain transformational leaders' actions. For example, Kotter and Heskett (1992) found that highly politicized or rigid cultures may prevent the selection of transformational leaders or limit their effectiveness, which further leads to poor organizational performance. Research efforts in public relations leadership also revealed similar findings in describing the relationships between organizational structure and leadership effectiveness (e.g., Berger and Meng, 2010; Kang and Berger, 2009; Meng, 2009). For example, Meng's (2009) study confirmed the strong impact organizational structure and culture can have on the effectiveness of leadership in public relations practice. Kang and Berger (2009) also suggested that an open and participative communication system facilitates effective practice in public relations leadership.

One central aspect of organizational culture is internal communication, which some have argued is the most "fundamental driver of business performance" (Gay *et al.*, 2005, p. 11) and one of the most dominant and important activities in organizations (Harris and Nelson, 2008). A growing body of evidence suggests that effective internal communication can help increase employee commitment, trust, learning, productivity, and morale (e.g., Cheney and Christenson, 2001; Meng and Berger, 2012). Effective internal communication can also improve organizational communication climate and relationships with publics, and enhance quality, revenues, and earnings of the corporation. Most important here is that internal communication patterns often reflect the communication style, practices, and preferences of the senior leader. Smidts *et al.* (2001) studied the role of communication climate in leveraging perceived external prestige (reputation) and found that an attractive communication climate, which encourages active participation, involvement, and information sharing for each employee, can contribute significantly to the long-term success and build a strong corporate reputation.

Deetz *et al.* (2000) underscored the importance of leaders and communication in constructing organizational culture and suggested that their importance increases when they must lead their organizations through change or environmental uncertainty. Leaders are crucial because they model desired behaviors, construct and share vision, frame meanings and interpretations of change, and encourage and motivate employees to adopt to change and engage initiatives. Thus, while culture is complex and includes many components, executive leadership and corresponding internal communications in organizations affect the climate for communication and the extent to which employees may identify with their organizations and engage in work and problem solving. These, in turn, appear linked to productivity, quality of relationships with customers and other external groups, financial performance, and corporate reputation.

From Leadership to Reputation: A Contingent View

Our analysis of executive leadership suggests that the responsibilities of the CEO and top executives in an organization are vital, complex, and closely linked to organizational performance and reputation. Executive leaders often represent their organizations in media coverage, take crucial strategic decisions, allocate resources, and help shape the communication climate and culture of organizations. Thus, the study of top executives, their leadership styles, and the decisions they make is fundamental to understanding the communication flows, strategy formulation, and reputation management of the organization.

Today, organizations face significant challenges when coping with rapidly changing environments and the diffusion of information across industries. Such challenges require even more visionary and supportive executive leadership. To conclude our chapter, we propose a contingent view to understanding and describing the interdependent relationships among three interrelated domains (strategic leadership, organizational performance, and corporate reputation) that seem pivotal to organizational effectiveness and sustainability in a dynamic marketplace. Based on this view, we argue that effective strategic leadership requires multiple levels of involvement and a mixture of contingent factors across the organization to help it achieve a high level of performance and reputation.

The contingency approach of studying strategic leadership is not novel, and many scholars have argued that the appropriate leadership style largely depends on situational contingencies (Fiedler, 1963; Vroom and Yetton, 1973). However, when proposing sets of contingent variables affecting effective leadership styles, it is hard for scholars to reach complete agreement about what such factors were. For example, Fiedler (1963) introduced two sets of contingent factors: the relationship between the leader and the followers and the power of the leader. Other than the leader–follower relationship, Vroom and Yetton (1973) believed that the nature of the task (e.g., being arrayed along a dimension of "certainty" to "uncertainty") and the group's decision-making style (e.g., autocratic, consultative, or group based) present as other essential sets of contingent factors.

Though it is important to focus on the nature of the task and the predispositions of the group's members, other factors can also affect the leader's activities and styles. This is particularly true when the situation is not just about the completion of the task, but more centered on the organization's reputation. Assessing sets of contingent variables in determining the effectiveness of strategic leadership, organizational performance, and corporate reputation is much more complicated than the traditional contingent approach focusing on the leader–follower relationship and the task itself (Fiedler, 1963; Vroom and Yetton, 1973).

Based on the research we have reviewed, we suggest that there are five sets of contingent factors to be recognized when the purpose of research is to link effective communication, executive leadership, and corporate reputation. We briefly describe each factor and some corresponding research implications. First, the CEO's dynamics must be analyzed. This process includes identifying the bases of their influence (e.g., values, visions, other sets of executive psychology, and competence) and how power is distributed within the organization. Research in this approach could focus on how senior executives' communication style and leadership strategies help them gain respect, influence, and rewards, which eventually lead to a high level of employee engagement and the organizational success in terms of reputation management.

Second, there must be an assessment of the interaction between the CEO and his or her TMT. The top leadership group must understand the organization's goals and use their expertise and specializations to help the organization transform toward the strategic direction. Some interesting research points could be the investigation of possible determinants and consequences of CEO-TMT interactions and how the interactions would affect strategic decision making and perceived public reputation. In addition, much more research is required to develop acceptable TMT-level measures such as team member power relations, team-level functioning, inter- and intrapersonal communication among team members and across the organization.

Third, there must be an alignment between the leader's tasks and the organization's goals. The strategic decision-making process is a reflection of negotiation and consensus within the TMT about the best choice among a set of alternative strategies to accomplish the task and achieve the goal. We believe that the greater the congruence between the leader's tasks and the organization's goals, the more likely the followers could match their expectations to the competence of their leader. Therefore, to advance efforts, future research could focus on developing more complex frameworks in predicting factors that might contribute to a higher level of congruence, along with other moderating contextual influences such as the environment, the specific task, and the CEO.

Fourth, there must be a supportive, two-way communication system – a culture for communication – regardless of the organizational complexity, for example, the size and/or the structure. As a direct consequence of the culture for communication, followers would echo more supportive behaviors and functional outputs. The importance of applying a new set of indirect assessments of nonfinancial factors such as employee motivation, satisfaction, engagement, responsiveness, and other user-generated content should be recognized from the internal communication perspective. This type of recognition at the individual level can be linked to a long-term competitive advantage at the organizational level. This is consistent with Barney's (2001) resource-based theory of effective organizations, which mainly argues that the organization that emphasizes the importance of using employees as a source of competitive advantage would highly likely to increase its success. Effective use of an organization's internal resources can generate significant nonfinancial benefits for the organization, including increased organization knowledge and confidence, expanded support for organizational strategies, and strengthened corporate reputation.

Finally, there must be a participative organizational culture and workplace environment that supports leadership initiatives and the qualities of the leader–follower relationship, no matter whether the task is certain. This participative process encourages open communication between the leader and his or her followers, which could further reduce the feeling of uncertainty toward the task. Accordingly, to assess the importance of executive leadership to

organizational culture, we need to examine the importance of executive leadership in terms of its ability to facilitate effective internal communication. If the concept of executive leadership was initially considered for its significance for effective internal communication, when and how do the concept and leader-related behavior infuse communication with effectiveness?

By proposing these five sets of factors, we hope the contingent view can facilitate our understanding of strategic leadership and its functions in improving organizational performance, facilitating effective corporate communications, and building positive corporate reputations.

As indicated earlier, assessing organizational performance and corporate reputation begins with the empowerment of strategic leadership from top executives. This includes an understanding of CEOs' and top executives' psychological attributes, such as executive values, cognitive models, and other dimensions of executive psychology and experiences performed at the individual level. The empowerment of strategic leadership cannot ignore the top leadership group and group-based actions. As Finkelstein *et al.* (2009) have explained, TMT members are more than simply collections of senior executives. Their interrelationships, experiences, expertise, and power distribution have unique implications for decision making and strategy selection. Consequences of the CEO-TMT interface are reflected in the strategic decision-making process, especially the process of strategy formulation and implementation. Once corporate strategy and direction are aligned with the organization's goals and objectives, they are more likely to spur a transformational process for the organization.

However, executive leadership does not end with strategy formulation and implementation. The top leadership group must also build a culture and coherent communication system that facilitates effective corporate interactions and communications and engages employees in the change process. Only in this way can the organization hope to encourage more supportive behaviors from both internal and external audiences, and to acquire crucial knowledge about stakeholder needs and issues. When more functional outputs are carried out along with the organization's communication initiatives, the organization is more likely to achieve strong financial performance and win other noneconomic assessments by multiple stakeholder groups. In short, corporate communications significantly contribute to the organization's reputational capital (van Riel and Fombrun, 2009).

Top executives engage in the management of strategies, communications, and reputations to maximize their functions, their power, and organizational performance. Different dimensions and elements of strategic leadership are often closely interrelated in practice. Though strategic leadership has been widely studied, its importance in facilitating effective corporate communications and building strong and positive corporate reputations has been limited. Our review and analysis suggest that the study of strategic leadership and top executives has great theoretical and practical implications for organizational communication, for understanding executives' behaviors within organizations, and for evaluating the consequences of their behaviors for effective internal communication, organizational performance, and reputation building.

We hope this synthesis provides a comprehensive research agenda for public relations and communication scholars interested in studying top executives, the leadership styles they adopt, and the influences they have on both corporate reputations and corporate communication systems. This could provide a new approach to advancing our research efforts in measuring the impact and success of public relations and communications, as well as to creating more alignment and integration between strategic leadership and corporate communications. For example, researchers can explore how to measure the effectiveness of corporate communications when creating strategies and how building reputations have been aligned both internally and externally.

Just as van Riel and Fombrun (2009) suggested, corporate reputation is a multi-stakeholder social construct that is particularly appropriate for measuring the effectiveness of an organization's communication system. This statement further reveals the mutually interdependent relationship between effective corporate communication and corporate reputation. Effective corporate communication helps an organization to create distinctive and appealing images with its various stakeholder groups, build a strong corporate brand, enhance organizational performance, and develop reputation capital (Dowling and Roberts, 2002; Fombrun, 1996). At the same time, successful reputation management is an indicator of open, supportive, two-way symmetrical corporate communication systems (van Riel, 1995). The contingent approach sketched out here may enable top executives and those who work closely with them to better understand their functions and roles in facilitating such relationships in different situations. It is of particular interest to study how executive leadership may augment effective internal communication and thereby affect the long-term success of an organization and its reputation.

References

Barney, J.B. (2001) Resource-based theories of competitive advantage: A ten-year retrospective on the resource-based view. *Journal of Management, 27*, 643–650.

Bass, B.M. (1985) *Leadership and Performance Beyond Expectations.* New York: Free Press.

Berger, B.K. and Meng, J. (2010) Public relations practitioners and the leadership challenge. In R.L. Heath (ed.), *The SAGE Handbook of Public Relations.* Thousand Oaks, CA: Sage Publications, pp. 421–434.

Berger, B.K. and Reber, B.H. (2006) *Gaining Influence in Public Relations: The Role of Resistance in Practice.* Mahwah, NJ: Lawrence Erlbaum Associates.

Boal, K.B. and Hooijberg, R. (2000) Strategic leadership research: Moving on. *The Leadership Quarterly, 11*, 515–549.

Bolman, L.G. and Deal, T.E. (1991) *Reframing Organizations: Artistry, Choice, and Leadership.* San Francisco, CA: Jossey-Bass.

Burns, J.M. (1978) *Leadership*. New York: Harper & Row.

Cheney, G. and Christenson, L.T. (2001) Organizational identity: Linkages between internal and external communication. In F.M. Jablin and L.L. Putnam (eds), *The New Handbook of Organizational Communication*. Thousand Oaks, CA: Sage Publications, pp. 231–269.

Colbert, A.E., Kristof-Brown, A.L., Bradley, B.H., and Barrick, M.R. (2008) CEO transformational leadership: The role of goal importance congruence in top management teams. *Academy of Management Journal*, 51, 81–96.

Conger, J.A. (1999) Charismatic and transformational leadership in organizations: An insider's perspective on these developing streams of research. *The Leadership Quarterly*, 10, 145–179.

Conger, J.A. and Kanungo, R.N. (1998) *Charismatic Leadership in Organizations*. Thousand Oaks, CA: Sage Publications.

Cyert, R.M. and March, J.G. (1963) *A Behavioral Theory of the Firm*. Englewood Cliffs, NJ: Prentice Hall.

Daily, C.M. and Johnson, J.L. (1997) Sources of CEO power and firm financial performance: A longitudinal assessment. *Journal of Management*, 23(2), 97–117.

Datta, D.K. and Guthrie, J.P. (1994) Executive succession: Organizational antecedents of CEO characteristics. *Strategic Management Journal*, 15, 569–577.

Davis, S.M. (1984) *Managing Corporate Culture*. New York: Ballinger.

Deetz, S.A., Tracy, S.J., and Simpson, J.L. (2000) *Leading Organizations through Transition: Communication and Cultural Change*. Thousand Oaks, CA: Sage Publications.

Dowling, G.R. and Roberts, P.W. (2002) Corporate reputation and sustained superior financial performance. *Strategic Management Journal*, 23, 1077–1093.

Fiedler, F.E. (1963) *A Contingency Model for the Prediction of Leadership Effectiveness*. Champaign, IL: University of Illinois Press.

Finkelstein, S. and Hambrick, D.C. (1996) *Strategic Leadership: Top Executives and Their Effects on Organizations*. St. Paul, MN: West Publishing Company.

Finkelstein, S., Hambrick, D.C., and Cannella, A.A. Jr. (2009) *Strategic Leadership: Theory and Research on Executives, Top Management Teams, and Boards*. New York: Oxford University Press.

Fombrun, C.J. (1996) *Reputation: Realizing Value from the Corporate Image*. Boston: Harvard Business School Press.

Foster, L.G. (1990) The CEO connection: Pivotal for the '90s. *Public Relations Journal*, 46(1), 24–25.

Gaines-Ross, L. (2000) CEO reputation: A key factor in shareholder value. *Corporate Reputation Review*, 3, 366–370.

Gary, J.G. Jr. (1986) *Managing the Corporate Image*. Westport, CT: Quorum.

Gay, C., Mahoney, M., and Graves, J. (2005) *Best Practices in Employee Communication: A Study of Global Challenges and Approaches*. San Francisco, CA: IABC Research Foundation.

Geletkanycz, M.A. (1997) The salience of "culture's consequences": The effects of cultural values on top executive commitment to the status quo. *Strategic Management Journal*, 18, 615–634.

Hambrick, D.C. (1989) Putting top managers back into the strategy picture. *Strategic Management Journal*, 10, 5–15.

Hambrick, D.C. (1998) Corporate coherence and the top management team. In D.C. Hambrick, D.A. Nadler, and M.L. Tushman (eds), *Navigating Change: How CEOs, Top Teams, and Boards Steer Transformation*. Boston: Harvard Business School Press, pp. 123–140.

Hambrick, D.C. and Fukutomi, D.S. (1991) The seasons of a CEO's tenure. *Academy of Management Review*, 16, 719–742.

Hambrick, D.C. and Mason, P.A. (1984) Upper echelons: The organization as a reflection of its top managers. *Academy of Management Review*, 9, 193–206.

Harris, T.E. and Nelson, M.D. (2008) *Applied Organizational Communication: Theory and Practice in a Global Environment*. New York: Lawrence Erlbaum Associates.

House, R.J., Gupta, V., Dorfman, P.W., Javidan, M., and Hanges, P.J. (2004) *Culture, Leadership, and Organizations: The GLOBE Study of 62 Societies*. Thousand Oaks, CA: Sage Publications.

Judge, T.A. and Piccolo, R.F. (2004) Transformational and transactional leadership: A meta-analytic test of their relative validity. *Journal of Applied Psychology*, 89, 755–768.

Kang, J. and Berger, B.K. (2009) Organizational environment, autonomy, and the ethics counsel role of public relations. Paper presented at the Annual Conference of the International Communication Association, Chicago, IL.

Kotter, J.P. (1996) *Leading Change*. Cambridge, MA: Harvard Business School Press.

Kotter, J.P. and Heskett, J.L. (1992) *Corporate Culture and Performance*. New York: Free Press.

Meng, J. (2009) Excellent leadership in public relations: An application of multiple-group confirmatory factor analysis models in assessing cross-national measurement invariance. Doctoral dissertation. Retrieved from ProQuest Dissertations and Theses Database (UMI No. 3369756).

Meng, J. and Berger, B.K. (2010) Cultural influence on the perceptions of effective leadership in public relations. Paper presented at the 60th Annual Convention of the International Communication Association, Singapore.

Meng, J. and Berger, B.K. (2012). How top business communicators measure the return on investment of organization's internal communication efforts. *Journal of Communication Management*, *16*, 332–354.

Meng, J., Berger, B.K., Gower, K., and Heyman, W. (2012) A test of excellent leadership in public relations: Key qualities, valuable sources, and distinctive leadership perceptions. *Journal of Public Relations Research*, *24*, 18–36.

Miller, D. (1991) Stale in the saddle: CEO tenure and the match between organization and environment. *Management Science*, *37*, 34–52.

Miller, D. and Droge, C. (1986) Psychological and traditional determinants of structure. *Administrative Science Quarterly*, *31*, 539–560.

Miller, D. and Toulouse, J. (1986) Chief executive personality and structure in small firms. *Management Science*, *32*, 1389–1409.

Nutt, P.C. (1993) Flexible decision styles and the choice of top executives. *Journal of Management Studies*, *30*, 695–721.

Nutt, P.C. and Backoff, R.W. (1997) Facilitating transformational change. *The Journal of Applied Behavioral Science*, *33*, 490–508.

Nye, J.S. (2008) *The Power to Lead*. New York: Oxford University Press.

Nye, J.S. (2010) Power and leadership. In N. Nohria and R. Khurana (eds), *Handbook of Leadership and Practice*. Boston: Harvard Business School Press, pp. 305–332.

Peterson, R.S., Smith, D.B., Martorana, P.V., and Owens, P.D. (2003) The impact of chief executive officer personality on top management team dynamics: One mechanism by which leadership affects organizational performance. *Journal of Applied Psychology*, *88*, 795–808.

Porter, M.E. and Nohria, N. (2010) What is leadership? The CEO's role in large, complex organizations. In N. Nohria and R. Khurana (eds), *Handbook of Leadership Theory and Practice*. Boston: Harvard Business School Publishing, pp. 433–473.

Smidts, A., Pruyn, A.T.H., and van Riel, C.B.M. (2001) The impact of employee communication and perceived external prestige on organizational identification. *The Academy of Management Journal*, *49*, 1051–1062.

Thomas, A.B. (1988) Does leadership make a difference to organizational performance? *Administrative Science Quarterly*, *33*, 388–400.

Tyler, B.B. and Steensma, H.K. (1998) The effects of executives' experiences and perceptions on their assessment of potential technological alliances. *Strategic Management Journal*, *19*, 939–965.

van Riel, C.B.M. (1995) *Principles of Corporate Communication*. London: Prentice Hall.

van Riel, C.B.M. and Fombrun, C.J. (2009) *Essentials of Corporate Communication: Implementing Practices for Effective Reputation Management*. New York: Routledge.

Vroom, V.H. and Yetton, P.W. (1973) *Leadership and Decision-Making*. Pittsburgh, PA: University of Pittsburgh Press.

Waldman, D.A. and Yammarino, F.J. (1999) CEO charismatic leadership: Levels-of-management and levels-of-analysis effects. *Academy of Management Review*, *24*, 266–285.

Wiersema, M.F. and Bantel, K.A. (1992) Top management team demography and corporate strategic change. *Academy of Management Journal*, *35*, 91–121.

Yukl, G.A. (2002) *Leadership in Organizations* (5th ed.). Upper Saddle River, NJ: Prentice Hall.

Yukl, G.A. and Falbe, C.M. (1991) The importance of different power sources in downward and lateral relations. *Journal of Applied Psychology*, *76*, 416–423.

Zaccaro, S.J. and Klimoski, R. (2002) The interface of leadership and team processes. *Group and Organization Management*, *27*(1), 4–13.

27

Corporate Reputation and Workplace Environment

Hua Jiang
Towson University, USA

This chapter reviews prior studies on the conceptualization and measurement of corporate reputation and examines workplace environment as one of its important attributes. In particular, it examines three underlying dimensions of the attribute: internal communication management and employee–organization relationships; corporate culture; and an organization's ability to attract, develop, and retain top talent. It discusses the underlying theoretical frameworks that have been used for the attribute's dimensions and reports the empirical findings prior studies have yielded. This chapter also presents some other dimensions that have been revealed in prior research but have not been fully examined in the extant literature, and calls for future studies to establish a more complete and comprehensive list of workplace environment's indicators. It then suggests future directions for research in terms of concept and measurement. The chapter ends with a brief discussion of implications for many disciplines other than communication.

Workplace Environment as an Attribute of Corporate Reputation

This chapter focuses on workplace environment as an attribute of corporate reputation.

The workplace environment attribute deals with the extent to which various strategic constituencies believe that a company "is well organized," "looks like a good company to work for," and "looks like a company that would have good employees" (Fombrun *et al.*, 2000, p. 253). The workplace environment must be exciting, encouraging, engaging, empowering, and inspiring, characteristics which lead to employees' peak performance and reinforce a strong and stable favorable reputation (Dortok, 2006). On the basis of prior studies related to this attribute, this chapter examines the following key indicators of workplace environment: (1) a company's quality of communication management and relationship building with employees, (2) its robust and human corporate culture, and (3) its ability to attract, develop, and retain top talent.

Employee–organization relationship is one type of organization–public relationship (OPR). In an

The Handbook of Communication and Corporate Reputation, First Edition. Edited by Craig E. Carroll.
© 2013 John Wiley & Sons, Inc. Published 2015 by John Wiley & Sons, Inc.

employee–organization relationship, the behaviors of one party result in consequences for the other party in different states of the relationship (e.g., Grunig *et al.*, 2002; Hon and Grunig, 1999; Huang, 1997, 2001; Hung, 2002). Distinct from its antecedents and consequences, an employee–organization relationship is dynamic and can be measured using perceptions of either or both parties regarding four "indicators representing the quality of [employee-organization] relationships" or "relationship outcomes" – satisfaction, trust, commitment, and control mutuality (Grunig and Huang, 2000, p. 42) – at specific points of time.

Management scholars have also examined the significant effect of quality relationships between an organization and its strategic stakeholders on favorable organizational reputation (e.g., Fombrun, 1996; King, 1999; Schultz *et al.*, 2000). As Fombrun (1996) argued, positive and enduring corporate reputation relies on managers' efforts at building, developing, and maintaining good relationships with their organizations' strategic constituents, such as employees (p. 57). Corporations' relational behaviors – their behaviors to establish relationships with their stakeholders – influence reputation positively in the long term. Fombrun and van Riel (2004) emphasized the significance of organizations' relationships with employees, and suggested that socially responsible behaviors of corporations would result in positive corporate reputation.

One study related to employee–organization relationships is that of Carmeli and Freund (2002). They examined the relationship between work attitudes (e.g., altruistic and compliance organizational citizenship behavior (OCB)), workplace attitudes (e.g., affective and continuance commitment, job satisfaction, and turnover intentions), and employees' perceptions of external stakeholders' views of corporate reputation. They defined OCB as organizational members' behavior beyond their formal role requirements (p. 55). OCB enhances organizational performance through (1) promoting collegial atmosphere and managerial productivity; (2) coordinating communication between team members and across working teams; (3) improving an organization's ability

to attract and retain talented people; and (4) enhancing an organization's sustainable development and improving its adaptability to changing environments (p. 55). Carmeli and Freund used altruistic OCB to describe helping behaviors targeted at specific persons and compliance OCB to denote another set of behaviors aimed not at specific persons but at helping the whole system of workplace environment (p. 56). Based on data collected from randomly selected employees of law firms in Israel, this study conducted multiple hierarchical regression analyses to test its hypotheses. Results indicated that affective organizational commitment, compliance OCB, and job satisfaction significantly predicted employees' perceptions of external views of corporate reputation.

Corporate Reputation and Culture

Although scholars and practitioners have emphasized corporate reputation's strong economic value to companies, reputation has an intangible noneconomic institutional side (Brown and Perry, 1994; Fombrun and Shanley, 1990). An important institutional component of reputation is corporate culture (Barnett *et al.*, 2000; Carmeli and Tishler, 2004; Dutton and Dukerich, 1991; Flatt and Kowalczyk, 2000; Kowalczyk and Pawlish, 2002). Cultural values including responsibility, reliability, credibility, and trustworthiness are at the core of perceptual representations of corporate reputation (Fombrun, 1996). Scholars have spent increasing effort on examining how corporate culture and corporate reputation are conceptually related (e.g., Dutton *et al.*, 1994; Hatch and Schultz, 1997, 2002).

Conceptualization of Corporate Culture

Many approaches to defining corporate culture exist in the literature (e.g., Collins and Porras, 1994; Daft, 1998; Hochschild, 1983; Kotter and Heskett, 1992; Schein, 1992; Smircich, 1983; Tushman and O'Reilly, 1997). One way of defining the concept is to use the "person" metaphor in assessing internal views of an organization. For instance, researchers have used the characteristics of learning, authoritarian, controlling, and totalitarian to describe corporate culture (Schwartz, 1987; Senge, 1990). Organizations can also be personified as having gender (Alvesson and Billing, 1992; Hofstede, 1991). However, a more common way of conceptualizing culture is to view it as a collection of fundamental underlying beliefs, values, assumptions, material and behavioral artifacts, and symbols that prescribe and guide organizational members' behaviors (Alvesson, 2002; Flatt and Kowalczyk, 2000; Frost *et al.*, 1991; Kowalczyk and Pawlish, 2002; Martin, 2002; Schein, 1992; Wilkins and Ouchi, 1983). Culture is multifaceted, complex, and significant for an organization's sustainable development and business success (Schein, 1999). Organizational culture embodies "the heritage of the company and communicate[s] its meanings to its members; culture manifests itself in the ways employees all through the ranks feel about the company they are working for" (Hatch and Schultz, 2003, pp. 1047–1048). It is a symbolic context in which organizational members' interpretations of organizational identity are formulated and their intentions to influence external stakeholders' cognitive perceptions of the organization's reputation are constructed (Hatch and Schultz, 1997, p. 360). It is important for an organization to align the values of corporate culture and corporate reputation (de Chernatony and Harris, 2000) and communicate its culture to external audiences (Barney, 2002; Gioia *et al.*, 2000).

Measurement of Corporate Culture

Researchers have established diverse instruments to measure organizational culture (e.g., Denison, 1996; Hofstede *et al.*, 1990; Sackmann, 1992). For example, scholars have assessed organizational culture using scale items of personality characteristics, such as concern, aggression, creativity, innovation, supportiveness, dominance, risk taking, competitiveness, and social responsibility (Xenikou and Furnham, 1996). Chatman and Jehn (1994) constructed a culture scale with seven dimensions to assess the cultures of organizations in different industries: (1) innovation (i.e., an organization's willingness and likelihood to experiment new ideas and take risks); (2) stability (i.e., the extent to which an organization's behavior and performance is predictable and secure); (3) people orientation (i.e., the degree to which an organization practices fair decision-making procedures and respect employees' rights); (4) outcome orientation (i.e., the extent to which an organization focuses on achieving certain outcomes); (5) easygoingness (i.e., an organization's traits of being agreeable, calm, and reflective); (6) detail orientation (i.e., an organization's preciseness and analytical ability); and (7) team orientation (i.e., how much emphasis an organization puts on collaboration and teamwork).

One of the most widely used instruments is the Organizational Culture Profile (OCP) (O'Reilly *et al.*, 1991), which encompasses 54 cultural attributes that can be classified into a taxonomy of eight underlying dimensions: (1) innovation, (2) attention to detail, (3) outcome orientation, (4) aggressiveness, (5) supportiveness, (6) emphasis on rewards, (7) team orientation, and (8) decisiveness (O'Reilly *et al.*, 1991). The OCP gauges the intensity of the key cultural values and the extent of agreement on such values among organizational members (Flatt and Kowalczyk, 2000). Many studies have validated the OCP measurement and pointed out that the eight factors are actually similar to those which prior studies (Hofstede *et al.*, 1990; Sackmann, 1992) have suggested (Chatman and Jehn, 1994).

The Link between Corporate Culture and Reputation

Fombrun (1996) suggested that values such as credibility, reliability, trustworthiness, and responsibility are central to multiple stakeholders' perceptions of an organization's reputation. Therefore, corporate reputation is closely related to an organization's culture, character, and personality (Hatch and Schultz, 1997; Kowalczyk and Pawlish, 2002). Researchers have further pinpointed the importance of studying both internal and external perceptions of corporate culture (e.g., Kowalczyk and Pawlish, 2002). To achieve stakeholders' positive assessment of corporate reputation, an organization needs to become transparent through its organizational performance, its employees' interactions with external constituents, and its media visibility (Hatch and Schultz, 2000).

Internal influences on reputation

An organization's culture impacts the values, beliefs, and assumptions that employees embrace. The culture also guides employees' internal and external behaviors (Bettencourt and Brown, 1997; Kotter and Heskett, 1992; Wilkins and Ouchi, 1983). Both management and rank-and-file employees need to be aware of consistency between organizational core values and their behaviors because any inconsistency may result in stakeholders' negative perceptions of corporate reputation (Harris and de Chernatony, 2001).

Scholars have examined the link between organizational personality and corporate reputation through internal views (Gioia and Chittipeddi, 1991). How an organization treats its employees influences their perceptions of corporate culture and, in turn, impacts their evaluations of corporate reputation (Fox and Amichai-Hamburger, 2001). Fox and Amichai-Hamburger specifically discussed the treatment of employees in the context of an organizational change. During an imperative organizational change process, it is paramount for the organization to listen to its employees' concerns, opinions, and even objections sincerely and sympathetically. The trust developed through this gesture makes employees perceive their employer as being open, competent, and reliable, and therefore, they think of it as a good company to work for. An organization's

character of being communicative or a good communicator is critical for building a good reputation (Downs and Adrian, 2004). Management needs to keep dialogic communication with employees and to behave ethically and appropriately. Internal communication, if not handled properly, can have devastating effects on reputation management. In summary, corporate culture as an important indicator of workplace environment is closely related to employees' perceptions of corporate reputation.

External influences on reputation

Researchers have analyzed how the congruence between organizational culture and corporate reputation magnifies external stakeholders' sense of who the organization is and thereby enhances their perceptions of reputation (de Chernatony, 2001; Dowling, 2001; Hatch and Schultz, 2001, 2003).

Organizational culture exerts its external influences on reputation in different ways. First, many organizations have been managing their corporate reputation through different means of identity-based communication – for example, advertising, public relations techniques, marketing communication, and customer relations management (Hatch and Schultz, 1997). Within the organizational cultural context, managerial behaviors are expected to impact external stakeholders' perceptions of an organization's reputation as well as internal members' interactions with external constituents (Hatch and Schultz, 1997). To achieve favorable impressions of reputation, the external communication of top managers and organizational spokespersons tend to be deliberate and influential (Barich and Kotler, 1991; Dowling, 1993). For example, when Body Shop's reputation as a green retailer was challenged by media allegations, Anita Roddick's public lectures deliberately preserved internal organizational identity and defused negative external reputation (Hatch and Schultz, 1997, p. 361).

Second, in order to successfully manage reputation, it is essential to reach inside an organization and teach employees how to communicate key values to external publics: employees' awareness and knowledge of their own culture makes them competent to "communicate the non-imitable intangibles of the company and provide the foundation for a distinct and credible corporate image" (Hatch and Schultz, 2003, p. 1050). When an organization successfully uses its communication to impress external stakeholders, they are more likely to perceive it favorably and judge it as being innovative, trustworthy, and admired (Hatch and Schultz, 1997). In the Body Shop's case, the cultural value statements that Anita Roddick made in her internal communication greatly impacted the opinions and ideas of employees and facilitated internal constituents' interactions with external audiences in their daily work.

Empirical findings

To test the correspondence between organizational culture and corporate reputation, Flatt and Kowalczyk (2000) used the reputation instrument that *Fortune* Magazine developed. To measure organizational culture, they selected the OCP scale (O'Reilly *et al.*, 1991). In this study, 486 business students at a large university participated and "map[ped] cultural attributes onto the eight attributes of the AMAC [*Fortune* Magazine's America's Most Admired Companies annual survey]" (p. 354). In this process, the participants, using 54 cultural value attribute cards, assigned each of the cards into one of nine categories corresponding to the eight *Fortune* survey attributes and the ninth one labeled as "fits nowhere" (p. 354). This study used "a hypergeometric probability distribution" methodology to assess the significance of the overlap between AMAC's attributes and the OCP's factors (p. 354). Results showed a statistically significant correspondence between five cultural value attributes and five reputational factors. This suggested that stakeholders' impressions of corporate reputation actually reflect their perceptions of an organization's culture.

Kowalczyk and Pawlish (2002) also adopted an instrument based on the OCP scale and recruited 179 industry professionals as partici-

pants who rated six well-known companies (Apple Computer, Cisco Systems, Hewlett Packard, Oracle, Sun Microsystems, and 3 Com) on eight dimensions of organizational culture. The authors then evaluated perceptions of those companies' reputations using Fombrun *et al.*'s (2000) Reputation Quotient^{SM} (RQ) survey. Based on regression analysis, 11 out of 48 correlations between culture and reputation dimensions were statistically significant. The data collected from the six participant companies indicated that reputation as an organization's strategic intangible resource partially reflects external perceptions of organizational culture (p. 159).

Summary

Organizational reputation involves external stakeholders' interpretations and sensemaking of what an organization is, and in turn, it has an influence on internal cultural identity formation (Hatch and Schultz, 1997). First of all, organizational members can be members of external audiences, such as users of their organizations' products and/or services and media consumers of reports on the organizations. Thus, their sensemaking and interpretations of who their organizations are (i.e., organizational identity) in the symbolic context of organizational culture can be compared to their external understanding and perceptions of corporate reputation, resulting in both consensus and discrepancy. On the other hand, external constituents' appraisals of organizations and their members make internal audiences reconsider organizational cultural values and reconstruct organizational identity, leading to possible feedback from reputation to culture. Finally, the leadership and vision of top management are exposed to external influences when it comes to the management of corporate reputation. The vision statements, values, beliefs, and norms that top management communicates to internal constituents are influenced by the responses received from external stakeholders, which subsequently affects organizational culture and identity (p. 362).

In brief, congruence usually exists between organizational culture (i.e., the values demonstrated through organizational members' behaviors) and the ideal corporate image an organization aspires to create. In order to manage a favorable corporate reputation, an organization ought to listen to multiple stakeholders' views, confront them with organizational culture, and narrow the gap between the ideal and actual images that its external stakeholders perceive (Dutton and Dukerich, 1991; Gioia *et al.*, 2000; Hatch and Schultz, 2003).

Corporate Reputation and the Ability to Attract, Develop, and Retain Top Talents

Attracting top job applicants and keeping highly motivated and skilled employees have become very important steps toward an organization's sustainable development and success (Offermann and Gowing, 1990). Corporate reputation affects the composition of the workforce because job applicants' attraction to organizations is highly influenced by their perceptions of reputation (Cable and Graham, 2000; Ou, 2007). An organization's corporate social performance (CSP) influences its reputation, which is highly determinative of whether the organization can attract and retain excellent human resources (Fombrun and Shanley, 1990; Lado and Wilson, 1994; Wright *et al.*, 1995). To contribute to organizational competitiveness and success, the human resource (HR) management of a given organization should help to build the competence and motivation of employees who will, in turn, lead to positive corporate reputation through their interactions with external stakeholders (Friedman, 2009). To achieve this goal, HR needs to partner with top management and implement strategic HR and communication practices to promote corporate reputation (Ulrich and Brockbank, 2005).

Reputation and Job Applicants' Attraction to Hiring Organizations

The stakeholder perspective on reputation and social identity theory

Previous literature has identified organizational attributes related to financial success as key predictors of executives' perceptions of corporate culture (Cable and Graham, 2000). Some scholars believe that perceptions of reputation are constant across multiple stakeholders, but the stakeholder perspective on corporate reputation suggests that different constituencies actually view corporations differently. Social identity theory proposes that employees are more closely connected to their employers than many other stakeholder groups and, therefore, develop self-concepts compatible with the values and beliefs of their employing organizations (Ashforth and Mael, 1989; Dutton *et al.*, 1994). Job applicants strongly value the potential consistency or connection between their own self-concepts and an organization's reputation (Popovich and Wanous, 1982). Therefore, the criteria that job applicants use in assessing a potential employer's reputation are likely to be organizational attributes associated with their personal needs and self-concepts – for example, career development opportunities and a friendly and encouraging work environment (Cable and Graham, 2000).

Consistent with the stakeholder perspective on reputation and social identity theory, studies have found that jobseekers used different criteria than executives in evaluating hiring organizations' reputations (Cable and Graham, 2000). Examples of the criteria include (1) HR employment-at-will policies and compensation packages (Schwoerer and Rosen, 1989); (2) job applicants' familiarity with the employing organization (Gatewood *et al.*, 1993); (3) an organization's profitability, institutional behaviors related to employee relations, treatment of workplace environment, quality of products, and women and minorities issues (Turban and Greening, 1997); and (4) working atmosphere, customers, and product image (Highhouse *et al.*, 1999).

CSP as a critical source of competitive advantage for an organization

Behrend *et al.* (2009) discussed the close tie between CSP and organizational reputation. According to Turban and Greening (1997), "An organization's social policies and programs may attract potential applicants by serving as a signal of working conditions in the organization" (p. 659). As a consequence, jobseekers may perceive that an organization with good CSP will care for the well-being of its employees. Accordingly, a firm's CSP positively influences potential employees' perceptions of organizational reputation (Brammer and Millington, 2005; Turban and Greening, 1997).

CSP consists of a corporation's actions to fulfill its responsibilities to employees and other strategic constituents (Donaldson and Preston, 1995; Shrivastava, 1995; Turban and Greening, 1997). A company's CSP is largely determined by its social policies and programs, including those related to diversity issues in the workplace environment (e.g., women and minorities, work–life balance), employee relations, and community relations (Behrend *et al.*, 2009; Williams and Bauer, 1994). In addition, the training opportunities for employees and policies about personal leave signal an organization's norms and values of HR management (Turban and Greening, 1997). By informing the values and norms of a company, CSP can lead to prospective employees' perceptions of the company's image and reputation (Fombrun and Shanley, 1990; Greening and Turban, 2000; Rynes, 1991).

Empirical findings

Large corporations including IBM, General Motors, Microsoft, Coca-Cola, DuPont, and Lucent advertise their CSP efforts on corporate web sites to prospective and current employees. Research has examined the effects of CSP on employees' perceptions of organizational images.

The higher the ratings of employee relations (a CSP dimension), the more positive employees' perceptions of a company's reputation are (Turban and Greening, 1997). Brammer and Pavelin (2006) conducted a survey and found that CSP was a significant predictor of large global corporations' reputation.

Based on the results of a qualitative study, an experimental policy-capturing study, and a field study of recruiting organizations, Cable and Graham (2000) identified the following factors influencing job applicants' perceptions of organizational reputations: (1) industry (i.e., the products and services of a company, product diversity, and workforce composition); (2) opportunities for growth (i.e., training and career development opportunities); (3) organizational culture (i.e., organizational members' shared values, beliefs, and assumptions); (4) familiarity/previous exposure (i.e., prior knowledge and experience with the recruiting company); (5) history (i.e., historical information about a company); (6) endorsement (i.e., validation from someone who knows about the company and is trusted by job applicants); (7) size of the company (i.e., the number of employees, the amount of revenues, and the number of locations and offices); (8) legitimacy (i.e., the consistence between organizational behaviors and the prevailing norms in the industry); (9) global presence (i.e., the overseas branches or offices of a company); (10) financial profitability (i.e., strength of a company's financial position); (11) diversity (i.e., demographic composition of a company's workforce); (12) corporate headquarters (i.e., the locations of the companies' headquarters) (pp. 933–935); and (13) pay level (pp. 937–939).

To test their hypotheses on the relationships between CSP, corporate reputation, and organizations' attractiveness to job applicants and employees, Turban and Greening (1997) drew a sample of organizations from Kinder, Lydenberg, Domini, & Co. (KLD) Company Profiles, a database that has been used by previous researchers (e.g., Graves and Waddock, 1994). Turban and Greening used data from its 1992–1993 database, which consisted of ratings for 633 organizations (p. 661). Results of this study supported the hypotheses and indicated that CSP is related to corporate reputation and an organization's attractiveness to job applicants and current employees. "Such results add to the growing literature suggesting that CSP may provide firms with competitive advantages" (p. 658).

Develop and Retain Talented Employees through Strategic HR Practices and Internal Communication

The competence and knowledge of employees is closely related to organizational performance and reputation (Hurley, 2002). HR strategic practices can influence the extent to which employees identify with their employers. Employees' identification, in turn, motivates them to behave as ambassadors of their organizations and be involved in supportive actions in interactions with external stakeholders (Dortok, 2006; Edwards, 2005; Fombrun, 1996; Fombrun and van Riel, 2004).

Training

Innovative employee training can build organizational identities effectively because training allows organizations to assimilate the important new identities, increase employee satisfaction, and ultimately enhance corporate reputation (Mitki and Herstein, 2007). Strategically implemented training, mentoring, and timely career development programs develop employee capabilities, increase their marketability, and upgrade employees' skills that improve the qualities of products and services, an important dimension of corporate reputation (Friedman, 2009). Employee training programs can also be leveraged to benefit a company's customer relations and business partnerships with collaborators (Krell, 2001). For instance, Xerox Corporation has long integrated its customer training curriculum into its comprehensive employee training programs. Through classes,

seminars, and online materials on workflow and database analysis, technical training, and business planning, Xerox has attempted to establish a high level of customer loyalty, increase profitability and revenue, and promote corporate reputation (Friedman, 2009). Similarly, AT&T provides training sessions to help employees build long-term business relationships and obtain competitive advantage (Krell, 2001).

Partnership between HR and top leadership

Apart from implementing training programs, HR management forms partnerships with top management through aligning its objectives with an organization's business goals. Accordingly, the strategic partnership with organizational leadership should focus on the dimensions of reputation related to the interests of employees, as well as to organizational goals (Friedman, 2009). Fox (2007) singled out the collaboration between HR and senior management of Coca-Cola Company as an excellent example for developing corporate reputation. In 2004, the HR teams of Coca-Cola conducted quantitative and qualitative research with top management and identified the key issues existing in the organization. In 2005, HR helped the organization establish a new organizational mission, values, and goals, and communicated these to employees through various means of communication, including face-to-face meetings, intranet, and Web TV. The new initiative incorporated one significant dimension of corporate reputation in the Reputation Institute's RepTrak™ – workplace environment, basically, strategic internal communication and engagement. After the initiative was successfully executed, Coca-Cola became widely recognized as a reputable employer to work for that implements excellent diversity policies, work–family balance policies, employee safety and health programs, and its Occupational Safety and Health Administration Voluntary Protection Program (Friedman, 2009). Another prototype is General Electric (GE), which established a reward system that engages employees in the new product development process. GE used internal communication programs to promote the engagement program, which is a very effective way to achieve positive corporate reputation (Fombrun and van Riel, 2004).

Employee champion role of HR

HR management practices also contribute to positive corporate reputation through responding to the concerns and needs of employees (Friedman, 2009; Ulrich, 1997). The so-called "employee champion role" (Friedman, 2009, p. 237) addresses a wide range of concerns and needs – for example, pay equity, employee benefits, sexual harassment in the workplace, safety, and job satisfaction. The employee champion role promotes employee growth and advancement opportunities, and this, in turn, enhances corporate reputation.

Researchers and practitioners have reviewed the employee champion role that HR plays at Wegmans,[1] Google, and FedEx, and discussed how the HR practices have enhanced these firms' corporate reputations. Wegmans provides its employees with generous benefits, including a scholarship program that encourages employees to pursue their degrees, increases their marketability and upward mobility, and retains talent for the organization. Wegmans also earned its high rank on *Fortune*'s best companies to work for, owing to its orientation programs, training and rewards programs for employees, and policies on flexible working schedules (Friedman, 2009). Google has been widely acknowledged for its efforts devoted to establishing a friendly and nurturing workplace environment (Friedman, 2009; Hansell, 2007). Google provides its employees with opportunities and allotted time to design and implement independent creative projects, leading to greater productivity, loyalty, creativity, commitment, and satisfaction. Moreover, Google has a relatively low turnout rate and attracts a great number of jobseekers every month, an indicator of its favorable corporate reputation. Another example is FedEx, which has a flexible benefits plan that allows its employees to select their customized package

of health, life, retirement, tuition assistance, stock purchase, and global travel experiences (*Fortune* Datastore, 2007; Friedman, 2009).

Internal communication

To help build a long-term, stable, positive reputation, internal communication cannot take the one-way information disseminating approach. Instead, it should focus on establishing two-way symmetrical relationships with employees and using communication strategies that align the interests, needs, and expectations of employees with the business objectives of an organization. "The extent to which the company is appreciated is affected by the value attached by the company to its employees and the rights it provides for them" (Dortok, 2006, p. 338). Dortok hypothesized a positive correlation between internal communication and corporate reputation. Prior qualitative research has found that organizations with positive reputation and those with negative reputation think differently of the link between reputation and internal communication. Based on data collected from the top 10 and the bottom 10 companies listed in the *Capital* Magazine's Most Admired Companies study, Dortok discovered statistically significant findings that supported the hypothesis. The top 10 companies highly acknowledged the strong impact of internal communication on corporate reputation management and believed that commitment of employees was a significant predictor for business success.

Limitations of Research on Workplace Environment

One major limitation of the extant research on workplace environment is that researchers and practitioners have suggested a great variety of underlying dimensions that can be contained within the category. Unfortunately, however, little effort has been spent on theorizing the classification and generating a complete and comprehensive list of indicators for future research to examine. Apart from the three dimensions that this chapter scrutinizes, prior studies have suggested the following indicators but failed to clearly define and explore them in detail: (1) quality of management (Dortok, 2006; Grunig, 1992); (2) social benefits and rights of employees, payment policy and wage ranges, improvement of employee qualifications, communications and PR, employee qualifications, and employee satisfaction (Dortok, 2006); and (3) employee development and training, workplace relations and remuneration, organizational culture and diversity, and occupational health and structure (Inglis *et al.*, 2006), among many others. Such lists could, of course, always be expanded, but the challenge for future researchers is to devote more effort to conceptualizing and measuring workplace environment systematically.

Concept and Measurement: Future Research on Communication, Reputation, and Workplace Environment

Prior studies have proposed two important directions for future research on communication and reputation in the context of workplace environment: the conceptualization and measurement of corporate reputation.

More research is needed on the conceptualization of corporate reputation in studying workplace environment and communication with employees. A positive reputation allows a company to attract top jobseekers and strengthen employees' morale and loyalty (Boyd *et al.*, 1995; Vergin and Qoronfleh, 1998). It has become a central goal of communication professionals to help today's organizations build, develop, and maintain a stable and favorable reputation, and to have jobseekers and their employees closely networked and connected to the organizations (Sohn, 2009). Scholars have conceived of corporate reputation as a multidimensional attitudinal construct (i.e., attitudes toward an organization) (Meijer and Kleinnijen-

huis, 2006), which consists of (1) cognitive and (2) affective components.

The cognitive part of corporate reputation refers to employees' knowledge-based perceptions of tangible organizational attributes such as quality of products and services and business performance. The affective component describes employees' intrinsic psychological states and emotional dispositions toward an organization's tangible traits (Sohn, 2009). Other scholars have identified functional reputation and social reputation as two cognitive components of corporate reputation (de Castro *et al.*, 2006). This functional–cognitive dimension refers to an evaluation of an organization's accomplishment of its specific performance goals. On the other hand, the social–cognitive component of reputation describes employees' perceptions of an organization's adherence to social norms, values, and ethics (Sohn, 2009). That is why employees are becoming more conscious of their employers' internal and external socially responsible behaviors (Tucker and Melewar, 2005). Clearly, social reputation, as manifested by an organization's socially responsible and ethical corporate performance, plays a significant role in stakeholders' overall assessment of organizational reputation (e.g., Brammer and Millington, 2005; David *et al.*, 2005; Schnietz and Epstein, 2005). As for the affective dimension of reputation, it encompasses stakeholders' emotions and feelings toward an organization (Sohn, 2009).

In summary, corporate reputation encompasses (1) the functional–cognitive components of corporate performance and actions; (2) the social–cognitive factors based on ethics, integrity, and social responsibility; and (3) the affective emotional appraisal of sympathy and attractiveness (Sohn, 2009, p. 5). Unfortunately, many prior workplace environment studies only generally defined corporate reputation as an intangible organizational asset and as stakeholders' collective perceptions of organizational performance and behaviors over time (e.g., Barnett *et al.*, 2006), but never dissected the internal components in the conceptualization of the construct. Little research has examined how the cognitive and affective parts of reputation may influence internal communication with employees and employees' assessment of reputation-related workplace environmental elements or features.

More Research on the Measurement of Corporate Reputation in Studying Workplace Environment and Communication with Employees

Despite the wide use of *Fortune* Magazine's annual ratings and the RQ in empirical research, scholars and practitioners have started to challenge the methodological dominance of this model and seek alternative measures of reputation. This opens new avenues for assessing reputation in examining employee communication and their perceptions of workplace environment.

Many researchers have bemoaned the operational definition of reputation used by the well-known measures, such as *Fortune* Magazine's reputation index and RepTrak™. It assumes that individual stakeholders' perceptions toward an organization can be "averaged," and there is one single "aggregated" corporate reputation (Yang and Mallabo, 2003). Nevertheless, scholars have found empirical evidence supporting the argument that an organization can have multiple aggregate reputations because stakeholders have unique and idiosyncratic impressions of an organization based on their own individual experiences (Bromley, 1993, 2000). In line with this argument, Bromley (2000) conceptualized reputation as "collective representations" (p. 244) and asserted that reputation as a collective phenomenon can be represented as the distribution of individual stakeholders' impressions. Bromley (2000) further pointed out that the collective representations (i.e., second-order representations) are constructed through individual stakeholders' impressions (i.e., first-order representations) in either "distributed" or "undistributed" ways

(p. 245). According to Bromley, distributed representations are characterized by a consensus among stakeholders' individual impressions, whereas undistributed representations contain the feature of disconformity between individual stakeholders.

In addition to quantitative research, scholars have proposed that reputation can be evaluated through qualitative open-ended questions, along with a quantitative content analysis of the responses (Bromley, 1993). For example, participants in this type of research can be asked to write a paragraph or paragraphs about an organization that they know. Then, their feedback can be coded into different attributes of the focal organization. Grunig and Hung (2002) adopted Bromley's (1993) measurement of reputation and identified a taxonomy of cognitive representations using objects and attributes: (1) an object–attribute representation means objects and attributes are linked through an isa[2] connection – an example in the context of internal communication and workplace environment would be, "My organization is a large company"; (2) an object–object representation, which refers to the association between one object and another via an isa connection – for example, "XXX XXX is president of my organization"; (3) a behavioral representation that describes the connection between the first object and a second object through the first one's behaviors or actions on the recipient – for instance, "My organization fired 2000 workers this year"; and (4) an evaluative representation which can be an object–attribute, object–object, or a behavioral cognitive representation that includes an evaluative or attitudinal component – an example would be, "My company is an evil company" (Grunig and Hung, 2002, p. 23; Yang and Mallabo, 2003, p. 13).

Implications for Other Disciplines

Scholars in many other disciplines have contributed to the blossoming literature on corporate reputation: reputation as "traits and signals" that describe a company's behavior (economy), "intangible assets that are difficult for rivals to imitate, acquire, and substitute" (strategy), "intangible assets that are difficult in measure but create value for companies" (accounting), "the corporate associations that individuals establish with the company name" (marketing), "corporate traits that develop from relationships companies establish with their multiple constituents" (communication), "cognitive representations of companies that develop as stakeholders make sense of corporate activities" (organizational theory), and "social constructions emanating from the relationships firms establish with stakeholders in their shared institutional environment" (sociology) (Fombrun *et al.*, 2000, p. 243).

Fombrun and van Riel, (2004) proposed six key factors explaining the significance of corporate reputation in the marketplace: (1) globalization, (2) information availability, (3) product commoditization, (4) media mania, (5) ad saturation, and (6) stakeholder activism. Globalization has given rise to fierce local and international competition or rivalry among corporations. They need to retain favorable reputations to outperform others in the marketplace. The proliferation of media, including print media, broadcast media, and the Internet, has given rise to the instantaneous transmission of information about products and services that are important to various stakeholders. An organization with positive corporate reputation practices interactive communication with different stakeholder groups and obtains their trust and loyalty. Corporate reputation has become a critical source of differentiation and competitive advantage when product commoditization has diminished variances and increased homogeneity in products and services offered across different markets. The media have become a powerful influence in today's society. Therefore, corporations strive to maintain favorable reputations and secure their visibility in the media. The overload of corporate advertising has overwhelmed their strategic stakeholders. Those who strive to build favorable and stable reputations have "an edge for influencing

[different stakeholders'] perceptions and cutting through the crowded media marketplace" (Hung and Wun, 2006, p. 5). When organizations behave badly, activist groups may criticize, attack them, and pressure them to change. Some of the organizations are actually the most visible, economically powerful, and reputable in the world.

Obviously, reputation management remains a major concern for different types of organizations and a topic of great research interest for scholars in diverse fields, such as information studies, management, marketing, advertising, mass media, industrial studies, economy, strategy, and organizational studies. Employees play a significant role in all the six factors that Fombrun and van Riel (1997, 2004) set forth in explaining the significance of corporate reputation. Scholarship on employees, workplace environment, and reputation in other disciplines can be informed by (1) the internal communication and management of employee–organization relationships that communication scholars have discussed; (2) the interdependence between organizational culture and corporate reputation that researchers in organizational studies have examined; and (3) the contributions of HR communication, monitoring, policy making, and enforcement that management scholars have investigated.

Notes

1 A privately owned grocery chain store with its headquarters in Rochester, New York.
2 "Organizations also can be linked to other objects and associated with attributes through what Anderson and Lebiere (1998) called an 'isa' statement (p. 23)" (Grunig and Hung, 2002, p. 22).

References

Alvesson, M. (2002) *Understanding Organizational Culture*. London: Sage.
Alvesson, M. and Billing, D.Y. (1992) Gender and organization: Towards a differentiated understanding. *Organization Studies, 12/13*, 73–102.

Anderson, J.R. and Lebiere, C. (1998) *The Atomic Components of Thought*. Mahwah, NJ: Lawrence Erlbaum Associates.

Ashforth, E. and Mael, F. (1989) Social identity theory and the organization. *Academy of Management Review*, 14, 20–39.

Barich, H. and Kotler, P. (1991) A framework for marketing image management. *Sloan Management Review*, 94, 94–104.

Barnett, M.L., Boyle, E., and Gardberg, N.A. (2000) Towards one vision, one voice: A review essay of the 3rd international conference on corporate reputation, image and competitiveness. *Corporate Reputation Review*, 3, 101–111.

Barnett, M.L., Jermier, J.M., and Lafferty, B.A. (2006) Corporate reputation: The definitional landscape. *Corporate Reputation Review*, 9, 26–38.

Barney, J.B. (2002) *Gaining and Sustaining Competitive Advantage* (2nd ed.). Upper Saddle River, NJ: Prentice Hall.

Behrend, T.S., Baker, B.A., and Thompson, L.F. (2009) Effects of pro-environmental recruiting messages: The role of organizational reputation. *Journal of Business Psychology*, 24, 341–350.

Bettencourt, L.A. and Brown, S.W. (1997) Contact employees: Relationships among workplace fairness, job satisfaction and prosocial behaviours. *Journal of Retailing*, 73, 39–61.

Boyd, B.K., Caroll, W.O., and Dess, G.G. (1995) Determining the strategic value of firm reputation: A resource-based view. Paper presented at the Annual International Conference of the Strategic Management Society, Mexico City, Mexico, October.

Brammer, S. and Millington, A. (2005) Corporate reputation and philanthropy: An empirical analysis. *Journal of Business Ethics*, 61, 29–44.

Brammer, S.J. and Pavelin, S. (2006) Corporate reputation and social performance: The importance of fit. *Journal of Management Studies*, 43, 435–455.

Bromley, D.B. (1993) *Reputation, Image, and Impression Management*. Chichester, UK: John Wiley & Sons.

Bromley, D.B. (2000) Psychological aspects of corporate identity, image, and reputation. *Corporate Reputation Review*, 3, 240–252.

Brown, B. and Perry, S. (1994) Removing the financial performance halo form Fortune's "Most Admired" Companies. *Academy of Management*, 37, 1347–1359.

Cable, D.M. and Graham, A.M.E. (2000) The determinants of job seekers' reputation perceptions. *Journal of Organizational Behavior*, 21, 929–947.

Carmeli, A. and Freund, A. (2002) The relationship between work and workplace attitudes and perceived external prestige. *Corporate Reputation Review*, 5, 51–68.

Carmeli, A. and Tishler, A. (2004) The relationships between intangible organizational elements and organizational performance. *Strategic Management Journal*, 25, 1257–1278.

Chatman, J.A. and Jehn, K.A. (1994) Assessing the relationship between industry characteristics and organizational culture: How different can you be? *Academy of Management Journal*, 37, 522.

Collins, J. and Porras, J. (1994) *Built to Last*. New York: Harper Collins Business.

Daft, R.L. (1998) *Organization Theory and Design* (6th ed.). Cincinnati, OH: South-Western College Publishing.

David, P., Kine, S., and Dai, Y. (2005) Corporate social responsibility practices, corporate identity and purchase intention: A dual-process model. *Journal of Public Relations Research*, 17, 291–313.

de Castro, G.M., Navas López, J.E., and López Sáez, P. (2006) Business and social reputation: Exploring the concept and main dimensions of corporate reputation. *Journal of Business Ethics*, 63, 361–370.

de Chernatony, L. (2001) *From Brand Vision to Brand Evaluation*. Oxford, UK: Butterworth & Heinemann.

de Chernatony, L. and Harris, F. (2000) Developing corporate brands through considering internal and external stakeholders. *Corporate Reputation Review*, 3, 268–274.

Denison, D. (1996) What is the difference between organizational culture and organizational climate? A native's point of view on a decade of paradigm wars. *Academy of Management Review*, 21, 619–654.

Donaldson, T. and Preston, L.E. (1995) The stakeholder theory of the corporation: Concepts, evidence, and implications. *Academy of Management Review*, 20, 65–91.

Dortok, A. (2006) A managerial look at the interaction between internal communication and corporate reputation. *Corporate Reputation Review*, 8, 322–338.

Dowling, G.R. (1993) Developing your company image into a corporate asset. *Long Range Planning*, 26, 101–109.

Dowling, G.R. (2001) *Creating Corporate Reputations – Identity Image, and Performance*. Oxford, UK: Oxford University Press.

Downs, C.W. and Adrian, A.D. (2004) *Assessing Organizational Communication: Strategic Communication Audits*. New York: The Guilford Press.

Dutton, J.E. and Dukerich, J.M. (1991) Keeping an eye on the mirror: Image and identity in organizational adaptation. *Academy of Management Journal*, 34, 517–554.

Dutton, J.E., Dukerich, J.M., and Harquail, C.W. (1994) Organizational images and member identification. *Administrative Science Quarterly*, 39, 239–263.

Edwards, M.R. (2005) Organizational identification: A conceptual and operational review. *International Journal of Management Reviews*, 7, 207–230.

Flatt, S.J. and Kowalczyk, S.J. (2000) Do corporate reputations partly reflect external perceptions of organizational culture? *Corporate Reputation Review*, 3, 351–358.

Fombrun, C.J. (1996) *Reputation: Realizing Value from the Corporate Image*. Boston: Harvard Business School Press.

Fombrun, C.J. and Shanley, M. (1990) What's in a name? Reputation building and corporate strategy. *Academy of Management Journal*, 33, 233–258.

Fombrun, C.J. and van Riel, C.B.M. (1997) The reputational landscape. *Corporate Reputation Review*, 1, 5–13.

Fombrun, C.J. and van Riel, C.B.M. (2004) *Fame & Fortune: How Successful Companies Build Winning Reputations*. Upper Saddle River, NJ: Prentice Hall.

Fombrun, C.J., Gardberg, N.A., and Sever, J.M. (2000) The Reputation Quotient^SM: A multi-stakeholder measure of corporate reputation. *Journal of Brand Management*, 7, 241–255.

Fortune Datastore (2007) Fortune corporate reputation industry reports. Retrieved from http://www.timeinc.net/fortune/datastore/reputation/cr_report.html (last accessed September 25, 2012).

Fox, A. (2007) Refreshing a beverage company's culture. HR Magazine, November, pp. 58–60.

Fox, S. and Amichai-Hamburger, Y.T. (2001) The power of emotional appeals in promoting organizational change programs. *Academy of Management Executive*, 15(4), 84–93.

Friedman, B.A. (2009) Human resource management role implications for corporate reputation. *Corporate Reputation Review*, 12, 229–244.

Frost, P.J., Moore, L.F., Louis, M.R., Lundberg, C.C., and Martin, J. (1991) *Reframing Organizational Culture*. London: Sage.

Gatewood, R.D., Gowan, M.A., and Lautenschlager, D.J. (1993) Corporate image, recruitment image, and initial job choice decisions. *Academy of Management Journal*, 36, 414–427.

Gioia, D.A. and Chittipeddi, K. (1991) Sensemaking and sensegiving in strategic change initiation. *Strategic Management Journal*, 12, 433–448.

Gioia, D., Schultz, M., and Corley, K. (2000) Organizational identity, image, and adaptive instability. *Academy of Management Review*, 25, 63–81.

Graves, S.B. and Waddock, S.A. (1994) Institutional owners and corporate social performance. *Academy of Management Journal*, 37, 1034–1046.

Greening, D.W. and Turban, D.B. (2000) Corporate social performance as a competitive advantage in attracting a quality workforce. *Business & Society*, 39, 254–268.

Grunig, J.E. (1992) What is excellence in management? In J.E. Grunig (ed.), *Excellence in Public Relations and Communication Management*. Hillsdale, NJ: Lawrence Erlbaum Associates, pp. 219–250.

Grunig, J.E. and Huang, Y.-H. (2000) From organizational effectiveness to relationship indicators: Antecedents of relationships, public relations strategies, and relationship outcomes. In J.A. Ledingham and S.D. Bruning (eds), *Public Relations as Relationship Management: A Relational Approach to the Study and Practice of Public Relations*. Mahwah, NJ: Lawrence Erlbaum Associates, pp. 23–53.

Grunig, J.E. and Hung, C.F. (2002) The effect of relationships on reputation and reputation on relationships: A cognitive, behavioral study. Paper presented at the PRSA (Public Relations Society of America) Educator's Academy 5th Annual International, Interdisciplinary Public Relations Research Conference, Miami, FL, March.

Grunig, L.A., Grunig, J.E., and Dozier, D.M. (2002) *Excellent Public Relations and Effective Organizations: A Study of Communication Management in Three Countries*. Mahwah, NJ: Lawrence Erlbaum Associates.

Hansell, S. (2007) Google answer to filling jobs is an algorithm. Retrieved from http://nytimes.com/2007/01/03/technology/03google.html (last accessed September 25, 2012).

Harris, F. and de Chernatony, L. (2001) Corporate branding and corporate brand performance. *European Journal of Marketing, 35*, 441–456.

Hatch, M.J. and Schultz, M. (1997) Relations between organizational culture, identity and image. *European Journal of Marketing, 31*, 356–365.

Hatch, M.J. and Schultz, M.J. (2000) Scaling the Tower of Babel: Relational differences between identity, image and culture in organizations. In M.J. Schultz, M.J. Hatch, and M.H. Larsen (eds), *The Expressive Organization: Linking Identity, Reputation and the Corporate Brand.* Oxford, UK: Oxford University Press, pp. 11–35.

Hatch, M.J. and Schultz, M. (2001) Are the strategic stars aligned for your corporate brand. *Harvard Business Review,* February, 128–134.

Hatch, M.J. and Schultz, M. (2002) The dynamics of organizational identity. *Human Relations, 55*, 989–1018.

Hatch, M.J. and Schultz, M. (2003) Bringing the corporation into corporate branding. *European Journal of Marketing, 37*, 1041–1064.

Highhouse, S., Zickar, M.J., Thorsteinson, T.J., Stierwalt, S.L., and Slaughter, J.E. (1999) Assessing company employment image: An example in the fast food industry. *Personnel Psychology, 52*, 151–172.

Hochschild, A. (1983) *The Managed Heart.* Berkeley, CA: University of California Press.

Hofstede, G.H. (1991) *Culture and Organization: Software of the Mind.* New York: Harper Collins Business.

Hofstede, G.H., Neuijen, B., Ohay, D., and Sanders, G. (1990) Measuring organizational cultures: A qualitative and quantitative study across twenty cases. *Administrative Science Quarterly, 35*, 286–316.

Hon, L.C. and Grunig, J. (1999) *Guidelines for Measuring Relationships in Public Relations.* Gainesville, FL: The Institute for Public Relations.

Huang, Y.H. (1997) Public relations strategies, relational outcomes, and conflict management strategies. Unpublished doctoral dissertation, University of Maryland, College Park, MD.

Huang, Y.H. (2001) OPRA: A cross-cultural, multiple-item scale for measuring organization–public relationships. *Journal of Public Relations Research, 13*, 61–90.

Hung, C.F. (2002) The interplays of relationship types, relationship cultivation, and relationship outcomes: How multinational and Taiwanese companies public relations and organization-public relationship management in China. Unpublished doctoral dissertation, University of Maryland, College Park, MD.

Hung, C.-J. and Wun, F. (2006) Reputation Quotients[SM]: The evaluation of corporate reputation in Hong Kong. Paper presented at the Annual Convention of the International Communication Association, Dresden, Germany, June.

Hurley, R.F. (2002) Putting people back into organizational learning. *Journal of Business & Industrial Marketing, 17*, 270–281.

Inglis, R., Morley, C., and Sammut, P. (2006) Corporate reputation and organizational performance: An Australian study. *Managerial Auditing Journal, 21*, 934–947.

King, A. (1999) The social performance uncertainty principle. *Corporate Reputation Review, 2*, 43–46.

Kotter, J.P. and Heskett, J.L. (1992) *Corporate Culture and Performance.* New York: The Free Press.

Kowalczyk, S.J. and Pawlish, M.J. (2002) Corporate branding through external perception of organizational culture. *Corporate Reputation Review, 5*, 159–174.

Krell, E. (2001) Training earns its keep. *Training, 38*(4), 68–74.

Lado, A.A. and Wilson, M.C. (1994) Human resource systems and sustained competitive advantages: A competency-based perspective. *Academy of Management Review, 19*, 699–727.

Martin, J. (2002) *Organizational Culture: Mapping the Terrain.* Thousand Oaks, CA: Sage.

Meijer, M.M. and Kleinnijenhuis, J. (2006) Issue news and corporate reputation: Applying the theories of agenda setting and issue ownership in the field of business communication. *Journal of Communication, 56*, 543–559.

Mitki, Y. and Herstein, R. (2007) Innovative training in designing corporate identity. *Industrial & Commercial Training, 39*, 174–179.

Offermann, L.R. and Gowing, M.K. (1990) Organizations of the future: Changes and challenges. *American Psychologist, 45*, 95–108.

O'Reilly, C., Chatman, J., and Caldwell, D. (1991) People and organizational culture: A Q-sort approach to assessing person-organization fit. *Academy of Management Journal, 34*, 487–516.

Ou, W.M. (2007) Moderating effects of age, gender, income and education on consumer's response to corporate reputation. *Journal of American Academy of Business, 10*, 190–194.

Popovich, P. and Wanous, J.P. (1982) The realistic job preview as persuasive communication. *Academy of Management Review*, 7, 570–578.

Rynes, S.L. (1991) Recruitment, job choice, and post-hire consequences: A call for new research directions. In M.D. Dunnette and L.M. Hough (eds), *Handbook of Industrial and Organizational Psychology* (2nd ed., Vol. 2). Palo Alto, CA: Consulting Psychologists Press, pp. 399–444.

Sackmann, S. (1992) Culture and subcultures: An analysis of organizational knowledge. *Administrative Science Quarterly*, 37, 140–161.

Schein, E.H. (1992) *Organizational Culture and Leadership*. San Francisco, CA: Jossey-Bass.

Schein, E.H. (1999) *The Corporate Culture Survival Guide: Sense and Nonsense about culture Change*. San Francisco, CA: Jossey-Bass.

Schnietz, K.E. and Epstein, M.J. (2005) Exploring the financial value of a reputation for corporate social responsibility during a crisis. *Corporate Reputation Review*, 7, 327–345.

Schultz, M., Hatch, M.J., and Larsen, M.H. (2000) *The Expressive Organization: Linking Identity, Reputation, and the Corporate Brand*. Oxford, UK: Oxford University Press.

Schwartz, H.S. (1987) On the psychodynamics of organizational totalitarianism. *Journal of Management*, 13(1), 41–54.

Schwoerer, C. and Rosen, B. (1989) Effects of employment-at-will policies and compensation policies on corporate image and job pursuit intentions. *Journal of Applied Psychology*, 74, 653–656.

Senge, P.M. (1990) *The Fifth Discipline: The Art and Practice of the Learning Organization*. New York: Doubleday Currency.

Shrivastava, P. (1995) Ecocentric management for a risk society. *Academy of Management Review*, 20, 118–137.

Smircich, L. (1983) Concepts of culture and organizational analysis. *Administrative Science Quarterly*, 28, 339–358.

Sohn, Y. (2009) The interrelationships between corporate reputation, trust and behavioral intentions: A multi-stakeholder approach. Paper presented at the Annual Convention of the International Communication Association, Chicago, IL, May.

Tucker, L. and Melewar, T. (2005) Corporate reputation and crisis management: The threat and manageability of anti-corporatism. *Corporate Reputation Review*, 7, 377–387.

Turban, D.B. and Greening, D.W. (1997) Corporate social performance and organizational attractiveness to prospective employees. *Academy of Management Journal*, 40, 658–672.

Tushman, M.L. and O'Reilly, C.A. (1997) *Winning through Innovation: A Practical Guide to Leading Organizational Change and Renewal*. Boston: Harvard University Press.

Ulrich, D. (1997) *HR Champions*. Boston: Harvard Business Press.

Ulrich, D. and Brockbank, W. (2005) *The HR Value Proposition*. Boston: Harvard Business School Press.

Vergin, R. and Qoronfleh, M. (1998) Corporate reputation and the stock market. *Business Horizons*, 41(Jan-Feb), 19–26.

Wilkins, A.L. and Ouchi, W.G. (1983) Efficient cultures: Exploring the relationship between culture and organizational performance. *Administrative Science Quarterly*, 28, 468–481.

Williams, M.L. and Bauer, T.N. (1994) The effect of managing diversity policy on organizational attractiveness. *Group & Organization Management*, 19, 295–308.

Wright, P., Ferris, S.P., Hiller, J.S., and Kroll, M. (1995) Competitiveness through management of diversity: Effects on stock price valuation. *Academy of Management Journal*, 38, 272–287.

Xenikou, A. and Furnham, A. (1996) A correlational and factor analytic study of four questionnaire measures of organizational culture. *Human Relations*, 49, 349–371.

Yang, S.-U. and Mallabo, J. (2003) Exploring the link between the concepts of organization-public relationships and organizational reputations: A relational approach. Paper presented at the Annual Convention of the International Communication Association, San Diego, CA, May.

28

Corporate Reputation and the Practice of Corporate Governance

Justin E. Pettigrew and Bryan H. Reber
University of Georgia, USA

Little has been written about the concept of corporate governance from a communications or reputation perspective. This chapter provides a brief history of corporate governance; different roles of executive boards for a corporation; relevant theories that pertain to corporate governance, communication, and reputation; and an overview of past research that has been done regarding corporate boards and communication. While research in this area usually focuses on CEO compensation and the legal and financial reporting issues that differ from country to country (Conyon and Schwalbach, 1997; Lannoo, 1999), this chapter attempts to examine corporate governance and its impact on communication and corporate reputation. The chapter also provides some suggestions for future research in the field.

Introduction

In the twentieth century, the publicly owned corporation has emerged as the dominant form of business in the United States. From a historical perspective, the success of capitalism in the United States created opportunities for businesses to grow larger. A driver of this growth was the opportunity for investors to unite their capital in pursuit of projects and new enterprises. In return, these investors received shares in the businesses in which they invested, and have come to be known as shareholders. These larger businesses became too complex to be governed by proprietors or partnerships. In the twentieth century, the publicly owned corporation emerged as the dominant legal form for business enterprises.

The term "corporate governance" derives from an analogy between the governance of cities, nations, or states and the governance of corporations. Obviously, governance has existed since the dawn of civilization. The modern concept of corporate governance operates as a form of representational government (Colley *et al.*, 2005). The owners (shareholders) elect directors as their representatives to manage the affairs of the business. The elected

The Handbook of Communication and Corporate Reputation, First Edition. Edited by Craig E. Carroll.
© 2013 John Wiley & Sons, Inc. Published 2015 by John Wiley & Sons, Inc.

directors then provide broad oversight and control of the corporation, and are accountable to the shareholders (Colley *et al.*, 2005).

Boards of directors seem to be increasingly aware of what the actions of individual executives and directors and the governing body collectively communicate to stockholders, other stakeholders, and regulators. Boards have rewritten their policies on proxy statement to reflect more open communication with various publics. In many instances, the secretary to the board now engages in a regular outreach effort to engage shareholders and other interested parties in a dialog about the company's governance practices. Boards are finding more value in communications committees to keep their publics informed (Miller, 2010). Some corporations now have vehicles that allow publics to communicate directly with board members via their web sites. In the wake of corporate shenanigans by Enron and WorldCom, which led to the Sarbanes–Oxley Act of 2002, and more recently the gross errors, if not misdeeds, of corporate giants within the financial industry, effective communication about corporate governance has never been more important.

The concept of "representative government" through a corporate board is an important advantage of corporations over partnerships. However, there is still little agreement in scholarship and practice as to how representative of the parties involved corporate governance structures really are, or even whom it should represent. Different perspectives advocate everything from having top management on the board to having no representation from top management on the board, having "professional" board members whose sole job is to serve on various corporate boards, to a range of attitudes about board involvement in the day-to-day operations of a corporation.

Background

In March 2010, *The Review of Financial Studies* devoted an entire volume to corporate governance. Bebchuk and Weisbach (2010) wrote, "Interest in corporate governance has been rapidly growing, both inside and outside academia, together with recognition of its importance. In the academic world, the interest in corporate governance has been truly interdisciplinary, with much work being undertaken by researchers not only from economics and finance but also from law, management, and accounting" (p. 939). The authors noted that in 2009, the term "corporate governance" appeared as a key word in 987 article abstracts on the Social Science Research Network.

The definitional issue of corporate governance is necessarily taken on by the journal *Corporate Governance: An International Review*. The journal's editors define corporate governance "as the exercise of power over corporate entities so as to increase the value provided to the organization's various stakeholders, as well as making those stakeholders accountable for acting responsibly with regard to the protection, generation, and distribution of wealth invested in the firm."

Definitions of corporate governance vary, but they have the foundation of directors' responsibilities in common. The 1992 Report of the Committee on the Financial Aspects of Corporate Governance, commonly referred to as The Cadbury Report, named for the committee's chair, Adrian Cadbury, defined corporate governance:

> Corporate governance is the system by which companies are directed and controlled. Boards of directors are responsible for the governance of their companies. The shareholders' role in governance is to appoint the directors and the auditors and to satisfy themselves that an appropriate governance structure is in place. The responsibilities of the board include setting the company's strategic aims, providing the leadership to put them into effect, supervising the management of the business and reporting to shareholders on their stewardship. The board's actions are subject to laws, regulations, and the shareholders in general meeting. (The United Kingdom's Shareholder's Association, 1992, p. 7)

The Organisation for Economic Co-operation and Development, a consortium of 34 countries dedicated to global development, defines corporate governance as "[A] set of relationships between a company's management, its Board, its shareholders and other stakeholders [...] also (providing) the structure through which the objectives of the company are set, and the means of attaining those objectives and monitoring performance are determined" (Organisation for Economic Co-operation and Development, 2004, p. 11).

There is a dearth of research on corporate governance and corporate reputation from a communication perspective. What has been written frequently focuses on the role of corporate social responsibility (CSR) in corporate governance. Deetz (2007) wrote that governance models have historically focused on "some combination of managerial stewardship, governmental regulation, and consumer choices to make operant wider social values" (p. 267).

In summary, corporate governance is a growing concern for organizations and academics. Its definition focuses on control, resource management, accountability, and stewardship. From a communication perspective, corporate governance is inextricably linked to corporate reputation and how it is perceived by varied stakeholders.

What Does Corporate Governance Mean?

Corporate governance is generally assumed to mean the work by boards of directors in collaboration with organizational executives. Adams *et al.* (2008) note that the perception of literature on corporate governance is that it is largely empirical (p. 4). They argue, however, that general and "off-the-shelf" theories are often applicable to corporate governance, especially as it relates to boards of directors.

Corporate governance is unavoidably linked to the composition and work of boards of directors. Doh and Stumpf (2005) wrote,

> governance mechanisms typically take three principal forms: (1) establishment of an independent board of directors that oversees the

activities of top management; (2) the presence of a large block of shareholders who take an active interest in the activities of top management; and (3) a market for corporate control that serves to discipline managers for poor performance. (p. 11)

Adams *et al.* (2008) note that directors' primary tasks are making decisions about the hiring and firing of the CEO and setting strategy. Mace (1971) concluded that "directors serve as a source of advice and counsel, serve as some sort of discipline, and act in crisis situations" – especially in a crisis in which a change of CEO becomes necessary (p. 178). Pfeffer and Salancik (1978) identified two distinct functions of boards: advice and counsel, and oversight and control (p. 170). Parum (2006) noted that boards should review and guide strategy, major action plans, and risk policy as well as set performance objectives. She further wrote that directors should "oversee the process of disclosure and communications, ensuring the integrity of financial and non-financial reporting" (p. 559).

Despite the fact that most executives see directors' task as monitoring, hiring, and firing executive staff (most notably the CEO), a survey by Demb and Neubauer (1992) revealed that two-thirds of directors saw their role as setting strategic direction for the organization (p. 43). This notion of corporate governance being linked to strategic direction is reinforced by research that has exhibited a shift from passivity, especially in disciplinary matters, to activism (Adams *et al.*, 2008, p. 7).

Boards are generally structured with two key groups – inside directors, those who are full-time employees of the organization, and outside directors, those who bring special skill sets to the directors' table (e.g., bankers, lawyers, the politically connected, and investors). The demands on directors have increased as regulations such as Sarbanes–Oxley have increased. Board composition and size, directors' term length, and CEO membership as chairman of the board all affect board action (Adams *et al.*, 2008). While research has generally labored under the assumption that boards should be independent from management if they are to be most effective, Westphal (1999) found that a lack of independence (e.g., preexisting friendships between prospective board members and management) can actually increase board involvement and organization effectiveness. Hermalin (2005) provides a model that suggests the value of independent boards on CEO performance. He argues that independent boards are more likely to make external CEO hires and are more likely to monitor the CEO with vigilance. This puts upward pressure on CEO compensation. The issue of primary interest to us, however, is Hermalin's modeling of how independent boards affect CEO selection and monitoring.

In 1996, Johnson, Daily, and Ellstrand wrote that despite a strong and growing interest in corporate governance in both the academic and business communities, there was still no "convergence around a specified role set for directors" (Johnson *et al.*, 1996, p. 409). In their review of corporate governance, they classified directors' responsibilities into roles of control, service, and resource dependence (p. 411). It should be noted here that the first role, control, is rooted in the concept of an independent board; the others, service and resource dependence, are grounded in a more active view of the board as counsel to top management and active participants in corporate change and growth.

Control

The relative volume of research devoted to the different board roles is predominantly in the area of control. Most theories of corporate governance identify the board of director's control role as conceptually and normatively important (Bainbridge, 1993; Fama, 1980; Mizruchi, 1983; Zahra and Pearce, 1989). It should be noted, however, that the theoretical support for board monitoring as a form of corporate control is rooted in agency theory (Jensen and Meckling, 1976). According to this perspective, the function of boards is to reduce agency costs resulting from the delegation of strategic decision making, or "decision management" to top executives by exercising "decision control,"

which involves monitoring managerial decision making and performance (Westphal, 1999).

Walsh and Seward (1990) identify several internal control mechanisms for corporations, for which boards of directors are responsible. The board of directors needs to assess both the ability and efforts of the top management of their organization. A problem can arise when boards have little information about how managers behave, as the board usually convenes only once a year and is "presented" with information about management from management. However, a top manager's job is complex and ambiguous (Kotter, 1982). It can be difficult to be specific about appropriate or inappropriate managerial behaviors before and after the fact. Usually, communications professionals are involved in annual board presentations, so it is essential that they are aware of how information is presented to the board to reflect accurate corporate performance.

The board is also responsible for conducting an assessment of the environmental effects, for example, actions by competitors or regulators, before taking any action regarding the management team or changing the practices and policies of a corporation. Business communicators at the corporation can assist management in providing the board with an overview of issues that may be of interest or have an impact on decisions that are to be made.

Much debate has centered on the ability of directors to effectively fulfill the control role. Directors who may feel beholden to management for their positions on the board potentially face some difficulty in evaluating this same management (Gilson and Kraakman, 1991), especially when management performance is not up to standards. It should also be noted that in many cases, director candidates are often selected on the basis of their willingness to support management decisions (Goforth, 1994).

Service

The service role addresses directors' provision of advice and counsel to the CEO (Lorsch and McIver, 1989). Many organizations, particularly those with more influence from outside sources, such as regulators or labor markets, may choose to tap into the breadth of knowledge that outside board members provide to complement the depth of organization-specific knowledge of inside directors or C-level executives (Kesner and Johnson, 1990). Pearce and Zahra (1991) proposed a typology of boards based on the underlying dimensions of CEO power and board power. Survey data showed that organizations with powerful boards, especially participatory boards which are characterized by high board power and high CEO power, outperformed firms with weaker boards.

The service role of boards seems to be growing as more corporations recognize the value of more direct board involvement in a corporation's activities. While the provision of advice has been recognized as a potentially important form of board involvement, empirical researchers have neither explicitly modeled advisory relations nor examined how social factors may enhance a board's ability to exercise this function (Westphal, 1999). The greatest support for the service role of board members exists in the form of directors' self-reports that devote a considerable portion of their board-related time and effort to contributing to corporate decision making (Johnson *et al.*, 1996). The emerging development of this role in corporate boardrooms could potentially motivate further development and theory of the service role. An exploration of this area could be useful for the development of communication theory and practice.

Resource dependence

The resource dependence perspective views the board as one of a number of instruments that management may use to facilitate access to resources critical to the firm's success (Johnson *et al.*, 1996). Much of the research in this area is centered on the board as a source of capital. To date, research has supported the hypothesis that board membership may be used as a tool to facilitate access to capital.

Pearce and Zahra (1992) proposed several determinants of board composition (the proportion of affiliated and unaffiliated outsiders)

and board size. They argued that features of the environment, strategy, and past financial performance would partially determine board characteristics, which in turn would impact future financial performance (Johnson *et al.*, 1996). Contextual variables may also impact the resource dependence role of the board. Smaller firms may benefit from appointing a prestigious director to their board, who can help to provide access to needed resources. There is an opportunity for research in the resource dependence role of boards, in that much of the work that has been done in this area has neglected to address other resources the board may be able to provide, such as potential partnerships, opportunities for community outreach, and contacts.

Theoretical Frameworks

For the context of our interest (i.e., the relationship of communication and reputation to corporate governance), we will examine theoretical frameworks traditionally used in corporate governance research.

Agency theory

Agency theory is among the theories most frequently linked to the importance of board monitoring. In fact, most of the research that exists in the area of corporate governance is grounded in agency theory. Agency theory is based on the potential for self-interest when ownership and control of the firm are disparate (Johnson *et al.*, 1996). The crux of agency theory is that principals (shareholders) delegate authority to agents to act on their behalf (Davis *et al.*, 1997). It is this delegation that "allows agents to opportunistically build their own utility at the expense of the principals' utility (wealth)" (p. 23). Agency theorists specify an intermediate condition of control that minimizes the potential abuse of the delegation of authority by corporate boards (Jensen and Meckling, 1976). According to agency theory, boards' role is to reduce agency costs by delegating and monitoring strategic decision making (Fama and Jensen, 1983a, p. 303). Hillman *et al.* (2011) noted that "such monitoring helps to reduce agency costs and improve firm performance because absent such activities managers may pursue self-interest at the expense of shareholder interests" (p. 2). They go on to note that scholars have even argued that corporate governance and agency theory are equivalent. An inherent problem here is that agency theory is primarily focused on maximizing shareholder wealth, and does not take into account what some consider moral "obligations" of a corporation. Applied to corporate governance, agency theory poses a problem, as directors may face conflicts between their legal duty to effectively monitor firm management and their professional and personal associations with management. As we link corporate governance to corporate reputation, we will see that agency theory does not provide an adequate underpinning for a thorough examination of the roles of corporate board members.

Lan and Heracleous (2010), in their extension of agency theory, argue that

> the role of the board is not to be a monitor but, rather, a mediating hierarch – someone who balances the often competing claims and interests of the groups that contribute to the team production process, makes decisions on the allocation of team surpluses, and is legally ultimately in control of a corporation's assets and key strategic decisions. (p. 295)

From an early stage, theorists were aware that boards of directors, as the stewards of the shareholders, would not be effective monitors of management if this relationship was tainted by self-interest (Fama, 1980; Fama and Jensen, 1983a,b).

Another limit of agency theory is determined by its model of mankind. Agency theory assumes that individuals are self-serving and individualistic. Jensen and Meckling (1976) criticized this model as unrealistic and not reflective of actual human behavior. Doucouliagos (1994) argued that labeling all motivation as self-serving does not explain the complexity of human action, and Frank (1994) suggested

that this model of mankind does not suit the demands of a social existence.

Agency theory provides a useful way of explaining relationships where the interests of the parties are at odds and may be brought into more agreement through proper monitoring (Davis *et al.*, 1997).

Stakeholder theory

Stakeholder theory is a theory of organizational management and ethics (Phillips *et al.*, 2003). Stakeholder theory is another lens through which corporate boards are examined. Board members are stakeholders in the corporation, but their role is to protect and govern in the best interests of other stakeholders, primarily shareholders. Stakeholder theory is distinct because it addresses morals and values explicitly as a central feature of managing organizations (Phillips *et al.*, 2003). Managing for stakeholders involves attention to more than just maximizing wealth. Attention to the interests and well-being of those who can assist or hinder the achievement of the organization's objectives is the central thrust of the theory. While stakeholder theory provides a useful lens through which to examine corporate boards, there is still much debate as to its usefulness. One view holds that independent directors – those not in the employ of the firm – have no stake in the organization and are therefore independent (Dalton *et al.*, 2007). Nonindependent directors – those either affiliated with or in the employ of the firm – do have a stake in the organization and therefore can be influenced by pressures from inside the corporation. Upon further investigation, boards, regardless of their composition, are never truly independent (Dalton *et al.*, 2007).

Parum (2006) noted that "Stakeholders can be defined as any group or individual who is affected by or can affect the achievement of an organization's objectives" (p. 559). She differentiated between stakeholder analysis and stakeholder management. Stakeholder analysis includes identifying key stakeholders and their needs, and tapping them for ideas that can be integrated into a corporation's strategic management. "Stakeholder management," she wrote, "includes communicating, negotiating, contracting and managing relationships with stakeholders and motivating them to behave in ways that are beneficial to the organization and its other stakeholders (Harrison and St. John, 1998)" (Parum, 2006, p. 560). Parum's notions of stakeholder theory are thoroughly linked to communication, and especially external communication, by corporate boards of directors.

Resource dependence theory

Resource dependency theory asserts that the board is an essential link between the company and important resources it needs to conduct business and maximize performance (Pfeffer, 1973; Pfeffer and Salancik, 1978). The exact nature of a resource is variable. Specific resources that have been studied because of their perceived value to the firm include information, finance, or capital links to key suppliers, customers, and other significant stakeholders (Nicholson and Kiel, 2007). Central to this concept is power, which, in this instance, is control of resources. Resource dependence theory can be useful in examining board composition, in that external board members may have more access to resources outside the company than inside directors. While resource dependency theory may make sense from a performance perspective, one could conclude from one study that outside board membership is declining. In a recent study by James Drury Partners (JDP) (2011), 70% of active _Fortune_ 500 CEOs served on outside boards in 1990, while only 45% of active CEOs served on outside boards in 2010, filling only 288 seats. While the study focused on only America's 500 largest companies, it could serve as the starting point for future research in this area.

Stewardship theory

Stewardship theory is rooted in psychology and sociology, and was designed for researchers to examine situations in which executives as stewards are motivated to act in the best interests

of their investors (Donaldson and Davis, 1989, 1991). According to agency theory, people are rooted in economic rationality. Argyris (1973) argued that humans placed in an environment where they are restricted by a purely economic view suppress their level of aspiration. Such a view is based in the early work of McGregor (1960). In stewardship theory, the performance of a steward is affected by whether the structural situation in which he or she is located facilitates effective action. Therefore, if the executive's motivation fit the model of mankind underlying stewardship theory, then empowering governance structures and mechanisms are appropriate (Davis _et al._, 1997). Stewardship theory has many potential influences on corporate board governance, particularly on ways to structure a CEO's compensation package. Stewardship theory rests on the assumption that a steward who successfully improves the performance of the organization generally increases internal work motivation, and higher levels of performance as well as satisfaction with work (Davis _et al._, 1997). The major distinction between agency and stewardship theories is on the focus of extrinsic versus intrinsic motivation. For corporate boards, stewardship theory suggests that boards are less a control mechanism for a corporation and more of a guiding force in all areas, not just financial performance.

Summary

The responsibilities of the board and communication's role in them

To further understand corporate governance, we now turn to a review of the various responsibilities of the corporate board, and the role that communications may play in the various functions.

The bylaws

The bylaws of any corporation set out the rules under which the board will operate. While not an exhaustive list, below are some of the issues bylaws usually address:[1]

- The rules by which persons standing for election are voted on by the shareholders.
- How persons standing for elections will be elected.
- The number of directors on the board.
- The number of "inside" directors and "outside" directors.
- The term length of a director.
- The conditions under which directors may be removed from office, and any limitations, such as age, conflicts of interest, and misconduct that might result in board members being asked to resign.
- The board and corporate officer titles and duties, and the procedures for electing them.
- The level of compensation for directors.
- The board committees and their charges.
- Details about the annual meeting of shareholders.
- Details about special meetings of the shareholders, and who can call for them for what reasons.
- The conditions under which voting proxies will be issued to the shareholders.
- Authority to call a board meeting and the notice required.
- Frequency of board meetings.
- How the agenda will be prepared and by whom.
- Definition of a quorum.

It is important that a corporate communications team, especially if they are involved in investor relations, has access to and clear understanding of the bylaws, earnings reports, and other business-related documents of the corporation (Colley, 2005). Communications personnel may be asked to review bylaws and other documents for clarity and conciseness of communication. Such a review may be necessary to free bylaws of legalese and abide by the Securities and Exchange Commission's (SEC) requirement that business communication be written in "plain English."

Annual meetings of shareholders

The annual meeting of shareholders is probably the biggest responsibility placed on corporate communication teams. The shareholders' meeting is a major event for public corporations, scheduled after the close of business at the end of a corporation's fiscal year and following the availability of audited financial statements, usually 90–120 days after the end of the fiscal year. It plays a role in building and maintaining an organization's reputation, especially from the perspective of investors. Prior to the meeting, the corporation provides the shareholders with the annual report, which provides not only the results of the previous year's performance, but also an outlook for the future.

Corporate communicators are actively involved in the creation of the annual report, writing much of the more editorial portions of the document. Corporate communications departments are usually involved in the look, feel, and theme of the document as well, working with designers and printers to produce the finished piece. The report is usually delivered to shareholders prior to the annual meeting. Increasingly, annual reports may be delivered in several forms. Corporations now provide the extended 10-K report required by the SEC both within the annual report and as a freestanding document. Additionally, most corporations are sending printed versions of annual reports only to shareholders who request them, because the annual report and 10-K report are available on the corporate web site.

Annual meetings can vary from short legal formalities to large, extravagant events that promote the company as a good investment. They normally deal with the election of board members and any matters that require stockholder vote approval, such as executive compensation plans, including stock option plans, authorization of the sale of new stock, or the adoption of new plans that might affect stockholders.

Board meetings

The board meeting is the cornerstone of a board's activities. An effective board meeting begins with careful preparation. Communication professionals are usually involved with creating management presentations to brief the board on topics or issues of interest, or to present proposals to the board for actions. Communication managers must be able to counsel and support the CEO prior to board presentations. Members of the communications team are also often involved in arranging details of the board meeting, creating events for the board's interaction outside the boardroom, assisting in the preparation for board committee breakouts, and providing on-site support on the day of the meeting. It is also important that communications managers review the minutes of board meetings once they are approved, as they become the official record of the deliberations and actions of the board.

Corporate Governance and Doing the "Right Thing"

Research and practice provide evidence that corporate governance and corporate behavior are increasingly intertwined. Jamali *et al.* (2008) wrote,

> Under the umbrella of CG [corporate governance], companies are encouraged to promote ethics, fairness, transparency, and accountability in all their dealings. They are expected to continue generating profits while maintaining the highest standards of governance internally. A firm's decisions should also be aligned with the interests of different players within and outside the company (Freeman, 1984). Hence, businesses have to also keep their activities attuned to society's ethical, legal, and communal aspirations. (p. 444)

Gill (2008) argued that corporate governance has become increasingly important as a means to incorporate social and environmental issues into the corporate decision-making apparatus. Corporate governance "is being linked more and more with business practices and public policies that are stakeholder-friendly," Gill wrote.

Money and Schepers (2007) noted that the "triple bottom line" of profitability, social concerns, and environmental performance is a new norm of evaluation (p. 2). Increasingly, Money and Schepers argued, there is a substantial overlap between shareholders and stakeholders. Money and Schepers wrote, "A substantial body of literature argues that a new corporate governance paradigm is appearing; it shifts from a shareholder-based to a stakeholder-based approach" (Money and Schepers, 2007, p. 4).

Mackenzie (2007) researched the work of corporate boards in the United Kingdom as regards CSR. Company boards are essential to ensuring that CSR standards are met because boards should set standards and values for companies (Mackenzie, 2007, p. 936). In Great Britain, regulations explicitly require company directors to address the impact of the company on its community and environment, Mackenzie noted. Following a survey of board activities of Britain's 20 largest companies, Mackenzie found that several of those boards had specific CSR committees. Mackenzie reported that boards' CSR committees tend to focus on six priorities: (1) reviewing CSR issues, (2) identifying and monitoring nonfinancial risks, (3) establishing policies and standards, (4) monitoring CSR compliance, (5) reviewing company reporting of CSR activities, and (6) overseeing corporate philanthropy (Mackenzie, 2007, p. 939).

As various publics come to expect more from corporations than just profits and goods and services, boards need to be aware of the importance of attending to both stakeholders and shareholders in order to maintain a positive reputation for the corporation they oversee. This supports theories of governance beyond agency theory, and points to a more active role of the board in all aspects of corporate performance and for publics beyond investors.

Looking Ahead: Corporate Governance in Corporate Reputation Research and Practice

Research

Corporate governance has had a rich examination in the financial, managerial, and organization literature. More research is warranted in the areas of board communication and communication activities surrounding and on behalf of the corporate board. Work in this area can assist communicators in learning how to deal more effectively with boards, and how to assist boards in their communications both internally and externally.

One example of research linking corporate governance and communication is Parum (2006). She took an initial look at questions that have additional rich potential for corporate governance communication research. She examined the extent of external communication by publicly traded companies, what and why an organization's dominant coalition communicates regarding corporate governance, whether external communication leads to increased transparency in corporate governance, and whether the results of external communication include a clear and strong corporate identity (p. 562). Because her research involved only Danish corporations, the potential exists to extend and enlarge this line of research.

Research from a communication perspective might increase the focus on stakeholder versus shareholder relations as viewed by boards of directors. Because of the dearth of research in the area of communications and corporate governance, it seems appropriate to build a foundation of qualitative research such as case study analysis or, if possible, direct observation.

Content analysis of mission statements, bylaws, annual reports, social responsibility objectives, press releases, and so on, would be useful in terms of understanding the communication strategies of publicly held corporations. Press release archives provide a rich data set from which to draw conclusions about how corporations communicate with the press. Some research has been done on sustainability reports, but this remains a field with rich potential for understanding corporate and board strategy in stakeholder relations. This material is easily accessible via public records (e.g., SEC) or corporate web sites.

In-depth interviews with directors and executives, including corporate communications officers, may shed light on the role of communications in corporate governance. Following in-depth interviews, surveys might be developed to get at similar questions with a generalizable sample. One of the reasons such research has not been conducted is the difficulty in "getting to" board members and other high-level executives. Many board members are reluctant to speak about their participation on corporate boards, and corporate executives may not see the work of researchers pursuing primary research of this kind as important, and thus requests get ignored or pushed to the side.

However, because so little has been done in this area, the potential for meaningful research in corporate governance communication is as broad as the researcher's imagination.

Practice

Similarly, the potential for improving organizational practice is extensive. Communicators' role in corporate governance is often limited to investor relations, particularly related to annual reports and annual meetings. As we examine and more fully understand the role of communication, especially external communication to shareholders and other stakeholders, we can begin to make the case for additional involvement for corporate communications to be an active part of the corporate governance process, perhaps even serving as nonindependent directors.

Analysis and understanding of external communication tactics of other corporations can inform an organization's practice. How accessible are the board and the CEO and by what means are they accessible? What are the typical contents of mission statements within an industry? How are reputation activities communicated? Are they typically part of the annual report or do they warrant their own standalone report?

As with any relationship that requires management, management of the relationship of the board of directors with its key constituents is improved by identifying and incorporating best practices from within and across industries. Recognizing that board activities are an important part of the overall reputation strategy of a corporation is imperative. The role of corporate boards is changing, and corporate communicators should be able to adapt to an environment in which boards are more than control mechanisms.

Because communication has moved from the back seat to the front seat in corporate governance, the potential for increased influence and improved practice for corporate communicators is tremendous. As practitioners seek to expand their influence in the management boardroom, careful attention to board practices and activities is one way in which corporate communication can assert itself as integral to the success of a corporation. A study by Westphal and Deephouse (2011) suggested that CEOs and other top executives can influence the reputation of their company by developing interpersonal relationships with journalists. Could the same be true for board members of those same corporations?

In conclusion, it is impossible to cover all of the aspects of corporate boards and communications from the board in one chapter. What is evident is that much work can be done to improve our understanding and improve practice. Readers are encouraged to seek out avenues for research in this understudied field, and practitioners are called on to improve their knowledge and find ways to utilize and capitalize on the activities of corporate boards. Such work furthers the professionalization of public relations, and provides valuable resources in the ever-changing world of corporate business.

Note

1 Adapted from "How an Effective Board Organizes Its Work" from *What Is Corporate Governance?* (Colley, 2005).

References

Adams, R., Hermalin, B.E., and Weisbach, M.S. (2008) The role of boards of directors in corporate governance: A conceptual framework and survey. Cambridge, MA: National Bureau of Economic Research, Working Paper 14486.

Argyris, C. (1973) Organizational man: Rational and self-actualizing. *Public Administration Review*, 33, 354–357.

Bainbridge, S.M. (1993) Independent directors and the ALI corporate governance project. *George Washington Law Review*, 61, 1034–1083.

Bebchuk, L.A. and Weisbach, M.S. (2010) The state of corporate governance research. *The Review of Financial Studies*, 23(3), 939–961.

Colley, J.L. Jr., Doyle, J.L., Logan, G.W., and Stettinus, W. (2005) *What Is Corporate Governance?* New York: McGraw-Hill.

Conyon, M.J. and Schwalbach, J. (1997) *European Differences in Executive Pay and Corporate Governance*. E-Books on Demand, books to ebooks. eu.

Dalton, D.R., Hitt, M.A., Certo, S.T., and Dalton, C.M. (2007) The fundamental agency problem and its mitigation: Independence, equity, and the market for corporate control. *The Academy of Management Annals*, 1, 1–64.

Davis, J.F., Schoorman, F.D., and Donaldson, L. (1997) Toward a stewardship theory of management. *Academy of Management Review*, 22(1), 20–47.

Deetz, S. (2007) Corporate governance, corporate social responsibility, and communication. In May, S., Cheney, G., and Roper, J. (eds), *The Debate Over Corporate Social Responsibility*. Oxford, UK: Oxford University Press, pp. 267–278.

Demb, A. and Neubauer, F.-F. (1992) *The Corporate Board*. Oxford, UK: Oxford University Press.

Doh, J.P. and Stumpf, S.A. (2005) Towards a framework of responsible leadership and governance. In Doh, J. and Stumpf, S.A. (eds), *Handbook on Responsible Leadership and Governance in Global Business*. Cheltenham, UK: Edward Elgar, pp. 3–18.

Donaldson, L. and Davis, J.H. (1989) CEO governance and shareholders returns: Agency theory or stewardship theory. Paper presented at the Annual Meeting of the Academy of Management, Washington DC.

Donaldson, L. and Davis, J.H. (1991) Stewardship theory or agency theory: CEO governance and shareholder returns. *Australian Journal of Management*, 16, 49–64.

Doucouliagos, C. (1994) A note on the evolution of homo economicus. *Journal of Economics Issues*, 3, 877–883.

Fama, E.F. (1980) Agency problems and the theory of the firm. *Journal of Political Economy*, 88, 288–307.

Fama, E.F. and Jensen, M.C. (1983a) The separation of ownership and control. *Journal of Law and Economics*, 26, 301–325.

Fama, E.F. and Jensen, M.C. (1983b) Agency problems and residual claims. *Journal of Law and Economics*, 26, 327–345.

Frank, R.H. (1994) *Microeconomics and Behavior*. New York: McGraw-Hill.

Freeman, R.E. (1984) *Strategic Management: A Stakeholder Approach*. Boston: Pitman Publishing.

Gill, A. (2008) Corporate governance as social responsibility: A research agenda. *Berkeley Journal of International Law*, 26(2), 452–478.

Gilson, R.J. and Kraakman, R. (1991) Reinventing the outer director: An agenda for institutional investors. *Stanford Law Review*, 43, 863–906.

Goforth, C. (1994) Proxy reform as a means of increasing shareholder participation in corporate governance: Too little, but not too late. *The American University Law Review*, 43, 397–465.

Harrison, J.S. and St. John, C.H. (1998) *Strategic Management of Organizations and Stakeholders*. St. Paul, MN: West Publishing Company.

Hermalin, B.E. (2005) Trends in corporate governance. *Journal of Finance*, 60(5), 2351–2384.

Hillman, A.J., Shropshire, C., Certo, S.T., Dalton, D.R., and Dalton, C.M. (2011) What I like about you: A multilevel study of shareholder discontent with director monitoring. *Organization Science*, 22(3), 675–687.

Jamali, D., Safieddine, A.M., and Rabbath, M. (2008) Corporate governance and corporate social responsibility synergies and interrelationships. *Corporate Governance*, 16(5), 443–459.

James Drury Partners (2011) McDonalds tops new corporate governance study. [Press release]. Retrieved from http://www.jdrurypartners.com/Media_and_Press/JDP_News/Event_Detail/7 (last accessed September 26, 2012).

Jensen, M.C. and Meckling, W.H. (1976) Theory of the firm: Managerial behavior, agency costs and ownership structure. *Journal of Finance Economics*, 3(4), 305–360.

Johnson, J.L., Daily, C.M., and Ellstrand, A.E. (1996) Boards of directors: A review and research agenda. *Journal of Management*, 22(3), 409–438.

Kesner, I.F. and Johnson, R.B. (1990) An investigation of the relationship between board composition and stockholder suits. *Strategic Management Journal*, 11, 327–226.

Kotter, J. (1982) *The General Managers*. New York: Free Press.

Lan, L.L. and Heracleous, L. (2010) Rethinking agency theory: The view from law. *Academy of Management Review*, 35(2), 294–314.

Lannoo, K. (1999) A European perspective on corporate governance. *Journal of Common Market Studies*, 37(2), 269–294.

Lorsch, J.W. and McIver, E. (1989) *Pawns or Potentates: The Reality of America's Corporate Boards*. Boston: Harvard Business School Press.

Mace, M.L. (1971) *Directors: Myth and Reality*. Boston: Harvard Business School Press.

Mackenzie, C. (2007) Boards, incentives and corporate social responsibility: The case for a change of emphasis. *Corporate Governance*, 15(5), 935–943.

McGregor, D. (1960) *The Human Side of the Enterprise*. New York: McGraw-Hill.

Miller, K.L. (2010) What does a board communications committee do? Retrieved from http://NonprofitMarketingGuide.com (last accessed September 26, 2012).

Mizruchi, M.S. (1983) Who controls whom? An examination of the relation between management and boards of directors in large American corporations. *Academy of Management Review*, 8, 426–435.

Money, K. and Schepers, H. (2007) Are CSR and corporate governance converging? *Journal of General Management*, 33(2), 1–11.

Nicholson, G.J. and Kiel, G.C. (2007) Can directors impact performance? A case based test of three theories of corporate governance. *Corporate Governance: An International Review*, 15(4), 585–608.

Organisation for Economic Co-operation and Development (2004) OECD Principles of Corporate Governance, Organisation for Economic Co-operation and Development, Paris.

Parum, E. (2006) Corporate governance and corporate identity. *Corporate Governance*, 14(6), 558–567.

Pearce, J.A. and Zahra, S.A. (1991) The relative power of CEOs and boards of directors: Associations with corporate performance. *Strategic Management Journal*, 12(2), 145–153.

Pearce, J.A. and Zahra, S.A. (1992) Board composition from a strategic contingency perspective. *Journal of Management Studies*, 29(4), 311–438.

Pfeffer, J. (1973) Size, composition, and function of hospital boards of directors: A study of organization-environment linkage. *Administrative Science Quarterly*, 18, 349–364.

Pfeffer, J. and Salancik, G.R. (1978) *The External Control of Organizations*. New York: Harper & Row.

Phillips, R., Freeman, R.E., and Wicks, A.C. (2003) What stakeholder theory is not. *Business Ethics Quarterly, 13*(4), 479–502.

The United Kingdom's Shareholder's Association (1992) The Financial Aspects of Corporate Governance (The Cadbury Report). Retrieved from http://www.kantakji.com/fiqh/Files/Companies/w127.pdf (last accessed October 22, 2012).

Walsh, J.P. and Seward, J.K. (1990) On the efficiency of internal and external corporate control mechanisms. *Academy of Management Review, 15*(3), 421–458.

Westphal, J.D. (1999) Collaboration in the boardroom: Behavioral and performance conse-

quences of CEO-board social ties. *Academy of Management Journal, 42*(1), 7–24.

Westphal, J.D. and Deephouse, D.L. (2011) Avoiding bad press: Interpersonal influence in relations between CEOs and journalists and the consequences for press reporting about firms and their leadership. *Organizational Science, 22*(4), 1061–1086.

Zahra, S.A. and Pearce, J.A. (1989) Board of directors and corporate financial performance: A review and integrative model. *Journal of Management, 15*, 291–334.

29

Synthesizing Relationship Dynamics: An Analysis of Products and Services as Components of Corporate Reputation

Pan Ji

Nanyang Technological University, Singapore

Paul S. Lieber

University of Canberra, Australia

To date, explorations into product and service reputation and its communication often existed on theoretical islands, with economical, sociological, and/or relational explanations viewed in near isolation. Moreover, sister communication determinants in international commerce – for example, brand value, country of origin, and new media – were ignored in such inquiries. This chapter attempted to synthesize these separate theoretical paradigms, and with it identify key, overlapping communication variables to explain product and service reputation in the current, global marketplace.

Introduction

New communication technologies and an accelerated, international flow of goods and services (Post and Berman, 2001) combine to profoundly change the way global business is conducted (Logsdon and Wood, 2005). Both products/services and the marketing information about them now spread faster, wider, and in more diverse forms. In this more complex business environment, immense opportunities and consequences await corporations capable of establishing and/or preserving reputation as suppliers of and communicators about high-quality services and/or products. This chapter synthesizes existing theory on corporate, product and service, and relational definitions of reputation in hopes of addressing this modern business and communication reality.

Corporate Reputation

Economic reputation

From an economic viewpoint – whereby the economic value of a corporation is regarded as its main criteria – corporate reputation is

The Handbook of Communication and Corporate Reputation, First Edition. Edited by Craig E. Carroll.
© 2013 John Wiley & Sons, Inc. Published 2015 by John Wiley & Sons, Inc.

defined as an organization's communication, organizational, and product assets within a marketplace of goods and services (Barney, 1986; Caves and Porter, 1977; Dowling, 2004; Milgrom and Roberts, 1982), ones likely to bring financial or social gains in the future (Deephouse, 2000; Roberts and Dowling, 2002). Conceived within this perspective, corporate reputation is defined by (1) a company's internal strengths, (2) its history of interaction and business transactions with customers as known to others, and (3) a corporation's mission statement (Barney, 2001; Dowling, 2002; Dutton and Dukerich, 1991; van Riel and Balmer, 1997).

Thus, corporate reputation worth arguably lies in its effect on consumer perception of a company's past communication and commercial actions to inform present decision making. This economic conception of corporate reputation is derived according to a corporation's "true value" (Clark and Montgomery, 1998; Weigelt and Camerer, 1988a). Higher corporate value can enhance a company's profitability by inducing customers to buy from it, investors to purchase its securities, and employees to take its jobs (Fombrun, 1996; Fombrun et al., 1999; Nguyen and Leblanc, 2001).

As a corporation's main target as well as a key stakeholder group, consumers often base the evaluation of a company's market value on a combination of direct experiences with the company plus other forms of communication and symbolism about the entity. Thus, a corporation's interactions and subjective comparison with rival firms are also considered in a purchase decision-making process.

To consumers, corporate reputations can signal either a broad-based goodness or something more specific about a certain company and/or particular sentiments about the products/services it produces. To maintain the credibility and efficacy of an established corporate reputation, organizations need to proactively demonstrate commitment to produce and communicate about quality products/ services, with reputations validated and verified periodically among customers (Schultz *et al.*, 2000). Accordingly, Fombrun (1996) discov-

ered that the "combination of lower prices and a strong reputation attract most customers to an offering" of products and services. Corporate reputations are outcomes of a competitive process, during which a firm promotes its strengths to consumers to maximize its economic status and values (Fombrun and Shanley, 1990; Fombrun and van Riel, 1997) against similar products within the same market (Barney, 1986). Not only will customers prefer organizations with better reputation and an ability to communicate such strengths; they are also disinclined to accept negative information about an organization already blessed with good reputation (Wartick, 1992), reducing that corporation's transaction costs (Castro *et al.*, 2004; Walsh and Beatty, 2007) and enhancing trust and loyalty to it (Dowling, 2001; Foumier and Yao, 1997; Keller and Aaker, 1998). Conversely and even with extended communication efforts, when customers develop a negative perception of a certain company, profits and sales of the company sink (Gray and Balmer, 1998), and doing business becomes difficult if not entirely impossible (Table 29.1).

Sociological reputation

Alternatively and from a sociological point of view, communication takes on even greater prominence. From this perspective – whereby the dynamics of interpersonal relationships is the focus – corporate reputation is regarded as an organization's "total prestige," or value when analyzing a social system surrounding both a firm in particular and its industry at large (Rao, 1994; Shapiro, 1987). Corporate reputation is therefore the collective communication representation of an organization, one reconstructed through historical–social interactions driven by established values and belief systems in a community of stakeholders (Gardberg and Fombrun, 2002, 2006). Within these systems, current priority needs of a company – and more broadly, of a greater society the company resides within – selectively drive the buildup and reconstruction of collective memories associated with a corporation and its products.

Table 29.1 Conceptions of Corporate Reputation (CR).

CR conceptions	Economic	Sociological
Criteria	Value of corporation	Dynamics of CR-related Social Interactions
Propositions	1. CR as corporate asset in marketplace	1. CR as collective image/memory and relationship
	2. CR, pricing, and competition predict consumer attitude/decision and profit	2. Social interaction, value, and beliefs cultivate CR
	3. Corporate strength, mission, and interaction history predict CR	3. Social/corporate needs predict CR reconstruction
	4. CR needs to be verified	4. Culture expression, norm, and identity predict CR
	5. Competition results predict CR	5. History, communication, and corporate investment predict quality of CR as relationship

Viewed through a sister theoretical lens of symbolic interactionism, Albert and Whetten (1985) argued that corporate reputation is a product of mutual acculturation and identification toward and within an organization. It is rooted in an organization's self-expressions, evident not only in the symbolism of its logo and brands (see the sub-section "Brand value"), but also in its belief systems, cultural norms (Schultz *et al.*, 2000), and shared perceptions of that corporation's products or services (Collins and Porras, 1994). Sirgy (1985) argued that some products and services (see the section "Product and Service Reputation") could be conceptualized as having distinct personality images such as being "modern," "friendly," or "fashionable." Customers who associate positive personality images with a company's products and services are more likely to form a positive attitude toward the producer.

Corporate reputation can also be deemed a composite of corporate traits that help forge the relationship between a company and its consumer constituents (Fombrun and Gardberg, 2000) or between different companies (Dollinger *et al.*, 1997). Prior contact between professional representatives of a corporation and customers (Fombrun and Shanley, 1990) and word-of-mouth communications within customer social networks as well as corporate

investments into pricing, advertising, and PR campaigns (Milgrom and Roberts, 1986; Shapiro, 1988) have all been posited to impact the quality and strength of business relationships between a corporation and its customers, according to an extended literature review by Brown *et al.* (2006). This combination of experiences arguably defines not only the feedback loop inherent in successful two-way communication, but also the structural integrity of this loop.

Product and Service Reputation

Among the attributes of corporate reputation as measured by the Reputation Institute's (2011) Global RepTrak™ and the Reputation Quotient^SM (Fombrun, 2001a,b; Fombrun and Gardberg, 2000; Fombrun *et al.*, 1999; Gardberg and Fombrun, 2002), a company's products and services constitute one of the most important determinants in positive corporate reputation. Within this formula, however, different types of corporate reputation are affected by products and services ... and to different extents. Per earlier discussion, a company's reputation encapsulates the history of other people's shared experiences with it (Dowling,

Table 29.2 Dimensions of Products/Services (P/S).

Cognitive dimension (theoretical mechanism)	Relational dimension (theoretical mechanism)
1. Perceived rewards/risks predict P/S value, thereby behavior (expectancy value model). 2. Brand predicts perceived value of products (trust; cognitive dissonance theory) 3. Corporate image predicts perception of P/S (priming/framing theory) 4. Salient P/S cues predict purchase and attitude (elaboration likelihood model (ELM)) 5. Established perception of P/S and producer predicts introduction of innovative products 6. National image predicts evaluation of products (third-person effect, ELM)	1. Credibility/reliability of P/S predicts relationship/trust/dependence maintenance 2. Synchronous information diffusion; interactivity and higher uncertainty influence product-related ties 3. Commodification of communication experience; further integration of products and services as well as the appearance of proactive service options

2001). Therefore, different stakeholders also assign different weights to various reputational aspects of the same corporation (Helm, 2007; Wartick, 1992, 2002).

Scholars found that perceived rewards and risks associated with a purchase can significantly predict how consumers evaluate said purchase, and thereby behavior intentions in the market. Quantifying this concept – and borrowing from the expectancy value model (as an information processing mechanism, see Table 29.2) – the satisfaction that consumers are able to obtain from product or service experience can be derived from (1) one's beliefs about the likelihood of achieving a desired consequence through purchasing the product or service, weighted by (2) the evaluation of the expected outcome for the actor (Ajzen, 1991; Ajzen and Fishbein, 1980; Foumier and Mick, 1999; Triandis, 1977).

Evaluations and opinions derived from large groups of consumers – with whom a company may or may not have direct experience – form its "generalized reputation." Similarly, perceptions of small groups of consumers within the same geographic community of the corporation constitute what is called "direct reputation." Investment in human and/or social capital add to the "generalized reputation," whereas investment in product quality and business relationships with consumers produce its local

(generalized) equivalent (Petkova *et al.*, 2008; Wiedmann and Buxel, 2005).

When a company is positively evaluated by its various key stakeholders both within and outside the organization, its corporate reputation grows stronger (Rindova *et al.*, 2005, 2007). When a business consistently provides high-quality, reliable products or services, consumers are apt to spread positive evaluations within their network of social relationships (Shapiro, 1988), resulting in a much better reputation and more opportunities for the company and its line of brands (Rindova *et al.*, 2006). Conversely, when a company is perceived by stakeholders as a vendor of poor services or shoddy products, it literally pays the price. Not only will current customers avoid further purchases, they also tend to engage in negative, word-of-mouth communication about the corporation among prospective future buyers (Yang, 2007).

From these perspectives, perceptions of products and services – often the financial lifeline of a company – are integral attributes of corporate reputation and its communication strategies in general. A company's marketplace image is therefore a critical asset in the survival and development of any modern business (Roberts and Dowling, 1997). Moreover – and as a by-product of increased and speedy information flow – corporate reputation could substantially grow or ruin a business literally overnight. For instance, organizations perceived as having consistent and positive corporate reputation can benefit financially in the equity market (Srivastava *et al.*, 2001; Szwajkowski and Figlewicz, 1999); charge a premium price for their products and services from customers (Fombrun, 1996; Fombrun and Shanley, 1990; Weigelt and Camerer, 1988b); attract a larger base of consumers (Barnett *et al.*, 2006; Gardberg and Fombrun, 2002; Gotsi and Wilson, 2001); and enjoy higher esteem among the general public.

Apart from image, other heuristics are often processed as cognitive shortcuts during consumers' product and service decision-making process. For instance, the purchase of expensive items, such as a car or a personal computer, is normally the outcome of a more comprehensive deliberation process, during which many aspects of alternative products are compared.

However, when purchasers face complex decision problems of less significance, salient attributes of products and services – including brands, design, or even physical features – serve as potential heuristics to reduce information barriers of entry (Argenti and Druckenmiller, 2004; Kohli and Jedidi, 2007; Muzellec and Lambkin, 2006; Payne *et al.*, 1993; Yee *et al.*, 2007). When a product is of relatively low importance or relevance to the consumer – and borrowing from the elaboration likelihood model – cognitive shortcuts, or heuristics, could be employed to facilitate fast, accurate, and robust decision making (Petty and Wegener, 1999). This mechanism is especially applicable in instances when consumers have little expert knowledge about the product or service (Hoeffler and Ariely, 1999) and/or information is not completely available (Martignon and Hoffrage, 1999).

Brand value

When the image of a particular brand – an outcome of extended communication experiences over time – is perceived to resonate with the characteristics of products or services, the resulting increase in brand value can flow to the perceived value of the products or services themselves. On the contrary – and in line with cognitive dissonance theory where individuals avoid information encounters creating reasoning discord (see Table 29.2) – conflicts between brand value and consumer firsthand and/or vicarious experience with the product/services are likely to change brand perception and purchase in the opposite direction. However, even when the image of a brand is neither resonant nor conflicting with the characteristics of products or services, the credibility of brands – trustworthiness of people and the expertise systems behind a product or service – could still affect consumer perception (Ind, 1998).

For some globally recognized brands – that is, Coca-Cola, Nike, and Apple – branding is synonymous with the names of and cognition toward respective producers. In these instances, empirical studies found that changing the name of a corporation could affect consumer perceptions of the companies, but not necessarily the evaluation of individual products or services they produce. However, when a product's image sports similarities or associations with that of the producing corporation, they can enhance or undermine each other (Rotfeld, 2008). Under such circumstances, predictions – derived from priming theory context of being "primed" toward particular reasoning (see Table 29.2) – suggest that what an individual already knows or feels about a producer or service vendor can set the tone for cognition and behavioral responses to its products or services (Brown, 1998; Yoon *et al.*, 1993).

Nevertheless, not every attribute of a product/service carries equal weight, salience, or usefulness as a heuristic in consumer decision making. It was stressed that two components (Myers and Alpert, 1968) are important to assess the impact (i.e., the determinacy) of a product's attribute on the final decision of consumers: (1) consumer attitude toward a certain feature (i.e., its general relevance) and (2) perceived differences of this attribute among considered competitors in the marketplace. A remarkably positive or negative corporate reputation could influence both attitude and perceived difference. Yet, when certain product or service attributes are considered "nondeterminant" (with respect to Myers and Alpert's definition), consumers are very likely to ignore these product or service attributes (Scholz et al., 2010).

Contextualizing this relationship between corporate reputation and consumer cognition of its products/services, it was discovered that people's perception of a company could help it launch new product offerings (Garud and Lampel, 1997; Podnar, 2004; Waarts, 1999). In specific, corporate reputation, prior financial successes, and aggressiveness in the market all impact new product reception (Hultink et al., 2000), with information source (Waarts, 1999) especially salient. This remains true even for next generation, niche product launches, ones often at high-cost, high-risk, but also high-return purchase potential (Garud et al., 2002; Grulke and Silber, 2000; Wuyts et al., 2004).

For service-oriented brands in particular, communication is the single greatest predictor of financial success. A company's corporate reputation trumps the substantive goods themselves as a determinant of consumer evaluation (Klaus and Maklan, 2007). Meaning, while a vendor may feature a large variety of service offerings, consumers tend to perceive all as components of a single reputable brand and company. Similarly, as prepurchase evaluation of a service is usually based on incomplete information (Hall, 1993; Parasuraman et al., 1988; Walsh and Beatty, 2007), reputation – or communication history – becomes a critical surrogate indicator for the quality of services and trustworthiness of service providers (Bennett and Gabriel, 2001; Dawar and Parker, 1994; Hardaker and Fill, 2005; Stern et al., 2001). Reputations become a "quality promise," one which incentivizes a firm to focus on providing high-quality goods and services (Grossman and Stiglitz, 1980).

Consumers, however, do not exist on an island. The social–economic status of consumers themselves, their priority needs, and lifestyle as well as affective and cognitive responses combine to alter consumers' outcome expectations about products and services, and ultimately behavioral responses. Therefore and not

surprisingly, three types of crises – accidents, quality scandals, and product/service safety incidents – trigger drastic changes in consumer outcome expectation and evaluation about products or services (Phillips et al., 1983). Equally unsurprising is that all three are often accompanied by sophisticated communication exchanges between consumer and provider.

Therefore and even in these dramatic instances, communication trumps all. Consumer satisfaction with a company's products or services can still mediate the relation between actual quality of a product or service offering and the reputation of its producer (Carmeli and Asher, 2005). Related and when available products and services are similar to each other and/or the quality of particular products and services are not immediately transparent to prospective consumers, producer/service vendor reputation becomes a powerful communication-based differentiator (Fombrun, 1996; Oliver and DeSarbo, 1988).

Country-of-origin effect

With today's marketplace being a global one, a product's national origin can be an equally potent, reputational differentiator (Han and Terpstra, 1988; Sohail, 2005; Thakor and Lavack, 2003). Country-of-origin information – to include foreign corporate reputation (Hong and Kang, 2006) – can exert a significant impact on the profitability of a company's line of products within foreign markets. Perhaps not surprisingly, research finds consumer ethnocentrism (Shimp and Sharma, 1987), sense of patriotism (Peterson and Jolibert, 1995), and animosity toward the originating country (Klein et al., 1998) all contribute to the country-of-origin effect (Papadopoulos and Heslop, 1993).

In an empirical study on this topic, price cuts on goods labeled as "manufactured in South Korea" could not sway consumers away from more expensive, Japan-made competitors commonly believed to be of higher quality (Speece and Nguyen, 2005). Moreover – and depending on the national identity of consumers within a market – a third-person effect (where message impact on others is perceived as greater than one's self) was also empirically documented among consumers when evaluating recalls of food products produced by foreign corporations (Wei and Lo, 2010).

From an elaboration likelihood model context, country-of-origin effect can also stimulate extensive and comprehensive judgments about products or services attributes (Hong and Wyer, 1990). For instance, when capacity or motivation to evaluate a product or service properly is low, consumers are more likely to turn to country-of-origin information – perhaps the lowest denominator of available communication – as a convenient heuristic for judgment formation. In such circumstances, disperse prior information about multiple products manufactured in the same country – even different genres – is likely to affect consumers' present country-of-origin evaluations (Canli and Durairaj, 2000).

Still, consumers' prior knowledge about the product/service, access to information, and/or expertise about a product category can moderate a country-of-origin effect (Maheswaran and Shavitt, 2000). Thus and once again, communication between producer and consumer is of greatest value. Consumers with more product-related knowledge tend to base their evaluations on the strength of products/services versus origin and vice versa. More knowledgeable consumers applied country-of-origin cues only to selectively process and recall nonorigin, product attribute information they received earlier. In contrast, their less informed and communicated to counterparts applied country-of-origin information to frame future knowledge about product/service attributes. However, and even when country-of-origin information was used for evaluation purposes, these sentiments did not always translate to nonpurchase situations (Hong and Wyer, 1989).

Relational Reputation

Product or service information can also be regarded as a symbolic form of communication, one capable of developing and maintaining social relationships between consumers and producers or between peer consumers (Mooy and Robben, 2002). This relational dimension of products and services starts from a premise that these items – akin to country-of-origin effect – comprise a complex amalgamation of functional and expressive values. Functional values emphasize how a product/service makes consumers feel or think about them, which subsequently affects individual cognitive and affective responses. In contrast, expressive values address what a certain product or service tells others about (1) the consumer within his or her social network, (2) the producer, and (3) the social relationship between the two.

Therefore and in general, the credibility and reliability consumers perceive a product or service to possess will impact future commitment to the same producer (Omar and Heywood, 2010). Referenced earlier, consistency in branding is essential, as it promotes said commitments, also a foundation of trust (Kralingen, 1999) for future interactions. Communication consistency can reduce cognitive, economic, or psychological risks associated with consumption, likewise buoy expressive, affective, or functional purchase motivations. The latter so much so, that the perceived uniqueness of high-quality product or service can engender a dependency relationship between consumers and producers.

New media and reputation building

New media – especially mobile and Internet technologies – exert a profound effect on these consumer-to-business relationships (Gorry and Westbrook, 2009). Specifically, elevated synchronicity, interactivity, and uncertainty of social interactions mediated by these technologies exert a huge impact on the way product-related relationships are developed and maintained. New media technologies have given rise to new venues of mediated social interaction including consumer blogs, BBS systems, consumer review/feedback systems, or social network sites, conduits which enable consumers to share with others information and/or feelings about individual experiences at any time, any place.

Sharing of product-related information or feelings could be synchronous, enabling positive or negative product image experiences to spread instantaneously and like wildfire. While an array of theoretical models (see Table 29.2) attempt to predict and/or explain the pattern of information flow via new media, a current shortage exists on its specific link to reputation.

Even with minimal research, capabilities of new media technology are evident. The hyperconnectivity and interactivity of new media technologies encourage product- or service-centered consumer communities to form en masse in cyberspace. Within such communities, ones comprised of group identities, symbolism, and expressive values become paramount. Third – and in environments ripe with anonymous participation and limited, nonverbal social cues – trust between sources of product- or service-related information (including producers, advertisers, or other consumers) and consumers as information receivers is built on grounds quite different than with traditional communication.

This relational aspect of new communication technologies has also brought rise to a new platform of transaction, where the provision of products and related services is fully integrated. Responding to Friedman's (2005) proclamation that "we are finally witnessing the birth of a flat world where equal economic opportunities await the qualified urbanities," communication experiences with producers or service vendors have evolved from a support for core business models to one where such interactions are the primary commodity themselves (Chitty, 2002, 2009).

Thus, integrated media made an evolutionary frog leap toward "transactional venues," becoming simultaneous channels of both communication and distribution (Baker, 2003). This evolution – in tandem – diminished the social and psychological distance between consumers and producers. Customers are now significantly more likely to have direct communication with representatives of a company, also to receive online and/or other auxiliary services as a bonus incentive to products of their choice (Standifird et al., 2004).

Viewed from a relational perspective, the quality, presentation, and delivery of products – as well as related services – can be considered constituent components in a relationship between producers and consumers (Yoon et al., 2008). Within such transaction platforms, it becomes possible for corporate producers to proactively initiate product-related services for customers, efforts that both manufacture positive mental frames for their target audiences and foster a mentality more receptive to business relationships (Goutam et al., 2009).

In a series of interviews with nine focus groups comprised of 94 managers in both business-to-business and business-to-consumer settings, Goutam proposed three forms of proactive product service to enhance potential outcomes for businesses. All are derived from increased communication efforts: (1) proactive prevention whereby producers preempt possible product failures by contacting consumers (Barker et al., 2005; Bolton and Verhoef, 2008; Tax et al., 2006); (2) proactive education whereby producing companies advise consumers on the correct use of products (Grapentine, 2006); and (3) proactive feedback seeking, whereby corporate organizations solicit consumer feedback proactively (Berry and Leighton, 2004; Best, 2005; Crie, 2003).

Synthesizing Reputation

One step toward achieving these proactive outcomes is to reconceptualize corporation communication, specifically reputation, via a synthesized context. First and most generally, a comparison of the two discussed (economic and sociological) product/service dimensions primarily ignore the impact of relational, emergent technologies on consumer experiences. New media technology empowers advanced options for mediated social interactions, while begging for additional, more substantive explorations into its effects on product/service-based, economic relationships. While descriptive analyses are the norm at early stages of social science theoretical development, it is imperative that both concept and scope conditions of validated scientific theories are sufficiently adapted to explain new phenomena in the era of new media. Therefore, more inquiries are sorely needed linking conduit to communication, joining the impact of new communication technologies with the relational aspect of products and services.

In addition – and as presented in Table 29.2 – conceptual instruments currently dominate examination into the cognitive and relational dimensions of products and services. For instance and when exploring a dependent variable such as perceived product value, various theoretical frameworks and mechanisms (i.e., expectancy value and/or cognitive dissonance models) are used to predict outputs. Thus, to truly advance knowledge on this topic, research should ideally shift toward physically manifested, relational aspects of products/services. In doing so, such research could explore the development and maintenance of product-based social relationships, ones featuring different qualities and strengths (based on individual offering nuances) also near-limitless inquiry potential.

Third, and building on the premise that products and services constitute an important attribute of corporate reputation – both of which mutually influence each other – this chapter bridged theoretical conceptualizations of corporate communication and reputation to the various dimensions of products and services. This was premised on a belief that the parent communication concept can shed light on investigations of its constituent attributes. The following three research questions are proposed for future synthesis exploration:

> RQ1: Does consumer cognition and evaluation of products/services predict the social and economic values of its parent corporation? If so, how and under what communication conditions?
> RQ2: Does market competition between corporations and functionally equivalent products affect consumer relational cognition about a product/service? If so, how and under what communication conditions?

> RQ3: Does memory of prior experience with a product/service predict consumer perception of these entities as attributes of corporate reputation? If so, how and under what communication conditions?

Economic syntheses

Discussed earlier, economic conceptions of corporate reputation typically emphasize (1) corporate values as criterion and (2) products/services as integral attributes of corporate reputation. Therefore, (3) consumers' subjective construction of a product and service could theoretically affect perceived value of a corporate producer within a group of like-minded purchasers. Importantly, these can occur independent of behavioral, purchase intent.

Economic conceptions of corporate reputation also suggest consideration of market competition and time frames when examining opinion evolution of consumers about a product or service (Rindova and Fombrun, 1999). Existing research already argues for corporate reputation to be verified over time, with changes in value often a result of a dynamic competitive process among rival companies located in the same market and communication sphere. Still, this same research – to date – fails to examine either the cognitive dynamics of market competition or the explanatory power of a product's history in the social construction of products/services. A possible future query in this economic area:

> RQ4: Do products/services function as signifying symbols in collective memory, and – if so – how does this collective memory affect the quality and strength of business relationships? If so, how and under what communication conditions?

Sociological syntheses

When relational dimensions of products and services – notably new media – are contrasted with sociological conceptions of corporate reputation, multiple lacunas likewise reveal themselves. To begin, a sociological conception of corporate reputation suggests that a certain product or service could be regarded as symbolic versus market item in the collective memory among a purchase community. Collectively shared memories built around common product/service experiences can – over time – enhance both solidarity and identity of different consumer groups.

Trust is this bankable asset. Producers could maximize existing engagements with consumers by tapping trust foundations built over longer term. This could occur through extended communication and/or marketplace outreach. In tandem, consumers with limited information about a product/service might derive trust from new media, engagement mechanisms where both interaction and communication is aplenty. Finally and perhaps most importantly, organizations that choose to invest in a consumer trust relationship would now take into account how the reverse valuate and communicate about them. Therefore, further investigations on this topic could include the following:

> RQ5: Are there similarities in trust perceptions between producers and consumers and vice versa? If so, how and under what communication conditions?
>
> RQ6: Do sociological norms affect the strength and/or nature of product-based relationships between (a) consumers and producers, (b) consumers and consumers, and (c) consumer and nonconsumers? If so, how and under what communication conditions?

From a more macroscopic point of view, a sociological synthesis on corporate reputation implies that social structures plus consumer culture norms both need to be acknowledged when examining product/service-related social ties. Therefore, social ties between both peer consumers and those between consumers and nonconsumers arguably deserve at least as much attention as consumer–producer relationships. Inspired by this same sociological approach, it can also be suggested that emergent technologies – that is, synchronous and interactive communication – should be conceived as constructed by and constitutive of modern social institutions. These technologies,

by their very nature (of limited, nonverbal cues), foster higher social uncertainty even when communication increases. Ergo, they might be explored as social–psychological constructs linked to validated theoretical propositions. Future sociological research possibilities include the following:

1 Extend investigation of the relational dimension of products/services as an attribute of corporate reputation from phenomenon descriptions to more communication theory-based propositions.
2 Apply multiple communication theoretical frames toward constructing a focused set of dependent reputational variables on relational dimension of products and services.
3 Employ sociological factors – that is, cultural norms, priority relational needs – as potential predictors of cognitive bonds both among consumers and between consumer and producers, as well as the role of communication.

Finally – and when examining the cognitive dimension of products/services from a sociological conception of corporate communication and reputation – rather than focusing exclusively on individual's psychological factors, sociological factors (i.e., cultural norms, social or political beliefs, and community identities) could alternatively be employed to predict consumer product-related cognitions, decision making, and ultimately communication about these aspects. Similarly, when the relational dimension of products/services is contrasted with economic conceptions of corporate reputation, the development and maintenance of new forms of mediated business relationships – ones supported by recently introduced communication technologies – should be included as both antecedent and consequence of a corporation's financial and social values in the marketplace. This inclusion should note not only the aforementioned increased channels of new media but also their relational limitations. This dual recognition is critical in an era of product/

service and information globalization. Two last research questions are offered:

RQ7: Does new media technology influence the way consumers relate to each other and with product providers? If so, how and under what communication conditions?

RQ8: Do new media ties both among consumers and producers: consumers contribute to the economic or social value of corporations? If so, how and under what communication conditions?

Conclusion

As with any theoretical synthesis, next research steps multiply exponentially. Combining similar yet disparately researched communication concepts can produce a wealth of new independent and dependent variables, ones capable of further segmenting audience reasoning and decision making, also knowledge potential about these practices. In its exploration into product and services as an attribute of corporate communication and reputation, this chapter argued for the increased relevance of relational variables, specifically about products and services. In doing so, it proposed conceiving new media-based relationships – one with more channels but less context – on an equal playing field with traditional definitions of reputation founded in market conditions. In the future, more robust and empirical explorations become vital. Technology and global trade environments are comprised of conduits and reach, ones whose impact is only marginally understood to date.

References

Ajzen, I. (1991) The theory of planned behavior. *Organizational Behavior Human Decision Making Processes, 50*, 179–211.

Ajzen, I. and Fishbein, M. (1980) *Understanding Attitudes and Predicting Social Behavior.* Englewood-Cliffs, NJ: Prentice Hall.

Albert, S. and Whetten, D.A. (1985) Organizational identity. In L.L. Cummings and B.M. Staw (eds), *Research in Organizational Behavior* (Vol. 7). Greenwich, CT: JAI Press, pp. 263–295.

Argenti, P.A. and Druckenmiller, B. (2004) Reputation and the corporate brand. *Corporate Reputation Review, 6*(4), 368–374.

Baker, S. (2003) *New Consumer Marketing: Managing a Living Demand System.* Chichester: John Wiley & Sons.

Barker, W.O., Lane, J.R., Holbrook, D.P., Vadrevu, N.R., and Padalino, L.T. (2005) Preventative maintenance: A proactive customer service. *Bell Labs Technical Journal, 9*(4), 187–200.

Barnett, M.L., John, J.M., and Lafferty, B.A. (2006) Corporate reputation: The definitional landscape. *Corporate Reputation Review, 9*(1), 26–38.

Barney, J.B. (1986) Organizational culture: Can it be a source of sustained competitive advantage? *Academy of Management Review, 11*, 656–665.

Barney, J.B. (2001) Resource-based theories of competitive advantage: A ten-year retrospective on the resource-based view. *Journal of Management, 27*(6), 643–650.

Bennett, R. and Gabriel, H. (2001) Reputation, trust and supplier commitment: The case of shipping company/seaport relations. *Journal of Business & Industrial Marketing, 16*(6), 424–438.

Berry, L.L. and Leighton, J.A. (2004) Restoring customer confidence. *Marketing Health Services, 24*, 14–19.

Best, R.J. (2005) *Market-Based Management: Strategies for Growing Customer Value and Profitability.* Upper Saddle River, NJ: Pearson/Prentice Hall.

Bolton, R.N. and Verhoef, P.C. (2008) Expanding business-to-business customer relationships: Modeling the customer's upgrade decision. *Journal of Marketing, 72*, 46–64.

Brown, T.J. (1998) Corporate associations in marketing: Antecedents and consequences. *Corporate Reputation Review, 1*(3), 215–233.

Brown, T.J., Dacin, P.A., Pratt, M.G., and Whetten, D.A. (2006) Identity, intended image, construed image, and reputation: An interdisciplinary framework and suggested terminology. *Journal of the Academy of Marketing Science, 34*(2), 99–106.

Canli, Z.G. and Durairaj, M. (2000) Determinants of country-of-origin evaluations. *Journal of Consumer Research, 1*, 96–108.

Carmeli, A. and Asher, T. (2005) Perceived organizational reputation and organizational performance: An empirical investigation of industrial enterprises. *Corporate Reputation Review*, 8(1), 13–30.

Castro, M.C., Saez, P.L., and Lopez, J.E.N. (2004) The role of corporate reputation in developing relational capital. *Journal of Intellectual Capital*, 5(4), 575–585.

Caves, R.E. and Porter, M.E. (1977) From entry barriers to mobility barriers. *Quarterly Journal of Economics*, 91, 421–434.

Chitty, N. (2002) Mapping know-ware land. In N. Chitty (ed.), *Mapping Globalization: International Media and a Crisis of Identity*. Penang: Southboud, pp. 1–13.

Chitty, N. (2009) Frames for internationalizing media research. In D. Thussu (ed.), *Internationalizing Media Studies*. Oxon: Routledge, pp. 61–74.

Clark, B.H. and Montgomery, D.B. (1998) Deterrence, reputations, and competitive cognition. *Management Science*, 44(1), 62–82.

Collins, J.C. and Porras, J.I. (1994) *Built to Last*. New York: Harper Business.

Crie, D. (2003) Consumers' complaint behavior: Taxonomy, typology and determinants: Towards a unified ontology. *Journal of Database Marketing and Customer Strategy Management*, 11, 60–79.

Dawar, N. and Parker, P. (1994) Marketing universals: Consumers' use of brand name, price, physical appearance, and retailer reputation as signals of product quality. *The Journal of Marketing*, 58(2), 81–95.

Deephouse, D.L. (2000) Media reputation as a strategic resource: An integration of mass communication and resource-based theories. *Journal of Management*, 26(6), 1091–1112.

Dollinger, M., Golden, P., and Saxton, T. (1997) The effect of reputation on the decision to joint venture. *Strategic Management Journal*, 18(2), 127–140.

Dowling, G.R. (2001) *Creating Corporate Reputations: Identity, Image, and Performance*. New York: Oxford University Press.

Dowling, G.R. (2002) *Creating Corporate Reputations: Identity, Image, and Performance*. New York: Oxford University Press.

Dowling, G.R. (2004) Corporate reputations: Should you compete on yours? *California Management Review*, 46(3), 19–38.

Dutton, J.E. and Dukerich, J.M. (1991) Keeping an eye on the mirror: Image and identity in organizational Adaptation. *Academy of Management Journal*, 34, 517–554.

Fombrun, C.J. (1996) *Reputation: Realizing Value from the Corporate Image*. Boston: Harvard Business School Press.

Fombrun, C.J. (2001a) Corporate reputation as economic assets. In M. Hitt, R. Freeman, and J. Harrison (eds), *Handbook of Strategic Management*. Malden: Blackwell, p. 2001.

Fombrun, C.J. (2001b) Corporate reputation: Its measurement and management. *Thexis*, 4, 23–26.

Fombrun, C.J. and Gardberg, N. (2000) Who's tops in corporate reputation. *Corporate Reputation Review*, 3(1), 13–17.

Fombrun, C.J. and Shanley, M. (1990) What's in a name? Reputation building and corporate strategy. *Academy of Management Journal*, 33(2), 233–258.

Fombrun, C.J. and van Riel, C.B.M. (1997) The reputational landscape. *Corporate Reputation Review*, 1(1/2), 5–13.

Fombrun, C.J., Gardberg, N., and Sever, J. (1999) The Reputation Quotient[SM]: A multi-stakeholder measure of corporate reputation. *The Journal of Brand Management*, 7(4), 241–255.

Foumier, S. and Mick, D.G. (1999) Re-discovering satisfaction. *Journal of Marketing*, 63, 5–23.

Foumier, S. and Yao, J.L. (1997) Reviving brand loyalty: A re-conceptualization within the framework of consumer-brand relationships. *International Journal of Research in Marketing*, 14, 451–472.

Friedman, T.L. (2005) *The World Is Flat: A Brief History of the Twenty First Century*. Waterville: Thorndike Press.

Gardberg, N.A. and Fombrun, C.J. (2002) The global Reputation Quotient[SM] project: First steps towards a cross-nationally valid measure of corporate reputation. *Corporate Reputation Review*, 4(4), 303–307.

Gardberg, N.A. and Fombrun, C.J. (2006) Corporate citizenship: Creating intangible assets across institutional environments. *Academy of Management Review*, 31(2), 329–346.

Garud, R. and Lampel, J. (1997) Product announcements and corporate reputation. *Corporate Reputation Review*, 1(1–2), 114–118.

Garud, R., Jain, S., and Kumaraswamy, A. (2002) Orchestrating institutional processes for technology sponsorship: The case of Sun Microsystems and Java. *Academy of Management Journal*, 45, 196–214.

Gorry, G.A. and Westbrook, R.A. (2009) Winning the internet confidence game. *Corporate Reputation Review*, 12, 195–203.

Gotsi, M. and Wilson, A.M. (2001) Corporate reputation: Seeking a definition. *Corporate Communications: An International Journal*, 6(1), 24–30.

Goutam, C.R.V., Venkatesh, R., and Kohli, A.K. (2009) Proactive post-sales service: When and why does it pay off? *Journal of Marketing, 73,* 70–87.

Grapentine, T. (2006) Unconventional wisdom. *Marketing Research, 18,* 27–31.

Gray, E.R. and Balmer, J.M.T. (1998) Managing corporate image and corporate reputation. *Long Range Planning, 31*(5), 695–702.

Grossman, S. and Stiglitz, J. (1980) On the impossibility of informationally efficient markets. *The American Economic Review,* (70)3, 393–408.

Grulke, W. and Silber, G. (2000) Ten lessons from the future. @One Communications, Johannesburg.

Hall, R. (1993) A framework linking intangible resources and capabilities to sustainable advantage. *Strategic Management Journal, 14*(8), 607–618.

Han, C.M. and Terpstra, V. (1988) Country-of-origin effects for uni-national and bi-national products. *Journal of International Business Studies, 16,* 235–256.

Hardaker, S. and Fill, C. (2005) Corporate services brands: The intellectual and emotional engagement of employees. *Corporate Reputation Review, 7,* 365–376.

Helm, S. (2007) One reputation or many? Comparing stakeholders' perceptions of corporate reputation. *Corporate Communications: An International Journal, 12*(3), 238–254.

Hoeffler, S. and Ariely, D. (1999) Constructing stable preferences: A look into dimensions of experience and their impact on preference stability. *Journal of Consumer Psychology, 11,* 113–139.

Hong, S. and Kang, D.K. (2006) Country-of-origin influences on product evaluations: The impact of animosity and perceptions of industriousness brutality on judgments of typical and atypical products. *Journal of Consumer Psychology, 16*(3), 232–239.

Hong, S. and Wyer, R.S. (1989) Effects of country-of-origin and product-attribute information on product evaluation: An information processing perspective. *The Journal of Consumer Research, 16*(2), 175–187.

Hong, S. and Wyer, R.S. (1990) Determinants of product evaluation: Effects of the time interval between knowledge of a product's country of origin and information about its specific attributes. *The Journal of Consumer Research, 17*(3), 277–288.

Hultink, E.J., Hart, S., Robben, S.J., and Griffin, A. (2000) Launch decisions and new product success: An empirical comparison of consumer and industrial products. *Journal of Product Innovation Management, 17,* 5–23.

Ind, N. (1998) The company and the product: The relevance of corporate associations. *Corporate Reputation Review, 2*(1), 88–92.

Keller, K.L. and Aaker, D.A. (1998) The impact of corporate marketing on a company's brand extensions. *Corporate Reputation Review, 1*(4), 356–378.

Klaus, P. and Maklan, S. (2007) The role of brands in a service-dominated world. *Brand management, 15*(2), 115–122.

Klein, J.G., Ettenson, R., and Morris, M.D. (1998) The animosity model of foreign product purchase: An empirical test in the People's Republic of China. *The Journal of Marketing, 62*(1), 89–100.

Kohli, R. and Jedidi, K. (2007) Representation and inference of lexicographic preference models and their variants. *Marketing Science, 26,* 380–399.

Kralingen, R. (1999) Superbrands: Myth or reality. *Corporate Reputation Review, 2,* 178–187.

Logsdon, J. and Wood, D. (2005) Global business citizenship and voluntary codes of conduct. *Journal of Business Ethics, 59,* 55–67.

Maheswaran, D. and Shavitt, S. (2000) Issues and new directions in global consumer psychology. *Journal of Consumer Psychology, 9*(2), 59–66.

Martignon, L. and Hoffrage, U. (1999) Why does one-reason decision making work? A case study in ecological rationality. In G. Gigerenzer, P.M. Todd, and the ABC Research Group (eds), *Simple Heuristics That Make Us Smart.* New York: Oxford University Press, pp. 119–140.

Milgrom, P. and Roberts, J. (1982) Limit pricing and entry under incomplete information: An equilibrium analysis. *Econometrica, 50*(2), 443–459.

Milgrom, P. and Roberts, J. (1986) Price and advertising signals of product quality. *Journal of Political Economy, 94*(4), 796–821.

Mooy, S.C. and Robben, H.S.J. (2002) Managing consumers' product evaluations through direct product experience. *Journal of Product & Brand Management, 11*(7), 432–446.

Muzellec, L. and Lambkin, M. (2006) Corporate rebranding: Destroying, transferring or creating brand equity? *European Journal of Marketing, 40*(7/8), 803–824.

Myers, J.H. and Alpert, M.I. (1968) Determinant buying attitudes: Meaning and measurement. *Journal of Marketing, 32,* 13–20.

Nguyen, N. and Leblanc, G. (2001) Corporate image and corporate reputation in customers' retention decisions in services. *Journal of Retailing and Consumer Services*, 8(4), 227–236.

Oliver, R.L. and DeSarbo, W.S. (1988) Response determinants in satisfaction judgments. *Journal of Consumer Research*, 14, 495–507.

Omar, A.J. and Heywood, C.A. (2010) Corporate real estate management's credibility-positioning status: Preliminary investigation of a branding model in practice. *Journal of Corporate Real Estate*, 12(3), 185–195.

Papadopoulos, N.G. and Heslop, L. (1993) *Product-Country Images: Impact and Role in International Marketing*. New York: Routledge.

Parasuraman, A., Ziethaml, V., and Berry, L. (1988) SERVQUAL: A multiple-item scale for measuring consumer perceptions of service quality. *Journal of Retailing*, 64(1), 12–40.

Payne, J., Bettman, R., and Johnson, E.J. (1993) *The Adaptive Decision Maker*. Cambridge, UK: Cambridge University Press.

Peterson, R.A. and Jolibert, A.J.P. (1995) A meta-analysis of country-of-origin effects. *Journal of International Business Studies*, 26(4), 883–900.

Petkova, A., Rindova, V., and Gupta, A. (2008) How can new ventures build reputation? An exploratory study. *Corporate Reputation Review*, 11, 320–334.

Petty, R.E. and Wegener, D.T. (1999) The elaboration likelihood model: Current status and controversies. In S. Chaiken and Y. Trope (eds), *Dual Process Theories in Social Psychology*. New York: Guilford Press, pp. 41–72.

Phillips, L.W., Chang, D.R., and Buzzell, R.D. (1983) Product quality, cost position and business performance: A test of some key hypotheses. *Journal of Marketing*, 47, 26–43.

Podnar, K. (2004) Is it all a question of reputation? The role of branch identity (the case of an oil company). *Corporate Reputation Review*, 6(4), 1363–3589.

Post, J.E. and Berman, S.L. (2001) Global corporate citizenship in a dot.com world: The role of organizational identity. In J. Andriof and M. McIntosh (eds), *Perspectives on Corporate Citizenship: Rights, Responsibility, Accountability*. London: Greenleaf Publishing.

Rao, H. (1994) The social construction of reputation: Certification contests, legitimation, and the survival of organizations in the American automobile industry: 1895–1912. *Strategic Management Journal*, 15, 29–44.

Reputation Institute (2011) The RepTrak™ System. Retrieved from http://www.reputationinstitute.com/advisory-services/reptrak (last accessed September 26, 2012).

Rindova, V.P. and Fombrun, C.J. (1999) Constructing competitive advantage. *Strategic Management Journal*, 20, 111–127.

Rindova, V.P., Williamson, I.O., Petkova, A.P., and Sever, J.M. (2005) Being good or being known: An empirical examination of the dimensions, antecedents and consequences of organizational reputation. *Academy of Management Journal*, 48(6), 1033–1049.

Rindova, V.P., Pollock, T.G., and Hayward, M.L.A. (2006) Celebrity firms: The social construction of market popularity. *Academy of Management Review*, 31, 50–71.

Rindova, V.P., Petkova, A.P., and Kotha, S. (2007) Standing out: How new firms in emerging markets build reputation. *Strategic Organization*, 5(1), 31–70.

Roberts, P.W. and Dowling, G.R. (1997) The value of a firm's corporate reputation: How reputation helps attain and sustain superior profitability. *Corporate Reputation Review*, 1, 72–76.

Roberts, P.W. and Dowling, G.R. (2002) Corporate reputation and sustained superior performance. *Strategic Management Journal*, 23, 1077–1093.

Rotfeld, H.J. (2008) Brand image of company names matters in ways that can't be ignored. *Journal of Product and Brand Management*, 17(2), 121–122.

Scholz, S.W., Meissner, M., and Decker, R. (2010) Measuring consumer preferences for complex products: A compositional approach based on paired comparisons. *Journal of Marketing Research*, 27, 685–698.

Schultz, M., Hatch, M.J., and Larsen, M.H. (2000) *The Expressive Organization: Linking Identity, Reputation, and the Corporate Brand*. Oxford, UK: Oxford University Press.

Shapiro, B.P. (1988) What the hell is market oriented? *Harvard Business Review*, 66(6), 119–125.

Shapiro, S. (1987) The social control of impersonal trust. *The American Journal of Sociology*, 93(3), 623–658.

Shimp, T.A. and Sharma, S. (1987) Consumer ethnocentrism: Construction and validation of the CETSCALE. *Journal of Marketing Research*, 24, 280–289.

Sirgy, M.J. (1985) Using self-congruity and ideal congruity to predict purchase motivation. *Journal of Business Research*, 13(3), 195–206.

Sohail, M.S. (2005) Malaysian consumers' evaluation of products made in Germany: The country of origin effect. *Asia Pacific Journal of Marketing and Logistics, 17*(1), 89–105.

Speece, M. and Nguyen, D.P. (2005) Countering negative country-of-origin with low prices: A conjoint study in Vietnam. *Journal of Product & Brand Management, 14*(1), 39–48.

Srivastava, R.K., Fahey, L., and Christensen, H.K. (2001) The resource-based view and marketing: The role of market-based assets in gaining competitive advantage. *Journal of Management, 27,* 777–802.

Standifird, S.S., Roelofs, M.R., and Durham, Y. (2004) The impact of eBay's buy-it-now function on bidder behavior. *International Journal of Electronic Commerce, 9*(2), 167–176.

Stern, B., Zinkhan, G.M., and Jaju, A. (2001) Marketing images, construct definition, measurement issues, and theory development. *Marketing Theory, 1*(2), 201–224.

Szwajkowski, E. and Figlewicz, R.E. (1999) Evaluating corporate performance: A comparison of the *Fortune* reputation survey and the Socrates social rating database. *Journal of Managerial Issues, 112,* 137–154.

Tax, S.S., Colgate, M., and Bowen, D.E. (2006) How to prevent your customers from failing. *MIT Sloan Management Review, 47,* 30–38.

Thakor, M.V. and Lavack, A.M. (2003) Effect of perceived brand origin associations on consumer perceptions of quality. *Journal of Product & Brand Management, 12*(6), 394–407.

Triandis, H.C. (1977) *Interpersonal Behavior.* Monterey, CA: Brooks/Cole.

van Riel, C.B.M. and Balmer, J.M.T. (1997) Corporate identity: The concept, its measurement and management. *European Journal of Marketing, 31*(5/6), 340–355.

Waarts, E. (1999) Managing competitive response to new product introduction: Making use of effective market signals. *Corporate Reputation Review, 2*(2), 137–148.

Walsh, G. and Beatty, S.E. (2007) Customer-based corporate reputation of a service firm: Scale development and validation. *Journal of the Academy of Marketing Science, 35,* 127–143.

Wartick, S.L. (1992) The relationship between intense media exposure and change in corporate reputation. *Business & Society, 31,* 33–49.

Wartick, S.L. (2002) Measuring corporate reputation definition and data. *Business Society, 41*(4), 371–392.

Wei, R. and Lo, V. (2010) The third person effect of tainted food product recall news: Examining the role of credibility, attention and elaboration for college students in Taiwan. *Journalism and Mass Communication Quarterly, 87*(3–4), 598–614.

Weigelt, K. and Camerer, C. (1988a) Reputation and corporate strategy: A review of recent theory and applications. *Strategic Management Journal, 9,* 443–454.

Weigelt, K. and Camerer, C. (1988b) Reputation and corporate strategy: A review of recently theory and applications. *Strategic Management Journal, 9,* 443–454.

Wiedmann, K.P. and Buxel, H. (2005) Corporate reputation management in Germany. Results of an empirical study. *Corporate Reputation Review, 8*(2), 145–163.

Wuyts, S., Dutta, S., and Stremersch, S. (2004) Portfolios of interfirm agreements in technology-intensive markets: Consequences for innovation and profitability. *Journal of Marketing, 68,* 88–100.

Yang, S.-U. (2007) An integrated model for organization – Public relational outcomes, organizational reputation, and their antecedents. *Journal of Public Relations Research, 19*(2), 91–121.

Yee, M., Dahan, E., Hauser, J.R., and Orlin, J. (2007) Greedoid-based non-compensatory inference. *Marketing Science, 26*(July-August), 532–549.

Yoon, E., Guffrey, H.J., and Kijewski, V. (1993) The effects of information and company reputation on intentions to buy a business service. *Journal of Business Research, 27*(3), 215–228.

Yoon, D., Choi, S.M., and Sohn, D. (2008) Building customer relationships in an electronic age: The role of interactivity of e-commerce web sites. *Psychology and Marketing, 25*(7), 602–618.

30

Corporate Social Responsibility, Reputation, and Moral Communication: A Constructivist View

Friederike Schultz

Free University of Amsterdam, The Netherlands

Conditions and notions of corporate reputation underwent in the last years a fundamental change. Economic and technological processes of globalization, modernization, and rationalization enforced the institutionalization of corporate social responsibility (CSR) in the corporate world. It is often assumed, that CSR positively affects corporate reputation and leads to financial benefits, although empirical evidence and an appropriate conceptualization of reputation are often missing. This chapter discusses the relation between CSR and reputation by taking a meta-perspective: it presents and critically discusses insights from instrumental perspectives (PR, marketing, management research) and from political–normative perspectives (legitimacy, business ethics). It alternatively develops a constructivist communication view on CSR, building on the "communication constitutes organizations" perspective and a non-dualist turn. It argues that CSR is a symbolically mediated, communicative event, which, based on the underlying dynamics of moral communication, does not simply produce reputation, but also result in dysfunctional effects.

Introduction

Conditions and notions of corporate reputation underwent in the last years a fundamental change. Economic and technological processes of globalization, modernization, and rationalization enforced an intense discourse on the social (Carroll, 1999) and environmental (Elkington, 1997) responsibilities of business toward society, which is accompanied by an increasing institutionalization of corporate social responsibility (CSR) in the corporate world.

A central question in the diverse academic research on CSR (see Gond and Matten, 2007) is indeed how CSR can be used to react on these changed expectations and how it affects the corporate reputation (Eisenegger and Schranz, 2011). But neither a common understanding of the CSR concept itself (Margolis and Walsh, 2003) nor of its effects on reputation could be developed so far. How-to-do-it and early academic literature emphasizes a positive relationship between CSR and reputation, assuming that CSR increases the reputation (see Mutch and Aitken, 2009), motivation, and identifica-

The Handbook of Communication and Corporate Reputation, First Edition. Edited by Craig E. Carroll.
© 2013 John Wiley & Sons, Inc. Published 2015 by John Wiley & Sons, Inc.

tion of employees (e.g., Turban and Greening, 1997), and herewith purchase intentions (Brown and Dacin, 1997; Sen and Bhattacharya, 2001) and financial benefits (McWilliams and Siegel, 2001; Porter and Kramer, 2003). In the last years, such functionalist assumptions were increasingly criticized because they lack theoretical and empirical evidence (Margolis and Walsh, 2003; McWilliams *et al.*, 2006). Alternative perspectives developed, which point more to the widely neglected institutional and power determinants, by which CSR is socially constructed (Gond and Matten, 2007). Attempts to overcome these limitations can be observed not only in management studies (e.g., Scherer and Palazzo, 2007), but also in sociology and communication science (Ihlen *et al.*, 2011). By taking a broader, epistemological, and sociological perspective, authors pointed, for example, to the *risks* of the moralization of communication and reality through CSR and its potentially dysfunctional and delegitimizing effects (Schultz, 2011; Schultz and Wehmeier, 2010).

This chapter contributes to shed light on the relation between CSR and reputation. After discussing definitions and drivers of CSR, it presents insights from the dominant instrumental perspective as applied in management, marketing, and public relations research. It elaborates on the normative–political perspective, which developed in the last years, and proposes an alternative, epistemologically reasoned perspective – a communication perspective – which takes the role of communication and media more into account ("CCO"). According to this third view, CSR can be defined as a symbolically mediated, societal construct and communicative event instead of as reputation tool. This perspective tackles especially the dysfunctional effects of CSR on reputation.

CSR and Reputation: Development, Definitions, Drivers

The core idea of the CSR concept is that corporations have not only economic and legal responsibilities, but also ethical, philanthropic (Carroll, 1999), or environmental responsibilities (Elkington, 1997). Instead of following the owners' interests and increasing profits as argued in the liberal market paradigm (Friedman, 1970), corporations shall contribute to the "common wealth" of society and ethical aims. Especially in the last years, the liberal market moves again toward a temptation of capitalism and remoralization of the economy, in which products and consumerism are morally attributed and new norms are manifested in society (Stehr, 2007). Corporations initiate and bind themselves to mission statements, visions, ethic codices, or behavior guidelines, based on which they change products, services, processes. They identify themselves as "corporate citizen," which is a metaphor for their political orientation independent from their core field of activities (Wood and Lodgson, 2001). And they document social initiatives in social or CSR reports, building on a broad range of standards, certificates, audits, and guidelines (e.g., AA1000, Global Reporting Initiative). Accordingly, CSR is not only related to the strategic and operative management, but also part of external and internal corporate communications (public relations, marketing, advertising, etc.).

The academic discourse on CSR grows steadily since several years. Although it is marked by a variety of definitions of CSR, ranging from instrumental–functionalist, to political–normative, to integrative, ethical (see Garriga and Melé, 2004), and socioconstructivist ones (see Gond and Matten, 2007), it often relates CSR to reputation as an independent, dependent, or mediating variable. Reputation in turn is implicitly and explicitly affiliated with the discourse on social responsibility, as social and environmental responsibility is seen as one reputation determinant besides others (Fombrun *et al.*, 2000a; see also Eberl and Schwaiger, 2005; Eisenegger and Schranz, 2011). Not only CSR, but also reputation and therefore the relation between both remains fuzzy, as reputation is in instrumental perspectives often regarded as resource to produce tangible benefits (Fombrun and Shanley, 1990), whereas sociological perspectives point to the role of audiences (e.g., Fombrun and van Riel, 2003), organizational fields, and internal sensemaking processes for the construction of reputation (Bebbington *et al.*, 2008). To better understand the relation between reputation and CSR, it is therefore fruitful to shed light on these external processes and drivers of CSR. The following part presents different causes for the institutionalization of CSR (see for the following part, Schultz and Wehmeier, 2010).

CSR is of course institutionalized based on *economic* processes such as competition and partially regarded as a prerequisite for attracting global capital. Acting in turbulent environments, corporations are often not knowing whether they benefit from CSR or not, but follow innovators, branch leaders, guidelines, rating systems, or consultancies who frame CSR as strategic tool and offer "rationalizations" for the contested "win-win" situation of public and corporate values (*mimetic institutionalization*). Second, the institutionalization of CSR is also driven by *regulation* and the pressure of political actors such as states or the European Commission, which promotes CSR with strategy papers and campaigns in order to strengthen Europe economically and politically (European Commission, 2001). CSR is regarded as instrument for social engineering – for increasing the efficiency of societal processes, building feelings of community and influencing individuals. Also, nongovernmental, supra-governmental, and political organizations foster the implementation of standards and codes that are getting more and more legal status (Crane *et al.*, 2008; Rieth, 2011). With the global expansion of commercial activities into nonregulated areas and the withdrawal of state actors from political areas, corporations are expected to become political actors. Third, CSR institutionalizes due to changing expectations and understandings of business, for which *public pressure* on corporations and protest moralizations such as in the worldwide financial crises are symptomatic. Based on the diagnoses of societal disintegration, fragmentation and crises protest actors and publics increasingly criticize the liberal market system (see Schultz, 2011) and boycott corporations (see Shamir,

2005) via new communication technologies such as the Internet, which in turn helps them to organize and mobilize their peers.

This analysis documents that, not only purely economic drivers (increasing reputation) but also other drivers are fundamental for the institutionalization of CSR, and that therefore also the relationship between CSR and reputation need not necessarily be positive. In line with the different drivers and building on earlier attempts (e.g., Gond and Matten, 2007; Schultz & Gond, 2011), the following part can now develop divergent perspectives on the relation between CSR and reputation: an instrumental–functionalist view, a normative–political view, and a third view called constructivist view.

Instrumental–Functionalist View: Positive Relation between CSR and Reputation

The instrumental or functionalist perspective is quite dominant not only in management research, but also in marketing and PR research. It (1) considers corporations as the main unit of analysis; (2) searches for a unified and integrative measurable construct; and (3) tries to demonstrate that CSR increases financial performance (Gond and Matten, 2007). In line with the interpenetrating subsystems model theorized by Parsons (1966), CSR is seen as a function for the managed adaptation of societal and corporate goals (p. 12), based on which CSR is discussed in terms of "win-win" situations. Such a perspective is developed in different academic disciplines, such as *management research*, *marketing research*, and *public relations research*, which will now be discussed in more detail.

Management research: CSR as strategic tool and inherent part of the company

In *management research*, instrumental and functionalist views focus mainly on the organizational level, the corporation. CSR is seen as a strategic tool (Porter and Kramer, 2003) and discussed with regard to its effects on the financial performance. By building on a positivist framework, research tends to identify causal relationships between social activities and financial performance (Orlitzky *et al.*, 2003; Waddock and Graves, 1997; see Margolis and Walsh, 2003), and accordingly justifies social initiatives economically (critically Scherer and Palazzo, 2007). The "business case for CSR" argument is based on the idea that CSR creates long-term value (McWilliams and Siegel, 2001; McWilliams *et al.*, 2006; Porter and Kramer, 2006), purchase intentions (Murray and Vogel, 1997), and herewith financial performance (Orlitzky *et al.*, 2003), although investigations on such a positive relationship between both remain largely inconclusive (Margolis and Walsh, 2003). Also, reputation is often discussed in this instrumental–functionalist perspective. It is seen as an asset that can be improved through CSR (e.g., Brown and Dacin, 1997; Fombrun and Shanley, 1990; Orlitzky *et al.*, 2003; Waddock and Graves, 1997), or as a mediator between CSR and financial performance (see the meta-analysis by Orlitzky *et al.*, 2003). CSR in this field is also analyzed as an instrument to protect the reputation (Fombrun and Shanley, 1990; Luo and Bhattacharya, 2009), especially in crisis situations, and to influence the loyalty and motivation of employees (Turban and Greening, 1997), attract better employees and hereby increase financial benefits (Davis, 1973; Waddock and Graves, 1997).

Especially in the last years, more differentiated views on this relation between CSR, reputation, and financial performance developed, taking other moderators into account: organizational age, diversity of served market segments and networks, third parties such as watchdog agencies, mass media (Brammer and Pavelin, 2006; Rhee and Valdez, 2009), and industries, sectors, or national cultures. For example, it is argued that reputational effects vary across sectors (Brammer and Pavelin, 2006) and national cultures (Wright and Rwabizambuga, 2006), and that philanthropy has "a significantly larger effect on reputations in industries that exhibit significant social exter-

nalities, such as the alcoholic drink and tobacco sector, than it does in other sectors" (Brammer and Millington, 2005, p. 40). Furthermore, it is often argued that there needs to be a "fit" among different types of corporate social performance and the firms' stakeholder environment. For example, a high environmental performance enhances or damages reputation according to Brammer and Pavelin (2006), depending on whether the firm's activities "fit" the environmental concerns of stakeholders. And also, assumptions on the positive effects of corporate volunteering on reputation are questioned. Involving employees through volunteering might motivate especially internal stakeholders, but generates less reputational payoffs than cash giving (Brammer and Millington, 2005).

Marketing research: CSR as marketing tool to influence consumers

In *marketing research*, the discourse on CSR as led in academic journals such as *Journal of Marketing Communications* and *International Journal of Advertising* concentrates on the question, to what extent a moralization of marketing and advertising increases purchase intentions and is profitable for corporations. A huge amount of studies analyze the impact of CSR on brand value, reputation, and sales, and focus on aspects such as corporate giving and philanthropy (Brammer and Millington, 2005; Williams and Barrett, 2000), cause-related marketing (Brønn and Vrioni, 2001), social marketing (Chattananon *et al.*, 2007), or sustainable consumption. In the center of marketing research are consumers and their perceptions. CSR is here often regarded as marketing instrument, which leads to a more positive reputation and attitude toward the corporation and its products, a better brand awareness (Brønn and Vrioni, 2001) and brand credibility (Brown and Dacin, 1997), and finally more purchases (e.g., Bhattacharya and Sen, 2004; Kotler and Lee, 2005; Pomering and Dolnicar, 2009; Sen and Bhattacharya, 2001), which safeguard the competitive advantage of corporations (Jahdi and

Acikdilli, 2009; Webb and Mohr, 1998; Williams and Barrett, 2000).

Also, marketing research pointed in the last years to dysfunctional effects of CSR promotion and conditions and requirements for positive effects of CSR on reputation (see also Eisenegger and Schranz, 2011), such as the alignment of CSR to core corporate activities, a stable CSR history (Vanhamme and Grobben, 2009), source credibility, a lack of skepticism (Jahdi and Acikdilli, 2009), a positive prior evaluation of the organization and its motives, the branch (Yoon et al., 2006), and general opinions about and awareness for CSR (Brown and Dacin, 1997; Pomering and Dolnicar, 2009; Sen and Bhattacharya, 2001). For example, the proliferation of ethical and green claims by companies can contribute more to growing consumer skepticism of greenwashing (Jahdi and Acikdilli, 2009) and accordingly does not result in a higher amount of purchases. Also, general trust and skepticism in the corporation moderates the effects of CSR on reputation and purchases in that way, that low trust and high skepticism lowers reputation and purchases (Brønn and Vrioni, 2001; Webb and Mohr, 1998; Yoon et al., 2006). If the reputation of the corporation is based on its abilities directly, the impact on the perceptions of the corporation is higher (Brown and Dacin, 1997). And motives for the CSR activity and the communication source determine perceptions, as shown by Yoon et al. (2006, p. 382). "CSR activities only improved company evaluations when sincere motives were attributed [...] and consumers learned about it from a neutral source. Conversely, the CSR activity backfired when consumers had reason to doubt the company's motives, namely, when the company supported a cause with high benefit salience and they learned about it from the company itself."

Public relations research: CSR as PR instrument to influence reputation

An instrumental–functionalist perspective is also often applied in research on public relations and corporate communications. In contrast to management and marketing research, this research field focuses on CSR-related content of internal and external communication (Morsing and Schultz, 2006), on the role of media and the relation between corporations and publics by taking a broader range of stakeholders such as employees, consumers, political actors, or protest actors into account (Morsing et al., 2008; Nielsen and Thomsen, 2007). It concentrates on analyzing, often case-study based, the modes, instruments, and channels of CSR communication, such as social or environmental reporting (Golob and Bartlett, 2007; Nielsen and Thomsen, 2007), and hereby on strategic aspects such as reputation risk management (Unerman, 2008; critically Bebbington et al., 2008).

CSR communication is also in this view seen as protection shield against reputational damage (Fombrun et al., 2000b; Klein and Dawar, 2004) and as strategic instrument to integrate corporations in the local communities. Especially corporate social reporting is regarded as a tool to respond to external demands and positively influence public's perceptions of the corporation (Hooghiemstra, 2000). For example, environmental legitimacy is positively influenced by the quality of economic-based segments of annual reports, by reactive instead of proactive environmental press releases (Aerts and Cormier, 2009), and by their quality (Hasseldine et al., 2005). Also here, other factors that moderate the effect on reputation are more and more discussed, such as a corporations' prior performance (Fombrun and Shanley, 1990) and size. Large firms with greater name recognition face more reputational risks than smaller firms, which are per se stronger related to local communities (Nielsen and Thomsen, 2009). Organizations with a higher visibility exhibit greater concern to improve the corporate image through social responsibility information disclosure in annual reports and on the Internet (Branco and Rodrigues, 2006), than small- and medium-sized corporations, which implement CSR less strategically and with strong emphasis on the internal dimension.

In contrast to the marketing perspective, research on PR also highlights the dysfunctional and reputational risks of nonconformative behavior based on this broader perspective on organizations. It takes into account the huge criticism on CSR failures and the impact of "moral corporations" or protesters in organizational environments, which increasingly question the credibility of CSR activities and result in feelings of hypocrisy. Based on the insight that the promotion of good deeds backfires and evokes skepticism ("self-promoter's paradox"; Ashforth and Gibbs, 1990; see also Pomering and Johnson, 2009), the content and mode of CSR communication is in the center of the PR debate. Especially symbolic practices and promotional communications are seen as less credible than indirect communication via third parties such as experts or employees (Pomering and Dolnicar, 2009), and therefore as less effective (Morsing and Schultz, 2006; Morsing *et al.*, 2008; Schultz and Wehmeier, 2010). In line with the normative paradigm of PR (Grunig and Hunt, 1984) and the idea of *adaptation*, scholars stress the necessity of stakeholder involvement and dialog for the building of trust and reputation (Morsing and Schultz, 2006). As dialog allows in contrast to asymmetrical two-way communication ("stakeholder response strategy") consensus finding, mutual understanding, and a concurrent negotiation of reality, it is regarded as the most ethic and effective CSR communication strategy (Morsing and Schultz, 2006).

To summarize, instrumental–functionalist perspectives often state a positive relation between CSR and reputation, which results in better financial performance. The institutionalization of CSR is rationalized as an attempt to maintain or enhance corporate reputation. Although these functional effects are more and more questioned, potential dysfunctionalities deriving out of the complexity of communication processes are not sufficiently reflected.

Normative–Political View: CSR as Instrument to Build Legitimacy

In contrast to the instrumental–functionalist view, the normative or sociopolitical view on

CSR regards CSR mainly as power relationship and discusses especially the political role of corporations in today's societies (see Gond and Matten, 2007): rooted in an objectivist tradition, its goal is to uncover the "real" agendas of corporations and depict the organization–society interface as a political arena, which is characterized by power struggles, goal conflicts, and domination. CSR is in this view often described as critical, as a ceremonial exercise (Kuhn and Deetz, 2008), and as an ideology to maintain a capitalist status quo, and framed in terms of "greenwashing" (Elving, 2010), window dressing, or green rhetoric (e.g., Starkey and Crane, 2003). This in turn reflects the growing cynicism and distrust within society and from journalists and policy makers toward corporate claims of responsibility.

In the center of this normative perspective is the concept of "legitimacy" instead of reputation, which is herewith strongly related, but not interchangeable (Deephouse and Carter, 2005; see Bebbington *et al.*, 2008). Legitimacy is seen as a condition, in which organizations conform with societal norms, values, and expectations (Palazzo and Scherer, 2006). Legitimacy also provides an explanatory rationale for public relations and social and environmental disclosure. Accordingly, the impact of CSR is in this view discussed by building on the legitimacy theory, which derives like the stakeholder theory from political economy literature (see Bebbington *et al.*, 2008; Golob and Bartlett, 2007), or the institutional theory (Dowling and Pfeffer, 1975; Meyer and Rowan, 1977), which focuses especially on the constraints and conditions under which corporations can gain legitimacy.

In contrast to the instrumental–functionalist perspective, the normative–political perspective promotes a new understanding and role of corporations in society. Instead of being depoliticized private business actors who try to influence public political processes, corporations are regarded as politically responsible for not only implementing political norms, but also setting and developing them (Flohr *et al.*, 2010). In their "new theory of the firm," Palazzo and Scherer (2006), for example, discuss the new role of the firm as a (responsible) political actor with regard to legitimacy. Building on Suchman (1995) and Ashforth and Gibbs (1990), they argue that corporations need mainly "moral legitimacy," which they can get not only through deliberative politics, but also through a form of dialogic communication. Corporations become in this view, objects of moral legitimacy claims (Palazzo and Scherer, 2006; Scherer *et al.*, 2006).

To summarize, this normative perspective focuses on the power and the hegemony of discourses. Although it also discusses communication implicitly and takes a more critical perspective, it follows a normative ideal and partly shares functionalist ideas of communication (e.g., as dialog to improve society), which then tend to neglect the role of interpretation, sensemaking, and especially conflict. The following part contrasts both prior views by introducing a third and more communicative perspective, which is called constructivist view.

Toward a Communicative View: CSR and Reputation as Communicative Events

In this constructivist perspective, CSR is regarded as "socio-cognitive construction" (Gond and Matten, 2007, p. 18). The relationship between corporations and society and the concept of CSR itself are framed as negotiated stabilized compromises developed in processes of social construction. Accordingly, this view discusses the sensemaking processes, and institutional logics constructions are rooted in. The epistemological perspective of social constructivism is only rarely used in management research and often in communication research. But only recent studies explicated such an understanding of CSR as social construction, which is filled with different meanings by different actors and translated based on their context of interpretation (e.g., Schultz and Wehmeier, 2010). This perspective focuses on media, public, and organizational communication processes, and is in line with more recent approaches, which point to the communicative

constitution of organizations (CCO) (e.g., Taylor & van Every, 2000). This perspective challenges classic understandings of reputation as cognitive representation of a company's actions, as they build on linear and unidirectional models of communication instead of regarding communication as a dynamic, reciprocal process (see critically Christensen and Cornelissen, 2011).

Media research: Media logic and negativity bias

The media perspective contributes to overcome the deficit of earlier reputation research and the instrumental–functionalist perspective, which describes the relations of CSR, reputation, and financial performance based on meso-perspectives. It acknowledges that norms, expectations on corporations, and reality are medially negotiated in the public (*mediatization*): there is an increasing orientation of organizations on media logics, interference of media and social reality, and public observation of corporations, in which also the modes of media selection and interpretation changed (Krotz, 2007; Lundby, 2009; Eisenegger and Schranz, 2011). Media coverage, media content, and media reputation (Deephouse, 2000) reflect *and* influence the public's constitution of CSR and reputation (e.g., Carroll and McCombs, 2003; Lee and Carroll, 2011; Wang, 2007).

Also, the development of new communication technologies such as the Internet plays a crucial role for the effects of CSR. Social media platforms (blogs, Facebook, Twitter, etc.), which allow more, faster, and more direct interactions and distributions of ideas, are often used by critical protest actors, who organize and mobilize their peers online, promote their alternative vision of society, and gain more power than on traditional ways. Accordingly, research on the relation between CSR and reputation has to take the role of the public sphere (Ihlen, 2008) and traditional (Lee and Carroll, 2011) and new media more into account. So far, their role remains underexplored, and also the dominant idea that companies should strive for mutual adaptation with their stakeholders instead of for news remains unchallenged (for a general critique, see Meijer and Kleinnijenhuis, 2006).

Although communication research, mainly from the field of public relations, analyzes macro level processes, such as the influence of PR activities on news (e.g., Kiousis *et al.*, 2007), of news on reputation (Carroll, 2004), or the mediating role of news in the effect of public relations on reputation (Carroll, 2010), only few studies examine this social construction of CSR and responsibility in the media and at the macro level theoretically (Eisenegger and Schranz, 2011; Schultz, 2011; Schultz and Wehmeier, 2010; Siltaoja and Vehkaperä, 2010) or empirically (Einwiller *et al.*, 2010; Lee and Carroll, 2011). Theoretical studies argue that moral misbehavior is often instrumentalized for scandalization in the news (Eisenegger and Schranz, 2011; Schultz and Wehmeier, 2010), as journalists actively select topics that allow moral attributions of esteem and disesteem in order to receive attention (Luhmann, 1996). Accordingly, the institutionalization of CSR is based on this moral(ized) communication, which raises based on reductions of societal complexity expectations on corporations, that in turn binds them to promises they can hardly fulfill (entrapment, see Schultz, 2011).

Empirical studies partially support theoretical assumptions, but also show contradicting results. Whereas Kiousis *et al.* (2007) argues that the attention to a corporations' CSR in the media correlates positively with its reputation, Lee and Carroll (2011) show that with increasing attention for CSR in the US media in the last 25 years, the most prevalent valence of opinion pieces were negative, and the amount of such negative pieces is increasing. Furthermore, it is an accepted insight that a negative framing of CSR efforts decreases the reputation, whereas positively framed CSR news do not evoke strong reactions. Because of the "negativity bias" (e.g., Sen and Bhattacharya, 2001), negative CSR news affect corporations, whereas the benefit from positive

CSR news is quite small. Wang (2007) documents more detailed, that a negatively framed news report did not influence the participants' judgments, when they are not primed with CSR, and that their own position toward the organization moderates the negativity effect of framing, but not the priming effect (Wang, 2007). Besides discussing dysfunctional effects, media research points especially to vice versa effects of media on corporations. It is known that media reporting leads to increases in a corporation's prosocial CSR activities but not decreases in negative ones (Zyglidopoulos *et al.*, 2012), and that higher news coverage on environmental issues puts pressure on corporations to increase their environmental reporting (Aerts and Cormier, 2009).

The following chapter elaborates now more on the role of moralization and morale communication as constitutive element for CSR and reputation.

Organizational communication research: CCO and moral communication

In this last perspective, CSR can be regarded as socially and based on moral and moralized communication constituted, empty concept (Schultz, 2011). It is *translated* by different actors, filled with different meanings, and publicly negotiated (Schultz and Wehmeier, 2010). CSR is not a fixed script or tool that might be used by corporations to produce legitimacy, but represents instead a dynamic continuum of meanings, a "symbolic resource" that is often competitively used by a variety of actors. Publics and organizations develop within their interplay different narrations, and corporations co-constitute as polyphonic actors such narrations through their variety of individuals (Wehmeier and Schultz, 2011).

The idea of the communicative constitution of CSR is in line with a theoretical perspective that developed in the past 30 years and is most recently debated under the moniker of CCO (see Ashcraft *et al.*, 2009). Inspired by the linguistic turn in social theory, it argues that organizations emerge in communication (Taylor and Van Every, 2000) and points to the formative effect of language in sensemaking processes and the representation of institutions in such communications, too (Ashcraft *et al.*, 2009; Putnam and Nicotera, 2008; see also Christensen and Cornelissen, 2011). The article discusses CSR in line with the CCO perspective, when opting for overcoming the dualism of realism/materialism – idealism through concepts such as "constitutive entanglement" (Ashcraft *et al.*, 2009), but even stronger proposes an explicit epistemological shift towards a *nondualistic perspective* (Schultz, 2011). This nondualist perspective challenges both dominant epistemological paradigms – realism and constructivism – by arguing that reality is directly integrated into communication, which in turn is mainly performative in character (Cassirer, 1944; Mitterer, 1992). Especially narrations reduce complexity and organize social reality by moralizing constructions of reality and applying the frames of good and bad. Building on this epistemological perspective, three conclusions can be drawn.

First, it can be concluded that CSR and reputation are both *communicative events*. They are constituted communicatively, whereas perceptions or constructions of CSR and reputation, but also related metaphors such as transparency and authenticity, are symbolically and communicatively mediated. Although CSR does not exist as an ontological event, it is getting real for actors and here enfolds effects by leading and legitimizing actions. Each analysis of the interplay of CSR and reputation therefore has to take into account that CSR and reputation are both part of societal narratives, which in turn are coproduced by a multiplicity of actors in a variety of complex interactions and discourses (see also Bebbington *et al.*, 2008, for reputation). From this follows that reputation is not simply produced by organizations, but provided by publics, who both coproduce public policies and agendas (Nothhaft and Wehmeier, 2007), and both enact the discourse on CSR that legitimates organizations. This perspective offers space for CSR and reputation research, as it acknowledges the form of com-

munication that underlies both – *moral* and *moralized communication* (see Schultz, 2011): Whereas moral communication is in the functionalist view regarded as mechanism to integrate and lead social processes, it is in the communicative view, first of all, a form of communication, in which actors refer on oversituational valid values, something abstract, polysemantic, and undetermined that has no fixed meanings while at the same time hides the contingency it claims to abolish. For example, CSR and reputation, but also "social" and "responsible," are quite fuzzy terms, which have very different and no fixed meanings and are associated with divergent assumptions, for example, on their effects. At the same time, they produce semantic traps.

From this follows *second*, that constructions of CSR as manifested in corporate communications are institutionalized for other than purely functional reasons (increase reputation, persuasion) or normative reasons (becoming ethical). Also, reputation is not a fixed script or variable that can be affected or employed singularly by CSR. Building on the conceptualization of moral communication (Schultz, 2011), it can instead be argued that CSR and also the notion of reputation are both introduced in discourses as means to reduce complexity, variety, and ambiguity, and keep the idea of unity, causality, and controllability alive. They are both due to their fuzziness, partly mythical in character, and used to overcome insecurities of action by the performative creation of new rooms of action in the sense of alternative realities, on which decisions and differences shall now be based. In this sense, CSR serves to maintain the self-organization or autopoiesis of organizations and societies. It is used on different levels (individuals, organizations, societies) as a vehicle to increase self-esteem and part of the symbolic production of identity. In a similar vein, Bebbington *et al.* (2008) concluded that corporate reports are filtered through the eyes of individuals who may be struggling to provide themselves with a narrative about the impact of the corporation. As moral communication secures follow-up communication and, as moralized communication, breaks up communication and disintegrates (Schultz, 2011), and since organization surfaces in communication (Ashcraft *et al.*, 2009), the institutionalization of CSR also does not simply aim at producing reputation. Instead, CSR and the discourse on reputation are expressions of organizational and societal changes and iteratively change societal norms and expectations.

Third, it can be assumed that the proclaimed loss of reputation can become a self-fulfilling prophecy (see Schultz, 2011): as the moralization of reality leads to the breakdown of communication and of reality negotiations (moral paradox), it produces delegitimacy as well. As the *moralized, second reality* invisibilizes societal, economical, organizational, and communicative processes, differences, and contingencies, and excludes them from the discourse – or "ex-communicates" – without being able to exclude these realities – it contributes even further to the decoupling of reality. This might, in the case of CSR, lead to a downward spiral of legitimacy (see also Schultz and Wehmeier, 2010; Crane and Livesey, 2003).

Discussion and Conclusion

The chapter documents that the relation between CSR and reputation is differently described based on the applied perspective. Only from a functionalist perspective, morale and ethic can be regarded as integrative mechanism to increase reputation, identification, and loyalty. Accordingly, functionalist views as developed in management, marketing, and PR research with focus on the meso level tend to overestimate a positive relationship. This chapter followed others who already proposed a stronger integration of meso and macro (Eisenegger and Schranz, 2011) as well as micro perspectives (Schultz and Wehmeier, 2010) and build on the pluralistic framework of Gond and Matten (2007) to cluster research perspectives and furthermore detect research deficits. In contrast to functionalist perspectives and also political–normative views, constructivist perspectives take processes of mediatization

on the macro level, and sensemaking and communication on the micro level as well as paradoxes of moralized communication into account. It shows that CSR practices and communications bear not only opportunities, but also risks for corporations. As discussed, social reality is rarely negotiated not only by rational argumentations, but also by emotionalized and moralized communications, which do not necessarily aim at finding a consensus, but might aim at breaking up the communication.

Future research needs to investigate the relation between CSR and reputation from these three and additional perspectives (e.g., culturalist) and contribute especially to the constructivist one. It needs to analyze, for example, how corporations are as social or political actors communicatively constructed, and how CSR institutionalizes based on macro institutional effects and micro sensemaking processes. Furthermore, the role of media and new and social media has to be taken more into account. Especially the rise of social media extended opportunities to comment, share, or forward corporate communications, which also affect the corporate reputation even more. For these analyses, different empirical methods, such as social and semantic network analyses, could be used to better analyze the use, spread, and shift of CSR and reputation as metaphors in public and organizational discourses, the translation of meaning in corporations, and the role of new media and protest actors in their public constitution.

References

Aerts, W. and Cormier, D. (2009) Media legitimacy and corporate environmental communication. *Accounting, Organizations and Society, 34,* 1–27.

Ashcraft, K.L., Kuhn, T., and Cooren, F. (2009) Constitutional amendments. "Materializing" organizational communication. *The Academy of Management Annals, 3*(1), 1–64.

Ashforth, B.E. and Gibbs, B.W. (1990) The double-edge of organizational legitimation. *Organization Science, 1*(2), 177–194.

Bebbington, J., Larrinaga, C., and Moneva, J.M. (2008) Corporate social reporting and reputation risk management. *Accounting, Audition & Accountability Journal, 21*(3), 337.

Bhattacharya, C.B. and Sen, S. (2004) Doing better at doing good: When, why and how consumers respond to corporate social initiatives. *California Management Review, 47*(1), 9–24.

Brammer, S.J. and Millington, A. (2005) Corporate reputation and philanthropy: An empirical analysis. *Journal of Business Ethics, 61*, 29–44.

Brammer, S.J. and Pavelin, S. (2006) Corporate reputation and social performance: The importance of fit. *Journal of Management Studies, 43*(3), 436–455.

Branco, M.C. and Rodrigues, L.L. (2006) Communication of corporate social responsibility by Portuguese banks. A legitimacy theory perspective. *Corporate Communications: An International Journal, 11*(3), 232–248.

Brønn, P.S. and Vrioni, A.B. (2001) Corporate social responsibility and cause-related marketing: An overview. *International Journal of Advertising, 20*, 207–222.

Brown, T.J. and Dacin, P.A. (1997) The company and the product: Corporate associations and consumer product responses. *Journal of Marketing, 61*, 68–84.

Carroll, A.B. (1999) Corporate social responsibility. Evolution of a definitional construct. *Business and Society, 38*, 268–295.

Carroll, C.E. (2004) *How the mass media influence perceptions of corporate reputation: Exploring agenda-setting effects within business news coverage.* Unpublished doctoral dissertation, The University of Texas, Austin, TX.

Carroll, C.E. (2010) Should firms circumvent or work through the news media? *Public Relations Review, 36*(3), 278–280.

Carroll, C.E. and McCombs, M.E. (2003) Agenda-setting effects of business news on the public's images and opinions about major corporations. *Corporate Reputation Review, 6*(1), 36–46.

Cassirer, E. (1944) *An Essay on Man. An Introduction to a Philosophy of Human Culture.* London: Yale University Press.

Chattananon, A., Lawley, M., Trimetsoontorn, J., Supparerkchaisakul, N., and Leelaouthayothin, L. (2007) Building corporate image through social marketing programs. *Society and Business Review, 2*(3), 230–247.

Christensen, L.T. and Cornelissen, J. (2011) Bridging corporate and organizational communication: Review, development and a look to the future. *Management Communication Quarterly, 25*(3), 383–414.

Crane, A. and Livesey, S. (2003) Are you talking to me? Stakeholder communication and the risks and rewards of dialogue. In Andriof, J., Waddock, S., Husted, B. and Rahman, S.S. (eds), *Unfolding Stakeholder Thinking 2: Relationships, Communication, Reporting and Performance.* Sheffield: Greenleaf, pp. 39–52.

Crane, A., McWilliams, A., Matten, D., Moon, J., and Siegel, D.S. (eds) (2008) *The Oxford Handbook of Corporate Social Responsibility.* Oxford, UK: Oxford University Press.

Davis, K. (1973) The case for and against business assumption of social responsibilities. *Academy of Management Journal, 16*(2), 312–322.

Deephouse, D.L. (2000) Media reputation as a strategic resource: An integration of mass communication and resource-based theories. *Journal of Management, 26*(6), 1091–1112.

Deephouse, D.L. and Carter, S.M. (2005) An examination of differences between organizational legitimacy and organizational reputation. *Journal of Management Studies, 42*(2), 329–360.

Dowling, J. and Pfeffer, J. (1975) Organizational legitimacy: Social values and organizational behavior. *Pacific Sociological Review, 18*, 122–136.

Eberl, M. and Schwaiger, M. (2005) Corporate reputation: Disentangling the effects on financial performance. *European Journal of Marketing, 39*(7/8), 838–854.

Einwiller, S., Carroll, C.E., and Korn, K. (2010) Under what conditions do the news media influence corporate reputation? The roles of media systems dependency and need for orientation. *Corporate Reputation Review, 12*(4), 299–315.

Eisenegger, M. and Schranz, M. (2011) CSR – Moralisierung des Reputationsmanagements. In J. Raupp, S. Jarolimek, and F. Schultz (eds), *Handbuch CSR, Kommunikationswissenschaftliche Grundlagen, disziplinäre Perspektiven und methodische Herausforderungen.* Wiesbade: VS-Verlag, pp. 71–97.

Elkington, J. (1997) *Cannibals with Forks: The Triple Bottom Line of 21st Century Business.* Oxford, UK: Oxford University Press.

Elving, W. (2010) CSR as greenwashing. Paper presented at the Euprera Conference, Jyvyskylä.

Etzioni, A. (1988) *The Moral Dimension.* New York: Free Press.

European Commission (2001) *Promoting a European framework for corporate social responsibility.*

Green Paper, Industrial Relations and Industrial Change Series, Office for Official Publications of the European Communities, Luxembourg.

Flohr, A., Rieth, L., Schwindenhammer, S., and Wolf, K.D. (2010) *The Role of Business in Global Governance: Corporations as Norm Entrepreneurs.* Basingstoke: Palgrave MacMillan.

Fombrun, C.J. and Shanley, M. (1990) What's in a name? Reputation building and corporate strategy. *Academy of Management Journal, 33,* 233–258.

Fombrun, C.J. and van Riel, C.B.M. (2003) *Fame and Fortune: How the World's Top Companies Develop Winning Reputations.* New York: Pearson Publishing/Financial Times.

Fombrun, C.J., Gardberg, N.A., and Sever, J.M. (2000a) The Reputation Quotient^SM: A multistakeholder measure of corporate reputation. *Journal of Brand Management, 7*(4), 241–255.

Fombrun, C.J., Gardberg, N.A., and Barnett, M.L. (2000b) Opportunity platforms and safety nets: Corporate citizenship and reputational risk. *Business and Society Review, 205*(1), 85–106.

Friedman, M. (1970) *The social responsibility of business is to increase its profit.* The New York Times Magazine, September 13, pp. 32–33, 122–126.

Garriga, E. and Melé, D. (2004) Corporate social responsibility: Mapping the conceptual territory. *Journal of Business Ethics, 53,* 51–71.

Golob, U. and Bartlett, J.L. (2007) Communicating about corporate social responsibility: A comparative study of CSR reporting in Australia and Slovenia. *Public Relations Review, 33*(1), 1–9.

Gond, J. and Matten, D. (2007) *Reconsidering the organization-society interface: A pluralistic framework on corporate social responsibility.* International Centre for Corporate Social Responsibility ICCSR Research Paper Series, No. 47-2007 Nottingham University Business School, United Kingdom.

Grunig, J.E. and Hunt, T.T. (1984) *Managing Public Relations.* New York: Harcourt Brace Jovanovich College Publishers.

Hasseldine, J., Salama, A.I., and Toms, J.S. (2005) Quantity versus quality: The impact of environmental disclosures on the reputation of UK Plcs. *The British Accounting Review, 37,* 231–248.

Hooghiemstra, R. (2000) Corporation communication and impression management – New perspectives why companies engage in corporate social reporting. *Journal of Business Ethics, 27,* 55–68.

Ihlen, Ø. (2008) Mapping the environment for corporate social responsibility. Stakeholders, publics and the public sphere. *Corporate Communications: An International Journal, 13*(2), 135–146.

Ihlen, Ø., Bartlett, J.L., and May, S. (2011) *The Handbook of Communication and Corporate Social Responsibility.* Oxford, UK: Wiley Blackwell.

Jahdi, K.S. and Acikdilli, G. (2009) Marketing communications and corporate social responsibility (CSR): Marriage of convenience or shotgun wedding? *Journal of Business Ethics, 88,* 103–113.

Kiousis, S., Popescu, C., and Mitrook, M. (2007) Understanding influence on corporate reputation: An examination of public relations efforts, media coverage, public opinion, and financial performance from an agenda-building and agenda-setting perspective. *Journal of Public Relations Research, 19*(2), 147–165.

Klein, J. and Dawar, N. (2004) Corporate social responsibility and consumers' attributions and brand evaluations in a product-harm crisis. *International Journal of Research in Marketing, 21,* 203–217.

Kotler, P. and Lee, N. (2005) *Corporate Social Responsibility. Doing the Most Good for Your Company and Your Cause.* Hoboken, NJ: Wiley.

Krotz, F. (2007) *Mediatisierung: Fallstudien zum Wandel von Kommunikation (Mediatization: Case Studies in the Change of Communication),* Wiesbaden: VS.

Kuhn, T. and Deetz, S. (2008) Critical theory and CSR: Can/should we get beyond cynical reasoning? In A. Crane, A. McWilliams, D. Matten, J. Moon, and D. Siegel (eds), *The Oxford Handbook on Corporate Social Responsibility.* Oxford, UK: Oxford University Press.

Lee, S.Y. and Carroll, C.E. (2011) The emergence, variation, and evolution of corporate social responsibility in the public sphere, 1980–2004: The exposure of firms to public debate. *Journal of Business Ethics, 104,* 115–131.

Luhmann, N. (1996) *Die Realität der Massenmedien* (2nd ed.). Opladen: Westdeutscher Verlag.

Luo, X. and Bhattacharya, C.B. (2009) The debate over doing good: Corporate social performance, strategic marketing levers, and firm-ideosyncratic risk. *Journal of Marketing, 73,* 198–213.

Margolis, J.D. and Walsh, J.P. (2003) Misery loves companies: Rethinking social initiatives by business. *Administrative Science Quarterly, 48*(2), 268–305.

McWilliams, A. and Siegel, D. (2001) Corporate social responsibility: A theory of the firm perspective. *Academy of Management Review, 26*, 117–127.

McWilliams, A., Siegel, D., and Wright, P. (2006) Corporate social responsibility: Strategic implications. *Journal of Management Studies, 43*, 1–18.

Meijer, M.M. and Kleinnijenhuis, J. (2006) News and corporate reputation: Empirical findings from the Netherlands. *Public Relations Review, 32*, 341–348.

Meyer, J.W. and Rowan, B. (1977) Institutionalized organizations: Formal structure as myth and ceremony. *American Journal of Sociology, 83*(2), 340–363.

Mitterer, J. (1992) *Das Jenseits der Philosophie. Wider das dualistische Erkenntnisprinzip.* Wien: Passagen.

Morsing, M. and Schultz, M. (2006) Corporate social responsibility communication: Stakeholder information, response and involvement strategies. *Business Ethics: A European Review, 4*, 323–338.

Morsing, M., Schultz, M., and Nielsen, K.U. (2008) The "catch 22" of communicating CSR: Findings from a Danish study. *Journal of Marketing Communications, 14*(2), 97–111.

Murray, K.B. and Vogel, C.M. (1997) Using a hierarchy-of-effects approach to gauge the effectiveness of corporate social responsibility to generate goodwill toward the firm: Financial versus nonfinancial impacts. *Journal of Business Research, 38*(2), 141–159.

Mutch, N. and Aitken, R. (2009) Being fair and being seen to be fair: Corporate reputation and CSR partnerships. *Australasian Marketing Journal, 17*(2), 92–98.

Nielsen, A.E. and Thomsen, C. (2007) Reporting CSR – What and how to say it? *Corporate Communications: An International Journal, 12*(1), 25–40.

Nielsen, A.E. and Thomsen, C. (2009) Investigating CSR communication in SMEs: A case study among Danish middle managers. *Business Ethics: A European Review, 18*(1), 83–93.

Nothhaft, H. and Wehmeier, S. (2007) Coping with complexity: Sociocybernetics as a framework for communication management. *International Journal of Strategic Communication, 1*(3), 151–168.

Orlitzky, M., Schmidt, F.L., and Rynes, S.L. (2003) Corporate social and financial performance: A meta-analysis. *Organization Studies, 24*(3), 403–441.

Palazzo, G. and Scherer, A.G. (2006) Corporate legitimacy as deliberation: A communicative framework. *Journal of Business Ethics, 66*(1), 71–88.

Parsons, T. (1966) *Societies. Evolutionary and Comparative Perspectives.* Englewood Cliffs, NJ: Prentice Hall.

Pomering, A. and Dolnicar, S. (2009) Assessing the prerequisite of successful CSR implementation: Are consumers aware of CSR initiatives? *Journal of Business Ethics, 85*, 285–301.

Pomering, A. and Johnson, L.W. (2009) Advertising corporate social responsibility initiatives to communicate corporate image. Inhibiting skepticism to enhance persuasion. *Corporate Communications: An International Journal, 14*(4), 420–439.

Porter, M.E. and Kramer, M.R. (2003) The competitive advantage of corporate philanthropy. *Harvard Business Review on Corporate Responsibility.* Boston: Harvard Business School, pp. 27–64.

Porter, M.E. and Kramer, M.R. (2006) Strategy and society. The link between competitive advantage and corporate social responsibility. *Harvard Business Review, 12*, 78–92.

Putnam, L.L. and Nicotera, A.M. (eds) (2008) *Building Theories of Organization: The Constitutive Role of Communication.* Oxford, UK: Routledge.

Rhee, M. and Valdez, M.E. (2009) Contextual Factors surrounding reputation damage with potential implications for reputation repair. *Academy of Management Review, 34*(1), 146–168.

Rieth, L. (2011) CSR aus politikwissenschaflicher Perspektive: Empirische Vorbedingungen und normative Bewertungen unternehmerisch en Handelns. In J. Raupp, S. Jarolimek, and F. Schultz (eds), *Handbuch Corporate Social Responsibility, Kommunikationswissenschaftliche Grundlagen und empirische Fallstudien.* Wiesbaden: VS-Verlag, pp. 395–418.

Scherer, A.G. and Palazzo, G. (2007) Toward a political conception of corporate responsibility: Business and society seen from a Habermasian perspective. *The Academy of Management Review, 32*(4), 1096–1120.

Scherer, A.G., Palazzo, G., and Baumann, D. (2006) Global rules and private actors: Toward a new role of the transnational corporation in global governance. *Business Ethics Quarterly*, *16*(4), 505–532.

Scheufele, D.A. and Tewksbury, D. (2007) Framing, agenda-setting, and priming: The evolution of three media effects models. *Journal of Communication*, *57*(1), 9–20.

Schultz, F. (2011) *Moral – Kommunikation – Organisation. Normative Konzepte und Theorien der Organisationskommunikation des 20. Und 21. Jahrhunderts.* Wiesbaden: VS-Verlag.

Schultz, F. and Wehmeier, S. (2010) Institutionalization of corporate social responsibility within corporate communications. Combining institutional, sensemaking and communication perspectives. *Corporate Communications: An International Journal*, *15*(1), 9–29.

Sen, S. and Bhattacharya, C.B. (2001) Does doing good always lead to doing better? Consumer reactions to corporate social responsibility. *Journal of Marketing Research*, *XXXVIII*, 225–243.

Shamir, R. (2005) Mind the gap: Commodifying corporate social responsibility. *Symbolic Interaction*, *28*, 229–253.

Siltaoja, M.E. and Vehkaperä, M.J. (2010) Constructing illegitimacy? Cartels and cartels agreements in Finnish business media from critical discourse perspective. *Journal of Business Ethics*, *92*, 493–511.

Starkey, K. and Crane, A. (2003) Toward green narrative: Management and the evolutionary epic. *Academy of Management Review*, *28*, 220–243.

Stehr, N. (2007) *Die Moralisierung der Märkte. Eine Gesellschaftstheorie.* Suhrkamp: Frankfurt am Main.

Suchman, M.C. (1995) Managing legitimacy: Strategic and institutional approaches. *Academy of Management Review*, *20*(3), 571–610.

Taylor, J.R. and Van Every, E.J. (2000) *The Emergent Organization: Communication as Its Site and Surface.* Mahwah, NJ: Erlbaum.

Turban, D.B. and Greening, D.W. (1997) Corporate social performance and organizational attractiveness to prospective employees. *Academy of Management Journal*, *40*(3), 658–672.

Unerman, J. (2008) Strategic reputation risk management and corporate social responsibility reporting. *Accounting, Auditing & Accountability Journal*, *21*(3), 362–364.

Vanhamme, J. and Grobben, B. (2009) Too good to be true! The effectiveness of CSR history in countering negative publicity. *Journal of Business Ethics*, *85*, 273–283.

Waddock, S.A. and Graves, B. (1997) The corporate social performance-financial performance link. *Strategic Management Journal*, *18*, 303–319.

Wang, A. (2007) Priming, framing, and position on corporate social responsibility. *Journal of Public Relations Research*, *19*(2), 123–145.

Webb, J.D. and Mohr, L.A. (1998) A typology of customers' responses to cause related marketing: From skeptics to socially concerned. *Journal of Public Policy and Marketing*, *17*(2), 226–239.

Wehmeier, S. and Schultz, F. (2011) Corporate social responsibility and corporate communication: A storytelling perspective. In Ø. Ihlen, J. Bartlett, and S. May (eds), *Handbook Communication and Corporate Social Responsibility.* Boston: Blackwell.

Williams, R.J. and Barrett, J.D. (2000) Corporate philanthropy, criminal activity, and firm reputation: Is there a link? *Journal of Business Ethics*, *26*(4), 341–350.

Wood, D.J. and Lodgson, J.M. (2001) Theorising business citizenship. In J. Andriof and M. McIntosh (eds), *Perspectives on Corporate Citizenship.* Sheffield: Greenleaf.

Wright, C. and Rwabizambuga, A. (2006) Institutional pressures, corporate reputation, and voluntary codes of conduct: An examination of the equator principles. *Business and Society Review*, *111*(1), 89–117.

Yoon, Y., Gürhan-Canli, Z., and Schwarz, N. (2006) The effect of corporate social responsibility (CSR) activities on companies with bad reputations. *Journal of Consumer Psychology*, *16*(4), 377–390.

Zyglidopoulos, S., Georgiadis, A., Carroll, C.E., and Siegel, D. (2012) Does media attention drive corporate social responsibility? *Journal of Business Research*, *65*(11), 1622–1627.

31

Reputation or Financial Performance: Which Comes First?

Alexander V. Laskin

Quinnipiac University, USA

This chapter examines the relationship between financial performance and corporate reputation, and the role that communication plays in this relationship. Financial performance is viewed as an important attribute for evaluating corporate reputation. In fact, several corporate reputation measures rely on financial performance as the most important indicator. Financial performance, usually measured through profitability, investment risk, competition, and future anticipated financial performance, is nevertheless largely based on the perceptions of the financial community. In other words, what really counts is how all four of these financial performance areas are being interpreted by the company's stakeholders. Thus, when considering financial performance's contribution to corporate reputation, it is impossible to ignore the role of corporate communications in the process. As a result, it becomes imperative to discuss how stakeholders perceive financial performance, how companies can manage these perceptions through corporate communications, and what relationship exists between these efforts and the overall corporate reputation.

Financial Performance as an Attribute of Corporate Reputation

Financial performance is widely accepted as an indicator or attribute of corporate reputation. Some ratings of corporate reputation even treat financial performance as the most important indicator of corporate reputation (Brown and Perry, 1994; Flanagan *et al.*, 2011; Fombrun *et al.*, 2000). A study by Fryxell and Wang (1994) analyzed the methodology behind the *Fortune* Corporate Reputation Index, a well-regarded ranking of companies based on their reputations, and concluded that the index is almost exclusively based on financial performance rather than any other indicators of corporate reputation: "Taken together, these findings have important implications about what the *Fortune* data actually measure, or, stated differently, what these firms have a reputation for.

The Handbook of Communication and Corporate Reputation, First Edition. Edited by Craig E. Carroll.
© 2013 John Wiley & Sons, Inc. Published 2015 by John Wiley & Sons, Inc.

We conclude that the dominant factor underlying the database appears to be predominately financial in its construct domain" (p. 11).

The authors of the *Fortune* Index recognized the heavy influence of financial performance on corporate reputation by accepting that financial performance is responsible for almost 50% of the index's overall score ("America's Most Admired Corporations," 1993). In other words, despite the fact that the *Fortune* Index promises to measure corporate reputation in such areas as quality of management, quality of products and services, ability to attract and keep talented employees, and so on, the financial performance of the company dominates the reputational result in the end.

Fombrun *et al.* (2000) actually suggest that not just *Fortune*, but many other corporate reputation measurements also focus exclusively on financial performance. In fact, after Fombrun *et al.* (2000) reviewed such reputation rankings as *Fortune*'s America's Most Admired Companies, *Fortune*'s Global Most Admired Companies, *Financial Times*' World's Most Respected Companies, *Industry Week*'s Best Managed Companies, *Far Eastern Economic Review*'s Asia's Leading Companies, *Management Today*'s Britain's Most Admired Companies, *Asian Business*' Asia's Most Admired Companies, and *Manager Magazine*'s Ranking of German Manufacturing and Service Firms, they claimed that reputation measures are mostly "developed by the business media" and tend "to define reputations on the basis of the perceptions of a restricted set of financially oriented stakeholders (CEOs and analysts)" (p. 254).

Given the strong influence of financial performance on corporate reputation, it is important to understand what financial performance means and how it can affect organizational reputation. At first sight, it seems like an easy task. Most of the organization's stakeholders are quite likely to agree what constitutes positive reputation in the area of financial performance and what constitutes negative. Indeed, shareholders clearly want the company to succeed financially, but the same is also true for the company's employees. The local community would also prefer to have a financially successful company as its tax-paying neighbor. A company's suppliers and customers would also prefer to do business with a financially stable organization rather than with a firm teetering on the verge of bankruptcy. This is true for many other stakeholders. Unfortunately, financial success can be defined using different metrics. And at this point, different stakeholders would prefer focusing on different metrics as measures of financial success.

In addition, corporate reputation resides in the minds of company's stakeholders. Although a company's actions are important, reputation is essentially built on the stakeholders' perceptions of these actions rather than on the actions themselves. Fombrun and Shanley (1990) explain that "Publics construct reputations from available information about firms' activities originating from the firms themselves, from the media, or from other monitors. Publics use and propagate information they deem important for assessing firms' successes and failures at acquiring resource inputs, improving throughputs, and sustaining outputs" (p. 234). This makes communications about a company's financial performance as important, or even more important, than financial performance itself.

Thus, measuring financial performance can become a complex task in itself. In fact, the Reputation Quotient^{SM}, the most widely used tool for measuring corporate reputation, relies on four sub-attributes to allow the survey respondents to describe the financial performance of a company:

- strong record of profitability
- investment risk
- outperforming competitors
- prospects for future growth.

Respondent assessments of a firm on each of these four sub-attributes are then combined to provide an overall indication of a firm's financial performance in relation to its reputation.

The first sub-attribute of financial performance focuses on the company's "strong record of profitability" (Fombrun *et al.*, 2000, p. 253). However, profitability itself is not a simple unidimensional concept – it can mean different things to different stakeholders, and different indicators can be used to measure profitability. Generally Accepted Accounting Principles (GAAP), an accounting standard used in the United States, requires companies to report four types of income: income from continuing operations, income from discontinued operations, extraordinary gains or losses, and adjustments. Clearly, selling land or buildings that a company owns may lead to significant profits on the income statement, but this profit is not sustainable – in other words, sooner or later, the company will run out of land and buildings to sell. As a result, a better description of corporate financial performance is not based on one-time transactions, or on discontinued operations and adjustments, but based on its long-time performance, usually reflected in the income from the operations section of a financial statement. Indeed, if a company can demonstrate profitability from its main business activities, this will lead to growth in profits over time, which, in turn, leads to a positive evaluation of a firm's financial performance, and this, in the end, contributes to an enhanced corporate reputation. Thus, it seems that focusing on the income from continuing operations is the best option in evaluating a company's financial performance.

Yet, measuring income in absolute terms can be misleading – companies with larger resources and selling more products would always seem to be more profitable. Thus, another approach to measuring profitability is comparing a company's net profits to its equity. Indeed, shareholders of the company, as well as other financially oriented stakeholders, want to know how much income managers can generate from every dollar that was invested in this company. This allows shareholders to easily see what investment is the most promising – if one dollar invested in company A can generate more income than one dollar invested in company B, then investment in company A should be more profitable.

In addition to these approaches, financial analysts and professional investors use many more techniques to evaluate the profitability of companies in order to control for other factors that can influence a company's operations. All of these issues may make evaluating corporate profitability a daunting task that can affect our confidence in the overall evaluation of a company's reputation.

The second sub-attribute of a company's overall financial performance as an indicator of corporate reputation asks the respondents to evaluate a company's "investment risk" (Fombrun *et al.*, 2000, p. 253). Corporations can operate because of the capital supplied by investors. In return, investors receive an ownership interest in the firm, thus becoming shareholders. The shareholders expect the price of the stock they own to go up as the company grows and increases its profitability. However, if the company goes bankrupt, shareholders stand to lose all or most of their investment in the corporation. As a result, shareholders always face a risk of losing their investment. Investment risk can simply be defined as uncertainty about the future. Damodaran (2003) defines risk as "the likelihood that in life's games of chance, we will receive an outcome that we will not like" (p. 14).

The third sub-attribute of financial performance focuses on evaluating the company's track record at "outperforming competitors" (Fombrun *et al.*, 2000, p. 253). An important caveat in measuring a firm's financial performance is that managers cannot control every variable that affects the company's performance. In fact, other events can cause a company's financial performance to drop or rise. Events such as an economic downturn, fluctuations in oil prices, availability of various resources, sociopolitical changes, and even weather and climate change, can have an impact on the company's bottom line. The drop in demand for offshore drilling rigs following BP's Gulf of Mexico tragedy undoubtedly affects the entire drilling rig industry. Yet, the drilling rig manufacturers are not to blame for the disaster as they were not the ones operating the rigs in the Gulf. Nevertheless, the moratorium on new offshore drilling has resulted in a decline in new orders of drilling rigs and a sharp drop in revenues for the entire industry. As a result, it is important to look at companies in the same industry, often known as a peer group, since these peers would be affected in a similar manner by outside factors. A company's ability to show extraordinary returns versus its peers, thus, may lead to higher corporate reputation because it serves as a statement of a company's superior advantage.

Finally, the fourth sub-attribute of financial performance reads, "Looks like a company with strong prospects for future growth" (Fombrun et al., 2000, p. 253). This indicator is quite different from the first three indicators in that it asks respondents to evaluate the future financial performance of the firm as opposed to the firm's past performance. Indeed, Laskin (2009) claims that investors are most interested in what is going to happen with the company in the *future* rather than what happened with it in the *past*. The main reason for investing in a company's stock is the expectation that growth of a company's business will result in an increase in the company's share price. As a result, evaluating a company's prospects for future growth is an important measure of a company's financial performance.

It should be noted that a company's current financial performance does not always correlate perfectly with its long-term financial performance. Companies may carry heavy investment burdens that are expected to produce benefits over time. For example, a pharmaceutical company's research and development (R&D) expenses, incurred in an effort to create a new cancer-fighting drug, can have a negative impact on financial performance in the year when they occurred and portray the company as underperforming in comparison with its competitors. Yet, such a drug can lead to extraordinary profits in future periods. Ittner and Larcker (2000) explain that "Even when the ultimate goal is maximizing financial performance, current financial measures may not capture long-term benefits from decisions made" (p. 2). They provide several examples, including investments in customer satisfaction: "investments in customer satisfaction can improve subsequent economic performance by increasing revenues and loyalty of existing cus-

tomers, attracting new customers and reducing transaction costs" (p. 2). As a result, when looking at the financial performance's contribution to corporate reputation, future growth prospects add an important attribute to such evaluation.

In conclusion, financial performance and its sub-attributes are generally recognized as an important contributor to corporate reputation, particularly in the formation of impressions among financially oriented stakeholders (Fombrun et al., 2000). The first sub-attribute of financial performance evaluates the company's record of profitability. The second sub-attribute looks at the risk associated with investment in this company. The third sub-attribute compares the company with its main competitors. Finally, the fourth sub-attribute gauges future anticipated financial performance. Taken together, these four sub-attributes provide for a holistic view of a company's financial performance. Yet, what really counts is how all four of these financial performance areas are being interpreted by the company's stakeholders. Thus, when considering financial performance's contribution to corporate reputation, it is impossible to ignore the role of corporate communications in the process.

The Role of Communications in Evaluating Financial Performance

Laskin (2011) studied the role that investor relations, a specialty area of corporate communication, plays in communicating financial information to investors, shareholders, and analysts. His research indicates that prime function of investor relations is in managing the expectations of a company's stockholders. Indeed, generating the same profit in dollar terms can be perceived as a success for one company, while it can be viewed as a failure for another organization. In other words, each one of the four indicators of financial performance described earlier is meaningless taken out of the context of corporate communications. For example, an increase in corporate profits can be perceived as a negative event if such an increase is below the level of profits expected by investors or the level promised earlier by the company. Thus, communication about financial performance becomes the key factor in how this performance is actually evaluated.

It is important to review once again the four sub-attribute of financial performance – but now by looking at the effects that corporate communication has on them. The first sub-attribute, profitability, is constantly managed through communication efforts. Most commonly such management occurs through the use of "earning guidance." Earning guidance is a statement released by a company's management that provides a projection of the company's future revenue and earnings. Earning guidance can have various time frames, but most typically companies release quarterly earning guidance and annual earning guidance, thus coinciding with the periods of financial reporting for corporations. Often earning guidance is expressed as the company's projected earnings per share for some future period, such as the next quarter or next year. The idea behind earning guidance is to help investors and financial analysts evaluate the future performance of the company – managers have the best access to the information and thus they are believed to be the most qualified in making accurate predictions, thus reducing market volatility.

Earning guidance has a strong influence on how corporate profitability is perceived. Indeed, a company making millions of dollars in profits can be perceived as a failure if earlier earning guidance promised profits in the billions. Conversely, the same company can be perceived as a success if its earlier earnings guidance only promised profits in the thousands. Some companies choose to err on the conservative side, making their earning predictions smaller and thus easier to attain. This, however, is not always a winning strategy. Conservative guidance is perceived as being a vote against the company's future prospects and can lead to a dip in the stock price when the guidance is released to the market. Apple Inc., for example, is known for providing conservative earning guidance, often "lowballing" its earnings forecasts. In addition, too high or too low guidance sends a strong negative signal to the investment community that a company's management does not really understand what drives the company's profits and does not have a good grasp of the business. This can also lead to a negative perception of a company's financial results.

Investment risk, the second sub-attribute of financial performance, is also evaluated through a prism of corporate communications. In fact, every publicly traded company has to issue Management Discussion and Analysis (MD&A) information, in which the management of a company tries to explain to its stakeholders what the organization's financial performance really means. The US Securities and Exchange Commission instructs publicly held companies that "MD&A should be a discussion and analysis of a company's business as seen through the eyes of those who manage that business" (Securities and Exchange Commission, 2003). A key part of MD&A is a discussion of risk. Companies are expected to communicate about their loans and other ways of financing the business, the financial ratios and what they mean for business, the quality of loans, and the various risks associated with them. Furthermore, management is expected not just to report the risk, but also estimate its impact on the future of the company and how the company can mitigate such impact.

Shareholders, investors, financial analysts, and other company's stakeholders review these discussions of risk carefully. Such discussions serve an important mediating role in how the risks are actually perceived and how they will affect the perception of financial performance and thus corporate reputation. Extensive and competent evaluation of future risk, coupled with confident presentation of strategies to address these risks, should have a positive impact on the corporate reputation, while ignoring the risks, not understanding their significance, or an inability to develop a strategy for addressing risk will be perceived negatively.

Thus, corporate communication, once again, becomes a key factor in evaluating a sub-attribute of financial performance.

Interpretation of the third and fourth sub-attributes of financial performance, outperforming competitors and prospects for future growth, are also rooted in corporate communications. Both of these areas have prominent roles in MD&A, annual reports, quarterly reports, and corporate news releases. A corporation is expected to carefully present its views on the overall industry, its market position in this industry and its market share, comparisons with competitors, competitive advantages and disadvantages, entry barriers into the industry, and overall market strategy for the future with the prospects for future growth. Company management is also expected to discuss the assumptions on which these predictions are made and evaluate their soundness. Needless to say, such extensive communications about these two metrics of financial performance frame the way financial performance is perceived and evaluated and can help the company manage the expectations of the stakeholders.

This managing of performance expectations among stakeholders is an important job of corporate communications. It helps corporations put their performance in the context of various internal and external environments – some of which are out of the company's control. It also helps build a management team's credibility with stakeholders. Fombrun (1996) elaborates:

> As investors, we expect companies to be credible. We ask that managers live up to the claims and commitments they make in press releases, annual reports, and other communications. Having entrusted them with our hard-earned savings, we demand that they show good faith in their dealings with us. We want them to accurately convey the risks of their strategies, warn us of impeding problems, and disclose material facts that might influence our assessment of their performance. (pp. 64–65)

It is important to underline that communication plays an even larger role than simply modifying the perception of financial performance in general and perceptions of these sub-attributes of financial performance. It also educates stakeholders on who and what stands behind the numbers and also builds relationships with stakeholders. Investors want to understand what the numbers actually mean. If a company increased its profits, investors want to understand if that was caused by an increase in sales or a decrease in expenses; was it related to the changes in industry or seasonal fluctuations; or was it because of the changes in the domestic or international markets; and so on. The process of communicating this information can affect investors' perceptions significantly.

Besides, many companies today are extremely complex: internationally diverse, technologically advanced, and resource dependent. Investors and shareholders are for the most part company outsiders, yet they are expected to make reliable evaluations regarding the corporation's financial performance. Therefore, corporate communications have to educate stakeholders about the complexities of a company's business.

Often, however, such communications efforts are missing. Several research projects conducted by Baruch Lev and his colleagues indicate that investors systematically misprice the shares of corporations (Lev, 2004). The question, however, arises as to why this mispricing occurs? Who or what is responsible for that? Lev wonders, "Underpricing securities and misallocating corporate resources mean that both companies and investors are leaving substantial value on the table" (p. 111).

The answer might lie in an inability of investors, outsiders of the company, to fully grasp the value of complex business capabilities, or in the time constraints of financial analysts who have to cover many corporations and digest large amounts of information to present their recommendations to the investors and thus often resort to simplified financial models. Often, however, the answer seems to lie in corporations' lack of voluntarily disclosing corporate information beyond the required disclosure of financial forms. Such shortage of information can no doubt harm stakeholders' understanding and, subsequently, evaluation of companies (Laskin, 2010).

The lack of communication about what stands behind the numbers is likely an important contributor to the problem. Another issue, however, is the complexity and difficulty of communicating such information. One might argue that the burst of the dot-com bubble was partially caused by the inability of financial analysts and investor to correctly evaluate business models and understand what stands behind the numbers. Indeed, one thing is establishing the value of 100 barrels of oil by consulting oil market price; a quite different exercise is evaluating a person's idea to let people write on their friends' virtual walls with no market prices or even any comparables in existence.

At the same time, companies that *are successful* in their corporate communication efforts not only enhance their reputation among stakeholders, but may be awarded a higher market valuation. For example, Laskin (2011) concluded that investor relations enhances investors' understanding of the company's business drivers; furthermore, it becomes a basis for improving the company's stock market value.

Laskin (2007) also observes that corporate communication can help build relationships with various stakeholders, particularly shareholders. This relationship, in turn, can have a mediating role in how the financial performance is interpreted:

> The rewards of this relationship can be significant. Value gaps tend to diminish because investors believe management can accomplish what it says. Positive events and development earn higher stock gain rewards. A flat or down quarter isn't an automatic sell signal. Investors look for explanations and, when convinced that fundamentals are still strong and growing, are more likely to hold their shares or even increase their positions. Patience is more likely to be accorded. (p. 21–22)

In other words, the financial performance of a company is interpreted through the lenses of relationships between the company and its stakeholders. Once an excellent relationship is established, stakeholders may be more forgiving when they learn of negative company news related to financial performance and more rewarding regarding positive news. Thus, building such relationship becomes an important goal of corporate communications.

These observations suggest that corporate communication plays a vital role in helping stakeholders evaluate the financial performance of companies. Based on a national study of investor relations practices at *Fortune* 500 companies, Laskin (2009) concluded that communications can enhance corporate value. He explained that communications "provide investors with the information they need, thus reducing uncertainty and lowering the risk premium that investors demand for their investment. In other words . . . it decreases investors' risk and subsequently decreases the cost of capital for the company" (p. 227). Through communications, companies manage the expectations of stakeholders, frame the company's performance, help stakeholders understand what the financial numbers actually mean, educate stakeholders on the complexities of their business models, and, finally, establish and maintain relationships with various stakeholders. All these factors have a positive effect on interpreting the financial performance by various stakeholders and that, in turn, leads to a positive corporate reputation.

The Influence of Corporate Reputation on Financial Performance

Having discussed financial performance as a factor in forming, building, and protecting corporate reputation, it is also important to look at the reverse relationship – the influence of corporate reputation on the company's "bottom line" profitability. In fact, much discussion among academics and professionals focuses on the issue of corporate reputation: companies invest resources in improving their image, devote efforts to maintaining positive relationships with their stakeholders, and attempt to manage their positive standings in the mass media. But do all of these efforts pay off? In other words, can positive corporate reputation help companies be more successful financially? Is there a causal link between shifts in corporate reputation and changes in financial performance?

Fombrun *et al.* (2000) claim that corporate reputation has a strong influence in a variety of areas:

> To economists, reputations are traits that signal a company's likely behavior. To strategists, a company's reputation is a barrier to rivals, a source of competitive advantage. To accountants, reputations are an intangible asset, a form of goodwill whose value fluctuates in the marketplace. To marketers, reputations are perceptual assets with the power to attract loyal customers. To students of organization, reputations are an outgrowth of a company's identity, a crystallization of what the company does, how it does it, and how it communicates with its stakeholders. (p. 241–242)

But does that influence lead to actual increases in revenues and heightened profitability? The answer to this question remains elusive despite the fact that various studies have looked at reputation as a predictor variable (Bauer, 2010; Fombrun and van Riel, 2004; Roberts and Dowling, 2002).

Steven Wallman, a former Securities and Exchange Commission (SEC) commissioner, argues that the effect of intangibles, such as reputation, on corporate financial results is very significant and is getting more and more important every day. In fact, Wallman (2003) posits that our whole economy is becoming an economy of intangibles: "When historians look back at the turn of the century, they will note one of the most profound economic shifts of the era: The rise of Intangible Economy" (p. v). Hand and Lev (2003) elaborate on this increasing role of intangible assets: "Wealth and growth in modern economies are driven primarily by intangible assets" (p. 1). Laskin (2010) goes even further and proposes that "not only the role of intangibles is increasing, but the role of tangible assets is simultaneously diminishing

as they become less and less capable of creating a competitive advantage and, thus, providing above-average returns" (p. 49).

The reputational assets play an important role among these intangible assets and can contribute to the company's financial performance. One of the most widely accepted explanations for the reputation's contribution to financial performance is grounded in the resource-based theory (Boyd *et al.*, 2010; Roberts and Dowling, 2002). The resource-based theory stipulates that companies that possess strategic resources will enjoy a competitive advantage and will be able to demonstrate above-average financial results, outperforming companies that do not possess these strategic resources. Not every resource, however, can be considered strategic. In fact, for a resource to be strategic, it must meet several requirements. First of all, the resource must be valuable – in other words, it must have a significant influence on the bottom line (Roberts and Dowling, 2002; Shamsie, 2003). Second, a resource must be rare. In other words, some companies should have positive reputations and some should lack it and the difference between those with good reputation and those with a poor reputation should be clear. A resource must also be inimitable to be considered strategic. If a resource is easy to substitute with something else that is easy to acquire or easy to imitate, it cannot be considered strategic. There is hardly any doubt that reputation meets this requirement. Reputations are developed over a long period of time in interactions with stakeholders and based on performances in many areas (Barney, 1991; Lin *et al.*, 2009; Reed and DeFillippi, 1990). Finally, an organization must be able to take advantage of this resource to earn above-average returns in order for such resource to be considered strategic. In other words, if a company has a reputation for outstanding employee policies, it should be able to take advantage of this reputation to hire a better workforce than its competitors or exhibit better employee productivity than its competitors.

As a result, as a valuable, rare, and inimitable resource, reputation may in fact improve a company's financial performance if such a company is well positioned to benefit from its positive reputation. Positive reputation can help a company raise capital (Beatty and Ritter, 1986), hire talented workers (Fombrun, 2001), or charge premium for its products and services (Shapiro, 1983). Several scholars even conclude that reputation is not just one of the strategic resources that can help companies earn above-average returns, but one of the *most important* ones (Boyd *et al.*, 2010; Deephouse, 2000; Flanagan and O'Shaughnessy, 2005; Hall, 1992).

Another commonly accepted explanation for the influence of reputation on financial results is based on signaling theory (Fombrun and van Riel, 1997; Puncheva, 2008; Wartick, 1992). Signaling theory suggests that information deficiencies exist between corporations, and their stakeholders and parties often have to draw conclusions and make decisions in an environment of uncertainty. Spence (1973, 1974, 2002) suggested that a company could send information signals to its stakeholders to compensate for the lack of information. Having received these signals, stakeholders would rely on this information to help them make decisions.

For example, consumers cannot observe directly how the laptops are produced; often consumers do not even know the country of origin where a laptop's key components, such as motherboards, memory sticks, processors, and graphic adapters, were produced. In this situation, the laptop manufacturer's reputation can serve as a signal about the manufacturing process itself and compensate for the lack of direct information about the production process. Thus, a customer may be willing to pay a premium price for an Apple-branded laptop rather than a competing brand, even though the laptops may all have similar specifications. A company's reputation as a manufacturer of good quality products serves as a signal to consumers, allowing the company to generate above-average returns.

Furthermore, corporate reputation can be a reflection of the overall quality of a firm's management team. Since reputation is one of the resources, managers are expected to manage it

the same way as they manage other resources available to the company. Thus, positive reputation indicates that managers are successful in managing the reputational resource, and this sends a signal that managers are overall capable of running the business. If reputation is, however, negative, that may indicate incompetence of the management team in other areas altogether as well. Acquaah (2003), following Petrick *et al.* (1999), claims that "a firm's corporate reputation is a signal of its corporate management skills, expertise and effectiveness in managing the value creating process for shareholders" (p. 384).

As a result, corporate reputation can be viewed as a strategic resource that can generate above-average returns for a firm. Corporate reputation can also be used as a signal to stakeholders about the aspects of the firm's performance not observable directly. Finally, corporate reputation can serve as a litmus test for the company's management – if executives are successful in managing this highly visible resource, they can be believed to be successful in other areas as well.

However, relationship between financial performance and corporate reputation is not unidirectional, but rather one of mutual influence. Priem and Butler (2001) note that there is a certain "chicken and the egg" dilemma in discussing the value of reputation – whether reputation leads to better financial performance or financial performance leads to better reputation seems very difficult to determine. It is more likely that both of these variables are positively linked and co-influence each other with prior financial performance having an effect on the reputation, which in turn affects future financial performance. Perhaps to better understand the value of reputation as a strategic resource, one should look for a mediating relationship rather than a direct cause-and-effect link (Sirmon *et al.*, 2007). Ketchen *et al.* (2007) illustrate the point: "Customers do not mail checks to a company just because the company possesses certain resources" (p. 962). One of the rare studies that actually looked at reputation as a moderating variable is a research conducted by Acquaah (2003) who discovered that corporate reputation serves as an intermediary variable between organizational competencies such as employee value-added and technological development on one side and firm-specific Tobin's q, "a stock market's valuation of a firm's ability to earn current and future profits relative to its major competitors" (p. 384) on the other.

Conclusions

This chapter discussed the relations between corporate reputation and financial performance of a company. The accumulated research suggests that financial performance is a meaningful contributor to the evaluation of a firm's corporate reputation. In fact, research indicates that stakeholder perceptions of financial performance may in fact be the most important contributor to corporate reputation, when the evaluator is a financially oriented stakeholder, such as corporate executives, analysts, and investors (Fombrun and Shanley, 1990; Roberts and Dowling, 2002). Research indicates that nonfinancial stakeholders are driven more by other attributes of reputation, such as evaluations of products and services and social responsibility, rather than financial performance or vision and leadership (Einwiller *et al.*, 2010; Fombrun and van Riel, 2004; van Riel and Fombrun, 2007). As explained by van Riel and Fombrun (2007), "the public cares little for financial performance and leadership, in contrast to financial and managerial stakeholders who tend to place performance and leadership above all others" (p. 250). This being said, even non-financially-oriented stakeholders are not likely to evaluate favorably a company with visibly lackluster financial performance on the verge of insolvency.

However, financial performance can be measured using a variety of different approaches and techniques. As a result, the influence of financial performance on the corporate reputation, although important, is hard to estimate precisely. Fombrun and Shanley (1990) conclude that "a limited bivariate analysis linking short-term profitability to reputation would be misleading" (p. 252). Future research is needed to establish more reliable measures of such relationships.

Short-termism is, in fact, another factor making measuring the influence of financial performance on corporate reputation difficult. In fact, the influence of financial performance on corporate reputation usually exhibits itself over long periods of time. Thus, cross-sectional studies or longitudinal studies based on a short time span are not capable of identifying the relationship. At the same time, short-term influences can also exist – the announcement of a bankruptcy filing is likely to have a strong effect on the company's reputation. As a result, once again, although reputation seems to be based on both short-term and long-term financial performance, it proves to be difficult, if not impossible, to measure precisely the ratio of long-term to short-term contributions. Once again, more research is needed to establish the influences of long-term and short-term effects.

Both of these tasks, however, are complicated by the fact that financial performance may have more of an indirect influence – rather than direct influence – on corporate reputation. Financial performance may serve as a moderating variable among other influences. Interplay among many variables influencing reputation and each other all at the same time seems to be a better explanation. However, identifying these influences requires elaborate date sets and complex multivariate models.

Finally, corporate reputation is based on the perceptions of stakeholders. Yet, companies have various stakeholder groups with different interests, different access to information about the firm, and different capabilities of interpreting such information. Thus, firms may have different reputations among different stakeholders and different reputations for different attributes. Deephouse (2000) provides an example of a bank donating to charity. These donations decrease the bank's profits, thus leading to a decline in the financial performance measure of reputation. However, this same donation can lead to a positive story in the media and positive perception in the local community. Thus, more customers might open accounts in the bank and more loans might be requested. This can, in turn, have a positive effect on the financial performance measure of corporate reputation. Yet, "determining the order, direction, and magnitude of these effects is an important issues for future research" (Deephouse, 2000, p. 1107). Communications with stakeholders, as a result, play an important role in evaluating financial performance's influence on corporate reputation. Laskin (2010) suggests that corporate communication should take charge of managing stakeholders' expectations in various performance areas, including financial performance. Even positive performance can be interpreted negatively if it falls below expectations.

Another important observation involves the classical dilemma of "the chicken and the egg." Although financial performance influences corporate reputation, corporate reputation also influences financial performance. Corporate reputation is a strategic resource and, as a result, it can help companies earn above-average returns. Corporate reputation also sends a signal about the firm's performance and can have a positive impact on future financial performance as well. Thus, cross-influences between corporate reputation and financial performance undoubtedly exist. Future research will be required to separate and measure these effects.

References

Acquaah, M. (2003) Organizational competence and firm-specific Tobin's q: The moderating role of corporate reputation. *Strategic Organization*, *1*(4), 383–411.

America's Most Admired Corporations (1993) *Fortune*, February 8, pp. 44–53.

Barney, J.B. (1991) Firm resources and sustained competitive advantage. *Journal of Management*, *17*, 99–120.

Bauer, T.N. (2010) Looking back: Reputation research published in the Journal of Management. *Journal of Management*, *36*, 585–587.

Beatty, R.P. and Ritter, J.R. (1986) Investment banking, reputation, and the under pricing of initial public offerings. *Journal of Financial Economics*, *15*, 213–232.

Boyd, B.K., Bergh, D.D., and Ketchen, D.J. (2010) Reconsidering the reputation–performance relationship: A resource-based view. *Journal of Management*, *36*, 588–609.

Brown, B. and Perry, S. (1994) Removing the financial performance halo from *Fortune*'s "Most Admired" Companies. *Academy of Management Journal*, *37*(5), 1347–1359.

Damodaran, A. (2003) *Investment Philosophies: Successful Strategies and the Investors Who Made Them Work*. Hoboken, NJ: John Wiley & Sons.

Deephouse, D.L. (2000) Media reputation as a strategic resource: An integration of mass communication and resource-based theories. *Journal of Management*, *26*, 1091–1112.

Einwiller, S.A., Carroll, C.E., and Korn, K. (2010) Under what conditions do the news media influence corporate reputation? The roles of media dependency and need for orientation. *Corporate Reputation Review*, *12*(4), 299–315.

Flanagan, D.J. and O'Shaughnessy, K.C. (2005) The effect of layoffs on firm reputation. *Journal of Management*, *31*, 445–463.

Flanagan, D.J., O'Shaughnessy, K.C., and Palmer, T.B. (2011) Re-assessing the relationship between the *Fortune* reputation data and financial performance: Overwhelming influence or just a part of the puzzle? *Corporate Reputation Review*, *14*(1), 3–14.

Fombrun, C.J. (1996) *Reputation: Realizing Value from the Corporate Image*. Boston: Harvard School Press.

Fombrun, C.J. (2001) Corporate reputations as economic assets. In M.A. Hint, R.E. Freeman, and J.S. Harrison (eds), *The Blackwell Handbook of Strategic Management*. Oxford, UK: Blackwell Publishers, pp. 289–312.

Fombrun, C.J. and Shanley, M. (1990) What's in a name? Reputation building and corporate strategy. *The Academy of Management Journal*, *33*(2), 233–258.

Fombrun, C.J. and van Riel, C.B.M. (1997) The reputational landscape. *Corporate Reputation Review*, *1*(1 and 2), 1–13.

Fombrun, C.J. and van Riel, C.B.M. (2004) *Fame and Fortune: How Successful Companies Build Winning Reputations*. Upper Saddle River, NJ: Prentice Hall.

Fombrun, C.J., Gardberg, N.A., and Sever, J.M. (2000) The Reputation Quotient[SM]: A multi-stakeholder measure of corporate reputation.

The Journal of Brand Management, 7(4), 241–255.

Fryxell, G.E. and Wang, J. (1994) The *Fortune* Corporate "Reputation" Index: Reputation for what? *Journal of Management*, 20(1), 1–14.

Hall, R. (1992) The strategic analysis of intangible resources. *Strategic Management Journal*, 13, 135–144.

Hand, R.M. and Lev, B. (2003) *Intangible Assets: Values, Measures, and Risks*. New York: Oxford University Press.

Ittner, C.D. and Larcker, D.F. (2000) Non-financial performance measures: What works and what doesn't. October 16. Financial Times: Mastering Management. Knowledge@Wharton Web site. Retrieved from http://knowledge.wharton. upenn.edu/article.cfm?articleid=279 (last accessed September 27, 2012).

Ketchen, D.J., Hult, G.T., and Slater, S. (2007) Toward greater understanding of market orientation and the resource-based view. *Strategic Management Journal*, 28, 961–964.

Laskin, A.V. (2007) *The Value of Investor Relations: A Delphi Panel Investigation. Institute for Public Relations Research Reports*. Gainesville, FL: Institute for Public Relations.

Laskin, A.V. (2009) A descriptive account of the investor relations profession: A national study. *Journal of Business Communication*, 46(2), 208–233.

Laskin, A.V. (2010) *Managing Investor Relations: Strategies for Effective Communication*. New York: Business Expert Press.

Laskin, A.V. (2011) How investor relations contributes to the corporate bottom line. *Journal of Public Relations Research*, 23(3), 302–324.

Lev, B. (2004) Sharpening the intangibles edge. *Harvard Business Review*, 82(6), 109–116.

Lin, Z., Yang, H., and Arya, B. (2009) Alliance partners and firm performance: Resource complimentarity and status association. *Strategic Management Journal*, 30, 921–940.

Petrick, J.A., Scherer, R.F., Brodzinski, J.D., Quinn, J.F., and Ainina, M.F. (1999) Global leadership skills and reputational capital: Intangible resources for sustainable competitive advantage. *Academy of Management Executive*, 13, 58–69.

Priem, R.L. and Butler, J.E. (2001) Is the resource-based "view" a useful perspective for strategic management research. *Academy of Management Review*, 26, 22–40.

Puncheva, P. (2008) The role of corporate reputation in the stakeholder decision-making process. *Business Society*, 47(3), 272–290.

Reed, R. and DeFillippi, R.J. (1990) Causal ambiguity, barriers to imitation, and sustainable competitive advantage. *Academy of Management Review*, 15, 88–102.

Roberts, P.W. and Dowling, G.R. (2002) Corporate reputation and sustained superior financial performance. *Strategic Management Journal*, 23, 1077–1093.

Securities and Exchange Commission (2003) Interpretation: Commission guidance regarding management's discussion and analysis of financial condition and results of operations. December 19. Retrieved from http://www.sec.gov/rules/interp/33-8350.htm (last accessed September 27, 2012).

Shamsie, J. (2003) The context of dominance: An industry-driven framework for exploiting reputation. *Strategic Management Journal*, 23, 199–216.

Shapiro, C. (1983) Premiums for high-quality products as returns on reputations. *Quarterly Journal of Economics*, 98, 659–681.

Sirmon, D.G., Hitt, M.A., and Ireland, D.R. (2007) Managing firm resources in dynamic environments to create value: Looking inside the black box. *Academy of Management Review*, 32, 273–292.

Spence, M.A. (1973) Job market signaling. *Quarterly Journal of Economics*, 87(3), 355–374.

Spence, M.A. (1974) *Market Signaling: Informational Transfer in Hiring and Related Screening Processes*. Cambridge, MA: Harvard University Press.

Spence, M.A. (2002) Signaling in retrospect and the informational structure of markets. *American Economic Review*, 92(3), 434–459.

van Riel, C.B.M. and Fombrun, C.J. (2007) *Essentials of Corporate Communication: Implementing Practices for Effective Reputation Management*. New York: Routledge.

Wallman, S. (2003) Foreword. In R.M. Hand and B. Lev (eds), *Intangible Assets: Values, Measures, and Risks*. New York: Oxford University Press, pp. v–vi.

Wartick, S.L. (1992) The relationship between intense media exposure and change in corporate reputation. *Business & Society*, 31(1), 33–49.

32

Who's in Charge and What's the Solution? Reputation as a Matter of Issue Debate and Risk Management

Robert L. Heath
University of Houston, USA

Whereas in its inception, issues management, and a bit later risk management, dealt primarily with public policy matters, a companion to that theme developed over time. That companion theme was reputation management through the logics of issues and risk management. The link is legitimacy. If the legitimacy as reputation for a company or other organization, even industry, is sufficiently called into question, public policy initiatives are likely to be offered as a way of bringing the organization up to standards that warrant its legitimacy. One of the reasons that legitimacy becomes a problem results when the organization, through crisis or some other activity, violates (or even seems to) key stakeholder expectations. Once that occurs, corrective strategies are required. Thus, proactively and reactively, issues and risk management offer strategic protocols and commitment to corporate social responsibility as means for protecting and advancing reputation.

Issues and Risk Management

Featuring issues in the title, and conceptualization of this chapter, raises an important question. If issues (or issue) management is the disciplinary keeper of matters relevant to corporate reputation, when did corporate reputation become a featured aspect of that discipline? To lay the foundation for answering that question and developing a coherent statement on issues, risk, and corporate reputation, we can turn the clock back to the late 1970s and early 1980s to examine the footprint set by W. Howard Chase as he pioneered what he and others have called issue management.

In his 1984 book, Chase took an emerging issue and proactive response posture. In what can be viewed as the front piece to *Issue Management: Origins of the Future*, he observed that the function is "To *manage* both profit and policy by disciplined process – not by visceral impulse." He offered this objective for the book and discipline: "To *participate* in formation of public policy that affects an institution,

The Handbook of Communication and Corporate Reputation, First Edition. Edited by Craig E. Carroll.
© 2013 John Wiley & Sons, Inc. Published 2015 by John Wiley & Sons, Inc.

instead of being the end of the crack-the-whip line dominated by external, and usually adversarial forces." Both of these statements helped him establish the goal of the book: "To *provide* both the rationale and discipline for effective issue/policy management" (np, italics in the original).

The point of this brief review of the icon of issue management is to note that the discipline began with proactive and disciplined attention to issues relevant to public policy challenges that surround businesses. No matter how important reputation might be to the warranting of those conditions or the policy implications for reputation, reputation was not the original staking point of issue management. Thus, if we are to look for when issues and reputations, as well as risk management and communication, came together, we have to look later than 1984.

This introduction, anchored in the mists of the history of modern issues management, is offered to set the foundation for the current chapter which asks that, within the context of issues management and risk, attention be given in that context to communication and corporate reputation. Thus, we begin with a review of the strategic issues management (SIM) literature to justify applying its concepts, originally developed for public policy discussions, to matters relevant to building corporate reputation. In that discussion, the essence of each issue as a contestable matter will be applied to reputation framed in terms of corporate social responsibility (CSR) set in the dynamics of changing conditions including matters of legitimacy. Then, we discuss risk, in which we reason that the rationale of society, in which reputation plays a role, is the collective management of risk.

As such, the case will be made that an organization's reputation in small or large part depends on its contribution to society's collective ability to manage risk. Along the way, these themes will be connected to discussions of corporate society responsibility, credibility, and legitimacy; stakeholder expectations; and the mix of management and communication principles to make society more fully functioning.

In all of that analysis, a staking point will be the argument that organizations' reputations, by whatever metrics, come down to their ability to earn and justify the community franchise to operate as an artificial citizen by aligning their interests with those of others and in doing so meeting the expectations of those others.

Issues Management: Managing in Response to Issues

Examining what he believed to represent the history of modern management through the lens of issue management, Chase (1984) claimed that the fourth revolution bringing business to where it was in the mid-1980s could be summarized in the following way: "The fourth revolution is the growing recognition that management of policy is as important as the management of people and profit, that it requires new and teachable skills, and that the disciplines of issue/policy management are vital to corporate and institutional survival in a politicized age" (p. xiii). A decade later, advocates of issues management would incorporate reputation into the corpus of what needs to be managed, along with people, profit, and policy/issue. In fact, one could argue that even in the 1980s, reputation was becoming an "issue" or issues raised by business critics were having reputational impact. In fact, that was the battleground of the emerging disciplines of business ethics and CSR.

Although discussed primarily as business ethics by business executives and academics, CSR was entering the SIM literature as well. Chase (1984) noted that "by 1983 more than 200 companies (of the *Fortune* 1,000) have formally published their creeds of 'Corporate Social Responsibility' and maintain Board-level committees by the same or related names" (p. 13). In this sense, responses by management to changing operating conditions were reactionary, not proactive:

> But what they had failed to understand was that the *definition* of corporate social

responsibility was largely the creature of their adversaries. The problem became how to write such a creed in terms that would be acceptable to the Ralph Naders and the ubiquitous corporate critics. (p. 13, italics in the original)

The battle lines were drawn over whether businesses were or were not structured and operating in the public interest. Chase framed the case as questions addressed to managements by activists: "Why should the public trust them to assume leadership in social decision-making? Who appointed them trustees in behalf of the public interest?" (p. 14). In short, although this is not how Chase and others framed the case, we came to ask do businesses have the kind of reputation, as social responsibility, to define the public interest and assert satisfactorily that they know what it is and appreciate the means needed to serve it? Is the private sector reputation positive to the public interest?

In short, if their structures, policies, and behaviors fall short of serving the public interest they must be condemned to have a "bad" corporate reputation. As such, they should be controlled from outside through regulation, legislation, and adjudication. Thus, the allegation is that business is unfit and incapable to control itself to meet or exceed the standards of CSR held by internal (employees, especially whistleblowers) and external stakeholders. Either the private sector has to reduce the legitimacy gap (Sethi, 1977) between corporate behavior and public(s)'s expectation or it will suffer the arrows of scorn, regulation, legislation, and adjudication.

By this logic, a powerful rationale had been established for issues management as a discipline – even applying it to reputation and brand equity. It could contest the issues that were being debated relevant to corporate performance. These could be featured as fact, value/evaluation, and policy. Later (Heath, 2006; Heath and Palenchar, 2009) identification was added to the list of focal considerations for issues management as was the challenge of treating brand equity as both the matter of issue contest and the grounds for justifying an

organization, through its reputation as being worthy of the brand equity it wished to deserve with customers, competitors, and critics.

Issues and Managements' Response

In the midst of an ebullient sense of private sector self-efficacy following the Great Depression and the allied victory in WWII, criticism came from every point of view to damn the legitimacy of business and its impact on society. This burst of criticism caught managements off guard. The criticism centered on public policy lapses and violations of the public trust. Although the criticism centered on public policy challenges, typically calls for higher standards of regulation, close attention to the discourse of the era would reveal that corporate reputation was also on the line.

Early on, as it associated issues management with public affairs, the Public Affairs Council (1978) described it as "a program that a company uses to increase its knowledge of the public policy process and enhance the sophistication and effectiveness of its involvement in that process" (p. 1). The Council endorsed the now-standard issues management model that consists of (1) monitoring the public policy arena to determine what trends will demand a reorientation of corporate policy and communication, (2) identifying those issues of greatest potential importance to the organization, (3) evaluating their operational and financial impacts through issues analysis, (4) prioritizing and establishing company policy positions by coordinating and assisting senior management decision making, (5) creating the company response from among a range of issue-change strategy options, and (6) implementing the plans through issue action programming.

Such language and strategy at the inception of corporate issues engagement centered on public policy battle with reputational undercurrents. The reputational dimension as such was nearly 20 years down the road. First, the task was to both influence public policy and learn how to respond to it as a changing operating environment in a way that served the public interest above and through businesses' self-interests. The search was for order, collaboration, and interdependence.

What is an issue? That question is essential to public policy, but not irrelevant to discussions of reputation. Taking a rhetorical stance, Heath and Nelson (1986) focused on issues as contestable matters of fact, value, and policy. Thus, debates over public policy addressed what is true and known to be the case, such as environmental damage. Controversy also centered on evaluative/value standards, perhaps reducible to broad categories of safety, fairness, equality, and environmental quality – even quality of life. Each of these has a reputational component, as does fact if we include factual battles over what organizations do or do not do as part of their operations. For instance, we do not debate product safety, but the debate can center on whether a product – especially its ingredients or design – is safe. Thus, by 2010, we agree as a society that lead at "significant levels of dose response" is unsafe as an ingredient in paint, especially that which one finds on children's toys. But what about phthalates or bisphenol A (BPA)?

Finally, in terms of the issue troika mentioned earlier, we come to the matter of policy, what should or must be done if a legitimacy gap exists – either the organization at the dysfunctional end of that model must change what it does and how it operates to reduce the gap, or the expectations used to judge business activities needs to be changed. A third option is to correct misperceptions (inaccurate interpretations) of what the organization does because mistaken understanding results when a company is "not guilty" as charged of some violation of expectation. As such, policy can be public: regulation, legislation, or judicial restraint. It can also be individual, such as decisions to buy/not buy products that are seen as violating customers' CSR standards, such as safety. It could also be a matter of employee choice; companies with better reputations are believed to be better places to work. Both of the individual policy choices, however, can be limited by the availability of competing products/services and choices for employment. Sometimes individual choice is simply not a corrective, especially if the decision chain lacks transparency or alternatives are not available. But, making alternative products available, for instance, in such commercial situations is a way for organizations to recover their reputation or improve it, even to create it. More on that topic will be discussed later.

The logic that developed along these lines is that public policy solutions are sought to reduce legitimacy gaps when key publics (even inter- and intra-industry) doubt the willingness and/or ability of private sector organizations (and governmental as well as nonprofit) to operate or change operations in proper and constructive ways. Thus, not only were the reputations of key businesses such that stakeholders disfavored them but the critics also believed that organizations were incapable or unwilling (or both) to change without external influence and control. As such, part of the battle over crisis is the concern for businesses' ability and willingness to control themselves in ways that do not damage their legitimacy and reputations.

Setting the foundation for contemporary discussion of SIM, Jaques (2010) observed that "When issue management was becoming established in the late 1970s and early 1980s, its founders explicitly envisaged a discipline that would enable corporate and business associations to proactively deal with issues that affect them, rather than merely reacting to such issues" (p. 435). Jaques reasoned that "*issue management is not about how to manage an issue, but how to manage because of an issue*" (p. 435, italics in the original). That distinction in the evolution of the discipline is crucial.

The key to that process is for managements not to presume that the business sector can "manage" issues to its exclusive or narrow benefit, but in fact must adapt to changing conditions through its strategic business planning and the set of CSR principles it adopts and implements (see also Heath, 1997; Heath and Palenchar, 2009).

Early in the evolution of this discipline, Chase (1984) defined an issue as "an unsettled matter which is ready for decision" (p. 38). Set against this definition, Jaques analyzed what he called the disputation approach – the definition of issues as contestable matters. In addition to those choices, he found the expectation gap theme, based on competing CSR standards and the perceived willingness and ability of the targets of criticism to achieve constructive change. Jaques also considered what he called the impact theme which is based on Brown's (1979) seminal discussion for the Conference Board. Brown's discussion reads as follows: "An issue is a condition or pressure, either internal or external to an organization that, if it continues, will have a significant effect on the functioning of the organization or its future interest" (p. 1). One can view Brown's analysis as not discounting the other versions of issues, but it adds the important feature that change motivation may not only be the result specifically of dispute or contested CSR standards, but may also result from "conditions" or "pressures" that can dramatically change management challenges and strategic responses. This latter position makes salient the discussion of factors relevant to strategic business management, including reputation management.

Such analysis makes a solid bridge to discussions of risk, the theme of the next section. It also connects our discussion to a trend in the C-Suite starting in the 1990s, at least, which led to the discipline relevant to strategic management called risk management. These "conditions" can challenge management and become part of the discourse that defines issues specifically as well as contests in the wrangle over public policy and private sector strategic management policy. How issues work out through discourse becomes part of a dynamic set of conditions to be addressed by management teams employing issues management as part of strategic management, including the dynamics of changing stances on mission, vision, and CSR. From this foundation, it is a small step to connect, or reconnect, reputation to the equation. But first, we add to our analyti-cal foundation by further discussion of risk management and communication.

Risk and Managements' Response

Risk became part of the issues management process through specific analysis in the 1990s (Heath, 1997; see especially chapter 20; see also Heath and Palenchar, 2009). Following key events in the 1980s (Three Mile Island, MIC release in India, oil spill off the California coast, and the Exxon Valdez), risk as a topic and rationale for strategic management response became a vital aspect of management, governmental, activist, and academic discussion.

Essential to this discussion is the proposition that the rationale for society is its role in the collective management of risk. Authors, especially Mary Douglas (1992) and Ulrich Beck (1992, 1999), reasoned that society organizes as it does for the collective management of risk. Risk is a matter of uncertainty. It is event or outcome specific and follows the logic that risk is traditionally defined by uncertainty: what can happen, at what probability, to which risk bearers, in what way and when, and to what magnitude? Here lies the challenge of risk that demands applications of sound science generated and discussed with stakeholder culture implications. How such issues work themselves out can affect the image/reputation and product acceptance in marketing and public policy contexts.

Central to issues of risk management, assessment, and communication, researchers have asked what level of risk is safe enough (Fischhoff *et al.*, 1978). Beyond this challenge, or taking the next step by combining CSR and risk management/communication, another question is asked, how fair is safe enough (Rayner and Cantor, 1987)? Within or because of these parameters, risks can become issues, issues can become risks, and issues can become crises, crises can become issues. Crises can be defined as risks manifested. So, we have the logic for treating issues, risks, and crises as corners of an analytic triangle (Heath, 1997; Heath and Palenchar, 2009).

That connection is not only the basis for the latest positioning of SIM for public policy adjustments, but it also lays the foundation for connecting SIM and reputation, which was not the original intention of the pioneers. But by the mid- to late 1990s, practitioners were making a connection between issues and image/reputation, especially on a risk and crisis management foundation. The logic was that as attacks/discussions of ethical performance, CSR, abounded in general and specific to each business, they or it was vulnerable for discourse having a negative effect on profit and share value. Violations of expectations for risk management could bring the ire of critics to assault businesses' reputations. Under such analysis, share value could suffer and appeals for regulation could become salient.

The logic was this: issues must be monitored and responded to for their general operating environment implications and specific impacts – including reputation. Impact was defined as reputation based, and that was measured by rising or falling share value. During this decade, crisis was becoming a salient theme in public relations, and made this SIM topic even more salient, especially as it was issue oriented. Thus, we might have attacks calling for increased regulation which in turn could increase the cost of doing business but not increase revenue. Thus, at a specific company, or by industry, regulation (legislation or litigation) might result in a lowered share value. More specific to crisis per se, the logic was that either because of attack or blunder on the part of the organization, its policies/management actions could result in discrediting financial analyst assessment, and thereby lowered share value. Consultancies offered cases where attacks and blunders caused millions of dollars of share value decline, and even the end to businesses. One of the cases of the latter kind was Union Carbide, the company responsible for the MIC release in India. It was eventually bought by Dow.

Also, the literature, academic and professional, was full of cases related, for instance, to tobacco and asbestos. Bankruptcies, trusts, superfund sites, and other business activities became part of the business and public policy culture. Matters of the cost of regulation, litigation, and judicial decisions became part of the trend to globalization of markets and the motives for companies and industries to flee certain regulatory environments. It was even the case that new plants in a developing country were cheaper than rebuilding and remediating in the United States, for instance. The dynamics of the private sector began to change dramatically. Risk, crisis, and issues were a troika pulling the private sector cart.

Parallel to those trends was another, to feature reputation and reputation management, as a major concern for the C-Suite, consultancies, and eventually academics. We find emerging discussions linking reputation and SIM, as was the case for Heath's (2002) chapter entitled "The Importance of Issues Management and Environmental Scanning for Corporate Image." This sort of analysis continues and is updated by new editions and discussion in journals such as *Corporate Reputation Review*.

Heath's discussion, often typical of others, focused on the legitimacy gap: companies that do not suffer a legitimacy gap have a good reputation; those that suffer a legitimacy gap have a bad one. The sorts of cases Heath (2002) offered in his analysis of the connections between issues and reputation centered on business blunders, crises, where companies were found to be at fault in their efforts to help stakeholders manage risks. One case was the co-branding initiative by Intel where it encouraged computer manufacturers to use Intel components and note that fact on packaging – co-branding. Intel was riding high, an excellent company with little or no legitimacy gap. Then, a computer expert found flaws in Intel chips through analysis requiring repeated computations by multiple computers. This analysis revealed computational errors – a legitimacy gap. Another case addressed the issue of consumer safety created by Playtex Company.

Considered one of the best companies for creating and marketing products to be used with children, it developed and marketed what were called sippy cups. They were child and parent friendly because they were spill proof. These cups added to the brand equity of Playtex because they reduced and eliminated spills while allowing beverage on demand for small children. The legitimacy indictment was twofold. One was that parents could load the cups with sugary liquids, making them available to children all day – leading to dental problems. Second, cups could be left in places where the contents could spoil – hot cars and under furniture. Parents could find children consuming liquids that were not fresh. Such legitimacy problems are tricky. The product worked as Playtex claimed and parents desired. But it led to other risks, and to crisis.

Regulation, legislation, and litigation were unneeded. The marketplace would serve as the correction. Reputation was on the line. Playtex had to aggressively communicate with parents and caregivers to monitor the cups. Do not load them with sugary drinks; use water to hydrate children. Do not let the contents become soured and spoiled. Quick and proactive recovery was the salve needed for reputation management. That was not the normal circumstances for SIM as conceptualized, but led to a very real application of the logics discovered and researched over two decades. Also, if reputation is maintained or recovered, then regulation and other sanctions is less needed; so the logic went.

Thus, we have the tools and philosophies of SIM augmented by attention to crisis and risk communication and management. Rather than being defensive and resistant to change, change management was the solution. How could the need for change be determined early enough to avoid substantial reputational damage, and even the prospect of regulation – such as banning products? Issues monitoring and high CSR standards coupled to effective issue communication were the solution to reputation management in a risk and crisis context. As Jaques (2010) noted, issue management implies managing because of an issue not "managing the issue" to the narrow and exclusive interest of the enterprise. Thus, we have the logics of risk management coming to the rescue, as C-Suite planning and management as well as proactive communication. All of this is set in the context that companies are reputationally committed to serving society's effort to collectively manage risk – or they should be. Failing to do so puts the enterprise itself at "risk" – because of a daunting legitimacy gap.

Reputation and Managements' Response

By definition, an issue is a point of controversy, a dispute – and/or a set of conditions. From the early years in the life of modern issues management, the discipline was built on issues relevant to stakeholder participation, savvy management based on high standards of corporate responsibility, issue monitoring, and issue communication. As such, reputation, identity, image, or brand equity, as the case might be, was destined to be a matter of how the organization, especially businesses, behaved and how well it communicated – meeting others' expectations relevant to issues, CSR standards, and/or conditions. This analytical foundation is simple to say, but daunting to sustain given the plethora of critics and the absence of universal CSR standards to define legitimacy. So, part of communication was and continues to be devoted to discourse relevant to such standards, as well as whether and how organizations meet or fall short of such standards as stakeholder expectations. Therein is the substance (content and meaning) of corporate reputation management.

From the early years, issue communication was in various ways claimed by experts in advertising. In part, the assumption was reputation was the battleground. If a company or industry was thought to be "good," having a positive reputation, then no issue indictment would be sustainable. Such was the logic because part of the early rationale for issues management was that once key publics learned more and "came to their senses," they would realize that business was "actually doing a good job" at least in the opinion of senior managements.

Factors that key stakeholders use to assess a company's image may not be controversial. The controversy may more specifically result from failures of specific businesses and/or industries to meet stakeholder definitional expectations of reputation. If controversy exists regarding an organization's image, it may be less of a matter of which criteria should be used to judge it than concerns about whether the organization meets those criteria. Considering ingredients relevant to the attitudes that constitute corporate image, Garbett (1981) voiced an agentic approach to the matter as he defined corporate image advertising by stressing its unique outcomes:

1. To educate, inform, or impress the public with regard to the company's policies, functions, facilities, objectives, ideals, and standards.
2. To build favorable opinion about the company by stressing the competence of the company's management, its scientific know-how, manufacturing skills, technological progress, product improvements, and contribution to social advancement and public welfare; and, on the other hand, to offset unfavorable publicity and negative attitudes.
3. To build up the investment qualities of the company's securities or to improve its financial structure.
4. To sell the company as a good place in which to work, often in a way designed to appeal to college graduates or to people with certain skills. (p. 13)

Thus, as early as the beginning of the 1980s, after the Public Affairs Council's definition of SIM but before the publication of Chase's (1984) book, counselors were attempting to sort the mix of image, issues, and legitimacy.

As noted earlier, some focused primarily, even exclusively on public policy battles, but others saw the challenge to be centered on image or reputation. To some extent, the difference in perspective is central to that between advertising and public relations/public affairs. The former tended to feature image and reputation, whereas the latter saw public policy positions as central although not independent of reputation and especially legitimacy.

In the early years of modern SIM conceptualization, image and issue were cloudy or confusing matters, but relevant topics for considering during the early years of this discipline, and the rationale for its growth. Some of the controversy focused on what is issue communication and what is image communication. Those categories – however different, overlapping, and inseparable – were in part based on standards created by and implemented through the Internal Revenue Service, the Federal Trade Commission, and the Federal Communications Commission (Heath and Nelson, 1983a,b, 1985, 1986). Simplifying a very complex matter, suffice it to say here that image communication was tax deductible, issue communication was not. However, issue communication is protected speech and image is not. Thus, managements and regulators were confronted with sorting chaff from wheat – or apples from oranges.

Without a templated definition of image, reputation, or reputation management, one is left to select and self-define this matter (within guidelines of regulatory bodies). That may not be the best approach to participating in a coherent discourse on this topic. But, then, common threads seem to appear in the fabric of that topic, which is such contested ground that a chapter could be devoted to the analysis, comparison, rejection, refutation, repudiation, and synthesis of a huge body of literature relevant to the nature of and role of image, identity, and reputation to corporate performance. Realizing that image (reputation, identity, and such) is relevant to the literature on evaluative perception, in general, discussants see it variously as powerful/trivial, based on fact/totally manipulated, and definitionally relevant to brand equity and selling points. In a word, image and/or reputation as a point of discussion is supported by literature, a vast literature, that considers attitude as a combination of evaluation and subjective belief, both of which are variously and interdependently relevant to proof and conjecture.

As attitude, image (and its relevant substitutes) is a term with motivational implications. As a subjective belief, it is relevant to empirical substantiation. It is both the foundation of and result of identification. And to the extent that human cognition cannot operate without the phenomena associated to what is called attitude with its attachment to perception and understanding, the field of psychology and communication, including marketing, advertising, and public relations, simply cannot ignore the concept or dismiss it.

O'Connor (2005) drew on materials specific to the topic of reputation management to define it as "the strategic use of corporate resources to positively influence the attitudes, beliefs, opinions, and actions of multiple corporate stakeholders, including consumers, employees, investors, and the media" (p. 745). One cannot proceed in such discussions by ignoring the fact that reputation can be "negative" and cannot actually be controlled or managed but can be influenced by what organizations do and say, and what is said about them and done in regard to them. In fact, scandal has reputational impact which is perhaps the result of failed management and/ or reputation management – or even malicious and unfounded attack. We also need to cautiously keep in mind agentic efforts by managements to control and shape image set in the context of community agency where such matters follow the chaos and vagaries of public (and private) discourse.

Broadly, Carroll (2008) observed that

> corporate (or organizational) reputation refers to what is generally said about an organization. Corporate reputation is different than organizational identity by its focus on what other people say about the organization, rather than what the organization itself or its members say. Corporate reputation is distinguished from organizational image in the sense that it is generally more durable and substance-based rather than fleeting and impression-based. (p. 1019)

In his analysis, Carroll acknowledged that a tension (and therefore correspondence or difference) can occur between the actional nature of the organization (what is factual about what it does and says) and the interpretation of the organization through key publics' perceptual screens.

The paradox opens the door exactly to the connection between SIM and corporate reputation. Recall the discussion earlier that issues are relevant to fact, evaluation, policy – actional responses whether public policy or individual actions including buying or consumer behavior – and identification (association or disassociation, as well as the propensity of humans to share perspectives with what they believe to have positive reputation and vice versa). Thus, the fact (empirical rationale) of what the organization does, the conditions it creates and responds to, can produce highly subjective beliefs or those that can be demonstrated and verified. Thus, for instance, the excellent performance of a computer chip can be measured and judged empirically.

Evaluations (attitudes and values) are central to reputational attribution because of the potentiality of defining the organization in terms that have positive or negative (even neutral) valence. These are standard assumptions relevant to attitudes, as is the likelihood that beliefs associated with positive or negative valence predict behavioral intention and/or action. Humans tend to prefer that which is positive and avoid that which they deem negative (although that construct is not universal). And, we know that individuals can experience cognitive involvement (the desire to create and use attitudes to guide choice toward rewards and away from negative outcomes; see especially Petty and Cacioppo, 1986) on both a positive valence (support) or negative valence (oppose) as well as paying attention to and giving consideration of communication sources both by low- and high-involved individuals (Heath and Douglas, 1990, 1991).

The upshot of such action then is to be able (in whatever persona) to judge an organization's reputation as being worthy/unworthy of earning resources it needs or being denied them. All of this fits and derives from the legendary work by Martin Fishbein and Icek Azjen to develop and prove the theories of information integration (Fishbein and Azjen, 1975), of reasoned action (Azjen and Fishbein, 1980), and of planned behavior (Azjen, 1985, 1991), as well as the theory of identification and terministic screens argued by Kenneth Burke (1968, especially chapter 3, 1969). (For extensive discussion of the relevant persuasion theory and research, see Dillard and Pfau, 2002; O'Keefe, 2002.)

Simply put, humans cannot act without judgmental or decision-relevant perceptions of reality. Especially insofar as humans have linguistic skills, their terms as well as even the possibility of nonlinguistic perceptions help or facilitate decision making. Moreover, assessments of legitimacy, the foundational essence of corporate reputation, depends on the ability to "know" something about an organization and thereby judge whether that "knowledge" warrants support or opposition (in varying degrees, not as a binary decision) relevant to the expectations (attitudes) of various stakeholders and stakeseekers.

As additional theoretical foundation for the perspective taken in the chapter, it is important to consider how critics of image, reputation, and identity as topics can be dismissive for various reasons rather than insightful and analytical. One of the first problems is to attribute agentic power to organizations. This assumption looks at such matters from the strategic perspective of managements of organizations. Reputation-sensitive judgments can be and are based on attributions about companies and other organizations. The rationale for using communication to manufacture reputation, image, and identity can result from the desire to forge opinions even against the cognitive decision-making preferences of highly involved audiences.

As the overview discussed earlier suggests, it is best to look at the "persuasive influence" and role of persuasion (even manipulation and control) from the audiences' (stakeholders, publics, markets, critics, targets, etc.) perspectives. The logic of such analysis is that people

for various reasons create impressions, opinions, perceptions, attitudes, beliefs, intentions, and support/opposition because they must, and not because the organizations must control or even shape them.

The entire logic, for instance, of an epistemic or cognitive approach to communication, as in the case of the uncertainty reduction theory of interpersonal communication, reasons that people require and therefore make attributions about relational partners. If this is true, and it is, for interpersonal communication, then it is also true of organizational communication – whether based on messages or actions/performance or both. Conrad (1992) provided one of the best analyses using attribution theory as he discussed management efforts relevant to corporate image or reputation management in the context of investor relations. He offered case analysis that managements in that context apply the classic logic of attribution in their annual reports and other financial communication. They attribute success to their management acuity and place blame on external conditions if their plans, or as their plans, fail to produce results favorable to analyst evaluations and recommendations to buy, hold, or sell publicly traded stock.

Whether soundly or not, based on evidence and reason or pure myth and conjecture, humans need anchoring perceptions in relationships. Thus, and for that reason, they acquire and consider information as it is relevant to making decisions that lead to positive outcomes and away from negative ones. As such, therein lies the overarching rationale for corporate reputation. And, as risk management is an individual, corporate, and community incentive, individuals who judge and respond to corporate entities do so in the context of risk assessment, management, and communication. As the rationale for such cognitions, behavioral intention, and behaviors, we find then the role for issues management coupled with risk management and communication as the rationale for collective thought, communication, and action in society. Society is organized on the rationale that it serves individual and collective risk management. Businesses and other organizations are thought to be legitimate to the extent to which they help stakeholders manage risks.

Applications: Reputation as Legitimacy Is Always a Bumpy Road Fraught with Contention and Uncertainty

To finalize the analysis established earlier, the applications of SIM to reputation management will be explored with special attention to legitimacy. In such matters, we need to realize that reputation, as they say, is as reputation does – and how it is perceived and attributed. That means that not every audience, market, public, and such will hold the same perception and evaluation of any organization's corporate reputation. Also, some will be positive, others will be relatively neutral. Others may be quite negative. Lots of people will be able to make some judgment of various and all organizations, perhaps with some priming or cuing, but some of the reputations are irrelevant to the issue at hand. For instance, many businesses, especially those specific to business-to-business (B-2-B) marketing, might be outside of specific radar of most people. Those reputations, then, are relevant only to the context of B-2-B marketing.

For instance, there are many oil field services companies. Three became well known during the BP Maconda Prospect well explosion, fire, and massive release in the Gulf of Mexico in 2010. They are Halliburton, Transocean, and Cameron. Most people had little or no opinion and knowledge of these companies, or the government agencies that were variously involved in the event, except the Coast Guard. Nevertheless, with varying degrees of cognitive involvement, people judged the reputation of various organizations. BP took the biggest hit, although one member of the United States House of Representatives apologized for the massive levy placed against BP for the cost of clean up. People, such as those who live in Houston, Texas, would have various opinions

of the key companies because of their proximity to the oil industry. Other people around the globe would have little or no opinion, but could be triggered to have an opinion either by each company's association with the blowout or with the cue that they are oil field services companies, serving "big oil." As well as knowledge, evaluation, and policy positions on this matter, people held various identifications with the companies, and federal or state government agencies. So, reputation is complex. And, in truth, the perceptions as the foundation for reputations might have little to no consequence on matters, except to the degree that key observers held stakes, which they could grant or withhold to the various companies.

Since BP is the only retail player in the mix, it is the only company, for instance, that customers could punish. It is unlikely that the vast array of supporters or opponents relevant to the matter held resources that Transocean, Halliburton, or Cameron needed. Thus, we can argue that reputation is as reputation does.

As a matter of SIM, reputation relates to legitimacy and is a contestable matter, whether disputation, expectation, or impact (Jaques, 2010), as discussed earlier. In such matters, reputation (and its variation, image) depends on varying degrees of support – factual justification either from the point of the organization (agentic), those who are making the perceptual judgment based on attribution, and commentators (supporters and opponents) in the agency of the community.

Setting a critical perspective for this matter seen through the lens of image, Cheney (1992) pointed to logics of a Western managerial philosophy that can be dysfunctional to meaningful image (reputation) in the effort to be and be seen as legitimate. Cheney observed, "we live in an image dominated culture" (p. 170). "Our large organizations invest time, money, and energy in crafting appropriate and compelling images for their various publics, defining identities as well as styles" (pp. 170–171). Drawing on the work of Baudrillard (1988), Cheney noted how image could be crafted with varying degrees of factual justification in a manner that has implications for the legitimacy of the organization in light of its reward dependency.

Parsing the concept of image, Baudrillard (1988) reasoned that at least four levels could be conceptualized: (1) image as reality – the extent to which it reflects or represents reality – capable of empirical judgment and corresponding attributional frames; (2) a mask or perversion of reality, as in the case that the asserted image or its enactment simply and profoundly does not fit with empirical reality (a lie; the organization is not what it asserts itself to be); (3) a mask that is substituted or proposed in the absence of empirical proof, the test of reality (a crafted image for which evidence is asserted but the evidence is not probative); and (4) the sort of asserted image that bears no relationship to empirical reality and so the image becomes its own crafted reality (see Cheney, 1992, pp. 172–173, for extended description and critical analysis). The question, then, is what is the organization, as in the sense that it is what it is, but what is it? And, is that sense of the organization justification for its alleged and/or needed test of legitimacy?

Among the several (and reputation is like a many prismed gem) aspects of legitimacy which is a normative matter, Boyd (2009) featured two: "in order for an organization to be seen as operating in a manner consistent with social norms, it must be perceived as useful (competent) and responsible" (p. 157). These two dimensions of acceptance (usefulness and responsibility) are keenly relevant to the underpinning rationale for the organization to exist and operate in "the public interest," the corporate rationale for its approved existence. As such, it is legitimate to the extent that it participates appropriately/responsibly and effectively (usefully) in the collective management of risk. Thus, legitimacy, issues, and risk are fundamentally interconnected as a singular, but multidimensional rationale for organizations' resource dependency.

Keeping in mind Boyd's (2009) two dimensions of legitimacy (utility and responsibility), we can add to that list and or see those concepts through various prisms. Thus, Vaara *et al.* (2006) distinguished five "legitimation strate-

gies: (1) normalization, (2) authorization, (3) rationalization, (4) moralization, and (5) narrativization" (p. 789). These critical attributions offer guidelines to help us understand what can or must be achieved as we decide which and when enactment and discursive strategies serve effectively and ethically as legitimacy cues. Their analysis is based on this premise: "Legitimacy is a prerequisite for institutionalization and institutionalization is key to understanding the resources of legitimacy" (p. 791). The key to understanding this paradox rests with language and co-created, shared meaning. "From this perspective, *legitimacy means a discursively created sense of acceptance in specific discourses or orders of discourse*" (p. 793, italics in the original).

Based on this foundation, Vaara *et al.* featured the importance of their five dimensions. (1) Legitimacy by normalization "seeks to render something legitimate by exemplarity" (p. 798). (2) "Authorization is legitimation by reference to authority" (p. 799). As such, legitimacy is derived from the imprimatur of one or more empowering agencies. (3) "Rationalization is legitimation by reference to the utility or function of specific actions or practices" (p. 800). (4) "Moralization is legitimation that refers to specific values" (p. 801). (5) Narrativization is legitimation that occurs when "telling a story provides evidence of acceptable, appropriate, or preferential behavior" (p. 802). The potency of narrativization results from dramatic structures that make some matter concrete and thematic. Thus, the power bases of legitimacy become the result of and the playing out of narratives that define the norms of influence and shape interpretations (Heath, 1994) used as the rationale for enlightened choice relevant to one of more contestable matter, a matter of ethics/CSR, and/or impact under specific conditions – the ability of the organization to manage risks it creates or those created by contextual events.

One of the salient themes in a narrative approach to corporate communication and reputation management is the role that others' expectations play in the enactment of organizations as narratives. Although organizations certainly participate in the shaping of the framing expectations relevant to perceptions of legitimacy and reputation, the challenge of enactment is to know the expectations others hold relevant to organizational behavior. Those expectations need to be central to strategic planning and management, based in substantial ways on alignment of interests through wisely enacted missions/visions. Herein lies the challenge of knowing and accomplishing alignment of interests in ways that demonstrate an organization's usefulness and its willingness and ability to shoulder responsibility to resource management.

On the matter of corporate reputation, as this book attests, many perspectives can be and are taken to help us understand this complex topic. The view advanced here, within the tradition of SIM, features the concept of legitimacy. It does not discount the agentic role of each organization to design (largely through its mission and vision as the rationale for its existence as an artificial citizen) and enact its reputation (often through marketing and advertising). But, a SIM perspective prefers to see that matter as the product of multiple dimensions, fact based, and in the context of multiple voices reflecting and expressing many perspectives, variously supportive and opposing.

With the dimensions identified (but likely not definitive) earlier, we can pose a matrix. One axis is composed of the four key conditions of issues management action and discourse as multivocal rhetorical enactment (Heath, 2001). The conditions on that axis are platforms of (1) fact, (2) evaluation, (3) policy as resource management in the public and private sectors, and (4) identification (the processes of identity matching and interest alignment). On the continuum, we ask by what facts can a reputation be disputed, evaluated, and translated into the rationale of support/opposition and identification?

The other axis consists of conditions of legitimacy, starting with utility and responsibility (Boyd, 2009). These factors or conditions on that axis relate to risk management: is the organization's enactment of its mission and vision responsive to CSR standards that lead key stakeholders to assess it as willing and able to meet its responsibility as cocreated or codefined and to what extent is it willing and able to serve the utility of risk management in service of each community where it operates? That last question, but not ignoring the first, includes matters of product and service design and marketing. It is easy to imagine that marketing is judged by the standards of legitimacy relevant to risk management. Here we can think quickly of matters of operational and product safety, as well as the efficacy of products and services to reduce risks and produce benefits. That applies, for instance, in a range of business conditions from cold remedies, to banking services, and to the production of energy that benefits the community and does not harm it. (Thus, we have pharmaceutical product efficacy claims, but lists of potential risks associated with product use.)

To these items, we can add those proposed by Vaara et al. (2006): normalization, authorization, rationalization, moralization, and narrativization.

Normalization refers to the process by which an organization works to demonstrate itself as exemplary – therefore deserving mission/vision relevant resources – because of its ability to bring about desired results. Here we have the tradition of the A student, not merely competent but outstanding and therefore deserving of special recognition and regard as part of its reputation.

Authorization refers to the process by which an organization is justified by the authority of others' judgment and affirmation or opposition – especially government agencies. The organization withstands the legitimacy test of deserving affirmation by public and private sector voices for accomplishing what it is designed and managed to do. Here the test of the organization arises as it works to meet the standards set by the community through the authority of its regulatory, legislative, and judicial systems.

Rationalization features the pragmatics of utility. This is the attribute of heavy lifting, the ability to hold its own and do what needs to be done. The legitimacy arises from and justifies its enfranchisement. As mentioned earlier, we have oil field services companies, as those involved in the Deep Horizon event in the Macando Prospect. Can the organizations discover hydrocarbons through seismic investigation and drilling processes and produce those products safely (to humans and the environment) in ways that serve the needs for energy which have been developed as collective management of risk?

Moralization is the process of knowing as well as meeting or exceeding the legitimacy standards of value judgment. The SIM tradition has featured fairness, equality, safety, and environmental quality – quality of life as molar concepts to ethical judgment. Here we have the rhetorical tradition of the organization seeking first to be good by doing good, being worthy of praise rather than censure or blame. As in the rhetorical tradition, organizations – like people – earn praise and blame for their actions, and the outcomes and impacts of those actions. Here is an important ethical dimension of legitimacy.

Narrativization is the process of engaging with other voices in the cocreation of socially constructed interpretations of reality. In one sense, this legitimacy dimension responds to the dramatic lines of "once upon a time" and leading to the continuing best-case scenario of "happily ever after." As organizations, private sector businesses not only enact narratives relevant to their legitimate operations, but also work with other voices to cocreate those narratives. One dimension of the legitimacy battle is to work against or seek to avoid competing and conflicting narratives. Such narratives, as their substance, can and do feature variations of the legitimacy themes mentioned in other dimensions: responsibility, utility, normalization, authorization, rationalization, and moralization.

Thus, by postulating this matrix, with its two axes, we set the groundwork for developing complex analytical and research relevant conditions to study and refine the processes of corporate reputation as SIM.

Conclusions

The approach to corporate reputation championed in this chapter features the concept as dynamic and the process surrounding it, from within each key organization to the voices of the community around it, as resting on the premise that the process is dynamic, not static. It is essentially the process of dynamic change management as organizations adapt to and shape the community expectations where they operate, and as relevant to that community's risk management.

As rhetorical enactment (Heath, 2001), the discourse has its agentic moment as each organization, through what it says and does, asserts the rationale for its reputation into the community where resources reside to be sought and allocated. Each organization asserts itself into the lifeworld of interested parties, in a manner that is recurring and (re)presentational. And, thus, the reputation that is hammered out on the anvil of social acceptability as legitimate is the result of assertion, counter assertion: action, reaction, and the lesson learned. In this way, the process is inherently dialogic although various organizations invariably work to make it monologic.

One of the icons in the development and refinement of issues management, Ewing (1987) reasoned: "Issues management is about power. It is about the power that controls the new bottom line of all American corporations – optimal profits and public acceptance" (p. 1). As he continued, he observed:

> It is about management of the legitimate power a corporation has over its total environment, when it is willing to use it. And it is about the power others have over the same environment and future of the corporation – power that can be shared through foresight and informed planning. (p. 1)

As such, the power the organization has depends on its ability to derive from its communities of operations the resources it needs to continue, and even to prosper, as legitimately deserving of those resources.

In the discussion of corporate reputation, some can rightly be concerned – even outraged – by attention to power on the part of private sector organizations. However contentious such matters are, they rightly address the willingness and ability of organizations to earn through reduced legitimacy gap the power resources they need to operate in the public interest – the ultimate rationale for organizations whether public and private. The challenge to management, Ewing cautioned, centers on the worst of management failures. "The ignorance in question is management's lack of knowledge of what is going on in all the corporation's relevant environments, the social and political as well as the economic" (p. 2). As said, it is not enough to seek power but to know the price of such resources. That price is the opinion in the collectivity where the organization operates. Savvy management begins with knowing that price and being willing to pay it. As the saying goes, and it is relevant for corporate reputation management, one must know and be willing to pay the piper's price if one wants to dance.

Such insight is the bottom line of SIM's approach to corporate reputation management, a key element of change management through risk management in a community of many voices. Those voices define the expectations and examine the extent to which corporations' reputations are a good fit or collide with key stakeholders' expectations. As such, reputation is not sender oriented or agentic alone, but a product of community dialog. Such dialog addresses in various ways relevant matters of concern, CSR standards, and the conditions that serve as incentives, constraints, and rationale for reward allocation.

References

Azjen, I. (1985) From intentions to actions: A theory of planned behavior. In J. Kuhl and J. Beckman (eds), *Action Control: From Cognition to Behavior*. Berlin: Springer-Verlag, pp. 11–39.

Azjen, I. (1991) The theory of planned behavior. *Organizational Behavior and Human Decision Processes*, 50, 179–211.

Azjen, I. and Fishbein, M. (1980) *Understanding Attitudes and Predicting Social Behavior*. Englewood Cliffs, NJ: Prentice Hall.

Baudrillard, J. (1988) Simulacra and simulations. In M. Poster (ed.), *Jean Baudrillard: Selected Writings*. Stanford, CA: Stanford University Press, pp. 166–184.

Beck, U. (1992) *Risk Society: Towards a New Modernity*. London: Sage.

Beck, U. (1999) *World Risk Society*. Cambridge, UK: Polity Press.

Boyd, J. (2009) 756* The legitimacy of a baseball number. In R.L. Heath, E.L. Toth, and D. Waymer (eds), *Rhetorical and Critical Approaches to Public Relations II*. New York: Routledge, pp. 154–169.

Brown, J.K. (1979) *The Business of Issues: Coping with the Company's Environments*. New York: Conference Board.

Burke, K. (1968) *Language as Symbolic Action: Essays on Life, Literature, and Method*. Berkeley, CA: University of California Press.

Burke, K. (1969) *A Rhetoric of Motives*. Berkeley, CA: University of California Press [originally, 1950].

Carroll, C.E. (2008) Corporate reputation. In W. Donsbach (ed.), *The International Encyclopedia of Communication*. Malden, MS: Blackwell, pp. 1019–1021.

Chase, W.H. (1984) *Issue Management: Origins of the Future*. Stamford, CT: Issue Action Publications.

Cheney, G. (1992) The corporate person (re)presents itself. In E.L. Toth and R.L. Heath (eds), *Rhetorical and Critical Approaches to Public Relations*. Hillsdale, NJ: Lawrence Erlbaum Associates, pp. 165–183.

Conrad, C. (1992) Corporate communication and control. In E.L. Toth and R.L. Heath (eds), *Rhetorical and Critical Approaches to Public Relations*. Hillsdale, NJ: Lawrence Erlbaum Associates, pp. 187–204.

Dillard, J. and Pfau, M. (eds) (2002) *The Persuasion Handbook: Developments in Theory and Practice*. Thousand Oaks, CA: Sage.

Douglas, M. (1992) *Risk and Blame*. London: Routledge.

Ewing, R.P. (1987) *Managing the New Bottom Line: Issues Management for Senior Executives*. Homewood, IL: Dow Jones-Irwin.

Fischhoff, B., Slovic, P., Lichtenstein, S., Read, S., and Combs, B. (1978) How safe is safe enough? A psychometric study of attitudes towards technological risks and benefits. *Policy Sciences, 8*, 127–152.

Fishbein, M. and Azjen, I. (1975) *Belief, Attitude, Intention, and Behavior: An Introduction to Theory and Research.* Reading, MA: Addison-Wesley.

Garbett, T. (1981) *Corporate Advertising: The What, the Why, and the How.* New York: McGraw-Hill.

Heath, R.L. (1994) *Management of Corporate Communication: From Interpersonal Contacts to External Affairs.* Hillsdale, NJ: Lawrence Erlbaum Associates.

Heath, R.L. (1997) *Strategic Issues Management: Organizations and Public Policy Challenges.* Thousand Oaks, CA: Sage.

Heath, R.L. (2001) A rhetorical enactment rationale for public relations: The good organization communicating well. In R.L. Heath (ed.), *Handbook of Public Relations.* Thousand Oaks, CA: Sage, pp. 31–50.

Heath, R.L. (2002) The importance of issues management and environmental scanning for corporate image. In P.S. Brønn and R. Wiig (eds), *Corporate Communication: A Strategic Approach to Building Reputation.* Oslo, Norway: Gyldendal Norsk Forlag, pp. 133–150.

Heath, R.L. (2006) A rhetorical theory approach to issues management. In C. Botan and V. Hazleton (eds), *Public Relations Theory II.* Mahwah, NJ: Lawrence Erlbaum Associates, pp. 63–100.

Heath, R.L. and Douglas, W. (1990) Involvement: A key variable to people's reaction to public policy issues. *Journal of Public Relations Research*, 2, 193–204.

Heath, R.L. and Douglas, W. (1991) Effects of involvement on reactions to sources of messages and to message clusters. *Journal of Public Relations Research*, 3, 179–193.

Heath, R.L. and Nelson, R.A. (1983a) An exchange on corporate advertising: Typologies and taxonomies. *Journal of Communication*, 33(Autumn), 114–118.

Heath, R.L. and Nelson, R.A. (1983b) Image/issue advertising tax rules: Understanding the corporate rights. *Public Affairs Review*, 4(94–101), 104–105.

Heath, R.L. and Nelson, R.A. (1985) Image and issue advertising: A corporate and public policy perspective. *Journal of Marketing*, 49(1), 58–68.

Heath, R.L. and Nelson, R.A. (1986) *Issues Management: Corporate Public Policy Making in an Information Society.* Beverly Hills, CA: Sage.

Heath, R.L. and Palenchar, M.J. (2009) *Strategic Issues Management: Organizations and Public Policy Challenges* (2nd ed.). Thousand Oaks, CA: Sage.

Jaques, T. (2010) Embedding issue management: From process to policy. In R.L. Heath (ed.), *SAGE Handbook of Public Relations.* Thousand Oaks, CA: Sage, pp. 435–446.

O'Connor, A. (2005) Reputation management. In R.L. Heath (ed.), *Encyclopedia of Public Relations.* Thousand Oaks, CA: Sage, pp. 745–746.

O'Keefe, D.J. (2002) *Persuasion: Theory and research* (2nd ed.). Thousand Oaks, CA: Sage.

Petty, R.E. and Cacioppo, J.T. (1986) *Communication and Persuasion: Central and Peripheral Routes to Attitude Change.* New York: Springer-Verlag.

Public Affairs Council (1978) *The Fundamentals of Issue Management.* Washington, DC: Author.

Rayner, S. and Cantor, R. (1987) How fair is safe enough? The cultural approach to technology choice. *Risk Analysis*, 7(1), 3–9.

Sethi, S.P. (1977) *Advocacy Advertising and Large Corporations: Social Conflict, Big Business Image, the News Media, and Public Policy.* Lexington, MA: D.C. Heath.

Vaara, E., Tienari, J., and Laurila, J. (2006) Pulp and paper fiction: On the discursive legitimation of global industrial restructuring. *Organizational Studies*, 27(6), 789–810.

33

Form Following Function: Message Design for Managing Corporate Reputations

Peter M. Smudde and Jeffrey L. Courtright

Illinois State University, USA

This project examines the role of specific message-design strategies for the management of corporate reputations. Message design for reputation management is the catalyst for an organization's communication, and this project combines Fombrun and van Riel's (2004) platforms for corporate transparency with Courtright and Smudde's (2009) genre-based analysis of corporate reputation management into a systematic and practical method to understand and create corporate reputation discourse. This chapter establishes a holistic process model of the development of corporate communication texts that are key to an organization's successful and strategic presentation of messages about its reputation and the relationships between organizations and their audiences. The chapter covers culture-based influences that guide message design and discourse selection as cases warrant. The chapter presents a systematic and practical method to understand and create corporate reputation discourse, which would be useful in both academe and industry.

Corporate reputations "reflect how companies are perceived across a broad spectrum of stakeholders" (Fombrun and van Riel, 2004, p. xxvii). What organizations do to ensure their reputations are sound is referred to as "reputation management," and this organizational activity is necessarily communication based and therefore typically handled by corporate communications departments, often in conjunction with other functional areas such as marketing, legal staff, and board of directors. Positive and negative events in the life of any organization reflect on its reason for being as well as direct

people's attention to salient matters about what and why an organization does what it does – for example, financial reporting, product safety, employee satisfaction, and customer relationships. Reputations, then, are earned through organizational action – primarily communicative action – with various stakeholders.

Although scholars have given some attention to communication's role in reputation management (e.g., Brønn and Berg, 2005; Schultz *et al.*, 2000), that role has been, in the main, broadly construed. This is not surprising because this literature of necessity has focused

The Handbook of Communication and Corporate Reputation, First Edition. Edited by Craig E. Carroll.
© 2013 John Wiley & Sons, Inc. Published 2015 by John Wiley & Sons, Inc.

on defining and demarcating the key terms of identity, image, and reputation. Attention to particular communication concerns has been paid to several areas (e.g., visual identity (e.g., van den Bosch *et al.*, 2005); how narratives may build reputation (Dowling, 2006; Vendelø, 1998); the media's role in influencing corporate reputation (Dowling and Weeks, 2008); and how messages chosen during crises relate to reputation (e.g., Coombs, 2007)). The mitigating factor in these areas of reputation management is establishing and maintaining relationships between organizations and their stakeholders, and doing so on as much of an individual basis as possible.

Message design, then, is at the heart of reputation building in such a way that any rhetorical or communication theory (see Ihlen, 2004) may be employed to deepen our understanding of how messages may shape identity in order to influence stakeholders' images and change or sustain corporate reputation (Courtright and Smudde, 2009). What is needed in the literature, however, is examination of the role of specific message-design strategies that work best in the management of corporate reputations. Such strategies also have culture-based influences that guide message design and discourse selection, and these influences are also not well developed in the literature. This project fills this need and extends our work on the intersection of communication tactics, message design, and strategic planning (Smudde and Courtright, 2012).

Published scholarship about corporate reputation makes up a sizable body of knowledge that can and should be reexamined for new insights about message design. This project, then, fills a gap in the literature by showing scholars and practitioners how corporate communication texts (i.e., "corporate discourse genres") are key to the successful and strategic presentation of messages about an organization's reputation and the relationships between organizations and their stakeholders. Two central concepts, trust and transparency, are important to reputation and fold into one another. Trust is a precious commodity that organizations need but can lose in an instant.

As Kiley and Helm (2009) stated in their *BusinessWeek* article, "Trust is the most perishable of assets. Polling in recent months shows that increasing numbers of consumers distrust not just the obvious suspects – the banks – but business as a whole" (p. 38). Indeed, reputation is typically seen as a function of trust, and both are simultaneously cultivated by public relations activities and supported by marketing efforts.

Corporate Reputation Messages and Discourse Creation

As long as internal and external stakeholders need to understand why an organization can be worthy of their trust, those same people demand ways to obtain evidence for trustworthiness in many areas. Organizations, especially large corporations, have been seen as faceless, monolithic things, and that view has not been useful in many ways, especially to understand corporate performance and social value. The concept of transparency emerged and became the framework by which stakeholders virtually "see into" an organization, primarily for how it does what it does and why. As Fombrun and van Riel (2004) argued, "A transparent company allows stakeholders to gain access to all pertinent information needed to make an accurate assessment of the company's current operations and future prospects" (p. 185). The reporting of organizational performance of its operations must be done in a comprehensive, timely, relevant, reliable, and comparable manner, typically according to the rule of law (federal, state, and local). Underlying all these criteria for transparency is forthrightness, or an organization says and does the right thing at the right time in the right ways for the right reasons for the right people. The concept of transparency, then, takes us back to trust because it "enables interested stakeholders to verify the company's claims – thereby guarding against puffery and self aggrandizement" (p. 189).

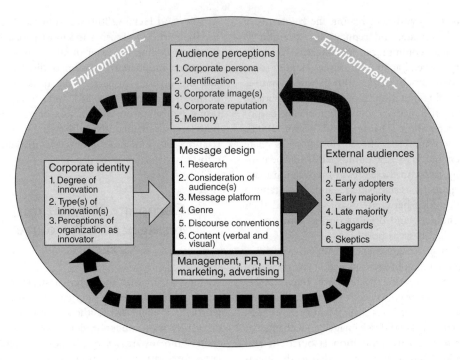

Figure 33.1 Rhetorical model of the reputation management process for innovative organizations. PR, public relations; HR, human resources.

Through it all, organizations manage their reputations through communication. Because the predominant province of reputation management is public relations, the essential knowledge and skillfulness (i.e., "discourse competence") in the ethical use of particular discourse types is key. Moreover, the choice of discourse is driven by rhetorical purpose, not the other way around. In other words, form literally follows function. Smudde and Courtright (2012) argue, in tune with McLuhan and Fiore (1967), that the medium is not necessarily the message: medium and message work together in rhetorical ways that organizations use to inspire cooperation with their stakeholders while also inviting them to celebrate their common ground.

Putting these ideas together about reputation management – trust, transparency, and public relations discourse competence – is the core of this project. We propose a systematic and practical method to understand the rhetorical process for creating specific kinds of

corporate discourse that successfully and strategically present an organization's reputation-related messages within the context of the relationships between organizations and their publics. The method is based on a combination of Fombrun and van Riel's (2004) platforms for corporate transparency with Courtright and Smudde's (2009) rhetorical model of corporate reputation management shown in Figure 33.1. We will explain the model within the context of two reputation-management situations: organizations known for (or wanting to be known for) innovation and organizations facing product recalls.

The corporate reputation literature clearly indicates that corporate identity is an expression of what organizational members explicitly recognize as what the organization stands for – its "unique characteristics – which are rooted in the behaviors of the organization" (van Riel and Balmer, 1997, p. 341). The "identity mix" (communication, symbolism, and behaviors) influences the perceptions of organizational members and external audiences. The model, shown in Figure 33.1, reflects a rhetorical point of view of the process of reputation management for organizations focused on themselves as innovators. The model, first presented by Courtright and Smudde (2009), is comprised of four principal components: corporate identity (i.e., the actual degree of innovation or other salient matter that is literally part of an organization's identity that is enacted and/or recognized by its own members), message design (i.e., the type(s) of innovation(s) or other salient matter that members of selected corporate groups view as central to their organization), external audiences' disposition toward innovation, and audiences' perceptions of the organization.

The left side of the model begins with corporate identity and its link to innovation as an example of one of many salient matters of corporate identity that can be literally tied to an organization. As Cheney and Christensen (2001), Gioia *et al.* (2000), and Hagen (2008) have demonstrated, corporate identity has a reflexive nature as both the product of and influence on organizational communication. So the degree and types of salient matters of corporate identity create perceptions within the organization, and its members have come to associate with the organization's distinctiveness. These perceptions directly influence (indicated by the light gray arrow) the message design process. Only the most competent communication professionals can be successful in this vital part of the reputation management process, for it requires expertise in all matters of planning, writing, execution, and evaluation of corporate discourse.

Message design includes six areas of activity: (1) research about an organization and its situation as perceived internally and externally, which includes extant (even proprietary) studies completed about the organization's environment and personal experiences and expertise in making sense of the salient matters facing any corporate rhetorical exigence; (2) consideration of audiences and their disposition toward the organization and situations it may face, including documented insights from new and/or pre-vious studies about an organization's audiences and stakeholders; (3) key message platform that outlines the core ideas about a particular exigence that must be echoed in all discourse according to (a) a single, central theme or slogan and (b) "proof" points that support the theme/slogan; (4) communication genre choice based on the purposes for communication (i.e., form follows function); (5) discourse conventions/rules to ensure what is said is conveyed in the best way that fits the communication purposes; and (6) content development of messages in both visual and verbal ways according to discourse conventions.

Instrumental in this message-design process and augmenting Courtright and Smudde's (2009) original design is Fombrun and van Riel's (2004) platform for corporate transparency, which concerns an organization's products and services, financial performance, leadership and vision, corporate citizenship, and workplace environment (pp. 197–207). This platform is useful at all points as communication professionals consider the degree to which any or all of these five matters of transparency are necessary in the messages (verbal and visual) given both the organization's objectives and the audiences' needs. Moreover, language choices can intensify, minimize, or otherwise reframe corporate reputation matters, which thereby direct audience attention to evidence and reasoning in support of those matters (see Courtright and Smudde, 2009; Rowland and Jerome, 2004). Fombrun and van Riel's platform is instrumental in this place in the model because it provides an audience-centered basis for decision making about communication in every respect, from the key message platform to the production of final discourse. Indeed, Fombrun and van Riel's platform for transparency works well early in the rhetorical process behind reputation management shown in the model because its components bridge matters of purpose (from the organization's point of view) and understanding (from the audiences' point of view). In other words, the incorporation of the transparency platform into the model for message design ensures that form follows function.

Once the final discourse is created and disseminated to audiences (as indicated by the medium-gray arrow), those audiences have control over if and how messages get applied. The focus becomes audiences' receptivity to salient messages about corporate reputation based on their dispositions on the adoption curve (i.e., being an innovator, an early adopter, a part of the early majority, member of the late majority, a laggard, or a skeptic), not an organization's own view of itself and its messages. Outcomes of corporate reputation communication are the final measurement of success – whether and how well audiences responded according to the plan. Perceptions of an organization and its reputation are based on past experiences, current communication and action, and future expectations and assumptions. The top box in Figure 33.1, then, shows that audiences not only process information about a corporate reputation, but they also process whether the organization's identity *as communicated* is consistent with (1) the persona conveyed (implicitly or explicitly) through the message plus (2) their memories and present knowledge about the organization. Indeed, an awareness of individual and group memories can influence message design because, given Finlay *et al.*'s (2000) and Larson's (2010) work in the field of psychology, verbal cues can trigger certain memories, presumably those that are the most relevant and salient to the exigence an organization faces. There can be multiple identifications achieved by audience perceptions (in the form of images and memory traces). The most enduring of these images and memories create and sustain corporate reputation, and the product-recall example we cover in this chapter will demonstrate this point.

An important dynamic in Figure 33.1 is the "convection" of all discursive actions (written and oral) in the rhetor–audience relationship indicated by the broken and solid arrows between blocks and their effects on an organization and message design. The model, then, necessarily leads us back to the organization's corporate identity, because feedback from audiences and evaluations of communication efforts influence how the organization communicates

in the future, but those perceptions also influence how the organization's members view the organization (because they are also members of external audiences as well as being internal audience members). Moreover, the broken arrows account for the fragmentary nature of contemporary discourse (McGee, 1990), for publics and individuals select, from what they receive, only bits and pieces of what an organization has said and done, and what they remember of those and competing messages in the marketplace necessarily constitute different impressions. The production and reproduction of corporate identity, therefore, includes attempts to identify with audiences and resulting identifications that build and reinforce reputation.

Message design concerns all corporate reputation matters. Message design is thus the linchpin in the creation and maintenance of organizational culture and identity as well as external image(s) and reputation. Corporate identity is conveyed through message design in the form of a desired image, a corporate persona. The model in Figure 33.1 illustrates the process of corporate rhetors charged with the responsibility and authority to manage organizational reputations through discursive actions, including those that enlighten image and identity. Moreover, the model recognizes the intended and unintended consequences of corporate communication through effective message design because no communication act is perfect, but the discourse competence of corporate rhetors is absolutely essential to achieve objectives that strengthen reputation, not weaken it. We have argued that message design, therefore, is central to reputation building. Now we turn to the category of recalls to illustrate the model's utility.

Recalls as an Example

Although the public relations literature has emphasized product recalls of crisis proportions, the number of recalls per year would suggest that not all recalls are dramatic. Over the past 35 years, the United States Consumer Product Safety Commission (2008), for example, has issued 4006 recalls, which averages nearly 115 recalls a year – and the large majority of them were not high profile. The 2009 European Commission report on nonfood recalls documents gradual increases every year from 2003 to 2008, with peak levels in 2008 in 10 of 28 countries reported. Thus, product recalls figure prominently among the many strategic communication concerns of today's organizations. In this section, we employ modest, routine recalls as well as the dramatic, highly publicized ones in recent years as examples.

Basic textbooks provide convenient labels for types of audiences, and many writings on crisis communication provide a typology of crisis types (e.g., see Seeger *et al.*, 2003, for a review of three such classification schemes). The same is true of product recalls. Coombs and Holladay (2004), following Lerbinger (1997), use two general categories: product recalls caused by a technical error and those caused by human error. In the business literature, Berman (1999), from three different sources, generates seven categories: design flaw, production defect, new scientific data about dangers from products or materials originally sold as safe, accidental contamination, product tampering, unforeseen misuse of the product by consumers, and failure to meet safety standards. However, our focus in this section concerns the choice of media channel (i.e., discourse type), the issue of formal message pattern, and the design, purposes, and functions of product recall messages.

Writings regarding the form and structure of product recall messages range from the formulaic to the sophisticated. How to conduct a product recall and how to structure the accompanying message are the stuff of government documents (e.g., Great Britain. Department of Trade and Industry, 1999, cited in Gurău and Serban, 2005). A Google search of "product recall procedures" results in documents available from, among others, the United States Consumer Product Safety Commission (1999), the Food and Drug Administration (United States Food and Drug Administration, 2007), and state government agencies (e.g., State of California, 2011). Likewise, step-by-step procedures and tips for handling and communicating recalls can be found in many trade/academic publications (e.g., Berman, 1999; Gibson, 1995, 1997, 2000; Smith *et al.*, 1996).

Although somewhat focused on more obvious components of product recall messages such as the size and "official" look of the message, Gibson (1997) does suggest four other elements that unify product recall advertisements: "limited apology, minimization of risk or harm, provision of consumer instructions . . . and reassuring tone" (p. 46). Although his article is based on a very small convenience sample of four different media channels, Gibson's first three characteristics suggest substantive elements of product recall communication, and reassuring tone may be one choice or one component of the genre's style.

Closely related to a product recall message's discursive elements is the purpose the message must accomplish. Basing their assumptions on discourse analysis, Gurău and Serban (2005) argue that product recall messages embody action, knowledge, and situation. First, product recall texts tell audiences the "what, why, when, and how" of the product and its recall; second, these texts transmit information to audiences about potential dangers; third, the message must be carefully designed and disseminated in order to respond to – and shape – the situation and "have the desired impact on the target audience" (p. 327). Smith *et al.* (1996) make similar recommendations regarding media channel usage, also, as part of their emphasis on planning, include communicative concerns, for example, to "keep customers properly informed and persuade them to complete the necessary changes" (p. 109). A second key concern for the authors is that recall planners recognize that "customer communications can reinforce the company's image as a responsible organization" (p. 109). After a recall, the authors recommend a focus on image repair and reputation maintenance: "restoring and strengthening the company's reputation and the reputation of the product in question" (p. 109). Taken together, the purposes of product recall messages can be reduced to two main points. Product recall messages simultaneously attempt "(1) to provide the practical nature regarding the defective product, and the operational process of recalling it; and (2) to defend the reputation of the affected firm" (Gurău and Serban, 2005, p. 328, citing Jefkins, 1995).

In addition to the prescriptive recipes presented in several articles mentioned earlier, case studies in the public relations and organizational rhetoric literatures – even those that center on discourse with application of Benoit's (1995a,b) image restoration theory – have focused most on these pragmatic concerns. The success stories illustrate how to keep customers informed (Benson, 1988; Thomsen and Rawson, 1998; see also Taylor and Kent, 2007, recommendations for the use of web sites), and many provide examples of how to present clearly the information consumers need to participate in the recall (e.g., Sellnow *et al.*, 1998). Negative cases reveal failures to do so (e.g., Blaney *et al.*, 2002; Ihlen, 2002; Venette *et al.*, 2003). Perrier, for example, after the discovery of benzene in its sparkling water, withdrew the product completely from grocery shelves but failed to offer a coherent, single explanation as to why the recall was necessary (Pratt, 1994).

How audiences might perceive recall messages, of course, is also of concern. Gurău and Serban (2005), citing Jefkins (1995), observe that public relations messages are designed to turn public hostility to sympathy, prejudice to acceptance, apathy to interest, and ignorance to knowledge. In the case of food, there is already a general disconnect between what organizations know about their products and the lack of information consumers have in making purchases (Verbeke, 2005), and the literature indicates that product recalls draw attention to that asymmetrical relationship and focus consumer uncertainty. Van Waes and van Wijk (2000–2001) show how companies faced with a product recall are in a precarious position that must balance audience concern with corporate image to maintain relationships. In particular, the authors argue that being more indirect with audiences, using language to soften the threat,

and use of passive voice can be pluses in cases of mild to moderate risk, making a recall message more acceptable, thus capturing the nature and scope of the situation while also instilling appreciation, acceptance, and perception of the organization and its corrective action. In contrast, greater care must be used in framing messages to deal with high-risk situations because politeness strategies actually may be perceived negatively.

It is clear from the corporate *apologia* literature that organizations may use product recalls as a part of broader efforts to maintain audience focus on product quality and relate it to a positive corporate reputation. For example, cooperation with government agencies is a dominant theme in food safety and recall literature (e.g., Sellnow *et al.*, 1998; Tompkin, 2001). In general, product recalls, like other organizational crises, may be turned into opportunities (Smith *et al.*, 1996). Johnson & Johnson's introduction of sealed packaging of Tylenol and introduction of childproof caps is but one examplar (Berg and Robb, 1992). In such cases, product recall and subsequent messages may allow organizations to use model/ antimodel arguments (Sellnow and Brand, 2001). The organization's past practices – and perhaps the industry's – become the antimodel, the old way of doing things. The organization's corrective actions beyond the recall itself, such as implementing new policies or procedures to prevent a recall situation's reoccurrence, becomes the model argument that establishes the organization as an industry leader rather than the scapegoat.

These concerns reflected in what we would argue to be the discourse conventions of product recall messages parallel Rowland and Jerome's (2004) reconceptualization of organizational *apologia*. The actual recall serves an image-repair function – to rectify the problem, decrease consumer uncertainty, and provide accurate information so that consumers can follow clear instructions on how to participate in the recall. The recall message also serves an image-maintenance function – to improve credibility with consumers, strengthen product position, and maintain or even improve the

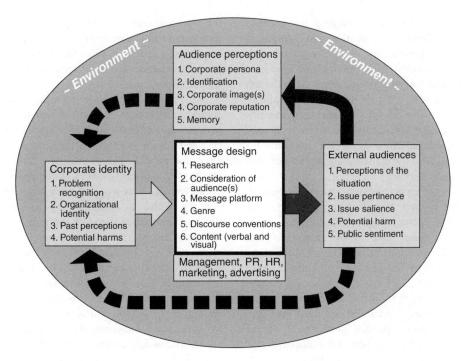

Figure 33.2   Rhetorical model of the reputation management process during product recalls. PR, public relations; HR, human resources.

organization's reputation. Also, among the several observations that Rowland and Jerome make is the importance of the organization's environment and its attendant situation constraints to be an important consideration. The demands of recalls vary from industry to industry, or, in theoretical terms, from one argument field to another (for more information on argument fields, see Rowland and Jerome, 2004; Toulmin, 1958).

One consideration hidden in this literature is the fact that many, if not most, of the recalls cataloged by federal agencies do not rise to the level of public awareness that product recall crisis situations entail. Certainly, more information about product recalls today is communicated via the Internet or through direct contact (electronic or otherwise) with affected consumers. Moreover, not all recalls are considered newsworthy. If we are to understand the dynamics of recall messages as driven by strategic use of tactics, recalls of *all* levels of

importance warrant our attention, not just the recalls that garner news coverage.

Adjusting Figure 33.1 based on the previous section, Figure 33.2 maps corporate reputation messaging for product recalls. Keys to both figures are the components that change and those that do not. Specifically, the components of corporate identity and external audiences change while the others do not. The reason is simple: the exigence is different, which affects corporate rhetors' approach to it and external audiences' disposition toward it. So at the left of the model, we assume the organization's recognition of the situational need for a recall (problem recognition) and its interaction with how the organization thinks about itself (organizational identity) in relation to the audiences' perceptions and memories about the organization and reactions to the situation at hand. Information related to product problems then are necessarily filtered through people's memories about the organization and past exigencies, what the organization has communicated about itself in the past (corporate persona), perceptions of the organization's current image(s) with publics and corporate reputation (note the dotted arrow from the top of the model) vis-à-vis audience perceptions, and their prior influence on corporate identity. Additionally, organizational decision makers and communicators gauge the potential for harm to both the audience and reputation that the problem poses.

As noted earlier, message design thus entails further research regarding the problem, publics, and choice of genre, discourse conventions, content, and media channel(s) (see Smudde and Courtright, 2012). As part of the research regarding publics, corporate communicators must gauge the following factors (found at the right of the model under "external audiences"): organizations must take into account various publics' perceptions of the situation; the pertinence and salience of the problem to them, including the potential of danger; and each public's sentiments regarding the organization, ranging from hostility to patience/forbearance. Such attention to detail thus can help organizations more effectively manage recall communications.

Discussion

Recall communications exhibit the classic problem–solution pattern to allay the audience's fears while simultaneously assert why the audience must become involved in the situation. This rhetorical nature of recall communications underscores the motives behind and effects sought by an organization and constitute the classic argument stock issue of *solvency* (i.e., how well the solution addresses the problem). We suggest that proper explanation of the problem precipitating a recall lends credibility to the organization because it is taking responsible action, assigning jurisdiction to itself, and claiming the right to assess harm and inherency. Regardless of the level of blame – for organizations may take responsibility for harms

they did not cause – these responsible actions then extend to the essential tasks of providing a solution, a cure that will address the level of harm to audiences and incur certain cost to the organization.

The product recall itself provides affected audiences with clear instructions that they can perform (again, cure), such as contact a physician and return products to the store of purchase for refund. Taken together, then, the fear-control elements of recall communications assign responsibility to (1) the organization to cure the ill and (2) audiences to participate in the cure. Sometimes the recall message may be necessary but not sufficient to control public fears, such as the recall of Dole packaged spinach in the summer of 2006. In such cases, it is essential that the recall message document the harm credibly and ethically. Reducing ambiguity for audiences may not be that hard for some recall messages, but to get an audience's attention, the messages must be targeted carefully and crafted so as to address risk with the appropriate level of fear inducement and ability to reduce audience uncertainty. Matters of language intensity are paramount at this level, and there are means for effectively using language in recall communications.

A problem–solution approach that frames the recall and its corrective action depends on an effective pattern of language intensity that garners attention to the problem, inspires cooperation, and then elicits participation in the solution. High language intensity (e.g., emotional appeals, startling statistics) draws journalists' attention to matters (sometimes through purposeful hyperbole) to make them more "sexy" and thereby can increase the likelihood of media coverage and audience compliance. This approach is typical of the most dramatic and publicly notable of product crises, including those typically seen in the corporate *apologia* literature. Communicators must be careful, however, not to overemphasize facts and statistics at the expense of honestly communicating the level of harm and/or inherency. Next, neutral language intensity can be used to communicate factual information so audiences know what procedures they should follow to participate in the recall, which cures the problem. For example, recognition of food product codes and instructions to destroy tainted products are commonplace and therefore require little drama, if any (e.g., LU Général Biscuit Belgique, 2008). Proper use of the fear-appeal elements coupled with stylistic choices may help to cut through all the other competing messages to reassure audiences, emphasize the idea that things will be righted, and focus on product and organizational reputation in purposefully, strategically chosen discourse types.

The most important aspect to remember about the use of any discourse type is its strategic value in the big picture of a product recall. Audience compliance with the recall in any regard is seen as a tactical concern about how people ultimately respond to actual communication texts. That is, strictly tactical thinking is focused on just "getting the word out." But truly effective and successful communications depends on strategic thinking that focuses on the bigger picture, making tactics subservient to larger objectives that tie directly to an organizational mission and vision. This is the realm of discourse competence, which includes an acute sensibility about the use, benefits, and risks of any medium that may be used. Being mindful of and implementing an organization's overall strategic plan is the responsibility of all organizational members, especially its leaders and, in particular, its communication professionals.

Secondary to addressing the product problem, although by no means less important, is image management or repair (Rowland and Jerome, 2004). How an organization handles a recall may affect reputation, if the situation rises to crisis levels. However, we also suggest that the day-to-day management of routine recalls may be treated in the same way. The organization must satisfy, through its messages and actions, legal requirements, and audiences' expectations. Even then, public memory is not just fragmentary but short. What remains in collective memory depends not only what the organization says but also the social and historical contexts in which events occur and how

they are perceived in the flow of time, in the context of previous messages, whether from the organization itself or from other sources (see Gronbeck, 1998, for a discussion of how past rhetoric impinges on the present, and Rowlinson *et al.*, 2010, for a critique of social memory studies).

Instrumental in this satisfaction is the concept of power between organizations and their publics. Here we mean power not in the typical sense of control, dominance, or influence. We view power as "a community-based phenomenon that people confer on each other through their relationships with one another based on hierarchical positions they hold, the rhetorical manifestation and recognition of relationships and positions through communicative acts, and the social implications these dimensions have on individual and, especially, communal views of the system of relationships that exist and evolve among people" (Courtright and Smudde, 2010, p. 177). In this view, an organization and its audiences/stakeholders exercise power through words and deeds that affect trust and transparency in the course of the relationship. Trust and transparency are created, sustained, and transformed through symbolic action. Either party may impose rewards or hardships/constraints on the other in ways that are commensurate with the situation. For example, a class of consumers may demand reparations for an alleged faulty product, and the company that produced it may or may not comply with the demand by issuing a recall or taking other actions, depending on the preponderance of evidence about the product. Conversely, an organization may independently and proactively impose a recall because quality-assurance measures confirmed a potential problem in a product it produced and distributed for sale. In both cases, the organization must ethically address the situation and its cure within the power relationship context.

On another level, the inherent demands of certain organizational fields may facilitate different power dynamics in organization–audience relationships. For example, the US Department of Homeland Security has established and maintains a high degree of power through low transparency because citizens do not demand transparency, thereby increasing trust by meeting public expectations. In the banking industry, however, transparency is expected, especially in light of recent scandals and congressional bailouts, which greatly decreased trust in both fields. Organizational fields (see Fligstein, 2001; Greenwood *et al.*, 2002), then, offer an additional audience-centered viewpoint for message design that could guide strategic planning, message design, and discursive action about corporate exigencies, including product recalls. A product recall therefore is more than just a series of steps or a matter of filling in the discursive blanks. Strategy, not just tactics, is key.

Strategy is necessary in the full range of strategic communication efforts, from the simplest announcement to the most complicated crisis. Tactics, like press releases and news conferences, are only means to an end. In terms of recalls, communication professionals must be mindful of the organization–audience power relationship and act in accordance with (1) an annual plan for the operation of all communications efforts that is synchronized with the organization's strategic plan, (2) ad hoc or campaign plans tied to the annual communication plan, and (3) contingency plans for unplanned but high-risk situations like crises, issues, and recalls that can put an organization's image, reputation, and financial position in jeopardy (see Smudde, 2004, 2007, 2011; Smudde and Courtright, 2012; see also Botan, 2006; Ferguson, 1999; Oliver, 2007). Specific discourse types should be prescribed and drafted in template form in contingency plans so that key information can be added and arrangements can be made depending on the situation for the benefit of both the organization and its audiences/stakeholders.

Conclusion

This project's unique focus fills an important research niche by demonstrating the function–form synergy of corporate reputation messages

and final communication discourse. The model of the rhetorical communication process for reputation management shows it to be a holistic one that relies on strong discourse competence of communication professionals. The specific kinds of texts that organizations may choose to manage their reputations with audiences and stakeholders will vary from one occasion to the next. Message design for reputation management is the catalyst for an organization's communication, and Fombrun and van Riel's (2004) platform for corporate transparency (i.e., platforms about products and services, financial performance, leadership and vision, corporate citizenship, and workplace environment) is a useful taxonomy for message design, which is the heart of the rhetorical process of reputation management. Combining Fombrun and van Riel's work with that of Courtright and Smudde (2009) can provide a systematic and practical method to understand and create specific kinds of corporate discourse that successfully and strategically present an organization's reputation-related messages within the context of the relationships between organizations and their stakeholders.

Author Notes

Part of the work in this project was supported by a Pretenure Faculty Initiative Grant from Illinois State University's College of Arts and Sciences for the first author.

The authors wish to thank Charles Conrad for his helpful feedback on an early version of this chapter, which was presented as a paper at the National Communication Association's 2011 Convention in New Orleans.

References

Benoit, W.L. (1995a) *Accounts, Excuses, and Apologies: A Theory of Image Restoration Strategies.* Albany, NY: State University of New York Press.

Benoit, W.L. (1995b) Sears' repair of its auto service image: Image restoration discourse in the corporate sector. *Communication Studies, 46,* 89–105.

Benson, J.A. (1988) Crisis revisited: An analysis of strategies used by Tylenol in the second tampering episode. *Communication Studies, 39,* 49–66.

Berg, D.M. and Robb, S. (1992) Crisis management and the "paradigm case". In E.L. Toth and R.L. Heath (eds), *Rhetorical and Critical Approaches to Public Relations.* Hillsdale, NJ: Erlbaum, pp. 93–109.

Berman, B. (1999) Planning for the inevitable product recall. *Business Horizons, 42*(2), 69–78.

Blaney, J.R., Benoit, W.L., and Brazeal, L.M. (2002) Blowout!: Firestone's image restoration campaign. *Public Relations Review, 28,* 379–392.

Botan, C. (2006) Grand strategy, strategy, and tactics in public relations. In C.H. Botan and V. Hazleton (eds), *Public Relations Theory II.* Mahwah, NJ: Erlbaum, pp. 223–247.

Brønn, P.S. and Berg, R.W. (eds) (2005) *Corporate Communication: A Strategic Approach to Building Reputation* (2nd ed.). Oslo, Norway: Gyldendal.

Cheney, G. and Christensen, L.T. (2001) Organizational identity: Linkages between internal and external communication. In F.M. Jablin and L.L. Putnam (eds), *The New Handbook of Organizational Communication: Advances in Theory, Research, and Methods.* Thousand Oaks, CA: Sage, pp. 231–269.

Coombs, W.T. (2007) Protecting organization reputations during a crisis: The development and application of situation crisis communication theory. *Corporate Reputation Review, 10,* 163–176.

Coombs, W.T. and Holladay, S.J. (2004) Reasoned action in crisis communication: An attribution theory-based approach to crisis management. In D. Millar and R.L. Heath (eds), *Responding to Crisis: A Rhetorical Approach to Crisis Communication.* Mahwah, NJ: Erlbaum, pp. 95–115.

Courtright, J.L. and Smudde, P.M. (2009) Leveraging organizational innovation for strategic reputation management. *Corporate Reputation Review, 12,* 245–269.

Courtright, J.L. and Smudde, P.M. (2010) Recall communications: Message genres, symbolic charging, and message design. *International Journal of Strategic Communication, 4,* 58–74.

Dowling, G.R. (2006) Communicating corporate reputation through stories. *California Management Review, 49*(1), 82–100.

Dowling, G.R. and Weeks, W. (2008) What the media is *really* telling you about your brand. *MIT Sloan Management Review, 49*(3), 27–34.

Ferguson, S.D. (1999) *Communication Planning: An Integrated Approach.* Thousand Oaks, CA: Sage.

Finlay, F., Hitch, G.J., and Meudell, P.R. (2000) Mutual inhibition in collaborative recall: Evidence for a retrieval-based account. *Journal of Experimental Psychology: Learning, Memory & Cognition, 26,* 1556–1567.

Fligstein, N. (2001) Social skill and the theory of fields. *Sociological Theory, 19,* 105–125.

Fombrun, C.J. and van Riel, C.B.M. (2004) *Fame & Fortune: How Successful Companies Build Winning Reputations.* New York: Prentice Hall.

Gibson, D.C. (1995) Public relations considerations of consumer product recall. *Public Relations Review, 21,* 225–240.

Gibson, D.C. (1997) Print communication tactics for consumer product recalls: A prescriptive taxonomy. *Public Relations Quarterly, 42*(1), 42–46.

Gibson, D.C. (2000) The cyber-revolution in product recall public relations. *Public Relations Quarterly, 45*(2), 24–28.

Gioia, D.A., Schultz, M., and Corley, K.G. (2000) Organizational identity, image, and adaptive instability. *Academy of Management Review, 25*(1), 63–81.

Great Britain. Department of Trade and Industry (1999) *Customer Product Recall: A Good Practice Guide.* London: Author.

Greenwood, R., Suddaby, R., and Hinings, C. (2002) Theorizing change: The role of professional associations in the transformation of institutionalized fields. *Academy of Management Journal, 45*(1), 58–80.

Gronbeck, B.E. (1998) The rhetorics of the past: Rhetoric, history, and collective memory. In K.J. Turner (ed.), *Doing Rhetorical History: Concepts and Cases.* Tuscaloosa, AL: University of Alabama Press, pp. 47–60.

Gurău, C. and Serban, A. (2005) The anatomy of the product recall message: The structure and function of product recall messages published in the UK press. *Journal of Communication Management, 9,* 326–338.

Hagen, Ø. (2008) Seduced by their proactive image? On using auto communication to enhance CSR. *Corporate Reputation Review, 11,* 130–144.

Ihlen, Ø. (2002) Defending the Mercedes A-class: Combining and changing crisis-response strategies. *Journal of Public Relations Research,* *14,* 185–206.

Ihlen, Ø. (2004) Norwegian hydroelectric power: Testing a heuristic for analyzing symbolic strategies and resources. *Public Relations Review, 30,* 217–223.

Jefkins, F.W. (1995) *Public Relations Techniques* (2nd ed.). London: Butterworth-Heinemann.

Kiley, D. and Helm, B. (2009) 100 best global brands: The great trust offensive. *BusinessWeek, 4148,* 38–42.

Larson, J. (2010) *In Search of Synergy.* New York: Psychology Press.

Lerbinger, O. (1997) *The Crisis Manager: Facing Risk and Responsibility.* Mahwah, NJ: Erlbaum.

LU Général Biscuit Belgique (2008) Avis de rappel de produit [Product recall advisory]. September [News release]. Retrieved from http://www. securite-alimentaire.public.lu/actualites/alertes/ 2008/09/avis_de_rappel_de_produit_lu/Avis_ Rappel_Prduit_LU.PDF (last accessed September 28, 2012).

McGee, M.C. (1990) Text, context, and the fragmentation of contemporary culture. *Western Journal of Speech Communication, 54,* 274–289.

McLuhan, M. and Fiore, Q. (1967) *The Medium Is the Message.* New York: Bantam.

Oliver, S. (2007) *Public Relations Strategy* (2nd ed.). London: Kogan Page.

Pratt, C.B. (1994) Applying classical ethical theories to ethical decision making in public relations: Perrier's product recall. *Management Communication Quarterly, 8,* 70–94.

Rowland, R.C. and Jerome, A.M. (2004) On organizational apologia: A reconceptualization. *Communication Theory, 14*(3), 191–211.

Rowlinson, M., Booth, C., Clark, P., Delahaye, A., and Procter, S. (2010) Social remembering and organizational memory. *Organization Studies, 31,* 69–87.

Schultz, M., Hatch, M.J., and Larsen, M.H. (eds) (2000) *The Expressive Organization: Linking Identity, Reputation, and the Corporate Brand.* London: Oxford.

Seeger, M.W., Sellnow, T.L., and Ulmer, R.R. (2003) *Communication and Organizational Crisis.* Westport, CT: Praeger.

Sellnow, T.L. and Brand, J. (2001) Establishing the structure of reality for an industry: Model and anti-model arguments as advocacy in Nike's crisis communication. *Journal of Applied Communication Research, 29,* 278–295.

Sellnow, T.L., Ulmer, R.R., and Snider, M. (1998) The compatibility of corrective action in organizational crisis communication. *Communication Quarterly, 46,* 60–74.

Smith, N.C., Thomas, R.J., and Quelch, J.A. (1996) A strategic approach to managing product recalls. *Harvard Business Review, 74*(5), 102–112.

Smudde, P.M. (2004) Implications on the practice and study of Kenneth Burke's idea of a "public relations counsel with a heart". *Communication Quarterly, 52,* 420–432.

Smudde, P.M. (2007) Public relations' power as based on knowledge, discourse, and ethics. In J.L. Courtright and P.M. Smudde (eds), *Power and Public Relations.* Cresskill, NJ: Hampton Press, pp. 207–238.

Smudde, P.M. (2011) *Public Relations as Dramatistic Organizing: A Case Study Bridging Theory and Practice.* Cresskill, NJ: Hampton Press.

Smudde, P.M. and Courtright, J.L. (2012) *Inspiring Cooperation and Celebrating Organizations: Genres, Message Design, and Strategies in Public Relations.* New York: Hampton Press.

State of California (2011) Product recall. Retrieved from http://www.takechargeca.ca.gov/besafe/ product_recalls.shtml (last accessed September 28, 2012).

Taylor, M. and Kent, M.L. (2007) Taxonomy of mediated crisis responses. *Public Relations Review, 33,* 140–146.

Thomsen, S.R. and Rawson, B. (1998) Purifying a tainted corporate image: Odwalla's response to an *E. coli* poisoning. *Public Relations Quarterly, 43*(3), 35–46.

Tompkin, R.B. (2001) Interactions between government and industry food safety activities. *Food Control, 12,* 203–207.

Toulmin, S.E. (1958) *The Uses of Argument.* New York: Cambridge University Press.

United States Consumer Product Safety Commission (1999) Recall handbook. May. Retrieved from http://www.cpsc.gov/businfo/8002.html (last accessed September 28, 2012).

United States Consumer Product Safety Commission (2008) CPSC recall announcements and product safety alerts. Retrieved from http://www. cpsc.gov/cpscpub/prerel/prerel.html (last accessed September 28, 2012).

United States Food and Drug Administration (2007) Regulatory procedures manual March 2007. Chapter 7. Recall procedures. March. Retrieved from http://www.fda.gov/ora/compliance_ref/ rpm/pdf/ch7.pdf (last accessed September 28, 2012).

van den Bosch, A.L.M., de Jong, M.D.T., and Elving, W.J.L. (2005) How corporate visual identity supports reputation. *Corporate Communications: An International Journal, 10*(2), 108–116.

van Riel, C.B.M. and Balmer, J.M.T. (1997) Corporate identity: The concept, its management and management. *European Journal of Marketing, 31*, 340–355.

Van Waes, L. and van Wijk, C. (2000–2001) The influence of politeness on the perception of product recall notices. *Document Design, 2*, 272–279.

Vendelø, M.T. (1998) Narrating corporate reputation: Becoming legitimate through storytelling.

International Studies of Management and Organizations, 28(3), 120–137.

Venette, S.J., Sellnow, T.L., and Lang, P.A. (2003) Metanarration's role in restructuring perceptions of crisis: NHTSA's failure in the Ford-Firestone Crisis. *Journal of Business Communication, 40*, 219–236.

Verbeke, W. (2005) Agriculture and the food industry in the information age. *European Review of Agricultural Economics, 32*, 347–368.

Section 4

Contexts of Reputation

34

Contrabrand: Activism and the Leveraging of Corporate Reputation[1]

Jarol B. Manheim and Alex D. Holt

The George Washington University, USA

The authors adopt the perspective of anticorporate or other contrarian activists to review literature relating to corporate reputation as a factor that impacts on the style, content, objectives, and likelihood of success of campaigns directed against a particular company or industry. In this view, reputation conveys potential strengths and vulnerabilities, some obvious but others less so, that help to shape strategy, and even to select among the available targets. Topics include the social construction of activism and of the corporation in areas such as branding, framing, and enemy construction; networking and digital activism; and issue-centered activism in such areas as labor relations and socially responsible investing. They conclude that the growing volume and sophistication of anticorporate activism represents a major challenge, not only to corporations themselves, but to the assumptions that both companies and scholars make about the role and significance of corporate reputation.

Much of the present volume emphasizes the analysis, refinement, encouragement, rewarding, and general promotion of corporate reputation as a social good with the potential for ancillary economic benefits. The present chapter is not merely different; it is contrapuntal. That is because, either explicitly or implicitly, anticorporate activists treat corporate reputation, whether positive or negative, central or peripheral, as a target attribute – a characteristic of a company or an industry that might increase or decrease the utility of launching an attack, define its strategy and tactics, and determine its likelihood of success. Bartley and Child (2009), for example, examined the factors that open corporations to campaigns of naming and shaming. Those that are leaders in globalization are most likely to be targeted, these authors found in a study focusing on the apparel and shoe industries, but a strong secondary determinant is reputation, and more particularly, the extent of a company's dependence on maintaining a good one. Large companies with branded consumer products and patterns of globalization, they suggested, are the most vulnerable.

The Handbook of Communication and Corporate Reputation, First Edition. Edited by Craig E. Carroll.
© 2013 John Wiley & Sons, Inc. Published 2015 by John Wiley & Sons, Inc.

As an indicator of susceptibility to influence, reputation is nonlinear. Companies with poor reputations are potentially attractive targets because their reputation is a weakness that may at once legitimize the activism itself and limit such companies' ability to resist outside pressure. But companies with especially strong reputations are also potentially attractive as targets if and to the extent that internally generated pressure for reputation maintenance renders them disproportionately willing to yield to activists' demands. Activism feeds off of reputation per se and is largely indifferent to its niceties.

Activists communicate through branding, framing, messaging, audience segmentation, channel selection, and the many other means of generating, controlling, and disseminating information (see, e.g., Allan *et al.*, 2000; Bennett, 2004; Cashore *et al.*, 2004; DeLuca, 1999; Gamson, 1990; Gregory *et al.*, 2005; Jordan *et al.*, 2004; Martin, 2004; Ryan, 1991; Salzman, 2003; and Shaw, 1996, on the application of basic communication strategies to activism). But, as the label implies, they also communicate through actions – actions that extend beyond messaging to such things as the staging of events or the formation and activation of alliances and networks (Arquilla and Ronfeldt, 2001; Bandy and Smith, 2005; Della Porta and Tarrow, 2005; DeMars, 2005; Diani and McAdam, 2003; Keck and Sikkink, 1998; Oppenheimer and Lakey, 1964; Smith and Johnston, 2002; Tarrow, 2005). To a surprising extent, activists are guided by such underlying conceptual frameworks as the stakeholder theory of the firm, power structure analysis, persuasion, media effects, and social network analysis (Manheim, 2011).

Activists of interest to corporations have a clear point of view: they tend to be antiestablishment and anticorporate (see, e.g., Bakan, 2004; Danaher and Mark, 2003). Some are pragmatists, focused on trying to change corporate policies or behaviors. Some are ideologues, trying to disrupt, undermine, and displace the corporation as a form of social and economic organization. And finally, activists are almost invariably weaker than the corporations they seek to affect. Whether economically, politically, or by some other standard, activists lack the wherewithal to impose their wishes on the companies they target, and are thus forced to employ communication and action as force multipliers, and the reputation of their target as a point of leverage. Companies are generally not well served when closely associated with risk, uncertainty, or instability; for them, reputation is a potential line of defense. But activists are not only well served by such things; they actually thrive upon them. Their own reputations are enhanced by their ability to generate conflict or discord – to undermine the reputation and stability of their targets. The iterative clash of these competing values and interests often amounts to a form of reputational warfare.

In this chapter, then, we offer an examination of how activists focus on corporate reputation and employ it to their own ends. We will focus on activism itself, looking first at its general outlines and dynamics, second at its evolution in recent years, and third at its application in selected areas of particular concern to corporations.

Vogel (1978) anticipated many of the challenges to the business community that would arise from then-developing forms of activism, identifying many of the actors, actions, and emphases that have since emerged, including the politicizing of the corporation, the emphasis on transparency, the emergence of shareholder-based activism, internationalization, and the use of codes of conduct. In a series of subsequent books Vogel (1989, 1995, 1996) explored the sources, applications, and limitations of corporate political power before returning to a more direct examination of activism in *The Market for Virtue: The Potential Limits of Corporate Social Responsibility* (Vogel, 2005), in which he examined the business case for socially responsible behavior in the context of a range of issues and advocacy efforts.

As Vogel's work makes clear, the political context in which anticorporate activism occurs is essential both to its practice and to the analysis thereof. Bakir (2006), for example, employed the Greenpeace–Shell–Brent Spar case to study nongovernmental organizations' (NGOs) use of the media to impact the public policy agenda, finding that the media were primarily effective in shaping public perception of risk and policy makers' perception of public opinion, but not in shaping policy preferences themselves. Similarly, Salmon *et al.* (2003) argued that the goal of the so-called public will campaigns is to "alter the policy potential of a social problem in such a way that it moves from having a relatively low profile on the unstructured and somewhat amorphous public agenda to a much higher profile on the more structured and concrete policy agenda" (p. 4). They went on to argue that it is the power, resources, and skill of those who seek to influence the public to support social change, far more than the objective characteristics of the social problems being addressed, that lead to success in mobilizing the public will.

Friedman (1999) detailed the use and success–critical aspects of a traditional component of much anticorporate activism, the consumer boycott, giving examples from the labor movement and religious, environmental, and civil rights campaigns, among others. Klein *et al.* (2004) focused less on the critical factors in boycotts than on the motivations that draw consumers into conflicts that are not always their own.

The Social Construction of Activism and Its Targets

We will examine three major factors contributing to the perceived reality of anticorporate activism and campaigns – branding, framing, and enemy construction and the setting of standards of conduct.

Branding

Bennett (2004) argued that in a globalized world of inexpensive or otherwise undifferentiated products, companies set themselves apart primarily through branding, and that brand becomes extremely valuable to a given company. That enhanced value, in turn, leads activists to

target the brand through grassroots campaigns and boycotts in order to apply pressure to the company. The activists might be a diffuse group, and the costs of their actions minimal, but the effects on the brand can be catastrophic and damaging to the company behind the brand. The problems arising from these attacks, however, are not limited to their targets. As Bennett also pointed out, there are significant disadvantages for the attackers as well. Because they tend to be leaderless and unstructured, these efforts tend to lack coordination; so many messages may be drowned out in the noisy information environment both within any given campaign and among different campaigns. And if there is no leader to a movement, with whom is a company to negotiate when it is willing to change its practices? No less importantly, who guarantees that the boycott or other action will stop if the company improves its behavior? The emerging importance of brands as transcendent points of leverage against corporate reputations has led, in the view of some scholars (see Micheletti *et al.*, 2004), to the empowerment of consumers, whether acting in their own interests or as agents of activists who are able to mobilize them.

Ultimately, an attack on a corporate brand is either an avenue toward or a stand-in for an attack on that company's legitimacy. For that reason, Suchman's (1995) taxonomy of legitimacy and delineation of the various strategies available for developing, maintaining, and, where required, restoring it may be of particular interest in the present context.

Framing

Entman (1993) has provided a unifying definition of framing: "To frame is to select some aspects of a perceived reality and make them more salient in a communicating text, in such a way as to promote a particular problem definition, causal interpretation, moral evaluation, and/or treatment recommendation for the item described" (p. 52). Snow *et al.* (1986) provided a critical linkage between framing and participation in social movements through the mechanism of frame alignment processes. These include frame bridging, or the connection of two or more ideologically congruent frames through their application to a common issue; frame amplification, or the clarification and "invigoration" of a frame as it applies to a given issue; frame extension, or making explicit the relationship between the frame and important values and beliefs; and frame transformation, or redefining the objectives of a movement or organization so that they are not undermined by established interpretive frames.

Hansen (1991) argued that "cultural resonance" and linkage to powerful underlying symbolic attachments were essential to understanding why some environmental issues register strongly among the public while others do not. In a later study, Hansen (2000) employed the Brent Spar controversy to examine the framing of environmental disputes, finding, in that instance, that Greenpeace did demonstrate the ability to generate media coverage of its claims, but that this success did not translate into an ability to influence the frames employed in the resulting news coverage. Huxham and Sumner (1999) studied the competing messages and frames in the same campaign, and determined that Shell frequently appealed to expert opinion and rationality while Greenpeace appealed to populism, ignorance, and emotionality. A few years earlier, Lange (1993) analyzed competing information campaigns, in that instance between environmental groups and timber companies over the spotted owl and old growth forests. He found that the opposing groups tended to "mirror and map" one another in a "logic of interaction" with little or no direct communication between the two. Both groups utilized strategies of framing, selecting extreme statistics, vilification, simplification, dramatization, and continuous reframing to keep arguments fresh.

Payne (2001) examined the role of what he termed "norm entrepreneurs" in constructing frames designed to maximize audience resonance while in a competitive environment where that resonance is merely an intermediate step on the way to producing desired policy outcomes. Payne viewed frame construction, then, primarily as a means to create a power resource – not new power, but a new or stronger connection with an existing power structure – that can be employed to construct new social norms. Drawing on this, and on some more general research into the impact of competition on framing (Chong and Druckman, 2007a,b, 2010), Ihlen and Nitz (2008) examined the competition between opposing interests – environmentalists and the petroleum industry – to frame media portrayals of an oil exploration project in Norway in 2003. They determined that the media ignored all of these efforts, focusing instead on the competition itself, the "horse race," as the dominant frame. Echoing Hansen, Ihlen and Nitz concluded that advocates might be more successful in establishing their frames if they were to rise above a single-issue emphasis and focus on overarching master frames with broader cultural resonance.

Reber and Berger (2005) examined the Sierra Club's framing of three core environmental issues – oil drilling in the Arctic, coal-fired electricity generation, and urban sprawl – in chapter newsletters as well as in regional and national newspapers. They found that the newsletters tended to follow framing guidance more than the newspapers, though not as closely as one might expect, but that all of these media provided competing frames. In something of a contrast from a different policy arena, Martin (2004) identified five dominant frames within which labor issues tended to be presented – consumerism and choice, the absence of a public interest in production, the driving role of business leaders and entrepreneurs in the economy, the workplace as a meritocracy, and a negative view of collective economic action – which, he concluded, were not meaningfully competitive and which served to undermine the claims and interests of labor.

Enemy construction and standards of conduct

The construction of enemies is a core element of the rhetoric of agitation (Bowers *et al.*, 1993). Edelman (1988) provided a systematic general view of the rationale for enemy construction and the mechanisms through which it can be achieved. Bullert (2000) highlighted the importance of enemy construction – in this case, Nike Corporation and CEO Phil Knight – in the success of the anti-sweatshop movement. A related phenomenon in activist campaigns is the use of celebrities, either in support of a given movement, cause, or campaign, or as a personification of the target. Meyer and Gamson (1995) found that celebrity involvement in social movements can be either constructive or deleterious. While celebrities can bring hard-to-achieve attention, marquee value for fund-raising, and other resources to the cause, they can also be sources of distraction or moderation, and can even eclipse the issue frames around which activists are organized. Thrall *et al.* (2008) studied the role of more than 200 celebrities in issue advocacy and news-making, finding that they have relatively little impact on the shaping of traditional news, but do influence the increasingly important nontraditional media.

Enemy construction is one side of a coin, the reverse of which is the establishment of affirmative standards of conduct, which activists seek to impose on corporations as continuing points of leverage. Clawson (2003), for example, illustrated the use of codes of conduct and the associated rhetoric in living wage and anti-sweatshop campaigns. Grant and Taylor (2004) examined the development of the Kimberley Process, a regulatory framework, to govern and ultimately end the trade in the so-called conflict diamonds, while Bartley (2007a) argued that such transnational systems of private regulation of corporate labor and environmental practices, which arise from political conflicts involving states, NGOs, and other actors, have emerged as important non-market-based institutional by-products of globalization, as, for example, in the forest products and apparel industries. Bartley (2007b) then used the case of forest certification to illustrate how foundations used their grant-making to establish a whole new field of activity, populate it with social movement organizations, and leverage the resultant protest activity to advance their goals. Seidman

(2005) reflected on the development of corporate codes of conduct and of international regimes for monitoring and enforcement, concluding that such efforts have limitations, and benefit from the active engagement of governments and their regulatory systems. Manheim (2000) identified the sequential stages of code-related public debate, each of which represents a potential pressure point at which activists may confront a given corporation.

Activist Networking and Digital Activism

Activist networking

The past 20 years have seen an emergent emphasis on network construction by activists of all stripes, including those challenging corporations, with much of this literature (e.g., Bandy and Smith, 2005; Della Porta and Tarrow, 2005; Demars, 2005; Keck and Sikkink, 1998; Smith and Johnston, 2002; Tarrow, 2005) centering on transnational activists and transnational advocacy networks (TANs). In their seminal study of TANs, Keck and Sikkink (1998) studied human rights activists in Latin America, environmental activists, and those combating violence against women, and found that domestic decision makers in countries where violations are occurring tend to be unreceptive to external NGOs' calls for change. In order to combat this, the authors argued both descriptively and prescriptively, activists have used, and should use, what they termed a "boomerang model." In this model, NGOs in the offending Country A partner with NGOs from a more liberal, Western Country B. Those NGOs pressure the government of Country B, or some other third party, to adopt their position and to serve as their agent in pressuring the offending Country A. In effect, this amounts to moving a domestic NGO preference onto the international agenda, where it is taken up by a government or an intergovernmental organization, which then applies its own, presumably greater, leverage to press for change. Although the initial conceptualization of the model applied mainly to pressuring governments, companies are often targets in these transnational campaigns. Keck and Sikkink themselves, for instance, point to an advocacy campaign targeting Nestle in an effort to stop poor women in developing countries from feeding their newborns infant formula. According to the authors, the campaign singled out Nestle because the company was transnational and could productively be attacked in more developed countries. Keck and Sikkink found that TANs tend to be effective in such areas as agenda setting and framing, pushing actors to make certain commitments, changing the structure or procedures of an organization, influencing a targeted actor to change policy, or modifying behavior.

Bob (2005) offered important insights into the bottom-up internal dynamics by which TANs are sometimes formed, and into the central role played by NGOs, whose recruitment as sponsors and primary participants is often crucial to TANs' success. Examining two cases – the Zapatista insurrection in southern Mexico and the Ogoni people's efforts, centering on Shell Oil and other petroleum producers, to control environmental damage in Nigeria – Bob found that fledgling social movements in the developing world must compete for attention in a crowded information environment by "marketing" themselves to prominent NGOs in the developed world. Through the construction of coalitions, global NGOs force the social movements in developing countries to adapt their goals, ideals, and tactics in order to satisfy the wishes of the Western NGOs. Peizer (2006) used his insider's knowledge of the networks and systems employed by organizations associated with George Soros to illuminate the uses of information and communication technologies (ICTs), as well as business models and marketing, to impose efficiency and productivity on these civil society organizations. Juska and Edwards (2005), in a case study of a joint US–Polish campaign against Smithfield Foods, found that the existence of strong national activist movements, a favorable political environment, and strategic, charismatic leadership were essential to campaign success.

Demars (2005) offered a structural theory of transnational NGOs, arguing that NGOs derive their power, not from wealth or force, but from their partnerships, and should therefore be understood primarily as conduits of latent messages and norms across nations and societies. Because the messages are latent, he asserted, NGOs are both unpredictable and potentially dangerous destabilizing forces. Demars also argued that because NGOs are private actors ostensibly acting in the public interest, they are prone to surreptitious exploitation by various external parties, and that they may institutionalize political conflict by acting as a medium through which actors fight for influence and control.

States and corporations both have hierarchical structures that were developed in, and may be better suited to, an analog era, and are often unable to adapt quickly enough to respond to activists waging what Arquilla and Ronfeldt (2001) term a "netwar." In their view, netwar is characterized by a diffuse, networked structure and by the rapidity with which resources can be mobilized to create a swarming effect. Ronfeldt and Arquilla (2001) portrayed the Zapatista insurgency in Mexico, with its fluidity, its adaptability to the information environment, and its ability to transcend regional and national boundaries through both technology and the near-instantaneous formation of a global coalition, as a quintessential example of this new phenomenon. Similarly, Robb (2007) argued that hierarchical institutions are at an inherent disadvantage in the age of open-source warfare because insurgents are able to focus their limited resources on systems disruption, where their costs are low and the potential return on investment is quite high indeed.

In his account of the "Battle of Seattle" protests in 1999, which centered on these business-related themes, De Armond (2001) described how an unstructured network of activists totally overwhelmed the police and brought the city of Seattle to a halt for days. Companies, typically hierarchical, are increasingly likely to confront similar tactics directed against both their operations and their corporate reputations.

Digital activism

The pace of change in digital technologies themselves has energized, and been reflected in, the pace of change in the social application of these technologies by anticorporate activists. Writing just before the emergence of the Web, Myers (1994) saw computer-based technologies as enhancing the integration of geographically dispersed social movements, providing means for enhanced message control, creating the ability to generate virtual density for a given movement, and forming and coordinating coalitions. Price (2000) reviewed some of the ways this new form of activism was already affecting the business community, both directly and through public policy initiatives. Rheingold (2002) and Karpf (2009) explored the use of one such technique, the so-called smart mobs or flash mobs, swarms of activists who can be mobilized on short notice and deployed to a physical location or a virtual one.

Scholars have also begun examining the use of specific cyber-strategies and tactics in anticorporate activism. Pickerill (2001), for example, examined the use of the Internet by environmental activists in the United Kingdom, focusing on problems associated with Internet access, the risks of Internet surveillance of activism, the potential of the Internet as a mobilizing force, and the development of online tactics. She found that through the Internet, activists were better able to control the content and distribution of their messages and reach a far wider audience, all at a lower cost, than through traditional media; to avoid containment, either by states or by multinational corporations, through nonhierarchical forms of organizing; to increase the cohesion of their movement both by reinforcing movement networks in the physical world and by engaging in virtual actions; to employ "swarming" and other new tactics; and to communicate and act more quickly and more frequently, unconstrained by geographical boundaries and distances.

Similarly, Michelleti and Stolle (2004) studied emails generated in a 2001 "culture jam" – in effect, a pseudo-event challenging the company on its self-expressed values – targeting Nike on the issue of sweatshop labor as part of a larger campaign that was by then in its tenth year. The precipitating event was a request by an activist that Nike produce a pair of customized shoes with the name "Sweatshop" on them. The resulting email exchange, which the activist shared with a few friends, spread virally to an estimated 11 million people around the world, producing the unsolicited responses studied by Michelleti and Stolle. They concluded that traditional examinations of social movements were increasingly outmoded because, with their tendency to focus on formal organizations and governmental institutions, they overlooked the emerging, viral, and less institutionalized phenomenon of "discursive political consumerism," facilitated by new media, which treats the marketplace as a political arena in which to target not only corporations, but also lifestyles and social values.

Feldner and Meisenbach (2007) studied the use of a web site, SaveDisney.com, to challenge the legitimacy of a major corporation, but not by the traditional type of corporate critic. Rather, the challengers were former insiders, including Roy Disney and another former director, who formed an alliance of shareholders to challenge management on a matter of corporate governance. The campaign employed general themes of transparency and empowerment centered on a highly interactive web site, and succeeded in forcing the resignation of the company's CEO. And in one recent effort to generalize about specific forms of cyber-activism, Karpf (2008) offered a four-part typology of blogging by activists on the Internet, using the dimensions of the underlying software platforms (open or closed authorship) and the source of the blog's reputation (personal or institutional), then mapped the top 25 progressive and conservative blogs into the resulting two-dimensional space.

Many of the established and then-emergent capabilities of digital activism were brought together by the contributors to Van de Donk *et al.* (2004). But while considerable research on digital activism has focused on the use of technology to facilitate or expand traditional forms of activism, cyber-activism does have a less-explored dark side. Denning (2001), for example, though writing in the context of regime-level conflicts, explored the phenomenon of "hacktivism," or the use of sophisticated digital capabilities to attack the Web resources of a target. Her work thus anticipated later anticorporate attacks that employed such elements as hijacking of web sites, denial of service, and theft and leaking of corporate data.

Though networked forms of activism continue to represent the dominant trend, and though they are clearly empowered by digital technologies, at the same time, networks are themselves being challenged by technological change. Bennett (2005), for example, has argued that the increasing reliance on digital communication and the expanding capabilities of that technology are leading to a type of less-structured, leaderless activism that nonetheless forms a global network, while Shirky (2008) has gone so far as to argue that the Internet and mobile telephony are empowering individuals at a level that rivals even governments. De Armond (2001) and Juris (2005) argued that the antiglobalization movement and its participants are often in the forefront of this new, peer-to-peer type of activism.

Activism by the Issues

In many of these efforts, the corporation is a target of opportunity or of necessity, but only as it affects the achievement of some broader objective such as environmental reform. We will conclude our essay by examining three topical foci – labor, social responsibility investing (SRI), and anticorporate activism – which are distinguished and united by an almost single-minded emphasis on corporations and industry, per se, as their primary targets.

Labor activism

Labor activism takes a variety of forms, including community- and campus-based efforts (Clawson, 2003). From the perspective of corporate reputation, however, the most signifi-

cant form is a specialized type of information and influence campaign that has variously been known as the coordinated campaign, the consolidated campaign, or the corporate campaign. We will adopt the latter term. A corporate campaign is a multidimensional, coordinated attack directed by a union against a corporation, usually for one of four purposes – to influence collective bargaining, to facilitate labor organizing (the most common), to influence corporate policy or practices on environmental or other issues, or to influence corporate engagement or positioning in the electoral or public policy arenas. Perry (1987) and Manheim (2001) have provided extensive analyses of such campaigns, including both strategic overviews and numerous case studies. Examining 28 corporate campaigns between 1976 and 1978, Jarley and Maranto (1990) found that corporate campaigns were most likely to be successful when they work in tandem with more traditional union organizing as opposed to supplementing bargaining. Campaigns supporting strikes were actually quite likely to fail. With regard to corporate reputation, the authors found that companies that were most concerned with their public images tended, other things being equal, to be the most responsive targets as conflict escalated. Manheim (2001) pointed out that, because unions suffer from negative public perceptions, they must form coalitions consisting of partners that carry higher levels of legitimacy.

Many case studies with an activist bent as well as a scholarly one either focus primarily on, or incorporate analyses of, corporate campaigns and associated forms of activism (e.g., Ashby and Hawking, 2009; Brisbin, 2002; Getman, 1998; Juravich and Bronfenbrenner, 1999; Rosenblum, 1998). And companies need not have labor issues of their own to become entangled in these attacks, as Ashby and Hawking (2009) make clear in their examination of the targeting of State Farm Insurance as a secondary or even tertiary pressure point on A.E. Staley, which was the real focal point of the campaign in question.

Such campaigns have an increasingly global dimension. Bronfenbrenner's (2007) anthology, for example, contains numerous case studies of unions from the industrialized world partnering with their counterparts in emerging economies to pressure corporations to improve the rights of workers in both the developed and developing worlds. Snell (2007) noted that unions are sometimes wary of boycotts and divestment campaigns in developing countries because they worry about the effects on the workers in those countries.

Coalition building in these campaigns not only enhances the influence of unions in dealing with employers, but also contributes to the integration, or perhaps the reintegration, of organized labor with other activist movements. Studying the labor-initiated anti-sweatshop movement, for example, Kelly and Leftkowitz (2003) noted how the campaign brought together the labor and social justice movements, which found common ground on the issue.

Social responsibility investing

This area of activism originated partly in the labor movement of the 1970s, and partly in the antiwar movement of the 1960s. The first of these gave rise to an appreciation of the potential power of such activism, while the second gave it form and purpose.

Drucker (1976) pointed out that the proliferation and growing scale of pension fund investments in which workers had a beneficial interest meant that the United States had become the first truly socialist country in the world – workers were effectively the principal owners of numerous American companies. He argued that, through a combination of directed investment and systematic proxy voting, these holdings could be used directly to change corporate behavior, and indirectly to affect the American political system. Rifkin and Barber (1978) contended that pension funds would become a new leverage point used by unions in negotiations with companies. In a related development within the European context, Furlong (1977) detailed the concept of code-termination as practiced in West Germany, whereby both workers and stockholders sat on

corporate boards of directors. Fung *et al.* (2001) provided a detailed analysis of the resources available to the labor movement for these purposes and an overview of the leverage provided by the equities markets. Chakrabati (2004) analyzed the factors that lead to successful union shareholder initiatives, finding that unions tend to be more successful if they build coalitions with nonunion shareholders and that Institutional Shareholder Services, a proxy advisory firm, can be a particularly influential ally. The strategic use of proxy votes and the emphasis on influencing corporate governance are cornerstones of labor activism in the United States today, where the trillions of dollars invested in union-controlled or union-influenced pension funds are seen as a counterweight to the decline of labor's share of the workforce (Manheim, 2005a).

Corporate governance is but one of the areas of corporate behavior that activist shareholders seek to influence. Others include all manner of policies and operations – from product lines or lines of business to environmental practices and workplace policies – through which companies interact with their communities. Activist mutual funds, companies, and foundations try to leverage their investments (or their threats to divest) to influence these outcomes, often through the mechanism of "social screening," or the direction of investment toward only those companies who are in acceptable industries and engage in acceptable practices. Vogel (1978) traced the development of this form of activism to strategies employed by the American civil rights movement and an investment approach developed for religious congregations that sought to separate themselves from the Vietnam War.

Price (2004) offered several examples of prominent companies attempting to deal proactively with corporate shareholder activism. In sharp contrast, Entine (2005) saw a serious danger in the possibility of activists increasing their influence at the top levels of corporations. One contributor to the volume edited by Entine, Manheim (2005b), examined social investment as an application of power-structure analysis. An illustration of this is provided by Ganzi *et al.* (1998), environmental activists who published what is effectively a "how-to" guide for applying leverage to the financial services sector in order to achieve broad policy objectives. This document identified eight distinct segments of the financial services industry and recommended specific, stakeholder-based tactics for use by activists to generate pressure on these companies.

Though they are not for the most part major investors, activist foundations have played an important role in developing and channeling much of this investor activism, and much of the political activism that has been employed to produce certain regulatory changes that have facilitated its growth. These foundations, together with other nonprofit advocacy NGOs, benefit from income tax exemptions that require them to operate in a nonpolitical manner. At the invitation of a group of foundations, Colvin (1993), in an obscure but highly influential monograph, set forth six models of activism that they might employ and yet preserve their tax-exempt status.

Anticorporate activism

Even as they attack corporate reputations and pressure corporate policies and actions, labor advocates and activist investors have one essential objective in common: the preservation of those corporations they seek to improve. The same cannot be said for anticorporate activists and the campaigns in which they engage. Whereas labor and investment activists tend to be at least somewhat pragmatic, anticorporate activists are fundamentally ideological. They dislike and distrust the corporation as a social institution, and many are openly anticapitalist. Therefore, although their activism often takes familiar forms, their objectives are quite different, and extend, in some instances, to what Danaher and Mark (2003) have characterized as "dismantling corporate rule" (p. 299). Similarly, Hayduk (2003) characterized the goals of the closely related and equally ideological antiglobalization movement as ending what these activists perceive to be the "domination" of the corporation, establishing local sovereignty, and eliminating throughout the world the income disparity that they attribute to the power of globalized corporations and the governments that aid their advance.

As noted, anticorporate campaigns use many of the same strategies and tactics as do their labor-based counterparts, but often reflect the view, at least implicitly, that the world would be better off without the target corporation (and its ilk). These campaigns may be organized around a policy focus such as the environment, human or indigenous rights, or antiglobalization, but they often incorporate an ideological component and recruit like-minded allies. Because of their ideological bent, these activists are willing to take actions that their more conservative counterparts invariably eschew. As a result, they can be significantly more dangerous to corporations, because anticorporate campaigns theoretically pose an existential threat. It is anticorporate campaigners, not labor activists, who hang by ropes from bridges and buildings to garner attention, and anticorporate campaigners, not activist investors, who challenge legislatures to rescind corporate charters (Manheim, 2004). Rosenkrands (2004) analyzed a number of anticorporate web sites, concluding that, even though they were operated in the commercial sphere, their content was primarily political. And Wright (2004) assigned a central role to digital activism in what he saw as an emerging wave of anticapitalist movements.

Conclusion

Anticorporate activism has enjoyed significant growth over recent decades, powered by the twin engines of technological and social networking that have also driven its rapid transformation from a traditional, boots-on-the-ground style of action to a mix that is increasingly dependent on digital interaction. Along with these changes has come a growing sophistication in the conceptual underpinning of activists' strategies and tactics, and the adoption of nonhierarchical forms that pose special challenges to corporations and other institutional targets alike. In the end, however, the key to the success of any activism lies in its messaging, and more particularly, in the ability of activist appeals to resonate with the public, to mobilize allies, and to generate pressure on the target. It is in this context that the importance of corporate reputation, and both the strength and the vulnerability that it represents, is best understood.

Note

1 Portions of this chapter are derived from Manheim (2011, pp. 194–273).

References

Allan, S., Adam, B., and Carter, C. (eds) (2000) *Environmental Risk and the Media*. London: Routledge.

Arquilla, J. and Ronfeldt, D. (eds) (2001) *Networks and Netwars: The Future of Terror, Crime, and Militancy*. Santa Monica, CA: Rand Corporation.

Ashby, S.K. and Hawking, C.J. (2009) *Staley: The Fight for a New American Labor Movement*. Urbana, IL: University of Illinois Press.

Bakan, J. (2004) *The Corporation: The Pathological Pursuit of Profit and Power*. New York: Free Press.

Bakir, V. (2006) Policy agenda setting and risk communication: Greenpeace, Shell, and issues of trust. *Harvard International Journal of Press/Politics*, 11, 67–88.

Bandy, J. and Smith, J. (eds) (2005) *Coalitions Across Borders: Transnational Protest and the Neoliberal Order*. Lanham, MD: Rowman & Littlefield.

Bartley, T. (2007a) Institutional emergence in an era of globalization: The rise of transnational private regulation of labor and environmental conditions. *American Journal of Sociology*, 113, 297–351.

Bartley, T. (2007b) How foundations shape social movements: The construction of an organizational field and the rise of forest certification. *Social Problems*, 54, 229–255.

Bartley, T. and Child, C. (2009) Shaming the corporation: Globalization, and the dynamics of anti-corporate movements. An earlier version of this paper was presented at the Annual Meeting of

American Sociological Association, New York City, August 2007. Retrieved from http://www.indiana.edu/~tbsoc/SM-corps-sub.pdf (last accessed October 24, 2012).

Bennett, W.L. (2004) Branded political communication: Lifestyle politics, logo campaigns, and the rise of global citizenship. In M. Micheletti, A. Follesdal, and D. Stolle (eds), *Politics, Products, and Markets: Exploring Political Consumerism Past and Present*. New Brunswick, NJ: Transaction Books, pp. 101–125.

Bennett, W.L. (2005) Social movements beyond borders: Understanding two eras of transnational activism. In D. Della Porta and S. Tarrow (eds), *Transnational Protest and Global Activism*. Lanham, MD: Rowman & Littlefield, pp. 203–226.

Bob, C. (2005) *The Marketing of Rebellion: Insurgents, Media, and International Activism*. Cambridge, UK: Cambridge University Press.

Bowers, J.W., Ochs, D.J., and Jensen, R.J. (1993) *The Rhetoric of Agitation and Control* (2nd ed.). Long Grove, IL: Waveland Press.

Brisbin, R.A. Jr. (2002) *A Strike Like No Other Strike: Law & Resistance during the Pittston Coal Strike of 1989–1990*. Baltimore, MD: Johns Hopkins University Press.

Bronfenbrenner, K. (2007) *Global Unions: Challenging Transnational Capitalism through Cross-Border Campaigns*. Ithaca, NY: Cornell University Press.

Bullert, B.J. (2000) Strategic public relations, sweatshops and the making of a global movement (Working Paper No. 2000-14). Cambridge, MA: Shorenstein Center, Harvard University. Retrieved from http://www.hks.harvard.edu/presspol/publications/papers/working_papers/2000_14_bullert.pdf (last accessed October 1, 2012).

Cashore, B., Auld, G., and Newsom, D. (2004) Legitimizing political consumerism: The case of forest certification in North America and Europe. In M. Micheletti, A. Follesdal, and D. Stolle (eds), *Politics, Products, and Markets: Exploring Political Consumerism Past Present*. New Brunswick, NJ: Transaction Books, pp. 181–202.

Chakrabati, M. (2004) Labor and corporate governance: Initial lessons from shareholder activism. *Working USA: The Journal of Labor and Society*, 8, 45–69.

Chong, D. and Druckman, J.N. (2007a) A theory of framing and opinion formation in competitive elite environments. *Journal of Communication*, 57, 99–118.

Chong, D. and Druckman, J.N. (2007b) Framing public opinion in competitive democracies. *American Political Science Review, 104,* 663–680.

Chong, D. and Druckman, J.N. (2010) Dynamic public opinion: Communication effects over time. *American Political Science Review, 101,* 637–655.

Clawson, D. (2003) *The Next Upsurge: Labor and the New Social Movements.* Ithaca, NY: Cornell University Press.

Colvin, G.L. (1993) *Fiscal Sponsorship: 6 Ways to Do It Right.* San Francisco, CA: Study Center Press.

Danaher, K. and Mark, J. (2003) *Insurrection: Citizen Challenges to Corporate Power.* New York: Routledge.

De Armond, P. (2001) Netwar in the Emerald City: WTO protest strategy and tactics. In J. Arquilla and D. Ronfeldt (eds), *Networks and Netwars.* Santa Monica, CA: Rand Corporation, pp. 201–235.

Della Porta, D. and Tarrow, S. (eds) (2005) *Transnational Protest and Global Activism.* Lanham, MD: Rowman & Littlefield.

DeLuca, K. (1999) *Image Politics: The New Rhetoric of Environmental Activism.* Mahwah, NJ: Lawrence Erlbaum Associates.

Demars, W.E. (2005) *NGOs and Transnational Networks: Wild Cards in World Politics.* London: Pluto Press.

Denning, D.E. (2001) Activism, hacktivism, and cyberterrorism: The internet as a tool for influencing foreign policy. In J. Arquilla and D. Ronfeldt (eds), *Networks and Netwars.* Santa Monica, CA: Rand Corporation, pp. 239–288.

Diani, M. and McAdam, D. (eds) (2003) *Social Movements and Networks: Relational Approaches to Collective Action.* Oxford, UK: Oxford University Press.

Drucker, P.E. (1976) *The Unseen Revolution: How Pension Fund Socialism Came to America.* New York: Harper & Row.

Edelman, M. (1988) *Constructing the Political Spectacle.* Chicago, IL: University of Chicago Press.

Entine, J. (ed.) (2005) *Pension Fund Politics: The Dangers of Socially Responsible Investing.* Washington, DC: American Enterprise Institute.

Entman, R.M. (1993) Framing: Toward clarification of a fractured paradigm. *Journal of Communication, 43,* 51–58.

Feldner, S.B. and Meisenbach, R.J. (2007) SaveDisney.com and activist challenges: A Habermasian perspective on corporate legitimacy. *International Journal of Strategic Communication, 1,* 207–226.

Friedman, M. (1999) *Consumer Boycotts: Effecting Change through the Marketplace and the Media.* New York: Routledge.

Fung, A., Hebb, T., and Rogers, J. (eds) (2001) *Working Capital: The Power of Labor's Pensions.* Ithaca, NY: Cornell University Press.

Furlong, J. (1977) *Labor in the Boardroom: The Peaceful Revolution.* Princeton, NJ: Dow Jones Books.

Gamson, W.A. (1990) *The Strategy of Social Protest* (2nd ed.). Homewood, IL: Dorsey Press.

Ganzi, J., Seymour, F., and Buffet, S. (1998) *Leverage for the Environment: A Guide to the Private Financial Industry.* Washington, DC: World Resources Institute.

Getman, J. (1998) *The Betrayal of Local 14: Paperworkers, Politics, & Permanent Replacements.* Ithaca, NY: Cornell University Press.

Grant, A. and Taylor, I. (2004) Global governance and conflict diamonds: The Kimberley process and the quest for clean gems. *The Round Table: The Commonwealth Journal of International Affairs, 93,* 385–401.

Gregory, S., Caldwell, G., Avni, R., and Harding, T. (eds) (2005) *Video for Change: A Guide for Advocacy and Activism.* London: Pluto Press.

Hansen, A. (1991) The media and the social construction of the environment. *Media, Culture, and Society, 13,* 443–458.

Hansen, A. (2000) Claims-making and framing in British newspaper coverage of the "Brent Spar" controversy. In S. Allan, B. Adam, and C. Carter (eds), *Environmental Risk and the Media.* London: Routledge, pp. 55–72.

Hayduk, R. (2003) From anti-globalization to global justice: A twenty-first-century movement. In J.C. Berg (ed.), *Teamsters and Turtles? U.S. Progressive Movements in the 21st Century.* Oxford, UK: Rowman & Littlefield, pp. 17–50.

Huxham, M. and Sumner, D. (1999) Emotion, science, and rationality: The case of the Brent Spar. *Environmental Values, 8,* 349–368.

Ihlen, Ø. and Nitz, M. (2008) Framing contests in environmental disputes: Paying attention to media and cultural master frames. *International Journal of Strategic Communication, 2,* 1–18.

Jarley, P. and Maranto, C.L. (1990) Union corporate campaigns: An assessment. *Industrial and Labor Relations Review, 43,* 893–896.

Jordan, A., Wurzel, R., Zito, A., and Brückner, L. (2004) Consumer responsibility-taking and national eco-labeling schemes in Europe. In M. Micheletti, A. Follesdal, and D. Stolle (eds), *Politics, Products and Markets: Exploring Political Consumerism*. Somerset, NJ: Transaction Publishers, pp. 161–180.

Juravich, T. and Bronfenbrenner, K. (1999) *Ravenswood: The Steelworkers' Victory and the Revival of American Labor*. Ithaca, NY: Cornell University Press.

Juris, J.S. (2005) The new digital media and activist networking within anti-corporate globalization movements. *The Annals of the American Academy of Political and Social Science*, 597, 189–208.

Juska, A. and Edwards, B. (2005) Refusing the Trojan pig: The U.S.-Poland coalition against corporate pork production. In A. Juska and B. Edwards (eds), *Coalitions across Borders: Transnational Protest and the Neoliberal Order*. Lanham, MD: Rowman & Littlefield, pp. 187–207.

Karpf, D. (2008) Understanding blogspace. *Journal of Information Technology & Politics*, 5, 369–385.

Karpf, D. (2009) Why bowl alone when you can flashmob the bowling alley? Implications of the mobile web for online-offline reputation systems. Paper presented at the WebSci'09 Conference, Athens, Greece.

Keck, M.E. and Sikkink, K. (1998) *Activists beyond Borders: Advocacy Networks in International Politics*. Ithaca, NY: Cornell University Press.

Kelly, C. and Leftkowitz, J. (2003) Radical and pragmatic: United students against sweatshops. In J.C. Berg (ed.), *Teamsters and Turtles? U.S. Progressive Movements in the 21st Century*. Oxford, UK: Rowman & Littlefield, pp. 83–97.

Klein, J., Smith, N.C., and John, A. (2004) Why we boycott: Consumer motivations for boycott participation. *Journal of Marketing*, 68(3), 92–109.

Lange, J. (1993) The logic of competing information campaigns: Conflict over old growth and the spotted owl. *Communication Monographs*, 60, 240–257.

Manheim, J.B. (2000) *Corporate Conduct Unbecoming: Codes of Conduct and Anti-Corporate Strategy*. St. Michaels, MD: Tred Avon Institute Press.

Manheim, J.B. (2001) *The Death of a Thousand Cuts: Corporate Campaigns and the Attack on the Corporation*. Mahwah, NJ: Lawrence Erlbaum Associates.

Manheim, J.B. (2004) *Biz-War and the Out-of-Power Elite: The Progressive Attack on the Corporation*. Mahwah, NJ: Lawrence Erlbaum Associates.

Manheim, J.B. (2005a) *Power Failure, Power Surge: Union Pension Fund Activism and the Publicly Held Corporation*. Washington, DC: HR Policy Association.

Manheim, J.B. (2005b) The strategic use of social responsibility investing. In J. Entine (ed.), *Pension Fund Politics: The Dangers of Socially Responsible Investing*. Washington, DC: American Enterprise Institute, pp. 81–101.

Manheim, J.B. (2011) *Strategy in Information and Influence Campaigns*. New York: Routledge.

Martin, C.R. (2004) *Framed: Labor and the Corporate Media*. Ithaca, NY: Cornell University Press.

Meyer, D.S. and Gamson, J. (1995) The challenge of cultural elites: Celebrities and social movements. *Sociological Inquiry*, 62, 181–206.

Michelleti, M. and Stolle, D. (2004) A case of discursive political consumerism: The Nike e-mail exchange. In M. Boström, A. Føllesdal, M. Klintman, M. Micheletti, and M.P. Sørensen (eds), Political Consumerism: Its Motivations, Power, and Conditions in the Nordic Countries and Elsewhere: Proceedings from the 2nd International Seminar on Political Consumerism, Norden, Oslo, August 26–29.

Micheletti, M., Follesdal, A., and Stolle, D. (eds) (2004) *Politics, Products and Markets: Exploring Political Consumerism Past and Present*. New Brunswick, NJ: Transaction.

Myers, D.J. (1994) Communication technology and social movements: Contributions of computer networks to activism. *Social Science Computer Review*, 12, 250–260.

Oppenheimer, M. and Lakey, G. (1964) *A Manual for Direct Action*. Chicago, IL: Quadrangle Books.

Payne, R.A. (2001) Persuasion, frames, and norm construction. *European Journal of International Relations*, 7, 37–61.

Peizer, J. (2006) *The Dynamics of Technology for Social Change*. New York: iUniverse.

Perry, C.R. (1987) *Union Corporate Campaigns*. Philadelphia: The Wharton School of the University of Pennsylvania.

Pickerill, J. (2001) Environmental Internet activism in Britain. *Peace Review*, 13, 365–370.

Price, T. (2000) *Cyber Activism: Advocacy Groups and the Internet*. Washington, DC: Foundation for Public Affairs.

Price, T. (2004) *Activists in the Boardroom: How Advocacy Groups Seek to Shape Corporate Behavior*. Washington, DC: Foundation for Public Affairs.

Reber, B.H. and Berger, B.K. (2005) Framing analysis of activist rhetoric: How the Sierra Club succeeds or fails at creating salient messages. *Public Relations Review*, 31, 185–195.

Rheingold, H. (2002) *Smart Mobs: The Next Social Revolution*. Cambridge, MA: Perseus.

Rifkin, J. and Barber, R. (1978) *The North Will Rise Again: Pensions, Politics and Power in the 1980's*. Boston: Beacon Press.

Robb, J. (2007) *Brave New War: The Next Stage of Terrorism and the End of Globalization*. Hoboken, NJ: John Wiley & Sons.

Ronfeldt, D. and Arquilla, J. (2001) Emergence and influence of the Zapatista social netwar. In J. Arquilla and D. Ronfeldt (eds), *Networks and Netwars*. Santa Monica, CA: Rand Corporation, pp. 171–199.

Rosenblum, J.D. (1998) *Copper Crucible: How the Arizona Miners; Strike of 1983 Recast Labor-Management Relations in America* (2nd ed.). Ithaca, NY: Cornell University Press.

Rosenkrands, J. (2004) Politicizing Homo economicus: Analysis of anti-corporate websites. In W. Van De Donk, B.D. Loader, P.G. Nixon, and D. Rucht (eds), *Cyberprotest: New Media, Citizens, and Social Movements*. London: Routledge, pp. 57–76.

Ryan, C. (1991) *Prime Time Activism: Media Strategies for Grassroots Organizing*. Boston: South End Press.

Salmon, C.T., Post, L.A., and Christensen, R.E. (2003) Mobilizing public will for social change. Paper prepared for the Communications Consortium Media Center, Washington, DC.

Salzman, J. (2003) *Making the News: A Guide for Activists and Nonprofits*. Boulder, CO: Westview Press.

Seidman, G.W. (2005) Monitoring multinationals: Corporate codes of conduct. In A. Juska and B. Edwards (eds), *Coalitions across Borders: Transnational Protest and the Neoliberal Order*. Lanham, MD: Rowman & Littlefield, pp. 163–183.

Shaw, R. (1996) *The Activist's Handbook: A Primer for the 1990s and Beyond*. Berkeley, CA: University of California Press.

Shirky, C. (2008) *Here Comes Everybody: The Power of Organizing without Organizations*. New York: Penguin.

Smith, J. and Johnston, H. (eds) (2002) *Globalization and Resistance: Transnational Dimensions of Social Movements*. Oxford, UK: Rowman & Littlefield.

Snell, D. (2007) Transnational corporations, human rights abuse, and violent conflict in the Global South. In K. Bronfenbrenner (ed.), *Global Unions: Challenging Transnational Capitalism through Cross-Border Campaigns*. Ithaca, NY: Cornell University Press.

Snow, D.A., Rochford, E.B. Jr., Worden, S.K., and Benford, R.D. (1986) Frame alignment processes, micromobilization, and movement participation. *American Sociological Review*, 51, 464–481.

Suchman, M.C. (1995) Managing legitimacy: Strategic and institutional approaches. *Academy of Management Review*, 20, 571–610.

Tarrow, S. (2005) *The New Transnational Activism*. Cambridge, UK: Cambridge University Press.

Thrall, A.T., Lollio-Fakhreddine, J., Berent, J., Donnelly, L., Herrin, W., Paquette, Z., Wenglinski, R., and Wyatt, A. (2008) Star power: Celebrity advocacy and the evolution of the public sphere. *International Journal of Press/Politics*, 13, 362–385.

Van De Donk, W., Loader, B.D., Nixon, P.G., and Rucht, D. (eds) (2004) *Cyberprotest: New Media, Citizens, and Social Movements*. London: Routledge.

Vogel, D. (1978) *Lobbying the Corporation: Citizen Challenges to Business Authority*. New York: Basic Books.

Vogel, D. (1989) *Fluctuating Forces: The Political Power of Business in America*. New York: Basic Books.

Vogel, D. (1995) *Trading Up: Consumer and Environmental Regulation in a Global Economy*. Cambridge, MA: Harvard University Press.

Vogel, D. (1996) *Kindred Strangers: The Uneasy Relationship between Politics and Business in America*. Princeton, NJ: Princeton University Press.

Vogel, D. (2005) *The Market for Virtue: The Potential Limits of Corporate Social Responsibility*. Washington, DC: Brookings Institution.

Wright, S. (2004) Informing, communicating and ICTs in contemporary anti-capitalist movements. In W. Van De Donk, B.D. Loader, P.G. Nixon, and D. Rucht (eds), *Cyperprotest: New Media, Citizens and Social Movements*. London: Routledge, pp. 77–94.

35

Identity, Perceived Authenticity, and Reputation: A Dynamic Association in Strategic Communications

Juan-Carlos Molleda
University of Florida, USA

Rajul Jain
DePaul University, USA

This chapter explores the association among identity, perceived authenticity, and reputation – constructs that are relevant to a marketspace where organizations are competing for attention, a commodity in deficit. In a world saturated with information and fraught with skepticism and distrust, organizations must communicate a clear and consistent identity to gain attention of consumers and stakeholders. A solid organizational identity should contribute to achieve a desired reputation; both identity and reputation should help organizational claims and offerings be perceived as authentic. This chapter focuses on how organizations could build favorable and unique reputations in the minds of consumers and stakeholders by demonstrating consistency with their core values in their claims, actions, and decisions. The main construct that is analyzed is perceived authenticity, which has become a promising construct in public relations and strategic communication.

Introduction

Stakeholders, consumers, and organizations are constantly interacting within and between both local communities and communities worldwide. Personal, group, and organizational claims and offerings are competing for attention of their targeted audiences. In information-overloaded environments, attention has become a commodity in deficit. All actors make decisions, execute actions, and produce communication contents that are sought after, processed, or ignored in fluid and multidimensional analog and digital platforms. As a consequence, organ-izations, in particular, face a "marketspace" characterized by competing and contrasting voices; therefore, their voices progressively must be clear and consistent.

This chapter focuses on how organizations could achieve stronger and distinctive voices for the ultimate goal of attaining a desired reputation in the eyes and minds of consumers and other stakeholders. The main construct that will be analyzed and discussed here is perceived authenticity, which has become a promising and prominent construct in public relations and strategic communication. In particular, authenticity has peaked interest of public relations and

The Handbook of Communication and Corporate Reputation, First Edition. Edited by Craig E. Carroll.
© 2013 John Wiley & Sons, Inc. Published 2015 by John Wiley & Sons, Inc.

strategic communication professionals as evident from the Arthur W. Page Society's *Authentic Enterprise* report issued in 2007, the International Communication Association (ICA) conference panel held in Chicago in May 2009, and the special edition issued by the *Journal of Communication Management* in 2010 discussing authenticity and projecting it as a central construct in contemporary public relations practice and research ("The authentic enterprise," 2007; "Authentic influence," 2009; PR Industry Leaders, 2009). Furthermore, a Public Relations Society of America's (PRSA) Counselors Academy survey demonstrated that public relations professionals and industry leaders are calling authenticity one of the top three issues facing the profession (PR Industry Leaders, 2009). The construct of perceived authenticity offers a significant framework to analyze strategic communication practices, conduct research, and contribute to the evolving body of knowledge.

The understanding of the association between perceived authenticity and reputation is relevant because we are living in more demanding political and socioeconomic environments in which organizations aim to sustain their activities and operations with legitimacy and public acceptance. Moreover, "in the age of complexity, skepticism has become endemic" (Edelman, 2011, ¶ 21). Some of the trends we are experiencing in these environments are more active stakeholders and consumers; emergence of the experience economy; erosion of trust in institutions; greater demand for transparency, openness, and responsibility; expanded and sophisticated competition and communication media and channels; and the emergence of realities and consequences of economic difficulties of many nations during and after the global recession. Once again, attention has become the most important commodity and reality is defying fiction.

Perceived Authenticity

Authenticity is one of the five elements that, in theory, contribute to organizational reputation along with distinctiveness, transparency, visibility, and consistency (Fombrun and van Riel, 2004). Consumers and other stakeholders evaluate organizational claims and promises against its actions and behavior to form perceptions of authenticity. Therefore, authentic organizations must demonstrate consistency with their core values in actions, behaviors, decisions, and communication with internal and external stakeholders. This is a challenging task for organizations in the complex world where good intentions are not enough to gain stakeholder trust; organizations must prove themselves in their deeds (Fombrun and van Riel, 2004).

However, organizations that succeed in this challenging task win stakeholders' trust and commitment. An authentic person, object, or organization is considered "[e]ntitled to acceptance or belief, as being in accordance with fact, or as stating fact; reliable, trustworthy, of established credit" (The Oxford English Dictionary, 2010). In this sense, an authentic organization is perceived as credible, trustworthy, genuine, and honest (Gilmore and Pine, 2007; Molleda, 2010a; Molleda and Jain, 2011).

Much like reputation and transparency, authenticity is an important construct for the development of organizational identities and perceptions (Debreceny, 2010; Henderson and Edwards, 2010; Molleda, 2010a,b; Molleda and Jain, 2011). According to Zickmund (2007), "[a]uthenticity is a process of being true to one's own self, of living life according to one's own being" (p. 407). Fine's (2003) definition of authenticity reads, "[S]incere, innocent, original, genuine, and unaffected . . . linked to moral authority of the creator and simultaneously to the fact that the object was made by hand, not mechanically produced" (p. 155). From an advertising perspective, Beverland (2005) defined authenticity as "a story that balances industrial (production, distribution and marketing) and rhetorical attributes to project sincerity through the avowal of commitments to traditions (including production methods, product styling, firm values, and/or location), passion for craft and production excellence, and the public disavowal of the role of modern industrial attributes and commercial motivations" (p. 1008).

Thus, to be perceived as authentic, organizations must be consistent between what they say and what they are and, most importantly, what they do and the decisions they make. Moreover, efforts should be invested in developing an organizational identity that captures their values, principles, management philosophy, and motivations as well as their historical pledges of quality processes, productions, and deliveries. This organizational identity should be clearly and repeatedly communicated, over time, to consumers and other audiences with a distinctive voice and with the inclusion of effective mechanism of engagement with the targeted consumers and audiences.

Similar to other constructs, such as trust and credibility, authenticity is an experience and perception that is cocreated by the organization and its stakeholders as an ongoing negotiation of meaning and understanding. In this sense, authenticity is a function of perceived genuineness and positive evaluation of organization's actions and behavior (Trilling, 1972) and hence could determine the quality of organization–public relationships (Molleda, 2010a,b).

Also from its historical roots in Greek philosophy ("To thine own self be true"), where it was described as the quality of being true to oneself (Avolio and Gardner, 2005; Harter, 2002), authenticity has been used as the notions of correspondence and genesis. Traditionally, authenticity is built around the notion that communication plans, programs, or campaigns cannot achieve it unless the underlying object, person, or organization in its true essence represents an authentic being by manifesting its true identity in its actions, decisions, and philosophy of living up to its own and others' expectations and needs (Molleda, 2010a).

Applying this rationale, Molleda (2010a,b) has proposed a preliminary index of authenticity, which includes a range of indicators through which an organization's perceived authenticity could be evaluated. The purpose of the index is to measure the effectiveness of public relations efforts, techniques, and message system

by evaluating the perceived authenticity of organizations, including its actions, operations, products, services, and corporate spokespeople in the mind of internal or external stakeholders. Recently, Molleda and Jain (2011) expanded the conceptualization of authenticity and tested this index in their study involving the public relations efforts of a private cultural and eco-archeological park in the Mayan Riviera of Mexico. The authors found that overall experience with an organization, its products, services, and public relations claims, and active engagement of organizational publics are two dimensions that describe this multidimensional construct.

From a leadership perspective, authenticity "represents the extent to which a leader is aware of and exhibits pattern of openness and clarity in his/her behavior toward others by sharing the information needed to make decisions, accepting others' inputs, and disclosing his/her personal values, motives, and sentiments in a manner that enables followers to more accurately assess the competence and morality of the leader's actions" (Walumbwa *et al.*, 2010, p. 901). This perspective of an authentic leader could be extended to the context of organizational authenticity. It can be argued that an organization can portray itself as authentic by sharing periodic and accurate information with its consumers and other stakeholders, engaging them in a dialog by soliciting their feedback, and disclosing its personal values, motives, and beliefs in a manner that enable publics to more accurately assess the identity and integrity of an organization's actions. According to Gilmore and Pine (2007), authentic communication entails expressing the true values and traditions of an organization or brand with consumers or audiences they engage.

Similarly, Morgan (2009) explained that consistency in actions, motivations, and intentions foster perceptions of authenticity:

> We believe people are authentic when they are open with us in a sense that feels real. It has to do with transparency of motive and intention. We believe people are authentic when we

know what makes them tick – because they've told us and their actions bear it out. And it has to do with consistency of action. We believe that people are authentic when they keep the same agenda for a substantial period of time. (p. 10)

However, scholars suggested that there may be much more to authentic organizations than just being true to oneself (Jain and De Moya, 2011; Molleda, 2010a,b; Molleda and Jain, 2011; Molleda and Roberts, 2008). One often cited definition of the construct states that people tend to perceive as authentic that which exists in its natural form; is not artificial or synthetic; is original in design and not an imitation or copy; is executed exceptionally and extraordinarily well; refers or draws from heritage or history; and inspires people to a higher goal (Gilmore and Pine, 2007; Molleda, 2010a).

The Dynamic Association

Organizational identity

Organizational identity is a complex phenomenon that has received significant attention in business and communication literature, yet much like perceived authenticity, its nature remains debated. At its core, organizational identity deals with determining who the organization is. However, the answer to this question is not simple, since organizations can have multiple identities (Pratt and Foreman, 2000) that could evolve or be affected by external and internal operating environment changes (Brilliant and Young, 2004).

Albert and Whetten (1985) described organizational identity as those characteristics of an organization that members perceive as enduring, central, and unique about their organization. At the individual level, members may develop a schema of core attributes that uniquely identify an organization and are shared by its members (Dutton and Penner, 1993). This implies that organizational identity may vary depending on the attributes that members might associate with an organization.

While an organization might be known for its social responsibility efforts and community engagement, another might be identified for its quality of products and services. However, irrespective of what attributes uniquely characterize an organization, organizational identity is a subset of the collective beliefs that constitute an organization's culture (Dutton et al., 1994).

Along similar lines, Balmer and Greyser (2006) proposed that organizational identity is defined by a combination of organization's character, "what we indubitably are," and culture, "what we feel we are" (p. 735). The authors further elaborated that organizational philosophy and ethos, its products and pricing, distribution and sourcing mechanisms, quality of its products and services, its competitive positioning, and personality as exuded by its culture and employees, are the key elements of organizational identity. Other scholars also suggested that organizational mission statements, strategy, values, and beliefs are the foundation of its identity (Sha, 2009; van Riel and Balmer, 1997).

Examining the various perspectives approaching organizational identity, van Riel and Balmer (1997) characterized them into three main developments: visual identity using graphic design, integrated communication, and last, a multidisciplinary approach that draws from organizational behavior. Scholars have examined organizational identity from a graphic design perspective by analyzing visual elements such as symbols, logos, colors, and nomenclatures as manifestations of an organization's strategy, branding, and communication policies (Olins, 1978). From an integrated communication perspective, scholars such as Bernstein (1986), Grunig and Grunig (1992), and Schultz et al. (1994) argued that organizational identity is an outcome of integrated communication efforts on behalf of the organization with all its stakeholders. Finally, a multidisciplinary approach suggested that organizational identity is a set of unique characteristics that are rooted in the behavior of its members, that is, its culture. Furthermore, organizations can achieve a desirable identity by using communication and symbolism and through actual behavior.

From a corporate perspective, Melewar and Jenkins (2002) identified four subconstructs of organizational identity: communication and visual identity, behavior, corporate culture, and market conditions. The authors further elaborated that communication and visual identity is an outcome of corporate communications, uncontrollable communication, architecture and location of the firm, and corporate visual identity. Similarly, behavior represents corporate, management, and employee actions and behavior. Melewar and Jenkins (2002) described that corporate culture is manifested in the goals, philosophies, and principles of a firm; its nationality; history; and imagery. Finally, the nature of the industry and corporate or marketing strategies define market conditions of an organization, and are an integral part of its identity.

In sum, scholars conceive organizational identity as a collectively held frame by its members; however, identity is "objectively held – that is, it has a reality independent of individual observers – although it is subjectively arrived at" (Scott and Lane, 2000, p. 43). Thus, from a stakeholder's perspective, "organizational identity is best understood as contested and negotiated through iterative interactions between managers and stakeholders" (Scott and Lane, 2000, p. 44). This perspective demonstrates the key role public relations and other strategic communication disciplines perform in the development and maintenance of organization identity because "organizational communication is essentially a process through which meaning is created, negotiated, and managed" (Cheney and Christensen, 2000, p. 241).

Also, organizational identity often serves as an important reference point for stakeholders to evaluate an organization's actions, behavior, and communication claims (Dutton and Dukerich, 1991). For instance in their study, Dutton and Dukerich (1991) found that the more the members perceive an issue to be relevant to organizational identity, the greater is the perceived legitimacy of the issue and the perception of the feasibility of resolving the issue.

These scholarly discussions suggest that organizational identity is an important precedent to evaluate if an organization is acting according to its true self, or in other words identity, and thereby influence the opinions of stakeholders about organizational authenticity. Another closely related construct to identity, organizational reputation is an important precedent to perceived organizational authenticity, as discussed next.

Organizational reputation

Since most scholarly work has examined reputation in the context of corporations (Balmer, 1995; Balmer and Greyser, 2006; Bromley, 2001; Mahon, 2002), this chapter uses this perspective to operationalize organizational reputation. From a corporate perspective, reputation is defined as "the aggregation of a single stakeholder's perception of how well organizational responses are meeting the demands and expectations of many corporate stakeholders" (Wartick, 1992, p. 34). These aggregate perceptions are based on organizations' actions as well as stakeholders' memory and perceptions (Mahon, 2002). Similarly, Bromley (2001) defined reputation stakeholders' "overt expression of a collective image" of an organization. In other words, reputation is the way in which consumers and external stakeholders conceptualize an organization.

Along these lines, Balmer and Greyser (2006) explained that organizational reputation, "what we are seen to be," is an outcome of organizational communication, "what we say we are," organizational constituencies, "whom we seek to serve," and organizational covenant, "what is promised and expected" (p. 735). In other words, organizational communication, stakeholders' management, and brand promise shape and inform how an organization is perceived and what stakeholders expect from it. Furthermore, organizations that act consistent with stakeholders' expectations will be regarded as authentic (Gilmore and Pine, 2007; Molleda, 2010a,b; Molleda and Jain, 2011).

Scholars argued that while organizational identity and reputation are related constructs, they should be conceived as distinct constructs (Bromley, 2001; Fombrun, 1996). According to Fombrun (1996), identity is the foundation of reputation, and to "focus on a company's reputation also is to determine how it deals with all of its constituents; it is to focus on a company's character or identity" (p. 111). In other words, while identity is intended and constructed by organizations, reputation is an outcome of such efforts as perceived by its various stakeholders. Furthermore, Bromley (2001) proposed that while identity refers to the perceptions and mental associations about an organization held by its members, reputation is defined as the evaluations and perceptions of an organization held by others outside the organization.

Similarly, Camilleri (2008) conceptualized reputation as a function of organizational identity, in his examination of authenticity claims of a wine manufacturing company. The author emphasized that organizational identity is how organizations present themselves, whereas organizational reputation is how stakeholders perceive an organization. Similar to other scholars, Camilleri identified organizational mission, visual presentation, and corporate culture as the pillars of organizational identity, which is a precedent to stakeholder expectations from an organization. The author also highlighted the role of communication in building organizational reputation.

Reputation has been extensively examined in the business literature where it has been defined as opinions of market participants about an organization's strategic positioning (Weigelt and Camerer, 1988), salient characteristics that stakeholders associate with a firm (Fombrun and Shanley, 1990), the value that publics ascribe to an organization (Fombrun, 1996), media coverage and tone (Deephouse, 2000), and people's collective belief about an organization's identity and personality (Rao, 1994).

Reputations are formed through direct interaction (experience) with an organization, as well as through the information that publics have of their actions (Gotsi and Wilson, 2001). This process emphasizes the importance of objective-oriented communication in forming corporate reputation, and the key role played by public relations. Additionally, these concep-

tualizations illustrate that much like identity, reputation serves as a reference point for stakeholders to evaluate organizational authenticity assertions against its actions and behaviors.

While there are several measurements of organizational reputation in scholarly research (Black *et al.*, 2000; Carroll, 2004; Fombrun and Shanley, 1990; Nakra, 2000), the Reputation Quotient[SM] (Harris Interactive, 2009), is particularly useful for this. The instrument was used to compile an annual ranking of the most visible companies in the United States and their reputation, as well as to offer its clients insights into their reputation branding goals and designing messages and strategies. Since Gardberg and Fombrun's (2002) initial evaluation, this early index was validated through scholarly research as an accurate measure of stakeholder evaluations of organizations (Carroll, 2004; Carroll and McCombs, 2003; Kiousis *et al.*, 2007).

More recently, the Reputation Institute's RepTrak™ model evaluates corporate reputation using these dimensions: products and services, innovation, citizenship, governance, workplace, leadership, and financial performance (Reputation Institute, 2012). These dimensions, or reputational attributes, are measured on a 7-point scale, which provides the composite evaluation of the company's reputation. Similarly, Doorley and Garcia (2011) suggested nine reputation criteria, six of which are similar to the Reputation Quotient[SM], and three are unique: communicativeness (transparency), governance, and integrity (responsibility, reliability, credibility, trustworthiness).

Identity, reputation, and perceived authenticity

Fombrun and van Riel (2004) explained that an authentic organization is the one that acts consistent with its identity and established reputation. In other words, perceived organizational authenticity is the degree to which stakeholders perceive organization's offerings and claims to be consistent with its identity and reputation. Authentic organizations must "be grounded in a sure sense of what defines it – why it exists, what it stands for and what differentiates it in a marketplace [...] values, principles, beliefs, mission, purpose or value proposition – must dictate consistent behavior and actions" ("The authentic enterprise," 2007, p. 6).

In this sense, organizations have to be aware of their identity and reputation, should actively communicate it to their myriad of stakeholders, who then form a perception about the organization and who it really is, and ultimately, evaluate organization's claims of authenticity. Authenticity is considered an integral part of organizational reputation (Fombrun and van Riel, 2004) and is seen as firmly ingrained in an organization's identity (Gilmore and Pine, 2007). Along these lines, Molleda (2010a) suggested:

> Organisations progressively build their corporate personalities by highlighting and putting certain authentic features out to the scrutiny of their stakeholders who, at the same time, make selective interpretations and consequently judge these organisations' reputations. The consistency of what organisations do and say may result in a perceived reputation close to the carefully built corporate identity with the use of strategic public relations and communication management. (p. 225)

Along these lines, Fombrun and van Riel (2004) proposed that to be perceived authentic, organizations should engage in a "process of discovery" (p. 165) that involves identifying its core values and what it stands for and actively and consistently communicates it to its consumers and other stakeholders. Similarly, Gilmore and Pine (2007) explained that at any given time, an organization is in the "Here-and-Now" space (p. 182), which represents a progression of organizational identity over time, beginning with its origin and heritage, and leading up to what it is today. At this point, organizations face an execution zone of future strategic possibilities that determine a future course of action, and thereby, dictate the possibilities of rendering organizational authenticity by acting in accordance to an organization's established identity and who it has come to be known for.

This conceptualization illustrates the significant role that public relations could perform in helping organizations render authenticity. Scholars have suggested that organizations can portray themselves as authentic by being transparent, sharing periodic and accurate information with its publics, engaging them in a dialog by soliciting their feedback, and disclosing its personal values, motives, and believes in a manner that enable publics to more accurately assess the identity and integrity of an organization's actions (Gilmore and Pine, 2007).

Based on this theoretical formulation, we propose the following dynamic association between identity, perceived authenticity, and reputation (see Figure 35.1). Additionally, we also summarize how these three important constructs are conceptualized in the academic literature (see Table 35.1).

Conclusions

The main contribution of this chapter is the introduction of perceived authenticity as a construct that is closely associated with organizational identity and reputation. Perceived authenticity is becoming a promising construct in the various practices of strategic communication and is regarded as a construct with great potential to strengthen public relations and strategic communication practices and to conduct both trade and academic research.

Studies and conscious practical associations among identity, perceived authenticity, and reputation are relevant in a marketspace signaled by evolving communication technologies and globalization. The intense flow of communication, interactions, and all types of transactions demand organizations to cultivate and speak with a clear and consistent voice, a voice that need to capture the attention of consumer and stakeholders, a commodity in deficit. A solid organizational identity should contribute to achieve a desired reputation; both identity and reputation should help organizational claims and offerings be perceived as authentic. More specifically, organizational identity can be

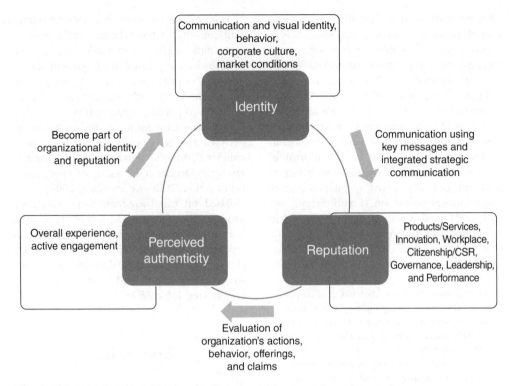

Figure 35.1 The dynamic association: identity, perceived authenticity, and reputation.

Table 35.1 Constructs in the dynamic association.

Construct	Conceptualization	Authors/study
Perceived authenticity	Overall experience Active engagement	Molleda (2010b) and Molleda and Jain (2011)
Identity	Four subconstructs: communication and visual identity, behavior, corporate culture, market conditions	Melewar and Jenkins (2002)
Reputation	Products/Services, Innovation, Workplace, Citizenship/CSR, Governance, Leadership, and Performance	

managed; that is, it is intended and constructed by organizations. Identity should endure and be central to the collective beliefs of organizational members and, therefore, its organizational culture. What the organization is should be reflected in how its consumers and stakeholders interpret the organization. In addition, to achieve and construct an intended identity, the organization must meet the demands and needs of consumer and other stakeholders. This

is a prerequisite to obtain the desired conceptualization of an organization by its external stakeholders, that is, the desired reputation. Identity and reputation serve as references to evaluate authentic claims, actions, and offerings of an organization.

The three constructs included in this chapter are dynamic in nature. They are in flux. They will change over time. Reason why organizations must invest conscious efforts to achieve consistency between actions, claims, offerings, and strategic communications that match their consumers and stakeholders needs, demands, and expectations. More than strategic communication efforts and techniques, organizations should seriously produce "experiences" for their consumers and stakeholders that allow them to be engaged with organizational members, facilities, brands, product, services, causes, and so on. Consistency over time and experiential elements would strengthen the synergistic association among identity, perceived authenticity, and reputation.

We encouraged scholars already interested in organizational identity and reputation to include perceived authenticity in their research projects. Practitioners have found the conceptualized association useful and strategic. The main inspiration of this chapter was the positive and constructive feedback obtained by the authors from public relations and strategic communications practitioners who have been exposed to the three constructs and their interactions in conferences and private workshops. Follow-up work should include case studies and scientific research to support or reject the claims made by the authors.

References

Albert, S. and Whetten, D.A. (1985) Organizational identity. In L.L. Cummings and B.M. Staw (eds), *Research in Organizational Behavior.* Greenwich, CT: JAI Press Inc.

Authentic influence with Ogilvy CEO Christopher Graves (2009) Retrieved from the Public Relations Society of America website http://www.prsa.org/Intelligence/TheStrategist/Articles/view/8961/102/Authentic_influence_with_Ogilvy_CEO_Christopher_Gr (last accessed September 29, 2012).

Avolio, B.J. and Gardner, W.L. (2005) Authentic leadership development: Getting to the root of positive forms of leadership. *The Leadership Quarterly, 16*(3), 315–338.

Balmer, J.M.T. (1995) Corporate branding and connoisseurship. *Journal of General Management, 21*(1), 24–46.

Balmer, J.M.T. and Greyser, S.A. (2006) Corporate marketing: Integrating corporate identity, corporate branding, corporate communications, corporate image and corporate reputation. *European Journal of Marketing, 40*(7/8), 730–741.

Bernstein, D. (1986) *Company Image & Reality. A Critique of Corporate Communications.* Eastbourne, UK: Holt, Rinehart and Winston.

Beverland, M.B. (2005) Crafting brand authenticity: The case of luxury wines. *Journal of Management Studies, 42*(5), 1003–1029.

Black, E., Carnes, T.A., and Richardson, V. (2000) The market valuation of corporate reputation. *Corporate Reputation Review, 3*(1), 31–42.

Brilliant, E. and Young, D.R. (2004) The changing identity of federated community service organizations. *Administration in Social Work, 28* (3/4), 23–45.

Bromley, D.B. (2001) Relationships between personal and corporate reputation. *European Journal of Marketing, 35*(3/4), 316–331.

Camilleri, C.S. (2008) The ecological modernisation of the Yalumba Wine Company. Unpublished doctoral dissertation, Deakin University, Victoria.

Carroll, C.E. (2004) How the mass media influence perceptions of corporate reputation: Exploring agenda-setting effects within business news coverage. Unpublished doctoral dissertation, The University of Texas, Austin, TX.

Carroll, C.E. and McCombs, M. (2003) Agenda-setting effects of business news on the public's images and opinions about major corporations. *Corporate Reputation Review, 16*(1), 36–46.

Cheney, G. and Christensen, L.T. (2000) Identity at issue: Linkages between "internal" and "external" organizational communication. In F.M. Jablin and L.L. Putnam (eds), *New Handbook of Organizational Communication.* Thousand Oaks, CA: Sage, pp. 231–269.

Debreceny, P. (2010) The authentic enterprise revisited: A relevant guide – Or a missed opportunity? *Journal of Communication Management, 14*(3), 186–188.

Deephouse, D.L. (2000) Media reputation as a strategic resource: An integration of mass communication and resource-based theories. *Journal of Management, 26*(6), 1091–1112.

Doorley, J. and Garcia, H.F. (2011) *Reputation Management: The Key to Successful Public Relations and Corporate Communications* (2nd ed.). New York: Routledge.

Dutton, J.E. and Dukerich, J.M. (1991) Keeping an eye on the mirror: Image and identity in organizational adaptation. *Academy Management Journal*, *34*, 517–554.

Dutton, J.E. and Penner, W.J. (1993) The importance of organizational identity for strategic agenda building. In J. Hendry and G. Johnson (eds), *Strategic Thinking: Leadership in the Management of Change*. New York: Strategic Management Society, Wiley, pp. 89–113.

Dutton, J.E., Dukerich, J.M., and Harquil, V.V. (1994) Organizational images and member identification. *Administrative Science Quarterly*, *2*(June), 229–263.

Edelman (2011) Reimagining Our Profession, Public Relations for a Complex World. Retrieved on from Institute for Public Relations website http://www.instituteforpr.org/events/distinguished/ (last accessed September 29, 2011).

Fine, G.A. (2003) Crafting authenticity: The validation of identity in self-taught art. *Theory and Society*, *32*, 153–180.

Fombrun, C.J. (1996) *Reputation: Realizing Value from the Corporate Image*. Boston: Harvard Business School Press.

Fombrun, C.J. and Shanley, M. (1990) What's in a name? Reputation building and corporate strategy. *Academy of Management Journal*, *33*, 233–258.

Fombrun, C.J. and van Riel, C.B.M. (2004) *Fame and Fortune: How Successful Companies Build Winning Reputations*. Upper Saddle River, NJ: Financial Times Prentice Hall.

Gardberg, N. and Fombrun, C. (2002) The global Reputation Quotient[SM] project: First steps towards a cross-nationally valid measure of corporate reputation. *Corporate Reputation Review*, *4*, 303–307.

Gilmore, J.H. and Pine, B.J. Jr. (2007) *Authenticity: What Consumers Really Want*. Boston: Harvard Business School Press.

Gotsi, M. and Wilson, A.M. (2001) Corporate reputation management: "Living the brand". *Management Decision*, *39*(2), 99–104.

Grunig, J. and Grunig, L. (1992) Models of public relations and communication. In J. Grunig (ed.), *Excellence in Public Relations and Communication Management*. Mahwah, NJ: Lawrence Erlbaum Associates, pp. 285–326.

Harris Interactive (2009) Corporate reputation. Retrieved from http://www.harrisinteractive.com/services/reputation.asp (last accessed September 29, 2012).

Harter, S. (2002) Authenticity. In C.R. Snyder and S. Lopez, (eds), *Handbook of Positive Psychology*. Oxford, UK: Oxford University Press, pp. 382–394.

Henderson, A. and Edwards, L. (2010) Guest editorial. *Journal of Communication Management*, *14*(3), 184–185.

Jain, R. and De Moya, M. (2011) Offering an "authentic" tourism experience: An investigation of nation branding of Costa Rica and The Dominican Republic. Paper presented at the 2011 International Public Relations Research Conference, Miami, FL.

Kiousis, S., Popespu, M., and Mirook, M. (2007) Understanding influence on corporate reputation: An examination of public relations efforts, media coverage, public opinion, and financial performance from an agenda-building and agenda-setting perspective. *Journal of Public Relations Research*, *19*(2), 147–165.

Mahon, J.F. (2002) Corporate reputation: A research agenda using strategy and stakeholder literature. *Business & Society*, *41*(4), 415–446.

Melewar, T.C. and Jenkins, E. (2002) Defining the corporate identity construct. *Corporate Reputation Review*, *5*, 76–90.

Molleda, J.C. (2010a) Authenticity and its dimensions in strategic communication research. In S. Allan (ed.), *Rethinking Communication: Keywords in Communication Research*. Cresskill, NJ: Hampton Press, pp. 53–64.

Molleda, J.C. (2010b) Authenticity and the construct's dimensions in public relations and communication research. *Journal of Communication Management*, *14*(3), 223–236.

Molleda, J.C. and Jain, R. (2011) Testing a perceived authenticity index with triangulation research: The case of Xcaret in Mexico. Paper presented at the Public Relations Society of America (PRSA) Educators Academy International Conference, Orlando, FL.

Molleda, J.C. and Roberts, M. (2008) The value of "authenticity" in "global" strategic communication: The new Juan Valdez campaign. *International Journal of Strategic Communication*, *2*(3), 154–174.

Morgan, N. (2009) *Trust Me: Four Steps to Authenticity and Charisma*. Hoboken, NJ: John Wiley & Sons, Inc.

Nakra, P. (2000) Corporate reputation management: CRM with a strategic twist? *Public Relations Quarterly*, *45*(2), 35–42.

Olins, W. (1978) *The Corporate Personality: An Inquiry into the Nature of Corporate Identity*. London: Design Council.

Pratt, M.G. and Foreman, P.O. (2000) Classifying managerial responses to multiple organizational identities. *Academy of Management Review*, 25(1), 18–42.

PR Industry Leaders (2009) PR industry leader see authenticity, ROI, social media mastery as top three issues facing the profession in 2009–10. Public Relations Society of America's website. Retrieved from http://media.prsa.org/article_display.cfm?article_id=1298 (last accessed September 29, 2010).

Rao, H. (1994) The social construction of reputation: Certification contests, legitimation, and the survival of organizations in the American automobile industry: 1895–1912. *Strategic Management Journal*, 15(Winter Special Issue), 29–44.

Reputation Institute (2012) The RepTrak™ System. Retrieved from http://www.reputationinstitute.com/thought-leadership/the-reptrak-system (last accessed October 25, 2012).

Schultz, D., Tannenbaum, S.J., and Lauterborn, R.F. (1994) *Integrated Marketing Communications: Pulling It Together and Making It Work*. Chicago, IL: NTC Business Books.

Scott, S.G. and Lane, V.R. (2000) A stakeholder approach to organizational identity. *Academy of Management Review*, 25, 43–62.

Sha, B.-L. (2009) Exploring the connection between organizational identity and public relations behaviors: How symmetry trumps conservation in engendering organizational identification. *Journal of Public Relations Research*, 21(3), 295–317.

The authentic enterprise (2007) Arthur W. Page Society's website. Retrieved from http://www.awpagesociety.com/images/uploads/2007AuthenticEnterprise.pdf (last accessed September 29, 2012).

The Oxford English Dictionary (2010) Authenticity. Retrieved from the Oxford English Dictionary website http://www.oed.com/view/Entry/13325?redirectedFrom=authenticity# (last accessed September 29, 2012).

Trilling, L. (1972) *Sincerity and Authenticity*. Cambridge, MA: Harvard University Press.

van Riel, C.B.M. and Balmer, J.M.T. (1997) Corporate identity: The concept, its measurement and management. *European Journal of Marketing*, 31(5), 340–355.

Walumbwa, F.O., Wang, P., Wang, H., Schaubroeck, J., and Avolio, B.J. (2010) Psychological processes linking authentic leadership to follower behaviors. *The Leadership Quarterly*, 21(5), 901–914.

Wartick, S.L. (1992) The relationship between intense media exposure and change in corporate reputation. *Business & Society*, 31, 33–49.

Weigelt, K. and Camerer, C. (1988) Reputation and corporate strategy: A review of recent theory and applications. *Strategic Management Journal*, 9, 443–454.

Zickmund, S. (2007) Deliberation, phronesis, and authenticity: Heidegger's early conception of rhetoric. *Philosophy and Rhetoric*, 40(4), 406–415.

36

Corporate Branding and Corporate Reputation

Esben Karmark

Copenhagen Business School, Denmark

Introduction

Branding and corporate reputation are inherently linked within the field of corporate communication. In virtually all of its conceptualizations, corporate reputation is conceived as the way in which constituents or stakeholders perceive, assess, and evaluate the organization in terms of its financial, social, and environmental performance over time (Barnett *et al.*, 2006). Such perceptions and evaluations are often taken to be based on the organization's branding (Gray & Balmer, 1998; Hatch and Schultz, 2008). Brands, in particular, corporate brands, are often seen as the nexus of the organization's integrated communication encapsulating the entire set of organizational *expressions* (Schultz *et al.*, 2000) towards both internal and external stakeholders and as instrumental in establishing corporate reputation among these stakeholders (Christensen and Cornelissen, 2010; Schultz *et al.*, 2005). Branding as a construct now encompasses multiple perspectives such as brand equity (Keller, 2000), employer branding (Martin *et al.*, 2005), and corporate branding (Balmer and Gray, 2003; Hatch and Schultz, 2008). Of these, corporate branding has emerged as the most multidisciplinary (Schultz,

2005) and as a branding perspective that, in terms of its key ideas, underlies many of the current thoughts on branding (Christensen and Cornelissen, 2010; Ghodeswar, 2008). Furthermore, corporate branding is also often taken to be the branding construct most closely linked to corporate reputation (Fombrun and van Riel, 2004; Schultz, 2005).

Corporate branding has been seen as developing in "waves" (Schultz *et al.*, 2005). This chapter explores the links between corporate branding and corporate reputation as they emerge in the context of three waves of corporate branding. It will highlight the way in which the two constructs have related to each other through organizational culture and identity, and how, although characterized by parallel developments, new ideas and models from a "third" wave of corporate branding challenge prevailing assumptions of corporate reputation particularly in terms of the assumptions that reputations emerge from authentic and transparent expressions of corporate brand identity (Fombrun and Rindova, 2000; Fombrun and van Riel, 2004). It will introduce notions that reputations, like corporate brands, may be considered as co-constructed by stakeholders, formed through multiple meanings and the

The Handbook of Communication and Corporate Reputation, First Edition. Edited by Craig E. Carroll.
© 2013 John Wiley & Sons, Inc. Published 2015 by John Wiley & Sons, Inc.

subject of stakeholder negotiation, and discuss such ideas in the context of a future research agenda for corporate brands and corporate communication.

Classical Branding

One frequently applied definition of a brand is that of the American Marketing Association. Here, a brand is taken to be a

> Distinguishing name and/or symbol (such as logo, trademark or package design) intended to identify the goods or services of either one seller or group of sellers and to differentiate those goods and services from those of competitors. (cf. Ghodeswar, 2008)

A key concept in branding is brand identity, a distinct and differentiating identity that connects the consumer to the brand through the associations and symbolic meanings that the brand evokes. For instance, Aaker (1996) suggested that the brand's identity in the minds of consumers was related to associations connected with such dimensions as the brand as a product as well as the brand's more symbolic meanings (an example is BMW, where the brand as product is associated with automotive performance, and the brand as symbol can be seen as evoking associations of a sophisticated urban lifestyle). A brand identity perspective is related to the idea that brands have value or equity. Brands become equitable based on the brand's degree of awareness among consumers, the quality consumers perceive the brand to represent, the broader set of *associations* that the brand evokes among consumers such as the "personality" of the brand, as well as through the *loyalty* that the consumer displays toward the brand. From such a perspective, brand management becomes a matter of seeking to manage brand associations through brand identity (Aaker and Joachimsthaler, 2000).

The brand identity/brand equity perspective on branding has been referred to as the "classical branding perspective." Schultz *et al.* (2005) suggested that such a classical view of

branding implies that the brand is primarily associated with the organization's products and is characterized by having a marketing-oriented and visual identity approach to branding. This implies that the brand is seen as a marketing tool creating symbolic distinction from other brands, and as the responsibility mainly of marketing and corporate communications function within the organization. The key issues for branding, thereby, become establishing the brand's identity and positioning in the mind of primarily the consumer as opposed to a wider set of stakeholders.

From the classical branding perspective, reputation connects to branding through the brand's ability to establish a distinct identity for the product and services it stands for:

> When brand faces aggressive competition in marketplace, brand personality and reputation of the brand help it distinguish from competing offerings. This can result in gaining customer loyalty and achieve growth. A strong brand identity that is well understood and experienced by the customers helps in developing trust which, in turn, results in differentiating the brand from competition. A company needs to establish a clear and consistent brand identity by linking brand attributes with the way they are communicated which can be easily understood by the customers. (Ghodeswar, 2008, p. 5)

Corporate Branding and Corporate Reputation

Under the corporate branding perspective, the brand is conceptualized as a key symbol or central idea capturing and expressing all aspects of the organization: its culture and identity, its employees and their behavior, the products and services, and its strategic vision (Balmer and Gray, 2003; Hatch and Schultz, 2003; Olins, 2004; Schultz *et al.*, 2005). Corporate branding further differs from classical branding in its conceptualization of the role of stakeholders and reputation. Whereas the former is mostly concerned with the consumer as a recipient of brand communication, corporate branding seeks to involve all the organization's internal and external stakeholders, and sees the organization's reputation among stakeholders as an integral element of the brand. For instance, Hatch and Schultz (2001, 2008), in their model of corporate branding, proposed that a corporate brand involves three key organizational dimensions: the organization's culture and identity, top management's strategic vision for the organization, and the organization's reputation among stakeholders. In their model, corporate brand management becomes a matter of aligning the organization's culture and identity with external stakeholders' expectations and evaluations of the organization on a number of dimensions relevant to reputation primarily its financial, environmental, and social performance (Barnett *et al.*, 2006; Hatch and Schultz, 2008). The reputational effect from a corporate brand is particularly related to the degree to which the corporate brand can foster identification with the brand among stakeholders (Fombrun and van Riel, 2004). The basis for identification with a brand is considered broader with a corporate brand compared with a product brand because of the inclusion of organizational values and cultural practices in the corporate brand expressions (Schultz, 2005). A further key element of corporate branding as opposed to classical branding is that it extends the notion that stakeholders identify with the brand's expressed values and identity to include organizational members. Thus, the degree to which organizational members identify with, or "live the brand" is considered key to "brand delivery," that is, the way in which organizational members communicate the brand through behavior and stakeholder interactions. In corporate branding, the notion that employees in this way become what has been referred to as "brand ambassadors" is seen as critical in ensuring corporate brand coherence or alignment between the organization's internal cultural practices and reputation among external stakeholders (de Chernatony and Harris, 2000; Hatch and Schultz, 2001; Ind, 2007).

"Waves" of Corporate Branding and Links to Corporate Reputation

Schultz *et al.* (2005) suggested that corporate branding is a concept that is continuously evolving in "waves," and this development can also be taken to influence the way corporate branding relates to corporate reputation. Under the "first wave" of corporate branding, this construct was usually seen as an extension of the product brand, the approach to communicating the brand was rooted in a stakeholder information or one-way communication perspective, and links between corporate branding and reputation were mainly from the perspective of "reputation as asset" (Barnett *et al.*, 2006). Such a perspective considers reputation as a resource or as an intangible, financial, or strategic asset to the organization. Consequently, under the "first wave," corporate branding and corporate reputation were often connected with financial performance, and the reputation of corporate brands were assessed mainly in rankings such as Interbrand's Best Global Brands, of which all top 10 in the 2011 ranking are corporate brands (http://www.interbrand.com).

Under the "second wave," corporate branding evolved into an interdisciplinary and dynamic perspective with insights from marketing, strategy, human resource management (HRM), organization theory, and corporate communication. One main difference in relation to the "first wave" is that, under the "second wave," corporate branding conceptualizations began to consider the brand corporate brand's long-term and dynamic relationship with multiple stakeholders. Hatch and Schultz (2003) suggested that the organization–stakeholder interrelationship is founded in the organization's identity, which then becomes an integrate part of the brand. Organizational identity was originally proposed by Albert and Whetten (1985) as a construct that encapsulated organizational members' perceptions of the central or core, distinct and enduring features of that organization. It builds on the notion that organizations, like individuals, possess identities, which develop through relational and social processes. Elaborating on the identity process for a corporate brand, Hatch and Schultz built on Mead's theory of social identity in which individual identity is formed through a conversation between the "I" and the "me," where the "me" represents the aspects of identity which develop through the impressions of a person from the outside world and the labels assigned to that person, whereas the "I" represents the person's inner perceptions of its "self." Extending social identity theory to the corporate brand, Hatch and Schultz' model takes corporate brand identity to be relational, built and maintained through balancing external stakeholders' perceptions and images of the organization with the organization's inner cultural values. The dynamic process or "conversation" between the organizational members and stakeholders occurs as organizational members respond or "listen" to what stakeholders say about the organization. Such reflections on the organization's reputation among stakeholders do not necessarily result in altered internal perceptions of identity or practices, however. Rather, the organizational culture provides a context for reflecting on the organizational members' own perceptions of "who they are as an organization" (Albert and Whetten, 1985), which may or may not lead to new perceptions of identity and practices depending on the organizational members' evaluation of the identity clues coming from the organization's external reputation (cf. Dutton and Dukerich, 1991).

In what can be seen as a parallel development of corporate branding and corporate reputation, such reflections on the organizational members' own identity perceptions are also taken to be significant in terms of building corporate reputation. In what we may refer to as "second wave" of corporate reputation (i.e., as opposed to the "reputation as asset" perspective), Fombrun and van Riel (2004) proposed a model of reputation consisting of five dimensions of corporate identity significant to building corporate reputations: visibility, dis-

tinctiveness, transparency, authenticity, and consistency. Such a model extends beyond the notion that corporate reputation represents financial and strategic value to the organization and primarily involves external stakeholders. By including dimensions such as the degree to which the organization is seen by stakeholders as authentic and transparent, this corporate reputation model connects to corporate branding in considering the role played by the organization's culture and identity in reputation formation. Accordingly, in the model, authenticity refers to a convincing constructed identity, based on a broad consensus within the organization, which is expressed to external stakeholders. In terms of reputation, organizations that are perceived to be authentic are seen as real, genuine, accurate, reliable, and trustworthy. Conversely, a misalignment or gap between the "promise" and "performance" of the organization and corporate brand (Bernstein, 2009) will lead to a lack of credibility and legitimacy in the eyes of stakeholders for that organization and the corporate brand. In Fombrun and van Riel's model, the reputation effect from transparency builds on the notion that the more transparent the organization, the more stakeholders will rely on its disclosures. Transparency is thus taken to increase trust in the organization and reduce uncertainty. The specific organizational elements and practices related to the transparency dimension include culture- and value-based aspects of the organization such as vision and leadership, corporate social responsibility, and the workplace environment. Such an assumption that organizations need to be transparent and disclose its internal practices in order to achieve a strong corporate reputation thereby reflects the ideas inherent in corporate branding that the culture and vision of the organization must be aligned with external stakeholders' expectations.

Despite these parallel developments in the conceptualizations of corporate branding and corporate reputation, however, both constructs tend to treat this interrelationship mainly from their own perspective, paying less attention to insights from the other. For instance, although

Fombrun and van Riel's model links corporate reputation to perceptions of identity held by organizational members, the dynamics of organizational culture and identity in this process are not considered in much detail. Similarly, in their conceptualizations of corporate branding, Hatch and Schultz tend to take a distinctively inside-out approach, emphasizing the internal organizational processes based on organizational culture and identity in their models of corporate branding. Here, corporate reputation becomes something of a black box, reduced to an outcome of these processes. Recent examples from organizations suggest that the corporate reputation and corporate branding constructs could be enriched by considering the dynamic interrelationship between the two constructs in more detail. The instance of a Goldman Sachs executive director publicly resigned from the global investment bank in the op-ed pages of *The New York Times* and the *International Herald Tribune* in March of 2012 citing the presence of a "toxic and destructive culture" in the organization and a lack of respect for clients' interests as his reasons is a case in point (Smith, 2012). First, although we may refer to the executive's act as a case of whistle-blowing (Gabriel, 2008), that is, a form of organizational resistance by an individual member of a large organization, it has had a much larger impact than we would usually expect from such an act. In terms of corporate reputation, the op-ed piece has affected not only that of Goldman Sachs, but also the reputation of the entire financial sector. Media coverage of the case referred to a public relations storm for Goldman Sachs as a result of the executive's letter as well as a potential wider recruitment crisis for Wall Street banks as young college graduates will increasingly be unwilling to be associated with the bank's reputations. Here, the ideas inherent in corporate branding would suggest that the organizational identity in Goldman Sachs has developed into a narcissistic identity (Hatch and Schultz, 2008) in which organizational members' reflections of who they are as an organization as well as the values and practices of the organization are disassociated from the demands placed on

the organization by external stakeholders. Such a perspective may well nuance the likely explanation given by corporate reputation. From this perspective, we might argue that Goldman Sachs has not expressed an authentic and transparent image of themselves to stakeholders, and that this is the key reason for the reputational crisis. The shortcoming of such an explanation, however, is that according to the former executive director, what he discloses is the authentic culture of the organization. This suggests that the corporate reputation construct could benefit from placing more emphasis on the dynamics involved in culture, identity, and identification, and the impact of these dynamics on reputations. One possible consequence for reputation of the Goldman Sachs case may well be that we need to consider reputation as this is held and interpreted by organizational members. Such a notion differs from reflections on culture and identity (as would be highlighted in the corporate branding models) in that these construct are more related to the organization's internal practices and historically developed values and perceptions of "who we are." Reputation is distinct from identity in that it comprises

> Observers' collective judgment of a corporation based on assessments of the financial, social and environmental impact attributed to the organization over time. (Barnett *et al.*, 2006, p. 34)

Reputation, thereby, is formed by the impressions that stakeholders have of an organization, and such impressions are also influenced by forces external to the organization including media coverage, governmental regulation, and, increasingly, activism (cf. the Occupy movement). The corporate branding literature under the second wave, however, to a large extent, still considers the corporate brand within the strategic control of the organization. For instance, Hatch and Schultz' (2001, 2003) models emphasize the need to manage the corporate brand through presenting stakeholders with an aligned and consistent brand, seeking to reduce "gaps" between the organization's culture and external reputation. Such gaps, however, may occur suddenly as we see in the Goldman Sachs case, making them highly difficult to manage. A stronger emphasis on the forces that shape reputations both inside and outside the organization may point us toward the meaning that the brand has for both internal and external constituents. Before elaborating on this as one suggestion for a future research agenda for the interrelationship between corporate branding and corporate reputation, however, we should consider the most recent developments within the corporate branding literature as these tend to place even more emphasis on the role of stakeholders, and thereby might point us to further aspects to further integrate corporate branding and corporate reputation.

The "Third Wave" of Corporate Branding

Corporate branding conceptualizations have recently entered into what we may refer to as a "third wave." This development can be distinguished from previous corporate branding models primarily in terms of control of the brand. Whereas previous models still considered the brand and stakeholder responses to the brand as largely within managerial control, a third wave model such as the "enterprise branding" model was proposed by Hatch and Schultz. In this model,

> The corporation is only part of the enterprise it serves. When the entire enterprise is included in brand management practices, the corporate brand is transformed from a tool of self-promotion into a symbol that focuses attention on what the company's stakeholders value, and a set of actions expressing and realizing those values (. . .) brands can no longer be considered financial assets, or branding only a tool of management. Brands are, and always have been, interpreted and judged by all who touch them. Branding practices determine how much of this diversity of meaning

is accepted and cherished with the organization. (Hatch and Schultz, 2009, p. 118)

The construct of enterprise branding, thereby, moves toward considering the stakeholders' values and their interpretations of the brand as inherent in the corporate brand. Elaborating on this construct, Hatch and Schultz (2009, p. 118) further suggested that

> Grasping how brand managers move down the path from corporate to enterprise branding involves reaching into the deepest layers of a company's reason for being. At the same time it involves extending the boundaries of the organization to include all stakeholders.

Key to the idea of extending the boundaries of the organization is the notion that brands have symbolic meanings for the stakeholders, and such meanings carried by brand symbols are what translate into "affection and support for the brand during its lifetime." More specifically, the organization is seen to extend its boundaries through a process in which

> Respect for the meaning brand symbols carry, and involvement with the processes by which these meanings shift and change, keep an organization in touch with its stakeholders and give it the best chance to respond to inevitable changes in expectations in timely and appropriate ways. (Hatch and Schultz, 2009, p. 121)

In terms of reputation, the enterprise branding models suggest that ranking the brand in equity measures such as awareness or loyalty will not necessarily capture the processes that lead to affection and support for the brand. Elaborating on this model, and building on their longitudinal study of the branding processes and practices of the LEGO Company, Hatch and Schultz (2010) proposed a theory of brand cocreation with implications for brand governance. In this model, the authors extended the concept of cocreation, an idea originally applied to user-driven innovation, to branding meaning that stakeholders and the organization together cocreate the brand identity:

The meaning of brands is most often defined in plural among a multiplicity of stakeholders who produce and reproduce and ever shifting and often ambiguous variety of brand interpretations. (Hatch and Schultz, 2010, p. 593)

Hatch and Schultz' theory of brand cocreation proposes that brand communities play a key role in engaging stakeholders in the creation of brand identity. Brand communities, or social relationships between stakeholders involved with a brand and the organization behind the brand, constitute contexts for engaging stakeholders in the brand cocreation process though social networking, information sharing, and the structuring of the relationships with the organization behind the brand. These processes, in turn, involve access and dialog between the brand organization and the members of the brand communities. Dialog occurs as community members provide feedback on product development as well as other aspects of an organization's behavior and impression management techniques that are connected with the brand. Hatch and Schultz provide the example of the LEGO Company brand community LUGNET, which grew out of the adult fans of the LEGO community (cf. Antorini, 2007). LUGNET is dedicated to the development and exchange of LEGO brick building concepts, and the community activities include an offline celebration of the LEGO brand and its products known as BrickFests. Hatch and Schulz suggested that engaging with such stakeholders have led not only to the implementation of user-driven innovations in the LEGO Company, but also to cultural change in the organization in terms of the way the brand is regarded. According to the LEGO CEO cited in the paper, the LEGO culture has become more user-centered and now encourages dialog with users on product innovation and brand meaning.

The development of corporate branding into a third wave suggests a number of implications for corporate reputation. One such implication concerns the notion that the more open and transparent the organization becomes through its branding and communication, the more the organization will also expose itself to external scrutiny. When engaging in brand cocreation with stakeholders, Hatch and Schultz (2010, p. 595) suggested that

Once stakeholders gain access to the organization, more of the organization becomes visible to them and consequently available to those in their extended network, thereby revealing more of the organization's culture, decision-making and management practices and the technical knowledge on which its business is based.

According to Hatch and Schultz, brand cocreation in this sense also becomes a reputation risk and the expression of authenticity and transparency something of a balancing act for the organization. Further reputation risks that result from the cocreation process include the risks of losing distinctiveness as competitors may copy cultural and management practices, as well as the general risk of loosing control of the brand and its expressions as a result of the dynamics of brand cocreation with stakeholders. These risks, Hatch and Schultz argued, must be balanced with the positive reputation gains from engaging in brand cocreation, which develop from the increase in organizational transparency and stakeholders' engagement in the brand. As argued by Schultz (2005), in order to be seen as legitimate, and thereby achieve a *license to operate* from general society, organizations and corporate brands must respond to stakeholder demands while simultaneously reflecting on their own culture and identity.

The third wave of corporate branding thereby poses a number of questions to the way in which a corporate brand connects to corporate reputation. First, it raises the issue of reputation as a risk thereby adding a new dimension to the clusters of reputation conceptualization identified by Barnett *et al.* (2006), that is, corporate reputation as awareness, assessment, and asset. Moreover, the corporate branding models point to the need for a conceptualization of corporate reputation to encompass the level of organizational transparency that arises from stakeholder involvement such as can be found in brand communities. In other words, it suggests that we may need to think also of reputations cocreated through organization–stakeholder interactions.

Recent contributions to the corporate reputation literature such as Ponzi *et al.* (2011) to some extent reflect this turn toward interpretation and meaning. In their measure of corporate reputation, these authors included stakeholders' emotions and beliefs, and suggested that corporate reputation can be seen as a corporate association and stakeholders' overall impression of an organization. The stakeholder feelings assessed in the measure included their degree of trust in the organization, the degree of admiration and respect for the organization as well as the sense that the organization has a good overall reputation. The assumption behind this corporate reputation measure, however, reflects the view that reputation represents a strategic competitive advantage for organizations as it provides the organization with a "rare, inimitable and valuable asset" (Ponzi *et al.*, 2011, p. 15; cf. Barney, 1991). The processes of cocreation as outlined by the third wave of corporate branding, however, would suggest that just as cultural values, vision, and leadership processes may potentially be imitated through the cocreation processes, this may also apply to reputational uniqueness.

In order to elaborate on the implications for the linkages between corporate branding and corporate reputation that result from the more recent corporate branding ideas and the questions that arise from these, we can look to more critical approaches to branding and corporate communication.

Critical Approaches to Corporate Branding and Corporate Reputation

Kärreman and Rylander (2008) studied the meanings related to corporate branding and reputation among organizational members in a large, international consultancy. Critiquing

mainstream approaches to branding including corporate branding for their strategic, marketing-oriented, and instrumental focus, Kärreman and Rylander (2008, p. 105) suggested that such approaches do little in terms of demonstrating how brands are "socially constructed, maintained, consumed and resisted." In their empirical study of a large, international consulting firm, these authors investigated branding as a process of "management of meaning that is, systematic efforts from top management to influence and shape frames of reference, norms and values among organizational members" (p. 108). Kärreman and Rylander's findings from the study suggest several implications for the way in which we can understand corporate branding and corporate reputation as interrelated multiple interpretations by stakeholders. First, the study found that the meanings ascribed to the corporate brand and the corporate reputation by stakeholders were highly ambiguous, abstract, and emotional. In relation to the reputation of the corporate brand among clients, presumably a key target group for the brand communication, the brand was seen as "charged with meaning," but not in a coherent and consistent way, and not attached to particular characteristics of the consultancy's services. Rather, the reputation of the consultancy's corporate brand appeared to be shaped by the "mystique" and perceived elitism assigned to the consultancy's culture and people by clients. The study found that this reputation was related to clients' vague perceptions of the consultancy's services – an unclear idea of "what they do" and "how they do it." Furthermore, this reputational vagueness was found to be in line with the consultancy's corporate brand strategy, which was seen as expressing being the best rather than being explicit about what the best was in relation to the needs of the client. The key strategic role of the consultancy's corporate reputation, the study suggests, seemed to be more related to recruiting and retaining talented employees. In the study, such ambiguity was also found to characterize the internally held meanings related to the corporate brand among the consultants. Here, the authors found that the branding discourse (reflecting corporate communication) and the discourse related to the consultancy's organizational identity (reflections on "who we are as an organization"; cf. Albert and Whetten, 1985) to be sometimes overlapping and sometimes contradictory depending on the context.

Christensen and colleagues, in their critique of the communicative "ideal" underlying corporate branding and corporate reputation models, have also considered ambiguity and polyphony in corporate communication over the "clarity, consistency, and coherence" in corporate communication that this ideal represents (Christensen *et al.*, 2008). Increasing global media interest in organizations, multiple roles for employees in- and outside the organization, and as the rise in organizations' communication of messages on their corporate values and corporate social responsibility, all render organizations more open to more scrutiny from stakeholders. In such a communication environment, wherein all aspects of an organization has the potential to become an object of communication, organizations are under pressure to present not only clear, consistent, and coherent communication to stakeholders, but also a coherent and shared organizational culture and brand (Christensen *et al.*, 2009; Hatch and Schultz, 2009).

In terms of corporate reputation, Christensen and Cornelissen (2010) suggested for instance that Fombrun and van Riel's (2004) model builds on the assumption that the visible, transparent, and consistent identity expressed by the organization will transfer into a coherent corporate reputation among stakeholders in a way that corresponds to the desired reputation and organizational self-presentation. Such an assumption, however, fails to take into account the multiple meanings that stakeholders are likely to make of such identity expressions. Rather,

> Receivers of corporate messages – internal or external – are not passive targets but mature, creative, and savvy partners in the production of identities and experiences (. . .) consumers frequently interpret and use corporate prod-

ucts and messages differently from their original purpose, reshape and adapt them to personal use, and modify and sometimes pervert their meanings in ways not imagined by their creators (. . .). Likewise, members of organizations creatively co-construct or deconstruct the meanings of corporate messages in ways not intended by management. (Christensen and Cornelissen, 2010, p. 391)

As illustrated by the Goldman Sachs executive's public resignation example, organizational members cannot always be expected to accept the organization's identity as established by managerial discourse. Such identities, despite the notion inherent in corporate branding and corporate reputation models that such identities are connected to a cultural and thereby authentic context, empirical studies have demonstrated that such discourses are often self-referential, and reflect management's desired identity than the actual identity of the organization (Christensen and Cheney, 2000). Again, such multiple identity interpretations held by organizational members may well transfer into multiple reputational meanings by stakeholders. In the Goldman Sachs example again, international media such as the *Financial Times* became the global forum for a discussion by other former employees of the validity of the former executive's claims about the characteristics of the Goldman Sachs culture (Mousavisadeh, 2012). Here, it would seem that both the corporate brand identity and the corporate reputation of Goldman Sachs are being "charged with meaning" not as intended by any corporate brand or reputation strategy, but rather by former employees in public media settings outside of management's control. Thus, we can assume that brand and reputation cocreation will occur not only in the form of interactions between the organization and its stakeholders, but also through stakeholder interactions independent of any participation by the organization. In that sense, the ownership of the meanings that brands and reputations carry is transferred from the control sphere of management to a much wider set of audiences, and become iconic of a larger culture, in this case, of the investment banking world (Holt, 2004).

As a further implication of the communications ideal of integrated communication underlying corporate branding and corporate communication, Christensen and Cornelissen (2010) proposed that this has the effect of actually rendering the organization inflexible and unresponsive in relation to stakeholders. Instead, these authors suggested that organizations instead embraced ambiguity and polyphony in their interaction with stakeholders. These principles imply that, rather than seeking to achieve coherence and consistency in corporate messages, organizations allow for a plurality of voices expressing the organizational values in diverse ways to multiple stakeholders. Building on the idea of strategic ambiguity (Eisenberg, 1984), Christensen and Cornelissen suggested that allowing for corporate messages to be expressed in vague and equivocal language may actually enable the organization to integrate a variety of members and stakeholders without alienating anyone.

Toward a New Agenda for Corporate Branding and Corporate Reputation

The developments related to corporate branding and corporate identity conceptualization and the ideas from the critical communications literature, thereby, point us toward new issues and agendas for corporate branding and corporate reputation. For corporate reputation, one issue that emerges is the issue of how to conceive of reputations as cocreated with and between multiple stakeholders. Current ideas about corporate reputation, in fact, assume that reputations are created by multiple stakeholders (including current and potential employees, the media, consumers, and the general public), and that reputation emerges from the interaction between these stakeholders including more informal interactions such as between employees and customers (Martin *et al.*, 2005). In many ways, relationship management can be seen as an underlying idea behind corporate

reputation models as such models emphasize openness, responsiveness, and credibility (Van Woerkum and Aarts, 2008). Current measure-based approaches to reputation (e.g., Ponzi *et al.*, 2011), however, while seeking to reflect multiple stakeholders emotions about the organization, do not seem to provide the organization with the ability to connect to stakeholders beyond a stakeholder-response approach (Morsing and Schultz, 2006). Such an approach implies that organizations will seek responses from stakeholders albeit on issues and questions that are predetermined by the organization. An example here is the reputation measure proposed by Ponzi *et al.* (2011), which assess reputation on predetermined issues such as their degree of trust in the organization. From a critical communication perspective, we might argue that, rather than seeking dialog with stakeholders, such measures actually lead to discursive closure (McClellan and Deetz, 2009) privileging managerially driven and strategic terms and dimensions in the assessment of corporate reputations over alternatives that might emerge from stakeholders.

Another issue for corporate reputation as it connects to corporate brandings is related to the pervasive idea within corporate reputation models (Fombrun and van Riel, 1997; Ponzi *et al.*, 2011) that corporate reputation constitutes a strategic competitive advantage for the organization. Here, the brand cocreation theory proposed the notion of reputation as a balancing act for corporate brand. The idea of reputation as a risk naturally challenges the conceptualization of reputation as a competitive advantage. To be a competitive advantage, a resource such as reputation must be rare, valuable, and difficult to imitate (Barney, 1991). Conceiving of reputation as a risk challenges the idea that reputations are valuable only. Furthermore, as pointed out by Hatch and Schultz (2010), cocreation may lead to excessive transparency for the organizational practices and identities. As these are seen to be the building block of corporate reputation as perceived and evaluated by outsiders, such a view also challenges the notion that reputations are always difficult to imitate. For instance, in a recent survey[1] of the reputation of Japanese brands among Chinese consumers, only three Japanese brands were found to be the most trusted. And this included categories such as television and cars, where Japan has traditionally held strong product brands (e.g., Toyota, Sony, and Panasonic). In the survey, what can be seen as newcomer brands within these categories, such as the Korean brand Samsung, had overtaken the Japanese brands in terms of reputation. This suggests that reputations are in flux, and just as branding has been seen to be driven by the "death of the USP" (or "unique selling proposition") for products due to the rise of technology and production capabilities that make products easy to imitate, we might consider a similar challenge to corporate reputation. Here, embracing the notion that reputations are cocreated by stakeholders and through interactions among stakeholders might aid the organization in keeping the corporate brand and reputation up-to-date with stakeholder perceptions. The corporate branding literature has pointed to another aspect that may help us in conceptualizing corporate reputation as a more equivocal phenomenon. Here, the concept of the "uniqueness paradox" suggests that corporate brands often fall in the trap of seeking to express uniqueness and distinctions by emphasizing features of the brand identity that are, in fact, not unique (Antorini and Schultz, 2005). Similarly, when corporate reputations are assessed in measures that are standardized across several types of organizations with a diverse set of stakeholders, such measures are likely to capture few unique characteristics of a corporate reputation.

Moreover, the Goldman Sachs case suggests that internally held reputations are important in establishing external reputation and to manage the potential risks that emerge from such corporate culture exposés. In corporate reputation and corporate branding models, however, culture is still conceptualized as internal to the organization, more specifically as a context for interpreting externally held views as expressed by the organization's stakeholders. In terms of the organization allowing for multiple interpretations to be included in corporate brands and corporate reputations in a cocreational manner, it could be argued that such a process is more relevant to certain types of organizations than others. In a review and discussion of "living the brand" models as a subset of corporate branding, this author argued that knowledge workers such as can be found in specialized organizational departments and high-expertise service organizations may be more attuned to identifying with brand values that are often communicated by top management in more abstract terms (Karmark, 2005; cf. Christensen and Cheney, 2000; Kärreman and Rylander, 2008).

Conclusion

Branding, in particular, corporate branding, is inherently linked to corporate reputation as reputation is built and maintained on the basis of stakeholders' long-term assessments and evaluations of corporate brand identity. A corporate brand expresses the cultural values of the organization and, as such, becomes the symbolic focal point for the stakeholders' identification with the corporate brand, as well as assessments of the degree to which the organization behind the brand is authentic, transparent, and trustworthy. New ideas emerging in the corporate branding literature and from critical approaches to the corporate communication raise new questions for the way in which corporate branding and corporate reputation interconnect. Such ideas were explored in this chapter, and include the notion that corporate branding and corporate reputation are ambiguous constructs that have multiple meanings and are cocreated by multiple stakeholders, that reputation may be considered a risk rather than an asset to the organization only. Consequently, both corporate reputation and corporate branding involve paradox, ambiguity, and dualities for the organization, all of which suggest new possibilities for cross-fertilizations between the two constructs.

Note

1   Nikkei Weekly, March 18th 2012.

References

Aaker, D.A. (1996) *Building Strong Brands*. New York: The Free Press.

Aaker, D.A. and Joachimsthaler, E. (2000) *Brand Leadership*. New York: The Free Press.

Albert, S. and Whetten, D.A. (1985) *Organizational Identity. Research in Organizational Behavior*. Greenwich, CT: JAL.

Antorini, Y.M. (2007) *Brand Community Innovation – An Intrinsic Study of the Adult Fans of LEGO Community*. Copenhagen: Samfundslitteratur.

Antorini, Y.M. and Schultz, M. (2005) Corporate branding and the "conformity trap". In M. Schultz, Y.M. Antorini, and F. Csaba (eds), *Corporate Branding – Purpose, People, Process*. Copenhagen: Copenhagen Business School Press.

Balmer, J.M.T. and Gray, E.R. (2003) Corporate brands: What are they? What of them? *European Journal of Marketing*, 37(7/8), 972–997.

Barnett, M.L., Jermier, J.M., and Lafferty, B.A. (2006) Corporate reputation: The definitional landscape. *Corporate Reputation Review*, 9, 26–38.

Barney, J. (1991) Firm resources and sustained competitive advantage. *Journal of Management*, 17, 99–120.

Bernstein, D. (2009) Rhetoric and reputation: Some thoughts on corporate dissonance. *Management Decision*, 47(4), 603–615.

Christensen, L.T. and Cheney, G. (2000) Self-absorption and self-seduction in the corporate identity game. In M. Schultz, M.J. Hatch, and M.H. Larsen (eds), *The Expressive Organization: Linking Identity, Reputation, and the Corporate Brand*. Oxford, UK: Oxford University Press.

Christensen, L.T. and Cornelissen, J. (2010) Bridging corporate and organizational communication: Review, development and a look to the future. *Management Communication Quarterly*, 25(3), 383–414.

Christensen, L.T., Morsing, M., and Cheney, G. (2008) *Corporate Communications: Conventions, Complexity, and Critique*. Los Angeles, CA: Sage.

Christensen, L.T., Firat, A.F., and Cornelisssen, J. (2009) New tensions and challenges in integrated communications. *Corporate Communications: An International Journal*, 14(2), 207–219.

de Chernatony, L. and Harris, F. (2000) Developing corporate brands through considering internal and external stakeholders. *Corporate Reputation Review*, 3(3), 268–274.

Dutton, J.E. and Dukerich, J.M. (1991) Keeping an eye on the mirror: Image and identity in organizational adaptation. *Academy of Management Journal*, 34, 517–554.

Eisenberg, E. (1984) Ambiguity as strategy in organizational communication. *Communication Monographs*, 51, 227–242.

Fombrun, C.J. and Rindova, V.P. (2000) The road to transparency: Reputation management at Royal Dutch/Shell. In M. Schultz, M.J. Hatch, and M.H. Larsen (eds), *The Expressive Organization: Linking Identity, Reputation and the Corporate Brand*. Oxford, UK: Oxford University Press, pp. 77–98.

Fombrun, C.J. and van Riel, C.B.M. (1997) The reputation landscape. *Corporate Reputation Review*, 1, 5–13.

Fombrun, C.J. and van Riel, C.B.M. (2004) *Fame and Fortune: How the World's Top Companies Develop Winning Reputations*. New York: Pearson.

Gabriel, Y. (2008) Spectacles of resistance and resistance of spectacles. *Management Communication Quarterly*, 21, 310–326.

Ghodeswar, B.M. (2008) Building brand identity in competitive markets: A conceptual model. *Journal of Product & Brand Management*, 17(1), 4–12.

Gray, E.R. and Balmer, J.M.T. (1998) Managing Corporate Image and Corporate Identity. *Long Range Planning*, 31(5), 695–708.

Hatch, M.J. and Schultz, M. (2001) Are the strategic stars aligned for your corporate brand? *Harvard Business Review*, 79, 128–134.

Hatch, M.J. and Schultz, M. (2003) Bringing the corporation into corporate branding. *European Journal of Marketing*, 37(7/8), 1041–1064.

Hatch, M.J. and Schultz, M. (2008) *Taking Brand Initiative: How to Align Strategy, Culture and Identity through Corporate Branding*. San Francisco, CA: Jossey-Bass-Wiley.

Hatch, M.J. and Schultz, M. (2009) From corporate to enterprise branding. *Organizational Dynamics*, 38(2), 117–130.

Hatch, M.J. and Schultz, M. (2010) Toward a theory of brand co-creation with implications for brand governance. *Brand Management, 17*(8), 590–604.

Holt, D. (2004) *How Brands Become Icons*. Boston: Harvard Business School Press.

Ind, N. (2007) *Living the Brand – How to Transform Every Member of Your Organization into a Brand Champion*. London: Kogan Page.

Karmark, E. (2005) Living the brand. In M. Schultz, Y.M. Antorini, and F. Csaba (eds), *Corporate Branding – Purpose, People, Process*. Copenhagen: Copenhagen Business School Press.

Kärreman, D. and Rylander, A. (2008) Managing meaning through branding – The case of a consulting firm. *Organization Studies, 29*(01), 103–125.

Keller, K.L. (2000) Building and managing corporate brand equity. In M. Schultz, M.J. Hatch, and M.H. Larsen (eds), *The Expressive Organization: Linking Identity, Reputation, and the Corporate Brand*. Oxford, UK: Oxford University Press.

Martin, G., Baumont, P., *et al.* (2005) Branding: A new performance discourse for HR? *European Management Journal, 23*(1), 76–88.

McClellan, J. and Deetz, S. (2009) Communication and critical management Studies. In H. Willmott, T. Bridgman, and M. Alvesson (eds), *Handbook of Critical Management Studies*. Oxford, UK: Oxford University Press, pp. 433–453.

Morsing, M. and Schultz, M. (2006) Corporate social responsibility communication: Stakeholder information, response and involvement strategies. *Business Ethics: A European Review, 15*(4), 323–338.

Mousavisadeh, N. (2012) Separate myth from reality at Goldman. *Financial Times*, March 16.

Olins, W. (2004) *On B@and*. New York: Thames & Hudson.

Ponzi, L.J., Fombrun, C.J., and Gardberg, N.A. (2011) RepTrak™ pulse: Conceptualizing and validating a short-form measure of corporate reputation. *Corporate Reputation Review, 14*(1), 15–35.

Schultz, M. (2005) A cross-disciplinary perspective on corporate branding. In M. Schultz, Y.M. Antorini, and F. Csaba (eds), *Corporate Branding – Purpose, People, Process*. Copenhagen: Copenhagen Business School Press.

Schultz, M., Antorini, Y.M., and Csaba, F. (2005) *Corporate Branding – Purpose, People, Process*. Copenhagen: Copenhagen Business School Press.

Schultz, M., Hatch, M.J., and Larsen, M.H. (eds) (2000) *The Expressive Organization: Linking Identity, Reputation, and the Corporate Brand*. Oxford, UK: Oxford University Press.

Smith, G. (2012) Why I am Leaving Goldman Sachs. *New York Times*, March 14.

Van Woerkum, C. and Aarts, N. (2008) Staying connected. The communication between organizations and their environment. *Corporate Communication: An International Journal, 13*(2), 197–211.

37

Corporate Reputation and Corporate Speech

Robert Kerr

University of Oklahoma, USA

With 2010's *Citizens United v. Federal Election Commission*, the United States Supreme Court for all practical purposes placed corporate political media spending (often referred to as "corporate speech") beyond the reach of government regulation aimed at preventing corruption of political campaigns. By thus permitting, via the First Amendment, greater influence of corporate money on democratic processes than at any time since the Gilded Age, the US Supreme Court also squarely placed ultimate control over whatever reputational interests may be advanced through that power henceforth squarely within the domain of corporate management. What this brand new age of such absolute lack of restraint on that type of spending will mean for American democracy remains to be seen. But it offers a burgeoning frontier for both descriptive and normative research on this realm of corporate reputation and its now incalculable potential for political, economic, and social influence.

Since the beginnings of the business corporation's rise in nineteenth-century America as a dominant institution, an intense societal debate has been waged over the degree to which reputation as advanced through corporate political spending should be mandated by law. Though the nature and extent of that regulation evolved over the course of more than a century, the balance of power to define the terms of such corporate political spending remained ultimately in favor of democratic governance throughout. In 2010, that changed dramatically.

With *Citizens United v. Federal Election Commission*, the US Supreme Court for all practical purposes placed corporate political media spending (often referred to as "corporate speech") beyond the reach of government regulation aimed at preventing corruption of political campaigns. By thus permitting, via the First Amendment, greater influence of corporate money on democratic processes than at any time since the Gilded Age, the US Supreme Court also squarely placed ultimate control over whatever reputational interests may be advanced through that power henceforth squarely within the domain of corporate management. What this brand new age of such absolute lack of restraint on that type of spending will mean for American democracy remains

The Handbook of Communication and Corporate Reputation, First Edition. Edited by Craig E. Carroll.

to be seen. But it offers a burgeoning frontier for both descriptive and normative research on this realm of corporate reputation and its now incalculable potential for political, economic, and social influence.

Corporate Political Media Spending and the First Amendment

The story of how regulation of corporate political media spending became the subject of a series of major First Amendment cases is by and large the story of what has been described as "the corporate free-speech movement" (Kerr, 2008). The term "corporate speech" is often used to distinguish corporate media spending that seeks to influence political outcomes or social climate from "commercial speech" – media efforts that promote products or services. Each has generated a distinct body of First Amendment law, and in that context, all corporate speech is not *commercial*, and neither is all commercial speech *corporate*. This chapter for the most part avoids references to corporate speech in favor of terminology that is more representative of what has been at issue in the cases of the corporate free-speech movement: *corporate political media spending*.

In literal meaning, a corporation cannot of course actually "speak" in the way that human beings can, given that it is an "artificial being . . . existing only in contemplation of law," as Chief Justice John Marshall so succinctly put it in the majority opinion of the seminal corporation case of US law, *Dartmouth College v. Woodward* (1819, p. 636). It can only spend – pay someone to express messages on its behalf (through the spending decisions of corporate management). Beyond that, the use of the term "corporate speech" also represents a rather disingenuous act of rhetorical framing, creating the impression that something that does not in fact actually exist is an everyday reality. Legal scholar Linda Berger (2004, 2007) has focused much work on the way that the metaphors society and the legal

system choose to focus on in regard to corporate spending demonstrate contrasts in understanding of the corporate role in a democratic society and can even influence judicial outcomes. As the late Chief Justice Rehnquist – who authored a substantial body of opinions consistently focused on the reality of corporate political media spending in contrast to the rhetoric of corporate speech – once emphasized, to treat the institutional messages of corporations the same in the First Amendment law as those of natural persons "is to confuse metaphor with reality" (*Pacific Gas & Electric Co. v. Public Utilities Commission of California*, 1986, p. 33).

The series of the First Amendment cases on this subject represent a relatively recent chapter in efforts over more than a century to restrain corporate political corruption in the United States. In the second half of the nineteenth century, as the United States reinvented the corporate form on a previously unimagined scale, many Americans had begun to see large business corporations as a threat to the balance of social forces, the very sort of excessive centralized power that American founders had sought to prevent through the Constitution's checks and balances. The alarm that such developments engendered in American public opinion has been described by historian Roland Marchand (1998) as "a crisis of legitimacy" for big business, as in barely a generation's time, corporate expansion suddenly dwarfed traditional institutions of family, church, and local community (p. 2–4). Efforts to regulate the excesses of the giant corporations and trusts began as early as the 1870s, with the United States becoming the first nation to enact regulatory legislation directed specifically against big businesses. After massive contributions from corporations to political candidates late in the nineteenth century sparked major reform efforts (Lammers, 1982, p. 3), corporations were prohibited from direct financial involvement in federal elections by the 1907 enactment of the Tillman Act, which was replaced by the stronger Federal Corrupt Practices Act in 1925. That legislation was aimed at protecting political processes from both the reality and appearance of undue influence by economic interests and at protecting corporate shareholders from having their investments used for political purposes that they might not support (Matasar, 1986, pp. 7–8). It remained the centerpiece of such regulation until more comprehensive regulations were enacted after revelations of numerous illegal contributions to Richard Nixon's 1972 presidential campaign, resulting also in the establishment of the Federal Election Commission to monitor campaign finance.

The 1970s also saw the beginnings of a series of First Amendment challenges to the campaign-finance regulations as well as a sharp rise in corporate efforts to influence public opinion and political processes. It was a period in which the government–business relationship went through great evolution with the rise of public-interest activism sparked at least in part by corporate roles in environmental, consumer, and civil-rights problems, followed by the economic decline of 1970s – the nation's worst since the 1930s. The late 1960s and early 1970s brought the enactment of a number of major regulatory initiatives to protect the environment, consumers, and workers, followed by vigorous executive and judicial enforcement. In response, big businesses in the 1970s dramatically revamped their manner of engaging the political process.

Between 1968 and 1978, the number of corporations with their own public-affairs offices in Washington increased from some 100 to more than 500. By 1980, more than 80% of the *Fortune* 500 companies had their own Washington offices, with more than half of them having been created since 1970 (Vogel, 1989, pp. 195–197). The unprecedented mobilization of business interests focused on successfully defeating major regulatory bills in Congress and effectively lobbying to influence the drafting of others. The era of heightened regulatory activity thus faded markedly, beginning during Jimmy Carter's late 1970s presidency and ending with the inauguration of Ronald Reagan, elected on an antigovernment, probusiness platform in 1980. Rutherford (2000) characterized the heightened corporate advocacy efforts in the 1970s as part of a broader effort to "restore order" on the part of authority interests whose hegemony had been challenged in the 1960s (p. 48–67).

It was also a period in which corporate advocacy advertising increased significantly. Such advertising is also often called issue advertising or corporate advertising, although the latter tends to refer to a broader sort of corporate communications that may not necessarily involve advocating a position on political and social issues (Sethi, 1977). Most prominent among that trend was Mobil Oil's editorial-advocacy campaign, focused particularly on the op-ed page of *The New York Times*. Over the course of the decade, the oil company made that campaign the focus of a groundbreaking advocacy strategy to promote interests that went far beyond its immediate business objectives. Mobil vigorously essayed to legitimize corporate speech as an activity fully embraced by the First Amendment, utilizing discourse that consistently framed the corporate role in democratic processes as identical to that of the individual citizen. Heath's (1997, p. 208) assessment of Mobil as "the most visible – and feistiest – corporate practitioner of advocacy communication" for the past quarter century is typical of its characterization in corporate-advocacy literature.

The successful public-interest reform efforts of the 1960s and early 1970s were a key factor in Mobil's decision to create its editorial-advocacy campaign in response (Warner and Silk, 1979). Herbert Schmertz, vice president for public affairs and an aggressive, articulate practitioner of public relations, was the architect of Mobil's editorial-advocacy campaign, said that a motivating factor for the company was to compete with the news media of the day. "The media was abrogating to itself all First Amendment claims, which we certainly did not agree with," he said (H. Schmertz, personal communication, August 13, 2002). Disseminating messages to influence public opinion rather than directly generate commerce became a practice increasingly adopted by other corporations in the 1970s. Corporate spending on advocacy advertising climbed from $154 million in 1970 to more than $500 million in

1979 ("Taking a stand," 1980). *Ad Forum* called Mobil "the leading practitioner" of such advertising in the 1970s ("Mobil's Warner," 1981).

Mobil's efforts stood out in part because it was willing earlier than most corporations of the period to take controversial political positions and also because of the way its messages reflected a rhetorical coalescing of the corporation into the discursive process idealized in marketplace of ideas concepts but previously considered most often in terms of individuals. Mobil called for more corporations to speak out, to recognize what it considered to be a duty to compete not only in the economic marketplace but also in the political marketplace: "For a long time now, we've been raising our voice in ads like this one. The trouble is, not enough other businesses follow suit" ("The soapbox," 1975). Equating the interests of the corporation with the interests of the people in its op-ed messages, Mobil invariably characterized regulatory efforts as threatening the rights of individuals.

Near the end of the decade, it published what could serve as a manifesto for its efforts to justify the corporation as a vital participant in democratic processes protected by the First Amendment. The statement summarized the core assertions of Mobil's editorial-advocacy framing of the corporation as politically engaged citizen: "Mobil provokes, needles, challenges . . . to stir free-wheeling dialogue in the public prints. Saying what we think needs saying on issues that matter to people. Inflation. Jobs. Energy. Environment. . . . Voices of business balance other voices. Stifling any voice distorts the democratic process. The people must be able to weigh all the evidence . . . so future decisions in our participatory democracy will be based on the noblest wisdom of the past – the First Amendment" ("Imagine tomorrow," 1979).

The year before, in *First National Bank of Boston v. Bellotti*, the US Supreme Court established a degree of First Amendment protection specifically for political media spending by corporations. It represented the culmination of a

16-year struggle between the legislature and corporate interests over a ban that Massachusetts (like many other states at the time) imposed on corporate spending aimed at influencing referendum questions that did not materially affect corporate interests. In a five-to-four decision, the majority held that corporate spending on communications that seek to influence the outcome of referenda is protected by the First Amendment from government regulation. Justice Lewis F. Powell, Jr.'s majority opinion asserted that "if the speakers here were not corporations, no one would suggest that the State could silence their proposed speech. It is the type of speech indispensable to decisionmaking in a democracy." Powell declared that statement "no less true because the speech comes from a corporation rather than an individual," and that "self-government suffers when those in power suppress competing views on public issues 'from diverse and antagonistic sources'."

Indeed, it was critical to Justice Powell's assertions to focus them on "views" rather than spending. For example, he contended that the Massachusetts regulation would have meant that "much valuable information which a corporation might be able to provide would remain unpublished because corporate management would not be willing to risk the substantial criminal penalties" that could be imposed on them (*First National Bank of Boston v. Bellotti*, 1978, pp. 767–769, 777, 785). In reality, corporate management actually would have risked criminal penalties under such regulation only if it spent corporate revenues to influence referenda. The managers would have faced no risk of that sort if they simply participated in referenda campaigns like other citizens as individuals, with none of the special, wealth-generating advantages (perpetual life, limited liability, and tax treatment) that are granted by the government to the corporate form – but not to individuals. The question of permitting corporate management to transfer those advantages from the economic marketplace directly over to the political marketplace would not draw scrutiny from a majority on the Court until later cases on corporate political media spending, however.

Thus, in the 1970s, corporate efforts to reshape the fundamental nature of the marketplace of ideas advanced significantly, providing corporate political media spending much greater legitimacy in American democracy than before that period. As *Bellotti* and related cases unfolded, the sort of movement they represented grew more evident. It could be seen in the way so many of the proponents in the effort to win greater First Amendment protection for corporate political media spending began to champion it with rhetoric that characterized corporate expenditures made to influence political outcomes as simply another form of citizens' speech. Government regulation of such expenditures was consistently represented as a looming threat to the wider society. The brief for the plaintiffs in the *Bellotti* case (a group of five corporations doing business in Massachusetts) argued exactly that (Brief for Appellant, 1978, pp. 35–36), and amicus briefs asserted the point in other ways. Northeastern Legal Foundation and Mid America Legal Foundation (organizations focused on corporate legal issues), for example, warned that "the lessons of history tell us that when a fundamental right is taken from one group in society, that right will not be long enjoyed by others" (Brief for Northeastern Legal Foundation, 1978, pp. 3, 5, 10). The US Chamber of Commerce depicted the political speech of "incorporated enterprise" to be as equally vital to "the free, frank, and robust expression of public opinion" fostered by the First Amendment as any other source of such speech (Brief for Chamber of Commerce of the United States of America, 1978, pp. 3–5).

Careful Adjudication of the Balance of Power

Although the *Bellotti* ruling opened the door to a series of US Supreme Court cases that would further weigh the balance of power

appropriate for defining the terms of corporate reputation as advanced via political spending, for more than two decades, the Court declined to shift that balance so as to fully equate such spending with human expression in regard to First Amendment protections. Most significant were a group of cases decided over the course of the 1980s in which the Court carefully and steadily walled off corporate political media spending in candidate elections when it was done from corporate treasuries advantaged by the special, state-created protections of perpetual life, limited liability, and special tax advantages. That process was deeply grounded in the priorities of more than a century of legislative and judicial judgment. With key support from justices in the *Bellotti* majority, the Court established a precisely balanced doctrine that fully protected political expression and unlimited political expenditures not only by individuals but also by associations of individuals who wished to engage in such expression through similarly unlimited media spending via political action committees or ideological corporations. Thus, it put in place a doctrine that effectively maximized political expressive freedom by individuals and associations of individuals and minimized encroachment upon that freedom by structurally advantaged corporate spending of stockholders' money by corporate managers.

That series of cases began with *Federal Election Commission v. National Right to Work Committee*. In that 1982 ruling, the Court had unanimously upheld a section of the Federal Election Campaign Act that prohibited corporations or labor unions from soliciting contributions for separate segregated funds (political action committees) from sources outside a committee's legally allowable membership (*Federal Election Commission v. National Right to Work Committee*, 1982, p. 211). The Court accepted the government's argument that Congress had acted to prevent corporations from using their general treasury funds to influence federal elections "only after it became aware of widespread abuses that were thought to present imminent danger of corruption to the federal election process, resulting in a decline of public confidence in the integrity of elected officials and the fair operation of government" (Brief for Appellant, 1982, pp. 17–18).

The federal government successfully argued that it had a compelling interest in ensuring that the "substantial aggregations of wealth" accumulated through the special legal advantages granted the corporate form (*United States v. Morton Salt Co.*, 1950, p. 652) would not be converted into political "war chests" – the deployment of which could incur political debts from candidates in elections, as the Court had established a quarter century before (*United States v. United Auto Workers*, 1957, p. 579). The Court also noted that the interest of protecting individuals who invested in a corporation for economic purposes from having their money used for political purposes had been well established for some three decades (*United States v. Congress of Industrial Organizations*, 1948, p. 113). In accepting that the asserted interests were compelling and thus outweighed the First Amendment rights asserted by the National Right to Work Committee (NRWC), the unanimous Court declared: "The governmental interest in preventing both actual corruption and the appearance of corruption of elected representatives has long been recognized and there is no reason why it may not in this case be accomplished by treating unions, corporations and similar organizations differently from individuals" (*Federal Election Commission v. National Right to Work Committee*, 1982, pp. 210–211).

The ruling emphasized that preventing both real and apparent corruption was "of almost equal concern as the danger of actual quid pro quo arrangements" because of its potential eroding impact on confidence and participation in political processes (*Buckley v. Valeo*, 1976, p. 27). It should also be noted that Justice Powell, the author of *Bellotti*, joined the opinion in full, and no justices wrote separately to qualify or challenge the majority opinion in any way. Indeed all four of the justices from the *Bellotti* majority still on the Court – Justices Warren Burger, Harry Blackmun, John Paul Stevens, and Powell (the fifth, Potter Stewart, having

retired the year before) – joined the *NRWC* holding.

Thus, the *NRWC* – and the body of case law it reaffirmed – glaringly contradicts the assertion that Justice Anthony Kennedy made in his *Citizens United* majority opinion that "*Bellotti*'s central principle" means "the First Amendment does not allow political speech restrictions based on a speaker's corporate identity" (*Citizens United v. Federal Election Commission*, 2010, p. 902). Similarly contradicted is Justice Kennedy's declaration in *Citizens United* that another crucial case it overruled (*Austin v. Michigan Chamber of Commerce*, 1990) had "identified a new governmental interest" in "preventing 'the corrosive and distorting effects of immense aggregations of wealth that are accumulated with the help of the corporate form'" (*Citizens United v. Federal Election Commission*, 2010, p. 902). That contradiction is most starkly highlighted – as detailed earlier – by the fact that eight years before *Austin*, the author of *Bellotti* and the remainder of his *Bellotti* majority accepted just such restrictions in *NRWC*. In doing so, a unanimous Court in 1982 thus recognized as long established the interest that Justice Kennedy 28 years later would represent as having been "new" in 1990s *Austin*.

Three years after the crucial *NRWC* ruling, in striking down of limits on campaign expenditures by political action committees, the Court declared that it did so because such expenditures did not represent the same threat of real or apparent corruption as those of business corporations. It emphasized that the speech interests of individuals joined together for the purpose of expressing viewpoints were protected and distinguished from the economic interests represented by funds accumulated in corporate treasuries through the special advantages of the business corporate form (*Federal Election Commission v. National Conservative Political Action Committee*, 1985, pp. 495–496, 500–501).

A year after that, the Court still again distinguished spending made directly via such treasuries as fundamentally different from human First Amendment expression in holding that regulations of independent political expenditures applied to ideological corporations (rather than business corporations) were unconstitutional. The economic advantages provided to the business corporate form can create "an unfair advantage in the political marketplace," the Court declared, because the "resources in the treasury of a business corporation . . . are not an indication of popular support for the corporation's political ideas. They reflect instead the economically motivated decisions of investors and customers." *Massachusetts Citizens for Life, Inc.*, established a three-part test to distinguish between the two types of corporations, a test that critically emphasized why such ideological corporations could not accept contributions from business corporations – so as to prevent the former from serving as conduits into the political marketplace for spending from the latter (*Federal Election Commission v. Massachusetts Citizens for Life Inc.*, 1986, pp. 257–264).

Thus, it actually seemed anticlimactic – rather than "new" – four years later when the majority once again recognized the interests already established as compelling in *NRWC* and *Massachusetts Citizens for Life Inc.* (*Austin v. Michigan Chamber of Commerce*, 1990, pp. 659–660), for its holdings reflected a doctrine clearly articulated by the Court over the course of the previous decade. By walling off spending from corporate treasuries advantaged by special, state-created protections (perpetual life, limited liability, and tax advantages), the Court had reached a carefully balanced doctrine that fully protected political expression and unlimited political expenditures by any human individual, as well as that of any association of such individuals who wished to engage in such expression collectively through the similarly unlimited media spending of political action committees or ideological corporations. That doctrine arguably represented as close to a nearly perfect balance as possible between maximizing human political expressive freedom and minimizing encroachment on that freedom by structurally advantaged corporate spending – a balance that preserved the priorities of more than a century of legislative and judicial judgment.

Debating Corporate Reputation and Political Media Spending

In terms of the debate over corporate reputation as potentially advanced through political media spending, some scholarly discourse has focused on a laissez-faire interpretation of the right to receive information in arguing that government should not have any role in regulating corporate political media spending. Martin Redish, for example, has contended that the First Amendment prohibits government from blocking any opinions or ideas relevant to the governing process, including those disseminated through political expenditures made by corporate managers. He contended that "to exclude corporate expression from the scope of the free speech clause, then, would be unwisely to shut out from public debate a substantial amount of relevant, provocative, and potentially vital information and opinion on issues of fundamental importance to the polity" (pp. 235–236, 256–257).

However, that is countered by the assertion that regulation of political spending directly from corporate treasuries by those managers in no way shuts out the information and opinion those managers wish to contribute to public debate as citizens. The US Supreme Court has emphasized that such regulation seeks only to deny corporate management the advantage of tapping into funds generated through the "economically motivated decisions of investors and customers" and then spending that money in the political marketplace so as to "influence unfairly the outcome of elections" (*Austin v. Michigan Chamber of Commerce*, 1990, pp. 668–669).

Or as Greenwood (1998) has characterized it, a business "corporation is not a banding together of citizens but rather best understood as a pot of money . . . an institution we have created to serve us in a particular area and for a particular purpose" (pp. 1062–1063). That is, in terms of the doctrine articulated by the US Supreme Court over the course of the decade of the 1980s, the corporate form of business is endowed through legislative action with powerful economic advantages, such as limited liability, perpetual life, and favorable treatment of the accumulation and distribution of assets. Those advantages are provided so that corporate managers may "enhance their ability to attract capital and to deploy their resources in ways that maximize the return on their shareholders' investments," the US Supreme Court has said, not dominate democratic decision making (*Austin v. Michigan Chamber of Commerce*, 1990, pp. 658–659).

The debate on corporate political media spending has generated a considerable body of scholarly literature. One vein condemns virtually all efforts at campaign finance reform – including that aimed at corporate spending – in some cases to the point of arguing that money does not truly represent a corrupting political force and that those who support laws to prevent any such corruption are not acting in the public interest. John Samples (2006) has stated flatly, "I do not believe that campaign contributions have corrupted representation or American political culture in any significant way. I do not believe that Congress creates campaign finance laws to attain the public interest or the common good." He calls campaign finance reform "a delusion. It purports to reform the world for the better but in reality affirms the status quo for better or worse" (pp. 13, 290). Sheppard (2007) argues that the structural relationship between the Federal Election Commission and elected officials who benefit from its activities diminishes its effectiveness, contending "the primary group of 'winners' and 'losers' regarding campaign finance policy are the same elected officials that create the 'rules of the game' that administer, implement, and enforce these regulations" (p. 111).

This school of thought seems to consider the main motivation for campaign finance reform to be redistribution of wealth – as if there could be no other reason for opposing domination of political processes by the few over the many. Smith (2001) declares, for example, that "[t] here can be no doubt that many of those active in the campaign finance reform movement despise the inequalities of wealth that a system

of democratic capitalism produces" (p. 201). Smith concludes that although "campaign spending is important, it does not 'buy' elections, and limits on spending seem to destroy electoral competition. Far from corrupting the legislature, campaign contributions seem to have remarkably little effect on legislative behavior" (p. xi). Some analysis argues that convictions of elected officials selling votes for campaign contributions are rare and that states with stronger campaign-finance regulation have no more impact on reducing corruption or appearance of corruption than states with weaker campaign-finance regulations (Nemeroff, 2006).

Such assertions have been countered with arguments that such empirical data fail to tell the full story because most legislative action occurs outside of the formal voting process, away from the trade-off of an up-or-down vote on a discrete issue that a moneyed interest might support or oppose (Hohenstein, 2007, p. 254). Multiple scholarly efforts have documented evidence of the corrupting influence of corporate spending in relation to democratic processes (Easley, 1983; Lagasee, 1995; Shockley, 1985). The literature addressing the Court's jurisprudence on corporate political media spending also includes a substantial body of work asserting support for its soundness in terms of law, philosophical grounding, political and social benefit, and consistency with fundamental principles of American freedom of expression (Joo, 2001; Lassman, 1992; Lipson, 1995; Sitkoff, 2002). Others argue against virtually all of that (Dana, 2000; Geary, 1992; Ramler, 1991; Schofield, 1991).

In the discourse that matters most in terms of the current law of the land, the most recent debate at the US Supreme Court turned on a five-to-four vote in early 2010 that President Barack Obama said gave "a green light to a new stampede of special interest money in our politics" (Liptak, 2010). Senate Minority Leader Mitch McConnell of Kentucky called the decision "an important step in the direction of restoring the First Amendment rights of these groups by ruling that the Constitution protects their right to express themselves about political candidates and issues" (Liptak, 2010, p. 1). Lawrence M. Noble, an attorney at a major Washington firm and former general counsel of the Federal Election Commission, said that the ruling meant that lobbyists would now be able to tell lawmakers, "We have got a million we can spend advertising for you or against you – whichever one you want" (Kirkpatrick, 2010, p. 1).

In its *Citizens United v. Federal Election Commission* ruling, the US Supreme Court declared a provision in the Bipartisan Campaign Finance Act (BCRA) banning corporate-funded broadcasts targeting specific candidates within 30 days of a primary or 60 days of an election (*Citizens United v. Federal Election Commission*, 2010, p. 913). However, it also overturned 1990's *Austin v. Michigan State Chamber of Commerce* and its broad affirmation of the constitutionality of regulations on corporate political media spending in candidate elections (p. 902). Justice Kennedy asserted that the majority had applied "ancient First Amendment principles" in reaching those holdings, arguing that "before *Austin*, the Court had not allowed the exclusion of a class of speakers from the general public dialogue" (pp. 886, 889). Justice Stevens wrote for the four dissenting justices, however, that the majority was rejecting "a century of history" by treating "the distinction between corporate and individual campaign spending as an invidious novelty," (p. 930). Chief Justice John G. Roberts, Jr., maintained in a concurring opinion that the majority ruling "properly" asserted that the "First Amendment protects more than just the individual on a soapbox and the lonely pamphleteer" (p. 917).

The majority opinion relied heavily on its reading of *First National Bank of Boston v. Bellotti* as establishing unequivocally that "the First Amendment does not allow political speech restrictions based on a speaker's corporate identity" (p. 903). That reading contradicted the analyses of the majorities on the Court that decided *Austin* in 1990 and in the preceding 1980s cases that provided the set of holdings establishing its foundation (all holdings, to reemphasize, that *Bellotti* author Justice Powell joined). Justice Stevens – the only

justice in 2010 who had been on the Court for every one of the corporate political media spending cases and other campaign-finance cases since 1975 – all but hooted at the *Citizens United* majority's contention that earlier rulings had decisively rejected the possibility of distinguishing corporations from natural persons. "It just so happens that in every single case in which the Court has reviewed campaign finance legislation in the decades since, the majority failed to grasp this truth. The Federal Congress and dozens of state legislatures, we now know, have been similarly deluded," he wrote (p. 957).

Nevertheless, the five justices in the 2010 majority declared that henceforth "the Government may not suppress political speech on the basis of the speaker's corporate identity" (p. 913). Justice Kennedy's majority opinion characterized the regulations that *Citizens United* swept away as having making political expression felonious "solely because a corporation" spent money in opposition to or support of candidates. "Governments are often hostile to speech, but under our law and our tradition it seems stranger than fiction for our Government to make this political speech a crime," he wrote. Although the Court "must give weight to attempts by Congress to seek to dispel either the appearance or the reality" of corrupting influences, he asserted, the "remedies enacted by law, however, must comply with the First Amendment; and, it is our law and our tradition that more speech, not less, is the governing rule." Thus, in the majority's assessment, the Court was obligated to reject such legislative interference as restrictions on corporate political media spending because "civic discourse belongs to the people, and the Government may not prescribe the means used to conduct it" (pp. 916–917).

To what degree future courts and legislatures may ultimately challenge the *Citizens United* majority opinion's dismissal of corporate political media spending as irrelevant to anticorruption legislation will shape the role such spending may play in terms of corporate reputation in the years to come. Justice Stevens provided an extensive base for such challenges in a dissenting opinion that by itself was roughly equal in length to the majority opinion of Justice Kennedy and the concurrences authored by Chief Justice Roberts and Justices Antonin Scalia and Clarence Thomas combined. Justice Stevens pointed out that the "fact that corporations are different from human beings" had been so deeply established in legislation and jurisprudence that it was "unremarkable" when Justice William Rehnquist wrote for a unanimous Court in 1982's *Federal Election Commission v. National Right to Work Committee* that Congress' "careful legislative adjustment of the federal electoral laws . . . to account for the particular legal and economic attributes of corporations . . . warrants considerable deference," and "there is no reason why it may not . . . be accomplished by treating . . . corporations . . . differently from individuals." In making that point, Justice Stevens was writing with the authority of having been a member of the Court at that time, just as he was in his assertion that "all six members of the *Austin* majority had been on the Court at the time of *Bellotti*, and none so much as hinted in *Austin* that they saw any tension between the decisions" (pp. 950–955, 960, 971).

In sweeping terms, Justice Stevens characterized the majority opinion in *Citizens United* as "backwards in many senses. It elevates the majority's agenda over the litigants' submissions, facial attacks over as-applied claims, broad constitutional theories over narrow statutory grounds, individual dissenting opinions over precedential holdings, assertion over tradition, absolutism over empiricism, rhetoric over reality." Indeed, in Justice Stevens' assessment of *Citizens United*, the majority did not so much decide the case as *create* it, pointing out as he did that whether "corporations' electoral expenditures may not be regulated any more stringently than those of individuals" was "not included in the questions presented to us by the litigants" and was "argued here only in response to the Court's invitation." Thus, in his assessment: "Essentially, five Justices were unhappy with the limited nature of the case before us, so they changed the case to give

themselves an opportunity to change the law" (pp. 931–932, 979).

Future Directions of Research

At this point in time, scholars cannot know whether future courts and justices will fully embrace the jurisprudence of the five justices in the *Citizens United* majority or will work to constrain or even reject it ultimately. That aspect of the subject will continue to offer opportunities for research contributions, much as it did in the decades leading up to the ruling. For the foreseeable future, it can be expected that those particular five justices will hold firm at the US Supreme Court on the precedents of *Citizens United*, given the fact that even though it is a narrow majority, by all evidence, it is likely to remain firmly in place for some time to come.

Perhaps the most fertile new ground for scholars to plow lies in consideration of future efforts to enact expanded requirements for disclosure of the source of corporate political media spending. Too often, as the courts have noted, such spending is conducted "behind dubious and misleading names like: 'The Coalition – Americans Working for Real Change' (funded by business organizations opposed to organized labor), 'Citizens for Better Medicare' (funded by the pharmaceutical industry)" (*McConnell v. Federal Election Commission*, 2003, p. 237). The great potential for research to contribute to such efforts can be seen in the fact that the only element of *Citizens United* that did not split the Court five-to-four down the middle was support for regulation that would greatly expand such disclosure. All the justices except for Justice Thomas joined Justice Kennedy in providing the Court's blessing for such regulation in the future: "Even if the ads only pertain to a commercial transaction, the public has an interest in knowing who is speaking about a candidate shortly before an election" (*Citizens United v. Federal Election Commission*, 2010, pp. 913–916).

Ideally, that would include regulation that requires corporate managers to notify their stockholders in advance of such spending when they intend to use company profits on expenditures for political candidates – a form of disclosure quite specifically endorsed in Justice Kennedy's majority opinion: "With the advent of the Internet, prompt disclosure of expenditures can provide shareholders and citizens with the information needed to hold corporations and elected officials accountable for their positions and supporters. Shareholders can determine whether their corporation's political speech advances the corporation's interest in making profits, and citizens can see whether elected officials are " 'in the pocket' of so-called moneyed interests." Justice Kennedy seemed to be envisioning a world in which both citizens and corporate investors will be provided with extensive resources through which they may derive an accurate understanding of corporate reputation on the basis of how political media spending may contribute to its formation. For Justice Kennedy and seven other justices currently serving, disclosure of that sort would permit "citizens and shareholders to react to the speech of corporate entities in a proper way. This transparency enables the electorate to make informed decisions and give proper weight to different speakers and messages" (p. 916).

References

Austin v. Michigan Chamber of Commerce, 494 US 652 (1990).

Berger, L.L. (2004) What is the sound of a corporation speaking? How the cognitive theory of metaphor can help lawyers shape the law. *Journal of the Association of Legal Writing Directors*, 2, 169–208.

Berger, L.L. (2007) Of metaphor, metonymy, and corporate money: Rhetorical choices in Supreme Court decisions on campaign finance regulation. *Mercer Law Review*, 58, 949–990.

Brief for Appellant. *First National Bank of Boston v. Bellotti*, 435 US 765 (1978).

Brief for Appellant. *Federal Election Commission v. National Right to Work Committee*, 459 US 197 (1982).

Brief for Chamber of Commerce of the United States of America. *First National Bank of Boston v. Bellotti*, 435 US 765 (1978).

Brief for Northeastern Legal Foundation. *First National Bank of Boston v. Bellotti*, 435 US 765 (1978).

Buckley v. Valeo, 424 US 1 (1976).

Citizens United v. Federal Election Commission, 130 S.Ct. 876 (2010).

Dana, S.W. (2000) Restrictions on corporate spending on state ballot measure campaigns: A re-evaluation of Austin v. Michigan Chamber of Commerce. *Hastings Constitutional Law Quarterly*, 27, 309–367.

Dartmouth College v. Woodward, 17 US 518 (1819).

Easley, A.K. (1983) Buying back the first amendment: Regulation of disproportionate corporate spending in ballot issue campaigns. *Georgia Law Review*, 17, 675–758.

Federal Election Commission v. Massachusetts Citizens for Life Inc., 479 US 238 (1986).

Federal Election Commission v. National Conservative Political Action Committee, 470 US 480 (1985).

Federal Election Commission v. National Right to Work Committee, 459 US 197 (1982).

First National Bank of Boston v. Bellotti, 435 US 765 (1978).

Geary, S.T. (1992) Austin v. Michigan Chamber of Commerce: Freedom of expression issues implicated by the government regulation of corporate political expenditures in candidate elections. *Boston University Law Review*, 72, 825–840.

Greenwood, D.J.H. (1998) Essential speech: Why corporate speech is not free. *Iowa Law Review*, 83, 995–1070.

Heath, R.L. (1997) *Strategic Issues Management: Organizations and Public Policy Challenges*. Thousand Oaks, CA: Sage.

Hohenstein, K. (2007) *Coining Corruption: The Making of the American Campaign Finance System*. DeKalb, IL: Northern Illinois University Press.

Imagine tomorrow without argument. (1979) *The New York Times*, August 16, sec. 1, p. 23.

Joo, T.W. (2001) The modern corporation and campaign finance: Incorporating corporate governance analysis into First Amendment jurisprudence. *Washington University Law Quarterly*, 79, 1–87.

Kerr, R.L. (2008) *The Corporate Free-Speech Movement: Cognitive Feudalism and the Endangered Marketplace of Ideas*. New York: LFB Scholarly.

Kirkpatrick, D.D. (2010) Lobbyists get potent weapon in campaign finance ruling. *The New York Times*, January 22, sec. A, p. 1.

Lagasee, D.R. (1995) Undue influence: Corporate political speech, power and the initiative process. *Brooklyn Law Review*, 61, 1347–1397.

Lammers, N. (1982) *Dollar Politics*. Washington, DC: Congressional Quarterly.

Lassman, P.M. (1992) Breaching the fortress walls: Corporate political speech and Austin v. Michigan Chamber of Commerce. *Virginia Law Review*, 78, 759–792.

Lipson, M. (1995) Autonomy and democracy. *The Yale Law Journal*, 104, 2249–2275.

Liptak, A. (2010) Justices overturn key campaign limits. *The New York Times*, January 22, sec. A, p. 1.

Marchand, R. (1998) *Creating the Corporate Soul: The Rise of Public Relations and Corporate Imagery*. Berkeley, CA: University of California Press.

Matasar, A.B. (1986) *Corporate PACs and Federal Campaign Financing Laws: Use or Abuse of Power*. Westport, CT: Quorum Books.

McConnell v. Federal Election Commission, 251 F. Supp. 2d. 176 (2003).

Mobil's Warner energizes advocacy advertising. (1981) *Ad Forum*, February.

Nemeroff, M.A. (2006) The limited role of campaign finance laws in reducing corruption by elected public officials. *Howard Law Journal*, 49, 687–715.

Pacific Gas & Electric Co. v. Public Utilities Commission of California, 475 US 1 (1986).

Ramler, D.M. (1991) Austin v. Michigan Chamber of Commerce: The Supreme Court takes a "less speech, sounds great" approach to corporate political expression. *Federal Communication Law Journal*, 43, 419–449.

Rutherford, P. (2000) *Endless Propaganda: The Advertising of Public Goods*. Toronto, Canada: University of Toronto Press.

Samples, J. (2006) *The Fallacy of Campaign-Finance Reform*. Chicago, IL: University of Chicago Press.

Schofield, M. (1991) Muzzling corporations: The Court giveth and the Court taketh away a corporation's "fundamental right" to free political speech in Austin v. Michigan Chamber of Commerce. *Louisiana Law Review*, 52, 253–271.

Sethi, S.P. (1977) *Advocacy Advertising and Large Corporations: Social Conflict, Big Business Image, the News Media, and Public Policy*. Lexington, MA: Lexington Books.

Sheppard, M.C. (2007) *The Federal Election Commission: Policy, Politics, and Administration*. Lanham, MD: University Press of America.

Shockley, J.S. (1985) Direct democracy, campaign finance, and the courts: Can corruption, undue influence, and declining voter confidence be found? *University of Miami Law Review*, 39, 377–428.

Sitkoff, R.H. (2002) Management and control of the modern business corporation: Corporate speech and citizenship. *The University of Chicago Law Review*, 69, 1103–1166.

Smith, B.A. (2001) *Unfree Speech: The Folly of Campaign Finance Reform*. Princeton, MJ: Princeton University Press.

Taking a stand on the issues through advertising. *Association Management*, December.

The soapbox is a lonely place. (1975) *The New York Times*, May 8, sec. 1, p. 39.

United States v. Congress of Industrial Organizations, 335 US 106 (1948).

United States v. Morton Salt Co., 338 US 632 (1950).

United States v. United Auto Workers, 352 US 567 (1957).

Vogel, D. (1989) *Fluctuating Fortunes: The Political Power of Business in America*. New York: Basic Books.

Warner, R. Jr. and Silk, L. (1979) *Ideals in Collision: The Relationship between Business and the News Media*. Pittsburgh, PA: Carnegie Mellon University Press.

38

Corporate Reputation Management and Issues of Diversity

Damion Waymer

Virginia Tech, USA

Sarah VanSlette

Southern Illinois University Edwardsville, USA

Although valuing diversity in the corporate context should be a societally moral ascription, on a pragmatic level, diversity makes smart business sense. Scholars have made similar arguments. In fact, research about US workplace environments has shown that, on at least two demographic dimensions of diversity, ethnically diverse female employees desire flexible policies and workplaces that cater to them and their cultural needs (Buzzanell *et al.*, 2007). Companies would be wise to take these diverse perspectives into account if they want to retain a diverse workforce. This chapter aims to make the mentioned business case for diversity more clear, specifically, by contributing to the growing body of scholarship on diversity in the corporate landscape. Via three diversity-related case studies, we make this contribution by focusing on a very specific dimension of business management and diversity: the intersect of diversity and reputation management.

Those who perceive diversity as exclusively a moral imperative or societal goal are missing the larger point. Workforce diversity needs to be viewed as a competitive advantage and a business opportunity. . . . Diversity is about recognizing, respecting and valuing differences based on ethnicity, gender, color, age, race, religion, disability, national origin and sexual orientation. It also includes an infinite range of individual unique characteristics and experiences, such as communication style, career path, life experience, educational background, geographic location, income level, marital status, military experience, parental status and other variables that influence personal perspectives. . . . Superior business performance requires tapping into these unique perspectives. If we are to form lasting business relationships with our customers and become a true global leader in the industry, we must understand our customers' diverse cultures and decisional processes, not merely their languages. To do so, we must begin with a diverse workplace. . . . To remain competitive for talent and for customers, it is imperative that we attract and value diverse talent and enable that talent to attract and value diverse customers. (Chubb, 2011)

The Handbook of Communication and Corporate Reputation, First Edition. Edited by Craig E. Carroll.
© 2013 John Wiley & Sons, Inc. Published 2015 by John Wiley & Sons, Inc.

As this quote illustrates, the business case for diversity is a rather simple one: although valuing diversity should be a societally moral ascription, on a pragmatic level, diversity makes smart business sense. Scholars have made similar arguments. In fact, research about US workplace environments has shown that, on at least two demographic dimensions of diversity, ethnically diverse female employees desire flexible policies and workplaces that cater to them and their cultural needs (Buzzanell *et al.*, 2007). Companies would be wise to take these diverse perspectives into account if they want to retain a diverse workforce. This chapter aims to make the mentioned business case for diversity more clear, specifically, by contributing to the growing body of scholarship on diversity in the corporate landscape. We make this contribution by focusing on a very specific dimension of business management and diversity: the intersect of diversity and reputation management.

We begin by discussing the inherently communicative nature of reputation. Next, we establish a link between reputation and diversity; we present a few cases that demonstrate the import of giving issues of diversity greater scholarly focus in organizational reputation research, and finally, we draw conclusions and provide directions for future research.

Reputation: A Cocreated Construct

Reputation has been widely recognized as a valuable intangible asset for companies that can generate lasting competitive advantage (Fombrun *et al.*, 2000), and from a public relations perspective, of which we both teach and research, scholars have argued that reputation, as a major public relations outcome, interacts with other outcome variables such as trust, credibility, and relationship, to affect public relations efforts' return on expectation (ROE) and return on investment (ROI) for organizations (Stacks, 2010).

Although we agree, in principle, with scholars who have sought to look for concepts and constructs, such as reputation, to demonstrate public relations' effectiveness, philosophically, we articulate the position that the processes of creating, erecting, and sustaining an organizational reputation asset are inherently communicative (Gotsi and Wilson, 2001) – dare we say even rhetorical (it should be noted that the principle and the philosophical positions are not necessarily at odds). Through communication processes of dialog, advocacy, statements, and counterstatements among organizations and their myriad stakeholders, stakeholders and organizations define, cocreate, and agree upon the tenets (Heath, 1993) of what constitutes favorable and/or unfavorable reputations, what factors or events will undo favorable reputations, or what actions must be undertaken to repair tarnished reputations. Viewing reputation management as a form of issues communication (Heath and Palenchar, 2009), we can also argue that legitimacy is the cornerstone of a strong organizational image, brand, and reputation.

Watson (2010) argued that "reputation was, is, and always will be of immense importance to organizations, whether commercial, governmental, or not for profit" (p. 339). Whether making product choices, career decisions, or even investigating investment opportunities, corporate stakeholders and publics often rely on organizations' reputations to aid in their decision-making processes. It is important for companies to present accurate, balanced depictions of themselves and their activities in this regard because reputation researchers have found that "reputations signal publics about how a firm's products, jobs, strategies, and prospects compare to those of competing firms" (Fombrun and Shanley, 1990, p. 233). Hence, publics are interpreting various signs and messages from organizations and then making a variety of decisions based on their interpretation of those symbols. Watson captured the cocreated nature of reputation when he defined it as the "sum of predictable behaviors, relationships, and two-way communication undertaken by an organization as judged affectively and cognitively by its stakeholders over a period of time" (p. 340).

Reputation and Issues of Diversity

Both the majority of research on reputation and definitions of reputation, according to Watson (2010), "tend to favor the positive, with emphasis placed on being well thought of, in public esteem, and delivering on promises. But reputation has two sides" (p. 341) – good and bad. Despite Gardberg and Fombrun's (2002) study of companies' reputations that included a sample of companies considered to have the best and worst corporate reputations, most research and practical analysis still tend to focus on the benefits of a favorable reputation such as the ability for corporations to charge premium prices, attract better applicants, enhance their access to capital markets, and attract investors. Even so, little attention has been paid to the role diversity might play in further building or detracting from an organization's reputation.

Organizations, however, are now attempting to accrue further reputational assets by investing in and promoting their activities in and around the area of diversity. One means by which it appears organizations are attempting to establish a favorable reputation in the area of diversity is to be rated as "highly committed to diversity" by outside entities.

DiversityInc.com

DiversityInc is a magazine that features news and information about how various issues of diversity and specific diversity initiatives affect different organizations. Since 2001, the magazine presents annually its "DiversityInc Top 50 Companies for Diversity." The magazine's web site describes the methodology it uses to rank the organizations. *DiversityInc* derives data and lists from a more than 300-question survey that is sent to all organizations desiring participation in the study. Questions on the survey include topics such as CEO commitment, corporate and organizational communications, and supplier diversity; per their web site, any company that does not offer same-sex domestic-partner

benefits is automatically disqualified from the *DiversityInc* Top 50 list and any of the other lists that it creates (DiversityInc, 2011). Other lists include (1) The DiversityInc Top 10 Companies for Recruitment & Retention; (2) The DiversityInc Top 10 Companies for Supplier Diversity; (3) The DiversityInc Top 10 Companies for Blacks; (4) The DiversityInc Top 10 Companies for Latinos; (5) The DiversityInc Top 10 Companies for Asian Americans; (6) The DiversityInc Top 10 Companies for Executive Women; (7) The DiversityInc Top 10 Companies for LGBT Employees; and (8) The DiversityInc Top 10 Companies for People with Disabilities (DiversityInc, 2011).

Working Mother Magazine

Similarly, *Working Mother* Magazine – under the umbrella of Working Mother Media – "reaches 2.2 million readers," "is the only national magazine for career-committed mothers," and is a vehicle the parent company uses to demonstrate its focus on "culture change for working moms, women and diversity in the workplace" (Working Mother, 2011a). Moreover, per the their web site, "2010 marked 25 years of Working Mother's signature research initiative, Working Mother 100 Best Companies, the most important benchmark for work life practices in corporate America, and the launch of the Working Mother Research Institute" (Working Mother, 2011a). *Working Mother*'s data and lists are generated from "more than 650 questions on workforce representation, child care, flexibility programs, leave policies and more" (Working Mother, 2011b).

So what does it matter to be listed on one of these magazines' lists? For one, organizations are taking these rankings seriously. Coca-Cola (ranked twelfth on the 2011 DiversityInc list) has its ranking along with all of its diversity-related awards featured prominently on its "Our Progress" tab on its web site. Sodexo (ranked second on the 2011 DiversityInc list) has many of its diversity-related rankings and award featured on its "About Us" tab on its web page. Some of the awards include

Named a "Best Company for Hourly Workers" by *Working Mother* magazine

Named a "Best Company for Multicultural Women" by *Working Mother*

Ranked #1 among "Top 50 Companies for Diversity Inclusion" by *DiversityInc*

Named One of the 2009 DiversityInc Top Ten Employers for LGBT Workers

Named a 2010 Straight for Equality in Business Awardee by PFLAG

Ranks Second on the 2009 DiversityInc Top Ten Companies for Latinos. (Sodexo, 2011)

It appears that these rankings at least matter enough to these organizations for them to submit the materials needed to be evaluated by these independent raters as well as for these organizations to post (and boast about) their successful rankings and awards on their web sites.

Rationale for Diversity and Reputation

There is evidence that the image of an organization affects potential applicants' initial job decisions (Turban and Greening, 1997). In order to attract, recruit, and retain the best talent (and diverse clientele), organizations must not only seek diverse applicants for their workplaces, but also help to foster an environment that is welcoming, inclusive, and sensitive to diversity. If diverse workplaces are deemed desirable workplaces, then it makes sense for organizations to attempt to build strong reputations in the area of diversity. Competition has been and continues to be fierce among specialized and technical corporations for qualified applicants due to the variety of employment choices desired applicants may have (Albinger and Freeman, 2000). Highly skilled persons from underrepresented minority groups as well as historically marginalized groups, however, might simultaneously experience greater choice in employment opportunities as well as self-imposed opportunity constraint. They may limit their job searches to organizations that have strong reputations in the area of diversity.

Given the limited information available to applicants early in the job search process, initial application decisions are heavily based on general impressions of the organization (Rynes, 1991). Because "the individual uses the information obtained from a recruitment source to decide whether or not to pursue possible employment with an organization" (Gatewood *et al.*, 1993, p. 414), a major component of attracting employees is establishing a favorable reputation in the eyes of publics. Attracting and retaining diverse talent is important because as the opening vignette suggests, a diverse workforce likely leads to the creation of a welcoming environment that espouses diversity of thought; this diversity of thought might ultimately yield an organization many dividends – one notably being the ability to reach and attract the widest range of publics including customers. To further explicate the rationale for diversity and reputation, a brief case summary is provided.

Deloitte

Then-chairman and CEO of Deloitte Michael Cook stated:

> The firm invests millions of dollars recruiting and training these talented people, and if they leave prematurely we have, in effect, squandered our investment. Not only that, but clients aren't served as well if you pick your partners out of half the people hired. You want all the best people to stay with you, men and women. (quoted in Williams, 2000, p. 88)

At the time, Deloitte had an employee retention problem because it had developed a reputation of being unreceptive to the needs of its women employees. Deloitte had been hiring approximately the same number of women and men into entry level positions since the early 1980s (Molina, 2005). The company assumed that by hiring equal number of women and men, it had assured that more women would reach the partner ranks within 10–12 years; however, a decade later, only 10% of that year's partner candidates were women (Molina, 2005). Cook sought to find the cause of this attrition. Via independent research, Deloitte discovered that nearly 70% of the women that left the company were working full time at other companies, and 20% were working part time (Molina, 2005). Thus, women were not leaving Deloitte because they wanted to stay home with children; rather, they were leaving the company because they did not want to work at Deloitte (Molina, 2005). Reasons former employees gave for leaving Deloitte include (1) the company was not considered to value women's ways of perception and relating to others; (2) the company did not provide sufficient opportunities for women to advance; and (3) the company excluded women from informal networks and mentoring (Molina, 2005).

Deloitte's story, however, is not all bad. Today, Deloitte is highlighted as a success story. It was once a company that was affected adversely (lost lots of money and could not retain good talent) because it had a negative reputation in terms of gender equity; Cook made achieving gender equity an organizational imperative. He made systematic changes to the organizational structure to make Deloitte a more inclusive work environment. Almost two decades later, Deloitte is considered one of the top 10 companies to work for in 2011 by *DiversityInc*. Deloitte is proud of this achievement as evidenced by its supplying this ranking to *PR Newswire* in the form of a press release (Deloitte, 2011). In this press release, Deloitte is celebrated for its diversity efforts including receiving some of the following awards and accolades: 12 consecutive appearances on *Fortune* Magazine's "100 Best Companies to Work For" ranking as well as being recognized by *Fortune* for its focus on diversity; a top five ranking on the "Best Companies for Multicultural Women" by *Working Mother* Magazine as well as a top 10 employer on *Working Mother's* "100 Best Companies for Working Mothers" (Deloitte, 2011).

This brief case is important for the following reason. Because reputation is based on a company's performance, its identity programs, as well as how multiple stakeholders perceive the company's behavior (Argenti and Drucken-

miller, 2004), past crises – especially those centering on difference or discrimination – can form a reputational threat to corporations at varying levels of intensity (Coombs, 2004). Simply put, organizations would be wise to be reflective, as well as to engage in precrisis communication efforts that are sensitive to diverse populations (Waymer, 2012). Moreover, such efforts might mitigate backlash from "emergent publics" when a crisis hits (Waymer and Heath, 2007). Sadly, many organizations wait until diversity issues/crises occur before they choose to address organizational diversity issues. Although Deloitte waited until it had lost several employees before it attempted to change its organizational culture, this example highlights what organizations can do to shed a negative reputation in terms of diversity, as well as shows how over time these organizations can create new diversity-oriented reputations. So this chapter addresses the following question:

RQ: How do some organizations, in the wake of diversity-based reputational threats, respond?

In this chapter, we explore this question by analyzing two current cases to gauge how organizations respond *during* these times of diversity-oriented reputational threats. We also assess whether there is some modicum of public outcry surrounding these diversity-related incidences. The two cases are chosen for both their timeliness and for the fact that they represent vastly different industries:

1   *Lowe's*. In December of 2011, Lowe's pulled advertising for the TV show "All-American Muslims"; Lowe's has had a history of discriminatory practices (EEOC, 2009, 2010) and this PR gaffe with "All-American Muslims" could be the latest manifestation of a systemic diversity problem at Lowe's.

2   *Abercrombie & Fitch*. In June 2011, CBS News reported that a 20-year-old Muslim, claiming she was fired for refusing to remove her headscarf while on the job, sued the company (Glynn, 2011). In the

same year, another Muslim woman won a lawsuit against the company (EEOC, 2011b).

Each of the two companies' web sites is studied. Specifically, we study the sites and analyze their specific diversity pages and other diversity-related content. Company web sites are used because these web sites serve an important public relations function and are easily accessible. Scholars in the discipline have discussed the potential for public relations and the Internet (Hallahan, 2004; McAllister-Spooner, 2009). Hallahan (2004) argued that the Internet has changed, dramatically, the ways that practitioners "distribute information, interact with key publics, deal with crises and manage issues" (p. 255). Because of the increased importance and visibility of the Internet to organizations' strategic management efforts, an analysis of organizational web sites allows us to gauge the public relations diversity initiatives that organizations have or do not have in place and/or public statements about their commitment or lack thereof to diversity. Moreover, Holtz (2002) opined that corporate communicators believe that the Internet is one of the most promising public relations tools available to them in defending organizational interests – including reputations.

In addition to corporate web sites and their diversity pages, we searched the Web and published news reports for statements the organizations might have made in defense of their actions as well as for statements from individuals and/or collectivities speaking against these corporations and their actions.

The Case of Two Diversity Missteps

Lowe's

The only public statement by Lowe's on diversity and inclusion can be found under its Social Responsibility web page. In this 318-word statement, they claim that "Lowe's is committed to treating each customer, employee, community, investor and vendor with respect and dignity" (Lowe's, 2011a, para. 2). They have a Diversity Advisory Council as well as Diversity Leadership Teams who regularly meet to evaluate diversity and inclusion initiatives. They describe their supplier diversity program and commitment to equal opportunity employment, claiming that their "inclusive work force helps provide our diverse customer base with the products and services they need" (Lowe's, 2011a, para. 4). Interestingly, they claim that their diverse workforce is what ensures an inclusive environment for customers of diverse cultures. They say, "Recruiting, developing and retaining a diverse work force ensures a welcoming customer experience" (Lowe's, 2011a, para. 1). That begs the question, is commitment to a diverse and inclusive workplace enough to develop a positive relationship with diverse customers?

Lowe's has a history of discrimination lawsuits filed by the U.S. Equal Employment Opportunity Commission (EEOC). In August 2009, Lowe's paid a $1.7 million settlement to three female employees from Washington who experienced "rampant sexual harassment" over a six-month period. The harassment included repeated acts of "physical and verbal abuse which culminated in one instance of sexual assault" (EEOC, 2009). In addition to the monetary payment, Lowe's agreed to provide sexual harassment training to all managers in the region. In September 2011, Lowe's paid a $120,000 settlement to an employee in Tennessee who was forced to work on the Sabbath, a violation of his sincerely held religious belief. In addition to the payment, Lowe's had to amend its human resources management guide to include a statement on religious bias, and had to provide discrimination awareness training to all managers in the region (EEOC, 2011a).

In December of 2011, their commitment to diversity was tested yet again. Lowe's caved to pressure from the Florida Family Association (FFA) and pulled its advertising for the TLC reality TV show "All-American Muslim." The FFA, whose mission is to "educate people on what they can do to defend, protect and promote traditional, biblical values"(FFA, 2011a), mounted a full-scale campaign to get corporations to pull their advertising from the program, as the show misled Americans into believing that Muslims were just "ordinary folks." The FFA accused the show of deception because it did not feature any of the "many Islamic believers whose agenda poses a clear and present danger to liberties and traditional values that the majority of Americans cherish" (FFA, 2011b). According to DiversityInc.com, only Lowe's and Kayak.com succumbed to the FFA campaign ("Lowe's Muslim publicity," 2011). In the days that followed, word spread about the advertisements that were pulled from All-American Muslim, and a public firestorm erupted. While some lauded the company for taking a stand against the show, many were outraged.

On Saturday, December 10, 2011, Lowe's published a statement on their official Facebook page, explaining their decision to distance themselves from All-American Muslim. They said,

> Individuals and groups have strong political and societal views on this topic, and this program became a lighting [sic] rod for many of those views. . . . As a result we did pull our advertising on this program. We believe it is best to respectfully defer to communities, individuals and groups to discuss and consider such issues of importance. (Collins, 2011, para. 3)

This post spurred over 28,000 comments on their Facebook page in the next four days, many of which were bigoted, hate-filled rants against Muslims, and Lowe's neither responded to the bigotry nor did they remove the offensive comments from the page. Their silence was deafening, and the Council on American-Islamic Relations (CAIR) publicly wondered if Lowe's was intentionally leaving up the hate-filled anti-Muslim rhetoric because they supported it ("Lowe's Muslim publicity," 2011). Finally, on Wednesday, December 14, Lowe's took down their original Facebook post about the advertisements and all the related com-

ments. They put up a new post that apologized to anyone who was offended by their original business decision or the offensive comments that people left on Lowe's Facebook page. They explained that, "out of respect for the transparency of social media, we let the debate continue. However, we have seen a large volume of comments become more pointed and hateful. As a result, we have taken the step of removing all previous posts and will more tightly filter future comments on this topic" (Lowe's, 2011b). As of December 22, 2011, there were almost 14,000 comments under that Facebook post, many of which voiced support for Lowe's and their decision to pull the ads.

As DiversityInc.com points out, their weak position on diversity and inclusion (as reflected in their brief and vague statement on Lowe's web site) could have caused this latest PR mess: "by having no demonstrable understanding of diversity management practices and no stated clarity on its own values, Lowe's was incapable of making good decisions. By bending to a hate group (the Florida Family Association), Lowe's became their ally" ("Lowe's Muslim publicity," 2011, para. 13). In addition to the public scolding by CAIR, Rep. Keith Ellison (the first Muslim elected to Congress), Rep. John Conyers (MI), Senator Ted Lieu (CA), actress Mia Farrow, and organizations like Muslim-Matters.org all expressed their disagreement with the store's decision and some called for boycotts of Lowe's.

Abercrombie & Fitch

At Abercrombie & Fitch (A&F), exclusion is institutionalized. The multibillion dollar clothing retailer is open about its policy to only hire good-looking young people to be salesclerks (or "models," as they are called at A&F). On their corporate web page, the job description for "models" reads: "Models protect and project the image of the brand through personal style, providing customer service and maintaining presentation standards" (Abercrombie & Fitch, 2011b, para. 1). To its credit, A&F does include "diversity awareness" as one of the traits they look for in a model. Others include "Sophistication, aspiration, sense of style . . . integrity, applied learning, outgoing personality and communication skills" (Abercrombie & Fitch, 2011b, para. 2). A&F has a corporate "look book" that explains what new sales representatives should look like, and they require that managers send in mug shots of their new hires for corporate's approval (Edwards, 2003). A writer for *The Times* of London, who was invited to visit the corporate headquarters in Ohio, called A&F "the Fourth Reich in flip-flops" (Collard, 2003). This exclusion is strategic and is central to the brand, according to the A&F CEO, Mike Jeffries. After interviewing him, one reporter put it this way: "As far as Jeffries is concerned, America's unattractive, overweight or otherwise undesirable teens can shop elsewhere" (Danizet-Lewis, 2006, para. 23).

When the CEO was asked if the company's practice of hiring people based on their "style" was exclusionary, he defended his position: "If I exclude people, absolutely, [I'm] delighted to do so" (Edwards, 2003). In 2006, Jeffries elaborated on this position when he told a writer from Salon.com,

> We go after the cool kids. We go after the attractive all-American kid with a great attitude and a lot of friends. A lot of people don't belong [in our clothes], and they can't belong. Are we exclusionary? Absolutely. Those companies that are in trouble are trying to target everybody: young, old, fat, skinny. But then you become totally vanilla. You don't alienate anybody, but you don't excite anybody, either. (Danizet-Lewis, 2006, para. 23)

The same writer asked him about the company's notoriously offensive T-shirt designs (including shirts that read "Who Needs a Brain When You Have These?," "Gentlemen Prefer Tig Ol' Bitties," and "Do I Make You Look Fat?"). Jeffries replied, "Listen, do we go too far sometimes? Absolutely. But we push the envelope, and we try to be funny, and we try to stay authentic and relevant to our target customer. I really don't care what anyone other

than our target customer thinks" (Danizet-Lewis, 2006, para. 36).

In 2004, a group of nine former employees or job applicants (all minorities) won a $50 million settlement against the company, arguing that they were either denied employment or they were forced to work in the stockroom or take night shifts because they did not fit the "Abercrombie look" (EEOC, 2004). As part of the settlement, A&F agreed to hire and promote women and minorities into managerial positions. They agreed to hire a vice president for diversity, provide diversity training to all managers, and agreed to ensure that its web site and marketing materials would reflect diversity. In a statement about the settlement, the EEOC stated, "The retail industry and other industries need to know that businesses cannot discriminate against individuals under the auspice of a marketing strategy or a particular 'look'" (EEOC, 2004, para. 5).

While the company is openly committed to only hiring "stylish" people, they do have (likely as a result of this EEOC lawsuit settlement) a page on their "Careers" web site that is devoted to diversity. On that page, under the heading "Measurement and Accountability," they tout these accomplishments.

Since the start of the initiative, we have seen marked improvement in the diversity of our in-store staff. We continue to work at this and other aspects of our initiative, but here are a few key facts as of April 30th, 2010 that we are proud of.

- Our in-store workforce, as a whole is 50.22% people of color
- Our in-store models are 48.44% people of color
- Our in-store managers-in-training are 41.04% people of color (Abercrombie & Fitch, 2011a, para.1)

Based on this statement, and the adjacent photo stream of extremely attractive ethnically diverse young people, one can only assume that diversity at A&F is limited to racial diversity.

This narrow focus on race (to the exclusion of other types of diversity) could explain the nature of A&F's most recent diversity-related lawsuits. In 2009, a British girl who was missing a part of her arm was forced to work in the stockroom instead of on the sales floor because her prosthetic arm did not fit the "looks policy" of A&F (BBC News, 2009). She was awarded £9000 for harassment and wrongful dismissal ("Student with prosthetic," 2009). Also in 2009, a Minnesota judge fined the retailer $115,264 for discrimination against a customer with autism after employees refused to allow the girl's parents to accompany her into a changing room (Baran, 2009). And in 2011, a Federal judge ruled for the plaintiff in an EEOC lawsuit against A&F on behalf of a Muslim woman who was not hired because of her headscarf (EEOC, 2011b). The EEOC alleged "that Abercrombie & Fitch refused to accommodate the applicant's religious beliefs by granting an exception to its 'Look Policy,' an internal dress code that includes a prohibition against head coverings" (EEOC, 2011b, para. 2).

It seems that while A&F's profits, like many other retailers, have slipped in the past few years, they are poised for a comeback in 2012 (O'Brien, 2011). Apart from the plaintiffs in the (seemingly never-ending) string of lawsuits alleging discrimination, there seems to be very little public uproar about the brand or its policies. It remains a popular brand among high school and college-aged kids, and has even developed a cult-like following among gay men (Danizet-Lewis, 2006). This popularity among gay men is particularly fascinating given the company's open eschewing of nonmainstream cultures and their brand's push for a "rugged and masculine" ideal man (Danizet-Lewis, 2006). The consistent popularity is perhaps not surprising when you consider the target market of the store: the "cool kid." Why would a young person want to publicly announce that he does not feel included or welcomed by A&F? By protesting the store, its clothing, or its hiring practices, that person is admitting that he is uncool, unattractive, and an outsider.

Conclusion

As the earlier discussed corporate cases demonstrate, the damage to reputation sustained by companies embroiled in diversity scandals is inconsistent. Deloitte was able to right their ship, and learn valuable lessons about the interests and expectations of its employees. Deloitte's Top 10 rank on DiversityInc (2011) Top 50 Companies for Diversity list is a testament to how a company can work diligently to change its culture, and will reap the benefits of that hard work. Lowe's could take a page from the Deloitte playbook, as they do not appear to have learned much yet from their diversity scandals and lawsuits. If the thousands of people who signed petitions asking Lowe's to reverse their decision or vowed to boycott the store, actually stopped shopping at Lowe's, their cultural insensitivity could have major financial repercussions. Shoppers in need of home improvement supplies have other options (Home Depot, Ace Hardware, etc.), and the zero-sum game of retail means that Lowe's competitors will quickly profit off their angry customers.

The target audiences of Lowe's and A&F are very different. This difference in markets could explain why A&F, despite a record of diversity problems that puts Lowe's to shame, does not seem to absorb the impact of any of its numerous EEOC lawsuits. While some of A&F's monetary settlements have been expensive, and millions of dollars in settlements can certainly have an effect on the bottom line, the lack of an organized public protest against the company's openly discriminatory practices is fascinating. The people who hate what the A&F brand stands for and are sensitive to discrimination issues were probably not going to shop at A&F in the first place. As we hypothesized earlier, A&F targets kids who want to be cool, stylish, and to belong. Kids who want to be cool and belong (perhaps the majority of young adults) typically will not protest the store that sells coolness. Those who feel the clothes are not made for them will feel a sense of shame in not fitting in (literally and figuratively), and they will not be inclined to admit that they have been excluded.

Future studies could be done on the different strategies that companies use to repair their images after they have lost a discrimination lawsuit. On December 21, 2011, Bank of America (BofA) agreed to pay $335 million to settle allegations that its subsidiary, Countrywide Financial, discriminated against minority homebuyers by charging them higher interest and higher fees than white customers with comparable credit scores and incomes. The discriminatory lending took place when the housing market was at its peak and before BofA acquired Countrywide in January of 2008. Despite Countrywide's discriminatory practices, BofA was ranked eleventh on the DiversityInc (2011) Top 50 Companies for Diversity. This ranking underscores the success BofA has had in distancing itself from Countrywide's questionable practices, and at the same time using the lawsuit as a platform from which to remind people of BofA's commitment to diversity issues. Currently, the BofA web site features a number of pages that tout its commitment to diversity. They are currently expanding their outreach to help customers at risk for foreclosure (Bank of America, 2011c), and in August of 2011, they announced a number of initiatives that would preserve affordable housing in underserved communities (Bank of America, 2011b). And not coincidentally, they also released their first corporate social responsibility report in July of 2011 (Bank of America, 2011a). When the $335 million settlement was announced and the media put BofA and "discriminatory lending" in the same headlines, a BofA spokesperson took that opportunity to remind the public that Countrywide's discriminatory loans happened prior to BofA's acquisition of the company. He also stressed that BofA is "committed to fair and equal treatment of all our customers, and will continue to focus on doing what's right for our customers, clients and communities. . . . We discontinued Countrywide products and practices that were not in keeping with our commitment" (Savage, 2011, para. 6). This is a great example of a company that used a potentially damaging PR crisis as an opportunity to highlight what the company stands for and to strengthen its public commitment to diversity.

Although race has been considered one of the most pressing social issues of the day – especially in public relations research and scholarship (Waymer, 2010) – those with their eyes on the horizon of workplace diversity issues have predicted the diversity-issue trends that we should expect. Phil Harlow, the Chief Diversity Officer at Xerox, believes that sexual orientation and religion will emerge as key areas for companies to manage (Whitelaw, 2010). He adds, "The issues and sensitivity associated with the gay and lesbian community will be picking up increased momentum in the next few years when it comes to expectations and putting systems in place to support the sensitivities those groups have" (para. 15). In 2010, the *International Herald Tribune* reported that a record number of lawsuits are being filed on behalf of Muslims who are experiencing discrimination at the workplace. From 2005 to 2009, Muslims' complaints of hostility in the workplace jumped 60% (Greenhouse, 2010). The A&F lawsuit previously discussed is not an isolated case. Hertz, for example, was sued by Muslim employees for religious discrimination. Hertz claims that the employees were fired because they did not clock out when they went to midday prayers, but the employees claim that their labor contract did not require them to clock out and coworkers were not required to clock out when they took smoke breaks (Myers, 2011).

As Coombs (1999) argued, crises are predictable yet untimely events – meaning that it is not a question of if a crisis is going to befall an organization but rather when. Although much research has been conducted on crisis communication and management, far less research has looked at crises and diversity matters. Scholars and corporations alike concerned with reputation would be negligent if they do not take matters of diversity seriously. Organizations would be prudent to conduct social audits to determine the vulnerability of their image and reputation regarding issues/challenges/crises of diversity that could emerge or should they arise. This chapter demonstrates that in some cases, proactive measures for encountering diverse publics are not only needed but warranted. If reputation management is as important as practitioners and scholars alike articulate, then it is paramount that we collectively continue to seek understanding as to the ways that reputation can be studied, managed, built, maintained, enhanced, or damaged.

References

Abercrombie & Fitch (2011a) Diversity and inclusion. Retrieved from http://www.abercrombie.com/anf/careers/diversity.html (last accessed October 2, 2012).

Abercrombie & Fitch (2011b) Store opportunities: Model. Retrieved from http://www.abercrombie.com/anf/careers/model.html (last accessed October 2, 2012).

Albinger, H.S. and Freeman, S.J. (2000) Corporate social performance and attractiveness as an employer to different job seeking populations. *Journal of Business Ethics*, 28, 243–253.

Argenti, P.A. and Druckenmiller, B. (2004) Reputation and the corporate brand. *Corporate Reputation Review*, 7, 368–374.

Bank of America (2011a) Bank of America releases first corporate social responsibility report. July 12. Retrieved from http://ahead.bankofamerica.com/featured/bank-of-america-releases-corporate-social-responsibility-report/ (last accessed October 2, 2012).

Bank of America (2011b) Preserving affordable housing in underserved communities. August 26. Retrieved from http://ahead.bankofamerica.com/supporting-communities/preserving-affordable-housing-in-underserved-communities/ (last accessed October 2, 2012).

Bank of America (2011c) We are expanding our outreach to help customers at risk of foreclosure. Retrieved from http://ahead.bankofamerica.com/featured/were-committed-to-working-with-our-homeowners-in-need-of-assistance/ (last accessed October 2, 2012).

Baran, M. (2009) Abercrombie and Fitch fined for discrimination against girl with autism. September 9. Minnesota Public Radio. Retrieved from http://minnesota.publicradio.org/display/web/2009/09/09/abercrombie-and-fitch-discrimination-suit/ (last accessed October 2, 2012).

BBC News (2009) Disabled woman sues clothes store. June 24. Retrieved from http://news.bbc.co.uk/2/hi/8116231.stm (last accessed October 2, 2012).

Buzzanell, P., Waymer, D., Tagle, M., and Liu, M. (2007) Different transitions into working motherhood: Discourses of Asian, Hispanic, and African American women. *Journal of Family Communication*, 7, 195–220.

Chubb (2011) Business case for diversity. Retrieved from http://www.chubb.com/diversity/chubb4450.html (last accessed October 2, 2012).

Collard, J. (2003) Camp America. *The Times (London)*, April 5. Retrieved from LexisNexis.

Collins, S. (2011) Lowe's hit by furor in "All-American Muslim" ad flap. *Los Angeles Times*, December 12. Retrieved from http://latimesblogs.latimes.com/showtracker/2011/12/lowes-hit-by-furor-in-all-american-muslim-ad-flap.html (last accessed October 2, 2012).

Coombs, W.T. (1999) *Ongoing Crisis Communication: Planning, Managing, and Responding*. Thousand Oaks, CA: Sage.

Coombs, W.T. (2004) Impact of past crises on current crisis communication. *Journal of Business Communication*, 41, 265–289.

Danizet-Lewis, B. (2006) The man behind Abercrombie & Fitch. Salon.com, January 24. Retrieved from LexisNexis.

Deloitte (2011) Deloitte earns no. 8 position for demonstrated leadership in cultivating diverse talent. *PR Newswire*, March 16. Retrieved from http://www.prnewswire.com/news-releases/deloitte-rises-to-the-top-10-on-the-diversityinc-top-50-companies-for-diversity-118074329.html (last accessed October 2, 2012).

DiversityInc (2011) Diversity management: DiversityInc top 50 methodology. Retrieved from http://diversityinc.com/the-diversityinc-top-50-companies-for-diversity/diversityinc-top-50-methodology-2 (last accessed October 2, 2012).

Edwards, J. (2003) Whitewash? AdWeek. October 6, Retrieved from http://www.adweek.com/news/advertising/whitewash-67532 (last accessed October 2, 2012).

EEOC (2004) EEOC agrees to landmark resolution of discrimination case against Abercrombie & Fitch. November 18. Retrieved from http://www.eeoc.gov/eeoc/newsroom/release/11-18-04.cfm (last accessed October 2, 2012).

EEOC (2009) Rampant sex harassment costs Lowe's $1.7 million in settlement of EEOC lawsuit. August 21. Retrieved from http://www.eeoc.

gov/eeoc/newsroom/release/8-21-09.cfm (last accessed October 2, 2012).

EEOC (2010) EEOC sues Lowe's Home Centers for religious discrimination. March 30. Retrieved from http://www.eeoc.gov/eeoc/newsroom/release/3-30-10.cfm (last accessed October 2, 2012).

EEOC (2011a) Lowe's Home Centers to pay $120,000 to settle EEOC religious bias and retaliation lawsuit. September 20. Retrieved from http://www.eeoc.gov/eeoc/newsroom/release/9-20-11.cfm (last accessed October 2, 2012).

EEOC (2011b) Court finds for EEOC in religious discrimination suit against Abercrombie & Fitch. July 15. Retrieved from http://www.eeoc.gov/eeoc/newsroom/release/7-15-11a.cfm (last accessed October 2, 2012).

FFA (2011a) About us. Retrieved from http://floridafamily.org/full_article.php?article_no=94 (last accessed October 2, 2012).

FFA (2011b) Campbell's Soup and Hershey's show strong support for All-American Muslim while 87 companies decline. Retrieved from http://floridafamily.org/full_article.php?article_no=108 (last accessed October 2, 2012).

Fombrun, C.J. and Shanley, M. (1990) What's in a name? Reputation building and corporate strategy. *Academy of Management Journal*, *33*, 233–258.

Fombrun, C.J., Gardberg, N.A., and Sever, J.M. (2000) The Reputation Quotient^{SM}: A multi-stakeholder measure of corporate reputation. *The Journal of Brand Management*, *7*, 241–255.

Gardberg, N.A. and Fombrun, C.J. (2002) For better or worse: The most visible American corporate reputations. *Corporate Reputation Review*, *4*, 308–315.

Gatewood, R.D., Gowan, M.A., and Lautenschlager, G.J. (1993) Corporate image, recruitment image, and initial job choice decisions. *Academy of Management Journal*, *36*, 414–425.

Glynn, C. (2011) Muslim woman sues Abercrombie & Fitch, says she was fired over hijab. *CBS News*, June 28. Retrieved from http://www.cbsnews.com/8301-504083_162-20075051-504083.html (last accessed October 2, 2012).

Gotsi, M. and Wilson, A.M. (2001) Corporate reputation: Seeking a definition. *Corporate Communications*, *6*, 24–30.

Greenhouse, S. (2010) U.S. Muslims ill at ease on the job: Complaints of hostility in the workplace jump 60% over 4 years. *International Herald Tribune*, September 24. Retrieved from LexisNexis.

Hallahan, K. (2004) Protecting an organization's digital public relations assets. *Public Relations Review*, *30*, 255–268.

Heath, R.L. (1993) Toward a paradigm for the study and practice of public relations: A rhetorical approach to zones of meaning and organizational prerogative. *Public Relations Review*, *19*, 141–155.

Heath, R.L. and Palenchar, M.J. (2009) *Strategic Issues Management: Organizations and Public Policy Challenges* (2nd ed.). Thousand Oaks, CA: Sage.

Holtz, S. (2002) *Public Relations on the Net: Winning Strategies to Inform and Influence the Media, the Investment Community, the Government, the Public, and More* (2nd ed.). New York: Amacom.

Lowe's (2011a) Diversity and inclusion. Lowe's website. Retrieved from http://www.lowes.com/cd_Diversity+and+Inclusion_616526113 (last accessed October 31, 2012).

Lowe's (2011b) Facebook post. December 14. Retrieved from https://www.facebook.com/lowes (last accessed October 2, 2012).

Lowe's Muslim publicity gaffe serves as a case study of what not to do (2011) DiversityInc.com. Retrieved from http://diversityinc.com/generaldiversityissues/lowes-publicity-gaffe-snowballs-company-appears-paralyzed/ (last accessed October 2, 2012).

McAllister-Spooner, S.M. (2009) Fulfilling the dialogic promise. A ten-year reflective survey on dialogic Internet principles. *Public Relations Review*, *35*, 320–322.

Molina, V.S. (2005) Changing the face of consulting: The women's initiative at Deloitte. *Regional Review Q1*. Retrieved from http://www.bos.frb.org/economic/nerr/rr2005/q1/section3d.pdf (last accessed October 2, 2012).

Myers, L.L. (2011) Hertz to fight Muslim workers' suit over prayer breaks. *Reuters*, December 9. Retrieved from http://www.reuters.com/article/2011/12/09/us-muslims-hertz-lawsuit-idUSTRE7B80TN20111209 (last accessed October 2, 2012).

O'Brien, B. (2011) Don't ditch Abercrombie & Fitch. *Barron's*, December 20. Retrieved from http://online.barrons.com/article/SB50001424052748704872704577110923257048062.html?mod=BOL_da_wt (last accessed October 2, 2012).

Rynes, S.L. (1991) Recruitment, job choice, and post-hire consequences: A call for new research directions. In M.D. Dunnette and L.M. Hough (eds), *Handbook of Industrial and Organizational Psychology*. Palo Alto, CA: Consulting Psychologists Press, pp. 399–444.

Savage, C. (2011) Countrywide will settle a bias suit. *The New York Times*, December 21. Retrieved from http://www.nytimes.com/2011/12/22/business/us-settlement-reported-on-countrywide-lending.html?_r=2 (last accessed October 2, 2012).

Sodexo (2011) About us. Retrieved from http://www.sodexousa.com/usen/aboutus/aboutus.asp (last accessed October 2, 2012).

Stacks, D.W. (2010) *Primer of Public Relations Research* (2nd ed.). New York: Guildford.

Student with prosthetic arm awarded £9000 after Abercrombie & Fitch "banished her to stockroom". (2009) *The Daily Mail*, August 13. Retrieved from http://www.dailymail.co.uk/news/article-1206332/Disabled-student-wins-Abercombie-Fitch-case-store-banished-stockroom.html (last accessed October 2, 2012).

Turban, D.B. and Greening, D.W. (1997) Corporate social performance and organizational attractiveness to prospective employees. *Academy of Management Journal, 40,* 658–672.

Watson, T. (2010) Reputation models, drivers, and measurement. In R.L. Heath (ed.), *The SAGE Handbook of Public Relations*. Thousand Oaks, CA: Sage, pp. 339–351.

Waymer, D. (2010) Does public relations scholarship have a place in race? R.L. Heath (ed.). *The SAGE Handbook of Public Relations*. Thousand Oaks, CA: Sage, pp. 237–246.

Waymer, D. (2012) Crisis management and communication: Pre-crisis preparation that is sensitive to diverse populations. In B. Olaniran, D. Williams, and W.T. Coombs (eds). *Pre-Crisis Management: Preparing for the Inevitable*. New York: Peter Lang, USA, pp. 281–298.

Waymer, D. and Heath, R.L. (2007) Emergent agents: The forgotten publics in crisis communication and issues management research. *Journal of Applied Communication Research, 35,* 88–108.

Whitelaw, K. (2010) Defining diversity: Beyond race and gender. NPR, January 13. Retrieved from http://www.npr.org/templates/story/story.php?storyId=122327104 (last accessed October 2, 2012).

Williams, J. (2000) *Unbending Gender: Why Family and Work Conflict and What to Do About it*. New York: Oxford University Press.

Working Mother (2011a) About working mother media. Retrieved from http://www.workingmother.com/other/about (last accessed October 2, 2012).

Working Mother (2011b) 2011 100 best methodology and application. Retrieved from http://www.workingmother.com/best-companies/2011-100-best-methodology-and-application (last accessed October 2, 2012).

39

Corporate Reputation in Emerging Markets: A Culture-Centered Review and Critique

Rahul Mitra and Robert J. Green
Purdue University, USA

Mohan J. Dutta
National University of Singapore, Singapore

In this chapter, we review and critique the literature pertaining to corporate reputation in emerging markets. Drawing from the culture-centered approach, we interrogate how the concepts of "corporate reputation" and "emerging markets" are constructed. Five main themes of corporate reputation are evident: resource or asset owned by the firm, stake socially managed by stakeholders, crisis management tool, social responsibility, and social capital. Emerging markets are represented through four broad lenses: lack of engagement with sociohistorical specificities, depictions of corruption and instability, strict authoritarianism, and strangely outlandish cultural customs. We close by suggesting a critical program of research, with specifically five directions for future scholarship: decenter the corporation to examine subaltern viewpoints, examine the political constitution of reputation by bringing the State under purview, probe the emerging public sphere(s), consider how corporate reputation constitutes strategic management, and critique corporate dialog.

Corporate reputation, described as "a cognitive representation of a company's actions and results that crystallizes the firm's ability to deliver valued outcomes to its stakeholders" (Fombrun *et al.*, 2000, p. 87), is an important concept for organization studies, public relations, and organizational communication. Good corporate reputation leads to better recruitment/retention of employees, favorable coverage by stock market analysts and the media, a better relationship with State regulating agencies, leverage with source/partner/distributor networks, and a more saleable brand

for consumers (Fombrun and Shanley, 1990; Wang *et al.*, 2006; Zhang and Rezaee, 2009).

Owing to the increased relevance of the so-called emerging markets like the BRIC countries (Brazil, Russia, China, and India) in global commerce, so that transnational companies (TNCs) from the "emerged" global North increasingly permeate them, emerging market TNCs gradually probe emerged nations, and various corporate/noncorporate organizations become ever-more intricately connected worldwide, there is a strong impetus to examine corporate reputation in emerging markets. Thus, several practitioners and scholars have targeted their sights on how corporate reputation is constituted in these locales, the cultural/national implications for corporate reputation, and how it influences firm financial performance here (e.g., Anand, 2002; Chetthamrongchai, 2010; Fombrun and Pan, 2006; Gök and Özkaya, 2011; Mitra, 2011). Despite the interest, this body of research largely seeks to apply Eurocentric theories, without adequately deconstructing contextual complexities of the emerging countries, so that we outline in this chapter a suitable research trajectory for the same.

The culture-centered approach (CCA) (Dutta, 2008, 2011) we adopt in this chapter attends to the power structures and systems of organizing that limit subaltern possibilities at the margins. Specifically, it helps us interrogate how culture–structure–agency are implicated in the communicative constitution of corporate reputation in non-Western, emerging economy situations. We thus take corporate reputation to be informed by the local forces of various emerging markets interacting dialogically with global discourses of marketization. Two main implications follow for our review of the corporate reputation in emerging markets literature. First, we take a critical stance in decentering the corporation and deconstructing both the concepts of "corporate reputation" and "emerging markets." We note how corporations often use their reputational and financial clout to dominate communities in developing countries; enter into strategic linkages with institutions such as State agencies, media conglomerates, and nongovernmental organizations; and co-opt discourses originating from these communities to further neoliberal interests (Dirlik, 1997; Dutta, 2009; Garvey and Newell, 2005; Munshi and Kurian, 2005). Thus, rather than focus solely on corporate actions and interests, we privilege the *communicatively enacted* relationships within which firms are embedded and reputations are created. Our hope is to foreground alternatives to neoliberal organizational practices.

Second, we argue that mainstream conceptualizations of emerging markets are rooted in neocolonial logics of development, democracy promotion, and paternalism. Specifically, the term "emerging markets" implies a perennial "not-yet-ready" stance toward these nations, vis-à-vis the global North; presumes that the goal of such "emergence" is establishing a capitalist system like that in the United States, while ignoring the possibility of any alternative economic framework; reduces sociohistorical conflict to market-oriented changes, while ignoring their accompanying social costs; and employs an Orientalist frame that others these nations (Bardhan and Patwardhan, 2004; Chakravarty, 2000; Hussein, 2005). That is, we argue that *the context's constitution* itself influences how corporate reputation is propagated here.

Our chapter is organized into three sections. First, we outline the CCA that guides this review and deconstruct the "emerging markets" concept itself. Second, we analyze the extant research on corporate reputation in emerging markets to outline the contributions of and limitations faced by this body of work. Our analysis focuses on areas generally emphasized by this literature: China, India, and countries of the former Soviet Bloc in Eastern Europe. Finally, we suggest directions for future research to critique and reconstruct both "corporate reputation" and "emerging markets."

Theoretical Foundations and Definitional Terrains

Drawing on its postcolonial theory and subaltern studies roots, the CCA interrogates the hegemonic practices that configure structures of global neoliberalism through the erasure of subaltern stakeholders (Dutta, 2008, 2009, 2011; Dutta and Pal, 2011). The framework attends to the intersections among academic knowledge structures, corporate strategies, and structures of national governance, which determine the global, national, and local policies that shape interventions carried out in the name of development, modernization, and structural adjustment. Organizational practices, such as public relations, issues management, lobbying, corporate advocacy, reputation management, and corporate social responsibility (CSR), are situated within broader geopolitical terrains to examine how relationships of power, control, profit, and exploitation are constituted within these terrains, resulting in the epistemic erasure of subaltern voices. Of particular relevance is the critique of these organizational practices within the broader perspective of development, attached to "free market" conceptualizations of democracies and nation states conducive to the functioning of TNCs, so that democracy promotion and nation building often become technologies for creating global political climates favorable to TNCs (Dutta-Bergman, 2005).

The CCA theorizes social transformation by attending to *culture, structure,* and *agency. Culture* refers to the dynamic, contested, and contextually situated web of meanings that offers the immediate framework for localized actions. In contrast to most studies on corporate reputation that understand culture in terms of universalized (and universalizing) Hofstedian (Hofstede, 1980) dimensions (i.e., power distance, collectivism, masculinity, uncertainty avoidance, and long-term orientation), the CCA emphasizes a contextually centered play of local and global flows, whereby organizations and stakeholders engage in communicative meaning making. On the one hand, it offers a broader context for localized communicative practices; on the other hand, it is through the constitutive role of culture that subaltern communities co-construct symbols, rituals, and meanings that are transformative in their agendas.

Structures refer to the roles and rules within social, economic, and political systems that provide the bedrock for specific forms of organizing. They are played out communicatively through the constellations of organizational practices that enable organizations to maximize their resources and manage relationships with their stakeholders. For instance, "best practices" of measuring corporate reputation and its effectiveness vis-à-vis corporate stakeholders would be a form of structure in the CCA. While structures constrain the capacities of subaltern

communities to participate in relationships with mainstream organizations, the fissures, cracks, and openings within them create opportunities for subaltern political involvement. *Agency* refers to the complex array of individual and collective capacities of local subaltern actors to actively engage in negotiating existing structures and thus participate in processes of social change. It is enacted through processes of solidarity building, alternative organizing, and resistance directed at changing extant organizational, national, and international policies/ practices. The CCA is thus sensitized to the possibilities of cocreating alternative principles of communication practices that challenge the inequities perpetuated by exploitative organizational practices.

Culture, structure, and agency interact to set up specific terrains of political engagement, in the backdrop of mainstream market economics directed toward organizational efficiency and profiteering. Reading organizational practices such as reputation management within the dialectical ambits of culture, structure, and agency, the CCA creates spaces for interpretive frames attentive to the enactment of subaltern agency to negotiate social change. Our critique of corporate reputation management in the backdrop of emerging markets thus focuses on cocreating spaces of transformative politics, negotiated in the relationships forged by subaltern publics with corporations, national and local governments, and transnational political spheres.

The term "emerging markets" appeared in the 1980s when the World Bank played a key role in defining economies seen as excellent sources of profit, and which simultaneously had more risks than the economically "developed" countries of the United States, Western Europe, and Japan (Char, 2009; Khanna and Yafeh, 2007). It was seen as a replacement for the "less economically developed countries" label, capturing *transitioning* economies seen to be on the path of economic progress. For Duhé and Sriramesh (2009), emerging markets have the potential for phenomenal growth in their transition from centralized political economies toward free-market ideologies of governance and communication. This definition is rooted in the World Bank's (2011) categorization of countries as per capita income, so that emerging markets are the lower and upper-middle class income nations (with per capita income of $996–$3945 and $3946–$12,195, respectively) that are transitioning out of poverty to upper-middle or high-income status. The Washington, D.C.-based Institute for International Finance classifies countries from four different regions of the world as "emerging": Asia/Pacific, Latin America, Europe, and Africa/Middle East. The region of Asia/Pacific is represented by countries such as India, Indonesia, Malaysia, the Philippines, South Korea, and Thailand; Latin America contains Argentina, Brazil, Chile, Colombia, Ecuador, Mexico, Peru, Uruguay, and Venezuela; Europe comprises of Bulgaria, the Czech Republic, Hungary, Poland, Romania, Russia, Slovakia, and Turkey; and Africa/Middle East includes Algeria, Egypt, Morocco, South Africa, and Tunisia.

An emerging market can thus be defined and described as a space where political economies, civil societies, and cultural practices are moving toward neoliberal principles and practices. Public relations and reputation management largely play a normative role in establishing the means to and ends of transition to neoliberal democracy (Dutta, 2009; Dutta and Pal, 2011). Public relations practitioners assist "business, government, and civil society organizations in reconciling conflicting interests, influencing public opinion, and communicating with a variety of stakeholders affected by globalization in ways that must be tailored to the unique expectations of each country" (Duhé and Sriramesh, 2009, p. 40).

Although the economic basis of measuring progress takes precedence in categorizing countries as emerging (or not), implicit here is the coupling of democracy and capitalism within free-market logics. Crucially important is a political configuration that offers stability to the investments made by TNCs (Saxer, 2009). The minimization of risks in the market environment, establishment of a supposedly participative public sphere, and the creation of sociopolitical stability are key indicators of "progress." However, as Dutta-Bergman (2005) notes, civil society ideals of the (Western) public sphere often fall short, favoring dominant institutionally backed players over subaltern agents, rarely allowing them to articulate their concerns – an aspect little considered in World Bank circles or mainstream scholarship on emerging economies (see also Mitra, 2013).

Moreover, the dominant framework on emerging markets reflects a deep-seated neocolonial logic of development (Dutta, 2011). Chakravarty (2000) argues that such discourses of development place emerging nations into the anteroom of development so that they do not ever reach cultural, political, and economic maturity. Until a nation supposedly reaches political and economic adulthood, characterized by self-regulating civil society processes, the civil societies of emerging markets depend heavily on American and Western European governments, nongovernmental organizations (NGOs), and independent donors (Taylor, 2009). The mainstream discourse emphasizes a pedagogical relationship of the developed world as teacher, forever teaching the developing world, which is forever adolescent. It perpetuates specific politico-economic interplays of power through classifying the world's nations as per economic markers, and then utilizes these to set in motion projects conducive to TNC profit making.

Emerging Markets and Corporate Reputation Scholarship

In this section, we first review the extant literature to see how "corporate reputation" is framed as an organizational practice in emerging market contexts, and then how the "emerging market" concept is constructed. Five main themes of corporate reputation are evident: resource or asset owned by the firm, stake socially managed by stakeholders, crisis management tool, social responsibility, and social capital. Meanwhile, emerging markets are represented through four broad lenses: lack of engagement with sociohistorical specificities, depictions of corruption and instability, strict authoritarianism, and strangely outlandish cultural customs.

Corporate reputation as organizational practice

In the organizational studies and public relations literature, corporate reputation is largely conceptualized as a *resource* or *asset* to be managed by organizational leaders. Grunig and Hung (2002) define reputation as an intangible asset that is a valuable "composite of all of the cognitions and attitudes of all stakeholders" (p. 17). These cognitions and attitudes are not created through the mere circulation of positive representations; rather, organizations facilitate positive reputation when they identify and respond to the various problems confronting them over time (Zhang and Rezaee, 2009). In Barnett's (2010) study on the impact of the Union Carbide disaster at Bhopal, India, on the chemical industry companies' reputation, the researcher notes reputation and legitimacy as resources exchanged between firms and their stakeholders. Although both are assumed to be fairly stable, Barnett argues that a firm's action "can sometimes trigger resource holders to re-examine this presumption and can lead to a loss of legitimacy" (p. 5). Moreover, corporate reputation does not always translate to positive outcomes; for instance, Gök and Özkaya (2011) found that despite corporate reputation being recognized as a valuable asset by companies, a portfolio of highly admired firms in Turkey earned about 10% less than the market's overall portfolio annually.

As resource, corporate reputation may be manifest in the "codes of conduct" voluntarily enacted by companies and showcased to stakeholders. For instance, Barnett (2010) traces how the implementation of the "Responsible Care" platform by the American Chemistry Council following the Bhopal debacle significantly assuaged risk perception for American chemical companies (p. 11). Such codes of conduct constitute responsibility as a voluntary and unenforceable organizational practice.

Treating corporate reputation as a resource provides a fair degree of insurance against global risks. Stohl *et al.* (2007), for example, note that Enron evaded charges of corruption and irresponsibility in India until 2001 because of its established reputation in the United States. At the same time, there is a limit to how much companies may get away with for their irresponsibility. Royal Dutch Shell in South America, for example, was forced to actively consult with local communities in its corporate plans, after international scrutiny revealed its top-down, profit-centered operations in Nigeria, in collusion with an arguably oppressive national government (Livesey, 2002).

Second, corporate reputation often involves a *social process of reputation management*, whereby "various stakeholders selectively process the various informational cues or signals provided by the organization to judge the effectiveness of that organization for satisfying their interests and needs" (Riordan *et al.*, 1997, p. 402). Traditionally, practitioners and theorists seek to cultivate the conditions for positive reputational development by identifying strategic publics to build mutually beneficial relationships between firms and stakeholders through symmetrical dialog (Grunig, 1993; Grunig and Hung, 2002; Yang and Grunig, 2005). Enhancements and/or crises in reputation may influence others with whom the firm is aligned, or even other nonaligned firms operating in the same industry. Conceptualizing of a "reputations commons" accordingly, Barnett (2010) notes the import of gauging the degree to which corporate errors – consistently poor strategic choices or unplanned mistakes – may produce significant consequences for both allies and rivals.

Based on his study of Google's operations in China, Wu (2007) takes reputation (together with "perception") to be one of the three "stakes" held by stakeholders of a corporation. Although reputation is claimed by the corporation, Wu argues that it is actually "owned by those primary or periphery constituents" of the firm, and consists of both financial and "non-business-oriented issues, such as social responsibility and democratic ideology" (p. 422). He links perception and reputation to the other two stakes of "policy and regulation" (linked to procedural issues) and "product and revenue" (that concern the bottom line) of the company. These generally predetermine the status, performance, and function of the higher-level reputation and perception stakes, so that a financially sound, well-functioning, and managed corporation normally gets "accommodative policy support and positive media coverage" (p. 423). At the same time, reputation constantly influences the other stakes, so that a firm's good reputation creates a friendly environment for it to operate and affords it the benefit of doubt during crises.

Third, the extant literature often constrains the value of corporate reputation to instances of *wrongdoing* or *crises*, rather than an everyday mechanism for social good and stakeholder relations. In their take on why the Nigerian financial industry suffers from a disreputable image, Pratt *et al.* (2011) suggest ways to restore reputation: personalize stakeholder experiences, integrate ethics at the workplace and in communications, sponsor training sessions on applied ethics, use integrated branding, and conduct outcome assessments (pp. 72–73). The end result of such reputation management is financial growth and "managing, sustaining and expanding [the banks'] market share" (p. 71). Similarly, Collins *et al.* (2004) discuss the implications of the California Supreme Court's decision to categorize Nike's reputation management as "commercial speech," in the aftermath of allegations that Nike's developing country workers operated under sweatshop conditions, arguing that such a legal verdict places too great a responsibility on corporate shoulders. The researchers appeal to bottom-line incentives, rather than the alternative and marginalized voices that may welcome such a reframing of reputation management.

Despite Collins *et al.*'s (2004) protests, corporate reputation has long been linked to *social responsibility and trust* in both emerging and emerged markets. In their study of consumer perceptions of the top 100 Chinese companies (27 of them privately owned, 33 State owned, and 40 TNCs operating in China), Fombrun

and Pan (2006) find that corporate reputation is comprised of mainly four aspects: good feeling, admiration and respect, trust, and positive regard. Anand (2002) also links corporate reputation to social responsibility. He recounts case studies from his career as a reputation practitioner to show how Indian companies use cause-related marketing to be "perceived as a company with a heart" (p. 72) and entrench themselves with key customers/stakeholders. Similarly, Sagar and Singla (2004) argue that corporate reputation in India is understood as trust and respect, both steeped in the country's rich sociohistorical traditions. A chief limitation of their essay is that while they highlight several aspects of reputation as trust and respect, like the "overall quality, top management leadership, depth of talent, belief in transparency, ethics, social responsiveness, environmental consciousness, etc." (p. 285), they focus only on CSR, instead of considering how these interplay together.

Finally, another aspect of corporate reputation evident in the literature – especially those works focused on China – is that of social capital. Reputation as *social capital* is distinct from the resource aspect noted earlier, since it involves a direct consideration of the social networks the firm and organizational members are embedded in, rather than a discrete resource owned by any entity. Drawing from the importance of *guanxi* in Chinese contexts, Standifird (2006) locates corporate reputation in social networks formed communicatively and relationally. Although common interests among stakeholders and organizational members are important to establish *guanxi*, they are not sufficient in themselves. Moreover, good network placement does not automatically establish favorable corporate reputation, so that long-term investment in authentic dialog with stakeholders is called for: "It is through the network of connections to potentially important others that one establishes themselves as reputable" (p. 180). Since *guanxi* is an individual-based relationship, organizations may not actually have good *guanxi* themselves, but employ employees' *guanxi* as an asset when they are willing to use it to fulfill organizational objectives

(Standifird, 2006, p. 176). The social network perspective thus suggests an amalgamation of reputation as resource managed by the company and as stake negotiated by the stakeholders, keeping in mind the structural conditions of placement. It actively considers the quality of the communicatively enacted ties between organizational members and stakeholders, assuming that all such ties are unique, rather than uniform. However, managerial interests rather than subaltern concerns are still paramount in this framework.

Images of emerging markets

Extant scholarship has largely used a cultural sensitivity lens to examine corporate reputation in emerging markets. While the CCA is committed to building theories and applications from *within* subaltern communities, a cultural sensitivity approach adapts messages to the cultural markers of a target audience with the goal of unilaterally changing audience attitudes (Dutta, 2007). Even where there is a call for specific, contextual knowledge of corporate reputation management, these contexts and their cultures are nevertheless defined with respect to the measured distance from dominant Anglo-American perspectives. A representative example is Chetthamrongchai's (2010) study that tested and revalidated the Reputation Quotient[SM] and Corporate Character Scale, developed originally in the global North, among 385 customers of Thai retail giant Tesco Lotus, with some minor tweaks but hardly defined by the specific context. Thus, in much of the literature, emerging markets' sociohistorical particularities are either completely ignored, or Orientalized as "never-quite-ready" locales mired in corruption and instability, ruled by totalitarian regimes, and steeped in customs alien to Anglo-Americans.

In Barnett's (2010) study of the Bhopal gas disaster's impact on American chemical firms, India is merely the remote site of an unfortunate accident with financial repercussions for a US-based industry, and little else. There is no nuanced grappling with how the disaster's geographical location or impacted communities'

socio-politico-cultural issues might influence stakeholder perceptions and otherwise affect the chemical industry, or even a consideration of the work done by similar firms in other emerging countries. Collins *et al.* (2004) treat "developing nations" as an aside in their discussion of what reputation management by an American company means for the company and its (Western) stakeholders in the face of a crisis. In such examples, the nuanced nature of the emerging market is hardly considered.

In several studies that *do* consider emerging market culture(s), there is very little deconstruction of sociopolitical history. For instance, Fombrun and Pan (2006) mention *guanxi* only briefly in speculation:

> At this point, most Chinese companies still view reputation management as a system for "face-saving" rather than as a driver of performance, corporate expediency and core organizational function. In doing so, they rely on Guanxi to steer away immediate obstacles for short-term gain rather than focus on building institutional and lasting stakeholder relationship for long-term sustainability. (p. 170)

Moreover, we contend that it is not enough to simply state that firm legitimacy depends on "changes in societal expectations" (Barnett, 2010, p. 7), because such a perspective takes societal expectations to be stable and even rigid, or allows for change "abruptly following a shock" (p. 7). This perspective is, in fact, in keeping with mainstream managerial discussions of culture, noted Dirlik (1997), which posit relatively stable and generalizable components of culture in the Hofstedian tradition (e.g., China as collectivist and the United States as individualist). Hofstede's (1980) analysis stemmed from a study of IBM, a TNC that tapped the international division of labor to dominate global markets, so that such a view of culture arguably already privileges TNC domination. The avowed goal in such work is to break down a culture into its particular components, so that dominant corporate interests may be legitimized via "culturally sensitive boundary spanners" who tailor products, services, and messages to the local public to produce trust

(Bardhan and Patwardhan, 2004; Burke, 1994). For example, although Sagar and Singla (2004) highlight *respect* as "an intrinsic part of Indian culture" (p. 284) in their piece, they do not examine its everyday communicative constitution or its implications for corporate reputation as a complex long-term social process. Instead, respect becomes essentialized as one of "the pillars upholding the symbiotic relationship between the community and businesses in India" (p. 289), the demonstration of which by TNCs will supposedly help their corporate reputation and eventual financial performance.

Relatively few studies engage in a deeper understanding of culture and communication, while examining corporate reputation in emerging markets. Zhang *et al.* (2009) eschew an essentialist treatment of Chinese *guanxi* to produce a nuanced analysis of it being negotiated by public relations professionals working for foreign TNCs in China. Instead of viewing *guanxi* as static or simplistic bribery (as is very common in Western scholarship), they note how it builds long-term relationships between/within publics through a "delicate process of maintaining these connections" and "treating your 'connections' as ends rather than means to ends" (p. 230). Similarly, Standifird (2006) notes the overlap of *guanxi* with Western traditions of networking, challenging the poles-apart framework of much intercultural research. Simultaneously, *guanxi* is distinct from mainstream network theory, with its focus on face/representation, dialectical harmony, long-term exchange, and reciprocity (pp. 171–172).

The literature also tends to downplay the deliberative public spheres and institutions of government operating in emerging markets, and highlights the bribery, corruption, and inefficient administration as the costs of doing business here. Drawing from the recent controversy of Google's planned pullout from China, Wu (2007) outlines a framework for stakeholder positioning that is largely based on the constraints imposed by the Chinese State. In an earlier work, he went so far as to suggest that China did not have "a public," owing to centuries of "an elite-authoritarian governing political and social system that prevented citizens from participating in political decision-making" (Wu, 2002, p. 17). In another example, Nigeria emerges as the site of severe banking irregularities and unethical practices (Pratt *et al.*, 2011). In Eastern European countries, "emergence" is reified as the transition from supposedly deviant or imperfect market and political systems to a Western model of liberal democracy and capitalism (Ferguson, 1998; Hiebert, 1992, 1994). Gruban (1995) idealizes public relations principles of symmetrical communication as a means to change "the political system and social structure" (p. 21) here away from an authoritarian asymmetrical model, while Kent *et al.* (2006) describe a transition economy as "one in which the ownership and direction of the economy is moved by market forces rather than governmental directives" (p. 11).

Such efforts are inevitably guided by a cultural sensitivity approach that manages the transition to "capitalism with a human touch" (Lawniczak, 2007, p. 385). Tampere (2008) proposes a pedagogical role for public relations practice in post-Soviet countries, teaching organizational members, stakeholders, and the public at large the value of idealized symmetrical communication model that frames agency within the transition to the structures and cultures of free-market democracy. More than 20 years after the fall of the Berlin Wall and several "successful" civil society interventions later, Eastern European countries are still described as spaces of transition. In some cases, neo-imperialism appears more marked, as in the advocated import of "foreign values" in Russian business and public relations to combat a perceived culture of corruption and anti-Western nationalist sentiment (Guth, 2000, pp. 205–206).

Implications for Future Research

We conclude this chapter by pointing out the limitations of extant research on corporate reputation in emerging markets. Additionally, we draw on the CCA to suggest important directions for future communication research in this area.

An important drawback of the prior literature is the seeming lack of detailed empirical research on the meanings and implications of corporate reputation. Most studies uses surface-level descriptive case studies or quantitative tools (to suggest theoretical/analytical models in some cases), so that there is a paucity of advanced qualitative methods, such as "narrative analysis methodology, appreciative community planning, participatory rapid assessment, and public consultations" (Hussein, 2005, p. 335). What corporate reputation means – its underlying drivers and restraints, contextual considerations, and implications – is rarely engaged with in detail. The usual measures for corporate reputation performance (e.g., stock market price, consumer perceptions) are largely company or industry centered, effectively marginalizing stakeholders who are not located within the conventional market framework, such as impacted communities who may not buy/sell a company's products or stock.

Second, the literature has rarely been critical in tone and intent: it tends to be highly appreciative of managerial efforts rather than deconstructive, reduces corporate reputation to one-off activities instead of examining accountability of regular business operations, or uses "given" cultural standards (e.g., Hofstede, 1980) to apply in particular contexts rather than from the ground-up. Third, corporate reputation is often understood as a static outcome or by-product of organizational practice, instead of constitutive or processual. For instance, by placing reputation at the highest tier of the "stake pyramid," Wu's (2007) model suggests that the corporation – as the "decision making center" for reputation (p. 423) – needs to address reputation only after first looking at product/revenue and policy/regulation issues. Finally, the literature focuses almost exclusively on TNCs originating in the West/North. Little interest is given to homegrown companies in emerging markets, or how TNCS from emerging markets negotiate corporate reputation outside their home countries. An important exception is Maktoba *et al.*'s (2009) case study

of Chinese TNC Haier's introduction of its corporate logo in the United States, but this work adopted mainly a generalist approach to corporate reputation without probing the complexities of emerging market competition.

Given these limitations, we offer the CCA as a baseline to reexamine corporate reputation as a concept and embark on new trajectories of research relevant to both emerging markets and the global North. Our consideration of how culture, structure, and agency act together, both restraining and reinforcing the impacts of the others, reframes how scholars may conceptualize reputation, organizational practices, stakeholders, deliberative spheres, and the neoliberal politico-economic system itself.

First, scholars should consider *decentering the corporation to examine alternative perspectives* that both reify and challenge reputation (Dutta, 2009, 2011; Dutta and Pal, 2011). This is crucial, given that reputation is a multiplayer process, so that even as firms attempt to portray a particular image, how that image is received and interpreted depends on various stakeholders (Fombrun and Shanley, 1990; Fombrun *et al.*, 2000). Barnett (2010) notes the existence of "a reputation commons" and "legitimacy commons" (p. 17), in that firms and industries are interconnected as far as reputation and public trust go. Moreover, corporate reputation is intrinsically linked to larger issues of accountability; Mitra (2011) notes the thematic interconnections between corporate reputation and responsibility in India, in terms of the institutionalization of ethical codes, eco-friendly and resource-efficient technological upgrades, historical legitimacy, and nation building. Since firms in emerging markets hone their reputation through ties with noncorporate entities such as NGOs and the media, reputation becomes both a corporate *and* noncorporate agenda (Mitra, 2010, 2013). Future research should thus examine how different players interact in corporate reputation, and how corporate reputation affects their legitimacy.

Second, *the State* and its political agents deserve much greater study. Government policy is crucial to organizational practice, despite the "free market" rhetoric spouted by its proponents (Dirlik, 1997), and it assumes special significance in emerging markets, given the ongoing transition in political and economic structures (Duhé and Sriramesh, 2009; Keister and Zhang, 2009; Mitra, 2011, 2013). Emerging market TNCs are increasingly judged according to which countries they originate from (e.g., are Chinese companies less committed to product quality than Indian, are boards of East European companies more corrupt than Chinese?), and private sector companies are often the bulwark of public diplomacy (e.g., lobbyists, tourism agencies, or even bellwether companies of a nation). Moreover, scholars must be attuned to potentially new combinations, permutations, and appropriations of the political economy as nations and their communities transform, rather than expect replications of Western style neoliberal capitalism.

Third, research on corporate reputation should *critically reexamine conditions of deliberation and the public sphere* in emerging markets, since these are vital to the formation of reputation. Rather than bemoaning the lack of Western-style deliberation here, scholars should study how deliberation *does* occur in nonliberal democratic contexts that may be unfamiliar to the global North. For instance, concepts like "authoritarian deliberation" in China (Jiang, 2010) should be critically engaged with to examine how authoritarianism and participation may co-occur in situations hitherto impervious to grassroots participation. Such grounded analyses explode the myth of "ideal" liberal democratic forms of organizing, which are rife with hidden inequities themselves (Dutta, 2011; Dutta-Bergman, 2005). As Zhang *et al.* (2009) note, the "Chinese people seem to have a different understanding of public" (p. 230), teasing out the implications of which is crucial.

Fourth, while extant scholarship largely takes corporate reputation as the (static) outcome or by-product of organizational practices, we suggest an inversion of this relationship to also *consider how corporate reputation constitutes particular styles of strategic management*. This follows from our CCA-based view of corporate reputation as an ongoing communicative process, constantly being reified and challenged, influenced by and in turn influencing organizational practices. For instance, scholars should study how corporate and noncorporate stakeholders may use social networks (*guanxi* in the Chinese context, or otherwise) to organize themselves and co-constitute reputation, which in turn may give rise to related organizational practices such as branding and sales. Zhang *et al.* (2009) note that Chinese practitioners "tailored Western strategies to the Chinese industry, which gave rise to an *emerging Chinese strategic management*" (p. 230, italics added). Conversely, the experiences of emerging market TNCs in the West/North should be traced, given their increasing global footprint (e.g., Maktoba *et al.*, 2009), so that how home and host cultures influence reputation management strategies of both emerging and emerged market TNCs, their intersections, and subsequent appropriation deserve closer study.

Finally, we *urge caution in terms of favoring dialog and participation* while examining corporate actions. All too often, dominant institutional players provide the appearance of participation and use the language of dialog to co-opt and silence the concerns of impacted stakeholders (Dutta, 2009; Dutta and Pal, 2011; Garvey and Newell, 2005; Mitra, 2013; Munshi and Kurian, 2005). Accordingly, reputation scholars should be acutely critical of the underlying processes at play, rather than pandering to managerial concerns. Hussein (2005) suggests, "The first prerequisite for a dialogue is *introspection*, a tool that enables me to confess, confront, and analyse my state of affairs, and then take corrective measures through an *intervention*" (p. 334). Although his advice is meant for practitioners of public diplomacy in Islamic emerging markets like Pakistan, it is also valid for scholars of corporate reputation. Even as we decide on our project of inquiry (our "intervention"), it is crucial to be self-reflexive about our interests and aims, what/who we are trying to promote, what ends we are serving, and whether they are socially *just*. Reflexivity is crucial while both reexamining the research methods and measures employed, and the terminology adopted (Dutta, 2008, 2011). From our review, we find that stakeholder-oriented and in-depth qualitative methods like discourse analysis, grounded theory, and ethnography are especially underutilized in corporate reputation research. Researchers should also be aware of the postcolonial and neo-imperialist implications of the "emerging market" taxonomy (Chakravarty, 2000). Accordingly, scholars like Mohanty (2003) suggest alternative phrasing, such as "two-thirds world," to recognize conditions of inequity even within so-called emerged nations and foster solidarity among marginalized populations worldwide. Thus, although the prevalence of the "emerging/emerged" market terminology makes it hard for scholars and practitioners to resist it, they should at least be attuned to alternative modes of organizing, deliberating, and acting.

Conclusion

The critique of organization studies, including strategic management, organizational communication, and public relations, as a US-centric, manager-oriented enterprise is not new. Several scholars have called for the consideration of alternative views and interests, for instance, Elmer (2007) argued that the future relevance of public relations depends on reintegrating subaltern knowledge, so that "public relations needs to become unmanaged" (p. 366). In the spirit of this call, we have drawn on the culture-centered framework to interrogate how corporate reputation and emerging markets are largely constructed, and suggested some alternative frames. Specifically, we have advanced five directions for future research: decenter the corporation to examine subaltern viewpoints, examine the political constitution of reputation by bringing the State under purview, probe the emerging public sphere(s), consider how corporate reputation constitutes strategic management, and critique corporate dialog. In sum, we suggest a critical program of research that is open to diverse stakeholder concerns,

attuned to postcolonial and subaltern marginalization by dominant corporate interests, and self-reflexively aware of the changes wrought through communicative practices.

References

Anand, V. (2002) Building blocks of corporate reputation: Social responsibility initiatives. *Corporate Reputation Review*, 5, 71–74.

Bardhan, N. and Patwardhan, P. (2004) Multinational corporations and public relations in a historically resistant host culture. *Journal of Communication Management*, 8, 246–263.

Barnett, M.L. (2010) Tarred and untarred by the same brush: Exploring interdependence in the volatility of stock returns. *Corporate Reputation Review*, 10, 3–21.

Burke, J. (1994) Training MNC employees as culturally sensitive boundary spanners. *Public Relations Quarterly*, 39(2), 40–44.

Chakravarty, D. (2000) *Provincializing Europe: Postcolonial Thought and Historical Difference*. Princeton, NJ: Princeton University Press.

Char, S. (2009) Emerging markets: Need for a taxonomy. *Journal of Emerging Knowledge on Emerging Markets*, 1, 129–141.

Chetthamrongchai, P. (2010) Revalidating two measures of reputation in Thailand. *Corporate Reputation Review*, 13, 209–219.

Collins, E.L., Zoch, L.M., and McDonald, C.S. (2004) When [professional] worlds collide: Implications of Kasky v. Nike for corporate reputation management. *Public Relations Review*, 30, 411–417.

Dirlik, A. (1997) *The Postcolonial Aura: Third World Criticism in the Age of Global Capitalism*. Boulder, CO: Westview Press.

Duhé, S.C. and Sriramesh, K. (2009) Political economy and public relations. In K. Sriramesh and D. Verčič (eds), *The Global Public Relations Handbook: Theory, Research, and Practice*. New York: Routledge, pp. 22–46.

Dutta, M.J. (2007) Communicating about culture and health: Theorizing culture-centered and cultural-sensitivity approaches. *Communication Theory*, 17, 304–328.

Dutta, M.J. (2008) *Communicating Health: A Culture-Centered Approach*. London: Polity Press.

Dutta, M.J. (2009) Theorizing resistance: Applying Gayatri Chakravorty Spivak in public relations.

In Ø. Ihlen, B. van Ruler, and M. Fredrikson (eds), *Social Theory on Public Relation*. London: Routledge, pp. 278–300.

Dutta, M.J. (2011) *Communicating Social Change: Structure, Culture, and Agency*. New York: Routledge.

Dutta, M.J. and Pal, M. (2011) Public relations and marginalization in a global context: A postcolonial critique. In N. Bardhan and K. Weaver (eds), *Public Relations in Global Cultural Contexts: Multi-Paradigmatic Perspectives*. New York: Routledge, pp. 195–225.

Dutta-Bergman, M.J. (2005) Civil society and public relations: Not so civil after all. *Journal of Public Relations Research*, *17*, 267–289.

Elmer, P. (2007) Unmanaging public relations: Reclaiming complex practice in pursuit of global consent. *Public Relations Review*, *33*, 360–367.

Ferguson, D.P. (1998) From communist control to *glasnost* and back?: Media freedom and control in the former Soviet Union. *Public Relations Review*, *24*, 165–182.

Fombrun, C.J. and Pan, M. (2006) Corporate reputations in China: How do consumers feel about companies? *Corporate Reputation Review*, *9*, 165–170.

Fombrun, C.J. and Shanley, M. (1990) What's in a name? Reputation building and corporate strategy. *Academy of Management Journal*, *33*, 233–258.

Fombrun, C.J., Gardberg, N.A., and Barnett, M.L. (2000) Opportunity platforms and safety nets: Corporate citizenship and reputational risk. *Business and Society Review*, *105*, 85–106.

Garvey, N. and Newell, P. (2005) Corporate accountability to the poor? Assessing the effectiveness of community-based strategies. *Development in Practice*, *15*, 389–404.

Gök, O. and Özkaya, H. (2011) Does corporate reputation improve stock performance in an emerging economy? Evidence from Turkey. *Corporate Reputation Review*, *14*, 53–61.

Gruban, B. (1995) Performing public relations in Central and Eastern Europe. *Public Relations Quarterly*, *40*(3), 20–23.

Grunig, J.E. (1993) Image and substance: From symbolic to behavioral relationships. *Public Relations Review*, *19*, 121–139.

Grunig, J.E. and Hung, C.J. (2002) The effect of relationships on reputation and reputation on relationships: A cognitive, behavioral study. Paper presented to the Public Relations Society of America Educator's Academy, Miami, FL.

Guth, D.W. (2000) The emergence of public relations in the Russian Federation. *Public Relations Review*, *26*, 191–207.

Hiebert, R.E. (1992) Public relations and mass communication in Eastern Europe. *Public Relations Review*, *18*, 177–187.

Hiebert, R.E. (1994) Advertising and public relations in transition from communism: The case of Hungary, 1989–1994. *Public Relations Review*, *20*, 357–369.

Hofstede, G. (1980) *Culture's Consequences*. Beverly Hills, CA: Sage.

Hussein, Z. (2005) Arab/Muslim image world-wide: A case for introspection, and intervention. *Public Relations Review*, *31*, 333–337.

Jiang, M. (2010) Authoritarian deliberation on Chinese Internet. *Electronic Journal of Communication*, *20*(3&4).

Keister, L.A. and Zhang, Y. (2009) Organizations and management in China. *The Academy of Management Annals*, *3*, 377–420.

Kent, M.L., Taylor, M., and Turcilo, L. (2006) Public relations by newly privatized businesses in Bosnia Herzegovina. *Public Relations Review*, *32*, 10–17.

Khanna, T. and Yafeh, Y. (2007) Business groups in emerging markets: Paragons or parasites? *Journal of Economic Literature*, *45*, 331–372.

Lawniczak, R. (2007) Public relations role in a global competition "to sell" alternative political and socio-economic models of market economy. *Public Relations Review*, *33*, 377–386.

Livesey, S.M. (2002) The discourse of the middle ground: Citizen Shell commits to sustainable development. *Management Communication Quarterly*, *15*, 313–349.

Maktoba, O., Williams, R.L. Jr., and Lingelbach, D. (2009) Global brand market-entry strategy to manage corporate reputation. *Journal of Product & Brand Management*, *18*, 177–187.

Mitra, R. (2010) Organizational colonization and silencing strategies in the Indian media with the launch of the world's cheapest car. *Communication, Culture, & Critique*, *3*, 572–606.

Mitra, R. (2011) Framing corporate responsibility-reputation linkage: The case of Tata Motors in India. *Public Relations Review*, *37*, 392–398.

Mitra, R. (2013) The neo-capitalist firm in emerging India: Organization-State-Media linkages. *Journal of Business Communication*, *50*, 3–33.

Mohanty, C. (2003) *Feminism without Borders: Decolonizing Theory, Practicing Solidarity*. Durham, NC: Duke University Press.

Munshi, D. and Kurian, P. (2005) Imperializing spin cycles: A postcolonial look at public relations, greenwashing, and the separation of publics. *Public Relations Review*, *31*, 513–520.

Pratt, C.B., Ademosu, E.A., Adamolekun, W., Alabi, A.L., and Carr, R.L. (2011) Managing a crisis of confidence in Nigeria's banking and financial industry. *Public Relations Review*, *37*, 71–73.

Riordan, C.M., Gatewood, R.D., and Bill, J.B. (1997) Corporate image: Employee reactions and implications for managing corporate performance. *Journal of Business Ethics*, *16*, 401–412.

Sagar, P. and Singla, A. (2004) Trust and corporate social responsibility: Lessons from India. *Journal of Communication Management*, *8*, 282–290.

Saxer, M. (2009) Performance matters: Challenges for the democratic model and democracy promotion. FES Briefing Paper 6, Berlin.

Standifird, S.S. (2006) Using *guanxi* to establish corporate reputation in China. *Corporate Reputation Review*, *9*, 171–178.

Stohl, M., Stohl, C., and Townsley, N.C. (2007) A new generation of global corporate social responsibility. In S.K. May, G. Cheney, and J. Roper (eds), *The Debate Over Corporate Social Responsibility*. New York: Oxford University Press, pp. 30–44.

Tampere, K. (2008) Stakeholder thinking and a pedagogical approach in public relations processes: Experience from transition societies. *Journal of Public Relations Research*, *20*, 71–93.

Taylor, M. (2009) Civil society as a rhetorical public relations process. In R.L. Heath, E.L. Toth, and D. Waymer (eds), *Rhetorical and Critical Approaches to Public Relations II*. New York: Routledge, pp. 76–91.

Wang, Y., Kandampully, J.A., Lo, H.P., and Shi, G. (2006) The role of brand equity and corporate reputation in CRM: A Chinese study. *Corporate Reputation Review*, *9*, 179–197.

World Bank (2011) How we classify countries. Retrieved from http://data.worldbank.org/about/country-classifications (last accessed October 2, 2012).

Wu, X. (2002) Doing PR in China: A 2001 version – Concepts, practices and some misperceptions. *Public Relations Quarterly*, *47*(2), 10–18.

Wu, X. (2007) Stakeholder identifying and positioning (SIP) models: From Google's operation in China to a general case-analysis framework. *Public Relations Review*, *33*, 415–425.

Yang, S.U. and Grunig, J.E. (2005) Decomposing organizational reputation: The effects of organization-public relationship outcomes on cognitive representations of organizations and evaluations of organizational performance. *Journal of Communication Management*, *9*, 305–325.

Zhang, A., Shen, H., and Jiang, H. (2009) Culture and Chinese public relations: A multi-method "inside out" approach. *Public Relations Review*, *35*, 226–231.

Zhang, R. and Rezaee, Z. (2009) Do credible firms perform better in emerging markets? Evidence from China. *Journal of Business Ethics*, *90*, 221–237.

The Power of Social Media ar Influence on Corporate Reputation

Tina McCorkindale

Appalachian State University, USA

Marcia W. DiStaso

Pennsylvania State University, USA

Social media has had a tremendous impact on corporate reputation as organizations are investing more time, money, and resources into engaging and managing relationships with various stakeholders. With the ever-changing digital landscape, a wide variety of stakeholders, such as customers, employees, and the media, are creating and curating content as well as serving as spectators. As evidenced in numerous case studies, a reputation can be damaged in a matter of minutes, thanks to the community nature and rapid speed of information dissemination on social media. With this comes added opportunities and challenges for companies, and the biggest of both is corporate reputation. This chapter explores facets of corporate reputation as it impacts social media such as trust, transparency, and engagement. This chapter also discusses how organizations are measuring and monitoring social media accounts to draw insights that influence decision making. Finally, best and worst practices of various social media tools, including blogs, wikis, microblogs, social networking sites, and video-sharing sites, are included.

"Your online reputation is your reputation" (Fertik and Thompson, 2010, p. 16). In the past 10 years, social media has transformed the great Internet landscape. Previously, companies were limited to communicating online primarily through web sites and e-mail (Springston, 2001). Now companies have the opportunity to engage and inform stakeholders who have the ability to create and share content online almost instantaneously through the use of social media. According to a Pew Internet and American Life Project (2011) study, 59% of American Internet users used at least one social networking site, more than doubling the 26% finding from two years earlier. Of the social networking users, 92% used Facebook, 29% used MySpace, 18% used LinkedIn, and 13% used Twitter.

As more and more people use social media, its impact on companies becomes stronger. Every aspect of a company has the potential to be affected by some aspect of this new landscape from customers to employees and suppliers. With this comes added opportunities and challenges for companies and the biggest of both is corporate reputation.

The Handbook of Communication and Corporate Reputation, First Edition. Edited by Craig E. Carroll.
© 2013 John Wiley & Sons, Inc. Published 2015 by John Wiley & Sons, Inc.

The purpose of this chapter is to analyze the impact and power social media has on corporate reputation. In addition, the effects of best and worst practices of companies' social media efforts on corporate reputation are explored.

Why Social Media Matters

Fombrun (1996) defined corporate reputation as "the overall estimation in which a particular company is held by its various constituents" (p. 37). Ettenson and Knowles (2008) took it a step further and defined corporate reputation as "a company-centric concept that focuses on the credibility and respect that an organization has among a broad set of constituencies" (p. 19). Central to both, and most definitions, is the idea that corporate reputation does not belong to the company itself, but is determined in large part by its stakeholders (Aula, 2011) on whom the company's success or failure depends (Cutlip *et al.*, 1999). Corporate reputation includes a comparison of companies (Deephouse and Carter, 2005; Schreiber, 2008) comprised of the combined images about a company (Yang and Grunig, 2005). Therefore, corporate reputation is a type of feedback received by a company from its stakeholders. Ultimately, it can be said that corporate reputation is cocreated by companies and their stakeholders.

Having a favorable corporate reputation does not necessarily come easily, but it has been found to be the driving force behind many "successful" companies (Hutton *et al.*, 2001). According to Fombrun and van Riel (2003), one of the strongest factors in determining a favorable corporate reputation is the visibility of a company as perceived by its stakeholders. Aula described corporate reputation as having six dimensions: a company's culture and management, its product and services, success, corporate responsibility, public image, and its ability to change and develop.

The level of trust in US companies continues to remain low (Edelman, 2011), so companies looking to differentiate themselves should focus on a strategic approach to communication (DiStaso *et al.*, 2009). The latest Edelman Trust Barometer (Edelman, 2011) study found that the factors important to corporate reputation are high quality or services, transparent and honest business practices, being a company that people can trust, treating employees well, communicating frequently, and pricing fairly. More so today than ever, companies are under public scrutiny, and stakeholders are demanding that companies be good corporate citizens (Aula and Mantere, 2008; DiStaso, 2012; Laurence and Blakstad, 2001). With the increased focus on corporate responsibility and corporate governance, companies must be aware of how they are perceived through their "online reputation."

Pitt and Papania (2007) found that companies communicate a certain "personality" on their web sites, whether intentional or unintentional. These personality traits are demonstrated more so on social media sites, which allow companies to engage in one-on-one conversations with stakeholders. Hallahan (2010) suggested that these online technologies should redefine the role of public relations professionals as those who oversee relationships as opposed to managing them.

Managing corporate reputation should take into consideration both internal and external stakeholders. Employees play an important role in contributing to a company's reputation (Helm, 2011). Internal stakeholders often present a company's "face" and share information, both personally and professionally, on social media sites. Because of this, companies are increasingly implementing social media policies to protect themselves from the sharing of proprietary, secure, or unfavorable information, by providing guidelines for employee use.

Social media has changed the way companies do business. It diminishes the control companies have on their corporate reputation as stakeholders are now influencing the rules of reputation management (Bulmer and DiMauro, 2009; Laurence and Blakstad, 2001). Research has also found that the medium has a greater effect on corporate reputation than the message (Aula, 2011). These networks give companies an opportunity to engage with various stake-holders and listen to their online commentary to help develop strategy. Plus, with the reach of social media, local issues have now become global issues.

The two factors of online communication that have the biggest impact on corporate rep-utation are a company's products/services and its public image (Aula, 2011). The nature of participation, the lack of exclusivity, as well as the rapid and efficient dissemination of infor-mation on social media sites may pose a risk for a company's reputation (Aula, 2010). Risks can include a poorly handled natural disaster, a financial crisis, a seemingly minor customer service issue, or a product recall (Cunningham and Hunt, 2010). Customers will use social media outlets to complain about an issue the company is failing to address, which in turn can create reputational problems (Tripp and Gregoire, 2011). Due to the nature of social media, crises can disseminate rapidly and create long-term damage to a company's reputa-tion in a matter of minutes. Properly and proactively managing one's reputation and pre-sence on social media sites can help companies manage issues and respond appropriately in crisis situations.

Crises are publicly played out on social media sites. For example, Primark, a retailer based in the United Kingdom, was receiving negative attention on review sites, YouTube, and blogs surrounding ethical issues with their suppliers. Instead of using traditional media, the company set up a microsite to effectively and publicly communicate with their stakeholders (Jones *et al.*, 2009). The campaign helped the recov-ery of Primark's reputation.

Fertik and Thompson (2010) identified several ways corporate reputations can be attacked online: the simple lie, the half-truth, the manip-ulated photo, the breach of privacy, and harass-ment and hoaxes. Missing from this list, though, is when a company is attacked because they have done something to violate the trust of a stakeholder or if they acted irresponsibly. When this occurs, many stakeholders take to social media channels to air their frustration and seek a resolution. However, the public

nature of social media can damage a company's reputation after only one individual's post goes viral.

Barnes (2008) found that more than 70% of active Internet users relied on social media to learn about customer care prior to a product or service purchase. Social media allows individu-als to become a collective, which can have both a positive and negative impact on a company. While other touted benefits of social media include its cost-effectiveness (Pavlik, 2007), its widespread dissemination, and its ability to connect with stakeholders, companies must strategically integrate these technologies into their company's communication plan to help enhance and protect its reputation.

Social media empowers stakeholders to help distribute information about companies that quickly influences public opinion (Conway *et al.*, 2007). The instant transmission and speed of how information is delivered is one of the most powerful aspects of social media (Kinzey, 2009). Using social media, companies can quickly disseminate information to a broad and specialized audience allowing interaction with stakeholders at a level higher than ever before.

There are several aspects of social media that make it unique for corporate reputation man-agement. Schiller (2010) noted that social media communications are usually viewed outside the time and place in which they occurred. Another aspect, which is rarely addressed in the literature, is permanence. With social media, conversations and comments are recorded and preserved on the Internet. Therefore, resolutions and negoti-ations must also be carried out online. The power of the permanency of online communi-cations cannot be underestimated. Similar to this is the power of anonymous posters on social media. Historically, the legal system has favored these anonymous posters over a company's rep-utation (Fertik and Thompson, 2010). When dealing with trolls, or individuals who personally attack or aggravate others online, Brogan and Smith (2009) suggest ignoring them as the best recourse.

While some scholars contend that brand and corporate reputation can be used interchange-ably, others suggest that while both concepts are intertwined, confusing the two can result in costly mistakes (Ettenson and Knowles, 2008). In one study of how online and offline corporate brand images differ, respondents reported that the online image of a bookstore was seen to be more informal and innovative than the offline brand images (Alwi and Da Silva, 2007). However, it should be noted, that while there are differences between how offline behavior versus online behavior is perceived, both are equally important and should not be regarded separately.

Externally, there are many company stakeholders that can influence corporate reputation, and many of which are using social media. Social media is not just used for engagement with consumers and other businesses, but also allows companies to interact and engage with other stakeholders, such as the media, the community, and the government (Barnes, 2010a). Argenti (2011) wrote, "Stakeholder empowerment, as it has come to be known, has shifted the corporate hierarchy of corporate influence from the hands of elite business executives to their audiences" (p. 2). Social media melds stakeholders previously regarded as separate entities, which makes companies transparent to everyone (Ettenson and Knowles, 2008). Research indicates that even though there are different stakeholders, there is no difference in terms of criteria as to how different types of stakeholders, such as customers, employees, and consumers, perceive corporate reputation (Helm, 2007).

While the early 2000s saw the start of online communities mobilizing on web sites and discussion boards to boycott companies, such as in the case of the French multinational food and beverage company, Danone (Hunter *et al.*, 2008), stakeholders are now frequently using social media to quickly and efficiently organize. The power of Facebook was demonstrated during the Egyptian uprising as activists used the site as their primary means of coordinating protests. According to Burns (2007), the Internet also allows activists to influence public opinion, build international coalitions, as well as gain support from politicians.

Building a good corporate reputation online takes time, but it can be lost overnight (Aula, 2011). Also, if stakeholders perceive a company to be poor in one area, research has shown that they typically believe that the company may be poor in other areas as well (Aula, 2011). According to Aula and Mantere (2008), "images, symbols, stories, myths, and rumors both fabricate and challenge the organization's reputation" in social media and refer to it as "ambient publicity" (p. 47). Even so, they should be regarded as online conversations and tools for engagement.

Social media poses a constant threat to a company's reputation if it is not managed properly. According to Walsh (2002), "reputations are made or destroyed online by any of the many different kinds of stakeholders who now have inexpensive and effective means to do it" (p. 38). While companies invest millions of dollars to build their reputation online, the same companies can see their reputation damaged or destroyed in a short period of time. Companies must invest in proactive communication and use issues management to protect their valuable yet fragile corporate reputation (Aula, 2010; Fertik and Thompson, 2010; Omar and Williams, 2006).

Social Media Variables That Impact Corporate Reputation

Trust

Following multiple corporate crises, financial scandals, and global turmoil, public scrutiny of companies is rampant, and trust is possibly more important than ever. Although there lacks one widely accepted definition of trust (Watson, 2005), two definitions are especially important to consider when considering social media and companies. Zucker (1986) viewed trust as a "set of expectations shared by all those involved in an exchange" (p. 54). This indicates that trust in a company is not just based on the actions of the company but also everyone involved. Hon and Grunig (1999) identified trust as "one party's level of confidence in and willingness to open oneself to the other party" (p. 3). To build a corporate reputation through social media, companies and their stakeholders need to trust each other.

In Edelman's latest Trust Barometer Report (Edelman, 2011), trust in credentialed spokespeople is in higher demand while trust in media has declined. Search engines were the top source where people first go for news about a company followed by online news sources. Stakeholders are trusting companies less and relying more on other stakeholders, thereby demonstrating the importance of managing corporate reputation on social media sites.

Companies must be diligent in establishing and maintaining trust, which in turn affects corporate reputation and ultimately stakeholder decisions such as recommending or purchasing goods or services. Brand perceptions and purchasing decisions are often traded by customers online (Jansen *et al.*, 2009). Even when company information is available, people often gravitate to other sources of information. Cheong and Morrison (2008) found in a qualitative study that participants were more likely to trust in product information generated from fellow consumers than manufacturer-generated information. These online word-of-mouth platforms can have a big impact on companies.

Although trust in CEOs has increased recently (Edelman, 2011), research has found that stakeholders may be skeptical of executive disclosure. Waddock (2008) found that the skepticism in organization-generated corporate responsibility reports has led to more companies hiring third-party groups to produce the reports and other documents. It should be noted that the growing trend to disclose information encouraged in part by regulations such as Sarbanes–Oxley has not created greater levels of trust (Dando and Swift, 2003). The current trust deficit encourages stakeholders to rely more on trust agents, defined as "non-sales oriented, non-high pressure marketers" (Brogan and Smith, 2009, p. 15). Typically, these agents are genuinely interested in people

and building true relationships online using social media.

According to Dr. Judy Olson, an expert in online collaboration, online communication is different than face-to-face communication, because when only text is available, trustworthiness is based on responsiveness (see Ferenstein, 2010). Olson also indicates that video is better than audio, and audio is better than an online chat window. This relates to how a message is conveyed versus what is said.

Trust has also been found to influence how stakeholders rationalize information. Edelman (2011) found that 57% of those surveyed felt they would believe negative information about a company they do not trust after hearing it just once or twice. This dropped to 25% agreeing that they would believe negative news about a company they do trust after hearing it once or twice. Positive information was perceived the same way, with less people stating they would believe good news about a distrusted company. "These findings send a strong signal that corporate leaders would be well advised to create a trust foundation so that positive information has an echo chamber in which to resonate" (p. 7).

Social media provides companies another medium for building trust. Having a corporate blog and allowing stakeholders to comment not only provides companies a wealth of information but also garners trust. Furthermore, through transparent communication and engagement on social media sites, trust can be further instilled.

Transparency

When a lack of trust exists in a relationship, transparency is needed to repair it (Jahansoozi, 2006). Companies must engage in creating dialog with various stakeholders while communicating transparently and authentically to build their corporate reputation (Molleda, 2010). Shih (2011) wrote, "Companies have no choice but to become transparent, responsive, or collaborative, or else risk going out of business" (p. 14). Rawlins (2009) defined transparency as the deliberate attempt to make available all legally releasable information – whether positive or negative in nature – in a manner that is accurate, timely, balance, and unequivocal, for the purpose of enhancing the reasoning ability of publics and holding organizations accountable for their actions, policies, and practices. (p. 75)

Transparency is not easy for companies because it is unending and new information constantly needs to be provided (Gower, 2006). Just disclosing information does not constitute transparency. Rawlins (2009) identified three important elements of transparency: (1) being truthful, substantial, or useful; (2) having participation of stakeholders; and (3) being objective, balanced, and accountable. These elements include a range of behaviors such as trusting employees to communicate with publics and communicating company information that helps others understand what the company does and why.

The 2009 Arthur W. Page Society and Business Roundtable Institute for Corporate Ethics report on the dynamics of public trust in business looked at what they called the crisis of transparency in business. They ask for a new kind of dialog created by embracing and welcoming transparency. Wakefield and Walton (2010) suggest that translucency may be a better and, in some cases, a more ethical approach where not all information is revealed, but only what the public needs. For example, disclosing some information may cloud certain key messages and overwhelm stakeholders with unnecessary details. The key is making sure all stakeholders have the information they need to make decisions.

In social media, transparency takes on a new level. Most researchers accept that social media can help companies increase transparency, but where a company draws the line can be challenging. Company executives cannot be 100% transparent. The Securities and Exchange Commission and Financial Accounting Standards Board have rules and regulations about disclosing financial and other information that may impact the stock, but beyond that, it is tricky.

An example of a company grappling with transparency is Domino's Pizza and their 2010 Pizza Turnaround campaign. This campaign caused quite a stir in the social media world because it was centered around Domino's employees admitting that their pizza was bad. They created a blog and posted videos of company chefs and executives talking about the pizza – for example, one said "Domino's pizza crust is to me like cardboard." This was a bold and very transparent move. The campaign played out over social media on their blog (that they controlled), and over Twitter, YouTube, and Facebook where they took an active role in conversations. A new pizza was created and Domino's stock rose more than 150% and domestic same-store sales climbed 12.9% since the start of the campaign (Gelles and Rappaport, 2011).

Engagement

The community nature of social media allows companies to create and engage in content building, as opposed to traditional one-way communication tactics that merely disseminate information to stakeholders. Through two-way sharing and engagement, companies and their stakeholders cocreate corporate reputation. According to Paine (2011a), "engagement means that someone has taken an additional step beyond just viewing what you tossed out there" (para. 5). This includes activities like rating a video, commenting on a blog, participating in a conversation on Facebook, and responding to tweets.

It is to the benefit of companies to develop a social media presence so that people can talk to them not just about them. A 2009 Pew study found that almost 40% of Americans say they have doubted a medical professional's opinion or diagnosis because it conflicted with information they found online (Fox and Jones, 2009). That gives an indication into how much faith people place in what they learn on the Internet. Companies need to be a part of those conversations, and through this engagement, they may be able to successfully avoid crises and help manage corporate reputations.

By engaging communities, companies have been successful in building trust and ultimately increasing profits. Admittedly, engagement does place a company in some risk, but the benefits are considered to outweigh the risks. It can be used to gauge reactions to messages and products, test message understanding, enable calls to action, and simply to learn about audiences and their needs. For example, when J&J subsidiary LifeScan used social media to answer questions about its prototype iPhone app for diabetics to monitor glucose levels, their replies far exceeded the content of press release (Kane *et al.*, 2009).

While much of the research on social media suggests companies should engage in dialog with various stakeholders, Stoker and Tusinski (2006) suggest that balancing dialog with information dissemination is the most ethical approach. Demanding a quid pro quo relationship and asking stakeholders to participate may possibly restrict their freedom and integrity in the communication process. Communicating on social media sites should be akin to having a conversation where both listening and conversing are employed. Companies should not be solely focused on generating dialog.

Corporate Social Media Actions

Monitoring social media

Monitoring or listening is an important social media action for companies and is critical for building and maintaining one's corporate reputation. According to Bonini *et al.* (2009),

> Organizations need to enhance their listening skills so that they are sufficiently aware of emerging issues; to reinvigorate their understanding of, and relationships with, critical stakeholders; and to go beyond traditional [public relations] by activating a network of supporters who can influence key constituencies. (p. 75)

To manage corporate reputation, companies must monitor and scan the social media environment using appropriate metrics (Kietzmann *et al.*, 2011). Companies must constantly monitor the social media sphere to help address any issues that threaten their reputation (Bonini *et al.*, 2009; Conway *et al.*, 2007) or that may potentially turn into a crisis.

Lariscy *et al.* (2009) found that almost half of the public relations professionals they surveyed handled their social media monitoring in-house, but the most frequent percentage of the budget spent on monitoring and using social media was 1%. They also found that 49% felt that social media should be monitored daily for rumors or other negative information, and that 41% felt that monitoring social media was as important as monitoring traditional media.

Given the lack of control over the conversations about their companies, public relations professionals are facing an increasing need to monitor public opinion. This is especially important when you consider the use of social media by journalists.

Measuring social media

According to a study by DiStaso *et al.* (2011), social media measurement is one topic that communication executives felt they had "more questions than answers" (p. 7). Measuring social media can be tricky. Paine (2011b) believes that "from a measurement perspective, this social media revolution requires an entirely new way of thinking about what we do and how we define marketing success" (p. 69). One of the big changes is in how success is quantified. Measuring hits (or as Paine calls it How Idiots Track Success) on a web site is simply not enough.

Metrics must be used that move beyond merely counting one's number of followers or likes on social media sites. Instead, social media metrics should encompass more relationship building by using tools to analyze conversations, such as those tracking sentiment that evaluate how and what various stakeholders are saying both about the company as well as its competitors. This includes web analytics and content analysis. Traditional tools such as surveys, polls, and focus groups are necessary to truly measure corporate reputation and relationships. It is important to note that there are multiple tools available purporting to measure social media, which are in fact, not valid measures. Bottom line,

> to do measurement you have to have goals, metrics, a benchmark and a timeline. You have to build it into your plan, not just add it on at the end. Real measurement involves actually doing something with the results. Drawing conclusion, making decisions and actually looking into the accuracy and meaning of the data. (Paine, 2011a, para. 3)

Today's Social Media Tools

Blogs

There are more than 160 million blogs on the Internet (NielsenWire, 2012), and 23% of *Fortune 500* companies have corporate blogs (Barnes, 2010b). Most corporate blogs allow users to post comments and subscribe to the blogs, which lends itself to transparency. According to Logan Williams from MWW Group (as cited in Brown, 2008), "blogs can enhance a company's reputation while giving a name, face, and personality to an otherwise single corporate entity" (p. 24). While individual bloggers may be viewed as fragmented, they are still very powerful and have a tremendous amount of influence on a company's reputation due to the ability of blogs to be aggregated (Gonzalez-Herrero and Smith, 2008).

One of the most significant factors to a blog's success is a blogger's credibility (Yang and Lim, 2009). Smudde (2005) in his piece on ethical blogging suggests that companies must be candid and open while creating dialogic communication, but not engage in unethical practices such as paying for blog content or disclosing proprietary information. He suggested that the benefit of companies and stakeholders engaging in blogs "fosters dialogue about the good, the bad and anything in between, which should help stakeholders to identify with an organization and its messages, build community rapport,

and maintain image, reputation, and credibility" (p. 38).

While some companies have stand-alone blogs, other companies partner with prominent bloggers to improve their corporate reputation. For example, in 2010, Kellogg partnered with TheMotherhood and BlogHer bloggers to create a campaign to improve the perception of cereal, which was receiving a lot of negative attention in the press thanks to consumer complaints of high sugar content as well as high-fructose corn syrup. According to Ketchum (2011) who managed the campaign and won a PRSA Silver Anvil, the initiative drove 374 blog posts and 41,804 comments, generating 27 million earned digital engagements. The company also increased good nutrition/nutritious mentions online by 150% and increased Kellogg's online share of voice by 8%.

Complaints as well as a lack of transparency in blogs can also negatively impact a company's reputation. In a white paper, several public relations firms analyzed traditional and online media coverage after Jeff Jarvis blogged about his negative customer service experience with Dell (Marketsentinel, Analytica, & Immediate Future, 2005). The researchers found that the blog was a key online source for others who also had a negative experience and Dell had little influence on the topic. Another issue that perpetuates the difficulty of companies breaking the blog realm is that bloggers tend to act in packs and frequently reference one another further spreading messages.

When creating a blog, companies must be transparent. In 2006, a writer and photographer ventured across America staying in Walmart parking lots every night and blogging about their experience in the campaign, "Walmarting across America" (Burns, 2008). While the two who took the trip were real, the campaign was sponsored by Working Families for Walmart, a front group created by the public relations firm Edelman. This made the public question Walmart and Edelman's ethics in both traditional and online media and resulted in the President and CEO Richard Edelman openly apologizing for the gaffe and lack of transparency.

Collaboration

Wikipedia

This online collaboratively edited encyclopedia has become one of the world's most popular web sites since it was founded in 2001. It is currently the seventh most popular web site in the world and the sixth in the United States and on average, visitors spend about five minutes per visit (Alexa.com, 2011). As of May 2010, 14% of worldwide Internet users access Wikipedia on a daily basis, and 53% of American Internet users look for information on Wikipedia (Zickuhr and Rainie, 2011). Oftentimes, Wikipedia is one of the top sites provided when searching for companies using prominent search engines (DiStaso and Messner, 2010). This easy and frequent access places Wikipedia in a position to potentially influence public opinion.

The collaboration concept of this social media is what makes it different than other types of encyclopedias. Any Internet user can contribute or modify any topic, not just experts. This means that the public is creating the content available on topics, including companies. Articles are edited by many people and have been found to be largely neutral in content (DiStaso and Messner, 2010).

A corporate Wikipedia article looks like it may be sponsored by the company because it contains the logo, history of the company, and links directly to the company web site, but in reality, a company has very little involvement in the content on their Wikipedia article. It is actually strongly suggested by Wikipedia that company representatives refrain from editing their articles and instead appeal to the Wikipedia community through posting on the discussion boards of their articles with any edits they feel are necessary. The content in Wikipedia is to be supported with credible resources. This means that any content with a credible reference cannot be removed resulting in topics available in corporate Wikipedia articles that companies would rather people forget about. This includes topics of scandals and legal problems that have the potential to influence corporate reputation long after their discussion has waned in mainstream media and even in other social media.

Internet forums and message boards

Internet forums and message boards are online discussion sites where people engage in conversation. Stakeholders use Internet forums or message boards for a variety of reasons including sharing information, seeking or giving support for an issue, or building relationships. They often have a moderator who is responsible for overseeing the forum or board to ensure their rules and policies. It is common for Internet forums or message boards to have a main topic that draws people together for the purpose of discussing relevant issues. The topics vary greatly from the The Vegan Forum to the Truckers Trucking Forum to Raging Bull: The General Electric Company Message Board.

While Internet forums and message boards provide companies with a wealth of information about specific groups, they are also an online tool that can impact corporate reputation. Park and Lee (2007) found that a single negative comment on an online news forum impacts corporate reputation. Therefore, in most cases when dealing with a frustrated stakeholder, the company should visibly respond to the content of not only online news sites, but individual forum posts as well. Companies, such as Cymfony (2005), track message boards and discussion groups on behalf of clients to track perceptions, fine-tune messages, identify influencers, and investigate misinformation in an effort to manage a company's reputation.

Companies must be careful about engaging in Internet forums and message boards that they do not sponsor. If any company representatives are participating, being transparent about who they are is critical. For eight years, CEO John Mackey of Whole Foods Market, Inc., was anonymously posting messages to the Yahoo! Financial message boards boasting about his company while disparaging competitor, Wild Oats (Reder, 2009). This incident raised questions of corporate governance, including the impact on a company's information security and corporate reputation.

Microblogging

Twitter

Twitter allows users to post text-like updates of up to 140 characters to a list of their self-selected followers. One of the key differences between Twitter and many social networking sites like Facebook is "following" the updates of people you do not personally know is acceptable, while on Facebook, an individual's friends are more likely to be people the user has some sort of personal connection with even if it is a distant one. This characteristic allows companies to connect with stakeholders they do not have a personal relationship with which highlights the possibilities of Twitter in a corporate social media plan.

In May 2011, Twitter had nearly 28 million unique visitors, and was the thirty-first most visited site on the Internet in the United States (Compete, 2011). In 2010, 60% of *Fortune 500* companies had a Twitter account with recent tweets, and of those, one-third were engaging in dialog with stakeholders through the @replies or retweet function (Barnes, 2010b). Rybalko and Seltzer (2010) found in their study that 60% of the companies responded to others, while nearly one-third attempted to stimulate discussion.

A 2009 Weber-Shandwick study found that most *Fortune 100* companies were missing the opportunities Twitter offered as most were still only disseminating information. The public relations company suggested that companies do four things:

- Create a companywide engagement strategy
- Demonstrate a consistent and comprehensive brand presence
- Build a dialogue that paves the way to new relationships with stakeholders
- Generate loyalty with new and existing communities. (p. 8)

Companies use Twitter for a variety of reasons such as implementing crisis communication, communicating internally, engaging in dialogic communication, disseminating information, and responding to customer service

issues (Jacques, 2009; McCorkindale, 2012; Stewart, 2008), all of which directly impact corporate reputation. For example, Virgin Media uses Twitter to communicate internally, both professionally and socially. In addition, the company uses Twitter for external stakeholders to answer questions, to collaborate, as well as to help spot and solve customer queries (Signorelli, 2009). Nonprofit organizations are also using Twitter; for example, the American Red Cross uses Twitter for disaster-related announcements as well as fund-raisers (Stewart, 2008).

Schultz *et al.* (2010) found that using Twitter had less negative crisis reactions than blogs and newspaper articles. Moreover, due to the ease of "retweeting," Twitter users are more likely to disseminate the company's message more than blogs and newspapers. In an analysis of Twitter, researchers found that while more than half of mentions of a brand on Twitter were positive, one-third were critical of a company or product; this word-of-mouth communication directly impacts a company's reputation (Jansen *et al.*, 2009). Therefore, to encourage transparency and build positive relationships in an effort to enhance corporate reputation, companies should have an established Twitter account that names the tweeter who manages it (McCorkindale, 2012; Park and Lee, 2011).

The wide distribution possibilities of Twitter can also work against a company. In February 2011, @KennethCole posted the following tweet during the Egyptian revolution, "Millions are in uproar in #Cairo. Rumor is they heard our new spring collection is now available online at http://bit.ly/KCairo." After receiving flak on Twitter, which quickly spread to other social media sites and mainstream media, the company issued an apology.

Dell is often considered a leader in social media, and Twitter is a tool they utilize successfully (Sernovitz, 2011). Dell devotes a great deal of its communication resources to managing social media. Sarah Richardson, Communications Senior Adviser who helps manage Dell's social media accounts, said their Twitter accounts (@Dell for managing corporate reputation and @DellCares for managing customer support) are two of the most important social media accounts for their company (personal interview, June 30, 2011). The @Dell account provides information from the corporate communications department, including links to blog posts, earnings, and helpful information for journalists, analysts, customers, and other important stakeholders. Other than disseminating information, the tweeters who are listed on Dell's Twitter page, engage in dialog with their followers.

Social networking

Facebook

Public relations professionals reported that Facebook is the most important new communications for public relations messages in 2010 and 2011, replacing search engine marketing in 2009 (Wright and Hinson, 2011). As of 2010, 56% of *Fortune 500* companies had a Facebook profile (Barnes, 2010b). While research in 2009 found that companies were not taking advantage of Facebook's potential (McCorkindale, 2010), companies have been jumping on the bandwagon since then to improve their social media presence.

In July 2011, one of the most popular Facebook pages was Coke with 31 million likes (Allfacebook.com, 2011). Coke's page has videos, links to its social responsibility efforts, a virtual gift giver for a user's friends, and interactive tools featuring their international "happiness goes around" campaign.

While Facebook allows companies to communicate and establish a dialog with users, Vorvoreanu (2009) suggests that this may not be the best approach, especially with the millennial generation, who may not want companies to engage in dialog with them. Research also suggests that posting too much information can also cause Facebook fans to turn off a company's updates (McCorkindale and DiStaso, 2011).

To help repair or manage corporate reputations, companies must also decide how to best respond to negative online comments. In some cases, a response to a negative comment may create more damage to the reputation (Samuels *et al.*, 2009). In 2010, Greenpeace posted a video on Nestle's Facebook page accusing the company's palm oil supplier of rainforest deforestation and destroying the orangutan's habitat. When Nestle responded rudely to posters on their Facebook page and appeared to be more concerned with alterations of their Kit Kat logo than to the deforestation issue, the issue spread to other social media sites and to the mainstream media. This was one of the first times comments on a corporate Facebook page created a crisis. As a result, Nestle (2010) released a statement of its goal to use fully sustainable palm oil within the next five years, showing the power of online activist publics in achieving desired change.

Video social media

YouTube

YouTube is a video sharing service that receives more than 100 million daily views on their mobile site while their web site reached 700 billion playbacks in 2010 (YouTube, 2011). In public relations, YouTube can be used to kick off a campaign, respond to a crisis, uncover communities, extend a brand, and connect with the media and bloggers. Depending on the content, a video that goes viral can either benefit or be detrimental to a company.

In fact, the rise of digital video production and online distribution through sites such as YouTube provides companies a means to communicate directly with publics without traditional media gatekeepers. Wright and Hinson (2011) found that 71% of the public relations professionals they surveyed felt that video sharing like YouTube was important to their company's overall communication efforts compared to 29% in their 2009 study.

In 2010, Old Spice took to YouTube to refresh their brand with their Old Spice Guy Campaign when it created YouTube ads that attracted 34 million viewers in a week. Next, they used Twitter to provide fans with an opportunity to ask questions of the "Old Spice Guy" and he responded to 186 of the questions with videos. The campaign has been considered a wide success and truly highlighted the power of video.

Ford Motor Company has also used YouTube successfully. On their YouTube channel, Ford's Spokesperson Mike Rowe narrates videos of the company's F-150 being subjected to various torture tests. The videos, also posted on Ford's web site, have received more than 2.5 million views on YouTube alone. More companies are now creating videos to help provide information to various stakeholders to help manage and improve their corporate reputation in a transparent manner.

The most famous example of a video that hurt a company was created in 2008 when United Airlines refused to reimburse passenger Dave Carroll for breaking his $3500 guitar. Carroll posted a music video on YouTube, "United Breaks Guitars," that earned 10.5 million views, launched Carroll's singing career, and caused a reputation crisis for United.

Domino's Pizza also experienced negative attention both online and in the mainstream media when an employee uploaded a video of another employee "contaminating" a customer's food. The viral video sent Domino's scrambling to a variety of social media channels to help repair its brand reputation.

Conclusion

Companies should strategically integrate their social media channels to build trust by ensuring that stakeholders receive a consistent message while being transparent and engaging. Even though there are risks involved with engaging stakeholders online, companies must do so ethically and without fear of retribution while using principles of trust and transparency. To properly manage these social channels, companies must also monitor and measure social media. Goodman and Hirsch (2010) suggest that "a healthy skepticism about the use of these tools by corporations is a rational response . . . it will be a bold – perhaps even foolhardy – company that doesn't become deeply familiar with the opportunities and challenges [social media] present" (p. 57). Companies must overcome their skepticism

and embrace these technologies especially in terms of the impact social media can have on a company's reputation.

References

Alexa.com (2011) Wikipedia.org. Retrieved from http://www.alexa.com/siteinfo/wikipedia.org (last accessed October 3, 2012).

Allfacebook.com (2011) Facebook page leaderboard. Retrieved from http://statistics.allfacebook.com/pages/leaderboard/ (last accessed October 3, 2012).

Alwi, S.F.S. and Da Silva, R.V. (2007) Online and offline corporate brand images: Do they differ? *Corporate Reputation Review*, 10(4), 217–244.

Argenti, P. (2011) Digital strategies for powerful corporate communications. Retrieved from the European Financial Review from http://www.europeanfinancialreview.com/?p=2581 (last accessed October 3, 2012).

Arthur W. Page Society and Business Roundtable Institute for Corporate Ethics (2009) The dynamics of public trust in business – Emerging opportunities for leaders. Retrieved from http://www.darden.virginia.edu/corporate-ethics/pdf/public_trust_in_business.pdf (last accessed October 3, 2012).

Aula, P. (2010) Social media, reputation risk, and ambient publicity management. *Strategy and Leadership*, 38(6), 43–49.

Aula, P. (2011) Meshworked reputation: Publicists' views on the reputational impacts of online communication. *Public Relations Review*, 37, 28–36.

Aula, P. and Mantere, S. (2008) *Strategic Reputation Management*. New York: Taylor & Francis.

Barnes, N. (2008) Exploring the link between customer care and brand reputation in the age of social media. *Journal of New Communications Research*, 3(1), 86–91.

Barnes, N.G. (2010a) The 2010 Inc. 500 update: Most blog, friend, and tweet, but some industries still shun social media. Retrieved from Society for New Communications Research from http://www1.umassd.edu/cmr/studiesresearch/2010inc500.pdf (last accessed October 3, 2012).

Barnes, N.G. (2010b) The *Fortune* 500 and social media: A longitudinal study of blogging, Twitter, and Facebook usage by America's largest companies. Retrieved from Society for New Communications Research from http://

www1.umassd.edu/cmr/studiesresearch/2010 F500.pdf (last accessed October 3, 2012).

Bonini, S., Court, D., and Marchi, A. (2009) Rebuilding corporate reputations. *McKinsey Quarterly*, *3*, 75–83.

Brogan, C. and Smith, J. (2009) *Trust Agents: Using the Web to Build Influence, Improve Reputation, and Earn Trust*. Hoboken, NJ: Wiley & Sons.

Brown, L.M. (2008) Internet protocol: Agency professionals discuss best online media practices. *Public Relations Tactics*, *15*(5), 24–26.

Bulmer, D. and DiMauro, V. (2009) The new symbiosis of professional networks: Social media's impact on business and decision-making. Retrieved from Society for New Communications Research from http://sncr.org/sites/default/files/new_symbiosis_research_report_brief.pdf (last accessed October 25, 2012).

Burns, K.S. (2008) The misuse of social media: Reactions to and important lessons from a blog fiasco. *Journal of New Communications Research*, *3*(1), 41–54.

Burns, T. (2007) Holding companies accountable in cyberspace: The threat posed by Internet-based, anti-corporate campaigners. *International Review of Law Computers & Technology*, *21*(1), 39–57.

Cheong, H.J. and Morrison, M.A. (2008) Consumers' reliance on product information and recommendations found in UGC. *Journal of Interactive Advertising*, *8*(2), 1–29. Retrieved from http://jiad.org/article103 (last accessed October 3, 2012).

Compete (2011) Site profile for Twitter.com. Retrieved from http://siteanalytics.compete.com/twitter.com/ (last accessed October 3, 2012).

Conway, T., Ward, M., Lewis, G., and Bernhardt, A. (2007) Internet crisis potential: The importance of a strategic approach to marketing communications. *Journal of Marketing Communications*, *13*(3), 213–228.

Cunningham, W.H. and Hunt, J. (2010) Online, you are your reputation. *Risk Management*, *57*(8), 28.

Cutlip, S., Center, A., and Broom, G. (1999) *Effective Public Relations* (8th ed.). Englewood Cliffs, NJ: Prentice Hall.

Cymfony (2005) How marketers are using consumer generated content and online discussion. Retrieved from http://blog.cymfony.com/2005/09/the_nytimes_pub.html (last accessed October 3, 2012).

Dando, N. and Swift, T. (2003) Transparency and assurance: Minding the credibility gap. *Journal of Business Ethics*, *44*, 195–200.

Deephouse, D.L. and Carter, S.M. (2005) An examination of differences between organizational legitimacy and organizational reputation. *Journal of Management Studies*, *42*(2), 329–360.

DiStaso, M.W. (2012) The annual earnings press release's dual role: An examination of relationships with local and national media coverage and reputation. *Journal of Public Relations Research*, *24*(2), 123–143.

DiStaso, M.W. and Messner, M. (2010) Forced transparency: Corporate image on Wikipedia and what it means for public relations. *The Public Relations Journal*, *4*(2), 1–23.

DiStaso, M.W., Stacks, D.W., and Botan, C.H. (2009) State of public relations education in the United States: 2006 report on a national survey of executives and academics. *Public Relations Review*, *35*(3), 254–269.

DiStaso, M.W., McCorkindale, T., and Wright, D.K. (2011) How public relations executives perceive and measure the impact of social media in their organizations. *Public Relations Review*, *37*(3), 325–328.

Edelman (2011) 2011 Edelman Trust Barometer. Retrieved from http://www.edelman.com/trust/2011 (last accessed October 3, 2012).

Ettenson, R. and Knowles, J. (2008) Don't confuse reputation with brand. *MIT Sloan Management Review*, *49*(2), 19–21.

Ferenstein, G. (2010) The science of building trust with social media. Mashable. Retrieved from http://mashable.com/2010/02/24/social-media-trust/ (last accessed October 3, 2012).

Fertik, M. and Thompson, D. (2010) *Wild West 2.0: How to Protect and Restore Your Online Reputation on the Untamed Social Frontier*. New York: AMA.

Fombrun, C.J. (1996) *Reputation: Realizing Value from the Corporate Image*. Boston: Harvard Business School Press.

Fombrun, C.J. and van Riel, C.B.M. (2003) *Fame & Fortune: How Successful Companies Build Winning Reputations*. Upper Saddle River, NJ: Prentice Hall.

Fox, S. and Jones, S. (2009) The social life of health information. Pew Internet & American Life Project. June. Retrieved from http://www.pewinternet.org/Reports/2009/8-The-Social-Life-of-Health-Information.aspx?r=1 (last accessed October 3, 2012).

Gelles, D. and Rappaport, A. (2011) Domino's eats humble pie to boost sales. Financial Times, May 6. Retrieved from http://www.ft.com/cms/s/0/f8178fa2-7804-11e0-b90e-00144feabdc0.html#axzz1SBSFo9aC (last accessed October 3, 2012).

Gonzalez-Herrero, A. and Smith, S. (2008) Crisis communications management on the web: How Internet-based technologies are changing the way public relations professionals handle business crises. *Journal of Contingencies and Crisis Management*, *16*(3), 143–153.

Goodman, M.B. and Hirsch, P.B. (2010) *Corporate Communication: Strategic Adaptation for Global Practice*. New York: Peter Lang.

Gower, K.K. (2006) Truth and transparency. In K. Fitzpatrick and C. Bronstein (eds), *Ethics in Public Relations*. Thousand Oaks, CA: Sage, pp. 89–106.

Hallahan, K. (2010) Thinking inside the box. Retrieved from the Institute for PR from http://www.instituteforpr.org/2007/10/kirk-hallahan-thinking-inside-the-box/ (last accessed October 3, 2012).

Helm, S. (2007) One reputation or many? Comparing stakeholders' perceptions of corporate reputation. *Corporate Communications: An International Journal*, *12*(3), 238–254.

Helm, S. (2011) Employees' awareness of their impact on corporate reputation. *Journal of Business Research*, *64*, 657–663.

Hon, L.C. and Grunig, J.E. (1999) Guidelines for measuring relationships in public relations. Retrieved from http://www.instituteforpr.org/wp-content/uploads/Guidelines_Measuring_Relationships.pdf (last accessed October 3, 2012).

Hunter, M.L., Menestrel, M.L., and de Bettignies, H.C. (2008) Beyond control: Crisis strategies and stakeholder media in the Danone boycott of 2011. *Corporate Reputation Review*, *11*(4), 335–350.

Hutton, J.G., Goodman, M.B., Alexander, J.B., and Genest, C.M. (2001) Reputation management: The new face of corporate public relations. *Public Relations Review*, *27*, 247–261.

Jacques, A. (2009) Get shorty: The business applications for Twitter. July. Retrieved from Public Relations Tactics from http://www.prsa.org/Intelligence/Tactics/Articles/view/8116/101/Get_shorty_The_business_applications_for_Twitter (last accessed October 3, 2012).

Jahansoozi, J. (2006) Organization-stakeholder relationships: Exploring trust and transparency. *Journal of Management Development*, *25*(10), 942–955.

Jansen, B.J., Zhang, M., Sobel, K., and Chowdury, A. (2009) Twitter power: Tweets as electronic word of mouth. *Journal of the American Society for Information Sciences and Technology*, *60*(11), 2169–2188.

Jones, B., Temperley, J., and Lima, A. (2009) Corporate reputation in the era of Web 2.0: The case of Primark. *Journal of Marketing Management*, *25*(9–10), 927–939.

Kane, G.C., Fichman, R.G., Gallaugher, J., and Glaser, H. (2009) Community relations 2.0. *Harvard Business Review*, *87*(November), 45–50. Retrieved from http://hbr.org/2009/11/community-relations-20/ar/1 (last accessed October 3, 2012).

Ketchum (2011) Kellogg Company delivers the facts about cereal. Retrieved from PRSA from http://www.prsa.org/SearchResults/Download/6BE-1102C20/0/Kellogg_Company_Delivers_the_Facts_about_Cereal (last accessed October 3, 2012).

Kietzmann, J.H., Hermkens, K., McCarthy, I.P., and Silverstre, B.S. (2011) Social media? Get serious! Understanding the functional building blocks of social media. *Business Horizons*, *54*, 241–251.

Kinzey, R. (2009) Managing your reputation in a social media world. The Business Journal. Retrieved from http://www.bizjournals.com/triad/stories/2009/07/27/smallb2.html (last accessed October 3, 2012).

Lariscy, R.W., Avery, E.J., Sweetser, K.D., and Howes, P. (2009) Monitoring public opinion in cyberspace: How corporate public relations is facing the challenge. *The Public Relations Journal*, *3*(4), 1–17.

Laurence, A. and Blakstad, M. (2001) Managing reputation in the digital age. In A. Jolly (ed.), *Managing Corporate Reputations*. London: Kogan Page, pp. 12–19.

Marketsentinel, Analytica, & Immediate Future (2005) Measuring the influence of bloggers on corporate reputation. December. Retrieved from http://www.onalytica.com/Measuring BloggerInfluence61205.pdf (last accessed October 25, 2012).

McCorkindale, T. (2010) Can you see the writing on my wall? A content analysis of the *Fortune* 100's Facebook social networking sites. *The Public Relations Journal*, *4*(3), 1–13.

McCorkindale, T. (2012) Twitter me this, Twitter me that: A quantitative content analysis of the

40 Best Twitter Brands. *Journal of New Communications Research*, 43–60.

McCorkindale, T. and DiStaso, M.W. (2011) "Like" or "unlike": How millennials are engaging and building relationships with organizations on Facebook. Paper to be presented at the Association for Education and Journalism Convention, St. Louis, MO.

Molleda, J.C. (2010) Authenticity and the construct's dimensions in public relations and communication research. *Journal of Communication Management*, 14(3), 223–236.

Nestle (2010) Update on deforestation and palm oil. Retrieved from http://www.nestle.com/Media/Statements/Pages/Update-on-deforestation-and-palm-oil.aspx (last accessed October 3, 2012).

NielsenWire (2012) Buzz in the blogosphere: Millions more bloggers and blog readers. Retrieved from http://blog.nielsen.com/nielsenwire/online_mobile/buzz-in-the-blogosphere-millions-more-bloggers-and-blog-readers/ (last accessed October 25, 2012)

Omar, M. and Williams, R.L. (2006) Managing and maintaining corporate reputation and brand identity: Haier Group logo. *Journal of Brand Management*, 13(4/5), 268–275.

Paine, K.D. (2011a) Lies and consequences in KDPaine's PR Measurement Blog. Retrieved from http://kdpaine.blogs.com/ (last accessed October 3, 2012).

Paine, K.D. (2011b) *Measure What Matters. Online Tools for Understanding Customers, Social Media, Engagement, and Key Relationships.* Hoboken, NJ: Wiley & Sons.

Park, H. and Lee, H. (2011) The use of human voice as a relationship building strategy on social networking sites. Paper presented at the IPRRC Conference, Miami, FL.

Park, N. and Lee, K.M. (2007) Effects of online news forum on corporate reputation. *Public Relations Review*, 33, 346–348.

Pavlik, J.V. (2007) Mapping the consequences of technology on public relations. Retrieved from the Institute for Public Relations from http://www.instituteforpr.org (last accessed October 3, 2012).

Pew Internet and American Life Project (2011) Social networking sites and our lives: Summary of findings. Retrieved from http://www.pewinternet.org/Reports/2011/Technology-and-social-networks/Summary.aspx (last accessed October 3, 2012).

Pitt, L.F. and Papania, L. (2007) In the words: Managerial approaches to exploring corporate intended image through content analysis. *Journal of General Management*, 32(4), 1–16.

Rawlins, B. (2009) Give the emperor a mirror: Toward developing a stakeholder measurement of organizational transparency. *Journal of Public Relations Research*, 21(1), 71–99.

Reder, M. (2009) CEO postings – Leveraging the internet's communication potential while managing the message to maintain corporate governance interests in information security, reputation and compliance. *DePaul Business & Commercial Law Journal*, 7, 179–202.

Rybalko, S. and Seltzer, T. (2010) Dialogic communication in 140 characters or less: How *Fortune* 500 companies engage stakeholders using Twitter. *Public Relations Review*, 36(4), 336–341.

Samuels, C., Newson, A., and Patten, J. (2009) Online reputation. In A. Newson (ed.), *Blogging and Other Social Media*. Burlington, VT: Gower Publishing, pp. 171–180.

Schiller, K. (2010) Getting a grip on reputation. *Information Today*, 27(10), 1–46.

Schreiber, E.S. (2008) Reputation. Retrieved from http://www.instituteforpr.org/topics/reputation/ (last accessed October 3, 2012).

Schultz, F., Utz, S., and Gortiz, A. (2010) Is the medium the message? Perceptions of and reactions to crisis communication via Twitter, blogs, and traditional media. *Public Relations Review*, 37, 20–27.

Sernovitz, A. (2011) Andy's answers: How Dell finds ROI from social media. Smart Blog on Social Media. April 6. Retrieved from http://smartblogs.com/socialmedia/2011/04/06/andys-answers-how-dell-generating-roi-from-social-media/ (last accessed October 3, 2012).

Shih, C. (2011) *The Facebook Era*. Boston: Pearson.

Signorelli, A. (2009) How Virgin Media uses Twitter for collaboration. *Strategic Communication Management*, 13(4), 8–9.

Smudde, P.M. (2005) Blogging, ethics, and public relations: A proactive and dialogic approach. *Public Relations Quarterly*, 50(3), 34–38.

Springston, J.K. (2001) Public relations and new media technology: The impact of the internet. In R. Heath (ed.), *Handbook of Public Relations*. Thousand Oaks, CA: Sage, pp. 603–614.

Stewart, J. (2008) How companies are using and responding through the social networking tool. *Public Relations Tactics*, 15(10), 17.

Stoker, K.L. and Tusinski, K.A. (2006) Reconsidering public relations' infatuation with dialogue: Why engagement and reconciliation can be more ethical than symmetry and reciprocity. *Journal of Mass Media Ethics*, 21(2&3), 156–176.

Tripp, T.M. and Gregoire, Y. (2011) When unhappy customers strike back on the internet. *MIT Sloan Management Review*, 52(3), 37–44.

Vorvoreanu, M. (2009) Perceptions of corporations on Facebook: An analysis of Facebook social norms. *Journal of New Communications Research*, 4(1), 67–86.

Waddock, S. (2008) The development of corporate responsibility/corporate citizenship. *Organization Management Journal*, 5, 29–39.

Wakefield, R. and Walton, S. (2010) The translucency corollary: Why full transparency is not always the most ethical approach. *Public Relations Journal*, 4(4). Retrieved from the Institute for Public Relations from http://www.prsa.org/intelligence/prjournal/documents/2010wakefieldwalton.pdf (last accessed October 25, 2012).

Walsh, T. (2002) *The Reputation Vortex: Online Reputation Management*. London: Spiro Press.

Watson, M.L. (2005) Can there be just one trust? A cross-disciplinary identification of trust definitions and measurement. Retrieved from http://www.instituteforpr.org/wp-content/uploads/2004_Watson.pdf (last accessed October 3, 2012).

Weber-Shandwick (2009) Do *Fortune* 100 companies need a Twittervention? Retrieved from http://www.webershandwick.com/resources/ws/flash/Twittervention_Study.pdf (last accessed October 3, 2012).

Wright, D.K. and Hinson, M.D. (2011) A three-year longitudinal analysis study measuring new communications media use by public relations practitioners. Paper presented at the Association for Education in Journalism and Mass Communication Convention, St. Louis, MO.

Yang, S.U. and Grunig, J.E. (2005) The effects of organization–public relationship outcomes on cognitive representations of organizations and overall evaluations of organizational performance. *Journal of Communication Management*, 9(4), 305–325.

Yang, S.U. and Lim, J.S. (2009) The effects of blog-mediated public relations (BMPR) on relational trust. *Journal of Public Relations Research*, 21(3), 341–359.

YouTube (2011) Statistics. Retrieved from http://www.youtube.com/t/press_statistics (last accessed October 3, 2012).

Zickuhr, K. and Rainie, L. (2011) Wikipedia, past and present. January 13. Retrieved from http://www.pewinternet.org/Reports/2011/Wikipedia.aspx (last accessed October 3, 2012).

Zucker, L.G. (1986) Production of trust: Institutional sources of economic structure (1840–1920). In B.M. Staw and L.L. Cummings (eds), *Research in Organizational Behavior* (Vol. 8). Greenwich, CT: JAI Press.

The Reputation of Corporate Reputation: Fads, Fashions, and the Mainstreaming of Corporate Reputation Research and Practice

Magda Pieczka

Queen Margaret University, UK

Theodore E. Zorn

Massey University, New Zealand

The corporate reputation construct has generated enormous popular interest and academic attention. Its rapid emergence and widespread adoption raises the question of whether it may be a passing fad or fashion. In this chapter, we examine corporate reputation discourse in relation to the characteristics of management fashions. While it is too early to determine if, like other fashions, it will decline in popularity, corporate reputation discourse shares many of the qualities of fashions.

The recent surge of interest in the notion of corporate reputation prompts us to ask some critical questions about its emergent popularity as an explanation for organizational effectiveness and as a framework for strategic action. While we do not question that reputations are important to organizations, we think it is appropriate to raise questions whenever a framework or trend emerges that is used – and perhaps overused – to explain organizational phenomena.

Within the past 20 years or so, corporate reputation has emerged as a major focus of interest for the business press and for scholars of organizations (Carroll, 2008). While pinpointing a precise starting point for the phenomenon is problematic, Carroll identifies the genesis of corporate reputation as the 1983 launch of *Fortune* Magazine's list of Most Admired Companies. The launch of a journal specifically devoted to the issue is another important milestone: *Corporate Reputation Review* was launched in 1997. And a recent review points to only the past decade as the formative phase (Lange *et al.*, 2011) for research on the issue. Regardless of differences as to exactly when corporate reputation emerged as

The Handbook of Communication and Corporate Reputation, First Edition. Edited by Craig E. Carroll.
© 2013 John Wiley & Sons, Inc. Published 2015 by John Wiley & Sons, Inc.

an important construct, there has clearly been an upsurge of interest and activity related to the issue in recent years.

The rapid growth of interest among businesses and scholars in the corporate reputation construct raises the question of whether there is a certain faddishness to adopting it. The focus of this chapter is to examine the extent to which the current interest in corporate reputation is simply the latest in a series of management fads and fashions, or whether instead it is a more stable and permanent fixture on the scene. We compare the characteristics of management fashions to those of corporate reputation and argue that the latter has most of the qualities typically associated with fashions. A crucial question, however, is whether interest in and activity related to corporate reputation will demonstrate the bell-shaped curve typical of fashions – that is, a rapid rise in interest followed by an equally dramatic decline. Thus far, interest – as demonstrated by the number of academic publications and the formation of organizations dedicated to corporate reputation and related concepts – seems to be on the rise. We also discuss the implications of corporate reputation's fashion-like characteristics for practice.

Management Knowledge and Management Fashion

The question of whether corporate reputation fits the criteria for management fashions is important beyond simply categorizing the concept. The more compelling issue is whether practices that have the potential to create more effective organizations are subject to the "next big thing" mentality that originally accompanied now nearly forgotten business practices such as management by objectives (MBO), quality circles, and total quality management (TQM), or alternatively, whether these practices can be permanently woven into the fabric of organizational and societal life.

The present chapter draws on literature addressing the diffusion of management practices and the social construction of management knowledge. This literature has been concerned with deconstructing management thoughts and practices such that the modernist view of management as a linear progression of increasingly sophisticated knowledge of organizational reality and increasingly effective ways to manipulate and control that reality is recast as discursive constructions that are continually renegotiated to produce meaningful accounts of organizational practice (Parker, 1992). As du Gay (1996) argued, "The dispositions, actions and attributes that constitute 'management' have no natural form, and for this reason must be approached as a series of historically specific assemblages" (p. 264). Management practices, thus, are seen as normative belief structures, and their diffusion is influenced by social and political pressures rather than simply as the logical march of progress or the "rational" advance of knowledge (see Fiss and Zajac, 2004). In our previous research, we have raised similar questions about other recent management phenomena, including knowledge management (Zorn and Taylor, 2004), sustainable business and corporate social responsibility (Zorn and Collins, 2007), and dialog (Pieczka and Escobar, 2010).

A number of streams of research have called attention to the transitory nature of management practices. For example, research emanating from institutional theory has empirically documented how practices become established as a result of organizations' desire to be seen as legitimate members of a particular organizational field motivating responses to pressures from various sources (Scott, 1991; Tolbert and Zucker, 1983; Van de Ven and Hargrave, 2004). These pressures include "mimetic" pressures, or the perceived need to imitate the practices of other organizations. Similarly, management fashion theory (Abrahamson, 1996, 1997; Abrahamson and Fairchild, 1999; Jackson, 2001; Rolfsen, 2004) and guru theory (Clark and Salaman, 1998) have identified the tendency of organizations to adopt the latest popular management programs (e.g., TQM, business process reengineering, knowledge management) and then to gradually discard these programs in favor of newer ones. Finally, discourse theorists (Thompson and Davidson, 1995; Zorn *et al.*, 2000) have explained how being immersed in sociocultural discourses promoting particular values and practices leads managers to draw on these discourses as resources in developing and selling strategic organizational changes and leads staff to see such changes as logical "best practice."

These perspectives all point to the notion that, rather than seeing current management practices as the culmination of knowledge that has resulted in steady improvements or progress, contemporary practices reflect transitory beliefs influenced by social pressures and discourses, including a substantial amount of hype by management "gurus," journalists, consulting firms, and business schools. The notion of *management fashion* has been used to describe these trends; like any metaphor, *fashion* foregrounds certain features while masking others. Abrahamson (1996) defined management fashions as "transitory collective beliefs that certain management techniques are at the forefront of management progress" (p. 254) and Spell (2001) defined them as "transitory beliefs that if certain management techniques and practices are pursued, organizational performance will increase" (p. 358).

Of course, to tag a management practice with the term *fashion* is to frame it in a particular way. As Benders and Van Veen (2001) argued, terms such as *fad* and *fashion* are used mainly pejoratively. *Fashion* suggests frivolousness, an emphasis on aesthetics (particularly superficial or surface aesthetics), a concern with image over substance, emotive or nonrational decision making, and short-term or temporary changes rather than long-term, permanent, or stable changes. One can contrast the label of management fashion with alternative ways of framing newly adopted practices: *management knowledge* (or *wisdom*), *best* (or *leading edge*) *practice*, *industry standards*, or *new paradigm*. Thus, our attempt to consider corporate reputation as a fashion could be seen as an attempt to disparage the notion. While certainly we intend to cast a critical eye over organizational practice, we do so not to dismiss the notion of corporate reputation, but in the hope that our efforts will encourage scholars and practitioners to evaluate more carefully their acceptance and use of arguments related to it. Also, it is important to recognize that to say that a concept has characteristics of a management fashion does not mean that it is necessarily misguided or useless. Management tools become successful fashions in part because they highlight ideas that are appealing and sensible. Regarding TQM, for example, who can argue against the idea of improving the quality of products and services by continuously examining and adjusting them?

Since our interest is to identify whether in fact corporate reputation has characteristics of a management fashion, we need to identify the criteria for making such a determination. Table 41.1 summarizes the key characteristics gleaned from the literature. These characteristics reflect substantive features (e.g., *has a management technique, practice, or concept at its heart*), typical rhetorical means of presenting fashions persuasively (e.g., *presented as universally applicable*), as well as fashions' origination and diffusion.

To ask whether or not a particular managerial technique can be understood in terms of a fashion means to enquire about its content, the manner in which it seeks to legitimize itself, its visibility for the network of its producers/users, and the way in which the technique is diffused – or, to put it differently, the way in which it is circulated within the network of those with an interest in its promotion or adoption.

Corporate reputation as a management fashion

To assess the fashion-like qualities of corporate reputation, we focused on the characteristic features of the management fashion listed in Table 41.1. Specifically, we started with a quantitative analysis of scholarly articles devoted to corporate reputation in order to gauge the visibility and the dissemination pattern of the concept – that is, to assess the degree to which the literature demonstrates a bell-shaped popularity life cycle. This approach is combined with a textual analysis of key sources (selected

Table 41.1 Characteristics of management fashions.

Characteristic	Source(s)	Refers to
Has a management technique, practice, or concept at its heart	Abrahamson (1996); Jackson and Rigby (2000)	Substance
Over time, demonstrates a bell-shaped adoption or popularity life cycle	Jackson and Rigby (2000); Spell (2001)	Origins and dissemination
Provides a clear recipe for action	Rolfsen (2004)	Substance
Has its own distinctive lexicon and signifiers	Jackson and Rigby (2000)	Substance and rhetoric
Claimed to enhance organizational performance, often dramatically, if adopted	Benders and Van Veen (2001); Spell (2001)	Rhetoric
Presented as being at the forefront of management progress	Jackson and Rigby (2000)	Rhetoric
Presented as universally applicable	Benders and Van Veen (2001)	Rhetoric
Presented as timely, innovative, and future oriented	Benders and Van Veen (2001)	Rhetoric
Is actively disseminated by the management fashion industry	Jackson and Rigby (2000)	Origins and dissemination
Resonates with problems and concerns that are particularly prominent in an era	Rolfsen (2004)	Rhetoric
Presented as imperative to adopt to prevent disaster or crisis	Benders and Van Veen (2001); Rolfsen (2004)	Rhetoric
Presented as easily understandable with a catchy title or memorable abbreviations of three letters (e.g., TQM, MBO)	Benders and Van Veen (2001); Rolfsen (2004)	Rhetoric
Presented as strategically ambiguous to enable interpretive viability	Benders and Van Veen (2001); Rolfsen (2004)	Rhetoric
Launched in the East Coast of the United States, in particular, by professors from Harvard or MIT	Rolfsen (2004)	Origins and dissemination

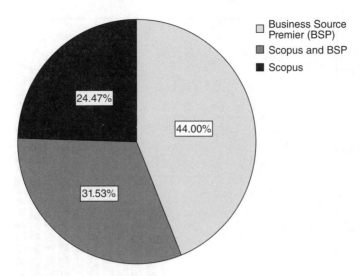

Figure 41.1 Sample structure.

books, articles, and organizational documents) to establish the extent to which certain key fashion characteristics are displayed in corporate reputation discourse.

The life cycle

Despite the well-recognized limitations of the bibliometric analysis used to produce the bell-curve representation of a fashion's life cycle (Benders and Van Veen, 2001; Clark, 2004; Giroux, 2006), it remains widely used in research investigating management fashions, partly because of the logistic and cost barriers to investigating such a large-scale and complex phenomenon as the diffusion of management knowledge (see Nijholt and Benders, 2007, pp. 648–649). If deficient as evidence of the adoption of a particular set of ideas and techniques in practice, bibliometric analysis still offers a useful indication of the popularity of a concept. Like Giroux (2006, p. 1236), we accept here Kieser's (2002) point that "to turn into a management fashion a concept *must* become an object of public discourse" (p. 169).

Our quantitative data come from a combination of two databases: Business Source Premier (BSP) and Scopus. We searched for the presence of "corporate reputation" in abstracts. The BSP search returned 335 articles in aca-

demic journals and 245 in trade and news publications; and the Scopus search returned 255 journal articles and 6 in trade journals. The analysis then focused on the scholarly articles: the relevant parts of the two sets of results were combined and cleaned producing the final sample of 425 items. Figure 41.1 shows the structure of our final sample: 134 of the articles were common to both databases, and the remaining articles were found in one or the other of them (187 in BSP; 104 in Scopus). The differences in coverage are accounted for by two main factors: the inclusion of journals in the database and the extent of their coverage *at the time*. For example, *Strategic Communication Management* was indexed by BSP, but not by Scopus; *Corporate Reputation Review*, although included in both databases, was covered less extensively by Scopus, with some years missing. Although proper care was taken to proceed in a systematic way, these methodological issues lead us to advocate some caution in dealing with the numerical results. It is the overall pattern of the findings that is meaningful rather than any of the findings' constituent parts taken out of context.

Our bibliometric analysis found that the frequency distribution of the journal articles can be represented as a curve that fits the general

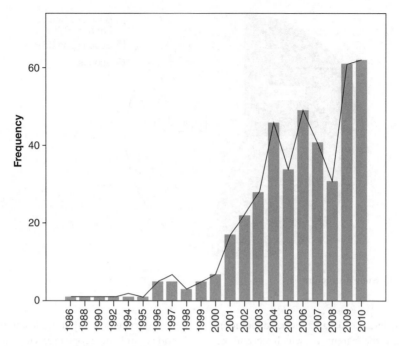

Figure 41.2 Frequency distribution of articles.

pattern for the early stages of a management fashion (see Figure 41.2).

The graph attests to the pattern of very little activity in early 1990s, followed by an increase in the mid-1990s and a surge of interest in corporate reputation from 2001. Whether the interest is currently at its peak or is still growing will only become clear with time. Comparing the life cycle of corporate reputation with those of other fashions offers further support to our proposition: the pattern of distribution would not look out of place among graphs presenting an overview of 36 management fashions tracked in the period of 1950–1995 (Ghemawat, 2000, cited in Rost and Osterloch, 2009, p. 120). Its overall shape, with a long thin run-in time until the mid- to late 1990s, looks similar to that of pay-for-performance (Rost and Osterloch, 2009, p. 122) and even more similar to that of knowledge management, with its thin tail plotted from 1975 until the fashion takes off around 1995 on an incline less steep than that of pay-for-performance (Raub and Rüling, 2000, p. 114).

Our data also help us to think about academic communities who lay claim to the concept of corporate reputation. Spell (2001) used quantitative analysis to provide "a finer grained" picture of the emergence of several management fashions, aiming to identify the role played by "sub-fields or sectors" (p. 337) within the literature, distinguishing between popular business press and academic journals. We use quantitative data generated in this study to answer the question about the importance of corporate reputation for the academic division of labor and constitution of academic disciplines. In order to establish which academic disciplines engage with the concept and how intensely they do so comparing across the disciplines, we coded all the journals in our sample into three disciplines on the basis of the keywords in journal titles: business, management, and accountancy (BMA); communication; and marketing. To compare the disciplines in a more meaningful way, that is, to get round the fact that disciplines might be represented by very different number of journals, we offer a

Table 41.2 Intensity of usage.

Discipline	No. of journals	No. of articles	Average
Corporate reputation	1	64	64
Business ethics	4	27	6.6
BMA (including corporate reputation and business ethics)	68	331	4.9
Communication (including public relations and advertising)	19	78	4.1
BMA (excluding corporate reputation and business ethics)	63	240	3.8
Marketing	15	45	3.0
Other	23	36	1.56

measure of the intensity of usage of the concept, calculated as an average number of articles per journal in a given discipline. As Table 41.2 shows, corporate reputation is part of the knowledge base for business and management, but also for communication and marketing scholars. Within business and management, it is more central to business ethics, understood here as a distinct subdiscipline with its own journals, and is marked as a specialist subject in its own right by the existence of the *Corporate Reputation Review* journal.

To illustrate this intensity of interest in the subject in another way, Table 41.3 lists top 10 journals in terms of the contribution they have made to the visibility of the subject in the academic sphere. *Corporate Reputation Review* accounts for 15% of all the articles in our sample and, together with two communication journals, for over a quarter of the sample. What this analysis shows is that although *corporate reputation* is incorporated into disciplinary knowledge and practices of distinct academic disciplines with different degrees of importance to those disciplines, as a fashion in academic research and publishing, it owes much of its visibility specifically to communication in addition to those in business and management who identify their expertise using the term.

Reputation as discourse

Our exploration of the concept of corporate reputation has revealed that its popularity grew in the pattern characteristic of a management fashion. In this section, we focus on a relatively small amount of purposefully selected material representing different genres of writing about corporate reputation in order to examine the discursive features of corporate reputation, including the constitution of the key entity (corporate reputation); the recipes for action highlighted in the literature; and the strategies of promotion that engender widespread adoption. Our analysis weaves together the discussion of academic exposition, popular exposition in the form of a book aimed at managers/practitioners, and the credentials pitch from consultancy web sites.

The key text in the formative years of the corporate reputation construct was without any doubt Charles Fombrun's (1996) *Reputation: Realizing Value from the Corporate Image*. The book, its author's name, authority, and ideas are directly or indirectly recognized in many subsequent texts and in practice, most visibly in the work of the Reputation Institute. We also chose other texts representing the genre of popular exposition that offer an insight into the practitioner discourse on corporate management. Three criteria guided the selection: the authors spoke from practical experience, they addressed an audience of managers, and the industry or professional endorsement of the ideas presented is clearly signaled in the publication. For example, Haywood's (2005) *Corporate Reputation* bears the logo of the Chartered

Table 41.3 Key journals: journals with the highest frequency of corporate reputation articles 1986–2010.

	Journal title	Frequency	Percent	Cumulative percent
1	Corporate Reputation Review	64	15.1	15.1
2	Strategic Communication Management	15	3.5	24.2
3	Journal of Communication Management	11	2.6	26.8
4	Public Relations Review	11	2.6	29.4
5	Business & Society	10	2.4	31.8
6	Corporate Communications	10	2.4	34.1
7	Management Decision	9	2.1	36.2
8	Australasian Marketing Journal	8	1.9	38.1
9	Industrial Marketing Management	8	1.9	40.0
10	Journal of Product and Brand Management	8	1.9	41.9

Institute of Marketing on the cover. CIM describes itself as "the world's largest organization for professional marketers [with] a key role in training, developing and representing our profession" (http://www.cim.co.uk/about/home.aspx). Griffin's (2008) *New Strategies for Reputation Management* was published in association with the Chartered Institute of Public Relations (CIPR), a key industry body in the United Kingdom. The author is the chief executive of Regester Larkin, "a specialist reputation strategy and management consultancy" (http://www.regesterlarkin.com/). Finally, Gaines-Ross (2008), the author of *Corporate Reputation*, "leads Weber Shandwick's global reputation consulting services and thought leadership development" (http://www.webershandwick.com/Default.aspx/People/LeslieGaines-Ross). The books were published during the decade 2000–2010 so that they offer some opportunity to observe stability and change over time. Finally, they are all highly accessible, as they are promoted and sold through Amazon.com, a leading online bookseller.

The discussion that follows deals with all three dimensions of the management fashion identified earlier (see Table 41.1): its substance, origins and dissemination, and rhetoric.

Substance: The corporate reputation concept: For corporate reputation to be seen as a management fashion, we must establish that it has a management technique, practice, or concept at its heart (Abrahamson, 1996; Jackson and Rigby, 2000). This is clearly the case. In fact, definitions of *corporate reputation* are constructed with reference to its three key features, all of which point to its essence as a management practice: its content, its function, and the set of techniques used to manipulate or manage it. An example of defining the concept in terms of content is Fombrun's early definition, "[corporate reputation consists of] perceptions held by people inside and outside company" (1996, p. 57), or Diermeier's assertion that "reputation is widely considered a core asset, and its protection is near the top of the CEO's agenda" (2011, p. xi).

Defining corporate reputation in terms of function may be seen in numerous authors' lists of advantages and examples of costly failures. Fombrun's (1996) version reads as follows: "Favorable reputations produce tangible benefits: premium prices for products, lower costs of capital and labor, improved loyalty from employees, greater latitude in decision making, and a cushion of goodwill when crises hit" (p. 57). Other authors follow this approach and list specific benefits that can be derived from a good reputation (Doorley and Garcia, 2011; Gaines-Ross, 2008), or express the point more generally, like Haywood: "A good reputation pays. The factors that shape reputation can be managed. The investment in these management initiatives can reap major dividends. And a failure to address reputation issues can be a painful, expensive and even a terminal error" (2005, p. xi).

Finally, corporate reputation is sometimes defined in terms of a set of techniques, or more specifically, measurement techniques. The next section will explore these techniques in more detail, but the important point here is that corporate reputation is viewed as having a set of management techniques at its core. As Fombrun put it, corporate reputation "calls for practices that measure and monitor how the company is doing with its four top constituencies: employees, investors, customers, and communities" (1996, p. 57).

Looking ahead to the discussion of the rhetorical features of corporate reputation, it is important to show at this stage how difficult it may be to draw a clear line between the substance (concept) and the rhetoric employed to present it. Fombrun's work in developing the concept in relation to its organizational functions is careful to position this knowledge in a way that resonates with well-established managerial preoccupations with productivity, profit, product, and the nature of organizations' social legitimacy. This feature is displayed in the commentary that accompanies Fombrun's tabular representation of the concept: "Companies . . . have amassed goodwill and good reputation from pursuing 'excellent' practices in each of four domains: maintaining good workplaces, producing strong financial results, selling good products, and acting like good citizens" (1996, pp. 136–137). Thus, this explanation of corporate reputation could be seen as incorporating the audience it addresses into the definition of the phenomenon by the way in which its key features are chosen. The credibility of *corporate reputation* may depend partly on the way in which the knowledge it articulates about the world can be fitted into the existing managerial discourse and, equally importantly, on the way in which the definition can support the development of systematic managerial practices.

In defining the key concept, the sources we have analyzed also reflect that corporate reputation has its own distinctive lexicon and signifiers,

another key characteristic of management fashion (Jackson and Rigby, 2000). For example, Fombrun (1996) offers *reputational capital*, *reputational risk*, and *reputational audit*, and Gaines-Ross (2008) proposes *reputation recovery*; in fact, *reputation management* itself comes to function as a technical term. Mahon and Mitnick's (2010) contribution of *reputation shifting* and *reputational actions* is an example of continuing efforts to develop and apply the concept in new ways. The effects of this specialist lexicon can be understood as creating entities amenable to expert handling and thus delineating the expert field by means of technical mastery. Both of these play a part in the circulation of the ideas.

Substance: recipes for action

Like all good management fashions (Rolfsen, 2004), corporate reputation textbooks also strive to offer a clear recipe for action. The previous section has demonstrated that corporate reputation was given a clear, if not necessarily narrow, meaning that supports the development of a set of techniques making it usable and useful to managers. Here, we focus on these techniques, or "recipes for action." There are a number of variations offered in the literature that prescribe orchestration of reputation-generating efforts through the use of a sequenced reputation management process. Prominent within these recipes – and elsewhere in the corporate reputation literature – is the importance of measurement of an organization's reputation to establish what action needs to be taken. Therefore, we will first consider the general recipe and then discuss the issue of measurement more specifically.

Corporate reputation management appears to demand a structured sequence of steps: for Morley (1998, p. 15), the process consists of 13 steps; Haywood claims that the concept can be turned into "practical policies" by 20 "key actions" (2005, p. 16); for Gaines-Ross (2008), corporate reputation management is achieved in 12 steps, as the title of her book states. Despite superficial differences – the number of steps, the starting point of the sequence, and the level of generality – there is much that is shared and very familiar in these prescriptions. The underlying model in these schemes is captured by research, action, communication, and evaluation (RACE; Marston, 1979) or Cutlip *et al.*'s (1985) four-step process model of public relations management: problem definition, planning, action and communication, and evaluation. Both models have been staples in public relations textbooks since the 1970s and have been widely adopted in training as well as in education. Both use research at the beginning and at the end of the sequence; in both, action is directed by goals derived from data analysis; and both can be looped back, creating a continuous process, and thus the need for continuous specialist engagement. The various recipes with multiple steps work in precisely such a generic way. For example, Haywood's first six steps list the types of people and types of information to be included in the initial research (or problem definition); steps 7–17 are concerned with action and communication – specifically, policies and their organization-wide implementation; step 18 goes back to research and evaluation to loop the process back to the strategic level of continuous policy adjustment. What is striking in these explanations is the way in which they both reuse and extend the existing practical knowledge: familiar ways of acting and existing practices, such as crisis and issues management, are blended with the newer ideas – integrating reputation into the familiar network of phenomena and concepts – in order to create a distinct new practice of corporate reputation management.

While measurement is typically part of the structured recipes for action discussed earlier, the prominence of measurement in the corporate reputation literature suggests the need to consider it further. Researching the development of corporate reputation measurement, we found two different ways in which the story has been told: a popular, early account (Fombrun, 1996) and slightly later, academic accounts (Berens and van Riel, 2004; van Riel and Fombrun, 2002). The first of these focuses on the popularity of corporate contests and rankings for all manner of products and companies

introduced by trade bodies and business magazines, most significantly here, *Fortune* Magazine's annual rankings of Most Admired Companies established in 1983 (Fombrun, 1996, pp. 166–191, 1997). Their public visibility and resonance attracted much attention (Fombrun *et al.*, 2000, p. 241), including analyses conducted by Fombrun and Shanley (1990a,b) and Shanley and Fombrun (1993). This work led to the identification of two main reputation factors – a company's economic record and its institutional record – and, in 2000, after three years of collaborative work, the launch of the Reputation Quotient^{SM} (RQ) methodology and more recently the RepTrak^{TM} system by the Reputation Institute (van Riel and Fombrun, 2002).

Academic literature tells the measurement story differently: first, the time horizon is extended beyond the popular interest in reputation in the 1980s and 1990s to academic publications going back to the 1950s; second, the discussion reveals a range of conceptual choices and a number of ways in which the focal concepts have been operationalized in existing research (Berens and van Riel, 2004; van Riel and Fombrun, 2002; Walsh *et al.*, 2009). Berens and van Riel's discussion organizes this work into three approaches built around concepts of social expectations, corporate personality, and trust. Each of these, in turn, offers a number of instruments. For example, the RQ RepTrak^{TM} is based on the concept of social expectations, measuring them across five dimensions: products and services, innovation, workplace, governance, citizenship, leadership and financial performance. This approach is markedly similar to the measurement developed in the 1950s by the Opinion Research Corporation (Berens and van Riel, 2004, p. 169). Other authors approached corporate reputation by measuring expectations in two (Brown and Dacin, 1997) or three (Winters, 1986), rather than five, dimensions. The discussion of the remaining two mainstreams of research, similarly, identifies the most widely known instruments, the early work on conceptualization, and the differences between them, explained by the way in which they operationalize the key concept. For example, Davies *et al.*'s (2001) work is seen as key to the corporate personality measurement, while work based on *trust* encompasses a related concept of corporate credibility and its measurement developed by Goldsmith (Lafferty and Goldsmith, 1999; Newell and Goldsmith, 2001).

The main conclusion to draw from this discussion is that corporate reputation fits yet another criterion of a management fashion – it offers clearly articulated recipes for action. Measurement of reputation is a particularly important component of these recipes. Measurement tools provide a concrete basis for action that may be taken up by virtually any organization.

Origins and dissemination: the management fashion industry

The next step in our discussion is to attend to the question of how the concept of and practices associated with corporate reputation originated and spread. Parts of the answer have already emerged: we have identified some of the important texts, people, and institutions, including business media, universities, and consulting organizations. Literature on management fashions has long recognized the key role played by consultants/management practitioners and academics in creating and sustaining fashions (Bos and Heusinkveld, 2007) and noted the presence of the business media and academic journals in their creation and circulation (Fombrun, 1996, 1997; Spell, 2001).

The life cycle curve of *corporate reputation* (see Figure 41.2) shows that academic engagement with the subject intensified from around 2001 onward, coinciding with a heightened interest among practitioners, judged by the number of popular management books on the subject in the last decade (e.g., Alsop, 2004; Dalton and Croft, 2003; Diermeier, 2011; Doorley and Garcia, 2011; Gaines-Ross, 2008; Griffin, 2008; Haywood, 2002, 2005). However, these developments follow earlier, important events: the publication of *Reputation* (Fombrun, 1996) and, on the back of this work, the establishment of the Reputation Institute, and the launch of *Corporate Reputation Review*, both in 1997. Each of these played an important role in the development of the fashion: laying the conceptual and normative basis for the practice; developing and promoting technical tools; and providing a clearly focused academic space for reputation research activity, as our quantitative analysis has shown. The definition, tooling, and circulation of this fashion have been driven jointly by academics and consultants. However, both of these groups recognize that the spark for the intense interest in reputation came from *Fortune*'s annual Most Admired Companies ranking started in 1983.

The third fashion setter to consider is thus the business media. Magazines and business magazines, in particular, are an under-researched area. As Johnson (2007) points out, there is hardly any "industrial" (p. 523) research available in the public domain to help understand business strategies of magazine publishers. Knowledge extracted from media comments and reports from periodical publishers' trade bodies allows us to view the Most Admired Companies ranking as a competitive tactic rather than an intentional addition to managerial knowledge (Speedup, 1978). That is, *Fortune*, *Forbes*, and *Business Week* had traditionally been close competitors in the same market (Carmody, 1994) and each had had success in publishing "top" lists or rankings. For example, *Forbes* launched its ranking of 400 richest Americans in 1982 and *Business Week* published its first annual rating of business schools in 1988. Such rankings have an intuitive appeal and thus enhance circulation and advertising, and also serve to build and extend the magazine's brand (see American Business Media's white papers at http://www.americanbusinessmedia.com/).

Fashion setters operate as a network of organizations and individuals with different interests that find common ground in creation and exploitation of a fashion (Abrahamson, 1996; Perkmann and Spicer, 2008). The interests of each of them – consultancy, academia, and the business media – can be understood in terms of competition for a market position, or as position taking within a professional field.

Magazines traditionally compete for readers and advertisers, but they also work to transform themselves into brands that can be exploited through non-media-content products; consultants compete for business by acquiring and selling specialist knowledge; and academics progress in their careers by demonstrating a track record of research and publishing within the competitive field of their disciplines.

There are a number of ways in which these interests can be shown to overlap in corporate reputation work: the production and exploitation of rankings; acquisition and exploitation of knowledge about the phenomenon of reputation in relation to industry- or sector-relevant issues; the production and exploitation of proprietary instruments for reputation measurement; and publication of books. For example, *Fortune*'s World's Most Admired Companies has been produced by Hay Group, a management consultancy, since 1997. The rankings themselves are published in the magazine and on its online portal CNNMoney. Hay Group further exploits this work by conducting additional research "to find out what business practices make these companies so successful" (Hay Group, 2011). Such research, in turn, builds Hay's perceived expertise and thus increases demand for their services. For example, a Hay Group's newsletter described how the analysis of *Fortune*'s Most Admired Companies led to a better understanding of the strategies used by these companies for executive pay structures gave them a competitive advantage (Wise, 2008).

Rankings can also be useful in the academic context to help establish an expert position and advance one's career, as exemplified by Michael Brown, Professor for Corporate Reputation and Strategy, coauthor of *The Admirable Company*, but more importantly, the expert responsible for Britain's Most Admired Companies research published annually in *Management Today* since 1992, and published prior to that in *The Economist* (Brown and Turner, 2008; "Dr Michael Brown," 2008). Charles Fombrun's and Cees van Riel's professional careers are the most visible examples of the way in which the work on developing *corpo-*

rate reputation could be utilized across both academia and consultancy in ways appropriate to these different fields. Both men have impressive academic records, professorships, publications, editorial involvement with academic journals, not least *Corporate Reputation Review*. Both men are central figures in the Reputation Institute – Fombrun as the founder and chairman, and van Riel as the vice chairman – and have lent their expertise to the development of tools fundamental to the operation of their consulting business (see http://www.reputationinstitute.com/about/index.php).

Corporate reputation thus has been created and circulated in the ways described by the management fashions literature: involving a group of fashion setters, creating and using the knowledge and techniques for their own purposes consistent with the logic of the fields in which they operate. While we have shown the work done at the conceptual and technical level, we have so far not paid much attention to the rhetorical strategies employed by the fashions setters.

Rhetoric: Legitimizing corporate reputation: This section examines the ways in which the fashion for corporate reputation has sought to justify its own existence. There are three primary ways this is done. First, proponents promote the concept as universally applicable and particularly appropriate to the challenges of the times. Second, ambiguity and paradox are employed to gloss over counterarguments and maintain interpretive viability (Benders and Van Veen, 2001). Third, well-known literary and classical references are used to further enhance the wisdom and timelessness of corporate reputation principles.

Universality and timeliness: Management fashions are typically presented as having relevance to a wide variety of organizations, a feature central to their popular appeal (Benders and Van Veen, 2001). The universal applicability of *corporate reputation* is shown in three ways. First, explicit statements are made about the subject. Perhaps the most far reaching of those can be found in Diermeier's (2011) *Reputation Rules*: "The principles of reputation management do not apply only to corporations. They also hold for nonprofits, government agencies, politicians, celebrities, and many others" (p. 29).

Second, the choice of the case study material routinely used in writing about the phenomenon illustrates its relevance to different types of entities. The combined lists of examples found across the popular texts we have selected contain hundreds of names of well-known companies from all sectors of the economy. For example, Fombrun (1996) put together cases drawn from very different sectors: fashion, banking, and education (specifically, business schools). If corporations are the main target for the expertise promoted, there are also examples to show how the concept applies more generally, to give just one example: Gaines-Ross (2008, p. 5) referred to the impact of the botched response to Hurricane Katrina on President Bush's reputation.

Finally, the assessment instruments used in the reputation improvement process suggest universal relevance. For example, the Reputation Institute's Country RepTrak™, City RepTrak™, and Global RepTrak™, by highlighting the applicability of corporate reputation measures to different entities (specifically, countries, cities, and firms, respectively), illustrate further the versatility of the concept.

In addition to its universality, management fashions are rhetorically constructed as timely (Benders and Van Veen, 2001) and resonant with problems and concerns currently prominent (Rolfsen, 2004). Corporate reputation advocates argue that the concept works because it, uniquely, can solve profound and urgent problems faced by the world of business. In particular, corporate reputation is heralded as the solution to the vulnerability created by corporate scandals and failures. Gaines-Ross (2008) highlights the impact of such spectacular corporate failures around the turn of the twenty-first century, and the resulting focus on reputation: "During this post-dot-com and post-Enron period, the ruins of once-heralded industry leaders, corporate failures, and lost

investments defaced a formerly pristine business landscape. Suddenly, all corporations and CEOs were vulnerable. Corporate propriety became a matter of overriding concern" (p. xv).

Dalton and Croft (2003, p. 4) and Griffin (2008), however, paint a picture of the world in which corporate scandals are only one of a number of factors relevant to need for improved corporate reputation management. Globalization, privatization, technological change, trade liberalization, consumer confidence, and the role played by nongovernmental organizations (NGOs) also contribute to an environment in which reputation becomes crucial. Diermeier (2011) reiterates this argument in his new book to conclude that "there will be no return to a 'normal' business environment; instead, the intense scrutiny that companies have been facing over the last decade is the new normal. The underlying forces that elevate reputational concerns are not transitory" (p. ix).

Such an understanding of the contemporary world is, in fact, constructed as a counterpoint to a rather nostalgic view of the past as more rational and controllable, structured in terms of traditional hierarchies and modern values. The view is not unique to this context; the same discourse of a simpler past and a turbulent present that requires new solutions was found in a study of public relations professional training and subsequently conceptualized as part of the structure of public relations professional expertise (Pieczka, 2002). Commonly articulated justifications, thus, can be seen to rely on constructing a shared experience of the world faced by CEOs and organizational leaders.

Ambiguity and paradox: Literature on management fashions has pointed out the fashion's ability to adapt and to travel across different settings (Benders and Van Veen, 2001); *corporate reputation* is no different in this respect as it relies on ambiguity and paradox to sustain its interpretive validity. Let us illustrate this dynamic.

Fombrun's (1996) *Reputation* points out the paradox at the heart of the concept. Corporate reputation is about creating and sustaining uniqueness (pp. 24–27), yet the way to this goal leads through "mundane management" (pp. 20–29). Reputation has powerful and far-reaching consequences, and can be constructed, managed, and measured; at the same time, it is fragile and can be shattered by one false step, by bad luck, or a momentary lowering of the corporate guard (pp. 5–10). The numerous quotations from famous, classical sources present throughout the book send a message that the idea is old and venerable; yet it is also newly discovered – this is what the books, models, and measurement instruments are all about. We have an instinctive understanding of what reputation is: it has a direct, common-sense appeal (p. 4). Yet it is also hard to explain in unambiguous ways. As Griffin (2008) puts it, "We know it's important but we can't agree on exactly what reputation is and what reputation management entails" (p. 12).

The simplicity and the immediate appeal of the concept of corporate reputation are thus juxtaposed with the complexity and opacity of the concept, and it is this paradox that creates the need for expert knowledge and intervention. This ambiguity is central to the continued development of the practice: it allows a diversity of approaches within the practice and powers a continuous search for new explanations and new tools.

Referencing the classics: A distinct feature of the corporate reputation rhetoric is the use it makes of a range of classical sources, most notably Shakespeare. Fombrun's (1996) *Reputation* opens with a quotation from Shakespeare's *Richard II*, "The purest treasure mortal times afford/Is spotless reputation . . ." establishing thus one of the key themes of the book and of much of subsequent work – the value of reputation. In fact, each chapter is preceded by a quotation from a range of Western classics, modern authors, or men of note in the world of politics, business, or sport. Shakespeare is the most frequent source, but we also find Aristotle, Blaise Pascal, Benjamin Disraeli, Robert Frost, Arthur Ash, J.P. Morgan, and Kenneth Boulding, to name just a few. While the use of successful companies' or business leaders' names can be seen as an established way of symbolically

transferring success and credibility onto a fashion (Pieczka and Escobar, 2010), the references to the classics of Western literature or philosophy play a different role: they display cultural capital, that is, cultural and intellectual assets that are associated with high status (Bourdieu, 1986). Fombrun's book is the most elaborate example, but such references occur also in other books, papers, or even conference web sites. "The purest treasure" quotation is, for example, used by Doorley and Garcia (2011); it appears prominently on the web site for the 12th International Conference on Corporate Reputation, Brand, Identity and Competitiveness (http://reputationcapital.org/lang/en/events/id/12th-international-conference-on-corporate-reputation-brand-identity-and-competitiveness-322/), and in a number of other similar contexts revealed by a Google search.

The practice of corporate reputation is thus associated not only with business success; it can also become a mark of social distinction, in the sense given to the term by Bourdieu (1984), thus establishing the difference and hierarchy within the field of management.

Implications

Our discussion has shown that corporate reputation fits the key criteria of a management fashion in the way in which it is defined, applied, disseminated, and supported by its rhetorical features. Is it, therefore, merely a transitory phenomenon, as definitions of a fashion offered at the start of our discussion suggest? As Perkmann and Spicer (2008, p. 813) point out, little research has been done to understand if all fashions are just passing fads, or if some can become more permanent additions to management knowledge and practice. Their work suggests that fashionable practices and ideas may acquire more permanence through institutional work, provided that work uses a mixture of political, cultural, and technical types of institutional work and is conducted by a range of actors, with a range of skills appropriate for the different types of institutional work. In the case of corporate reputation, we see both technical and cultural work conducted at different times by different actors partaking in the process. The crafting of categorizations and tools, creation of models (technical work), as well as grounding of the practice in a broader normative framework (cultural work) (Perkmann and Spicer, 2008, p. 818) are shared between academics and consulting practitioners and, to an extent, by publishers of business magazines, textbooks, as well as academic journals. This suggests that corporate reputation is likely to show a degree of permanence and become part of managerial knowledge.

The extent to which management fashions represent innovation has been contested in the literature, and critics of management fashions tend to see fashions as "old wine in new bottles," merely recycling old ideas. This criticism can be applied to the reputation management process. Clearly, the corporate reputation literature – both popular and scholarly – has borrowed extensively from earlier sources, in particular, literature and practice in public relations. On the other hand, the development of reputation measurement instruments, such as RepTrak™ illustrates a more creative aspect of this putative fashion, pointing again to a greater degree of its permanence.

References

Abrahamson, E. (1996) Management fashion. *Academy of Management Review*, 21(1), 254–285.

Abrahamson, E. (1997) Technical and aesthetic fashion. In B. Czarniawska and G. Sevon (eds), *Translating Organizational Change*. Berlin: Walter de Gruyer, pp. 117–137.

Abrahamson, E. and Fairchild, G. (1999) Management fashion: Lifecycles, triggers, and collective learning processes. *Administrative Science Quarterly*, 44(4), 708–740.

Alsop, R. (2004) *The 18 Immutable Laws of Corporate Reputation: Creating, Protecting & Repairing Your Most Valuable Asset*. London: Kogan Page.

Benders, J. and Van Veen, K. (2001) What's in a fashion? Interpretative viability and management fashions. *Organization*, 8(1), 33–53.

Berens, G. and van Riel, C.B.M. (2004) Corporate associations in the academic literature: Three

main streams of thought in the reputation measurement literature. *Corporate Reputation Review*, 7(2), 161–178.

Bos, R. and Heusinkveld, S. (2007) The guru's gusto: Management fashion, performance and taste. *Journal of Organizational Change Management*, 30(3), 304–325.

Bourdieu, P. (1984) *Distinction: A Social Critique of the Judgment of Taste* [R. Nice, trans.]. London: Routledge.

Bourdieu, P. (1986) The forms of capital. In J. Richardson (ed.), *Handbook of Theory and Research for the Sociology of Education*. New York: Greenwood, pp. 241–258.

Brown, R. and Turner, P. (2008) *The Admirable Company: Why Corporate Reputation Matters So Much and What It Takes to Be Ranked among the Best*. London: Profile Books.

Brown, T. and Dacin, P. (1997) The company and the product. Corporate associations and consumer product responses. *Journal of Marketing*, 61(1), 68–84.

Carmody, D. (1994) The business: A shaper of magazines retires. The New York Times, May 2. Retrieved from http://www.nytimes.com/ (last accessed October 3, 2012).

Carroll, C. (2008) Corporate reputation. In W. Donsbach (ed.), *The International Encyclopedia of Communication* (Vol. 3). Oxford: Wiley-Blackwell, pp. 1018–1021.

Clark, T. (2004) The fashion of management fashion. *Organization*, 11(2), 297–306.

Clark, T. and Salaman, G. (1998) Telling tales: Management gurus' narratives and the construction of managerial identity. *Journal of Management Studies*, 35(2), 137–161.

Cutlip, S., Center, A., and Broom, G. (1985) *Effective Public Relations* (6th ed.). Englewood Cliffs, NJ: Prentice Hall.

Dalton, J. and Croft, S. (2003) *Managing Corporate Reputation*. Thorogood Professional Insight Report. London: Thorogood.

Davies, G., Chun, R., Vinhas Da Silva, R., and Roper, S. (2001) The personification metaphor as a measurement approach for corporate reputation. *Corporate Reputation Review*, 4(2), 113–127.

Diermeier, D. (2011) *Reputation Rules: Strategies for Building Your Company's Most Valuable Asset*. New York: McGraw-Hill.

Doorley, S. and Garcia, H. (2011) *Reputation Management: The Key to Successful Public Relations and Corporate Communication*. London: Routledge.

Dr Michael Brown and Britain's Most Admired Companies. (2008) Nottingham Business School [News story], December 15. Retrieved from http://www.ntu.ac.uk/nbs/news_events/News_archive/75344.html (last accessed 25 January 2013).

du Gay, P. (1996) *Consumption and Identity at Work.* London: Sage.

Fiss, P.C. and Zajac, E.J. (2004) The diffusion of ideas over contested terrain: The (non)adoption of a shareholder value orientation among German firms. *Administrative Science Quarterly, 49,* 501–534.

Fombrun, C. (1996) *Reputation: Realizing Value from the Corporate Image.* Boston: Harvard Business Press School.

Fombrun, C. (1997) Indices of corporate reputation: An analysis of media rankings and social monitors' ratings. *Corporate Reputation Review, 1*(4), 327–340.

Fombrun, C. and Shanley, M. (1990a) What's in the name? Reputation building and corporate strategy. *Academy of Management Journal, 33*(2), 233–258.

Fombrun, C. and Shanley, M. (1990b) Keeping score: Institutional assessment of corporate performance. Working Paper, New York University, New York.

Fombrun, C., Gardberg, N., and Sever, J. (2000) The Reputation Quotient SM: A multi-stakeholder measure of corporate reputation. *Journal of Brand Management, 7*(4), 241–255.

Gaines-Ross, L. (2008) *Corporate Reputation: 12 Steps to Safeguarding and Recovering Your Reputation.* Hoboken, NJ: John Wiley & Sons.

Ghemawat, P. (2000) Competition among management paradigms: An economic analysis. Harvard Business School Working Paper HBS 01-011, 1–28.

Giroux, H. (2006) "It was such a handy term": Management fashions and pragmatic ambiguity. *Journal of Management Studies, 46*(6), 1227–1260.

Griffin, A. (2008) *New Strategies for Reputation Management.* London: Kogan Page.

Hay Group (2011) Success uncovered: *Fortune's* World's Most Admired Companies. [Brochure]. Retrieved from http://www.haygroup.com/ (last accessed October 3, 2012).

Haywood, R. (2002) *Manage Your Reputation: How to Plan Public Relations to Build and Protect the Organization's Most Powerful Asset* (2nd ed.). London: Kogan Page.

Haywood, R. (2005) *Corporate Reputation, the Brand and the Bottom Line: Powerful Proven Communication Strategies for Maximizing Value* (3rd ed.). London: Kogan Page.

Jackson, B. (2001) *Management Gurus and Management Fashions: A Dramatistic Inquiry.* London: Routledge.

Jackson, B. and Rigby, D. (2000) Bringing e-business to New Zealand: The role of the "Big Five" management consulting firms. Paper presented at the European Institute for Advance Studies in Management, Brussels, November 14.

Johnson, S. (2007) Why should they care? The relationship of academic scholarship to the magazine industry. *Journalism Studies, 8*(4), 522–528.

Kieser, A. (2002) Managers as marionnettes? Using fashion theories to explain the success of consultancies. In M. Kipping and L. Engwall (eds), *Managing Consulting: Emergent Dynamics of Knowledge Industry.* Oxford, UK: Oxford University Press, pp. 146–163.

Lafferty, B. and Goldsmith, R. (1999) Corporate credibility's role in consumers' attitudes and purchase intentions when a high versus a low credibility endorses is used in the ad. *Journal of Business Research, 44*(2), 109–116.

Lange, D., Lee, P.M., and Dai, Y. (2011) Organization reputation: A review. *Journal of Management, 37,* 153–184.

Mahon, J. and Mitnick, B. (2010) Reputation shifting. *Journal of Public Affairs, 10,* 280–299.

Marston, J. (1979) *Modern Public Relations.* New York: McGraw-Hill.

Morley, M. (1998) *How to Manage Global Reputation: A Guide to the Dynamics of International Public Relations.* Basingstoke, UK: Macmillan.

Newell, S. and Goldsmith, R. (2001) The development of a scale to measure perceived corporate credibility. *Journal of Business Research, 52*(3), 235–247.

Nijholt, J. and Benders, J. (2007) Coevolution in management fashions: The case of self-managing teams in the Netherlands. *Group and Organization Management, 32*(6), 628–652.

Parker, M. (1992) Post-modern organizations or postmodern organization theory. *Organization Studies, 13,* 1–17.

Perkmann, M. and Spicer, A. (2008) How are management fashions institutionalized? The role of institutional work. *Human Relations, 61*(6), 811–844.

Pieczka, M. (2002) Public relations expertise deconstructed. *Media, Culture and Society*, *24*(3), 301–323.

Pieczka, M. and Escobar, O. (2010) Fashion for dialogue: Dialogue as a management fashion. Paper presented at the Annual Conference of International Communication Association, Singapore, June 2010.

Raub, S. and Rüling, C.-S. (2000) The knowledge management tussle – Speech communities and theoretical strategies in the development of knowledge management. *Journal of Information Technology*, *16*, 113–130.

Rolfsen, M. (2004) The tyranny of trends? Towards an alternative perspective on fads in management. In D. Tourish and O. Hargie (eds), *Key Issues in Organizational Communication*. London: Routledge, pp. 112–129.

Rost, K. and Osterloch, M. (2009) Management fashion pay-for-performance for CEOs. *Society and Business Review*, *61*, 119–149.

Scott, W.R. (1991) The organization of societal sectors. In W.W. Powell and P.J. DiMaggio (eds), *The New Institutionalism in Organizational Analysis*. Chicago, IL: University of Chicago Press.

Shanley, M. and Fombrun, C. (1993) The market impact of reputational rankings. Working Paper, Stern School of Business, New York University, New York.

Speedup. (1978) *Columbia Journalism Review*, March/April, p. 9.

Spell, C.S. (2001) Management fashions: Where do they come from, and are they old wine in new baskets. *Journal of Management Inquiry*, *10*(4), 358–373.

Thompson, P. and Davidson, J.O.C. (1995) The continuity of discontinuity: Managerial rhetoric in turbulent times. *Personnel Review*, *24*(4), 17–33.

Tolbert, P.S. and Zucker, L.G. (1983) Institutional sources of change in the formal structure of organizations: Diffusion of civil service reform, 1880–1935. *Administrative Science Quarterly*, *28*, 22–39.

Van de Ven, A.H. and Hargrave, T.J. (2004) Social, technical, and institutional change: A literature review and synthesis. In M.S. Poole and A.H. Van de Ven (eds), *Handbook of Organizational Change and Innovation*. New York: Oxford University Press, pp. 259–303.

van Riel, C.B.M. and Fombrun, C. (2002) Which company is most visible in your country? An introduction to the special issue on Global RQ-project nominations. *Corporate Reputation Review*, *4*(4), 296–302.

Walsh, G., Mitchell, V., Jackson, P., and Beatty, S. (2009) Examining the antecedents and consequences of corporate reputation: A customer perspective. *British Journal of Management*, *20*, 187–203.

Winters, L. (1986) The effect of brand advertising on company image. Implications for corporate advertising. *Journal of Advertising Research*, *26*(2), 54–59.

Wise, D. (2008) Fortune's Most Admired Companies: Executive compensation practices. The Executive Edition [Newsletter]. Retrieved from http://208.254.39.65/haygroupusmkting/e_000216960000085824.cfm?x=b11,0,w (last accessed 8 December 2012).

Zorn, T.E. and Collins, E. (2007) Is sustainability sustainable? CSR, sustainable business, and management fashion. In S.K. May, G. Cheney, and J. Roper (eds), *The Debate about Corporate Social Responsibility*. Oxford: Oxford University Press, pp. 405–416.

Zorn, T.E. and Taylor, J.R. (2004) Knowledge management and/as organizational communication. In D. Tourish and O. Hargie (eds), *Key Issues in Organisational Communication*. London: Routledge, pp. 96–112.

Zorn, T.E., Page, D., and Cheney, G. (2000) Nuts about change: Multiple perspectives on change-oriented communication in a public sector organization. *Management Communication Quarterly*, *13*(4), 515–566.

42

Reputation and Legitimacy: Accreditation and Rankings to Assess Organizations

Jennifer L. Bartlett
Queensland University of Technology, Australia

Josef Pallas
Uppsala University, Sweden

Magnus Frostenson
Uppsala University, Sweden

A key perspective on reputation is that of assessment. Much of the communication literature focuses on the influence organizations have on impression formation. In this chapter, however, we suggest that in order to understand reputation assessment, it is also important to understand the related concept of legitimacy. We address two approaches to understanding reputation in this chapter: accreditation and ranking. Accreditation alludes to concepts of legitimacy in which firms may acquire credibility by meeting formalized standards of certification. Ranking deals with categorizing and rating organizational reputations so that they may be assessed relative to one another. The chapter explores the various ways in which the mechanisms of accreditation and ranking operate and the role of social actors in developing and applying them. Ranking systems that provide the mechanism for comparing organizations and assessing their relative value are also explored.

The notion of corporate reputation has developed since the 1980s into a concept that is widely used both in the academy and in practice. While scholars differ on the specifics of defining the term *reputation* (Fombrun and van Riel, 1997), there is greater consensus around how it has been used in the literature.

Barnett suggests that the multitude of reputation definitions have been used in three ways: awareness, assessment, and as an asset. The predominant perspective is of reputation as assessment (Barnett *et al.*, 2006). Such a perspective reflects Fombrun and van Riel's (1997) assertion that "a corporate reputation is a col-

The Handbook of Communication and Corporate Reputation, First Edition. Edited by Craig E. Carroll.
© 2013 John Wiley & Sons, Inc. Published 2015 by John Wiley & Sons, Inc.

lective representation. . . . It gauges a firm's relative standing both internally with employees and externally with stakeholders" (p. 10).

Relative assessment of organizations, however, suggests that first organizations meet standards in order to then be judged in relation to each other. One way to consider this two-part phenomenon is to consider the related concepts of legitimacy and reputation (Deephouse and Carter, 2005). On the one hand, reputation is about the assessment of future value and relativity (Fombrun and Shanley, 1990). Legitimacy, on the other hand, relates to meeting social expectations (Deephouse and Carter, 2005). To date, much of the communication literature has focused on an instrumental perspective of maximizing the way organizations can influence the impressions it makes on others and therefore its reputation (van Riel, 1997). This chapter pays particular attention to social expectations (legitimacy) as the assessment process occurs. We do this by examining the relative standing of organizations (reputation), and the processes of accreditation and ranking that achieve this. We also pay attention to the roles of various social actors in this process: the role of organizations in shaping perceptions and the role of external social actors, particularly those that can exert soft regulatory pressure on organizations and ranking systems.

Fombrun and van Riel's (1997) seminal piece on the reputational landscape noted that there are multiple approaches to corporate reputation – economic, strategic, marketing, organizational, sociological, and accounting. Marketing and organizational approaches tend to favor personalized assessment and subjective perceptions of a firm. Economic and strategic approaches incorporate both the antecedents and consequences of reputation for firm values. The accounting model focuses on both accounting for and reporting on reputation, which also includes attempts to quantify and account for intangible firm assets such as reputation. For sociologists, the interest is in prestige and status and how reputation, with its emphasis on comparative stature, is conceptualized. To shed light on legitimacy, reputation, accreditation,

and ranking, we draw on a sociologically informed perspective. This provides insights into the mechanisms of how socially agreed standards emerge against which organizations and their reputations are compared and rated. It also yields insights into the social actors involved in this process and the implications for research into reputation. The reputation literature has focused on the raft of proprietary models organizations used in practice to make such assessments (Hillenbrand and Money, 2007), and we consider the role of these models in the accreditation and ranking process.

We address two approaches to understanding reputation in this chapter: ranking and accreditation. *Ranking* is about categorizing and ranking organizational reputations so that they may be considered in comparison to others. *Accreditation* alludes to concepts of legitimacy in which firms may acquire credibility by meeting formalized standards of certification. Central to understanding this perspective on reputation is the concept of legitimacy, which is widely used in sociological perspectives of organization studies. Using this as a theoretical underpinning, the chapter explores the various ways in which these mechanisms operate and the role of social actors in developing and applying them. Ranking systems provide the mechanism for comparing organizations and assessing their relative value; theoretical and empirical work around reputation assessment is presented and tensions revealed. Finally, directions for future research are discussed.

Legitimacy and Reputation

Legitimacy is the central imperative of neo-institutional theory, the dominant perspective in organization theory (Greenwood *et al.*, 2008). Institutional accounts dealing with the issue of legitimacy tend to emphasize that legitimacy for groups of organizations depend on the adaptation of organizational practices or structures to "symbolic myths" reflecting normative ideas or assumptions in society (Meyer and Rowan, 1977). While this discussion often focuses on groups of organizations or the overarching field, legitimacy has in recent decades become a concept that is looked on strategically in the management literature. Typical of the management literature is the treatment of legitimacy as a strategic resource (Pfeffer and Salancik, 1978). This means that legitimacy, whether moral (building on value correspondence), pragmatic (resting on self-interested assumptions), or cognitive (reflecting meaningfulness or comprehensibility), is understood at the organizational level as something that could and should be managed in order to get hold of other resources (Suchman, 1995). Research on legitimacy has, one could claim, gone through a "strategic turn" in which the concept has been transformed into something that the individual organization can, at least to some extent, actively manage through manipulation or other strategic activities (Deephouse and Suchman, 2008; Suchman, 1995). This development has also implied the proximity of legitimacy to the concept of reputation, which is also dependent on evaluations made in the organizational environment (Fombrun, 1998).

The link between legitimacy and reputation is clear. For instance, Suchman (1995, p. 574) defined legitimacy as "a generalized perception or assumption that the actions of an entity are desirable, proper, or appropriate within some socially constructed system of norms, values, beliefs, and definitions," and Deephouse and Suchman (2008, p. 59) described reputation as "a generalized expectation about a firm's future behavior or performance based on collective perceptions (either direct or, more often, vicarious) of past behavior or performance." While the generation and sources of both legitimacy and reputation are more or less similar, reputation seems to be an issue at the organizational level that involves, to a higher degree than legitimacy, future expectations on behavior. Reputation, thus, is a continuous measure that is also relative to other organizations in a certain sector or other sectors. Its essence lies in comparison among organizations, according to Deephouse and Carter (2005). As they noted in a study of commercial US banks, in line with traditional assumptions about legiti-

macy, isomorphism (the pressure to create similar structures and processes within a field) increases legitimacy. But this does not imply effects on reputation for each organization active in the specific field; rather, the reputation of an organization is relative to other organizations in the sector. Deephouse and Carter also noted that higher financial performance tends to increase reputation, but does not increase the legitimacy of high performing banks.

The strategic turn in legitimacy research underscores the fact that legitimacy can be understood at different levels. Societal legitimacy is closely linked to the existence of overarching ideas – those that are successful or popular with a strong capacity of diffusion. By adopting or conforming to such ideas (often in a modified or "translated" form, see Sahlin and Wedlin, 2008), organizations are perceived as legitimate in a social context. What is striking when one turns to organizational legitimacy at the micro level is the fact that organizations adopt different strategies whose outcomes are dependent on the ruling or dominant master idea, such as shareholder value or the ideology of globalization. This means that there is always a discursive backdrop to organizational processes for legitimacy.

Mazza and Alvarez (2000) suggested that legitimacy is a concept that is also valid for management ideas or practices. Their analysis, much like accounts of management ideas as fads (e.g., Abrahamson, 1996), suggests that organizations can, to some extent, obtain legitimacy by adopting management concepts or practices that are in vogue. This is a form of indirect legitimation of organizations, where the adoption or existence of a certain practice (cf. activities related to corporate social responsibility (CSR)) may in itself contribute to organizational legitimacy. Management ideas may originate at some authoritative center (Røvik, 2004) and are diffused through management education institutions, consultants, the popular press, or other actors. From a managerial point of view, it is, perhaps paradoxically enough, possible for organizations with high legitimacy to deviate from established practices (Sherer and Lee, 2002). Legitimacy thus enables change and provides a degree of freedom for developing new practices or structures. One consequence of this is that legitimacy – most easily gained by conforming to environments (Suchman, 1995) – may itself be a resource that allows for heterogeneity rather than homogeneity. If so, there is a possibility for business schools, taking them as an example, to develop programs, practices, or structures deviating from standards.

The concept of legitimacy allows us to consider the role organizations play in seeking to manage the way others see them and, as such, lays the foundations for assessing organizational reputation relative to others. Accreditations and rankings play an integral role in reputational assessment.

Accreditations and Rankings: The Signals of Legitimacy and Reputation

Contemporary organizations are subjected to organizational as well as institutional pressures to be accountable for their activities. These pressures are not only expressed in terms of financial and economic effectiveness and adjustment to legal and regulatory constraints; the organizations are also expected to project and justify their commitments to moral values and social norms and expectations (Djelic and Sahlin-Andersson, 2006; Engwall et al., forthcoming). In many cases, these expectations have traditionally been the domain of other societal institutions (Beck et al., 1994), which expose the organizations to a number of reputational and legitimacy risks (Power et al., 2009; Solove, 2007). This is especially important in times when organizations operate in an environment characterized by increased distrust and lack of confidence in corporate affairs (Frostenson et al., 2010).

The institutional demands come, however, only partly in terms of coercive measures. Instead, they take a form of soft regulation – rules and norms that emerge through the work of nonhierarchical actors that scrutinize,

monitor, and evaluate organizations and their activities (Jacobsson and Sahlin-Andersson, 2006, p. 259; Mörth, 2004). Regulation, both hard and soft, has led to the emergence of a wide variety of external evaluations and audits that describe and assess how well organizations deal with and respond to the different pressures and expectations (Power, 1997; Wedlin, 2007). These external audits are central to what Suchman (1995) described as evaluative and cognitive dimensions of legitimacy (see also DiMaggio and Powell, 1983; Meyer and Rowan, 1977). Such external auditing, in its various forms, operates as a tool for defining the constitutional properties of organizations. That is to say, auditing reflects organizational ability to gain or defend a favorable position in relevant societal contexts such as industries, fields, or entire societies (Power, 2007; see also Deephouse and Carter, 2005; DiMaggio and Powell, 1983).

Societies are not static or monolithic, however, and the evaluative processes do not represent absolute or consistent values and norms. In this context, the various auditing firms and agencies take an active role in production of codes, rankings, certifications, and accreditations through which organizations such as business firms, universities, museums, and political parties are assessed and evaluated (Sahlin-Andersson and Engwall, 2002; Wedlin, 2007).

In the following section, we will focus on two major forms of external audits – accreditations and ranking – and the way they signal the legitimacy and reputational status of organizations. In line with Deephouse and Carter's (2005) discussion of the difference between legitimacy and reputation, we see ranking as mainly based on the "relative standing or desirability" of an organization, whereas accreditation focuses on "meeting and adhering to the expectations of a social system's norms, values, rules and meanings" (Deephouse and Carter, 2005, p. 331).

Similarly, Hedmo et al. (2006) argued that rankings and accreditations differ with respect to the underlying principles of what they focus on: "while accreditation rests on inclusion, ranking rest on exclusion. A ranking puts in place a hierarchy between those included, and the inclusion of some means the exclusion of others" (p. 322). Thus, rankings not only provide an external assessment of organizational reputation, but also signal the positional status of an organization vis-à-vis its different stakeholders (Sauder, 2006). This means that whereas some forms of auditing – such as accreditations and certifications – emphasize legitimacy as based on conformity with prevailing institutional values and norms, other forms – such as rankings and awards – work on the basis of how well an organization scores on these values and norms relative to other organizations sharing same institutional environment (Wedlin, 2007, p. 25).

The legitimacy signals expressed by accreditation processes testify to an organization's ability and desire to imitate the models and prescriptions included in the accreditation criteria (Hedmo *et al.*, 2006, p. 203). By their inclusive and imitative function, accreditations serve to spread and stabilize prevailing institutional values, rules, models, and ideas among organizations occupying same social landscape (cf. DiMaggio and Powell, 1983, p. 152; Hedmo *et al.*, 2006, p. 309).

Ranking and its impact on an organization's reputation influence the status positions of organizations and embeds organizations in status hierarchies that shape relations within relevant fields (Rao, 1994; Sauder, 2006). Ranking and reputational status thereby also signal an organization's propensity to actively adopt and respond to revised or innovative methods, criteria, and principles for assessment (Sauder, 2006). Thus, rankings order organizations with respect to their abilities, values, and assumptions not only of what is considered proper and legitimate but also of what is considered competitive and distinctive (Elsbach and Kramer, 1996; Rao, 1994).

Ranking Systems

Much of the work on rankings in the reputation literature involves identifying and understanding the various ranking systems available. While there have been various forms of public rankings of organizations conducted especially through the media, the surge of interest in and proliferation of ranking systems has emerged concurrent with the emergence of reputation in the literature. The Reputation Institute identified 183 ranking systems across 38 countries (Fombrun, 2007). The majority of the lists were based on whether an organization was a good place to work, or on overall reputation. The remaining public lists rated or ranked firms on the basis of citizenship, performance, innovation, governance, or products (Fombrun, 2007). The reputation rankings are not based on financial performance but on "soft(-er)" factors such as citizenship and governance (Fombrun, 2007).

The variety of reputation ranking lists and the criteria on which they assess firms are in themselves the subject of study (Campbell and Sherman, 2010). One of the chief issues with the reputation ranking lists is being able to compare the outcomes for each firm. There are two key reasons for the differences in ranking outcomes for firms between ranking systems. The first is the methodology used to assess reputation. The second is the differences in the criteria on which firms are assessed (Schultz *et al.*, 2001). These differences create significant variation between which organizations feature high on the lists and raise questions about the value of reputation rankings as a measure of organizational performance and value.

From a communicative perspective however, high rankings are an important indicator that communicate with stakeholders about the organization's relative worth. As such, achieving a ranking, especially a high level one, provides a distinctive attribute that forms part of an organization's identity. Such symbols of status provide useful references to facilitate identification and alignment with an organization by both insiders and outsiders to the organization (Hatch and Schultz, 1997). This again highlights the strategic turn organizations have taken in seeking to manage legitimacy and reputation.

Strategic Action around Reputation

If reputation is relative and future looking, accreditation and rankings play important roles in the mechanisms of reputation. These roles rely on two elements, which we will now discuss – the strategic communication work of organizations to show that they are legitimate and to highlight the dimensions in which they are distinctive, and the assessment work by a variety of social actors to rate organizational legitimacy.

Organizations' strategic attempts to manage legitimacy

The journal *Corporate Reputation Review* highlights the fact that understanding reputation is a multidisciplinary arena which brings together various views around the concept (Fombrun and van Riel, 1997). Earlier in this chapter, we focused on the contribution that sociological perspectives and organization theory make to understanding the accreditation and ranking dimensions of reputation. This literature noted the strategic attempts of various social actors to shape perceptions of organizational compliance and alignment with social standards and to make comparisons between organizations and their attributes. This highlights the role of communication in the phenomena surrounding reputation, a role considered in both the management and communication literatures.

Within the management literature, one stream of legitimacy research focuses on the rhetoric for obtaining legitimacy for action. As Erkama and Vaara (2010) noted, legitimacy is actively sought through different rhetorical strategies. The dynamics of legitimation involve justifying actions, decisions, and structures by means of well-known rhetorical strategies such as *logos* (rational arguments), *pathos* (emotional arguments), and *ethos* (reference to authority), as well as what these authors call *autopoeisis* (autocommunication or self-invented narratives about who we are, for

example, correspondence with self-formulated strategies or visions) and *cosmos* (a reference to "predetermined" inevitable change mechanisms at a higher societal level). Such strategies are of course not only a possibility for management, but also a possibility for individuals or groups trying to resist management action or plans, for example, those related to shutdowns of production sites. From this perspective, legitimacy is a resource emanating from a discursive struggle. As Vaara and Tienari (2008) noted, such a struggle may involve the use of different discursive elements like *authorization* (legitimation by referring to authority), *rationalization* (legitimacy based on perceived utility of action), *moralization* (values-based legitimation), and *mythopoesis* (legitimation through narratives). Erkama and Vaara (2010) see a particularly prominent role for *autopoeisis* as a strategy for advancing legitimacy in a sensitive shutdown case of a production site. This strategy has to do with what the organization formulates its nature and identity to be. Institutions that have deeply rooted self-images (such as educational institutions) often try to strengthen this identity through spelling out codes and other documents that endorse this self-image.

Communication scholars have also contributed to our understanding in numerous ways. *Corporate Reputation Review* emphasizes the role of corporate communication in managing reputation. Van Riel (1997) suggested that strategic and integrated corporate communication is one of the most promising ways for organizations to manage their reputation. Van Riel (1995) argued that coordinated communication activities from advertising, marketing, and public relations departments within the organization are significant contributors to perceptions of the organization. This view suggests that communication about the organization's identity results in images of the organization. From this perspective, the images held by multiple stakeholders over time create the reputation of an organization (van Riel, 1995).

Such communication is not only an externally focused matter. Communication to employees is also the subject of significant attention in the literature. Research on image and identity highlights the integral role of employees in the process. This was first noted with the suggestion that employees play a significant role in influencing the image of an organization (Kennedy, 1977). Every time an employee has an interaction with another stakeholder, especially one outside the organization, he or she is bringing to life the identity of that organization (Hatch and Schultz, 1997). Employees play an active role both in presenting the corporate identity to those outside the organization and in translating insights about the organizational image back into the organization, which can further shape the identity and identity symbols (Hatch and Schultz, 2002). For example, Dutton *et al.* (1994) showed in the Port Authority case that when an organization's legitimacy was questioned, the employees' individual identity was also challenged. In the Port Authority case, employees were active in influencing management to change corporate practices to influence the organization's legitimacy. This suggests that organizations need to actively substantiate their reputation with employees across the organization. Fombrun (2007) argued that it is imperative to communicate reputation to managers as well as how to use it and what it means for them. Similarly, Dowling (2004) discussed the importance of storytelling with employees in order to continue to highlight and substantiate the distinctive elements of the organization's reputation, and to therefore replicate these areas of differentiation.

This focus on the role of corporate communication in influencing reputation has also led to suggestions that this organizational function is in fact responsible for reputation. This is an assumption and claim made often by practitioners and is reflected in the number of public relations firms that describe their practices as reputation management (Bartlett and Hill, 2007). However, this claim is problematic as it can lead to claiming responsibility for aspects of reputation which are outside the control of the communication professional (Hutton *et al.*, 2001). Hutton *et al.* (2001) noted that because reputation is considered on a range of organizational attributes such as product quality,

governance, leadership qualities, and the like, the communication professional cannot be responsible for such attributes and therefore for reputation as a whole.

Particular attention has been paid to the role of the media in relation to legitimacy, reputation, and ranking. This has been examined from two perspectives. The first has focused on the influence of the media as a communication channel on reputation. Given the prior discussion on corporate communication, this perspective views the role of the media in firms' strategic communication attempts to influence and manage reputation. The second perspective, which we will discuss later, focuses on the media as social actors in their own right. This allows us to consider the media's role in ranking reputations.

As Deephouse and Suchman (2008) noted, studies are increasingly using different sources through which legitimacy can be measured or estimated – for example, media statements, certification, licensing, endorsements, and links to prestigious organizations. This management perspective highlights the role of media in disseminating information about organizational attributes that in turn contribute to the perception of an organization's legitimacy. From the communication perspective, Carroll and McCombs (2003) elaborate on the influence of media coverage on reputation. Drawing on the influential work on the role of media agenda setting, Carroll and McCombs posited that just as media agendas can influence the salience and attributes of political issues and opinions, media coverage can also influence opinions about corporate reputation. For example, media coverage about an organization achieving a particular certification or accreditation then influences opinion about that organization. The individual level effects on opinions contribute not only to how organizations and corporate activities are perceived to comply with social and institutionalized norms (accreditation), but also to a cognitive ranking schema of organizations in relation to one another.

The news media also play a role as social actors in their own right in shaping perceptions of an organization and influencing elements related to reputation. Through this lens, the media are playing a purposive role in reputation and legitimacy management. In the organization theory literature, the role of the media has been understood as that of a legitimating agent (Deephouse and Suchman, 2008), conferring legitimacy on organizations and corporate practices. This provides a useful perspective from which to consider the role of both accreditation and ranking. Rather than seeing the media as merely providing information about an organization for individual audience members to make sense of, this perspective highlights the role of the media as social actors in determining what is appropriate at a societal level.

In such a view, the role of the media is emphasized – alongside those of other institutional intermediaries such as academia, consultants, and industry associations – as central for building an organization's reputation. The extent and patterns of media coverage are directly involved in the way an organization's reputation accumulates and evolves, not least by way of the media's varying focus on different reputational components such as visibility, level of distinctiveness, and tenor (cf. Greenwood *et al.*, 2005; Rindova *et al.*, 2007). As Pollock and Rindova (2003) found, media visibility has a strong effect not only on name recognition of a firm, but also on the firm's market and financial performance (see also Jonsson and Buhr, 2011; Jonsson *et al.*, 2009).

The ability of the media to influence the social status of individual organizations (e.g., reputation) is in this context intimately related to the proliferation of media products such as rankings, certifications, and accreditations (Fombrun, 1998; Power *et al.*, 2009). These are often mentioned as major drivers of the way organizations are perceived, evaluated, and acted on (Deephouse, 2000; Fombrun, 1998; Pollock and Rindova, 2003). Rhee and Valdez (2009), in discussing how organizational age and diversity of market segmentation influence stakeholders' perception of an organization, included media-based quality ratings, winning awards, and certifications as contributing both to reputational damage and to organizational ability to retain a positive stand (p. 154).

As discussed earlier in the chapter, ranking and accreditations work differently in their ability to discriminate between organizations sharing joint social contexts (ranking) and the extent to which organizations are perceived as following normative prescriptions and constraints (accreditations). Through publishing of ranking lists, awards, and accreditations, the media's involvement in reputation building is connected to their function to (1) affiliate organizations with prominent/deviant field members and (2) spread and proliferate moral and professional norms, values, and expectations (Carey, 1992; Jonsson and Buhr, 2011; Jonsson *et al.*, 2009; Rao *et al.*, 2000; Wry *et al.*, 2006).

The later form of media involvement in reputation building – the creation, translation, and distribution of models, ideas, and other normative thoughts about what an organization is, should be, or want to be – is also a part of the identity formation of individual organizations as well as the contexts (e.g., organizational fields) that the organizations are a part of (Sahlin-Andersson and Engwall, 2002). Media-framed identity formation and its evaluation and categorization is a central part of reputational status because it addresses the increasing need of organizations to clarify and communicate who they are, what they stand for, and what moral standards they are built on (Schultz *et al.*, 2000).

The way in which organizations can access and influence media and their coverage has far-reaching consequences not only for their immediate market and financial performance but also for their long-term ability to build institutional foundations – such as reputation and legitimacy – for their survival (Motion and Weaver, 2005; Pallas and Fredriksson, 2011). Meijer and Kleinnijenhuis (2006) showed in the context of business news how the second-level effect of agenda setting influence reputation of organizations. They not only confirmed earlier findings concerning the way news about a certain issue stimulated the salience of that issue, but also introduced an ownership perspective, suggesting that if organizations are perceived as not controlling the issue, they may also suffer reputation losses (see also Eisenegger and Imhof, 2008; Schultz *et al.*, 2001).

Nongovernmental organizations (NGOs), consultants, and other social actors

Ranking the reputation of organizations has also been taken up by NGOs and business consultancies and contributes to the plethora of ranking systems. The notion of transparency as a business imperative around social and environmental activities has evolved from the central neoliberal market principle that open information facilitates efficient markets (Nadesan, 2011). While governments have not regulated this sector as they have financial markets, they have supported the role of NGOs in providing checking and monitoring systems for business activity (Nadesan, 2011) that might contribute to reputation.

Rindova *et al.* (2005) conceptualized reputation as including two elements: economic and marketing attributes that illustrate an organization's ability to generate desirable products and services and thereby economic profit, and institutional recognition placing organizations in a context of larger societal settings such as organizational fields (see also Wedlin, 2006). Even though the latter has been found to be more decisive in terms of effect on organizational reputation (Rindova *et al.*, 2005, p. 1044), contemporary research suggests that both of these components are necessary to understand the accumulative/historical and relative evaluation of organizational performance (Jonsson and Buhr, 2011; Rindova *et al.*, 2006).

Ranking is also a commercial arena where different actors compete with each other to establish their own criteria for inclusion and exclusion. It is notable, for instance, that ranking indices are managed by private consulting firms. One example is the Dow Jones Sustainability Indices, where the Swiss consulting firm SAM plays a constitutive role in assessing the sustainability performance of companies from all industries. Following a best-in-class approach, companies are evaluated against a number of long-term economic, social, and environmental criteria. Indices may also be values based (only including companies living up to certain values) or compiled according to other criteria. Often, commercial actors like KLD combine these indexing and rating services with the screening of companies according to social or environmental investment criteria with other traditional consulting services. It is evident that corporate ranking and reputation has created a commercial industry marked by active product and service innovation. For companies and other ranked or rated institutions, the downside of this is not only the risk of reputational loss but also the burden of information placed on them by the actors in the field. Nonsynchronized forms and questionnaires from a variety of competing actors must be filled out, and this task becomes in itself a full-time duty for employees, for example, at the communications or CSR departments (cf. Dubbink *et al.*, 2008).

One should also bear in mind that media rankings are often carried out with the assistance of commercial actors. One example is the *Newsweek* 2010 Green Ranking, an assessment of the largest companies in the United States and in the world. These rankings were the result of teamwork between *Newsweek* and three commercial research organizations within the environmental field. This also shows that there is a connection not only between the media and NGOs when it comes to monitoring companies (Grafström *et al.*, 2008), but also between commercial organizations and the media in terms of ranking and rating.

One corollary of the expansion of the ranking industry is that intermediaries such as consultancies play a dual role when it comes to ranking and reputation. They are part of the ranking industry while at the same time benefitting from the existence of the ranking industry because they assist commercial actors and others in the quest for improving reputations. And recently, a new arena for consultants has been created by the rise of social media, where the ranking and rating industry to some extent becomes privatized.

Academic literature on the relationship between social media and reputation is still limited, but parallels can be made; social media provides a broadcast form of word of mouth that has impacts in terms of both dissemination of information in the same way that traditional mass media have functioned. However, social media has an added dimension of personal influence in that the information from person to person influences the perceptions of the subject (Katz and Lazarsfeld, 1964). If we consider reputation as largely based on perceptions, then social media raises numerous issues about organizations' ability to attempt to manage perceptions of the organization. It also allows a range of social actors to influence large numbers of people about organizations and organizational attributes.

Scholarly Tensions and Future Research

While reputation has been a central concern for practitioners, there is relatively little attention paid to accreditation and ranking in the communication literature. As noted earlier, much of the literature around reputation arises from an applied area of corporate communication that encompasses public relations, integrated marketing communications, and employee communication. There is also an arm of marketing literature devoted to image, identity and branding, and reputation that is significant. Media and reputation work is arguably the most theoretically sophisticated. The concept of the reputation ranking process, however, is inherent within all these discussions, as previously mentioned, in terms of their role in capturing future expectations (Deephouse and Suchman, 2008) and relativity (Deephouse and Carter, 2005).

Much of the existing work has considered the role of reputation – which is inherently work on rankings – as an antecedent or consequence of various organizational performance factors. For example, the relationship between financial performance and reputation has been noted. These are not overtly the domain of communication scholars. The role of communication has centered more on the communication or

dissemination of reputation attributes, accreditations, and rankings to influence the perception of an organization. Van Riel (1995), for example, suggested that this is one of the most important contributors to reputation for an organization. This process, however, can be understood at multiple levels. The first is from the organization's perspective, focusing on their strategic approach to communicating the distinctive attributes of their business while also managing the legitimacy of their business or alignment with existing rules. The second focuses on the role of the channels of this communication. The third focuses on the perception formation of the communicated attributes and on reputation.

Strategic communication, reputation, rankings, and accreditation

The role of communication in seeking to strategically manage reputation is prominent in the literature, which leads us to consider the structure-agency debate. At present, the applied communication perspective of communication and reputation reflects a largely instrumental approach to the phenomena surrounding reputation which emphasizes the agentic approach. However, the implication at a macro level is that multiple organizations engaging in the reputation ranking competition creates effects in its own right. At one level, the largely instrumental approach institutionalizes the emphasis on organizational performance on nonfinancial measures which aligns with the CSR movement and the triple bottom-line imperative for organizations. It is also related to governance and transparency movements where, again, a range of organizational matters are of importance for executives.

Channel

The internal–external dimension of employees' impacting how their firm is perceived also opens up a host of research opportunities for examining the role of employees as channels of communication related to reputation. Hatch and Schultz (1997, 2002) have discussed the intertwining of the internal and external aspects of how organizations seek to construct what is distinctive about them, and also the role of employees in interpreting and enacting those desired images. There is also a literature on "dirty work" (Ashforth and Kreiner, 1999) and the role of employees in managing their own and the organization's reputation when that reputation is very poor. This highlights the paradox of organizations that can continue to operate and be considered legitimate, while at the same time having a poor reputation.

This requires us to consider the implications of rating and accreditations in the perception formation process. Accreditations and ratings are evaluated and awarded by specific social actors (e.g., formal accreditation bodies, the media, NGOs). The question is how the achievement of accreditation and ranking is communicated to others, how perceptions are formed, and what the implications are for other relationships and dimensions of the organization–stakeholder relationship. There is an assumption that a good ranking leads to greater access to resources. This further suggests that the perceptions of some stakeholders are more important than those of others, particularly in relation to their ability to provide access to resources. Therefore, the instrumental suggestion that good employee communication is important for reputation requires far deeper exploration and understanding. This might relate to how knowledge of accreditation and ranking may boost the identification between employee and organization and, in turn, higher levels of service provision, third-party endorsement, and problem solving.

The existing consideration of the role of employees in the third-party endorsement process also requires extension as the boundaries of organizations continue to expand. As noted earlier, to date, there has been limited empirical research on the role of social media in relation to reputation, and while there is considerable interest in the topic, this work remains in its nascent stages. However, social media opens up organizational boundaries in two ways. First, social media gives stakeholders who are perceived to have credible knowledge about an organization a platform from which their views may be constructed, accessed, and disseminated. This is particularly so in an environment characterized by increased distrust and lack of confidence in organizational operations (Frostenson *et al.*, 2010). Second, the potential reach in disseminating information about the organization through social media is global.

Role of evaluating organizations

Constructing the guidelines for accreditation and ranking organizations opens up important questions about communication – not for the focal organizations who are the subject of reputation rankings, but for those organizations creating and employing the guidelines. These groups often include NGOs, media, and social movement groups (Engwall *et al.*, forthcoming). The management literature has paid little attention to these groups, particularly in relation to legitimacy (Deephouse and Carter, 2005). The role of these groups in the broader process of constructing the norms underpinning accreditation and ranking also opens up theoretical research opportunities. The social constructionist perspective, for example, can be useful in this task. Because societies, legitimacy, and evaluation standards are constantly evolving (Meyer and Rowan, 1977), the role of communication in the processes through which this takes place offers important opportunities for further research. One perspective is on the role of communication as organization (Cooren, 1999) so that communication constitutes the organization and the meaning of its attributes. Lammers and Barbour (2006) also suggested that the insights on the social construction of reality from institutional theory (Meyer and Rowan, 1977/1991) can also add macro level perspectives to understanding communication phenomena. These perspectives allow communication and management studies to inform each other in relation to how communication studies allow us to understand the ways that social norms develop and how accreditation and ranking systems evolve. Doing this allows a shift in the exploration of reputation away from the instrumental perspective, which is largely at the level of the organization and management of perceptions, to a broader perspective from which legitimacy and reputation as social norms and organizational differentiation can be studied.

Conclusion

In this chapter, we have examined the role of accreditation and rankings in relation to studies of corporate reputation. Given that reputation is a matter of relative standing between organizations, accreditation and ranking provide ways to examine the inclusion and exclusion of organizations, as well as the order of standing among competitors. We noted that both the management and communication literatures have been involved in research on these topics, and both provide insights into the reputation process. The two literatures also suggest a host of interesting and important future studies which offer greater understanding of the dynamics of reputation ranging from the micro, across the meso, and up to the macro level of analysis. Given the emphasis in industry on the importance of reputation, and the claims by the public relations industry in particular in regard to reputation management, there are significant opportunities for the academic research to further inform this area of organizational life.

References

Abrahamson, E. (1996) Management fashion. *Academy of Management Review*, 21, 254–285.

Ashforth, B.E. and Kreiner, G.E. (1999) How can you do it?: Dirty work and the challenge of constructing positive identity. *Academy of Management Review*, 24(3), 413–434.

Barnett, M.L., Jermier, J.M., and Lafferty, B.A. (2006) Corporate reputation: The definitional landscape. *Corporate Reputation Review*, 9(1), 26–38.

Bartlett, J.L. and Hill, H. (2007) Footprints in the sand: Insights into the public relations profession in Queensland. *Asia Pacific Journal of Public Relations*, 8(1), 109–120.

Beck, U., Giddens, A., and Lash, S. (1994) *Reflexive Modernization: Politics, Tradition, and Aesthetics in the Modern Social Order*. Stanford: Stanford University Press.

Campbell, K. and Sherman, W.R. (2010) Lists and more lists: Making sense of corporate reputations. *Journal of Business and Economics Research*, 8(7), 47–58.

Carey, J.W. (1992) *Communication as Culture: Essays on Media and Society* (Repr. ed.). New York: Routledge.

Carroll, C.E. and McCombs, M.E. (2003) Agenda-setting effects of business news on the public's images and opinions about major corporations. *Corporate Reputation Review*, 6(1), 36–46.

Cooren, F. (1999) *The Organizing Property of Communication*. Amsterdam: John Benjamins.

Deephouse, D.L. (2000) Media reputation as a strategic resource: An integration of mass communication and resource-based theories. *Journal of Management*, 26(6), 1091–1112.

Deephouse, D.L. and Carter, S. (2005) An examination of differences between organizational legitimacy and organizational reputation. *Journal of Management Studies*, 42(2), 329–360.

Deephouse, D.L. and Suchman, M.C. (2008) Legitimacy in organizational institutionalism. In R. Greenwood, C. Oliver, K. Sahlin, and R. Suddaby (eds), *The SAGE Handbook of Organizational Institutionalism*. London: Sage, pp. 49–77.

DiMaggio, P.J. and Powell, W.W. (1983) The iron cage revisited: Institutional isomorphism and collective rationality in organizational fields. *American Sociological Review*, 48(2), 147–160.

Djelic, M.-L. and Sahlin-Andersson, K. (2006) *Transnational Governance: Institutional Dynamics of Regulation*. Cambridge, UK: Cambridge University Press.

Dowling, G.R. (2004) Corporate reputations: Should you compete on yours? *California Management Review*, 46(3), 19–36.

Dubbink, W., Graafland, J., and van Liedekerke, L. (2008) CSR, transparency and the role of intermediate organizations. *Journal of Business Ethics*, 82, 391–406.

Dutton, J.E., Dukerich, J.M., and Harquail, C.V. (1994) Organizational images and member identification. *Administrative Science Quarterly*, 39, 239–263.

Eisenegger, M. and Imhof, K. (2008) The true, the good and the beautiful: Reputation management in the media society. In A. Zerfass, B. Ruler, and K. Sriramesh (eds), *Public*

Relations Research. Wiesbaden, Germany: VS Verlag für Sozialwissenschaften, pp. 125–146.

Elsbach, K.D. and Kramer, R.M. (1996) Members' responses to organizational identity threats: Encountering and countering the business week rankings. *Administrative Science Quarterly*, *41*(3), 442–476.

Engwall, L., Grünberg, J., Pallas, J., Sahlin, K., Strannegård, L., Wedlin, L., Hägg, I., Buhr, H., Jonsson, S., Frostenson, M., Romani, L., Windell, K., and Buhr, K. (forthcoming) *Corporate Governance in Action: A Field Approach*.

Erkama, N. and Vaara, E. (2010) Struggles over legitimacy in global organizational restructuring: A theoretical perspective on legitimation strategies and dynamics in a shutdown case. *Organization Studies*, *31*, 813–839.

Fombrun, C.J. (1998) Indices of corporate reputation: An analysis of media rankings and social monitors' ratings. *Corporate Reputation Review*, *1*(4), 327–340.

Fombrun, C.J. (2007) List of lists: A compilation of international corporate reputation ratings. *Corporate Reputation Review*, *10*(2), 144–153.

Fombrun, C.J. and Shanley, M. (1990) What's in a name? Reputation building and corporate strategy. *Academy of Management Journal*, *33*, 233–258.

Fombrun, C.J. and van Riel, C.B.M. (1997) The reputational landscape. *Corporate Reputation Review*, *1*(1–2), 5–13.

Frostenson, M., Helin, S., and Sandström, J. (2010) Understanding internal processes for sustainability in retail: Corporate disclosure or concealment? Nordic Retail and Wholesale Conference 2010, Gothenburg.

Grafström, M., Göthberg, P., and Windell, K. (2008) *CSR: Företagsansvar I förändring*. Malmö, Sweden: Liber.

Greenwood, R., Li, S.X., Prakash, R., and Deephouse, D.L. (2005) Reputation, diversification, and organizational explanations of performance in professional service firms. *Organization Science*, *16*(6), 661–673.

Greenwood, R., Oliver, C., Sahlin, K., and Suddaby, R. (eds) (2008) *The SAGE Handbook of Organizational Institutionalism*. London: Sage.

Hatch, M.J. and Schultz, M. (1997) Relations between organizational culture, identity and image. *European Journal of Marketing*, *31*(5/6), 356–365.

Hatch, M.J. and Schultz, M. (2002) The dynamics of organizational identity. *Human Relations*, *55*(8), 989.

Hedmo, T., Sahlin-Andersson, K., and Wedlin, L. (2006) The emergence of European regulatory field of management education. In M.-L. Djelic and K. Sahlin-Andersson (eds), *Transnational Governance: Institutional Dynamics of Regulation*. Cambridge, UK: Cambridge University Press, pp. 308–328.

Hillenbrand, C. and Money, K. (2007) Corporate responsibility and corporate reputation: Two separate concepts or two sides of the same coin? *Corporate Reputation Review*, *10*(4), 261–277.

Hutton, J., Goodman, M., Alexander, J., and Genest, C. (2001) Reputation management: The new face of corporate public relations? *Public Relations Review*, *27*(3), 247–261.

Jacobsson, B. and Sahlin-Andersson, K. (2006) Dynamics of soft regulations. In M.-L. Djelic and K. Sahlin-Andersson (eds), *Transnational Governance: Institutional Dynamics of Regulation*. Cambridge, UK: Cambridge University Press, pp. 247–265.

Jonsson, S. and Buhr, H. (2011) The limits of media effects: Field positions and cultural change in a mutual fund market. *Organizational Science*, *22*(2), 464–481.

Jonsson, S., Greve, H.R., and Fujiwara-Greve, T. (2009) Lost without deserving: The spread of legitimacy loss in response to reported corporate deviance. *Administrative Science Quarterly*, *54*(2), 195–228.

Katz, E. and Lazarsfeld, P.F. (1964) *Personal Influence: The Part Played by People in the Flow of Mass Communication*. New York: Free Press.

Kennedy, S.H. (1977) Nurturing corporate images: Total communication or ego trip? *European Journal of Marketing*, *11*(3), 120–164.

Lammers, J.C. and Barbour, J.B. (2006) An institutional theory of organizational communication. *Communication Theory*, *16*(3), 356–377.

Mazza, C. and Alvarez, J.L. (2000) Haute couture and Prêt-à-porter: The popular press and the diffusion of management practices. *Organization Studies*, *21*(3), 567–588.

Meijer, M.-M. and Kleinnijenhuis, J. (2006) Issue news and corporate reputation: Applying the theories of agenda setting and issue ownership in the field of business communication. *The Journal of Communication*, *56*(3), 543–559.

Meyer, J.W. and Rowan, B. (1977) Institutionalised organizations: Formal structure as myth and ceremony. *The American Journal of Sociology*, *83*(2), 340–363.

Meyer, J.W. and Rowan, B. (1977/1991) Institutionalized organizations: Formal structure as myth and ceremony. In W.W. Powell and P.J. DiMaggio (eds), *The New Institutionalism in Organizational Analysis*. Chicago, IL: The University of Chicago Press, pp. 41–62.

Mörth, U. (2004) *Soft Law in Governance and Regulation: An Interdisciplinary Analysis*. Cheltenham, UK and Northampton, MA: Edward Elgar.

Motion, J. and Weaver, C.K. (2005) The epistemic struggle for credibility: Rethinking media relations. *Journal of Communication Management*, 9(3), 246–255.

Nadesan, M.H. (2011) Transparency and neo-liberal logics of corporate economic and social responsibility. In Ø. Ihlen, J.L. Bartlett, and S. May (eds), *Handbook of Communication and Corporate Social Responsibility*. Oxford, UK: Wiley-Blackwell, pp. 252–275.

Pallas, J. and Fredriksson, M. (2011) Providing, Promoting and co-opting: Corporate media work in a mediatized society. *Journal of Communication Management*, 15, 165–178.

Pfeffer, J. and Salancik, G.R. (1978) *The External Control of Organizations*. New York: Harper & Row.

Pollock, T.G. and Rindova, V.P. (2003) Media legitimation effects in the market for initial public offerings. *Academy of Management Journal*, 46, 631–642. Academy of Management.

Power, M. (1997) *The Audit Society. Rituals of Verification*. Oxford, UK: Oxford University Press.

Power, M. (2007) *Organized Uncertainty: Designing a World of Risk Management*. Oxford, UK: Oxford University Press.

Power, M., Scheytt, T., Soin, K., and Sahlin, K. (2009) Reputational risk as a logic of organizing in late modernity. *Organization Studies*, 30 (2–3), 301–324.

Rao, H. (1994) The social construction of reputation: Certification contests, legitimation, and the survival of organizations in the American automobile industry: 1895–1912. *Strategic Management Journal*, 15(1), 29–44.

Rao, H., Davis, G.F., and Ward, A. (2000) Embeddedness, social identity and mobility: Why firms leave the NASDAQ and join the New York stock exchange. *Administrative Science Quarterly*, 45(2), 268–292.

Rhee, M. and Valdez, M.E. (2009) Contextual surrounding reputation damage with potential implication for reputation repair. *Academy of Management Review*, 34(1), 146–168.

Rindova, V.P., Williamson, I.O., Petkova, A.P., and Sever, J.M. (2005) Being good or being known:

An empirical examination of the dimensions, antecedents, and consequences of organizational reputation. *Academy of Management Journal*, 48(6), 1033–1049.

Rindova, V.P., Pollock, T.G., and Hayward, M.L.A. (2006) Celebrity firms: The construction of market popularity. *Academy of Management Review*, 31(1), 50–71.

Rindova, V.P., Petkova, A.P., and Kotha, S. (2007) Standing out: How new firms in emerging markets build reputation. *Strategic Organization*, 5(1), 31–70.

Røvik, K.A. (2004) *Moderna Organizationer – Trender Inom Organizationstänkandet vid Millennieskiftet*. Malmö, Sweden: Liber.

Sahlin, K. and Wedlin, L. (2008) Circulating ideas: Imitation, translation and editing. In R. Greenwood, C. Oliver, K. Sahlin, and R. Suddaby (eds), *The SAGE Handbook of Organizational Institutionalism*. London, California, New Delhi, Singapore: Sage, pp. 218–242.

Sahlin-Andersson, K. and Engwall, L. (eds) (2002) *The Expansion of Management Knowledge: Carriers, Flows, and Sources*. Stanford, CA: Stanford University Press.

Sauder, M. (2006) Third parties and status systems: How the structures of status systems matter. *Theory & Society*, 35, 299–321.

Schultz, M., Hatch, M.J., and Holten Larsen, M. (eds) (2000) *The Expressive Organization: Linking Identity, Reputation, and the Corporate Brand*. Oxford, UK: Oxford University Press.

Schultz, M., Mouritsen, J., and Gabrielsen, G. (2001) Sticky reputation: Analyzing a ranking system. *Corporate Reputation Review*, 4(1), 24–41.

Sherer, P.D. and Lee, K. (2002) Institutional change in large law firms: A resource dependency and institutional perspective. *Academy of Management Journal*, 45(1), 102–119.

Solove, J.D. (2007) *The Future of Reputation: Gossip, Rumor, and Privacy on the Internet*. Yale: Yale University Press.

Suchman, M.C. (1995) Managing legitimacy: Strategic and institutional approaches. *Academy of Management Review*, 20, 571–610.

Vaara, E. and Tienari, J. (2008) A discursive perspective on legitimation strategies in MNCs. *Academy of Management Review*, 33(4), 985–993.

van Riel, C.B.M. (1995) *Principles of Corporate Communication*. London: Prentice Hall.

van Riel, C.B.M. (1997) Research in corporate communication: An overview of the emerging field.

Management Communication Quarterly, 11(2), 288–309.

Wedlin, L. (2006) *Ranking Business Schools: Forming Fields, Identities, and Boundaries in International Management Education*. Northampton, MA: Edward Elgar Publishing.

Wedlin, L. (2007) The role of rankings in codifying a business school template: Classifications, diffusion and mediated isomorphism in organizational fields. *European Management Review*, 4(1), 24–39.

Wry, T., Deephouse, D.L., and McNamara, G. (2006) Substantive and evaluative media reputations among and within cognitive strategic groups. *Corporate Reputation Review*, 9, 225–242.

43

Hidden Organizations and Reputation

Craig R. Scott[1]

Rutgers University, USA

Despite the attention to organizations that focus heavily on their reputations, the complex society of the twenty-first century is also characterized by organizations that either shun reputations or manage them in rather different ways in order to conceal themselves. We can refer to these collectives as *hidden organizations*, where key parts of the collective's identity are concealed by management or other members, for a variety of reasons, from various audiences. This chapter examines the major categories of hidden organization (secret societies, criminal organizations, informal economy, terrorist organizations, secret government agencies, and other), with special attention to aspects suggesting implications for reputation. The chapter closes with a set of conclusions about reputation in these hidden organizations.

A recent international survey of executives argues that reputation now matters more than it has for decades (Bonini *et al.*, 2009). Amid such claims, it is not surprising to find reputational studies ranking everything from the top colleges and universities to the best steak houses on earth, and from the top 10 golf courses to America's top 100 Teddy Roosevelt terrier breeders. These lists exist for corporations as well as major nonprofits, and they may include global organizations or be conducted separately for each major nation. Similar lists of the least reputable organizations can also be found. In all cases, the names that appear on these lists are relatively well known to large numbers of us. Without question, many organizations dedicate substantial efforts to provide a highly recognizable name and visual identities that enhance their reputation, all of which creates an assumption that organizations wish to be clearly identified to various others. That is an assumption that may, at first glance, seem quite reasonable to most consumers and citizens. Indeed, much of our theory and research about organizations tacitly accepts this claim as well in that most of our definitions, frameworks, and methods have privileged highly visible and generally recognized organizations.

That assumption, however, needs to be questioned. Not all organizations seek to promote

The Handbook of Communication and Corporate Reputation, First Edition. Edited by Craig E. Carroll.
© 2013 John Wiley & Sons, Inc. Published 2015 by John Wiley & Sons, Inc.

their identity and establish a reputation with the general public or other audiences. What about the vast majority of businesses and other organizations without an extensive public relations or corporate communication arm to constantly engage in image/identity management – or even those that might use such resources to conceal their identity and thus limit their reputation? Consider all those organization that do not have much of a reputation at all, and actually prefer that (if not depend on it). How important is reputation for those organizations that do not produce a product or service relevant to most of the public and who may not want other organizations in their community to know much about them either? Consider what reputation might mean for organizations wishing to keep a low profile as they operate under the radar.

For obvious reasons, one is hard-pressed to find a list of those organizations published in *Fortune* or *Forbes* or elsewhere. Yet, the complex society of the twenty-first century is characterized by increasingly diverse organizations that either shun reputations or manage them in rather different ways. As Alvesson (2004) observed, we live in a world filled with organizations most of whom are barely known. I refer to these collectives as *hidden organizations.* Unfortunately, we as citizens, consumers, and students of organizations have failed to adequately consider these various forms of hidden organizations – creating both missed opportunities and potential dangers. Our focus on the familiar organizational foreground of predominantly large for-profit businesses, easily recognized governmental agencies, and a few high-profile nonprofits and nongovernmental organizations (NGOs) contributes to a lack of vision on what may be an even larger arena of other less visible collectives. Commentary about such organizations is sometimes linked to the fringe and marginal; but, these hidden organizations are far more common and consequential than previously thought. As a result, they also need to be better incorporated into mainstream thinking about organizations by scholars, policy makers, and everyday citizens.

As scholars interested in the study of reputation, we need to more fully consider this broader range of organizations in our theorizing and research about reputational processes. As a step in that direction, I will begin with a brief comment on the current focus of reputation research. From there, I provide an overview of research on various hidden organizations, with special attention given to reputation implications associated with each. The chapter closes with some conclusions and suggestions for moving forward. The goal here is not to minimize or discount the valuable research that exists on corporate reputation already; instead, I contend that future work in this area needs to expand to consider these other more hidden organizations where reputation processes may often differ.

Revisiting Reputation

Reputations are actual perceptions of outsiders about core characteristics of the organization; furthermore, they tend to develop and last over periods of time rather than exist as a short-term impression (see Fombrun and Rindova, 2000; Spittal and Abratt, 2009). These perceptions may be revealed to the organization and others through various means – company rankings, comments by analysts, media coverage, feedback provided directly by consumers, and so on. A great deal has been written about the importance of reputation for a number of very positive organizational outcomes (see review by Walker, 2010); thus, it is not surprising that management values it greatly and substantial attention has been paid to attacks on one's reputation.

Tadelis (2003) suggests that a firm's name symbolizes its reputation. When negative reputation feedback is about one's core identity, there is much greater concern and higher likelihood of response (Dukerich and Carter, 2000). Certainly, organizational members and other stakeholders will link reputational assessments with the organization's identity (or at least one of its identities) – reminding us again of the processual nature of identity development as an organization and its members communicate with various audiences. Additionally, organizations may have more than one reputation as assessed by various others (see Padanyi and Gainer, 2003).

Reputation is regularly linked to how well an organization communicates with others, which usually means being very transparent with and expressive to stakeholders about the organization (see Fombrun and Rindova, 2000). Some work has even explicitly linked favorable reputations to organizational transparency – even in contexts where bureaucratic secrecy is also a source of power (Moffitt, 2010). In general, this work reflects an orientation that reputations can and must be managed for key audiences – which may regularly involve the clear and transparent communication of information about the organization to relevant stakeholders. As we have already seen, such assumptions may work well for some organizations but less so for others. It is not clear in the reputational literature how we are to understand organizations whose identity is so secret that few if any efforts are made to project an image to which various others might respond. In such situations where there is an absence of identity-related communication, is a reputation formed at all? How is the hidden nature of the organization assessed when we are at least somewhat aware of its existence? In societies that value openness and transparency, does the lack of identifying information lead to negative assessments of those organizations by many? Conversely, does the ability of a hidden organization to hide its identity from certain others lead to a positive reputation among those who value or benefit from that secrecy?

One potential reason we generally lack answers to these and other related questions can be found in broader critiques about our continued reliance on outdated organizational theory even amid recognition of widespread changes. Davis (2009) offers an informative critique in arguing that large corporations have lost their central place in American social structure as we move from an industrial to postindustrial economy, where "the applicability of several of our existing theories is called into question" (p. 41). Davis's work here is important because it suggests the benefit of a different approach that breaks from the focus on formal corporate organizations. This critique is also echoed by Mayntz, who notes that "organization studies have come to concentrate increasingly on one specific type: economic organizations, or firms" to "the neglect of clandestine illegal organizations" (2004, p. 5). In some ways, we can make the same critique about corporate reputation studies that have focused theory and research on certain collectives to the neglect of others. However, a contemporary view of corporate reputation broadly considered has to look beyond the large corporation and the formal organization to consider other types that may be far less visible, but for whom reputational issues are still relevant.

Hidden Organizations

Hidden organizations are ones where key parts of the collective's identity are concealed by management or other members, for a variety of reasons, from various audiences. This does not refer to those organizations who are hidden only because they have not yet achieved their desired discovery by others (e.g., underground musical band still trying to get noticed) or those who have been ineffective in their intended efforts to promote themselves (e.g., new business that fails to advertise enough to draw in customers). So what are these hidden organizations who actively seek to maintain some degree of anonymity? Most exotic among them are the undercover units, shadow governments, clandestine groups, terrorist cells, crime cartels, and other dark networks. We can also add to that a variety of brotherhoods, cults, orders, sects, enclaves, and various secret societies. Perhaps less exotic, but similarly hidden from view, are the various clubs, establishments, parlors, and other groups who may

Table 43.1   Types of potentially hidden organizations.

General Type	Example
Anonymous support/hate groups	Narcotics Anonymous
Front organizations	Get Government Off Our Backs
Gangs	Gangster Disciples
Fraternal orders	Freemasonry
Government intelligence agencies	Central Intelligence Agency (CIA)
Hackers/Hacktivists	Computer Chaos Club
Informal economy organizations	Sweatshop
New religious movements/cults	Church of Scientology
Organized crime groups	Yakuza
Political fund-raising organizations	527s
Secret societies	Skull and Bones
Select small businesses	W R Cold Storage Business
Stigmatized/backstreet businesses	Men's bathhouse
Terrorist organizations	al-Qaeda

front for criminal organizations or be elements of the shadow economy – all of whom benefit from reduced exposure to others. We can also potentially add a variety of backstreet, behind-the-scenes, under-the-radar, unmarked, and/or unpublished businesses that remain largely invisible to not only the public, but to many organizational scholars as well. In this section, I examine the major categories of hidden organization with special attention to aspects suggesting implications for reputation. Table 43.1 provides examples of several hidden organizations.

Secret societies

Despite contemporary fascination with secret societies in much of popular culture, these organizations date back centuries. Some groups seem linked to criminal or subversive activities, whereas others are better understood as under-ground resistance to illegitimate power, with still yet others being more social and apolitical in nature. These organizations are defined in significant part by the premium they place on secrecy:

> What unites them is not any one purpose of belief. It is, rather, secrecy itself: secrecy of

purpose, belief, methods, often membership. These are kept hidden from outsiders and only by gradual steps revealed to insiders, with further secrets always beckoning, still to be penetrated. (Bok, 1982, p. 46)

Indeed, one of Simmel's (1906) claims is that control of information and knowledge, especially about one's secrets, is vital to these organizations. In his view, a great deal depends on trusting members not to endanger the organization by revealing the true nature of the group and its activities. Others have argued that the power of these organizations depends on the ability to control information (Tefft, 1992). "Secret societies prevent or restrict com-munication, and distribute information and knowledge in ways that create nuanced struc-tures of knowing and not knowing, of awareness and ignorance" (Anheier, 2010, p. 1356). Thus, the very information on which others might assess reputation is itself concealed.

However, these societies are not all alike in form or in the degree to which that information is restricted. Hazelrigg (1969) suggests that secret organizations take one of two forms: those where everything is secret including the organization's existence; or, those which only some aspects such as membership, goals, and so on, remain secret. MacKenzie's (1967) edited volume offers what amounts to a classification of organizations into four types based on degree of secrecy. *Open* organizations have no secrets from insiders or outsiders; *limited* organizations select members, but outsiders know the organization's activities; *private* organizations restrict membership and activities are largely secret; and *secret* organizations have very strict limits on membership and strong efforts to shield organizational activities from public gaze. In short, these secret societies vary substantially. As a result, they may manage themselves in ways that limit reputation to certain audiences, create reputations that emphasize the secret nature of the organization, potentially try to downplay reputations that describe them as overly secretive and mysterious, and/or seek to avoid having enough visibility to even have a reputation.

Criminal organizations

For obvious reasons, research into many aspects of organized crime is also a challenge considering the potential threat (for both members and victims) of revealing information to outsiders and the largely underground nature of so much of this work. Criminal organizations have historically been involved with activities such as drug trafficking, money laundering, counterfeiting, gambling, prostitution, weapons, stolen goods, and human trafficking. Today, organized crime also involves cybercrime and markets for organs, antiquities, and wildlife.

Defining organized crime can be challenging, but one of the key issues revolves around the identity of organizations and members. In fact, some work has even linked secret societies with criminal organizations, arguing that secret societies initially created to resist/overthrow unpopular governments or provide protection may later turn to criminal activity (e.g., Mafia, Chinese Triads). This has specifically been observed with Chinese criminal organizations that bear resemblance to secret societies (Xia, 2008). Whether a secret society or not, secrecy characterizes many criminal organizations (Paoli, 2002), where rituals/oaths and

information about organizational activity are withheld from nongroup members (which also creates a special loyalty and cohesion among organizational members). Various rituals, secretive gestures, and signs of recognition help convey a criminal group's collective identity (Paoli, 2002; Xia, 2008). Criminal organizations are also hard to locate physically as they seemingly disappear into the communities in which they operate through efforts to "have no precise physical presence and to avoid drawing unnecessary attention" (Thorne, 2005, p. 10). The key for staying at least somewhat hidden is not only the existence of such secrets, but also the silence about those secrets. If an organization is engaged in criminal activities, its members cannot risk revealing secret arrangements publicly even when complaints arise between cartel members (van de Bunt, 2010). For example, "omerta" refers to a code of silence found in mafia organizations. It is an extreme form of loyalty where one's silence shows commitment (and being an informant does not). In such organizations, reputation may also have much to do with an ability to keep information about the organization quiet.

By far the most relevant examination of communication in organized crime is Gambetta's (2009) *Codes of the Underworld*. Though it is more about criminals than their organizations, several points are directly relevant. Gambetta claims there are three fundamental problems that stem from the inherent secrecy of organized crime. First, the *communication problem* is the need to interact with known colleagues without rivals or law enforcement intercepting and understanding the message. Second, the *identification problem* is about the ability to identify other organization members (and being identifiable to them) while not being recognized by a third party. Third, the *advertising problem* stems from the fact that criminal organizations cannot promote their goods and services in traditional ways despite the need to attract interested others. Interestingly, Gambetta suggests that names and trademarks matter for organized crime too, because they need them to establish a reputation among customers/clients and other criminal organizations – but such reputations are harder to establish for organizations than for individuals; furthermore, no outside entity can protect a criminal organization's use of trademarks or other identifying information (allowing other organizations to potentially borrow or mimic that identity). Though difficult to establish, Gambetta argues that the Mafia name does matter in the "protection" market – though the use of the term "Mafia" is very rare even by its own members.

Another useful example is to look at some of the research on street or youth gangs. As Valdez claims, "some gangs placer high importance on monikers, colors, symbols, and hand signs, which are used for self-identification. Although this type of gang may be involved in illegal activities such as drug dealing, its primary goal is to protect the gang's honor, turf, and solidarity" (2003, p. 15). For these gangs, reputation among other gangs and in the community matters, but the management of that reputation is almost certainly different than what we find in a for-profit corporation.

Informal economy

The informal economy is often described as involving those entities that are hidden for tax and/or welfare purposes, but which are otherwise legal or as part of the gross domestic product that is not reported or underreported officially (see Habibullah and Eng, 2006; Williams and Windebank, 2004). There is relatively little organizational research related to the informal economy, with management scholars noting "little research has focused on organizations operating outside of laws and regulations in different societies or on how institutions can encourage ventures to transition from the informal to the formal economy" (see Webb *et al.*, 2009, p. 506). Although it has at times been linked to and confused with organized crime – because both may be involved in some illegal activities and both have a need for secrecy – there are also clear differences. Considering both the *legality* and the societal *legitimacy* of means and ends, the formal economy (where both means and ends are legal

and legitimate) is in direct contrast with the renegade economy (where both means and ends are illegal and illegitimate); however, the informal economy is viewed as legitimate – but either the means or ends (or both) are viewed as illegal (Webb *et al.*, 2009).

Indeed, the sometimes illegal work involved here necessitates these organizations being less visible to various audiences. Existing research (not to mention many of the other names given to this sector: shadow, twilight, underground, black, hidden, nonobserved, unrecorded, subterranean, etc.) points to such issues as clearly relevant. For example, Portes and Haller (2005) argue that the success of informal organization in highly repressive situations (e.g., strong state regulations) depends heavily on avoiding detection by authorities. Periodic rites of solidarity, trust, and community enforcement are viewed as important for keeping such secrets – which can include entirely clandestine factories, for example, in such network organizations. Research sponsored in part by the Aspen Institute (Losby *et al.*, 2002) argues that "The viability of informal enterprise relies considerably on being able to operate under the regulatory radar screen" (p. 10). The extent to which informal activity is concealed varies; in other words, in more developed areas where regulations are more extensive, those engaged in such activity have to do more to conceal themselves (Portes and Haller, 2005).

As an example, at least part of the complex sex industry involves an informal aspect that seeks to avoid taxation and regulation that is of relevance as part of the informal economy. These various organizations may include escort services, massage parlors, health clubs, bathhouses, brothels in various establishments, after-hours clubs, hourly hotels and hotel party groups, and organizations that are merely a front for various sexual services (see Raymond *et al.*, 2001). Though some of these organizations advertise widely, many keep a relatively low profile so as not to attract unwanted attention, and others take extreme measures to remain completely under the radar of authorities. For the more hidden organizations operating in this informal economy, reputation issues are relevant in that they not only may relate to gaining business, but also have to be managed in ways that avoid unwanted detection by law enforcement and certain other groups opposed to the industry's efforts.

Terrorist organizations

One of the most important commonalities among terrorist organizations and other hidden collectives we have mentioned here is their secretiveness:

> Terrorists and international organized criminals depend on secrecy as a foundational concept for their organizations. This includes secret membership, secret locales, secret leadership, and secret communications. The organizers of their activities are hard to identify, and both groups use all forms of modern information technology to execute their operations with minimal risk of disclosure. (Shelley and Picarelli, 2002, p. 3)

Stohl and Stohl (2011) define clandestine organizations, which include terrorist groups, based on three characteristics that help ensure their concealment more so than we find for other types of organizations: members agree to keep their own and others' affiliations secret, internal structures operate outside public knowledge, and external traces of the organization only become visible over time. They may be illegal or not, working for or against the state, and their secrecy can be to maintain freedom of action, disguise relations with others, and/or enhance organizational effectiveness. Furthermore, clandestine organizations vary in terms of how known and acknowledged they are – and to whom they are known/unknown. Thus, reputation may be relevant to some groups more so than others.

Some research about these organizations has examined issues of visibility and awareness, which may have clear links to reputation. For example, al Qaeda even changed its name several years ago as part of its effort to strengthen itself globally and establish increased public awareness – while also maintaining local connections (Marret, 2008). Morrill *et al.*

(2003) used the notion of social visibility to describe the degree to which interests and actions are known (though this work is more about internal conflict). Most terrorist attacks are anonymous – since 1968, 64% of attacks worldwide have been conducted by unknown groups; furthermore, those numbers have grown since September 11, 2001, with three of every four attacks now done anonymously (Abrahms, 2008). The identity of the sponsor of terrorist acts is a key issue. Jenkins (2003) argues that attribution is vital for understanding terrorist actions. However, sometimes multiple groups will claim responsibility while the actual attackers may remain hidden. In some cases, these are "false flags" used for various reasons. One such motive Jenkins terms deniability, where a terrorist organization may create a separate front organization that carries out its terrorist activities (the use of the Izz al-Din al-Qassam brigades by Hamas), is the political party able to negotiate with an enemy state (the use of Sinn Fein by the Irish Republican Army), or is a bogus front group on which unpopular acts can be blamed (use of Black September by the al-Fatah) – all of which may minimize damage to one's reputation. A second type of false flag is known as stigmatization, where an especially heinous crime is committed with the goal of blaming another enemy organization to tarnish its reputation.

Even as they operate in hidden ways, these organizations may use online tools to promote themselves and their identity in ways that help establish reputation. In fact, extremist groups were some of the first to use early computer bulletin boards to promote their ideas (Zhou *et al.*, 2005). They at times even use the Internet as a means of image control so as to highlight certain aspects of the organization over others (Caiani and Parenti, 2009; Zanini and Edwards, 2001). Indeed the relationship between the offline organization and its online presence may be complex. A study of Hamas (see Mozes and Weimann, 2010) has noted that some of their migration online has used the traditional offline Hamas brand; however, for the Palestinian Information Center web site, Hamas created a new brand that concealed the link to Hamas offline (at least in non-Arabic language sites).

Secret government agencies

The research here covers state intelligence agencies, covert and clandestine counterterrorism operations, secret police, and other hidden organizations (both public and private) working against various enemy groups. The work of these agencies may involve the establishment of fake organizations and work histories as part of covers for organizational members. It may also require the organization and/or its member(s) to "go dark" (where the member cannot obviously reveal his/her ties to the investigating agency and even the agency itself may remain masked). These actions provide the organization behind them with plausible deniability as needed. Like other areas of research on hidden organizations, this research can be difficult to conduct – for the additional reasons that information may be classified and mis/disinformation is more common. Furthermore, this is an area where very little research appears about the organizations, their communication, and their image/reputation. As one business scholar advocating such linkages has noted,

> Agencies relating to intelligence, counterterrorism, warfare, defence procurement, policing and so on can be understood as organizational apparatuses which could be studied in similar ways to any other organization. In fact, such studies are rare when compared to almost any other sector. (Grey, 2009, p. 311)

Although covert intelligence and secret government groups have existed through much of history in many parts of the globe (e.g., Sparta had secret police in the fourth century BC, and the Culper Spy Ring played an essential role for the United States during its revolutionary war), the more sophisticated efforts during and following WWII have received special attention – especially in book length treatments of specific organizations. Great Britain's Bletchley Park, as described in Smith's (1998) book *Station X*

and Conant's (2008) book *The Irregulars*, which examined the British Security Coordination, represents two such examples. Today, in the United States, we think of the National Security Agency (NSA) and the Central Intelligence Agency (CIA) as two relatively well-known entities in the government intelligence community – but who are also filled with secret organizations and practices that complicate their reputations. For example, Bamford (2001) describes an assassination unit within Division D of the CIA that operated with great secrecy (until it was discovered and then banned), the secret 303 committee of the NSA that reviews covert operations, the Special Collection Services (alternately led by CIA or NSA) that plants eavesdropping equipment and attempts to recruit key foreign communication personnel, and the Joint Functional Component Command for Network Warfare, which is a highly secretive hacking organization within the US Strategic Command.

Additionally, when it comes to counterterrorism, the US Joint Special Operations Command (JSOC) is itself very secret, and branches within it such as the Strategic Support Services may be even more hidden (see Scahill, 2009). JSOC is the primary covert operations force within the US military and controls covert groups generally known as Delta Force and SEAL Team 6. Other examples of these hidden counterterrorism efforts in the United States include the Office of Special Plans – which has been described as a "Pentagon-within-the-Pentagon" (p. 49) – and the National Counterterrorism Center – which remains hidden amid high-rise office buildings (Schmitt and Shanker, 2011, p. 49). Government groups may have special considerations when it comes to managing reputation considering what information should be disclosed and what is classified (knowing it may later be declassified and scrutinized). Additionally, efforts to maintain a positive reputation that ensures funding without revealing much about its identity that might threaten operations (or damage reputation) may also require careful reputation management practices.

Other hidden organizations

Scholarly research on other organizations not fitting into these broader categories exists as well. Notably, Simon's (1996, 2009) books on *Hidden Champions* reveal a whole range of formal businesses that passively or actively seek to remain obscure even as they perform quite well. Simon captures this group well:

> They shy away from publicity, some through explicit policies of not dealing with the press – or, by the way, with academic researchers! As an executive of a leading manufacturer of material processing equipment said, "We are not interested in revealing our success strategies and helping those who have recently neglected their business." Another hidden champion CEO wrote, "We don't want to be on your list. We strongly prefer to remain hidden." And the chief of the world market leader in a critical component for vibration control equipment remarked, "We want neither our competitors nor our customers to know our true market share." The young chief of a service company commented, "We have cherished our anonymity for years and feel very comfortable about it. Nobody has noticed our niche." (Simon, 1996, pp. 3–4)

These hidden champions do not depend heavily on a reputation given that they often do not deliver products directly to consumers; in fact, their lack of reputation outside their own industry may even help them from being distracted. Furthermore, they may share some things in common with small businesses generally. The Aspen Institute notes that very small enterprises (fewer than 10 employees) and microenterprises (fewer than 5 employees) account for three-fourths of US establishments and appear to be an enduring feature of the organizational and economic landscape (see Losby *et al.*, 2002). "These enterprises are largely invisible or operate at low levels of visibility" (p. 36), and that may even be to their advantage as they allocate limited resources elsewhere.

As a different type of example, front groups help the actual organization behind such entities remain hidden to the public and other audiences. This can be especially important for organizations and industries whose image is tarnished (e.g., tobacco industry; see Apollonio and Bero, 2007). The reputation of the secretive front organization may hide or help overcome problematic reputations for the organization being fronted. Hudson and Okhuysen (2009) examine another type of organization with a tarnished image. They have researched men's bathhouses as a core-stigmatized organization (a collective whose central outputs, processes, or customers violate social norms), finding that patrons regularly try to hide membership. Furthermore, they conclude that these organizations often used discreet locations, limited signage, and other boundary management conditions – which we might also describe as reputation management efforts – designed to make "bathhouses nearly invisible and anonymous" (p. 141). For such organizations, it is possible that remaining out of sight and without a reputation is generally desirable.

Other examples exist as well. Research has begun to examine hacker organizations, online hate groups, various support organizations, new religious movements, and even political groups (501c4 organizations and 527s). Arguably, reputation issues are problematic in all these organizations as they seek to protect themselves and their members from certain forms of unwanted attention while still attempting to establish some legitimacy as an organization. As a couple final examples, a sizable body of research exists on alcoholics anonymous and other 12-step groups modeled after it, though the role of anonymity appears to rarely be a focal point of scholarly interrogation. These organizations appear to enjoy their generally positive reputation in part by not promoting themselves extensively. Additionally, the organized efforts of the Underground Railroad – which helped move thousands of US slaves to freedom via cover of night, coded messages, disguises, and a network of secret hiding places – would represent another example where concealment of the organization and its members was vital (Siebert, 1898). The movement needed enough reputation that it would be used, trusted, and supported – but not one that would attract unwanted attention from authorities and others wishing to expose it.

Conclusions and Suggestions for Future Work

Having described these various hidden organizations and some of the reputational issues relevant to them, we can make some tentative conclusions about them (even knowing that these hidden organizations are not all alike and that they vary in terms of just how hidden they are). In a few ways, their reputation concerns are like those of almost any organization. For example, many of them have complex and multiple reputations to consider as they interact with different audiences. In other ways, there reputational concerns are at least somewhat unique. Regardless, we can claim that reputation is not irrelevant for these hidden organizations as a group; it is just manifested and managed in somewhat different ways. Table 43.2 highlights some of these reputation-related conclusions about hidden organizations.

In general, it is more difficult for others to assess a hidden organization's reputation because too much information is concealed. This may lead to lack of reputation or attribu-

tions made by the evaluator on the basis of other clues (e.g., distrust if I assume the organization is foreign and I do not trust foreigners). We can also suggest that hidden organizations may strategically seek to avoid reputations and awareness by tightly managing communication with external audiences. Organizations remain hidden through concealing information about their identity. When we know of a hidden organization, but know little about who they really are, the hidden/secretive nature of the organization may be the basis for reputation (i.e., reputation as a secretive club). In many cases, a less than positive reputation may result if one is aware of the organization but is suspicious of the lack of information about it. We can also say that these hidden organizations will have more favorable reputations in contexts where secrecy is valued but less favorable reputations when the relevant audience expects transparency and openness.

With so much focus on the strategic communication of identity and image in the existing literature, it is interesting that reputation for many hidden organizations also depends to some degree on silence of their members. Keeping silent can reinforce certain identities and further conceal information; it also helps the organizations more uniformly manage reputations. The reduced information not only

Table 43.2 Tentative conclusions about reputation in hidden organizations.

Harder for others to assess their reputation because too much information is concealed.

Organization may strategically seek to avoid reputations and awareness by tightly managing communication with external audiences.

Hidden/secretive nature of organization may be basis for reputation (i.e., reputation as a secretive club).

Have more positive reputations in contexts where secrecy is valued than in contexts where transparency/openness is expected.

Reputation may depend to some degree on silence rather than active promotion of organization.

Reputation is harder to firmly establish and harder to protect when attacked.

Avoid reputations that attract unwanted attention from authorities.

Reputation among other similar organizations may matter substantially more than general/public reputation.

Front organizations used to enhance reputation or obscure negative reputations.

Online presence can help establish reputation while still protecting an organization's identity.

Organizations that obsess about reputation management are actively concealing identity information from others.

Reputation problem: creating enough of a favorable reputation to attract needed resources without disclosing core information that could reveal organization.

makes reputation harder to firmly establish in these hidden organizations, but it is very difficult to protect it when attacked. Others may claim responsibility for certain actions or falsely accuse others of activity that is damaging to their reputations. The more informal, unregulated nature of many contexts where hidden organizations are found can create real challenges for adequately maintaining (or avoiding) a certain reputation. In many cases, hidden organizations avoid reputations that attract unwanted attention from police, tax officials, the media, and even certain critical publics.

To the extent that a reputation is promoted, it may be done so among other similar organizations more so than with the general public. We may wish to have a certain reputation among rival groups or in certain industries, but prefer not to be in the general public's eye. In some cases, organizations will hide behind front organizations to avoid their own negative reputations or create somewhat obscure and hidden fronts that help build the reputation of the organization backing them. Few organizations are so hidden that they have no visible online presence; instead, the Internet is used for (among other things) helping establish enough of a reputation to benefit the organization but still creating a shield (with the lack of physical presence, encrypted messages, etc.) that protects the organization's identity. In a few cases, we may even see hidden organizations that obsess about reputation management – but unlike their more visible counterparts that push their identity at every turn, the obsession here involves extreme efforts to conceal identity information from others so that the organization can remain very dark to nearly all others.

Finally, in the spirit of Gambetta's (2009) description of the communication, identification, and advertising problems he sees as stemming from the secrecy of organized crime, I also suggest these hidden organizations suffer from a *reputation* problem. These organizations often have to create enough of a favorable reputation to attract needed resources (money, members, clients, etc.), but they have to do so without disclosing core information that could reveal the organization. As many of our other examples illustrate, there is a real tension here between a need for some visibility amid various degrees of anonymity.

Considering these tentative conclusions, it seems clear that reputational issues are relevant for this entire range of organizations that corporate reputational scholars have scarcely begun to address. This is exciting because it suggests a number of new avenues for theory and research. Admittedly, studying hidden organizations is, for obvious reasons, not always easy; but, accessing reputations of them by various audiences may be more feasible. Those efforts, combined with case studies of various hidden organizations and their efforts to manage reputations, should be quite informative. In an age where every day is filled with news of clandestine government operations, often unclaimed terrorist organization attacks, alleged organized crime activities, offers of help from anonymous online support groups, groups hacking into computers, and outsourcing of work ultimately to underground sweatshops – combined with an awareness of all the efforts that various organizations take to ensure we do not hear about their work – we need to take a closer look at the hidden organizations around us. Attempting to better understand various processes related to how they manage their reputation is a key part of that important endeavor.

Note

1   Portions of this chapter draw from Scott's (2013) book on *Anonymous Agencies, Backstreet Businesses, and Covert Collectives: Rethinking Organizations in the 21st Century* (Stanford University Press).

References

Abrahms, M. (2008) What terrorists really want: Terrorist motives and counterterrorism strategy. *International Security, 32*(4), 78–105.

Alvesson, M. (2004) Organization: From substance to image? In M.J. Hatch and M. Schultz (eds), *Organizational Identity: A Reader.* Oxford, UK: Oxford University, pp. 161–182.

Anheier, H.K. (2010) Secret societies. In H.K. Anheier and S. Toepler (eds), *International Encyclopedia of Civil Society* (Part 19). New York: Springer Science, pp. 1355–1358.

Apollonio, D.E. and Bero, L.A. (2007) Creating industry front groups: The tobacco industry and "get government off our back". *American Journal of Public Health*, 97, 419–427.

Bamford, J. (2001) *Body of Secrets: Anatomy of the Ultra-Secret National Security Agency from the Cold War through the Dawn of a New Century*. New York: Doubleday.

Bok, S. (1982) *Secrets: On the Ethics of Concealment and Revelation*. New York: Pantheon Books.

Bonini, S., Court, D., and Marchi, A. (2009) Rebuilding corporate reputations. *McKinsey Quarterly*, 3, 75–83.

Caiani, M. and Parenti, L. (2009) The dark side of the web: Italian right-wing extremist groups and the Internet. *South European Society and Politics*, 14, 273–294.

Conant, J. (2008) *The Irregulars: Roald Dahl and the British Spy Ring in Wartime Washington*. New York: Simon & Schuster.

Davis, G.F. (2009) The rise and fall of finance and the end of the society of organizations. *Academy of Management Perspectives*, 23(3), 27–44.

Dukerich, J.M. and Carter, S.M. (2000) Distorted images and reputation repair. In M. Schultz, M.J. Hatch, and M.H. Larsen (eds), *The Expressive Organization: Linking Identity, Reputation, and the Corporate Brand*. Oxford, UK: Oxford University Press, pp. 97–112.

Fombrun, C. and Rindova, V. (2000) The road to transparency: Reputation management at Royal Dutch/Shell. In M. Schultz, M.J. Hatch, and M.H. Larsen (eds), *The Expressive Organization: Linking Identity, Reputation, and the Corporate Brand*. Oxford, UK: Oxford University Press, pp. 77–96.

Gambetta, D. (2009) *Codes of the Underworld: How Criminals Communicate*. Princeton, NJ: Princeton University Press.

Grey, C. (2009) Security studies and organization studies: Parallels and possibilities. *Organization*, 16, 303–316.

Habibullah, M.S. and Eng, Y.K. (2006) Crime and the underground economy in Malaysia: Are they related? *The Journal of Global Business Management*, 2, 138–155.

Hazelrigg, L. (1969) A reexamination of Simmel's "The Secret and the Secret Society": Nine propositions. *Social Forces*, 47(3), 323–330.

Hudson, B.A. and Okhuysen, G.A. (2009) Not with a ten-foot pole: Core stigma, stigma transfer, and improbable persistence of men's bathhouses. *Organization Science*, 20, 134–153.

Jenkins, P. (2003) *Images of Terror: What We Can and Can't Know about Terrorism*. New York: Aldine de Gruyter.

Losby, J.L., Else, J.F., Kingslow, M.E., Edgcomb, E.L., Malm, E.T., and Kao, V. (2002) Informal economy literature review. Unpublished Working Paper, Aspen Institute, Washington, DC.

MacKenzie, N. (1967) *Secret Societies*. New York: Holt, Rinehart and Winston.

Marret, J. (2008) Al-Qaeda in Islamic Maghreb: A glocal organization. *Studies in Conflict & Terrorism*, 31, 541–552.

Mayntz, R. (2004) Organizational forms of terrorism. Hierarchy, network, or a type sui generis? Max Planck Institute for the Study of Societies, Cologne, Germany, May.

Moffitt, S.L. (2010) Promoting agency reputation through public advice: Advisory committee use in the FDA. *The Journal of Politics*, 72, 880–893.

Morrill, C., Zald, M.N., and Rao, H. (2003) Covert political conflict in organizations: Challenges from below. *Annual Review of Sociology*, 29, 391–415.

Mozes, T. and Weimann, G. (2010) The e-marketing strategy of Hamas. *Studies in Conflict & Terrorism*, 33, 211–225.

Padanyi, P. and Gainer, B. (2003) Peer reputation in the nonprofit sector: Its role in nonprofit sector management. *Corporate Reputation Review*, 6, 252–265.

Paoli, L. (2002) The paradoxes of organized crime. *Crime, Law & Social Change*, 37, 51–97.

Portes, A. and Haller, W. (2005) The informal economy. In N. Smelser and R. Swedberg (eds), *Handbook of Economic Sociology* (2nd ed.). New York: Russell Sage Foundation, pp. 403–428.

Raymond, J.G., Hughes, D.M., and Gomez, C.J. (2001) Sex trafficking of women in the United States: International and domestic trends. Unpublished report. Coalition Against Trafficking in Women, Amherst, MA.

Scahill, J. (2009). The secret U.S. war in Pakistan. *The Nation*, December 21/28, pp. 11–18.

Schmitt, E. and Shanker, T. (2011) *Counterstrike: The Untold Story of America's Secret Campaign against Al-Qaeda*. New York: Times Books.

Scott, C.R. (2013) *Anonymous Agencies, Backstreet Businesses, and Covert Collectives: Rethinking*

Organizations in the 21st Century. Palo Alto, CA: Stanford University Press.

Shelley, L.I. and Picarelli, J.T. (2002) Methods not motives: Implications of the convergence of international organized crime and terrorism. *Police Practice and Research, 3,* 305–318.

Siebert, W.H. (1898) *The Underground Railroad: From Slavery to Freedom.* New York: Russell & Russell.

Simmel, G. (1906) The sociology of secrecy and of secret societies. *The American Journal of Sociology, 11,* 441–498.

Simon, H. (1996) *Hidden Champions: Lessons from 500 of the World's Best Unknown Companies.* Boston: Harvard Business School Press.

Simon, H. (2009) *Hidden Champions of the 21st Century: Success Strategies of Unknown World Market Leaders.* Bonn, Germany: Springer.

Smith, M. (1998) *Station X: The Codebreakers of Bletchley Park.* London: Channel 4 Books.

Spittal, R. and Abratt, R. (2009) The impact of geographic expansion on intended identity of an organization. *Journal of General Management, 35,* 65–78.

Stohl, C. and Stohl, M. (2011) Secret agencies: The communicative constitution of a clandestine organization. *Organization Studies, 32,* 1197–1215.

Tadelis, S. (2003) Firm reputation with hidden information. *Economic Theory, 21,* 635–651.

Tefft, S.K. (1992) *The Dialectics of Secret Society Power in States.* Atlantic Highlands, NJ: Humanities Press.

Thorne, K. (2005) Designing virtual organizations? Themes and trends in political and organizational discourses. *Journal of Management Development, 24*(7), 580–606.

Valdez, A. (2003) Toward a typology of contemporary Mexican-American youth gangs. In L. Kontos, D. Broutherton, and L. Barrios (eds), *Gangs and Society: Alternative Perspectives.* New York: Columbia University Press, pp. 12–40.

van de Bunt, H. (2010) Walls of secrecy and silence: The Madoff case and cartels in the construction industry. *Criminology and Public Policy, 9,* 435–453.

Walker, K. (2010) A systematic review of the corporate reputation literature: Definition, measurement, and theory. *Corporate Reputation Review, 12,* 357–387.

Webb, J.W., Tihanyi, L., Ireland, D.R., and Sirmon, D.G. (2009) You say illegal, I say legitimate: Entrepreneurship in the informal economy. *Academy of Management Review, 34,* 492–510.

Williams, C.C. and Windebank, J. (2004) The heterogeneity of the underground economy. *International Journal of Economic Development, 6*(2), 1–23.

Xia, M. (2008) Organizational formations of organized crime in China: Perspectives from the state, markets, and networks. *Journal of Contemporary China, 17*(54), 1–23.

Zanini, M. and Edwards, S.J.A. (2001) The networking of terror in the information age. In J. Arquilla and D. Ronfeldt (eds), *Networks and Netwars: The Future of Terror, Crime and Militancy.* Santa Monica, CA: Rand, pp. 29–60.

Zhou, Y., Reid, E., Qin, J., Chen, H., and Lai, G. (2005) U.S. extremist groups on the web: Link and content analysis. *IEEE Intelligent Systems, 20,* 44–51.

Section 5

Communication Research and Evaluation

44

Corporate Reputation Measurement and Evaluation

Don W. Stacks, Melissa D. Dodd, and Linjuan Rita Men

University of Miami, USA

This chapter reviews previous evaluation methods and advances a public relations/corporate communications model that focuses on reputational outcomes associated with both subjective and objective measures and statistical models. However, it should be noted that much of the quantitative research done on reputation is *atheoretical* and inductive, rather than deductive and based on established models of reputational change. Taking a best practices approach to reputation suggests that research should center on both objective (financial) and subjective (nonfinancial or "soft") variables to produce reliable and valid evaluation based on rigorous methodological and statistical testing.

The role of reputation in today's business world is undoubtedly a major driver of success or failure. Perhaps, this is best evidenced in the words of renowned investor Warren Buffett who said, "Lose money for the firm, and I will understand; lose a shred of reputation for the firm, and I will be ruthless" (1995, p. 409). What exactly constitutes reputation and how it can be assessed, however, is controversial. Over the past decades, there has been a movement from a subjective evaluative approach to establishing reputation to a more quantitative and objective evaluation of what constitutes reputation today. In today's world, simply having a CEO on the cover of an industry magazine does not "count" as much as it used to. Today,

reputation is multidimensional and is tied closely to credibility, trust, and relationship and confidence. Additionally, the relationship of reputation to return on investment (ROI) from the public relations/corporate communications function has taken on increased importance and can be formally stated as

$$\text{Reputation} = \{B_{ij} \pm \text{credibility}_{ij}{}^{x} \\ \pm \text{relationship}_{ij}{}^{x} \\ \pm \text{trust}_{ij}{}^{x}\} \\ \times \{\text{confidence}_{ij}{}^{x}\},$$

where B is some constant as modified by the variables influencing reputation (see Figure 44.1). Indices of these variables now include employee,

The Handbook of Communication and Corporate Reputation, First Edition. Edited by Craig E. Carroll.
© 2013 John Wiley & Sons, Inc. Published 2015 by John Wiley & Sons, Inc.

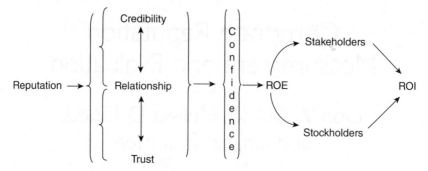

Figure 44.1   Conceptual model of reputation.

stakeholder, stockholder, and regulatory perceptions of the organization. Furthermore, the advent of social media means that those variables that predict reputation can change quickly and without notice.

This chapter will differentiate between the three major sources of reputation that stem from the public relations/corporate communicate communications function in a business context. First, there are the reputation drivers – the *outputs* associated with the function; these are the "physical" things the function does in daily activity (e.g., press releases, blogs, video news releases). Second, there are the *outtakes* or mediating variables (e.g., credibility, relationship, trust, and confidence) that may be manipulated to change target audience perceptions of the company. And, finally, there are *outcomes* – supportive behaviors driven by the public relations/corporate communications function – that influence a company's reputation and ROI.

This chapter reviews previous evaluation methods and advances a public relations/corporate communications model that focuses on reputational outcomes associated with both subjective and objective measures and statistical models. However, it should be noted that much of the quantitative research done on reputation is *atheoretical* and inductive, rather than deductive and based on established models of reputational change. Taking a best practices approach (Michaelson and MacLeod, 2007) to reputation suggests that research should center on both quantitative and qualitative methods

and economic and social variables to produce reliable and valid evaluation based on rigorous methodological and statistical testing.

Defining Reputation

As previously mentioned, what constitutes reputation is controversial. Despite this, definitions of reputation are ubiquitous and appear across several streams of research, most notably business, organizational, marketing, and public relations/communication. In fact, Fombrun and van Riel (1997) called for an integrative definition of reputation, citing six approaches for which reputation research was being cited: the economist view, the strategic view, the marketing view, the organizational view, the sociological view, and the accounting view. The authors further examined the major tenants of each of the viewpoints they identified, confirming a previously suggested integrative definition: "A corporate reputation is a collective representation of a firm's past actions and results that describes the firm's ability to deliver valued outcomes to multiple stakeholders. It gauges a firm's relative standing both internally with employees and externally with its stakeholders, in both its competitive and institutional environments" (Fombrun and Rindova, 1996, as cited in Fombrun and van Riel, 1997, p. 10).

Although Fombrun and Rindova (1996) offered this integrative definition (further confirmed by Fombrun and van Riel, 1997), which has widely been acknowledged and/or accepted by many scholars, the lack of an agreed-upon definition of reputation has persisted throughout the past two decades. Perhaps, the confusion surrounding the definition of reputation has been furthered by terminology used synonymously for reputation, that is, image, prestige, goodwill, esteem, identity, and standing, for example. However, as will be further addressed in this chapter, reputation is most commonly used synonymously with image and identity. A review by Barnett *et al.* (2006) filtered through hundreds of relevant articles and books, resulting in 49 sources with unique definitions of reputation. The authors concluded that among the sources, three distinct clusters of meaning in the reputation definitions existed: reputation as a state of *awareness* (definitions indicating that stakeholders held a general awareness but lacked judgment about organizations), reputation as an *assessment* (definitions indicating that stakeholders assessed or judged an organization), and reputation as an *asset* (definitions indicating that reputation was equivalent to something of value or significance, that is, an asset, for an organization).

Furthermore, the authors used the aforementioned clusters of meaning to differentiate between terminologies that are often used interchangeably with reputation. Briefly, the authors explain that corporate identity is a "collection of symbols" that distinguishes an organization's central features from other organizations (p. 33). Next, corporate image refers to "impressions of the firm" generated by both internal and external observers and factors such as media coverage, for example (p. 33). Corporate reputation, then, refers to "judgments by observers" (p. 33) that are "rooted in perceptions of the firm's identity and impressions of its image but often occurs as a consequence of a triggering event" (p. 34). Importantly, Barnett *et al.* (2006) further suggest that as the aforementioned judgments accumulate throughout time, "reputation capital ebbs and flows," that is, the economic property of reputation changes as a result (p. 34). The authors conclude that corporate reputation is best defined as "observers' collective judgments of a corporation based on assessments of the financial, social, and environmental impacts attributed to the corporation over time" (p. 34). This is, however, just one of several definitions offered for corporate reputation, as well as those terms that are used interchangeably with the concept (see, e.g., Gotsi and Wilson, 2001; Markwick and Fill, 1997; and Saxton, 1998).

It is also important to mention that in addition to controversy surrounding definition and confusion in terminologies, the concept of corporate reputation is further complicated by those researchers who seek to create a hierarchy among the concepts of image, identity, and reputation. Fombrun (1996) suggests that reputation is part identity and part persuasive efforts; however, Wei (2002) argues that if reputation is partly persuasive, then it should be subsumed by image, and not vice versa. However, specific to the public relations field, Grunig (1993) argued that

> Theories of research and research on schemas, therefore, show that the grand designs that many public relations practitioners have for shaping, changing, projecting, and polishing images generally only have incremental effects on the breadth of cognitive processes . . . Once people accumulate cognitions and attitudes, they continue to store them in long-term memory and associate them when they have reason to think about an organization. A "reputation" – if that term is equated with schema – has a long life. (pp. 134–135)

In other words, Grunig seems to suggest that the short-term image be subsumed within the more long-term reputation construct in regard to cognitive and attitudinal representations of stakeholders.

Clearly, definitions of corporate reputation diverge according to area, view, and terminology, among other things. However, despite the divergence in definition, it seems that there may be one thing that can be generally agreed upon: public relations professionals and scholars are commonly thought as those with the most responsibility regarding reputation, both in practice and research. For example, Hutton *et al.* (2001) stated, "Reputation management, if it is to emerge as a significant business function, clearly rests on a foundation of what is traditionally termed 'public relations'" (p. 248). Furthermore, Barnett *et al.* (2006) suggest that public relations professionals are those who are responsible for the transition between (their definitions of) corporate identity and corporate image. Thus, public relations scholars Stacks and Watson (2007) have generally defined reputation as "the historical relationship between organizations and publics" (p. 69). More specifically, this relationship is steeped in confidence, credibility, relationships, and trust (oft examined variables in public relations research) and affects the "return of expectation" or ROE of stakeholders and stockholders, which in turn affects the ROI for an organization (see Figure 44.1). Furthermore, from a public relations/corporate communication standpoint, this chapter proposes that the following assertions can be gleaned from the relevant literature surrounding corporate reputation:

1 Reputations are fragile: they are hard to make and easy to lose.
2 They are historical.
3 They are perceptual.
4 They differ according to publics or audiences.
5 Definition, measurement, and evaluation are difficult.

By this point, it should be clear that even presenting a general definition of corporate reputation is problematic and controversial. Most importantly, however, to the definition of corporate reputation is in its implications for measurement. In other words, definition implies measurement (Stacks, 2010), such that the variation apparent among the many definitions of reputation ultimately results in differences in the measurement of the construct. As will be detailed throughout the remainder of this chapter, the measurement of reputation is as ubiquitous as the definition. This should not be surprising since measures of reputation are derived from the various aforementioned definitions, that is, operationalizations of reputation. Nevertheless, it is important for this chapter to provide a detailed historic account of the measurement of reputation, concluding with a proposed model for the future of corporate reputation measurement for public relations/corporate communication. Figure 44.2 details a historical and contemporary overview of the measurement of reputation.

A Historical Overview of the Measurement of Reputation

Regardless of the disparity apparent among the definition and subsequent measurement of reputation, research and measurement of the

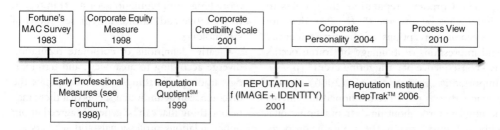

Figure 44.2 Timeline for the measurement of corporate reputation.

construct have persisted. Thus, this section provides a historic overview of the measurement of reputation within its earliest forms, that is, prior to the twenty-first century. First, an examination of the variety of methodologies used for the assessment of reputation is presented. Next, the most well-recognized measure of reputation and the grand aggregation approach common to many measures of reputation are presented, and, finally, several professional measures of reputation are mentioned, most notably the corporate equity measure within the public relations/corporate communication discipline.

Methodologies

While both historic and contemporary measures of reputation rely heavily on surveys or attitude scale methodologies across both professional and academic measures, several other approaches have been apparent in the literature, and these are worthy of note. van Riel *et al.* (1998) sought to determine if different methods apparent in the reputation literature resulted in different measures and if different methods were better in certain circumstances than in others. They looked at the differences between using what they termed "closed-end" and "open-end" measures of corporate image (no distinction was made between image and reputation). Closed-end measures used to measure corporate reputation (image) included attitude scales and Q-sorts. Briefly, attitude scales refer to corporate reputation as the result of attitudes toward the organization and thus are measured by obtaining scores (typically on Likert and semantic differential scales). Often, attitude scales are then weighted according to salient features rated by participants in the research. Next, Q-sort methods are a comparative method used to identify the applicability of statements about an organization and the rank order of those statements. Participants begin with a large amount of statements, and gradually, statements are sorted based on each participant's identification of the applicability and rank.

Likewise, the open-end measures identified and used by van Riel *et al.* (1998) to measure corporate reputation (image) included the Kelly Repertory Grid (KPG), natural grouping, laddering, and photosorts. The KPG method identifies dimensions for an organization's reputation measure by asking participants to view three alternatives (often company names or brands) and decide which two of the three are most similar. Once dimensions are created, participants are then asked to rank the organization on these dimensions. Next, natural grouping asks participants to sort a large number of corporate names into two subsets and then describe why they placed organizations in each subset. The criteria that participants use to separate organizations into subsets comprise the dimensions of the reputation measure, and these dimensions are considered more important the earlier they are mentioned by participants in the explanation. Similarly, laddering simply refers to an in-depth interview where participants are asked to articulate thoughts they have associated with an organization. Again, the thoughts that participants express are used as the dimensions of the reputation measure, and these dimensions are considered more important the earlier in the interview that they are mentioned by participants. And last, photosorts are the presentation of photos to participants who are then asked to assign the photos to an organization (or indicate if the photo does not fit with any of the organizations offered by the research). Next, photos are again shown to participants, and they are asked to indicate for which photos they feel an affinity.

The researchers used each of the six methods, concluding that "closed-end techniques provide more convergence across industries and are better for studies where the objective is monitoring one's image over time and comparing it to relevant competitors" (pp. 325–326). On the other hand, open-end methods "provide considerably more qualitative descriptions that can be used as input for closed methods and are more helpful in eliciting [reputation] dimensions" (pp. 325–326).

The most admired companies survey and the grand aggregation approach

Again, both historic and traditional measures of reputation rely heavily on survey or attitude scale methodologies across both professional and academic measures. One of the first and most prominent survey or attitude scale methodologies is attributable to *Fortune* Magazine. *Fortune* Magazine's survey of America's Most Admired Companies (i.e., MAC survey) "spawned a veritable industry devoted to profiling corporate reputations" (Fombrun, 1998) and still persists today, although it has expanded to an international level and is now called the World's Most Admired Companies (see *Fortune*, 2011). The MAC survey has been published annually since 1983 and represents the top companies per industry based on revenue and ranked on a number of reputation indicators (e.g., investment value and social responsibility) by industry professionals, specifically upper-level executives. The MAC survey uses a grand aggregation approach to the measurement of reputation from which many of the "veritable spawn" of the MAC adopted their own methodologies. Additionally, many of the contemporary measures of corporate reputation continue to use a grand aggregation approach.

The grand aggregation approach aggregates the dimensions of reputation (regardless of what the indices have defined them as) to create the construct of reputation. However, there are clear measurement problems associated with such an approach. For example, in the case of the MAC survey, reputation is ranked only by industry professionals. Thus, the reputation of *Fortune* organizations is not assessed in regard to a host of other stakeholders (stockholders, employees, etc.) who undoubtedly build and detract from organizations' reputations. In fact, Wartick (2002) argued that the grand aggregation approach "loses substantial informational content unless multiple, and a nearly exhaustive list of, stakeholder groups could possibly be surveyed" (p. 377). However, even when the data can be collected from multiple stakeholder groups of the organization, it is still difficult to

gauge overall stakeholders' perceptions. In other words, information is often lost on how one single constituency perceives the organization when the ratings are aggregated. Under different circumstances or in light of different situations (e.g., if the organization is experiencing a crisis, if the organization is still in its developmental stages, or even industry type), certain stakeholder groups may become more salient than others. The grand aggregation approach does not take into consideration the fact that reputation resides in the eyes of different stakeholders and that stakeholders are normally not equally important for the organization. Furthermore, when aggregating different attributes of reputation to generate a single reputation rating, the quality of information may be suspect because the multiple dimensions of reputation may have different weights in predicting the construct of reputation depending on the sampled organizations. Thus, it is recommended that based on the importance of the stakeholder or dimension to the reputation and organization, weighting of different stakeholder groups and dimensions be administered. However, the weighting of stakeholder groups and dimensions present its own methodological problems such as the subjective assignment of importance to different groups.

Early professional measures

As previously mentioned, the development of the MAC survey resulted in a variety of alternative professional measures for reputation (see Fombrun, 1998, for a full review), most borrowing their methodological foundation from the MAC survey. For example, on a global level, reputational measures using a similar methodology to that of the MAC survey appeared in Asia (*Asian Business*: Asia's Most Admired Countries), Great Britain (*Management Today*: Britain's Most Admired Companies), and Europe (*Financial Times*: Europe's Most Respected Companies). Additionally, specialized magazine and book publications (*Business Ethics*, *Working Mother Magazine*, The 100 Best Companies to Work for in America, The Best Companies for Minorities, The Best Companies for Women, and The 100 Best Companies for Gay Men and Lesbians) and social monitors (Council on Economic Priorities; Kinder, Lydenberg Domini & Company, Inc.; Ethical Investment Research Service; Frankline Research and Development Corporation; Interfaith Center on Corporate Responsibility; Investor Responsibility Research Center) also created their own methodologically similar measures of reputation and reported them diligently to their interested publics. However, according to Wartick (2002), it should be noted that for the majority of these early professional measure of reputation, "the methods underlying these ratings had little to do with reputation . . . and it seemed to have more to do with the author's attempt to manipulate or artificially construct reputation" (p. 382).

Importantly, Fombrun (1998) analyzed the characteristics of a majority of professional reputation measures at the time, concluding that the following six criteria converged across lists as criteria dominant to the assessment of reputation: financial performance, product quality, employee treatment, community involvement, environmental performance, and organizational issues (e.g., equal opportunity, diversity, and ethical issues). Fombrun (1998) tended to agree with Wartick's (2002) assertion that

> Based on the review of existing reputational ratings, the author suggests that a suitable conceptual framework within which to examine corporate reputations should recognize (1) the multiple stakeholders whose assessments aggregate into collective judgments; (2) the different but overlapping financial and social criteria according to which stakeholders judge companies. A true reputational index – if it is to provide managers and researchers with an accurate barometer of corporate reputations – can only result from sampling a representative set of stakeholders on a conceptually relevant set of criteria. (p. 338)

Corporate equity

Director of research at leading global public relations firms Burson-Marsteller, Leslie Gaines-Ross under the direction of managing partner

at Yankelovich Partners, John Gilfeather, created what was termed a "groundbreaking" measure of corporate reputation in 1998 (Gaines-Ross, 1998). The measure, part of a major research project termed *Leveraging Corporate Equity*, assessed both attitudes toward the organization across a broader range of executive constituencies (senior and middle management of industries) than the MAC survey and behaviors directed in support of that corporation, in order to determine reputation. Prior to *Leveraging Corporate Equity*, measures of corporate reputation neglected to include those outcome measures of interest (e.g., behaviors toward organizations).

Corporate equity scores were studied using the following dimensions: awareness, familiarity, overall impression, perceptions, and supportive behaviors. The measure's dimensions were then combined and weighted to determine each individual organization's overall corporate equity score. Wartick (2002) mentioned that the measure shows great promise and addresses previous concerns associated with the MAC survey (i.e., the high reliance of the MAC on financial indicators of performance). Wartick (2002) also notes that the corporate equity score measure seems to get at the "strength of reputation" with the addition of the supportive behaviors dimension apparent in the measure (p. 384).

Contemporary Measurement of Reputation (2000 to Present)

As evidenced by the previous discussion, reputation has historically been measured by a variety of organizations and scholars; however, it was not until the early twenty-first century that reputation research really gained momentum, with the average number of scholarly articles on corporate reputation increasing fivefold during the period of 2001–2003 as compared to the period of 1990–2000 (Barnett *et al.*, 2006).

The Reputation Quotient^{SM} (RQ) and the RepTrak^{TM}

Charles Fombrun at New York University and the Harris Interactive Research Company in New York jointly developed the RQ in 2000. This measure was developed based on Fombrun's previous academic work on corporate reputation (e.g., Fombrun, 1996, 1998). Adopted by numerous reputation scholars in public relations and business, the RQ has been proved to date as "a valid, reliable, and robust tool for measuring corporate reputation" (Gardberg and Fombrun, 2002). According to Fombrun *et al.* (2000), the RQ is measured with 20 attributes. The reputation rating for a certain organization can be calculated by aggregating the ratings of each attribute. As noted by Wartick (2002), the RQ showed promise because it measured the perception of a general public who may or may not be the companies' key stakeholder group. Therefore, it did not need to tackle with the stakeholder weighting problem as the MAC survey had. Additionally, created as a second-order multidimensional construct of reputation, the RQ underscores various indicators of reputation. However, one problem that might concern reputation researchers regarding the RQ is that, similar to other grand aggregation approaches, it may lose substantial information from one particular stakeholder group (e.g., customers, or employees). Fombrun and the Reputation Institute produced an updated version called the RepTrak^{TM} focusing on seven dimensions: products/services, innovation, workplace, governance, CSR/citizenship, leadership and financial performance.

Reputation = f(Image + Identity)

Another representative reputation measure using the grand aggregation approach reconciled the use of analogous terms such as image and identity. As summarized by Wartick (2002), although often used synonymously, the constructs of image and identity can be distinguished from reputation with a close examination. While image is related mostly to external stakeholders (e.g., customers, the media, the community), identity focuses more on internal stakeholders (e.g., employees, managers). By contrast, reputation is the overall evaluation of the organization by both internal and external stakeholders. To incorporate both internal and external stakeholder perspectives into measuring reputation, Davies *et al.* (2001), developed the formula of reputation as Reputation = f(Image + Identity). This aggregation ends up with an all-encompassing definition of reputation and meanwhile underscored the differentiation between image, identity, and reputation.

Other major approaches

Other contemporary approaches adopted by scholars in measuring corporate reputation are represented by the corporate personality measure and trust-based measure, as concluded by Helm (2005) and Wartick (2002). Davies *et al.* (2001, 2003) identified the concept of corporate personality. In this approach, reputation is measured through a number of indicators that underlie people's personality traits, which can also be attributable to organizations, such as exciting, interesting, well liked, warm and friendly, superficial, and arrogant (Dowling, 2004). The trust-based measure of reputation is represented by the corporate credibility scale developed by Newell and Goldsmith (2001). Hereby, the evaluation of the honesty, reliability, and benevolence aspects of an organization indicates the evaluation of the organization's reputation. In the similar vein, Stacks (2010) and Stacks *et al.* (2010) also pointed out that as a major public relations outcome, reputation interacts with other indicators such as trust, credibility, and relationship to affect public relations efforts' ROE and ROI for organizations.

A Process View of Reputation Measures

Through a comprehensive review of reputation measures from different approaches in the business and communication literatures, it should be noted that reputation has been measured as a reflective construct in a process. As noted by Stacks (2010), what companies do (i.e., outputs) are drivers or antecedent factors for the reputation building. Reputation in the eyes of stakeholders measured with key indicators is what the stakeholders actually understand (i.e., outtakes). What the stakeholders understand in turn determines what they do (i.e., outcomes), which is directly related to business outcomes.

Key drivers/antecedents (outputs)

Quite a number of themes have come up after extensive scholarly attempts to seek for reputation drivers. A detailed discussion of an exhaustive list of these reputation drivers is beyond the scope of this chapter, but some of the key factors that are widely recognized across academia and the commercial world include effective two-way communication (Fombrun and van Riel, 2004; Murray and White, 2005), providing good value and quality products and services (Dowling, 2004; Fombrun and van Riel, 2004; Fombrun *et al.*, 2000; Helm, 2005), effective leadership (e.g., CEO) and management (Dowling, 2004; Fombrun *et al.*, 2000; Helm, 2005), strong financial performance (Fombrun *et al.*, 2000), workplace environment (i.e., quality people, fair treatment of employees) (Dowling, 2004; Fombrun and van Riel, 2004; Fombrun *et al.*, 2000), and social responsibility and accountability (Fombrun *et al.*, 2000; Helm, 2005).

Further analysis can categorize these factors into three main domains: communication, corporate capability, and social responsibility. While the corporate capability in providing quality products, innovation, and maintaining competitive advantage lays the foundation for a favorable representation, continuous and symmetrical communication efforts are a central plank in building favorable perceptions among stakeholders and protecting reputation (Murray and White, 2005). According to Fombrun and van Riel (2004), companies rated high on the RepTrak™ tend to more readily disclose information about themselves and engage stakeholders in direct dialogs than do those less regarded companies. Communica-

tion increases the probability that an organization is perceived as genuine and credible. Finally, social responsibility plays a key role demonstrating to the general public that the organization is an accountable citizen (Fombrun and van Riel, 2004).

Key indicators (outtakes)

One should note that there is no fine line between the reputation drivers and their indicators. Since reputation is measured as a reflective construct, some of its antecedent factors also serve as indicators to measure reputation. For example, an organization's product and services, financial performance, work environment, and social responsibility as organizational outputs contribute to reputation building; meanwhile, as indicators of the Reputation Institute's RepTrack™, these aspects can be rated by stakeholders to evaluate an organization's reputation. Integrating major perspectives in measuring reputation, a list of key indicators of reputation can be summarized as follows:

Visibility. According to Fombrun and van Riel (2004), there is no real reputation without visibility. "Top-regarded companies are more than simply familiar – but they are definitely visible" (p.105). With that said, enhanced reputation can be achieved when the organization conveys a clear and visible image with the public most of the time. Dowling (2004) also noted that a prominent market and media presence of the organization acts as a descriptor of corporate reputation.

Credibility. Defined as the extent to which consumers, investors, or other stakeholders believe in an organization's trustworthiness and expertise (Newell and Goldsmith, 2001), corporate credibility has been recognized as a key determinant of corporate reputation (Fombrun, 1996; Lafferty *et al.*, 2002; Newell and Goldsmith, 2001). Corporate credibility forms part of the organization's image and also plays an important role in shaping corporate identity (Lafferty *et al.*, 2002), which in turn defines corporate reputation. Stacks (2010) also points out that how people rate an entity, individual, or brand in terms of believability, namely, credibility, interacts with other stakeholder expectations such as trust, relationship, and confidence.

Authenticity. According to Fombrun and van Riel (2004), authentic companies are seen as real, genuine, accurate, reliable, and trustworthy. The authentic values and behaviors an organization endorses are appreciated by its stakeholders. It returns in a form of emotional appeal created among stakeholders by the organization, which is another key driver for corporate reputation (Fombrun _et al._, 2000). Additionally, authenticity is an indispensable part of social accountability (Dowling, 2004). Therefore, directly or indirectly, authenticity shapes reputation.

Transparency. As a reputation trait, transparency was defined to encompass integrity, respect, and openness (Rawlins, 2009). A transparent organization is characterized by disseminating truthful, accurate, timely, balanced, and substantial information; stakeholder participation to identify the information they need; and objective and unbiased reporting of corporate activities and policies which hold the organization accountable (Balkin, 1999; Rawlins, 2009). Stakeholders ascribe strong reputation to the organization when it is transparent in the conduct of its affairs. On the contrary, if the organization avoids communication with stakeholders or provides only minimal, incomplete, or untruthful information to stakeholders, it loses ground in the court of public opinion (Fombrun and van Riel, 2004). As other reputation indicators, transparency is strongly tied to trust, credibility, corporate social responsibility, and ethics (Rawlins, 2009).

Trust. With respect to reputation, trust can be defined as stakeholder expectations that the business of the organization will be reliable, dependable, and continue to act in their interests even in an uncertain future (MacMillan _et al._, 2005). Helm (2005) noted that perceptions of an organization's honesty,

reliability, and benevolence are regarded as indicators of reputation. Similarly, Stacks (2010) also discussed the positive interrelationship between trust and reputation in his public relations measurement model.

Relationship. Defined as stakeholders' perception of association with the organization (Stacks, 2010), relationship is another key concept underlying reputation. According to Hon and Grunig (1999), quality relationship is characterized by mutual trust, commitment, satisfaction, and balance of power control. A close and quality relationship between stakeholders and the organization highly associates with the corporate reputation (Yang, 2007).

Confidence. Dowling (2001) suggested that the reputation of an organization is the combination of the admiration, respect, trust, and confidence in the organization's actions. Stacks (2010) also noted that stakeholder expectations such as reputation, trust, credibility, and relationship are _modified_ by stakeholder confidence before they demonstrate effects on stakeholder outcomes (ROE) and corporate ROI. Confidence is influenced and influences corporate reputation.

Although it is not an exhaustive list, these indicators discussed interact with each other jointly defining reputation. As a multidimensional construct comprising various stakeholder outtakes, reputation contributes to stakeholder and business outcomes.

Key outcomes

As recognized across academia and business communities, reputation leads to supportive stakeholder behavior and beneficial business outcomes. Externally, a good corporate reputation attracts customers to its products, investors to new investment, and media journalists to favorable press coverage. Internally, a good corporate reputation helps employees internalize corporate values, commit to their work and the organization, and engage in dialogs, cooperation, and citizenship behaviors (Caruana, 1997;

Fombrun and van Riel, 2004), which in turn lead to superior work performance.

In his public relations measurement model, Stacks (2010) demonstrated that reputation interacts with other nonfinancial indicators (i.e., trust, credibility, relationship, and confidence) to determine the return on stakeholders' expectation (ROE), which, in turn, contributes to economic ROI. Fombrun and van Riel (2004) also built the connection between reputation and financial values by arguing that stakeholder support are dramatically intertwined with financial indicators such as sales, revenues, and profits. Serving as an intangible asset with tangible values, reputation creates competitive advantage for the organization to outstand in the market.

Figure 44.3 lays out a process model of reputation. It establishes a linear relationship between the aspects where public relations/corporate communications tactical outputs could emphasize, leading to perceptual changes in an organization's reputation, and then the outcomes expected from the function.

Online Reputation Management

Furthermore, it is important to briefly note that reputation in the Digital Age has emerged as an entirely new area for research, definition, and measure. Internet communication specialist Alan Jenkins stated, "Your brand is no stronger than your reputation and will increasingly depend on what comes up when you are Googled" (cited in Phillips and Young, 2009, p. 154). The measurement of online reputation has borrowed from traditional, offline measures of reputation; however, more attentiveness to online reputation are required than traditionally was necessary. While online reputation remains a multidimensional construct, many of the major tenants of what we have come to understand as offline reputation appear to have been changed. For example, today, it takes only a single blogger or solitary Tweet to catch fire and influence an organization's reputation. As the agency WeberShandwick (http://www.online-reputations.com) explains,

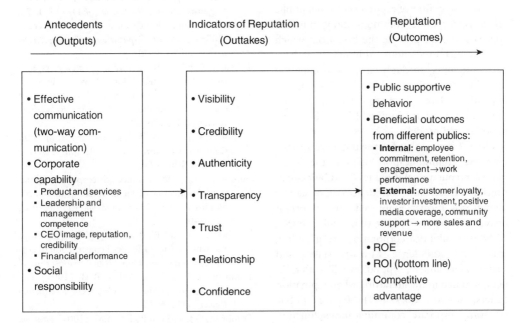

Figure 44.3 A process view of reputation.

Companies are now finding that they must attend to a diverse and all-powerful portfolio of stakeholders that now include online media, environmental groups, bloggers, Twitterers and citizen journalists that constantly command attention. Armed with little more than a computer and an opinion, some of these online word-of-mouth transmitters and receivers can undo a company's reputation by disseminating misinformation and innuendo instantly.

As a result, online reputation management has become an important factor for organizations to consider today.

Conclusion

Although it is tempting to conclude that there is one or more measures and methods that best predict the effect of an organization's reputation on corporate ROI, that is simply not possible given today's measurement and theoretical quandaries. The number of different measurement schemas employed and the lack of a clear definition of reputation from a public relations/corporate communications function approach do not provide the base from which to make such predictions. Although there have been attempts through structural equation modeling to imply some sort of causal modeling, there have been too few underlying theoretical models from which to base the hypothesized model.

What is clear is that for the public relations/corporate communication function, the "soft" or social reputational variables (credibility, relationship, trust, and confidence) in whatever definitional format employed are important drivers of corporate reputation. Quite simply, without credibility, a corporation's relationship, trust, and confidence with its stake- and shareholders and its reputation will suffer. As demonstrated in the literature, when reputation suffers, so too does ROI. Hence, public relations/corporate communications function ability to impact on ROE cannot be underestimated and should be at least one line of

research in better understanding the relationship between what is communicated by an organization and its impact on reputation and ultimately ROI.

References

Balkin, J.M. (1999) How mass media simulate political transparency. *Cultural Values*, 3, 393–413.

Barnett, M.L., Jermier, J.M., and Lafferty, B.A. (2006) Corporate reputation: The definitional landscape. *Corporate Reputation Review*, 9(1), 26–38.

Berens, G. and van Riel, C.B.M. (2004) Corporate associations in the academic literature: Three main streams of thought in the reputation measurement literature. *Corporate Reputation Review*, 7, 161–178.

Buffett, W. (1995) *Buffett: The Making of an American Capitalist*, R. Lowenstein (ed.). New York: Random House, Inc.

Caruana, A. (1997) Corporate reputation: Concept and measurement. *Journal of Product and Brand Management*, 6(2), 109–118.

Davies, G., Chun, R., da Silva, R.V., and Roper, S. (2001) The personification metaphor as a measurement approach for corporate performance. *Corporate Reputation Review*, 4(1), 113–127.

Davies, G., Chun, R., da Silva, R., and Roper, S. (2003) *Corporate Reputation and Competitiveness*. London: Routledge.

Dowling, G.R. (2001) *Creating Corporate Reputations*. Oxford, UK: Oxford University Press.

Dowling, G.R. (2004) Journalists' evaluation of corporate reputations. *Corporate Reputation Review*, 7(2), 196–205.

Fombrun, C.J. (1996) *Reputation: Realizing Value from the Corporate Image*. Boston: Harvard Business School Press.

Fombrun, C.J. (1998) Indices of corporate reputation: An analysis of media rankings and social monitors. *Corporate Reputation Review*, 1(4), 327–340.

Fombrun, C.J. and Rindova, V. (1996) Who's tops and who decides? The social construction of corporate reputations. Unpublished manuscript.

Fombrun, C.J. and van Riel, C.B.M. (1997) The reputational landscape. *Corporate Reputation Review*, 1(1), 5–13.

Fombrun, C.J. and van Riel, C.B.M. (2004) *Fame & Fortune*. Upper Saddle River, NJ: Pearson Education, Inc.

Fombrun, C.J., Gardberg, N.A., and Sever, J.M. (2000) The Reputation Quotient^SM: A multi-stakeholder measure of corporate reputation. *The Journal of Brand Management*, 7(4), 241–255.

Fortune (2011) World's Most Admired Companies. Retrieved from http://money.cnn.com/magazines/fortune/mostadmired/2011/full_list/ (last accessed October 5, 2012).

Gaines-Ross, L. (1998) Leveraging corporate equity. *Corporate Reputation Review*, 1(1, 2), 51–56.

Gardberg, N. and Fombrun, C. (2002) The global Reputation Quotient^SM project: First steps towards a cross-nationally valid measure of corporate reputation. *Corporate Reputation Review*, 4, 303–315.

Gotsi, M. and Wilson, A.M. (2001) Corporate reputation: Seeking a definition. *Corporate Communications*, 6(1), 24–30.

Grunig, J.E. (1993) Image and substance: From symbolic to behavioral relationships. *Public Relations Review*, 19(2), 121–139.

Helm, S. (2005) Designing a formative measure for corporate reputation. *Corporate Reputation Review*, 8(2), 95–111.

Hon, L.C. and Grunig, J.E. (1999) Guidelines for measuring relationships in public relations. Institute for Public Relations. Retrieved from http://www.instituteforpr.org/topics/measuring-relationships/ (last accessed October 29, 2012).

Hutton, J.G., Goodman, M.B., Alexander, J.B., and Genest, C.M. (2001) Reputation management: The new face of corporate public relations? *Public Relations Review*, 27, 247–261.

Lafferty, B.A., Goldsmith, R.E., and Newell, S.J. (2002) The dual credibility model: The influence of corporate and endorser credibility on attitudes and purchase intentions. *Journal of Marketing Theory and Practice*, 10(3), 1–12.

MacMillan, K., Money, K., Downing, S., and Hillenbrand, C. (2005) Reputation in relationships: Measuring experiences, emotions and behaviors. *Corporate Reputation Review*, 8(3), 214–230.

Markwick, N. and Fill, C. (1997) Towards a framework for managing corporate identity. *European Journal of Marketing*, 31(5/6), 396–409.

Michaelson, D. and Macleod, S. (2007) The application of "best practices" in public relations measurement and evaluation systems. *Public Relations Journal*, 1(1), 1–14.

Murray, K. and White, J. (2005) CEO's view of reputation management. *Journal of Communication Management*, 9(4), 348–358.

Newell, S.J. and Goldsmith, R.E. (2001) The development of a scale to measure perceived corporate credibility. *Journal of Business Research*, 52, 235–247.

Phillips, D. and Young, P. (2009) *Online Public Relations*. London: Kogan Page Limited.

Rawlins, B. (2009) Give the emperor a mirror: Towards developing a stakeholder measurement of organizational transparency. *Journal of Public Relations Research*, 21(1), 71–99.

Saxton, K. (1998) Where do reputations come from? *Corporate Reputation Review*, 1(4), 393–399.

Stacks, D.W. (2010) *Primer of Public Relations Research* (2nd ed.). New York: Guildford.

Stacks, D.W. and Watson, M.L. (2007) Two-way communication based on quantitative research and measurement. In E.L. Toth (ed.), *The Future of Excellence in Public Relations and Communication Management*. Mahwah, NJ: Lawrence Erlbaum Associates, Inc.

Stacks, D.W., Dodd, M.D., and Men, L.R. (2010) Public relations research and planning. In T. Gillis (ed.), *The IABC Handbook of Organizational Communication* (5th ed.). San Francisco, CA: Jossey-Bass, Inc.

van Riel, C.B.M., Stroeker, N.E., and Maathuis, O.J.M. (1998) Measuring corporate images. *Corporate Reputation Review*, 1(4), 313–326.

Wartick, S.L. (2002) Measuring corporate reputation: Definition and data. *Business & Society*, 41(4), 371–392.

Wei, Y.K. (2002) Corporate image as collect ethos: A poststructuralist approach. *Corporate Communications*, 7(4), 269–278.

Yang, S.U. (2007) An integrated model for organization – Public relational outcomes, organizational reputation, and their antecedents. *Journal of Public Relations Research*, 19(2), 91–121.

45

Corporate Reputation and Return on Investment (ROI): Measuring the Bottom-Line Impact of Reputation

Yungwook Kim and Jungeun Yang

Ewha Womans University, South Korea

This chapter deals with economic returns as the meaning of bottom-line contribution. Relating corporate reputation to the company's bottom line deserves more scientific explication rather than that based on common sense or intuition. Considering the weakness of the current evaluation system in public relations, the development of truly scientific evaluation might be possible by clarifying the causal links between reputation as public relations value and contribution to the bottom line. The chapter is composed of five parts. First, the need for return on investment (ROI) measurement of communication is discussed in the context of communication evaluation. Second, the reasons why reputation can be a legitimate goal of communication relations and how communication can contribute to the bottom line by achieving the goal are explained. Also, the relationship between reputation and financial performance is reviewed. Third, the possible ROI measure models are introduced and the results in the previous study are reviewed. Fourth, the preventive function of reputation is suggested and the full model for measuring the bottom-line impact is discussed. Fifth, the result of replication study with current data is presented and the implication and the extension of the theory are discussed. The results of the 1999 study and the results of the replication study with 2008–2010 data consistently proved the significant effect of reputation on revenue. Among the three models, the double-log model showed better explanatory power than the other models with easy application of reputation elasticity. Future empirical study should be extended to include the preventive effect of reputation and how it contributes to the bottom line. Based on the results, other theoretical ramifications are discussed.

Introduction

The need to demonstrate the effectiveness of communication work beyond clip counts has long been argued (Baskin *et al.*, 2010). Grunig (2006) stated that showing the return on

investment (ROI) of communication through the intangible assets would prove the value of communication. Applying the concept of marketing expenditure in contributing revenue growth and other quantifiable strategic objectives has been prioritized by businesses of all

The Handbook of Communication and Corporate Reputation, First Edition. Edited by Craig E. Carroll.
© 2013 John Wiley & Sons, Inc. Published 2015 by John Wiley & Sons, Inc.

sizes (Baskin *et al.*, 2010), and communication is no exception to this (Philips, 2001; Radford and Goldstein, 2002).

Measuring effectiveness in communication as attitudinal or behavioral change has been already discussed in the context of organizational impact (Dozier and Ehling, 1992; Grunig, 2006). However, the direct relationship between those impacts and the company's returns has rarely been tested in communication (Kim, 2000, 2001; Lee and Yoon, 2010). In other management fields, the relationship between reputation and financial performance has been tested, but its implication for communication has been very limited (Carmeli and Tishler, 2005; Graham and Bansal, 2007; Roberts and Dowling, 2002). Reputation in the perspective of publics has been introduced as long term and often intangible bottom-line contributions (Grunig, 1992; Hutton *et al.*, 2001). However, more concrete bottom-line contributions should be measured in terms of strategic and organization-level benefits such as revenue or financial returns (Ehling, 1992; Kim, 2000; Lee and Yoon, 2010).

Grunig (1998) argued that the economic contribution of communication is one dimension of explaining communication's value. Grunig and his colleagues conducted surveys of communication executives and CEOs and in-depth case studies to explore communication's value (Grunig, 1998). They found that communication's value is the integration of economic returns and maintaining good relationships with publics.

This chapter deals with economic returns as the meaning of bottom-line contribution. Relating communication value, such as reputation to the company's bottom line deserves more scientific explication rather than that based on common sense or intuition. Considering the weakness of the current evaluation system in communication, the development of truly scientific evaluation might be possible by clarifying the causal links between reputation as communication value and contribution to the bottom line.

The chapter is composed of five parts. First, the need for ROI measurement of communica-tion is discussed in the context of communication evaluation. Second, the reasons why reputation can be a legitimate goal of communication and how communication can contribute to the bottom line by achieving the goal are explained. Also, the relationship between reputation and financial performance is reviewed. Third, the possible ROI measure models are introduced and the results in the previous study are reviewed. Fourth, the preventive function of reputation is suggested and the full model for measuring the bottom-line impact is discussed. Fifth, the result of replication study with current data is presented and the implication and the extension of the theory are discussed.

Communication Evaluation and the Need of ROI Measures

In comparison with general evaluation research (Rossi and Freeman, 1993; Scriven, 1991), evaluation in communication can be categorized into six cells by three dimensions (formative/ summative evaluation, program/organizational level, effectiveness/efficiency). From Table 45.1, while formative evaluation (cell 1 and cell 2) and program-level evaluation (cell 3 and cell 4) being the most frequently conducted evaluations in the communication field, organizational-level evaluation (cell 5 and cell 6) rarely has been focused among practitioners and scholars, except for some effectiveness studies (Grunig, 1998, 2006; Grunig *et al.*, 1992) and efficiency studies (Ehling, 1992; Kim, 2000, 2001; Lee and Yoon, 2010).

General problems of communication evaluation can be summarized. First, effectiveness and evaluation have been used interchangeably. Effectiveness is one of the components of evaluation. Thus, measuring effectiveness does not mean a comprehensive evaluation. Second, the definition between effectiveness and efficiency is unclear. Sometimes effectiveness has been interpreted in a cost-efficient manner.

Table 45.1 The categorization of public relations evaluation.

	Effectiveness	*Efficiency*
Formative evaluation	Cell (1) Assessing expected program effectiveness Modifying the program through program assessment Identifying strategic constituencies	Cell (2) Selection of a cost-efficient program The application of media planning strategy such as message-vehicle cost per thousand Budgeting and decision making
Summative/program context	Cell (3) Media coverage Number of clippings Number of participants Cognitive effect Attitude change Behavioral-intention change after conducting the program	Cell (4) Program efficiency Material cost-effectiveness Cost-effectiveness of the program compared to other programs Cost–benefit analysis of programs
Summative/ organization context	Cell (5) Impact assessment to the organization Attitude–behavior change about the organization The measurement of public relations effectiveness to the organization such as reputation, relationship, and public opinion	Cell (6) Cost–benefit analysis in the organizational level Cost-effectiveness analysis in the organizational level Economic impact of public relations expense to the company's bottom line

While efficiency describes cost-effectiveness, effectiveness is related to goal achievement. Third, researchers have misused "quantification" in evaluation research. It is not impossible to quantify communication activities in view of evaluation research. For example, perceptions and attitude changes can always be quantified with psychometric scales. Yet, what is really difficult is measuring the relationship between communication activities and their contributions to the organization as presented in cell 6 in Table 45.1.

The reason for pursuing efficiency assessment lies in the presence of limited resources in the organization. Without presenting cost-efficiency, communication expense will always be curtailed when the organization faces economic recession and downsizing (Hon, 1997a; Kim, 2000, 2001). Also, it is better to evaluate communication activities with an organization's own objective standard, rather than depend on other managerial standards. Measuring efficiency at the organizational level is an

inevitable task for both practitioners and scholars (Kim, 2000, 2001; Lee and Yoon, 2010).

Bottom line can be defined as measurable benefits to the organization such as "enhanced cash flow, improved share price and shareholder value, greater productivity, more sales, better market shares, less employee turnover and higher earnings per share" (Webster, 1990, p. 18). In this chapter, ROI implies the bottom-line impact of communication value such as reputation (Kim, 2000). Measuring ROI implies the organization-level efficiency evaluation of communication activities (cell 6). This efficiency measure connects effectiveness (cell 5) and efficiency (cell 6) to evaluate the value of communication with economic sense of mind. Measuring the ROI impact is to materialize the achieved communication value (effectiveness) on the organization's bottom line with the consideration of cost (efficiency). ROI was investigated once in the Excellence study. It found averages of 184% ROI and 300% ROI in the case of excellent companies. However, since these results were derived from interviews with CEOs in an arbitrarily subjective way, it implies that quantitative data were not considerably used for measuring ROIs.

Reputation as the Communication Goal

Measuring the ROI impact of communication is based on the goal-attainment perspective. This perspective is presented in the discussion of organization effectiveness (Grunig *et al.*, 1992; Hon, 1997b). Setting goals for evaluation is a widely accepted methodology in communication evaluation (Gregory, 2001; Hon, 1997b). This tradition goes back to Grunig and Hunt's (1984) mention about applying the same principle of management by objective (MBO) to communication evaluation. The goal-attainment approach is the most focused approach of organization effectiveness in the Excellence study (Dozier and Ehling, 1992; Grunig, 2006). Researchers have defined effective communication as achieving its goal through communication activities (Hon, 1997b).

In this regard, setting up appropriate and measurable goals can be the first step of measuring the ROI impact of communication. By doing this, causal relationships between the communication goal and the organizational goal can be empirically tested to connect effectiveness and efficiency.

Among communication goals, reputation manifests communication value in an embracing manner (Clark, 2000; Hon, 1997b; Hutton *et al.*, 2001; Kim, 2000). Reputation represents what communication management should achieve in the end (Clark, 2000). Thus, measuring the ROI impact of communication value implies returns on reputation, which can be called the "reputation ROI." Then the important question lies on how a company's reputation impacts its bottom line.

It should be noted that the term reputation has been used interchangeably with other terms such as image and identity. In review of the past reputation literatures, Walker (2010) differentiated reputation with organizational identity and organizational image. Reputation, in contrast to organizational image, refers to actual public perceptions. Reputation is also different from organizational identity in that it is the perception by both internal and external stakeholders, while identity is the actual perception by the internal publics (Walker, 2010). Reputation is also different from image in that it takes time to build (Mahon, 2002). For this reason, image is considered flexible, while reputation is relatively stable and enduring, since it takes time to build (Gray and Balmer, 1998).

Extending Fombrun's (1996) definition on reputation, Walker (2010) summarized the attributes of reputation based on the previous reputation literatures. Reputation (1) is based on perception, (2) is the aggregate perception of all stakeholders (Wartick, 2002), (3) is inherently comparative (Fombrun, 1996), (4) can be positive or negative (Brown *et al.*, 2006), and (5) is stable and enduring (Gray and Balmer, 1998; Roberts and Dowling, 2002). For this reason, reputation has often been argued to be closely related to communication (Clark, 2000; Hutton *et al.*, 2001; Kim, 2000).

On the relationship between communication and reputation, Clark (2000) argued that reputation management is often referred as another name of public relations. Hutton *et al.* (2001) found that public relations practitioners consider reputation management as one of the most important communication goals. Obtaining good reputation is considered as a key communication goal (Kim, 2000). Reputation studies in communication have two research directions in recent years. First, the impact of media visibility and framing on reputation and the company's performance has been investigated (Carroll and McCombs, 2003; Kiousis *et al.*, 2007; Mahon and Wartick, 2003). Media coverage has a very close relationship with reputation. Not only the amount of coverage but the issue salience of media coverage also influenced a company's reputation (Carroll and McCombs, 2003). Kiousis *et al.* (2007) extended the relationship between media coverage and reputation, and found that the public relations messages in news were related to the company's financial performance.

Second, the influence of the company's corporate social responsibility (CSR) on reputation and social performance was another area showing the relationship between communication and reputation. Numerous studies have explored how CSR contributed to create and increase intangible corporate assets, including reputation (Brammer and Pavelin, 2006; David *et al.*, 2005).

Based on the review, it can be construed that building reputation is regarded as a pivotal goal of communication. Studies on the relationship between communication and corporate reputation have been extended to include the bottom-line effect of various public relations activities, mediated by corporate reputation (Kim, 2001; Kiousis *et al.*, 2007). Thus, measuring the reputation ROI became a prerequisite for providing the bottom-line impact of communication.

Reputation and Financial Performance

Grunig *et al.* (1992) argued that communication objectives should be connected to broader organizational goals. Other researchers and practitioners also agreed with the importance of that task (Grunig, 2006; Hon, 1997b). The reputation ROI research is also in line with the assumption that communication goals should be connected to organizational goals to measure the contribution of communication to the organization.

Organizational contribution can be defined as achieving organizational goals (Grunig, 2006). Campbell (1977) defined 30 organizational effectiveness measures such as productivity, efficiency, profit, control of the environment, and revenue growth. In the context of economic value, profitability and revenue are the most common indicators of organizational goals (Gregory, 2001). In the multiple-goal theory, which suggested various goals in each stage of organizational efforts (Kim, 1999), profitability

and revenue were listed as the ultimate goals in the organization.

In relation to communication, reputation acted either as a mediating or moderating variable that influences the financial performance of the company. Deephouse (2000) found that positive media coverage was connected to increased financial performance for commercial banks. Kiousis *et al.* (2007) compared public relations content, news media coverage, public opinion, and corporate financial performance in 28 US companies from the Reputation Quotient. As a result, describing or mentioning corporate vision and leadership in *The Wall Street Journal* was significantly related to company revenues, profits, and assets. Lee and Yoon (2010) examined the relationship between economic outcome and international investment of communication in the United States. After controlling the economic size of the countries, they found that more public relations contracts resulted in higher US imports from the countries, US direct investment on other countries, and the number of US tourists visiting other countries.

The financial value of intangible assets has been studied from various management fields (Schnietz and Epstein, 2005). The impact of corporate reputation on corporate financial performance has been empirically investigated. Black *et al.* (2000) suggested that nonfinancial, intangible assets such as reputation create market value, even after controlling the halo effects of the financial performance of the company. Roberts and Dowling (1997, 2002) further examined the relationship between reputation and financial performance by decomposing reputation into financial (a component predicted by previous financial performance) one and the residual ones. Empirical results showed that firms with better corporate reputations were better able to sustain superior financial outcomes over time. Good reputations also helped even the poor performing firms to reset their profitability on standard. It was true that it was not only a firm's financial reputation that had consistently strong impact on profit persistence, but also its residual reputation.

Duhe (2009) testified the relationship between reputation and bottom line. Analyzing 706 firms over a 21-year time frame revealed that three attributions of reputation – that is, management quality, financial soundness, and social responsibility – made consistently positive contributions to several measures of a firm's financial performance. Eberl and Schwaiger (2005) divided reputation into cognitive (sympathy) and affective (competence) dimensions. Even after controlling the past performance, both reputation dimensions significantly influenced future financial performance. Strategic value of reputation also evidences in the company's abilities to attract, attain, and operate physical, financial, and intellectual resources for creating sustainable competitive advantage (Smaiziene, 2008). There is no doubt that consumers utilize corporate reputation as a strategic weapon for seeking lower costs for better purchase of credit terms, using greater bargaining power of theirs. Also, reputation can be exploited for better firm performance such as stock price (Vergin and Qoronfleh, 1998).

Socially desirable performance proves to generate financial value in many studies (Hillman and Keim, 2001; Waddock and Graves, 1997). The mediating role of reputation between CSR and financial performance was examined as well. Surroca *et al.* (2010) found that the effect of CSR is mediated by intangible assets such as innovation, human capital, culture, and reputation. Similarly, Luo and Bhattacharya (2006) also found that the effect of CSR on firm value was mediated by corporate reputation.

The financial performance of reputation has been conceptualized and measured in various ways. Sabate and Puente (2003) conducted a review of literatures on the relationship between corporate reputation and financial performance. In the review, financial performance was defined as return on assets (ROA), market share, revenue growth rate, share value, return on invested capital (ROIC), and Tobin's q. In this chapter, measuring the reputation ROI implies the impact of reputation on the company's financial performance. In communication literature, the company's financial performance was often measured by revenue or revenue change (Kim,

2000, 2001, 2006; Kiousis *et al.*, 2007). Studies in other fields also utilized revenue data as the company's financial performance (Carmeli and Tishler, 2005; Deephouse, 1997).

The Previous Reputation ROI Research and Possible Models

The reputation ROI research has been rare in communication studies. In the pilot study, Kim (1997) found a positive relationship between the company's reputation and returns across all industries. By using economic linear and nonlinear models, the considerable amount of the variance in revenues could be explained by reputation. The most important indication of this study is the exhibition of a positive relationship between reputation and revenue.

Assigning an economic value to the company's reputation can be an initial step for developing more sophisticated and scientific methodologies of measuring contributions of communication. However, economic modeling is different from the cost–benefit analysis, which directly assigns the monetary value of communication goals. Assigning the monetary value, as Grunig (1998) indicated, depends on intersubjective reliability and is less than objective. However, coefficients from the economic model testing can represent the weighted relationship between the company's reputation (the communication goal) and returns (the organizational goal) in a specific category. These coefficients can be used in the next step to assign the monetary value of goal achievement.

Previous studies (Kim, 1999, 2000, 2001) were an initial step to materialize communication values in an empirical way. Reputation was set as the communication goal, and the company's revenue is chosen as the organizational goal. The previous research on the reputation ROI (Kim, 1999) was conducted as follows.

First, the previous study accepts *Fortune*'s approach that utilized an instrument measuring relational image and represented the symmetrical worldview. Thus, reputation data were

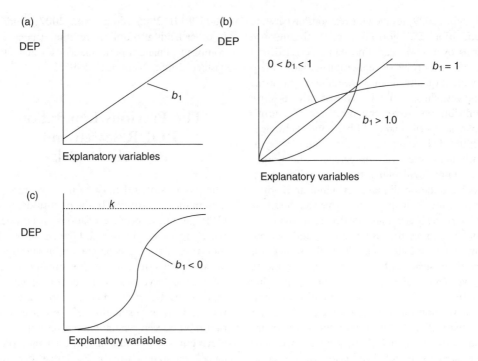

Figure 45.1 Three possible models for measuring each relationship: (a) linear model; (b) double-log model; (c) log reciprocal model.
DEP, dependent variables.

collected from the results of *Fortune*'s annual corporate reputation survey 1996–1998. Reputation is measured by eight key attributes: quality of management; quality of products or services; ability to attract, develop, and keep talented people; value as a long-term investment; use of corporate visible and invisible assets; financial soundness; innovativeness in corporate culture; and community and environmental responsibility. Reputation data were computed into increasing and decreasing rates from previous scores.

Second, other economic variable data such as revenues and market share were collected from existing databases. For measuring contributions to the organization, there are two options: profitability and revenue. Revenue was chosen for measuring the direct impact of reputation following previous research. Revenue data collected from *Fortune*'s 1996, 1997, and 1998 revenue change (%) item were used as a final dependent variable in the models.

By analyzing data from 157 companies, both linear and nonlinear regression models for the relationship between reputation and revenue were tested. The previous study proposed three models based on the communication and other management literatures (Kim, 1999, 2000). These are the linear model, the double-log model, and the log reciprocal model (refer to Figure 45.1).

Three possible economic models can be specified:

1. the linear model: $REV = b_0 + b_1\,REP + b_2\,MS$,
2. the double-log model: $REV = \exp^{b0} \times REP^{b1} \times MS^{b2}$,
3. the log reciprocal model: $REV = \exp^{b0 + b1/REP + b2\,MS}$,

where REP = reputation, MS = market share, and REV = revenue.

Looking at the relationship between reputation and revenue in the linear model, revenue indefinitely increases as reputation increases (Figure 45.1a). Once again in the double-log model, indefinite revenue growth occurs but this time with decreasing slope in a concave down form $(\partial Y/\partial X > 0,\ \partial^2 X/\partial Y^2 < 0)$ (Figure 45.1b). This explains that revenue never reach the speed of increasing reputation. In the log reciprocal model, revenue increases up to the k level. It also shows an overall of positive slope, but with an evidence of a change in slope from a concave up shape (increasing slope) to a concave down shape (decreasing slope) $(\partial Y/\partial X > 0,\ \partial^2 X/\partial Y^2 >$ and $<0)$ (Figure 45.1c). Theoretically, the nonlinear models seem to explain revenue increase better than the linear model because in reality revenue cannot increase proportionately with increasing reputation (Kim, 2000).

All three of the models showed the positive effect of the company's reputation on the company's revenue with the one-year data (Kim, 1999). In the linear model, reputation indicated a positive relationship $(b_1 = 0.637)$ that was statistically significant $(t = 2.345)$. In the double-log model, reputation had a positive impact on revenue and was a statistically significant explanatory variable $(b_1 = 0.298,\ t = 2.805)$. Interestingly, the linear model $(R\text{-squared} = 0.119)$ and the double-log model $(R\text{-squared} = 0.109)$ indicated similar explanatory power. With the three-year data $(n = 417)$, the double-log model $(R\text{-squared} = 0.047)$ indicated better explanatory power than other models (refer to Table 45.2). The log reciprocal model did not show any statistical significance both in the one-year and the three-year data. This result demonstrates that the impact of reputation on revenues has a diminishing increasing rate. It is important to note that the increasing rate of the company's revenue can be different by the level of reputation increase. Nevertheless, the most important point is that all three models indicated the positive impact of the company's reputation on the company's revenue. This result confirms what was indicated by the literature review.

Another study on the reputation ROI measurement was conducted for service industries from *Fortune* companies (Kim, 2000). The results also showed positive impact of reputa-

Table 45.2 Regression results with three-year (1996–1998) data $(n = 417)$.

Variable	Coefficient	Standard error	t-Statistic
a) The linear model (REV = $b_0 + b_1$ REP + b_2 MS)			
C	10.477	1.322	7.923
REP	0.276	0.140	1.970
MS	0.208	0.070	2.992
F-statistic (zero slopes) = 6.840			
R-squared = 0.0320			
b) The double-log model (REV = $\exp^{b0} \times$ REP $^{b1} \times$ MS^{b2})			
C	1.685	0.241	7.003
LREP	0.220	0.068	3.215
LMS	0.094	0.0927	1.013
F-statistic (zero slopes) = 5.743			
R-squared = 0.0468			
c) The log reciprocal model (REV = $\exp^{b0 + b1/\text{REP} + b2\,\text{MS}}$)			
C	1.911	0.091	21.109
RREP	−0.028	0.043	−0.665
MS	0.501E-02	0.470E-02	1.066
F-statistic (zero slopes) = 0.768			
R-squared = 0.381E-02			

REV, revenue; REP, reputation; LREP, log (reputation); RREP, 1/reputation; MS, market share; LMS, log (market share).

tion on revenue increase. Although the sample only included companies in the service industry, the results showed a positive relationship between corporate reputation and ROI. The beta coefficients of reputation were 3.470 in the linear model $(R\text{-squared} = 0.0570)$ and 1.970 in the double-log model $(R\text{-squared} = 0.139)$. In the log reciprocal model $(R\text{-squared} = 0.129)$, it was −10.101, signifying positive relationship between reputation and revenue. All coefficients in the three models were statistically significant. Therefore, the results confirmed that stronger reputation did contribution to the corporate ROI.

The Prevention Effect as Another Reputation ROI

Building reputation was used as the communication goal in the previous test (Kim, 1999,

2000, 2001). However, communication can contribute to a company's bottom line by preventing reputational crises. These activities include environmental scanning, issue management, and crisis containment. However, these prevention effects are not normally measured as the bottom-line effect even though they are closely related to the company's survival and profitability in modern society. Therefore, these multifaceted aspects of communication impact should be considered.

Fombrun (2001) explained reputation acts like a "reservoir of goodwill," implying that reputation works as a form of insurance of the company. Previous studies found that firms with good reputation survive crises (Fombrun, 1996; Gregory, 2001). In this regard, reputation's impact on financial performance does not come from increasing financial performance but from insulation from negative financial performance (Schnietz and Epstein, 2005). On the basis of the role in the process of creating corporate values, reputation has a significant role in treating potential and current conflicts between a company and its environment (Grof, 2001; Waddock and Smith, 2000).

In the analysis of the 1999 Seattle World Trade Organization (WTO) meeting, Schnietz and Epstein (2005) found that firms with a reputation for social responsibility appear to have been less harshly penalized by investors than those firms without it. They concluded that reputation for social responsibility yielded tangible financial benefit during the crisis of the Seattle meeting. Jones *et al.* (2000) also found that *Fortune*'s "Most Admired Companies" suffered lower market valuation losses in the 1989 stock market plunge than did the firms with lower *Fortune* reputation ratings.

Also, issue management activities were considered to contribute to the creation of corporate reputation by preventing crisis (Yoon, 2002). Fombrun (2001) claimed that reputation had considerable hidden value as a form of insurance. Firms with good reputation withstand crises with lesser economic loss (Fombrun, 1996; Knight and Pretty, 1999).

In the comprehensive sense, the reputation ROI can be specified as follows:

The reputation ROI
= the influence of reputation on the company's revenue
+ the preventive effects of reputation crises
+ other contextual considerations.

For the reputation ROI, the contribution of reputation is obtained from the regression result, which can be analyzed through the company's own cumulated data. And the preventive effect of reputation can be achieved by calculating the expected revenue loss after similar issue case studies in the same industry. For the final judgment, other contextual factors should be considered, and some of the possible considering factors include world economic crises, oil price hikes, and other external emergencies.

The calculation of preventive effects can be estimated by listing all the issues of a company and collecting the issues that actually did not happen. Preventive effects can be calculated based on the similar previous event. For example, if a certain company faced issues like food tampering, accidents, and rumors, and if the company prevented them from happening, with expected loss of US$5 million, US$1 million, and US$2 million each, the total preventive effect could be estimated as US$8 million. And this is the economic value that the corporate reputation protected from the potential crises.

Replication with Current Data and Applications

A replication study of Kim (1999) was conducted in order to reconfirm the effect of reputation on ROI. *Fortune*'s "Most Admired Companies" were chosen for the samples. The 50 Most Admired Companies for three years (2010, 2009, and 2008) were selected. After omitting unavailable data, the total of 140 data were prepared for the testing. For the reputation and revenue data, increasing rates compared to those of the previous year were used. This time market share was not included as a variable, since *Fortune*'s industry division had become too segmented to calculate comparable data. Also, for the purpose of the replication that was more about determining the effect of reputation on ROI, the model was simplified for application. However, in the future study, in order to increase the explanatory power, variables such as market share, past financial performance (Eberl and Schwaiger, 2005; Roberts and Dowling, 2002), and other contextual variables might be included. This replication was more concentrated on showing the predictive power of reputation in a simple way, rather than on increasing the overall explanatory power of the model.

The three models were tested again with current data and results are summarized in Table 45.3.

Both the linear model and the double-log model showed the positive impact of reputation on revenue, and the direction of the effect remained the same as the previous study. In the linear model, reputation indicated a positive relationship ($b_1 = 0.230$, $p = 0.184$) though not statistically significant. In the double-log

Table 45.3 Regression results with three-year (2008–2010) data ($n = 140$).

Variable	Coefficient	Standard error	t-Statistic
a) The linear model (REV = $b_0 + b_1$ REP + b_2 MS)			
C	5.181	1.356	3.822
REP	0.230	0.1720	1.335
F-statistic (zero slopes) = 1.783			
R-squared = 0.013			
b) The double-log model (REV = $\exp^{b0} \times \text{REP}^{b1} \times$ MS^{b2})			
C	0.208	0.080	2.611
LREP	0.280	0.102	2.749
F-statistic (zero slopes) = 7.555			
R-squared = 0.052			
c) The log reciprocal model (REV = $\exp^{b0 + b1/\text{REP} + b2\,\text{MS}}$)			
C	0.161	0.080	2.003
RREP	0.076	0.060	2.262
F-statistic (zero slopes) = 1.592			
R-squared = 0.011			

REV, revenue; REP, reputation; LREP, log (reputation); RREP, 1/reputation; MS, market share.

model, reputation had a positive impact on revenue ($b_1 = 0.280$) that is statistically significant ($t = 2.749$, $p = 0.007$). Therefore, by the replication test, the positive impact of reputation on ROI has been reconfirmed.

The double-log model for the year 2008–2010 data showed consistent results when compared to the previous studies conducted for year between 1996 and 1998. Reputation coefficients and explanatory powers (R-squared) showed similar outcomes in both models. This consistency implies that revenue cannot increase proportionately as the level of reputation increases. The increasing rate of the company's financial performance is slowly decreasing. Thus, when a company obtains a high level of reputation among publics, maintaining the current level should be its priority objective of all.

Also, the double-log model showed the possible use of reputation elasticity for measuring the bottom-line impact of communication activities. By transferring to the log model, the reputation elasticity of revenue can be automatically computed. In this regard, this variable can be termed *reputation elasticity*.

Reputation elasticity can be expressed as the following:

$$\text{Elasticity } (\eta) = \partial \text{ Revenue}/\partial \text{ Reputation} \times \text{Reputation}/\text{Revenue}.$$

From the double-log model, we can derive the reputation elasticity. If we transfer the double-log model using log (Gujarati, 1995),

$$\log(\text{Revenue}) = b_0 + b_1 \log(\text{Reputation}) + b_2 \log(\text{Market share}).$$

By getting a derivation, b_1 becomes reputation elasticity of revenue:

$$\partial \text{ Revenue}/\partial \text{ Reputation} = b_1(\text{Revenue}/\text{Reputation}),$$

$$b_1 = \partial \text{ Revenue}/\partial \text{ Reputation} \times \text{Reputation}/\text{Revenue}.$$

This formula can be easily used to calculate the bottom-line impact of reputation. If one company has its own cumulated time-series data, its reputation elasticity can be calculated through the double-log model with ease.

To apply the model in the real world, the communication department may establish the communication goal (reputation) based on the company's yearly policy. If the company policy is very aggressive toward the market and demanding a challenging goal, the communication department should set up an appropriate increasing rate of reputation based on the previous three- or five-year cumulated trends. Practitioners can use the proposed testing model as a starting point. With the company's own time-series data, practitioners can easily derive parameter estimates that can explain the bottom-line impact of reputation based on empirical outcomes.

If a hypothesized case for company A is given, the coefficients for variables can be estimated from the testing model. If the communication goal of company A for this year is to increase the current level of reputation by 10% and the regression coefficient between reputation and the company's revenue is 0.3, the company could expect a bottom-line impact of a 3% increase in the company's revenue when the goal is achieved. Also, if company A faces several issues and manages well to prevent reputational crises, the monetary value saved from successful issue managements should be counted to draw a full picture of the reputation ROI. When the monetary value is assigned for successful issue and crisis managements, similar cases of previous experience in the same industry should be used as a reasonable reference point. Other contextual variables should also be considered in this juncture.

If there existed an electronic company A with total revenue of 100 million dollars and its yearly reputation goal is fully achieved, the reputation impact is 3 million dollars. Then the company faced several issues this year. The crises include product tampering, accidents, and managerial misbehavior, and these issues were partly or fully managed by the company. They were compared to similar crises that occurred in the same industry and assigned dollar values accrued from the monetary value

saved from successful issue and crisis managements. The total monetary value saved is 3 million dollars, aggregating 1, 1.5, and 0.5 million for each crisis issue. Thus, the total reputation value is 6 million dollars. In case the communication budget was 3 million dollars, 200% reputation ROI is achieved for company A this year:

$$
\begin{aligned}
&\text{Total} \\
&\text{reputation} \\
&\text{value} \\
&\text{(6 million} \\
&\text{dollars)}
\end{aligned}
=
\begin{aligned}
&\text{reputation} \\
&\text{impact} \\
&\text{(3 million} \\
&\text{dollars)}
\end{aligned}
+
\begin{aligned}
&\text{prevention} \\
&\text{effects} \\
&\text{(3 million} \\
&\text{dollars)}
\end{aligned}
+
\begin{aligned}
&\text{other} \\
&\text{factors}
\end{aligned}
$$

$$
\begin{aligned}
&\text{The} \\
&\text{reputation} \\
&\text{ROI} \\
&(200\%)
\end{aligned}
=
\left(
\frac{\text{total reputation}}{\text{value/communication}}{\text{expenses}}
\right) \times 100.
$$
$$[(600/300)\times 100]$$

Overall, the validity and reliability of this method can be reinforced if the company uses its own cumulated data to extract the impact coefficient. Economic modeling can be elaborated by accommodating special circumstances each company should consider. The impact of specific changes such as crisis situations and a surge in competition can be recorded for future use. After one fiscal year, practitioners can also provide CEOs with results based on longitudinal analysis. In highly regarded companies, maintaining the current level of reputation can be a goal. Also, after a crisis situation, restoring the company's reputation becomes a goal. The proposed approach can be a starting point for all of these evaluation approaches.

Conclusion

Measuring the bottom-line impact of reputation is important since it is related to the effort to develop the efficiency measure in communication evaluation. Reputation should be considered as a legitimate goal of communication, and the contribution of communication to revenue can be estimated through reputation. Past studies on the effect of media coverage on financial performance or the effect of social responsibility on financial performance show that reputation mediated the effect of communication activities.

Direct relationship between reputation and the financial performance was tested by linear and nonlinear analyses using existing *Fortune* data. The results of the 1999 study and the results of the replication study with 2008–2010 data consistently proved the significant effect of reputation on revenue. Among the three models, the double-log model showed better explanatory power than the other models with easy application of reputation elasticity. Future empirical study should be extended to include the preventive effect of reputation and how it contributes to the bottom line.

Theory Extension and Implications

The relationship between communication expense and the communication goals should be supplemented to make the economic value model more complete. Given this reality, communication studies have tried to develop the two-step measurement systems to demonstrate the economic value of communication activities (Figure 45.2) (Kim, 2001). But not much research has been conducted to finalize the appropriate model so far.

In the previous study, the positive relationship between communication expense and reputation was supported (Figure 45.2) (Kim, 2001), and the influencing coefficient was statistically significant. This outcome implies that, as the unit of communication expense increases, a positive effect on the company's reputation

can be expected. In addition, the positive relationship between reputation and the company's revenue was also supported.

Thus, by integrating the results, a two-stage model for measuring the economic impact of communication activities was accomplished. Communication expense affects the company's reputation positively and reputation impacts the company's revenue positively. Thus, communication expense indirectly affects the company's revenue. As discussed in the literature review, measuring the economic impact of communication activities was the integration of the effectiveness measure (between communication activities and the company's reputation) and the efficiency measure (between reputation and the company's revenue) at the organizational level. This proposed two-stage model was successfully supported through hypothesis testing and model fitting (Kim, 2001).

This line of study suggests an inventive methodology compared to previous research such as Ehling's (1992) work. Ehling's work tried to assign subjective utilities of public relations activities. However, the introduction of an empirical methodology can enlarge the scope of communication evaluation research by showcasing measurable impact. Obviously, communication practitioners can use this methodology to present tangible results of communication activities on the company's bottom line.

Also, as confirmed in the test, measuring the impact of communication expense directly on the bottom line was not empirically supported (Kim, 1999). This result implies that communication can contribute to the bottom line best by achieving the communication goal. This two-stage model validates the unique importance of reputation as the communication goal

Figure 45.2 The two-stage model of measuring the economic value of public relations in the organizational level.

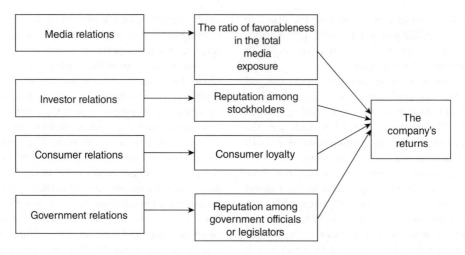

Figure 45.3   The example of measuring the bottom-line impact of each public relations function.

in the economic value model. However, this line of study should be continued for empirical verification. Generalizing communication impact through a meta-analytic approach becomes possible only when enough empirical data have been accumulated.

Communication data from research organizations (such as A.C. Nielsen in the advertising field) would be indispensable for national-data cumulating and reliability checks. Also, the most imminent task of communication academicians and practitioners is to find mutually agreeable constructs for the communication goal. And the development of models can be accelerated through application for diverse industry and product categories.

Halo effects and long-term effects (Black *et al.*, 2000) in evaluative measures were not considered at this stage. Cumulative components of evaluation measures should be reflected in a future model. Longitudinal data contain the lagged effects of communication activities and reputation. In addition, the possibility of interaction effects among explanatory variables is an important consideration that should be investigated in future study.

The economic value model has broad applications to communication management and education. First, all corporate communication activities can be measured together in the

detailed model (Figure 45.3). For example, if one company performs several communication functions such as media relations, investor relations, consumer relations, and government relations, several mediating variables can be included. Some examples of those variables might be ratio of favorable stories to total media exposure, reputation among stockholders, level of consumer loyalty, and reputation among government officials or legislators. By testing all of these outcomes of communication activities in the detailed model, the impact of each activity can be compared. This enables executives or CEOs to have a comprehensive view of the impact of all of their corporate communication activities, broadening their usual way of depending on just one measurement. This scenario is described in Figure 45.3.

Second, the economic value model can provide insights for an integrated marketing communications (IMC) evaluation model. Communication and advertising effects can be integrated into the same goals of contribution to the organization. This integration is possible only in view of the organizational goal. Doing so eliminates conflicts over communication dominance or advertising dominance, either of which impairs the full function of effective communication activities for the organization (Thorson and Moore, 1996). Public relations

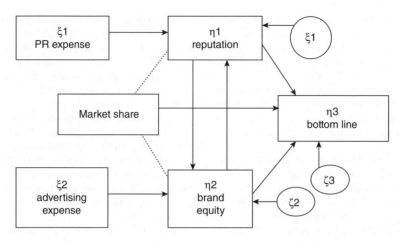

Figure 45.4   A model for IMC evaluation.

and advertising have their independent goals – reputation and brand equity. When each domain of communication activities works toward its specific goals and maintain its independence, communication activities in the organization are optimized and the bottom-line impact is maximized (see Figure 45.4). The empirical evidence showed that both the company's reputation and brand equity have significant impact on the company's revenue (Kim, 2002). Also, reputation and brand equity showed the positive relationship in the proposed model. For communication practitioners, the results provide the opportunity to demonstrate the value of communication within an IMC approach beyond mere product publicity.

Third, practitioners can legitimately choose communication programs based on tangible results estimated by the economic value model. This tangible justification provides the basis for scientific communication budgeting process in the organization. Fourth, the proliferation of Internet and social network services has diverse ramifications for the economic value model. Social network service produces various tangible data that can be converted into the economic model and reinforces the validity of data collection.

Lastly, communication evaluation in the classroom should be covered in a more comprehensive manner. In addition to existing effectiveness measures such as attitude change and

behavioral intention, efficiency measures such as cost–benefit analysis and cost-effectiveness analysis should be introduced to the classroom. Also, organization-level evaluation such as impact assessment to the organization and cost-efficiency at the organizational level should be addressed. Discussing the totality of evaluation will enhance the scientific measurement of communication. As Ehling (1992) explained, the social value and economic value of communication are both important topics in the classroom.

References

Baskin, O., Hahn, J., Seaman, S., and Reines, D. (2010) Perceived effectiveness and implementation of public relations measurement and evaluation tools among European providers and consumers of PR services. *Public Relations Review*, *36*, 105–111.

Black, E., Carnes, T., and Richardson, V. (2000) The market valuation of corporate reputation. *Corporate Reputation Review*, *3*(1), 31–42.

Brammer, S. and Pavelin, S. (2006) Corporate reputation and social performance: The importance of fit. *Journal of Management Studies*, *43*(3), 435–455.

Brown, T.J., Dacin, P.A., Pratt, M.G., and Whetten, D. (2006) Identity, intended image, construed image, and reputation: An interdisciplinary framework and suggested terminology. *Journal of the Academy of Marketing Science*, *34*(2), 99–106.

Campbell, J.P. (1977) On the nature of organizational effectiveness. In P.S. Goodmand and J.M. Pennings (eds), *New Perspectives on Organizational Effectiveness*. San Francisco, CA: Jossey-Bass, pp. 235–248.

Carmeli, A. and Tishler, A. (2005) Perceived organizational reputation and organizational performance: An empirical investigation of industrial enterprises. *Corporate Reputation Review*, 8(1), 13–30.

Carroll, C.E. and McCombs, M. (2003) Agenda-setting effects of business news on the public's images and opinions about major corporations. *Corporate Reputation Review*, 6(1), 36–46.

Clark, C.E. (2000) Difference between public relations and corporate social responsibility: An analysis. *Public Relations Review*, 26(3), 363–380.

David, P., Kline, S., and Dai, Y. (2005) Corporate social responsibility practices, corporate identity, and purchase intention: A dual-process model. *Journal of Public Relations Research*, 17(3), 291–313.

Deephouse, D. (1997) The effect of financial and media reputations on performance. *Corporate Reputation Review*, 1(1/2), 68–72.

Deephouse, D. (2000) Media reputation as a strategic resource: An integration of mass communication and resource-based theories. *Journal of Management*, 26(6), 1091–1112.

Dozier, D.M. and Ehling, W.P. (1992) Evaluation of public relations programs: What the literature tells us about their effects. In J. Grunig (ed.), *Excellence in Public Relations and Communications Management*. Hillsdale, NJ: LEA, pp. 159–184.

Duhe, S. (2009) Good management, sound finances, and social responsibility: Two decades of U.S. corporate insider perspectives on reputation and the bottom line. *Public Relations Review*, 35, 77–78.

Eberl, M. and Schwaiger, M. (2005) Corporate reputation: Disentangling the effects on financial performance. *European Journal of Marketing*, 39(7/8), 838–854.

Ehling, W.P. (1992) Estimating the value of public relations and communication to an organization. In J. Grunig (ed.), *Excellence in Public Relations and Communications Management*. Hillsdale, NJ: LEA, pp. 617–638.

Fombrun, C.J. (1996) *Reputation: Realizing Value from the Corporate Image*. Boston: Harvard Business School Press.

Fombrun, C.J. (2001) Corporate reputation as economic assets. In M. Hitt, R. Freeman, and J. Harrison (eds), *Handbook of Strategic Management*. Oxford, UK: Blackwell.

Graham, M. and Bansal, P. (2007) Consumer's willingness to pay for corporate reputation: The context of airline companies. *Corporate Reputation Review*, 10(3), 189–200.

Gray, E.R. and Balmer, J. (1998) Managing corporate image and corporate reputation. *Long Range Planning*, 31(5), 695–702.

Gregory, A. (2001) Public relations and evaluation: Does the reality match the rhetoric? *Journal of Marketing Communication*, 7, 171–189.

Grof, A. (2001) Communication in the creation of corporate values. *Corporate Communications*, 6(4), 193–198.

Grunig, J.E. (ed.) (1992) *Excellence in Public Relations and Communication Management*. Hillsdale, NJ: LEA.

Grunig, J.E. (1998) The value of public relations. Manuscript submitted for publication.

Grunig, J.E. (2006) Furnishing the edifice: Ongoing research on public relations as a strategic management function. *Journal of Public Relations Research*, 18(2), 151–176.

Grunig, J.E. and Hunt, T. (1984) *Managing Public Relations*. New York: Holt, Rinehart and Winston.

Grunig, L., Grunig, J.E., and Ehling, W. (1992) What is an effective organization? In J. Grunig (ed.), *Excellence in Public Relations and Communication Management*. Hillsdale, NJ: LEA, pp. 65–90.

Gujarati, D.N. (1995) *Basic Ecometrics* (3rd ed.). New York: McGraw-Hill.

Hillman, A. and Keim, J. (2001) Shareholder value, stakeholder management and social issues: What's the bottom line? *Strategic Management Journal*, 22(2), 125–139.

Hon, L. (1997a) Demonstrating effectiveness in public relations: Goals, objectives, and evaluation. Paper presented at the Annual Meeting of the AEJMC, Chicago, IL.

Hon, L. (1997b) What have you done for me lately? Exploring effectiveness in public relations. *Journal of Public Relations Research*, 9, 1–30.

Hutton, J.G., Goodman, M.B., Alexander, J.B., and Genest, C.M. (2001) Reputation management: The new face of corporate public relations? *Public Relations Review*, 27, 247–261.

Jones, G., Jones, B., and Little, P. (2000) Reputation as reservoir: Buffering against loss in times of economic crisis. *Corporate Reputation Review*, 3(1), 21–29.

Kim, K. (2006) Corporate communications and reputation building. Paper presented at the International Communication Association, 2006 Annual Meeting.

Kim, Y. (1997) Measuring efficiency: The economic impact model of reputation. Paper presented at the Annual Conference of the Public Relations Society of America, Nashville, TN.

Kim, Y. (1999) An organization-level public relations evaluation model in the context of economic value. A dissertation submitted to the graduate school of the University of Florida.

Kim, Y. (2000) Measuring the bottom line impact of corporate public relations. *Journalism and Mass Communication Quarterly*, 7(2), 273–291.

Kim, Y. (2001) The economic value of public relations. *Journal of Public Relations Research*, 13, 3–26.

Kim, Y. (2002) The impact of brand equity and the company's reputation on revenue: Testing an IMC evaluation model. *Journal of Promotion Management*, 6(1/2), 89–111.

Kiousis, S., Popescu, C., and Mitrook, M. (2007) Understanding influence on corporate reputation. *Journal of Public Relations Research*, 19(2), 147–165.

Knight, R. and Pretty, D. (1999) Corporate catastrophes, stock returns and trading volume. *Corporate Reputation Review*, 2(4), 363–378.

Lee, S. and Yoon, Y. (2010) Return on investment (ROI) of international public relations: A country-level analysis. *Public Relations Review*, 36, 15–20.

Luo, X. and Bhattacharya, C. (2006) Corporate social responsibility, customer satisfaction, and market value. *Journal of Marketing*, 70, 1–18.

Mahon, J.F. (2002) Corporate reputation: A research agenda using strategy and stakeholder literature. *Business and Society*, 41(4), 415–445.

Mahon, J.F. and Wartick, S. (2003) Dealing with stakeholders: How reputation, credibility and framing influence the game. *Corporate Reputation Review*, 6(1), 19–36.

Philips, D. (2001) The public relations evaluationists. *Corporate Communications*, 6(4), 225–237.

Radford, G. and Goldstein, S. (2002) The role of research methods in corporate communication. *Corporate Communications: An International Journal*, 7(4), 252–256.

Roberts, P. and Dowling, G. (1997) How do reputations affect corporate performance? The value of a firm's corporate reputation: How reputation helps attain and sustain superior profitability. *Corporate Reputation Review*, 1(1), 72–76.

Roberts, P. and Dowling, G. (2002) Corporate reputation and sustained superior financial performance. *Strategic Management Journal*, 23, 1077–1093.

Rossi, P.H. and Freeman, H.E. (1993) *Evaluation: A Systematic Approach*. Newbury, CA: Sage.

Sabate, J. and Puente, E. (2003) Empirical analysis of the relationship between corporate reputation and financial performance: A survey of the literature. *Corporate Reputation Review*, 6(2), 161–177.

Schnietz, K.E. and Epstein, M.J. (2005) Exploring the financial value of a reputation for corporate social responsibility during a crisis. *Corporate Reputation Review*, 7(4), 327–345.

Scriven, M. (1991) The methodology of evaluation. In R. Tyler, R. Mies, and M. Scriven (eds), *American Educational Research Association Monograph Series on Curriculum Evaluation. Perspectives of Curriculum Evaluation*. Chicago, IL: Rand McNally, pp. 39–83.

Smaiziene, I. (2008) Revealing the value of corporate reputation for increasing competitiveness. *Economics and Management*, 13, 718–723.

Surroca, J., Tribo, J., and Waddock, S. (2010) Corporate responsibility and financial performance: The role of intangible resources. *Strategic Management Journal*, 31, 462–490.

Thorson, E. and Moore, J. (1996) *Integrated Communication: Synergy of Persuasive Voices*. Mahwah, NJ: Lawrence Erlbaum Associates.

Vergin, R. and Qoronfleh, M. (1998) Corporate reputation and the stock market. *Business Horizons*, 41(1), 19–26.

Waddock, S. and Graves, S. (1997) The corporate social performance-financial performance link. *Strategic Management Journal*, 18(4), 303–319.

Waddock, S. and Smith, N. (2000) Relationships: The real challenge of corporate global citizenship. *Business and Society*, 105(1), 47–63.

Walker, K. (2010) A systematic review of the corporate reputation literature: Definition, measurement and theory. *Corporate Reputation Review*, 12(4), 357–387.

Wartick, S. (2002) Measuring corporate reputation: Definition and data. *Business and Society*, 41(4), 371–392.

Webster, P.L. (1990) What's the bottom line? *Public Relations Journal*, 46, 18–21.

Yoon, Y. (2002) Exploring preventative roles of public relations. Paper presented at the ICA, Seoul.

46

The Future of Communication Research in Corporate Reputation Studies

Craig E. Carroll
New York University, USA

In graduate school seminars devoted to communication research and theory, students are often told the story about the six blind men and the elephant – but do you know the story about the six blind elephants and the man?

Six blind elephants were discussing what humans were like. After arguing among themselves, they decided to find a human and determine what he or she was like by direct experience. The first blind elephant found a man and after patting him down thoroughly with his feet declared, "Humans are flat." The other blind elephants took turns patting the man down the same way, and they all agreed.

To some degree, this inversion of the blind men and the elephant story illustrates what has occurred over the past twenty years in corporate reputation scholarship. Across academic disciplines, including the field of communication, scholars privately delight in the wide variety of definitions and ways of measuring reputation. As long as there is agreement that the verdict is out, there is room, time, and need for further debate and study. Nevertheless, we have another elephant in the room. It concerns our taken-for-granted consensus on the reasons for studying corporate reputation and the benefits for organizations of investing in reputation management. It also concerns our preference for particular theories and academic disciplines for studying corporate reputation, the particular definitions of what counts as a reputation attribute, and our delimitation of inquiries in terms of antecedents, dimensions, and consequences.

The inversion of the story about the blind men and the elephant points to the dangers of establishing authoritative descriptions or definitions and then rushing to judgment too soon. We may draw premature conclusions that are not very satisfying, kill the subject of interest in the process, and fail to learn what we need to know. With premature assessments that are unsatisfying, empirical results that are anticlimactic, and a subject of interest that is dead, we may conclude that further study is not warranted. But if our subject were given time and voice to speak, we might discover that the most interesting questions, stories, contexts, and applications have yet to be revealed. Such are the possibilities of studying corporate reputation from a communication standpoint.

A Multifaceted Subject and a Multiplicity of Research Approaches

This handbook details the current state of research on corporate reputation from the per-

The Handbook of Communication and Corporate Reputation, First Edition. Edited by Craig E. Carroll.
© 2013 John Wiley & Sons, Inc. Published 2015 by John Wiley & Sons, Inc.

spective of communication, most notably human and mass communication perspectives. The opening chapter begins with a communication rationale for studying corporate reputation and offers a communication-based definition of the concept (Carroll, 2013). The chapter contributors were commissioned to describe the disciplinary frameworks associated with their sub-disciplines of communication and to tease out areas of inquiry and disciplinary assumptions that enrich and/or constrain the study of corporate reputation. As a result, readers have immediate access to a wide range of communication studies, including perspectives that might otherwise be overlooked.

However, the volume stops short of imposing this communication-based definition on the rest of the chapters or defining any particular paradigm. Instead, these chapter contributors were selected because of their previous research and writing, regardless of their paradigm. Some scholars were chosen because they have programs of research specifically focused on corporate reputation from communication perspectives. Others were chosen because readers will see the connections between their chapters and the concept of reputation, even if the contributing scholars do not consider reputation to be their primary focus (e.g. Kim et al., 2013). Still other scholars were chosen because their areas of inquiry – such as organizational learning and renewal (Sellnow et al., 2013), management fashions (Pieczka and Zorn, 2013), and hidden organizations (Scott, 2013) – offer new doorways, paths, and possibilities for corporate reputation researchers.

Despite the wide range of interests in corporate reputation that this volume demonstrates exists across the field of communication, the study of corporate reputation from communication perspectives is still in its infancy. Thus, collating the research and identifying where there is an abundance and where there is a lack of research on corporate reputation from communication perspectives became more important than offering a unified, normative stance. As extensive as this volume is, it became clear even as the chapter contributors excavated existing and potential programs of reputation research from communi-

cation perspectives that more theories, contexts, and applications – and even additional communication disciplines – merited attention. Additional disciplinary perspectives that should be included in the future include rhetoric, intercultural communication, computer-mediated communication, and nonverbal and political communication, to name a few. Ilhen's (2013) chapter on rhetoric, for instance, deals with theories of rhetoric, and points to the need for a more extensive treatment from the perspective of rhetoric as a communication discipline itself. The combination of nonverbal and computer-mediated communication, for example, has the potential to shed light on how stakeholders may read communication channel access and availability as nonverbal signals. An organizational stakeholder's perceptions of channel availability for interacting with an organization can be read as cues about the organization's ability and willingness to engage with stakeholders in general or the individual stakeholder in particular. Such nonverbal cues have the potential to affect stakeholders' perceptions of the organization's willingness to receive feedback on areas of concern. Fewer communication channels increase the communicative risk, thereby increasing the likelihood that a stakeholder will share concerns with others he or she encounters rather than with the organization itself. Intercultural communication theories (specifically cultural dimensions and face negotiation) can help explain cultural differences in reputation formation processes. Finally political communication perspectives help communication scholars transcend the debate about the relative importance of reputation to organization-public relationships (see Kiousis and Strömbäck, 2011).

Recommendations for Future Research Topics, Styles, and Approaches

The following recommendations grow out of this volume of literature reviews. Future researchers will benefit from considering them as they embark on corporate reputation studies from communication perspectives.

First, communication scholars should reflect upon the rhetoric of reputation valorization and the needs and interests served by offering insights into reputation-related phenomena, and work towards the development of a communication paradigm. Valorization is the process of increasing value, respect, and/or dignity for some concept, attribute idea, or cause. An examination of the rationales that many communication studies (broadly defined) currently offer for researching corporate reputation reveals an unreflective endorsement of the financial and instrumental benefits that organizations can achieve by having good or strong reputations. These rationales often entail charging a premium price for goods or services, attracting a more talented workforce, or being able to weather crises. What often goes unexplored and evaluated is the degree to which organizations achieving these benefits use them for less than noble purposes. For example, attracting a more talented workforce may mean paying employees less than a desirable wage and expecting them to work longer hours because of the assumed personal benefits they may accrue from being affiliated with a highly reputable organization. In other words, organizations may sometimes treat the ability to "bask in the glory" of the organization's reputation as if it were part of the employee's compensation package. Communication research should be prepared to comment on such justifications for studying reputation, and offer case studies illustrating the consequences of such rationales being taken too far.

Most of the research done on corporate reputation comes from a functional paradigm, and communication research on reputation is no exception. In fact, much of our research embraces business and commercial values to the neglect of communication values, pursuing research questions that seek to establish links between corporate reputation and organizational financial performance. Financial performance should not be the only, or even the primary focus, even from a functional perspective. It is time for communication scholars studying corporate reputation and those considering communication research on reputation to reflect upon the field's foundational values and the disciplinary assumptions embedded in their sub-disciplines for what these may contribute to our understanding of reputational benefits and limitations. There is also an opportunity to move beyond the functional focus on reputational attributes and consider what we can learn from interpretive and postmodern perspectives. For example, critical reflection on what it means to have a good reputation or a strong reputation for a particular attribute is needed. Enron, the name now synonymous with scandal, accounting fraud, corporate abuse and excess, was a company known for its innovation. Indeed, it was Enron's "innovation" that contributed to its corruption and led to the company's eventual collapse. So, there are opportunities here for critical scholars to illuminate the often unexamined nature of reputation attributes.

Second, scholars interested in what the communication field offers the study of corporate reputation need to become familiar with a variety of communication's sub-disciplinary perspectives. This handbook has focused on 14 sub-disciplines within the field of communication, making a strong case for multi-disciplinary communication perspectives on corporate reputation. These perspectives show the wide array of lenses through which scholars can study corporate reputation. Each sub-discipline brings disciplinary tools and biases that simultaneously illuminate and hide aspects of the concept being studied, making a multi-disciplinary communication perspective on reputation all the more important. Some sub-disciplines, such as public relations, have a rich history of reputation research. Others, such as organizational communication, have less history in this area. I do not suggest that each sub-discipline should embark upon inquiry into corporate reputation – only that researchers risk too narrow of a field of vision if alternative or supplementary sub-disciplinary perspectives, theories, contexts, and applications are not considered. Furthermore, new researchers can greatly expand their contributions and increase the speed at which they offer them by cross-fertilization. Scholars may import these dimensions back to their sub-disciplinary homes or they may decide to create a new home, drawing out the connections, associations, and implications for the sub-discipline they visit.

Third, scholars interested in what the communication field offers corporate reputation study should consider multiple points of interest. The second section of this handbook has offered ten theoretical perspectives on corporate reputation. These theories illustrate a wide variety of viewpoints on the concept of corporate reputation. Some theories were born within communication studies, such as agenda-setting theory (e.g., Ragas, 2013), whereas others – for example, institutional theory (Lammers and Guth, 2013) and social capital theory (Luoma-Aho, 2013) – have been imported from other academic disciplines such as sociology. Some chapters discussed theories that have a long tradition of application to corporate reputation, whereas others broke new ground, being the first elaborations of the perspective they offer. The handbook has not sought to promote the view that more favorable and stronger corporate reputations is the be-all, end-all focus of reputation scholarship – a view often found in research from management and organizational theory perspectives, where "reputation as a strategic asset" dominates. The chapter on the Excellence tradition (Kim, *et al.*, 2013) provides a balancing force to remind us that not all research on corporate reputation needs to be pro-reputation as the focus of our endeavors. Moreover, communication studies would encourage organizational agents to move beyond simply using communication for reputation defense (Benoit, 2013; Coombs, 2013; Ihlen, 2013) and consider how reputation can function as feedback that can help organizations to change, develop, learn, and take corrective action (Sellnow, Veil, and Anthony, 2013). As noted above, scholars who become familiar with the disciplinary assumptions of their sister sub-fields will have a more complete understanding of the role communication plays in the different stages and facets of reputation as a phenomenon.

To illustrate the importance of these two recommendations, one might consider the concept of transparency. Scholars, practitioners, organizational and communication critics, and first-hand organizational observers implicitly see the relevance of transparency for reputation. Transparency is a central concept of interest to a number of sub-disciplines within communication, as noted by chapter contributions on corporate (Brønn, 2013), marketing (Varey, 2013), and visual communication (Alesandri, 2013), as well as law (Gower, 2013). Transparency is also a subject of interest for reputation scholars from other disciplines (Eccles, Grant, and van Riel, 2007). Transparency, then, is one topic among many on which communication scholars can contribute to scholarship about corporate governance as a reputation attribute, as Pettigrew and Reber (2013) observe in their chapter. Yet the path to this contribution remains wide and varied. From a public relations perspective, Rawlins (2008) recently highlighted transparency reputation traits (integrity, respect for others, openness) and four transparency efforts (participation, substantial information, accountability, and secrecy). Organizational communication scholars may recognize transparency as a concept with a long history; scholars have discussed the limits and excesses associated with too wide of a focus on transparency (Eisenberg and Witten, 1987), as well as how transparency itself is strategically ambiguous (Eisenberg, 1984). Familiarity with multiple sub-disciplines and the theoretical frameworks associated with them has the potential to help scholars recognize alternative viewpoints, previous research paths, and the blind spots associated with their sub-disciplinary orientation. As a result of such cross-familiarity, scholars may develop a stronger footing for their studies and expedite the rate at which they make theoretical and empirical contributions.

Fourth, corporate reputation scholars need to move beyond their focus on performance and achievement attributes as the focus of their investigation. Attributes help answer the question, reputation for *what?* The answer generally concerns corporate conduct (or misconduct) or corporate performance and achievement (or the lack thereof). As Einwiller (2013, p. 297) notes, there is a distinction between the concrete and objectively verifiable attributes and the abstract or subjective attributes. Nevertheless, Murphy and Gilpin (2013) remind us that attributes need to be understood in terms of their rhetorical power via specific audiences and that they cannot be judged solely on their fit with reality. The present volume focuses primarily on performance and achievement attributes of reputation because that is what the body of research in corporate reputation currently focuses on. Reputation scholars have typically given little systematic attention and reflection to the study of reputational attributes across the disciplines; this is true for communication studies, organizational studies, management, marketing, finance, psychology, sociology, economics, and other fields. What little attention is paid to reputation attributes is guided more by business disciplines and by the popular press than by scholarly disciplines (see Bartlett, Pallas, and Frostenson, 2013; Pieczka and Zorn, 2013).

As this chapter makes clear, focusing solely on performance and achievement attributes is a matter of searching for something only by looking where it is easiest to find. The body of research from other organization-related disciplines has built up a wealth of knowledge about these attributes. It is time for communication studies to expand the focus into new areas, examining reputational attributes that may offer as much or more insight into what corporate reputation is and how it is formulated, managed, and changed. Future research (and practice, for that matter) should consider laying out *organizational communication performance* dimensions that can function as reputation attributes, enabling the discussion, reflection, benchmarking, and rewarding of organizations systems, practices, and processes that create more desirable organizations, workplaces, products and services, and contributions to society.

Communication scholars should consider how other organizational characteristics relate to corporate reputation, including the role of communication. To illustrate, consider the impact of organizational demographics on measuring corporate reputation. Organizational demographics are frequently used as control variables in advanced statistical analyses about reputation. Controlling for the influence of demographics suggests that they have some influence on the perception of reputation. Understanding the role demographics play in corporate reputation is important because organizations have the least amount of control over them; this suggests that there are some aspects of organizational identity that may need to be accepted, rather than attempting to change the unchangeable. Given the lack of attention to demographics in reputation construction in general, scholars may need to do more work in this area before offering assessments (see Stacks, Dodd, and Men (2013). Other attributes warranting attention for how they contribute to corporate reputation-related phenomena include organization-level psychographics, anthropomorphic traits, technical efficiency, and most importantly, organization-level communicative traits, both verbal and nonverbal. Communicatively, it would be interesting to know whether and how stakeholders' satisfaction with one reputation attribute relates to their perceptions of and concerns about other dimensions of the organization's reputation.

Fifth, communication scholars studying corporate reputation should consider the communication-related consequences of corporate reputation. One particular type of consequence identified earlier in this chapter is *stakeholders' communicative risk*. Communicative risk refers to a stakeholder's perceptions of certainty or uncertainty about the potential for adverse consequences he or she will experience if he or she attempts to engage the organization through communication. Communicative risk may vary by particular communication channel. Thus, communicative attributes become important for determining an organization's capacity to receive feedforward from its stakeholders. If, for example, a stakeholder feels comfortable enough to share feedback with an organization while a problem or issue is in the latent stage, the organization may successfully learn from the stakeholder and resolve the issue while it is still in the latent stage. Thus the need for the stakeholder to share the issue with other stakeholders is mitigated, thereby potentially preventing a problem from becoming a part of the organization's reputation. There are a number of other communication consequences of corporate reputation that offer fertile fields for research. Some of these include organizational identification, workplace democracy, workplace civility, communicative virtues, participation, authenticity, empowerment, engagement, communication satisfaction, transparency, honesty, decision-making processes, social support, and organization-public relationships.

Summary

This volume encourages communication researchers studying reputation to return to the core values and disciplinary assumptions underlying their sub-disciplines to see how they shed light on the concept and its relations to organizational phenomenon. Articulating our core communication assumptions and disciplinary biases – both helpful and unhelpful – will further illuminate the concept, expose the limitations of each sub-discipline, and perhaps even the limitations and assumptions of 'reputation' as a concept that may need to be challenged. Such a searching self-examination will also help us as scholars to be more open to concepts and theories from other sub-disciplines. Further, we should move beyond organization-centric viewpoints to consider individual-, group-, network-, public-, and population-centered viewpoints. Moreover, it is time for communication researchers to think about what interpretive, critical, cultural, postmodernist, and post-structuralist theories have to offer to communication perspectives on reputation. We must not lose sight of the fact that reputation attributes themselves are socially constructed, legitimized, and reified, not only by organizations and their publics but by researchers across academic fields. What the communication field needs, however, is an articulation of reputation attributes that are more common, familiar, and central to our discipline – and more central to the lived experience of those who encounter organizations in their daily lives.

In sum, this volume has the potential to help scholars avoid reinventing the wheel, recognize the limitations, delimitations, and blind spots associated with their sub-disciplinary orienta-

tion, develop a stronger footing for their studies, and increase the speed at which they contribute. Drawing these disciplines together into a volume that connects them to numerous theories, attributes, contexts, and measurement issues gives rise to the identification of other communication disciplines that scholars should consult in future research.

References

Allesandri, S.W. (2013) Corporate Reputation and the Discipline of Visual Communication Corporate Reputation Measurement and Evaluation. In C.E. Carroll (ed.) *The Handbook of Communication and Corporate Reputation*. Malden, MA: Wiley-Blackwell, pp. 130–140.

Bartlett, J., Pallas, J. and Frostenson, M. (2013) Reputation and Legitimacy: Accreditation and Rankings to Assess Organizations. In C.E. Carroll (ed.) *The Handbook of Communication and Corporate Reputation*. Malden, MA: Wiley-Blackwell, pp. 530–544.

Benoit, W. (2013) Image Repair Theory and Corporate Reputation. In C.E. Carroll (ed.) *The Handbook of Communication and Corporate Reputation*. Malden, MA: Wiley-Blackwell, pp. 213–221.

Brønn, P.S. (2013) Corporate Reputation and the Discipline of Corporate Communication. In C.E. Carroll (ed.) *The Handbook of Communication and Corporate Reputation*. Malden, MA: Wiley-Blackwell, pp. 53–61.

Carroll, C.E. (2013) Corporate Reputation and the Multi-Disciplinary Field of Communication. In C.E. Carroll (ed.) *The Handbook of Communication and Corporate Reputation*. Malden, MA: Wiley-Blackwell, pp. 1–10.

Coombs, W.T. (2013) Situational Theory of Crisis: Situational Crisis Communication Theory and Corporate Reputation. In C.E. Carroll (ed.) *The Handbook of Communication and Corporate Reputation*. Malden, MA: Wiley-Blackwell, pp. 262–278.

Eccles, R.G., Grant, R.M., and van Riel, C.B.M. (2007) Reputation and transparency: Lessons from a painful period in public disclosure. *Long Range Planning*, 69(4), 353–359.

Einwiller, S. (2013) Corporate Attributes and Associations. In C.E. Carroll (ed.) *The Handbook of Communication and Corporate Reputation*. Malden, MA: Wiley-Blackwell, pp. 262–278.

Eisenberg, E.M. (1984) Ambiguity as strategy in organizational communication. *Communication Monographs*, 51(3), 227–242.

Eisenberg, E.M., and Witten, M.G. (1987) Reconsidering Openness in Organizational Communication. *Academy of Management Review*, 12(3), 418–426.

Gower, K.K. (2013) Corporate Reputation and the Discipline of Corporate Communication Law. In C.E. Carroll (ed.) *The Handbook of Communication and Corporate Reputation*. Malden, MA: Wiley-Blackwell, pp. 141–150.

Ihlen, Ø. (2013) Relating Rhetoric and Reputation. In C.E. Carroll (ed.) *The Handbook of Communication and Corporate Reputation*. Malden, MA: Wiley-Blackwell, pp. 293–305.

Kim, J.N., Hung-Baesecke, C.F., Yang, S.U., and Grunig, J.E. (2013) A Strategic Management Approach to Reputation, Relationships, and Publics: The Research Heritage of the Excellence Theory. In C.E. Carroll (ed.) *The Handbook of Communication and Corporate Reputation*. Malden, MA: Wiley-Blackwell, pp. 197–212.

Kiousis, S. and Strömbäck, J. (2011) Political public relations research in the future. In J. Strömbäck and S. Kiousis (eds.), *Political Public Relations*. New York, NY: Routledge, pp. 314–323.

Lammers, J.C. and Guth, K. (2013) The Institutionalization of Corporate Reputation. In C.E. Carroll (ed.) *The Handbook of Communication and Corporate Reputation*. Malden, MA: Wiley-Blackwell, pp. 222–234.

Luoma-aho, V. (2013) Corporate Reputation and the Theory of Social Capital. In C.E. Carroll (ed.) *The Handbook of Communication and Corporate Reputation*. Malden, MA: Wiley-Blackwell, pp. 279–290.

Murphy, P. and Gilpin, D.R. (2103) Complexity Theory and the Dynamics of Reputation. In C.E. Carroll (ed.) *The Handbook of Communication and Corporate Reputation*. Malden, MA: Wiley-Blackwell, pp. 279–290.

Pettigrew, J. and Reber, B. (2013) Corporate Reputation and the Practice of Corporate Governance. In C.E. Carroll (ed.) *The Handbook of Communication and Corporate Reputation*. Malden, MA: Wiley-Blackwell, pp. 334–346.

Pieczka, M. and Zorn, T.E. (2013). The Reputation of Corporate Reputation: Fads, Fashions, and the Mainstreaming of Corporate Reputation Research and Practice. In C.E. Carroll (ed.) *The Handbook of Communication and Corporate Reputation*. Malden, MA: Wiley-Blackwell, pp. 513–529.

Ragas, M.R. (2013) Agenda-Building and Agenda-Setting Theory: Which Companies We Think About and How We Think About Them. In C.E. Carroll (ed.) *The Handbook of Communication and Corporate Reputation*. Malden, MA: Wiley-Blackwell, pp. 334–346.

Rawlins, B. (2008) Give the Emperor a Mirror: Toward Developing a Stakeholder Measurement of Organizational Transparency. *Journal of Public Relations Research*, 21(1), 71–99.

Scott, C.R. (2013) Hidden Organizations and Reputation. In C.E. Carroll (ed.) *The Handbook of Communication and Corporate Reputation*. Malden, MA: Wiley-Blackwell, pp. 545–558.

Sellnow, T.L, Veil, S.R. and Anthony, K. (2013) Experiencing the Reputational Synergy of Success and Failure through Organizational Learning. In C.E. Carroll (ed.) *The Handbook of Communication and Corporate Reputation*. Malden, MA: Wiley-Blackwell, pp. 235–248.

Stacks, D.W., Dodd, M.D., and Men, L.R. (2013) Corporate Reputation Measurement and Evaluation. In C.E. Carroll (ed.) *The Handbook of Communication and Corporate Reputation*. Malden, MA: Wiley-Blackwell, pp. 561–589.

Varey, R. (2013) Corporate Reputation and the Discipline of Marketing Communication. In C.E. Carroll (ed.) *The Handbook of Communication and Corporate Reputation*. Malden, MA: Wiley-Blackwell, pp. 334–346.

Author Index

The Handbook of Communication and Corporate Reputation, First Edition. Edited by Craig E. Carroll.
© 2013 John Wiley & Sons, Inc. Published 2015 by John Wiley & Sons, Inc.

Subject Index

The Handbook of Communication and Corporate Reputation, First Edition. Edited by Craig E. Carroll.
© 2013 John Wiley & Sons, Inc. Published 2015 by John Wiley & Sons, Inc.